W9-CLD-030

THE CHALLENGE OF SLUMS

First published in the UK and USA in 2003 by Earthscan Publications Ltd
for and on behalf of the United Nations Human Settlements Programme (UN-Habitat)

Copyright © United Nations Human Settlements Programme (UN-Habitat), 2003

All rights reserved

United Nations Human Settlements Programme (UN-Habitat)
PO Box 30030, Nairobi, Kenya
Tel: +254 2 621 234
Fax: +254 2 624 266
Web: www.unhabitat.org

DISCLAIMER

The designations employed and the presentation of the material in this publication do not imply the expression of any opinion whatsoever on the part of the Secretariat of the United Nations concerning the legal status of any country, territory, city or area, or of its authorities, or concerning delimitation of its frontiers or boundaries, or regarding its economic system or degree of development. The analysis, conclusions and recommendations of the report do not necessarily reflect the views of the United Nations Human Settlements Programme, the Governing Council of the United Nations Human Settlements Programme or its Member States

HS/686/03E

ISBN: 1-84407-037-9 paperback
         1-84407-036-0 hardback

Page design and typesetting by MapSet Ltd, Gateshead, UK
Printed and bound in the UK by Thanet Press Ltd, Margate, Kent
Cover design by Amrik Kalsi and Danny Gillespie
Cover photographs © Amrik Kalsi/UN-Habitat

For a full list of publications please contact:

Earthscan Publications Ltd
120 Pentonville Road, London, N1 9JN, UK
Tel: +44 (0)20 7278 0433
Fax: +44 (0)20 7278 1142
Email: earthinfo@earthscan.co.uk
Web: www.earthscan.co.uk

22883 Quicksilver Drive, Sterling, VA 20166-2012, USA

Earthscan is an editorially independent subsidiary of Kogan Page Ltd and publishes in association with WWF-UK and the International Institute for Environment and Development

A catalogue record for this book is available from the British Library

Library of Congress Cataloging-in-Publication Data

The challenge of slums : global report on human settlements, 2003 / United Nations Human Settlements Programme.
       p. cm.
    Includes bibliographical references and index.
    ISBN 1-84407-037-9 (pbk.) — ISBN 1-84407-036-0 (hardback)
    1. Slums. 2. Slums—Case studies. 3. Slums—Government policy. 4. Urban poor—Housing. 5. Urban poor—Statistics. I. United Nations Human Settlements Programme

HV4028.C48 2003
307.3'364—dc21

                                                                                                          2003013446

This book is printed on elemental chlorine free paper

DEC 0 5 2003

FOREWORD

Almost 1 billion people, or 32 per cent of the world's urban population, live in slums, the majority of them in the developing world. Moreover, the locus of global poverty is moving to the cities, a process now recognized as the 'urbanization of poverty'. Without concerted action on the part of municipal authorities, national governments, civil society actors and the international community, the number of slum dwellers is likely to increase in most developing countries. And if no serious action is taken, the number of slum dwellers worldwide is projected to rise over the next 30 years to about 2 billion.

In the United Nations Millennium Declaration, world leaders pledged to tackle this immense challenge, setting the specific goal of achieving 'significant improvement in the lives of at least 100 million slum dwellers by the year 2020'. This means addressing not only the needs of slum dwellers for shelter, but also the broader problem of urban poverty, especially unemployment, low incomes and a lack of access to basic urban services.

The Challenge of Slums: Global Report on Human Settlements 2003 presents the results of the first global assessment of slums by the United Nations since the adoption of the Millennium Declaration. The report proposes an operational definition of slums and, on this basis, provides the first global estimates of the numbers of urban slum dwellers. It discusses the local, national and international factors underlying the formation of slums. It analyses the social, spatial and economic characteristics and dynamics of slums. And it assesses the impact of the main policies towards urban slums adopted by governments, civil society groups and international organizations.

Slums represent the worst of urban poverty and inequality. Yet the world has the resources, knowhow and power to reach the target established in the Millennium Declaration. It is my hope that this report, and the best practices it identifies, will enable all actors involved to overcome the apathy and lack of political will that have been a barrier to progress, and move ahead with greater determination and knowledge in our common effort to help the world's slum dwellers to attain lives of dignity, prosperity and peace.

Kofi A Annan
Secretary-General
United Nations

INTRODUCTION

The Challenge of Slums: Global Report on Human Settlements 2003 is mainly concerned with the shelter conditions of the majority of the urban poor. It is about how the poor struggle to survive within urban areas, mainly through informal shelter and informal income-generation strategies, and about the inadequacy of both public and market responses to the plight of the urban poor. But the report is also about hope, about building on the foundations of the urban poor's survival strategies and about what needs to be done by both the public and non-governmental sectors, as well as by the international community, if the goal of adequate shelter for all is to have any relevance for today's urban poor.

Efforts to improve the living conditions of slum dwellers (especially within developing countries) have been feeble and incoherent over the last decade or so, having peaked during the 1980s. However, renewed concern about poverty has recently led governments to adopt a specific target on slums in the United Nations Millennium Declaration, which aims to significantly improve the lives of at least 100 million slum dwellers by the year 2020. As this report emphasizes, slums are a manifestation of the two main challenges facing human settlements development at the beginning of the new millennium: rapid urbanization and the urbanization of poverty. Slums areas have the highest concentrations of poor people and the worst shelter and physical environmental conditions.

Among the most important findings of *The Challenge of Slums* is the global estimate of the magnitude of the challenge of slums. The total number of slum dwellers in the world stood at about 924 million people in 2001. This represents about 32 per cent of the world's total urban population. At that time, 43 per cent of the combined urban populations of all developing regions lived in slums, while 78.2 per cent of the urban population in least developed countries were slum dwellers. In some developing country cities, slums are so pervasive that it is the rich who have to segregate themselves behind small gated enclaves.

This report explores both the negative and positive aspects of slums. On the negative side, the report shows that slums have the most intolerable of urban housing conditions, which frequently include: insecurity of tenure; lack of basic services, especially water and sanitation; inadequate and sometimes unsafe building structures; overcrowding; and location on hazardous land. In addition, slum areas have high concentrations of poverty and of social and economic deprivation, which may include broken families, unemployment and economic, physical and social exclusion. Slum dwellers have limited access to credit and formal job markets due to stigmatization, discrimination and geographic isolation. Slums are often recipients of the city's nuisances, including industrial effluent and noxious waste, and the only land accessible to slum dwellers is often fragile, dangerous or polluted – land that no one else wants. People in slum areas suffer inordinately from water-borne diseases such as typhoid and cholera, as well as more opportunistic ones that accompany HIV/AIDS. Slum women – and the children they support – are the greatest victims of all. Slum areas are also commonly believed to be places with a high incidence of crime, although this is not universally true since slums with strong social control systems will often have low crime rates.

On the positive side, the report shows that slums are the first stopping point for immigrants – they provide the low-cost and only affordable housing that will enable the immigrants to save for their eventual absorption into urban society. As the place of residence for low-income employees, slums keep the wheels of the city turning in many different ways. The majority of slum dwellers in developing country cities earn their living from informal sector activities located either within or outside slum areas, and many informal entrepreneurs operating from slums have clienteles extending to the rest of the city. Most slum dwellers are people struggling to make an honest living, within the context of extensive urban poverty and formal unemployment. Slums are also places in which the vibrant mixing of different cultures frequently results in new forms of artistic expression. Out of unhealthy, crowded and often dangerous environments can emerge cultural movements and levels of solidarity unknown in the suburbs of the rich. Against all odds, slum dwellers have developed economically rational and innovative shelter solutions for themselves. However, these few positive attributes do not in any way justify the continued existence of slums and should not be an excuse for the slow progress towards the goal of adequate shelter for all.

Many past responses to the problem of urban slums have been based on the erroneous belief that provision of improved housing and related services (through slum upgrading) and physical eradication of slums will, on their own, solve the slum problem. Solutions based on this premise have failed to address the main underlying causes of slums, of which poverty is the most significant. The report therefore emphasizes the need for future policies to support the livelihoods of the urban poor by enabling urban informal-sector activities to flourish and develop, by linking low-income housing development to income generation, and by ensuring easy geographical access to jobs through pro-poor transport and more appropriate location of low-income settlements. Slum policies should in fact be integrated within broader, people-focused urban poverty reduction policies that address the various dimensions of poverty.

The report identifies participatory slum upgrading programmes that include urban poverty reduction objectives as the current best practice. It emphasizes the need to scale up such slum upgrading programmes to cover whole cities, and to be replicated in all other cities, as well as for sustained commitment of resources sufficient to address the existing slum problem at both city and national levels. It also emphasizes the need for investment in citywide infrastructure as a pre-condition for successful and affordable slum upgrading and as one strong mechanism for reversing the socio-economic exclusion of slum dwellers. In this context, the report highlights the great potential for improving the effectiveness of slum policies by fully involving the urban poor, as well as the need for the public sector to be more inclusive in its urban policies.

The Challenge of Slums further recognizes the increasing emphasis, mainly by civil society and international organizations, on security of tenure (for both owner-occupied and rental accommodation) and on housing and property rights for the urban poor, especially their protection from unlawful eviction. For slum dwellers, security of tenure opens up possibilities of raising credit for livelihood related activities. The report emphasizes the need for governments and local authorities to build on these recent positive developments.

The United Nations Human Settlements Programme (UN-Habitat) is the focal point, within the United Nations system, for the implementation of the Millennium Declaration target on slums, as well as for global monitoring of progress towards this target. Slum upgrading has therefore become a very important area of focus for the organization, with increasing emphasis being placed on policy and operational support to the following areas: scaling up of slum upgrading projects and programmes, within the context of city development strategies and through more innovative international and national financing mechanisms; urban water supply and sanitation, mainly through region-wide operational programmes; and pro-poor planning and management of the urban economy, so as to enhance income-generation opportunities for the urban poor.

The Challenge of Slums: Global Report on Human Settlements 2003 provides a new impetus to all of these efforts. More importantly, it provides directions for the future that are worthy of consideration by national governments, municipal authorities, civil society organizations and international organizations concerned with improving the lives of slum dwellers. The report also provides a baseline for the long journey towards cities without slums, and should therefore be seen as the starting point of the task of global monitoring of the United Nations Millennium Declaration target on slums.

Anna Kajumulo Tibaijuka
Executive Director
United Nations Human Settlements Programme (UN-Habitat)

ACKNOWLEDGEMENTS

The United Nations Global Reports on Human Settlements are a product of the strong dedication of many people, whose knowledge and expertise help to produce them. The current volume, which is concerned with shelter and urban poverty, is based on full commitment to the goals of social equity and environmental sustainability in human settlement development. This approach determines the overall focus, tone and motif of the report.

The Challenge of Slums: Global Report on Human Settlements 2003 was prepared under the general guidance of Daniel Biau, Acting Director of the Global Division of UN-Habitat, Donatus Okpala, Acting Director of the Monitoring and Research Division and Nefise Bazoglu, Chief of the Urban Secretariat. Naison Mutizwa-Mangiza, Acting Chief of the Policy Analysis, Synthesis and Dialogue Branch, supervised the preparation of the report. The Research and Reporting Section had primary responsibility for the production of the report, with Iouri Moisseev coordinating its preparation.

Members of the UN-Habitat Senior Management Board provided strategic advice in the areas of their respective responsibility at different stages in the preparation of the report. These included: Alioune Badiane, Nick Bain, Nefise Bazoglu, Daniel Biau, William Cobbett, Jochen Eigen, Jorge Gavidia, Axumite Gebre-Egziabher, Antoine King, Lucia Kiwala, Sylvie Lacroux, Joseph Mungai, Toshi Noda, Jane Nyakairu, Donatus Okpala, Kalyan Ray, Lars Reutersward, Sharad Shankardass, Anathakrishnan Subramonia, Tomasz Sudra, Paul Taylor, Farouk Tebbal and Rolf Wichmann.

The initial step in the development of the report was a strategic paper prepared by Nefise Bazoglu. This was followed by a Workshop and an Expert Group Meeting to identify the focus and structure of the report, as well as to formulate a consistent operational definition of slums and establish procedures for estimation of the numbers of slum dwellers. These meetings were attended by Christine Auclair, Nick Bain, John Barreh, Nefise Bazoglu, Marjolein Benschop, Daniel Biau, Yves Cabannes, Fernando Cavallieri, Tanzib Chowdhury, William Cobbett, Anne Comolet, Selman Erguden, Jean Du Plessis, Alain Durand-Lasserve, Joe Flood, Erlinda Go, Joseph Guiebo, Tim Harris, Harvey Herr, Mark Hildebrand, Inge Jensen, Robert Johnston, Guenter Karl, Cecilia Kinuthia-Njenga, Miloon Kothari, Tony Lloyd Jones, Elisa Lustosa Caillaux, Rajeev Malhotra, Aman Mehta, Dinesh Mehta, Diana Meirelles Da Motta, Iouri Moisseev, Jay Moor, Eduardo Moreno, Naison Mutizwa-Mangiza, Pierre Ngom, Tumsifu Jonas Nnkya, S Onsare, Alberto Paranhos, Couglan Pather, Martin Raithelhuber, Robin Rajack, Shea Rutstein, Daniela Simioni, Farouk Tebbal, Raf Tuts,Willem van Vliet–, Patrick Wakely, Jane Weru, Stephanie Wilcock, Chris Williams, Saad Yahya, Yap Kioe Sheng and Nicholas You.

Following the experts' recommendations, a number of authors were commissioned to prepare city case studies on slums under the direction of Patrick Wakely and coordinated by Kate Clifford of the Development Planning Unit, University College London, UK. The Terms of Reference for city case studies were initiated by Jay Moor of UN-Habitat. The willingness of these authors to give of their time, and their responsiveness to requests for revisions at short notice, is very much appreciated. Case studies for the following cities were prepared: Abidjan (Kouame Appessika, Côte d'Ivoire) Ahmedabad (Mihir Bhatt, Foundation for Public Interest, India); Bangkok (Sopon Pornchokchai, Thai Appraisal Foundation, Thailand); Barcelona (Alex Walker and Bernardo Porraz, Development Planning Unit, University College London, UK); Beirut (Mona Fawaz and Isabella Peillen, Department of Urban Studies and Planning, American University of Beirut, Lebanon); Bogotá (Nicolás Rueda, Facultad de Arquitectura, Universidad de Los Andes, Colombia); Cairo (David Sims, consultant economist, Egypt, with contribution from Monija El-Shorbagi and Marion Séjourné, Centre for Economic, Juridical and Social Studies and Documentation, Egypt); Chengdu (He Hong, Tian Jun and Zhan Li, *Chengdu Daily*, China); Colombo (K A Jayaratne, SEVATHA Urban Resource Centre, Sri Lanka); Durban (Colin Marx and Sarah Sharlton, Built Environment Support Group, South Africa); Guatemala (Carlos Valladares, Urban Research, Guatemala); Havana (Jill Hamberg and Mario Coyula Cowley, Cuba's National Union of Artists and Writers, Cuba); Ibadan (Laurent Fourchard, French Institute for Research in Africa (IFRA), University of Ibadan, Nigeria); Jakarta (Paul McCarthy, Civil Society Consultant, World Bank, Indonesia); Karachi (Arif Hasan, Karachi Urban Resource Centre, Pakistan); Khartoum (Galal Eldin Eltayeb, Development Consultant, Khartoum); Kolkata (Nitai Kundu, Institute of Wetland Management and Ecological Design, India); Los Angeles (Neal Richman and Bill Pitkin, Advanced Policy Institute, University of California, US); Lima (Gustavo Riofrio, Urban Programme for DESCO, Peru); Lusaka (Chileshe Mulenga, Institute of Economic and Social Research, University of Zambia, Zambia); Manila (Junio M Ragragio, Metro Manila Urban Study Programme, Philippines); Marseille (Michel Teule, with the participation of Suzanne Benasson and Clothilde Benazet, Centre d'Etudes, de Recherche et de Formation Institutionelle du Sud Est, France); Mexico City (Priscilla Connolly, Universidad Autónoma Metropolitana-Azcapotzalco, Mexico); Moscow (Alexey Krasheninnikov, Moscow Institute of

Architecture, Russian Federation); Mumbai (Neelima Risbud, School of Planning and Architecture, Delhi, India); Nairobi (Winnie Mutulah, Institute of Development Studies, University of Nairobi); Naples (Matteo Scaramella, University of Rome, Italy); Newark (Mara S Sidney, Rutgers University-Newark, US); Phnom Penh (Pierre Fallavier, Asia Multimedia Resource Centre, Canada); Quito (Diego Carrión, Jaime Vásconez, with the collaboration of Nury Bermúdez, Centro de Investigaciones Ciudad, Ecuador); Rabat-Salé (Françoise Navez Bouchanine, Centre d'Etude et de Recherches sur l'Urbanisation du Monde Arabe (URBAMA), France); Rio de Janeiro (Helia Nacif Xavier, Instituto Brasileiro de Administração Municipal (IBAM), and Fernanda Magalhães, Universidade Federal do Rio de Janeiro, Brazil); São Paulo (Mariana Fix, University of São Paulo, Pedro Fiori Arantes, USINA – centre for human settlements, Giselle M Tanaka, Housing and Human Settlements Laboratory FAU-USP, Brazil); Shanghai (Zhu Linchu and Qian Zhi, Development Research Centre of Shanghai Municipal Government, China); Sydney (Joe Flood, Urban Resources, Australia). The case studies were edited by Alex Walker and Anna Soave of the Development Planning Unit, University College London, UK. The initial draft of the summary of case studies contained in Part IV of the report was prepared by Joseph Maseland and edited by Naison Mutizwa-Mangiza (UN-Habitat).

Background papers and drafts of sections were prepared by a number of eminent consultants: Joe Flood (Urban Resources, Australia), Alain Durand-Lasserve (Centre National de la Recherche Scientifique (CNRS), France), James Mutero (Housing Finance Consultant, Kenya), AbdouMaliq Simone (Graduate School of Public and Development Management, University of Witwatersrand, South Africa), Graham Tipple (University of Newcastle, UK), Willem van Vliet– (University of Colorado, US) and Patrick Wakely (Development Planning Unit, University College London, UK). Structural organization of the report and substantive editing of its chapters were carried out by Iouri Moisseev and Naison Mutizwa-Mangiza of UN-Habitat.

At UN-Habitat, a number of people provided vital support by reviewing and commenting on background papers and taking leadership in drafting additional sections of the report. Among them were: Cecilia Anderson, Clarissa Augustinus, Marjolein Benschop, Joseph Maseland, Dinesh Mehta, Jay Moor, Laura Petrella, Sabine Ravestijn, Roman Rollnick, Wandia Seaforth, Ananthakrishnan Subramonia, Seyda Turkmemetogullari, Brian Williams and Christopher Williams.

Several professionals of UN-Habitat made other valued contributions. In particular, the following staff provided their time amidst competing demands: Graham Alabaster, Jean-Yves Barcelo, Andre Dzikus, Mohamed El-Sioufi, Selman Erguden, Anne Fraser, Szilard Fricska, Jorge Gavidia, Guenther Gross, John Hogan, Inge Jensen, Amrik Kalsi, Cecilia Kinuthia-Njenga, David I Kithakye, Ole Lyse, Uwe Lohse, Kibe Muigai, Rainer Nordberg, Laura Petrella, Tatiana Roskoshnaya, Ali Shabou, Sharad Shankardass, Soraya Smaoun, Catalina Trujillo, Rafael Tuts, Rolf Wichmann and Nicholas You.

The following staff members of UN-Habitat were involved in the preparation of the Statistical Annex: Tanzib Chowdhury, Guenter Karl, Iouri Moisseev and Martin Raithelhuber. Christine Auclair and Eduardo Moreno assisted with data analysis and checking. The estimation of slum dwellers was conducted by the Global Urban Observatory (GUO) of UN-Habitat, under the technical guidance of Harvey Herr (consultant). Mugabi Nsibirwa assisted in data processing and in the formatting of the Data Tables. Phillip Mukungu provided technical assistance in data checking.

In addition, many other people were helpful in reviewing and commenting on drafts, making valuable contributions to the report, compiling data, preparing graphs, contributing information and in a variety of other ways. Among them the following names should be mentioned: Ronald Banks (Centre for Land Policy Studies, UK), Paul Barter (Department of Geography, University of Singapore, Singapore), Kate Clifford (Development Planning Unit, University College London, UK), Laurent Fourchard (IFRA, University of Ibadan, Nigeria), Simon Fraser (Graphic Design Consultant, Nairobi, Kenya), Pietro Garau (Millennium Task Force on Slums and University of Rome, Italy), Assunta Gleria (Vicenco, Italy), Talal Hourani (United Nations Economic and Social Commission for Western Asia (ESCWA)), Mathias Hundsalz (Trier University, Germany), Wanarat Konisranakul (Development Planning Unit, University College London, UK), Elena Mikoulina (Moscow Institute of Architecture, Russian Federation), Srdan Mrkic (United Nations Statistics Division (UNSD)), Babar Mumtaz (Development Planning Unit, University College London, UK), Kemer Norkin (Moscow City Government, Russian Federation), Jonas Rabinovitch (United Nations Development Programme (UNDP)), Elizabeth Riley (Development Planning Unit, University College London, UK), Lauren Royston (Development Works, South Africa), Elliott Sclar (Columbia University, US), AbdouMaliq Simone (New York University, US), Anna Soave (Development Planning Unit, University College London, UK), Vladimir Sosnovski (Moscow Institute of Architecture, Russian Federation), Oumar Malick Sy (United Nations Economic Commission for Africa (ECA)), Bernadia Irawati Tjandredewi (CityNet, Japan), Irina Voronova (International Union of Economists, US), Julian Walker (Development Planning Unit, University College London, UK), Emiel Wegelin (UrbAct, The Netherlands).

The report also benefited from consultations with colleagues in the United Nations Regional Commissions. These staff members shared generously their expertise – the comments and suggestions of Ousmane Laye (ECA), Daniela Simioni (United Nations Economic Commission for Latin America and the Caribbean (ECLAC)), Riadh Tappuni (ESCWA), Guennadi Vinogradov (United Nations Economic Commission for Europe (ECE)) and Yap Kioe Sheng (United Nations Economic and Social Commission for Asia and the Pacific (ESCAP)), in particular, are very much appreciated.

Sriadibhatla Chainulu, Katja Nilsson and Henk Verbeek of UN-Habitat and Josie Villamin of the United Nations Office at Nairobi (UNON) provided administrative support during the preparation of the report. Secretarial and general administrative support was provided by Florence Bunei, Mary Dibo, Josephine Gichuhi, Ramadhan M Indiya, Mary Kariuki, Pamela Murage, Stella Otieno and Lucy Waikwa of UN-Habitat and Esther Kimani of UNON.

Special thanks are due to the Governments of Germany, Italy and The Netherlands for their earmarked contributions to the United Nations Habitat and Human Settlements Foundation in support of research inputs to the Global Report series. Special thanks are also due to the people at Earthscan Publications Ltd, in particular its Publishing Director Jonathan Sinclair Wilson, Publishing Manager Frances MacDermott, copy editor Andrea Service and Akan Leander, Helen Rose and Jennifer Poole.

CONTENTS

Foreword   *v*
Introduction   *vi*
Acknowledgements   *viii*
List of Figures, Boxes and Tables   *xviii*
List of Acronyms and Abbreviations   *xxi*

Key Findings and Messages   XXV

Prologue: Urban Growth and Housing   xxix
    Population Explosion and Urban Expansion   xxxi
    Accommodating Growth   xxxi
    The Focus of this Report   xxxii
    Notes   xxxiv

PART I

SHARPENING THE GLOBAL DEVELOPMENT AGENDA

1   Development Context and the Millennium Agenda   5
    Cities Without Slums?   5
        The failure of governance   5
        Institutional and legal failure   6
    The Millennium Development Agenda   7
    Understanding Slums   8
        The notion of slums   9
        Defining and measuring slums   10
        Characteristics of slums   11
            Lack of basic services   11
            Substandard housing or illegal and inadequate building structures   11
            Overcrowding and high density   11
            Unhealthy living conditions and hazardous locations   11
            Insecure tenure; irregular or informal settlements   11
            Poverty and social exclusion   11
            Minimum settlement size   11
        Operational definition of slums   12
        Number of slum dwellers: assessments and estimations   12
        Trends in numbers of slum dwellers   13
    Notes   16

2   Urbanization Trends and Forces Shaping Slums   17
    Socio-Economic Inequality   17
        Spatial organization and residential differentiation   17
            The ecological school and the neo-classical model   17
            Factorial ecology   18
            Measuring spatial inequality and separation   20
            Spatial concentration of poverty   20
        Urban form and disadvantage   22
            Mosaic post-modern cities in the developing world   22
            Measuring urban development and disadvantage   23

Challenges to Sustainable Urbanization   **23**
   Demographic changes and slum formation   23
      Urban growth   24
      Rural–urban migration   25
      International migration   27
      Declining areas and depopulation   27
   Poverty   28
      Poverty and slums   28
      Defining poverty   29
      Measurement of poverty incidence   30
      Targeting of poverty reduction programmes   31
Notes   **31**

3   Cities and Slums within Globalizing Economies   34
Inequality and Poverty   **34**
   Inequality: a recent history   35
   Globalization: poverty amid affluence   39
   Trade, globalization and cities   40
      Trade theory and inequality   40
      Trade: the reality   40
      Finance, information and economic volatility   41
      Labour markets under free trade regimes   42
      Africa: economic stagnation in a globalizing world   43
The Retreat of the State   **43**
   Privatization of utilities   44
   Structural adjustment, cities and poverty   45
The Local and the Global   **46**
   Insecurity and the diffusion of the local   47
   Subsidiarity and the weakening of national governments   48
   Transurban cooperation and integration: towards new urban economies 50
   Slums and globalization   52
   Looking ahead   52
Notes   **54**

PART II

ASSESSING SLUMS IN THE DEVELOPMENT CONTEXT

4   Social Dimensions   62
Historical Context and Evolution of Social Stratification Patterns   **62**
   Views on inner-city slums   63
      Slums and urbanization   64
      Slums and capitalism   64
      Slums and reformism   65
      Are slums inevitable?   65
   Social diversity of contemporary slums   66
Social Attributes and Functions of Slums   **67**
   Accommodation of low-cost labour   67
   Network for migrant absorption   68
   Mobilization of political power   68
   Environmental externalities   69
   Service provision   70
Slums within Urban Society   **70**
   Contribution to cultural developments   71
   Co-location and social aspects of poverty   71
   Health issues   72
      Slums and disease   74
   Crime issues   75
      Community risk factors   75
      Findings of recent research on crime   76
Notes   **77**

5	Territoriality and Spatial Forms	79
	Slums Formation Processes and Spatial Types	80
	Inner-city slums	80
	Slum estates	81
	Squatter settlements	82
	Illegal settlements and subdivisions	83
	Diversity of slums' spatial forms and associated opportunities	84
	Origins and Age	85
	Historic city-centre slums	85
	Slum estates	86
	Consolidating informal settlements	87
	Recent slums	87
	Location	88
	Central	88
	Scattered slum islands	89
	Peripheral	90
	Size and Scale	90
	Large slum settlements	90
	Medium-sized slum estates	91
	Small slums	91
	Legality, Vulnerability and Spatial Forms	92
	Illegal	92
	Informal	92
	Development Dynamics	92
	Ongoing individual and community-led development	93
	Intervention-led improved slums	93
	Upgraded slums	93
	Lacking community incentives for improvement	95
	Incipient slum creation	95
	Notes	95
6	Economic Dynamics	96
	Labour Force Growth	96
	The creation and distribution of income	96
	The global labour force	97
	Unemployment and underemployment	98
	Labour market abuses	99
	Informality within Urban Settings	100
	The informal economy	100
	Defining the informal sector	100
	The nature of informal-sector enterprises	101
	The reasons for the informal sector of the economy	102
	The scale of the informal sector	103
	Informal housing	104
	Slums in the Housing Sector	104
	Tenure and security: the formal–informal housing continuum	105
	Formal home-ownership	105
	Formal private rental	105
	Informal home-ownership: squatting	105
	Informal home-ownership: illegal subdivisions	106
	Public rental	106
	Informal rental	106
	Customary tenure	106
	Tenure distribution	106
	Slums and tenure insecurity	106
	Renting in slums	107
	Home-ownership in slums	109
	Land prices	112
	Adequacy: extent of housing disadvantage	112

Networked services 113
Water 113
Waste management 114
Adequacy of housing and inadequacy of planning 114
Notes 115

PART III

SEARCHING FOR ADEQUATE POLICY RESPONSES AND ACTIONS

7 New Policy Developments at the National and Global Levels 123
Search for Affordable Alternatives at the National Level 123
Public housing in developing countries 124
Assisted self-build and slum-improvement programmes 125
Housing capital subsidies 127
Past and Present Approaches to Slums at the National and Local Levels 128
Negligence 129
Eviction 130
Self-help and *in situ* upgrading 130
Enabling policies 131
Resettlement 131
Current best practice: participatory slum improvement 132
Recent Contextual Changes 133
Increased inequality within and between cities 133
New political influence of cities 135
International Actors Dealing with Slums and Their Priorities 136
Range of actors 136
The shifting priorities 136
Bilateral cooperation: diversity of political objectives 136
Multilaterals: a growing convergence 136
Inter-institutional programmes and initiatives: emphasis on slum upgrading, innovative partnerships and
local development 139
The Cities Alliance 139
The Urban Management Programme (UMP) 140
The Municipal Development Programme (MDP) 140
Emerging common themes 141
Integrated approaches to slums 141
The promotion of partnerships and inter-institutional networks 141
Decentralized cooperation 142
Sectors addressed 142
Urban management and finance 142
Urban land management and tenure 143
Service provision and delivery 143
Environment and public health 143
Housing delivery 144
Population and social issues 144
Capacity building, research activities and knowledge exchange 144
Pressing Issues 145
Financial constraints 145
Contradictions between economic and social objectives 145
Coordination and cooperation 145
Notes 146

8 Civil Society in Action 148
Residents in Action 148
The strategies of slum households 148
Inside the household 149
Reciprocity and remittance 150
Vulnerable households 150

Community-Based Organizations in Action 151
    The growth and range of community-based organizations (CBOs) 151
    Working with CBOs 152
Non-Governmental Organizations (NGOs) in Action 153
    Defining NGOs 153
    The growth of NGOs 155
    The range and diversity of NGOs 156
    The increasing power and decreasing autonomy of NGOs 158
Urban-Sector CBOs and NGOs 159
The Challenges Faced by NGOs and CBOs 161
Notes 163

9   **Towards Inclusive Cities: Reconsidering Development Priorities** 164
Policy Issues and Strategies for Inclusive Cities 165
    From slum upgrading to cities without slums 165
        Lessons learned from past experiences of upgrading 165
        The Cities Without Slums action plan 167
    Tenure issues and access to land for the urban poor 167
        Security of tenure: a key to the 'inclusive city' 168
        Alternative approaches to security of tenure 170
        Diversity of situations and objectives requires diversity of responses 171
    Inclusive infrastructure: making the connections between transport and housing security 172
        Dilemmas of housing security versus access 172
        Resistance to displacement and negotiated outcomes 172
        Increasing housing choice through greater mobility for the poor 173
        Impacts of transport and land-use regulation 173
        Impacts of the location of housing for the urban poor 174
    Improving the livelihoods of slum dwellers 175
        Poverty, governance and empowerment 175
        Generating employment from shelter development programmes and civil works 176
    Mobilizing finance for urban development 178
        Financing slum upgrading and shelter development: current challenges 178
        Improving municipal finance for investment in low-income residential areas 179
        Improving housing finance for low-income shelter development 180
Enabling Local Policy to Work 182
    Good urban governance and the 'inclusive city' 182
        Sustainability in all dimensions of urban development 183
        Subsidiarity of authority and resources to the closest appropriate level 183
        Equity of access to decision-making processes and the basic necessities of urban life 183
        Efficiency in the delivery of public services and in promoting local economic development 183
        Transparency and accountability of decision-makers and stakeholders 183
        Civic engagement and citizenship 183
        Security of individuals and their living environment 183
    Enhancing development potential through partnerships 183
        Capacity building 185
        Low-income households as financial and political partners 185
        Local businesses, city elites and local media as partners 185
        NGOs as partners 185
        Women's participation 186
        Self-help and management of projects 186
        Scaling-up and spreading the movement 186
        Partnerships based on trust 186
        Horizontal partnerships 186
    Effective policy coordination 186
Notes 187

Epilogue: Looking Forward – Moving Ahead   189
    Towards Cities Without Slums: Turning the Dream into Reality   189
    Action Needed to Tackle the Current Trends   189
    Notes   192

PART IV

SUMMARY OF CITY CASE STUDIES

Overview of Case Studies   195
    Origin of Slums   195
    Slum Definitions   196
    Types of Slums   196
    Tenure in Slums   197
    Slum Dynamics   197
    Slum Socio-Political Characteristics   197
    Policy Actions Taken or Proposed   198
    Policy Impacts and Development Prospective   198
    Notes   199

Case Study Highlights   200
    Abidjan, Côte d'Ivoire   200
    Ahmedabad, India   201
    Bangkok, Thailand   201
    Barcelona, Spain   202
    Beirut, Lebanon   203
    Bogotá, Colombia   205
    Cairo, Egypt   205
    Chengdu, China   206
    Colombo, Sri Lanka   208
    Durban, South Africa   208
    Havana, Cuba   209
    Ibadan, Nigeria   211
    Jakarta, Indonesia   211
    Karachi, Pakistan   212
    Kolkata, India   213
    Los Angeles, US   214
    Lusaka, Zambia   215
    Manila, Philippines   215
    Mexico City, Mexico   216
    Moscow, Russian Federation   218
    Nairobi, Kenya   219
    Naples, Italy   220
    Newark, US   221
    Phnom Penh, Cambodia   222
    Quito, Ecuador   223
    Rabat-Salé, Morocco   224
    Rio de Janeiro, Brazil   225
    São Paulo, Brazil   226
    Sydney, Australia   227
    Notes   228

PART V

STATISTICAL ANNEX

Technical Notes   231
    Explanation of Symbols   231
    Country Groupings and Statistical Aggregates   231
    Nomenclature and Order of Presentation   234
    Definition of Statistical Terms   234
    Sources of Data   239
    Notes   240

Methodological Notes   241
    Slum Dweller Estimations at the Global and Regional Levels   241
    The *Global Urban Indicators Databases*   245
    Notes   245

Data Tables   246
    Regional-Level Data
        A.1 Demographic indicators   246
        A.2 Housing indicators   247
        A.3 Economic and social indicators   248
    Country-Level Data
        B.1 Size and growth of total population and households   249
        B.2 Urbanization trends, size and growth of urban and rural population   252
        B.3 Housing-ownership and water and toilet facilities, selected countries   255
        B.4 Access to improved water sources and sanitation   258
        B.5 Energy and transport   260
        B.6 Economic development indicators   262
        B.7 Social indicators   264
    City-Level Data
        C.1 Urban agglomerations: population size and growth rate   267
        C.2 Households' living conditions, selected cities   273
        C.3 Housing indicators, selected cities   274
        C.4 Environmental infrastructure, selected cities   277
        C.5 Transport and environment indicators, selected cities   280
        C.6 Social indicators, selected cities   283
        C.7 Urban governance indicators, selected cities   287

References   *290*
Index   *301*

LIST OF FIGURES, BOXES AND TABLES

FIGURES

1.1	Slum population by region, 2001	14
1.2	Slum dwellers as a percentage of urban population by region, 2001	15
1.3	Proportion of slum dwellers in urban population by region, 2001	15
1.4	World distribution of slum dwellers by region, 2001	15
2.1	Inequality, poverty and slum formation	17
2.2	Ecological schema for Chicago	18
2.3	Areas of disadvantage in Sydney	19
2.4	Socio-economic clusters in Sydney	23
2.5	Annual increment in total and urban population	24
2.6	Urban and rural populations in more and less developed regions, 1950 to 2030	24
2.7	Estimated urban population increment by city size	25
2.8	Percentage unauthorized housing and infrastructure deficiency, city-size ranges, 1993	26
3.1	Booms and busts: stylized long wave	35
3.2	The invisible hand: ratcheting of inequality in booms and busts	35
3.3	Ratio between richest and poorest nations' GDP per person, 1800 to 2000	36
3.4	Gini coefficient, world (unweighted), 1950 to 1998	37
3.5	Growth of trade by region, 1980 to 2001 (1980 = 1.00)	41
4.1	Progression of an inner-city slum, Surry Hills, Sydney	66
4.2	Life expectancy at birth for the world and development groups, 1950 to 2050	72
4.3	Urban child mortality by City Development Index (CDI) quintile, 1993 and 1998	72
6.1	Labour force participation rates, 1950 to 2010, selected regions	97
6.2	Employment in agricultural sector, 1950 to 1990, selected regions	97
6.3	Housing tenure, 1998	107
6.4	World security of tenure	109
6.5	Land price to income ratio	111
6.6	Permanent dwellings and housing in compliance, by development level	112
6.7	Access to networked infrastructure by City Development Index (CDI) quintile	113
6.8	Connections to networked infrastructure, informal and all developing cities, 1998	114
6.9	Networked services in Africa, formal and informal settlements	114
9.1	Linkages between housing and transport	175

BOXES

1.1	Scope of Millennium Development Goals and Targets	8
1.2	Terms in use in Manila	10
1.3	Combining the indicators	13
1.4	Nairobi slum study	13
2.1	Highlights of urbanization trends	25
2.2	The constituents of urban poverty	30
3.1	Measuring global inequality	38
3.2	Cost recovery in water in South Africa	44
4.1	Diversity in education levels and occupation types among residents of slums in Pune, India	67
4.2	Civil society organizes against forced evictions in Metro Manila	69

5.1	Barcelona inner-city slums	80
5.2	Bogotá inner-city slums	81
5.3	Hostels in South Africa	81
5.4	Chawls in Mumbai, India	81
5.5	The 'recent public city' of Naples	82
5.6	Informal settlements in Durban	83
5.7	Illegal construction in Naples	84
5.8	Illegal subdivision of agricultural land around Cairo	84
5.9	Illegal subdivisions in Quito	85
5.10	Ibadan's historical centre slums	86
5.11	Old Havana	86
5.12	The *medinas* of Morocco: Rabat-Salé	87
5.13	Consolidating *favelas* in Rio de Janeiro	87
5.14	Consolidating informal settlements in Bogotá	88
5.15	Recent slums in Phnom Penh	88
5.16	Centrally located slums in Colombo	89
5.17	Centrally located slums in São Paulo	89
5.18	Scattered slum islands in Beirut	90
5.19	Peripheral slum islands in Ibadan	90
5.20	Karachi: women's access to employment	91
5.21	Mexico City: Valle de Chalco Solidaridad	91
5.22	Mumbai: Prakash Nagar Pavement Community	92
5.23	Phnom Penh: living in the grounds of a pagoda	92
5.24	Illegal districts in Rabat-Salé, Morocco	93
5.25	Informal areas in Cairo	93
5.26	Mexico City: Ciudad Netzahualcóyotl	94
5.27	'Incipient slums' in Moscow	95
6.1	Informal-sector workers in Quito, Ecuador	102
7.1	Aviles, Spain: integration of slum households within existing neighbourhoods	124
7.2	Singapore: a successful public housing programme	125
7.3	Building urban China, 1949 to 1990	126
7.4	The First Home Owners Scheme (FHOS) in Australia	128
7.5	South Africa's right-based housing policies and demand-side subsidies	129
7.6	Participatory relocation in Samambaia, Brazil	132
7.7	Social Inclusion in Santo André, Brazil	133
7.8	Urban Community Development Fund (UCDF), Thailand	134
7.9	The range of actors dealing with slums	135
7.10	United Nations Housing Rights Programme	138
7.11	Cities Alliance	140
7.12	City Consultation Methodology	141
8.1	Unequal relations in the household	149
8.2	Vulnerable minority groups	151
8.3	Community-based organizations dealing with housing insecurity in the Philippines	151
8.4	Organizing for land and housing, social inclusion and human development, Quezon City, Philippines	152
8.5	Shack/Slum Dwellers International (SDI)	153
8.6	Nairobi Vikundi vya Kujisaidia (NAVIKU: self-help groups, Nairobi, Kenya)	154
8.7	Popular Habitat Programme in San José, Costa Rica (FUPROVI)	157
8.8	Increasing urban focus of NGOs	158
8.9	CARE-Zambia: Project Urban Self-Help (PUSH II)	158
8.10	*The Habitat Agenda* commitment on enablement and participation	160
9.1	Slum upgrading actions	165
9.2	Slum networking: Indore, India	167
9.3	Cities Without Slums action plan: six key actions necessary to meet the goal	168
9.4	Conventional responses to irregularity	169
9.5	Recent responses to irregularity	171

TABLES

1.1	Attributes of selected slums	12
1.2	Indicators and thresholds for defining slums	12
1.3	Total urban and estimated slum population by major region, 2001	14
2.1	Distribution of urban population and growth by city-size category	26
2.2	Population living below US$1 per day at 1993 purchasing power parity (PPP), by region	31
3.1	Changes of distribution of household income in Canada during two downturns: earned income	36
3.2	Per capita GDP by region, 1820 to 1998 (1990 international dollars)	37
4.1	Mortality rates, world, 1998	73
4.2	Health indicators: under the age of five mortality and life expectancy, 1998	74
5.1	Major categories of slum spatial analysis	85
5.2	Summary of opportunities linked to tenure	94
6.1	Urban economic indicators by City Development Index (CDI) quintile, 1998	96
6.2	Estimated number of children in unconditional worst forms of child labour	99
6.3	Broad tenure categories, 1998 (percentages)	107
6.4	Insecure tenure by region (percentages)	109
6.5	Changes in annual rent and household income of renters, 1993 to 1998	110
6.6	Housing affordability by region: house prices and household incomes	111
6.7	Housing adequacy, by region and development level, 1993	112
6.8	Connections to infrastructure (percentage)	113
6.9	Connections to infrastructure: informal settlements (percentage)	114
6.10	Urban waste management by region and development level, 1998 (percentage)	115
7.1	The dos and don'ts of slum upgrading	142
8.1	Seven values and principles underpinning community development	155
8.2	Six types of NGOs	155
8.3	Main categories of urban-sector NGOs	161
8.4	Urban-sector NGOs by region	161
10.1	Issues covered in slum definitions	197
11.1	Component loadings	244
11.2	List of indicators corresponding to *The Habitat Agenda* key areas of commitment	246

LIST OF ACRONYMS AND ABBREVIATIONS

ABO	area-based organization
ADB	Asian Development Bank
AHUR	Australian Housing and Urban Research Institute
AIDS	acquired immune deficiency syndrome
AIMF	International Association of Mayors and Leaders of Wholly or Partially French-speaking Capital Cities and Metropolitan Areas
AIT	Asian Institute of Technology
AMC	Ahmedabad Municipal Corporation
ANC	African National Congress
ANZRSA	Australia and New Zealand Regional Science Association
APHRC	African Population and Health Research Centre
ASDB	Asian Development Bank
ASEAN	Association of Southeast Asian Nations
AU	African Union
AusAID	Austrian Agency for International Development
BANANA	build absolutely nothing anywhere near anyone
BIT	bilateral investment treaty
BMR	Bangkok Metropolitan Region
BMZ	German Ministry for Economic Cooperation and Development
BOOT	build–own–operate–transfer
BOT	build–operate–transfer
CBD	central business district
CBO	community-based organization
CDC	Community Development Committee
CDI	City Development Index
CDS	city development strategy
CARDO	Centre for Architectural Research and Development Overseas (UK)
CIDA	Canadian International Development Agency
CIS	Commonwealth of Independent States
CMC	Calcutta Municipal Corporation
CNRS	Centre National de la Recherche Scientifique (France)
CODATU	Cooperation for the continuing development of urban and suburban transportation
COHRE	Centre on Housing Rights and Evictions (Switzerland)
Comecon	Council for Mutual Economic Assistance
COPE	Community Organization of the Philippines Enterprise
CPF	Central Provident Fund (Singapore)
CPRC	Chronic Poverty Research Centre
CRESEM	Comisión para la Regulación del Uso del Suelo del Estado de México
DAC	Development Assistance Committee (OECD)
DANIDA	Danish International Development Agency
DAWN	Development Alternative for Women in a New Era
DFID	Department for International Development (UK)
DHS	Demographic and Health Survey
DINKY	double income no kids yet
DRC	Democratic Republic of Congo
EBRD	European Bank for Reconstruction and Development
EC	European Commission
EDSA	Epifanio de los Santos avenue (Manila)

EIUS	Environment Improvement in Urban Sector (Kolkata)
EGM	Expert Group Meeting
EU	European Union
FAO	Food and Agriculture Organization of the United Nations
FDI	foreign direct investment
FHOS	First Home Owners Scheme (Australia)
FIABCI	International Real Estate Association
FIG	International Federation of Surveyors
FINEZA	Fideicomiso de Ciudad Nezahualcóyotl (Mexico City)
FINNIDA	Finnish International Development Agency
FMCU	World Federation of United Cities
FUPROVI	Foundation for Housing Promotion (Costa Rica)
GATT	General Agreement on Tariffs and Trade
GCST	Global Campaign for Secure Tenure
GCUG	Global Campaign for Urban Governance
GDI	Gender-Related Development Index
GDP	gross domestic product
GEM	Gender Empowerment Measure
GIS	geographical information systems
GNI	gross national income
GNP	gross national product
GPI	genuine progress indicator
GSS	Global Strategy for Shelter to the Year 2000
GTZ	German Development Agency
GUID	*Global Urban Indicators Database*
GUO	Global Urban Observatory (UN-Habitat)
Habitat II	second United Nations Conference on Human Settlements (Istanbul, 1996)
HDAs	housing development authorities
HDB	Housing Development Board (Singapore)
HDI	Human Development Index
HDR	*Human Development Report*
HIC	high income country
HSD	Human Settlements Development
IADB	Inter-American Development Bank
IDA	International Development Association
IDAs	international development agencies
IDB	Inter-American Development Bank
IDB	International Development Bank
IDP	internally displaced person
IDRC	International Development Research Centre
IEA	International Energy Agency
IFI	international financial institution
IFPRI	International Food Policy Research Institute
ILO	International Labour Organization
IMF	International Monetary Fund
IRF	International Road Federation
IRGLUS	International Research Group on Law and Urban Space
ISD	informal subdivisions of state land (Pakistan)
ISIC	International Standard Industrial Classification
ISSC	International Social Science Council
IULA	International Union of Local Authorities
JMP	Joint Monitoring Programme
LA	Los Angeles
LAC	Latin America and the Caribbean
LDA	land development agency
LDC	least developed country
LDMQ	Law of the Metropolitan District of Quito
LDR	less developed regions
LEARN	Link Environmental and Academic Research Network

LGC	Local Government Code (Manila)
LGU	local government unit (Manila)
LLDC	landlocked developing country
MDA	Millennium Development Agenda
MDG	Millennium Development Goal
MDP	Municipal Development Programme
MDR	more developed regions
MICS	Multiple Indicator Cluster Surveys
MMDA	Metropolitan Manila Development Authority
MOST	Management of Social Transformations (UNESCO)
MPP	Municipality of Phnom Penh
MSEs	micro- and small-scale enterprises
N-AERUS	Network Association of European Researchers on Urbanization in the South
NATO	North Atlantic Treaty Organization
NAVIKU	Nairobi Vikundi vya Kujisaidia (self-help group, Kenya)
NCC	Nairobi City Council
NESDB	National Economic and Social Development Board (Thailand)
NGC	National Government Centre (Philippines)
NGCHC	National Government Centre Housing Committee (Philippines)
NGO	non-governmental organization
NHA	National Housing Authority (Bangkok)
NHDA	National Housing Development Authority (Sri Lanka)
NIC	newly industrialized countries
NIMBY	not in my backyard
NMV	non-motorized vehicle
NORAD	Norwegian Agency for International Development
NSDF	National Slum Dwellers' Federation (India)
NSDP	National Slum Development Programme (Kolkata)
NUREC	Network on Urban Research in the European Union
OBCs	other backward casts
ODA	Overseas Development Agency
OECD	Organisation for Economic Co-operation and Development
OHCHR	Office of the United Nations High Commissioner for Human Rights
OUP	Office of University Partnerships
PANA	Participatory Appraisal and Needs Assessment
PAR	Programa de Arrendamento Residencial (Brazil)
PCA	Principal Components Analysis
PD	Population Division
PHASE	People's Housing Alternative for Social Empowerment (Philippines)
POs	people's organizations
PPPs	public–private partnerships
PPP	purchasing power parity
PPPUE	Public–Private Partnerships for the Urban Environment (UNDP)
PPS	probability proportional to size
PRI	Revolutionary Institutional Party (Mexico City)
PROSPECT	Programme of Support for Poverty Elimination and Community Transformation
PRUSST	Urban Renewal and Local Sustainable Development Programme (Naples)
PUSH	Project Urban Self-Help (Zambia)
RDC	residential development committee (PUSH)
SAP	structural adjustment programme
SAR	Special Administrative Region
SCs	scheduled casts
SDC	Swiss Development Cooperation
SDI	Shack/Slum Dwellers International
SEWA	Self-Employed Women's Association
SFNV	National Housing Financing System (Costa Rica)
SIDA	Swedish International Development Agency
SIDS	small island developing states
SNA	System of National Accounts

SPARC	Society for the Protection of Area Resource Centres (Mumbai)
SSE	small-scale enterprise
STDP	Small Town Development Programme
TFYR	The former Yugoslav Republic
UCDF	Urban Community Development Fund (Thailand)
UCDO	Urban Community Development Office (Thailand)
UDHA	Urban Development and Housing Act (Manila)
UE	Urban and Environmental Credit Program (USAID)
UIS	Institute for Statistics
UK	United Kingdom
UMP	Urban Management Programme
UNCHR	United Nations Commission on Human Rights
UNCHS	United Nations Centre for Human Settlements (Habitat) (*now* UN-Habitat)
UNCTAD	United Nations Conference on Trade and Development
UNDG	United Nations Development Group
UNDP	United Nations Development Programme
UNEP	United Nations Environment Programme
UNECA	United Nations Economic Commission for Africa
UNECE	United Nations Economic Commission for Europe
UNECLAC	United Nations Economic Commission for Latin America and the Caribbean
UNESCAP	United Nations Economic and Social Commission for Asia and the Pacific
UNESCO	United Nations Educational, Scientific and Cultural Organization
UNESCWA	United Nations Economic and Social Commission for Western Asia
UNFPA	United Nations Population Fund
UN-Habitat	United Nations Human Settlements Programme (*formerly* UNCHS (Habitat))
UNHCR	United Nations High Commissioner for Refugees
UNHRP	United Nations Housing Rights Programme
UNICEF	United Nations International Children's Fund
UNIFEM	United Nations Development Fund for Women
UNON	United Nations Office at Nairobi
UNRISD	United Nations Research Institute for Social Development
UNSD	United Nations Statistics Division
UNV	United Nations Volunteers
UPRS	Urban Poverty Reduction Strategy (Phnom Penh)
US	United States
USAID	United States Agency for International Development
UTO	United Towns Organization
UVA	Union of African Towns
WACLAC	World Assembly of Cities and Local Authorities Coordination
WEOG	Western European and Other States Group
WHO	World Health Organization
WMO	World Meteorological Organization
WOCSOC	World Civil Society Conference
WRI	World Resources Institute
WTO	World Trade Organization

KEY FINDINGS AND MESSAGES

Following the adoption of the Millennium Declaration by the United Nations General Assembly in 2000, a Road Map was established identifying the Millennium Development Goals and Targets for combating poverty, hunger, disease, illiteracy, environmental degradation and discrimination against women and for improving the lives of slum dwellers. *The Challenge of Slums: Global Report on Human Settlements 2003* presents the first global assessment of slums. Starting from a newly accepted operational definition of slums, the report first presents global estimates of the number of urban slum dwellers, followed by an examination of the global, regional and local factors underlying the formation of slums, as well as the social, spatial and economic characteristics and dynamics of slums. Finally, it identifies and assesses the main slum policies and approaches that have guided responses to the slum challenge in the last few decades.

From this assessment, the immensity of the challenge posed by slums is clear and daunting. Without serious and concerted action on the part of municipal authorities, national governments, civil society actors and the international community, the numbers of slum dwellers are likely to increase in most developing countries. In pointing the way forward, the report identifies recent promising approaches to slums, including scaling up of participatory slum upgrading programmes that include, within their objectives, urban poverty reduction. In light of this background, the key findings and messages of this issue of the *Global Report on Human Settlements* are presented below.

THE MAIN FINDINGS

In 2001, 924 million people, or 31.6 per cent of the world's urban population, lived in slums. The majority of them were in the developing regions, accounting for 43 per cent of the urban population, in contrast to 6 per cent in more developed regions. Within the developing regions, sub-Saharan Africa had the largest proportion of the urban population resident in slums in 2001 (71.9 per cent) and Oceania had the lowest (24.1 per cent). In between these were South-central Asia (58 per cent), Eastern Asia (36.4 per cent), Western Asia (33.1 per cent), Latin America and the Caribbean (31.9 per cent), Northern Africa (28.2 per cent) and Southeast Asia (28 per cent).

With respect to absolute numbers of slum dwellers, Asia (all of its sub-regions combined) dominated the global picture, having a total of 554 million slum dwellers in 2001 (about 60 per cent of the world's total slum dwellers). Africa had a total of 187 million slum dwellers (about 20 per cent of the world's total), while Latin America and the Caribbean had 128 million slum dwellers (about 14 per cent of the world's total) and Europe and other developed countries had 54 million slum dwellers (about 6 per cent of the world's total).

It is almost certain that slum dwellers increased substantially during the 1990s. It is further projected that in the next 30 years, the global number of slum dwellers will increase to about 2 billion, if no firm and concrete action is taken. The urban population in less developed regions increased by 36 per cent in the last decade. It can be assumed that the number of urban households increased by a similar ratio. It seems very unlikely that slum improvement or formal construction kept pace to any degree with this increase, as very few developing countries had formal residential building programmes of any size, so it is likely that the number of households in informal settlements increased by more than 36 per cent. However, it is clear that trends in different parts of the world varied from this overall pattern.

In Asia, general urban housing standards improved during the decade, and formal building kept pace with urban growth, until the financial crisis of 1997. Even after the crisis, some countries like Thailand continued to improve their urban conditions. In India, economic conditions also improved in some cities such as Bangalore. However, it is generally considered that urban populations grew faster than the capacity of cities to support them, so slums increased, particularly in South Asia.

In some countries of Latin America, there was a wholesale tenure regularization and a large drop in numbers of squatter households, which would reduce the number of slums under most definitions. Also, urbanization reached saturation levels of 80 per cent, so that slum formation slowed. Still, housing deficits remain high and slums are prominent in most cities.

Most cities in sub-Saharan Africa and some in Northern Africa and Western Asia showed considerable housing stress, with rents and prices rising substantially while incomes fell, probably corresponding to higher occupancy rates. In addition, slum areas increased in most cities, and the rate of slum improvement was very slow or negligible in most places. In South Africa, a very large housing programme reduced the numbers in informal settlements significantly.

More than half of the cities on which case studies were prepared for this Global Report indicated that slum formation will continue (Abidjan, Ahmedabad, Beirut, Bogotá, Cairo, Havana, Jakarta, Karachi, Kolkata, Los Angeles, Mexico City, Nairobi, Newark, Rabat-Salé, Rio de Janeiro and São Paulo). A few (Bangkok, Chengdu, Colombo and Naples) reported decreasing slum formation, while the rest reported no or insufficient data on this topic (Durban, Ibadan, Lusaka, Manila, Moscow, Phnom Penh, Quito and Sydney).

There is growing global concern about slums, as manifested in the recent United Nations Millennium Declaration and subsequent identification of new development priorities by the international community. In light of the increasing numbers of urban slum dwellers, governments have recently adopted a specific target on slums, ie Millennium Development Goal 7, Target 11, which aims to significantly improve the lives of at least 100 million slum dwellers by the year 2020. Given the enormous scale of predicted growth in the number of people living in slums (which might rise to about 2 billion in the next 30 years), the Millennium Development target on slums should be considered as the bare minimum that the international community should aim for. Much more will need to be done if 'cities without slums' are to become a reality.

Slums are a physical and spatial manifestation of urban poverty and intra-city inequality. However, slums do not accommodate all of the urban poor, nor are all slum dwellers always poor. Based on the World Bank poverty definitions, it is estimated that half the world – nearly 3 billion people – lives on less than US$2 per day. About 1.2 billion people live in extreme poverty, that is on less than US$1 per day. The proportion of people living in extreme poverty declined from 29 per cent in 1990 to 23 per cent in 1999, mostly due to a large decrease of 140 million people in East Asia during the period 1987 to 1998. However, in absolute terms, global numbers in extreme poverty increased up until 1993, and were back to about 1988 levels in 1998.

Despite well-known difficulties in estimating urban poverty, it is generally presumed that urban poverty levels are less than rural poverty and that the rate of growth of the world's urban population living in poverty is considerably higher than that in rural areas. The absolute number of poor and undernourished in urban areas is increasing, as is the share of urban areas in overall poverty and malnutrition. In general, the locus of poverty is moving to cities, a process now recognized as the 'urbanization of poverty'.

Slums and poverty are closely related and mutually reinforcing, but the relationship is not always direct or simple. On the one hand, slum dwellers are not a homogeneous population, and some people of reasonable incomes live within or on the edges of slum communities. Even though most slum dwellers work in the informal economy, it is not unusual for them to have incomes that exceed the earnings of formal sector employees. On the other hand, in many cities, there are more poor people outside slum areas than within them. Slum areas have the most visible concentrations of poor people and the worst shelter and environmental conditions, but even the most exclusive and expensive areas will have some low-income people. In some cities, slums are so pervasive that rather than designate residential areas for the poor, it is the rich who segregate themselves behind gated enclaves.

The majority of slum dwellers in developing country cities earn their living from informal sector activities located either within or outside slum areas, and many informal sector entrepreneurs whose operations are located within slums have clienteles extending to the rest of the city. Most slum dwellers are in low-paying occupations such as informal jobs in the garment industry, recycling of solid waste, a variety of home-based enterprises and many are domestic servants, security guards, piece rate workers and self-employed hair dressers and furniture makers. The informal sector is the dominant livelihood source in slums. However, information on the occupations and income generating activities of slum dwellers from all over the world emphasizes the diversity of slum populations, who range from university lecturers, students and formal sector employees, to those engaged in marginal activities bordering on illegality, including petty crime. The main problems confronting the informal sector at present are lack of formal recognition, as well as low levels of productivity and incomes.

National approaches to slums, and to informal settlements in particular, have generally shifted from negative policies such as forced eviction, benign neglect and involuntary resettlement, to more positive policies such as self-help and *in situ* upgrading, enabling and rights-based policies. Informal settlements, where most of the urban poor in developing countries live, are increasingly seen by public decision-makers as places of opportunity, as 'slums of hope' rather than 'slums of despair'. While forced evictions and resettlement still occur in some cities, hardly any governments still openly advocate such repressive policies today.

There is abundant evidence of innovative solutions developed by the poor to improve their own living environments, leading to the gradual consolidation of informal settlements. Where appropriate upgrading policies have been put in place, slums have become increasingly socially cohesive, offering opportunities for security of tenure, local economic development and improvement of incomes among the urban poor. However, these success stories have been rather few, in comparison to the magnitude of the slum challenge, and have yet to be systematically documented.

With respect to the issue of crime, which has long been associated with slums and has accounted for much of the negative views of slums by public policy-makers, there is an increasing realization that slum dwellers are not the main source of crime. Instead, slum dwellers are now seen as more exposed to organized crime than non-slum dwellers as a result of the failure of public housing and other policies that have tended to exclude slum dwellers, including in matters of public policing. The result is a growing belief that most slum dwellers are more victims than perpetrators of crime. While some slums (especially traditional inner-city slums) may be more exposed to crime and violence, and may be characterized by transient households and 'counter-culture' social patterns, many are generally not socially dysfunctional.

THE MAIN MESSAGES

In facing the challenge of slums, urban development policies should more vigorously address the issue of livelihoods of slum dwellers and urban poverty in general, thus going beyond traditional approaches that have tended to concentrate on improvement of housing, infrastructure and physical environmental conditions. Slums are, to a large extent, a physical and spatial manifestation of urban poverty, and the fundamental importance of this fact has not always been recognized by past policies aimed at either the physical eradication or the upgrading of slums. Future policies should go beyond the physical dimension of slums by addressing problems underlying urban poverty. Slum policies should seek to support the livelihoods of the urban poor, by enabling urban informal sector activities to flourish, linking low-income housing development to income generation, and ensuring easy access to jobs through pro-poor transport and low-income settlement location policies.

In general, slum policies should be integrated with, or should be seen as part of, broader, people-focused urban poverty reduction policies that address the various dimensions of poverty, including employment and incomes, food, health and education, shelter and access to basic urban infrastructure and services. It should be recognized, however, that improving incomes and jobs for slum dwellers requires robust growth of the national economy, which is itself dependent upon effective and equitable national and international economic policies, including trade.

Up-scaling and replication of slum upgrading is among the most important of the strategies that have received greater emphasis in recent years, though it should be recognized that slum upgrading is only one solution among several others. The failure of past slum upgrading and low-income housing development has, to a large extent, been a result of inadequate allocation of resources, accompanied by ineffective cost-recovery strategies. Future slum upgrading should be based on sustained commitment of resources sufficient to address the existing slum problem in each city and country. Proper attention should also be paid to the maintenance and management of the existing housing stock, both of which require the consistent allocation of adequate resources. Slum upgrading should be scaled up to cover the whole city, and replicated to cover all cities. Up-scaling and replication should therefore become driving principles of slum upgrading, in particular, and of urban low-income housing policies in general. Some countries have made significant strides by consistently allocating modest percentages of their national annual budgets to low income housing development, for example Singapore, China and, more recently, South Africa.

For slum policies to be successful, the kind of apathy and lack of political will that has characterized both national and local levels of government in many developing countries in recent decades needs to be reversed. Recent changes in the global economic milieu have resulted in increased economic volatility, decreasing levels of formal urban employment (especially in developing countries) and growing levels of income inequality both between and within cities. At the same time, economic structural adjustment policies have required, among other conditionalities, the retreat of the state from the urban scene, leading to the collapse of low-income housing programmes. Much more political will is needed at both the national and local levels of government to confront the very large scale of slum problems that many cities face today and will continue to face in the foreseeable future. With respect to urban poverty and slums, greater state involvement is, in fact, necessary now more than ever, especially in developing countries, given increasing levels of urban poverty, decreasing levels of formal employment and growing levels of income inequality and vulnerability of the urban poor.

There is great potential for enhancing the effectiveness of slum policies by fully involving the urban poor and those traditionally responsible for investment in housing development. This requires urban policies to be more inclusive and the public sector to be much more accountable to all citizens. It has long been recognized that the poor play a key role in the improvement of their own living conditions and that their participation in decision-making is not only a right, thus an end in itself, but is also instrumental in achieving greater effectiveness in the implementation of public policies.

Slum policies should seek to involve the poor in the formulation, financing and implementation of slum upgrading programmes and projects, building on the logic of the innovative solutions developed by the poor themselves to improve their living conditions. Such involvement, or participation of the poor, should also extend to the formal recognition of the non-governmental organizations (NGOs) working with the urban poor at both the community and higher levels, and their formal incorporation within the mechanisms of urban governance. Further, slum solutions should build on the experience of all interested parties, that is informal sector landlords, land owners and the investing middle class. This should be done in ways that encourage investment in low-income housing, maximize security of tenure and minimize financial exploitation of the urban poor.

Many poor slum dwellers work in the city, ensuring that the needs of the rich and other higher-income groups are met; the informal economic activities of slums are closely intertwined with the city's formal economy; and informal services located in slums often extend to the whole city in terms clientele. Clearly, the task is how to ensure that slums become an integral, creative and productive part of the city. The broader context, therefore, has to be good, inclusive and equitable urban governance. But inclusive and equitable urban governance requires greater, not less, involvement of the state at both the national and local levels. Particularly needed in this respect are equitable policies for investment in urban infrastructure and services.

It is now recognized that security of tenure is more important for many of the urban poor than home ownership, as slum policies based on ownership and large scale granting of individual land titles have not always worked. A significant proportion of the urban poor may not be able to afford property ownership, or may have household priorities more pressing than home ownership, so that rental housing is the most logical solution for them - a fact not always recognized by public policy-makers. Slum policies have therefore started placing greater emphasis on security of tenure (for both owner-occupied and rental accommodation) and on housing rights for the urban poor, especially their protection from unlawful eviction. There is also increasing focus on the housing and property rights of women. Improving security of tenure and housing rights of slum dwellers lie at the heart of the norms of the Global Campaign for Secure Tenure (GCST), although several international organizations, especially bilateral, still place emphasis on formal access to home ownership and titling. However, it is clear that future policies should incorporate security of tenure and enhance housing rights of the poor, with specific provisions for poor women. For the poorest and most vulnerable groups unable to afford market-based solutions, access to adequate shelter for all can only be realized through targeted subsidies.

To improve urban inclusiveness, urban policies should increasingly aim at creating safer cities. This could be achieved through better housing policies for the urban low-income population (including slum dwellers), effective urban employment generation policies, more effective formal policing and public justice institutions, as well as strong community-based mechanisms for dealing with urban crime. Evidence from some cities, especially in Latin America and the Caribbean, points to the need to confront the underlying causes of urban crime and violence and making slums safer for habitation. During the 1960s and 1970s, the greatest fear among slum dwellers in some Latin American cities, especially those in squatter settlements or *favelas*, was of eviction either by government or private landowners. Today, this has been replaced by fear of violence and crime, including shootings related to drug trafficking. While more globally representative empirical evidence on the linkages between crime and slums is needed, some recent analyses (as indicated earlier) suggest that slum dwellers are not a threat to the larger city, but are themselves victims of urban crime and related violence, often organized from outside slum areas. Slum dwellers are, in fact, more vulnerable to violence and crime by virtue of the exclusion of slums from preventive public programmes and processes, including policing.

To attain the goal of cities without slums, developing country cities should vigorously implement urban planning and management policies designed to prevent the emergence of slums, alongside slum upgrading and within the strategic context of poverty reduction. The problem of urban slums should be viewed within the broader context of the general failure of both welfare oriented and market-based low-income housing policies and strategies in many (though not all) countries. Slums develop because of a combination of rapid rural-to-urban migration, increasing urban poverty and inequality, marginalization of poor neighbourhoods, inability of the urban poor to access affordable land for housing, insufficient investment in new low-income housing and poor maintenance of the existing housing stock.

Upgrading of existing slums should be combined with clear and consistent policies for urban planning and management, as well as for low-income housing development. The latter should include supply of sufficient and affordable serviced land for the gradual development of economically appropriate low-income housing by the poor themselves, thus preventing the emergence of more slums. At the broader national scale, decentralized urbanization strategies should be pursued, where possible, to ensure that rural-to-urban migration is spread more evenly, thus preventing the congestion in primate cities that accounts, in part, for the mushrooming of slums. This is a more acceptable and effective way of managing the problem of rapid rural-to-urban migration than direct migration control measures. However, decentralized urbanization can only work if pursued within the framework of suitable national economic development policies, inclusive of poverty reduction.

Investment in city-wide infrastructure is a pre-condition for successful and affordable slum upgrading, as the lack of it is one strong mechanism by which the urban poor are excluded, and also by which improved slum housing remains unaffordable for them. At the core of efforts to improve the environmental habitability of slums and to enhance economically productive activities is the provision of basic infrastructure, especially water and sanitation, but also including electricity, access roads, footpaths and waste management. Experience has shown the need for significant investment in city-wide trunk infrastructure by the public sector if housing in upgraded slums is to be affordable to the urban poor and if efforts to support the informal enterprises run by poor slum-dwellers are to be successful. Future low-income housing and slum upgrading policies therefore need to pay greater attention to the financing of city-wide infrastructure development.

Experience accumulated over the last few decades suggests that *in-situ* **slum upgrading is more effective than resettlement of slum dwellers and should be the norm in most slum-upgrading projects and programmes.** Forced eviction and demolition of slums, as well as resettlement of slum dwellers create more problems than they solve. Eradication and relocation destroys, unnecessarily, a large stock of housing affordable to the urban poor and the new housing provided has frequently turned out to be unaffordable, with the result that relocated households move back into slum accommodation. Resettlement also frequently destroys the proximity of slum dwellers to their employment sources. Relocation or involuntary resettlement of slum dwellers should, as far as possible, be avoided, except in cases where slums are located on physically hazardous or polluted land, or where densities are so high that new infrastructure (especially water and sanitation) cannot be installed. *In-situ* slum upgrading should therefore be the norm, with justifiable involuntary or voluntary resettlement being the exception. Easy access to livelihood opportunities is one of the main keys to the success of slum upgrading programmes.

URBAN GROWTH AND HOUSING

The *Global Report on Human Settlements 2003* is about slums – the places where poor people struggle to make a living and bring up their families, and the places where about one third of the world's urban population live. This report is, therefore, about poverty and housing and about poor housing policy.

Ever since there have been cities there have been poor quarters but only since the 16th century have there been slums, places that are 'squalid, overcrowded and wretched'. Slums have been the only large-scale solution to providing housing for low-income people. It is the only type of housing that is affordable and accessible to the poor in cities where the competition for land and profits is intense, and the places where they must live if they have little income or no other options.

A few citations from the case studies prepared for this report provide striking highlights on the diversity of slums and the different ways in which they reflect global and local political and economic trends.[1]

From historical times, industrialization in the city of Kolkata has attracted a cheap labour force from the rural hinterland who found accommodation in the low-cost settlements in the slums. Information shows that more than 41 per cent of households have lived in slums for more than 30 years. More than 70 per cent of the households have lived in slums for more than 15 years. About 16 per cent of the population have been living in slums for 6 to 15 years. New entrants in slums, with duration of stay of up to 5 years, constitute only 4 per cent of the sample surveyed.[2]

Who lives in slums? A very rough estimate of the total slum population, compiled from existing data and estimates, reveals that in total there are around 300,000 slum dwellers in the 24 listed slums, that is over 20 per cent of the population of the capital city. Four groups (rural migrants, displaced persons, refugees and foreign workers) constitute the majority of these dwellers, all of them generally living in particularly precarious conditions (eg daily/unstable employment, illegal papers, etc). These do not, however, constitute all those living in poverty in Beirut, neither do they constitute all those living in poor conditions in

this city, since many shacks are spread out all around Beirut and its suburbs, outside slums as well as inside them.[3]

A woman from the neighbourhood (aged 35), born in the central part of Quito, married for 12 years (3 children, aged 11, 9 and 6), has been living at Corazón de Jesús for the last 10 years. Unemployed since she got married, domestic chores consume all her time. As her husband works as a carpenter on building sites, he is away from home for several days or even weeks, and she has to rule the household and manage the family budget. She only studied until the third year of secondary school and has discarded the possibility of finishing her studies. However, she would like to receive some training or assistance to set up a productive business, in order to complement the family income.[4]

About two-thirds of the population of Mexico City live in what might be called a slum: in owner-occupied or rented housing in irregular settlements at various stages of consolidation, in traditional vecindades, *in pauperized public housing projects or in other types of minority dwellings on rooftops or in shacks on forgotten bits of land here and there.*[5]

Slums in Nairobi are homes to urban residents who earn comparatively low incomes and have limited assets. Livelihoods are earned through different forms of economic activities, which include: employment as waiters, barmen and barmaids, drivers, watchmen, shop assistants, casual labourers in factories and construction sites, artisans, small business owners, and other income-generating activities such as herbalists, entertainers and carriers of goods.[6]

Walter Cordoba, 36 years old, from Población La Hondonada, Santiago de Chile, says: 'People identify themselves with the area and commit themselves to the place but they have no aspirations, there is no way to show their children that there could be another way of living. The settlements in the surrounding areas are the worst, they are also poor and that has an impact on our children because they see the world as the settlements are, a world aggressive, with overcrowding, with drugs, all those things.'[7]

The favelas *in São Paulo, unlike in Rio de Janeiro, are a recent phenomenon, less than 50 years old and whose current, sharp, growth dates back to 1980, with their share of the population having jumped from 5.2 per cent to 19.8 per cent since then. Their appearance is associated with peripheral patterns of urbanization for the working class and the impoverishment resulting from the end of uninterrupted economic growth since 1950. About 60 per cent of the population growth was absorbed by São Paulo's* favelas.[8]

Slum areas are also a refuge for women who are fleeing difficult situations created by divorce or marital disputes. This is the case for Jeanne: 'I was married to a young man from my region. After six children, he decided that we would not have any more. I accepted this. Without me knowing, he then started having a relationship with another woman, who became pregnant. I discovered this and we quarreled. I left my children to escape the hatred of my in-laws. I came to Abidjan. As I could no longer return to my parents, I came here to be independent. I do not want to get into a serious relationship with a man. However, I have a boyfriend. Thanks to his help and my small business, I can cover my needs.'[9]

Overcrowding in the slum areas of Ahmedabad leads to high levels of waste, making these areas highly pollution prone. In addition, absence of an adequate sanitation network causes sewage to accumulate in open areas. The condition becomes precarious during the monsoons. More than 30 per cent of the population does not have access to underground sewers for waste disposal. Often the drinking water facilities are not at a distance from the drainage sites. This, coupled with the location of slums near the city's industrial areas and their polluting units, compounds the health hazards faced by the slum dwellers. The indices of diseases caused by polluted air or water or both rise rapidly in the slum areas. On the whole, the quality of the local environment is very poor and the population is susceptible to water-borne diseases, malaria and other contagious diseases.[10]

These are interesting findings. All slum households in Bangkok have a colour television. The average number of TVs per household is

1.6. There is only one household that has a broken TV with an unclear picture. Almost all of them have a refrigerator. Two-thirds of the households have a CD player, a washing machine and 1.5 cell phones. Half of them have a home telephone, a video player and a motorcycle. However, only one-fourth (27 per cent) own an automobile. Only 15 per cent of them own an air-conditioning unit and a hot water machine in a bathroom. It should be noted that television and refrigerator are considered common necessities for day to day life. Cell phones are very popular in Thailand.[11]

The life conditions of poor people in Bogotá constantly change according to the place in which they live, their work and the people they are in charge of. Depending on the location of their neighbourhood, they could live in high-risk zones exposed to floods and landslides, in places located far from the main roads or in some very insecure places. If they are large families the incomes tend to be more limited and the possibilities to access education are fewer. Some household heads have not had any access to education, which makes it more difficult to find a job and supply the needs of their families, while others have the possibility to get other kinds of jobs in which they will receive a better payment.[12]

It was a shock for Um Ishaq when she first saw her new house in Manshiet Nasser. Although the house has two floors, each with two sleeping rooms, a living room, a kitchen and a toilet on a total floor size of 50m^2, once she steps out of the house, she finds herself surrounded by garbage. All streets adjacent to the house are covered with non-recyclable waste and sacks with plastic, paper, metal and glass waste are piled up the walls of the houses. Goats, chickens and cats search through the garbage for food. The house is located in the Zabaleen area where most of Cairo's garbage collectors live. 'The biggest problem are the mice and the snakes which come with the garbage. You just can't get rid of them', says Um Ishaq, 'but what can we do, we have to live somewhere and we couldn't afford a house somewhere else.'[13]

Women in a slum community in Colombo formed a small group savings and credit programme. The programme has grown well and the women now get loans for their self-income activities. After six months, they networked their group with the other groups in the area and now they have their own Women's Bank. One woman received a loan of Rs.100,000 for building a small house for her family and another Rs.80,000 for buying a three-wheeler for her son to start his own business. Now poor women don't need to go to moneylenders. They have their own bank. [14]

POPULATION EXPLOSION AND URBAN EXPANSION

Rapid urbanization, one of the greatest socio-economic changes during the last five decades or so, has caused the burgeoning of new kinds of slums, the growth of squatter and informal housing all around the rapidly expanding cities of the developing world. Urban populations have increased explosively in the past 50 years, and will continue to do so for at least the next 30 years as the number of people born in cities increase and as people continue to be displaced from rural areas that are almost at capacity. The rate of creation of formal sector urban jobs is well below the expected growth rate of the urban labour force, so in all probability the majority of these new residents will eke out an informal living and will live in slums.

At the time of the first United Nations Conference on Human Settlements in 1976, there were just over 3.5 billion people in the world. Two decades later, when the second United Nations Conference on Human Settlements took place, there were already 6 billion people worldwide. The world's urban population had doubled in only two decades. The developing world has been predominantly rural but is quickly becoming urban. In 1950 only 18 per cent of people in developing countries lived in cities. In 2000 the proportion was 40 per cent, and by 2030 the developing world is predicted to be 56 per cent urban. Future urban growth in developing countries will be absorbed by urban centres, which have a high average annual urban population growth rate of 2.3 per cent, in contrast to the developed world's rate of 0.4 per cent.

The *Global Report on Human Settlements 1996, An Urbanizing World*, highlighted that while there is no evidence that a threshold population size exists beyond which cities generate more negative than positive effects for their countries, in many cities the rapid pace of population growth and enormous size of the population have overwhelmed the capacity of municipal authorities to respond.[15] Millions of people in the developing country cities cannot meet their basic needs for shelter, water, food, health and education

The 'new urban revolution' – explosive growth of cities in developing countries – presents a serious challenge for national and local authorities. How can the capacity of governments be enhanced to stimulate the investment required to generate jobs and to provide the services, infrastructure and social supports necessary to sustain liveable and stable environments? Developing countries will also face intensified environmental problems due to urbanization. How can living conditions be improved for the millions of people densely packed into cities without destroying the natural resource base on which improved living standards depend? Meeting the challenges posed by rapid urbanization could be as important for the future as addressing rapid population growth itself has been over the last 50 years.

ACCOMMODATING GROWTH

The incomes of slum dwellers are mostly too low for formally regulated markets to provide them with any kind of permanent housing. They have acted to solve their own problems by building their own dwellings, or by building informal rental accommodation for each other. Rather than being assisted in their efforts by governments, they have been hounded and their homes frequently demolished, they have been overlooked when basic services are provided, and they have been ignored and excluded from normal opportunities offered to other urban citizens.

It is a mistake to think that slums are an unnecessary or extraneous part of the city, that slums are just for poor people or that they are all the same. In the developing world, slums are in fact the dwelling places of much of the labour force in their cities, they provide a number of important services and are interesting communities in their own right. They are melting pots for different racial groups and cultures. Many of the most important movements in music, dance and politics have had their origins in slums. Many people who are not so poor also live in slums.

For the most part, however, people in slums are among the most disadvantaged. Slums are distinguished by the poor quality of housing, the poverty of the inhabitants, the lack of public and private services and the poor integration of the inhabitants into the broader community and its opportunities. Slum dwellers rate far lower on human development indicators than other urban residents, they have more health problems, less access to education, social services and employment, and most have very low incomes.

Slums are a staging ground for people moving to the city or for people who are temporarily in trouble, a place where they can live cheaply until they establish themselves. The long-term aim of most slum dwellers is to make some money and find a better place to live. Many succeed, many others do not. Particularly for the increasing number of those without stable employment, who live a hand-to-mouth existence in the rapidly growing informal sector, life is hard and always uncertain. Social exclusion, lack of empowerment, illness or living in a precarious and illegal situation make it very difficult for slum dwellers to do more than survive, sometimes in reasonable, if insecure, conditions, but just as often in poverty and despair.

The drab vistas of slums that occupy many large cities of the developing world, and the amorphous, polycentric patchworks of commercial concrete buildings and informal markets is far from the dream of modernist urban planners who sought to design 'garden cities' of harmony and light, or who speculated about ultra-high-rise futuristic cybercities. In many cities around the world, there is growing wealth for some but also abject poverty for many others; gated communities whose residents have access to all the amenities and conveniences that make life comfortable and pleasant are now a common feature but there are also sprawling slums that fail to meet even people's most basic needs, that are used as dumping grounds for hazardous wastes and other socially undesirable externalities, and where lack of access to safe water and adequate sanitation pose serious health risks and create life-threatening conditions.

The main problem is that very few countries, cities or agencies have recognized this critical situation, and outside of a few rapidly advancing countries, very little development effort is going into providing jobs for the rapidly expanding urban population, or planning for land, housing and services that 2 billion new urban residents will need. Slum dwellers lack access to water supply, sanitation, storm water drainage, solid waste disposal and many essential services. However, there is very little forward planning to address even the current problems, let alone the expected future doubling of demand.

Some of the national development policies currently in favour have actually acted to reduce employment and increase inequality. They have made the conditions in cities of the developing world worse and must take some responsibility for the dramatic expansion of slums over the last 30 years. Formal sector employment opportunities are not expected to expand greatly under these policies, and the majority of new residents are expected to work in the informal sector and live in slums, in the absence of any concerted intervention.

Poor or biased policies with regard to land are also an enormous obstacle in the path of the poor in their search of a place to live, as in many developing countries the legal and regulatory frameworks, particularly with regard to land markets and land acquisition, including land registry, land valuation, and legal instruments to facilitate land acquisition, are ineffective. Furthermore, the poor often do not have access to the financial resources needed to buy houses, as the existing housing finance system are not accessible to them and subsidies for housing are not properly targeted. Without significant improvements in the legal, regulatory, and financial systems, the problem of current slums is only a glimpse of an even worse future.

In general, slums are the products of failed policies, bad governance, corruption, inappropriate regulation, dysfunctional land markets, unresponsive financial systems and a fundamental lack of political will. Upgrading of existing slum and squatter settlements addresses the backlog of urban neglect but many cities, especially in Africa and Asia, will face an onslaught of new urban residents over the next several decades, many of whom will be poor.

Increasingly, however, coalitions are being formed between international agencies, cities and action groups which wish to improve the situation, and they are acting in a concerted way and with the benefit of knowledge of past successes and failures to deal with the challenge of slums. Holistic approaches to the life situation of slum dwellers are being developed as part of city strategies and with the direct participation of the slum dwellers themselves. These responses are considerably more sophisticated than the simple engineering solutions or slum clearances of the past, which often created more problems than they solved. They take into account income generation, social services, location, environmental, economic and political sustainability, governance and community cohesion, as well as the straightforward physical upgrading of the slum itself. Replicating these efforts on a large and continuing scale is the challenge which action groups and international agencies now face.

THE FOCUS OF THIS REPORT

Over the course of the next two decades, the global urban population will double, from 2.5 billion to 5 billion. Almost all of this increase will be in developing countries. Understanding and managing dynamics of urbanization and addressing issues of secure land tenure are also critical elements in any comprehensive poverty reduction policy... The World Bank and Habitat are building a global alliance of cities and their development programme includes the Cities Without Slums action plan, whose patron is President Nelson Mandela. The aim of the programme is to improve the living conditions of 100 million slum dwellers in the developing countries by 2020.[16]

This report is the fourth issue of the Global Report series, the established goal of which is to provide a complete review of the condition of human settlements, including an analysis of major forces and trends accounting for their development, maintenance and improvement. The specific objectives of the series are to:

- provide a basic source of information on global and regional conditions of human settlements and trends that would be of value to individual countries and international agencies in shaping their policies and programmes;
- encourage and maintain a general interest in, and contribute to, the understanding of the evolving nature of human settlements, the interrelationship of their parts and the significance of settlement systems in providing settings for human, social, economic and environmental development;
- provide a periodic updating and synthesis of all information that may be relevant to the above objectives.

The current Global Report is a response to the historical decision of the Millennium Assembly to address the problem of slums. The purpose of the issue is several-fold. To begin with, it is the first attempt ever to document the extent and the diversity of slums worldwide. Although a comprehensive assessment must await completion of continuing work on the estimation of numbers of slum dwellers, this report provides useful indications in this regard. Secondly, this report examines the aetiology of slums. It explores the underlying dynamics that give rise to the formation and expansion of slums in different parts of the world. Thirdly, the report reviews the various approaches that have been adopted in the past concerning the challenges posed by slums as well as the approaches that are currently being pursued. Finally, the report aims to draw lessons from the experiences in dealing with slum problems. It seeks to learn about policies and programmes that have worked and how they might be adapted to address similar challenges elsewhere. The review and analyses presented in this report focus in particular on innovative approaches and make the case for their positive potential, while also stressing their limitations and cautioning against seeing them as a panacea for all problems faced by slum dwellers.

Broadly speaking, this Global Report focuses on urban poverty and slums. Within this wider context, there is a more specific concern with the role of different actors in developing solutions for the pressing problems of inadequate access to housing and basic services. A conclusion of the 2001 Global Report, *Cities in a Globalizing World*, concerned the emergence of broad-based partnerships that involve not only the public and private sectors, but also civil society groups.[17] The current report shows that in this regard the participation of people living in poverty and their representative organizations as empowered and equal partners is crucial for effective problem solving. Evidence presented in the chapters that follow demonstrates how such broad-based partnerships work in innovative and supplemental ways, freeing up productive potential and helping mobilize necessary resources. In short, the aims of this report are to:

- assess slums, globally, in terms of their extent and form;
- determine the forces underlying the emergence and shaping the development of slums;
- assess the social, spatial and economic characteristics and functions of slums;
- identify and assess policy responses to slums, including those of the public sector, international organizations and civil society; and
- explore future policy directions aimed at realization of the goal of the Cities Without Slums action plan.[18]

Part I of the report establishes why slums are important in the global agenda, and the global changes that have been occurring in demographics, poverty, inequality, trade policy and informal networks, all in the context of liberalization and globalization. It looks at international agreements and coalitions seeking to improve the situation of slum dwellers, and at possible definitions and means of enumerating them. It also considers the processes of formation of slums and the external and internal forces that lead to the segregation and deterioration of particular areas. These include market forces within cities, inappropriate government interventions and

regulations, global economic changes and changes in the orientation of policy that have led to greater inequality and have inadvertently expanded the urban informal sector while failing to deliver affordable and secure housing, as well as urban services.

Part II is concerned with slums, their form, their role in the city and their living conditions. The impacts of slums on ill health and the life chances of slum citizens, the danger to slum dwellers from criminal activities and the lack of basic urban services in different parts of the world are discussed. The different types of slums are described, drawing from the city case studies commissioned for the report. The discussion shows the great variety in form, location and legal status that may occur, the means that people use to try to establish their legality, and different interventions including the gradual upgrading of better-situated informal settlements. Changes in the global labour force are examined, including the rapid fall-off in agricultural employment in all regions. The informal sector is described, particularly its roles in providing employment for many slum dwellers. The effects of illegality and insecure tenure on slum dwellers are also considered, along with an assessment of the extent of housing inadequacy. Finally, the role of governance and urban management in improving the situation of slum dwellers is described, particularly the lack of any real policy to deal with the problems of current and future slums in many cities.

Part III examines the various attempts to deal with the problems of slums, and critically reviews the changing priorities and assumptions of the various stakeholders responsible for improving the situation, and the problems they have faced in practice. Both public-sector and market-based attempts to improve the situation in developed and developing countries are considered, along with their successes and failures over many decades of experience. These policies have ranged from neglect or eviction, through to slum upgrading, public housing and aided self-help. Several recent large-scale interventions through direct subsidy are considered, alongside the now standard international response of slum upgrading accompanied by inclusive strategies of partnership and participation and a much greater concern for environmental and social sustainability. The role of non-governmental organizations (NGOs) and community-based organizations (CBOs), which have been essential in facilitating and managing the self-help process, is also considered. Finally, broader policies, including attempts to improve the lives of slum dwellers through better governance, income generation, transport policy, access to finance and overall 'inclusive city' approaches are discussed.

If there is a single conclusion from such a complex web of concerns and responses, it is that cities and countries that have admitted what the problems of slums are and that have come to a social consensus about how to solve them with a clear vision and consistent strategy have generally found that the problems *can* be solved and will partly solve themselves through the efforts of everyone involved in meeting that vision.

NOTES

1   Specifically for the purposes of this report, 37 case studies were commissioned. The full text of 34 of these studies is available electronically from UN-Habitat and a short summary of 29 of the case studies is contained in Part IV of this report. The authors of the case studies are listed in the Acknowledgements.

2   Case study – Kolkata, 2002.

3   Case study – Beirut, 2002.

4   Case study – Quito, 2002.

5   Case study – Mexico City, 2002.

6   Case study – Nairobi, 2002.

7   Case study – Santiago de Chile, 2002.

8   Case study – São Paulo, 2002.

9   Case study – Abidjan, 2002.

10 Case study – Ahmedabad, 2002.

11 Case study – Bangkok, 2002.

12 Case study – Bogotá, 2002.

13 Case study – Cairo, 2002.

14 Case study – Colombo, 2002.

15 UNCHS (Habitat), 1996a.

16 Kofi A Annan, Secretary-General of the United Nations (2000) *Common Destiny, New Resolve. Annual Report on the Work of the Organization*. United Nations, New York.

17 UNCHS (Habitat), 2001a.

18 For details of Cities Without Slums, see Cities Alliance, 1999. See also Boxes 7.11 and 9.3 in this report.

PART I

SHARPENING THE GLOBAL DEVELOPMENT AGENDA

The major concern of this report is the growing challenge of slums, in the context of unprecedented urban growth and increasing poverty and inequality. During the next 30 years, urban growth will bring a further 2 billion people into the cities of the developing world, doubling their size. This is largely because the world's rural population has essentially reached its peak, so that almost all further population growth will be absorbed by urban settlements. The main problem is that very few countries, cities or agencies have recognized this critical situation, and outside of a few rapidly advancing countries, very little development effort is going into providing jobs for these people, or planning for land, housing and services that these 2 billion people will need.

This first part of the *Global Report on Human Settlements 2003* highlights the importance of the global agenda as a framework for human development, including improvement of the lives of slum dwellers. Definitions and means of enumerating slum dwellers are discussed in this part. It also considers the processes of formation of slums and the external and internal forces that lead to the segregation and deterioration of particular areas, especially market forces within cities, inappropriate government interventions and regulations, global economic changes and changes in the orientation of policy that have led to greater inequality and have inadvertently expanded the urban informal sector, while failing to deliver affordable, secure housing and urban services.

Chapter 1 begins by briefly covering the major issues – the urbanization crisis, the growth of urban poverty, failures of governance, including institutional and legal failure, and the way in which these conspire to exacerbate the situation of poor people. The Millennium Goals, the principal outcome of a series of major United Nations conferences of the 1990s, have included goals on slum improvement, and on water and sanitation supply.

The goal to improve significantly the lives of at least 100 million slum dwellers by 2020 has prompted a close examination of the possible definitions of slums, from a historical and cultural perspective, and to develop means of measuring numbers of slum dwellers. The conclusion is that slums are a multidimensional concept involving aspects of poor housing, overcrowding, lack of services and insecure tenure, and that indicators relating to these can be combined in different ways to give thresholds that provide estimates of numbers of slum dwellers.

A recent estimate using a slum definition of this type is that about 924 million people lived in slums worldwide in 2001, or about 32 per cent of the global urban population. Slums are seen in practically all parts of the world but with higher concentration in the developing world cities – about 50 per cent of slum dwellers were in South-central and Eastern Asia combined, and 14 per cent in Latin America and 17 per cent in sub-Saharan Africa. The proportion in Africa is rising rapidly as populations increase and urban housing shortages continue, while it is falling in Latin America due to regularization and slum improvement. In Asia, where economic conditions improved overall during the 1990s, the proportion of slum dwellers appears to have fallen, although the absolute number has increased.

Chapter 2 is concerned with the forces shaping slums – brought about by global socio-economic trends and by internal forces within the city, generated by markets and governing institutions.

Theories of residential differentiation began with the Chicago School of the 1930s, which saw city growth as a colonization of different 'quarters' by different income and ethnic groups. Their successors, the neo-liberal urban economists, regarded slums as the natural response of the market in providing housing for poor people: the housing that they can afford. Poor people needed to live at high densities in poor quality dwellings in order to afford housing accessible to income earning opportunities. A number of other reasons have also been suggested as to why poor people are segregated in space: regulation; public spending; and separation of work places for the rich and poor.

Post-modern theories of urban spaces are seen to be more appropriate to the multi-centred and fragmented cities of the 21st century. Many cities are now divided by different occupation groups: the very rich; the affluent professionals, the suburban middle class; the unskilled workers; the informal workers; and the residual or marginalized 'underclass'. Each has a clear part of the city to themselves, supported by housing and distribution networks, but overlaying each other rather than necessarily confined to clear 'quarters'. Methods of designating slum areas and measuring spatial disadvantage using factorial ecology indices, geographical information systems and other techniques can distinguish these groups in space.

The major challenges facing cities are urbanization and poverty. The world is entering a significant stage in a history of urbanization. During the next 30 years, the urban population in the developing world will double to about 4 billion people, at the rate of about 70 million people per year. Rural populations will barely increase and will begin to decline after 2020. Several regions – Europe and the Americas – are already 80 per cent urbanized. Rural–urban migration has slowed but is still very significant, while international migration accounts for many of the most marginalized people in cities and is a major risk factor for slum formation. Oddly enough, depopulation of certain

areas, particularly in Europe, is starting to be an important issue and may contribute to slum development in the future.

Poverty and slums are closely related and mutually reinforcing. As poverty reduction is now the major objective of development agencies, they have conducted considerable work in defining and measuring poverty. Poverty, like slums, is a multifaceted concept; but some simple income proxies have come into general use. Some 1.2 billion people globally live below the World Bank US$1-a-day extreme poverty line and about half the world's population lives below US$2 a day. Poverty increased very rapidly from 1975 to 1993, but since then the numbers have barely increased. This disguises considerable regional variation: the biggest changes in poverty during the 1990s were in the transitional countries following liberalization, where extreme poverty increased from 14 million to 168 million – countered by an equivalent fall in poverty in China and Southeast Asia. Global urban poverty estimates are not currently available, and it is very difficult to survive in cities on less than a dollar a day; but there is evidence that about one third of slum dwellers in South Asia and Africa live in extreme poverty.

Chapter 3 updates the subject of the previous issue of the Global Report series, *Cities in a Globalizing World*, but from the particular perspective of inequality and poverty, and their impacts on slum formation. Much of the economic and political environment in which globalization has accelerated over the last 20 years has been instituted under the guiding hand of a major change in economic paradigm – neo-liberalism, which is associated with the retreat of the national state, liberalization of trade, markets and financial systems and privatization of urban services. Globally, these neo-liberal policies have re-established a rather similar international regime to that which existed in the mercantilist period of the 19th century when economic booms and busts followed each other with monotonous regularity, when slums were at their worst in Western cities and colonialism held global sway.

This chapter also presents a brief history of inequality over the last two centuries. Since 1800, the ratio of gross domestic product (GDP) per person between the richest and the poorest countries has expanded from 3:1 to almost 100:1. Inequality within societies has also continued to increase, except for the period of 1945 to 1978, when governments intervened to redistribute income and maintain full employment and minimum wages. In the period of 1978 to 1993, inequality between countries and within those countries that adopted liberalization regimes increased very rapidly. The contrast between the rich and poor in these countries has become stark, especially in less developed countries where being in the lowest income groups is associated with starvation and misery.

The rise of neo-liberalism is associated with the growth of international trade, the privatization of goods and services, the reduction of public welfare expenditure and the reform of regulation. Each of these has substantial

impacts on the urban poor – in most cases, very negative impacts. Within countries, neo-liberalism has found its major expression through Structural Adjustment Programmes (SAPs), which have weakened the economic role of cities throughout most of the developing world and have placed emphasis on agricultural exports, working against the primary demographic direction where all new workers are locating in towns and cities. In most countries, these policies have not resulted in the promised economic growth and have led to a crippling burden of debt. These global and national policies, as much as anything else, have led to the rapid expansion of the informal sector in cities, in the face of shrinking formal urban employment opportunities.

The final part of Chapter 3 discusses the phenomenon of 'bottom-up' globalization, or the spread in scope of informal networks through cheaper travel and greater ease of communication. These international connections provide opportunities to carve out a broader spectrum of 'hybrid practices' in economic, social and cultural spheres; but they are rather threatening to local communities and their social cohesiveness. Some networks allow cities or groups with a 'commonality of interest' to associate; others are a series of informal business transactions that can span continents and are often mediated through the core economies. These are small in scale compared with the massive structures of formal international transactions; but they do provide a necessary 'informal infrastructure' that later may manifest itself as more substantial linkages.

Major highlights of the first part of the report are:

- The world is rapidly moving towards 'maximum urbanization', which has already largely been completed in Europe and North and South America. Mostly, the population growth will be absorbed by the cities of the developing world, which will double in size by 2030. Three-quarters of the growth will be in cities with populations of 1 to 5 million or in smaller cities under 500,000 people. There is little or no planning to accommodate these people or provide them with services.
- In response to this and other challenges to sustainability, the Millennium Declaration of the United Nations has established targets for 'improving the lives of at least 100 million slum dwellers by 2020' by reducing poverty and improving water and sanitation. These objectives require global and regional estimations of existing conditions and trends, through an associated set of indicators, and a close examination of what is really happening to disadvantaged people in the world's cities.
- People often have clear perceptions as to which areas are slums; but slums can only be rigorously defined through combining different dimensions of housing, urban services, overcrowding and tenure insecurity. A recent estimate of numbers of slum dwellers

indicates that, globally, 32 per cent of urban residents live in slums (compared with about 20 per cent in informal settlements, which are the most visible slums). The incidence of slums in African cities and many smaller cities in other parts of the developing world is over 50 per cent.
- Asia has about 60 per cent of the world's slum dwellers. Africa has about 20 per cent, but this is growing quickly. Latin America has 14 per cent.
- Slums arise from poor people's need to find affordable and accessible housing. They are created by the market or by the people themselves when increasing numbers of people in poverty meet inadequate housing and planning responses. Slum conditions are worsened by economic decline, increasing inequality, loss of formal-sector jobs, rapid immigration, poor governance and exclusionary actions.
- Inequality contributes not just to poverty, but makes it more difficult for subsequent economic growth to have an effect on poverty. Regular booms and busts have contributed in the past not just to 'ratcheting' inequality upwards, but they have been directly associated with slum formation and dilapidation in cities exposed to global trade. It seems probable that this will, once again, begin to happen in a globalized, deregulated world.
- The largest improvements in urban conditions and poverty alleviation over the last 20 years have been in China and East Asia. During the 1990s, these were almost exactly countered by a major decline in the living conditions of people in the former socialist countries of Europe and Central Asia, following rapid liberalization. Real incomes in many African countries are still below the levels of the mid 1970s, as, indeed, they are for the bottom third of households in the US and a number of other countries exposed to liberalization during the period.
- World trade has grown rapidly during the 1980s and 1990s, but is still dominated by a small group of countries. Contrary to popular belief, the West has not lost its manufacturing share; rather, it is the less developed countries who have lost their share of manufacturing employment and trade to a small group of countries in Asia.
- The powers and functions of national governments in the developing world have been considerably weakened through subsidiarity and other liberalization prescriptions. This potentially has benefits in local accountability and the mobilization of local resourcefulness, but has dangers in that a system of government is imposed from outside as part of a global hegemony of uniform ideas and cultures.
- Informal networks of various kinds have become widespread in space and within 'commonalities of interest' as globalization has reduced transaction

costs and governments have withdrawn from action and regulation. In the short term, these networks are meagre compared with the large-scale transactions of the formal international economy; but they may form the basis of future activity.

- A case can be made that the primary direction of both national and international interventions from 1975 has actually increased urban poverty and slums, increased exclusion and inequality, and weakened urban elites in their efforts to use cities as engines of growth. This has been partially counterbalanced by the recognition of self-help and the informal sector as a legitimate strategy, and a slow reduction in the persecution of the urban poor in their attempts to create a better life and environment.

1

DEVELOPMENT CONTEXT AND THE MILLENNIUM AGENDA[1]

The 20th century was a time of great change, and the greatest of those changes was in the numbers of people on the globe and where they lived. Since 1950, mankind has endured its most rapid expansion, from 2.5 billion to 6 billion people. Sixty per cent of this gain has been in urban areas, particularly in the urban areas of the developing world, where the urban population has increased more than sixfold in only 50 years. Humanity is only about half way through this great transformation to urban living. During the next 30 years, the global urban population will increase by more than 2 billion while rural populations will be almost static.[2] The greatest impact will be felt in the developing world, and nowhere more so than throughout South and South-eastern Asia and sub-Saharan Africa. During the next 15 years, many large cities in Asia and Africa will nearly double their population.

The huge increase in urban populations amounts to a crisis of unprecedented magnitude in urban shelter provision. Every year, the world's urban population is increasing by about 70 million, equivalent to seven new megacities. These people all need to be provided with shelter, with employment and with urban services. The stretched capacity of most urban economies in developing countries is unable to meet more than a fraction of these needs, so that the informal sector is providing most of the new employment and housing in environments that have come to be known as informal settlements or slums, where more than half of the population in many cities and towns of developing countries are currently living and working.

CITIES WITHOUT SLUMS?

It has been estimated that one third of the world's urban population today do not have access to adequate housing, and lack access to safe water and sanitation. These people live in overcrowded and unserviced slums, often situated on marginal and dangerous land. They lack access to clean water, for which they will pay a premium. Their waste not only remains untreated, it surrounds them and their daily activities and affects their health, especially their children's.

This situation is not new. Since humanity first began to live in cities, the problems of inadequately serviced and overcrowded urban housing in which the poorer members of urban society live have been recognized as undesirable aspects of urban living. The more developed parts of the world have already undergone their primary urbanization, albeit at a smaller scale and at a considerably slower pace.

The crisis that these changes engendered in society in Europe and elsewhere from the 17th to the 19th centuries has been documented in a huge literature describing slum conditions possibly worse and more degrading than those currently prevailing in the developing world, accompanied by more profound political and social unrest.

Although modern technology, improvements in social attitudes and in organization, and the existence of a large pool of wealth in the developed countries should make it possible to weather the remainder of this global challenge under better conditions than prevailed in the first phases of urbanization, this is, in fact, not happening. The situation is being exacerbated by two factors – an almost complete lack of planning or preparation for urban growth in most parts of the world, and a rapid increase in both inequality and poverty, which is compounded by policies intended to improve growth, but which have mostly not done so because they have tried to fight the key urbanization dynamic rather than work with it.

As this report will show, it has been possible for a very few countries to urbanize without the wholesale expansion of slums and informal employment that is the norm. While this has tended to occur in political situations that are not replicable, they do show that it is possible, and that directed policy and planning can substantially improve the situation, particularly where it is applied consistently over an extended period. What is happening in most cases is the reverse: piecemeal, undirected or impractical policies that cannot be implemented or which, in practice, benefit only those in power.

The failure of governance

An important message of this report is that slums and urban poverty are not just a manifestation of a population explosion and demographic change, or even of the vast impersonal forces of globalization. Slums must be seen as the result of a failure of housing policies, laws and delivery systems, as well as of national and urban policies.

The most important factor that limits progress in improving housing and living conditions of low-income groups in informal settlements and slums is the lack of genuine political will to address the issue in a fundamentally structured, sustainable and large-scale manner. There is no doubt that the political will to achieve long lasting and structured interventions constitutes the key to success, particularly when accompanied by local ownership and leadership, and the mobilization of the potential and capacity

During the next 30 years, the urban population will increase by more than 2 billion. The greatest impact will be felt in the developing world

Since humanity first began to live in cities, the problems of inadequately serviced and overcrowded urban housing have been recognized as undesirable aspects of urban living

Slums must be seen as the result of a failure of housing policies, laws and delivery systems, as well as of national and urban policies

The nuts and bolts
of urban governance
have become a
central issue of
development

of all the stakeholders, particularly the people themselves. Lessons from several countries underscore the importance and the fundamental role of sustained political will and commitment in improving or reducing slums.

The failure of policy is at all levels – global, national and local. At the global level, policies that have weakened national governments without any countervailing central control appear to be leading to an unrestrained globalization that is accommodating greater inequality and marginalization. At the national level, liberalization and the sectoral fragmentation of policy and analytical and institutional frameworks have failed to support the urban–rural and cross-sectoral dynamics that are critical both to sustainable economic growth and the distribution of its opportunities. At the local level, a startling lack of capacity to cope with, or manage, the situation has left many slum citizens in a no-man's land of illegality, insecurity and environmental degradation.

The *Global Report on Human Settlements 2001* was concerned largely with globalization and its effect on urban settlements. Much of the economic and political environment in which globalization has accelerated over the last 20 years has been instituted under the guiding hand of a major change in economic paradigm – that is, neo-liberalism. Globally, these policies have re-established a rather similar international regime to that which existed in the mercantilist period of the 19th century when economic booms and busts followed each other with monotonous regularity, when slums were at their worst in Western cities, and colonialism held global sway. Nationally, neo-liberalism has found its major expression through Structural Adjustment Programmes (SAPs), which have tended to weaken the economic role of cities throughout most of the developing world and placed emphasis on agricultural exports, thus working against the primary demographic direction moving all of the new workers to towns and cities. These policies, as much as anything else, have led to the rapid expansion of the informal sector in cities, in the face of shrinking formal urban employment opportunities.

It has been
estimated that one
third of the world's
urban population
today do not have
access to adequate
housing

A case can be made that the primary direction of both national and international interventions during the last 20 years has actually increased urban poverty and slums, increased exclusion and inequality, and weakened urban elites in their efforts to use cities as engines of growth. This has been partially counterbalanced by the neo-liberal recognition of self-help as an effective strategy, and a slow reduction in the persecution of the urban poor in their attempts to create a better life and environment.

It is a paradox that the greatest global challenges – urbanization and the growth of poverty, including the feminization of urban poverty – are increasingly being managed at the local level. In those parts of the developing world that are already substantially urbanized, cities of all sizes are faced with demands and responsibilities for which they are mostly ill equipped and ill resourced. Policy and legal frameworks, regulatory authority, planning authority, human skills, revenue base, accounting and accountability are as much in demand as raw land. Lip service is paid to decentralization without providing the means to make it

The urban poor are
trapped in an
informal and 'illegal'
world – in slums
that are not
reflected on maps,
where waste is not
collected, where
taxes are not paid
and where public
services are not
provided

work. The nuts and bolts of urban governance have become a central issue of development, though generally lacking support and direction from higher levels of government where the resources actually lie.

Ultimately, the poor suffer most from the lack of governance and political will, as weak urban governance meets the impact of growing inequality, corruption and imbalances in resource allocation. The problem stems from a failure of national and city governments to recognize that their primary reality is one of rapid urbanization; that their primary task is to ensure that jobs, shelter and services are provided to the new generations of urban dwellers who are their national future; or even where the problem is recognized, to act in a concerted and systematic way to ensure that slum living and illegality is not the fate of the vast majority of new urban residents.

Institutional and legal failure

The urban poor are trapped in an informal and 'illegal' world – in slums that are not reflected on maps, where waste is not collected, where taxes are not paid and where public services are not provided. Officially, they do not exist. Although they may reside within the administrative boundary of a town or city, their local authority may well be a slumlord or mafia leader, rather than city council staff, who often no longer attempt to assert their jurisdiction or even enter the slums. As illegal or unrecognized residents, many of these slum dwellers have no property rights, nor security of tenure, but instead make whatever arrangements they can in an informal, unregulated and, in some respects, expensive parallel market.

In the majority of cases, slum dwellers exist outside of the law where they live and work. They are not able to access most of the formal institutions of society, and lacking a legal address they are often unable to access social services such as subsidized health care or education, which are largely used by the more affluent. Governments, in many cases, refuse to provide them with services on the grounds that their settlements are not legal, even though these may have been in place for over 50 years and comprise a majority of the population. Rather than helping them or trying to provide for them, governments actually hound them and restrict them in their attempts to provide the fundamentals of life – shelter and livelihood – and they live in a state of permanent insecurity and illegality.

The institutions that are failing slum dwellers are not just those of government and law, but also the private and commercial systems. Slum dwellers' 'life chances' are low; they are rarely able to obtain formal-sector jobs because of their lack of social capital, including lack of education, lack of patronage and contacts, and a general exclusion from 'regular society' that is mediated by signifiers of social class and a lack of empowerment. Slum dwellers are also not able to access regular sources of finance to develop their own businesses. Banks do not usually have branches in slums, and if they do, the lack of legally registered collateral will exclude all but the most well-off slum dwellers from obtaining loans. Slum entrepreneurs are forced to draw on informal sources of finance at exorbitant rates and very short repayment periods.

The lack of access to finance is at its most critical in housing provision. Conventional housing finance is usually only available to higher-income groups, resulting in the highly segmented housing markets that separate informal and formal housing markets throughout the developing world. Housing is usually available – often with high vacancy rates – at the high-quality, high-cost and high-income segment of the market. Meanwhile, the low end of the market is extremely tight, with low or no vacancy rates and a progressive increase in densities as more people occupy each available room.

The poor-, low- and even middle-income majority of the population in developing countries cannot afford a loan for even the least expensive, commercially built housing units. This is why so much slum housing is built by landlords – but many of these people are often not particularly well off and cannot obtain loans at normal rates for new dwellings in slum neighbourhoods, restricting rental supply. The remaining low- or middle-income owner-occupier households build their own houses progressively over long periods, primarily starting from a makeshift base, as money slowly becomes available to permit them to extend their simple dwellings (presuming that land is available to do so). Their squatter or partly legal housing has been the main target of public harassment.[3]

THE MILLENNIUM DEVELOPMENT AGENDA

In the face of these and other global challenges, world leaders met at the special Millennium Summit of the United Nations in September 2000 to establish a series of goals for humanity in the 21st century, based on the key policy documents from the series of major United Nations conferences held during the previous decade, including *Agenda 21* and *The Habitat Agenda*.[4] The summit's Millennium Declaration also outlined a wide range of commitments in human rights, good governance and democracy. At the General Assembly session following this Millennium Declaration, a Road Map was established with a set of 8 specific global goals (the Millennium Development Goals or MDGs) and 18 targets (MDG targets) for combating poverty, hunger, disease, illiteracy, environmental degradation and discrimination against women (see Box 1.1).[5] These were to be measured through 32 indicators (the MDG indicators).

The MDGs provide a framework for the entire United Nations system to work coherently towards common ends. The United Nations Development Group (UNDG) will help to ensure that the MDGs remain at the centre of those efforts. The United Nations is on the ground in virtually every developing country and is uniquely positioned to advocate for change, to connect countries to knowledge and resources, and to help coordinate broader efforts at the country level.

UN-Habitat has been given responsibility for operationalizing, collecting and measuring some of the MDG targets and indicators, which is a complex task given that the assigned indicators include ones that are possibly the most difficult to define and operationalize, and which are not part of the statistical system used by agencies or national statistical offices.

The most important target from the point of view of this report is Target 11: *By 2020, to have achieved a significant improvement in the lives of at least 100 million slum dwellers*, which builds upon the Cities Alliance's Cities Without Slums initiative.[6,7] The Cities Alliance was launched in 1999 by the World Bank and UN-Habitat, and now has expanded to 18 members, including the leading global associations of local authorities, ten bilateral agencies and four multilateral agencies.[8]

Within the context of several MDGs competing with each other for the attention of policy-makers, and the world's limited financial resources for international development, it is an important political signal from the international development community to have adopted the goal on slums. No matter how top-down and prescriptive global goals may seem, they have proven to have enormous impact both at global and local levels because they provide a mission and unifying objective. Thus, 'measurement of universal indicators' is not just a technical exercise, but also a major political tool, in obtaining consensus and direction.

The MDGs, targets and indicators of importance to this report, together with a brief assessment of progress, include:

Goal 1: Eradicate extreme poverty and hunger

Target 1: Halve, between 1990 and 2015, the proportion of people whose income is less than US$1 a day

Indicator 1: Proportion of population with income below US$1 a day
The proportion of people living in extreme poverty – defined by the World Bank as average per capita consumption of US$1 a day or less – declined from 29 per cent in 1990 to 23 per cent in 1999, although this masks significant regional differences.[9] During the same period, East Asia has seen the proportion of people living on less than US$1 a day drop from 28 per cent to 15 per cent. South Asia, where nearly half of the world's very poor still live, has seen a more modest drop from 44 per cent to 40 per cent, while in Africa the drop has only been from 48 per cent to 47 per cent. Overall, progress is too slow to meet the target.[10]

Goal 7: Ensure environmental sustainability

Target 10: Halve, by 2015, the proportion of people without sustainable access to safe drinking water

Indicator 30: Proportion of population with sustainable access to an improved water source, urban and rural
During the period of 1990 to 2000, the percentage of the world population with access to improved water sources rose from 77 per cent to 82 per cent. Although rural areas have seen the greatest improvements in coverage – from 64 per cent to 71 per cent – compared

The Millennium Declaration outlined a wide range of commitments in human rights, good governance and democracy

A Road Map was established with a set of specific global goals and targets for combating poverty, hunger, disease, illiteracy, environmental degradation and discrimination against women

Box 1.1 Scope of Millennium Development Goals and Targets

Goal 1: Eradicate extreme poverty and hunger
- Reduce by half the proportion of people living on less than US$1 a day.
- Reduce by half the proportion of people who suffer from hunger.

Goal 2: Achieve universal primary education
- Ensure that all boys and girls complete a full course of primary schooling.

Goal 3: Promote gender equality and empower women
- Eliminate gender disparity in primary and secondary education, preferably by 2005, and at all levels by 2015.

Goal 4: Reduce child mortality
- Reduce by two-thirds the mortality rate among children under five years' old.

Goal 5: Improve maternal health
- Reduce by three-quarters the maternal mortality ratio.

Goal 6: Combat HIV/AIDS, malaria and other diseases
- Halt and begin to reverse the spread of HIV/AIDS.
- Halt and begin to reverse the incidence of malaria and other major diseases.

Goal 7: Ensure environmental sustainability
- Integrate the principles of sustainable development within country policies and programmes; reverse loss of environmental resources.
- Reduce by half the proportion of people without sustainable access to safe drinking water.
- Achieve significant improvement in the lives of at least 100 million slum dwellers by 2020.

Goal 8: Develop a global partnership for development
- Develop further an open-trading and financial system that is rule based, predictable and non-discriminatory. This includes a commitment to good governance, development and poverty reduction – nationally and internationally.
- Address the least developed countries' special needs. This includes tariff-free and quota-free access for their exports; enhanced debt relief for heavily indebted poor countries; cancellation of official bilateral debt; and more generous official development assistance for countries committed to poverty reduction.
- Address the special needs of landlocked and small-island developing states.
- Deal comprehensively with developing countries' debt problems through national and international measures to make debt sustainable in the long term.
- In cooperation with the developing countries, develop decent and productive work for youth.
- In cooperation with pharmaceutical companies, provide access to affordable essential drugs in developing countries.
- In cooperation with the private sector, make available the benefits of new technologies – especially information and communications technologies.

The term 'slum' is used in this report to describe a wide range of low-income settlements and/or poor human living conditions

with urban areas – from 94 per cent to 95 per cent – they remain poorly served in terms of access to safe water.[11] The overall progress seen in the period of 1990 to 2000 shows that the target is attainable if the current rate of increase is sustained.[12]

Target 11: By 2020, to have achieved a significant improvement in the lives of at least 100 million slum dwellers

Indicator 31: Proportion of urban population with access to improved sanitation
Over the period of 1990 to 2000, access to improved

sanitation increased from 51 per cent to 61 per cent globally. Despite these gains, in 2000 about 2.4 billion people still lacked access. Sanitation coverage data are not specifically available for urban slum dwellers.[13]

Indicator 32: Proportion of households with secure tenure
Measurement has been held up by lack of an agreed definition for security of tenure. There are many complex forms of housing tenure, and security can mean different things, ranging from the existence of national legal rights to subjective assessments of security, through to actual evictions.[14]

Assessment of the progress towards Target 11 is addressed in more detail later in this chapter.

The world is making progress toward the MDGs – but it is uneven and too slow. A large majority of nations will reach the MDGs only if they get substantial support – advocacy, expertise and resources – from outside. The challenges for the global community, in both the developed and developing world, are to mobilize financial support and political will, re-engage governments, re-orient development priorities and policies, build capacity and reach out to partners in civil society and the private sector.[15]

Political assessment suggests that progress must be made on a much broader front, otherwise the ringing words of the Millennium Declaration will serve only as grim reminders of human needs neglected and promises unmet. It was estimated that meeting the MDGs would cost an additional US$50 billion in annual aid.[16] At the Monterrey Conference on Financing for Development, the US pledged to increase aid spending by 50 per cent, or US$5 billion a year, and the European Union (EU) promised an additional US$7 billion a year. Efforts to achieve the MDGs have been further boosted by additional targets and initiatives launched at the World Summit on Sustainable Development in Johannesburg in September 2002. These include a target to halve the proportion of people without access to basic sanitation, and to match the Millennium Declaration target of halving the proportion of those without access to clean water.

UNDERSTANDING SLUMS[17]

The term 'slum' is used in this report and in the MDGs in a general context to describe a wide range of low-income settlements and/or poor human living conditions. These inadequate housing conditions exemplify the variety of manifestations of poverty as defined in the Programme of Action adopted at the World Summit for Social Development.

'Slum', at its simplest, is 'a heavily populated urban area characterized by substandard housing and squalor'.[18] This definition encapsulates the essential characteristics of slums: high densities and low standards of housing (structure and services), and 'squalor'. The first two criteria are physical and spatial, while the third is social and behavioural. This spread of associations is typical, not just for the definition of slums but also of our perceptions of them. Dwellings in such settlements vary from simple shacks to more permanent structures, and access to basic services and infrastructure tends to be limited or badly deteriorated.

The definition of the term 'slum' includes the traditional meaning – that is, housing areas that were once respectable or even desirable, but which have since deteriorated as the original dwellers have moved to new and better areas of the cities. The condition of the old houses has then declined, and the units have been progressively subdivided and rented out to lower-income groups. Typical examples are the inner-city slums of many towns and cities in both the developed and the developing countries.

Slums have, however, also come to include the vast informal settlements that are quickly becoming the most visible expression of urban poverty in developing world cities, including squatter settlements and illegal subdivisions. The quality of dwellings in such settlements varies from the simplest shack to permanent structures, while access to water, electricity, sanitation and other basic services and infrastructure is usually limited. Such settlements are referred to by a wide range of names and include a variety of tenure arrangements.

Although the term 'slum' is considered an easily understandable catch-all, it disguises the fact that within this and other terms lie a multitude of different settlements and communities. However, slums can be divided into two broad classes:

1   *Slums of hope*: 'progressing' settlements, which are characterized by new, normally self-built structures, usually illegal (eg squatters) that are in, or have recently been through, a process of development, consolidation and improvement; and
2   *Slums of despair*: 'declining' neighbourhoods, in which environmental conditions and domestic services are undergoing a process of degeneration.

Unfortunately, the history of inner-city slum areas in Europe, North America and Australia has shown that, in the absence of appropriate interventions, slums of hope may all too easily yield to despair, a self-reinforcing condition that may be maintained for a very long time. A more detailed typology of slums, including their origins, age and legal status, is given in Chapter 5.

The notion of slums

Since its first appearance during the 1820s as part of the London cant, the term 'slum' was used to identify the poorest quality housing and the most unsanitary conditions; a refuge for marginal activities including crime, 'vice' and drug abuse; and a likely source for many epidemics that ravaged urban areas – a place apart from all that was decent and wholesome.

During the major part of the 19th century, the word appeared in the written language in quotation marks mostly as 'back-slum(s)'. At the end of the 19th century, slum meant 'a street, alley, court, situated in a crowded district of a town or city and inhabited by people of a low class or by the very poor; a number of these streets or courts forming a thickly populated neighbourhood or district where the houses and the conditions of life are of a squalid and wretched character... a foul back street of a city, especially one filled with a poor, dirty, degraded and often vicious population; any low neighbourhood or dark retreat – usually in the plural, as Westminster *slums* are haunts for thieves (*Dickens*).'[19]

The Housing Reform Movement in England during the 1880s changed a popular word that once described an awkward phenomenon to a general operational concept as 'a house materially unfit for human habitation', and made possible the delimitation of 'slum areas' on city maps for planning purposes. It became a common word in the Anglophone world, used, for example, in India in order to designate without distinction the *bustees*, *chawls* or *cheris* of Mumbai, Delhi or Chennai.

The 20th century made the word obsolete in contexts requiring more precise and rigorous terms, such as 'tenement house', 'tenement district' and 'deteriorated neighborhood', because of legislation from the 1890s and 1930s authorizing the eradication of the so-called slums, and imposing technical and legal definitions and standards for such actions. At the same time, the social movement generated new words, such as 'neighbourhoods' or 'communities', to qualify the designated slums in order to 'rename' the socially stigmatized slum areas. As with most euphemisms, alternative terms were eventually subsumed into the argot and served to maintain rather than counteract the negative prejudices against slum dwellers. The polite 'neighbourhood' has become shortened to 'hood', a badge of youthful 'attitude' in Los Angeles.

Today, the catch-all term 'slum' is loose and deprecatory. It has many connotations and meanings and is banned from many of the more sensitive, politically correct and academically rigorous lexicons. It can also vary considerably in what it describes in different parts of the world, or even in different parts of the same city.

In developing countries, the term 'slum', if it is used, mostly lacks the pejorative and divisive original connotation, and simply refers to lower-quality or informal housing. Large, visible tracts of squatter or informal housing have become intimately connected with perceptions of poverty, lack of access to basic services and insecurity. Terms such as slum, shanty, squatter settlement, informal housing and low-income community are used somewhat interchangeably by agencies and authorities. The coverage of settlement types is even more complex when one considers the variety of equivalent words in other languages and geographical regions:

*   French: *bidonvilles, taudis, habitat précaire, habitat spontané, quartiers irréguliers*;
*   Spanish: *asentamientos irregulares, barrio marginal, barraca* (Barcelona), *conventillos* (Quito), *colonias populares* (Mexico), *tugurios* and *solares* (Lima), *bohíos* or *cuarterias* (Cuba), *villa miseria*;

Slums can be divided into two broad categories: slums of hope; and slums of despair

The problem with measuring slums starts with the lack of an agreed definition

- German: *Elendsviertel*;
- Arabic: *mudun safi, lahbach, brarek, medina achouaia, foundouks* and *karyan* (Rabat-Sale), *carton, safeih, ishash, galoos* and *shammasa* (Khartoum), *tanake* (Beirut), *aashwa'i* and *baladi* (Cairo);
- Russian: *trushchobi*;
- Portuguese: *bairros da lata* (Portugal), *quartos do slum, favela, morro, cortiço, comunidade, loteamento* (Brazil);
- Turkish: *gecekondu*;
- American English: 'hood' (Los Angeles), ghetto;
- South Asia: *chawls/chalis* (Ahmedabad, Mumbai), *ahatas* (Kanpur), *katras* (Delhi), *bustee* (Kolkata), *zopadpattis* (Maharashtra), *cheris* (Chennai), *katchi abadis* (Karachi), *watta, pelpath, udukku* or *pelli gewal* (Colombo);
- Africa: *umjondolo* (Zulu, Durban), *mabanda* (Kiswahili, Tanzania).

In Karachi, the local term *katchi abadi* (non-permanent settlements) is used, as well as the English 'informal subdivisions of state land'.[20] Terms such as *villa miseria* are specific to Argentina, *favelas* to Brazil, *kampungs* to Malaysia and Indonesia, and *bidonvilles* to France and Francophone Africa – describing precarious settlements made out of iron sheets and tins (*bidons*).

In Egypt, the term *aashwa'i* is the only one used officially to indicate deteriorated or underserved urban areas.[21] It actually means 'random' on the basis that these areas are unplanned and illegally constructed. The areas are not necessarily slums, although being informal/illegal, they tend to be the least well served in terms of infrastructure and public services, and they suffer from poor accessibility and high levels of overcrowding. Both government officials and the local press ascribe to *aashwa'i* settlements various social problems of crime, drugs and anti-social behaviour.

Some authorities have attempted to address the damaging effect of prejudice against slums. In Peru and other Latin American countries, in an attempt to do away with the pejorative connotations associated with the word *tugurio*, official terminology has tried to popularize terms such as 'young settlements' (*pueblos jovenes*).

Box 1.2 Terms in use in Manila

If Eskimos have many words for snow, some languages have many words for poor accommodation. In Manila the majority of the housing stock would be regarded as of poor quality and inadequately serviced. 'Slum' has no direct equivalent in the local language, and slums are better referred to in descriptive Tagalog words, such as:

- *iskwater* (a physically disorganised collection of shelters made of light and often visually unappealing materials where poor people reside);
- *estero* (narrower than sewers and associated with a bad smell);
- *eskinita* (alleys that fit only one person at a time);
- *looban* (meaning inner areas where houses are built very close to each other and often in a manner not visible to the general view of the city);
- *dagat-dagatan* (areas frequently flooded);
- "*Bedspacer*" (subtenant occupants of bunk bedding rental accommodation, four or six to a small room, usually young women who have come to the city looking for work).

Defining and measuring slums

The problem with measuring slums starts with the lack of an agreed definition. As a result, enumeration of slums has not yet been incorporated within mainstream monitoring instruments, such as national population censuses, demographic and health surveys, and global surveys. Some surveys provide proxies or related variables, such as 'proportion of unauthorized housing' or 'proportion of squatters'. Participatory poverty assessments in many least developed countries (LDCs) generally provide only qualitative information on urban poverty. The generic definition suggests that a slum is:

> ...a contiguous settlement where the inhabitants are characterized as having inadequate housing and basic services. A slum is often not recognized and addressed by the public authorities as an integral or equal part of the city.[22]

Other similar definitions are provided in many policy documents; for example the Cities Alliance Action Plan describes slums as follows:[23]

> Slums are neglected parts of cities where housing and living conditions are appallingly poor. Slums range from high-density, squalid central city tenements to spontaneous squatter settlements without legal recognition or rights, sprawling at the edge of cities. Slums have various names, favelas, kampungs, bidonvilles, tugurios, yet share the same miserable living conditions.

These general definitions meet the common perception of what a slum is; yet, as it stands, they are not associated with operational definitions that would enable one to ascertain whether or not a particular area is a slum.

In practice, what has happened when it has been necessary to operationalize the concept is that areas have been designated specifically as slums, usually by planners making impromptu surveys or following popular usage.[24] This was the case during the Housing Reform in the UK, and subsequently in many other countries.[25] More recently, definitions developed in 1993 in India use housing conditions and availability of facilities as the main basis for defining areas as slums – areas with dense, poorly built or mostly temporary housing, with inadequate sanitary and drinking water facilities.[26]

Clearly, it would be better for a number of purposes to have a more universal and objective definition – particularly when global measurement and MDG targets are involved. Yet, the most important indicators associated with UN-Habitat work – slums, insecure tenure and poverty – are terms that do not have clear or universally agreed definitions.

Efforts to propose a more 'quantitative' definition of slums have only recently been started, not only because of divergent opinions as to what constitutes the key determinants of slums, but because of several features of the concept:

- *Slums are too complex* to define according to one single parameter.
- *Slums are a relative concept* and what is considered as a slum in one city will be regarded as adequate in another city – even in the same country.
- *Local variations* among slums are too wide to define universally applicable criteria.
- *Slums change too fast* to render any criterion valid for a reasonably long period of time.
- *The spatial nature of slums* means that the size of particular slum areas is vulnerable to changes in jurisdiction or spatial aggregation.

What is agreed is that slums, like poverty and secure tenure, are multidimensional in nature. Some of the characteristics of slums, such as access to physical services or density, can be clearly defined, and others, such as social capital, cannot. Even with well-defined indicators, measurement can be very problematic, and acceptable benchmarks are not easy to establish.

Characteristics of slums

A review of the definitions used by national and local governments, statistical offices, institutions involved in slum issues and public perceptions reveals the following attributes of slums.

■ Lack of basic services

Lack of basic services is one of the most frequently mentioned characteristics of slum definitions worldwide. Lack of access to sanitation facilities and safe water sources is the most important feature, sometimes supplemented by absence of waste collection systems, electricity supply, surfaced roads and footpaths, street lighting and rainwater drainage.

■ Substandard housing or illegal and inadequate building structures

Many cities have building standards that set minimum requirements for residential buildings. Slum areas are associated with a high number of substandard housing structures, often built with non-permanent materials unsuitable for housing given local conditions of climate and location. Factors contributing to a structure being considered substandard are, for example, earthen floors, mud-and-wattle walls or straw roofs. Various space and dwelling placement bylaws may also be extensively violated.

■ Overcrowding and high density

Overcrowding is associated with a low space per person, high occupancy rates, cohabitation by different families and a high number of single-room units. Many slum dwelling units are overcrowded, with five and more persons sharing a one-room unit used for cooking, sleeping and living. Bangkok requires at least 15 dwelling units per *rai* (1600 square metres).

■ Unhealthy living conditions and hazardous locations

Unhealthy living conditions are the result of a lack of basic services, with visible, open sewers, lack of pathways, uncontrolled dumping of waste, polluted environments, etc. Houses may be built on hazardous locations or land unsuitable for settlement, such as floodplains, in proximity to industrial plants with toxic emissions or waste disposal sites, and on areas subject to landslip. The layout of the settlement may be hazardous because of a lack of access ways and high densities of dilapidated structures.

■ Insecure tenure; irregular or informal settlements

A number of definitions consider lack of security of tenure as a central characteristic of slums, and regard lack of any formal document entitling the occupant to occupy the land or structure as *prima facie* evidence of illegality and slum occupation. Informal or unplanned settlements are often regarded as synonymous with slums. Many definitions emphasize both informality of occupation and the non-compliance of settlements with land-use plans. The main factors contributing to non-compliance are settlements built on land reserved for non-residential purposes, or which are invasions of non-urban land.

■ Poverty and social exclusion

Income or capability poverty is considered, with some exceptions, as a central characteristic of slum areas. It is not seen as an inherent characteristic of slums, but as a cause (and, to a large extent, a consequence) of slum conditions. Slum conditions are physical and statutory manifestations that create barriers to human and social development. Furthermore, slums are areas of social exclusion that are often perceived to have high levels of crime and other measures of social dislocation. In some definitions, such areas are associated with certain vulnerable groups of population, such as recent immigrants, internally displaced persons or ethnic minorities.

■ Minimum settlement size

Many slum definitions also require some minimum settlement size for an area to be considered a slum, so that the slum constitutes a distinct precinct and is not a single dwelling. Examples are the municipal slum definition of Kolkata that requires a minimum of 700 square metres to be occupied by huts, or the Indian census definition, which requires at least 300 people or 60 households living in a settlement cluster.

Table 1.1 shows how slum areas may vary in their disadvantages, in different parts of the world or even within the same city.

The experience of 'living in a slum', according to slum dwellers, consists of a combination of these multiple dimensions, not only one. Many slum areas may show only a few of these negative attributes, while the worst may have them all. The 'worst type of slum household' is prone to all of the above disadvantages, which, to an extent, also constitute some of the main obstacles that have to be

Slums, like poverty and secure tenure, are multi-dimensional in nature

A review of the definitions used by national and local governments, statistical offices, institutions involved in slum issues and public perceptions reveals a number of common attributes

Example of a slum	'Slum' parameters					
	Services	Structure	Density	Location	Poverty and exclusion	Security of tenure
Ibadan, Bodija Market	Poor	Fair	High	Hazardous	Poor	Secure
Dhaka railways	Fair	Poor	High	Hazardous	Severe	Insecure
Karachi invasion of state land	Poor	Fair	High	Not hazardous	Severe	Secure
Karachi ad-hoc settlements	Poor	Poor	High	Hazardous	Poor	Insecure
Cairo highrises	Fair	Good	High	Not hazardous	Poor	Secure
Durban 'informal' settlements	Poor	Poor	Medium/low	Not hazardous	Severe	Secure

Source: adapted from UN-Habitat, 2002b.

Table 1.1

Attributes of selected slums

overcome in realizing the right to adequate housing: one that has no services, has poor-quality housing on fragile land, does not have secure tenure, and where the occupants are poor, marginalized and belong to a vulnerable group. Less badly affected households may carry one or more of these burdens.

Operational definition of slums

The operational definition of a slum that has been recently recommended (by a United Nations Expert Group Meeting (EGM) held in Nairobi from 28 to 30 October 2002) for future international usage defines a slum as an area that combines, to various extents, the following characteristics (restricted to the physical and legal characteristics of the settlement, and excluding the more difficult social dimensions):

Table 1.2

Indicators and thresholds for defining slums

- inadequate access to safe water;
- inadequate access to sanitation and other infrastructure;
- poor structural quality of housing;
- overcrowding;
- insecure residential status.

The proposed indicators and thresholds in Table 1.2 are based on the MDG indicators, where possible.

These indicators are provisional and subject to international field-testing for appropriateness, robustness and compliance with available sources, before reliable baseline global estimates of the numbers of people living in slums are obtained. It is also intended that local modifications of the indicators should be used as long as they are applied consistently over time.

Number of slum dwellers: assessments and estimations[27]

Slum dweller estimation, like any other estimation, depends on data availability as well as on criteria established. Several preliminary estimates have been undertaken. The starting point was the measurement of security of tenure, which focused on the proxy measure of tenure status (eg the type of tenancy: owner, renter or squatter). Empirical tests of this approach showed that this measurement method was not a reliable indicator of the legal basis for occupancy and the broader concept of security of tenure. Subsequently a Secure Tenure Index was developed in 2002, focusing on

Characteristic	Indicator	Definition
Access to water	Inadequate drinking water supply *(adjusted MDG Indicator 30)*	A settlement has an inadequate drinking water supply if less than 50% of households have an improved water supply: • household connection; • access to public stand pipe; • rainwater collection;[i] with at least 20 litres/person/day available *within an acceptable collection distance.*
Access to sanitation	Inadequate sanitation *(MDG Indicator 31)*	A settlement has inadequate sanitation if less than 50% of households have improved sanitation: • public sewer; • septic tank; • pour-flush latrine; • ventilated improved pit latrine. The excreta disposal system is considered adequate if it is private or shared by a *maximum of two households.*
Structural quality of housing	a. Location	Proportion of households residing on or near a hazardous site. The following locations should be considered: • housing in geologically hazardous zones (landslide/earthquake and flood areas); • housing on or under garbage mountains; • housing around high-industrial pollution areas; • housing around other unprotected high-risk zones (eg railroads, airports, energy transmission lines).
	b. Permanency of structure	Proportion of households living in temporary and/or dilapidated structures. The following factors should be considered when placing a housing unit in these categories: • quality of construction (eg materials used for wall, floor and roof); • compliance with local building codes, standards and bylaws.
Overcrowding	Overcrowding	Proportion of households with more than two persons per room. The alternative is to set a minimum standard for floor area per person (eg 5 square metres).
Security of tenure	Security of tenure *(MDG Indicator 32)*	• Proportion of households with formal title deeds to both land and residence. • Proportion of households with formal title deeds to either one of land or residence. • Proportion of households with enforceable agreements or any document as a proof of a tenure arrangement.

Note: i 'Well' and 'spring' are considered acceptable sources in the original MDG indicator but are almost certain to be polluted in urban areas.

Sources: adapted from UN-Habitat, 2002a, 2002b.

the comparatively well-measured physical representation of secure tenure that better estimates the magnitude of slum populations (see Methodological Notes in Statistical Annex). Using this approach, the baseline year (1993) estimate of global slum population was 712 million and the straight-line projection for 2001 based on the urban population projection was 837 million.

During the next stage of slum population estimation, the relative definitions of secure tenure and slums were refined in consultation with participants in the United Nations EGM mentioned earlier and their related networks of professionals. Furthermore, a set of guidelines was produced containing operational definitions and questionnaires for household surveys and censuses on secure tenure and slums. As mentioned earlier, the EGM slum definition broadened the concept of slum dweller. A slum dweller was deemed to have one or more of the following attributes: insecurity of tenure; low structural quality/durability of dwelling; poor access to safe water; poor access to sanitation facilities; and insufficient living area/space (see Table 1.2).

The estimates presented in Table 1.3 are based on this operational definition of slums and on a revised estimation procedure based on the recommendations of the EGM.

These new estimates were achieved using existing household survey and census data. Furthermore, the data used for the estimates are of a higher quality and were collected at the household level. Box 1.4 illustrates how this revised estimation procedure was applied in one particular city, Nairobi. These global estimates are the latest and most reliable. However, they should be seen as an outcome, at a particular stage, of a continuous process of improvement towards more accurate and reliable estimates of slum dwellers. The estimations in this table are presented by the established MDG regions (see composition of regional aggregates for MDG indicators in the Statistical Annex).

These estimates show that as many as 31.6 per cent of the urban population in 2001 were living in inadequate housing conditions. Developing country cities have an estimated 43 per cent of urban residents living in slums, while for developed country cities the estimate is 6 per cent. Notable is Sub-Saharan Africa, where 71.9 per cent of the urban population is estimated to be living in slums. This unfortunate reality is in line with findings on Africa for higher consumption poverty and higher under-five mortality rates. Although slum dwellers and the urban poor are largely co-located, not all slum dwellers may be classified as poor.

As Figure 1.4 shows, Asia dominates the global picture, having about 60 per cent of the total world's slum dwellers in 2001, Africa had 20 per cent, Latin America and the Caribbean (LAC) had 14 per cent of the world's slum dwellers, while Europe and other developed countries combined, had about 6 per cent.

The multidimensional method used in arriving at the above estimations is undergoing systematic refinement and improvement, and a standardized, representative global survey is planned that will permit much more accurate estimates according to the agreed definitions.

Box 1.3 Combining the indicators

There are a number of different ways in which multidimensional concepts are combined for measurement and ranking purposes; where possible, these will be used in testing the slum definitions that have been established for the MDGs.

Geographical information systems (GIS)

Where cities have formal, computerized geographical information systems (GIS) established at the small tract or enumerator district level, it is possible to overlay maps of the various indicators, finding areas where there are simultaneously high concentrations of various negative characteristics that are associated with slums. The advantage of this method is that a variety of thresholds can readily be tested, and specifically tailored local thresholds can be established – for example, areas having the bottom 20% of values for different indicators can be mapped.[i]

Instrumental or proxy variables

A single variable can be chosen to act as a proxy for the combined effect of the various dimensions. For example, the World Bank uses an income of US$1 a day as a simple proxy for more legitimate poverty measures. This has disadvantages (in that urban poverty is substantially underestimated by the method) but is very simple to use at the household level.

Indices or multidimensional methods

A common method for dealing with multidimensional concepts is to create an index using weighted linear combinations of the different variables. This is used by the United Nations Development Programme (UNDP) in the well-known Human Development Index (HDI), and in UN-Habitat's City Development Index (CDI). In this way a 'Slum Index' or Housing Disadvantage Index can be created.

Multi-criteria approaches

Households that fail one, two or three of the various conditions associated with slums can be regarded as slum households. This approach has been widely used in defining inadequate housing conditions, and is likely to be used in the MDG testing process. It has the advantage that individual households can be evaluated; therefore, it is tract independent.

Note: i Mapping of this kind has been undertaken in Johannesburg, Mexico City and Rio de Janeiro – generally with donor support.

Trends in numbers of slum dwellers

Until recently, there has been no agreed definition of slum, and firm base-year levels still have to be established; as a result, quantitative estimates of trends cannot yet be made.

Box 1.4 Nairobi Slum Study

UN-Habitat in cooperation with the Government of Kenya, Central Bureau of Statistics and the Nairobi City Council identified the slum areas of the city. The purpose of this identification was to permit disaggregation of the recent census data by slum and non-slum, as well as to identify slum areas for inclusion in future household samples, such as the forthcoming Demographic and Health Survey (DHS). An earlier study of Nairobi's slums by the African Population and Health Research Centre (APHRC) used the DHS survey instrument exclusively in the slum areas. This study and an analysis of the Kenya census data were revealing.

In the year preceding the census, approximately 150,000 persons arrived in the identified slum areas (some of these could be temporary residents captured by the census). 85% to 90% of these persons did not have access to safe sanitation. 60% lived in a one-room dwelling unit. More than 95% of the new arrivals came from Kenya's rural areas. Individuals who had been resident in the identified slum areas between five and ten years had not improved their access to safe sanitation, 60% still lived in one room and nearly all continued to use charcoal, wood or paraffin for cooking. The data does not tell us how many slum dwellers have managed to improve their lot and leave; but it does tell us that the slum areas are not improving. It suggests that the factors affecting increased morbidity and mortality in the slum areas are not being addressed.

Major area, region	Total population (millions)[a]	Urban population		Estimated slum population	
		(millions)[a]	Percentage of total population[a]	(thousands)[b]	Percentage of urban population[b]
World	6134	2923	47.7	923,986	31.6
Developed regions	1194	902	75.5	54,068	6.0
Europe	726	534	73.6	33,062	6.2
Other	467	367	78.6	21,006	5.7
Developing regions	4940	2022	40.9	869,918	43.0
Northern Africa	146	76	52.0	21,355	28.2
Sub-Saharan Africa	667	231	34.6	166,208	71.9
Latin America and the Caribbean (LAC)	527	399	75.8	127,567	31.9
Eastern Asia	1364	533	39.1	193,824	36.4
South-central Asia	1507	452	30.0	262,354	58.8
South-eastern Asia	530	203	38.3	56,781	28.0
Western Asia	192	125	64.9	41,331	33.1
Oceania	8	2	26.7	499	24.1
Least developed countries (LDCs)	685	179	26.2	140,114	78.2
Landlocked developing countries (LLDCs)	275	84	30.4	47,303	56.5
Small island developing states (SIDS)	52	30	57.9	7,321	24.4

Sources: a Total and urban population: World Urbanization Prospects: The 2001 Revision, Table A.1. *b Slum population and percentages calculated by UN-Habitat using data from DHS (1987–2001); MICS (1995–2000); WHO/UNICEF JMP (1998–1999).*

Table 1.3

Total, urban and estimated slum population by major region, 2001

Recent estimates show that as many as 31.6 per cent of the urban population in 2001 were living in inadequate housing conditions

Urban populations in less developed regions increased by 36 per cent during the decade (from 1439 million in 1990 up to 1964 million in the year 2000). It is likely that the number of slum households increased by a higher proportion

As will be shown in Chapter 3, it has taken a great deal of research and argument to determine whether easier indicators, such as income inequality or income poverty, increased or decreased worldwide in the rather mixed decade of the 1990s, and the same will certainly be true of slums.

The difficulties are both definition and data related. Different definitions will have different impacts on slum incidence.[28] Even when there is a firm definition, it is difficult to say what happened during the 1990s. Service delivery, especially water, improved markedly during the decade (as shown in Chapter 6), which would reduce the incidence of slums under the present definition. However, new immigrants tend disproportionately to be poor and urgently need new housing, which would increase the slum incidence.

The lack of accurate data is also a major problem. As long as many cities have no idea of how many dwellings are within their urban areas, and choose to exclude slum dwellings from statistics, particularly those in peri-urban areas, it will be difficult to estimate baseline numbers definitively. As cities change their boundaries, the numbers will increase (and, probably, the incidence as well, given that housing in peri-urban areas tends to be informal).

Whatever the definition, it seems almost certain that slum dwellers increased substantially during the 1990s. Urban populations in less developed regions increased by 36 per cent during the decade. Unless overcrowding increased in existing settlements, it can be assumed that the number of urban households increased by a similar ratio. It seems very unlikely that slum improvement or formal construction kept pace to any degree with this increase, as very few developing countries had formal residential building programmes of any size. Therefore, it is likely that the number of slum households increased by more than 36 per cent. However, it is clear that these changes were very different in different parts of the world.

Very little is known about what happened to irregular settlements during the 1990s, even in well-studied megacities. However, what is known or suspected about particular regions could be summed up in the following ways:

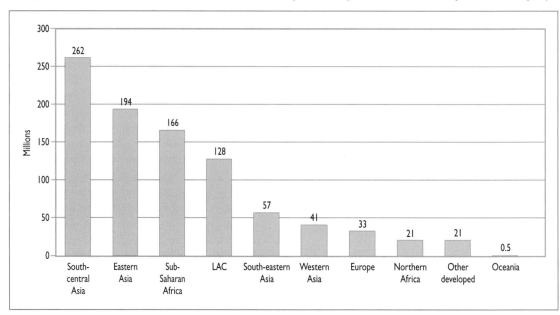

Figure 1.1

Slum population by region, 2001

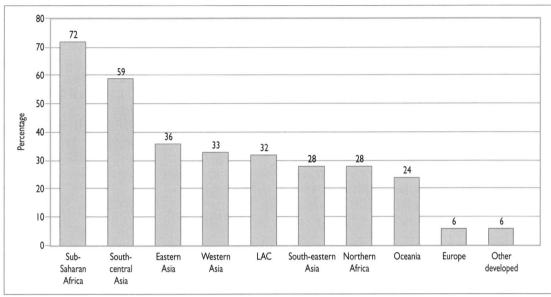

Figure 1.2

Slum dwellers as a percentage of urban population by region, 2001

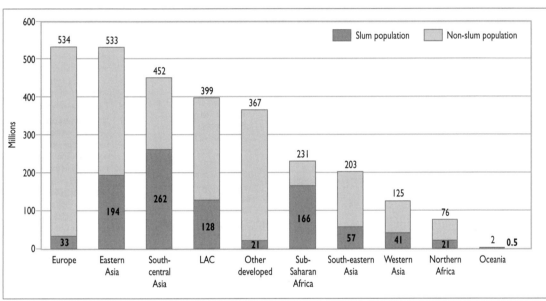

Figure 1.3

Proportion of slum dwellers in urban population by region, 2001

- In Asia, general urban housing standards improved considerably during the decade, and formal building kept pace with urban growth. This was also the case in much of Southeast Asia until the Asia Crisis of 1997. Even after the crisis, some countries such as Thailand continued to improve their urban conditions. In India, which has about one third of the world's slums, economic conditions also improved in some cities such as Bangalore. However, it is generally considered that urban populations grew faster than the capacity of cities to support them; therefore, slums increased, particularly in South Asia.

- In some countries of Latin America, there was a wholesale tenure regularization and a large drop in numbers of squatter households, which would reduce the number of slums under most definitions. Furthermore, urbanization reached saturation levels of 80 per cent, so that slum formation slowed. Nevertheless, housing deficits remain high and slums are prominent in most cities.

- Cities in sub-Saharan Africa and in some Arab states showed considerable housing stress, with rents and prices rising substantially while incomes fell, probably corresponding to higher occupancy rates. As well, slum areas increased in most cities, and the rate of

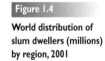

Figure 1.4

World distribution of slum dwellers (millions) by region, 2001

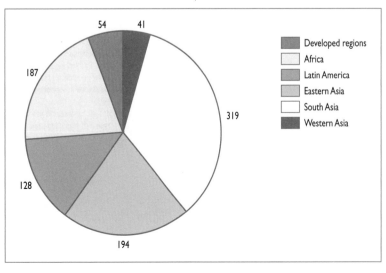

slum improvement was very slow or negligible in most places. In South Africa, a very large housing programme reduced the numbers in informal settlements significantly.

All of these factors and regional differences are discussed more fully in succeeding chapters and are the key to understanding what is happening globally. Accuracy in global estimates can most easily be obtained by focusing on areas with the greatest concentration of slums and the fastest urbanization – especially in South and South-eastern Asia, where nearly half of the world's slums are located and where improvements are beginning to occur. The work of

estimating changes in numbers of slum residents accurately for purposes of the MDG targets is very complex as there is currently no representative data, so authoritative results will not be obtained for several years.

Finally, it should be noted that estimation of such a complex concept will always be somewhat arbitrary and definition driven. Nevertheless, by using the same, consistent slum definition in the same places at different points in time, genuine changes may be observed – particularly when broad averages are 'drilled down' to examine the underlying changes in real conditions in individual cities.

NOTES

1   This chapter draws primarily on outcomes of the Workshops and Expert Group Meetings, organized by UN-Habitat during the period of January to October 2002, as well as on background papers prepared for the report by the core group of consultants and staff of the UN-Habitat. The Cities Alliance's *2002 Annual Report* has also been taken into consideration.

2   United Nations Population Division, 2001; 2002.

3   Hardoy and Satterthwaite, 1989.

4   UNCHS (Habitat), 1996.

5   See www.development goals.org and www.undp.org/ mdg/goalsandindicators.html.

6   The goal refers to improvement in situ. Slum dwellers are improving their own situation by moving to better locations.

7   UN-Habitat, 2002a; 2002b.

8   International Union of Local Authorities (IULA), Metropolis, World Federation of United Cities, World Association of Cities and Local Authorities Coordination (WACLAC), Canada, France, Germany, Italy, Japan, The Netherlands, Norway, Sweden, the UK and the US, the Asian Development Bank and the United Nations Environment Programme (UNEP). From UN-Habitat's perspective this initiative is part of a broader effort that also includes the Global Campaign for Secure Tenure (UNCHS (Habitat), 2001), the Global Campaign on Urban Governance; and Managing

Water for African Cities (see United Nations, 2001, p24, para 120).

9   Based on 1989 US$ values at purchasing power parity. The definition was recently changed somewhat, which has made comparisons rather difficult, as Chapter 3 shows.

10   See Table B.7 in the Statistical Annex.

11   The MDG indicator sets an extremely low standard that is likely to be automatically observed in urban areas. In fact, there has been a very substantial improvement in urban water supply, as Chapter 6 shows.

12   See Table B.4 in the Statistical Annex.

13   See Table B.4 in the Statistical Annex.

14   The indicator was initially proposed by the World Bank and was further elaborated within the objectives of the Global Campaign on Secure Tenure (GCST). An Expert Group Meeting, organized by UN-Habitat in Nairobi ironed out most of the issues, establishing definitions and a set of indicators covering most aspects of secure tenure. The worldwide tenure situation is described in Chapter 6. See UN-Habitat, 2002c, d.

15   The UNDP coordinates the MDG campaign and country-level monitoring activities, which include practical assistance in support of country priorities; country-and global-level monitoring; research leadership; and advocacy. The UN system and

its international and civil society partners are aiming to spearhead a series of awareness-raising Millennium Campaigns within countries, based on national strategies and needs. In the developed countries, the campaigns' primary focus will be on galvanizing public opinion as a means of boosting development assistance, trade, debt relief, technology and other support needed to achieve the MDGs. In the developing world, the aim is to build coalitions for action and to help governments set priorities, including in their budgets, and to use resources more effectively.

16   In a report prepared in 2001 for the Secretary-General by a panel headed by former Mexican President Ernesto Zedillo, and including former US Treasury Secretary Robert Rubin.

17   This section draws on papers prepared by Joe Flood, Nefise Bazoglu, Patrick Wakely, Harvey Herr, Guenther Karl, Christine Auclair, and Martin Raithelhuber. See UN-Habitat, 2002c, d and e.

18   *The Merriam-Webster Dictionary* (1994) Merriam-Webster Inc.

19   *The Oxford English Dictionary* (1989), Second edition, Clarendon Press, Oxford.

20   Case study – Karachi.

21   Case study – Cairo.

22   UN-Habitat, 2002c.

23   Cities Alliance, 1999.

24   One example is the infamous 'windscreen survey' in Melbourne, Australia, during

the 1960s, when two planners drove around and designated particular streets as slums for demolition without getting out of their car.

25   In fact, administrative fiat may not be an unreasonable procedure if socially negotiated: areas in a number of countries are designated as urban or rural in this way.

26   Case study – Ahmedabad.

27   During this report preparation, two other methods have been suggested for estimating slum population. The first method equates slums for most parts of the world with informal settlements, which has as a good proxy variable the proportion of dwellings not in compliance with local building regulations, or 'unauthorized dwellings'. However, a multi-criterion or multidimensional definition is preferred for what is a multidimensional concept. The second method for estimating numbers of slum dwellers combines housing status and condition with lack of service provision. These estimates show that of the order of 480 million to 490 million people lived in unauthorized housing or slums in 1993, or close to 20 per cent of the world's urban population. If the proportion of slum dwellers in developing countries has been sustained, the number of people living in slums has risen to around 645 million by 2003.

28   Incidence – the proportion of urban dwellers in slums.

2

URBANIZATION TRENDS AND FORCES SHAPING SLUMS[1]

Slums do not occur in a vacuum. Despite the easily recognizable similarities in terms of physical and social conditions and attitudes that surround slums, there are also very great differences between slums that reflect local cultures and conditions, accidents of history or politics, and topography or the built environment. Some slum areas are working communities in their own right, with their own economy and social structure, whereas others are 'black holes of misery and despair'.

Slums, however, do have a number of things in common wherever they occur, and these include the economic, social and spatial forces that create and shape them and differentiate them from the rest of the city. This chapter deals with these forces.

The first part of this chapter examines the theories of spatial distribution, residential differentiation and ecological succession that have been developed by urban researchers to understand why people live where they do, why cities have particular forms, and why poor people congregate in particular locations. It also looks at the methods that have been used to measure spatial inequality. These theories have largely been developed to explain market-driven cities, where land use is determined by economic competition, and they are less applicable to many of the cities of the developing world that are still undergoing transitions from more traditional exchange and land tenure regimes. However, as with Western cities, the cities of the developing world are gradually adopting the rules of market forces, and the advanced methods of urban spatial analysis help to understand these trends.

The second part of the chapter considers the macro or external forces acting on cities that are responsible for slum formation – primarily those that operate at the national level. The chapter is devoted to discussing these forces: firstly, urbanization, migration and other demographic changes, and, secondly, poverty, its measurement and incidence. Chapter 3 continues the discussion by looking at the new international regime of economic liberalization and globalization and its effects on urban inequality and slum formation.

SOCIO-ECONOMIC INEQUALITY

Slums result from a combination of poverty or low incomes with inadequacies in the housing provision system, so that poor people are forced to seek affordable accommodation

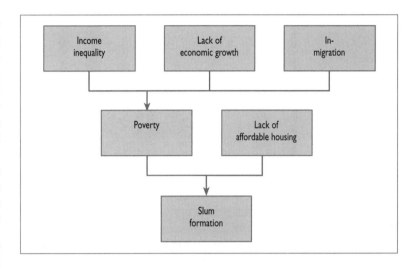

Figure 2.1

Inequality, poverty and slum formation

and land that become increasingly inadequate. The numbers of urban people in poverty are, to a large extent, outside the control of city governments, and are swelled by a combination of economic stagnation, increasing inequality and population growth, especially growth through in-migration. The situation is depicted in Figure 2.1.

Spatial organization and residential differentiation

An essential part of city life is constant change: building and rebuilding, the succession and occupation of different groups, the relocation of industry and commerce, and processes of marginalization and impoverishment. In the capitalist city, this is largely driven by the search for higher returns and optimal land use, and this has led to the physical expression of inequality in built form, of which slums lie at the lowest socio-economic level. In developing cities, where land use is still partially dictated by traditional uses or controlled by governments, slums have tended to sit outside of the formal market system, to some extent, acting as a residual for older market systems of exchange and income generation rather than the specialized shops of formal urban-distribution systems.

■ The ecological school and the neo-classical model

Theories of city form that have been current in urban geography, until the post-modern paradigm shift during the 1980s, stem originally from the ideas of Burgess, Hoyt and others during the 1920s and 1930s, collectively known as the 'Chicago School'. They lived in an urban environment

Slums do not occur in a vacuum. They result from a combination of poverty or low incomes with inadequacies in the housing provision system

Great differences between slums reflect local cultures and conditions, as well as accidents of history or politics

Figure 2.2

Ecological schema for Chicago

Source: Burgess, 1925

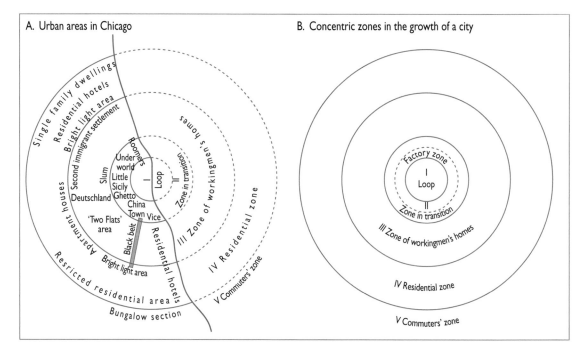

A. Urban areas in Chicago

B. Concentric zones in the growth of a city

where the inner city had largely been vacated by families who had moved outward to the suburbs in rings and wedges from the downtown centre, leaving the decaying inner city to the most disadvantaged groups. The Chicago School saw the internal spatial organization of cities as an outcome of 'ecological' competition for niches between social classes who behaved like different species in terms of their endowments and wants, and who would compete for different land uses, with the strongest groups taking the most desirable positions and the weaker groups occupying residual spaces. As society and transport technology changed, and as the circumstances of the groups altered or housing became inadequate, they would vacate particular areas, leaving them for new immigrants or social groups who would occupy, in their turn.

The Burgess spatial schema for Chicago is shown in Figure 2.2. The zones of most interest in the diagram are those designated as 'working men's housing' and 'zones in transition'. Earlier generations of 'working men's housing' were slowly being taken over by warehouses, immigrants and the urban poor, as better-off households vacated for the suburbs. These zones in transition were the ghettos, slums and 'bright light areas'.

The picture is, in fact, apt for many (though not all) larger industrial cities in the Western world – with the proviso that, since the 1960s, a new form of urban succession has emerged. Yuppies and childless couples are moving back into the centre of cities, where they share it with the poor, remodelling the slums by renovating older dwellings and converting factories and warehouses, and, in some cases, displacing the poor to other areas.

The Chicago schema was put on a more rigorous footing with the advent of neo-classical economics, – in particular, the Alonso-Muth-Mills model, which demonstrated how the 'rent gradient' of declining land prices and rents away from the centre could be calculated from first economic principles, and the location of various groups could be predicted. In the model, residents are considered to have

a trade-off between transport costs or time and living space. Each group has a 'bid rent curve' for the amount that they are prepared to pay per square metre for particular locations, and the group with the steepest curve will win. Poorer people, for example, could beat the rich by taking much smaller plots of land at a higher price, accepting higher crowding as the price for location. The poor are where they are because, even with their low incomes, they are outbid by the rich for the areas in which they live, and they pay more than the rich would be prepared to pay to live there.[2]

As far as it goes, the model is reasonably accurate in determining social change in a centralized city with a reasonable level of residential mobility. Gentrification can be predicted using the model because of the steepening of the rent gradient, a phenomenon that has been steadily observed in most Western cities.[3] This steepening has occurred in different places because of:[4]

- *Limiting growth impact of the city perimeter.* If the area of the city does not expand while the population increases, so that population densities increase, land prices and rents will increase with a bias towards the centre.

- *Increase in smaller households.* Smaller households need less space, so they buy in the centre.

- *Increase in multiple-income households.* If there are two commuters in a household, they will tend to locate more centrally in order to minimize transport costs, as these are a higher proportion of their budget.

- *Households with high valuation on travel time or travel cost.* The richest households tend to locate centrally because they put a high valuation on travel time, while the poor locate centrally because they cannot afford to travel. If inequality increases, both groups put pressure on the best-located areas for different reasons.

- *Consumer taste changes* (more interest in 'integrated living', mixed use, historical precincts, public space as opposed to private, etc). The value of the central

The poor are where they are because, even with their low incomes, they are outbid by the rich for the areas in which they live, and they pay more than the rich would be prepared to pay to live there

city increases for all groups, and central values increase in relative terms.

The centralizing tendency of all of these factors can be deduced from the model and, more significantly, have all been observed empirically.[5] The net result is that the poor are outbid in the central area by the new affluent bidders, and either will share the space or move outwards to more affordable areas.[6]

■ Factorial ecology

During the 1970s, a new quantitative paradigm came to dominate urban science, made possible by computers and the availability of detailed urban census data, and with some basis in Chicago School theory. The major new technique was called *factorial ecology*, and it was based on a multivariate analysis of the various socio-economic indicators distinguishing small areas in the city, calculating indexes that would distinguish these areas from each other. The results were quite startling. In every city that was studied in widely different parts of the developed world, the spatial separation was due, in large part, to three factors, usually known as socio-economic status, familism and ethnicity.[7]

Socio-economic advantage was an 'index of advantage' that combined factors such as income, education and occupation; and measured the extent to which households well endowed with these factors were separated from those poorly endowed.

Familism concerned the effect of family type; households with children and non-working wives in the 1970s tended to seek suburban bungalows, while single persons were more inclined to live in apartments in central cities.

Ethnicity usually measured the proportion of those born outside of the country, but could also represent the separation of particular ethnic or religious groups.

The three factors were of different strengths in different cities and cultures, and had different weightings on the variables; but they were, invariably, the three major factors determining city social structure.

Factorial ecology lapsed along with other quantitative approaches in the post-modern disciplinary fashion of the 1980s and 1990s; but the method has been recently revisited to show that the factorial division holds as strongly as it ever did, with many factors very similar to 30 years ago. The new factors reflect the current realities, and are critically involved with change in work and in household demographics in the intervening period.[8]

In line with the theses of globalization, people working in producer-service industries and university graduates are stronger determinants of *socio-economic advantage*.[9] The social divide is no longer between 'white collar' and 'blue collar' occupations, but between professionals and the rest.

Familism has now become more closely related to *urban lifestyles*, distinguishing areas with apartment living, lack of a car, walking to work and small family size from

In widely different parts of the developed world, the spatial separation in cities was due, in large part, to three factors, usually known as socio-economic status, familism and ethnicity

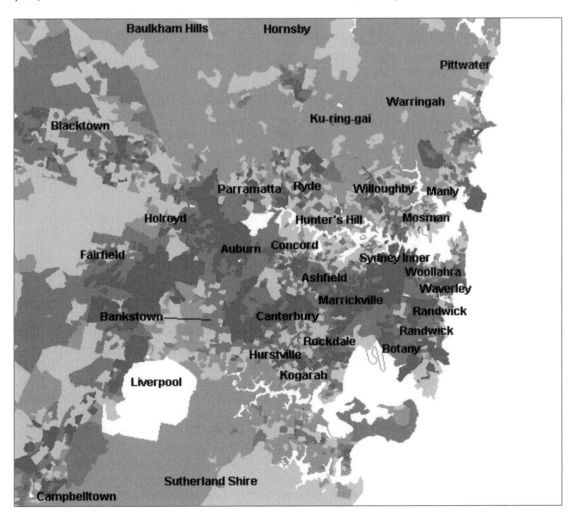

Figure 2.3

Areas of disadvantage in Sydney

family households who live in the suburbs and commute. Familism in 1995 had less to do with wives without formal employment, home ownership and living in single houses than it did during the 1970s, and was more concerned with having children, being part of extended families and staying in the same location.

By simplifying the methods of earlier work, it has been shown that instead of socio-economic advantage and familism, the two principal factors are, in fact, an *accessibility/space* trade-off and *socio-economic disadvantage*.[10]

Accessibility/space distinguishes between households who want accessibility and households who want space. Accessibility can be afforded either through high incomes, small family size or crowding. The factor is identical with the trade-off that is the starting point of neo-classical urban economics.[11]

Socio-economic disadvantage is the flip side of advantage, and shows how households who suffer from unemployment are single parents, have little education, receive welfare or belong to marginalized ethnic groups and are separated from the rest.

The index of disadvantage is the measure that describes what is thought of as a traditional slum, and most slums or former slums have very high values on this index.[12]

Figure 2.3 shows the parts of a city that are disadvantaged. In this case (Sydney), it is a long, sweeping dragon-shaped area to the south and south-west, where most of the industry, immigrants, lower-income people and welfare recipients are located.[13]

Another advantage of this kind of analysis is that it can easily distinguish when 'divided cities' are forming. In Sydney, for example, a separation can be made between a 'global city' sitting astride the harbour and a more conventional US-style city with a low-income centre about 20 kilometres west of the central business district (CBD), surrounded by rings of suburbs.[14]

■ Measuring spatial inequality and separation

A number of measures are in common use for distinguishing the level of inequality or unevenness of distribution of sub-populations across space. The best known and simplest of these is the index of segregation or dissimilarity.[15] It measures the proportion of the sub-population that would need to move in order for it to be equally represented in all areas.[16] It is used most often for racial groups, but also for low-income earners. Surprisingly, the index of dissimilarity for low-income people has proven to be remarkably stable over an extended period in some cities such as Sydney.[17]

The question of whether or not the poor and rich have moved further apart, and therefore whether they are more or less segregated over time, is not clear. The very deliberate suburbanization separating the middle class from the poor and defining the traditional slums during the 1880s to 1950s may have marked a period of greatest residential differentiation of income groups in a number of developed countries.[18] Greater mobility and social acceptance of different groups also act to reduce spatial separation.[19] With gentrification and with a retreat from rigid planning guidelines that separated dwelling types and sizes and other urban activities until quite recently – and a move away since the 1970s from the policy of construction of large peripheral public housing estates – rich and poor have moved closer together in space in many places.[20] However, the growth of large areas of disadvantage towards the edge of some cities, while the wealthy have continued to occupy areas of prime accessibility or amenity, would militate against a general assumption of reduced spatial separation.

The very obvious increase in gated communities discussed at length in *Cities in a Globalizing World: Global Report on Human Settlements 2001* might be an indication that the rich and poor have been moving closer together in space.[21] If violent crime has not increased, then the closing off of high-income precincts or buildings would be a sign that the rich have no longer been able to separate themselves spatially from the poor, or have lost control of the streets, retreating into small areas where their particular needs are catered for. To some extent, it is the perception that crime has increased, due to a constant media barrage, rather than any actual crime increase, that has prompted the elderly and affluent to withdraw in this manner.[22]

Even in specific countries, the figures on change in spatial inequality can be quite confusing. For example, recent studies have shown that income segregation increased within each of white, black and Hispanic populations in the US between 1970 and 1980 and between 1980 and 1990.[23] However. racial segregation in the US is at its lowest level since the 1920s. Key questions for the present report are whether spatial inequality is increasing within cities, and whether areas of social disadvantage, particularly slums, are expanding in population or area in the world, as a whole. There seems to be very little research done, even within individual cities, on the extent to which this is happening in recent years or whether it is happening at all. Research is needed; but it seems likely that the results will differ from city to city. It may well be the case in the high income countries (HICs) that if income inequality is increasing due to withdrawal of welfare, or the boom-bust ratcheting of inequality described in Chapter 3, then this might find a spatial expression, and the spatial separation between rich and poor might be increasing in many parts of the world. The rapid expansion of developing cities would seem to make this a foregone conclusion in the developing world.

■ Spatial concentration of poverty

It has been clearly demonstrated by factorial ecology that social advantage and social disadvantage are the major agglutinative forces in cities – possibly the major forces in Western cities, at least. The question is why. It is not immediately obvious in these days of cheap telephones and cheap transport why people of a similar economic or social status choose to live together. In many cities in the developing world, the separation in space so obvious in Western cities is not obvious at all; in others, it is very visible. It is fairly clear why particular ethnic groups choose to cluster together for access to social networks, speciality shops and facilities; but why do social classes congregate in particular areas?

A case may be advanced that the rich or middle class act to exclude the poor because they no longer need them around and have an antipathy towards them. In the case of the gated communities of the US, Brazil and the Philippines, this exclusion is very obvious and direct – but many countries do not have gated communities, except for those housing the elderly. Identifying the specific mechanisms by which the poor are excluded is the question that needs to be answered. Most of the social separation has been visible for centuries in the older Western cities, accelerating during the suburbanization phase during the first half of the 20th century and, it would appear, partly reversing during the last 30 years due to gentrification.[24]

The conventional neo-classical explanation for residential differentiation is based largely on *housing and land costs*, as expressed in the Alonso-Muth-Mills model. Lower-income people live in particular areas because they can outbid the rich for the kind of housing that is there – it would be too expensive or undesirable for the rich to convert it to other uses. This argument is reasonable but not really satisfactory. Why are the rich not interested in this valuable inner-city land and converting it to profitable uses, such as the development of condominiums?

A related argument suggests that *employment opportunities* for the rich and poor are not consanguineous, so that the rich tend to locate near, for example, office areas, while the poor locate near, for example, factories or markets. This argument once had considerable merit; but in an era of cheap transport, it is no longer applicable (though for some high-income households, the 'cost' of 'travel time' has replaced 'transport cost' as a residential location factor).[25] In fact, it has been argued in the US that the move of industry to outer areas has disadvantaged the inner city poor and worsened slum areas, since now there are no jobs in their vicinity, and this is contributing to unemployment.[26] The loss of jobs and businesses may start early in the decline cycle of an inner-city slum and is an ongoing contributor to its deterioration.[27]

The second argument refers to *amenity*. Slums, it is believed, begin on fragile or poor-quality land subject to flooding, landslip and other disadvantages, while the rich locate in areas of high amenity – ocean views, pleasant, slightly hilly areas of good soil and aspect.[28] This amenity is self-reinforcing in that both public and private investment suited to each class tends to locate accordingly and attracts more people of a similar socio-economic profile – particularly at the upper-class end. Private schools, elite shopping centres, and social and business services tend to follow their clientele. Services for the poor also tend to cluster – for example, welfare agencies, food distribution and public medical facilities. A need to be near these kinds of services attracts the homeless, in particular.

In places where taxation is collected locally, in particular, spending on *local public goods* will be much higher because of the much better revenues, further accentuating inequality. Local governments in slum areas have almost no revenue base and cannot find money to either construct or maintain infrastructure and other services, and the whole system goes downhill, causing the more affluent residents and formal businesses to move out thus further lowering revenue potential. The push for decentralization and own-source revenue generation in many developing countries could increase spatial inequality accordingly.

The third argument relates to *exclusionary zoning*, which is seen as the main factor distinguishing different cities, and is probably responsible for most of the more visible tract-wide spatial separation of the classes. The 'wrong side of the tracks' is actually enshrined in local laws and regulations that prevent poor people from building the kinds of houses that they can afford in rich areas, or conducting the kinds of informal income-generating activities that are necessary for their livelihood. Home-based enterprises, street markets or the raising of chickens, for example, are expressly forbidden in most of the affluent suburban areas of the world.[29] Local democracy exacerbates the situation, as the middle class will always vote to exclude activities that they do not conduct themselves.

In the meantime, exclusionary zoning affects amenity by pushing various negative externalities into low-income areas where the poor are not organized to resist. Factories and noxious or polluting industry, and possibly waste disposal facilities, are located within these areas, further pushing down land prices. Illegal activities are also pushed into these areas, through police 'turning a blind eye' and lack of organized local opposition to their presence. The partly extra-legal nature of income opportunities for the poor also discourages the kind of strict scrutiny and enforcement that occurs in middle-class areas.

Exclusionary regulation was once absolutely overt and designed specifically to keep the poor 'in their place'. Ethnic segregation, in particular, has taken extreme forms, such as apartheid or ghettos. Following the Chicago riots of 1919 in which white street gangs attacked blacks with impunity, blacks were excluded from the majority of open residential areas through 'restrictive covenants' from 1923 to 1947,[30] and the extreme racial separation resulting from white resistance to integration continues to the present. The arrival of a more liberal era that sought to encourage equality of opportunity, if not incomes, has considerably weakened these covenants to the point that they have been disallowed in many places. Affirmative action programmes, such as 'bussing' in the US, have sought to counter the exclusionary effects of segregation and differential spending on local public goods. The increased mixing of income groups in Western cities is largely due to the retreat of the local state and a loss of the social consensus for its powers to keep classes apart.

The final argument is the post-modern one of *cultural landscapes*, in which spatial distinctions are embedded in social constructs of what is real. Poverty and slums are, essentially, comparative notions that assign particular groups and particular places to the good, the rich and the successful, and the bad, the poor and the unsuccessful, and the paths of people's lives tend to follow these assigned constructs unless they can redefine their own self-worth. The reality of exclusion actually stems from an allocation of status to individuals at an early age. While initial

The conventional neo-classical explanation for residential differentiation is based largely on *housing and land costs*

Spatial distinctions are embedded in social constructs. Poverty and slums are, essentially, comparative notions that assign particular groups and particular places to the good, the rich and the successful, and the bad, the poor and the unsuccessful endowments of wealth will also play a large role, many of the personal choices and most of the social chances and opportunities will result from the part of the cultural landscape to which individuals are 'assigned', the 'signs' being accent, dress, self-confidence and reputation. It is in this way that social classes are reproduced, and why slums and poverty show such a high level of resilience and continuity through generations.[31]

Urban form and disadvantage

■ Mosaic post-modern cities in the developing world

Older European cities grew in an environment where market norms and feudal landholding systems had been well established since the Middle Ages, and dwellings could be readily traded by owners or landlords for alternative uses. They also grew, initially, during a time when most work was centrally located and people walked, then later expanded to suburbs along rail corridors, filling between these corridors as personal motor transport became universally available. However, the situation of cities that have emerged as substantial centres in the developing world during the past 50 years is often very different from that of a succession of land uses described by the Chicago School. Their business centres have often not been in the historic centre, but have been purpose built and multinucleated, with access to airports and to the residential zones of the more affluent. The shape of the city has been determined not by centralized rail networks but by minibuses and private cars.

The types of city forms to be found in many parts of the developing world do not usually show the classic Chicago pattern of cities with a decaying, possibly partly rejuvenated core, surrounded by rings of garden suburbs. They can be divided into several types:

The polycentric, interactive nature of the post-modern city is a result of more efficient transport systems that allow all except the very poorest to move freely in the city

- *Colonial-style cities*, with a well-built formal core, surrounded by large areas of informal settlements, some of which may have been there for 50 years. Many cities in Africa and South Asia have this form. The inner-city area was protected by the colonial powers from encroachment.[32] The design resembles the feudal European design of a castle or walled city with the poor beyond the walls.[33]
- *Planned ethnic separations* are an extreme example of urban social segregation.[34] For example, during the apartheid years, Soweto and other ethnic satellite cities of Johannesburg were made possible by cheap, subsidized daily bus transport for workers in the centre. The system is similar for Palestinians working in Israel.
- *Saucer* or hollowed cities are the norm for some countries in Eastern Europe. A low-rise centre is surrounded by public housing apartment buildings, which become progressively higher towards the rim, linked to the centre with rapid transit. Some Western European cities with a lot of high-rise public housing have aspects of the form.

- *Multi-centres*: many Southeast Asian and Latin American cities are multi-centred and amorphous, based on the style of Los Angeles, because they have been built almost from the beginning around motorized transport rather than walking. High-income areas often surround the concrete canyons of business districts into which few poor people venture, or are tucked away in areas of high amenity, or may form an 'edge city' technopolis. There may be large tracts of poor-quality low-income housing in older inner areas, in squatter zones on the fringe or on wedges and strips of fragile land.[35,36] In some Asian cities, palaces are quite literally next to hovels, and there are no large identifiable slum areas of more than a few blocks.

The amorphous, polycentric, interactive nature of the post-modern city is a result of more efficient transport systems that allow all except the very poorest to move freely in the city. It is also due to the withdrawal of the local state that previously formally divided the city into areas of exclusion, using planning controls. With the departure of ideological certainty as to its role in separating the classes, it no longer has the credibility or authority to do this. The separation is now accomplished by the private sector, as the preceding *Cities in a Globalizing World: Global Report on Human Settlements 2001* has eloquently explained.[37] Individual firms or investors can only gain control over relatively small spaces to direct them towards the consumption requirements of specific social classes. Therefore, development decreasingly involves tract-wide separations.

However (to preserve the ecological metaphor), the enclosing of habitats is in an almost virtual network, where it is possible to travel throughout the city on a spatial network designed for a particular social class while barely being aware of the adjacent networks used by other classes. Separation is no longer mediated by fiat but by hegemony: controls of expectation, social habit and, ultimately, purchasing power and commodification. The post-modern city still remains amenable to spatial socio-economic analysis.[38] The Global Report distinguishes five 'cities' with specified class actors and economic functions:

1. *The luxury city and the controlling city*, involving the groups for whom the city is a locus of power and profit, as well as consumption and relaxation.
2. *The gentrified city and the city of advanced services*, involving income-earning professionals and those involved in the 'knowledge economy'.
3. *The suburban city and the city of direct production* of the better paid blue-collar and white-collar non-professional workers and their factories and offices.
4. *The tenement city and the city of unskilled workers*, including the immigrant enclaves, the lower paid wage workers and the 'respectable poor'.
5. *The abandoned city and the residual city*, for the very poor and the permanently unemployed 'underclass' or 'ghetto poor', with income based on marginal or illegal activity, direct street-level exploitation, and

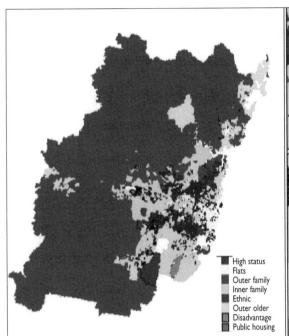

High status
Flats
Outer family
Inner family
Ethnic
Outer older
Disadvantage
Public housing

Figure 2.4

Socio-economic clusters in Sydney

denial of the public and private services of other parts of the city.

The last 'city' is the traditional Western slum; but in less developed countries, a sixth city must also be added:

6   *The informal city and the city of illegality*, which comprises the slums of the developing megacities and where the informal sector has its base; where services are poor or non-existent; where residents are invisible to legal status systems; and where harassment by authorities is commonplace.

In fact, the 'five cities' are more than a metaphor and can be distinguished by cluster analysis and geographical information systems (GIS). Figure 2.4 shows the division of Sydney into zones of similar socio-economic concentration. The analysis shows four of the five cities quite well, along with another 'retirement city' of older people on relatively low non-wage incomes in areas of high amenity and lower accessibility, often joined by other people on fixed incomes.[39] This sixth retirement city is likely to become more important in the West as populations age and the baby boomers retire.

■ **Measuring urban development and disadvantage**

Factorial ecology studies have not been attempted in cities of the developing world because of a lack of appropriately detailed data at the sub-city level. It is likely that the same factors defining urban difference would be found, but the components would be quite different. In particular, it might be expected that socio-economic advantage and disadvantage would be defined in terms of education, health, poverty and the physical factors of housing and urban services that formed part of the slum index approach described in Chapter 1.

A closely related technique to factorial ecology has been used to rank not just parts of a city on their socio-economic status, but cities themselves and their level of development. UN-Habitat has derived a City Development Index (CDI), paralleling the United Nations Development Programme (UNDP) Human Development Index (HDI), but including service provision and environmental management, as well as standard human development categories, that ranks cities on the basis of their level of development.[40,41]

CHALLENGES TO SUSTAINABLE URBANIZATION

Demographic changes and slum formation

The picture of developing megacities that is commonly painted in the popular imagination is of sprawling areas of crowded substandard housing and no facilities or sanitation, with numbers continually augmented by a hopeless stream of in-migrants from depressed rural areas who expect very little and receive less, building makeshift shelters on the edges of town or along rivers and trying to eke out a living.

In fact, while many of the larger cities do have these problems, the reality is far more complex. Most cities are vibrant and dynamic places, each with their own unique character. If not too crippled by the urban externalities of congestion, pollution and crime, they have interesting streetscapes, workspaces and residential spaces in which the majority are able to make an acceptable income and obtain an education, if they wish, while enjoying a better standard of living at a considerably lower risk of death and starvation than their rural counterparts.

The visible minority of street children and other extreme poor are not so fortunate, and in some cities where

Population growth was the main demographic issue of the 20th century and it continues to be the focus of attention in the developing world. Growth continues at a high but diminishing rate

Figure 2.5

Annual increment in total and urban population

Source: United Nations Population Division, 2002, Figure 1

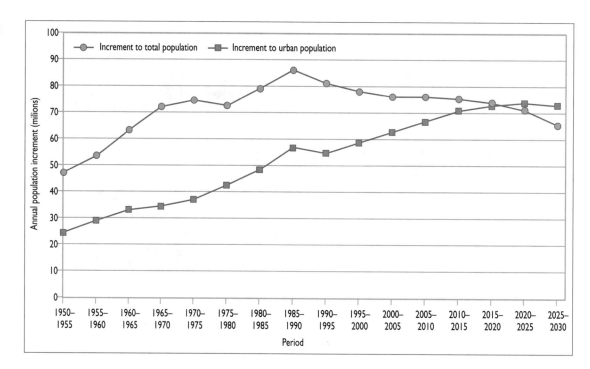

rescue organizations are poorly developed, opportunities are minimal, it is not possible to forage or grow own food as in the countryside, and starvation is not too far away. It remains a fact, however, that very few people die in the city streets any more because there is always someone to help them – and this is rarely the case in rural areas. Without the safety nets that have been painstakingly developed, there would be many more in extreme deprivation, and the corpses that once lay in the streets of Kolkata and Mumbai would be far more prevalent.

Cities are, by definition, concentrations of population; and these concentrations occur through in-migration and internal growth. It is now recognized that the bulk of urban growth in larger cities is due to net birthrates. Nevertheless, rural–urban flows continue in many parts of the world; and they tend to be larger where the cities are least able to

absorb immigrants: the poorer areas of South Asia and sub-Saharan Africa.

■ Urban growth

Population growth was the main demographic issue of the 20th century and it continues to be the focus of attention in the developing world. Growth continues at a high but diminishing rate, as Figure 2.5 shows. This growth is largely due to the extraordinary success of modern medicine in raising life expectancies by 40 per cent over the century – which must surely rate as the greatest human achievement of the period.[42] However, it has taken several generations for social behaviour to adjust to these new conditions by also reducing birthrates.

Over the past 50 years, great strides have been made by the urbanization process. Urban population has increased

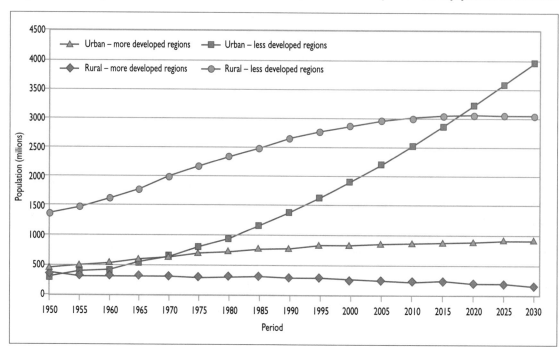

Figure 2.6

Urban and rural populations in more and less developed regions, 1950 to 2030

Source: United Nations Population Division, 2002

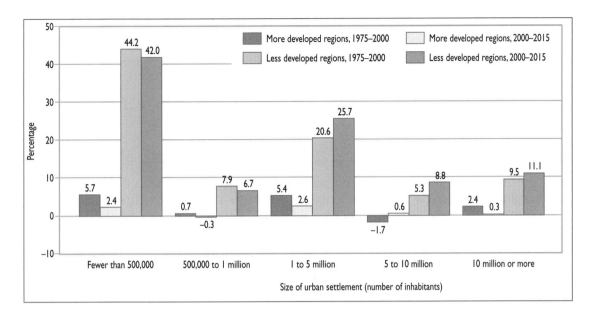

Figure 2.7

Estimated urban population increment by city size

Source: United Nations Population Division, 2002

by 20 to 30 per cent in most parts of the world. The Statistical Annex (Table B-2) contains data on the rate of urbanization for all countries around the world.

Other population trends, revealed by Box 2.1 and Figure 2.6, are rather startling. They imply that the world has a maximum number of rural dwellers who can be supported, and that number has almost been reached. The trends also imply that world urban populations will increase by the equivalent of 33 new cities of 2 million people per year for 30 years, or by 6 megacities per year, for the next 30 years.[43]

There are 19 megacities at the moment with populations of over 10 million. Eight per cent of the world's urban population lives in these very large cities, while over 50 per cent live in cities under 500,000 people (see Table 2.1 and Figure 2.7). Some megacities will grow very large (Dhaka, Mumbai, Sao Paulo, Delhi and Mexico City expect over 20 million by 2015); but none are projected to exceed the current size of Tokyo. Table 2.1 shows that the megacities are anticipated to take about one ninth of world population growth and will improve their share of global urban population somewhat.[44]

While the urban development focus on the teeming megacities has been very pronounced, with extensive research and many large-scale improvement projects, the major population growth is now in medium cities of 1 to 5 million people, and in smaller cities of under 500,000 people, which still have half of the world's population growth. Although these smaller cities do not have the vast areas of social exclusion, informality and unhealthy living conditions of the largest cities, they do have less in the way of urban facilities and development than larger cities, and this contributes to slum incidences that may exceed those of larger cities.

Figure 2.8 shows infrastructure deficiency and unauthorized housing for four city-size groups.[45] The availability of infrastructure increases with city size, while the proportion of authorized housing decreases.[46, 47] It is the middle-sized cities where both come together.[48]

▪ Rural–urban migration

Urbanization is perhaps the only enduring trend in human history. The high rate of urbanization that is now occurring throughout the developing world parallels that which occurred in England and some other European countries during their industrial revolutions in the 18th and 19th centuries. What is different now is that urbanization is not being accompanied by adequate economic growth in many developing countries.

The main features of contemporary urbanization have been determined by:[49]

- *political factors*: instability, civil war and repression;[50]
- *economic, environmental and social factors*:
  - *pushing*: environmental degradation and declining productivity of cropland; low rural incomes from agriculture; lack of new lands for farming; move to export rather than subsistence farming; enclosure and consolidation of farm holdings; limited off-farm employment;
  - *pulling*: higher incomes in urban areas; greater employment opportunities; economic safety nets; availability of social services, education and health care; improved water supply and other environmental services and infrastructure.

Box 2.1 Highlights of urbanization trends

- 47% of the world's population were located in urban areas in 2001, which will rise to 50% by 2007. Figure 2.6 shows the crossover for less developed regions, which will be in 2030.
- The average rate of world population growth will slow (see Statistical Annex Tables A.1, B.1 and B.2). Almost all of the population increase (90%) will be absorbed by the urban areas of the less developed regions, where the population will increase by 2 billion. This will mostly occur in Asia and Africa, where annual urban population growth is projected to be 2.4%.
- The rural population is projected to grow very slowly at just 0.2% per year and will remain nearly stable at about 3.2 billion.

Source: United Nations Population Division, 2002.

City size	Proportion of urban population			Proportion of increment	
	1975	2000	2015	1975–2000	2000–2015
10 million or more	4.4	7.9	8.8	11.9	11.4
5–10 million	7.9	5.9	6.8	3.6	9.4
1–5 million	21.5	23.6	24.8	26.0	28.3
0.5–1 million	11.4	10.1	9.2	8.6	6.4
Under 0.5 million	54.7	52.5	50.4	49.9	44.4

Source: United Nations Population Division, 2002.

Table 2.1

Distribution of urban population and growth by city-size category

The image of vast, spreading estates of makeshift housing self-built by recent arrivals is one of the most enduring in development; however, this is not the only way, or even the most common way, in which rural to urban migration takes place

Figure 2.8

Percentage unauthorized housing and infrastructure deficiency, city-size ranges, 1993

Source: UNCHS (Habitat), 1996c

Push factors: the relationship between rural productivity and population is complex. Land has a maximum carrying capacity and when it is exceeded, people will eventually be forced off the land. Modern technologies such as the Green Revolution have improved productivity on good quality land, generally staving off an overpopulation crisis.[51] This more productive farmland will support more people, but not in rural areas. Most productivity improvement technologies do not involve subdivision and sharecropping, which would support more families on the existing fixed supply of arable land, but actually involve enclosure of common lands or the creation of bigger estates for export-oriented crops. Projects that improve productivity per person also mean that less labour is required in rural areas.[52] Consequently, labourers are displaced, as are children of farmers, who go to seek work in the city. For the more prosperous farmers, their children receive an education, entitling them to a better paid professional job in the city.[53]

Pull factors: the question remains as to why poor rural populations continually move to the city, even when there are apparently no jobs for them and they have to live in slums with what might appear to be a lower quality of life, in a vulnerable situation and separated from everything they know. The 'bright lights' syndrome is the usual answer – there just seems to be a lot more going on in the city. Rural life is dull and backbreaking; there are few opportunities and little new arable land that can be developed, especially for women, who are often excluded from land occupancy upon death of, or divorce from, husband. The cities are uniquely able to create jobs, and if the formal sector does not have them, the informal sector can produce them.[54]

Life in the city is also not as risky as is often thought. Sanitation is generally now better; medical and social services are more readily available than in rural areas; life expectancies are higher; there is less risk of attack by brigands; and food availability is less dependent on the good health of working animals and the condition of crops, and less subject to the vagaries of the weather.[55] Famines are largely a rural phenomenon since it is fairly easy for aid agencies to ship supplies into cities, where it is in the interests of elites to ensure that they are distributed, and where levels of monitoring from well-informed and local action groups and the support agencies themselves are much higher. In rural areas or smaller urban areas, however, distribution channels are poor and there are many intervening opportunities for humanitarian aid to go astray. Cities are, in the end, a more controlled environment and life is less risky.

The separation between rural and urban life is also not as absolute as is often thought. For generations, informal settlements carry much of the atmosphere of the rural communities from which they have stemmed.[56] It is this rural imprint that gives them their unique, lively character, without the separations between home, work place and recreation that is the hallmark of 'modern' and middle-class society.

The image of vast, spreading estates of makeshift housing self-built by recent arrivals is one of the most enduring in development; however, this is not the only way, or even the most common way, in which rural to urban migration takes place. Transportation is no longer expensive; most immigrants have contacts or relatives in the city; they move backwards and forwards to live with friends until they are ready to make a permanent move; then they make a choice as to where and how they will live based on what they have learned. If there is affordable rental housing, they will pay for it until they can manage no longer. If there are new intrusions on unoccupied land, they will join in and build whatever they can afford. They will move in and out of backyard shacks or other informal accommodation until they have been there longer than anyone else and they become 'the resident'.

Another commonly held theory is the 'city as parasite' – that urban–rural migration is a result of differential taxation with an 'urban bias'.[57] The urban elite (particularly under colonialism) tax rural produce to pay for services in the city, which attracts people to the city. This allegedly causes a misappropriation of resources in favour of urban areas.

This theory is very difficult to substantiate. Very little tax is actually paid in rural areas, which is why rural local governments have such trouble in providing services that have to be largely paid for by central government transfers.

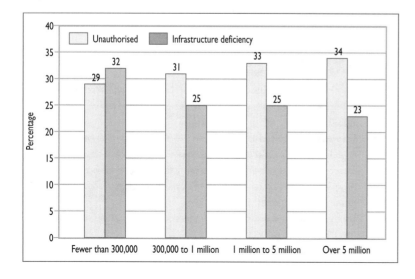

Most business and other taxes are paid in cities, and in many countries, rural areas receive high levels of subsidy.

Cities are so much more successful in promoting new forms of income generation, and it is so much cheaper to provide services in urban areas, that some experts have actually suggested that the only realistic poverty reduction strategy is to get as many people as possible to move to the city.[58] The fact is that higher incomes and more urbanization go hand in hand. As indicated earlier, improvement in rural productivity mean that less labour is required in rural areas. Increasingly, however, population growth in cities comes from within, and the larger urban spaces are no longer mandated by experience of the rural or the small town. As rural–urban migration slows and becomes less important, cities take on a truly urban character – the faceting and dividing of space between the social classes into a mosaic landscape of differences.

■ International migration

> *Give us your tired, your poor...the wretched refuse of your teeming shore.*[59]

The famous inscription on the Statue of Liberty welcoming immigrants to the New World may today be somewhat dated and, mostly, politically and factually incorrect; but it does stress that population movement is very often a response to deprivation and displacement. Immigration policy is, and remains, an incendiary issue in most countries. On the one hand, the reluctance of an increasingly educated youth to take on the 'difficult, dirty and dangerous' jobs has become a reason for increasing immigration in more affluent countries, while, on the other hand, a reluctance to 'dilute national character' and to pay various benefits and subsidies to immigrants tends to leave these people in a vulnerable state once they arrive.[60] Discriminatory attitudes towards foreigners persist as they have always done, and immigrant communities are always 'in the fishbowl', being examined for any signs of crime or deviant behaviour, while local perpetrators receive scant publicity. Attitudes towards multiculturalism softened somewhat in the new era of post-war liberalism; but the recent escalation of international terrorism has revived deep-seated xenophobic fears.

New immigrants tend to proceed directly to their own ethnic communities for support and advice, partly because they will often have networks of family and friends, partly because they will be able to communicate and operate under terms with which they are familiar, partly because they will have access to religious and retail facilities that meet their needs, but mostly because they will be welcomed without suspicion and 'shown the ropes'. The tendency to form ethnic neighbourhoods can, however, be part of the slum formation process, and if immigrants have few resources they may find themselves congregated in the poorer parts of town with few opportunities to join the wider community.[61] It is not an accident that ethnicity is usually a major component of disadvantage, and that the most disadvantaged areas in cities are usually found within bigger zones of high ethnicity.

In more developed countries, the succession of different groups of immigrants into traditional central slums forms much of the basis of the Chicago School ecological argument. Each new group of immigrants seeks the cheapest housing and replaces the last wave, who hopefully had been able to build up enough income after some years to leave the slums and find a better location.[62] The turnover of tenants, or even owners in low-cost premises, is high because considerable mobility out of the lowest income groups exists, and seeking temporary work requires frequent moves.[63]

In less developed countries, large numbers of international immigrants are refugees from neighbouring war-torn areas. Although refugee support agencies work hard to improve conditions, refugee camps can be among the most crowded, depressed and poor communities in the world – the 'slums of the slums'.[64] Refugees also face considerable prejudice if they enter the broader community; they can be subject to all sorts of slurs regarding their customs and appearance. If they are poor, they are accused of bringing disease and poverty; if they receive refugee allowances to which locals are not entitled, they are accused of being 'professional refugees' and are resented.

There are many examples of slums that have formed around an ethnic immigrant core or have later formed a primarily ethnic character. Harlem, New York, for black immigrants from the south or Puerto Ricans; 'Chinatowns' in many ports around the world; the Nigerian zones in Khartoum for pilgrims who have run out of money and been forced to interrupt their *hajj* to Mecca; 'little Italies' in Chicago and New York; the Gorbals in Glasgow; Kibera in Nairobi for demobbed Sudanese soldiers; the Palestinian refugee camps in Amman, Jordan; Dharavi in Mumbai, the 'world's largest slum', where Tamil is spoken as the main language; the Algerian *banlieus* in Paris and Lyons; and the Indian quarters of Southeast Asian cities are just a few examples.[65]

Immigration policy has toughened throughout the world, and large-scale population movements are not so much a part of the 'new globalization' as they were in the first globalization period of the late 19th century, or even in the post-war period.[66] There are no new frontiers to conquer. Nevertheless, international population movements have stepped up in recent years. A number of European countries that have been relatively closed and protected societies – for example, Austria, Belgium, Norway and Germany – have found themselves dealing with levels of international migration that they are poorly equipped to handle.[67]

■ Declining areas and depopulation

While urbanization and growth have received the bulk of attention in the slum literature, economic decline and loss of population, in fact, have taken up the greater part of the lifespan of most established traditional inner-city slums.[68] The decline and evacuation of inner cities and other places of urban blight have been the major feature of 'traditional' inner-city slums once they have passed their population peaks. Intra-urban flight is what causes the traditional slums: the 'abandoned city'. Both people and capital leave these residential areas to whoever is left behind or whoever is

There are many examples of slums that have formed around an ethnic immigrant core or have later formed a primarily ethnic character

International population movements have stepped up in recent years and a number of countries have found themselves dealing with levels of international migration that they are poorly equipped to handle

On a regional level, poverty and depression are also major features of areas that have lost their prime industries

While large numbers of dependent children were the main problem in earlier decades, and still are in many parts of the world, the ageing of the population and an increasing percentage of dependent-aged people is the looming demographic issue of the 21st century

Slums and poverty are closely related and mutually reinforcing, but the relationship is not always direct or simple

prepared to live within urban ruin. Property maintenance becomes uneconomic, and the 'slumlords' attempt to extract profits from whomever remains, usually obtaining good returns at no outlay on their largely depreciated capital, no matter how low the rents.

On a regional level, poverty and depression are also major features of areas that have lost their prime industries. Capitalism has its winners and losers, and there will always be declining regions where older people sit in genteel poverty as the young head towards the bright lights. Many parts of Europe and the 'rust belt' in the US have been in decline for extended periods. In these regions, it is loss of population and its associated effects – economic decline and capital withdrawal – that is the problem. In this case, the people who are left behind have few opportunities to improve or even maintain their situation as the heart falls out of their communities; and they become dependent on remissions from employed relatives in more dynamic areas, or government transfers and subsidies, in order to stay afloat. These decaying areas and industrial or mining 'ghost towns' can be most depressing. They are often, also, the site of environmental disasters because of inadequate environmental controls during earlier years.[69]

On a global scale, although urban in-migration will remain the primary dynamic for a considerable time, there are parts of the world in which the reverse is happening – and, as usual, it is the young with fewer ties to place who move most frequently, stripping areas of their future growth prospects. Emigration from cities often occurs when economic priorities change – as with the 'rust belts' in the US that lost most of their industrial jobs since 1970. Emigration from smaller cities to larger cities can also occur when the emphasis moves away from agriculture or mining, and new central city economic activities are strengthening under globalization pressures. The areas left behind become depressed zones with an ageing and often impoverished population as businesses close and capital migrates.

A demographic phenomenon that has been increasingly noticed in countries with a developed social security system has been exchange migration, where rural people seeking jobs (particularly young women) move to the city – often the partly gentrified central city – and people on fixed incomes move to lower-cost areas of high amenity, such as coastal regions. These are poor people on benefits, retirees and middle-aged rentiers. These people do not need access to employment and therefore prefer not to pay the higher housing and food costs of central areas, moving to coastal, mountain or other pleasant areas, often near the fringes of the cities, where house prices may be a third the cost and food 20 per cent less.[70]

Europe has already reached maximum population levels and the population of most European countries has begun to fall. The result of this depopulation, unless supplemented by immigration, will be economic stagnation on a national scale, similar to that already affecting areas based on the 'old economy'. However, many European countries are beginning to regret the pressure on their established social and cultural structures that immigration

has caused, and doors have been gradually closing to developing world immigrants for some time.

Dependency rates are a looming issue in a number of parts of the world, and here it is ageing and falling fertility rather than high birthrates that are of concern. A higher proportion of people in the work force is a great advantage to a country in improving incomes, reducing poverty and generating local savings and investment.[71] While large numbers of dependent children were the main problem in earlier decades, and still are in many parts of the world, the ageing of the population and an increasing percentage of dependent-aged people is the looming demographic issue of the 21st century.[72] Birthrates fell to well below replacement levels in most Organisation for Economic Co-operation and Development (OECD) countries during the 1990s, and 44 per cent of the world's population now lives in countries where population is below replacement levels.[73] As a result of falling fertility, it is estimated that by 2050, the proportion of population over 60 will more than double from 10 per cent to 21 per cent. Most of Europe and Japan will have around one third of their population over 60, and 9 per cent over 80, by that time.

The developing countries will not be spared the problem, though it will take longer to take effect. Improvements in health conditions are such that, in 2002, life expectancy at age 60 was 15 years in less developed regions (LDRs), and barely greater at 18 years in the HICs.[74] Once the current 'boom generations' reach 60, all countries will have the same ageing problem. Although it is still well in the future for much of the world, preparations must be made for the global problems that ageing populations will ultimately cause.

Poverty

■ Poverty and slums

Slums and poverty are closely related and mutually reinforcing, but the relationship is not always direct or simple. On the one hand, slum dwellers are not a homogeneous population, and some people of reasonable incomes choose to live within, or on, the edges of slum communities. Even though most slum dwellers work in the informal economy, it is not unusual for them to have incomes that exceed the earnings of formal-sector employees. On the other hand, in many cities, there are more poor outside slum areas than within them. Slums are designated areas where it is easiest to see poor people in the highest concentrations and the worst conditions; but even the most exclusive and expensive areas will have some low-income people.

Slum conditions are caused by poverty and inadequate housing responses, which are mutually reinforcing, to some extent. It is not surprising that the characteristics of the settlement or housing is often confused by act or by implication with the characteristics of the people living in them. The issues of living conditions, poverty and poor people's management of their own situation are amalgamated, and cause-and-effect relationships are confused. This presents a policy and delivery problem for programmes aimed at addressing slum conditions as part of an overall poverty reduction agenda. The converse is the case for non-housing poverty reduction programmes, which sometimes presume that their activities will result in improvements in housing, infrastructure and service delivery in slum areas – but 'trickle through' to housing may be extremely slow or non-existent unless the income improvements are substantial and sustained.

Although poverty in urban areas has been increasing for some decades and there are now higher numbers of the 'poorest of the poor' in urban centres throughout the world than at any previous time, the urban poor are usually able to help themselves more than their rural counterparts. Indeed, the immigrant urban poor have largely moved voluntarily in order to exploit actual or perceived economic opportunities. Opportunities manifest, in part, due to the growing urban informal sector, which is most spectacularly visible in the many growing and large-scale informal and squatter settlements in urban centres. In many cities, the informal sector accounts for as much as 60 per cent of employment of the urban population and may well serve the needs of an equally high proportion of citizens through the provision of goods and services.[75]

Yet, it cannot be assumed that those living in slums that appear physically uniform all have the same needs and demands. The necessity to distinguish between different levels of poverty has been recognized with a view to targeting and tailoring resources at those most in need. Women – widows in particular – children, unemployed youths and disabled people have all been identified as the most vulnerable amongst the poor, as have female-headed households and certain ethnic and religious groups. Where housing conditions are poor, such as in slums and informal urban settlements, it is the vulnerable who suffer most from environmental degradation and inadequate service provision.

Increasingly, the phenomenon of women-headed households is common in urban areas and especially in slums. Women-headed households constitute 30 per cent or more of the total households in urban low-income settlements in parts of Africa.[76] Women-headed households tend to have fewer income-earning opportunities than male-headed households and are generally poorer.[77] Typically, women have lower levels of education, work longer hours, retain responsibility for childcare as well as productive and community management roles, and have poorer diets and more restricted mobility than men.[78] In general, women-headed households will have narrower housing choices by virtue of their low incomes. Sometimes their low social and legal status limits their housing choices, in addition to their exclusion from holding title to land through either legal or cultural means.[79]

■ Defining poverty

Like slums, poverty is something that people believe they can easily distinguish; in fact, the concept is difficult to define. Urban poverty is often defined in terms of household income – for example, the proportion of a city's households who are earning less than what is needed to afford a 'basket' of basic necessities, or living on less than US$1 or US$2 a day.

Monetary measures of poverty have been used in many countries, but they do not capture the multidimensional nature of poverty.[80] People may be poor not just because of low incomes, but their poverty may derive from an inadequate, unstable or risky asset base needed as a cushion to carry them through hard times. They may be poor because their housing is overcrowded, of low quality or is insecure; because they do not have access to safe water, adequate sanitation, health care or schools; because they are lacking a supportive safety net; or because they are not protected by laws and regulations concerning civil and political, as well as economic, social and cultural rights, discrimination and environmental health, or because they are denied a voice within political systems. These and related aspects of poverty are shown in Box 2.2.

The different dimensions of urban poverty have been described as:[81]

- *Low income*: consisting of those who are unable to participate in labour markets and lack other means of support, and those whose wage income is so low that they are below a nominal poverty line;
- *Low human capital*: low education and poor health are the components of 'capability poverty' used in the UNDP HDI. Health shocks, in particular, can lead to chronic poverty;
- *Low social capital*: this involves a shortage of networks to protect households from shock; weak patronage on the labour market; labelling and exclusion. This particularly applies to minority groups;
- *Low financial capital*: lack of productive assets that might be used to generate income or avoid paying major costs (for example, a house, a farm or a business).

It is important to consider all of the inter-related aspects of poverty; merely addressing monetary resources or livelihoods may only be a temporary stop gap and may not deal with the many other aspects of poverty that may ensure a sustainable transition from poverty.

Other conceptual approaches to poverty are as follows.

Capability poverty has been defined as the lack of life chances and opportunities, defined particularly through ill health and lack of education – this has formed the underpinning of the UNDP HDI.[82] These more fundamental needs are paramount in the least developed countries in establishing the capability of individuals to improve their lives. Once these have been met, capability is somewhat more subtle and encompasses empowerment, work contacts and the ability to transcend social class. The concept of *social capital* is related to capability, but refers to the individual's ability to command or work within 'institutions, relationships and norms that shape the quality and quantity of a society's social interactions'.[83]

Chronic poverty: in the US, only about 50 per cent of those in poverty remain in this situation for more than two years.[84] A similar 50 per cent figure seems to apply in most countries. Approximately half of those in poverty are long-

Mobility has implications for pro-poor policies. Two kinds of programmes are necessary: safety nets for the transitory poor; and empowerment and capability raising programmes for the chronically poor

Women – widows in particular – children, unemployed youths and disabled people have all been identified as the most vulnerable amongst the poor, as have female-headed households and certain ethnic and religious groups

Box 2.2 The constituents of urban poverty

I   Inadequate income (and thus inadequate consumption of necessities including food and, often, safe and sufficient water; often problems of indebtedness, with debt repayments significantly reducing income available for necessities).

2   Inadequate, unstable or risky asset base (non-material and material including educational attainment and housing) for individuals, households or communities.

3   Inadequate shelter (typically poor quality, overcrowded and insecure).

4   Inadequate provision of 'public' infrastructure (eg piped water, sanitation, drainage, roads, footpaths) which increases the health burden and often the work burden.

5   Inadequate provision for basic services such as day care/schools/vocational training, health care, emergency services, public transport, communications, law enforcement.

6   Limited or no safety net to ensure basic consumption can be maintained when income falls; also to ensure access to shelter and health care when these can no longer be paid for.

7   Inadequate protection of poorer groups' rights through the operation of the law, including laws and regulations regarding civil and political rights, occupational health and safety, pollution control, environmental health, protection from violence and other crimes, protection from discrimination and exploitation.

8   Voicelessness and powerlessness within political systems and bureaucratic structures, leading to little or no possibility of receiving entitlements; of organizing, making demands and getting a fair response; or of receiving support for developing their own initiatives. Also, no means of ensuring accountability from aid agencies, NGOs, public agencies and private utilities or being able to participate in the definition and implementation of their urban poverty programmes.

Source: Satterthwaite, 2001.

term poor, while the other half are moving in and out of poverty.[85] In Australia, mobility is higher: about 80 per cent of those in the lowest quintile of household income move upwards within two years, and 15 per cent of these move into the highest quintile (students, unemployed professionals etc).

This mobility has implications for pro-poor policies. Two kinds of programmes are necessary: safety nets for the transitory poor, and empowerment and capability raising programmes for the chronically poor.[86]

■ Measurement of poverty incidence

Most countries have some way of measuring poverty (locally defined poverty). The common types of measures are those based on income, which include the following.

Absolute poverty: this comprises people who cannot afford to buy a 'minimum basket' of goods – which sometimes is just food and water for minimum nutrition, but should include other necessities, such as clothing, shelter and transport to employment, education or the means to obtain the basic necessities.

Relative poverty: this is the proportion of people below some threshold, which is often a percentage of local median income.

However, the World Bank has recently popularized a simple '*extreme poverty*' measure of US$1 a day or US$2 a day (both adjusted for purchasing price parity, or local costs). It is on this basis that most of their poverty figures since 1993 have been calculated.

These income-based measures substantially underestimate urban poverty because they do not make allowance for the extra costs of urban living (housing and

transport, plus the lack of opportunity to grow one's own food). They also do not reveal intra-household poverty in situations where there is unequal power among household members, so that it is possible for women and children to live in poverty even though the larger household of which they are a part is not classified as such. Research has shown that budgetary allocations are different in households where women act as the decision-makers. Measures of household income also do not reveal relevant background conditions; they do not, in themselves, provide information on the spatial distribution of poverty or its national context.[87] Nevertheless, the main results of recent Word Bank studies are worth recording, as they show broad trends, useful for reaching the Millennium Development Goals (MDGs).

Overall, half of the world – nearly 3 billion people – lives on less than US$2 dollars a day. As discussed in Chapter 1 in connection with Target 1 of the MDGs, the proportion of people living in extreme poverty of less than US$1 a day declined from 29 per cent in 1990 to 23 per cent in 1999, mostly due to a large decrease of 140 million people in East Asia during 1987 to 1998. In absolute terms, global numbers in extreme poverty increased up to 1993, and were back to about 1988 levels in 1998, as Table 2.2 shows. A recent study points to 'two main proximate causes of the disappointing rate of poverty reduction: too little economic growth in many of the poorest countries and persistent inequalities that inhibited the poor from participating in the growth that did occur'.[88]

The region where the increase in extreme poverty was the most pronounced comprised the former socialist countries of Eastern Europe and Central Asia. Poverty rates moved to over 50 per cent in half of the transitional countries in the transition period of 1988 to 1995; and persons in poverty increased from 14 million to 168 million in the region, as a whole. The number of people in poverty in Russia rose from 2 million to 74 million, in the Ukraine from 2 million to 33 million, and in Romania from 1.3 million to 13.5 million.[89] These massive changes were due to lower incomes, to increased income inequality and especially to inflation, which lowered purchasing power substantially.

Locally defined poverty increased in developed countries without adequate safety net systems during the period up to about 1995, and has decreased somewhat in the subsequent boom years.

There are no specific global estimates of urban poverty at this stage; but it is generally presumed that urban poverty levels are less than rural poverty. However, in India, there are equal proportions of about 15 per cent of the population in the extreme poverty category in both urban and rural areas.[90] Urban poverty has also been increasing its share in most countries subject to structural adjustment programmes, most of which are deliberately anti-urban in nature.[91] The absolute number of poor and undernourished in urban areas is increasing, as is the share of urban areas in overall poverty and malnutrition, and the locus of poverty is moving to cities.[92]

Further research is needed to determine the relationship between the two MDG targets of poverty reduction and assisting slum dwellers, and to delineate, in more specific terms, the extent to which slums are the

The absolute number of poor and undernourished in urban areas is increasing, as is the share of urban areas in overall poverty and malnutrition, and the locus of poverty is moving to cities

	Percent living in extreme poverty					Millions				
	1987	1990	1993	1996	1998	1987	1990	1993	1996	1998
East Asia	26.6	27.6	25.2	14.9	15.3	417.5	452.5	431.9	265.1	278.3
(excluding China)	23.9	18.5	15.9	10.0	11.3	114.1	92.0	83.5	55.1	65.2
Eastern Europe	0.2	1.6	4.0	5.1	5.1	1.1	7.1	18.3	23.8	24.0
Latin America	15.3	16.8	15.3	15.6	15.6	63.7	73.8	70.8	76.0	78.2
Middle East and North Africa	4.3	2.4	1.9	1.8	2.0	9.3	5.7	5.0	5.0	5.6
South Asia	44.9	44.0	42.4	42.3	40.0	474.4	495.1	505.1	531.7	522.0
Africa	46.6	47.7	49.7	48.5	46.3	217.2	242.3	273.3	289.0	290.9
Total	28.3	29.0	28.2	24.5	24.0	1183.2	1276.4	1304.3	1190.6	1198.9
(excluding China)	28.5	28.1	27.7	27.0	26.2	879.8	915.9	955.9	980.5	985.7

Sources: Chen and Ravallion, 2001; updated from Ravallion and Chen, 1997.

spatial manifestation of urban poverty, particularly in cities and on a global scale.

Targeting of poverty reduction programmes

The reduction of poverty in all of its forms is now the prime objective of development policy. The new 'poverty before growth' emphasis has resulted in a number of observations regarding the success of past programmes that were ostensibly pro-poor, particularly poorly targeted health, education or income-generation programmes, and issues surrounding governance.[93]

An evaluation of several recent programmes finds that it takes some time before benefits reach the poor in most broad interventions.[94] Early on, better connected groups can capture the benefits, particularly where outlays are small; but if the programme is well targeted in concept, targeting tends to improve as the programme expands. Similarly, during cutbacks such as structural adjustment programmes (SAPs), the poor are more adversely affected than higher-income people, so specific measures must be provided to assist poorer groups to weather downturns.

Corruption and other governance challenges become major issues once targeting becomes the main priority. Substantial proportions of funds intended for the poor or for general development have sometimes disappeared into the accounts of officials responsible for tendering contracts. Widespread corruption in all aspects of local service provision has also acted as an effective tax on the whole community, particularly the most disadvantaged. Another recent study, encompassing 41 countries, concludes that 'High and rising corruption increases income inequality and poverty by reducing economic growth, the progressivity of the tax system, the level and effectiveness of social spending, and by perpetuating an unequal distribution of asset ownership and unequal access to education.'[95]

Table 2.2

Population living below US$1 per day at 1993 purchasing power parity (PPP), by region

The reduction of poverty in all of its forms is now the prime objective of development policy

NOTES

1   This chapter is based on a draft prepared by Joe Flood, Urban Resources, Australia.

2   This is compounded by the higher risk profile of the poor, who default more regularly and move more frequently in search of work – which means that they have to pay higher rents in a competitive system.

3   This steepening simply means that land and housing prices rise faster towards the centre.

4   According to Flood, 1984, 2000c.

5   Fujita, 1989.

6   According to the model, poor households who value accessibility will not move to the edge of cities as some have thought, but instead immediately outward to the next ring.

7   There is a very large literature on factorial ecology. Some key references include Shevky and Bell, 1955; Berry and Kasarda, 1975; and, in the context of globalization, Wyly, 1999; Flood, 2000b.

8   Flood, 2000b.

9   Services are commonly divided into three classes: producer (services to industry, including finance), consumer (services to individuals) and social (education, health and other government services).

10   Flood, 2000b.

11   Muth, 1969; Fujita, 1989. Urban economics presume that households compete for space according to their incomes and their preference for space/accessibility, and locate accordingly in the city.

12   The Australian Bureau of Statistics sells indices of advantage and disadvantage that are devised using very similar methods to Flood, 2000b.

13   In Sydney, the inner-city slums that have been gentrified now have the highest scores on both advantage and disadvantage because the producer service graduates have now located there, but so have various special groups, including the homeless, the gay community and drug users. As

well, many of the original inhabitants are still around.

14   Case study – Sydney. This separation is partly due to the westwards movement of the natural population centre of the formerly coastal city; but it also represents a clear division of function.

15   A bibliography for indexes of segregation or dissimilarity is found at www.stat.psu.edu/~jkuha/msbib/node18.html.

16   It has the disadvantage that the smaller the areal subdivision, the larger the index tends to become, presuming that the sub-population is clumped together at a very small level, such as the city block or census collection area.

17   Flood et al, 1992.

18   According to Logan (2002), the suburban versus inner-city income inequality that is such a special feature of US cities actually increased during the prosperous 1990s. Poverty rates are twice as high in the cities as in the suburbs,

unchanged since 1990. In a few cities such as Seattle and Chicago, the very large existing income differentials have reduced somewhat. The opposite is the case in Australian cities, where inner cities have much higher average incomes and the differential with the (middle-class) suburbs is increasing. Although spatial income differentials have increased, this does not necessarily imply that income segregation has increased, because existing differentials between rich and poor have been reinforced rather than new areas of disadvantage appearing.

19   For example, blacks and whites have become more integrated during the 1990s in 60 out of 74 counties in Ohio, US; see www.ipr.uc.edu/Beyond/2001mar/btn_2001mar_table1.pdf. Rapid desegregation applies largely to smaller and newer areas, and segregation still remains very high in older US cities such as Detroit and Chicago. Figures for primary

school segregation in 2000 are given in www.mumford1.dyndns.org/cen2000/SchoolPop/SPsort/sort_d1.html.

20 Priemus (1998) shows that spatial inequality reduced in The Netherlands during the early 1990s.

21 UNCHS (Habitat), 2001a.

22 Caldeira, 1996a.

23 Jargowsky, 1996a; 1997.

24 Not in the US, where inner-city blight still rules and worsened in many cities, with increasing inequality, up to 1994.

25 Public housing in Adelaide, Australia, for example, was originally 'working men's housing' built in areas specifically designated for government factories.

26 Sanchez-Jankowski, 1999.

27 Bingham and Zhang (1997) find that 50 per cent of economic activities decline substantially in US city neighbourhoods once poverty reaches 10 per cent. At 20 per cent poverty, supermarkets and banks disappear and corner stores take their place, with the area effectively ghettoized. The housing stock declines somewhat later, at about 40 per cent poverty.

28 In Melbourne, for example, most of the early slums and warehouses were located in areas subject to flooding. The city divided clearly east and west of the Yarra River because of prevailing topographic conditions – the west is a flat basalt plain where few trees can grow; the east is pleasant rolling countryside with deep soils. The social east–west divide has lessened in recent years.

29 This does not apply to professional home-based work.

30 The website www.stu.cofc.edu/~mcgallig/#15 contains excellent footage of slum conditions of the period.

31 The reproduction of social classes is a major branch of sociology to which its founders, Marx, Weber, Durkheim, among many others, have contributed a substantial literature. More recently, post-modern approaches to space and social reproduction were introduced by Pierre Bourdieu, David Harvey, Edward Soja and Doreen Massey. A short bibliography is at www.eng.fju.edu.tw/Literary_Criticism/postmodernism/postmo_urban/biblio.htm#Cities.

32 In Nairobi, during the Mau Mau period, the 'white' city was actually ringed with barbed wire and passes were required. Passes are generally required in formal ethnic separations.

33 The growth of Mumbai followed this plan. See www.theory.tifr.res.in/bombay/history/slums.html.

34 These areas are often known as ghettos. Ethnic groups are forcibly separated and removed to these areas.

35 These peri-urban slum areas are often rapidly expanding in the face of urbanization (Briggs and Mwamfupe, 2000; Sutcliffe, 1997).

36 Typically, subject to flooding or landslip, or along transport corridors, as discussed in Chapter 1.

37 UNCHS (Habitat), 2001a.

38 UNCHS (Habitat), 2001a.

39 The 'city of power' has low population numbers and cannot easily be distinguished from residential characteristics alone.

40 UNDP, 2002.

41 Flood, 1997; 2001; ADB, 2001.

42 United Nations Population Division, 2002; www.un.org/esa/population/publications/wup2001/wup2001dh.pdf.

43 USAID, 2001.

44 For most places outside of Asia, urban growth rates were highest during 1960 to 1965. The actual increment in urban population will be highest around 2025 at 74 million per year (it is currently about 60 million per year).

45 The deficiency index is defined here as the average in each city of the proportion of houses that do not have water, sewerage and electricity. It is an index of the amount of work that remains to be done in networked infrastructure. 'Unauthorized housing' is a housing stock in urban areas that is not in compliance with current regulation.

46 The relationship is highly statistically significant and is at its strongest in the less developed regions: Africa and Southern Asia. It appears to be reversed only in China, where bigger cities may be in worse shape.

47 This relationship is quite weak and may not be significant.

48 The city-size effect on infrastructure availability is significant but does not compare with differences resulting from different levels of national development.

49 Derived from www.frameweb.org/meetings/urbanization.ppt.

50 Refugees usually flood into the cities where they feel relatively safe and can find accommodation and assistance. Except for specifically designated camps that are places of no opportunity, there is no place for them in the rural parts of their new countries.

51 Food production per head continues to fall in Africa, and very substantially in the former USSR; see www.fao.org/docrep/U8480E/U8480E05.htm#Rural-urban%20poverty%20indicators.

52 USAID, 2001.

53 Cambodia (2001) shows that 34 per cent of tertiary students were the children of land-owning farmers, which are only about 10 per cent of the population.

54 One study of Punjabi migrants to Delhi found that 94 per cent of them had found work within two months (USAID, 2001).

55 This was not the case even as late as the middle 20th century, where high density living was commonly regarded as the major source of epidemics of infectious disease, and where life expectancies were generally lower than in rural areas. The early phases of urbanization were the major motivation for the development of modern medicine and sanitation systems.

56 Kenyan urban folk who have lived in downtown Nairobi all of their lives, if asked where they come from, will say from Nyeri or Kiambu or Eldoret, even if they have never been to these places. They will be taken there to be buried on ancestral land when they die.

57 See, for example, Becker et al, 1994. Much of the value added of food exports actually takes place in cities, where it is taxed. Normally, there will only be a rural bias if food prices are frozen or directly subsidized.

58 Norconsult, 1996.

59 Statue of Liberty inscription.

60 For Japan, see Atoh, 2000.

61 A typical example of labour market abuses that immigrants, especially illegal immigrants, must endure is found in www.usinfo.state.gov/regional/ea/chinaaliens/kwongstory.htm.

62 For example, during the 1970s, and later in Melbourne, Australia, which is one of the most multicultural cities in the world, Southern European post-war immigrants were happy to sell their inner-city dwellings and head for much larger properties in the northern suburbs. A new wave of Vietnamese refugees moved in and established businesses, and streetscapes changed accordingly.

63 In the US, only about 50 per cent of those in poverty stay that way for more than two years, according to Bureau of the Census (2001). In Australia, about 80 per cent of those in the lowest quintile of household income move upwards within two years, and 15 per cent of these move into the highest quintile (students, unemployed professionals, etc).

64 Refugees in camps in the Gaza strip live at an average of nine per room. Few have any form of employment, and many families have been consistently there for 40 years.

65 The main languages in Mumbai are Marathi (official), Gujarati and Hindi.

66 US immigration was virtually unencumbered during the 19th century, when 32 million people crossed the Atlantic between 1840 and 1920; but now Green cards are the subject of stringent quotas. In the post-war period, Australia actually paid for millions of people to immigrate, with free sea fares and assistance with hostel accommodation. Now, non-refugee immigrants have to bring substantial funds with them and processes to obtain permanent residence are slow and expensive, as in other countries.

67 Charlotte Abney, in Euroviews 2002, writes on Norway's adjustment problems: www.manila.djh.dk/norway02.

68 See the discussion of Surry Hills in Sydney in Chapter 5.

69 Typical transitional economies have a 60 per cent reliance on manufacturing industry compared with less than 20 per cent in highly developed countries. Most of the industry is based on outdated technology and is not competitive.

70 The whole south-eastern seaboard of Australia now has an essentially urban population, with less than 2 per cent involved in agricultural pursuits. New small coastal towns of over 40,000 people are appearing for the first time in a century, and many of them have problems dealing with ecological damage and lack of urban services, since the new arrivals do not provide a strong economic base. One

town actually has an elected 'unemployed party' representative on the local government.

71 It has, for example, been argued that this was the primary reason for the 'Asian Miracle' economic growth of 1980 to 1995.

72 The proportion of dependent children is forecast to fall from 30 per cent of the population worldwide to 20 per cent in 2050 (United Nations Population Division, 2001).

73 See www.un.org/esa/population/publications/longrange/longrangeExecSum.pdf.

74 Differences in life expectancies at birth are very largely due to difference in the infant mortality rate.

75 Mumtaz and Wegelin, 2001, Chapter 6.

76 UNCHS (Habitat), 1996a; Chant, 1997. The Global Urban Indicators Database (GUID) (see UNCHS (Habitat) (1996c) and UH-Habitat (2002f)) shows several African settlements with 55 per cent women-headed households, generally where the men are absent for work, with a median of 24 per cent for African cities. Hanoi, cities in the Caribbean and a number of European capitals also show very high figures of up to 40 per cent.

77 Tacoli, 1999. This does not occur so much in Asia, where woman-headed households are richer, on average.

78 Wratten, 1995.

79 Kruekeberg and Paulsen, 2002, p240.

80 Authors who have discussed the multidimensional nature of poverty include Amis, 1995; Baulch, 1996; Chambers, 1997;

Courmont, 2001; Jones, 1999; Maxwell, 1999; Moser, 1996; Moser et al, 1993; Wratten, 1995.

81 Moser et al, 1993.

82 Nobel Prize winner Amartya Sen, 1997.

83 Collier, 1998; Grootaert, 1998.

84 According to US Bureau of the Census, 2001.

85 Amis, 2002.

86 World Bank, 2001a, b. Illife (1987), after Gutton, calls these 'conjunctural' and 'structural' poverty.

87 In addition, they often do not inform us about the distribution of households across a range of income groups.

88 Chen and Ravallion, 2001. Their methodology has been extensively criticized by Reddy and Pogge (2002) on the basis of the arbitrary poverty line, an inaccurate measure of

purchasing power parity (PPP), and through extrapolation from limited data. The rather arbitrary change in the poverty line by the World Bank between 1993 and 2000 also increased poverty by 8 per cent in Africa and decreased elsewhere.

89 Milanovic, 1998, Table 5.1.

90 Mehta, 2001.

91 Moser et al, 1993; World Bank, 2000a, 2001a, p66.

92 Haddad et al (1999) show the percentage of poor in urban areas increasing in eight sampled countries from the mid 1980s to the 1990s.

93 In what Ali and Sirivardana (1996) call the 'new development paradigm', poverty is to be dealt with, and growth treated, as incidental rather than the converse.

94 Ravallion, 2002.

95 Gupta et al, 1998.

CHAPTER 3

CITIES AND SLUMS WITHIN GLOBALIZING ECONOMIES[1]

This chapter revisits the subject of the previous *Global Report on Human Settlements* – globalization – from the particular point of view of inequality and poverty, and their potential impacts on slum formation. It pays particular attention to the impact of neo-liberalism on the major facets of globalization – trade, deregulated capital and labour markets – and the withdrawal of the state in its various forms. It deals with the growing realization that changes in the development policy paradigm have, in part, contributed to changes in poverty and inequality in both the developed and the developing world since the late 1970s, while failing to deliver much in the way of growth for all except a select group of countries, and then only for a minority of their citizens. The expansion of urban slums in the developing world during the period may also have roots in these conditions. On a more positive note, globalization is offering opportunities for cities to act in their own rights and to form communities of interest, and for entrepreneurs of modest means who would, in the past, have had little chance to conduct international business to move out into the wider world. The insecurities created by globalization, however, go much further than the economic, and so far any benefits to the poorer people of the world have largely been elusive.

INEQUALITY AND POVERTY

On the face of it, the last decade of the 20th century should have been one of great prosperity because of the opening up of world economies to the benefits of trade, an increasing rate of productivity improvement due to new technologies, and a peace dividend with the potential of diverting the massive military expenditures of the previous century to more productive uses.[2]

The 20th century had been one of the grimmest and most isolationist on record from the point of view of international affairs and trade. Two World Wars and a Great Depression were accompanied by a dramatic drop in international trade and an increase in protectionism. Trade fell from about 20 per cent of most national economies in the mercantile period of 1870 to 1914 to less than 10 per cent during the 1930s.[3] Although international trade increased substantially following 1945, insurrections meant that large areas of some countries were unusable during much of the period because of struggles based on ideological differences supported by Cold War politics. Many important land trade routes were closed in the developing world because of the activities of guerillas or insurgents. Trade in guns and weapons

took up a high proportion of the budget of many developing countries, with money loaned and equipment opportunistically provided by the developed countries.

The fall of the Iron Curtain in 1990 might have presaged a great period of peace and development. Certainly, the previous decade had seen progress in opening up economies. During the 20 years between 1970 and 1990, world trade tripled (though most of this activity was in East Asia and the developed world, and did not extend to the world as a whole).

During the 1990s, trade continued to expand at an almost unprecedented rate, no-go areas opened up, and military expenditure decreased. New communications technologies, such as the internet, reduced the tyranny of distance, improved productivity and made it possible for people in developing countries or remote areas to share in knowledge and engage in types of work that would have previously been unthinkable. All the basic inputs to production became cheaper, as interest rates fell rapidly, along with the price of basic commodities. Capital flows were increasingly unfettered by national controls and could move rapidly to the most productive areas. Under what were almost perfect economic conditions according to the dominant neo-liberal economic doctrine, one might have imagined that the decade would have been one of unrivalled prosperity and social justice.

But this is not what happened. The gap between poor and rich countries increased, just as it had done for the previous 20 years and, in most countries, income inequality increased or, at best, stabilized. In the boom years since 1993, the situation is more equivocal and uneven; inequality has increased sharply in some parts of the world and decreased or remained stable (albeit at high levels) in others. The fact is, however, that any improvements have been modest: the real incomes of the least developed countries (LDCs) have not regained 1978 levels, and the median real income in the US has also fallen since the mid 1970s.

At the end of the 20th century, there appeared to be a general mood of pessimism – a feeling that things had gone backwards, somehow, for the majority of people, that poverty seemed to have increased and social justice and the quality of life had diminished, while sustainability was increasingly threatened. So, what went wrong?

The main issues, most analyses agreed, were:

*   high levels of inequality and insecurity;
*   increasing globalization (especially in trade, finance and telecommunications);

During the 1990s the gap between poor and rich countries increased and, in most countries, income inequality increased or, at best, stabilized

- the retreat of the state from its protective and supportive roles;
- rapid urbanization and population growth under conditions of economic stagnation; and
- improved access of the 'local' to the 'global'.

These issues will be considered, in turn, in this chapter.

Inequality: a recent history

If the world behaved as predicted by the simple neoclassical growth model, the per capita incomes of countries with the same saving rate, technologies, government policies and population growth would eventually converge... [However], there is enough evidence in support of the view that the world seems to be converging towards two clubs: the rich and the poor countries... The question is why are some countries kept in the low income club, and can something be done to reverse this?[4]

Capitalism has long been recognized to be cyclical in nature, with periodic booms and busts, or periods of prosperity and recession, in several time scales. The longer cycles have a strong correlation with urban in-migration, stops and starts in house building, and with the development of slum areas.[5] The overall picture for a very long economic cycle (Kondratiev wave of 50 to 60 years) is shown in Figure 3.1. The upwave is a time of slow inflation, growth and relative economic stability; the downwave is an unstable disinflationary period of booms and busts.

Entrepôt free-trade ports have been particularly prone to cyclical growth patterns, such as those responsible for areas or rings of slums in internationally exposed cities such as Sydney and Liverpool during the recessions of the 1850s and 1890s.[6,7] In booms, large numbers of poorer quality formal-sector houses are built as entrepreneurs seek to recycle their capital quickly. During recessions, maintenance expenditure on dwellings and infrastructure fall, lowering stock quality. Lower-income people tend to congregate in the lowest cost dwellings and housing, as their circumstances drive them into poverty. Large areas of poor quality housing with low-income occupants result – and the traditional, formal-sector slums of the Western world have often appeared in this way.

What generally happens under the irregular boom/bust cycles of unregulated capitalism is shown in Figure 3.2. In *booms*, shown in the left half of the figure, the ratchet handle moves upwards. The richest few per cent gain most of the income and wealth because they hold most of the assets. Most booms happen in a situation of mild disinflation, which inflates asset prices well above the underlying productivity trend. Real estate and stock prices rise enormously. There is usually a drop in unemployment and in poverty – but the trickle-down effect is fairly minimal.

In *busts*, shown in the right side of the figure, the ratchet handle moves downwards from its post-boom position. The poor suffer disproportionately, as do women,

losing both income-earning opportunities and government support, as revenues drop.[8] Table 3.1 shows that during two recent downturns in Canada, for example, earned income for the lowest-income group was reduced drastically. The higher-income groups are generally able to protect their wealth, and may even use the situation to buy cheap assets for the next cycle.

When translating the changes after the bust back to the initial position, there has been a marked increase in inequality: the rich have gained and the poor have lost. This will be repeated in subsequent cycles.

The only time when inequality appears to decrease is during long, steady *growth periods*, such as 1945 to 1967, when slowly increasing excess demand for labour allows wages to rise and keeps unemployment low.[9]

With more cities opening to cyclical forces of international trade, it is likely that booms and busts will become more marked, and that slums associated with these economic cycles will continue to form in the rapidly developing areas of the world.

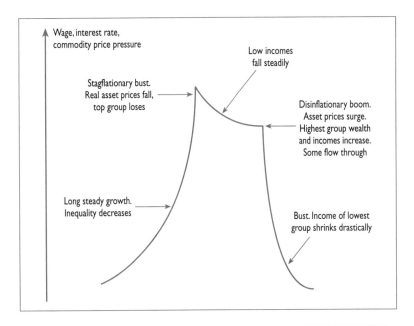

Figure 3.1

Booms and busts: stylized long wave

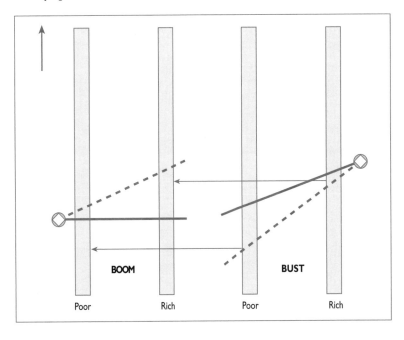

Figure 3.2

The invisible hand: ratcheting of inequality in booms and busts

Income group	1981–1984 (%)	1989–1993 (%)
1	-60	-86
2	-30	-45
3	-17	-21
4	-11	-16
5	-8	-14
6	-6	-11
7	-5	-7
8	-4	-6
9	-3	-5
10	2	-9

Note: 1 = lowest-income group.

Source: Curry-Stevens, 2001.

Table 3.1

Changes of distribution of household income in Canada during two downturns: earned income

During 1970, the top 20 per cent of the world's people in the richest countries had 32 times the income of the poorest 20 per cent, growing to 45 times in 1980, 59 times in 1989, and about 78 times at present

Figure 3.3

Ratio between richest and poorest nations' GDP per person, 1800 to 2000

Source: Maddison, 1995

In 1760, Indian per capita income was between 10 and 30 per cent inferior to the British per capita income, while in 1800, Chinese per capita income was equal to or higher than the British. Asia produced 56 per cent of world's gross domestic product (GDP), and Western Europe 24 per cent.[10] Figure 3.3 shows that during the long period of mercantile capitalism in the 19th century, the ratio between the GDP per person of the richest and the poorest nations steadily widened from 3 to about 10.[11] During 1970, the top 20 per cent of the world's people in the richest countries had 32 times the income of the poorest 20 per cent, growing to 45 times in 1980, 59 times in 1989, and about 78 times at present.[12]

Inequality decreased gradually in the long post-war growth period of 1945 to 1972. Wages and productivity rose steadily, and full employment was the norm. Economies were kept stable using the new techniques of Keynesian pump priming through the public sector. Under communist threat from the outside, and under pressure of growing social democratic and communist movements at home, the capitalist regimes, already enfeebled by the Great Depression, conceded to dramatic and far-reaching social reforms. The nature of wild capitalism of the 19th century changed with the introduction of unemployment benefits and pensions, paid vacations, the 40-hour week, guaranteed and free education and health care for all, and trade union protection of workers. In the developing countries that were liberated from colonial rule, dreams of industrialization and

'catching up' could be realistically entertained, and countries grew fast as import substitution became the dominant approach to development. Over the post-war growth period of 1950 to 1972, inequality primarily fell within countries, and during 1960 to 1978, divergence between countries slowed or lessened, as Figure 3.4 shows.

The oil price shocks of 1973 and 1980 increased costs radically for developing countries. Most of them ran up substantial debts to meet these costs, and interest rates were very high. In the developed countries, confidence in Keynesian government spending as the major tool of macro-economic policy ebbed, as a stagflationary spiral of high inflation and low growth proved resistant to all conventional measures. It was at this time that the neo-liberal group who had come to dominate economics schools with new theory but old remedies – a return to laissez-faire economics – gained ascendancy in the treasury departments and central banks of many countries. The social-democratic movement weakened, the collapse of communism eliminated the external threat and made global capitalism again, as in the 1870s, free to pursue unhindered its objectives of profit maximization – without much regard for social consequences. The neo-liberal agenda of state withdrawal, free markets and privatization achieved pre-eminence in English-speaking countries, and soon was exported to the world at large. This agenda was to have a very negative impact on income distribution and also, in a number of countries, an equally negative impact on economic growth and poverty. From 1973 to 1993, inequality, however measured, increased between countries, within most countries and in the world as a whole (see Box 3.1).

The 1980s were extremely uneven for development as what is now known as 'globalization' became evident under rapidly liberalizing international regimes. Latin America had had a 'miracle decade' in the 1970s; but the 1980s were known as the 'lost decade' as one financial and monetary crisis after another buffeted these insecure economies. In Asia, the 'tiger' economies opened their markets to private investment and began their own 'miracle', rapidly surpassing Latin America in growth and income, and with a significant drop in poverty.[13] China registered a remarkable growth, almost doubling its GDP per capita between 1965 and 1980, and then quadrupling it between 1980 and 1998.

Internally, inequality rose in most Organization for Economic Cooperation and Development (OECD) countries during the 1980s and into the early 1990s. Of 19 countries, only one showed a slight improvement. The deterioration was worst in Sweden, the UK and the US. In the UK, the number of families below the poverty line rose by 60 per cent during the 1980s, and in The Netherlands by nearly 40 per cent. In Canada, poverty increased by 28 per cent between 1991 and 1996. The city of Montreal had the nation's highest poverty rate at 41.2 per cent.[14] Extensive poverty existed even in the country that ranked first in the 2001 Human Development Index (HDI) for most of the 1990s.

Structural adjustment programmes (SAPs) were widespread in the developing world by this time; these austerity programmes involved substantial budget cuts and

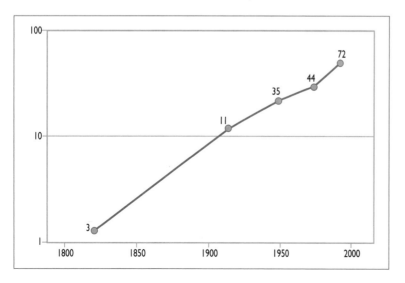

	1820	1870	1913	1950	1973	1998
Western Europe	1232	1974	3473	4594	11,534	17,921
Western offshoots[i]	1201	2431	5257	9288	16,172	26,146
Japan	669	737	1387	1926	11,439	20,413
Asia (excluding Japan)	575	543	640	635	1231	2936
Latin America	665	698	1511	2554	4531	5795
Eastern Europe and former USSR	667	917	501	2601	5729	4354
Africa	418	444	585	852	1365	1368
World	667	867	1510	2114	4104	5709
Inter-regional spread [ii]	3:1	5:1	9:1	15:1	13:1	19:1

Notes: i Western offshoots includes Canada, the US, Australia and New Zealand. ii Inter-regional spread is the ratio of the highest income to the lowest income for that year. For 1820, this is the ratio of Western Europe to Africa; for the remaining years, Western offshoots to Africa.

Source: Maddison, 2001, Table 3-1b, p126.

price rises, which impacted particularly strongly on the urban poor.[15] Africa was worst affected, and countries that had previously been quite buoyant began to slide into economic stagnation. In 24 African countries, real GDP per capita is less than in 1975, and in 12 countries even below the 1960s level.[16]

The economies of the Comecon countries of Eastern Europe and Central Asia stagnated or declined through most of the 1980s. Following the collapse of communism in 1990, the 'transitional' countries opened and liberalized their economies on the advice of Western neo-liberal advisers. This worked reasonably well for countries bordering on Western Europe, but was much more difficult in the former USSR, which had no earlier experience of markets and no immediate access to growth prospects. The GDP of the various republics fell by up to 60 per cent and a level of poverty and loss of quality of life ensued that would previously have been unimaginable. In the middle of 1990s, in Russia, electricity consumption fell by more than 20 per cent and construction activity fell by 70 per cent. The capital stock was only 60 per cent utilized, and the industrial work force fell by one third, with millions of workers on shortened day and compulsory leave. The severity of the contraction was much deeper and longer lasting than the Great Depression in the US.[17] Capital flight from Russia continues even after a decade of liberal 'reforms'.

Productive investment opportunities had begun to flag in the tiger economies of Asia during the early 1990s and money had begun to move into inflating asset prices and boom-level property and stock prices, which were no longer underpinned by growth. From 1994, Japanese and other international investors began to withdraw investment capital from the tiger economies, which left them vulnerable to attacks on their currencies. When the collapse came in 1997 in one country after another, all observers were caught by surprise.

From 1994, the withdrawal of capital back to the core economies, where investment in new communications technologies was required, paid immediate dividends. The US, in particular, entered a 'Goldilocks' era of falling interest rates, business and productivity growth, and rapidly inflating asset prices similar to Japan's a decade before – culminating in the 'tech-wreck' bubble. Profit rates rose to historic levels.

Official corporate strategy was not so much to invest in new job-generating activities, but instead to 'downsize', increasing profits through extensive programmes of layoffs, cost reductions and share buybacks. Nevertheless, conditions did improve for many during the period. In the US, unemployment rates fell to 4 per cent, the lowest for 40 years, and official poverty in 2000 also equalled the lowest level on record. The tiger countries of the Asia crisis recovered quite well from the fall in local currencies, which – after an initial debt shock and slump that put many enterprises in receivership and caused social hardship and unrest – gave them a competitive advantage to trade out of

Table 3.2

Per capita GDP by region, 1820 to 1998 (1990 international dollars)

The 1980s were extremely uneven for development as what is now known as 'globalization' became evident under rapidly liberalizing international regimes

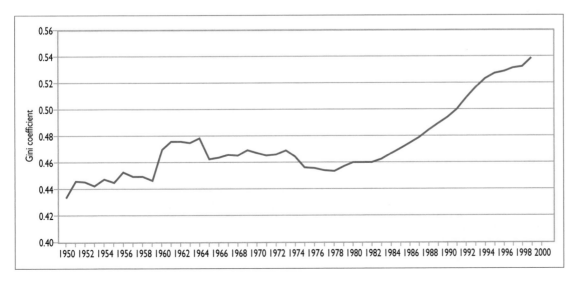

Figure 3.4

Gini coefficient, world (unweighted), 1950 to 1998

Note: The coefficient measures the percentage of area under a Lorenz curve of perfect equality that lies between it and the actual Lorenz curve of a society, with higher Gini coefficients indicating greater inequality.

Source: Milanovic, 2002a, Figure 4

Box 3.1 Measuring Global Inequality

World income inequality is very high: the Gini coefficient is 66 if one uses incomes adjusted for differences in countries' purchasing power, and almost 80 if one uses current dollar incomes. One can conjecture that such a high inequality is sustainable precisely because the world is not unified, and rich people do not mingle, meet or even know about the existence of the poor (other than in a most abstract way).[i]

There have been several typical ways of measuring global inequality. One way is by measuring inequality between countries, each treated as a single observation. Sometimes the distribution is weighted by population, so that each country is represented as if its whole population had the average national income.[ii] The best way, however, is to construct a global sample of individuals. This has been done by making use of a large collection of household surveys held by the World Bank.[iii]

It was found that between 1988 and 1993, mean per capita world income increased by 5.7% in real terms (or by 1.1% per annum on average). The increase – and more – went to the top income groups. Because of distributional change, the median income fell by 3%. The share of the bottom quintile of the population decreased from 2.3% of total world purchasing power parity (PPP) income to 2%, and that of the bottom half from 9.6% to 8.5%.

Some 85% of global inequality is explained by international differentials. Within-country inequality is relatively small on a global scale, accounting for only 1.3 Gini points, or 2% of total world inequality. In fact, lower-income people in the more developed countries have relatively high incomes: the lowest quintile of urban households in the high income countries (HICs) have five times the income of the top 20% of urban households in the least developed regions (LDRs).[iv]

The figure below shows how growth fell in all country income deciles during the period of 1978 to 1998, compared with the previous 20 years, with the good growth in middle-income

countries of 1950 to 1978 reversing, and only the higher income countries enjoying growth. While during the year 1960, there were 41 rich countries and 19 of them were non-Western, during the year 1998, there were 29 rich countries and only 7 of them were non-Western.

The experience of inequality differed substantially between regions, with the world appearing to converge into several widely spaced income blocs. Inter-country inequality went down between 1988 and 1993 in the HICs and in Latin America.[v] For the transition economies, the 1980s were a decade of stagnation, while the 1990s were not only a lost decade, but a decade of depression. In 1999, only three transition economies (Poland, Slovenia and Hungary) had a higher GDP per capita than in 1989.[vi] Very large increases in national Gini coefficients of up to 20 points were also recorded in some transitional countries.[vii]

The sudden increase in inequality from 1980 is usually attributed to domestic deregulation and economic liberalization. Recent studies reach the conclusion that:[viii]

…premature, poorly sequenced and unselective implementation under weak institutional and incomplete market conditions deliver not only inequality but low or negative growth…capital account liberalization appears to have had the strongest disequalizing effect, followed by domestic financial liberalization, labour market deregulation and tax reform. Privatization was found to be associated with rising inequality in some regions but not others, while trade liberalization had insignificant or mildly disequalizing effects.

Whether one accepts or not that this is the primary cause, it is a fact that any changes that took place during the period of 1980 to 1993 benefited only the richest countries, plus a handful of Asian countries, and in the former case, only the affluent people in these countries.

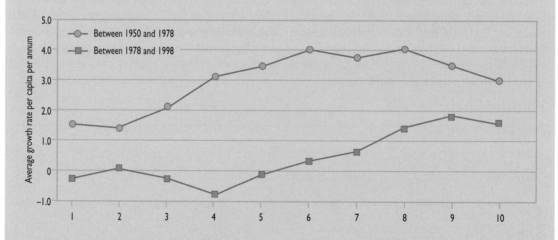

Average growth rate by decile, 1950 to 1978 and 1978 to 1998 [ix]

Notes: i Milanovic, 1999a. ii Recent results have been contradictory because of these different methodologies. Authors have said inequality is either decreasing (Boltho and Toniolo, 1999; Melchior et al, 2000), or is increasing (Milanovic, 1999a; Pritchett, 1997; Schultz, 1998; Maddison, 1995; Cornea and Kiiski, 2000). iii Milanovic, 1999a. iv UNCHS, 1996f, not adjusted for purchasing power. v The unweighted Gini coefficient of per capita GDPs of highly industrialized countries has almost continuously declined since the early 1950s in what is known as 'convergence', and is now only one half of its 1950 value. The conclusion must be that capital has sought to utilize all opportunities in the most conducive region before moving on to other new groups of countries, and has done so with relatively little risk, Milanovich, 1999. vi Milanovic, 2002a. vii Kanbur and Lustig, 1999. viii Cornea and Kiiski, 2001. ix Milanovic, 2002a, Figure 10.

trouble. While collapse was averted, a burden of debt now hangs over these countries that will limit their recovery in the medium term.

In the boom period of the late 1990s, a number of well-favoured countries advanced their economies on the back of the new information technologies, particularly countries with an educated population who had been suffering from isolation. Most obvious were Ireland, Finland and Australia,[18] while India and a few other countries developed indigenous software industries.[19] East Asia, particularly the Republic of Korea and the Shenzhen region in China, maintained global dominance in semiconductors and a number of other industrial activities.

From 2000, the economic downturn in the US began to hang ominously over the world economy. The tech-wreck collapse of dot-com share prices showed that internet technology had a long way to go before profitable online business models could be found. If the boom years of the 1990s, which should have been a time of healing and growth, had been uncertain and destabilizing, the prospects for the next decade began to look precarious.

Globalization: poverty amid affluence

From the mid 1940s, there has been considerable concern that globalization was exacerbating inequality worldwide – both at the global and the local level.[20] Almost 60 years on, there now seems to be little doubt about the matter. Increases in inequality can be traced almost directly to liberalization, which is also a proximate cause of globalization.

Despite a large number of studies, a consensus has not been reached as to how the interaction between growth or other macro-economic changes and inequality works, and many contradictory results have been obtained.[21] It is generally agreed that trade shocks and deterioration in the terms of trade are particularly bad for low income households.[22] It is also agreed that the more inequality, the harder it will be to stimulate growth and the less likely it is that poverty will be reduced when growth occurs.[23]

What happens within countries has been more an exercise in differential power than the operation of the invisible, equilibrating hand of the economy. Increasing incomes are not enjoyed equally within a country since, firstly, higher income people are in a better bargaining position and can appropriate some of the productivity gains of lower income people while keeping their own. Secondly, the higher earning producer service and information/ knowledge industries, which are the ones that have been increasingly generating wealth, have strong barriers to entry in terms of education, social class and contacts.[24] Economic returns to individuals from education have been increasing, and a good proportion of the population has been excluded from these high-leverage areas – instead, suffering a downgrade in their incomes, working conditions and job security.

Throughout the developing world, the contrasts between the elite who benefit or participate in globalization, and the rest of the population, are considerably more stark.

For example, in Angola, 40 per cent of urban children do not attend school. In its capital, Luanda, innumerable street children, amputees and destitute people sleep on the broken pavement amid heaps of rubbish, while the latest models of Mercedes Benz, BMW and Porsche zoom by, their cellphone-holding drivers nattily dressed in French and Brazilian couture.[25] Since 1994, the armed forces and police never received less than a 30 per cent share of the national budget, rising to 41 per cent in 1999, while the share to the social sectors (health, education, housing, social security and welfare) consistently dropped, from 15 to 9.4 per cent.[26]

Nigeria is potentially Africa's richest country. As the world's sixth largest producer of crude oil, with huge reserves of mineral and agricultural riches and human resources, it should be enjoying some of the highest global living standards. Until the 1980s, Nigeria failed to distribute its wealth to the poor, steering most investment into a few areas. Under a SAP between 1987 and 1992, real GDP increased by 40 per cent in terms of the local currency (but still was lower than during the early 1970s). Households in the top 30 per cent of incomes appropriated 75 per cent of the gain, while incomes of the bottom 10 per cent fell by 30 per cent. The Gini index increased by 20 per cent.

From 1980 to 1996, the percentage of Nigerians living in poverty rose from 28 per cent to 66 per cent. In absolute terms, the population living on less than US$1.40 a day rose from 17.7 million to 67.1 million. Those classified as the core poor (the poorest of the poor – living on about US$0.70 a day) increased from 6 per cent to 29 per cent of the population.[27] This steep rise in poverty occurred in spite of the fact that between 1970 and 1999, the country earned an estimated US$320 billion from the export of crude oil.[28]

In many LDCs, per capita incomes today are lower than they were in 1970.[29] Nearly 65 per cent of Africa's population lives below the poverty line. The Democratic Republic of Congo (DRC) fares worst, with 90.5 per cent below the poverty line.[30]

Poverty is also very much in evidence in the transition economies of Eastern Europe and the Commonwealth of Independent States (CIS), which have experienced the fastest rise in inequality ever. In Armenia, Russia, Tajikistan and Ukraine, the levels of inequality as measured by Gini coefficients have nearly doubled in the past decade.[31] Russia had the greatest inequality in 1999 – the income share of the richest 20 per cent was 11 times that of the poorest 20 per cent.[32] Many countries have experienced sharp declines in gross national product (GNP), large-scale unemployment, declining real incomes, and sharp increases in income poverty over the past decade. For example, in Hungary, the percentage of people living below the subsistence minimum was about 50 per cent higher in 1996 than in 1992.[33] In the seven CIS countries (Armenia, Azerbaijan, Georgia, Kyrgyzstan, Republic of Moldova, Tajikistan and Uzbekistan), more than half of the population lived in poverty in 1999.[34]

A recent UN-Habitat study stressed the grave implications of this deepening of inequalities – the growth of poverty amidst rising affluence.[35] This trend of polarization is also seen in Figure 3.3 and Table 3.2.

In the boom period of the late 1990s, a number of well-favoured countries advanced their economies on the back of the new information technologies

It is also agreed that the more inequality, the harder it will be to stimulate growth and the less likely it is that poverty will be reduced when growth occurs

Trade, globalization and cities

There is probably more confusion about trade and its effects on growth and inequality than any other aspect of globalization. This is because, on the one hand, there are several entrenched positions arguing their cases fiercely, and, on the other hand, trade acts in several different ways, some of which can reduce inequality between and within countries, and others which may increase it.[36]

■ Trade theory and inequality

According to neo-liberal trade theory, more trade, almost by definition, results in improved national wealth and incomes since arbitrage leads goods to be directed to their most productive use and sold where the best returns are to be had, both increasing producers' incomes and lowering consumers' costs, on average. As well as distributing goods more efficiently, trade also results in more production, since new markets open up for goods and services.

Conventional trade theories see increased trade and a liberalized trade regime as purely beneficial; but, as in all change, there are, in fact, winners and losers. Those participating in the active, growing areas of the world economy, or receiving (unreliable) trickle-down effects, benefit. Those who do not participate at best receive no benefits, but, in fact, are usually losers, since capital tends to take flight from their countries or their industries to more productive zones, reducing work opportunities and business returns as currencies and wages fall or jobs disappear.

There are several opposing trends associated with trade between richer and poorer countries or regions. On the one hand, *diffusion* allows new technologies, capital and jobs to trickle from the richer to the poorer areas where goods can be produced more cheaply. On the other hand, *concentration* causes people, capital and jobs to move to places of opportunity, draining less developed areas of human and financial resources and leaving them in a depressed state. Such areas will also have a great deal of difficulty establishing new industries in the absence of specific government interventions or subsidies, and this argument in favour of nurturing infant industries has become the major reason for the preservation of tariff walls.

Diffusion should not be underestimated since, realistically, it is one of the main processes that can lead to development. It is a major reason why wages for a given activity within a country tend to be relatively uniform and substantially different from other countries, because wages eventually diffuse through the country, which is a free trade area.[37,38] The transfer of industry to areas where labour costs less usually results in an increase in the overall number of jobs, and this can be very substantial.[39]

A third effect relating to international trade concerns *deterioration of the terms of trade*. Even in the active industries or countries, the stronger partner in the trade can benefit more (the basis of colonialism). In a case where productivity improves across the board, the higher income countries will receive all of the benefit of their own improvement, and also part of the benefit of the improvement in the less developed partner. This is because falling export costs due to productivity improvement lead to

a worsening in the terms of trade for the weaker partner (their currency falls), passing on extra benefits to the stronger partner.[40] The extremely strong US dollar in 2001 was at least partly due to this effect.

Falling commodity prices are a related phenomenon. The exceptional growth of the industrializing countries during much of the 20th century was fuelled, in part, by the availability of cheap agricultural and mineral products, which are the major outputs of the developing countries. Improved agricultural productivity, in particular, which is where the vast bulk of aid money went from 1985 onwards, turned out to be something of a two-edged sword. While it fed growing populations of less developed countries, it also cheapened their exports and worsened their terms of trade. At the same time, it released increasing proportions of the population from rural areas to the cities, where there were no jobs for them.

Other concerns relate to *structural* effects depending upon factor inputs. It is usually argued, for example, that tariffs increase inequality because they protect (urban) capital and profits at the expense of workers in more labour-intensive industries and export industries, such as agriculture. Conversely, if, as at present, trade relates to areas that require highly skilled or educated labour, as much of the producer services-driven expansion of the 1990s has done, the educated group will benefit accordingly at the expense of the others, and those countries with a higher proportion of educated people will benefit the most – the higher income countries.

It has been argued that the insistence on free trade has been destructive to fledgling industries in the developing world that hold out promise for much greater long-term growth than existing cash crops and are the only real path to development.[41] It is often pointed out that only countries with developed industries benefit from the luxury of free trade, and that the industrial countries in their early years operated under heavy regimes of protection (and still do, in many cases). The collapse of formal urban employment in the developing world and the rise of the informal sector is seen as a direct function of liberalization. By forcing the developing world to remove barriers through SAPs and other conditionalities is like someone trying to 'kick away the ladder' with which they climbed to the top. It has become very much a case of 'do what we say, not what we did'.[42]

■ Trade: the reality

A recent study argues at length that globalization and the shrinking of distance as a prevailing dynamic for changes in the world is largely an illusion since many of the changes that are being witnessed have historical precedents, and, in fact, the movement of goods and information remains quite regionalized.[43] World trade has increased from 7 per cent of world GDP in 1950 to at least 15 per cent over the period; but the reality is that trade has come to be largely confined to a smaller group of countries, a select club that includes the OECD and a few countries in Asia.[44] Figure 3.4 shows the growth of trade by region, with the proportion of world exports coming from the HICs steady at about 70 per cent

The collapse of formal urban employment in the developing world and the rise of the informal sector is seen as a direct function of liberalization

over the last 20 years, while Asian countries have almost doubled their share of exports from 9.5 per cent to 17 per cent, at the expense of the other developing countries.[45]

Neither Latin America, burdened by bad debt, nor stagnant African economies were attractive outlets for trade and investment during the period. The real consideration for countries in Africa and Latin America is, therefore, not whether trade increases inequality, but whether the loss of trade and investment share does.

The Asian tigers were mostly strong enough to secure reasonable terms of trade. However, where trade to the LDCs did take place, it was often under conditions that disproportionately benefited the domestic producers in exporting countries. The US and Europe have huge and increasing food subsidies and tariffs that exclude the agricultural products of other countries – the major exports of the LDCs.[46] The cash crops that these countries can easily produce and export, such as coffee, are at the expense of staple foods. In countries where nutrition levels were worsening during the period, the conversion to cash crops forces them, now, to import staples in many cases, weakening local food security.

The most dramatic turnaround in trade during the 1990s was in the transitional countries, where it was a major factor contributing to economic collapse. Trade between the Comecon countries had been a substantial part of their economies, and the Soviet system, in particular, had been predicated on specialized production in different republics. Following 'opening' of the region, trade sank to almost nothing – a huge shock to economies that were severely imbalanced and dependent on each other for particular goods. These countries had not previously been exposed to Western levels of quality and their goods were not competitive, so replacing this trade with world markets – or even maintaining their own share of local consumption – was going to take a very long time. Cuba, which, in fact, had several world-class export businesses, was subject to a US trade embargo that by 1990 had already lasted 25 years.[47] When Comecon trade collapsed, it was unable to seek other opportunities. Living conditions and human development decreased markedly, with the growth of poverty and of slums backing the historic Havana foreshore, which has World Heritage status.

In the developing countries, with their poorly policed borders, informal, unconventional or illegal trade has been commonplace, and may have replaced the declining share of formal-sector trade to some extent. Structural adjustment, globalization, political change and trade liberalization have come together to extend and intensify unconventional cross-border trade. Substantial amounts of capital and capacity are often deployed to find alternative ways and circuits to move raw materials and process consumables. This trade brings together a wide range of actors, including well-off business people, soldiers, militias, middlemen of various nationalities and petty traders. Unconventional trade is at its greatest in states where chronic political crisis has undermined regulatory systems, or where formal institutions function and retain some level of authority primarily through their participation in such unconventional trade.[48]

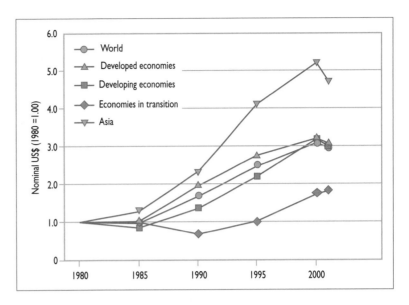

Figure 3.5

Growth of trade by region, 1980 to 2001 (1980 = 1.00)

Source: World Trade Organization (WTO), *World Trade Statistics 2001*, www.wto.org

It is definitely better to participate in increased trade opportunities, as the dramatic examples from East and Southeast Asia show. After they opened up their economies during the 1970s, growth spurted from low levels to averages of 10 per cent per year, in several cases rapidly moving these countries from low development to middle incomes – and it is definitely worse to lose trade, as the equally dramatic examples from the transitional countries and from the Great Depression show. However, it is difficult for the developing countries to participate in trade at all, and when they do it is from a position of disadvantage, converting to export crops that can threaten their own food security and have little long-term prospects for growth.[49]

Increased exposure to trade and the vagaries of international movements of capital almost guarantee that economies will become more volatile. The trouble is that rapid increases in national income are enjoyed less by low income earners, and rapid decreases are felt more, so just about any kind of rapid change is seen to be inequitable and will ratchet inequality upwards. The more unequal the society, the more this is felt – to the point that the lowest income groups may barely benefit at all from prosperity.[50]

■ Finance, information and economic volatility

A number of observers have considered that it is not physical trade that is so important in globalization, but the control over financial flows and information.[51] The opportunities and dangers presented by new communications technologies have been well documented.[52] On the one hand, access to cheaper telephone lines, faxes and the internet has dramatically reduced the times, costs and capital outlays required for doing international business, while giving people easy access to a range of information and opinions to which they would not previously have been exposed.

Many developing countries have rapidly expanding mobile phone systems, replacing obsolete, underdeveloped land-line technologies. Satellite dishes are widespread, and internet cafés can be found even in the isolated parts of the world. However, as with all new technologies, differential

Structural adjustment, globalization, political change and trade liberalization have come together to extend and intensify unconventional cross-border trade

access is even greater than access to more established facilities or technologies, and is largely restricted to the educated middle class.[53] The access to wider information has not been seen as a blessing by all – because of the dominance of English-language material on the internet and television, for example, some have seen these developments as a tool of 'cultural imperialism', attacking the social and moral foundations of long-standing cultures.

The enormous increases in the speed and flow of finance and capital around the world have been the most disconcerting feature of the new globalization. Rapid liberalization of financial systems during the 1980s within organizations ill prepared to handle the new norms of corporate governance led to a series of banking crises from 1985 to 1992. Technologies of fund transfer made it possible to transfer enormous sums of money within seconds, and exotic forms of derivatives could produce huge leverages against currencies and bonds. The failure of Barings Bank from the activities of a futures trader in 1995, and the rescue of Long Term Capital Management from bankruptcy in 1998, are two well-documented cases of the potential for corporate disaster.

More significant, however, were the activities of unregulated hedge funds during the 1990s in destroying the currency regimes of a number of countries. A conglomerate of hedge funds led by the financier George Soros in 1992 was able to muster more sterling than the Bank of England, selling down the currency and forcing the UK to exit the European exchange rate mechanism, devaluing sterling by 35 per cent, with an overnight profit in the billions of pounds for the traders. After this coup, the number of hedge funds doubled in the following year, with US$75 billion under management within 12 months.[54] Smaller operations were successfully mounted against Thailand, Malaysia and Indonesia during 1997, forcing them to float and devalue the currency by between 30 and 70 per cent and sending their economies into chaos.[55] However, the hedge funds met their match in Hong Kong, Special Administrative Region (SAR) of China, which had very deep pockets and, ultimately, chose to raise interest rates rather than devalue, causing Asian stock markets to plunge and precipitating the main events of the Asia crisis.[56]

It may well be the case that the economies had run out of steam and were overvalued, making the attack possible. Nevertheless, it is somewhat frightening to think that rogue traders were the proximate cause of events that brought whole countries to their knees and left millions in poverty.

Other key developments during the 1990s were the massive growth of pension funds and other financial institutions, which tended to place funds onto stock markets rather than other forms of more direct investment. In the name of diversification, these funds sought to invest on international markets, particularly as the tools became available to do it instantaneously. The much greater emphasis on foreign investment caused a flow of funds out of those countries where they had been previously used for local consumption or investment. In the short run, hasty removal of restrictions on international capital flows makes

it easier for wealthy citizens and international investors to take their wealth out of the country, while removal of 'capital controls' facilitates capital flight, further reducing productive investment, production, income and employment. This has happened repeatedly during the 1990s in Latin America and has been responsible for most of the many currency crises that have occurred throughout the region. As mentioned earlier, capital flight from Russia continues even after a decade of liberal 'reforms'.

■ Labour markets under free trade regimes

There has been very considerable debate regarding the extent to which globalization and trade have affected labour markets. Neo-liberal economic trade theory implies that opening economic barriers would benefit the factors in excess supply, or for which there was a comparative advantage.[57] For developed economies, this would be capital and highly skilled labour, and for developing countries, unskilled labour. The former is probably true, but the latter is not – skilled workers in developing countries have benefited more from improved trade.

A 1995 study, for example, found that 23 per cent of the increase in relative wages for skilled workers in developing countries during the period of 1986 to 1990 could be attributed to the reduction in tariffs and the elimination of import licence requirements.[58] Another study concluded that the increase in wage inequality can be attributed to the rapid increase in wages for more educated and experienced workers, while the wage increase was minimal among less skilled workers. The authors concluded that this trend is caused by a shift in demand, skewed in favour of higher skills.[59]

It is generally agreed that there is an across-the-board shift to higher returns to skills and education. Increased trade contributes only a very small part of labour force change, and the result is almost entirely due to increased mechanization of routine jobs in the manufacturing sector, and changes in consumer preferences as global incomes have increased in favour of products with more service and skilled inputs.[60] In addition, increased professionalization of the work force tends to be internally generated, rather than being specifically connected with international trade.[61]

There is very little for unskilled workers in LDCs to do in a globalized economy – so they join the informal sector and live in the slums. The LDCs are caught in a vicious cycle: the lack of skilled workers causes them to concentrate in sectors where limited skills are needed. This concentration, in turn, reduces the demand for more advanced skills – a process further intensified with trade liberalization.[62] Generating a demand for skill acquisition is perhaps the key area for governmental intervention – and, in some situations, is probably more important than macro-economic management and free trade.

Nevertheless, it is suggested in Chapter 6 that hybrid forms of formal–informal business interaction with a fair degree of local control have become commonplace in the cities of less developed regions. Although currently small, some potential may exist for the shaping of semi-formal

The enormous increases in the speed and flow of finance and capital around the world have been the most disconcerting feature of the new globalization

Removal of restrictions on international capital flows makes it easier for wealthy citizens and international investors to take their wealth out of the country, while removal of 'capital controls' facilitates capital flight, further reducing productive investment, production, income and employment

international opportunities that could, ultimately, benefit a wider range of actors and provide a 'filtering down' or even a 'bottom-up' response to globalization.

■ Africa: economic stagnation in a globalizing world

Despite notable successes registered by a few developing countries in adapting to, and actively engaging with, global changes, the LDCs have largely been 'left out' of most facets of globalization. In particular, the so-called new international division of labour has largely bypassed major parts of the African continent. Real incomes have fallen at an annual rate of 1 per cent since the 1980s and minimum wages have fallen between 50 per cent and 70 per cent during this time. It is likely that 22 million jobs will be created between 1985 and 2020, far short of the 380 million necessary to target unemployment to below 10 per cent. Africa's share of foreign direct investment (FDI) continues to decline. In 1997, 8 countries experienced net outflows of FDI and 22 other countries had inflows of only US$1 to US$2 per capita.[63]

The investments attracted have primarily been in mining and cash crop production. These sectors depend mainly on foreign technology, foreign expertise and foreign markets, and are characterized by few linkages with the internal market (labour and commodity, alike). The impact on the overall socio-economic development and technological innovation of foreign direct investments in Africa has therefore been negligible. Increasing capital outflows, poor economic growth, very high debt to export ratios (479 per cent in 1995) and the continent's paltry share of world trade (1.9 per cent in 1997) contribute to a process of institutional and socio-economic disintegration.

The continent has been largely unable to transcend its traditional functions in the world economy as a supplier of raw materials and a captive market for imported manufactured goods. This fact is central to Africa's current economic crisis. Even though an extensive period of import substitution-led industrialization was attempted, many of the firms established remained dependent upon the importation of critical inputs. As these firms were not oriented to produce goods for exports, they could not generate sufficient foreign exchange to cover their import costs.[64] While total export revenue increased by 5.9 per cent in 1997, Africa's share of world trade continues to decline, shrinking from 2 per cent in 1996 to 1.9 per cent in 1997.[65] Additionally, deterioration in the terms of trade is thought to account for a 0.7 per cent reduction in the African growth rate relative to other developing countries.[66]

The United Nations Economic Commission for Africa (UNECA) has adopted indicators that measure the capacity of countries to maintain long-term economic growth. According to these measures, there has been little improvement for the majority of Africans even in countries experiencing accelerated growth rates.[67] Only those countries which have substantial levels of resource endowment, coupled with small and highly skilled populations – for example, Botswana, Mauritius, South Africa, Tunisia and Equatorial Guinea – demonstrate any significant capacity to maintain long-term economic growth.[68]

THE RETREAT OF THE STATE

The main single cause of increases in poverty and inequality during the 1980s and 1990s was the retreat of the state. The redirection of income through progressive taxation and social safety nets came to be severely threatened by the ascendancy of neo-liberal economic doctrines that explicitly 'demanded' an increase in inequality. The neo-liberal ideology was based on individualism, competition and self-reliance, and collectivism in all except the most rudimentary forms was anathema. Markets were somehow regarded as being capable of delivering prosperity for all, and the major problem was regarded as governments who were sapping the ability of the people to generate wealth.

Typical neo-liberal policy panaceas were the reduction of all forms of government spending and government regulation, particularly those that might inhibit people being active in the market, and the reduction of top-level tax rates and support of high salaries, as these high income earners were somehow regarded as the most productive and required more incentive to produce. Following almost 50 years of government intervention and wealth redistribution under the Keynesian or socialist orthodoxies, these policies dramatically increased inequality and social exclusion wherever they took root.

For cities and housing, the major policy changes emerging from neo-liberal policy and the retreat of the state were:

- *The reduction of most forms of public 'welfare' expenditure.* In the developed world, this has been carried out under different spurs – under right-of-centre 'reformist' regimes; or under the terms of treaties such as the Maastricht Treaty in Europe. In the developing world, this was usually carried out under the terms of SAPs following fiscal crises.
- *The privatization of many forms of government enterprise.* The new rule was that the government should not be involved in anything that the private sector could do. The new role of government was to 'enable' the private sector, primarily by withdrawing from many spheres of life, but also by improving its institutions and its planning and supportive capabilities, rather than engaging directly in productive activity. The enterprises most affected were utility companies and public housing; however, there were also effects on employment through the retrenchment of large numbers of public-sector employees.
- *The reform of regulation.* In line with the primary neo-liberal goal of small government, large numbers of regulations and restrictions have been removed in many countries. The most important of these have been the *deregulation of the work force*, which has led to widespread labour casualization; the *reduction of trade barriers*, which has led to increased trade and economic restructuring; the *deregulation of financial systems*, which has allowed for considerably improved flows of capital at the cost of greater instability and less local control; *decentralization of government*,

Generating a demand for skill acquisition is perhaps the key area for governmental intervention

which can create its own problems by moving responsibility down the chain without adequate resources to fulfil them; and the *removal of planning restrictions*, which has generally allowed for more mixed-use areas and development at higher densities, but possibly involving the loss of affordable housing to the redevelopers.

Privatization of utilities

In the margin: *In some countries, attempts to facilitate cost recovery can have very unpleasant outcomes*

In general, it was the privatization of utility services that was most visible, although the virtual dismembering of public housing in a number of developed countries was also a feature of the reforms.[69]

The basic idea was that long-standing bureaucracies can become self-serving, and the development of formal rules for conduct of all activity, while in theory assisting with transparency, efficiency and safety, can eventually stifle innovation. Government bureaucracies have a tendency to expand until checked and to undercharge for their services. It was believed that the 'discipline of the market' would limit this and would stop government enterprises from becoming 'employers of last resort'. Pricing was also a key issue, since many bureaucracies provide services with a number of hidden subsidies, and it is in the interest of elected governments seeking popular support that they continue to

do so, which can be very economically inefficient and wasteful.[70]

Furthermore, beginning in the US where most utility provision was already private, competition between utilities was considered to benefit the consumer, and many elaborate structures have now been designed throughout the world for utilities such as electricity or water to:

* divide provision between wholesale and retail arms;
* ensure there are competing retailers;
* set up regulatory frameworks to ensure that prices do not rise, quality and safety standards are preserved, and statutory obligations to disadvantaged groups are met.

In the developing world, while pricing and employment were also major issues, the theme was often much simpler: the elimination of corruption. Actions such as the connection of services are often extraordinarily slow and inefficient in developing countries, with waiting times that can be indefinite and low-paid front-line employees who tend to extract payments from the public for 'speed money'. On the other hand, government enterprises were the favoured channel of highly placed officials or political leaders seeking to funnel loan moneys into their own bank accounts without trace. Government provision systems are also notoriously prone to patronage, and high-income areas and key electorates or tribal groups can be the major beneficiaries.

In countries where there have been 'payment strikes' by consumers, which governments are unwilling to risk conflict to deal with, privatization can be an instant solution to the almost zero-cost recovery that drains national budgets. Neo-liberal solutions enforcing cost recovery in these countries can have very unpleasant outcomes, as Box 3.2 shows, and sensitivity to the needs of the most disadvantaged must be paramount in successful privatizations.

In a number of cases, the conduct of privatization was done in a great hurry under overwhelming pressure from foreign advisers, and the result was 'outright theft'.[71] Public assets were sometimes sold to the private sector at a fraction of their true worth. 'Riots' against utility price rises have taken place in a number of places, most notably Ecuador.

The jury is still out on privatization. Privatized utilities are the same as all private enterprises; their primary aim is not the provision of service but the creation of profit for shareholders and rewards for top managers. Privatization generally results in big pay rises for the management and the sacking of many employees. Prices normally rise, and standards and safety may suffer unless strictly regulated and monitored. Financial stability is also at risk – it is relatively easy for a private provider to become insolvent, and protocols for their bailout without interrupting services citywide become necessary.

On the positive side, what can be said decisively is that privatization is a way of shaking up moribund organizations and improving operational efficiency. Service when provided is often better, particularly those such as connections that involve direct payment by the consumer;

Box 3.2 Cost recovery in water in South Africa

During apartheid, large sections of the population were moved to water-scarce homelands. In some places, water was being provided free – for example, following a drought in Kwazulu in 1983. The African National Congress (ANC) campaigned on a promise of a daily minimum of 50 litres per person. The *Urban Infrastructure Investment Framework*, drafted by the World Bank in 1994, provided for communal water taps and pit latrines where households earned less than 800 Rand (R800) (US$100) a month. Low volume infrastructure that limited supply to communal taps and 25 litres per day per person was, however, built. In 1996, the government adopted an austerity plan named *Growth, Employment and Redistribution*, which, like other structural adjustment efforts, has delivered most significantly on cutting budget deficits and inflation. As always, a major plank of the programme was to commodify water and other utilities.

From 1995, municipalities started cutting off water supplies to whole communities who could not pay. Major delivery non-governmental organizations (NGOs) such as the Mvula Trust tried full-cost recovery in the mid 1990s, but projects broke down. Even Pretoria achieved only 1% cost recovery and most taps ran dry. In Hermanus, which had introduced an escalating water scale and conservation strategy,[i] evictions and attachments of poor people's homes for non-payment began in 1999.[ii]

Originally the ANC had proposed a rising block tariff to larger users to fund water for the poor. In practice, most cities actually began charging higher rates for the lower consumption blocks – in line with the common situation in Africa that the poor pay more for water.

A more serious outcome was an outbreak of cholera in Kwazulu from 2000 to 2001, with about 106,000 infected, mostly people with no access to piped water. The epidemic began in a community that had its water cut off; inability to pay user fees was cited as the cause by NGOs.

Following the outbreak, and in line with ANC ongoing policy, free minimum allowances of water and electricity have now been implemented in a number of cities.

Notes: i www.hermanus.co.za/info/water.htm; www.hermanuswater.co.za.
ii www.qsilver.queensu.ca/~mspadmin/pages/Project_Publications/News/Bitter.htm;
www.qsilver.queensu.ca/~mspadmin/pages/Project_Publications/News/Project.htm.

but lack of coordination between different bodies and lack of transparency become even more of an issue. In less developed cities, probably the main issue is cost recovery, which public agencies seem to find inordinately difficult, and this is guaranteed under privatization unless subsidies are made explicit.

However, issues of equity then arise as poor people may no longer have access to services. Like everything else, the business goes where the money is. Cross-subsidization between different groups of consumers disappears, and higher levels of service tend to be provided to better-off consumers. Needs-based allocation disappears. As in the transitional countries, services can become completely unaffordable to the poor unless specific subsidies are paid, and such subsidies are subsequently a constant target for budget managers seeking to trim costs. Capital expenditure in slums is unlikely unless the residents can bear the full costs. Exactly as with housing, the kinds of service that they can afford are unlikely to meet the full standards of formal provision, and more informal, lower cost methods need to be tried.

Overall, it is hard to judge today what the net effect of privatized services will be, and no doubt many unanticipated problems will arise as these are implemented within developing countries, while others will be solved.

Structural adjustment, cities and poverty

From a position of leadership in national economies, and a magnet attracting people from the countryside, the city has become the focus of national depression.[72]

SAPs began in 1980 in the form of conditional loans to floundering economies. The conditions were a package that comprise the main points of the neo-liberal agenda:

* *Trade and exchange rate liberalization.* Tariffs are usually removed. The exchange rate is generally floated (normally causing a large devaluation, averaging 40 per cent, but up to 95 per cent).[73] Restrictions on the inflow or outflow of capital are removed, as well as what businesses or banks are allowed to buy, own or operate. These moves usually create a massive load of foreign-denominated debt, but make the economy much more outward looking.
* *Reduction in the role of the state.* Government spending is cut, particularly investment and through laying off staff, in order to reduce public deficits.
* *Public-sector and price management.* Cost recovery is sought on public enterprises by increasing their prices and laying off staff. Enterprises are privatized, if possible. Subsidies to both public and private enterprises are removed or reduced. Public-sector wages are frozen. Price controls on commodities and controls on labour and financial markets are removed, usually including environmental and safety standards.
* *Anti-poverty policies.* Various measures to protect the poor are often recommended, including 'work for food', targeted food subsidies, redirecting social expenditures to the poor etc.[74]

Most SAPs have been carried out in crisis situations, and the SAPs in their extreme 'crisis' form cause a sharp inflationary depression, throwing large numbers of people out of work and causing prices to rise sharply while wages fall substantially in real terms. Many of the economies undergoing structural adjustment in Latin America during the 1980s were in a state of economic crisis, with burgeoning public deficits, rampant inflation and capital flight, and were on the point of defaulting on international loan repayments. The Asian tigers in the years 1997–1998 were in a bust following a bubble economy. In these circumstances, the first SAP actions are always to quarantine the problem and protect the international financial system by rescheduling payments.[75] Other economies have simply been in a state of stagnation with net deficits. In these circumstances, SAPs are more measured and aim only to remedy structural deficiencies, rather than to shock the system into compliance and soothe international investors.

These adjustments have now been taking place for 20 years, and a great deal of experience has been gained. Certain things can be guaranteed from a SAP:

* The economy will be opened up and exports will improve (in amount, but not necessarily in dollar value).
* The money supply normally undergoes a severe tightening and interest rates skyrocket, so that investment stops and many smaller enterprises are unable to continue.[76]
* The informal economy will increase substantially due to the swelling unemployed and the removal of controls.[77]
* Enterprises will have a large burden of debt and the financial sector will be technically insolvent.
* The urban poor will bear a disproportionate share of the damage.[78]
* Safety nets will be directed to politically powerful groups who may be disadvantaged, and not to the poor who have a low priority on most national agendas.
* As with all neo-liberal programmes, social insecurity in all of its forms will increase.

Government enterprises dominated the economic scene prior to structural adjustment; they were highly inefficient and were often used as conduits for corruption. Ineffective restrictions were being applied to currency and import flows,[79] which were stifling new investment and the modernization of industry and which, in many cases, led to balance of payments crises. Many countries were fixing prices on food, cement and other staples, or granting monopolies to well-connected businesspeople – resulting in serious price distortions and artificial shortages.[80]

Unfortunately, what has replaced these manifestly inadequate systems has been worse. Economic growth, savings and capital investment have not resumed, even after 30 years in some cases.[81] As this is the major objective once financial stability has been restored, the validity of these

Privatization is a way of shaking up moribund organizations and improving operational efficiency. However, in a number of cases, the conduct of privatization was done in a great hurry and the result was 'outright theft'

SAPs, in their extreme 'crisis' form, cause a sharp inflationary depression, throwing large numbers of people out of work and causing prices to rise sharply while wages fall substantially in real terms

programmes, even according to their own parameters, must be questioned – as SAPs rarely have been. The balance of payments situation also did not necessarily improve because of debt servicing, and productivity gains are more likely to stem from worsened working conditions than new investment.[82] Government recurrent spending often increased because reductions of expenditure were matched by increases in the interest bill.[83] It has been observed that SAPs have contributed to the worsening of urban poverty, inequality and slums – although there is no unanimity on this.[84]

Public-sector employment, often the largest domain of formal employment in many African cities, has been severely curtailed under SAPs, with substantial retrenchment and attrition. Those who remain in the public sector have faced significant reductions in their earning capacity. The removals of explicit and hidden subsidies has left urban populations in increasingly precarious circumstances in terms of meeting basic needs.

Africa had 156 SAPs from the IMF during the 1980s, with 94 later tranches, or new programmes, and 52 structural adjustment loans from the World Bank.[85] In the DRC (formerly Zaire), for example, a SAP reduced the civil service from 429,000 in 1980 to 289,000 in 1985. About 80,000 health and education workers were cut from government payrolls. In 1985, Ghana employed 1782 doctors. In 1992, it employed 965. During the period of 1980 to 1985, the wages of top-level public-sector employees in Tanzania fell by 61 per cent in real terms; 72 per cent of urban residents in Dar es Salaam in a 1986 to 1987 survey were engaged in some form of secondary economic activity.[86]

The SAPs have not reduced the debt of LDCs, whose principal has been paid back many times over.[87] Debt service takes a major share of income that countries need in order to keep their people alive, and it also forces countries to keep their economies oriented to production of exports in order to earn foreign exchange. For every aid dollar received by Africa in 1993, US$3 left Africa in debt service; four-fifths of Uganda's export earnings go to debt service.

A specific feature of SAPs is that they have shifted the focus of policy in African countries away from urban areas. Because export crops were necessary to meet the interest bill, much of the policy effort has turned away from urban concerns. Some analysts believe that the major impact of SAPs is to correct 'urban bias'[88,89] by removing protection from import-competing secondary industry in favour of rural exports.[90] The price of food and other urban staples usually rises, making cities less attractive. Tight credit makes it difficult to establish urban businesses or create urban jobs. But, somehow, people keep moving to the city and will do so for the next century.

The overall picture following a typical structural adjustment in a poorer country is that the public budget is balanced, but the long-term economic picture is grim. Fledgling urban industries that might have had a chance for long-term growth are eliminated. Rural food crops have been exchanged for export agricultural commodities. The money earned from these is used entirely to pay off the debt, which

A specific feature of SAPs is that they have shifted the focus of policy in African countries away from urban areas

hardly decreases. There is little chance that export earnings will increase in the future with rising world incomes, as the demand for these products has a low income elasticity and competition is increasing due to other SAPs. With no chance for growth and high debt levels, foreign direct investment falls to practically nil.

In a form of neo-colonialism that is probably more stringent than the original (since the developed countries no longer have to make local investments for development), many developing countries have become steady state suppliers of raw commodities to the world and continue to fall further and further behind. As agricultural productivity improves, the surplus rural population moves to the cities to find work. Instead of being a focus for growth and prosperity, the cities have become a dumping ground for a surplus population working in unskilled, unprotected and low-wage informal service industries and trade. The slums of the developing world swell.

THE LOCAL AND THE GLOBAL[91]

Globalization has, unfortunately, tended to be treated in the literature as a kind of totalizing rubric or meta-narrative that sums up and provides an overarching order to recent history. This is not necessarily the case; there are, for a start, other spatial orders that are constantly in play – including regionalization and individuation.[92] All combine in various sometimes complementary and frequently contradictory ways to alter the means of governance, economic production and social formations.

The global makes possible a new visibility and articulation of localities, providing them with new instruments to reshape themselves. The 'nation' no longer monopolizes the mediation of 'inside' and 'outside'. Globalization reflects a process where localities become more significant at a global, rather than national, scale, and where institutions and mechanisms become more globalized through a more direct engagement of localities.[93]

Globalization has also, by default, been treated as being due to vast impersonal forces, so that governments have no freedom to move except where it takes them and can abdicate their responsibilities to their citizens. Countries do have the sovereign right to be different – but it is being exercised increasingly less frequently – and with increasing sanctions. These actions – the contraction of national functions and responsibilities, the withdrawal of subsidized production and consumption and the marketization of basic needs, which have caused globalization as much as they have resulted from it – have made life increasingly difficult for most urban citizens in the developing world. But what is less evident is the way in which proactive strategies to engage globalization processes or compensate for their more deleterious effects is generating a kind of bottom-up 'globalization' from the ground.

The most visible aspects of this 'pedestrian' globalization include direct actions by local bodies and individuals to participate in transnational economic activity. Urban localities link themselves into larger units and direct networks of association. Extending conventional notions of 'social economy', new modalities of integrating local human, physical and spatial resources are being deployed to maximize the scope of local economic initiatives and access to opportunities.[94] On some occasions, these efforts are tightly organized. During others, they entail more diffuse, open-ended networks of collaboration.

This section aims to highlight some of the dynamics of economic, social and governance linkages, both within and across cities. It seeks to establish the importance of transurban links among discrete cities as a necessary platform for their long-term economic viability. These links heighten the accessibility of a city, connecting it to flows of capital and people. Accessibility ultimately determines a city's potential as a generator of goods and information, and makes intensified transactions among households, firms, agencies and networks critical economic activities in their own right.[95] Cities are no longer just simply located within specific geographical and historical domains. They are also situated in complex matrices of exchange and movement, where the strength of the city is contingent on the extent to which it can involve itself in cities elsewhere.

Insecurity and the diffusion of the local

The insecurities created by globalization go well beyond income inequality and the demise of reassuring and stabilizing state structures. They extend into many aspects of the economy, social life and networks of support, and the signs and symbols upon which cultural identity is based.

In many respects, the operations of global economies make it very difficult for many people in less developed regions to continue functioning 'inside' their cities. These cities have been penetrated by seemingly arbitrary circulations of the 'unknown' – in other words, what makes people rich or poor; what is valued and why; and 'working assessments' of who is doing what to whom are viewed as more uncertain.

Under these conditions, the capacity to maintain recognizable and usable forms of collective solidarity and collaboration becomes difficult. This collective solidarity has been critical to the way in which traditional societies have been run, particularly those with tribal or strongly family-oriented leanings. Modifying reflections on *habitus*, this collective capacity can be viewed as the crucial means through which localities, as social territories, are marked and are experienced as self-contained, 'organic' environments.[96] National economic success is critically dependent upon establishing notions of trust so that transactions may be established on a wider basis and critical mass can be established in particular industries. In the absence of that trust or of unifying norms, it becomes difficult to be anything more than a satellite of distant powers and ideas – as in the colonial period.[97] In extreme cases, this weakening of traditional norms of behaviour can cause societies to become crime or graft ridden as social standards become increasingly threatened by the bewildering attraction of the 'new'.

Under the dislocating effects of globalization, when through the media or economic action the 'distant' can become nearer and more immediate than the next-door neighbour, a sense of being encompassed, drawn into and acting upon a circumscribed world of commonality becomes difficult, as the previously relied upon practices of forging social solidarity dissipate. Urban residents appear increasingly uncertain about how to spatialize their life chances: where will they secure livelihood; where can they feel protected and looked after; and where will they acquire critical skills and capacities? When children across most cities in the developing world are asked about what they will do with their lives, the answer usually entails a life trajectory carried out far away from 'home'.

But this state of being thrown out into a world far away from home is not only something that occurs by default or through media impressions of distant affluence. Given just how increasingly precarious life in urban Africa has become, residents who share a quarter must often find ways of not locking themselves into fixed commitments with each other – in order to pursue their own livelihoods and aspirations on a more individual basis. But, at the same time, they must engage each other in ways that maintain some semblance of local stability. A series of practices and institutions must be elaborated to effectively balance these divergent, yet interconnected, needs. As such, these practices are the beginnings of stable institutions that are capable of constituting new horizons of action and viable scales of economic activity that do not presume a fixed spatial arena – 'local', 'regional' or 'global' – but that entail elements of each.[98,99]

To a certain extent, the 'worlding' has been a process inherent in the very formations of cities. Because many cities in developing countries, especially in Africa, were essentially colonial cities, the urban 'accomplishments' of individuals were often recognized and supported somewhere else than the particular city in which they lived. In the case of the most successful, there was grudging recognition by colonial powers; but in the case of most, there was repatriation of their earnings back to rural or peri-urban areas and the status that this occasioned.[100] Most cities were shaped by an uneasy mixture of external imposition and local opportunism to carve out hybrid practices of urban life. As such, many colonial cities came to exist in a universe of being rooted 'everywhere and nowhere'. But, at the same time, they have an extensive history of being subject to often highly idiosyncratic compromises and social and economic arrangements that makes them very 'localized' despite the external networks to which they are connected.

Shrinking public-sector employment, overcrowding in informal sectors, increased competition for resources and services, and a growing survivalist orientation on the part of many urban residents re-localizes the ways in which people structure everyday work relationships.[101] Firms deal with those familiar to them. Transactions are conducted with those with whom one is in regular contact. For all of its problems – mutual resentments, obligations and loss of autonomy – family relations become the basis of business

The most visible aspects of 'pedestrian' globalization include direct actions by local bodies and individuals to participate in transnational economic activity relations. This is especially the case when particular sectors are unable to effectively absorb any new entrants.[102]

But there are also large elements of dissimulation and masking involved in this process. What appears to be increasingly parochial, narrowly drawn identities and practices may actually operate as markers in a complex social economy where actors attempt to participate in many different identities at the same time.[103] This is a 'game' where individuals become different kinds of actors for different communities and activities. Social actors use the heterogeneous, yet highly localized, residential domains of their cities to do two things at once. On the one hand, a largely kinship, neighbourhood-based solidarity is reiterated at 'home'.[104] At the same time, social actors are involved in very different ways of associating, doing business, gaining support, sharing information or performing their identities in other neighbourhoods across the city. Additionally, there is often a proliferation of 'officially' clandestine (but, in actuality, highly visible) economic arrangements.[105]

Here, actors from different religious, ethnic, regional or political affiliations engage in freewheeling collaboration. As a result, resources can often be put together and deployed with great speed and effectiveness. This is because the process is not excessively deliberated, scrutinized or subject to the demands and obligations usually inherent in kin and neighbourhood-based solidarity systems.

Urban quarters not only serve as platforms for popular initiative – for example, waste management, micro-enterprise development and shelter provision – but readapt local modalities of cohesion and sociality to more regional and global frameworks.[106] Some localities, such as Nima (Accra), Obalende (Lagos), Texas-Adjame (Abidjan) and Grand Yoff (Dakar) reflect a strong relationship between the elaboration of local associations and the generation of new economic activities and resources. In this context, associations become important in configuring new divisions of labour. They help coordinate the cross-border, small- and medium-scale trade of individual entrepreneurs and organize ways of pooling and reinvesting the proceeds of this trade to access larger quantities of tradable goods, diversify collective holdings and reach new markets.

In the more developed regions, the post-Fordist complexion of urban economic life leaves large areas of under-regulated and underutilized spaces intact. There are warehouses, suburbs and markets whose status may reflect their lack of functionality to the immediate local economic setting.[107] But in many instances, they are being seized upon by African and other developing country actors as sites for workshops and storerooms for artisan production to niche markets or as nodes in the trans-shipment of illegal commodities.[108]

As these businesses, community and other social associations grow in number and capacity, municipal politics will likely become more competitive and conflict ridden. Already in some cities, business associations, in particular, are going after political power as a way of protecting the interests of their members within restructured municipal regulatory frameworks. They are also going after political power because new associations

are developing all of the time, and the competition for members can get intense.

Subsidiarity and the weakening of national governments

One topic on which virtually all commentators on globalization agree is that the power of nation states has been substantially weakened. In most developing countries, this power has only been established relatively recently, in the post-colonial period from about 1965, and these countries have not had a great deal of time to build up a unified national pride and character, democratic institutions or a balanced national economy.

The weakening of nation states has occurred through several major mechanisms:

- The development of *multinational corporations* that now control most of the world's economic activity – these corporations exist beyond national boundaries and the control of governments, and can move their operations to anywhere that offers the most favourable input costs or subsidies and the least restriction to their activities.[109]
- The widespread availability of *contact and information* beyond national boundaries – this is achieved through the internet and rapidly cheapening telephone costs, so that entrepreneurs or small businesses can easily create international operations without the formal structures and state intermediation that larger businesses are subject to, and with little reference to the usual gatekeepers at national borders.
- The move of responsibility to lower levels of government, known as *subsidiarity* – in theory, this should strengthen national governments by enabling them to focus on their principal roles of centralized financial support, rather than the minutiae of local management or service delivery. In many more developed countries, this has, in fact, happened. However, this is not the case in a number of developing countries, where the central government is left in something of a vacuum, unable to articulate what its real role should be. This has been partly due to the reluctance to dismantle large bureaucracies, formerly responsible for service delivery, and to transfer the funds to local government. But it is also due to a sense of bewilderment in the face of rapid change, as long-standing channels of authority and support are dismantled.

Contributing to this loss of central autonomy are the activities of *international aid agencies*, which now also prefer to deliver their activities to the local level, generally through non-governmental organizations (NGOs) or city governments. This is partly because it is felt that many national governments have had their chance and have misdirected aid money to their own elites or according to different objectives than those of the agencies; partly because it is easier to monitor local projects and ensure they are being

All commentators on globalization agree that the power of nation states has been substantially weakened

targeted, through local organizations that have a vested interest in meeting international objectives of transparency and accountability; and partly due to the prescriptions of neo-liberal theory. Another very palpable advantage is that it permits widely different strategies to be tried in different places, allowing a whole range of possible strategies to determine good practice in activities where really nobody knows the answer.

These are considerable benefits. However, on the negative side, the whole, apparently decentralized, structure is foreign to the notion of national representative government that has served the developed world well, while it is very amenable to the operations of global hegemony. The dominant international perspective becomes the *de facto* paradigm for development, so the whole world rapidly becomes unified in the broad direction of what is supported by donors and international organizations.[110] National governments lose control over the direction of economic planning or policy, and the means to create a unified nation representing the will of the majority and the cultural, language and religious differences that are embedded in different societies.[111] Activities may also become piecemeal and disconnected, so that many different agencies are trying to achieve the same ends.[112] The typical bureaucratic failures of duplication and overlap, which so often occurs when different government agencies get involved in the same activities, are *writ miniscule* throughout the development administration as hundreds of different agencies take control – unless significant efforts are spent on coordination. The situation is not analogous to private service competitive delivery, where the 'discipline of the market' prevails to restore order. In this case, the paying clients for the executing bodies, such as local governments and NGOs, are not the public, who have no money to pay for such services, but the funding agencies, and successful delivery means meeting the norms of these agencies, which are established at the international level.

The danger, also, is that the successful local governments are no longer the ones who can follow national government policy and meet their requirements for good practice, but the ones who can put on a smooth front for donors and meet their norms, and have the capacity to put together first-rate proposals. The poorly governed have little chance in this system – and rarely do they have the chance to find out what they are missing out on and act upon it.[113]

A major tenet of neo-liberal thinking is that development can only proceed through a more proficient mobilization, organization and deployment of local and individual resources and resourcefulness. This mobilization can be assisted through a comprehensive decentralization of governmental authority and financial responsibility to the municipal level. At this level, it is hoped that citizens will be more aware of the rigidities or misdemeanors of government and will act directly or politically to improve the situation. Only when urban citizens take responsibility for the management of their political affairs, it is believed, will they feel secure enough to become proficient entrepreneurs and forward looking in their individual and collective initiatives.[114]

In this process of subsidiarity – that is, of bringing the management of public affairs and goods down to the most immediate and practical levels of where they actually take effect – municipal authorities are also supposed to act with increased fiscal autonomy. Municipal authorities are to take on more responsibility for covering larger shares of their operating costs. In this respect, nascent municipal governments in many cities are caught in a persistent bind: improvements in physical and administrative infrastructure are necessary in order to make people's activities more productive. By being more productive, these activities can generate increased amounts of revenue. Municipal governments can use this revenue to improve the overall urban environment. But as the tax base of most cities remains very limited, how do municipalities raise sufficient funds, in the interim, in order to have some kind of working capital to register such improvements? Trying to address this dilemma has been one of the main features of externally induced policy and project initiatives.

Local urban economic development has concentrated on putting into effect the locational decisions of foreign investment through offering tax breaks and other inducements to attract firms that would then create jobs. The fear of being uncompetitive has probably been the prime contributor to the weakening of labour market laws and industry protection throughout the HICs and a number of developing countries, creating the insecurity that has been the hallmark of the post-Keynesian period.[115] This struggle to offer inducements to international capital to locate or invest, and the desire to be 'competitive' at all costs became a rather pointless merry-go-round in which countries scrambled to give ever-greater inducements to multinational firms. An inordinate amount of time and money was spent on 'boosting' the attractions of a given city; but the payoff, in terms of the amount of investments secured, just was not there.

Offering direct subsidies to locating industries is now somewhat in decline, since recent WTO regulations prohibit any domestic subsidy that could displace inputs in domestic markets or other countries' exports in international markets. These regulations deter local governments from offering subsidies to specific industries within their jurisdictions or from using tax breaks to attract particular firms.[116]

The current trend is towards creating local economies of agglomeration – that is, basically taking what exists and finding new ways of organizing, linking and effecting it. Part of the strategy involves creating 'clusters' or areas that are amply provided with infrastructure, and where related firms can benefit from the presence of vertically or horizontally linked firms.[117] Another component is to foster greater links between education, training and job creation, which hopefully will result in a human capital base more closely aligned to the requirements of the labour market.[118,119]

Transurban cooperation and integration: towards new urban economies

In many respects, the focus on decentralization and the related production of urban infrastructure circumvents the broader issue of how discrete cities can move towards greater long-term economic viability of scale. What are the real economies that are potentially attainable? How are the developmental trajectories of discrete cities dependent upon expanding the possibilities of transurban interactions, while elaborating complementarity and niche functions within a larger nexus of regional economic growth?

As the economic activities of actors at various scales attempt to extend beyond local operations and national boundaries, it is important to learn more about how they operate and what prospects they have. It is vital to examine the relationships between long-established economic and cultural transurban corridors and the emergence of nascent ones. Cities throughout Europe have formed themselves into networks of influence. In Asia, the 'southern growth triangle' of Singapore, Johore Bahru in Malaysia and the Riau Islands in Indonesia is among the best known transnational clusters. The corridor that runs from Abidjan to Ibadan has over 70 million urban inhabitants with a long history of dealing with each other.

The critical point is the extent to which regionalist policies can engage with the fact that many adjacent regions are characterized by a substantial disarticulation from each other. It is easier to find goods from sub-Saharan Africa in San Francisco than in Egypt. It is easier to book travel in southern Africa in Sydney than in Nairobi. Many of the contexts in which cities in the LDCs have common goals are being mediated through the developed world rather than through direct contact – as they were during the colonial period.

This disarticulation extends to specific localities, where it reflects the fact that multiple forces – local, transnational and national – are interacting with each other in different ways. Consider the Kivu region in the DRC, with its patchwork of multinational extraction centres, militias and community-based smuggling networks. Or take the Foutou Jallon region of Senegal and Guinea, with its patchwork of gold and bauxite mining company towns, religious-cum-commercial centres, transportation hubs and isolated but culturally important mystical centres. Thailand, too, is a patchwork of the old and the new where the sharpest urban operations, factories and beachside tourist resorts rub shoulders with ancient shrines of meditation and peace and densely populated traditional rice-growing areas.

In these regions, markedly different capacities and local characters are forged in different towns and settlements. Different places, even neighbouring cities, are connected in very different ways to transnational capital, the national state, and regional social, cultural and economic networks. This process is especially the case in rapidly expanding urbanization on short-lived resource fronts – for example, temporary 'frontier' sites of intense cross-border smuggling, and timber and mining centres.

On an international scale, the role of migrants in facilitating trade with countries of origins has often been observed. Because of barriers of network, language, culture and government, it has been difficult to do business without intermediaries who understand the system. Education of developing world students in more developed countries continues to be a means through which international networks are preserved, particularly if the students return to their countries and take up key positions in government or industry. If, therefore, opportunities for international investment eventually appear, the long-term 'worlding' through population exchange of the elite will ultimately prove to be a valuable hidden resource.

Even outside of these more elite connections, one only has to witness the ways in which Djeddah, Dubai and Bombay are becoming 'Africanized' – as well as a number of European cities – to see the concerted efforts some urban Africans are making to 'reach the larger world'.[120] One only has to take note of Senegalese-based Mouride currency speculators and traders in cities across the world, and the spate of new banks and other facilities being constructed in Lagos, Malabo and Libreville, without funding from major multinationals or multilaterals. Chapter 6 will show how even the lowly informal sector can be enriched through international interchange. However small or limited these domains may be, they increasingly take on a public presence, even if the details of their operations may remain largely invisible.[121] Regional orientations have focused on preparing actors and institutions to act with greater flexibility and plurality across the sectors, localities and scales incumbent in reflexive capitalism.[122] Here, economic development becomes a matter of enriching and extending diverse institutional arrangements, and of being able to cohere various forms of intersections among the relational assets of specific communities, different productive sectors, institutions of governance, and private capital that can bring about development.

This flexibility is being demonstrated in the ways in which specific urban places, separated by marked physical and cultural distance, are being interpenetrated, in large part by the actions of individuals. For example, cities as diverse as Mbuji-Mayi, Port Gentile, Addis Ababa and Nouadibhou are being tied together through the participation of those who make them their base in an increasingly articulated system of counter trades involving mutual connections to Bombay, Dubai, Bangkok, Taipei, Kuala Lumpur and Djeddah.

These circuits, in turn, 'spin out' and link themselves to the more conventional migratory paths of West and Central Africans to Europe and, increasingly, to the US, and East Africans to North America and the UK.[123] While these circuits are organized around different commodities, a common profile has taken hold where valuable primary commodities, such as minerals, in particular, are diverted from 'official' national export structures into intricate networks where large volumes of underpriced electronics, weapons, counterfeit currencies, bonds, narcotics, laundered money and real estate circulate through various 'hands'.[124] The diversion can also include oil, agricultural products and timber.

As the economic activities of actors at various scales attempt to extend beyond local operations and national boundaries, it is important to learn more about how they operate and what prospects they have

If opportunities for international investment eventually appear, the long-term 'worlding' through population exchange of the elite will ultimately prove to be a valuable hidden resource

To a fair extent, this is a global extension of the 'bright lights' urbanization phenomenon, where migrants are seeking economic opportunity in the expanding service economies of the developed world and East Asia, or the purchase of cheap goods from urban markets in these regions. However, it is more than a dependence on remittances or the extension of hegemonic control from core economies. Instead, an intricate framework for operating at a 'world level' is being created. It is produced through individual travel, the cultivation of permeable boundaries through which goods and money can pass with minimal regulation, the incorporation of formal financial and political institutions within informal mechanisms of disposing goods and accessing markets, and a willingness to take substantial risks.

The question is who benefits from this internationalization of commerce? In which direction are the true benefits proceeding? This 'worlding' may be a constantly unstable and precarious practice, unable to substantially alter the positions and capacities of poorer cities within a globalized urban network.[125] Operations at this translocal level are limited to a small part of urban populations. Nevertheless, the attempts on the part of various associations, syndicates, and networks to articulate themselves and to access possibilities to act within this 'worlded' domain are not insignificant in the everyday social life of many cities in the LDCs.

In many ways, this 'worlding' ensues from the ways in which spaces of incapacity and marginality can be linked to reconsolidating political and economic power through a density of knowledge-based transactions represented by an elite cadre of urban centres. In one dimension of this articulation, one recent study refers to Africa's 'perverse connections' to the global economy.[126] Globalization entails speed, unimpeded capital flows, the hyper-reality of credit and fiscality, and the amplification of micro-dynamics and characteristics as key elements to profit-making. Accordingly, globalization provides new opportunities for economic and political actors to operate outside of increasingly outmoded laws and regulatory systems. While many of these activities may not be strictly legal, there may be much to learn from them that could be applied to more socially acceptable economic activities.

The critical question is how can geographically proximate cities be more effectively articulated in formal ways, given a history of largely informal connections? What we know about the potentials of transurban connections primarily comes to us through a growing understanding of informal, unconventional and sometimes illicit economies. How can we take these understandings and apply this knowledge to promote 'above-ground' articulations among developing country cities within specific regions? To begin addressing this task, the focus should be on some of the following questions:

- How can networks of inter-city exchanges be consolidated into ongoing policy and urban development fora that capitalize on historical, cultural or geographic connections as a means of developing economic blocs, trade zones or integrated markets?

- How could cities make more intentional use of such actual or potential inter-urban linkages as mechanisms to generate new development strategies and abilities to act in concert around issues deemed of mutual importance?

- On the more formal scale, by what means can cities or regions with mutual interests join together to prevent the process of 'divide and conquer' that global capital uses to weaken their already limited bargaining power and capacity to act independently in order to direct their economies for the benefit of their citizens?

- Can the official or quasi-official consolidation of transurban zones as planning and development entities in their own right have any strategic advantages? If so, what are the appropriate administrative forms that ensure a viable deployment of this critical mass and concomitant synergistic relationships?

- What kinds of concrete and complementary collaborations among municipal actors across sectors are possible in terms of beginning to consolidate a sense of shared urban space? In other words, what can local and national authorities, planners, city technicians and managers, NGO workers, activists and entrepreneurs start doing now to bring greater coherence and efficacy to the potentials inherent at such an urban scale? How are individual contributions to be managed; what rights and responsibilities will partners have?

Different institutions and spaces within different cities in the developing world are increasingly connected to cities around the world. This connection at a globalized urban scale is consolidated through a broad range of informational flows, financial transactions and inter-institutional affiliations that are negotiated within transnational private arenas. This consolidation, emerging from highly informalized processes, is increasingly subject to new notions of legality, private standards and norms that operate with substantial authority.[127]

Many aspects of economic governance shift from the public realm to transnational private arenas. Economic crises in the developing world have occasioned opportunities for the working out of highly innovative financial deals, structured by the collaboration of investment banks, accountants, international legal firms and public officials. These deals are then used to consolidate a primarily privatized domain of economic governance in which, unfortunately, local interests are rarely paramount or even considered, except to the extent that they assist with profits.[128]

The conventional idea remains that cities in less developed countries are largely made up of well-bounded local communities and that their strengthening is the key to development. But these communities are becoming increasingly tenuous and ineffective within a globalized urban world. The enclosure and sustenance of coherent local spaces increasingly depend upon the capacity to secure

International migration is a global extension of the 'bright lights' urbanization phenomenon, where migrants are seeking economic opportunity in the expanding economies

effective individual and corporate engagements with the wide range of networks and flows that make up translocal domains. To a large degree, communities can usually only come to this larger stage by using terms and practices that emerge from their own aspirations and logic.[129]

The less developed regions are not passive bystanders to the elaboration of transnational private arenas – unless they choose to be. Specific and long-standing traditions of social regulation and collective effort are being reworked as elements in elaboration of spaces of economic transaction, knowledge production and cultural influence. These spaces are translocal and transnational in terms that – although subsumed to the constellations of power that define the prevailing dynamics of what is 'global' – reflect substantial local control.

Slums and globalization

From the point of view of this Global Report, who are the winners from this dual-sided creation of transnational economies and spaces? Is globalization demolishing traditional institutions and corrupting social fabrics? Is it only the urban middle class and the most educated and skilled who benefit from globalization? Is escalating poverty and the often brutal deconstruction of polity and community in the developing countries worth the potential gain from a minimal trickle of international capital? Are there real opportunities from globalization that will ultimately benefit all of the world and all of its citizens?

At present, one direct benefit that slum dwellers receive from globalization is greater direct access of aid agencies to local aid NGOs and local governments and, therefore, better targeting of pro-poor programmes. Increased expectations of the possible might also be a benefit in that improved information might make some dwellers seek out livelihood solutions or opportunities that they had not previously considered. The more skilled or educated workers may be able to find jobs in international firms at advantageous pay rates – but these are unlikely to be slum dwellers.

Facing these very limited advantages is a truly formidable array of disadvantages – so many, in fact, that some national governments might be excused for not wishing to participate at all, if they genuinely have the welfare of the urban poor at heart. The major disadvantage is the wholesale *loss of formal-sector job opportunities* in both the public sector and the private import-substitution industries, so that informal-sector jobs, with no security and often with subsistence wages, are all that is left. As well, *inequality* increases as the part of urban society able to access global opportunities increases its income. This means that the prime resources of the city are increasingly appropriated by the affluent. And globalization is *inflationary* as the new rich are able to pay much more for a range of key goods, especially land. This is exacerbated by removal of price fixing on subsistence goods, and increased utility charges through privatization and the removal of cross-subsidy. The poor are *marginalized* in the worst parts of the city – the slums. The ability of national governments to act

on their behalf is curtailed, while local governments in poor areas have no tax base with which to assist. In addition, *social cohesion* is damaged through a bewildering array of new ideas, images and international norms, and through the general precariousness of existence, all of which undermine the traditional bases of authority.

'Trickle-down' theory has usually been advanced by the pro-growth theorists as a means by which entropy will eventually improve the incomes of the working poor. However, Kuznets-type theories have not been confirmed, and the consensus now is that any trickle down is confined to a relatively small part of society. Aid agencies such as the World Bank are now seeking to address the global problem of poverty quite directly.[130]

Overall, it would seem better for developing countries to participate in global opportunities than to isolate themselves in a 'splendid' poverty, as a very few countries have done. Nevertheless, countries might do well to emulate the examples of developed countries, who have been very choosy about allowing projects that have no local flow-on or tax benefits worth considering, or that do not benefit their citizens for other reasons. This requires a fair amount of sophistication on the part of governments – which very few local governments have.

Looking ahead

The poor have sometimes objected to being governed badly. The rich have always objected to being governed at all.[131]

The world, it would appear, has entered a new era of *laissez-faire* globalization, with everything that this implies – in particular, mercantile booms and busts that ratchet up inequality and distribute new wealth increasingly unevenly. In the past, this world system was responsible for creating the famous slum areas of major cities in the developed world; and it will, no doubt, do the same again in the developing world.

The long growth period from 1945 to 1973 was typified by falling inequality and improving equity. The situation then reversed: income inequality and poverty increased without respite during the recession years from 1978 to 1993, and real incomes actually fell for the bottom income groups in most countries and for the world as a whole – with a resulting increase in income poverty. The reasons are hotly contested. They include the withdrawal of the state; the cyclical nature of capitalism; increased demand for skilled labour; and the possible effects of globalization – all of which, in fact, are connected.

During the late 1990s, economic conditions improved in most of the HICs, with a typical asset boom concentrated in the fledgling information technology industries. The basic problem was that much of the increased wealth and income of the 1990s went to the very highest income groups, while low income groups at best stabilized their position or continued to go backwards, continuing a trend that had begun in the mid 1970s. The reason for this is quite simple: *except in situations where labour has strong bargaining power*

The policy question is what are the real opportunities from globalization that will ultimately benefit all of the world and all of its citizens?

and/or governments actively seek to redistribute wealth, the most powerful groups will always be in a position to take the lion's share.

To a large extent, it is not globalization *per se* that has caused countries and cities to abandon redistributive policies that benefit the majority of their citizens, but the *perception* that they need to be competitive. The fear of being overtaken by Asian low-cost producers led many countries to deregulate their labour markets and lower social spending. In fact, the trade position of the developed countries *strengthened*, if anything, and Asia's gain was at the expense of the rest of the developing world.

There has, therefore, been no particular need, as long as they are doing well, for cities and countries to damage the prospects of their low income citizens through adopting aspects of neo-liberal policies that redistribute incomes in favour of high income earners and business. Yet, that is what has happened, and that is what is responsible for most of the various phenomena that have come to be known collectively as globalization. The changes are somewhat mediated by new technology and falling transport and communication costs. The widespread feeling of insecurity that cities and countries are 'falling behind' and are in the grip of vast impersonal economic forces has provided an excuse to do nothing and to allow programmes of social redistribution and improvement to languish. In the end, the growth in inequality has happened because national governments have abdicated their responsibilities to their citizens to promote fairness, redistribution, social justice and stability in favour of a chimera of competitiveness and wealth for the few. It is also the outcome of international organizations that have adopted a dominant neo-liberal philosophy, which has failed to deliver on most of its promises almost everywhere that it has been applied. In the face of these failures, those organizations that have a mandate for aid, or are environmentally aware, have backpedaled rapidly since 1993 from a position of supporting growth for its own sake, and now have adopted poverty reduction as their imperative.

If a boom decade like the 1990s leaves the world with a gnawing feeling of insecurity and a reality of lack of social justice, then a bust decade will be many times worse. The cities most affected have been, and will be, in the half dozen or so new countries that have received an invitation to join the developed world because they are in the full path of global cycles. The fate of the remaining countries that are largely left out of this 'international gentrification' project remains uncertain, but it is not encouraging.

This globalization is now being performed against a background of urbanization flows that have peaked in rate, but will increase in absolute magnitude for the next 30 years – largely in the countries excluded from the development club. These countries will need a great deal of help to prevent their cities from going under due to congestion, environmental degradation and social unrest.

In the absence of a coordinated effort to address the crisis of urbanization and globalization, it will be left to the countries and cities themselves to try to articulate a role. If they are unable to establish working relations to ensure that they are not perpetually marginalized or exploited, then informal sector enterprises, including their international networks, will be the principal players. Unfortunately, these kinds of activities are less than fleas to the organized and coherent industrial and financial behemoths of the 'Centre'. They are, by definition, marginal, and although they are the only response possible, the chances of them amounting ultimately to a hill of beans are not great. Nevertheless, informal sector networks are, in fact, a key precondition for ultimate growth and integration into the Centre. It was in such humble beginnings that many of today's great corporations and industries had their origins; so if the cement of capital and resources can be found to enable the more directed of these loose configurations to adhere, anything is possible.

The medium-term prospect however, in the absence of a dramatic about-turn in policy, is for stagnation amidst urbanization in most of the developing world, and for the process that led to urban improvement in the developed world to continue in those countries benefiting from globalization. Even in this select group marked for success, it involves the growth of a middle class, the marginalization of certain areas increasingly occupied by impoverished minorities and disadvantaged groups, and their eventual recolonization by the middle class when it suits their economic interests. This process can, in fact, result in cities that are slum-free; but it has taken 150 years or more where it has occurred. This is rather too long for even the most extended policy horizons.

The answer, therefore, lies, as it has always done, with countries and city governments to decide what will benefit their people and to put together strategies in partnership with their citizens and donors that will enable these outcomes to be reached. Because slums are both a result and a manifestation of urban poverty, such strategies must address the fundamental problems of unemployment, lack of income-generation opportunities and rising income inequality. Put simply, the journey towards cities without slums must be part of the more difficult journey towards 'poverty eradication', which is essentially a search for sustainable urban livelihoods. It is up to the countries to articulate these aims and insist on them – without ignoring the realities of a global world, but not ultimately enslaved by it. Where goals are unequivocal and have universal support, the record is that they will be reached. Targets have already been reached to a fair extent with health, because everyone knew what had to be done. Good progress has also been made with connecting urban services, although there is still a long way to go. The same thing can happen with other social goals. In the end, social prosperity and economic development decisions should be in the hands of the people and their governments, and these rights must be exercised to maximize social welfare and to improve the fabric of the cities where all the change of the next decades is going to take place.

Decisions on social prosperity and economic development should be in the hands of the people and their governments, and these rights must be exercised to maximize social welfare and to improve the fabric of the cities where all the change of the next decades is going to take place

NOTES

1   This chapter is based on two backgrownd papers – 'Urban slums and poverty in context' by Joe Flood of Urban Resources and 'Towards the worlding of African cities: transurban approach to economic development' by AbdouMaliq Simone of the Graduate School of Public and Development Management, University of Witwatersrand, South Africa.

2   These factors were identified by Alan Greenspan, Chairman of the US Federal Reserve Board, on his presentation to US Congress, 12 September 2002.

3   Typical figures for trade as a fraction of GDP were UK 60 per cent from 1870 to 1914, 35 per cent in 1950. Tariff rates were about 5 per cent in Germany, Japan and Sweden in 1875 and 25 to 40 per cent by 1931. The US stayed protectionist with tariffs over 30 per cent throughout the period and trade rarely rose above 15 per cent of GDP (Held et al, 2000, pp158–159).

4   Kanbur and Lustig, 1999.

5   Berry, 1991, p2. Many conventional economists have dismissed the idea of a long, roughly periodic wave of inflation and deflation in human affairs; but the evidence is compelling. Certainly, the booms and busts of the 19th and early 20th century show a surprising regularity.

6   Case study – Sydney.

7   Less exposed cities such as Birmingham did not show this ring distribution.

8   Stiglitz, 1998.

9   Stagflationary episodes at the top of the cycle may also cause a sharp reduction in inequality since real wealth and capital income for those at the top of the distribution erode more quickly than jobs at this stage. This is one reason why inflation causes neo-liberal economists such huge concern.

10   Maddison, 2001.

11   Maddison, 1995, p22.

12   UNDP, 1992, p34; UNDP, 1999, pp36–38.

13   Hahnel (2001) writes: 'The truth is quite simple: international investment flooded into East Asia in the 1980s and 1990s because East Asia was a more profitable place to invest than anywhere else, and there was a sea of global wealth looking for dry land'.

14   See www.crd.bc.ca/poverty/abstract.htm.

15   See Jenkins, 1997.

16   Milanovic, 2002a.

17   Dolinskaya, 2001.

18   The Irish advance was a spectacular example of 'convergence', with many US firms locating their US production facilities there, encouraged by local incentives and low wages. Finland's Nokia became dominant in the rapidly growing mobile phone industry. While (or because) Australia had no significant involvement in new technologies, by 2002 it had the fastest growing economy in the OECD, encouraged by a favourable exchange rate and a lowering of transportation and communication costs.

19   Because of labour shortages, by 2000 it was estimated that up to one third of programmers in Silicon valley were from India or East Asia. At home, the growing software industry in Bangalore sat uneasily with worsening urban poverty.

20   Polyani, 1944.

21   For example, Sarel (1997) avers from a cross-sectional analysis of 15 medium- and high-income countries that controlling for other factors, growth and investment reduce income inequality, suggesting that lower-income households benefit relatively more from economic growth. Dollar and Kraay (2000) support this. However, longitudinal results, such as those for the US and Canada, do not bear this out. Kanbur and Lustig (2000) find from a literature survey that there is no discernible relationship.

22   Baldacci et al (2002) find that financial crises are associated with an increase in poverty and, in some cases, income inequality. Urban households, wage employees and households headed by very young and very old individuals are particularly hard hit.

23   Bruno et al, 1997. Cashin et al (2001) say: 'Comparative studies find that growth reduces poverty; but the estimated relationship varies widely. The effect is stronger in countries with less inequality, both of incomes and assets.'

24   Drennan et al, 1996; Brotchie et al, 1987.

25   For a detailed account of the chasm between the petro-diamond capitalism and wretched poverty found in Angola, see Hodges, 2001.

26   United Nations Integrated Regional Information Network (IRIN), 11 June 2002. Accessed at www.irinnews.org/report.asp?ReportID=28066&SelectR egion=Southern_Africa&Select Country=ANGOLA on 27 June 2002. The data come from a study conducted by Angola's National Institute for Statistics carried out with the United Nations children's agency (UNICEF) in 2001.

27   Thomas and Kanagarajah, 2002.

28   United Nations IRIN, 11 June 2002. Accessed at www.irinnews.org/report.asp?ReportID=28258&Select Region=West_Africa&Select Country=NIGERIA on 27 June 2002.

29   UNDP, 1999, p36.

30   See UNCTAD, 2002. Available at www.unctad.org/en/pub/ps11dc02.en.htm.

31   World Bank, 2001c.

32   UNDP, 1999, p36.

33   Lokshin and Ravallion, 2000.

34   IMF and World Bank, 2002.

35   UNCHS (Habitat), 2001; UNDP, 2000.

36   Bussolo and Solignac Lecomte, 1999.

37   Uniform government regulations and wage setting also play a major role, in practice.

38   One of the greatest advantages of the US is that internally it has been the largest highly developed free trade area in the world.

39   The worked example shows how the transfer of manufacturing jobs can easily create eight times the number of jobs in the recipient country. Goldsmith (1996), using a simpler reckoning, states that up to 40 times as many jobs could result.

40   For this reason among others, Latin America and Africa during the 1960s and 1970s conducted a regime of import substitution, which improves the terms of trade (at the expense of higher domestic prices if tariff walls are used). Australia also followed an import substitution policy for much of the century, for similar reasons. This argument has, however, fallen out of favour, and it is generally agreed that at least in the short term, the tiger economies have not suffered from a loss of trading power.

41   Michael, 1997.

42   Chang, 2002.

43   Hirst and Thomson, 1996. Held et al (2000) state that this is not strictly the case since trade is more extensive than ever before, with most pairs of countries engaging in some form of trade.

44   Held et al, 2000, p169.

45   Kaplinsky (2001) shows that trade has actually increased as a per cent of GDP in all regions since 1960; but the change is much larger in India and East Asia.

46   Stern (2000) estimates that trade embargos and subsidies by the developed world cost the developing world far more than the aid that is received.

47   Sugar, rum, tobacco and an excellent building design industry, particularly for holiday resorts.

48   Ellis and MacGaffey, 1996; Flynn, 1997.

49   Goldsmith (1996) argues eloquently that the world should be divided into free trading blocs of similar levels of development and wage costs.

50   Bruno et al, 1997.

51   'What the IMF has most to answer for is the leading role it has played in liberalizing the international credit system whose unrestrained dangers now frighten even those it was designed to serve' (Hahnel, 2001).

52   UNCHS (Habitat), 2001; UNDP, 2001.

53   This limited contact is, however, regarded as a threat to local culture and ideals in a number of developing countries, particularly the Arab states and China. Because of the US dominance of English internet content, it is seen as a medium for the more rapid spread of US-based culture.

54   This has now risen to US$270 billion, controlling flows of close to US$2 trillion. See www.business-times.asia1.com.sg/companies/story/0,2276,57529,00.html; www.pressreleasenetwork.com/newsletter/2000/main7_news29.htm.

55   See www.asiaweek.com/asia week/97/0228/biz4.html.

56   The hedge funds continued to harass Hong Kong for some time through expedients such as shorting the stock market and attacking the currency, taking profits when the Hong Kong government raised interest rates. Eventually, they were driven off by regulation.

57   The Samuelson-Stolper theorem.

58   Hanson and Harrison, 1995.

59   Cragg and Epelbaum, 1995.

60   Krugman, 1996; Krugman and Venables, 1995.

61   Hamnett, 1993.

62   Wood and Ridao-Cano, 1999.

63   UNCTAD, 1998.

64 Aryeety and Nissanke, 1997. Keeping currencies artificially high to protect local capital was also a necessary precondition.

65 UNECA, 1998a.

66 Elbadawi and Ndulu, 1996.

67 UNECA, 1999.

68 UNECA, 1999.

69 Forrest and Murie, 1988.

70 As an extreme example, almost free water supply in Uzbekistan, also used for cotton irrigation, led to the virtual emptying of the Aral Sea, while water sits in pools in the desert and over half the water supply leaks away.

71 Milanovic, 2002a; Stiglitz, 2000.

72 Riddell, 1997.

73 Thomas and Chhibber, 1989. Bolivia's currency depreciated by 93 per cent (Jenkins, 1997).

74 Subbarao et al, 1995.

75 This created a moral hazard for international lenders who had made unwise loans but were effectively insured by the IMF. It is fair to say that most SAPs are made on behalf of international lenders, not the countries, who do not end up with any long-term improvement in their financial situation but have a short-term cash flow problem averted.

76 Albert, 2001.

77 Riddell, 1997.

78 This has been conceded by many authors – for example, Illife, 1987; Moser et al, 1993; Amis, 1995, 2002; and, most significantly, the World Bank, 2000, 2001.

79 For example, even in the mid 1990s a few countries were recording the serial numbers of all foreign banknotes brought into the country. Travellers could gain the distinct impression that the local level of development was inversely related to the difficulty of entry to the country and the difficulty of conducting business there due to pointless government constraints.

80 The main effect of price fixing, monopolies and border controls is to create artificial scarcities – which, in the first case, can cause hardship for low-income producers and, in the latter cases, creates extra profits for local capitalists at the expense of consumers.

81 Killick, 1999.

82 Killick, 1999; Jenkins, 1997.

83 Humphreys and Jaeger, 1989.

84 Killick (1999) says that SAP agendas are somewhat peripheral to poverty and are unlikely to have much effect either way, but agrees that the programmes are associated with growing inequalities and have impacted particularly adversely on the urban working poor. Stern (2000) strongly opposes the idea that SAPs cause inequality, citing the (non-crisis) examples of Ghana, Uganda and Viet Nam.

85 Riddell, 1997.

86 Potts, 1997.

87 'The poorer the country, the more likely it is that debt repayments are being extracted directly from people who neither contracted the loans nor received any of the money' (Albert, 2000).

88 Riddell, 1997.

89 Becker et al, 1994; Potts, 1995.

90 Incidentally, but perhaps not coincidentally, this benefited industrial exporters from the West.

91 This section (and some others) draws on a paper prepared by AbdouMaliq Simone (2001) of the Graduate School of Public and Development Management, University of Witwatersrand, South Africa: 'Toward the "Worlding" of African Cities: Transurban approaches to economic development'.

92 Held et al, 1999.

93 Ould-Mey, 1994.

94 Develtere and Van Durme, 1999–2000.

95 Rimmer, 1996; Brotchie et al, 1985, 1987.

96 Bourdieu, 1990.

97 Fukuyama, 1995.

98 Jessop, 1999.

99 Brenner, 1998a.

100 Hopkins, 1973; Mabogunje, 1990; King, 1990; Cooper, 1994.

101 Mhone, 1995.

102 Kanji, 1995.

103 Berry, 1995.

104 An extreme example would be Masai businessmen or professionals who regularly return to their villages for ceremonies, or expatriate Indians who may lead a strongly family-oriented lifestyle but participate in complex international negotiations of the type Fukuyama (1995) regards as necessary for the conduct of extensive business.

105 Ellis and MacGaffey, 1996.

106 This is the conclusion of a broad range of initial field study reports under the auspices of the MacArthur Foundation Council for the Development of Social Science Research in Africa Programme on Africa's Real Economies.

107 Augé, 1999.

108 Carter, 1997; Kesteloot, 1995; Sassen, 1999.

109 Dunning, 1993.

110 This relates to the 'end of history' as Fukuyama (1993) has called the lack of effective counterbalance to the dominant paradigm.

111 This is a considerable plus, according to neo-liberals.

112 For example, in Thailand in 1999, some 12 different agencies were working on water supply, mostly supported by different donors and largely uncoordinated.

113 The city of Naga in The Philippines, which successfully instituted a People's Forum in the early 1990s (against government direction) and is regarded as the apotheosis of a well-run local government, has virtually had an aid-led prosperity, with five international projects going on at any one time, while few other local governments have

even one. The donors are, in fact, aware of over-targeting favourites and are seeking new prospective partners in poorer areas.

114 This attitude relates closely to the US political system and is not widely held in other parts of the HICs, where it is believed that a stable and responsible government – at all levels – is the key to economic security and development.

115 Krugman, 1996.

116 World Bank, 1999.

117 Porter, 1998.

118 These activities are intended to be largely outside of the public realm but, in fact, are carried out by governments almost everywhere.

119 Unfortunately, there are no guarantees, and some societies have become over-educated without the requisite professional jobs. Shop assistants in Manila mostly have college degrees, and signs in windows can be seen, such as 'Nightwatchman wanted: Criminology degree required'.

120 See Kloosterman and van der Leun, 1999.

121 African Economic Research Bulletin, Financial, Economic and Technical Series, 1997.

122 Storper, 1997.

123 Constantin, 1996.

124 Observatoire Geopolitique des Drogues, 1999; Bayart et al, 1999.

125 Herbst, 1996.

126 Castells, 1996.

127 Sassen, 1998.

128 Sassen, 1998.

129 Ranciere, 1998.

130 World Bank, 2000, 2001a, b. According to Ali and Sirivardana (1996), the move from growth to poverty reduction strategies is of sufficient significance to constitute a new aid paradigm. However, mainstream United Nations agencies, including UN-Habitat, have always had a pro-poor orientation.

131 G K Chesterton, English essayist (1874–1936).

PART II

ASSESSING SLUMS IN THE DEVELOPMENT CONTEXT

Slums play many roles in city life. As the place of residence of low-cost labour, they keep the wheels of the city working in many different ways. As a first stopping point for immigrants, they provide the low-cost housing that will enable the immigrants to save for their eventual absorption into society. They are adept at producing the services and commercial activities that the formal sector fails to provide through the mobilization of local enterprise and industry. They are places in which the vibrant mixing of different cultures frequently results in new forms of artistic expression, while – on the negative side – they are the recipients of the city's externalities: noxious industry, waste materials, ill health, crime and social dysfunction, and fragile, dangerous or polluted land that no one else wants.

Slums are extremely varied places that defy any one tight definition. Many are slums because they are unrecognized by the officials of the local authority and government. This lack of recognition – informality – is both a characteristic and cause of problems of inadequacy. Slums, poverty and the informal sector are closely related, but are by no means congruent.

Informal enterprise conducted from slums may be linked to formal enterprises in ways that are essential to the continued operation of the city. The screen-printer who provides laundry bags to hotels, the charcoal burner who wheels his cycle up to the copper smelter and delivers sacks of charcoal for the smelting process, the home-based crèche to which the managing director delivers her child each working morning, the informal builder who adds a security wall around the home of the government minister all indicate the complex networks of linkages between informal and formal. In Part II of this Global Report, the nature of the informal sector in employment and housing is discussed.

There is no intention to glamorize the life of slum dwellers. Many of them lack the most basic facilities for healthy and fulfilling lives and must draw upon internal wells of resilience just to cope each day. However, out of unhealthy, crowded and often dangerous environments can emerge cultural movements and levels of solidarity unknown in leafy suburbs.

The story of slums is, therefore, neither heterogeneous nor coherent and homogenous. It is a story of rich variety, great achievement and typical 21st-century urban life. When more than half of the urban population lives in them, the slums become the dominant city. This is the case in many countries and needs to be recognized so that slums

are awarded their rightful place in the centre of policies and politics.

Chapter 4 looks, firstly, at the history of slums in early capitalism, as urban areas swelled with low-income people seeking opportunity and enterprising developers and landlords sought to take advantage of the situation by subdividing dwellings or rebuilding to far higher densities. It considers the typical history of a slum over more than 100 years through 'working men's housing', steady exclusion and degradation, flight of all but the most desperate or indigent residents, and, finally, regeneration.

The functions of slums in providing cheap accommodation and informal low-cost services, a place for essential economic contributions by lower income people, and as a 'dumping ground' for unwanted aspects of urban life are discussed.

The cultural and occupational diversity of slums is stressed as places of origin of many important musical and dance movements of the 20th century. They have also been sources of political and social movements. The question, however, is whether slums are places of opportunity or places of desperation, poverty and social exclusion. Most slum areas have aspects of both and the balance determines the types of intervention that may be necessary. Most of the poor conditions in slums in developing countries are about differential access to power and resources, and this is expected to worsen under present strategies of fiscal decentralization and privatization, since slum dwellers cannot pay for services. They also cannot easily mobilize politically to divert social resources from elsewhere to improve their neighbourhoods.

Poor health is strongly associated with bad housing and overcrowding, and people in slum areas suffer inordinately from the killer diseases of the 20th century, including HIV/AIDS, tuberculosis and waterborne disease. Slum areas are commonly believed to be places with a high incidence of crime. This is not universally true; but in places of social dislocation with large numbers of unemployed young people, crime can be a serious problem for slum residents.

Chapter 5 describes a wide variety of slums, categorizing them by characteristics such as origin and age, location and scale, vulnerability and whether communities are involved in their improvement. Historically important city centres that have fallen on hard times and are run down are very different from peripheral new squatter settlements or illegal subdivisions. Tiny pockets of shacks on traffic islands need different treatment from neighbourhoods of traditional housing. The case studies carried out for the preparation of this report provide a rich source of information and experiences to demonstrate both how slums vary and how experiences are similar across national and continental boundaries, and what a rich variety there is amongst slums.

Some observations from the case studies are that the rapid growth of some slums may be a result of housing deterioration and poor previous building practices in times of economic downturn; some upgraded slums may subsequently have a considerably improved environment and status, while others have not attracted private investment or further upgrading and have fallen backwards into disrepair; and slums with heritage value increasingly have the possibility of being saved by improved upgrading technology that avoids wholesale clearance.

Inner-city slums are usually very overcrowded, representing long-term attempts to profit from their occupation, and are mostly well served with infrastructure. The main obstacle to improvement is not only resources but the complex and disputed systems of ownership, rent control and the 'externality' problem, in which owners may be reluctant to be the first to improve their dwellings. At the opposite extreme, newer 'makeshift' slums are the most likely to have housing of impermanent materials (because of the high risk of eviction) and to be on fragile land. As the land has not yet been commodified, housing markets may not exist and may be slow to start even after tenure regularization takes place.

Chapter 6 presents a discussion of economic aspects of slum formation, within the dynamics of city life. It starts with an examination of changes in the structure of the global labour force and the rapid growth of the informal labour force in developing countries, due largely to the significant demographic changes, rapid urbanization and liberalization trends highlighted in Part I.

This is followed by a discussion of the informal sector in the urban economy, in light of the very important role it plays in the livelihoods of slum dwellers. Most slum dwellers are employed within the informal sector, and virtually all of the employment provided within slums is informal. For this reason, it is important to understand the nature and extent of informal production and services in the urban economy, especially the small-scale, home- and street-based activities that constitute the main avenues of income generation for slum households.

The final section focuses on the economic position of slums in the housing sector, starting with the issues arising out of tenure insecurity, as these may limit access to services, the ability to build up assets (including housing) and networks, as well as community cohesion. Slum dwellers are lacking in access to water supply, sanitation, storm water drainage, solid waste disposal and to many essential services. However, there is a lack of forward planning to meet even the current problems, let alone the projected doubling of demand that is imminent. Appropriate solutions that are not overburdened with unsustainable regulations and which can involve the slum residents in planning and executing improvements need to be found and applied in a consistent way to meet the challenge of the remaining phase of urbanization.

Major highlights of Part II of the report are:

- Slum neighbourhoods have numerous economic, social, as well as infrastructure problems. Slum dwellers lack proper housing, water and sanitation, are exposed to serious health risks, and have limited access to credit and the formal job market due to stigmatization and discrimination and to geographic isolation. Furthermore, they have limited access to social and economic networks. Slum areas in cities have high population densities and high concentrations of social and economic deprivation, which may include broken families, unemployment, and economic, physical and social exclusion.
- Throughout the world today, a wide range of people live in slums, in a rich diversity of tenure, housing and employment types. The areas provide accommodation for urban workers of all kinds and are the sites of enterprises that have customers throughout the city. Slums provide low-cost housing and low-cost services for rapidly expanding low-income urban populations, and also serve as networks of social support for new migrants to the city.
- Early slum improvement efforts were a response to outbreaks of contagious diseases that were believed to originate in slums. There is a long literature linking housing deprivation with ill health later in life; even during the 1950s, morbidity rates in urban UK were higher than in rural areas. Many millions in slums suffer unhealthy living conditions, resulting in shorter life and chronic illness. The poorer general health of slum dwellers and the lack of access to medical attention increase their likelihood of dying from epidemic diseases such as AIDS and tuberculosis, while poor sanitation exposes them to waterborne diseases.
- Slums are often associated with crime; but in some places this is more a fabrication of the media than a reality. Places with strong social control systems will have low crime rates. The prevalence of both property crime and violent crimes is related to problems of economic hardship among the young, which increases during economic downturns. Violence against women is also related to economic hardship, but is also related to the low social status of women.
- Poor people suffer more from violence and petty theft, in cities where this is common, than rich people. In these circumstances, violence and security issues can be regarded by poor people as considerably more important than housing or income issues. The fear of crime has changed the nature of cities with a high level of violence, altering the open, interactive nature of the community, and enforcing segregation through gated communities and walled enclaves.

There are also added dangers of crime for slum dwellers, not necessarily because there are more criminals in slums than elsewhere but because their homes are less secure and there are likely to be fewer police on patrol than in wealthier areas.
- About 37 per cent of urban households in the developing world have piped water, 15 per cent have sewerage and 60 per cent have electricity. The levels of household connections to networked infrastructure are major indicators of urban adequacy and increase rapidly with city development. In least developed countries, only 8 per cent of wastewater is treated and only 12 per cent of solid waste is collected.
- Increases in poverty are associated with the appearance or growth of slums and homeless people. Following liberalization in Commonwealth of Independent States (CIS) countries and the subsequent rapid growth of poverty, large numbers of housing units are in urgent need of replacement or upgrading. Refugees and homeless beggars crowd railway stations, airports and subways, and migrants to the city are squatting in dilapidated and vandalized former municipal dormitories and in abandoned buildings.
- Slums are very varied, ranging from quite tolerable to filthy and dangerous, from tiny areas perched on a traffic island to huge sprawling areas with hundreds of thousands of people. An important distinction is between squatter slums (land invasion) and informal slums (with the permission of the owner, but not meeting regulations). The former are decreasing in importance as supervision of land increases, while the latter are increasing rapidly, often due to illegal subdivision or development.
- Although they may be very visible and have historic significance, inner-city slums have only a relatively small proportion of slum populations in developing countries. This change from the 19th century is due to the very rapid rates of urbanization – but it is also connected with today's much cheaper transport and decentralized work places, and the less stringent policing of land use at city edges in many places, which permits squatter construction.
- Public or 'new town' housing built near the edge of cities to re-house slum dwellers or poor people in several countries has itself become dilapidated and has joined the stock of slums – but with much less accessibility than the original. For this reason, these estates may end up being inhabited by only the destitute or desperate. Enterprise housing built to minimal standards for workers has even less chance of being adequately maintained, especially if the enterprises close.

- Secure tenure is one of the main concerns of shelter-based policies, and if security can be gained, neighbourhoods are likely to improve. Recent research has shown that tenure is not divided into formal and informal but is more nuanced and closer to a continuum from fully secure in perpetuity to highly insecure. It may also be that the landowner is secure but the users can be very insecure, at risk of of being moved off at hours' notice, sometimes violently.

- In many unauthorized settlements the residents regard themselves as de facto owners and usually have some form of title. A lively housing and rental market is usually in place. Illegal subdivision may act rather like incremental owner building in that initially unaffordable services may be improved as the community becomes more affluent – but, of course, there is no guarantee that subsequent upgrading will occur, unless facilitated by the government.

- Landlords, some of them similar to their tenants in terms of income, are providing most of the capital for housing development in slums. Their contribution is continually under-rated and blocked by rent control and other regulations, although they are doing exactly what the free market demands. Renting houses is probably the only retirement scheme available for slum households. A great deal more attention needs to be paid to involving informal landlords in slum improvement and in assisting them to mobilize capital and maintain standards.

- Since 1950 there have been 20 to 30 per cent falls in the proportion of people working in agriculture (in line with urbanization), while labour force participation rates have risen about 10 per cent since 1970 as birth rates began to level off. Both of these trends have enlarged the urban work forces of cities – during a period when the formal urban labour market was barely rising or even shrinking in most developing countries. The result has been an explosion in the informal sector (accompanied by poverty and slums).

- About 37 per cent of the urban work force in the developing world is in the informal sector. In sub-Saharan Africa, it accounts for about 78 per cent of non-agricultural employment and 42 per cent of gross domestic product (GDP). More than 90 per cent of additional jobs in urban areas in the next decade will be created in micro- and small-scale enterprises in the informal sector.

- There are two opposite and controversial positions on the informal sector. Many developing countries have regarded the informal sector, just like squatter housing, as something illegal to be eliminated since it undercuts the formal sector, which is required to comply with labour and safety laws and pay taxes. On the other hand, neo-liberals believe that reducing onerous regulations and dissolving large underproductive enterprises can unlock the creative power of micro-entrepreneurs and provide goods and services at the lowest cost. With assistance from development agencies that have sought to encourage poverty reduction and micro-enterprises, some countries have tried to support and empower the sector as a start-up part of the economy in which innovation can flourish.

- The growth in the urban labour force has imposed enormous strains on urban services, especially employment and housing. As formal urban development has failed to provide the factories, offices, market halls, transport facilities and housing required by the urban work force – and in most of the developing world has failed to provide the formal-sector jobs – the informal sector has taken up the slack. At the same time, the interaction with rural areas has become complex, and many so-called rural workers are dependent on cities for their livelihoods.

- Working conditions are very poor in slum areas, with long hours, unsafe work places and lack of rudimentary protection. Children are routinely employed. Some 8.5 million children are involved in work that is internationally condemned, including bonded labour, prostitution, child trafficking and drugs.

- Worldwide, squatters are about 20 per cent of all households, and about two-thirds are in insecure tenure. In total, around 28 per cent of households live in insecure tenure. Of these, one third are formal renters and half are squatters (equally divided between those who pay rent and those who do not).

- There is a great need for assistance for small-scale enterprises in the construction sector, which probably provide the majority of all new dwellings, so that their methods of supply are as efficient as possible. The poor are currently the largest producers of shelter and builders of cities in the world – and, in many cases, women are taking the lead in devising survival strategies that are, effectively, the governance structures of the developing world when formal structures have failed them. However, one out of every four countries in the developing world has a constitution or national laws that contain impediments to women owning land and taking mortgages in their own names.

- The difference among the levels of services in different cities is due largely to the availability of revenue. Cities in developed countries have (on average) 32 times as much money per person to spend on infrastructure and other urban services as cities in least developed countries. Nevertheless, the level of provision of urban services increased very rapidly during the 1990s across the whole development distribution, but particularly rapidly in cities of medium levels of development. This is a major achievement of the decade.

- Politically, slums can be an important source of votes and other forms of mutual support for local and national governments. In the absence of political mobilization, slums and squatter settlements may be demolished or, at least, neglected. Where residents act together, even evictions may be handled in a manner that includes and involves them

CHAPTER 4

SOCIAL DIMENSIONS[1]

Slums have grown as a seemingly inevitable part of modern urban life. Low-income people find the cheap accommodation helpful in their need to keep housekeeping costs low enough to afford. To do this, they tolerate much less than ideal conditions, no doubt hoping to improve and move to somewhere better. If the cheap accommodation is also well placed for employment, so much the better. Where they are not well placed for work or where formal work is not available or not sought, slum housing often plays host to a lively community of home-based enterprises of all sorts, providing the services and employment opportunities unfulfilled by planned cities.

Though the characteristics of slums may seem a problem to policy-makers, they also represent potential. Because slums exist, low-income households can survive and be ready to work in the city's economy. Slum housing can be used for profit by its owners as a source of rental income or as a location for home-based enterprises. The building and maintenance of low-cost housing and its infrastructure can provide large amounts of employment for semi- and unskilled workers if suitable technologies are used. At the same time, their residents endure much suffering. They have few political powers, seen often only as vote banks at election times, bought for an easy promise of better conditions.

Slums are very diverse and this is dealt with in more detail both here and in Chapter 5. They rarely fit stereotypes, being more marked for their diversity. They tolerate the worst environmental conditions and tend to share exposure to some environmental and human-made hazards related to transportation, industrial pollution, mudslides, garbage, fire and floods.

This chapter draws on material gathered in city case studies of slums around the world, as well as on other relevant research.[2] The case studies provide evidence and illustrations of many of the points made here and elsewhere in this report. The chapter discusses the social aspects of slums. The first section reviews the historical context and evolution of slums. It proposes a view that slums are an expression of urban stratification and explains how their spatial identity has become more distinct and more pronounced in recent centuries. It also examines the socio-economic diversity that characterizes slum populations in cities of the developing countries. The second section discusses, from another angle of social functions, three main attributes of contemporary slums – namely, accommodation of low-cost labour, absorption of migrants and mobilization

of political power. Environmental hazards to which most slum dwellers are exposed, as well as various informal means by which slum inhabitants provide services for both themselves and the wider urban society, are discussed in the third section. The final section focuses on slum contributions to culture and the implications of spatial concentrations of poor households in slums. It also discusses two major social problems that have, for as long as slums have existed, been the most immediate cause of public concern: health and crime.

HISTORICAL CONTEXT AND EVOLUTION OF SOCIAL STRATIFICATION PATTERNS

Cities are complex systems. As societies urbanize, their economies become increasingly differentiated. Their organization increasingly revolves around specialized activities in the production, consumption and trade of goods and services. Urban dwellers process, store and sell foodstuffs, repair equipment, loan money, build roads and structures, collect taxes, care for the sick, cobble shoes, tailor clothes, hold court, worship, run schools and government, enact and enforce laws, and – very significantly – operate markets.[3] These activities crystallize in particular professional and occupational roles. These roles, in turn, are attached to positions that help provide access to the things that people need or wish for in life, such as food, shelter, health care and education.

In varying degrees, these positions form hierarchical structures in which some people have more wealth and power than others. Cities are, therefore, not only complex systems; they are also stratified systems. The privileged stratum in pre-industrial cities included, at the minimum, the upper echelon of the interlocking political, military, religious and educational bureaucracies.[4] Relying on technology and coercion in the form of taxes and tributes, urban elites forced the peasantry to increase its food production and to surrender harvests.[5] They also arrogated to themselves luxury items and other means to set themselves apart and to support lifestyles and arrangements that further reinforced their power.[6] Religious leaders were instrumental in providing moral justification for a social order in which a privileged few dominated the rest of society. Places of worship often also served as schools, and

Cities are complex systems. As societies urbanize, their economies become increasingly differentiated. Their organization increasingly revolves around specialized activities in the production, consumption and trade of goods and services

religious functionaries frequently doubled as educators whose norms governed the academic curricula that sustained and propagated the elites.[7]

Urban stratification has multiple dimensions: economic, political, cultural, social, ethnic and, significantly, spatial. These stratifications find expression in various status markers. For example, people in different strata will often dress differently and they may use different vocabulary or pronunciation. There will also often be differences in what and how much they possess, the type and amount of food they consume, and their living environments. By tradition, status also prescribes certain behaviours and 'manners', including language used in communicating with those of different status, who sits where, who goes first through a door, who gives right of way on the street, and so forth. For example, in Tibetan cities, whenever political leaders mounted their horses, 'pedestrians were to stand aside, with their hats in their hands and their tongues hanging out'.[8]

Segregation by ethnic groups, which, in turn, were associated with specific occupations, occurred widely in pre-industrial cities. Ethnic quarters tended to be self-sufficient, physically and socially separated from the rest of the city. Often they had their own unique social structure, including political leaders and schools.[9] A description of 19th-century Canton lists dozens of streets, each restricted to the shops of artisans or merchants dedicated to making or selling a specific product. In many pre-industrial cities, streets were named after the occupation of the residents – street of the goldsmiths, street of the glass workers, and so on.[10] Rules for the layout of the ideal capital during the Ming and Qing periods in China reveal a clear pattern of strict spatial separation along lines of social class.[11] Similar, tightly regulated segregation between wards, housing different strata, characterized the social composition and spatial structure of Chang'an during the Tang period.[12] This behaviour is still a characteristic of many cities with large traditional quarters.

This localization of particular occupational activities in segregated quarters and streets was (and is) closely linked to a society's technological base. The rudimentary transport and communication media of former days demanded some concentration if markets were to operate. Proximity made it possible for producers, middlemen, retailers and consumers to interact. Sellers of hides would not have been able to do much business if their prospective customers, the leather workers, had their shops scattered randomly across the city. Moreover, the social organization, especially the guild system (itself largely interwoven with technology), encouraged propinquity, which, in turn, fostered community cohesion.[13]

Today's slums reveal the spatial dimension of contemporary urban stratifications. Historically, the spatial structure of many cities did not significantly reflect social and economic stratification. For example, in Pompeii and Herculaneum, there was considerable mixing of different population strata. Households tended to be large and consisted of many, often unrelated, individuals of diverse backgrounds, including patrician owners, as well as their slaves, freedmen and lodgers or tenants.[14] Similarly, research on European urban life in the Middle Ages has shown how apprentices and masters shared the same living quarters, and aristocrats shared their houses with an array of domestic servants.[15] These types of arrangements – with little spatial separation between members of different social classes – also existed in the imperial traditions of dynastic China, although the families of lower-class workers typically resided much farther away.[16] In other words, in earlier times, there existed more cross-cutting lines of occupational differentiation that mitigated the more extreme large-scale patterns of segregation that are now found in many cities.[17]

With the advent of the Industrial Revolution and the advances in transportation technology, this situation changed and it became increasingly possible for the privileged to separate themselves spatially from those in conditions of disadvantage. This trend of growing spatial segregation continues today and is accentuated further by advances in modern information and communication technologies that enable more affluent households to isolate themselves physically from what they see as less desirable parts of the city.[18]

Views on inner-city slums

Today, the vast bulk of areas with inadequate housing and slums is in the developing world; but it is important to remember that during the early years of urbanization and industrialization in the North, urban conditions were at least as bad as those anywhere today and slums were just as widespread.

The early history of slums in the North shows at least as much indifference, misery, exploitation, policy failure and bad governance as anything existing in the poorest country today. In fact, urban conditions were probably more hostile to life, in that urban life expectancies and general health were well below rural equivalents, even as late as the 1950s, whereas the reverse is mostly the case in the developing world today.[19] It is definitely the case that the developed world did less with more during these early years; real incomes were higher at the beginning of the urbanization period than in most developed countries today, conditions were often worse and improvements came much slower. Many mistakes were made in dealing with slums during centuries of indifference and bad policy, and a few good lessons were painstakingly learned. Eventually, affluence and effective interventions eliminated most of the slums in the West; but they can still be remembered by older people.

Although the circumstances and incomes of the highly industrialized countries may seem to be very different from those of the developing world, so that the solutions they have adopted are not affordable or appropriate in the developing world, salutary lessons may be learned from their past and present – both in terms of what can be done and what should not be done.

Urban stratification has multiple dimensions: economic, political, cultural, social, ethnic and spatial

Today's slums reveal the spatial dimension of contemporary urban stratification. This trend has been accentuated by advances in modern information and communication technologies that enable affluent households to isolate themselves from 'less desirable' parts of the city

■ Slums and urbanization

Slum areas were first defined by the 'regimen of congestion' that characterized the new mercantile cities of the 16th century as too many people began competing for too few dwellings and rooms.[20] The rapid influx to the cities of poor migrants looking for jobs created a huge need for accommodation. Much of the new housing for immigrants was developed or redeveloped by speculators seeking profits, and, in the absence of controls, was built to increasingly higher densities and poorer quality. If this new housing was not built quickly enough or was still not affordable, the obvious 'instant' solution for residents was to reduce the costs of housing by sharing the space and the rent with others. Landlords were quick to seize this opportunity, renting their properties out by the room and making a greater profit than they did from the same property rented out as a single unit.[21]

When this happened to more than just a few buildings in a neighbourhood, owner-occupiers, and even some of the other tenants, became concerned that the quality of the neighbourhood was being lowered and moved out. This provided the opportunity for these properties to be bought cheaply and subdivided for renting to new migrants and the expanding urban poor. This, in turn, further hastened the process, driving out the original residents and bringing in many times their number of yet poorer tenants. With increasing demand, the process did not stop there but was extended to subdividing rooms, and even sharing rooms between two or more families. So easy and profitable was the process that landlords took to building makeshift accommodation in the back gardens, specifically to rent out to yet more families.[22]

Needless to say, while the houses were being remodelled and subdivided, services were not extended, and the same facilities were shared by an increasing number of people. Given their financial means, the tenants had little choice but to accept ever-decreasing standards. Not surprisingly, repairs and maintenance, and even the day-to-day care and cleaning of the services and facilities, were non-existent since landlords were interested in extracting the maximum profit.

The downward decline into squalor was inevitable. In such poor conditions, the presence of so many people, inevitably poor and often desperate, helped to break down social order. The poor were easy prey for exploiters, and the crowded tenements became the haunts of thieves and other petty criminals. The link between slums, poverty and social stigmas was firmly established, at least in the popular imagination and common vocabulary.

> The link between slums, poverty and social stigmas was firmly established in the popular imagination and common vocabulary

■ Slums and capitalism

The growth of urban slums is intimately tied to the change from earlier economic systems to capitalism, and most of slums' worst features are intimately associated with conditions of inequality, profit seeking, exploitation and social disruption that occur until the institutions are slowly built that mollify the excesses of the new market system.

A ground-breaking study of the origins of cities observes that the appearance of slum areas was not only due to population pressure from the immigrant proletariat that began thronging the capitals of Europe, but was also due to the depersonalization of both people and space that occurred during these early centuries of capitalism.[23] Whereas most urban workers could earn a reasonable living as artisans or journeymen prior to this time, industrial production required a pool of very low-paid and undifferentiated labour, and income inequality increased rapidly at both ends of the spectrum. The new urban proletariat lived in a state of permanent insecurity, as inhabitants of informal settlements do today:

> *By the 17th century, destitution had been recognized as the normal lot in life for a considerable part of the population. Without the spur of poverty and famine, they could not be expected to work for starvation wages. Misery at the bottom was the foundation for the luxury at the top. As much as a quarter of the urban population in the bigger cities…consisted of casuals and beggars…the capitalist hired workers at will, or dismissed them on his own terms, without bothering as to what happened to either worker or city under such inhuman conditions.*[24]

The other aspect of depersonalization was the development of a formal market structure for land, and the rapid increase in prices and rents that this occasioned under conditions of population pressure. To a fair extent, land and house rents had been determined by traditional practices, and urban layouts had followed aesthetic ideals with a balance of open space and residential areas. Under the market system, both space standards and housing standards fell rapidly, and overcrowding became the norm as competing uses for urban land began to set the price of housing. Collective open spaces or courtyards disappeared as landlords sought maximum rents from people with falling incomes. By 1835, the first multi-family tenement block was erected in New York for the lowest income group, occupying 90 per cent of the block and incorporating standardized airlessness and unsanitary conditions. Within a generation, the premium for urban land was such that similar structures were being provided for the middle and upper classes.[25]

The periodic nature of economic booms and busts that occurred throughout the whole early capitalist period was also a major contributor to the formation of slums – the speculative poor-quality housing that was built during the boom years rapidly became the decaying slums of subsequent busts when very little money was to be had for any sort of urban improvement:

> *London is established upon commercial profit and financial speculation, and the pattern of its housing has followed similar imperatives. It has grown largely from speculative building, advancing in succeeding waves of investment and profit taking while being momentarily stilled in periods of recession.*[26]

Even in the heartlands of unbridled commercial development of the Industrial Revolution, it was still possible for some communities to develop in an orderly fashion. Amsterdam is often regarded as a model commercial city and an outstanding urban achievement. The city became the centre of the world's money markets from the mid 16th century, and quadrupled in size in 70 years. In the face of overcrowding, it instituted a City Building Ordinance that was so successful it was not changed for 300 years. Building inspectors examined building foundations before work could proceed, and sanitary and space requirements were strictly enforced. All urban improvements, including streets and footpaths, had to be paid for by plot holders.[27] The City Plan was constructed around transport corridors, which at that time were canals. Nevertheless, even in Amsterdam, the Jordaan area outside of the city to the south-west, on swampy land, formed a typical congested dumping ground for immigrants and the poorest workers. Jordaan was built as a speculation by merchants to far lower space and amenity standards, ensuring handsome profits for the developers and landlords. It was not until public housing was constructed in the 20th century that a solution to housing low-income earners was found.

■ Slums and reformism

The question arises as to why a notion of slum was developed only from the 1820s and not before, since slums had been around for several hundred years. This appears, partly, to be due to the fact that urban conditions had improved to such an extent by this stage that slums could actually be identified against a general background of better quality housing, which had not been the case in the early phases of the Industrial Revolution. Slums were, therefore, a term of the middle class to show how they had bettered their position.

The slum also appears to be a key part of the spatial expression of the great modernist project that began around that time and has lasted to the present day. The key idea of modernism was that rational and logical behaviour, planning and technology could improve the lot of humanity. The residential expression of modernism was the garden suburb, with its space, light and cleanliness, and the 'slum' was an opposite, everything that modernism was deemed not to be.[28] It is not coincidental that the term 'poverty' also seems to have been coined at this time, the idea being that once a problem has been identified and named, it can be solved.

Both slums and poverty are terms very much in the spirit of Christian reformism and later Western capitalism and a contrast to the modernist ideals of social and physical order, morality, health, spaciousness and urban quality. The commentaries of the 19th century lapse into colourful language such as 'filth, intemperance and depravity', 'debased', 'wretched' and 'vice' whenever slums are mentioned; and it is clear that the intention is to be outraged at the existence of these areas. Somehow, it was commonly believed, these areas of poor housing caused people to be bad or poor, and by eliminating the housing, the problem could be solved. In fact, the problem was the poverty of the inhabitants – coupled with much more intensive land use than had previously been the case.

Slums provided a focus for charity and reform efforts by religious groups, particularly temperance groups.[29] On the negative side, slums were (and still are) used as a populist focus to stigmatize particular social groups, most particularly immigrants and the poor. Once an area was designated a slum, most of the middle-income inhabitants would gradually leave, eventually circumscribing the area as a place of uniformly low incomes and a repository for the negative externalities of the city – illegal, polluting and dangerous activities.

Early reformist attempts to improve the situation generally made conditions rather worse. The poorhouses and hospitals of Dickens's era were almost as dangerous and unhealthy as the street, and the prisons were more so. Almost all early attempts at slum clearance and building of 'model housing' for the indigent displaced the poor and worsened their housing conditions. For example, the first model housing from the 1850s in New York had inside rooms that had no light except from a window opening to an outside room; the model tenement then became a favoured resort of thieves and prostitutes. The Peabody 'model housing' of the late 1800s, which was widely copied by public bodies, had a minimum of light, air and sanitation. The small court between the buildings was entirely paved and children were forbidden to play in it.

Failures of this kind have been endemic throughout the modern period as planners imposed their own ideas on what was an appropriate and affordable environment, without considering the real needs of poor communities. During the 20th century, modernism progressed to the ideas of the Bauhaus industrialized building and tower block residences designed by Le Corbusier, striding across the landscape, self-contained and surrounded by parkland. Ironically, deteriorated public-housing tower blocks now are a considerable blight on the skyline of many cities and are regarded by some as the 'new slums'.

■ Are slums inevitable?

The constant themes of this section arise throughout any discussion of slums: initial pressures due to population gain; increasing poverty and inequality; overcrowding as land prices rise; boom-and-bust construction; eventual marginalization and evacuation; and misguided reform efforts that only make the situation worse. The fact of the matter, as Chapter 7 will show, is that slums have vanished since the 1970s in all but a few developed countries as a result of increasing affluence, although affordable housing is still an issue everywhere.

Slums developed in much the same way not only in the Old World, but in new settlements throughout the New World. The history of inner-slum areas in Sydney is shown in Figure 4.1. An initial 30-year period of rapid expansion and substandard construction was followed by a slow deterioration and exclusion of these areas over 100 years. Once the neglect and depopulation of these areas reached its worst, an impromptu rejuvenation of the inner areas occurred over a fairly short period of about 30 years.

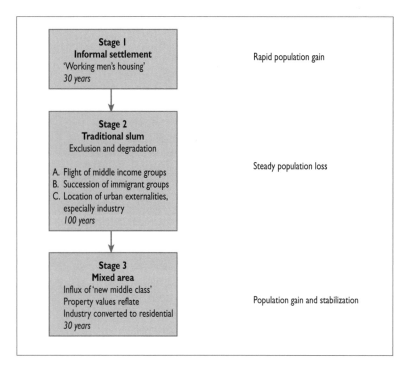

Figure 4.1

Progression of an inner-city slum, Surry Hills, Sydney

In the North, slums were not eliminated without a concerted public response coupled with a social climate that permitted civic engagement

In Sydney, which had fairly minimal planning interventions for much of its history, the overall urban decline and improvement strategy was never formally expressed since it operated largely through the private market, enabled by local officials. The process of decline involved, firstly, marginalizing certain areas so that the inhabitants with more resources would leave for bungalows in the suburbs; secondly, allowing noxious industries to locate there and to gradually replace much of the residential stock; and, finally, as a result of condemnation, clearing much of what remained of the housing a few properties at a time – or, in the mid 20th century, through wholesale block clearance.

It was ironic that during the latter part of the 20th century, what remained of the stock was preserved and gradually improved by gentrifying young professionals. The whole cycle of the informal shanty town of Surry Hills, its demonization as a slum and its recolonization as a mixed area took around 150 years, which is probably too long a time frame for most cities to be comfortable with.

This privately funded regeneration was not, in fact, led by profit seeking but by changing ideas of civic responsibility, coupled with a more responsible attitude to planning and heritage, and an effective private housing finance system that had followed from enabling interventions by government over an extended period. In European countries, the elimination of slums was effected by more blatant state interventions, including strict planning regimes, slum clearance and the widespread construction of public housing.

The moral to be drawn is that, in all examples, slums were not eliminated without a concerted public response, either directly through government enterprise, or through an enabling process that both protected citizens and broadened their access to markets that otherwise were available only to a privileged few, while providing subsidies to the most disadvantaged – coupled with a social climate that permitted civic engagement.

Social diversity of contemporary slums

There exists a common misperception that all slums are alike and that the people who live in slums conform to common stereotypes. In reality, however, there exists a wide range of people among slum residents. As regards tenure, information from the slum case studies reveals a rich diversity among slums and slum dwellers.[30] There are slums whose residents are exlusively or predominantly renters of units held in legal or semi-legal tenure. Units may be subject to rent control. In others, there is a mix of owners and renters. Sometimes land is rented from private owners or public entities. In others, there is illegal occupation of public land or private land. These few examples are but a brief indication of a large number of housing and land tenure categories found in slums worldwide. It is clear that these realities on the ground defy simplistic views of 'the slum'.

Slums and slum dwellers differ in many other ways, as well. Gender composition in the case studies ranges from an even balance of women and men in Ching Nonsee, Bangkok, to women making up less than 30 per cent of Skid Row in Los Angeles. Households headed by women account for 10 per cent of households in Karet Tensin *kampung* (Jakarta), 22 per cent of *favela* households in Sao Paulo, 50 per cent of the pavement community in Prakash Nagar (Mumbai), and 80 per cent of all households in Springfield/Belmont (Newark). Length of residence varies greatly, too. There are slums with a long history, whose residents have lived in the local community for a generation or more. In Barcelona, some slums are several centuries old, while others can be traced back to the mid 19th century. Bangkok's Chong Nonsee is 40 years old; but, at the other end of the spectrum, some of Durban's clandestine settlements emerged only during the late 1980s and early 1990s. There is great variety also within countries, and even within cities.[31] For example, some of Kolkata's slums are 150 years old, while others go back just a decade. Again, there is no simple way of characterizing slums.

The complexity of slums is further illustrated by information on the occupations and income-generating activities of slum dwellers. These span the gamut from university teachers and students (for example, Agbowo, Ibadan) to more marginal activities in slums, including petty crime, drug dealing, prostitution and arms trafficking – with markets and a clientele that extend to the rest of the city and the wider urban region (for example, Barcelona). They include informal jobs in the garment industry; packaging nuts and recycling solid waste (for example, Karachi); domestic servants; piece-rate workers and self-employed hair dressers (for example, Kolkata); furniture makers; and unskilled and semi-skilled carpenters and metal workers (for example, Lusaka); guards; and a variety of home-based enterprises (for example, Mumbai), among many others.

Using more objective criteria may reduce definitional ambiguity, but does not eliminate the diversity of slums. Indeed, this is one of the points stressed in this report. Box 4.1 presents additional evidence of diversity in educational levels and occupations in slums.

Box 4.1 Diversity in education levels and occupation types among residents of slums in Pune, India

The general occupational profiles of urban slum dwellers have not been systematically studied for most cities of the world. There are often fallacies held – by urban residents and policy-makers, alike – that slums are home to domestic servants, rag pickers, sex workers, manual labourers and criminals: people with very low or almost no education, and people with dysfunctional households or no households at all. Such fallacies have given rise to the idea that these settlements are 'urban sores' with almost no positive contribution towards the normal functioning of the city.

A recent survey conducted by a non-governmental organization, Shelter Associates, in partnership with a community-based federation of slum dwellers, Baandhani and the local municipal corporation in Pune (India) tells a different story. The survey conducted across 211 city slums revealed that the occupations vary from class IV government employees, ammunition factory employees, painters, drivers, small entrepreneurs or even office goers.[i] A majority of the women in slums work as housemaids, sweepers, vendors and even government employees. The survey also revealed the presence of a small number of computer professionals, teachers, nurses and doctors in some of the slums.

The average household size was found to be 4.7, with most households having incomes ranging from 2000 rupees (Rs2000) to Rs 6000 per month. For households where both husband and wife work, income ranged between Rs 6000 and Rs 7500. Some of the slums also revealed a healthier female–male ratio than the state average. While the ratio for the state has dipped to 922 females per 1000 males in the latest census, the Kamgar Putala slum, for example, has a ratio of 1004 females to 1000 males.

According to the estimates of the Pune Municipal Corporation, there are 503 slums in the city, out of which 322 have been declared official. Approximately 44% of the city's population live in slums, occupying less than 10% of its land.

The aim of this ongoing census is to compile a comprehensive directory of Pune's slums and slum dwellers, including an interactive spatial and statistical database using geographical information systems (GIS), as well as a book of fact sheets on every slum.

Note: i The survey is part of an ongoing census, a two-phase project which, when completed, will include over 400 slums located throughout the city of Pune. Work is in the final stages for phase 1 of the project, which covers 211 slums.

Source: This box was prepared with the assistance of Anirban Pal, based on information provided by Pratima Joshi, director, Shelter Associates.

These and many other differences are hilighted by the slum case studies. Together, this information makes abundantly clear that slums fall along a broad spectrum. They defy simplistic notions and misleading stereotypes. They have diverse histories, vary in spatial and environmental characteristics, and have widely different populations. Moreover, as is abundantly clear from the case studies, slums are not static; there are ongoing dynamics that, over a period of years, may turn an established urban area into a slum or that may lead to the redevelopment of an existing slum. Recognition of this variety is essential to the success of approaches aiming to improve the lives of slum dwellers.

SOCIAL ATTRIBUTES AND FUNCTIONS OF SLUMS

Urban slums and squatter settlements exist and continue to grow for a variety of reasons – economic, social, political and environmental. From an economic perspective, they are a source of (real or imagined) economic opportunity for a nation's poor, and of low-cost labour supply for the public and private production of goods and services. They are also a source of profit and capital accumulation for both internal and external property owners. Socially, slums provide low-cost housing and low-cost services for rapidly expanding low-income urban populations. They also serve as networks of social support for new migrants to the city. Politically, in democratic and quasi-democratic regimes, slums can be an important source of votes and other forms of mutual support for local and national governments. Alternatively, they can act as an organizational base for opposition to governments. These functions are discussed briefly below.

Accommodation of low-cost labour

Urban slums, in a wider sense of meaning, generate both economic opportunity and risks of exploitation for their residents. Even though a significant portion of rural-to-urban migration may be spurred by war, famine, government policy or natural disaster, the primary motivation of most voluntary in-migration is the hope for a better job and economic security.[32] Low-income housing, typically found in slums, accommodates pools of labour whose low-paid work restricts their living expenditures and, hence, the shelter burden that they can carry. Critics of the capitalist system have observed that slum housing thus enables capital to undervalue labour. At the same time, the demographic transition of the last two decades has generated unprecedented numbers of young workers needing gainful employment. In parts of the world, gender and class inequalities also appear to support rural–urban migration.[33]

Providing a supply of low-cost housing for the poor is an important economic and social function of slums. Workers attracted to urban areas need a place to live that is cheap and accessible to potential jobs. In order to achieve cheapness, households tolerate small spaces and crowding, poor physical conditions, poor access to services (often sharing them with many others), and relatively insecure tenure. A city's transportation infrastructure, especially a subsidized one that serves the slums and squatter settlements, may improve access to jobs for slum residents in either the formal or, more likely, the informal sector. However, as experience in, for example, Mumbai has shown, the improvement of access to jobs must be balanced by attention to other needs of slum residents – especially adequate housing.[34] Transportation and housing costs are often a trade-off. Better access to income-generating

Slums are not static; there are ongoing dynamics that, over a period of years, may turn an established urban area into a slum or that may lead to the redevelopment of an existing slum

Urban slums exist and continue to grow for a variety of reasons – economic, social, political and environmental

The demographic transition of the last two decades has generated unprecedented numbers of young workers needing gainful employment

activities typically means having to live in worse housing or even on pavements, by rail tracks or under bridges. By definition, slum housing is inadequate – with respect to some or all of the following:

- Location (on pavements, tracks, steep slopes, distant from jobs).
- Shelter from the elements (weather and natural or man-made hazards).
- Provision of urban services (especially water and sanitation).
- Security of tenure.
- Cost.

For a given type of work, education increases the potential wages to be received in the formal sector over the informal one. Conversely, employment opportunities in the informal labour market are enhanced when the wage gap between the formal and informal sectors grows.[35] Thus, to the extent that new migrants to the city (as well as current slum residents) have limited education, skills or economic resources, they provide an important source of supply for the (unregulated) informal job market at very low or below-subsistence wage rates.[36] When a large portion of an urban population resides in slums and squatter settlements (for example, in Mumbai, Mexico City or Dhaka), the hiring prospects for small industrial and service firms are enhanced because labour costs are kept low by severe job competition among a plentiful labour supply in the informal sector. The trade-off is that an expanding informal labour market increases wage instability, job turnover, the exploitation of women and children in low-wage jobs, and the income disparity between socio-economic groups. Currently, dominant globalization and the associated 'informalization' of the economy that is seen in many places is not only widening the chasm between rich and poor, but also generates 'a large growth in the demand for low-wage workers and for jobs that offer few advancement possibilities'.[37] Increasingly, the informalization of low-wage jobs becomes the burden of women and new immigrants.

The construction industry is particularly good at absorbing unskilled labour, thereby creating jobs for the lowest income sector in the economy.[38] In countries where labour is abundant, increased construction activity would be one sure way of increasing employment. The productive potential of the right kind of housing construction produces multiplier effects that yield further gains through backward and forward linkages. The benefits for development tend to be inversely proportional to cost. The highest accrue from housing built by the informal sector in areas uncontrolled by building and planning authorities. Low-income housing developments in the formal sector tend to be in the middle range of benefit for development, and high-income housing is the least favourable.[39]

The informal sector is particularly efficient in providing housing because its construction is simpler than in the formal sector and consumes less labour per unit cost. However, the lower unit cost means that investment of a given amount in informal housing tends to generate about one in five more jobs than in formal housing, besides contributing six times as many (lower-standard) dwelling units.[40] Labour supply and informal economy issues are discussed in more detail and from an economic perspective in Chapter 6.

Network for migrant absorption

Numerous studies in both developed and developing countries have documented the potential significance of slums as incubators for upward social and economic mobility.[41] However, the question of whether slums are networks of social and economic mobility or 'poverty traps' remains unresolved. The social capital of slums may serve two different functions: help for 'getting by' (social support) and help for 'getting ahead' (social leverage). Both may be, but are not necessarily, active in the same location.[42]

Globalization may facilitate social and economic mobility by expanding job opportunities and widening the opportunity networks of low-income urban residents. However, globalization and information technology can also help to create 'black holes of misery and despair' and 'truly fundamental social cleavages of the information age' that divide those with access to information and power from those without.[43] Whatever the case, the linkages of changing structures of low-cost labour markets to economic mobility are increasingly important.[44]

Upward mobility does not necessarily mean that people will move out of slums. *In situ* physical transformation in slum communities is, in many cases, evidence of socio-economic upgrading.[45] In this regard, support networks appear to be strongly conditioned by spatial proximity and cultural background.[46]

Mobilization of political power

One of the reasons that slums exist as places of poverty and inadequate services is the absence of political power among their residents.[47] The interaction between slums and local politics is shown by the success of *in situ* upgrading projects, thanks to the generation of significant political support and effective negotiating through community-based networks and partnerships.[48,49] In the absence of political mobilization, slums may be demolished or, at least, neglected in a perpetuation of the status quo.[50,51] Where residents can be mobilized, even the eviction may be handled in a manner that includes and involves them. Box 4.2 illustrates this.

On the other hand, regularization of land tenure in squatter settlements may provide a basis for social and political integration, or control and co-optation of the urban poor.[52] Slum upgrading and relocation programmes may be subverted to serve the narrow political interests of local and national governments. There is a long history of this, including support for the founding of societies for urban workers' housing during the 1850s in France, not so much for the benefit of the workers and their families, but to render the working class 'inaccessible to the seductions of

Providing a supply of low-cost housing for the poor is an important economic and social function of slums. Workers attracted to urban areas need a place to live that is cheap and accessible to potential jobs

In the absence of political mobilization, slums may be demolished or, at least, neglected in a perpetuation of the status quo. Where residents can be mobilized, even the eviction may be handled in a manner that includes and involves them

politics' and as a means of peacefully disarming resistance.[53] Rural–urban migration patterns can also have political underpinnings and may be exploited to support the inequities of pre-existing patronage networks.[54] An important point is that the internal and external political functions of slums do not exist in a vacuum, but interact with their other functions – economic, social and environmental.

Environmental externalities

Research provides many examples of the environmental risks and damage associated with slums and squatter settlements in both developed and developing countries.[55] The hazards identified in the case studies prepared for this report fall into the following categories:

- *Transportation.* Many communities are located on government land devoted to local transportation infrastructure – railroad or highway rights of way, airport runways or harbours. The physical danger from passing vehicles is particularly acute for children. All local governments in these examples are trying to remove these squatter settlements, but with only limited success.[56]
- *Industrial pollution.* Industrial pollution is a problem frequently encountered by the residents of adjacent slums. The most extreme example of these risks is the Bhopal community of Atal Ayub Nagar, where – in addition to the more than 8000 residents who died from the December 1984 release of lethal methyl isocyanate gas – people continue to die of complications or suffer from persistent health problems.[57]
- *Earth movements.* Many slums are located on land not deemed appropriate for permanent habitation because of its steep terrain or geological characteristics that make it prone to subsidence, landslides or mudslides.
- *Garbage dumps.* Slums are frequently 'receivers' of a city's negative externalities. Accumulations of solid waste in a city's rubbish dump represent one such negative externality. Such land has little or no economic value and, therefore, remains open to 'temporary' occupancy by immigrant families with nowhere else to go. Such settlements pose enormous risks to their residents from disease, from contaminated air, water and soil, and from collapse of the dump itself. One of the more extreme examples is provided by Payatas in Manila where the collapse of the rubbish dump killed 218 people in July 2000.[58]
- *Fires.* Massive fires are an all too frequent occurrence in many slum and squatter settlements because of the lack of publicly provided fire-fighting systems; the extreme proximity and high density of shelters; the narrow alleys impeding access by fire fighters; poorly wired electrical systems or the use of kerosene stoves and lamps; the lack of water sources to douse the flames; and the combustibility of construction

materials. The absence of municipal development controls to ensure acceptable levels of fire safety further amplifies fire risk. Many slums have experienced such disasters or continue to face serious risks in this regard. Descriptions of recent fire disasters in slums and squatter settlements make clear that arson may be used as a weapon, either by public or private interests to remove these communities in preparation for commercial development.[59]

- *Floods.* Floods are the most frequent of all natural disasters. Between 1947 and 1981, there were 343 flood disasters in which an estimated 200,000 people died.[60] Between 1900 and 1980, 339 million people were affected and 36 million people lost their homes.[61] Slums and squatter settlements are frequently constructed in low-lying areas subject to periodic flooding. The *tugurios* of the Paraguay River floodplain in Asunción, where 55,000 poor people live and are driven from their homes almost every other year, provide a typical example of the effect of such hazards on slums.

Slum dwellers are receivers of the city's negative externalities. Negative externalities are the costs of an action that accrue to people other than those directly responsible for the action. Because of their lack of resources and political clout, the residents of slums often have no choice but to occupy places otherwise unfit for habitation – for example, the rubbish dumps in Manila, the Philippines;[62] flood-prone lands in Dhaka City, Bangladesh[63] or Mumbai;[64] the polluted shorefronts of Asuncion, Paraguay; or the steep hillside *favelas* of Rio de Janeiro, Brazil.[65] In some cases, the social and economic costs sustained by slum residents as the

---

Box 4.2 Civil society organizes against forced evictions as Metro Manila

When local government didn't respond to protests over large-scale forced evictions in Manila, Philippines, an association of poor people's organizations, known as DAMPA, called on the Japanese government to investigate the violations of the rights of people displaced by a Japanese-funded public project. The project included a highway flyover, an aqueduct, a railway extension and an airport expansion. (The Philippines and Japan are both signatories to international treaties that prohibit funding of projects that violate the rights of displaced residents.)

In March 1996, a Japanese fact-finding team, including church, academic and non-governmental organization (NGO) representatives, made a much-publicized visit to Manila. They found that: people were evicted without prior consultation or notice; in relocation sites, people were left without basic services, water, electricity, schools and hospitals; people lost jobs in the relocation process; people were taken to relocation sites without the choice of where to go, resulting in community disorganization; and implementing agencies reneged on promises of compensation and support services.

The mission's findings were publicized in all of the local newspapers, along with its recommendations to the Japanese government: affected people, especially the poor, must be included in planning relocation programmes, and some of the project budgets should be allocated for relocation of displaced residents. The Japanese government subsequently decided to cancel funding for projects involving involuntary resettlement, and to investigate complaints of affected residents and rights violations.

Source: Asian Coalition for Housing Rights (1997) 'Creatively fighting transport-related forced eviction in Metro Manila', cited in *Habitat Debate* (2001) 7(3): 10.

result of these externalities are shared with the larger society through extensions of urban infrastructure (transportation systems, water and sewer improvements, etc) or through health programmes to reduce disease and other environmental health problems. However, in most cases they are not shared and the costs fall directly on the shoulders of the poor.

The irony of these negative externalities is threefold. Firstly, they derive from the short-term successes of urban job and wealth creation, which, in turn, attract new (poor) migrants to the city, thereby increasing the number of people exposed to environmental hazards. Secondly, a city's economic success, perhaps enhanced through globalization, frequently has the unintended side effect of driving up land rents and other living costs, making it less feasible for the urban poor to occupy decent, safe and sanitary housing in habitable neighbourhoods.

Finally, research suggests that if the full costs of negative environmental externalities associated with slums are taken into account, the costs of slum upgrading programmes in the informal housing sector will be the same as, or lower than, the cost of construction of new public housing for the same number of households.[66]

Service provision

In the absence of adequate formal provision of services within slums, there exist myriad examples of informal provision, ranging from illegal 'rented' electrical connections to squatter homes on the shorefront of Asunción, to unauthorized *jitney* bus services in Bogotá, to clandestine water taps, community wells and open sewers in Mexico City and Nairobi.[67]

When slums result from squatter invasions or illegal land subdivisions, they are usually informally laid out and rarely leave land for non-residential uses. However, slum residents are adept at producing the services and commercial activities that the formal sector fails to provide. Where there are no shops, residents sell convenience items from small shops set up in their homes. This is especially important when the absence of power in an area means that many households cannot refrigerate food to keep it fresh and wholesome. For example, in a peripheral area of Pretoria, South Africa, 'spaza shops' selling groceries, snacks, soft drinks and cigarettes are very common. Home-based small shops can offer high levels of service, throughout many hours of the day, selling quantities suitable for people with little cash, often on short-term credit.[68]

Home-based enterprises run by residents also provide personal services. Hairdressers and dressmakers are particularly common; but there are also agents for obtaining official documents and many other services that operate informally in low-income neighbourhoods, with little encouragement from city authorities. Because they do not have to pay high rents for formally designated commercial plots, such shops and services can operate profitably from very small beginnings, with very little working capital and almost no overhead. Thus, they need smaller client bases than a formal establishment and have fewer locational constraints.

While these services are vital for the livelihoods of the local residents, they often have a wider reach. People from all over the city use specialist shops and services operated by slum dwellers. Embroiderers in India, political memorabilia dealers in Indonesia, football repairers in Bolivia and motor mechanics in South Africa are some examples of services that attract city-wide and regional clienteles.

Access to informal, low-cost services, frequently provided by non-governmental organizations (NGOs), constitutes a relatively important social function of slums. It is relative because, as pointed out in a study of medical services in New Delhi slums, the services provided by informal practitioners may be inadequate or, ultimately, harmful to the intended beneficiaries.[69] In such situations, grass-roots NGOs play a critical intermediary role.[70] With appropriate technical assistance and financial support, they have demonstrated their ability to compensate for the budgetary constraints of local governments and the poverty of slum dwellers. Education is similarly critical for productivity, income generation and upward socio-economic mobility.[71] The value of education for improving life chances and empowerment – particularly among women – is widely recognized.[72] However, in many places, schools now require user fees, imposed as a result of structural adjustment policies, which have placed the education of children out of many parents' reach. In other cases, for example in Mumbai and New Delhi, the occurrence of slum children not attending school may have less to do with their families' economic circumstances than with the school system's shortcomings.[73] There is a severe scarcity of public schools that are accessible and affordable to the children living in slums and squatter settlements, and NGO educational programmes cannot make up for their absence.

SLUMS WITHIN URBAN SOCIETY

The role of slum areas in shaping the image of a city is important to its future. On the negative side, where the city appears to make few attempts to improve overall quality of life, this will be reflected in its image. Most cities at least pay lip service to poverty reduction and officials are mostly genuine in their efforts to improve their cities and their society. The debate on the extent to which place actually affects individual circumstances, rather than the reverse, remains unresolved; but this section examines the evidence.

The existence of slums, inequality and a poor or polluted urban environment is seen as a prime deterrent to international competitiveness and to the location choices of international firms and high-profile events such as the Olympic Games.[74]

The true problem to be tackled, however, is not the visibility of the poor but the condition of poor people. Poverty is the context within which slums are necessary and in the absence of which they might be replaced by better housing conditions. Lack of income lowers life chances directly and in a number of indirect, subtle ways. Poor health and lack of education are major impediments to individuals improving their circumstances and moving out of poverty.

In the absence of adequate formal provision of services within slums, there exist myriad examples of informal provision, ranging from illegal 'rented' electrical connections in Asunción's squatter homes, to unauthorized jitney bus services in Bogotá

Poverty is the context within which slums are necessary and in the absence of which they might be replaced by better housing

Lack of self-esteem or lack of contacts leads to lack of aspirations and limited employment choice. Many are still trapped in inner-city slums full of poor health, crime, drug abuse and misery.

Contribution to cultural developments

As described above, many so-called slums are not the social wastelands of the popular imagination at all, but provide livelihoods, social networks and a tolerable standard of living for the residents. The embedded sense of community participation, complex political mosaic and networks of support can be destroyed by clumsy slum clearance operations.

Although it is difficult for residents to have a sense of pride in their community when they are so marginalized, political action groups and manifestations of a 'class for itself' can develop in certain circumstances.[75,76] This has been a fear of elite groups since the Middle Ages; but it is quite exaggerated – the evidence is that poor people are less involved in their communities and more apathetic than affluent groups.[77] While riots and other manifestations of frustration and anger often arise, these are not often directed productively except in the presence of a cohesive force assisting to empower communities.

Some of the negative attributes of slums or the 'negative externalities' that they impose on others are social dysfunctions that may occur owing to:

- *Marginalization and dumping of the underclass, particularly in the North.* If poor people, the permanently unemployed or handicapped, and criminals are forced to live together through the repressive mechanisms of the state, the receiving neighbourhoods develop serious problems that spill over.
- *The mixing of disparate populations.* These populations come together through in-migration. They may well be foes; they may have a history of exploitation or fear, such as whites and blacks; or they may be groups that understand very little about each other's culture.
- *Family disruption.* The loss of one partner often not only substantially reduces the income of the family, so that it has to live in the cheapest housing, but it also makes the fulfillment of the care-giving and value-transmission role of the remaining parent very much harder, when livelihood must be their main concern. In addition, the trauma may sometimes disturb children and make them more vulnerable or attracted to socially undesirable behaviour.

It is hard to overestimate the contribution that slum dwellers have made to cultural life during the 20th century. Contributions have included some of the main musical and dance movements of the 20th century: jazz, blues, rock and roll, reggae, funk and hiphop music in the US; the ballads of Edith Piaf in France; breakdance in New York; *fado* in Portugal, *flamenco* in Spain and *rebetika* in Athens; township music and *soukuss* in Africa; and various Latin American dance crazes in Brazil and Argentina. Songs from many musical genres and countries have been located in slum settings: in rock, Bob Dylan's twisted urban landscapes in *Desolation Row* or *Visions of Johanna*; Bruce Springsteen's *Born to Run;* or Tracy Chapman's *Fast Car*; in folk music, Ewan McColl's *Dirty Old Town* or Dorothy Hewett's *Weevils in the Flour*; in mainstream pop, Elvis Presley's *In the Ghetto*, the Supremes' *Love Child* or musicals such as *West Side Story* and *Saturday Night Fever* have described aspects of or depicted scenes from slum life. The cityscapes of L S Lowry and the modern expression through graffiti are two ends of a continuum of art arising from slum life.

The literature of slum areas has ranged from deep social critiques of misery and crushed hopes, such as Tennessee Williams's *A Street Car Named Desire*; Zola in France; *Angela's Ashes* in Dublin; Charles Dickens and George Orwell in England; Saul Bellow, John dos Passos, James Baldwin and other black urban writers in the US, as well as Selby's grim *Last Exit to Brooklyn*; Maria de Jesus's *Beyond all Pity* or Meja Mwangi's novels of slum life and despair in Nairobi; to affirmations of the strength and moral character of people in adverse circumstances, such as Gershwin's *Porgy and Bess*. In the 1950s, a 'realist' romantic school sought to portray slum life as somehow more real, earthy, vibrant and productive (if always fragile and threatened by poverty) than emasculated and regimented middle-class life.[78] Internally, slums have developed their own communications: composite languages, creoles and local argots have originated from slums because of the needs of different groups thrown together to communicate or trade, or because exclusion has encouraged the development of local 'hip talk'.

Co-location and social aspects of poverty

It is generally presumed that the concentration of low-income people in particular locations is immensely detrimental to their well-being. However, this has been hotly debated as there are also certain advantages in service delivery, social cohesion and empowerment when low-income people have a critical mass in particular areas, rather than being scattered anonymously throughout the community.

In earlier years, many internationally driven housing and slum reform projects that simply concentrated on engineering and construction solutions failed because they were not sustainable or appropriate in developing country environments. They failed to consult with and involve the people for whom they were intended. They did not work with their organizations and meet their cultural requirements. In addition, they failed to take sufficient account of good governance issues and political will, without which little can be achieved and nothing sustained once the foreign experts have gone home. Social cohesion is critical for societies to prosper economically and for development to be sustainable.[79] Incorporating the poor within the design and implementation of development projects not only helps to produce more appropriate projects, but also ensures that

Social cohesion is critical for societies to prosper economically and for development to be sustainable

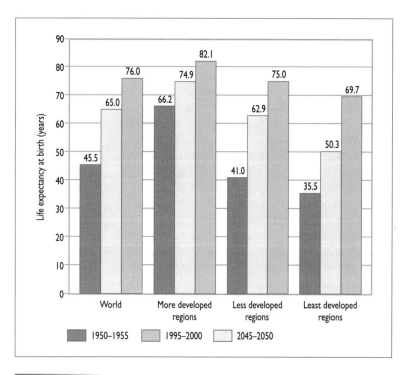

Figure 4.2

Life expectancy at birth for the world and development groups, 1950 to 2050

Source: United Nations Population Division (2001), World Populations Prospects 2000, Figure II.1

Figure 4.3

Urban child mortality by City Development Index (CDI) quintile, 1993 and 1998

they are better targeted to reach those with the greatest needs.[80] Including the poor from the outset helps to build confidence in, and loyalty to, improvement projects, as it was shown in work on participatory development in Sri Lanka and confirmed in many other projects.

There has been a substantial literature that has established that depressed slum environments are detrimental to health, life chances and social behaviour.[81] The US has affirmative action programmes specifically seeking to disperse slum dwellers to better neighbourhoods, and a number of studies have investigated whether this is socially beneficial. The conclusion is that households that move to better locations are substantially better off on a range of subjective and objective outcome measures, although this is not universal.[82,83,84]

The co-location of poor people is not, however, without its advantages. On the one hand, social melting pots and adversity can result in robust cultural expressions of all kinds. From the point of view of basic economics, it is

cheaper to provide targeted social services to poor people if they are concentrated – and, in fact, this can be a major attractive factor for certain locations. In addition, political and social action becomes possible where concentrations of poor people exists, which would not occur if they were dispersed and isolated throughout the community; spatial concentration thus provides the means for the poor to organize. Most NGO and community-based organization (CBO) groups that form such an important part of the political landscape of the developing world have their roots or support in poor communities, and are facilitated in their action against exploitation or social ills by having clear spatial constituencies.

Ultimately, most of the poor conditions in slums in developing countries are about differential access to power and resources, and this is expected to worsen under present strategies of fiscal decentralization and privatization.[85] Slum communities cannot of themselves raise the money to improve their localities. They also cannot easily mobilize politically to divert social resources from elsewhere to improve their neighbourhoods.

Health issues

Health is possibly the great success story of the 20th century, and a great deal has been written about aspects of urban health. Enormous strides have been made in health areas during the last half of the 20th century, with life expectancies increasing by up to 40 per cent in the least developed countries (LDCs), from much lower bases in 1900 – and infant mortality also declined by 60 per cent worldwide during the same period.[86,87] Higher death rates from infectious diseases in developing countries are partly matched by diseases of affluence in the developed world; for adults, there is now little difference in death rates in different parts of the world. The United Nations Development Programme (UNDP) has recorded consistent improvements in health and education at national levels throughout the 1990s – which shows what can be achieved when a consensus exists as to what should be done and when it is done.

There is absolutely no room for complacency, however. Child mortality remains a major problem, since 5.8 per cent of children in the developing world's cities die before reaching the age of five years, and more than 20 per cent in the LDCs overall, compared with 0.6 per cent in the higher income countries (HICs). The situation is improving, with the greatest improvements in the second quintile of cities, as Figure 4.3 shows; but there is still a long way to go.

Health indicators are more dependent on levels of development than on regional differences. In the lowest quintile of cities, almost 15 per cent of children die before reaching their fifth birthday, which is 16 times the death rate of those in the top quintile.

Table 4.1 shows that, in fact, death rates are about the same in the developed and developing countries. However, the causes of death are very different and people are dying much younger in the developing world. Life in the developing world is still a far more fragile and risky business. Mortality rates from infectious diseases are 15 times as high

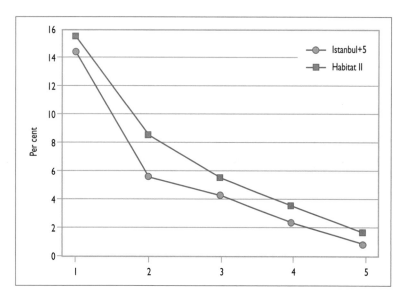

Table 4.1

Mortality rates, world, 1998

	Developed		Developing	
	Number (000)	Rate per 100,000	Number (000)	Rate per 100,000
TOTAL DEATHS	8033	885	45,897	922
Infectious and parasitic diseases	**122**	**13.4**	**9680**	**194.5**
Respiratory infections	309	34.0	3198	64.3
HIV/AIDS	32	3.5	2253	45.3
Diarrhoeal diseases	7	0.8	2212	44.4
Childhood diseases	10	1.1	1640	33.0
Tuberculosis	18	2.0	1480	29.7
Malaria	0	0.0	1110	22.3
Other diseases	55	6.0	1002	20.1
Maternal conditions	2	0.2	491	9.9
Peri-natal conditions	53	5.8	2102	42.2
Nutritional deficiencies	23	2.5	467	9.4
II. Non-communicable conditions	**7024**	**773.7**	**24,693**	**496.2**
Malignant neoplasms	2020	222.5	5209	104.7
Cardiovascular diseases	3592	395.7	13,098	263.2
Respiratory diseases	391	43.1	2604	52.3
Digestive diseases	322	35.5	1461	29.4
Diseases of the genitourinary system	139	15.3	626	12.6
Neuropsychiatric disorders	225	24.8	495	9.9
Diabetes mellitus	161	17.7	439	8.8
Congenital abnormalities	36	4.0	478	9.6
Other conditions	98	10.8	213	4.3
III. Injuries	**498**	**54.9**	**5266**	**105.8**
Unintentional	**327**	**36.0**	**3166**	**63.6**
Road traffic accidents	142	15.6	1029	20.7
Other accidents and injuries	185	20.4	2137	42.9
Intentional	**172**	**18.9**	**2100**	**42.2**
Self-inflicted	130	14.3	818	16.4
Violence	38	4.2	698	14.0
War	4	0.4	584	11.7

Source: WHO, 2000.

in the developing world, and comprise around one sixth of world deaths. Death rates from childhood diseases (such as diphtheria and polio) are 33 times as high; tuberculosis kills 1.5 million annually and is on the rise, and malaria now only occurs in the developing world. In the developing world, maternal deaths are many times higher and peri-natal deaths are nine times as common. Death rates from injuries are more than double in the developing world, and death by violence, including war, is six times as likely. Most of these deaths are preventable, were there less dangerous living conditions and appropriate systems of health care.

The AIDS pandemic continues unabated, with infection rates increasing in many new countries that were not previously exposed. Life expectancy reduced from 60 to 51 in Botswana during 1990 to 1997, and will further reduce by 6 to 11 years in the next decade in Kenya, Uganda, Zambia and Zimbabwe. In some areas of South Africa, 50 per cent of adults are estimated to be HIV positive; as a result, South Africa is the only African country expected to lose its population in the coming years. Global deaths were around 2.9 million in 2000, and rising rapidly, putting AIDS well ahead of diarrhoeal diseases as the greatest infectious killer. The people who die are usually of prime working age, leaving behind families who may themselves be affected. AIDS is estimated to take 1 per cent from GDP each year in the countries in which it occurs.

Poor housing conditions can be deadly for those suffering from a disease which destroys the victim's immune system. In addition to countries most affected by AIDS, life expectancy has stagnated or is declining in countries from one other region – the transitional countries.[88] The severe economic shocks that these countries have sustained have lowered human development across the board, not least through the demise of the formerly good medical services enjoyed in socialist countries. This is largely an urban problem because the cities have suffered disproportionately in the transition period, particularly the cities of Central Asia.

For a very long time, the threat of the outbreak of contagion from densely populated and vermin-infested slum locations has been a major incentive encouraging powerful groups to act forcibly in eliminating slums. The 'urban penalty' that caused death rates to be higher in cities than in the countryside, due to polluted water and crowding, has been reduced in many places; nevertheless, the threat of urban pandemics remains real. Most recently, the advent of globalization, de-industrialization and other neo-liberal policies, including structural adjustment programmes (SAPs) in Africa, are believed to have contributed to the increasing spread of various diseases, including AIDS and drug-resistant tuberculosis. Results of extensive studies indicate that the planned hollowing out of poor inner-city areas, coupled with increased mobility, have encouraged the rapid spread of emerging infections, which are a serious security threat in the US.[89]

Poor health, along with loss of wage employment, is the major shock dimension of urban poverty, while chronic

Region	Under the age of five mortality		Life expectancy	
	Urban	National	Urban	National
Africa	14.6	15.2	52.7	47.1
Asia and the Pacific	4.4	6.9	67.4	57.2
Latin America and the Caribbean	3.6	4.0	70.9	57.9

Source: UN-Habitat, 2002f; United Nations Population Division, 2000.

Table 4.2

Health indicators: under the age of five mortality and life expectancy, 1998

ill health is a major determinant of chronic poverty. Urban workers, reliant on wage labour, are particularly dependent on ongoing good health.[90] The inability of a principal wage earner to continue working, accompanied by the subsequent debt to meet medical costs, is enough to throw lower-income families into poverty for extended periods.

The principal outcome measures of health are life expectancy and infant or child mortality.[91] Table 4.2 shows that, on this basis, urban areas have better health on average than rural areas. However, while urban mortality rates are now below rural rates, on average, this is not true for the poor in the slums, or for smaller cities. Slums in Bangladesh, for instance, have child mortality rates much higher than in rural areas. Some small cities in Brazil, a middle-income country that contains areas indistinguishable from the HICs on all social measures, have mortality rates more typical of LDCs. Stunting rates for children in urban areas with low socio-economic scores are similar to rural averages in many less developed countries.[92]

In fact, poor people virtually everywhere have much worse health statistics than the rich. The illness or death of an urban breadwinner can be devastating to a poor family, and can lead them into deep poverty. Measures of human capability poverty include health as a prime component because, without good health, the chances of leaving behind poverty and the slums are negligible.

Urban health expenditure figures can also be quite misleading as they tend to be very poorly targeted in the developing world. The money is mostly spent on expensive health services and health clinics for the rich, who can be enjoying a higher-level income and lifestyle. In practically every country, disproportionately more health services are demanded and received by better-off people. The lower use of health services by poor people – due mainly to lack of financial resources, but also to lack of awareness and to perceptions that 'doctors are for rich people' – exacerbate poorer health to begin with, caused by poor diet and poor living environments. People from the slums may not even be entitled to attend public health clinics, since they may not have a registered address.

■ Slums and disease

Ill health in poor communities is normally associated with poor sanitation, lack of waste disposal facilities, the presence of vermin, and poor indoor air quality due to poor ventilation and the use of cheap fuels that emit particulate matter. Accidents, particularly involving children, are also far more common in households with open fires or accessible boiling water, and the results of these can be horrific when no medical care is available.

Even in the developed world, however, there is a long literature linking poor housing with ill health.[93] Health

Ill health in poor communities is associated with poor sanitation, lack of waste disposal facilities, the presence of vermin, and poor indoor air quality

concerns lay at the heart of the very first interventions in housing: the Public Health Acts in Britain during the late 19th century. The interventions in slum areas by the authorities were often less motivated by generosity or reformism than by the self-interest of the powerful. In the absence of modern transport networks, cities were much more condensed, and slum areas were contiguous with more expensive areas. The rich could not fully insulate themselves from exposure to areas that they considered undesirable, nor could they avoid interactions with the people living there. Lower health and sanitation standards meant that the rich were also exposed to the effluent from the poor. Diseases including cholera, small pox, tuberculosis, typhoid fever and other contagious diseases affected not only the people living in the slums, but were a threat to the health of more affluent people, as well.

In the UK, during the mid 1830s, over 21,000 people died of a cholera epidemic. The government finally acted in 1842, when Edwin Chadwick published his report on the country's public health. In 1848, after cholera had struck again, the Public Health Act was launched, with recommendations that water supplies and sewage facilities in towns and cities be improved. A second Public Health Act in 1875 compelled local authorities to provide sewage disposal facilities and clean water to all.[94] By 1900, the death rate had fallen dramatically and most towns had effective, hygienic sewers and water systems.

The poor and the rich thus shared a common fate. This intertwining prompted local government to regulate and intervene in the activities of landlords and speculative builders who were turning the centres of industrializing cities into insanitary slums.[95] For example, the City of London Sewer Act of 1851 prohibited cellar dwellings and the keeping of live cattle in courts; permitted condemnation and destruction of unwholesome property; and established inspection of common lodging houses for low-income households.[96] In the UK, therefore, during the period 1830 to 1860, the state was steadily taking more responsibility for wider control of private-sector enterprise in the interest of society as a whole. To enforce the legislation of control, a new division of government was being built up – the executive arm – imposing limits on the *laissez-faire* movement.[97]

In much the same vein, in 19th-century France, public health objectives for reform received attention only when connected to the larger social issues and economic transformations of the time, leading the Paris Commission on Unhealthful Dwellings to produce a report that criticized the absence of guidelines for new building and set forth specifications for residential construction.[98] As late as 1947, similar considerations underpinned legislation in the US that declared:

> *...such slum and blighted areas contribute to the development and cause an increase in, and spread of, disease, crime, infant mortality and juvenile delinquency, and constitute a menace to the health, safety, morals and welfare of the residents of the State.*[99]

A number of studies have connected overcrowded housing conditions in childhood with respiratory problems and infections not just at the time, but in later life. Using a long-term longitudinal sample, a recent study has shown that multiple housing deprivation can lead to a 25 per cent greater risk of disability or severe ill health across the life course, with the risk increasing if the exposure to poor housing was in childhood.[100]

As a result, wealthy individuals influenced policy (for better and for worse) in acknowledgment of the fact that they, themselves, would benefit from the availability of safe water and adequate sanitation for the poor. In 1902, Jacob Riis put it this way:

> *Justice to the individual is accepted in theory as the only safe groundwork of the common-wealth. When it is practised in dealing with the slum, there will shortly be no slum.*[101]

However, slum clearance and urban renewal, which were tacitly assumed to eliminate health hazards, have not proven completely successful.[102]

Crime issues[103]

Slum neighbourhoods experience various socio-economic hardships. They are a concentration of social and economic deprivations, high population density, high numbers of broken families, high unemployment, and economic, physical and social exclusion. These characteristics have been recognized as causes of crime and violence and therefore have the potential of a violent time bomb if found in combination in dense urban areas.

A great deal of research has been done on the incidence of urban crime and identification of its characteristics and causes. Of particular interest to an understanding of the relationship between slums and crime has been the idea of community risk factors.

■ Community risk factors

At the neighbourhood level, the causes of insecurity can be assessed through a classification of community risk factors, such as community composition, social structure, oppositional culture, legitimate opportunities, and social and physical disorder.

Community composition refers to the kinds of people who live in a community. The literature on this topic indicates that characteristics such as unemployment, broken families and school drop-out rates have been associated with higher rates of violent crime.[104] What is unclear in the literature is whether having more of these people simply produces a higher total of individual-level risk factors, or whether there is a 'tipping' effect associated with the concentrations of such people. Substantial findings on the effects of proportions of social groups have shown that the behaviour of entire communities changes when a proportion of one type of person goes beyond the tipping point.

Public policies contributing to the concentration of high-risk people in certain neighbourhoods could help tip the proportions of many communities towards a majority of persons or families at higher risk of crime. As long as those high-risk families or persons are in a minority, their low-risk neighbours are able to exercise a community protective factor against violent crime. When the high-risk families become a majority in any urban community, a spiral of crime and the fear of crime may lead to further loss of middle-class residents and jobs. This, in turn, increases the concentration of unemployed and poor people, followed by further increases in crime.

Independently of the kinds of people who live in a community, the way in which they interact may affect the risk of violent crime. Children of single parents, for example, may not be at greater risk of crime because of their family structure. But a community with a high percentage of single parent households may put all of its children at greater risk of delinquency by reducing the capacity of a community to maintain adult networks of informal control of children. The greater difficulty of single parent families in supervising young males is multiplied by the association of young males with other unsupervised young males, since delinquency is well known to be a group phenomenon. The empirical evidence for this risk factor is particularly strong, with violent victimization rates up to three times higher among neighbourhoods of high family disruption compared to low levels, regardless of other characteristics such as poverty.

Observers of high crime neighbourhoods have long identified the pattern of 'oppositional culture' arising from a lack of participation in mainstream economic and social life. Given the apparent rejection of community members by the larger society, the community members reject the values and aspirations of that society by developing an 'oppositional identity'.[105] This is especially notable in terms of values that oppose the protective factors of marriage and family, education, work and obedience to the law. As unemployment and segregation increases, the strength of the opposition increases. Efforts to gain 'respect' in oppositional cultures may then rely more upon violence than upon other factors.

Communities with very high rates of youth violence are places in which there are high concentrations of criminogenic commodities. Both alcohol use and drug use are highly correlated with violent crime, with drug use, especially, being linked to an oppositional culture.

Recent work on the 'broken windows' theory of community crime-causation claims that in communities where both people and buildings appear disorderly, the visual message that the community is out of control may attract more serious crime. This may happen by a spiral of increasing fear of crime among conventional people, who use the area less and thus provide less informal control. Communities who deteriorate in this respect over time are observed to suffer increased rates of violence.

All of these risk factors and more are recognized within the broader debates about welfare, social and economic exclusion and family life. These debates often ignore the extreme concentrations of these risk factors. The neighbourhoods that suffer high unemployment rates are also likely to suffer from weak social structure, high rates of alcohol abuse, drug abuse, frustrations and violent youth crime.

Slum areas in cities are a concentration of social and economic deprivations, high population density, high numbers of broken families, high unemployment, and economic, physical and social exclusion

The primary consequence is the development of a generalized, and not often objective, feeling of insecurity that is common in many urban populations. This perception crystallizes all of the fears of the population (such as insecurity with respect to employment, health, the future of children, domestic violence and the risk of impoverishment). It arises from an impression of abandonment, powerlessness and the incomprehension in the face of shocking crime, and the multiplication of minor acts of delinquency or vandalism. Because of its emotional character, this perception blows facts out of proportion, encourages rumour and can even cause social conflicts. The feeling of generalized fear can create a climate that may threaten the democratic foundation of a community or society, tearing apart the social fabric of the city.

■ Findings of recent research on crime

Some of the conclusions from recent research are:

- The prevalence of both property crime and violent crimes is related to problems of economic hardship among the young. Violence against women is also related to economic hardship, but is also inversely related to the social status of women.[106]
- While the above sentiments are widely held and appear to be correct, they are surprisingly difficult to support from comparative evidence. Total recorded crime at the international level is almost a proxy for the level of development. In the more developed countries, total convictions are typically 80 to 130 per 1000, whereas in developing countries the figure is more typically lower.[107] This is largely because:
  - the more developed countries are much more regulated, so that there are many more types of offences or fines that are strictly enforced;
  - the recording mechanisms are much more thorough;[108]
  - there are some crimes in developed countries that are committed a good deal more often, and which relate to the affluence and the much higher returns possible; these include drug crimes and burglary; and
  - the population has more confidence in the police force and is much more certain that something will be done if they report crimes; essentially, crime is reported when people believe that the police will do something about it.
- Crime rates vary substantially by region, even among countries with similar incomes.[109] For example, Asian countries (West Asian, in particular) show low crime levels, whereas Africa has quite high levels. Murder levels tend to be fairly constant in most places in the world, with lower figures in the HICs, and much higher figures in Latin America and a few other places such as South Africa and Jamaica where guns, social disruption or drugs are commonplace.

- National studies provide better evidence for a relationship between hardship and crime. There has been a spectacular fall in crime rates in the US since the end of the recessionary period in 1993, reversing a very long upward trend.[110] Demographics will affect crime levels, particularly the presence of large numbers of teenage boys in areas of social breakdown, and the fall in crime is also partly due to the ageing population.[111]
- There appears to be a higher incidence of theft when rich and poor are pushed closely together – when it becomes very obvious to the poor exactly how much they are denied.[112] Areas with tourists also attract thieves because tourists are easy targets as they are unfamiliar with local conditions and also are likely to carry valuables. These locations are not the traditional slum areas.
- Much violent crime stems from the weapons trade. Civil wars and insurrections distribute large numbers of guns that then lie in the hands of demobilized militias or are sold to bandits. Training in the use of guns, and willingness to use them, is also a feature of such places.[113] Countries that have higher firearm ownership rates also have higher firearm-related death rates, including homicide and suicide rates, although there are a few exceptions.
- Poor people suffer more from violence and petty theft, where this is common, than rich people. In these circumstances, violence and security issues can be regarded by poor people as more important than housing or income issues.[114]
- Strong social control systems can result in low crime rates in slums (for example, in Ghana and Indonesia).[115]

The most important mediating factor in this story may be the motivations of community residents. For example, the isolation of high poverty neighbourhoods from the legitimate job market may be critical in accounting for the lack of motivation among youth in these neighbourhoods. This also highlights that youth have difficulty in finding employment when they live in impoverished neighbourhoods without well-developed job connections.[116] The perceived returns to continuing in school or in acquiring human capital in other ways are low. This leads to low high-school graduation rates and high attrition in training programmes, maintaining the underinvestment in human capital of the previous generation in high poverty neighbourhoods.

Crime is commonly associated with the poorer, more seedy parts of cities and it has been their reputation as 'breeding grounds for crime' that has prompted slum clearance programmes. In particular, it is commonly alleged that an anti-establishment, or oppositional, culture prevails in slum areas, which is broadly supportive of all kinds of illegal activities. There is a lack of visible law and order; roaming teenage gangs, muggers, drug dealers, prostitutes and the indigent are evident, and marginal activities take place with impunity. However, this is by no means universal.

For example, slums in West Africa and the Middle East are unlikely to appear this way.

As the Sydney case study shows, these rumours are often (but not always) greatly exaggerated and depend more upon the biases of the media than upon statistics. Where they are true, it is once again a case of social exclusion deliberately pushing these activities into particular areas, where it is presumed that poor people 'will not care as much'. Obviously, those conducting low-level illegal activities such as drug dealing, prostitution and robbery would prefer to locate where the best clientele are likely to be – in the downtown or more affluent areas – but they are pushed into the excluded areas, where they will not bother 'decent citizens'. This puts the children of slum dwellers at considerable risk, as the visibility of these activities makes them commonplace, and access to these 'earning opportunities' is made much easier for the young and gullible. In some slum areas in some cities, the police are exceptionally visible and may harass residents, or are directly involved in supporting the activities as long as they do not stray from the designated zones.

Whatever the reality, the fear of crime has changed the nature of cities with a high level of violence, separating social groups, changing the open, interactive nature of the community, and enforcing segregation through gated communities and walled enclaves.[117]

Whatever the reality, the fear of crime has changed the nature of cities with a high level of violence, separating social groups, changing the open, interactive nature of the community, and enforcing segregation through gated communities and walled enclaves

NOTES

1   This chapter draws primarily on the drafts prepared by Willem van Vliet–, University of Colorado, US, and Joe Flood, Urban Resources, Australia, while the names of many others who contributed to this chapter's finalization are given in the Acknowledgements.

2   Evidence from the case studies are presented in many parts of the report; however, Part IV highlights major findings and contains a summary of the city case studies.

3   Urban markets are made possible by the workings of a cash economy that emphasizes people's ability to pay and that predisposes towards the commodification of housing and land. Market institutions are an essential defining characteristic in Max Weber's 1921 (1958) classic treaty on the city. See also Sjoberg, 1960, especially p111. For further references see Pirenne (1956), who calls attention to the role of defence in the establishment of medieval cities, and De Coulanges (1873), who stresses the role of religious aspects in the founding of ancient cities. However, many low-income groups do not take part in the commodification of housing for social or cultural reasons and, so, are increasingly excluded from any benefits that may accrue.

4   See Sjoberg, 1960, p118.

5   Sjoberg, 1960, p118. See also Rich and Wallace-Hadrill, 1991.

6   Rich and Wallace-Hadrill, 1991).

7   Rich and Wallace-Hadrill, 1991. See also Pirenne, 1956.

8   Shen and Liu, 1953, cited by Sjoberg, 1960, p126.

9   Sjoberg, 1960, p100; Breton, 1964.

10 The structural nature of urban stratification is implicit in De Coulanges's conceptualization of the ancient city as 'a confederation of groups, rather than an assemblage of individuals' (1873, p169).

11 Research by Ho Je Yu cited by Sit, 1995, Chapter 3.

12 See Kiang, 1999.

13 See Sjoberg, 1960, p101.

14 See Wallace-Hadrill, 1994, especially Chapter 5; Packer, 1971, especially Chapter 4.

15 Research on households in 15th-century Tuscany, Italy, and Coventry, UK, reported in Wallace-Hadrill (1994).

16 See Sit, 1995. The very name of the 'Forbidden City' reflects this exclusivity of household residence.

17 Segregation does not occur just along lines of income. As an example, in most US cities, upwards of 50 per cent of households would have to move in order to bring about a racially balanced population; see UNCHS (Habitat), 2001a, p36.

18 The quintessential form is that of gated communities, found in growing numbers in most countries around the world; see UNCHS (Habitat), 2001a, Chapter 2, especially p37.

19 Improved sanitation, medicine and attention to air and water quality have since redressed the health problems resulting from congestion. See Mumford, 1961, p467.

20 Mumford, 1961, p432.

21 Ackroyd (2000, p139) describes a cascading series of rental arrangements in which eight people who owned most of the housing in the London slum quarter of St Giles let it by the street, after which it was sublet by house and then by room.

22 Hence the term 'back slums'.

23 Mumford, 1961.

24 Mumford, 1961, p432.

25 Mumford, 1961, p433.

26 Ackroyd, 2000, p139.

27 Mumford (1961, p444) regards this example of responsible public direction as a 'happy bequest from the old mediaeval economy', which regarded corporate maintenance of standards as more important than profits, confirming that unbridled capitalism can only provide satisfactory housing for those on the 'inside', and that commercial success was ultimately equivalent to civic destitution. This Fabian interpretation is currently unfashionable, but deserves to be kept in mind by those seeking reduced government influence in urban planning.

28 The Sydney contribution describes how families in the early years of the 20th century were actively encouraged to desert the central areas, where high-density tenement living encouraged 'wantonness and idleness'.

29 At that time, the level of alcohol abuse was very high, due largely to the wide availability of cheap gin, and a high proportion of criminal charges were for insobriety.

30 Part IV highlights major findings and contains a summary of city case studies prepared for this report.

31 See Jargowsky, 1996.

32 See Brueckner and Zenou, 1999; Epstein and Jezeph, 2001; Meier, 2000.

33 See Srinivasan, 1997.

34 See O'Hare et al, 1998.

35 See Gong and van Soest, 2002.

36 See Cuervo and Hin, 1998.

37 See UNCHS (Habitat), 2001a, p72.

38 See Moavenzadeh, 1987.

39 See UNCHS (Habitat)/International Labour Organization (ILO), 1995.

40 See Sethuraman, 1985; UNCHS (Habitat)/ILO, 1995.

41 See Gans, 1962; Liebow, 1967; Suttles, 1972; Varela-Michel, 1997.

42 See Briggs, 1998, p178.

43 Castells, 1996, p346.

44 See Gong and van Soest, 2002.

45 McElroy, 1999; Tipple, 2000.

46 Erdogan et al, 1996.

47 See Amis and Kumar, 2000; Auyero, 1999.

48 Pikholz, 1997.

49 Appadurai, 2001.

50 See Goetz, 2000; Agbola and Jinadu, 1997.

51 See Goddard, 2001.

52 See Varley, 1998. Note also the experience of Singapore, where the government eradicated low-income neighbourhoods and relocated households on a large scale with the effect of dispersing spatial concentrations of ethnic groups that could otherwise have been powerful political forces opposed to government policies.

53 Shapiro, 1985. For more contemporary references, see Elmhirst, 1999; Pugh, 2000.

54 See Roy, 1999.

55 See DeSouza, 1997; El-Raey et al, 2000; Ferguson, 1996; Heywood et al, 1997; Sanderson, 2000.

56 Patel et al, 2002.

57 See Dinham and Sarangi, 2002.

58 See van Vliet–, 2002.

59 For example, see the reports of squatter settlements worldwide on www.innercitypress.org/icglobal.html. This is an excellent source of current information on these and related issues.

60 Blong, 1992.

61 Department of Humanitarian Affairs, 1993.

62 See van Vliet–, 2002.

63 See Rashid, 2000.

64 Patel et al, 2002.

65 See O'Hare, 2001.

66 See Ferguson, 1996.

67 See Zamberia, 1999.

68 The examples cited here are from the Centre for Architectural Research and Development Overseas (CARDO) research.

69 See De Zoysa et al, 1998.

70 See Madon and Sahay, 2002; Otiso, 2000.

71 See Swaminathan, 1997.

72 See Thapan, 1997.

73 See Banerji, 2000, p795.

74 This can have a serious negative effect. In Venice Beach, Los Angeles, some 200 homeless people, mostly schizophrenics, who live under structures or in makeshift shelters next to million dollar condominiums, are collected and forced to 'move on' in the dead of night for the annual Muscle Beach bodybuilding competition. Some 9500 homeless people in Atlanta were wrongfully arrested during the 1996 Olympics. Homeless people in downtown Sydney were given a fare and told to get out of town for the duration of the 2000 Olympics. These kinds of undesirable cosmetic actions – and Olympic bids, more generally – are strongly opposed by 'Bread not Circuses' activist coalitions (www.vcn.bc.ca/ioc/pdfs/).

75 It is common for young people from slums to disguise their addresses at work or with friends.

76 Marx's concept is of a social class that moves beyond socio-economic delineation to a politically active force, once a critical mass is achieved, in a situation where class interests are clearly articulated.

77 The ultimate expression was the French Revolution, which – while it had its constituency in the slums – was actually kick-started by the disenfranchised *bourgeoisie*.

78 For example, in Australia, plays and novels such as Ray Lawler's *Summer of the Seventeenth Doll*, Ruth Park's *Harp of the South* and Dorothy Hewett's *Bobbin Up* and *This Old Man Comes Rolling Home* were of this genre.

79 See www.worldbank.org/poverty/scapital/whatsc.htm.

80 Narayan, 1995.

81 See Brooks-Gunn et al, 1993, 1997; Wilson, 1987; Elliott et al, 1996; Coulton and Pandey, 1992; Cutler and Glaeser, 1997; Massey and Eggers, 1990; Massey and Denton, 1993; Tienda, 1991.

82 See Kaufman and Rosenbaum, 1992, for educational performance; Burby and Rohe, 1989, for crime and fear of crime; Lord and Rent, 1989, for public services and improved employment opportunities. Galster and Zobel, 1999, disputes that this is sufficient to justify the programmes.

83 The two main involuntary US programmes are the federal Hope VI programme, and the Moving to Opportunity, which requires poor households to use Section 8 vouchers in more affluent areas.

84 Goetz, 2002.

85 In fact, Amis (2002) suggests that the chronically poor are precisely those who are outside the system of governance and patronage. Getting on a local patronage network is one of the most sensible survival strategies for poor urban households.

86 Life expectancies increased from 40 to 64 years in the developing world from 1950 to 1995; WRI (1999).

87 United Nations Population Division, 2000.

88 Life expectancy for men fell from 63.8 to 57.7 in Russia during 1990 to 1994. Such a large change is unprecedented in peacetime, and appears to be owing to a combination of economic and social instability, high rates of tobacco and alcohol consumption, poor nutrition, depression, and deterioration of the health care system. See Notzon et al, 1998.

89 Wallace et al, 1999.

90 Ruel et al (1999) report that incomes decrease among outdoor occupations such as rickshaw drivers and construction workers during the rainy season in Dhaka, and this is partly due to ill health.

91 Other measures such as maternal mortality, malnourishment, and morbidity and mortality rates are also in common usage.

92 Haddad et al, 1999.

93 For literature review, see Lowry, 1991; Ineichin, 1993; Arblaster and Hawtin, 1993.

94 See 'Medicine through time: The industrial revolution and public health', www.bbc.co.uk/education/medicine/nonint/menus/inphmenu.shtml (accessed 27 May 2002).

95 It is significant that government intervention occurred first at the *local* level rather than the *national* level. For example, the Borough Police Act that Manchester Corporation promoted in 1844 imposed standards of housing and sanitation (including the prohibition of back-to-back housing), which it took more than a generation to enforce at the national level. See Deane, 1965, p219.

96 See Deane, 1965, p219.

97 See Deane, 1965, Chapter 13.

98 See Shapiro, 1985.

99 See Blighted Areas Redevelopment Act of 1947 (315 ILCS 5/), Section 2(b). Available at www.legis.state.il.us/ilcs/ch315/ch315act5.htm.

100 The survey is the National Child Development Study in the UK, which has collected data six times since 1958 on a cohort of about 17,000 individuals. See Marsh et al, 2000.

101 See Riis, 1902, 'Introduction: What the Fight is About'.

102 Easterlow et al, 2000.

103 This section draws on the paper ' Criminalisation of the social fabric', prepared for this report by Cecilia Andersson, Laura Petrella and Sabine Ravestijn, Safer Cities Programme of UN-Habitat.

104 Sherman et al, 1998.

105 Sherman et al, 1998.

106 UNODCCP, 1999, Chapter 1.

107 Seventh United Nations 'Survey on Crime Trends and the Operation of Criminal Justice Systems', June 2002, www.odccp.org/pdf/crime/seventh_survey/. The survey warns: 'to use the figures as a basis of comparison between countries is highly problematic'.

108 This is another example of the 'service-statistics paradox'.

109 The regional table of crime incidence from Global Urban Indicator Database 2 is reproduced in UNCHS (2001c).

110 It should, however, be noted that homicide rates are still about six times higher than they were in 1960 and all other crime rates are much higher: www.disastercenter.com/crime/userinc.htm.

111 Hirschfield and Bowers (1997), in a study of census tracts in UK cities, found that poor neighbourhoods that lacked social cohesion (on two different measures) had significantly higher crime levels. The two orthogonal measures of lack of cohesion were:

1   tracts with a high proportion of single parents and complaints about juveniles;

2   tracts with high mobility and ethnic and social mix.

These actually correspond to the two main kinds of disadvantaged areas identified in Sydney.

112 The site www.korpios.org/resurgent/L-gunownership.htm states 'absolute poverty levels do not correlate too significantly with the crime rate; income inequality does'.

113 UNODCCP, 1999.

114 Amis and Rakodi (1995) found that slum dwellers overwhelmingly identified this to be the 'main problem' in urban Kenya.

115 Tipple and Korboe (1998) report that in Kumasi, Ghana, this is vulnerable to outside pressures. Evidence from Surabaya, Indonesia, suggests that crime is so rare that home-based shops leave stock unattended with impunity.

116 Sherman et al, 1998.

117 Caldeira (1996a) writes: 'the talk of crime is the principal discourse in Sao Paulo everyday life'. The perception that the institutions of order, particularly the police, are also violent has magnified the fear and led to the growth of private guard systems.

5

TERRITORIALITY AND SPATIAL FORMS[1]

Spatial forms and the physical location of slums vary from region to region, from city to city and even within the same city. The working definitions of slums, suggested in Chapter 1, as non-complying with building regulations and standards, having inadequate basic services provision and insecure tenure status, leave a great deal of room for variation, from marginally inadequate in one feature to being a place of multiple insanitary and deprived conditions.[2]

Though the term slum includes the traditional meaning of housing areas that were once respectable or even desirable, but which have since deteriorated, it has come to include the vast informal settlements that are quickly becoming the most visual expression of urban poverty. Indeed, the majority of dwellings in most of the world's developing cities are in slums. Informal settlements come in many forms; but virtually all are either squatter settlements or illegal settlements and so it is important to distinguish between these even though they have an overwhelming range of similarities. The twofold tenure problem of squatters – that is, that they have neither the owner's permission nor the permission of the local authorities (while illegal settlements have the owner's permission) – tends to render life there more tenuous and to discourage investment.

Many important historic cities are in danger of terminal obsolescence. Fine traditional environments such as Old Cairo, Shahjahanabad (Old Delhi), the *medinahs* and *casbahs* of the Arab world, and the walled cities in Rajasthan, are just a few examples of important historic areas that now demonstrate the characteristics of slums. They are particularly sensitive areas as they may attract fervent loyalty from many citizens, provide accommodation for rich, traditionally powerful families or their retainers, harbour important traditional craft enterprises, and surround important religious and cultural edifices.

At the same time, many peripheral neighbourhoods, even in the same cities, are being constructed with the characteristics of slums from day one, or soon after. Some of these are government- or employer-built estates of low-cost housing, providing minimal accommodation for formal-sector workers. These often quickly deteriorate through lack of maintenance and unplanned levels of occupancy. Some are even built to standards of servicing that render them inadequate – for example, the Bastuhara housing at Mirpur, Dhaka, Bangladesh, where no toilets or water taps were fitted when the tiny dwellings were built in the 1970s.[3] Others are informally built, peripheral settlements that ring many developing cities. Some of the most spectacular can be seen in Rio de Janeiro, Caracas and La Paz, beginning in the lower slopes at the edge of the formal city and climbing to dizzying heights, often using the roof slab of a lower dwelling as their site. There is astonishing dynamism displayed in the founding and improvement of these settlements, and the lessons learned from them should not be ignored. At their earliest stage, they may be extremely poorly built and unserviced; but through the years they can develop into sturdy, well-serviced neighbourhoods. The transition from one to the other is not, however, automatic; encouragement and *de facto* security are important.

It is important to note that owners of dwellings in many slums are attached to them in a way that formal-sector house buyers may not be. If one has constructed a dwelling on empty land and seen a neighbourhood develop and improve, there is bound to be a tie to the dwelling that is strong. In central city areas, many dwellings are steeped in family history and are precious, although they are of little value. In addition, some households are so poor that even a ramshackle shack is more than they can bear to lose.

Many of the slums are very tiny, perched on a traffic island, on a small piece of back land in the business district, next to the railway goods depot. The issues they face may have less to do with servicing, as they can often free-ride on other people's water supply and sanitation. Instead, they have greater issues of security and recognition, and concerns about who will defend them against threats of eviction. At the same time, they may be holding up important development, or creating dangers for themselves and others. The task of solving the dilemma they present for city authorities is, therefore, beset with problems.

Were all of these slums simply illegal, then the tenure issue and their security would be much clearer. However, they possess many grades of security, leaving a much more complex context of intervention for the authorities and a more difficult future of improvement or decline to predict. This dynamic trajectory of the neighbourhood, whether it is in decline or progressing, was memorably expressed many years ago as the dichotomy of slums of despair or slums of hope.[4] The division by potential has, thus, been influential in policy. A neighbourhood in an old city centre area, which, seeing better days, has now been converted from palatial single-household dwellings into ever-cheaper rooming houses and small apartments with shared services, requires a different set of interventions to improve residents' livelihoods from those needed for a newly settled shack neighbourhood. Similarly, a relatively new government-built

The dynamic trajectory of the neighbourhood, whether it is in decline or progressing, was memorably expressed as the dichotomy of slums of despair or slums of hope

estate, in which the combination of poor maintenance and multiple social deprivation leads to rapid physical decline, is very different from an area where poor quality buildings have been erected on semi-legal subdivisions.

This chapter attempts to set out the range of neighbourhoods that fall under the classification of 'slums' and presents the context in which the later discussion can be understood. The criteria used encompass such diverse characteristics as origin and age; location; size; legality and vulnerability; and development dynamic, so there will inevitably be some overlap. However, this is a way of demonstrating the diversity of slums and the need for a multitude of approaches in order to improve the livelihoods of residents.

SLUM FORMATION PROCESSES AND SPATIAL TYPES

Despite a great range of varieties mentioned above, slums fall into two broad categories: declining areas and progressing settlements – each of which can, for the purposes of expanded analysis, be broken into:

- *Declining areas*:
    - 'old' city centre slums; and
    - 'new' slum estates.
- *Progressing settlements*:
    - squatter settlements; and
    - semi-legal subdivisions.

The process of the physical deterioration of central city housing stock can be reversed through processes of gentrification

In different ways, all four subcategories sustain the livelihoods of the urban poor and, at the same time, exacerbate their poverty in the ways described above. However, as described in the discussion of the Chicago Model of urban change and development, their impacts on the shape of cities and the strategic approaches to improving them differ significantly.[5] Not all central area slums and deteriorated housing estates are slums of despair, declining into worse and worse conditions. There is a cycle by which

slums are demolished and redeveloped for commercial use or renovated into upper-income housing. By the same token, not all self-built squatter settlements and other informally constructed housing are on the road to becoming integrated into the regular housing stock of the city, providing adequate space, amenity and services to their inhabitants and revenue to the city.

Inner-city slums

Inner-city slums gave birth to the concept of the slum: the process whereby central, prosperous residential areas of cities undergo deterioration as their original owners move out to newer, more salubrious and more fashionable residential areas. This is a commonplace and predictable consequence of the growth and expansion of cities, manifest by both an increase in the central commercial and manufacturing areas and activities, and the influx of migrants looking for employment opportunities. Initially, the housing vacated by the better-off is still structurally sound and serviceable, and provides an ideal housing opportunity for those willing to make do with less space and shared amenities. The location of buildings provides residents with good access to employment opportunities. Since the buildings were originally built for middle- and high-income groups, they are usually reasonably well serviced with urban infrastructure, though, over time, as dwellings are increasingly subdivided and the level of overcrowding grows, strain on those services can reach breaking point.

In general, occupants pay rent and often that rent is at relatively low levels, which in some cities is controlled by legislation, typically at levels below the economic cost of adequately maintaining the building and its services. This policy of rent freezing is widely recognized as contributing to the deterioration of tenement housing, making it uneconomical for owners to invest in the upkeep of their properties.[6] For example, the 1947 Bombay Rent Control Act was introduced to freeze rents at the 1940 level and to establish rights of tenants against evictions.[7] This meant that the construction of housing for workers became unprofitable for landlords, and also discouraged investment by owners in the repair and maintenance of existing buildings. Thus, these provisions had a negative impact on private investments in rental housing, and adversely affected property tax collection. The act was revised in 1986; later, in 1993, it became applicable only to new properties. Rent control was not exclusively applied to the city centre areas, however. In Beirut, slums generally have witnessed the development of large-scale rental markets, and renting has become, since 1982, the primary method of accessing housing and a main source of income for old property owners in slums.[8]

This process of the physical deterioration of central city housing stock can be reversed through processes of gentrification, as has been frequently seen in ex-slum neighbourhoods in Northern cities, where (usually young) professionals, themselves marginalized by the rising cost of 'acceptable' housing, are willing to move into a traditional slum, attracted by the architecture and cheap housing prices

---

Box 5.1 Barcelona inner-city slums

The district known as the Ciutat Vella, or old city, in Barcelona was the entire city until the mid 19th-century expansion. The old city had developed very high housing densities and had associated problems of lack of light, air and open space. As the city expanded, the more well-off population moved out. Slum conditions developed in various areas, and continue to the present day in several neighbourhoods, such as the Barri Gòtic, Santa Caterina and the Barceloneta. The highest concentration is found in the neighbourhood known as the Raval, and most specifically the Raval Sud, or Southern Raval. This area was traditionally known as the Barri Xino, or 'Chinatown', and, partly because of its proximity to the port, has been characterized by marginal activities and the highest levels of poverty in the city. It has also traditionally served as the gateway for new immigrants to the city, providing cheap lodging in very poor conditions, in the form of boarding houses, dormitories and subdivided apartments. The buildings in this area vary in age – some are several centuries old – and the existence of slum lodgings in the area can be traced back at least to the mid 19th century.

Source: Barcelona case study, 2002.

and, perhaps, encouraged by official renovation programmes. Gentrification can lead to a rapid shift in population, with poor tenants being pushed out to make way for wealthier occupants and new commercial and service developments – for example, in Morocco's development of medina areas in response to tourism and a conservation agenda.[9] However, gentrification in the cities of developing countries has been limited, and traditional slum housing remains very much the domain of the poor.

The Chicago Model of concentric rings of city growth that sees the development of central area slums is only common to the older, larger cities of Europe and the Arab States, the Americas and Asia. In most modern African cities that were developed as part of a colonial process, the houses of the rich were large sprawling bungalows, set in extensive grounds, usually kept at a distance from the 'old' or 'native' city. Rarely have these lost their value or attraction for those who can afford them.

Even where the process of the transformation of once desirable, centrally located residences has taken place in developing countries, it represents a relatively low proportion of a city's slums. The main reason for this is the high rate and scale of in-migration over the last 50 years. The stock of central area was unable to accommodate more than a very small fraction of the migrants, even when such dwellings are subdivided to house 10 or 20 families. Bogotá is one such example where the central areas represent a small proportion of the city area and population, compared with the growth of squatter settlements and illegal subdivisions elsewhere in the city.[10] The strategic location of such central areas, coupled with the visibility of physical and social degradation, have, however, drawn political attention to the area and prompted intervention in recent years.

Secondly, though it took almost 100 years, most of the cities of Europe and America were able to overcome the worst of the poverty and, therefore, were able to eradicate the slums through industrialization, colonization and, eventually, prosperity. More importantly, the rate and scale of in-migration and population growth was much lower than in developing countries, allowing the worst excesses of city centre degradation to be controlled.

The relatively slow pace of economic development in most countries of the South has also meant that the central slums of developing countries have yet to undergo the next phase of redevelopment: the replacement of slums by newer, taller buildings, often for commercial purposes. The major exception are the capitals of the 'tiger economies' of Southeast Asia, such as Jakarta in Indonesia, that went through a rapid rebuilding and renovation boom during the 1980s and early 1990s.[11]

Slum estates

This category differs from the traditional city centre slum in that the structures are relatively new and generally not in private ownership. Examples include both public housing estates and housing built by industry or to house industrial workers, such as the hostels for mine workers in Southern

---

Box 5.2 Bogotá inner-city slums

The inner-city slums of Mártires and Santa Fe are deteriorated zones in the centre of the city of Bogotá. As the city developed, some of the zones of the traditional downtown area were abandoned and progressively became occupied for low-income economic activity and housing. The buildings are tenement houses that were occupied in the mid 20th century by several families with independent rooms but collective kitchen, laundry and sanitary facilities. During the 1960s, the central tenement houses increasingly became lodgings for immigrants to the city, who took such accommodation for the first few years, then moved to unplanned settlements. The overuse of such houses has led to physical deterioration. Furthermore, while tenement housing still serves as temporary lodging, this is decreasing as families who live in less central areas increasingly provide rented rooms to supplement their household income.
Source: Bogotá case study, 2002.

Box 5.3 Hostels in South Africa

In South Africa, the 'hostel' accommodation provides one of the more extreme examples of housing-turned-slum. Hostels were built as predominantly single-sex accommodation to house and control (usually) male workers who were employed by institutions such as the railways, municipality or large industrial employers. The inadequacy of the buildings arises through gross overcrowding and a high intensity of use, which, combined with a lack of maintenance, has led to rapid deterioration. However, the tensions between rival political factions, particularly fuelled under the apartheid regime, have also led to notorious violence, intimidation and power struggles. Political and criminal control over the allocation of accommodation has led to a breakdown in formal systems of revenue collection and little formal reinvestment.
Source: Durban case study, 2002.

Africa and 'chawls' in India.[12] Both have experienced social problems arising from overcrowded and pressured conditions, making residents vulnerable to organized crime and political exploitation.

Ironically, in many cities, much of the public housing built between the 1950s and 1970s to re-house the residents of central city slums and squatter settlements, typically in four- to five-storey tenement blocks with minimal, if any, community amenities, has itself now joined the stock of slums. During the early 1990s in India, the Tamil Nadu Housing Board had a major programme to upgrade

---

Box 5.4 Chawls in Mumbai, India

In Mumbai, 'chawls' were rental tenements constructed by factory owners and landowners for low-income workers between 1920 and 1956. Later, the port authorities and a few other public-sector units began renting out similar tenements to their workers. Accommodation was designed as one room in a tenement with shared cooking and sanitary facilities, provided to house mostly single men for nominal rents. With the consolidation of male migrants in the city, their families joined them. Consequently, densities of these single-room tenements increased phenomenally and structures began to deteriorate rapidly. Rent control laws led to a halt in the supply of such accommodation; the same laws led to a lack of appropriate maintenance and worsened the degradation; and, in many cases, residential tenements were put to commercial/industrial use, resulting in excessive loading and damage to the structure. Environmental conditions of salinity and humidity also caused damp and corrosion in the structures. With such decay and dilapidation, conditions in chawls became very precarious, some collapsing during the monsoon every year.
Source: Mumbai case study, 2002.

Box 5.5 The 'recent public city' of Naples

The two zones in Naples of Ponticelli, in the east, and Scampia, in the north, can be termed the 'recent public city', together housing over 100,000 people. Entirely made up of public housing, they were planned during the 1960s and finished after the 1980 earthquake. Both are currently subject to renewal projects aimed at transforming them from dormitory quarters into normal city neighbourhoods. These quarters share a bad reputation. The decision to relocate large numbers of residents, already suffering from degrees of poverty, in a single area deprived of the social capital that they possessed in their original neighbourhoods encouraged marginalization and exploitation. Organized crime thrives in both quarters and opposes socio-economic development as a threat to its power over the population. The 'Sails', huge 20-storey housing blocks, were soon considered uninhabitable and two have already been demolished; the shared spaces are abandoned. The two quarters, and especially Scampia, are poorly linked to the rest of the city, and the distance from the centre presents a major problem for access to work, particularly for women.

Source: Naples case study, 2002.

tenements built by the Tamil Nadu Slum Clearance Board in Chennai less than 20 years earlier. Many apartment blocks built by the Tema (New Town) Development Corporation in Ghana during the early 1970s are in a precarious structural condition. Housing and living conditions in public housing estates have been further worsened through the lack of appropriate dweller control or involvement in the day-to-day management and maintenance of either individual dwelling units or the housing estates as a whole, including their public infrastructure. Often, this has also been accompanied by the omission, closure or breakdown of common amenities and facilities, usually due to shortages of resources to address the extent of need. Another common reason for the deterioration of relatively new public housing estates has been their peripheral location on the edges of cities where land was available, but access to work, markets, kin and social amenities was not. The relative isolation of such estates meant that the cost of transport was often unaffordable to the low-income inhabitants. As a result, they became abandoned by all but the most destitute and desperate.

Slum estates also embrace tied workers' housing that was built by employers, usually state industries, for the use of their work force during the period of their employment. These estates suffered even more than public housing estates from a lack of any form of occupant involvement in their management and maintenance, leading to their rapid deterioration. For example, in Chengdu, China, now that industry is no longer responsible for the provision of housing, units have been abandoned and left to private residents who, facing unemployment, are unable to maintain them. As a result, they face the possibility of serious deterioration.[13]

Squatter settlements

One of the most important components of the slum housing stock, and one that has attracted the most discussion during the last three decades, is squatter housing. Squatters are people who occupy land or buildings without the explicit permission of the owner. They often differ from other

Some of the public housing built between the 1950s and 1970s to re-house the residents of central city slums, typically in four- to five-storey tenement blocks with minimal community amenities, has itself now joined the stock of slums

informal settlements only in this particular. Thus, squatter settlements are settlements established by people who have illegally occupied an area of land and built their houses upon it, usually through self-help processes. Included in this category are settlements established illegally on pavements or rooftops. English language terms used to describe such settlements include self-help or self-built settlements; spontaneous settlements; marginal settlements; squatter areas; shanty towns; and slums. Terms in other languages include *barrios*, *tugurios*, *favelas*, *bidonvilles*, *gecikondus* and *kampungs*.

Squatter settlements are generally found in the towns and cities of developing countries. Some of them, in South and East Asia, date back to the 19th century; but most have much more recent origins. They are, primarily, though not exclusively, built on public land. They can be the result of organized 'invasions' of land, which may have occurred overnight (especially in Latin America), or they can be the result of a gradual process of occupation and incremental growth. Many land invasions and squatter settlements have grown to become municipalities in their own rights, housing hundreds of thousands of people. With them has come the commerce and services that characterize any town – although, perhaps taking a different form or on a different scale from that of the formal city. For example, Villa el Salvador in Peru started as an informal invasion of peri-urban land with pole and matting shelters in 1970 and is now a municipality of greater Lima with a population of nearly 300,000.[14] Ashaiman in Ghana was a village that, during the 1960s, provided shelter for the construction labourers and port workers in the new town of Tema, and is now a thriving town of 100,000. There are also the vast inner-city squatter areas of Asian cities, such as Dharavi in Mumbai and Orangi in Karachi, each with a population estimated at over 500,000.

Although the initial settlements may have been the result of the authorities turning a blind eye, particularly during the immediate post-independence inflow of migrants to the cities of Asia and Africa, squatting became a large and profitable business, often carried out with the active, if clandestine, participation of politicians, policemen and privateers of all kinds. In most cases, the prime target was public land or that owned by absentee landlords. In many cities, the process of illegally occupying public land has become highly organized. During the 1970s, political parties and organizations in many Latin American cities used the process of organized invasions of land as a political tool to build up a constituency or a power base.

Many squatter settlements, however, are small and makeshift. They may be located under bridges and flyovers, on vacant plots of land between formal buildings, or on pavements and dry-season riverbeds. In order to diminish the chances of immediate eviction, settlements frequently develop on land that is unsuitable for any other purpose, such as railway reserves; canal and river banks; steep (and unstable) slopes; flood-prone and swamp land; and garbage landfill sites. The size, location, condition and resilience of squatter settlements will be determined not just by the characteristics of their residents, but, more importantly, by the political context of official tolerance or intolerance towards them.

Contrary to popular belief, access to squatter settlements is rarely free and, within most settlements, entry fees are often charged by the person or group who exerts control over the settlement and the distribution of land. In Phnom Penh, for example, the majority of slum dwellers consider themselves owners of their plots; but the purchase of the plot is usually from local people with influence (such as the police, village chief and/or representatives of the Sangkat or Khan), who themselves have no prior ownership rights.[15] In some cases, the bribe paid is described as a registration fee for the 'right' to settle on a piece of public land.

Within settlements, there exists a range of actors from owner occupiers to tenants, subsistence landlords to absentee petty-capitalist landlords, and developers to rent agents and protection racketeers. Variety also exists in their legal status; while squatter settlements begin with an illegal occupation of land, over time some form of security of tenure, if not formally recognized legal title, can be transferred to the residents. In time, *de facto* legality can be implied by the simple fact of the settlements not being demolished, and/or public services being provided.[16] Since the 1970s, tolerance of squatter settlements by government and the public alike has grown and the numbers of forced evictions and demolitions have probably diminished, though they have certainly not ceased. This has enabled some of the more established squatter settlements to develop rapidly, with residents feeling sufficiently secure to invest in improving their homes and local environment. Where the state has also invested in settlements, through environmental and infrastructure upgrading projects and the provision of social services, the transformation can be such that, over time, the settlement loses its attributes as a slum. In this way, processes of gentrification can occur in squatter settlements as they do in city centre slums – although, in this case, the new occupants are likely to be lower-middle income groups, rather than an adventurous professional class.

Thus, squatter settlements in and on the fringes of cities in developing countries play an equivalent role to two forms of housing in Europe and North America in terms of providing accessible and affordable housing: the conventional central-area slum housing and low-priced suburban housing. Initially tolerated as a 'temporary' phenomenon by most city authorities, what started as a small-scale activity of largely self-built, makeshift housing by construction workers and other labourers very quickly mushroomed into a major settlement activity, far surpassing the formal housing efforts of most cities in most countries. In São Paulo, more than 60 per cent of the population growth in the 1980s is considered to have been absorbed by the *favelas*.[17]

Squatting, like living in conventional slums, provides a solution to the housing needs of those that cannot afford, or even find, alternative formal accommodation. As with conventional slum properties, some squatter settlements are cramped, high-density areas, with substandard construction

---

Box 5.6 Informal settlements in Durban

As a result of the colonial and apartheid eras, the predominant form of inadequate housing in Durban, as in many other African cities, is in informal settlements that have developed on marginal land that formerly lay beyond the city boundaries. In South Africa under apartheid, this land was under the jurisdiction of 'independent' states or on 'buffer strips' between areas designated for other use and the actual city boundary. In Durban, informal dwellings act as substitutes for about 75% of the metropolitan gross housing backlog of 305,000 units. The population living in informal areas is overwhelmingly African, and, indeed, nearly half of the black population of the entire municipal area lives in informal dwellings. While, in the past, there has been extensive harassment and physical destruction of informal dwellings, all such dwellings in existence in Durban in 1996 were granted some status and security from arbitrary eviction by the local authority. New settlement is, however, resisted by the municipality and attempts are made, with varying degrees of success, to keep vacant land free from occupation.

Source: Durban case study, 2002.

---

and inadequate levels of services and infrastructure. For instance, parts of Huruma settlement in Nairobi have residential densities of over 2000 people per hectare in single-storey structures.[18] However, others, especially those in newly developed peripheral areas, may be much more spacious.

The poor who occupy squatter settlements are often desperate and susceptible to pressure from organized crime. Their location, lack of services and poor infrastructure leave occupants prone to disaster, disease and disability. Like central-city slum dwellers, those who live in squatter settlements are widely perceived as petty criminals or under the control of organized crime, and a threat to society; but the reality is often very different, with a broad cross-section of people living under strong local social controls.

Illegal settlements and subdivisions

Not all of those who live in poor-quality, under-serviced housing areas are squatters, in the sense that they are occupying land to which they do not have rights. Unauthorized land developments or illegal subdivisions are widespread on the fringes of cities. Illegal subdivisions refer to settlements where the land has been subdivided, resold, rented or leased by its legal owner to people who build their houses upon the plots that they buy. The settlements are illegal owing to any combination of the following: low standard of services or infrastructure; breaches of land zoning; lack of planning and building permits; or the irregular nature of the land subdivision. Illegal subdivisions are very common in developing countries, but are not restricted to them or to occupation by people living in poverty, as the Naples example in Box 5.7 shows.

In some cases, farmers have found that the most profitable 'crop' for their land is housing. Peri-urban land is transformed from agricultural to urban use by landowners who divide it into plots for housing. The majority of these subdivisions are done without reference or recourse to the official urban planning mechanisms involving permission fees and licences. As informal and unrecognized settlements, they lack all but the most rudimentary public

Access to squatter settlements is rarely free and, within most settlements, entry fees are often charged by the person or group who exerts control over the settlement and the distribution of land

Squatting, like living in conventional slums, provides a solution to the housing needs of those that cannot afford, or even find, alternative formal accommodation

Settlements are illegal owing to any combination of low standard of services or infrastructure; breaches of land zoning; lack of planning and building permits; or the irregular nature of the land subdivision

Box 5.7 Illegal construction in Naples

Illegal building, which is elsewhere commonly associated with slums and poverty, is actually associated with middle-class neighbourhoods in Naples. The best-known case of illegal construction is Pianura, a neighbourhood that sprung up during the 1970s and 1980s, when five- to seven-storey buildings were built without authorization from the city in an area that the zoning plan classified as agricultural. They are illegal in the technical sense of having no building permits and violating the zoning plan; but the land was legally bought by private developers who respected building standards, and homes were placed on the market at prices only slightly (15–20%) below the cost of legal units. With the connivance of the authorities, they were linked to the public water and electricity system, and later to the sewerage system. Growth at Pianura is still strong – rising from 38,500 residents in 1981 to 54,000 in 1991, with young families, productive (although undeclared) businesses and higher homeownership rates than the city average. This type of illegal construction is widespread outside of the centre of Naples, but is usually limited to the expansion or construction of single-household homes. Many residential areas, of varying scale, have appeared spontaneously throughout the city.

Source: Naples case study, 2002.

infrastructure; however, this is what makes them affordable. Nevertheless, the housing built on them, while often substantial and constructed of permanent materials, in response to confidence in the security (legality) of the land sale process, rarely meets or is subjected to building and planning regulations and permissions. Though the conditions in these settlements are usually better than squatter settlements of the same age, they tend to have high densities since little provision is made for open space or access, and the plots themselves tend to be small, with high ratios of floor space to plot size.

In sub-Saharan Africa, customary landowners are often the main providers of land for housing, even if their right to the land is not formally recognized by the state. In many situations, the underlying issue is that customary law still applies and overlaps with statutory law. What distinguishes this form of development from squatting is that the sale of land is generally through a legal transaction, although not always formally registered. The land may not be recognized as suitable for urban development or housing, or the development may not comply with planning laws and

> Understanding and articulating the difference between slums is critical to developing effective strategies that address the problem

regulations, or with norms and standards regarding the provision of infrastructure and services.

As in squatter settlements, most occupants of illegal subdivisions build, extend and improve their own housing over time, and consider themselves to be owner occupiers, which, *de facto*, they are. Of course, not all dwellings in such settlements are owner-occupied. There are many unauthorized land developments where there is a vibrant rental housing market, controlled both by individual plot owners and by speculative developers and agents, sometimes on a fairly substantial scale. In Nairobi, Kibera – to the west of the city – is the largest uncontrolled settlement.[19] Its relative proximity to the main industrial area allows residents to save on transport costs and to walk to work; but shortages of accommodation mean both overcrowding and high rents.

Illegal and informal subdivision or change of land use are not limited to land on the urban fringes. It is also common to the process of raising densities in low- and medium-density inner-city areas as households, unable to acquire new accommodation for expanding families, or in order to benefit from rental income, extend and subdivide their properties. They may build in courtyards, gardens and circulation space, add floors, or extend onto flat roofs. Where housing is owner-occupied, this process tends to occur anywhere that the authorities allow it and often involves quite sophisticated neighbourly negotiations.[20] There is little evidence that such extensions lead to overloading of public infrastructure and services, although this may be expected. Where the dwellings are owner-occupied the chance of maintenance is increased.[21] Where houses are rented to many households, however, it is more likely that alterations and extensions carried out by tenants will be harmful as they will have little concern for the whole building.

Diversity of slums' spatial forms and associated opportunities

In general parlance, and in the official language, little differentiation is made between types of substandard housing. In practice, all and any of such housing is referred to as 'slums', or 'slums and squatter settlements', or 'slums and shanties', often interchangeably. Understanding and articulating the difference between them is critical to developing effective strategies that address the problems in slums, and to support the processes of improving settlements, alleviating the impacts of poverty within them and encouraging the spontaneous improvements that may follow, increasing wealth within them.

Each slum or area of poor housing possesses a number of attributes. For example, a slum on the urban periphery or in the city centre may be well established or relatively new. It may be large or small. Each of these conditions will endow it with certain qualities that reinforce both its strengths and its weaknesses, and may increase or decrease the potential to benefit from particular forms of upgrading or other improvement intervention.

The following section discusses a framework for analysing slums with reference to their settlement formation

Box 5.8 Illegal subdivision of agricultural land around Cairo

Over half of the population of Greater Cairo resides in private housing that is constructed on agricultural land purchased from farmers in areas where there were no subdivision plans and where building permits were not given. This constitutes almost half of the residential area. Since the 1960s, small agricultural areas on the fringes of 'formal' Cairo began to be subdivided by farmers and middlemen and sold to individual owner builders. This accelerated dramatically after the 1974 open-door policy was proclaimed, fuelled by ever increasing flows of remittances from the hundreds of thousands of Egyptians working mostly as labourers in the Gulf and in other oil-rich economies. Finances came from personal savings, remittances from relatives or conversion of other assets; as a result, incremental construction was a necessity. Plot coverage of 100% and incremental (room by room and floor by floor) reinforced-concrete construction are the norm. While the quality of construction of housing is generally good, there is a very common trend of increasing the density of areas over time and a parallel phenomenon of serious overcrowding.

Source: Cairo case study, 2002.

process, form, spatial organization and construction, strengths and weaknesses, and opportunities. A number of characteristics (see Table 5.1), used in combination, serve to identify issues pertaining to vulnerability, the social networks, physical and economic assets with the potential to improve livelihoods, and levels of and incentives for community organization and representation.

ORIGINS AND AGE

Origins and age indicate the legacy of a slum, such as its physical assets of building heritage, the root and speed of its formation, and the establishment of community. Given the pejorative associations with 'slum' discussed in Chapters 1, 2 and 4, this legacy will be fundamental to determining what initiatives and momentum will be required in order to effect change. There are clearly geographical and historical regional patterns to the world's cities. Nevertheless, many cities have some combination of old established slums, which may, indeed, be the original city itself. At the other extreme, there are the slums and areas of poverty that are currently forming; and between these are the remaining settlements of various vintage and degree of integration within the city.

Historic city-centre slums

Most cities in Asia and Africa that have a pre-colonial existence, also have some or all of that original settlement largely intact. The equivalent in Latin America are the colonial pre-independence cities, laid out according to the code of *La Lay de Indias*. In many instances, the original city is separated from the more modern city by its old defensive wall (for example, in Lahore, Pakistan) or a moat, or it is on a hill (such as Salvador, Bahia, Brazil), and often has a distinct name, such as the *kasbah* (for example, in Marrakesh, Morocco) or the old city (as in Old Delhi, India). It is a distinct neighbourhood or even a sub-city within the city. Many such neighbourhoods are a mixture of grand buildings and public spaces, many in semi-ruins, others taken over for private use. Those of the original inhabitants who could afford it have moved out to the new city, leaving the odd retainer, or even some members of the older generation, too set in their ways to move. Many of the buildings and places have been subdivided and let to poor households, perhaps employed in the old businesses and manufacturing units that remain, still producing the goods for which the city was once famous.

Many established historical city cores are classified as slums because they have high residential and commercial densities and overcrowding, as well as levels of services and infrastructure only suited to much smaller populations. This is especially evident in streets that are too narrow and irregular to accommodate cars, lorries and refuse-collection vehicles. In addition, the drains and water supply pipes often leak, and electricity and telephone cables, many of them unofficial, festoon the streets. In many, the once fashionable balconies now hang perilously, propped up by decaying posts, their facades blocked to provide additional rooms.

Box 5.9 Illegal subdivisions in Quito

In Quito, most low-income households are located on the urban periphery, in the *barrios periféricos*. During the last two decades, the Quito region has incorporated former minor urban centres and peripheral agricultural areas to form an agglomeration that covers the valleys of Tumbaco-Cumbayá, Los Chillos, Calderón and Pomasqui-San Antonio de Pichincha. Settlements such as Corazón de Jesús have evolved through a process of subdivision: the irregular topography influences both development and risks to the settlement. Housing is small and built with inadequate materials; some dwellings have latrines, but there is no drinking water or sewerage provision; waste collection service is non-existent or inefficient; and the main or secondary access roads and street lighting are in poor condition.

Source: Quito case study, 2002.

These are the classic inner-city slums; yet, each building often also represents a fortune, if not for what it manufactures, stores and sells, then for the rents it brings in from the many households that now share its once noble rooms. However, this economic return is often negated by rent control, which, in turn, encourages owners to withdraw maintenance and further accelerates decline. They are also often the subject of ownership disputes, feuds, claims and counterclaims. The many claimants and litigants make it difficult for these properties to be redeveloped; in the mean time, they go neglected and unmaintained. Slums of this kind are found in Karachi, Cairo and other established cities in the developing world.[22]

Nevertheless, these buildings, individually, and more so collectively, represent a part of the cultural heritage and generate claims for conservation, competing with those for demolition and modernization. Their strength also lies in their location within the city and in relation to the centres of commerce and production. The easy access to employment, real and potential, combined with cheap if run-down housing, are natural magnets for the poor.

The continued presence of the older generation, with ties and traditions that go back many years, is often an effective counterbalance to any socially disruptive tendencies. The continued presence of communities and community leaders, as well as the traditions and relationships between them, help to bind the newcomers, as well.

Run-down and inadequate infrastructure can be upgraded, and there are many technological advances that

---

Table 5.1

Major categories of slum spatial analysis

Origins and age	Historic city-centre slums
	Slum estates
	Consolidating informal settlements
	Recent slums
Location and boundaries	Central
	Scattered slum islands
	Peripheral
Size and scale	Large slum settlements
	Medium-size slum estates
	Small slums
Legality and vulnerability	Illegal
	Informal
Development stages: dynamic and diagnosis	Communities/individuals lacking incentive for improvement
	Slums with ongoing individual- and community-led development
	Intervention-led improved slums
	Upgraded slums

Box 5.10 Ibadan's historical centre slums

In Ibadan, the inner-city core area consists of the oldest, the lowest-quality and the highest-density residences of the city. During the 19th century, large compounds for Yoruba-extended families and warrior lineages constituted this part of the city. The area still has a strong cultural identity based on its heritage, and the presence of non-Yorubas in this part of the city is rare. Housing is constructed of mud, with virtually no sanitation facilities. It is highly residential, up to 90% in Elekuro ward, and the simultaneous presence of many old markets and street trading in the area cause traffic congestion and exacerbate overcrowding while providing essential employment and services. The colonial area developed beside the old city, making this area the worst case of deterioration less than 2 kilometres from the current city centre. Residents rent or squat. Some of the wealthier people of Ibadan, who were born in the core area, have kept their family house for cultural and familial reasons, although they now live in villas in the new government estates. However, the buildings and land that they occupy remain sacred to the original owning family and it is very difficult to change them from residential use. They are of little economic value but are precious to their multiple-related owners.

Sources: Ibadan case study, 2002; Amole et al, 1993.

Box 5.11 Old Havana

Old Havana has an irregular grid of narrow streets and small city blocks, with buildings sharing party walls and with inner courtyards: a coherent urban fabric with dominant squares and churches. As the city expanded during the 1700s, it developed typical *calzadas*: wide streets with tall porticoed pedestrian corridors opening into stores and dwellings above. However, in 1859, the new western suburb of El Vedado attracted the sugar-plantation aristocracy and, during the 1920s, a further upmarket area, Miramar, was developed close to the waterfront, which deliberately lacked stores and other amenities to discourage the less affluent. The mansions of the old city were turned into stores or subdivided as tenements with shared facilities: poverty masked behind classical facades.

About half of the residents of tenements with high ceilings have built *barbacoas* – makeshift mezzanines or loft-like structures that create an extra floor. They are often unsafe, poorly ventilated and their bricked up windows deform building facades. Moreover, *barbacoas* add considerable weight to load-bearing walls, already weakened by leaks, often leading to partial or complete building collapses. Another source of extra residential space, as well as extra building weight, are *casetas en azoteas* – literally, 'shacks on roofs' – which are usually wooden structures built on top of multi-household buildings. The Cuban regime's encouragement of development away from Havana has indirectly helped to shield Old Havana from some overuse; nevertheless, most slums are still concentrated in the inner-city municipalities of Old Havana (La Habana Vieja) and Centro Habana. The result of density, additions and poor maintenance is regular building collapse – Old Havana averages about two partial collapses every three days. In these cases, residents are usually assigned to emergency or existing transitional shelters, but are often reluctant to go there.

The restoration of Old Havana and San Isidro started after Havana became a World Historic Heritage site in 1982. In 1993, Havana's Historian's Office was granted the right to run its own profit-making companies in the real estate, building, retail and tourism fields, and to plough back part of its earnings into restoring the historic district. In addition, it could devote a portion of its own resources to financing community facilities and social programmes for local residents and to repair and rehabilitate dwellings, even in non-historic areas. Most residents remain in the area, and gentrification has been avoided, to some extent, since housing for local residents is included in the upper floors of restored buildings. Some, however, are displaced to apartments built and financed by the Historian's Office, where some residents welcome the more spacious, well-equipped new dwellings, while others find commuting extremely difficult. Temporary relocation housing is sometimes provided in Old Havana itself while rehabilitation is under way. Local economic development also takes place; some residents have received training and jobs as skilled construction workers for the restoration process, others have received incentives to produce crafts for sale to tourists, or obtained other employment in the tourist industry.

Source: Havana case study, 2002.

make this possible without endangering the structures. The inaccessibility of motorized transport may be a blessing, and the dilapidated structures can be refurbished. Very often, it is not the know-how or even the resources that prevent improvement of these areas, but the complexity of ownership and the economic risk of investing in a single building on the chances that the whole neighbourhood will be upgraded and allow the investment to be recovered. Where this does happen, of course, the poor are often denied access to affordable, centrally located housing and business premises.

Slum estates

From the time that the old city lost its place as the centre of attraction for the rich and the affluent, and was replaced by the new city, parallel developments for the less well off have emerged. Some of these have been in the form of formal public housing estates constructed relatively recently (at least three decades old in developing countries). The vast majority of others have been older illegal and informal settlements laying claim to land deemed unfit or unsafe for planned residential development.

As mentioned earlier, some slum estates have developed where relatively new estates, usually built for renting, have deteriorated quite quickly into areas where few would choose to live, but in which many low-income households are trapped through having no affordable alternative. Examples include government-built mass public housing estates, and housing built by industry or to house industrial workers, such as the hostels and estates of small dwellings for mine workers in Southern Africa, and 'chawls' in India.[23] Other examples include the 'new towns' of Cairo (Helwan, Moktam and Shubra), Ciudad Kenedy in Bogotá and the large State Housing Board developments that were constructed in virtually all of the major Indian cities during the 1970s and early 1980s.[24] Both have experienced social problems arising from overcrowded and pressured conditions, making residents particularly vulnerable to organized crime and political exploitation.

Another common reason for the deterioration of relatively new public housing estates has been their location on the edges of cities where land was available, but access to work, markets, kin and social amenities was not. The relative isolation of such estates means that the cost of transport is often unaffordable to the low-income inhabitants. They are, therefore, abandoned by all but the most destitute and desperate. In general, a lack of public resources is the most cited reason for the deterioration of physical conditions, as well as the conviction that, somehow, it is the culture of poverty of its residents that is the root cause.

Slum estates also include large amounts of housing built by employers as tied housing for workers. These vary from the tiny bungalows on featureless 'locations' in Southern Africa to the slab blocks in the former Communist bloc. They tend to be even more poorly maintained than publicly owned housing and may even be hated by their occupants. As many dwellings are transferred to occupier ownership, and many occupiers then lose their jobs in the decline of formal industries, conditions and the quality of life of the occupants decline in parallel. The Chengdu, China, case study shows that dwellings in public housing estates in the city are likely to suffer from serious deterioration.[25]

Consolidating informal settlements

Much of the urban development in rapidly developing cities of the South has been through informal settlements in which land has been informally subdivided and sold or leased to households who have built their own dwellings. Some of the land used in this way is deemed unsafe or unfit for planned residential development, such as the land occupied by the extensive informal settlements built on stilts over the tidal swamps of Guayaquil (Ecuador) and Cartagena (Colombia), and the Tondo Foreshore of Manila (Philippines). In some instances, it is land reserved for future development (by the sides of roads, railway tracks and canals, or even around airports and other facilities) that has been pressed into serving the needs of the otherwise unhoused.

Over time, some of the first of these settlements have been grudgingly recognized, tolerated and even accepted, such as Policarpa Salavarrieta, a large 1960s land invasion in central Bogotá, Colombia. There may have been attempts to dislodge these settlements; but there have also been interventions to improve them. Whether legal or not, their continued presence gives them a *de facto* right to exist and to develop.

In many countries, traditional authority structures have powers over land in tandem with the state and its agencies. Many areas are allocated by chiefs and traditional councils with or without the agreement of state institutions. Subsequent development may conform to some regulations but many do not fulfil all of the official requirements for housing neighbourhoods. These may be indistinguishable from, and treated in a similar way to, other informal subdivisions.

Although often not as substantial as in the more established slums, the majority of housing in informal consolidated areas is built of durable materials, though the piecemeal construction and improvement of such areas have given them a more chaotic (or organic) overall appearance than in formally developed areas. There are fewer public facilities, such as schools and playgrounds, and few formal commercial outlets than in the established slums. There are manufacturing and marketing activities; but these tend to be small-scale, family-operated enterprises. Similarly, though generally fairly accessible by road and public transport to the periphery, the internal streets of these settlements tend to be less adequate.

The general level of earnings and incomes is not the lowest, with more owner occupiers and self-employed residents than in newer, poorer settlements. The potential for improving such settlements is generally high as a result of the greater perceived and, to some extent, real benefits from upgrading for the residents. The most frequent constraint is the planning and zoning legislation that the

settlement contravenes, even though, in practice, the city government has learned to accommodate and adjust to the presence of these consolidating slum settlements. This occurs as it becomes apparent that political opposition militates against the demolition of such slums, and it is, therefore, in the interest of the city that they should be absorbed within the formal housing stock and improved in order to maintain the land values of the areas that surround them.

Recent slums

Recently developed slum neighbourhoods are often similar to the consolidated informal settlements, but are newer and unconsolidated. Their newness is expressed in poorer, less permanent materials, especially in settlements where residents are unsure of whether and for how long they will be allowed to stay before being evicted. In cities where evictions are common, or on sites where they are unlikely to be left alone, shacks are likely to be very rudimentarily built of recycled or very impermanent materials (such as straightened oil drums, used corrugated metal sheets, plastic and canvas sheets, cardboard cartons and discarded timber).

> In general, a lack of public resources is the most cited reason for the deterioration of physical conditions

> The potential for improving consolidated slums is generally high as a result of the greater perceived and, to some extent, real benefits from upgrading for the residents

---

Box 5.12 The *medinas* of Morocco: Rabat-Salé

The deterioration of some parts of the two *medinas* (the old neighbourhoods of the pre-colonial city) finds its origin, as in other Moroccan cities, in a double loss of affection: that of a housing model abandoned by middle- and well-off classes, who migrated to new neighbourhoods, and that of economic activities and craftworks that move elsewhere. The former leads to the densification and pressure on building fabric, and the latter directly impoverishes community members. In the twin cities of Rabat-Salé, rental, room by room, has led to rapid deterioration, and renewal movements are slow to appear. In other cities, concern for the historic building fabric has taken precedence over the livelihoods of the poor within them, and the policy was initially to 'depopulate' in order to promote the district for tourism. But greater recognition of socio-economic aspects is leading to investigation of alternatives. Some commercial and service activities remain, along with a number of craft businesses. However, those activities have been widely supplanted by the illegally built neighbourhoods in Rabat: Hajja and Maadid, and in Salé: Hay Inbiat. Thus, while the *medinas* at the moment continue to constitute a source of informal, irregular and provisory employment, for residents, the threats to livelihoods are yet to be addressed.

Source: Rabat-Salé case study, 2002.

Box 5.13 Consolidating *favelas* in Rio de Janeiro

The *favelas* of Rio de Janeiro have appeared throughout the city since the 1950s. There are now about 700 and they house an estimated 1 million inhabitants. The *favelas* are frequently on hilly sites and are primarily located in the suburbs, where public utilities are rarely available and environmental conditions are poor, owing to few connections to trunk infrastructure. Access to bus routes is reasonable; but they tend to be far from employment opportunities.[i] The dwelling is considered to be owner-occupied, though there is no security of tenure on the land. The *favela* movements of the 1970s and 1980s have helped to consolidate settlements and the *de facto* tenure, and a policy shift from settlement removal to upgrading has encouraged structural improvements as residents expect to remain there permanently.

Note: i However, the location of some, high up, overlooking the beautiful Atlantic coast and the rising sun, became valuable briefly as they were rented out to richer households wanting to celebrate the sunrise on the Millennium dawn.

Source: Rio de Janeiro case study, 2002.

Box 5.14 Consolidating informal settlements in Bogotá

Bogotá has had more than four decades of urban growth, largely based on 'illegal' development; although there are squatter settlements, Bogotá's slums, for the most part, have their origins in illegal subdivision. The localities of Ciudad Bolívar, Bosa and Usme are examples of 'slum' areas that, in their first stages of development, lacked water, drainage, sewerage and power infrastructure, along with education and health care facilities. However, the settlements have undergone consistent gradual improvement, partly through the installation of public services and the construction of roads, with the support of the city's administration and sometimes with the participation of the residents, and partly through individual initiatives of developing dwellings and space for informal economic activity.

Source: Bogotá case study, 2002.

Where authorities are more tolerant, or where such settlements are the norm for establishing new neighbourhoods (for example, around Lima), or if there are about to be elections, then the settlers are likely to build with more confidence, using more permanent materials and standards of construction. In either case, infrastructure is likely to be absent or only available through clandestine connections.

Box 5.15 Recent slums in Phnom Penh

Around 230,000 people or one quarter of Phnom Penh's inhabitants currently live in low-income communities or slums. All live on marginal, seasonally or permanently flooded land, or in multi-occupancy dilapidated buildings in the city centre. The rationale behind most locations is access to work. They are convenient for access to the city centre, main markets or the railway station. 35% of low-income settlements in Phnom Penh are located on 'empty' land, some 26% on riverbanks and canal sides, and the remainder are along railways and on roadsides, or on rooftops. The areas for settlement lack road access, water and power supply, sewerage and drainage, and are often insalubrious, situated above sewer lines, or near or on dumpsites. The public land on which settlements have developed includes relatively wide streets, railway tracks, riversides, and *boengs* (water reservoirs used to irrigate farmland during the dry season).

On private land, small clusters of households have settled in alleys of high-income districts, while other groups live as squatters in dilapidated, multiple-occupancy buildings in the centre of the city, where owners wait to sell the building for commercial development. Many people who lived in centrally located squatter settlements have now been evicted to the periphery to make way for commercial development. Thus, while squatter settlements developed primarily in the city centre until 1998, recent massive relocation programmes have contributed to establishing peri-urban zones of poverty. Allegedly, these relocations have also created more rental communities in Phnom Penh slums, as some relocated households cannot find work near relocation sites and have returned as renters in squatter settlements near employment areas.

Since 1995, rural migrants have developed squatter areas on the rural fringe of the city, on public land unsuited to construction where they expect that long-term occupation may provide them some tenure rights. Increasingly, the urban poor also informally purchase plots on the rooftops of large, mostly government, buildings where they live as squatters relatively close to their place of work. The settlements within or on top of old buildings have been created since 1985, when occupation rights were granted to all inhabitants. These rights are not ownership rights, and inhabitants could still be considered squatters and evicted; but they are recognized as stable residents and have a greater chance of obtaining some sort of compensation. Renters in Phnom Penh are either seasonal migrants who have a dwelling in the countryside and come to the city for a short time, or they are the poorest of the poor, who cannot afford to purchase a dwelling in a squatter settlement. They are under constant threat of eviction by their slum landlord. Single women head many of the renting households.

Source: Phnom Penh case study, 2002.

New or recently established slums tend to have lower densities as there are fewer constraints and less competition for the land; yet the individual plots and parcels occupied by each dwelling are unlikely to be any larger than in the more consolidated slums. This is because households tend to occupy only enough land for their individual needs, rather than explicitly seeking to profit from land holding and development.

Recently developed slums are generally found on the periphery of the built-up area of the city, or in pockets of even more marginal land than the more established slums. Increasingly, occupants of the newer slums often use the grid-iron layout, even without the assistance of external organization and support. There are several advantages in adopting grid layouts:

*   It is easy to lay out.
*   There is a stronger likelihood of obtaining urban services and recognition if the settlement is orderly.
*   There are likely to be fewer disruptions and demolitions when services are installed.

LOCATION

To some extent, as has been indicated above, there is a correlation between age and location, with older slums in the city centre and the newest on the periphery. Although this follows from the realities of a growing city, it is not always the case. For example, with a relatively young, but fast-growing, city, the oldest slum areas may well be outside of the centre. Regardless of age, the location of the slum endows it with certain attributes.

Central

As mentioned in the section on 'Inner-city slums,' central-city slums tend to have been formed by the classic process where central, prosperous residential areas of cities undergo deterioration as their original owners move out to newer, more salubrious and more fashionable residential areas. Initially, the housing vacated by the better-off, which generally has reasonable infrastructure and services, is ideal for those willing to trade off less space and shared amenities in exchange for access to employment opportunities.

Centrality of location does not necessarily imply the old city, or the central business or commercial centres of cities. As used here, it also embraces formal industrial areas, ports, wholesale markets and other areas of employment that are some distance from the central business district (CBD). Residents of slums that are located close to such zones are able to benefit from the high concentrations of employment opportunities, especially those related to unskilled and casual jobs. They are also likely to be better off in terms of transportation because of the tendency for cities to grow outwards radially and, therefore, to have roads and transport converging on centres of formal employment. This makes centrally located slums much more suitable for unskilled workers. If the neighbourhood originated in the old city centre, then it may also have the benefit of substantial buildings and a reasonable level of infrastructure and services, though it may have fallen into disrepair and infrastructure may be severely overloaded (see the case of Havana in Box 5.11).

The historic cores of many ancient cities (for example, Delhi, Dhaka, Cairo and Istanbul) are now in much reduced circumstances and would fit the description of city-centre slums; but these are dealt with separately as historic city slums.

As mentioned in 'Inner-city slums' on page 80, much of this housing is controlled by rent control legislation, which fixes rents at levels that are affordable by some measure, but which are usually unrelated to the value or replacement cost of the accommodation or to the economic cost of adequately maintaining the building and its services. Introduced in many countries during World War II, or in the economic upheaval caused by it, rent control is now widely recognized as contributing to the deterioration of the housing to which it applies as owners remove value from it by withdrawing maintenance or by converting it from residential to other uses (for example, cheap boarding houses).[26]

In West African cities, central areas are often dominated by traditional housing that is owned in common by many members of one lineage and is occupied by elderly or poor family members. This 'family housing' embodies a curious contradiction: it is both precious and valueless. It is sacred to the family and, thus, is precious. However, it suffers from multiple occupation by the people least able to maintain it; but it is not for sale and therefore is unlikely to develop into commercial or other uses to make economic use of the central location. Indeed, because of this, CBD functions tend to be spread around the city. These circumstances are unlikely to change without a major reappraisal of the function of housing in West African urban societies. This, in turn, could generate serious dysfunctions, which may be inimical to the cohesion of families and society there. Especially at risk are those who need the social safety net that free accommodation in the family house provides.[27]

Centrally located slums are most prone to being controlled by organized racketeers through their control over jobs, as well as property. The extent to which the *favelas* of central Rio de Janeiro, Brazil, are controlled by drug barons is legendary.[28] The majority of slum central-area dwellers tend to be wage earners, and are either on piece rates or are casually hired. The majority of them are tenants, renting or subletting from slum landlords, rather than owner occupiers living in dwellings that they have built themselves.

In more socially and economically mobile cities, notably in Latin America, many central-area slum dwellers, over time, move out to new and more peripheral locations, seeking less precarious and more permanent housing. They are the most likely candidates for official slum relocation programmes as they succumb to pressure and enticements from better-off households who want to move into the central locations once they have been improved or, in the more developed cities of the North, as part of the process of 'gentrification'.

> **Box 5.16 Centrally located slums in Colombo**
>
> The settlements commonly referred to as 'slums', 'tenement gardens' or '*mudukku*' in Colombo are the old deteriorating tenements or subdivided derelict houses located on high lands in the old parts of the inner-city areas. These old tenements were erected to accommodate the influx of a new labour force into the city during a period when a thriving plantation industry required labour for processing, packaging and storage, as well as handling and shipping. Tenement units normally consist of a single bedroom, a small veranda and a living area with common water taps and latrine facilities. They were usually built in back-to-back rows, on a block of land commonly referred to as a garden. These so-called tenements contain anything between a group of two or three units and a few hundred.
>
> Old residential buildings, mainly in older parts of north and central Colombo (for example, Pettah, Hultsdorp and Wolfendhal) were also turned into apartments for low-income workers. They were subdivided into small units, inadequately maintained and largely deprived of basic sanitary facilities.
>
> *Source:* Colombo case study, 2002.

Scattered slum islands

Scattered throughout cities are 'islands of slums', surrounded by formal housing and other officially sanctioned land uses. These islands may have been intended as open or green spaces, as the land was thought to be unsuitable for future housing, or locations that are physically or environmentally unsafe. Slum islands are typically small, as few as eight to ten dwellings. They often get their water from fire hydrants or neighbours in formal areas and dispose of their waste, both human and refuse, in the city's gutters and open spaces. They cannot support their own social infrastructure (school, clinic, etc); but use the facilities of the neighbourhoods in which they are located – unless they are denied access through social discrimination, which is quite common.

Slum islands that are closer to the centre share many of the advantages and attributes of the central slums described above. However, they are often physically isolated from the surrounding areas by barriers such as canals, storm drains, railway tracks or motorways, and, though close to urban facilities and opportunities, may not actually be able to benefit from them. Some islands may have started as rural communities that became engulfed by urban expansion; but this is rare, except towards the periphery.

> **Box 5.17 Centrally located slums in São Paulo**
>
> In São Paulo, *corticos* (rented rooms in a subdivided inner-city tenement building) are the traditional form of central slum housing. Most *corticos* are located in the central districts of the city, in areas that are deteriorated but near the city's jobs and services. Sacrifices of cramped, unhealthy and expensive housing are compensated for by the proximity of work and public services.
>
> *Favelas* sprout everywhere: in wealthy areas, poor areas, in the central region or in the periphery, wherever there is an empty and unprotected lot. Their appearance during the 1970s and 1980s mixed up the pattern of centre-periphery segregation in São Paulo. Public authorities constantly repressed and removed *favelas* in the areas valued by the market. The action of private property owners in regaining possession, moreover, has driven *favelas* to the poorest, most peripheral and environmentally fragile regions. Few remain in well-served regions, although the largest two, Heliópolis and Paraisópolis, are located in these areas.
>
> *Source:* São Paulo case study, 2002.

Box 5.18 Scattered slum islands in Beirut

In Beirut, in the Eastern Quarter, Hayy el Shaqi is located on an island in a major traffic intersection, below street level. One of the poorest settlements in the city, it was established during the 1950s after residents were displaced from a nearby zone where they had been squatting. Its residents originally came from Jabal el Druze (they were Syrian nationals from the Druze confession). Then, after 1982, most Syrian households left and were replaced by other foreign workers – Sri Lankans, Egyptians, Kurds and others. There are around 50 residents who run shops on the street. Construction is precarious, and this is the poorest of all of the city's slums. Dwellings are built with tin, wood, plastic sheets and other reused materials from the years of the Lebanon civil war. Being below street level, the slum also suffers from poor drainage, and several people have drowned there on days of heavy rain.

Source: Beirut case study, 2002.

Peripheral

Large slum settlements cannot rely on the services of the settlements around them and need their own, even to the extent of internal public transport systems.

Slums on the city fringes are, as described above, either squatter settlements in which households have invaded (usually public) land, or they occupy land that has been subdivided and for which they have paid or entered a rent-purchase arrangement with the developer or landowner. The urban periphery has distinct advantages over more central and urbanized areas as there is less competition for the use or control of land, especially if it is located outside of the municipal boundaries. Peripheral slums can be quite large settlements since they are rarely constrained by competing development.

In many cases, the quality of housing is relatively good – significantly better than is to be found in the adjoining rural areas – but the level of services is generally low. While this is not a great hazard to health and amenity when the overall density is low – as it can be during the early period of development – it can become a serious problem as the slum grows larger and denser. While dwellings are often owner-occupied, in many cities the provision of housing in peripheral settlements is controlled by a 'developer': a well-connected businessmen or politician who has the necessary power and resources to lay out and allocate land.

Box 5.19 Peripheral slum islands in Ibadan

Unplanned areas along the major roads in the outskirts of the city grew during the 1990s – notably, to the north, east and south of Ibadan. Some 30% of this informal unplanned housing is found more than 5 kilometres from the centre. While the inner-city slums have a predominantly Yoruba population, peripheral slums and their migrant settlers are much more heterogeneous in terms of ethnicity, religion or profession. Population densities in the outskirts are less than in the inner city, with a high turnover of occupants. The rental market thrives; landlords are often wealthy and living in other parts of town. Settlement is generally based on access to employment and other major activities. Agbowo, for example, is close to the university and is inhabited by students and junior staff. However, the shortage of accommodation on the university campus has resulted in a rental market where more than three students, on average, share a room, with up to eight students sharing in some cases. Housing conditions are also quite different from the inner city – dwellings form a heterogeneous pattern, built of cement, wood, or mud with cement plaster. Like the inner city, however, there is no potable water provision, water disposal or drainage, only occasional electricity supply. Routes are mostly impassable by motor vehicles.

Source: Ibadan case study, 2002.

An overriding problem facing peripheral slum dwellers is the low level of access and high cost of transport to jobs, markets, schools and the centres of administration of public services. Thus, households living in peri-urban areas can spend up to 30 per cent of their incomes on transport, or as much as three to four hours a day walking to and from work and school. Increasingly, middlemen are beginning to realize the potential offered by the women in these settlements by offering them piecework, bringing in the raw materials and collecting the finished products.

One of the main problems of home-based piece-working (home-working, as it is called in the literature) is that the 'invisible' workers can easily be exploited since control by labour authorities is very difficult.[29] When workers are scattered around new, unmapped areas, control is even more difficult, so exploitation is easier. In addition, the further that potential workers are from their jobs, the easier it is for exploiting employers to flourish.

A very significant feature of informal settlements on the urban periphery is their potential for efficient and effective upgrading through the provision of infrastructure and public services, especially if it is done before dwellings consume all of the available land. Increasingly, NGOs recognize this and are developing strategies to help new land invaders and informal developers to impose some discipline in the subdivision and layout of land in order to prepare for the installation of public infrastructure.

SIZE AND SCALE

The size of a settlement or slum area has obvious implications for what is, or is not, possible in terms of social organization, community cohesion and future intervention.

Large slum settlements

There are many slums around the world that are equivalent to cities in size. Dharavi in Mumbai, India, or Orangi in Karachi, Pakistan, house hundreds of thousands of households; Kibera in Nairobi, Kenya, has a population of 400,000 people.[30] To a large extent, this is a function of the size of the city of which they are part. However, it is possible for a slum or informal settlement to be larger than the city upon which it depends. For example, Ashaiman (in Ghana), referred to earlier, has a larger population (150,000) than Tema (140,000), the municipality of which it is formally part.

With such large slums, the need for local management and social organization becomes clear. Many different social groups may live and work within the slum's geographic boundary. While some large slums, such as Antop Hill in Mumbai, India, are organized spatially on ethnic lines, it is important for groups to cooperate with each other, whether or not it is traditional for their people to do so. Large slum settlements cannot rely on the services of the settlements around them and need their own, even to the extent of internal public transport systems.

With large numbers of slum dwellers, even though they are poor, there are substantial economies of scale and viable internal markets. It is possible for as many as 40 per cent of the population to find employment servicing and serving the needs of their own neighbours. The markets that spring up in large slums often attract custom from the surrounding formal settlements, as the produce tends to be cheaper than in formal-sector markets. The impacts and implications of such trends were discussed in Chapter 4.

Medium-sized slum estates

This is the most common situation, with neighbourhood-sized settlements developing in and around the city. The process of deteriorating conditions that led to falls in land and property values is self-perpetuating and, in many cities, relatively rapid. Of course, given the higher density of most areas that house the poor, a relatively small piece of land is required to house a community. Most often, the origins of such settlements is land that has been undeveloped or abandoned, since it was felt by the urban planners and developers to be difficult, if not impossible, to develop. These areas include swamps, marshes and steep slopes.

Medium or neighbourhood-sized slums are quite effective in resisting attempts to demolish or relocate them. In part, this is because they tend to form a cohesive community who support an active internal leadership, and because there are sufficient households to ensure that they have enough political and voting power to generate external political support.

Small slums

Scattered throughout cities are small, or even very small, slums that are surrounded by formal housing and other officially sanctioned land uses, sometimes on land designated for public or communal use, but most often on land left as reserves for future development or to serve or service roads and highways, waterways or railroads. The sites may have been intended as open or green spaces, or land thought to be unsuitable for future housing, or classified as locations that are physically or environmentally unsafe. These very small pocket-sized slums, characterized earlier as 'scattered slum islands', often contain as few as eight to ten dwellings. In many cases, occupants of neighbouring upper-income housing areas tolerate, or even protect, such slums as the residents often work as their domestic staff and other employees. Because of their small size, they cannot support their own social infrastructure (school, clinic, etc); but residents have easy access to public services from the neighbourhoods in which they are located. Sometimes, however, this is denied because of social discrimination. Where such settlements are not protected by their neighbours, they are vulnerable to exploitation and are ineffective at resisting eviction or relocation. These very small pocket-sized slums are often attractive to their residents because of their closeness to the centre. In the major cities of South Asia, very small pocket-sized slums occur through the occupation of pedestrian walkways. In Mumbai, India, it is estimated that there are more than 20,000 pavement dwellers who live in dwellings built on the pavements of the city centre, with residents using part of the carriageway as living space during the day.[31] Many of these dwellers have been there for 20 years or more.

Because of their small size, these slums have easy access to public services from the surrounding areas. On the other hand, where they are not protected, their small size makes them vulnerable to exploitation and less effective at resisting eviction or relocation. This precariousness is often responsible for the lack of substantial investment in housing, most of which is usually made from second-hand or recycled materials and components.

The markets that spring up in large slums often attract custom from the surrounding formal settlements, as the produce tends to be cheaper than in formal-sector markets

---

Box 5.20 Karachi: women's access to employment

The Khuda ki Bustee housing in Hyderabad, Pakistan, is located on the Karachi-Hyderabad Highway, on the edge of the city limits. While men were able to work, women were unable to find any employment locally and readily welcomed the approaches of middlemen to undertake piecework. Though this provided them with an income, the bulk of the money was kept by the middlemen. Consequently, when a local non-governmental organization (NGO) with experience of similar activities in Orangi, Karachi, offered to take on the role of the middlemen in providing raw materials and delivering to markets, the women joined readily, and now receive much more for their inputs. Similar stories of women succumbing to low wages are found in many low-income settlements in Pakistan, where the seclusion of women makes it difficult for women to enter the open labour market.

Box 5.21 Mexico City: Valle de Chalco Solidaridad

Valle de Chalco Solidaridad is a municipality that was created during recent years following massive settlement – in this case, in the agricultural municipality of Chalco, to the south-east of Mexico City. Agricultural land was originally appropriated after the construction of a canal during the 19th century. After the Mexican Revolution, the *haciendas* and other large agricultural properties were expropriated and distributed as *ejidos*, or agrarian communal properties, to the local communities.

By the late 1970s, Mexico City's growth began to affect the Chalco area. On the one hand, the demographic growth of the local communities meant that agriculture was increasingly unfeasible as a means of subsistence, on parcels of *ejidal* land averaging 1.7 hectares per household. On the other hand, demand for housing meant that the illegal sale of this land was an attractive proposition. In the case of Chalco, before 1984, many of the transactions were not handled by the *ejidatarios* themselves but by professional intermediaries or developers who bought the land from the individual *ejidatarios*, parcelled it out into lots of mostly between 120 and 250 square metres and sold them on credit. By this means the settlement process began between 1970 and 1980, when the population of the area now included in Valle de Chalco Solidaridad almost doubled from 44,000 to 82,000 individuals, living in about 18 *colonias*. During the following decade, it increased still more to about 220,000 reaching over 323,000 individuals in 2000.

The state embarked on an extensive regularization process, and a survey in 1998 found that 90% of the plots in Valle de Chalco had been regularized. Once this was underway, material improvements could be financed by the new federal poverty programme Solidaridad, which invested 407.9 million pesos (about US$160 million) in Valle de Chalco between 1989 and 1993, including street lighting, water mains and schools, then electrification, hospitals, pavements and main drainage. However, this regularization of tenure, public works and social investment programmes, as well as an influx of national and international NGOs and religious groups, is not reflected in the 2000 housing indicators: 78% of the dwellings have no inside tap; 40% have corrugated cardboard roofing; and 20% have only one room. Today, Valle de Chalco still contains some of the worst housing conditions in Mexico City.

Source: Mexico City case study, 2002.

Box 5.22 Mumbai: Prakash Nagar Pavement Community

This settlement originated 35 years ago; by 1998, it had 300 households who were made up of different ethnic groups. Most workers have daily wage-based activities on construction sites or domestic work. Dwellings are small and consist of plastic sheets precariously arranged on wooden poles. The community has faced demolition three to four times a year since 1985, generally without notice, including finally being evicted for the construction of a flyover in 1999. However, the community struggled to retain their foothold and has re-housed itself on a nearby privately owned plot, wishing to live in the vicinity in order to sustain livelihoods. Many households have filed applications for the necessary 'photo pass' in order to validate their residence in the community since 1994. Currently, the community is counter-claiming at the local courts and the National Human Rights Commission against their treatment by the authorities.

Source: Mumbai case study, 2002.

The threat of eviction is probably the most potent force in galvanizing communities – it can help to transform a heterogeneous group of households, settled in a particular locality, into a community

LEGALITY, VULNERABILITY AND SPATIAL FORMS

As has been pointed out above, not all slums are squatter or illegal settlements, and not all illegal or squatter settlements are slums. Therefore, legality and resident perception of its relative vulnerability are important considerations, both to the process and nature of viable development interventions. Indeed, it is commonly held that legality, or security of tenure to land and property, is the single most important criterion in any slum upgrading or regularization process.

Illegal

The informality that makes it easy to access land in these settlements and to build dwellings may make it more difficult to obtain credit or to transfer or sell these rights to others

There are settlements that are illegal, either because they are squatter settlements, without the right to be on or use the land, or the land on which they are settled has not been designated for housing and related activity in the statutory land uses of the city. Few cities in developing countries actually have up-to-date statutory land-use or zoning plans. In theory, residents of illegally occupied land are very vulnerable to being evicted as they have no right to occupy the land. However, what usually matters more, in practice, is the extent to which legality is enforced – and this may be not at all.

The literature on slums has made much of legality and the threat of eviction as the key to determining the level and extent of investment and other decisions. In practice, while the threat of eviction makes an enormous impact on the perceptions and, therefore, the behaviour and priorities of the slum dwellers, not all of their actions are governed exclusively by it. The threat of eviction is probably the most potent force in galvanizing communities – it can help to transform a heterogeneous group of households, settled in a particular locality, into a community. However, while the actual threat is there, it is likely to divert attention away from more long-term or development-oriented activities. If the threat is withdrawn, however, the community may be sufficiently enabled by the experience to undertake more development activities that require a collective effort, investment or the pooling of resources.

Many slums are built on land that is designated for housing, and the occupiers have a legal right to be there. However, the layout or type of housing may not have been given formal consent; often it may not have been sought! Essentially, dwellings in this type of settlement do not comply with municipal regulations. Consequently, these settlements may be denied access or connections to the urban infrastructure, or they may not have their land title registered or recognized. This will make it difficult or impossible for residents to obtain any form of certificate of title, access to housing finance and other such facilities. Thus, many settlements are unable to develop beyond basic structures and householders cannot use the value of their property as collateral for credit to invest in enterprises or development.

Informal

In many countries, the process of registering title to urban land and obtaining permission to develop it is a relatively recent introduction. Therefore, as has always happened in many rural areas, households settle and construct their dwellings without any thought to their formal recognition. For this reason, many well-established settlements are considered informal – this is a common occurrence in the peri-urban areas of many African cities. Thus, strictly speaking, these are illegal settlements; but, in practice, it is unlikely that urban authorities would test this in court and they prefer to adopt a more tolerant, *laissez faire* approach.

However, the informality that makes it easy to access land in these settlements and to build dwellings may make it more difficult to obtain credit or to transfer or sell these rights to others. While generally constraining, this has advantages in that it makes it equally difficult for settlers to give up their land at a lower-than-market price to cash buyers who are more aware of the potential of the particular location.

Box 5.23 Phnom Penh: living in the grounds of a pagoda

A settlement of 60 households has developed along a dirt lane leading to the pagoda because of the proximity to the city centre and jobs. Most heads of households are unskilled construction workers or vendors, and find work on nearby construction sites and markets. To settle on this public land, each household had to pay a bribe of US$10 to US$20 (approximately, one week's earnings) to the Sangkat authority as a 'registration fee'. The majority (around half) live in low-quality shelters with roofs and walls of palm, floors of recycled plywood, and doors and shutters of leaves. Around one third live in better dwellings with zinc roofs, thatched walls, wood floors, palm doors and shutters, and equipped with a bed, a table, a few dishes and pots, and a stove. The remainder are the poorest, often widows, sleeping on floors, living in shacks made of palm and old rice sacks, with no door or window, and furnished only with basic cooking utensils.

Source: Phnom Penh case study, 2002.

DEVELOPMENT DYNAMICS

Even within similar common geographical regions or contexts, settlements that share common characteristics in terms of age, origin, location and legality may still vary considerably. Different drivers and dynamics of development, both from internal (community) and external

(NGO or other agency interventions) will render living conditions vastly different.

The first two criteria within this category are based on the community's inherent perception of, and attitude towards, their ownership of the physical environment based on the origin of that settlement. The second two criteria cover the impacts of external or 'upgrading' interventions.

Ongoing individual and community-led development

Individual or household-led development is manifest in very many slum areas. Without perceived security of tenure, access to some means of generating livelihoods, and the necessary capacity to manage threats such as environmental hazards, the majority of slum dwellers are unlikely to make incremental improvements to their own housing and living conditions.

The extent to which there is community cohesion and organization to undertake broader development initiatives that serve the wider neighbourhood depends, partly, on the social structures of the neighbourhood and, partly, on either a supportive or a benign attitude by the authorities – which gives residents confidence that there will be no eviction. Where other settlements have experienced upgrading and improvements, there may be spin-offs as other neighbourhoods emulate the improvements. However, where settlements have been regularly subjected to evictions and demolitions, there may be a reluctance to take any action that would bring the neighbourhood to the notice of the authorities.

Intervention-led improved slums

These are settlements where some intervention has been made to improve one or more aspects of the settlement, housing or social and economic facilities and opportunities; however, they have not had a complete upgrading project.

The actual impact of such interventions is liable to vary, depending, in part, on what has been improved or introduced. More importantly, perhaps, is the way in which the improvements were performed. Often, they are part of a local politician's efforts to improve his/her standing and to win votes. This may have been done in a way that residents feel was only necessary; rather than being grateful, residents may see it for what it is: a bribe. Many settlements are very well aware of their voting power in countries where elections are regular occurrences (such as in India).

Ironically, where these improvements have been the result of a struggle that has taken time and effort, it probably also helps to create a greater sense of community. The resulting improvements, therefore, are more likely to have an enabling effect, empowering the residents to increase their efforts to further improve the settlements.

Upgraded slums

These are slums that have been the subject of a fairly comprehensive upgrading and improvement programme,

---

Box 5.24 Illegal districts in Rabat-Salé, Morocco

Illegal districts in the Rabat-Salé agglomeration have housing varying from concrete versions of traditional buildings to poor-quality dwellings. They are built on purchased plots of land, but without appropriate permits. Because they are illegal, these districts are also often deprived of the basic infrastructure; but conditions vary considerably. Older housing estates, for instance Hajja and Maadid in Rabat, appear less 'planned' but now include gardens and market gardens. More recently, larger settlements have been informally 'designed' in anticipation of achieving legal status. They appear similar to legal housing with respect to street network, division into blocks, and size and homogeneity of plots of land. Such is the case of the most recent part of Hay Inbiat and Oued ed Dehheb in Salé, or of Sidi Taibi. The last is a huge housing estate whose environment, currently, greatly benefits from its proximity to the rural environment.

Source: Rabat-Salé case study, 2002.

---

whether gradually over time or as a one-off intervention. Nevertheless, the intervention may not have reversed the basic conditions, or – if it did – there is no guarantee that improvements will last long. Furthermore, improved conditions can serve to attract more households to the settlement, increasing pressure on the housing and services to create, once again, slum-like conditions.

It is also often the case that, while a settlement may have had a project or a programme of upgrading, in practice, the application of the funds and efforts were superficial, and much of the funding might never have reached the settlement. In some cases, where such insensitive upgrading occurred, the neighbourhood condition has been worsened by it.[32] Most city authorities now recognize the need to address the problems of slums and squatter settlements in their cities and to do so in partnership with residents.

There is another possibility where, although a slum has been upgraded, the residents refuse to acknowledge the upgrading – not because the improvements have not happened, but because there are often positive-discrimination measures that benefit the slum dwellers who would lose those benefits if their settlement were no longer a slum. On the other hand, the fact that the settlement was once a slum may

---

Box 5.25 Informal areas in Cairo

In Cairo, informal areas have developed on former desert state-owned land. The history of the settlements varies according to location. For example, Manshiet Nasser began as a relocation site for slum dwellers and garbage collectors, and Ezbet El Haggana began as a hamlet for the households of coast guard soldiers stationed nearby. However, in each case, a core settlement was allowed to take hold, and expanded as the neglect of the government towards its own property became apparent. Usually, quite large plots on the fringes of the established core were walled, and then sub-parcels would be sold by these pioneers to other settlers. The rate of growth of individual communities varied greatly, with spurts of expansion at certain periods being quite common. The development process was completely informal, with no legal paper work and a total reliance on personal trust, mediated, when necessary, by the existing community, referred to as a 'hand claim' process. Although these areas are technically illegal, settlers have certain customary rights derived from interpretations of those portions of the civil code pertaining to hand claims on desert land. Residents tend to amass either the receipts from paying *tahkir* (a nominal rent imposed by a Governorate's Amlak (Properties) Department) or awayyid (property tax), from electrical connections, and from other items to establish as much paper legitimacy as possible.

Source: Cairo case study, 2002.

Table 5.2

Table 5.2

Summary of opportunities linked to tenure

	Characteristics	Opportunities for upgrading
Communities sited legally on public land – mainly owner-occupiers	Situated in the older and more central parts of the city.	Less likely to resort to community-based action if local municipality has provided a certain level of service.
	Standard of provision of infrastructure is moderate, though much of it may be run down and in a poor state of repair. Overcrowded.	However, housing upgrade schemes could be embraced – potential profits to be gained are a driving factor.
Communities sited legally on public land – mainly tenants	Occupied by low- and middle-income households in walk-up flats.	Tenants unwilling to pay more in rent to improve conditions.
	Maintenance and services are the responsibility of local government but are likely to be inadequate due to low-rental income.	Improvements possible if ownership and responsibility for conditions are transferred – this situation best supports the creation of housing and community associations to manage common areas and coordinate upgrading and repairs.
Communities sited illegally on public land – mainly occupiers of own structures/houses only	Comprises a variety of locations and sizes. Many such communities are able to remain on the land through the intervention of a local self-styled 'protector' with appropriate influence.	Communities keen to obtain security of tenure and legal title to their homes. Communities seek recognition for the whole group, with individual scope to buy their own title over time.
		Usually very keen to upgrade.
Communities sited illegally on public land – mainly renters of structures/houses	Few settlements of this type. Frequently, though not necessarily, made up of people who see themselves as temporary to the city – for example, seasonal workers.	Residents have little incentive to upgrade due to transitory nature and level of tenure insecurity.
Communities sited legally on private land – mainly owner-occupiers	Consisting of middle-income households keen to make an investment.	Forging 'community' difficult.
		Less keen on managing services themselves; prefer to 'buy' services.
Communities sited legally on private land – mainly tenants	High demand for security of tenure and willing to invest their time, money and effort into upgrading, in return for a guaranteed period of rent freezes and no eviction.	Landlords benefit from gradual upgrading of their property, though tenants may be apprehensive about resulting rent increase.
Communities sited illegally on private land – mainly occupiers of self-built structures/houses	Such squatter settlements are few but exist where there is a powerful patron, political leader or other intermediary to provide protection.	Securing tenure is the primary objective in these cases with any upgrading possibility that security of tenure provides.
Communities sited illegally on private land – mainly tenants	Less likely to be interested in security of tenure without, correspondingly, more secure economic situation. Distinction to be made between tenants temporary to the city and those unable to acquire their own housing.	Differential pricing required to cater to different characteristics of the tenants.

Box 5.26 Mexico City: Ciudad Netzahualcóyotl

Ciudad Netzahualcóyotl is a vast irregular settlement built on the Texcoco lake-bed. Since the draining of the lake in 1900, a series of government acts that dealt with selling and regaining the land, coupled with the existence of historic titles, rendered the legal tenure situation of plots and properties complex and ambiguous. However, the first settlements came about in the 1950s, after speculators 'sold' unserviced plots for development. Subsequent resale was legal in the sense that development was authorized by the state government. However, at the same time, this was illegal, because building failed to comply with state regulations for urban services – paved roads, street lighting, water and sewerage mains and areas for public facilities. Nevertheless, hundreds of thousands of unserviced plots were sold and resold to create a rectangular grid of plots averaging 150 square metres. Towards the end of the 1960s, the population was approaching 600,000.

Over half of the population was in *colonias*, without any form of drainage or water supply. Severe conflicts arose out of the irregular tenure and multiple sales of the same plot of land. The *colonos* (settlers) organized on a massive scale to form what was one of the first urban movements, the Movimiento Restaurador de Colonos, demanding incarceration of the land developers for fraud, expropriation of the land and regularization of tenure, together with the introduction of services. After a decisive monthly payment strike, the federal government stepped in with a solution that would eventually meet the demands of the *colonos*, but at a price. Some of the developers were jailed for fraud. But most of them cooperated with the government, putting their stake in the land – their portfolio of credits – into a specially created trust, Fideicomiso de Ciudad Nezahualcóyotl (FINEZA), set up in 1973, which would effectively regularize 43 of the 83 *colonias* in the municipality. After lengthy negotiation, an agreement was reached in 1977 on payments and, a year later, over 60,000 properties were regularized. In 1981, FINEZA, as a federal trust, was abolished, and the portfolio and functions were later handed over to the state government organization, Comisión para la Regulación del Uso del Suelo del Estado de México (CRESEM). Under CRESEM, regularization accelerated; by 1991, titles to a total of 159,000 lots had been issued. By the late 1990s, only an estimated 12% of the plots in Netzahualcóyotl had irregular land titles.

Most of the *colonias* in the municipality had electricity by the early 1970s. However, street lighting, paved roads, water and drainage were only introduced after the regularization process was under way, starting with the main thoroughfares. By 1980, most of the streets were paved and supplied with main water lines and drains. During this time, the population doubled to over 1.3 million, due to the influx of households who could pay higher prices for serviced land, and also to the proliferation of rented housing of all categories. During the 1990s, the population actually fell as Netzahualcóyotl was the principal exporter of population to other areas of Mexico City. The resident population is now highly mixed, as is the quality of housing: 63% of dwellings have inside tap water, for instance, while 15% have poor-quality roofing.

Consolidation resulted in more than improvement – albeit unequal – in housing conditions and diversification of social class. Over the past two decades, trees, banks, shops, offices, libraries, schools, universities, cinemas and even McDonalds have all appeared on the main streets of Netzahualcóyotl, which also has its own cathedral and Olympic sports stadium. What was once considered a 'slum dormitory' is now the place of employment of 262 thousand people: over 4% of Mexico City's economically active population.

Source: Mexico City case study, 2002.

carry a stigma that residents may not be able to shake off, even after the settlement has been upgraded.

Upgraded settlements are likely to have much better facilities and urban services than other slums. They may also have had the benefit of cash handouts or access to loans and other forms of financial assistance that would have enabled the residents to improve their housing and, indeed, their means of earning a livelihood. They may, even, have been 'promoted' out of slum status.

Lacking community incentives for improvement

There are instances when residents expect slums to provide only the bare minimum in terms of shelter, and the individual residents and owners have no incentive to undertake improvements. Where residents are temporary, pay little rent, do not feel part of a community network, and where the building itself is owned by an (absentee) landlord, there is little reason for individuals and households to invest in order to improve those living environments. The owners also often have little incentive, owing to rent control legislation, or where the asset no longer has economic potential in terms of location near industry. In the case of industry-provided housing – for example, chawls in India, hostels in Southern Africa – the building fabric does not easily lend itself to affordable conversion and upgrading.

Incipient slum creation

Where poverty is growing, there is a high probability of slum appearance. Many established historic city slums and others in the centre of cities fit this description. Where there is multiple ownership through inheritance (for example, family houses and old tenements), occupants are likely to be too poor to carry out major renovations and owners are unlikely to agree to pay, especially where rent control is in force. It is estimated that 5 per cent of Moscow's housing stock of 'first-generation' prefabricated apartment blocks built at the end of the 1950s falls into the category of housing that is in urgent need of replacement or upgrading. More than

---

Box 5.27 'Incipient slums' in Moscow

After Perestroika during the 1990s, Moscow's city authority experienced for the first time the difficulties of dealing with an influx of economic immigrants, particularly from former Soviet Republic states. Refugees and homeless beggars began to crowd railway stations, airports and subways, and migrants to the city sought temporary accommodation in 'squatter flats' and, to a lesser extent, in abandoned buildings awaiting demolition. The squatter flats are often in former municipal dormitories or barracks built in and around industrial zones in the middle belt of the city, during the 1950s, in order to provide temporary shelter for in-migrant workers, called *obschagi* (Russian jargon for 'dormitories'). Almost 700 dormitories currently exist, typically four- to five-storey high brick buildings, but occasionally one- or two-storey wooden or brick structures with a rudimentary infrastructure. They are overcrowded with refugees, illegal immigrants and seasonal workers. Present-day residents pay very little or no rent at all, often renting or sub-renting illegally and waiting for the alternative of state housing or support. Poor maintenance and vandalism has hastened their deterioration; but employers (they should, by law, provide accommodation for the incoming workers, such as a room or an apartment) have no incentive to invest in the repair and maintenance of buildings if they recognize that the housing is 'dilapidated'. The backlog of housing in Moscow, however, is such that municipal housing has a long waiting list and people will continue to live in deteriorated locales.

Source: Moscow case study, 2002.

318,000 households live in such housing. Box 5.27 gives additional details in this respect.

The deterioration and degradation of such housing estates has been hastened by the poor quality of construction and materials. In many instances, especially in Soviet-assisted and inspired economies, where prefabrication and mass production were widespread, poor attention to design details and the lack of adequate site supervision during the construction phase accounts for much of the rapid and dangerous deterioration in both structures and cladding. Around one third of Moscow's housing stock is of mass-industrial housing production built during the period 1955 to 1970. It is primarily located in the mid-zone between the central and peripheral districts. Typically, five-storey prefabricated concrete buildings, some 40 per cent of them, suffer from engineering and construction faults.[33]

NOTES

1 This chapter draws on an initial draft prepared by Patrick Wakely in collaboration with Babar Mumtaz and Kate Clifford, Development Planning Unit, University College London, UK.
2 See Chapter 1.
3 Tipple, 2000.
4 Lloyd, 1979.
5 See Chapter 2.
6 Tipple and Willis, 1991; Malpezzi and Ball, 1991.
7 Case study – Mumbai, 2002.
8 Case study – Beirut, 2002.
9 Case study – Rabat-Salé, 2002.

10 Case study – Bogotá, 2002.
11 Case study – Jakarta, 2002.
12 Case studies – Durban, Ahmedabad, Mumbai and Chengdu, 2002.
13 Case study – Chengdu, 2002.
14 Case study – Lima, 2002.
15 Case study – Phnom Penh, 2002.
16 Payne, 2002.
17 Case study – São Paulo, 2002.
18 Case study – Nairobi, 2002.
19 Case study – Nairobi, 2002.
20 A S Dasgupta, New Delhi, pers comm, based on his work in

public housing in Kalkaji and Lakshmi Nagar.
21 Tipple, 2000.
22 Case studies – Cairo and Karachi, 2002.
23 Case studies – Durban, Ahmedabad, Mumbai and Chengdu, 2002.
24 The extensive literature on segregation, spatial isolation and social exclusion in European cities includes Andersson, 1999; Bolt et al, 1998; Harth et al, 1998; Krantz et al, 1999; Lee, 1999; Lee and Murie, 1999; Madanipour et al,

1998; Musterd and Ostendorf, 1998; Power, 1997; Taylor, 1998.
25 Case study – Chengdu, 2002.
26 Tipple and Willis, 1991; Malpezzi and Ball, 1991.
27 Amole et al, 1993.
28 Case study – Rio de Janeiro, 2002.
29 Boris and Prügl, 1996.
30 Case studies – Mumbai, Karachi and Nairobi, 2002.
31 Case study – Mumbai, 2002.
32 Case study – Mexico City, 2002.
33 Case study – Moscow, 2002.

CHAPTER 6

ECONOMIC DYNAMICS[1]

People come together in cities for wealth creation, and the creation of income has been considered to be the prime measure of urban success until fairly recently, when quality of life concerns became more prominent

As Chapter 2 discussed, demographics, the economy and, ultimately, the environment, set the major frameworks in which cities flourish or struggle. The principal reason for cities to form in the first place is the generation of wealth and income, and their economic opportunities are why they continue to attract redundant agricultural labour away from rural areas.

As Chapter 3 pointed out, the formal economic sector is the major engine of city growth. But larger enterprises are backed up by very many much smaller ones, which are generally the principal source of employment for both skilled and unskilled labour. Except in the most regulated societies such as the highly industrialized countries have become, these smaller enterprises merge almost seamlessly into what is known as the informal sector of unregistered enterprises and people struggling to scrape a living through informal transactions. Where there are no social support systems, the urban informal sector supports the poor, the needy and new immigrants who have not yet been able to find more permanent employment.

While informal work, like poverty, is by no means confined to irregular housing or slums, in fact slums tend to form the epicentre or principal source of informal labour, and within slums most economic activity is informal. Following a general comparative discussion of incomes and changing labour market trends in different parts of the world, the chapter has as its principal topics: the informal or irregular urban sector in employment, its characteristics and anticipated future growth, and, finally, the importance of secure tenure for citizens to establish roots and opportunities within their communities.

LABOUR FORCE GROWTH

The growth in the global labour force has imposed enormous strains on urban settings, especially on employment and housing. As the formal sector has failed to meet such demands, the informal sector has taken up the slack

Poverty and lack of income, as discussed in the previous chapters, are among the most important factors in establishing and maintaining slums, and the labour market and the structure of livelihood opportunities becomes at least as important a concern as housing conditions. Many housing schemes have failed because they have ignored the community and livelihood basis of why people settle where they do in the dwellings they occupy. Income generation and credit schemes, in which the labour market and the structure of livelihood opportunities are the main concerns, have, accordingly, become an important part of the current generation of slum interventions. This section looks at what is known about employment for low-income earners, particularly those living in slums and working in the informal and private sectors.

The creation and distribution of income

Urban history shows that people come together in cities for wealth creation, and the creation of income has been considered to be the prime measure of urban success until fairly recently, when quality of life concerns became more prominent. In general, incomes and productivity are higher in urban areas, and this is borne out in the comparison of national gross domestic product (GDP) and average city product presented in Table 6.1.

It remains clear, however, that the largest gaps between developed and developing countries are in incomes, product and capital, and in the forms of consumption and investment that this permits. Average household income is about 17 times as great in cities in the developed countries as in the poorest 20 per cent of cities, and city product and GDP per person are 37 times as large.

Within countries, there may also be a tremendous differential in incomes. In Brazil in 1998, for example, average annual income in a relatively rich city such as Rio de Janeiro was about US$15,000, similar to smaller cities in Europe, whereas income in Icapui, a small, remote city, was

Table 6.1

Urban economic indicators by City Development Index (CDI) quintile, 1998

CDI quintile	GDP per capita (US$)	City product per person (US$)	Household income (US$)	Informal employment[i] (%)	Unemployment rate[i] (%)
1	606	571	1512	49	15
2	1571	1329	2593	51	16
3	2087	2409	3917	40	12
4	3230	3539	5521	26	12
5	11,822	12,842	16,743	19	7
All developing	2670	2988	4761	37	12

Note: i There is no clear distinction between informally employed (employed in unregistered enterprises) and unemployed, which relates to those actively seeking work in the formal sector. Quite often, officially unemployed people will work in the informal sector, so there may be double counting.
Source: UN-Habitat, 2002f.

US$1360, below that of many cities in least developed countries (LDCs). Within cities, average neighbourhood incomes can fluctuate by almost as much as this.

The global labour force

As Figure 6.1 shows, labour force participation rates in the developing world have been rising quite rapidly from low points around 1970. The most significant increases have been in Latin America, where participation rates have increased from 33 per cent to 43 per cent since 1970, and in East and Southeast Asia.[2] Here, they have risen from 42 per cent to almost 50 per cent since 1970, and are set to go higher than the high income countries (HICs) in the next ten years (which have a dependency rate of about 50 per cent). The falling dependency rates are thought to have allowed the savings that were responsible for the 'Asian Miracle' since 1980.[3]

Participation rates in South Asia and sub-Saharan Africa have been very similar over the period, and have still not come back to 1950 levels. North Africa and West Asia show much lower participation rates for cultural reasons that exclude women from the work force.

The breakdown by industry also shows very significant trends. Firstly, as expected from increasing agricultural productivity and urbanization, agricultural employment has diminished its share, from about 80 per cent to 60 per cent of the work force between 1950 and 1990, across all developing countries (this compares with 9 per cent in the more developed countries). About 12 per cent of the extra share has gone to services and 8 per cent to manufacturing.

Relative incomes have fluctuated over an extended period. The long growth period from 1945 to 1973 was typified by falling inequality and improving equity. The situation then reversed: income inequality and poverty increased without respite during the recession years from 1978 to 1993, and real incomes actually fell for the bottom-income groups in most countries and for the world as a whole – with a resulting increase in income poverty. The reasons are very much contested and are discussed in Chapters 2 and 3. They include the withdrawal of the state, the cyclical nature of capitalism, increased demand for skilled labour, and the possible effects of globalization – all of which are connected.

The level of non-agricultural employment in a country is a good proxy for the level of development – with the exception of Southern Africa, which has a substantial manufacturing sector, and East Asia, which still has a relatively lower level of urbanization.

Contrary to popular belief, industry has not lost its share of employment very much in the more developed countries overall since 1950, although it peaked around 1970 at 38 per cent. By comparison, less developed countries averaged 16 per cent. The vast bulk of manufactured goods are produced and exported from the more developed countries, as well as East and Southeast Asia. The service sector has at least doubled its share in every region and has been the main gainer everywhere. It is

those countries that have been able to turn their economies toward producer services, in particular, that have the high per capita incomes.[4]

The growth in the global labour force has imposed enormous strains on urban settings, especially on employment and housing. As the formal sector has failed to provide the factories, offices, market halls, transport facilities and housing required by the urban work force, the informal sector has taken up the slack. The location of work places is often in slum areas, and the conditions and characteristics of workers' accommodation have created slum areas.

At the same time, the interaction with rural areas has become complex, and many so-called rural workers are dependent on cities for their livelihoods. For example, in Thailand, people in the urban peripheries can travel to nearby urban areas very cheaply on good quality roads, so that informal traders commute up to 200 kilometres daily to set up stalls in Bangkok. Although 49 per cent of the labour force is still nominally engaged in agriculture, around two-thirds of income from farm households is from non-agricultural sources, directly or indirectly derived from urban activities.[5]

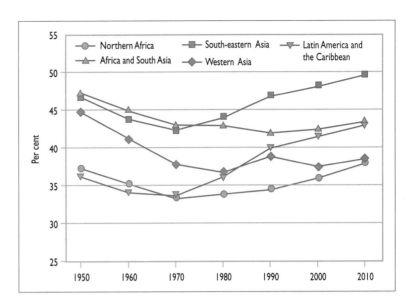

Figure 6.1

Labour force participation rates, 1950 to 2010, selected regions

Source: International Labour Organization (ILO) online database: www.ilo.org

Figure 6.2

Employment in agricultural sector, 1950 to 1990, selected regions

Note: Asia (South, Southeast and East) has agricultural employment very close to the developing country average

Source: International Labour Organization (ILO) online database: www.ilo.org

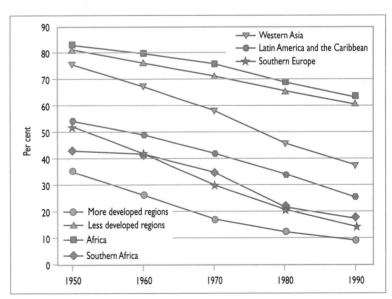

There have been considerable changes in the demographic and gender composition of the work force in the HICs, with many of the new jobs going to women. This has resulted in greater income inequality between households and changing spatial inequality. On the one hand, the dominant new family economic unit in the cities has become the 'double income no kids yet' (DINKYs), who have gentrified the centres of many cities.[6] Many married women with children, as well as young people, now have part-time jobs, and these lower earnings steepen the individual income profile. On the other hand, the number of low-income single parent households and single person households has increased, also skewing the income distribution.[7]

Most developed economies have substantially restructured their work forces, with an increasing professionalization, and this has been compounded by globalization.[8] The effect has been documented in many places as a 'hollowing out' of the work force. In much of the developing world, and particularly in slums, most of the employment is not formal wage labour at all, but takes place in a myriad of small, informal enterprises. Self-employment (mostly informal sector) is far higher in the developing countries, and social transfers are minimal. The informal or small enterprise 'competitive' economy has increased in size following the recession of the 1970s and subsequent liberalization.[9] Lay-offs have led to an increase in self-employment, casualization of the work force has led workers to seek supplementary earnings, and new immigrants, who tend to be excluded from more formal work opportunities, establish small businesses within an increasingly crowded and competitive economic environment.[10]

Owing to a lack of suitable workshops and commercial space (at costs that small firms can afford and locations close to home and customers), most informal-sector activities in slums take place in the streets and homes. Both are seen as a problem in official minds as they encroach on public circulation spaces and private living space. Their occurrence is so frequent that the idea of the neighbourhood as a factory has been posited and recent research work proposes that the inevitability of jobs occurring in slums should be acknowledged in service levels at the planning stage. Informal-sector entrepreneurs and employees are such an important sector of the adult population – the potential voters – that good governance is not served by ignoring them or, worse, harassing them. Recent social conflict in Nairobi was not between workers and employers (apart from teachers) but between informal-sector traders (hawkers) and the authorities. It is clear that the blanket condemnation of informal-sector employment opportunities within slums must cease and be replaced with the types of assistance and promotion available to formal-sector enterprises. The issue of the informal economy is taken up in more detail later in this chapter.

Unemployment and underemployment

Unemployment is part of the formal labour market, describing those people who are actively seeking work and are unable to find it. It is largely irrelevant in countries with large informal sectors because virtually everyone (including children) is involved in a number of economic activities in order to live, and the conceptual separation of workers and non-workers is meaningless.

In developed countries, however, unemployment levels are possibly *the* major indicator of the health of the economy. They are very politically sensitive and governments have fallen following changes in the indicator (though this fear is lessening somewhat with the casualization and deregulation of the work force). Since 1970, unemployment has risen very substantially in most Organisation for Economic Co-operation and Development (OECD) countries – from 'full employment' rates of less than 2 per cent to rates typically in excess of 8 per cent. It is this change that spurred governments to fight back with wage incentives that weakened their tax bases and their employment conditions during the period of 1980 to 1995.

Unemployment is also seen as a primary indicator of spatial disadvantage in developed countries – more commonly, in fact, than poverty – and social budgets have been directed at high unemployment areas using needs-based indicators. On the negative side, areas with high unemployment levels are often singled out as slums or proto-slums, sitting within the public gaze. The inability of people to join the core economy is seen as a primary sign of 'social parasitism' by those holding individualist philosophies: single mothers and the unemployed are easy targets for those looking for a victim to blame for any perceived inadequacy in society.

People often attach their self-worth to their job, and losing it can be deeply depressing, making it difficult for them to function properly or to find new work. In the current deregulated era, in which no one has a job for life and lay-offs and early retirement schemes are all too frequent, job insecurity has been the major cause of the anomie and perception of deep social insecurity that has repeatedly been expressed in consumer surveys. This is particularly the case for workers over 50 who now find it very difficult to be re-employed and may be forced into an involuntary premature retirement. The continuing malaise during the late 1990s might be considered surprising given the upbeat nature of many economies. In the boom period of the late 1990s, unemployment fell to low levels in some countries – 4 per cent in the US, for example – and labour markets became tight in industries in high demand, such as information technology.[11] Unemployment rates were fairly stable, with a slight decrease in unemployment in 24 of the 28 more advanced economies, while distinguishable increases occurred in only four countries in that grouping (France, Greece, Japan and Malta). Youth unemployment remained an unsatisfactory area. In many economies, the young labour force also found it difficult to find employment, just as they had during the previous two decades. In some of the OECD countries, Spain, Belgium, Finland and France, unemployment of those aged 15 to 24 remained above the 20 per cent mark. The falling unemployment rates in a number of industrialized economies, following the relatively sound period of economic growth during the last half decade of the 1990s, were, nonetheless, associated with an increase, or at least a stabilization, of rates

Most developed economies have substantially restructured their work forces, with an increasing professionalization. In much of the developing world, and particularly in slums, most of the employment is in a myriad of small, informal enterprises

Unemployment levels are possibly *the* major indicator of the health of the economy

of time-related underemployment. This indicated that the manner in which people attempted to adjust to downward changes in labour demand was to accept short-time work rather than not work at all.[12]

The transitional countries also knew unemployment for the first time during the 1990s. Bulgaria, Poland and Romania reported youth unemployment rates of over 30 per cent. Most of the damage was done in the period up to 1995. The International Labour Organization (ILO) reports that rates were fairly stable or decreasing for ten economies, while they increased for both men and women in ten others. Informal economic activity, including open-air markets, also substantially increased, as the anticipated more formal private markets failed to appear following the collapse of the Council for Mutual Economic Assistance (Comecon) and the disappearance of organized state markets and distribution channels.[13]

In the 17 Asian and Pacific economies with ILO data, where the economic crisis recently hit hard, the total unemployment rates increased in 11 economies, even doubling or more in the Republic of Korea and Thailand. It is interesting to note, however, that in many of these economies there was a corresponding increase in the labour force, implying that economic hardship was dealt with, in part, by individuals previously outside of the labour force (usually women) rejoining the work force in order to offset a loss of household income resulting from unemployment. Furthermore, the unemployment situation in the 'crisis' economies seems to have improved during the past couple of years. Men seem to have suffered worse unemployment than women in economies such as the Republic of Korea, which indicates that it was probably heavy industry (which is largely male-dominated) that was harder hit in these economies.

Among the 37 Latin American and Caribbean economies, unemployment rates increased in 15, decreased in 7, and remained relatively stable in the remaining economies. Twelve sub-Saharan African economies show high unemployment rates, with figures in the high double digits. Only Nigeria and Zimbabwe stated rates below 7 per cent after 1995 – but given the high informal employment in African countries, these figures are not very meaningful.

In most economies for which unemployment data are available, women tend to have higher unemployment rates than men, although notable exceptions during the past few years exist in the Baltic States, in parts of East Asia and in some highly industrialized economies, such as Australia, Canada, Japan, New Zealand and the UK. There are four possible reasons for this general trend, according to the ILO:

1　Women are more likely to leave and then re-enter the labour force for personal (often family-related) reasons. Because of their higher entry and exit rates at any one time, proportionally more non-employed women will be looking for a job.

2　Owing to the general crowding of women into fewer occupations than men, women may have fewer opportunities to find employment (in other words, there is greater competition for the jobs that are available to women).

3　Women in many economies are more likely than men to lack the level and range of education and training required for many types of employment.

4　Women may be the first to be affected by the lay-offs that usually accompany restructuring, perhaps owing to preconceived ideas concerning the 'breadwinner', and also because women tend to be more recent entrants into the labour force and will therefore be more affected by seniority rules.

Labour market abuses

Employees in developed countries have made very painful steps towards the rights that they enjoy, such as safe work places, fixed hours, wage awards, various benefits including pensions, and protection against harassment or unfair dismissal. These gains have involved work place solidarity, bitter union disputes or political activism over an extended period, and their weakening in the deregulated 1990s has been a bitter pill for many to swallow. It has also provided a major reason why globalization and the export of jobs has been so bitterly opposed by the left, since it is known that workers in the developing world have none of these benefits, have far lower wages and are believed to be exploited in performing the same work.

In fact, the labour market abuses in the developing world can be far worse than anything conceived of in the West, and any job with a foreign firm is usually seen as a stroke of luck since their conditions and pay are usually better than local employers give. Multinationals are rarely seen as overtly exploitative in local terms because of the scrutiny that they are under and their need to attract reliable labour.[14]

The most seriously regarded abuses are those affecting children, and countries have moved very quickly to ratify the ILO Worst Forms of Child Labour Convention 1999. The ILO estimates that 211 million children under the age of 15 were economically active in 2000, or about 18 per cent of the total, of which more than half were involved in hazardous work. About 30 per cent of children in Africa and 19 per cent of children in Asia were economically active in 2000. The worst abuses that are universally condemned and involve 8.4 million children are shown in Table 6.2.

The majority of these child labourers are in Asia, where forced and bonded labour is commonplace. Virtually all of these activities (except armed conflict) take place in urban areas and in the slums.

In most economies for which data are available, women tend to have higher unemployment rates

Table 6.2

Estimated number of children in unconditional worst forms of child labour

Type of abuse	Global estimate (000)
Trafficked children	1200
Children in forced and bonded labour	5700
Children in armed conflict	300
Children in prostitution and pornography	1800
Children in illicit activities (mostly drugs)	600
Total	8400

Source: ILO, 2002.

INFORMALITY WITHIN URBAN SETTINGS

It is important to understand the relationship between formal and informal sectors in the economy and housing in any discussion of slums. 'Informal' suggests a different way from the norm, one which breaches formal conventions and is not acceptable in formal circles – one which is inferior, irregular and, at least somewhat, undesirable. However, research and practice over the years have demonstrated that differences may not imply inferiority. While informal entrepreneurs may not follow legal requirements, their breaches may not outweigh the benefits that workers, neighbours and the economy draw from the enterprises. While informally constructed dwellings may not comply with building regulations and the occupiers may lack formal rights to the land, they provide accommodation that is unlikely to result in any other way in current circumstances. Although an informal settlement may be built on land zoned for industry and is, therefore, illegal, it provides accommodation, location and identity for its inhabitants at a cost that they can probably afford.

It is evident that the informal sector, in all its variations, is very large. Its contribution to national economies, especially in less developed countries, is very significant; more especially, its role in employment and survival in the poorer echelons of society is crucial. Without the ability to make a living that working in the home or street provides, many households would be in dire straits. Indeed, without the ability to run a business without paying for a specific building, much larger profits would be required for liquidity, let alone profit.

On the housing side, the informal sector delivers dwellings and accommodation at a price and in quantities that the formal sector fails to deliver. As profit-making is so difficult when low-cost housing and formal-sector institutions coincide, the formal housing delivery systems have rarely reached the low-income groups. The majority if not all poor households have been housed informally for many years in many countries.

In the past, the informality itself has often been enough to stigmatize enterprises and dwellings in the eyes of the authorities and to remove them from the purlieu of assistance programmes. This section discusses the nature and extent of informality in the economy, including the type of small-scale, home- or street-based economic activity that is predominant in slums.

The informal economy

■ Defining the informal sector

The term 'informal sector' has been used to describe a phenomenon that seems to be evident to most observers of economic development in rapidly growing cities: the generally small-scale industries and commercial activities that are not registered enterprises but provide large amounts of products and services that people use each day.

The early writings on the nature of the informal sector inferred separate and contrasting formal and informal sectors.[15] However, the reality is more complex as the two sectors are inter-linked in a number of ways. The term is now recognized to encompass very diverse enterprises that we know, intuitively, to be different from formal business and for which policies and programmes might be developed.[16]

The informal sector consists of units engaged in the production of goods or services with the following characteristics:[17]

*   Small-scale units, comprising, firstly, 'informal, own-account enterprises – that is, those unincorporated enterprises that are run without regular employees (but perhaps with unpaid family workers or occasional hired labour)'; and, secondly, enterprises of informal employers who employ one or more persons on a continuous basis.
*   Few barriers to entry: initial capital and skill requirements are low.
*   Informal skills acquisition: most entrepreneurs learn through informal apprenticeships in the sector, while a few have received vocational training.
*   Limited access to formal credit: capital needs are met informally from family, friends, money lenders and other business interests.[18]
*   An informal internal organization with a relatively flexible and informal hierarchy of work and roles: often the own account or self-employed worker is worker, manager and owner, all at once. They display little or no division between labour and capital as factors of production.[19]
*   Informal relationships with suppliers, clients and the state: few have licences or formal contracts, their hours of operation are flexible and contacts are irregular. They therefore tend to be 'invisible', unregulated and uncounted by official statistics, particularly by economic censuses. Thus, the entrepreneur avoids taxes, licence fees and requirements to conform to standards. Labour tends to be unprotected. Labour relations – where they exist – are based primarily on casual employment, kinship or personal and social relations, rather than on contractual arrangements with formal guarantees.
*   Combinations of different activities can exist in a single unit: these can exist simultaneously or by frequent change in activities, so it can be difficult to classify the business according to the standard industrial classification. Products may be made and sold in the same place and other producers' products may also be sold.
*   Predominance of an undercapitalized or labour-intensive process of production: the limited nature of the technology being used may hamper the ability of business to produce continuously and may limit the operator's ability to plan for investment and improved operation.
*   Consumption and production are not separated: part of what allows informal-sector businesses to keep operating is their use of personal and domestic assets,

While informally constructed dwellings may not comply with building regulations and the occupiers may lack formal rights, they provide accommodation that is unlikely to result in any other way in current circumstances such as living quarters, vehicles and furniture.[20] Furthermore, business expenditures, income, assets and labour are almost seamlessly linked to those of the household. This can be a problem for policy-makers who like to separate consumption and production as different spheres for statistical and taxation purposes.

Five theories, all of which are closely linked, explain why informal-sector activities persist in developing countries:[21]

1   The 'lack of growth' theory, in which the persistence of informal activities is owing to the lack of, or a decline in, the growth of GDP, particularly the lack of urban growth. This is based on the assumption that the share of the work force in modern or formal-sector employment increases as GDP per worker rises.
2   The 'jobless growth' theory, which assumes that capital-intensive technology and recent economic processes, such as privatization, deregulation and globalization, have led to two effects: the decline of formal-sector jobs or the informalization of certain formal-sector jobs.[22]
3   The 'growth from below' theory, which attributes some of the growth in GDP to the small-scale enterprise sector. This is based on the recognition that small-scale enterprises in the informal sector are growing faster in many countries than large-scale firms in the modern sector.
4   The 'period of adjustment' theory, which reflects how the informal sector grows when economies undergo structural adjustment, causing marked shifts from formal to informal employment.
5   Finally, there is simply the matter of institutional cost. The main justification for regulating enterprises is the extraction of business taxes and income tax. Conversely, regulation is an expensive business and it requires taxes on enterprises for it to succeed. If people are making so little money that there is no chance of taxing them, it seems pointless to register their enterprises. Furthermore, most informal enterprises have chosen not to register precisely because of the costs – in money and, especially, in time and harassment – of doing so.[23] However, informal entrepreneurs in many cities have to pay entry fees to informal-sector 'gate-keepers' and 'protection bribes' to local officials and the police.

■ The nature of informal-sector enterprises

The link between small-scale and informal-sector classification is so strong that a maximum of five or ten employees and a maximum turnover are often used to define enterprises as informal.[24] Micro-enterprises relate to the economy as a whole in three major groups:

1   The various forms of *casual work*, including temporary or seasonal activities. These include precarious survival activities such as carrying loads in the market and street vending at no fixed locale.[25]
2   Micro-enterprises that are *independent* and more or less stable, such as small shops and production operations, single-person firms in tailoring, wood- and metal-working, and repairing household paraphernalia and equipment.
3   *Subcontracting* micro-enterprises: this category is commonly referred to as 'outworking' or 'home-working'.

The 'independent' businesses tend to be the focus of most programmes that assist micro-enterprise; but many of the informal-sector workers most in need (especially women) are concentrated in the first and third groups.

There are informal-sector enterprises that compete with the formal sector and those that do not.[26] Those that compete with the formal sector do so without access to the technical advances and capital available to that sector. To survive, they must reduce incomes and profits (the returns to labour) and even use household assets for the business without compensation.[27] Those that do not compete directly with the formal sector tend to occupy 'niches' of economic activity that, for a variety of reasons, are not occupied by modern firms. These niches are constantly being changed, created and destroyed as the formal sector changes.[28] Both groups are subordinated to, and exploited by, the formal sector.[29] Even in the non-competing informal sector, many workers are successful informal entrepreneurs who run viable firms. Many entered the informal sector after a period as wage workers in the modern economy where they accumulated some savings, skills, equipment and/or contacts. By adopting the triple role of entrepreneur–capitalist–worker, they can achieve total incomes greater than comparable waged workers in the formal sector.[30]

A further two-way division of the informal sector can be made: those intent merely on subsistence, concentrating on the least risky or enterprising paths of development, and those that also have a capacity for accumulation. The latter have the potential to grow towards formal and modern entrepreneurship.[31] Though definitions may differ slightly at the margins, there is little separation in the literature between informal and small-scale or micro-enterprises, which are seen as inextricably linked. Typical informal-sector activities would be regarded as being 'small scale and characterized by low capital endowments, simple technologies, unremunerated family labour and flexible work sites'.[32]

Many of the characteristics of small-scale enterprises represent development strengths.[33] They tend to use labour-intensive methods and provide work for those living within local neighbourhoods (which may be far from formal work places). They tend to use a variety of local materials and a minimum of imported inputs. They develop from a very small scale, often in the home. They can give employment to skilled, unskilled and unemployed labour living in slums. Probably as important in times of a shrinking formal sector, they allow job opportunities for those with skills but without employment.

It is standard practice to include domestic service and many security tasks in the informal sector; but these tend

---

Box 6.1 Informal-sector workers in Quito, Ecuador

A study in Quito, in which informal-sector workers were enumerated according to their activity, shows clearly that domestic service is important as an informal employment source. Housekeepers are predominantly women; but cleaners, security guards and watchmen are predominantly men. Together, they form 30% of the informal-sector work force in Quito. Retailing is the largest source of work, with merchants and shopkeepers, their employees (sellers) and street vendors comprising 37% of all

informal-sector workers. Tailors, seamstresses, etc, and weavers, textile workers, etc, together constitute 9% of informal-sector workers in Quito. Mechanics, blacksmiths, craft-workers in wood, paper, leather, pottery, jewellery and fine metals are another substantial group. Most of the remainder offers personal services (hairdressing, shoe-shining, dry-cleaning and laundry) or cooked food.

Economic activity	Total workers	Percentage of women	Average monthly income (sucres)
Housekeepers	27,239	96.8	4031
Cleaning service, security guards and watchmen	11,277	26.3	9285
Small merchants and shopkeepers	33,427	63.0	12,279
Sellers, working in commerce and similar activities	10,113	42.8	8114
Street vendors	2841	72.6	5637
Mechanics, blacksmiths, locksmiths and plumbers	8671	0.9	11,597
Tailors, seamstresses, designers, furriers	8571	64.6	7411
Wood and paper craftsmen, carpenters and workers	6277	10.5	12,403
Leather craftsmen and workers	4843	13.7	9772
Weavers, textile workers and assistants	2285	58.3	9845
Goldsmiths, silversmiths, potters and jewellers	1987	18.0	11,081
Prepared food workers	1712	33.3	10,414
Barbers, salon stylists and related workers	3623	70.5	12,148
Shoe-shiners, delivery men	953	17.9	7168
Dry cleaning and laundry personnel	286	26.2	5750
Workers in unclassified services	2578	27.8	11,637
Total	126,683	54.9	–

Source: Bunivic, 1997.

---

to be qualitatively different employment experiences from being a working proprietor, an employee of a small-scale enterprise or a home-worker. They also employ quite large numbers of workers in many countries.

Some omissions from the Quito situation that would feature in Africa and Asia are transport workers (many cities rely on informal-sector operators of rickshaws, taxis and minibuses – for example, the *matatus* of Kenya or *tro-tros* of Ghana – and buses), and traditional medicine, divining and healing.[34]

■ The reasons for the informal sector of the economy

It is now generally accepted that the economic activity and employment in the urban informal sector are extremely important in developing countries where population and demand for jobs, goods and services are typically growing more quickly than national averages and too quickly for formal job creation to cope with. Indeed, years of structural adjustment and reduction in government employment have reduced formal-sector job opportunities in many urban areas. The informal sector creates many of the jobs needed by the growing work force and compensates for much of the formal sector's failure to provide goods and services.[35] It is predominant in slum neighbourhoods but occurs in higher income areas, as well.

As shown above, the roots of the informal sector have been argued over from several points of view. Neo-Marxists have emphasized the benefits that accrue when 'capital is

freed of the necessity to comply with its legal obligations'.[36] Thus, the capitalist producers of the formal sector can gain through exploiting informal-sector workers. Through it, they can reduce the costs of raw materials and inputs for formal-sector production, and they can keep formal-sector labour costs lower by providing wage goods to formal-sector workers more cheaply than the formal sector itself can generate.[37] This is especially evident with respect to women's contributions to the sector.

The structuralist approach, based on excess labour supply, holds that the bulk of those employed in the informal sector are working there because of lack of employment opportunities in the modern formal sector. Thus, many who seek employment in that sector are unable to find it and must create their own, often poorly paid, jobs in the informal sector. As the lack of opportunities is considered to derive from structural imperfections in the capital market and the segmentation of labour markets, it is often asserted that women suffer special disadvantages in this way. This is because they are more likely than men to be excluded from 'more desirable employment in the formal sector'.[38] The lack of productive resources, especially capital, to complement labour is also a feature of the informal sector and can inhibit the development of businesses in response to technological advances, reducing their competitiveness with the formal sector.

In the era of structural adjustment during the 1980s and 1990s, the neo-liberal approach became influential. It defines the informal sector as those firms that do not comply

---

The informal sector creates many of the jobs needed by the growing work force and compensates for much of the formal sector's failure to provide goods and services

with legal regulations, including licensing, minimum wage regulations and social security payments. Insofar as the administrative costs and regulations make it expensive and difficult to establish firms, businesses avoid them and the informal sector results.[39] It is obvious how strong a connection can be made here with the informality of the structures and neighbourhoods in which the workers in the informal sector live.

There are two opposite and controversial positions on how informal-sector enterprises relate to state institutions. On the one hand, there is the view that informal activities should be more strictly controlled in order to protect the modern enterprises from the threat of unfair competition from the informal sector, and (for unions) to preserve the rights of workers and their safe environments and pensions. On the other hand, there is the neo-liberal view that the regulatory system must be thoroughly reformed in order to free the initiative and economic potential of micro-enterprises and to release them from unnecessary costs of compliance.[40]

It took 289 days and cost US$1231 to legally set up a small garment factory, and 43 days and US$590 to set up a legal small shop in Lima.[41] Furthermore, another finding showed that the costs involved in complying with tax obligations and labour legislation could absorb US$77 out of every US$100 profit and only US$17.60 of this would go to pay taxes. As an alternative to this, in reality, informal enterprises spend 10 to 15 per cent of their gross income on avoiding penalties, while their formal-sector peers only spend 1 per cent.[42]

Women's informal-sector businesses are often subject to increased regulatory difficulties. Their access to credit and other inputs may be limited by their inferior legal status; they may have to obtain their husbands' signatures when applying for loans or they may have no independent control of property. Protective legislation that limits women's hours of work and provides them with maternity and other benefits not given to male workers also increases their exclusion from formal-sector employment, and may lead women to create their own employment opportunities.[43]

Neo-liberals argue that this implies that the informal sector arises from mistaken economic (and other) policies, or by the misguided actions of trade unions raising wages above their equilibrium level.[44] This would imply that removing minimum wages or destroying the power of trade unions will somehow solve the problem; but experience in Latin America has shown this not to be the case. Furthermore, eliminating or radically simplifying the regulations is unlikely to give rise to thousands of modern capitalist enterprises:

> *...the wood-worker who works with two pliers, three screwdrivers and a hammer will [not] be transformed into a capitalist entrepreneur just because regulations hindering establishment of modern firms are abolished.*[45]

Different countries have acted very differently in their attitudes to informality. In the developed countries, great efforts are made to eliminate the hidden economy since most of the tax base depends upon income tax and value-added tax from formal enterprises, and since many people involved also receive social security. Many developing countries have also regarded the informal sector, just like squatter housing, as something illegal to be exterminated (and something out of which the upper class cannot easily make money and which may even undercut their own legal enterprises). They have therefore harassed the informal sector in a variety of ways.

With support from international agencies that have sought to encourage poverty reduction and micro-enterprises, a few countries have tried to support and empower the sector as a start-up part of the economy in which innovation can flourish. In Kenya for example, the *jua kali* manufacturing enterprises have been fostered as an export industry, and political leaders often make statements in their favour.[46]

■ The scale of the informal sector

The informal sector plays a very important role in national economies and, more importantly – in the context of this report – is the livelihood of many slum dwellers. For example, in Uganda, small-scale trade is reported to contribute 95 per cent of the urban economy.[47] In Nigeria, it was estimated in 1993 that the informal sector adds between 20 and 30 per cent to the GDP.[48]

The informal employment sector tends to vary strongly with city development levels, ranging from about 54 per cent of all employment in Africa to 3 per cent or less in the HICs.[49] As indicated earlier, unemployment rates tend to be rather meaningless in countries with high levels of informal employment; but unemployment also falls away with increasing development levels.

In Africa, the informal sector accounts for about 20 per cent of GDP and employs about 60 per cent of the urban labour force. In sub-Saharan Africa, the informal sector accounts for 42.5 per cent of non-agricultural GDP and about 78 per cent of non-agricultural employment. It is also estimated that more than 90 per cent of additional jobs in urban areas there during the next decade will be created in micro-and small-scale enterprises in the informal sector.[50]

About 2 million people, or 16 per cent of the labour force, are employed in almost 1 million micro-enterprises and small enterprises in Kenya.[51] Recent studies in five sub-Saharan countries estimate that micro- and small-scale enterprises (MSEs)[52] employ an average of 22 per cent of the adult population, compared to only 15 per cent in the formal sector.[53] MSE employment in Kenya was over 1 million people in 1994, or one third of all working people. They contributed roughly 13 per cent of the GDP at that time. More than three-quarters of the enterprises had only one or two workers.

In Asia, the informal sector also accounts for a large percentage of all employment. In The Philippines, it accounts for 36 per cent of employment in urban areas. In Dhaka, Bangladesh, 63 per cent of all employed people are in the informal sector.[54] In Laos, the overall contribution of MSEs is estimated at 6 to 9 per cent of GDP.[55]

There are opposite and controversial positions on how informal-sector enterprises relate to state institutions

Different countries have acted very differently in their attitudes to informality

The informal employment sector tends to vary strongly with city development levels, ranging from about 54 per cent of all employment in Africa to 3 per cent or less in the HICs

Not all informal
housing can be
described as slums

The informal sector is also important in Latin America, where it constitutes the following fractions of employment: between 60 and 75 per cent in Guatemala, El Salvador, Honduras, Costa Rica and Nicaragua.[56] This comprises 1.7 million urban workers in these five countries. 89 per cent of commercial establishments in La Paz, Bolivia, in 1983 were in the informal sector; 76 per cent were in family units.[57]

Women are involved to a greater degree than men in small-scale commerce for the following reasons:[58]

- Self-employed commercial activities do not demand, in most cases, a stable schedule or a fixed location.
- Such work can be done in the home itself. Therefore, working as a micro-vendor does not necessarily have to conflict with the traditional female role of home-maker and child-rearer. Even in cases where the activity demands being outside of the home, working as a micro-vendor permits a certain flexibility in the work day and may include taking the children to the place of work.[59]
- The low levels of schooling and qualifications generally found among poor urban women limit their incorporation within other sectors of the labour market in which these attributes (among others) play an important role.[60]

Informal housing

Housing is described as informal when it does not conform to the laws and regulatory frameworks set up in the city in which it occurs. It can be informal at several levels. Housing can be provided through construction firms that are not licensed and whose work is not subject to guarantees. In turn, the housing is not likely to conform to the planning and building regulations in force or to be built in areas where there is no need to conform – for example, in 'semi-pucca' areas in Bangladesh or outside of city boundaries.

Housing that does not conform to rules may do so in several ways, including:

- being built on land intended for another use (even though the building itself may conform to the standards laid down in the regulations);
- not conforming to all of the standards laid down for that part of the city;
- not being subject to planning permission or building inspection (even though it may be eligible);
- being built on land not owned by the occupier and without permission of the owner.

Formal housing can become informal by the process of extension and alteration (transformation) by users without permission, or in ways that do not fulfil standards. This is now very common in government-built estates all around the world.

Not all informal housing can be described as slum housing. One of the few squatter areas in Ghana, on the site of the proposed National Stadium in Accra, is very high

Housing is possibly
the trickiest market
in which to
interfere, since well-
intentioned
measures can have
the opposite effects

The largest problem
is the lack of
recognition of slum
dwellers as being
urban citizens at all

quality housing, occupied by rich and influential people. The transformations which 'informalize' the government-built estates often represent better conditions (better physical conditions, more services, more space per occupant, higher value, better value for money) than the pre-existing housing.

SLUMS IN THE HOUSING SECTOR

The commonly accepted idea of a slum relates particularly to poor quality housing and residential infrastructure. The slum conjures up either a Dickensian vision of urban tenements, dire poverty and disease; a Chicago Southside of empty buildings and decay, suburban flight, roaming gangs and crack dealers; or a Calcutta or Jakarta, with endless vistas of makeshift shacks on the edge of town, filled with people in despair. In each case, the image suggests that the deprived urban environment has caused the poverty, when the reverse is mostly the case; people in poverty have sought out the accessible housing that they can best afford.

The misconception of some planning systems of the modernist tradition is that inadequate housing somehow breeds inadequate incomes, and middle-class distaste for poor housing has led quite frequently to dangerously inept policies. Housing is, in fact, possibly the trickiest market in which to interfere, since well-intentioned measures can have the opposite effects from what was intended. Comprehensive slum clearances have often eliminated better communities than they have created, at huge cost. Squatter evictions have created more misery than they have prevented. 'Indeed, it is now generally agreed that forced eviction represents a dimension of urban violence', and in 1996, all governments agreed to end illegal evictions when they adopted *The Habitat Agenda* in Istanbul.[61] Measures designed to limit costs in housing markets have, instead, ham-strung new investment in housing supply and maintenance, and caused residential investment to fall to nothing.

The distaste of more affluent urban citizens for slums impacts on every level – through slum clearance, harassment of informal-sector workers, and the unavailability of urban public and private services, finance or affordable housing. The largest problem is the lack of recognition of slum dwellers as being urban citizens at all. When services are not provided, the poor provide for themselves. The poor are currently the largest producers of shelter and builders of cities in the world – in many cases, women are taking the lead in devising survival strategies that are, effectively, the governance structures of the developing world, when formal structures have failed them.[62]

Housing issues almost inevitably refer to appropriateness (or adequacy), availability and affordability. These three issues take different forms in varied environments where standards are very different. They also interact with each other: sometimes in a trade-off, as affordability and adequacy usually do, and sometimes in concert, as availability and affordability mostly do.[63]

Tenure and security: the formal–informal housing continuum

The two most obvious problems facing people occupying informal-sector housing are related: tenure security and the provision of services. Obviously, providers of mains services are less willing to invest in pipes and other engineering works if dwellings in an area are likely to be removed. Furthermore, public authorities may use the availability of services as a weapon in the campaign against informal development. However, the old contrast between formal and informal is now much more clouded, resembling a continuum with many intermediary positions rather than a dichotomy:

> *The removal of tenure-insecurity related obstacles that prevent or constrain households from using their housing effectively as a productive asset is possibly the single most critical poverty reduction intervention.*[64]

The United Nations Millennium Goals have specifically articulated, as Indicator 31, the 'proportion of people with access to secure tenure'. The Global Campaign for Secure Tenure (GCST), a major international initiative since 1999, identifies the provision of secure tenure as essential for a sustainable shelter strategy, and as a vital element in the promotion of housing rights. It promotes the rights and interests of the poor, 'recognizing that the urban poor themselves provide the vast majority of their shelter'.[65] At its heart, the campaign addresses the outcomes of unstable tenure, including the inability to mobilize household capital, social exclusion and poor access to basic facilities. Lack of housing security makes it very difficult for people to participate in society, to establish firm roots and to build upon their networks and assets in order to obtain regular access to income-earning opportunities. People living in poverty are extremely vulnerable to changes in circumstances, and having safe, secure housing represents a substantial improvement in the quality of life for most. Without a fixed address it is almost impossible to have a formal-sector job, to receive any benefits that may be on offer, or to participate in political processes that might make a difference to local fund allocations for neighbourhood improvement.

Insecure tenure is one of the hallmarks of the informal sector, and gaining security can be the most important improvement for residents. Tenure can be complex, involving different bundles of rights over land or structure; but the main forms of tenure are discussed below.

■ Formal home-ownership

Formal home-ownership generally means that the owner of the structure has freehold or long leasehold title over the land, with the ability to sell or mortgage the improvements (in the present context, usually a dwelling), to leave it to descendants and to make any changes to the structure that are desired. However, there are other forms of titling for ownership, such as 'qualified titles' (Malaysia), 'provisional titles' (South Africa) and 'use right titles' (Indonesia). These may have different implications on inheritance and sale.

Home-ownership is undeniably the most secure tenure in that it provides the maximum control over dwelling and land within the confines of local planning and building regulations. While support for home-ownership has had an almost religious character in some countries, such as the US and Australia, its benefits are often exaggerated, and many affluent European countries have preferred a mix of social and private rental as their primary housing solution. As a pension scheme, home-ownership has considerable advantages in providing housing and assets for the aged, although it is often argued that a maldistribution of housing resources then occurs as an elderly couple or single person lives on in their family home.[66] Home-ownership is also alleged to contribute to participation and social activism,[67] although it often takes the form of not in my backyard (NIMBY)[68] action in order to exclude diversity of land use and of residents who do not fit the exclusive local profile.

■ Formal private rental

Formal private rental usually involves a lease or equivalent entitling the lessee to quiet enjoyment of the property for a fixed time, or until certain conditions are fulfilled, as long as the rent is paid and the property is maintained. There are no property rights inherent in most forms of lease, changes to the property cannot usually be made and, unless specifically legislated, most leases heavily favour the landlord in any dispute. In some cities, rental may also be more expensive in the long run than ownership.[69]

Private rental is dominant in cities in a diverse group of countries, including Germany, France, Denmark, many cities in Canada and the US; the Republic of Korea, Indonesia, Bangladesh and parts of India in Asia; Belize, Colombia and Jamaica in Latin America and the Caribbean (LAC); and in most African countries. However, in some it is discouraged or even illegal.

■ Informal home-ownership: squatting

Squatters are people who occupy land or buildings without the permission of the owner. Squatting occurs when an occupant has no claim to the land she or he occupies that can be upheld in law. In some countries, most squatting takes place in unused buildings, in which case the squatter has no legal claim to occupy the structure. In some countries and periods, squatting has been a legitimate way of occupying unused land. Examples include the settler periods in the US West and in parts of Australia, and, currently, desert land on the edges of Lima in Peru. Particularly in long-standing settlements, squatters, in many countries, have gained some form of informal title that is recognized by the community and can be traded in the housing market.[70] Squatters in self-built housing have been the primary focus of urban housing development programmes in the developing world over the last four decades.

Squatter housing generally divides into housing of poor quality or impermanent materials, and more established housing that may have been in place for a long period but has no official title to the land. In some countries such as Indonesia, Bangladesh, Kenya and parts of India, most squatter housing is rented from informal-sector landlords; in

Lack of housing security makes it very difficult for people to participate in society, to establish firm roots and their networks

other places, such as Latin America, it is typically occupied without cost.

■ Informal home-ownership: illegal subdivisions

Illegal subdivisions refer to settlements where the land has been subdivided, resold, rented or leased by its legal owner to people who build their houses upon the plots that they buy. These settlements are also illegal owing to the following additional factors: low standard of the services or infrastructure provided, breaches of land zoning, lack of planning and building permits, or the irregular nature of the land subdivision. Purchasers of land on illegal subdivisions often feel more secure than squatters because they have been through a process of buying the land from its owner and therefore do not fear that the owner will reclaim the land. This is a very common circumstance in rapidly developing cities.

■ Public rental

Public rental housing generally grants unlimited tenure, even to the next generation, at a subsidized rental; but it grants no property rights. Public rental was the social solution to housing during the inter-war and post-war periods in Europe and elsewhere, and very large housing estates were built – such as the Karl Marx Platz in Vienna, a housing block that is 5 kilometres long and includes many small businesses within its walls. In developing countries, the heyday of public rental housing was in the immediate post-World War II period when 'homes for heroes' and accommodation for the new urban workers were needed.

Along with other aspects of the state, public housing was originally available for everyone; but in many countries it is now increasingly targeted towards low-income earners and those with social problems. Large estates have, therefore, become major zones of exclusion, and the low incomes of the residents have damaged their financial viability so that increasing levels of subsidy have been required to meet basic costs such as maintenance. As shown in Chapter 5, these residualized areas have become recognized as the 'new slums' in some countries, with residents sometimes being ashamed to admit their addresses to outsiders.[71]

As one writer points out:

> *The British example demonstrates that the state, under certain conditions, can plan, produce and deliver high quality housing. It also demonstrates that, under other conditions, the state can become a slum landlord and can provide housing which is directly or indirectly a source of social exclusion and disadvantage.*[72]

On ideological grounds, the stock of public housing in many countries has either been sold off at a large discount to existing tenants (in the UK and many of its former colonies, and in some transitional countries where it was transferred outright) or semi-privatized into housing associations (in The Netherlands and the UK).[73] The results of this exercise are

still not clear; but lack of coordination and the ability to place tenants across the stock has become an issue.

■ Informal rental

Informal renting can take many forms, from occupying backyard shacks in public housing in South Africa, to subtenants in squatter housing in the *favelas* of Brazil, to pavement dwellers in India who make regular payments to someone in authority in order to keep their position. This group, along with new squatters, have the most fragile housing situation, short of having no shelter. They are able to live where they do until someone moves them along.

The subtenant category continues to be significant largely in sub-Saharan Africa. Backyard shacks and other forms of subletting are commonplace throughout much of sub-Saharan Africa. Some German and Venezuelan cities, as well as Trinidad and Kuwait, also have significant proportions of subtenants. Subletting appears also to be on the increase in those transitional countries where new housing investment has virtually been discontinued.

Private renting, both formal and informal, is the main alternative to home-ownership throughout much of the world. It is capable of providing accommodation not only to those with transient lifestyles, but also to those with limited resources who would not otherwise be able to afford the capital required for owner-occupied housing. However, most of the households who pay high proportions of their incomes on housing are private renters. While some countries make providing housing for rent difficult through rent controls, higher rates of tax on rental incomes, and legislation that makes recovering rented property from tenants very difficult, the importance of rental housing is likely to increase during the next few decades as incomes continue to fall behind the cost of providing formal-sector housing.

■ Customary tenure

Parts of many cities, particularly in Africa, have no state-formalized ownership of land and the land is not marketable. Instead, it is held by traditional leadership entities, such as chiefs, in trust for the community and its use is controlled through leases that allow rights of surface use for a fixed period (or in perpetuity to members of the local community). Some customary systems have central administrations in which documents are kept and can be consulted in case of dispute (as in the Asantehene's Lands Office in Kumasi, Ghana), while others do not. In the latter case, clouded titles (where the real owner or user is difficult to trace and there may be many conflicting claims) are a frequent problem. Customary and formal title can co-exist although this can cause much confusion.

■ Tenure distribution

Estimates of the incidence of different tenures worldwide are presented in Table 6.3 and Figure 6.3.[74] These estimates include all housing: slums and non-slums. It shows that about 19 per cent of households worldwide are in squatter housing (including those paying rent), about 42 per cent are in formal ownership and about 34 per cent are formal renters. On a

Region	Formal owner	Formal rental	Squatter (including informal rent-paying)	Other
Africa	25	23	38	15
Asia (without China)	29	19	45	7
China	35	50	9	6
Eastern Europe and Central Asia	65	34	1	3
Latin America and the Caribbean	48	21	25	6
Western Europe and others HICs	40	57	2	1
World	42	34	19	5

Source: Estimated from UNCHS (Habitat), 1996c and UN-Habitat, 2002f by Flood, 2001.

Table 6.3

Broad tenure categories, 1998 (percentages)

regional basis, ownership levels are now highest in the transitional countries because of the substantial privatization programmes that have taken place during the 1990s, and rental is highest in the developed countries. There is a small residual group of customary tenures, family houses, homeless people, etc, which is most significant in Africa.[75]

Squatter housing is most prevalent in Africa and South Asia and is now only a small proportion of the stock in South America, following substantial regularization programmes. Formal rental, both public and private, is most common in the high-income areas.

■ Slums and tenure insecurity

The relationship between slums and tenure insecurity is not immediately obvious, particularly in the Western world where slums actually developed within a context of defined tenure rights. However, the situation in the rapidly urbanizing developing world is rather different. Large visible tracts of squatter or informal housing have become intimately connected with perceptions of poverty, the negative effects of globalization, and lack of access to basic services and insecurity.

Many people living in informal settlements have been subject to continual harassment by authorities in their endeavours to provide themselves with appropriate and affordable housing. The unsatisfactory tenure of the majority of the urban poor has long been recognized, as access to secure tenure has often been a prerequisite for access to other opportunities, including credit, public services and livelihood. The ownership of land is a major area of gender discrimination. It is estimated that one out of every four countries in the developing world has a constitution or national laws that contain impediments to women owning land and taking mortgages in their own names. These are highest in Africa (41 per cent of cities), the Middle East and Northern Africa (29 per cent) and Asia and Latin America (24 per cent).[76]

Work in informal settlements in Peru and elsewhere was influential in encouraging international agencies to engage in large-scale formalization programmes.[77] For example, security of tenure issues received high priority in the housing sector policy development, emphasizing that its lack led to underinvestment in housing and reduced housing quality.[78] *The Habitat Agenda* stated unequivocally:

Access to land and security of tenure are strategic prerequisites for the provision of adequate shelter for all and the development of

sustainable human settlements. It is also one way of breaking the vicious circle of poverty.

One study identifies bureaucracy and elaborate red tape as major mechanisms that exclude the poor from participating in legal enterprises and legal ownership of dwellings.[79,80] These requirements mean that the poor do not have the resources to register enterprises or dwellings; therefore, they simply do not bother and stay outside of the legal system – thereby restricting legality only to the privileged few. An 'impenetrable bureaucracy bounds the formal economy' that is not interested in increasing wealth, just its redistribution.

A more recent study has taken the argument a stage further, stating that the granting of secure tenure is the single most important catalyst in mobilizing individual investment and economic development, since it is the foundation upon which capitalism has been established.[81] It argues that the substantial increase of capital in the West over the past two centuries is the consequence of gradually improving property systems. This has not happened in the developing world, where eight out of ten people hold their assets outside of the formal system, resulting in an estimated US$9.3 trillion of 'extra-legal' real estate assets in the form of 'dead capital', which is not transferable or fungible.[82] It cannot be accessed for other purposes, such as businesses, since it is held in a defective form without title.

A number of authors have been quick to refute the above arguments, saying that they misrepresent the situation in irregular settlements and underestimate the ability of informal systems to deliver, as follows:[83]

Figure 6.3

Housing tenure, 1998

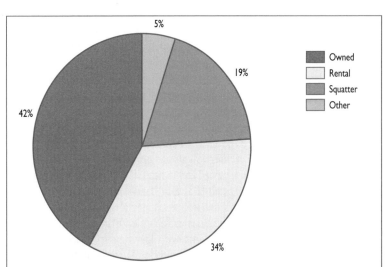

- Within most informal settlements, property is regularly traded according to some form of *de facto* titling system, which is based heavily on official systems. Formal titling is expensive, slow and subject to dispute where the land is privately owned in the formal system, and establishing formal title does not make much difference to the turnover of capital.[84] Housing turnover may not increase following legalization.[85] The importance and value of being able to transfer ownership rights increases with development, as skills become more hetero-geneous.[86]
- Access to informal credit is also a feature of most informal settlements. Formal finance is not forthcoming after legalization in the places where it has occurred.[87] The poor are, often for good reasons, suspicious about borrowing from banks in many countries.[88]
- Formal titling draws housing within the ambit of the land tax system, which the poor may not wish to pay.[89]
- While a minimum level of security is necessary before households will upgrade or undertake repairs, the literature showing the relationship between tenure and property maintenance is complex.[90]

The pro-tenure improvement arguments outlined above have also been said to misrepresent the situation in developed countries:

- Property and tenure rights in Europe grew from feudal and bourgeois concerns and not from any desire to tap the capital controlled by the poor. There have been healthy self-build and cooperative sectors in many developed countries; but most urban housing policy has concentrated on mobilizing the surplus income and capital of the middle class, either by building or subsidizing social housing with tax receipts, or by encouraging private landlords to invest in low-cost housing.[91]
- Home-ownership tends to be a preoccupation of formerly frontier societies such as the US and Australia, and of agricultural societies. Home-ownership is actually at lower levels in Europe than in most of the developing world. There is a well-known inverse relationship between levels of home ownership and GDP in Europe, with the richest countries tending to have the lowest levels of ownership.[92]
- Until the liberalization of mortgage markets during the 1980s, it was not an easy matter in most countries to borrow against owner-occupied housing for other purposes. This required high levels of equity and attracted penalty interest rates and other costs. Property rights and economic growth have tended to advance hand in hand. If anything, economic growth has acted as a precondition for distributing capital more widely, to the point, recently, where financial institutions have felt safe in providing universal instruments with low transaction costs, allowing households to access the capital in their homes for other purposes.[93]

Excessively complex, restrictive or inefficient systems of housing and land provision have a deleterious effect on both housing supply and housing prices and rents that, while appearing to improve conditions for existing occupants, actually reduce housing security for prospective and existing occupants.

Security of tenure and security of supply are, therefore, not necessarily complementary, since:

- There appears to be an upper limit beyond which increasing security of tenure may be counterproductive. In countries with formal supply systems, the poor have relatively few resources to invest in housing, and only the middle classes tend to supply housing capital. Many developed countries have, therefore, chosen to limit security of tenure in order to maximize housing supply, thereby encouraging the middle class to invest in housing for private tenants.
- As a particular example, the experience with draconian forms of rent control has been poor in all countries, resulting in poor supply, little or no housing maintenance or investment and overcrowding.[94]
- The practical experience with formal titling in irregular settlements has not been encouraging. As already discussed, some writers suggest that formal titling is of doubtful benefit to the poor, slowing and formalizing supply, and in some cases dramatically reducing affordability.[95] Better targeted partial changes to tenure rights can often avoid the undesirable effects of full-scale titling.
- There is no doubt that formal titling increases the value of properties; but there are cases where formal markets do not appear following regularization, and it is difficult for owners to realize the improved value.[96] There are too many areas where housing is not routinely marketable, especially in sub-Saharan Africa, for markets to be an assumed norm. Even where there are markets, regularization may simply raise the price of housing and reduce affordability across the board.

Legality is not particularly valuable to the poor; many of the outcomes of legality are desirable, but can be achieved in different ways.[97] There are differences between legitimacy and legality, and a number of tenure arrangements stop well short of formal titling while providing the desired benefits. Others discern a trend in interventions from tenure regularization towards security of tenure, recounting other strategies that achieve similar benefits to formal titling but without the costs:[98]

> *Secure* de facto *tenure is what matters to their inhabitants first and foremost – with or without documents. It is the security from eviction that gives the house its main source of value.*[99]

Not only is it unclear under what conditions improving formal security of tenure will improve the conditions of the majority of slum dwellers; but there are also very many people who do not live in slums and still have insecure tenure. Conversely, there are many individuals who live in slums who have legal tenure and/or are not poor. In addition, customary forms of tenure, which exist throughout sub-Saharan Africa and elsewhere, provide reasonably secure tenure even though these rights may not be recognized explicitly by the state.[100]

What is generally agreed is that secure tenure represents a bundle of different rights and is related to a number of other important issues. The specific legal rights to which tenure refers include the right to occupy/use/enjoy; to restrict who develops or uses the property; to dispose/buy/inherit; to cultivate/produce/sublet/sublet with fixed rent; to benefit from change in value; to access services; and to access formal credit. The tenure types that carry with them combinations of some or, ultimately, all of these are pavement dweller, squatter tenant, squatter 'owner', tenant in unauthorized subdivision, owner in an unauthorized subdivision, legal owner of an unauthorized building, tenant with a contract, leaseholder, and freeholder. These have progressively more rights.

The tenure figures in Table 6.3 have been used to obtain broad measures of insecure tenure, as in Table 6.4 and Figure 6.4. These estimates are bound to be approximate; but they are probably fairly indicative of the relative magnitude of the tenure types. About 28 per cent of households live in insecure tenure worldwide. Some 17 per cent of these are renters (7 per cent in informal tenure), while another 7 per cent are squatters who pay no rent.

In the light of the figures presented in Table 6.4, it may seem strange that so much attention has been lavished, over the past decade, on self-help for non-rent paying squatters. As there are so many more renters than squatters, it is strange that there are so few programmes that assist tenants with their rights and/or assist informal landlords to mobilize capital and participate in housing supply or estate improvement in various ways. It has been pointed out that helping someone to build their own dwelling is rather inefficient as it only results in one dwelling. Contrarily, if a successful self-builder decides to build dwellings for a business, the same agencies cannot help, and many official obstacles are put in the way of such small businesses.[101] There is a great need to assist small-scale enterprises in the construction sector – which probably provide the majority of all new dwellings – so that their methods of supply are as efficient as possible. At the same time, consumers need advice and knowledge on what represents good workmanship and value for money. The single householder–house interface represented by assisting self-help builders should be replaced by the twin interfaces of contractor–house and householder–contractor.[102]

While the importance of informal capital has been exaggerated, self-help has had the merit of producing innovative solutions to improve tenure conditions. The tenure data do not necessarily invalidate arguments regarding informal capital, although they clearly weaken them.[103] The few studies that have attempted to find out just where all of this informal capital for rental housing is coming from demonstrate that owners who build rental

	Squatters, no rent	Renters	Other	Total
Southern Africa	8	16	6	29
Rest of Africa	13	30	7	50
China	5	2	8	15
East Asia and Pacific, excluding Australasia	7	26	9	41
South and South-eastern Asia	14	31	5	50
Middle East	8	28	6	42
Western Europe	2	19	4	25
Northern America and Australasia	1	10	4	16
Latin America and Caribbean	11	17	6	34
World	**7**	**17**	**4**	**28**

Source: Flood, 2001.

Table 6.4

Insecure tenure by region (percentages)

rooms are often little better off than the renters, especially where traditional or shack housing is constructed. Most also continue to live in part of the house with their tenants, or close by.[104] Recent studies describe the considerable enterprise of slum dwellers; one major livelihood opportunity for women, in particular, is in providing rental housing.[105]

Aid programmes for rental tenure remain a neglected element of international assistance, and knowledge about informal landlords and tenants and the kinds of programmes that might benefit them are rare. Data relating to secure tenure are, overall, quite poor, even in those countries with established statistical systems, and the Millennium Goals programme offers a good opportunity to improve knowledge regarding housing tenure and the kinds of programmes that will improve the situation of those in insecure tenure.

Renting in slums

When their grandfathers and great grandfathers arrived in Sydney, they went, naturally, to Shanty Town, not because they were dirty or lazy, though many of them were that, but because they were poor. And wherever there are poor you will find landlords who build tenements, cramming two on a piece of land no bigger than a pocket handkerchief, and letting them for the rent of four.[106]

> There is a great need to assist small-scale enterprises in the construction sector – which probably provide the majority of all new dwellings – so that their methods of supply are as efficient as possible.

Figure 6.4

World security of tenure

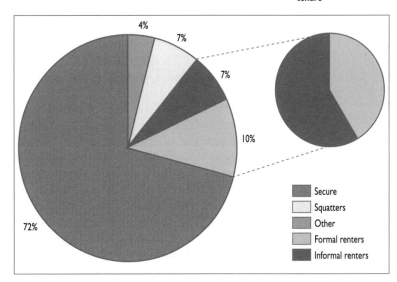

- Secure
- Squatters
- Other
- Formal renters
- Informal renters

Table 6.5

Changes in annual rent and household income of renters, 1993 to 1998ⁱ

Region	Median rent (US$)		Renter's median household income (US$)		Rent to income (%)	
	1993	1998	1993	1998	1993	1998
Africa	293	455	971	940	30.3	50.3
Asia and the Pacificⁱⁱ	4664	4792	3543	4237	82.0	71.7
Latin America and the Caribbean	881	1390	3098	3378	32.1	38.4

Notes: i Includes only those 69 cities for which all numbers were available or could be estimated. ii Includes a number of Korean cities. In the Republic of Korea, rents are primarily paid in a lump sum, which can be half the cost of the house (Hannah et al, 1993).

Sources: UNCHS, 1996c; UN-Habitat, 2002f.

The caricature of the exploitative landlord or landlady is as much a part of the mythology of the slum as the desperate battlers or the evil crimelord; but it is unwise to generalize. An early source writes:

> For the landlady to the London poor is too often a struggling, cheated, much-worried, long-suffering woman; soured by constant dealing with untrustworthy people; embittered by loss; a prey to the worst lodgers, whom she allows to fall into debt, and is afraid to turn out, lest she should lose the amount they owe her; without spirit or education to enable her to devise improvements, or capital to execute them – never able, in short, to use the power given her by her position to bring order into the lives of her tenants.[107]

Most people who rent out rooms in their own houses (for example, the 'bedspacers' of Manila or the backyard shack dwellers of Soweto) have been found to be as poor as their tenants or subtenants and often do not have better tenure security. Some studies that have researched the details of incomes of both landlords and tenants have found that landlords may have higher households than their tenants, but they are likely to have lower per capita incomes.[108] There is often little difference in incomes between those who do own a house (and can let rooms) and those who do not.[109] Such landlords perform a valuable service to the community and the labour market, giving slum dwellers a mobile base from which they can access fluid employment opportunities easily and cheaply, and providing affordable backup housing when formal or squatter building opportunities prove inadequate for urban growth. The supply of cheap rental housing is an essential component of the continued existence of a cheap urban labour force.[110]

However, while the informal landlord is an important player in new settlements, institutions, corporations and even the aristocracy tend to dominate the scene in more established slums. Christian churches and philanthropic institutions, in particular, have been major owners and on-leasers of tenement housing in the West. In economic recessions, the smaller landlords are more integrated within the community and are much less likely to have either the resources or the desire to evict tenants.[111] Consequently, they tend to fall by the wayside, lose their properties and are replaced by corporate and absentee landlords. Capitalist depressions, therefore, cause a shakeout in informal or small-scale landlordism. In the same way, they affect poor tenants disproportionately.

The previous section highlights the fact that the bulk of better-quality slum housing is built by landlords for profit, as a retirement scheme or because it is their only income-earning opportunity. Landlords have provided much of the capital for urban expansion in almost the same way that this occurred in the highly industrialized countries during their own periods of rapid urban expansion. Yet, until recently, their role has largely been ignored in aid programmes.[112]

This is probably because landlords who intend to make a profit from their tenants tend to be unacceptable beneficiaries of state-funded self-help programmes. Low-income owner occupiers, both *de facto* and *de jure*, are much more acceptable to both the left and the right and it is much easier to mobilize actors and appeal to popular support for them. However, lack of information about the situation has also contributed to the unpopularity of landlords, much as is the case of the developed world until the 1980s, when improved awareness of the role played by private rental housing led to a more sympathetic approach. Thus, assistance was given to private renters without inhibiting the ability of landlords to participate and invest in housing. This remains a major area for policy investigation in the developing world.[113]

Rents analyses also yield contradictory results. According to the figures collected internationally, rents have risen dramatically in many of the 69 cities for which data are available, as Table 6.5 shows. Of regions with a significant sample, only in the transitional countries are rents affordable (in fact, this represents a huge rise in rents over those during the socialist period). Furthermore, rents are very high compared with incomes: Latin America has median rents almost 40 per cent of median income of renters, and in Africa the figure is nearer to 50 per cent. However, where data on rents are available alongside income data for specific households, much lower rental levels than this are found. One extreme example is in Ghana where rents, under a long-standing rent-control regime, are typically between 2 per cent and 5 per cent of expenditure (a more accurate proxy for income than income data themselves).

The difference in the data presented in Table 6.5 is probably in how data are collected. It is likely that rents for formal-sector self-contained dwellings are collected rather than the sublet portion of the house, often a single room occupied by the household (73 per cent of households in Kumasi, for example).[114] Rents paid in Accra in 1992 were typically equivalent to UK£2 per month, which gives a figure of only about one twelfth of the 1993 figure in Table 6.5.[115] Other empirical studies in Africa have found low percentages of income spent on rent, even outside of rent

Table 6.6

Region	Median house price (US$)		Median household income (US$)		Price to income (%)	
	1993	1998	1993	1998	1993	1998
Africa	13,030	15,832	1419	1385	9.2	11.4
Asia and the Pacific	30,482	39,650	7354	9048	4.1	4.4
Latin America and the Caribbean	26,874	29,579	4851	5278	5.5	5.6

Note: i House prices are supposed to be obtained by taking a weighted average of formal and informal prices, and then dividing by median household incomes of occupants in each group. However, the figures indicate that this has not been done. The prices more nearly reflect the formal market than costs of informal dwellings.

Sources: UNCHS, 1996c; UN-Habitat, 2002f.

Housing affordability by region: house prices and household incomes[i]

control (in Lilongwe, this was 10 per cent; in Ibadan, 7 per cent; in Nairobi, 10 per cent; and 15 to 29 per cent in the private sector in Benin City, Nigeria).[116] In addition, we cannot assume that rents increase in real terms across the board through time. Rents decreased in Nairobi between 1975 and 1987.[117]

There can be no doubt about the importance of rental housing to low-income people in developing cities. Quite substantial majorities of low-income households, and even of all households, rent their rooms or dwellings. Although this might not be a very palatable idea after many decades of promoting owner occupation through loans, self-help schemes of various kinds and other initiatives, it remains likely that rental housing is the accommodation of choice or necessity for half of the world. While they might dream about owning a dwelling, the need to carry out much of the development through their own initiative, to pay cash and to build much more than a single room prevents most renters from fulfilling their dreams. Where they do manage to own, it is often in middle years after many years of renting.

In addition to renting, however, we must acknowledge the role of rent-free accommodation among the very poor. Many would-be households who share may not be included in this category, and so its size may be larger than statistics suggest. However, about one in four households in urban Nigeria[118] and in Kumasi,[119] 10 per cent in Pakistan[120] and 14 per cent in Bangkok live rent-free.[121] Most of these households are probably related to the house owner or are part owners in some tenuous way of an inherited property (a family house)[122] and are likely to be more common in slums than elsewhere. This tenure is a powerful welfare measure, ensuring that the old, the young and other households who would have difficulty in paying market or fixed rents are accommodated. Still others make the decision to eschew shelter altogether in order to save money and send it home to relatives or use it for other consumption (at the extreme, alcohol or drugs). Many street dwellers and rough sleepers find succour in slum streets and open spaces, especially in the inner-city areas.

Home-ownership in slums

There are two stories on housing affordability and they tend to be contradictory. The one that compares median household income to median house price shows serious problems. The one that examines current housing supply is more optimistic. These are taken in turn.

As can be seen from Table 6.6, housing is not at all affordable in most parts of the world, even for the median household (50 per cent up the income rank). Multiples of

more than about five times annual household income are not affordable to new market entrants, even when good housing finance systems are in place (and in most places they are not).

Table 6.6 shows that housing is not becoming more affordable. Of 100 cities included in both Global Urban Indicators Database (GUID) samples (1993 and 1998), 66 report rising house prices and 33 report stationary/falling prices. In Africa, the price increases have been accompanied by falling incomes in three-quarters of cities. Incomes have been falling in most transitional countries as well; but this has been accompanied, in a majority of cases, by falling house prices as populations decline and housing markets begin to develop. However, the fall in house prices has not matched the decline in incomes and, overall, prices have become less affordable. Rents are unequivocally more expensive – two-thirds of transitional cities showed rising rents and falling incomes between 1993 and 1998.

For the lowest-income groups, a formal serviced dwelling on its own plot is out of the question. These individuals have several options. They can build a dwelling themselves on vacant land for a cost of about a year's income, which is often affordable; the money can usually be borrowed from relatives or friends, or from loan sharks at exorbitant interest rates.[123] They can rent, choosing from one of the many options that are usually available. An option adopted by many households with incomes around the median and below, especially in sub-Saharan Africa, is to rent part of someone else's house, often a single room.[124] Work in Ghana found that renters of single rooms had relatively similar incomes to the owners of their multi-

Figure 6.5

Land price to income ratio

Note: Median land price of 1 square metre of urban land with various levels of services provided, divided by average annual household income

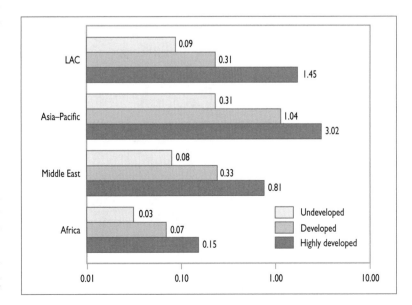

	Floor area per person (m²)	Permanent dwellings (%)	In compliance with regulation (%)
Region			
Sub-Saharan Africa	8.0	61.4	48.6
North Africa and Middle East	12.6	84.1	74.1
Asia	9.5	72.9	58.8
Latin America and the Caribbean	14.7	80.0	73.6
Development level (City Development Index, CDI)			
Low	6.8	50.7	43.9
Low to medium	8.3	70.8	48.7
Medium	10.3	73.1	64.9
High to medium	16.6	91.7	82.6
High	29.3	98.3	97.9

Source: UNCHS (Habitat), 1996c.

Table 6.7

Housing adequacy, by region and development level, 1993

household compounds, but very different incomes from owners of single household dwellings. Thus, it recommended that policies that encouraged renters to become owners of multi-occupied traditional compounds are likely to be much more successful than policies that advocate the building of single household dwellings.[125]

■ **Land prices**

Most cities have no strategy for the timely provision of land based on projections of household formation. The development of land can be a bureaucratic tangle involving dozens of agencies, each with their own requirements, delays and, possibly, bribes. This is reflected directly in unreasonably high formal land prices, with up to a 900 per cent markup on the direct costs of provision.[126] Only a few countries have developed an adequate system of bringing land onto the market in time for the people that need it – and that has taken a great deal of streamlining.[127] Land becomes available only after many years of frustration, and it is not surprising that most builders of dwellings find it less risky to bypass the law and occupy otherwise useless land. As the authorities are generally equally unsuccessful in finding out that this has been done, the squatters may have several years before they are questioned, by which time a substantial community will have arisen.

Figure 6.6

Permanent dwellings and housing in compliance, by development level

Even when adjusted for local variations in income, residential land prices vary a great deal by region. They tend to reflect investment pressure on land resources, which, in the developing world, is lowest in Africa and highest in Asia–Pacific. Relative land prices are 10 to 20 times as high in Asia as in Africa, while the transitional countries are somewhere near the geometric mean of the two.

It is not only the price of land that is a major concern, but also the registration of existing land. In many countries, local registration is held in the form of ancient volumes with no backup in the event of fire or war. The registrations are only spasmodically updated, which makes property tax impossible or uneconomic to collect. Transfers are also made difficult, thereby reducing supply, leaving local governments without any real income base or the means to fund local improvements. Only very recently have a few countries sought to improve, through various innovative approaches, or to computerize their cadastral records – although it is generally agreed that this is eminently achievable.[128] 'Weak cadastral registration and tenure records have made efficient land operations next to impossible.'[129]

Adequacy: extent of housing disadvantage

Housing disadvantage is a complex concept. It usually refers to the adequacy of the structure and associated services; but it may also include aspects of security of tenure and affordability. On a global basis, the only representative sources of information about cities and their facilities are the UNCHS (Habitat) databases GUID 1 (Base Year 1993) and GUID 2 (Base Year 1998), which were developed for Habitat II and Istanbul +5, respectively.[130]

The three most common indicators of housing adequacy are:

1 Space per person.
2 Permanent structures.
3 Housing in compliance with local standards.

The average value of each in different regions is presented in Table 6.7.

It is clearly evident from Table 6.7 that there is a strong and positive correlation between development level in a country and the quality of housing enjoyed by its citizens. Furthermore, the differences are very great: about fivefold in floor space per person between the very low and the highest. In addition, the physical quality of dwellings is much poorer in the countries with lower development indices. It is obvious, within this, that slums (impermanent dwellings and those without compliance) are a major part of the housing stock in the many countries with less than medium levels of development. The continent-wide data demonstrates how prevalent impermanent and non-complying housing is, especially in Africa and Asia.

Figure 6.6 shows that about half of the housing in least developed cities is made of non-permanent materials of various kinds. Such housing might be expected to last for less than ten years and must be replaced or substantially renovated quite soon. As in the developing world, about half

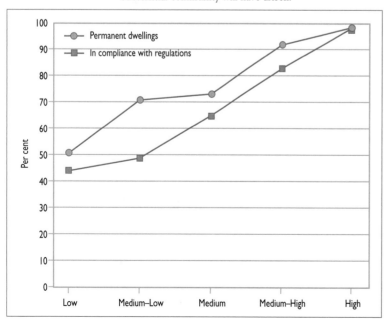

Table 6.8

Connections to infrastructure (percentage)

Region	Water connection	Sewerage	Electricity	Telephone	Access to water
Sub-Saharan Africa	48.4	30.9	53.9	15.5	73.5
North Africa and Middle East	79.1	65.9	91.8	42.0	88.0
Asia and the Pacific	65.9	58.0	94.4	57.1	94.8
Latin America and the Caribbean	83.7	63.5	91.2	51.7	89.1
City Development Index (CDI) quintile					
1	40.6	19.7	61.6	17.4	71.8
2	67.2	44.1	83.2	40.1	85.0
3	86.8	77.5	97.1	55.6	92.9
4	92.8	84.4	97.3	61.1	98.0
5	97.4	90.6	96.2	87.6	97.8
All developing countries	75.8	64.0	86.5	52.1	88.9

Note: Water connection refers to percentage of households with a piped water connection. Access to water means having potable water within 200 metres of the household (eg standpipes, wells, etc), and includes water connections (since most countries presume that piped water is potable).

of the housing is not in compliance with regulations; it seems evident that regulations are quite out of touch with local reality.[131] However, it does imply that by Western standards half of the housing in the world is inadequate according to this measure.

Networked services

The levels of household connection to networked infrastructure are major indicators of urban adequacy and the level of city development. The level of connection of each type of infrastructure tends to reflect the relative cost per household of providing that service and its relative importance to low-income households. Thus, access to potable water (which can be arranged fairly cheaply using communal standpipes) and electricity connections tend to advance most rapidly with development level. Sewerage (which is the most expensive) and telephone connections (which are something of a luxury item) increase more slowly, as Table 6.8 shows.

The difference among the levels of services largely owes to the availability of revenue. Cities in developed countries have 32 times as much money per person to spend on infrastructure and other urban services as cities in least developed countries. Dealing with service provision to large numbers of people has proved difficult because of the large capital investments required, inadequate cost recovery, use of inappropriately high standards and technologies, and little attention to maintenance and life-cycle issues. Nevertheless, the level of provision of urban services increased very rapidly during the 1990s across the whole development distribution, to the levels shown in Table 6.8. It was particularly rapid in cities of medium levels of development. This is a major achievement of the decade.

Connections to infrastructure in informal settlements are substantially lower than in cities, as a whole, as Table 6.9 shows. As seen in Figure 6.8, on average there is about half the level of connections to networked infrastructure in all categories.

Data are not available to calculate City Development Indices (CDIs) separately for informal settlements; but Figure 6.8 strongly indicates the differences between the poorer and the better parts of cities. The differences between informal and formal settlements become more

pronounced at lower levels of development, especially for the more expensive services. The relative proportions of connections are much the lowest in Africa, and in less developed regions more generally (see Figure 6.8).

Water

Water is one of the great necessities of human life. A supply of clean water is absolutely necessary for life and health; yet, many people of the world do not have access to clean water or can only obtain it at high prices in time and/or money. Many cities do not have a constant, potable water supply. Even in cities which are supplied with clean water, households in some informal areas that are not connected to the network can only buy water from vendors at up to 200 times the tap price, so that much of family income is spent on water.[132]

Availability of potable water in urban areas increases rapidly with development. Around 70 per cent of households have access to clean water in the developing country cities; but only 40 per cent of households in their informal settlements have access, as Tables 6.8 and 6.9 show, while almost everyone in developed cities has access. As with most other forms of consumption, water consumption is much higher in cities with higher incomes; but water price generally falls with the level of development. Typically, people

Most cities have no strategy for the timely provision of land based on projections of household formation

Figure 6.7

Access to networked infrastructure by CDI quintile

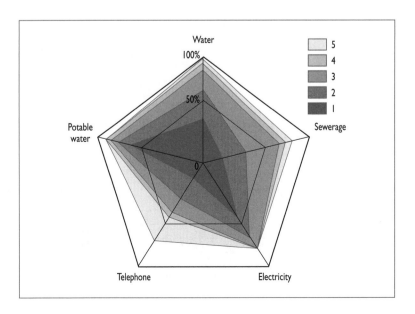

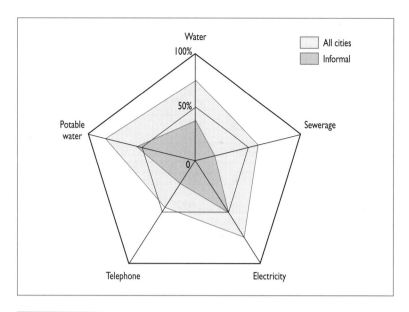

in developed cities use about 220 litres per day, while the average in Africa is 50 litres per day: less than one quarter.

Households in informal settlements use less than half of the amount of water as the average usage in the same cities, owing to poorer availability and greater costs. The median water price in informal settlements is almost five times the average price. This is primarily due to the high price of water in African informal areas.[133]

Although there has been substantial investment in water supply during the 1990s, there is some evidence that access to clean drinking water has not been keeping pace with urbanization. There was a growth of 30 per cent, or 62 million individuals, in the number of urban households without access to water during the decade.[134]

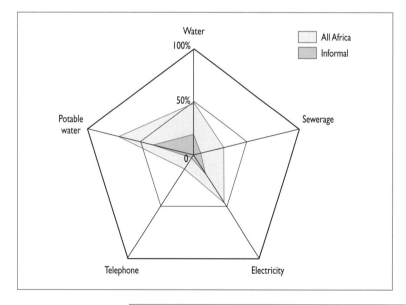

Waste management

Waste management is the component of the CDI that advances most slowly and is most difficult to improve with increasing development. While there are many advantages in urban living – primarily involving the cheaper provision of physical and social infrastructure and the greater availability of employment – the major disadvantages relate to congestion and to the problems of disposal of solid and liquid wastes from people living at high densities, as well as local environmental degradation and the propensity for health risks that this causes. Densely settled urban areas produce massive concentrations of environmental pollution, overwhelming the absorptive capacity of the natural ecosystem.[135] Human waste is the most toxic substance with which most people come into contact; so there is a great need for its disposal to be safe and efficient.

As with networked infrastructure, the effectiveness of environmental management increases rapidly with the level of development. Table 6.10 shows that only 8 per cent of wastewater is treated and 12.5 per cent of garbage is disposed of formally in the least developed cities. Even in a city such as Manila, out of a total of 4000 tonnes of garbage generated daily, only 1500 tonnes reach dump sites. The rest is left on the streets, dumped in storm drains, creeks and canals, burned (creating air pollution), collected and recycled by scavengers, or eaten by animals. High-income groups also contribute through the disposal of plastics and other wastes that cannot be recycled.[136] In cities of highly developed countries, 95 per cent of solid wastes are formally disposed of and 19 per cent are formally recycled. In transitional countries, 75 per cent of solid wastes are tipped onto open dumps. Industrialization also leads to the dumping of toxic wastes in many of the waterways of the world. Less than 35 per cent of cities in the developing world have their wastewater treated. In only one out of every five African and Latin American cities, and in one out of every three Asian cities, is wastewater undergoing some form of treatment. Of course, slum dwellers are the most vulnerable in this process, as they suffer not only their own uncollected garbage, but often that of richer people dumped near their homes as well.

Adequacy of housing and inadequacy of planning

Housing is generally regarded as a basic human need and an inalienable right; but a significant proportion of the urban housing in the world does not meet local regulations. Is this the fault of governments or of people, or simply a mismatch of expectations as to what can be achieved on very limited

Region	Water connection	Sewerage	Electricity	Telephone	Access to water
Sub-Saharan Africa	19.1	7.4	20.3	2.9	40.0
North Africa and Middle East	35.7	21.5	35.9	30.0	42.7
Asia and the Pacific	38.3	7.4	75.7	25.4	89.1
Latin America and the Caribbean	57.9	30.3	84.7	32.0	66.8
All developing regions	37.2	19.8	59.1	25.4	57.6

Note: This data may contain inaccuracies as sample sizes are small and measurement is uncertain.

incomes?

Adequacy is perceived very differently by different social groups and different cultures. A high rise flat would be regarded as an unacceptable place to bring up a family in Australia; but it is the usual thing in Lisbon, New York or Munich. Space of 10 square metres would not be enough for a child's bedroom in the US; but it would be regarded as adequate for a family in some developing countries. Houses with no water connection and a communal composting toilet would be unthinkable in urban Europe; but are acceptable in much of Africa and Asia.

In particular, formal housing is a middle-class preoccupation. Once adequate basic shelter is obtained and potable water and electricity are available, it has been repeatedly found that low-income households give higher priority to other needs, such as livelihood opportunities, consumer goods and education for their children, than to improving their housing conditions. Poor rural–urban immigrants, in particular, are so accustomed to self-built shacks, no facilities and crowded living with extended families that more than that can seem like an unnecessary luxury. This is not to say that low-income people do not want or should not have formal housing; but it does suggest that middle-class planners should not pre-judge the priorities of different social groups and should take account of their priorities in allocating scarce resources.

It would seem that most low-income earners, without subsidy and given a choice on how to spend their limited budgets, would choose the cheapest housing that meets their basic requirements for shelter, security and access to income and cultural opportunities. It is likely that such a choice would favour informal housing that does not meet the high building standards developed for more affluent households.[137] The housing stock of cities in less developed parts of the world reflects this profile.

However, the quality of housing occupied by a majority of the poor is not regarded as acceptable in most parts of the world. The gap between societally required and effectively demanded housing is known as 'housing needs', or the housing gap.[138] There are few cities that are prepared to endorse informal or self-help solutions to the housing problem, since they are not legal and not acceptable. It would make good sense for most countries to establish and monitor affordable health, environmental and building standards that are appropriate to local conditions. However, this would necessitate ensuring that land is available to meet projected housing needs, and providing advice and assistance to new arrivals in establishing first-stage housing. Instead, most cities tolerate the growth of illegal settlements that are substandard by any reckoning, then harass the inhabitants once they are established in their houses and communities through forced relocations and slum clearing. This is partly a problem of governance, since few lower-income countries have the staff or resources to establish locally inspired codes and monitoring frameworks. It is also based on misconceptions of what is appropriate to enable people to carry out their lives, and partly on a dislike of new settlers, in principle.

Where physical solutions using less-than-standard services or structures have been tried, they tend to be only pilot projects and are not directed at a resolution of the whole urban housing problem. They also tend to be unpopular with politicians who prefer high-profile 'modern' approaches that will provide a suitable monument to their efforts.[139] Thus, there is a significant problem of a lack of political will. In cities that have admitted what the problems are and that have come to a social consensus about how to solve them with a clear strategy, it has generally been found that the problems can be solved and will partly solve themselves through the efforts of everyone involved in meeting the consistent vision. Examples of some of these are contained in subsequent chapters.

Region	Wastewater treatment	Formal solid waste disposal
Sub-Saharan Africa	21.7	31.4
North Africa and Middle East	32.0	44.3
Asia and the Pacific	33.7	58.9
Latin America and the Caribbean	19.8	66.3
City Development Index (CDI) quintile		
1	7.8	12.5
2	13.0	40.5
3	30.9	43.0
4	65.5	54.5
5	82.4	85.2
All developing	34.6	46.4

Source: UN-Habitat, 2002f.

Table 6.10

Urban waste management by region and development level, 1998 (percentage)

In cities that have admitted what the problems are and that have come to a social consensus about how to solve them, the problems can be solved through the efforts of everyone involved in meeting the consistent vision

NOTES

1   This chapter draws on the background paper 'Urban Slums and Poverty in Context', prepared by Joe Flood of Urban Resources, Australia.

2   This is the proportion of the population that is economically active.

3   Bloom and Williamson, 1998.

4   Producer services are services to business, finance and real estate, including much of the knowledge economy. Drennan et al (1996) show that US cities that specialized in producer services were the big gainers during the 1980s, and this was the main source of income divergence between cities and regions.

5   Flood, 2000a.

6   DINKYs are households that usually have two professional-level incomes and substantial disposable income and bidding power for land, housing or other assets.

7   This is partly due to changing social attitudes towards the family and, paradoxically, to increasing overall wealth and better pensions, which have made it possible for even low-income people to live away from relatives.

8   Hamnett (1994) states that professionalization has been the major effect, and presents evidence to show that much of the restructuring would have occurred in any case, without the re-opening of global trade. This is confirmed in Sydney by Baum (1997).

9   Kesteloot and Meert, 1999.

10   Kloosterman et al, 1999.

11   Prior to the 'dot-com collapse'. It has been estimated that some 40 per cent of programmers in Silicon Valley have been imported from Asia, mostly India.

12   ILO (2002): www.ilo.org/public/english/employment/strat/kilm/kilm08.htm.

13   Sik and Wallace, 1999.

14   Te Velde and Morrissey (2001) find wages with international firms in five African countries to be 20–40 per cent higher; Lipsey and Sjöholm (2001) find an advantage for Indonesian non-production workers in

manufacturing enterprises; and Aitken et al (1996) find a similar result for Mexico and Venezuela. Dunning (1993) finds this to be generally true, though the use of more skilled workers and better capital equipment explains most of the difference.

15 Hart, 1970; ILO, 1972.

16 Peattie, 1987.

17 Berger, 1996; Sethuraman, 1976.

18 It would be a mistake to assume that all such enterprises are small in horizon. For example, traders from West Africa travel to Europe; collect money from contacts in London, Amsterdam, Frankfurt or Paris; purchase large amounts of clothing, car spares, second-hand goods, etc; air-freight them home; sell the produce; and return, sometimes twice a week. Many of the clothing manufacturers in Bolivia import cloth and designs, and export finished items of clothing all around Southern Latin America. Carpet manufacturers in Central Asia export throughout the world, as do better quality handicrafts from many countries.

19 ILO, 1993.

20 Tokman, 1978; Lipton, 1980.

21 Chen et al, 1999.

22 There are now more home-based enterprises in the growth information, financial advice and consultancy industries in the HICs. Taxation mechanisms have begun to tighten around small enterprises as a result, providing what many regard as an unacceptable compliance load.

23 Many other forms of registration or taxation have not proven financially worthwhile. In non-metropolitan areas of The Philippines, land titles can be many years out of date because of the costs of updating, and property taxes cost more to collect than they actually recover. In Kenya, highway taxes were discontinued because skimming by collectors was creating an overall loss.

24 Vega and Kruijt, 1994. This depends largely on the type of enterprise. A shop with five employees is quite large, while a manufacturer with ten may still be small; see Berger, 1996.

25 Featured by Bromley and Gerry, 1979.

26 Mezzera, 1996.

27 Tokman, 1978. A related phenomenon is the 'fast food delivery' industry in the HICs.

Initially, employers had a fleet of cars; but then it was discovered that parents would provide cars for their children to give them some work experience under conditions of high youth unemployment, thereby subsidizing delivery costs.

28 Robinson, 1977; Souza, 1979. These niches can be very large, indeed, even extending to, for example, all convenience retailing.

29 Tokman, 1978.

30 Mezzera, 1996.

31 Vega and Kruijt, 1994.

32 Moser et al, 1993.

33 UNCHS (Habitat)/ILO, 1995.

34 Gallagher, 1992.

35 During the structural adjustment in the Democratic Republic of Congo (then Zaire) in the 1980s, the civil service reduced from 429,000 in 1980 to 289,000 in 1985.

36 Vega and Kruijt, 1994.

37 Moser, 1978; Mies, 1986.

38 Moser, 1978; Mies, 1986.

39 de Soto, 1989.

40 This is most prominently expressed by de Soto, 1989. See also World Bank, 2000a.

41 de Soto, 1989.

42 Maldonaldo, 1995.

43 Berger, 1996.

44 For example, Mezzera, 1996.

45 Mezzera, 1996.

46 The term *jua kali* means 'hot sun'. Originally, this comprised metal-working and welding shops, conducted in the open. It now comprises all forms of informal manufacture, many of which have a good export base; Barasa and Kaabwe, 2001.

47 Uganda, Government of, 2001. In Kenya and Uganda, the 'informal sector' is defined as the same as small-scale industry.

48 *The Economist*, 1993.

49 Informal employment figures tend to be underestimated and concealed in developed countries because of compliance requirements.

50 UNESCAP, 2001.

51 According to Frijns and van Vliet–, 1999.

52 These are enterprises with less than 11 employees.

53 Cited by Daniels, 1999.

54 UNESCAP, 2001.

55 Daniels, 1999.

56 Funkhouser, 1996.

57 Escobar, 1996. Such data are subject to considerable errors, especially when used comparatively between countries or, over time, as collection practices vary. Funkhouser (1996) and

Mezzera (1996) argue that the informal sector (not including domestic service) remained roughly constant at about 20 per cent of non-agricultural employment in Latin America from 1950 to 1980.

58 Escobar, 1996. Women are also more likely than men to spend their earnings on family staples rather than on own entertainment (Levin et al, 1999), which limits the disposable income of women-headed households, but improves food security.

59 However, urban women are much more likely to leave children at home while they work; see Levin et al, 1999; urban women also make use of childcare arrangements with greater frequency (Ruel et al, 1999).

60 Levin et al, 1999.

61 Agbola and Jinadu, 1997.

62 UN-Habitat, 2001b.

63 Higher quality housing is inevitably more expensive; as a result, improving adequacy reduces affordability. Furthermore, if housing is more widely available it is usually cheaper from the functioning of supply and demand.

64 Moser, 1996.

65 See www.unhabitat.org/tenure/tenure.htm.

66 Flood and Yates (1989) note that, in Australia, home-owners aged over 65 have considerably more valuable housing than the general population, while renters aged over 65 occupy considerably less valuable housing than the average, although their average cash incomes are similar. However, the very large dwellings occupied by many owners after their children leave home could be regarded as a maldistribution of the stock. In developing country contexts, many elderly people actually extend their dwellings in their old age to house their grown-up children or to use the now vacant rooms as rented rooms to supplement their income; see Tipple, 2000.

67 UNCHS (Habitat), 1996a.

68 NIMBY suggests a desire for necessary urban externalities, or other activities that potentially reflect negatively on house prices, to be located elsewhere in the city. This is often complemented by the more obstructive BANANA: build absolutely nothing anywhere near anyone.

69 Private renters eventually end up paying the full capital cost of dwellings through their rent, as well as all of the other costs

of ownership. They also have to meet the management costs and risk/vacancy premium of the landlord, which an owner does not have to pay. Most significantly, they do not receive any direct benefit from capital gains and pay higher rents as property values inflate. In some cases, however, landlords do not make a good return from their rooms and sometimes voluntarily charge less than market prices for rooms out of social concern for renters. They may also allow family members to live rent-free. See Tipple and Willis, 1991; Willis and Tipple, 1991.

70 Payne, 2002.

71 Hall, 1997.

72 Murie, 1997.

73 Priemus and Dielemann, 1997, 1999.

74 It is clear that these estimates are not perfect, especially given the many intermediary positions in the formal–informal continuum; but they are the only ones available. Furthermore, housing tenure varies a great deal between otherwise similar or neighbouring countries, depending upon social attitudes and the policies that have been followed, so diversity is very considerable within each region. For example, home-ownership is around 70 per cent in North America and Australia, and is even higher in some countries where most people still live in rural areas; but it is under 50 per cent throughout Europe.

75 Amole et al, 1993.

76 UN-Habitat, 2002f.

77 Especially Turner, 1976; de Soto, 1989.

78 For example, World Bank, 1993.

79 de Soto, 1989.

80 In Egypt, acquiring and legally registering a lot on a state-owned desert land involves at least 77 bureaucratic procedures at 31 public and private agencies. In Peru, building a home on state-owned land requires 207 procedural steps at 52 government offices, says de Soto (1989). In The Philippines, establishing legal ownership takes 168 steps, and between 13 and 25 years. In Haiti, obtaining a lease on government land – a preliminary requirement to buying – takes 65 steps. Similar numbers of procedures surround the registering of legal business enterprises. In Mozambique, for example, registering a new business requires 19 steps and five

months, and costs more than the average annual income per capita (World Bank, 2001a).

81 de Soto, 2000.

82 This value was stated by de Soto (2000) without demonstrating the method, and has been criticized by Woodruff (2001), Gilbert (2001) and Payne (2002) as a considerable overestimate. However, the number is widely quoted in UNCHS (Habitat) (2001b): www.un.org/ga/Istanbul+5/32.pdf.

83 Including, Payne, 1998, 2002; Gilbert, 2001; Angel, 2001.

84 Payne, 2002. In fact, self-help housing is only rarely traded in Columbia, according to Gough (1998), and is not well suited to commodification.

85 Gilbert, 2001.

86 Deininger and Binswanger, 1998.

87 Gilbert, 2001.

88 Payne, 2002.

89 Angel, 2001.

90 Angel, 1983, 2001; Deininger and Binswanger, 1998.

91 The cooperative movements and assisted self-build initiatives have been widely encouraged in a number of countries in a situation of housing shortages.

92 For example, UNCHS (Habitat), 1996a.

93 It remains to be seen exactly what the effects of this relaxed lending regime will be; but the current high stock market

valuations can be partly attributed to liberalized mortgage and finance markets.

94 Malpezzi and Ball, 1991.

95 Angel, 2001; Fernandez, 1998; Payne, 1997, 2001, 2002.

96 Gilbert, 2001.

97 Payne, 2002.

98 Durand-Lasserve and Royston, 2002.

99 Angel, 2001.

100 Durand-Lasserve and Royston, 2002.

101 Usually on the grounds that public money would be helping a few entrepreneurs to make profits.

102 Tipple, 1994.

103 de Soto, 2000.

104 Kumar, 1996; Tipple and Willis, 1990.

105 de Soto, 2000; Gilbert, 2000.

106 Australian novelist Ruth Park (1948) in *The Harp of the South*.

107 Hill, 1883.

108 Tipple et al, 1999; Tipple, 2000.

109 Kumar, 1996.

110 UN-Habitat, 2002a.

111 According to Dennis, 1995.

112 UN-Habitat, 2002.

113 Kumar, 1996, 2001; Rakodi, 1995.

114 Malpezzi and Ball, 1991; Tipple and Willis, 1989.

115 Tipple et al, 1999.

116 Rakodi, 1995.

117 Amis, 1990.

118 Oruwari, 1990.

119 Tipple and Willis, 1991; Tipple and Korboe1989.

120 Kalim1990.

121 Wandeler and Khanaiklang, 1992.

122 Amole et al, 1993.

123 Self-building usually involves at least some input from tradesmen in the construction industry and is often entirely entrusted to small firms in the informal sector.

124 Tipple, 1994.

125 Tipple and Willis, 1991; Tipple and Korboe, 1989.

126 This entails agricultural land price plus cost of services.

127 In Australia and Malaysia, it took at least five years during the 1970s to pass through a web of over 50 bureaucratic hurdles before agricultural or government land could be formally occupied. Following substantial review, the time was brought down to three to six months by the 1990s.

128 This includes the creation of spatial information about the land prior to titling (Uganda) and the development of land administration systems where people's rights are adjudicated without titling (Mozambique), and the awarding of starter titles exclusive of planning and adjudication (Namibia).

129 UN-Habitat, 2002.

130 See UNCHS (Habitat), 1996c; UN-Habitat, 2002f.

131 For example, Yahya, Agevi et al, 2001.

132 UNCHS (Habitat), 1996c; UN-Habitat, 2002f.

133 UNCHS (Habitat), 2001c.

134 It is estimated that the rate of access to adequate water supplies fell from 91.8 per cent in 1990 to 90.7 per cent in 2000. Such estimates need to be treated with care since different countries use very different measures of adequacy. For example, in India all piped water is regarded as potable although it is generally not drinkable. In Thailand, which is regarded as having good water, most of the middle class use bottled water for drinking. The urban proportion with access to drinkable water according to Western standards would be less than 50 per cent.

135 UNESCAP, 1997, p37.

136 UNESCAP, 1997, pp59, 124.

137 It is surprising, given neo-liberal preoccupations, that studies examining the choice process and its urban outcomes have not been undertaken, given the large number of housing choice studies conducted in more developed countries. The extent to which lower-income households actually make the trade-off between location, housing quality and security of tenure, or even whether rational choices are made at all, rather than simply ones of expediency, is an unexplored area.

138 In Latin America, in particular, housing gap calculations are a major determinant of housing policy.

139 See Mackay, 1999.

PART III

SEARCHING FOR ADEQUATE POLICY RESPONSES AND ACTIONS

This third part of the Global Report builds on the preceding sections by examining who the different stakeholders responding to the growth and development of slums are, and reviewing the policy options and strategic alternatives that they have adopted, particularly inclusive strategies of partnership and participation.

Through this review, some of the past assumptions about the role and contribution of different actors are questioned, and many of the practical difficulties that they face are examined. The successes and failures that have characterized many decades of attempts to address slum conditions are highlighted. Recommendations encompass the need to adopt a flexible approach to the principal strategies, slum upgrading and secure tenure that can be tailored to specific contexts and that promote structures within which the different actors can cooperate and work together.

The chapters reveal a number of common themes that bring together the experience of the diversity of actors and policy approaches across the board. These are dealt with from a different angle in each of the three following chapters.

Chapter 7 looks at the shifting priorities and approaches of the variety of actors working with urban poverty and slums, including those of national governments, as well as of multilateral and bilateral development agencies. It starts with a review of the broad spectrum of interventions that have been used in slums in different countries, ranging from forced evictions and resettlement, through large-scale public-sector interventions of different kinds (including social housing and demand-side subsidies), to local pro-poor and inclusive approaches, such as upgrading, enabling and city development strategies.

In view of this changing context for urban development, the changes in priorities of the range of actors dealing with slums are reviewed. A number of emerging themes are highlighted, such as the extent to which the heavy reliance on purely market-based solutions to slums has increasingly been questioned by most actors, leading to a growing emphasis on human rights aspects of slums, and calling for better efforts to balance market-based approaches with a concern for social issues and equity for the urban poor. Positive trends are also highlighted: notably, encouraging examples of international networks and initiatives, as well as evidence of increasing efforts to adopt more integrated approaches to slum improvement.

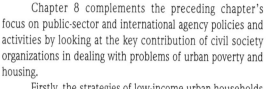

Chapter 8 complements the preceding chapter's focus on public-sector and international agency policies and activities by looking at the key contribution of civil society organizations in dealing with problems of urban poverty and housing.

Firstly, the strategies of low-income urban households themselves are examined, considering the barriers and sources of vulnerability faced by men, women and children in slums, and the responses of their community organizations. This discussion of poor households is used as a basis to define and examine the different components of civil society, including community-based organizations (CBOs) and non-governmental organizations (NGOs), highlighting the diversity of their structures, their motivations and their activities in slums. These range from the direct provision of resources and services to slum dwellers, to activities such as lobbying for policy change and mobilizing other actors who deal with slums.

In the light of this diversity, the chapter goes on to look at some of the implications of working with civil society organizations in efforts to address the problems of slums. In doing so, it highlights the important role of NGOs in representing and reaching the urban poor. At the same time, it questions some of the naive assumptions that are commonly held about civil society, leading to frequent failures to understand its scope for addressing urban poverty in many contexts. This is highlighted in issues such as lack of accountability or the existence of inequalities in power relations in communities, which may mean that the poorest and most vulnerable are excluded, and that the often conflicting relations between the state and civil society bodies are often not taken into account.

Chapter 9 draws together a number of issues relating to the 'inclusive city' and inclusive development strategies. The review of policy issues highlights a number of areas in which the major policy approaches need to be improved.

It continues from the previous chapter with an examination of the strategies and arrangements for replicating and broadening slum upgrading strategies before considering the key policy issue of security of tenure – for which there is a need to move from current strategies of regularizing tenure to more affordable and inclusive means of establishing housing security.

Infrastructure projects have rarely been approached in a way that meets the requirements of poor people or uses their labour. Poorly thought out transport policies have not been inclusive and have relocated the urban poor to remote areas and eliminated their means of accessibility in order to provide better access for affluent households with cars. Civil works, in general, often provide opportunities for small-scale enterprises and communities to improve their livelihoods through more labour-intensive appropriate technology approaches.

The mobilization of finance for small enterprise, civil works and housing has been a key concern for enabling approaches, as conventional banking or finance organizations rarely extend into slum areas because of perceived high costs and risks. Accessing novel instruments or sources to improve affordability and availability of funds generally requires government facilitation or support.

The second part of the chapter focuses on governance and inclusion, discussing the Campaign on Urban Governance, partnerships and cross-sectoral coordination. If inclusive policies are to be put into practice, participatory urban governance has a major role in reconciling the competing interests and priorities of urban actors from the public and private sectors and civil society, as well as in coordinating activities across a range of sectoral areas and levels of activity. Inter-sectoral coordination and the melding of bottom-up participatory planning with top-down national planning are critical to the success of participatory experiments.

Major highlights of the third part of the report are as follows:

- For a long time, neglect or forced evictions were the major response to urbanization in the developing world. A general consensus has slowly emerged that comprehensive slum upgrading schemes, forming part of larger development strategies, are the recommended best practice for less developed countries. Establishing secure tenure, public health and sustainability, advancing gender equality, and – especially – partnerships for poverty reduction are also major planks of the platform.
- Intra-household differences and inequalities (especially relating to the role of women) must be taken into account in defining strategies or interventions. Reciprocal relations between households that create support structures are vital parts of the operation of successful low-income communities. This explains why different ethnic groups cluster together. Keeping these relations intact must be addressed in all types of intervention.
- In a few places, the primary response to slums and areas of poor housing is now a combination of public or social housing, targeted housing allowances, and rebuilding through gentrification. Housing finance for low-middle income earners is supported by the secondary mortgage market or other government guaranteed funds. There have been considerable advances in public housing asset management and innovative housing and finance schemes for lower-income earners. Much public housing has been moved to housing associations (with NGO management). In many places, social housing is now quite diversified in order to meet the needs of a changing clientele, and is under tenant management or participation.
- The centrally planned economies met their primary urbanization with very large-scale, often high-rise,

public housing construction. China alone has provided up to 50 million enterprise-built dwelling units since 1950. These countries have had difficulty in meeting the challenges of asset management and diversification, partly because of the unsustainably low rents charged. By contrast, Singapore combined savings schemes with innovative asset-management practices to create sustainable organizations that supply most of the public and private housing.

- Chile and South Africa have conducted large-scale direct subsidy programmes, involving up-front payments to households to finance private-sector housing: South Africa has built over 1 million affordable houses in five years by this means. By and large, however, publicly assisted construction schemes have been a failure in the developing world, with poor execution and resources woefully inadequate to the task. Even aided self-help schemes, such as sites and services, have proved too expensive for lower-income households.

- The removal of regulations that harass poor people in earning their livelihoods or building housing, or that hamper the development of effective private markets, are a focus of some international agencies, including the World Bank and the US Agency for International Development (USAID). Others such as the Nordic countries focus on human development, sustainability and empowerment.

- In 1998, over 200,000 grassroots organizations were functioning in Africa, Asia and Latin America. These organizations are involved in organizing self-help activities, running community facilities, as well as a range of other local projects and activities.

- There are at least 50,000 NGOs working with poor communities in developing countries. They have been instrumental in obtaining and distributing resources, and in providing advocacy and diversity of response, and they have become the preferred channel for relief agencies to implement anti-poverty and self-help programmes. In many cases, non-profit organizations are preferred over the private sector in contracting out government services. They are seen to encourage democracy and accountability in countries where there has been increasing disillusionment with government. However, as they have gained in importance, they have also become less and less autonomous. The line between governments and NGOs has often become quite blurred. The understanding of what participation and partnership mean in practical terms remains open to wide interpretation. Participation and partnerships are often regarded as a cure-all for development problems, without careful thought being given to how best the complexity of, and barriers to, these goals should be addressed.

- Large-scale regularization of housing on public land has often failed to provide sufficient coverage and has failed to reach the poor. Regularization is often a difficult, costly, complex process, beset by corruption, which leads to situations in which the poorest residents may be squeezed out through market pressures after housing areas have been 'formalized'. Instead of heavy reliance on regularization programmes, therefore, Chapter 9 advocates a move to more locally tailored, flexible and incremental systems to upgrade tenure through, for example, temporary measures using cooperative ownership, or emphasizing occupancy rights rather than freehold titles through administrative or legal measures against forced evictions.

- Infrastructure development is a major cause of relocation of low-income households, often to remote locations without access to services or income opportunities. The equity implications of new transport initiatives must be part of project and programme plans – especially with regard to low-income transport and to relocated households.

- Upgrading and other infrastructure projects should use labour-intensive solutions involving small-scale enterprises rather than heavy equipment, where this is economically justified. Government incentives or subsidies to large contractors should be removed and legislation and training should support small enterprises. Building regulations should allow for more affordable technologies. Unpaid volunteer labour should only be used on the most local activities.

- Typical annual expenditures by local governments in Northern Europe are well above US$1,000 per person, while in the least developed cities the expenditure may be less than US$1. As a result, services are grossly inadequate. The lack of revenue is largely due to the poverty of the citizens, but is also compounded by poor governance and inefficient tax collection mechanisms.

- Micro-finance approaches used in informal enterprise lending have also been used for housing, but they are not ideal as terms are too short. A number of good practices in lending for cheaper or even informal housing exist; but they tend not to extend to the lowest-income households, including slum dwellers. The private financial system is unlikely to lend to the poorest groups. However, they can be encouraged to lend to middle-income households using various forms of guarantee or support, or through untapped sources of funds, such as credit societies or secondary mortgage markets, which takes off some of the pressure on housing markets. Interest rate subsidies or fixing are not recommended as they limit the supply and effective functioning of the housing finance system.

- The advantages of partnerships are in obtaining synergy, public efficiency and community participation. But partnerships must be inclusive and firmly within the domain of elected government. Partnerships may be developed for infrastructure or service provision, for planning, advocacy and the carrying forward of projects.
- Effective inter-sectoral cooperation requires the building up not just of mechanisms and committees, but of trust and a good knowledge of specific responsibilities and how they may be brought together. Obtaining a confluence of top-down and bottom-up approaches, effective coordination of decision-making and policies, as well as the building of a consensus and shared city vision, are prerequisites to the success of participatory governance.

7

NEW POLICY DEVELOPMENTS AT THE NATIONAL AND GLOBAL LEVELS[1]

Past slum policies and strategies pursued by governments and local authorities are generally well known and have been reviewed extensively.[2] This chapter is therefore more concerned with the forces that shape the sequence of slum policies implemented in both developed and developing countries, with emphasis on recent policy developments. As shown earlier in Chapters 4 and 5, the first experience of dealing with slums was in the now high-income, or developed, countries, starting in the late 19th century. This experience provided a starting point for developing countries as they sought to implement national urban low-income housing policies and, within that context, to address slum problems emerging in their rapidly expanding cities. In addition, slum solutions in developing countries have been increasingly shaped by the successive policies and approaches adopted by international agencies, both multilateral and bilateral.

In light of the above, this chapter first discusses the search for affordable and sustainable approaches to the provision of public-sector housing for low-income households in both developed and developing countries. This provides the necessary background to an understanding of the slum-specific policies pursued by governments, which are summarized in the second section. This is followed by a brief discussion of two recent contextual changes contributing to the shaping of new low-income housing and slum policies – that is, increased inequality within and between cities (earlier examined in more detail in Chapter 3) and the increasing relative political importance of cities. The fourth section analyses the roles and priorities of international actors who are partly responsible for shaping emerging slum policies, including both bilateral and multilateral agencies. The final section examines three current pressing issues that initiatives designed to improve the lives of slum dwellers should address – namely, financial constraints; contradictions between economic and social objectives; and coordination and cooperation, especially among international agencies working in slums.

SEARCH FOR AFFORDABLE ALTERNATIVES AT THE NATIONAL LEVEL

Periods of major housing stress have usually precipitated major changes in policy response. Demobilization following major military engagements has always led to a wave of owner-building. Unregulated 'wild settlements' sprang up around many European cities after World War I, and an international wave of owner-building occurred during the late 1940s, particularly in the US, Canada and Australia, where governments did not intervene quickly enough to deal with the huge housing shortages. Veterans' housing helped to set the post-war parameters for housing policy in these countries.

The most affected countries did, however, respond rapidly and effectively. From the 1930s to the 1970s, re-housing the poor was the focus through the construction of public housing, often in high rise blocks, that replaced existing 'slum areas', which often were perfectly viable heritage housing – for example, in Glasgow. The record of re-housing the existing residents remained poor – in Sydney less than 20 per cent of the residents of a tract demolished for a public housing block during the 1960s were re-housed. The blocks themselves often had the opposite of what was intended, in terms of effect, with no one having responsibility for the public spaces, and no interacting community to maintain order. The highly publicized demolition of the Pruitt Igoe block in Detroit, after only five years of operation, ranks with the Titanic as a testament to the folly of exaggerated claims.

A strong private commercial interest in developing and building these blocks through 'public–private partnerships' kept the building process alive for longer than their utility to the residents would have dictated. Only the collapse of several shoddily built blocks (notably, Ronan Point in Newham) stopped the march of the council behemoths in the UK.

From the 1980s, under neo-liberal theory, support for government construction or comprehensive subsidy was curtailed in favour of demand-side subsidies through payments to qualifying households to improve their housing-related income in order to make housing affordable. This was intended to enable the private sector to 'do its job' of building housing and supplying the capital for it. The full-scale neo-liberal agenda, as expressed in the US Housing Allowance Voucher Experiment of 1977, was never implemented; but, subsequently, universal housing allowances with a degree of tenure neutrality became a feature of most Western systems.

Critics of demand subsidies complained that low-cost housing was inelastically supplied, and that private rental lacked security and was inherently an unequal tenure, so that subsidies would primarily be absorbed as higher profits by landlords. Housing allowances would involve an ever increasing drain on government budgets that could never be removed, unlike capital expenditure that can be varied on an annual basis according to economic conditions. However, Keynesian-style pump-priming moved out of fashion, and budget flexibility ceased to be an issue. By the early 1990s, housing lost its own urban portfolio in government and was subsumed into social security in many countries. Expenditure on housing also fell substantially in many countries during the period: the extreme example was the US, where designated housing expenditure on low-income earners fell by 70 per cent in the 1980s.

In an attempt to maintain the low-income stock, different forms of public housing acquisition and control were tried: they paid more attention to social mix, had less uniformity of dwelling types and allowed for more tenant control. This included decentralization of control through housing associations, and alternatives such as shared ownership, spot purchase of existing dwellings to replace tenant sales and longer-term head-leasing from private landlords. Scattered site acquisition policies were begun in a number of countries.[3] These have had a mixed record of success. However, with increased inequality and a reducing or stationary stock, public housing as a fully viable alternative tenure, with cross-subsidy between generation groups and income groups, has become untenable. This public-sector housing tends to be residual and restricted to the most

During the 1990s, a number of governments stated their intention to reduce spatial inequality and to eliminate slums, often through partnership mechanisms, in a similar spirit to The Habitat Agenda

disadvantaged groups almost everywhere in the West, except perhaps in The Netherlands and the Nordic countries.

During the 1990s, a number of governments stated that their intention was to reduce spatial inequality or ethnic segregation and to eliminate slums, often through partnership mechanisms, in a similar spirit to *The Habitat Agenda*. Some countries, such as The Netherlands, have adopted legislation particularly to prevent spatial segregation of low-income earners – although this segregation had once enjoyed widespread policy support.[5] The US, which had spent more than a decade pressing forward with policies that had dramatically exacerbated spatial segregation and marginalization, adopted a number of affirmative action pilot initiatives from the late 1980s in order to improve spatial mix.[6] These housing responses were focused on individuals in the neo-liberal fashion, and scattered site-acquisition and housing-voucher programmes focusing on moving families from inner to suburban areas have been conducted on a fairly small scale in some cities.

In Europe, the dominant paradigm has become *social inclusion* rather than the underclass thesis[7] or discussions of poverty alleviation,[8] and what is to be done about excluded groups has become a key concern.[9] This has led to the adoption of area-based initiatives, which drew on the theory of social capital to develop social networks that become empowered in local governance situations.[10] This involved reforming governance structures to empower and include communities and individuals, rather than attempting to 'save' specific individuals by removing them from the influences of slums.[11] Tenure diversification on public estates, area-based interventions to empower local communities, tenant management, and the construction of more varied kinds of stock were other responses to reducing the increasing marginalization of those living in public housing as the state withdrew from direct intervention in parts of Europe (see Box 7.1).

Public housing in developing countries

The first attempts to solve the housing problem in developing countries, particularly during the 1960s and 1970s, copied European examples and began to build public housing. This rapidly stalled as it became clear that it would not provide a 100th of what was needed. It is estimated that no more than 100,000 dwellings were built in developing countries, and most of these went to government employees, such as police or teachers.

The places where public housing production succeeded in making a significant impact on total housing stock were in command economies with access to significant taxation revenues (see Boxes 7.2 and 7.3). In these places, the government was prepared to sequester a significant proportion of national income to meet housing costs. In the case of Singapore, self-sustaining programmes were created through housing sales and rents.

In the tiger economies of Asia and the oil economies of the Middle East, lobbying by private developers ensures that commercial high rise is still the major housing solution for low-income people. The housing that results is hostile to

Box 7.1 Aviles, Spain: integration of slum households within existing neighbourhoods

Aviles is a city on the coast of Asturias with an area of 25 square kilometres and a population of 85,000 inhabitants. In 1950, Aviles was an agricultural and stockbreeding area with a population of 21,000 inhabitants. During the 1960s, it became an industrial (iron and steel industry) city with a sharp economic growth that generated unplanned immigration. This migration brought urban speculation and the consequent socio-spatial segregation of the population. When the gypsy community arrived in Aviles, they settled in six shantytowns near the newly created housing states.

The gypsy community (about 500 people) progressively settled in certain impoverished areas with difficult access to basic services (housing, education, training and employment, health services). Since 1989, the eradication of the shantytowns and the integration of this group within the city has been one of the main political and social concerns. The Aviles local authority is working to achieve social inclusion by the end of 2003 and the figures show that from the 500 people who lived in six different shantytowns, currently there are only 125 living in four different shelters, and 160 are living in a 'promotional city'. The aim is to accommodate all of them (including the ones living in the promotional city) in 'normalized' conditions all over the city in order to ensure not only their access to decent housing, but also their access to other services and resources (for example, health, education and employment), thus facilitating social integration and multicultural coexistence.

The most important results are the resettlement of 75 families accommodated in 'normalized' housing all over the city and the eradication of two shantytowns (Villalegre and Divina Pastora). Others are the coexistence between the gypsy and non-gypsy population, induction into mainstream health care and education provision, and the creation of gypsies' associations – in particular, women and youth associations.

Among the contributing factors that have fanned the development of this project are social participation that is all inclusive, consensus within the community and, ultimately, the confluence in one territory of several plans, programmes and projects with complementary intervention objectives and strategies, involving different administrations and institutions.

Box 7.2 Singapore: a successful public housing programme

A great deal has been written about Singapore's successful public housing policy – for example, Yeh (1975), Wong and Yeh (1985), Pugh (1985, 1987), Castells et al (1990) and Lee et al (1993). It is one of the few countries that practices whole-housing sector development, with housing policies and institutions advancing systematically and comprehensively with the economy.[i]

By 1959, rapid population growth and neglect had led to deplorable housing conditions. As with most middle-income countries, market failure in mortgage finance was partly responsible.[ii] The Housing Development Board (HDB) was set up in 1960 to 'provide decent homes with modern amenities for all those who needed them'. Construction is tendered out to private companies. Slum and squatter settlements were cleared to make way for mostly high-rise apartment buildings.

Today, 82% of Singapore's housing stock has been built by the HDB. These dwellings are primarily sold to eligible households on a 99-year leasehold basis. Apartments have one to five rooms, including about 50,000 executive apartments and condominiums. They can be purchased, using funds from the Central Provident Fund (CPF), a forced savings scheme that receives a compulsory 20% of wages from all employees and 10% from employers. About 90% of the resident population have become owners, mostly through the HDB.

The CPF also provides mortgage loans, at concessional interest rates about 2% below the market rate, of up to 80 or 90% of the apartment price, which is also subsidized.[iii] It invests its money in government bonds. The private finance sector has also grown in recent years; but 63% of loans still originate from the public sector. From 1999, the HSB intended to start issuing bonds to meet 25% of its building programme.

There is a waiting list of about 2.5 years, and flats may not be resold for five years in order to curb speculative activity. Since 1994, one-off grants of about US$25,000 are available to eligible households to purchase resale flats. The public sector also dominates the land market, doubling its holdings to 80% of the island under the provisions of the draconian Land Acquisition Act of 1966. This was necessary to head off speculators who hoped to profit from public activity.

About 10% of the stock is held as minimum standard housing for the lowest-income households (less than US$5000 a year) and those awaiting apartment allocation.

An average of 9% of gross domestic product (GDP) per year has been allocated for housing (compared with around 4% in Organisation for Economic Co-operation and Development – OECD – countries). Savings have run at about 50% of gross national product (GNP) since 1975, most of which went into capital formation until the late 1980s. Housing expenditure has been used to pump-prime the economy in times of slowdown.

As in other countries with a large public building programme, by 1990, the stock of small apartments was inadequate to meet the needs of an affluent population. Entire blocks have been repossessed for retrofitting to larger size and higher quality. The costs of retrofitting apartments are shared with the owners. The option also exists for households to combine two adjoining small flats.

Notes: i Most of this description is from Phang (2001). ii Singapore was a middle-income country, at the time. Per capita GNP in 1997 was US$33,000, the fourth highest in the world. iii Prices are pegged to ensure that 90% of households can afford to buy a three-room repurchased flat or a four-room new flat.

traditional social patterns that make use of community and open space for lifestyle and income opportunities. The system-built dwellings are difficult for the occupants to repair or to expand as changing family circumstances dictate, and require expensive commercial interventions. This prohibitive repair bill was one problem that Russia faced before the authorities decided to hand the properties over to the residents.

A recent study concludes that there is no particular case favouring either public or private housing provision in terms of efficient production or management.[12] Appropriately configured not-for-profit producers can (and do) perform as efficiently and effectively as private producers, and actually enjoy an advantage in times of housing shortages or national trauma. However, it seems to be difficult for many developing countries to configure public delivery systems beneficially: corruption, political interference, inefficiency, inflexibility, unfair allocation and extensive delays are the rule rather than the exception.[13] Most importantly, resources available for housing are seldom sufficient to make more than a token dent in the housing problem – and it is very clear that public housing only works when it is carried out on a large scale with long-term government commitment.

Despite several well-publicized success stories, such as Singapore, government or even non-governmental organization (NGO) housing provision is largely out of favour in the developing world, and aided self-help remains the dominant paradigm, as it has been since the mid 1970s.

Assisted self-build and slum-improvement programmes

Slum clearance on the Western style has been the major response in many developing countries, despite its proven inadequacies – and for the same dubious reasons.[14] In Manila, attempts to re-house slum dwellers along the riverbanks into distant locations has not been a success – most of the beneficiaries, finding that they cannot make a livelihood on the edge of town, are back in place in a few months. Nevertheless, the Pasig River reclamation continues to be the major housing programme.

However, over a long period, other solutions that attempt to make use of the labour and resources of slum dwellers, and which seek to preserve and involve communities, have become the preferred solution to slum improvement.

It seems to be difficult for many developing countries to configure public delivery systems beneficially: corruption, political interference, inefficiency, inflexibility, unfair allocation and extensive delays are the rule rather than the exception

Box 7.3 Building urban China, 1949 to 1990

The example of China is like no other. It is possibly the only large country that has managed, so far, to urbanize rapidly without the creation of large slum areas or informal settlements. This has been done in ways that might not be acceptable or possible in other countries, and which have involved the unusual combination of centralized control over economic and social life, coupled with a great deal of decentralization. This grand experiment will probably never be replicated, requiring, as it does, tight control over the economy, a central planning system and the cooperation of a populace eager to build socialism and, therefore, to accept a more limited degree of personal consumption and property ownership than would be normal.

China's urbanization is an extreme example of a 'modernist' project, with urban influx controls related to jobs and almost complete uniformity of provision. From 1949, the new communist government provided the guaranteed basics of life to urban Chinese for the first time, and housing had a key place. The government instituted a regime involving economic expansion through state- or worker-controlled enterprises. Local management of the city and the enterprises was conducted by People's Committees, which also operated at the street level in setting up neighbourhood enterprises (for example, small goods workshops). Management within these committees was nominally democratic but was effectively controlled by the hierarchical network and the central planning process of the Communist party.

In return for accepting low wages, workers received many basic services, such as housing, utilities, education and health care, at a fraction of their cost.[i] The public enterprises provided most of the urban employment, and housing for the new employees was allocated to the project team, generally in the vicinity of the work place, which were usually large, walled, self-contained compounds.[ii] Initially, this was done through confiscating the housing of the middle and upper classes (about 35% of the private total), which was subdivided into shared room accommodation.[iii] From 1956, various forms of shared public–private ownership were instituted, which, after two years, reduced private housing to 23% of the stock in Xian.

Allocation was not based on needs or family circumstances but on work place status. The new workers were allocated 2 to 4 square metres each and were encouraged to keep their families in private accommodation. Essentially, housing was built through the profits of government enterprises as part of the reward system and was not operated on a sustainable basis. Rents were very low, well short of what was required for maintenance, and demolition and rebuilding, rather than refurbishing, became the norm. Up to 25% of urban capital spending was on new housing, but less than

1% was on urban maintenance. This remained a matter of concern for the central government, which sought to raise rents and even to transfer housing to the city governments; but the enterprises were continually seeking to lower rents in order to reward their employees.

By 1955, when the existing private stock had been filled, new construction began. The enterprises had an allocation of land (which was usually fixed) and a budget, and could build what housing they liked, subject to these constraints. The city government also built housing (about 6% of the urban total), and there was a small private sector of a similar size.

Initially, the new construction was single storey, low density, following the traditional style of courtyard single-storey dwellings in timber and sun-baked bricks.[iv] As enterprises expanded on a fixed land allocation, and since agricultural land was protected from urban expansion, the enterprises had to build to higher densities using the characteristic three- to five-storey rectangular buildings that would eventually become ubiquitous in urban China. Redevelopment of existing sites became a standard part of the urban scene.

China's urbanization between1949 and 1990, in which 300 million people were provided and re-provided with housing over a 50-year period without slum formation and without inequality, must rank as one of the great human projects of all time.[v] While the Great Wall can be seen from outer space, so can the urban lights of China. It was also the most equitable urbanization of all time; with the exception of a few senior party officials who received much better allocations, 'everyone was the same'.[vi] Some 2 billion square metres of housing were built during the period 1949 to 1990, and production continues at the rate of 240 million square metres per year, mostly built by enterprises and a few foreign developers. Oddly enough, this occurred within the context of a general 'anti-urban' policy of limiting urban growth in order to minimize urban consumption and to maximize savings and industrialization.[vii]

The execution was not faultless: the housing provided was far smaller than rural housing,[viii] and in comparison to other countries,[ix] allocation was often seen as unfair and untransparent,[x] while inadequate maintenance budgets and lack of forward thinking regarding future land and housing meant that housing had to be demolished and rebuilt, often not to community or aesthetic advantage. The almost total provision through enterprises (unlike Russia, where only 20% of housing was enterprise based) also created something of a production juggernaut that has been very hard to turn or stop, in the face of decentralization, economic liberalization and changing national priorities.

Notes: i Howell (1997). ii Gaubatz (1999). iii Taken from Wang (1995a, 1995b) and referring largely to the old capital of Xian. A similar procedure was followed in many other cities; but because of decentralization and local management, there were many differences. iv The old courtyard houses had their central open space filled in with extra bedrooms and communal facilities to form 'a maze of impossibly narrow passageways and dark tunnels' (Gaubatz, 1999). v Rosen and Ross (2000); 100 million workers and their households. vi Wang (2000); Wang and Murie (1998). vii Lin (1999). viii According to Lee (2000), average urban housing size was about 7.5 square metres per person in 1992, while rural housing averaged 18.9 square metres per person. ix The first household survey of housing conditions in 1985 revealed that 27% of the urban population were sharing their dwelling, 37% had a shared kitchen, 76% had a shared toilet and 27% had no running water (Xie, 1999). x It has become customary to stress these inequities; but they seem to have been very limited, compared with other countries.

Assisted self-build has been an acceptable form of intervention since colonial times.[15] Some studies encouraged the World Bank to intervene in housing through sites and services and slum upgrading.[16] The idea is based on observations in Peru and takes a benevolent view of communities, particularly of participatory and humanistic management, as opposed to coercive and 'scientific' administration. It holds that if governments can improve the environmental conditions of slums, and remove sanitary human waste, polluted water and litter from muddy unlit lanes, they need not worry about shanty dwellings. Squatters had already shown great organizational skill in managing to erect dwellings under difficult conditions, and could maintain the facilities once provided, while gradually bettering their homes.

Some sites-and-services schemes predated the involvement of the World Bank, which came to dominate the agenda. Notable among these is Bulangililo ('show piece'), developed in Kitwe on the Copperbelt of Zambia in 1967. Despite the then prevailing view of the World Bank, their first sponsored sites-and-services projects during the late 1970s turned out not to be replicable.[17] On the one hand, they were not popular with either residents or policy-makers; on the other hand, cost recovery was poor even in middle-income countries such as the Philippines, where they required 70 per cent subsidies.

The alternative that has come to be regarded as best practice in dealing with the problems of squatter slums is slum upgrading. Upgrading consists of regularization of the rights to land and housing and improving the existing infrastructure – for example, water supply (& storage), sanitation, storm drainage and electricity – up to a satisfactory standard. Typical upgrading projects provide footpaths and pit latrines, street lighting, drainage and roads, and often water supply and limited sewerage. Usually, upgrading does not involve home construction, since the residents can do this themselves, but instead offers optional loans for home improvements. Further actions include the removal of environmental hazards, providing incentives for community management and maintenance, as well as the construction of clinics and schools. Tenure rights are primarily given to the occupants. Those who must be moved to make way for infrastructure may be given sites and services plots.

Upgrading has significant advantages; it is not only an affordable alternative to clearance and relocation (which cost up to ten times more than upgrading), but it also minimizes the disturbance to the social and economic life of the community. The results of upgrading are highly visible, immediate and make a significant difference in the quality of life of the urban poor. An assessment of slum improvement programmes is presented later under 'self-help and *in situ* upgrading'.

From the late 1980s, with the launch of the Global Strategy for Shelter, self-help programmes reached a new level of sophistication based on neo-liberal principles of the withdrawal of government to a broadly facilitative role and the fostering of efficient markets.[18] It was decided that the resources of the private sector and the people themselves needed to be mobilized and that the role of the government would be to remove bureaucratic obstacles, provide plans and advice, and generally facilitate the process. The strategy was never really implemented on a significant scale, as it was something of an interim step on the way to the comprehensive poverty reduction programmes of the late 1990s. The 'enabling approach' is still official policy for many agencies and countries, although it tends to be honoured more in the breach than in the commission.[19]

Housing capital subsidies

The problem with self-help is that it is relatively slow to implement and depends upon the cooperation, goodwill and resources of residents, and their governments and other stakeholders. The example of the high income countries (HICs) must be kept in mind: self-help has only been an important feature of housing and service provision in circumstances where formal structures are unable to cope, such as post-war emergencies. Once the system has settled down and re-established itself, public and private formal suppliers have taken over.

Much of the developing world is, effectively, in a situation of urban housing emergency where formal structures have failed; but it is not surprising that, in some countries with rather more resources, wholesale attempts to solve the housing problem through direct intervention are being tried on a large scale. As public housing meets with such criticism from neo-liberal advisers, and from critics of one-solution-fits-all households, social housing is accordingly in retreat throughout the world and is no longer considered to be the logical option.

Some broad initiatives in line with neo-liberal principles have been tried in several countries.[20] Demand-side subsidies in the form of housing allowances and housing vouchers have been tried in Eastern Europe, although the scope of the programmes has been quite small – not comparable with the universal housing allowance schemes in place in a number of countries in Western Europe.[21]

The real test of demand-side subsidies in developing countries has come with large-scale cash grant schemes in Chile and South Africa. Similar cash grant schemes have been tried in Germany, Poland, and Australia, sometimes coupled with forced savings as in Singapore, as an adjunct to an already well-functioning housing provision system. However, applying cash grants to pay much of the cost of housing for a whole population in middle-income countries with partially developed provision systems is altogether a much more substantial and risky commitment.

The Chilean system of targeted housing subsidy was begun to replace the socialist public housing programmes. It is regarded as a best practice, and elements of the scheme later spread to Colombia, Costa Rica, Ecuador and Panama.[22] As with the first Australian scheme, a targeted programme provided a subsidy to lower-income families depending upon how much they were able to accumulate in savings. About 1.6 per cent of GDP was spent on the programme in 1998, and this has fallen in the current fiscal crisis. However, an average of about 90,000 subsidies a year was provided in

In high-income countries, self-help has only been an important feature of housing and service provision in circumstances where formal structures are unable to cope, such as post-war emergencies

Upgrading has significant advantages; it is not only an affordable alternative to clearance and relocation, but it also minimizes the disturbance to the social and economic life of the community

From the late 1980s, with the launch of the Global Strategy for Shelter, self-help programmes reached a new level of sophistication based on principles of the withdrawal of government to a broadly facilitative role and the fostering of efficient markets

Box 7.4 The First Home Owners Scheme (FHOS) in Australia

The First Home Owners Scheme (FHOS) in Australia has continued with occasional interruptions since the late 1960s. It involves a cash payment to eligible groups to assist with building or purchasing a first home, and is intended, partly, to fill the 'deposit gap' that households have to meet before they are eligible for finance. Conservative governments have started and stopped it according to housing market conditions and budget contingencies. It has always been immensely popular and has generally been associated with building industry and house price booms. In the mid 1980s, it was quite well targeted (Flood and Yates, 1986); but in its present incarnation of 2001 to 2002, it is not targeted at all (as it is intended to compensate for the effects of the new Goods and Services Tax on new housing): a number of millionaires have taken up the grant. Total outlays over two years have been 300,000 grants for US$250 million (an average of US$833), considerably more than is spent on public housing, and comparable to the spending on rent assistance.

The FHOS has always been attacked by housing activists on the major ground that very little of the money finds its way to the bottom 30% of the income scale or into cheap housing. Like concessionary home lending, it is, essentially, a programme for the lower middle class in order to move them into home-ownership when their market position seems to be weakening. As the votes of this group tend to control who is in power, any subsidy such as the FHOS that can be directly attributed to the incumbent party has good political support. When tied to new construction, as it has usually been, it is also a programme for the residential building industry, which has a strong lobby associated with the conservative political party.

the 1990s, covering some 22 per cent of the population.[23] A recent study concludes:

> *Chilean housing policy is exemplary. It is meeting many of the goals set by all developing countries, such as bringing an end to the illegal occupation of land, providing housing solutions for all families that need them (including the poorest), and making basic services available to almost the entire population.*[24]

In the case of South Africa, housing policy under apartheid was characterized by a 'fragmented patchwork of inequitable, unsustainable and disconnected interventions'.[25] The 'million homes programme' was a major election promise of the African National Congress (ANC) when it was swept into power in 1994. It had multiple objectives to reward people for what they had suffered under apartheid, to improve the housing stock, and to attract people out of a mishmash of public housing schemes where receipts were not even enough to meet the repair bill, where occupation had become informal and largely unregistered, and where utility bills were not being paid.

Up to 5 per cent of government budgets were to be spent on housing – primarily directly to developers on behalf of individuals whom they had 'signed up'. After six years of operation, the scheme provided 'secure tenure to the poorest of the poor in both urban and rural areas. The total number of houses that have been constructed is approximately 1,155,300, housing close to 5,776,300 people'.[26] This is a stunning achievement for a new programme. About 196,000 subsidies per year had been given by 2001.

The expenditure has, however, been lower than originally proposed, at less than 1 per cent of the national budget,[27] which was not particularly generous compared to a usual 2 per cent budget expenditure on housing in the developing world.[28] The subsidy of 18,000 rand per house was not enough, and not enough effort was put into establishing corresponding lending facilities to match the government grant or to obtain a contribution from the new owners so that, in the end, local governments have had to step in to make up the shortfall, particularly in the provision of infrastructure. The private sector has largely moved out of provision because of poor mark-ups on such cheap housing, and the bulk of 'subsidy housing' is now being built by government.

Much of the housing has been built to low standards because of its very low cost and the inexperience of new builders who rushed in to meet the huge surge in demand. Nevertheless, for once it was actually affordable to low-income earners. Some lower-income occupants were not prepared to meet the full cost of utilities and other home-ownership costs, preferring to sell their new houses, take the capital gains and move back to low-rent township housing. As with slum clearance and relocation, the failures have arisen because it has not been perceived that the problem is not one of housing, but of income generation in an informal setting.

These large-scale schemes in Chile and South Africa arose because the public housing systems that they replaced were almost bankrupt and something new had to be tried.[29] All of the examples have shown that a wholesale injection of funds into housing markets can produce a great deal of housing. The amount of expenditure can also be controlled, unlike housing allowances, and much of the money finds its way into owner-occupied rather than rental housing. The quality of this housing is at issue, the capacity to afford to occupy it is also in doubt for low-income earners, and the potential for diverting funds to enterprising but not necessarily competent developers has been substantial. Nevertheless, in terms of the number of new houses produced, these interventions are hard to beat.

PAST AND PRESENT APPROACHES TO SLUMS AT THE NATIONAL AND LOCAL LEVELS

Many policy approaches to slums have been attempted during the course of the last decades. They range from passively ignoring or actively harassing men and women who live in slums, to interventions aimed at protecting the rights of slum dwellers and helping them to improve their incomes and living environments. Comparative analysis of policy approaches to slums shows that, currently, cities are still practising many of those approaches that were in use decades ago. Approaches to slums that were employed even over 100 years ago may still be seen today. For instance, the use of summary eviction and slum clearance in 19th-century

Policy approaches to slums of the last decades range from passively ignoring or actively harassing those living in slums, to actions aimed at protecting the rights of slum dwellers and helping them to improve their incomes and living environments

---

Box 7.5 South Africa's right-based housing policies and demand-side subsidies

South Africa is one of some 30 countries that have included the right to housing in their constitutions. Its housing policy is also based on *The Habitat Agenda*. Section 26 of the constitution, adopted in 1996, states that all South Africans have the right to 'access to adequate housing'. A recent court ruling in South Africa, however, stressed that it is not an unqualified obligation on the state to provide free housing on demand, as the constitution states that 'The State must take reasonable legislative and other measures, within its available resources, to achieve a progressive realization of [Section 26: the right to have access to adequate housing]'. Moreover, the court ruled that there 'is an express recognition that the right to housing cannot be effected immediately'.

The South African government has taken a wide range of steps within the framework of a progressive realization of housing rights since the introduction of a democratic government. A wide range of legislation has been adopted to improve the housing conditions of the average citizen, in general, and of the most vulnerable and disadvantaged groups, in particular. Moreover, and in line with paragraph 61 of *The Habitat Agenda*, the legislation (the Housing Act) calls for monitoring and evaluation of the situation with regard to homelessness and inadequate housing. The South African Human Rights Commission is a major instrument in this context. It carries out and publishes an annual report on the realization of the rights enshrined in the constitution, including the right to adequate housing.

The main practical mechanism for implementing the new housing policy of South Africa is the use of a wide range of targeted subsidies. All households with incomes below certain minimum levels qualify for such subsidies. In fact, since the first democratic elections in 1994, the government – in collaboration with a wide range of civil society actors – has provided subsidies to more than 1,334,200 households for the poorest among the poor in rural as well as urban areas. By 2001, a total of 1,155,300

houses had been constructed, housing close to 5,776,300 people, in a country with some 40 million people – a remarkable achievement in so short a time.

The People's Housing Process is a major initiative addressing the shelter needs of the poorest and most vulnerable and disadvantaged groups. It makes a particular effort at involving women in decision-making and draws on their special skills and roles in the communities. The scheme contributes to the empowerment of communities and to a transfer of skills. This housing delivery approach relies on subsidies from the government and technical, financial, logistical and administrative assistance from non-governmental organizations (NGOs) and support organizations. The issue of quality control versus the quantity of units produced was being addressed in South Africa through the establishment of a National Home Builders Registration Council. Moreover, and rather importantly, it was recognized that a gradual approach to standards was necessary.

A number of lessons can be drawn from the South African experience with regard to the operationalization of the right to adequate housing. Among these are the need for national consensus on the definition of adequacy; the need to identify additional financial resources; and the need to improve the capacity of, and the efficiency among, all stakeholders in the housing delivery process. Moreover, there is a clear need to identify new and additional options in the housing markets in terms of quality of dwellings, as well as innovative tenure options that meet the requirements of the poorest groups.

Another, very significant, lesson from the South African experience is that a revision of national legislation is not a sufficient condition for creating the desired impact. Considerable financial commitment from government has proved to be necessary for a successful and significant impact, particularly in terms of alleviating the inadequate housing conditions of the most vulnerable and disadvantaged groups.

European cities can still be witnessed today somewhere in the world.

Frequently, policy approaches derive from the lessons learned and critical analysis of the previous endeavours and attempts. However, clear changes in the accepted wisdom of how best to deal with slums, and resulting changes in the approaches used, would be difficult to see as a straightforward process of policy evolution over time. While new policy approaches have been developed in response to the new requirements and to overcome the deficiencies of the past, many 'old' approaches, or at least some of their components, continue to be used today.

For example, educational and cultural issues were a key concern of programmes and policies premised on the post-war 'culture of poverty' perspective. Today, while this perspective is largely discredited, a focus on 'education' for slum dwellers is again evident, aiming at instilling appropriate values and behaviour modification, particularly in the context of current efforts to improve hygiene under unsanitary conditions.[30] Cultural factors are important in

many respects. Some are seen in attempts to create mixed-income communities, where middle-class households are expected to act as role models for neighbours who are unemployed. The work of the Culture in Sustainable Development group of the World Bank aims to support culture as a key element of social and economic development for poverty reduction, social inclusion and environmental protection.[31] Some of the policy approaches to slums that were used in the past (and all of which continue to be used today in various forms and contexts) are explored in more detail below.

Negligence

This approach predominated in most developing countries until the early 1970s. It is based on two basic assumptions: slums are illegal, and slums are an unavoidable but temporary phenomenon (mostly linked with accelerated rural–urban migration) that can be overcome by economic development in both urban and rural areas.

Negation of the reality of slums in cities – and, hence, of the rights of slums dwellers – was seen in the planning documents produced by urban central and local government planning institutions. More often than not, slums or informal urban settlements were not even placed on land-use maps, but were shown as blank spots denoting undeveloped land.

Such attitudes might be deeply influenced by the post-World War II reconstruction policy models that were heavily employed by the industrialized countries, especially in Europe, as shown earlier. These models where based on heavily subsidized low-cost housing programmes that, in the context of high and steady economic growth, brought improvement of housing conditions and resulted in elimination of urban slums. In an effort to achieve similar results, most developing countries responded to the housing needs of the poor through the formal provision of low-cost housing, rather than through policies of slum upgrading or integration. Making use of public land reserves and public subsidies, governments embarked on massive public housing schemes targeted, in principle, on low- and low middle-income groups, but actually allocated to the middle classes, government employees and political clienteles. The high cost of this approach was the main reason why the housing needs of the poor have not been met. In many countries, especially in sub-Saharan Africa, the situation was aggravated by post-independence economic constraints and resulted in increased social inequalities and spatial segregation in cities.

Eviction

This was a common response to the development of slums during the 1970s and 1980s, particularly in political environments predominated by centralized decision-making, weak local governance and administration, non-democratic urban management, non-recognition of civil society movements and lack of legal protection against forced evictions.[32] When it became clear to the public authorities that economic development was not going to integrate the slum populations, some governments opted for a repressive option with a combination of various forms of harassment and pressure on slum communities, leading to selective or mass eviction of slum dwellers.

Negotiations with slum dwellers (who were considered to be illegal squatters) were rare. Communities living in informal settlements were rarely offered viable alternative solutions, such as resettlement, and, more often than not, no compensation whatsoever was paid to evicted households. Evictions were usually justified by the implementation of urban renewal projects (especially during the redevelopment of city centres) and by the construction of urban infrastructures or for health, sanitary and security reasons. The highest pressure was therefore exerted on inner-city slum dwellers who occupied prime locations for development with better access to infrastructure.

This approach did not solve the problems of slums; instead, it shifted them to the periphery of the cities – to the rural urban fringes – where access to land was easier and planning control non-existent. The continuing spatial growth of cities brought about an endless cycle of new evictions and the creation of new slums at the periphery of cities, outside of the municipal boundaries, or it accelerated the overcrowding of dilapidated buildings within cities. Demand for land and housing from the urban poor during the 1970s and 1980s gave rise to the rapid development of informal markets and to the commodification of all informal housing delivery systems, including those in squatter settlements.

Self-help and *in situ* upgrading

This approach stemmed from the late 1970s, recognizing slums as a durable structural phenomenon that required appropriate responses.[33,34] It was based on the assumption of the diversity of local situations, of legal and regulatory frameworks,[35] and of the failure of responses based mainly on repressive options and the direct and highly subsidized provision of land and housing by the public sector for the poorest segment of the urban population. In addition, this new approach was fostered by increased awareness of the right to housing and protection against forced eviction at international level and the definition of new national and local political agendas in a context of an emergent civil society, as well as processes of democratization and decentralization.[36]

Self-help and upgrading policies tend to focus on three main areas of concern:

1   Provision of basic urban services.
2   Provision of secure tenure for slum dwellers and the implementation of innovative practices regarding access to land.
3   Innovative access to credit, adapted to the economic profile, needs and requirements of slums dwellers and communities.

Slum upgrading initiatives carried out during the earlier period of 1970 to 1990 were mostly no more successful or sustainable than sites and services. Certainly, slum upgrading appeared to be considerably cheaper than other alternatives. A 1980 study estimated World Bank upgrading projects to cost US$38 per household, compared with US$1000 to US$2000 for a core sites-and-services housing unit or US$10,000 for a low-cost public dwelling.[37] Early evaluation reports of the three largest upgrading programmes – in Calcutta (US$428 million), Jakarta (US$354 million) and Manila (US$280 million) – were glowing. For example, some 3 million people were assisted in Calcutta, and reported deaths from waterborne diseases fell by more than a half during the 1970s. *Kampung* improvement households in Jakarta invested twice as much in home improvements as other households.[38] The reclaimed Manila Tondo foreshore, where 200,000 squatters lived, underwent 'fantastic improvement' by 1981, with not only better environmental conditions, but also improved livelihoods, more recreational and health facilities, and greater stability and community cohesion.[39]

However, cheap solutions can have poor outcomes. Like other aid projects that focus purely on construction, the projects (although involving large numbers of households) existed in isolation from both government and the communities. Governments did not follow through with services, communities did not maintain the facilities, and governance structures disappeared once the international experts were gone. Later evaluations were less complementary, to the point where 'slum upgrading' disappeared from World Bank documents.[40] Overall, environmental conditions in these settlements were substandard. Environmental conditions remained extremely poor, with standpipes not functioning and other water sources suffering faecal contamination.[41] Most waste remained uncollected. Communal toilets and washing blocks were largely ineffective because of poor maintenance, unreliable water supply and poor location.[42]

Land acquisition was also always a problem – on private land, very considerable financial returns could be appropriated by the owner following development and upgrading. These owners had often originally engaged in informal or even illegal arrangements with invading groups and had made no attempt to improve the land themselves.

There has also always been a problem of poor governance. Poverty alleviation and slum upgrading were low on the real agendas of many governments. Many city governments seemed incapable of maintaining rudimentary urban services, enforcing cost recovery, or keeping land registries for property tax up to date – which further reduced their resources and their ability to act. In the worst cases, governments appeared to be largely a conduit for politicians and top officials to fleece the poor and the aid agencies. In such circumstances, citizen apathy rather than energy was the rule. It clearly would be much more difficult to implement slum upgrading in a sustainable way than originally thought. A number of different solutions were proposed, each with their own adherents and ideologues, and the resultant outcome was the 'enabling approach'.

Enabling policies

The progression of slum upgrading, dealing with the issues of secure titles and economic development in slums, brought an awareness of the need to involve slum dwellers not only in the construction processes of slum improvement, but also in the decision-making and design processes that establish priorities for action and support for implementation. Thus, from the mid 1980s to a culmination in *The Habitat Agenda* of 1996, the 'enabling approach' was developed to coordinate community mobilization and organization, and to make the argument for state withdrawal from the delivery of housing goods and services in favour of providing support for local determination and action. Enabling policies are based on the principles of subsidiarity and they recognize that, to be efficient, decisions concerning the investment of resources in domestic economic, social and physical development have to be taken at the lowest effective level.

For the majority of activities in connection with the improvement of slums, the lowest effective level is that of the community and the neighbourhood. However, it is recognized that for decisions to be rationally and responsibly

made at this level, many communities need support in the form of training, organizational assistance, financial help and managerial advice. The governance role, whether through local government or agencies of the central administration, is to ensure that such supports are provided. In cases such as the Sri Lanka Million Houses Programme during the 1980s, the government itself provided these supports. In many other situations, they fall to civil society organizations and NGOs.

The politics of devolution, decentralization and deregulation that is associated with such approaches is complex. The mechanisms for implementing such politics undermine many of the principles and practices upon which local bureaucracies are built. Furthermore, as will be discussed in the next chapter, communities are complex and rarely united. Thus, while there are many examples of effective and successful enabling strategies, the process is not easy.

Resettlement

Resettlement has been associated with virtually all types of approaches to slums. It embraces a wide range of strategies, though all are based on perceptions of enhancing the use of the land and property upon which slums are located or housed. At best, relocation is undertaken with the agreement and cooperation of the slum households involved, such as the resettlement of squatters on railway land in Mumbai, India, in conjunction with an NGO (Society for the Protection of Area Resource Centres, SPARC), the Railway Slum Dwellers Federation, Indian Railways and the World Bank, or the resettlement of squatters from Brasilia in Samambaia, Brazil, described in Box 7.6. At worst, resettlement is little better than forced eviction with no attempt at consultation or consideration of the social and economic consequences of moving people to distant, often peripheral, sites with no access to urban infrastructure, services or transport.

Despite and, in some cases, because of these approaches, except in those countries that have benefited from a high rate of economic development (mainly in Southeast Asia), the housing conditions of the poor have not improved significantly. In most cities, the numbers of urban dwellers living in slums remains stable or is increasing, except in countries that combine large-scale slum upgrading and tenure regularization programmes with the production of serviced sites and low-cost housing programmes.

However, this full range of approaches to slums continues to be used in different contexts today, including less enlightened approaches, such as neglect or summary eviction. It can, nonetheless, be argued that there has been an evolution of policy approaches to slums. Broadly, there has been a recognition that effective approaches must go beyond addressing the specific problems of slums – whether they are inadequate housing, infrastructure or services – and must deal with the underlying causes of urban poverty. Some of the recent developments in policy approaches to slums, and the context in which these new approaches operate, will be examined in the following sections.

There has been a recognition that effective approaches must go beyond addressing the specific problems of slums – whether they are inadequate housing, infrastructure or services – and must deal with the underlying causes of urban poverty

---

Box 7.6 Participatory relocation in Samambaia, Brazil

At a distance of 25 kilometres from Brasilia, the Samambaia Administrative Region occupies the southwestern region of the Federal District, covering a total of 104 square kilometres. The urban area of 26 square kilometres had only 5549 inhabitants in 1989 but grew to a population of approximately 163,000 inhabitants in 2000.

The residents of Samambaia are resettled squatters from Brasilia. Confronted with squatting on the extensive public open spaces and gardens that characterize the planned capital, Central Brasilia, the city authorities entered into a dialogue with the squatters. The authorities offered to resettle them in the Samambaia suburb, provided the squatting families agreed that land titles would be given in the name of wives rather than husbands. This was to safeguard against the sale of plots by men. Reportedly, ten years later, few, if any, families had sold their plots. The relocated squatters were assisted to move, sites and services were provided, but they had to build their houses themselves. In order to guarantee easy access to the city and employment, a subway has been constructed.

The consolidation of the city through government assisted settlement programmes spurred the transformation of the wooden shanties of the early phases into brick and mortar houses, now constituting 85% of the housing stock. The community structures and networks were kept as much as possible intact during the resettlement process. The city of Samambaia now has a high quality life, a vibrant local economy, a well established network of schools and a centre for professional skills training. It has ample public

open spaces and sports facilities, is well endowed with health facilities and has a good public transportation network.

With the approval of the Samambaia Local Structure Plan in 2001, a range of new initiatives are being executed by the Regional Administration of Samambaia. One of these innovative projects is the 'Linhão de Samambaia', which makes efficient use of a strip of land previously reserved for a power transmission line to accommodate approximately 68,000 additional urban residents. Another example is the 'Arrendar' project, consisting of 1350 units with rental housing contracts offering future purchase options, implemented in partnership between the Federal Government and the Government of the Federal District.

These projects are part of a new multi-faceted housing policy of the Federal District, designed to promote better use of existing urban land, to decentralize government action in the field of housing, to optimize employment generation and to ensure synergy with other sectoral policies. This is backed up with a new housing information system to effectively monitor the interventions programmed under the policy.

The Samambaia experience demonstrates the importance of secure tenure for the financing of projects and sustainability of project achievements, as people are more confident to invest their own savings if they have secure tenure. It also showed that a well articulated, multi-faceted housing policy integrated in a broader strategic planning framework is critical to expanding the range of housing options for all urban dwellers and can generate employment in the process.

Source: UNCHS (Habitat), 2001b, pp34–35.

Current best practice: participatory slum improvement

The best practice for addressing the challenge of slums in developing countries is now participatory slum improvement. However, so far, this has mostly been adopted on a limited scale or at the level of demonstration projects

The accepted best practice for housing interventions in developing countries is now participatory slum improvement.[43] However, so far, these have mostly been adopted on a limited scale or are demonstration projects.[44] The interventions are intended to work for the very poor, often in situations where there are no markets. The best examples are holistic approaches to neighbourhood improvement, taking into account health, education, housing, livelihood and gender. Government largely adopts a facilitative role in getting things moving, while maintaining financial accountability and adherence to quality norms. It is now good practice to involve the communities from the outset, often through a formalized process, and to require a contribution from the occupants, which gives them both commitment and rewards.[45] The more sustainable efforts appear to be those that are the main plank of a city development strategy with planned, rolling upgrades across the city and a political commitment to maintenance.[46] As a general rule, the more marginalized or culturally separate the group being assisted, the more participation and partnerships are necessary.

Many agencies have been involved in slum upgrading over the past 25 years in all regions of the world, along with thousands of local governments and NGOs. Much

organization, local goodwill and cohesion, and political will are necessary to make projects of this type work, and it remains to be seen whether they are replicable on a wider scale.

Some of the more sustainable examples of participative slum upgrading programmes include:[47]

- The Orangi Pilot Project in Karachi, where residents constructed sewers to 72,000 dwellings over 12 years during 1980 to 1992, contributing more than US$2 million from their own resources. It now includes basic health, family planning, and education and empowerment components.[48]
- Integrated programmes of social inclusion in Santo André municipality, São Paulo, a slum upgrading programme that has improved the living conditions of 16,000 *favela* inhabitants through partnerships with groups excluded from citizenship with local authorities and aid agencies (see Box 7.7).[49]
- Self-help partnership projects in Alexandria, Egypt, which are to be integrated, up-scaled and replicated throughout the country.
- The Urban Poor Community Development Revolving Fund in Thailand, which provides low interest rate loans for community development in poor areas (see Box 7.8).

Box 7.7 Social inclusion in Santo André, Brazil

Santo André, with a current population of 650,000, is part of the São Paulo Metropolitan Area. Santo André has been undergoing a period of transformation, from its industrial past to an expanding tertiary sector. The economic gap between the rich and poor has grown, exacerbated by the slowdown of the Brazilian economy during the 1990s. As a result, living conditions have deteriorated and a number of *favelas* – areas of extreme poverty – have emerged.

The municipality is promoting an Integrated Programme of Social Inclusion as a strategy to alleviate poverty. The objective of the programme is to establish new ways of formulating and implementing local public policies on social inclusion. Fourteen principal partners, local, national and international, are actively involved in the programme. Four areas were chosen for the pilot phase, selected through a participatory budgeting process, resulting in a total amount of US$5.3 million, which has been invested in the provision of urban infrastructure and services.

The project has seen the improvement of basic services in some of the worst neighbourhoods. Micro-credit facilities have been made available to small-scale entrepreneurs, while health care has been made more accessible through community health agents. Other social programmes have been implemented including literacy campaigns for adults and programmes aimed at street children. Recreational facilities have been made available, serviced plots have been transferred to families and low income families re-housed in apartment buildings. An index has been developed to measure social inclusion and data collection is carried out on a regular basis. One of the most important results has been the engagement of a wide range of actors and the creation of effective communication channels. All activities have taken into account gender participation and mainstreaming. The administration intends to extend the pilot programme to all slum areas in the city,

through differentiated slum upgrading projects while strengthening the approach towards regularization of land tenure. In addition, the programme will attend to all families facing situations of extreme economic exclusion through a revised minimum income policy and through the up scaling of existing programmes. Three initiatives from Santo André on Good Governance, Traffic Management and Administrative Reform are featured on the Best Practices database.[i]

The effective reduction of urban poverty and social exclusion in Santo André is based on a number of key principles:

- Well targeted government interventions in the urban sector can foster citizenship and enable people to create more productive urban livelihoods.
- The active participation of the urban poor in decision-making promotes effective formulation and implementation of local action plans.
- The participatory budgeting process, an innovative approach to urban governance and decision-making, provides a real voice for the urban poor in both the allocation and use of municipal and other resources.
- The Municipality of Santo André has shown that while effective leadership needs to be ensured by the local administration it, in turn, needs to devolve decision-making and implementation powers to the community.
- Inter-agency collaboration and effective channels of communication between various actors and stakeholders is critical to successful slum improvement and reduction of poverty and social exclusion.
- Principles of equity, civic engagement and security are key to success.

Note: i See www.bestpractices.org.

Source: UNCHS (Habitat), 2001b, pp34–5.

- Partnerships for upgrading in Dakar, Senegal, over the last five years, which have impacted more than 1 million inhabitants.
- The Holistic Upgrading Programme in Medellin, Colombia, which has addressed the needs of 55,000 slum dwellers in the first phase.

RECENT CONTEXTUAL CHANGES

This section examines some of the changes in the policy perspectives of the key actors involved in addressing the problem of slums, including those at the national and local levels examined earlier. It should be noted, however, that the emerging policy approaches proposed by these actors, as well as building upon the lessons learned from past successes and failures, are also evolving in response to recent changes in the cities in which slums exist. Over the last two decades, many global and urban development processes have had an impact on the nature of slums and on

the scope of different policy approaches for dealing with the problems and constraints faced by men and women who live in slums. Some key changes in the urban context include the increasing inequality within and between cities, and the growing autonomy and political influence of cities.

Increased inequality within and between cities

One of the many impacts of the increasingly globalized world economy, as Chapter 3 emphasizes, is that growing competition between cities to attract investments tends to increase inequalities between, and within, cities. Over the last decade, this issue has given rise to an abundance of literature[50] analysing the contradictory roles demanded of city governments as they seek to make their cities competitive in order to attract global investment (with incentives such as low labour costs or tax breaks), and attempt to combat the social and economic exclusion of many of their residents.[51] Furthermore, many policies promoted by the international financial bodies have been

Box 7.8 Urban Community Development Fund (UCDF), Thailand

The Urban Community Development Fund (UCDF) of Thailand was created as a tool for poverty eradication, empowering both the urban and rural poor. The project covers 53 provinces out of 75 throughout the country, and has resulted in about 950 community saving groups out of a total of 2000 urban communities, as well as more than 100 community networks.

The Urban Community Development Office (UCDO) was set up in 1992 in an effort by the Thai Government to take a new approach and develop new processes for addressing urban poverty. The government established a revolving fund of 1250 million baht (about US$28 million) through the National Housing Authority to set up a special programme and the new autonomous unit, UCDO, to address urban poverty nationally. The programme sought to improve living conditions and increase the organizational capacity of urban poor communities through the promotion of community savings and credit groups and the provision of integrated loans at favourable interest rates as wholesale loans to community organizations.

The UCDF was to be accessible to all self-organized urban poor groups. The idea, however, was not simply to provide low-interest loans to the poor. Community savings and credit activities were seen as a means for engendering a community's own holistic development, capable of dealing with the root causes of poverty. Of importance was the development of community managerial capacity and stronger community organizations to exercise leadership in various community development processes and to leverage external development resources. Thus the development process included community action planning and the creation of partnerships with other local development actors – especially municipalities.

Various kinds of low-interest, wholesale loans were offered to community savings and credit groups and networks throughout the country. They were allowed to add a margin to cover their expenses or the cost of other community development activities or welfare programmes. The organizations added certain margins so the members would receive the loans at a rate near to or slightly higher than the prevailing market rates, which in any case were still much lower than those in the informal money lending systems.

Between 1997 and 1999, the problems of the economic crisis affected the urban poor's savings and credit groups immensely and several community savings and credit groups came to the verge of collapse. This led UCDO to the new direction of bringing groups to work together and share risks and responsibilities through networking, thus widening communal responsibility for loan repayments. These new network processes were mobilized to deal with several other urban community issues such as infrastructure, housing, community planning, education, health and welfare.

The main achievements of the UCDF are:

- *Increased community organizations and networks:* UCDO has been able to expand its activities into 53 provinces throughout the country. About 950 community saving groups and more than 100 community networks have been set up.
- *Increased community assets and direct financial resources:* More than 1000 million baht (about US$22 million) have

been disbursed as various kinds of loans and more than half of the loans have been repaid. At the same time, community-based savings groups have, to date, mobilized more than 500 million baht (about US$11 million).

- *Increased community management and enterprising capacity:* Having established their resource base, communities, with the help of UCDO, have been able to create linkages and partnerships with other groups and develop the confidence necessary to initiate and implement activities to improve their living conditions and to form effective partnerships with local authorities.
- *More diverse housing solutions developed – from individual projects to city processes:* Several kinds of housing projects have been developed through loans to community initiatives, including buying existing slum land, resettlement schemes that are in close proximity to former communities, slum improvement and post-disaster housing repairs and reconstruction. As a result, the urban poor have a much wider range of options and the lessons learned have formed the basis for several city-wide housing development activities.
- *Development of large-scale community welfare activities:* Most of the community networks have developed their own community welfare programmes to take care of the more vulnerable groups in their midst. These welfare programmes have been completely designed and carried out by the networks, and include funds for school fees, for people who are sick, for the elderly, and for emergencies within communities.
- *The experiences of the UCDF have spread to other countries:* Several countries such as Cambodia, Laos, Viet Nam, India, South Africa, Namibia and Zimbabwe have developed similar approaches in their countries and there are now many similar community funds in operation.

Lessons learned from the UCDF experience include the following:

- The experience provides compelling evidence that access to credit is one of the main barriers preventing the urban poor from developing and extricating themselves from poverty. It also demonstrates that community-based savings and credit for housing is one of the most effective means to do so, as it allows people to lead more productive lives.
- The management of community funds or poverty reduction programmes should be designed on the basis of the conditions of the poor, not on the basis of market or bureaucratic exigencies. The wholesale lending system uses market rates and the resulting interest rates are much lower than those offered by informal credit systems.
- As poverty results from causes that are structural, it is necessary to develop ways in which the poor themselves can become stronger and have more confidence to initiate change, implement their own development activities and engage in partnerships and dialogue with public authorities. This process requires a long-term effort in capacity building.

Source: UNCHS (Habitat), 2001b, pp44–5.

criticized for their role in reinforcing social inequalities as they force weaker economies to cut costs by lowering prices and wages, which is invariably accompanied by longer working hours, deteriorating working conditions, reduced social security and increased informality.[52]

The patterns of inclusion and exclusion that result are not uniform; instead, some cities and some groups are successfully integrated within global trade systems through these strategies, albeit – at times – with a significant social cost, while others continue to be excluded from the global economy despite sacrifices in social welfare. The issue that this process raises for policies designed to deal with slums is that it is precisely those cities and groups that are excluded from the global economy that are likely to experience the problems of slums – at the same time that their financial capacity to deal with them is declining. Furthermore, as withdrawal of the state is a central aspect of the solution commonly advocated for the exclusion of cities or nations from the global economy, this raises the question of what the role of the state is in dealing with slums – and who should take on this role, if not the state?

New political influence of cities

At the same time, another factor that affects the scope and nature of new policy approaches to slums is the growing political influence of cities, many of which act with increasing autonomy from national governments. Various processes can be observed that have directly promoted this stronger role of city governments.

Firstly, international institutions and bilateral aid agencies have made efforts to promote local governance, which has meant that municipalities have become relatively more important. There is a growing consensus amongst such agencies that central governments should not be the only beneficiaries of international aid, and this has led to an increase in direct cooperation with local authorities and communities.[53]

Secondly, the decentralization policies that were promoted at the global level by bilateral and multilateral cooperation organizations from the late 1980s onwards have been key in raising the profile of city governments. This can be seen as a response to the perceived inability of central governments to respond to basic needs (such as land, housing and basic services), and the continuing state disengagement from the urban sector, in general, and from the housing sector, in particular. The increasing political influence of cities is accompanied by the development and strengthening of local authority networks and associations.

This increased influence of city governments has various implications for slum populations. One is the perceived stronger role of local (city) governments in promoting the social and economic inclusion of urban residents. For example, the Global Campaign on Urban Governance initiated by UN-Habitat is committed to the 'inclusive city' on the grounds that local democracy and decentralization are two inter-related norms, with inclusiveness being the 'red thread' between them.[54]

However, the danger of increased reliance on city governments to promote the inclusion of residents,

Box 7.9 The range of actors dealing with slums

International, multilateral and bilateral agencies

These include:

- International financial institutions (IFIs) – namely, the World Bank – and regional finance institutions, such as the International Development Bank (IDB) and the Asian Development Bank (ASDB).
- Organizations and programmes of the United Nations system, such as UN-Habitat, the United Nations Development Programme (UNDP), the United Nations Research Institute for Social Development (UNRISD) and the United Nations Environment Programme (UNEP), as well as regional commissions of the United Nations, that is the Economic and Social Commission for Asia and the Pacific (UNESCAP), the Economic and Social Commission for Western Asia (UNESCWA), the Economic Commission for Africa (UNECA), the Economic Commission for Latin America and the Caribbean (UNECLAC) and the Economic Commission for Europe (UNECE).
- Supra-national regional entities, such as the European Union (EU).
- Inter-agency programmes, such as the Urban Management Programme (UMP), the Municipal Development Programme (MDP) and the Cities Alliance.
- Regionally funded development programmes, such as UrbAl or AsiaUrbs, funded by the EU.
- Bilateral cooperation organizations: a few bilateral agencies have recently elaborated urban policy or strategy documents,[i] while a significant number of countries have no explicit urban strategy.[ii]

Networks

These include:

- International associations and networks of local authorities, such as the International Union of Local Authorities (IULA), CityNet, the United Towns Organization (UTO) and Metropolis.
- Professional associations, such as the International Real Estate Association (FIABCI), the International Federation of Surveyors (FIG) and the Cooperation for the Continuing Development of Urban and Suburban Transportation (CODATU).
- Foundations, associations, and national and international NGOs.
- Experts, researchers and academic international networks.

National and local bodies

These include:

- Central government entities, such as ministries and central administrations.
- Sub-national entities, such as states, regions and provinces.
- Government agencies, such as authorities and statutory bodies – for example, land development agencies(LDAs) and housing development authorities (HDAs).
- National and local finance institutions, such as housing banks and mortgage credit institutions.
- City and municipal governments and administrations.
- National and local partners of international networks and associations.
- National private-sector actors, such as real estate, infrastructure and service providers.
- National and local NGOs.
- Communities and community-based organizations (CBOs).

Notes: i DFID, 2001; BMZ, 2000; USAID, 2001; CIDA, 1998. In Australia: Flanagan and Kanaley, 1996; SIDA, 1995; SDC, 1995; The Netherlands Ministry of Foreign Affairs, 1994; DANIDA, 2000 (in Danish). ii For example, Belgium, Finland, France, Italy, Japan, Portugal and Spain.

including the poor, is that the increased political mandate of city governments (under decentralization) is often not supported by increased access to funds with which to act. In addition, while the scope of city governments to make decisions about how to promote the inclusion of citizens has grown, this is within the context of a global economy and unreformed international status quo – over which, it is argued, they have little or no influence.

INTERNATIONAL ACTORS DEALING WITH SLUMS AND THEIR PRIORITIES

Range of actors

A wide range of bodies and associations (see Box 7.9) is involved in aid and cooperation programmes in the urban sector. Some of these are directly involved in housing and slum-improvement projects and programmes, while others have an indirect impact on slums through interventions at global, national, city and settlement levels in areas such as sustainable urban development, decentralization, governance, capacity building, poverty alleviation and support to innovative partnerships.

The shifting priorities

Emerging strategies to improve the lives of slum dwellers attempt to address the underlying causes of poverty. There has been a shift to multi-sectoral approaches that consider the many inter-relationships between sectors

While the actors listed in Box 7.9 have a wide range of priorities, some general recent shifts in policy perspective can be observed that more or less cut across the board. Today, emerging policy strategies to improve the lives of slum dwellers attempt, for the main part, to avoid working through projects that merely target the manifestations of urban poverty in slums. Instead, they are becoming more supportive of approaches that address the underlying causes of poverty, and that involve the people who live in poverty and their representative organizations.

There is also a growing recognition that a great deal of improvement can result from simply eliminating regulations and policies that act against the interests of the poor men and women who live in slums, such as removing prohibitions against commercial, income-generating activities, relaxing unrealistic building codes and standards, and discontinuing eviction and displacement actions.

In addition, there has been a shift from approaches that are focused on a single issue, such as sanitation or upgrading of housing, to multi-sectoral approaches that consider the many inter-relationships between sectors. Perhaps most significantly, current developments include the emergence of new types of partnerships, supplementing conventional public–private partnerships with new forms of collaborative arrangements between civil society groups and the public and private sectors.

However, despite such common themes in current approaches to dealing with slums, many of the key actors working in this area have distinct priorities about, and approaches to, the problem. These are explored below.

■ Bilateral cooperation: diversity of political objectives

Bilateral cooperation policies in urban development reflect a diversity of priorities in accordance with the political objectives of each donor country and their view of the appropriate role of the public sector. Nonetheless, it is possible to group bilateral cooperation policies into three broad types:

1   Cooperation emphasizing accelerated economic liberalization, commodification of land and housing markets and integration of the informal sector within the sphere of the formal market. For example, USAID[55] takes a neo-liberal approach to housing and slums by promoting restricted public activity (seeing the state as an 'enabler'); strengthening the private sector; mobilizing private sources of funding; reducing public financing; improving local taxation systems; creating a framework for housing delivery by the private sector; and developing new municipal financing instruments.[56]
2   Cooperation emphasizing social integration objectives (the Nordic group and, to a lesser extent, Dutch, Canadian, Swiss and German cooperation agencies). The social-democratic position of the Nordic group gives strong support to municipal authorities aimed at improving their management capacity, and at coordination, funding and service delivery. It also strengthens the revenue base of municipalities within an appropriate policy framework.
3   Cooperation that combines these two objectives: the emphasis is on social or economic liberalization goals, depending upon local situations.[57]

■ Multilaterals: a growing convergence

The last few decades have seen multilateral cooperation agencies employ a range of activities that deal directly or indirectly with slums, revealing a sea change in their overall approaches to this issue. As is explored in detail below, the World Bank approach to slums has been subjected to significant changes over the last three decades, especially during recent years when the bank has begun to reasses the role of the state and the significance of social and environmental processes in slums, rather than focus only on markets as the solution for slums.

The United Nations approach to slums can be seen, in part, in the range of its initiatives, starting from the 1960s. The International Year of Shelter for the Homeless, 1987, was a significant stage in policy development, leading to the elaboration of the Global Strategy for Shelter to the Year 2000 (GSS). Several of the following United Nations world conferences showed increasing awareness of urban poverty issues and slums: the UN World Summit for Social Development, 1995, the UN-Habitat II Conference, 1996[58] and the UN Istanbul + 5, 2001.[59] In 1997, the International Forum on Urban Poverty formulated a set of policy principles that recognized that ongoing processes of global economic restructuring affect people living in poverty in urban areas, and stressed that policies on urban poverty cannot be formulated and applied at the city level alone.[60]

Overall, a review of the policy approaches of multilateral agencies reveals that their urban development priorities are increasingly in accord. At the same time, the role of international finance institutions and multilateral agencies in defining urban development and housing strategies is tending to increase as approaches to slums are generally situated within wider, integrated urban-development and anti-poverty programmes. Today, for international finance institutions, as well as cooperation and aid agencies, policies regarding slums must be seen as a component of the wider global urban-development strategy.[61] While some key differences in approach remain between the different multilaterals, there is, as will be illustrated below, a gradual convergence of approaches.

Since the 1970s, the World Bank has pursued a range of urban development operations (fluctuating between 3 per cent and 7 per cent of its lending), as is reflected in strategy papers and statements produced by the bank since the late 1970s.[62] Four main phases can be identified in the World Bank's strategy regarding urban, water and sanitation, and environment issues.

From the mid 1970s to the mid 1980s, the World Bank's urban development projects were predefined packages of multi-sectoral investments, primarily through central government agencies or specialized development authorities. This encompassed two approaches: sites and services, and slum upgrading, which were seen as more cost effective and socially acceptable than the approaches of slum clearance and relocation that prevailed in many countries.[63] The World Bank's assessment of the first decade of lending observed that these 'shelter projects' were limited in their coverage, benefiting directly an average of 25,000 households, but not replicated as city-wide or national programmes.[64] The main bottlenecks were found to be the existing regulatory frameworks and the complexity of projects, which were too difficult for the public agencies in charge of their implementation to deal with. A 1983 assessment[65] also stressed the need to address the structural distortions in housing markets, institutional finance and urban management in order to create conditions that favour greater replicability.[66]

By the mid 1980s, the World Bank's growing emphasis on structural adjustment took precedence over the earlier poverty orientation, shifting from multi-sectoral interventions targeted at low-income groups to a systemic approach. The focus for urban assistance moved to institutional development, the financial constraints impeding effective local service delivery, and to direct interventions that addressed poverty. The debt crisis contributed to this shift, leading to objectives such as improving the mobilization of resources and domestic savings, as well as cost recovery at project level. Institutional development was implemented in a global context of land and housing market liberalization and the setting-up of housing finance systems. However, many of these projects failed to extend programmes to the urban poor in a way that met their demands.

From the mid 1980s, many countries, with support from the World Bank, placed emphasis on a move to private-sector management of services, such as water and sanitation, housing, urban transport and solid waste management, as well as on incentive systems for formal-sector agencies. By the end of the 1980s, this process was expanded by a reassessment of the World Bank's lending policy. Emphasis was put on deregulation and privatization, and the disengagement of central governments from the urban service sector, moving to a 'minimal state' approach in which the state's role is limited to providing regulatory frameworks for areas such as health, fire hazards and certain kinds of waste. In many cities, the poorest segment of the population was directly affected by this set of measures, as the state withdrew from service provision in areas where the private sector would not cater for the poorest segments of the urban population.

The new urban strategy is directed at correcting sources of market failure in the urban economy, *as well as* government failure, paying particular attention to poverty and inequality issues.[67] This reflects the limits or failure of conventional aid and cooperation policies to deal with the growth of urban poverty (particularly in peri-urban areas), acknowledges the impact of urban poverty on social and political stability, and highlights the emergence of new social forces in cities. The new approach argues that cities must be sustainable and functional in four respects: they must be *liveable* (in order to ensure quality of life for all residents, including the poorest), *competitive*, *well governed and managed*, and *bankable* (financially sustainable). These objectives require:

- improvement in procedures through which donor institutions target and deliver subsidies;[68]
- support to institutional reforms, as 'poorly distributed assets may affect adversely the quality of institutions and their ability to solve problems';[69]
- development of partnership with informal institutions;
- improvement of housing finance mechanisms and support to micro-credit initiatives; and
- provision of security of tenure in informal settlements (though not necessarily through access to land ownership).

Four main activities are proposed in the renewed programme of the World Bank's urban support:

1   Formulating national urban strategies.
2   Supporting city development strategies.
3   Expanding assistance for capacity building.
4   Scaling up successful initiatives in services upgrading for the poor, including upgrading of low-income neighbourhoods.

This last activity requires wide support from beneficiaries and the originating institutions.[70] Finally, although the basic stance of the World Bank (market-oriented and recommending economic liberalization) has been constant over the decades, recent changes reveal an increasing concern for the economic, environmental and social sustainability of globalization and accompanying liberal urban-development strategies.[71]

The Habitat Agenda, of which UN-Habitat is the focal point within the United Nations system, reflects a consensual approach to shelter on the part of the international community, and focuses on shelter as a human right.[72] Implementing *The Habitat Agenda* depends upon the willingness of partner states and institutions. It acknowledges the global dimension of urbanization and the need for global responses to housing and shelter issues, and focuses on five strategy objectives of:

1 Adequate shelter for all.
2 Sustainable human settlements.
3 Enablement and participation.
4 Financing shelter and human settlements.
5 Integrating gender perspectives in human settlements-related legislation, policies, programmes and projects.

A 2001 report on the implementation of *The Habitat Agenda* emphasizes the:[73]

- central role of governments in improving the housing conditions of the most vulnerable and disadvantaged groups;

- strategic role of secure tenure;
- key importance of enabling policies, including community development, broad-based participation, and collaborative, cross-sectoral and participatory housing restructuring;
- need for targeted and transparent subsidies, and
- link between sustainability and income generation.

The United Nations and its constituent bodies' approach to slums reflects the unique capacity of the United Nations to set global norms and objectives (reflected in the international development goals that have been adopted over the past decade). Human rights are at the core of the United Nations approach to shelter. The focus on human rights comprises both normative and operational activities. Two strategic entry points have been chosen to help attain these goals regarding the rights of people living in poverty: the Global Campaign for Secure Tenure (GCST) and the Global Campaign on Urban Governance (GCUG). In tune with *The Habitat Agenda*, both campaigns aim to work closely with all levels of governments and representatives of civil society, especially those representing the urban poor, in order to raise awareness and improve national policies and local strategies to reduce urban poverty, as well as to enhance social inclusion and justice and to promote the role and equal rights of women – an essential factor for the success and sustainability of development.

The GCST was designed three years after the adoption of *The Habitat Agenda*. The campaign is based on the premise that security of tenure is a prerequisite to social and economic development and that its provision has long-lasting positive effects on a wide range of stakeholders. The campaign takes into account the social dimension of urban poverty and proposes a new strategy that involves the poor in the design of the solutions to their housing problems and their implementation.[74]

A significant development in recent years was the launching of the United Nations Housing Rights Programme (UNHRP) in 2002, a joint initiative by UN-Habitat and the United Nations High Commissioner for Human Rights (see Box 7.10).

At the 1995 World Summit for Social Development, poverty eradication was made the overriding priority of the UN organization – meaning that this body now has a clear role in improving the lives of the urban poor and slum dwellers. The UNDP's overall focus is on a range of activities, including building capacity for good governance, popular participation, and private- and public-sector development and growth with equity.

Using the framework of Sustainable Human Development, the UNDP is providing policy guidance and support in poverty eradication, employment and sustainable livelihoods. It also supports the mainstreaming of participatory approaches and the strengthening of civil society organizations. These advisory and support services reflect existing and anticipated demand from the developing countries.

In addition, the UNDP-initiated facility entitled Public–Private Partnerships for the Urban Environment

---

Box 7.10 United Nations Housing Rights Programme (UNHRP)

The United Nations Housing Rights Programme (UNHRP) was launched, in 2002, jointly by UN-Habitat and the Office of the United Nations High Commissioner for Human Rights (OHCHR). The establishment of the programme was a direct response to United Nations Commission on Human Settlements Resolution 16/7 and the United Nations Commission on Human Rights (UNCHR) Resolutions 2001/28 and 2001/34.

The objective of the UNHRP is to assist States and other stakeholders in implementing their commitments in *The Habitat Agenda* to ensure the full and progressive realization of the right to adequate housing as provided for in international instruments. This substantive focus is grounded in *The Habitat Agenda*, in particular paragraph 61, which states that 'Within the overall context of an enabling approach, Governments should take appropriate action in order to promote, protect and ensure the full and progressive realization of the right to adequate housing.'

The UNHRP is based on the mandates of both UN-Habitat and OHCHR, and operates as a fundamental tool for the Global Campaign for Secure Tenure (GCST). UNHRP is implemented in close consultation with the Special Rapporteur on Economic, Social and Cultural Rights. Civil society and non-governmental organizations, women's organizations, national human rights institutions, research and academic institutions and associations of relevant professions and local authorities are expected to play important roles as partners in the implementation of UNHRP.

The first phase of the UNHRP (2002–2004) focuses on five programme areas: advocacy, outreach and learning from partners; support for United Nations human rights mechanisms on housing rights; monitoring and evaluation of progress towards the realization of housing rights (including development of housing rights indicators); research and analysis on housing rights (promotion and development of relevant norms, standards and guidelines, as well as thematic research on housing rights); and capacity building and technical cooperation (assistance to states and other stakeholders in building capacities for implementing and monitoring housing rights).

(PPPUE) aims to bring together government, private business and civil society to pool resources and skills in order to improve basic services at local levels. Innovative partnership projects are conceived and designed by national and local governments, civil society organizations and private-sector associations, with the goal of improving the access of the urban poor to basic urban services such as water and sanitation, sustainable energy services, solid waste management and central municipal services.

UNRISD's recent research on urban issues has focused on the role of CBOs in confronting urban social problems, and the emerging form of cooperation and interactions between such organizations and local authorities. The purpose of this approach is to create a grassroots perspective on the problems and prospects for improving urban governance, and particularly the ability of marginalized groups (such as slum dwellers) to organize themselves in order to influence the flow of public and private resources for their benefit. Several recently formed partnerships and collaborations of this kind have already been designated as 'best practices', and have been promoted for replication in other communities and countries.

The interest of the European Union (EU) in urban issues of non-member state countries is relatively recent. For years, the EU cooperation strategy emphasized rural development as opposed to intervention in the urban sector. In response to requests from partner states, however, the European Commission (EC) has recently prepared an urban-strategy guidelines report.[75]

Although they have not yet been implemented, these guidelines provide an integrated framework for EU support to urban development, designed to ensure that sectoral projects in urban areas perform better and have a wider impact across other related sectors.

Emphasis is put on contradictions and linkages between economic development and social stability, justice and the environment. Furthermore, this is set in the context of the globalization of urban economies, which means that 'cities increasingly have to compete directly at global and regional levels for international investment to generate employment, revenues and funds for development'.[76]

The EU's development cooperation strategy is centred upon:

* supporting democratic participatory and transparent approaches to urban governance;
* formulating urban programmes and projects that are compatible with national or regional policies, as well as strategies undertaken with relevant agencies of central governments, in conjunction with other relevant development agencies at regional and local level; and
* decentralization.

Furthermore, in line with the IFIs, the EU approach is that direct public investment in housing is seldom efficient and is needed only exceptionally if all other initiatives have failed. However, the guidelines call for a reassessment of the relationship between the private sector and housing provision, noting that 'Although the emphasis has been, in recent years, to promote the role of the private actors, it should be clear that more creative processes of participatory actions between public, private and communal actors are to be stimulated'. The guidelines further stress that the public sector continues to have a key role in housing through guaranteeing access to resources, and ensuring norms and regulations for healthy, secure and affordable land and housing.

In terms of intervention in slums, the guidelines acknowledge that secure tenure is a prerequisite for stimulating investment in housing construction and improvement, and stress that evicting people is most often counter-productive as it only displaces a problem in addition to creating unnecessary social tensions. The guidelines also emphasize the need for managing and upgrading the existing housing stock; the need for preventive policies based on the provision of new sites for low-cost housing development, such as new types of sites and services projects, incremental housing and basic infrastructure provision projects; and the need to target interventions on poor communities.

Inter-institutional programmes and initiatives: emphasis on slum upgrading, innovative partnerships and local development

Many inter-institutional programmes and initiatives play significant roles within urban development. However, the policy foci and strategic approaches of the Cities Alliance, the UMP and the MDP are worthy of special attention.

■ The Cities Alliance

The creation of the Cities Alliance reflects new approaches to urban policy and management by four principal constituencies:

1. The urban poor themselves.
2. Local authorities and their associations, such as IULA, UTO and the World Assembly of Cities and Local Authorities Coordination (WACLAC).
3. National governments.
4. Bilateral agencies (ten countries) and multilateral agencies (the World Bank, UN-Habitat and UNEP).

Advancing collective know-how in working with cities is an objective of the Cities Alliance. Its partners have agreed to pool their resources and experience in order to focus on two key inter-related priorities for urban poverty reduction:

1. City development strategies (CDS), which link local stakeholders' vision for their city with clear priorities for action and investment.
2. City-wide and nation-wide slum upgrading that aims to contribute to the improvement of the living condition of at least 100 million slums dwellers by 2020, with an interim target of improving 5 million to 10 million lives by 2005 in accordance with the Cities Without Slums action plan (see Box 7.11).

Human rights are at the core of the United Nations approach to shelter. The focus on human rights comprises both normative and operational activities

Box 7.11 Cities Alliance

The Cities Alliance is a global alliance of cities and their development partners who are committed to improving the living conditions of the urban poor. It was launched in 1999 with initial support from the World Bank and the United Nations Human Settlements Programme (UN-Habitat), the political heads of the four leading global associations of local authorities, and ten governments : Canada, France, Germany, Italy, Japan, The Netherlands, Norway, Sweden, the UK and the US. The Asian Development Bank joined the Cities Alliance in March 2002, and UNEP joined in 2003. These Alliance partners have joined forces to expand the level of resources that reach the urban poor by improving the coherence of effort among on-going urban programmes, and by more directly linking grant-funded urban development cooperation with investment follow-up.

The Alliance was formed to realize the vision of Cities Without Slums, principally through action in two key areas:

1   CDSs, which link the process by which local stakeholders define their vision for their city, analyse its economic prospects and establish clear priorities for actions and investments.
2   City-wide and nation-wide slum upgrading to improve the living conditions of at least 100 million slum dwellers by 2020, in accordance with Millennium Development Goal 7, Target 11, and with the Cities Without Slums action plan.

Cities Alliance activities are organized around three strategic objectives:

1   Building political commitment and shared vision.
2   Creating a learning alliance to fill knowledge gaps.
3   Catalysing city-wide and nation-wide impacts.

In more specific terms, the Alliance achieves these strategic objectives by:

•   pooling the resources and experience of Alliance partners to foster new tools, practical approaches and exchange of knowledge in order to promote city development strategies, pro-poor policies and prosperous cities without slums;
•   focusing on the city and its region rather than on sectors, and recognizing the importance of cities and local authorities in the social and economic success of a country;
•   promoting partnerships between local and national governments, and those organizations that directly represent the urban poor;
•   promoting inclusive urban citizenship, which emphasizes active consultation by local authorities with the urban poor, with time being taken to develop a shared vision for the city;
•   scaling up solutions promoted by local authorities and the urban poor;
•   encouraging engagement of slum dwellers as partners, not problems;
•   promoting the role of women in city development; and
•   engaging potential investment partners in developing new public- and private-sector lending and investment instruments in order to expand the level of resources reaching local authorities and the urban poor, thus enabling them to build their assets and income.

The Alliance is currently working in partnership with the local and national authorities of Brazil, El Salvador, Madagascar, Mauritania, Nigeria, Rwanda, Swaziland, South Africa, Egypt, Morocco, Bangladesh, Cambodia, China, India, Indonesia, Nepal, Pakistan, Philippines, Viet Nam, Iran, Yemen, Mozambique, Kenya, Ethiopia, Jamaica and Bulgaria.

The Cities Alliance is playing a coordinating role in the operational implementation of the Cities Without Slums initiative, with particular attention to the GCST.

■ The Urban Management Programme (UMP)

The UMP, a joint UN-Habitat/UNDP global programme, gives advice to local and national governments on ways of improving the management of urban development in their countries. This is primarily through assistance in organizing 'city consultations' (see Box 7.12), promoting the participation of all stakeholders necessary to implement new approaches, and introducing new urban management policies and techniques.[77]

The strategy objectives of the UMP are to develop and apply urban management knowledge on participatory urban governance, alleviation of urban poverty and urban environmental management, and to facilitate the dissemination of this knowledge at city, country, regional and global levels.

Shifts in the UMP strategy have followed the commitments of *The Habitat Agenda*, with a growing focus on promoting and strengthening the role of local government and its relationship with civil society. In its current phase of activities (2001 to 2004) the UMP emphasizes coordination with other urban-sector programmes of the United Nations system, the strengthening of inter-agency cooperation, and the integration of the UMP within a new global strategic vision for urban development. It also aims to strengthen the links between the global campaigns on good GCUG and GCST, and programme activities. A stronger focus is being given to pro-poor governance and knowledge management activities that have direct impacts on the living conditions of the urban poor.

■ The Municipal Development Programme (MDP)

The MDP aims to facilitate dialogue between states and local governments on issues of decentralization in order to contribute to the development of African local governments, and to encourage decentralized cooperation between African local governments and local governments in other regions.

Although the MDP's main focus is on decentralization, one of its core activities (developing the supply of urban services in African cities) is directly related to slum upgrading programmes. The MDP's emphasis is on the ability of local governments to provide basic services on a sustainable basis – especially the management of solid waste, water supply and sanitation, and transport. The MDP has therefore been given the mandate to support communities in service delivery, and to help them develop new strategies.

Emerging common themes

As can be seen from the review of the priorities and activities of some of the main bilateral and multilateral actors who work on slum issues, a number of common themes appear to be emerging in their activities. These include a focus on integrated, cross-sectoral approaches to slums, efforts to promote partnerships and networking, and an emphasis on decentralization, including the promotion of decentralized cooperation. These themes are explored in more detail below.

■ Integrated approaches to slums

During the early 1990s, most donor agencies reconsidered their policies towards slums, replacing the use of 'pilot projects' with integrated projects and programmes. There is now a greater emphasis on cross-sectoral interventions for slums, mainly through integrated projects. While sectoral interventions continue to be used, they are more clearly understood as components of urban strategies.

For the World Bank, integrated policies that deal with slums are part of a more comprehensive urban development intervention model, addressing sources of both market and government failure. This stems from the financial logic of their urban development orientation during the 1990s, which focused on:[78]

- deregulation;
- privatization and public–private partnership (especially in the land and housing sectors and in the management of urban services);
- decentralization and urban management;
- housing finance; and
- enabling strategies.

However, as noted above, changes in the priorities of the World Bank over recent years have meant that it has also made efforts to factor in environmental and social criteria. The United Nations organizations have been more involved in sectoral interventions, which were partly designed to mitigate the social impacts of the market-oriented interventions promoted by the World Bank and other IFIs. In this light, United Nations organizations have their own rationale and objectives for integrated programmes, which relate broadly to the promotion of consensual mechanisms, calling for strategies such as:

- capacity building;
- community development;
- land management and tenure issues;
- the urban environment;
- poverty alleviation; and
- gender equity.

Realization of Target 11 of the Millennium Development Goals, 'By 2020, to have achieved a significant improvement in the lives of at least 100 million slum dwellers' – which clearly requires an integrated approach to slums – has catalysed the promotion of integrated approaches by United Nations agencies (see, for example UN-Habitat's approach, shown in Table 7.1).

Box 7.12 City Consultation Methodology

The City Consultation Methodology, initiated following the Habitat II Conference in Istanbul in 1996, is primarily intended to improve city policies, management and administration on poverty, environment and governance. The UMP City Consultation emphasizes partnerships with all urban stakeholders, both within and outside of city government. The UMP is working through this approach in a variety of regions, as outlined below.

Africa Region
During the recent wave of decentralization in Africa, local authorities and other stakeholders are working together to find ways of managing new responsibilities. This process has been facilitated by UMP activities through the Regional Office for Africa, and city consultation activities have been completed or are under way in 39 cities through regional anchor institutions and local partners.

Arab States Region
The UMP Arab States Office is working in 21 cities in the region and has been successful in improving the living conditions of the poor in many cities through the city consultation process. These successes have been made possible by the sustained collaboration between local UMP partners and the concerned municipalities, and by an advocacy approach that goes beyond the provision of technical advice. UMP Arab States has also made a concerted effort to include gender concerns within all of its activities. This effort has resulted in modified city consultation guidelines to include the gender dimension, and improved awareness and coverage of the issue by the local media.

Asia and the Pacific Region
In Asia and the Pacific, decentralization and local autonomy are gaining momentum; with this, interest in the capacity building of local governments is growing. The most recent experiences of UMP city consultations in Asia have shown that a participatory urban governance approach is essential for achieving improvements in existing urban conditions, processes and institutions. The UMP Asia Regional Office has undertaken 20 city consultations during Phase 3, and the outcome of these has indicated the acceptance of participatory urban governance in Asian cities. Many cities have been able to achieve significant success, which can be built upon and replicated.

Latin America and the Caribbean Region
The city consultation methodology is well suited to the current situation in the Latin America and Caribbean (LAC) region. Given the high rate of urbanization in the region (73%), urban areas in LAC have important lessons for other regions in the world in meeting the challenges of urbanization. The UMP LAC Regional Office has been active in 40 city consultations and has been successful in contributing to institutionalizing and formalizing participatory governance in the region, as well as having a positive impact on improving life and living conditions for poor and excluded communities. Mainstreaming a gender perspective has been an important component of UMP activities.

■ The promotion of partnerships and inter-institutional networks

Many of the actors involved in slum development activities have, over the last decade, worked hard to promote partnerships and networks that are designed to promote cooperation between those working in related fields. A range of activities to promote better cooperation can be observed over the last decade – for instance:

- an increasing emphasis on inter-agency programmes (as outlined above, the Cities Alliance, the UMP and

Table 7.1

The dos and don'ts of slum upgrading

Do	Don't
Promote good urban governance systems.	Assume that slums will disappear automatically with economic growth.
Establish enabling institutional frameworks involving all partners.	Underestimate the role of local authorities, landowners, community leaders and residents.
Implement and monitor pro-poor city development strategies.	Separate upgrading from investment planning and urban management.
Encourage initiatives of slum dwellers and recognize the role of women.	Ignore the specific needs and contributions of women and vulnerable groups.
Ensure secure tenure, consolidate occupancy rights and regularize informal settlements.	Carry out unlawful forced evictions.
Involve tenants and owners in finding solutions that prioritize collective interests.	Discriminate against rental housing or promote a single tenure option.
Adopt an incremental approach to upgrading.	Impose unrealistic standards and regulations.
Associate municipal finance, cross-subsidies and beneficiary contributions to ensure financial viability.	Rely on governmental subsidies or on full-cost recovery from slum dwellers.
Design and negotiate relocation plans only when absolutely necessary.	Invest public resources in massive social housing schemes.
Combine slum upgrading with employment generation and local economic development.	Consider slum upgrading solely as a social issue.
Develop new urban areas by making land and trunk infrastructure available.	Provide unaffordable infrastructure and services.

the MDP), as well as growth in partnership between multilateral and bilateral agencies in urban development projects (multi-bilateral projects);

* increasing efforts to work with international associations of local authorities;
* increasing importance ascribed to transnational networks and people/community-guided initiatives;
* growing recognition of the role of NGOs by international cooperation and aid agencies; and
* a growing role for decentralized cooperation among institutions, such as the World Federation of United Cities (FMCU).

The preparatory process of the Cities Summit (1996) gave rise to an unprecedented exchange of experiences, and the formal recognition of new urban stakeholders (CBOs and NGOs). However, Istanbul + 5 revealed a regression regarding some of the social commitments formulated in Istanbul.

Governments and partners in many countries in the South have also worked to promote partnerships and cooperation over the last decade. Relevant organizations include not only central government institutions and government agencies, but also local authorities (cities and municipalities), national stakeholders from the formal (and, to a lesser extent, the informal) private sector, communities and CBOs, and local NGOs, which are now more commonly recognized and accepted as partners in cooperation projects.

There has also been a significant growth in networking amongst research and training institutions. In recent years, bilateral cooperation agencies and/or the respective countries have established 'centres of excellence' that act as an 'intellectual, backstopping and think-tank resource'.[79] A number of research and training institutions have developed activities and programmes that relate to slums. They train staff from cities in developing countries, produce specific publications and establish networks for knowledge exchange. Some of them participate actively in the implementation of projects in slum areas.

■ Decentralized cooperation

Since the mid 1980s, central governments in the North have encouraged decentralized cooperation efforts. Almost all countries that have bilateral cooperation agencies and programmes also support decentralized cooperation, primarily in the form of municipal twinning (city-to-city cooperation), which can be seen as a 'mutual training process'.[80] However, this new kind of cooperation represents only a small proportion of official development assistance, and is often limited to technical cooperation and training; only in Spain does decentralized cooperation figure widely in bilateral urban activities.

Sectors addressed

As noted above, interventions to develop slums have, in recent decades been characterized by a move from sectoral, project-based approaches to more comprehensive urban and housing programmes. Nonetheless, a review of bilateral and multilateral agency policies over the last decade indicates that, within this more integrated comprehensive approach, seven main sectors of intervention remain important:

1. Urban management and finance.
2. Urban land management and tenure.
3. Service provision and delivery.
4. Environment and public health.
5. Housing delivery.
6. Population and social issues.
7. Capacity building, research activities and knowledge exchange.

Amongst the bilateral agencies, there is a clear convergence in their urban sectoral focus. Almost all of them are involved in six of the seven main sectors of intervention identified, with the exception of urban land administration and tenure. The specific approaches of bilaterals and other development actors to these sectors are examined in further detail below.

Urban management and finance

In this sector, the majority of bilateral agencies have focused particularly on decentralization, governance, local financial administration, and promoting capacity building at government and municipal levels. Various approaches to the sector may be observed.

The World Bank's new urban strategy is directed towards 'correcting sources of market failure in the urban economy, as well as government failure'. This involves a review of policy tools, such as targeted subsidies, basic land-use planning and urban transport management, to address social and environmental externalities in the urban economy. However, as noted earlier, this market-oriented approach is now coupled with the recognition that the market is not the only response to poverty and is not the most effective in all cases.[81] Emphasis is placed on market regulation, legal and regulatory frameworks, reassessment of financial assistance, planning, decentralization, governance, accountability, transparency and democracy.[82]

The United Nations system, EU and World Bank urban projects, since the late 1980s, have increasingly focused on policy reform and institutional changes, thus extending their dialogue further into issues of regulation, incentive systems and the pattern of relationships with urban stakeholders. This is based on the recognition that sustainable development requires approaches that reach across the physical environment, infrastructure, finance, institutions and social activities.

As discussed above, all multilateral institutions, and most bilaterals, support decentralized urban governance: the World Bank, the UMP (through its Institutional Anchoring Process Strategy), the MDP, as well as local authority associations and networks, such as the IULA, CityNet, the UTO and Metropolis.

Similarly, as noted above, most of the actors working on issues relating to slums have a strong concern with promoting partnership and participatory processes, which are of particular relevance to sectoral support for urban management. Thus, for example, the CDS of the Cities Alliance and the UMP work to develop participatory approaches for urban management and goal setting. Similarly, the UMP's City Consultation Methodology aims to develop and improve participatory decision-making and governance. Bilateral cooperation organizations have centred their intervention in slums on the strengthening of leadership at municipal and settlement levels, and on the empowerment of local authorities and CBOs, particularly concerning participation and population organization in slum upgrading programmes and projects. Urban planning, policies and practices have also been an important area of activity, involving the development and use of participatory planning procedures in slum interventions.

The reforming of legal and regulatory frameworks in the urban and housing sector has been a key activity of only a few bilateral agencies, such as the Austrian Agency for International Development (AusAID), CIDA, DANIDA, the German Development Agency (GTZ) and USAID. In slum interventions, some have targeted the redefining of norms and standards, and alternatives to evictions – for example, USAID and the GTZ.

■ Urban land management and tenure

Approaches to tenure, land management and titling issues reflect the ongoing debate on property rights. For UN-Habitat, adequate shelter for all requires the provision of legal security of tenure for all people, as well as transparent, comprehensive and accessible systems for transferring land rights.[83]

As noted above, the GCST is closely linked with policy intervention in slums. However – and despite the input of the GCST on the need for recognizing alternative and traditional rights to land and property in the debate on property rights – the EU, as well as the World Bank and the OECD, still emphasize formal access to home-ownership and titling. Professional associations, such as the FIG or the FIABCI are of the same opinion.

Bilateral cooperation agencies have increasingly focused on tenure (in particular, the UK, Danish, Canadian, German, Dutch and US agencies), examining appropriate land registration and titling procedures in informal settlements, tenure regularization[84] and securing tenure for the urban poor.[85]

■ Service provision and delivery

Although priority is increasingly given to the provision of basic urban services, few multilateral agencies are directly involved in their provision.[86] In contrast, their main objectives are to enable local urban stakeholders to provide and manage services on a sustainable basis, and to ensure the scaling-up of successful service provision initiatives.

With reference to the first objective, as noted above, the MDP has been given the mandate to support communities in service delivery and to help them develop new strategies, emphasizing partnership with other stakeholders. Regarding the second objective, the World Bank emphasizes scaling-up service upgrading for the poor, stressing the need for support from beneficiaries and local institutions (often CBOs or NGOs).[87]

In contrast, all bilateral agencies have directly provided or expanded basic infrastructure and social services. For example, in its Indian slum improvement programmes, the UK DFID has provided water supply on a city-wide scale,[88] while the Swiss have been engaged in assessing the need for social services in slums at city and settlement levels.[89]

■ Environment and public health

New emphasis is being put on the relationship between environmental problems and poverty alleviation policies.[90] However, for most agencies, the focus on environmental problems in slums (as opposed to more general urban environmental problems) has consisted of the provision of basic infrastructure, with an emphasis on the role of local authorities.

■ Housing delivery

As noted above, housing and tenure issues are a key focus of many of the actors who work with the urban poor. A central concern of the United Nations is promoting enablement and participation processes, including facilitating participation by tenants in managing public and community-based housing development.[91] Providing guidelines for innovative approaches to slums, in national and local contexts, and legitimizing the practices of urban stakeholders not usually associated in the decision-making process, are a major objective of UN-Habitat. This is a break with conventional policy responses to housing for the urban poor.[92]

The role of the formal private sector in housing and its articulation with the informal sector is currently being reassessed by the World Bank, the EU and the FIABCI. In particular, enabling housing strategies that were emphasized during the early 1990s are being reassessed by the World Bank, with particular attention to the demand from the poorest segment of the urban population.

Most bilateral agencies have worked less on housing policies and management, in general, than on concrete intervention in land and housing development. Some agencies have given direct support to the construction sector and to real estate developers, and have promoted public–private partnership for housing production and delivery (in particular, USAID). In slum-specific interventions, this has related to the involvement of private formal land and housing developers in providing low-cost serviced land and housing. Most bilateral cooperation activities have included the implementation of slum upgrading, the provision of basic urban services, and renewal and reconstruction programmes and projects, combined, in some cases, with relocation and resettlement programmes and policies. Italy, Norway, Spain and Sweden have applied their expertise to the alternative upgrading of city centres.

One key area of concern in the housing sector has also been housing finance systems. The World Bank and UN-Habitat emphasize the need for targeted and transparent subsidies. For the United Nations, financing shelter and human settlements requires the development of new housing finance instruments to address the financial needs of people with limited or no access to credit. This is performed through such approaches as community mortgage programmes that are accessible to people living in poverty.

Bilateral cooperation agencies, particularly the Swedish SIDA, the Canadian CIDA and USAID, have been active in setting up housing finance systems. The USAID approach has been based upon mortgage finance with the Urban and Environmental (UE) Credit Program, their major housing and infrastructure finance mechanism, which functions on a loan basis. However, this does not operate in the least developed countries (LDCs), as these countries cannot afford to borrow dollars at market rates and are generally eligible for concessional lending from the International Development Association (IDA).[93] In contrast, SIDA has developed a programme based on locally managed funds for loans adapted to slum dwellers' needs, coupled with a credit scheme for the promotion of micro-enterprises.

■ Population and social issues

For the main part, the core 'social issue' addressed by agencies working in slums is the overarching problem of poverty and inequality. The reduction of social inequalities

and elimination of poverty has been emphasized, as outlined above, by UN-Habitat and the World Bank, since the late 1990s. It has also become the core mandate of the UNDP, and is central to the EU urban strategy guidelines.

Urban poverty has been one of the principal goals of urban intervention by a large number of bilateral cooperation programmes since the early 1990s (for example, safety net measures that aim to reduce the social impact of structural adjustment policies (SAPs), followed by more articulated poverty alleviation programmes). Thus, employment and income-generating activities have become an important element of slum-specific interventions. Employment-generation activities and policies, and support to small-scale and home-based economic activities have formed part of most bilateral agendas. The Swiss have also concentrated on the integration of informal activities within the sphere of formal activities.[94]

Another key area of concern that is stressed by almost all institutions and agencies is gender equality, although the extent to which this concern is clearly operationlized in slum interventions is mixed. However, some bilateral agencies, notably SIDA, DANIDA and the GTZ, give particular attention to gender equality issues and the unequal treatment of women in many areas of policy and practice that relate to slums – in particular, women's access to land and housing programmes; their eligibility for relocation in slum upgrading and resettlement projects; their access to credit in slums; and the role of women in participatory slum-upgrading processes.

■ Capacity building, research activities and knowledge exchange

All agencies working with slums focus on the need for capacity building. The World Bank and the United Nations are currently expanding assistance for capacity building, and the EU is re-orienting development cooperation to include new approaches to urban research; awareness raising and capacity building; South–South cooperation; decentralized cooperation; and joint funding arrangements.

Almost all bilateral agencies are involved in capacity building at government and municipal levels. However, few (Canada, the US, Italy, Japan and the UK) have specifically undertaken socio-economic research on poverty and housing conditions relating to slums.

There has also been a rapid development of networking activities for research and knowledge exchange, including international knowledge exchange networks such as the International Research Group on Law and Urban Space (IRGLUS), Link Environmental and Academic Research Network (LEARN), and the Network Association of European Researchers on Urbanization in the South (N-AERUS). Cities Alliance has set up an urban upgrading data base in collaboration with a wide range of partners, including NGOs and CBOs, who have contributed information on a large number of slum upgrading programmes and are currently structuring a global effort to share perspectives, tools and experience on scaling-up slum upgrading.[95] Cities Alliance has also supported efforts to build communities of practices at regional level, especially in Africa and Central America.

A key area of concern that is stressed by almost all institutions and agencies is gender equality, although the extent to which this concern is clearly operationlized in slum interventions is mixed

Since 1995, UN-Habitat has developed a network database on 'best practices' relating to urban management, including a range of areas of key concern for slum initiatives. CityNet explores effective ways of supporting technical exchange and transfers of expertise and information from peer to peer in order to extend institutional capacities, and to influence the decision process at local, regional, national and international levels.

Many bilateral agencies, including those of France, Italy, Japan, Norway, Sweden and the US, actively support knowledge exchange and networking. They have set up knowledge-exchange programmes that are targeted at slums (including on preventive policies and direct interventions, innovative tools and practices, and adapted construction technology/materials).

PRESSING ISSUES

This review of the current priorities of the main national and international actors who are working on slum issues reveals that a number of lessons have been, and continue to be, learned in the effort to tackle the problems faced by women and men living in slums. These include the need to address social, environmental and human rights issues in addition to relying on markets; the need to take an integrated, multi-sectorial approach to slums and urban poverty; and the need to promote the participation of all key actors in tackling the problem of slums through processes such as decentralization, partnership and capacity-building activities.

Financial constraints

One of the main impediments to dealing effectively with the problems faced by urban slum dwellers has been financial constraints. This can be attributed, in part, to increased public-sector austerity in many countries in the South as a result of global economic inequalities and structural adjustment and liberalization programmes promoted by the IFIs. However, this problem has been exacerbated by a number of problems, including:

- lack or misuse of financial resources at national and city levels, including weak tax systems;
- increasing pressure on municipal budgets from new jurisdictions on their periphery;[96]
- lack of adequately trained personnel in most municipalities, resulting in the ineffective use of resources;[97]
- lack of access to credit for the poor, as well as appropriate housing finance systems; and
- the misuse and poor targeting of subsidies for the urban poor.

Furthermore, the financial impact of international aid should not be overestimated:

> *...at no time, in the past 30 years, has international aid exceeded US$60 billion a year... The reality is that US$60 billion for more than 2 billion very poor people in low- and*

> *middle-income countries is hardly likely to have a major impact on the global scale.*

Furthermore, urban aid has been a small proportion of total aid, and has been even smaller when compared to the efforts made by low-income and middle-income countries themselves.[98] An estimate during the early 1990s of investment in urban infrastructure concluded that total investment from public and private sources was about US$150 billion a year, with not more that US$6 billion a year coming from external sources.[99]

Contradictions between economic and social objectives

A key lesson that has been learned, and that is reflected in the increasing convergence between the market-oriented IFIs and the human rights-focused United Nations agencies is the contradiction between economic and social objectives. As noted above, there is a contradiction between market-oriented approaches that tend to increase the exclusion and marginalization of the urban poor, and socially oriented approaches that are limited in their impact and have been criticized for a heavy reliance on indebted public sectors and underfunded agencies.

However, even while there is increased awareness from both sides that there is a need to reconcile these two objectives, tensions between them persist. Even where attempts are made to link social and economic objectives, measures such as providing social safety nets and ongoing poverty alleviation programmes may be interpreted as a marginal response to the impact of neo-liberal urban and housing policies.

Coordination and cooperation

On a more optimistic note, the increasing convergence between actors who work in slums has led to more openings for cooperation, avoiding wastage of resources through duplication and competition, and promoting knowledge exchange. Agencies working on slums have been characterized by better coordination and collaboration in project implementation during recent years. Examples of such collaboration include the OECD–DAC (Development Assistance Committee) Group on Urban Environment (with active participation from Switzerland, the UK and Canada), the EU's Urban Experts Group, and the Programme Review Committee of the UMP (the meetings of which are limited to primary donor agencies and managers, and include Germany, The Netherlands, Sweden, Switzerland, the UK, the World Bank, UN-Habitat, the UNDP and, as an additional funder, Denmark). Some mutual consultation and coordination is also being practised within the Group of Nordic Countries, bringing together the Scandinavian agencies – SIDA, Finnish International Development Agency (FINNIDA), Norwegian International Development Agency (NORAD) and DANIDA – and the Utstein process that includes Germany, the Netherlands, Norway and the UK. Perhaps most significant of all is the Cities Alliance: a

'Learning Alliance' of the principal multilateral and bilateral agencies with enormous potential to influence support to urban poverty reduction and the improvement of slums. These forums provide guidance and monitoring to the programme, allow for direct involvement and participation of cooperation agencies, and create an opportunity for each participant to have improved knowledge of the other agencies' urban activities.

NOTES

1   This chapter is primarily based on a drafts prepared by Alain Durand-Lasserve, Centre National de la Recherche Scientifique (CNRS), France, and Joe Flood, Urban Resources, Australia.

2   Abrams, 1946; Mangin, 1967; Van Huyek, 1968; Wee, 1972; Stren, 1975; Dwyer, 1975; Peil, 1976; Tripple, 1976; King, 1976; Grimes, 1976; Doebele and Peattie, 1976, 1981; Turner, 1976; Laquian, 1977; Wegelin, 1977; Burgess, 1978; Keare and Parris, 1982; Ward, 1982; Amis, 1984; Malpezzi, 1984, 1989; Malpezzi and Mayo, 1987; Gilbert and Gugler, 1992.

3   This is known as 'spot purchase' in Australia, where policies to buy existing dwellings or building sites in established areas have been in place since the early 1980s in some states, so that comprehensive public housing construction has diminished substantially in importance.

4   For example, Wilson et al (1994) detail the accelerating rate of housing abandonment as an 'infection' that spread out from the core of Cleveland and other US cities from the late 1960s.

5   This is the dominant attitude in the US, which postulates that the undeserving poor are responsible for their own situation.

6   According to Marsh and Mullins (1998), a number of European states are hostile to the notion of poverty but are enthusiastic about social inclusion.

7   Marsh and Mullins (1998) attribute the concept as occurring since the mid 1970s from globalization concerns. It also has intellectual roots in the French post-structuralist movement and in post-modernism.

8   Parkinson, 1998.

9   Kearns, 2002. This attitude, in fact, dates back to the early attempts to rescue the deserving poor through suburbanization from 1880 to 1925.

10   Maclennan and More, 1997.

11   Server, 1996.

12   Werlin (1999) relates that due to the widespread prevalence of slum clearance during the 1970s, governments were annually destroying more low-income housing than they were building.

13   Serviced sites for self-build had been provided to black urban immigrants to Soweto – then known as Pimville – since the 1920s, according to Parnell and Hart (1999), as a parallel activity to the regimented and formally planned mass housing for workers that later formed the core of Soweto. Self-help housing was regarded as more suited to the African petty bourgeois elite.

14   Particularly Turner, 1966; Turner and Fichter, 1972.

15   World Bank, 1975; Pugh, 1997a, 1997b.

16   UNCHS (Habitat), 1992; Pugh, 1994, 1995; World Bank, 1993.

17   Strangely enough, in the returns to the Habitat II questionnaire in 1996, the only country to say that it did not have an enabling policy was Australia, which is possibly the only country to have successfully run a full-scale enabling policy for the housing sector over 50 years. This is because, with the enabling agenda completed, official housing policy is largely involved in the provision of public housing for the poorest households.

18   Neo-liberal theory is mostly concerned with avoiding economic distortions, which are considered to produce 'deadweight loss' in the economy. The theory predicts that one-off payments to individuals are the least distorting intervention, followed by income supplements, because these do not disrupt consumer choice or interfere with the private sector.

19   Primarily by USAID, in partnership with the Urban Institute, a think tank in Washington that had unsuccessfully tried to have similar demand-side measures introduced in the US during the 1970s. In the USSR, the housing benefit was being paid direct to utility-supply companies to help reduce costs.

20   Gilbert, 2002.

21   Gilbert, 2002.

22   Ducci, 2000, p149.

23   Rust and Rubenstein, 1996, p266.

24   RSA, Department of Housing, 2001.

25   In one year, expenditure reached 1.6 per cent of budget; but this included amounts rolled over from the previous year.

26   Renaud, 1999.

27   Gilbert, 2002.

28   For example, Abate et al, 2000.

29   See www.worldbank.org/research/conferences/culture/papers.htm for a list of papers presented at the Conference on Culture and Public Action, 30 June–1 July 2002; Rao and Walton, 2003 forthcoming.

30   Leckie, 1995.

31   Though it was first propagated by the likes of Abrams, Koenigsberger and John F C Turner more than a decade earlier.

32   Cohen, 1983; Badcock, 1984; Murphy, 1990.

33   Benton, 1994.

34   COHRE, 1999, 2002.

35   Churchill, 1980.

36   See Schubeler, 1996, for Calcutta and Jakarta.

37   Keare and Parris, 1983.

38   Kessides, 1997.

39   Mortality associated with diarrhoea in Jakarta is estimated to cost US$200 million a year, and the cost of boiling water a further US$50 million – 1 per cent of city product.

40   One of the authors of the background papers for this chapter, on a visit to an improved *kampung* in 1995, observed that a toilet block on the edge of the canal was not functioning; human waste was running directly down into the canal where a large group of children were swimming.

41   Luna et al, 1994; Amaral, 1994; Schubeler, 1996; Viloria et al, 1998. A good description of practice and problems is provided at http://web.mit.edu/urbanupgrading/upgrading/.

42   The site http://web.mit.edu/urbanupgrading/upgrading/ claims that this could be done easily for 1–2 per cent of GDP, including land acquisition and titling.

43   The participation manual by Goethert and Hamdi (1988) and the handbook by Hamdi and Goethert (1997) give the results of practice in different parts of the world.

44   See www.citiesalliance.org.

45   Some of these examples are described in UNCHS (Habitat), 2001b.

46   Ruel et al, 1999.

47   United Nations, 2001.

48   World Bank, 2002a; UNCHS (Habitat), 2001a.

49   Knox and Taylor, 1995.

50   Beall, 2002.

51   Randel and German, 1996.

52   Taylor, 1999.

53   USAID, 2001.

54   Kamete et al, 2001, p68.

55   DFID, French Cooperation.

56   UNCHS (Habitat), 1996.

57   25th special session of the General Assembly of the United Nations.

58   UNCHS (Habitat), 1998b.

59   Pugh, 1995; Querrien, 2000.

60   Cohen, 1983, 2001; Cohen and Sheema, 1992; Kessides, 1997; Mayo and Gross, 1987; World Bank, 1994, 2000a, 2000b, 2002a, 2002b.

61   Kessides, 1997.

62   Cohen, 1983.

63   Cohen, 1983.

64   Angel and Mayo, 1993.

65   World Bank, 2000a, 2000c.

66   Duebel, 2000, p34.

67   World Bank, 2003.

68   World Bank, 2000, p65.

69   World Bank, 2002b.

70   UNCHS (Habitat), 1996.

71   UNCHS (Habitat), 2001.

72   Tebbal and Ray, 2001.

73   European Commission, 2000.

74   European Commission, 2000.

75   UNCHS (Habitat), 1999.

76   World Bank, 1991.

77   Milbert 1999.

78   Milbert, 1999.

79   World Bank, 2002c.

80   World Bank, 2003.

81   *Habitat Debate*, 1997, 1999.

82   Huchzermeyer, 2002.

83   Fourie, 2000; Durand-Lasserve and Royston, 2002.

84   Satterthwaite, 1998.

85   World Bank, 2000, p65.

86   Milbert, 1999, p196.

87   Milbert, 1999, pp182–188.

88   Hardoy et al, 2001.

89   UN-Habitat, 2002a, 2002b.

90 UNCHS (Habitat), 1999c, 2001b.

91 Milbert, 1999, p209.

92 Milbert, 1999.

93 See http://web.mit.edu/ urbanupgrading.

94 Cohen, 2001, p47.

95 Cohen, 2001, p49.

96 Satterthwaite, 1998.

97 World Bank, 1991; Cohen, 2001, pp41–42.

98 Milbert, 1999, p176.

99 Kamete et al, 2001.

8

CIVIL SOCIETY IN ACTION[1]

Civil society has been a force on the ground for centuries as groups of men and women, workers and residents, practitioners and intellectuals have formed associations to protect and promote their interests. However, the last ten years have seen a shift in the attitudes of governments, international agencies, the media and the public towards the activities of civil society. It is now argued that civil society is central to raising the living standards of the poor and furthering processes of democratization in partnership with the state, rather than being seen as marginal to development, or an alternative to the state strategy for development.

The rise of neo-liberal economics and the dominance of theories of liberal democracy have accorded civil society this dual, though sometimes contradictory, role of service provider and social mobilizer. However, the complexity of organizations and associations that fall under the banner of civil society, and the diversity of roles they play, calls for an examination of some of the premises that underlie their growing popularity and importance.

The concept of civil society is the subject of much debate. A widely accepted definition is that civil society is 'an intermediate associational realm between state and family populated by organizations which are separate from the state, enjoy autonomy in relation to the state and are formed voluntarily by members of the society to protect their interests or values'.[2] However, this definition encompasses a huge variety of associational forms – such as trade unions; professional associations; organizations based on kinship, ethnicity, culture or region; formal and informal social networks based on patrimonial or clientelistic allegiances; and pressure or advocacy groups within, and outside of, the political system.[3]

Such a broad view of civil society is unhelpful to those who wish to work with it and encourage its growth, containing, as it does, those who are formal and informal, legal and illegal, hostile to and cooperative with the state. An alternative approach is to focus, instead, on the role that certain associations play in fostering norms of reciprocity, trust and social capital. Again, however, such a definition is too broad as the range of groups that contribute to social capital formation is too wide, including, for example, social and sports clubs, or religious groups. To make the issue less complicated, there is a tendency to separate political society from civil society so that it becomes 'possible to support democracy without becoming involved in partisan politics or otherwise interfering unduly in the domestic politics of another country'.[4] Nevertheless, as it is argued below, those

organizations that seek to bring about social and economic change are inevitably involved in politically sensitive activities; increasingly, the cooperation between civil society and government is blurring the line between the two.

The most widely adopted view of civil society among governments, donors and official supporters of civil society is that it consists only of voluntary associations that directly foster democracy and promote democratic consolidation:

These are associations that specifically seek interaction with the state, whether to advocate interests of the citizens, to oppose non-democratic behaviour of the state, or to hold states accountable to citizens for their actions.[5]

In this view, the range of associational groups that are seen as having a key role to play in development is more narrow and consists mostly of professionalized non-governmental organizations (NGOs) and community-based organizations (CBOs) that are located in those poor neighbourhoods, which are the subject of development initiatives:

Civil society actors, which supposedly seek to make their countries better by influencing government policies but not seeking power, can thus appear to make up an anti-political domain, a pristine realm in which a commitment to civic values and the public interest rules in place of traditional divisions, beliefs and interests.[6]

What will be seen below, however, is that those civil society organizations that seek to improve the lives of millions of people living in slum conditions do not make up a 'pristine realm'. Instead, they operate in an unavoidably politicized and conflictual realm, as they are not immune from the same contradictory pressures and forces that afflict political and social life.

RESIDENTS IN ACTION

The strategies of slum households

The current emphasis on strengthening civil society should not mean neglecting the importance of the activities of poor men and women as individuals and in households. A basic function of all households is to manage their resources and assets in order to maintain and reproduce the household as a social unit. In slums, where service provision by the state

Understanding how households devise and develop strategies to harness and manage resources is essential in the fight against poverty. Households are not static but are subject to changes in composition and social dynamic over time

and non-state actors is often very limited, and where residents are subject to the daily deprivations of poverty as well as sporadic shocks and crises, how the household manages its labour, time and energy is of crucial importance for the well-being and survival of all of its individual members. Understanding how households devise and develop strategies to harness and manage resources is, therefore, essential in the fight against poverty. There has been a tendency, however, to homogenize the household as a unit, overlooking the inequalities and conflicts that exist within it – instead, assuming that what benefits the poor household benefits all of its poor members equally. This is now widely recognized to be incorrect, and it is also accepted that households are not static but are subject to changes in composition and social dynamic over time: 'This "mini political economy" of decision-making about status, power, property and work between women and men, generations and kin is multi-faceted and dynamic in its formation and life'.[7]

Much more is now known about the strategies and structures of poor households than just ten years ago; yet, much of that knowledge remains in the realm of researchers and academics rather than in mainstream government agencies. Thus, for example, the majority of national census and survey data sets used by national policy-makers focus on household level data, and fail to reveal intra-household inequalities and relations. While policy-makers, private-sector service providers, NGOs and community organizations who work with poor households have begun to recognize the urgent need to reach within the household and target their interventions and services more effectively, success, so far, has been limited, and has centred on efforts to make women the primary recipients of resources. Thus, much more needs to be done to ensure that policy-makers and those who work with the poor understand how different households in different contexts function. Furthermore, a great deal more work needs to be done to ensure that their subsequent interventions actually respond to the unequal needs and the shifting dynamics of households in order to reduce poverty most effectively.

Inside the household

Internal division of power and status within the household between men and women, girls and boys, and generations and kin influence who makes what decisions and for whose benefit (see Box 8.1). Providing credit to women household members is now widely accepted to be more effective in benefiting the household as a whole, and especially its children, than when men are made the recipients of credit. Similarly, ensuring that women's names are on the deeds of land and house can serve to protect them and their children from homelessness in the event of family breakdown. Differences in power and status within each household depend upon a mix of individuals' behaviour and the given cultural norms of a particular society. For example, the decision-making status of elderly men and women in Asian households contrasts markedly with that in many Western societies, and the assumption in many countries that the

Box 8.1 Unequal relations in the household

A study of urban populations in Bengal looked at the different access of members of poor households to health care. This study indicated that the high cost of health-care treatment for poor households relative to income means that access to health services depends upon their status within the household and their resulting ability to make demands on household budgets. As a result, due to the relatively lower status of women and girls in Bengal, there tends to be less health expenditure on women and female children. This was clearly illustrated in the case of a cholera epidemic in Bangladesh, where female fatalities were three times higher than men's, not because women were more vulnerable to the disease, but, rather, because – in an effort to avoid expenditures on women's health – they tend to be taken to hospital when the disease is far more advanced.

Source: Guha Sapir, 1996.

man is the household head is highly inappropriate in many other countries.

The different tasks and responsibilities assigned to household members are linked to these differences in power, as well as to ideas about what is fitting to their social status and individual capabilities. For example, in many societies, women and girls living in peri-urban slums or urban slums are expected to obtain basic resources, such as water and fuel. These tasks can take up large amounts of time, to the detriment of women's and girls' income-earning and educational opportunities. In many slums, women explicitly or implicitly have considerable influence over decisions regarding investments in the home, as well as carrying out many of the maintenance tasks, while leaving the larger construction tasks to the men. The responsibilities assigned to boy children contrast markedly with those assigned to girl children in many societies, with the latter assuming many domestic duties, such as cleaning and child care, while, instead, the educational and leisure needs of boys are prioritized.

Intra-household relations and inequalities are not static, however, and shifts in the broader economy can have a profound impact on household composition and dynamics; 'the occupational mixes of lower-income households are reflective of broader economic trends, as well as cultural practices toward age and gender divisions of labour'.[8] In Southeast Asia, for example, the growth of export-oriented manufacturing has led to an influx of young single women to the cities, finding accommodation in dormitories and forming new types of household that contrast with the traditional concept of the nuclear or extended household. In Western European countries that have undergone rapid processes of de-industrialization, a marked shift in household power relations has occurred as the traditional male breadwinner has found himself unemployed and dependent upon the wages of his service-sector worker wife. Understanding just who does what and who gets what within the household, as well as how household structure and dynamics are changing, is therefore essential if the resources are to be targeted for maximum effect. For example, the provision of water standpipes may be far more effective in enabling women to undertake income-earning activities than the provision of skills training.

The different tasks and responsibilities assigned to household members are linked to ideas about what is fitting to their social status and individual capabilities

Reciprocity and remittance

Understanding what goes on within the household is, however, just a starting point. All households, and especially poor households, form part of networks of reciprocal relationships that can extend deep into the community and far beyond. The household is commonly defined as those members of a residential unit who share the same cooking pot; yet, the capacity of a poor household to manage its financial and material assets, to improve its immediate environment, and to enhance the opportunities of its individual members can be markedly improved if reciprocal exchange relations can also be established outside of the household, with, for example, neighbours, kin, friends and employers. A substantial share of poor households' income comes from within their immediate communities and neighbourhoods. For example, studies show that the material provisioning of households outside of the market (such as house construction and maintenance, and vegetable and fruit growing) takes place almost wholly in the community and can comprise as much as 30 per cent or more of the household income of the urban poor.[9] In squatter settlements, one of the most commonly recognized phenomena is the pooling of labour among family and neighbours in order to build houses. However, mutual exchanges can also revolve around financial assistance, child care and the care of the elderly, finding employment, education provision and improvements to communal spaces, to name just a few examples. These reciprocal relations can be essential during times of crisis when sickness reduces income-earning capacity and debts increase, or when evictions occur and the home and possessions are lost.

In many slum communities, households retain strong ties to their rural place of origin (or even across continents, owing to the spread of diaspora populations), and the reactions of those living many kilometres away may be considered when making decisions that affect the livelihoods and well-being of the household members. Urban workers can send money, and basic and luxury goods to their village relatives; marriages may be arranged and conducted in the rural home; and younger men and women may be sent to stay with urban family and friends in order to gain access to employment. Such relationships can make the difference between the success and failure of livelihood strategies.

Many government and donor-funded interventions rely upon the regular participation of poor households in activities such as the construction and maintenance of houses, toilets and communal buildings; yet, a common failing of such projects is the tapering off of residents' interest and the rapid deterioration of the infrastructure installed. In contrast, poor communities exercise a wide range of social sanctions to control relations of reciprocity and prevent free riders from taking advantage of others. Research in slum communities reveals that there are numerous ways in which small-scale social organizations have mechanisms, ranging from gossip to shunning and acts of violence, which are actively used to punish non-conformers and to ensure cooperative behaviour.[10] However, non-compliance may also be tolerated when those who are failing to contribute are known to have special circumstances, such as sickness, disability, bereavement and so on, that prevent them from taking an equal burden. In this case, support provided by the community can be essential to such disadvantaged households in coping and recovering.

Households need to remain in one place for a sufficient length of time if they are to build and maintain networks of reciprocal relations. The destruction of social networks that comes with evictions and forced resettlement is (along with disruption of livelihood activities by moving inhabitants far from their places of employment) one of the most common criticisms of resettlement and rehabilitation programmes that affect slum communities. Reliance on social networks explains why many slum communities reveal a remarkable homogeneity of place of migratory origin, and of ethnic or religious group. Such uniformity is not only attractive because it allows for a sense of belonging that migrants would otherwise not have upon arriving in a city, but because it also greatly facilitates the establishment of relations of support and reciprocity:

> *With the capacity to organize closely connected with social cohesion and the development of a 'we-consciousness', communities that do not have long histories of settlement or are characterized by a high degree of social, ethnical or political cleavage face particular difficulties in creating community-wide trust and cooperative association.*[11]

This is well illustrated by research undertaken amongst villagers resettled during post-independence land reforms in Zimbabwe, in which 71,000 households were resettled to new villages made up largely of strangers.[12] The research, using an investment game exercise, found that those villagers who had not been resettled showed far higher levels of trust and reciprocity – the lack of which in villages resettled as long ago as 1982 was due simply to less familiarity and the resultant greater uncertainty faced by resettled villagers when trying to predict each other's behaviour in strategic situations

Vulnerable households

Vulnerable households are often those who do not enjoy the support provided by networks outside of the household. Where a household has no security or socially recognized place within a community, debt, sickness and unemployment can be disastrous. Real or perceived security of tenure is thus essential if households are to put down roots and establish reciprocal relations of support. In addition, those who are recent migrants, those who belong to persecuted ethnic or religious minorities or to certain castes, or those who suffer the consequences of a particular social stigma can find themselves vulnerable and without support (see Box 8.2).

Furthermore, as relations within households are not equal, some individual members tend to be more vulnerable to the crises of poverty than others. These are usually women, children and the elderly who often enjoy a relatively

Reliance on social networks explains why many slum communities reveal a remarkable homogeneity of place of migratory origin, and of ethnic or religious group

Security of tenure is essential if households are to put down roots and establish reciprocal relations of support

small proportion of household resources, but contribute a substantial amount of their time and energy to household and community management activities. Especially vulnerable are single member poor households and single parent households that do not have the labour power and time to undertake many essential activities, such as cleaning, child care or house maintenance, as well as bringing in sufficient income for survival.

COMMUNITY-BASED ORGANIZATIONS IN ACTION

The growth and range of community-based organizations (CBOs)

In addition to individual and household strategies for livelihood management, collective social action is a key characteristic of poor communities, whether regular or sporadic, concerning leisure activities, the development and maintenance of public spaces and assets, or for the purpose of protest, advocacy or campaigning. To make such cooperative social action effective and sustainable, an organizational base is often essential, with a leadership that is sufficiently accountable and earns the respect of its members. Such CBOs, also known as grassroots organizations, are defined as locally based membership organizations that work to develop their own communities.[13] Again, this succinct definition covers a wide range of organizations. They vary in size, type and range of interests, management structure, size and nature of constituency, and level of interaction with other groups and actors (including the state).

The classification 'CBO' includes many types of group, such as community theatre and leisure groups; sports groups; residents associations or societies; savings and credit groups; child care groups; minority support groups; clubs; advocacy groups; and more. All reflect the heterogeneous nature of slum populations and their interests and needs. They can exist informally, entirely outside of the state, or they can be semi-official or have official legal status, perhaps with some senior members actually receiving government salaries. However, the vast majority of CBOs are not profit-making organizations. The two most common types of CBOs are local development associations, such as village councils or neighbourhood associations, which represent an entire community, and interest associations, such as women's clubs, which represent particular groups within a community. A third type includes borrowers' groups, pre-cooperatives and cooperatives, which may make profit, yet can be distinguished from private businesses due to their community development goals.

In 1998, it was estimated that there were probably over 200,000 grassroots organizations functioning in Asia, Africa and Latin America alone.[14] Their rapid growth over the last 20 years or so can be explained by broad structural changes in the way that global and, hence, local economies function, resulting in processes of democratization,

---

Box 8.2 Vulnerable minority groups

A participatory study with women from slums and chawls in Ahmedabad, Gujarat, which set out to identify the main sources of vulnerability for poor women, showed that one of the most at risk groups was women from the local Muslim minority. Many Muslim women had lost the productive assets that they relied upon for their livelihoods, such as rickshaws, handcarts, sewing machines and lathes, in communal (religious) riots, and were therefore forced to move into more poorly paid types of work that did not require equipment.

Source: Twigg and Bhatt, 1998.

---

privatization and government decentralization. Structural adjustment programmes (SAPs) from the 1980s onwards have led to the collapse of already meagre state support to some population groups, while de-industrialization in the North has left whole neighbourhoods and towns in recession. In response, many CBOs have been formed to deal with specific needs or problems faced by communities facing deprivation and crisis (see Box 8.3). Other CBOs form in response to a specific planned intervention by state or non-state actors (see Box 8.4). These single-issue organizations may fade once the need has been met or the problem dealt with; but some go on to diversify their demands and activities, widening their membership base accordingly. Cultural and religious institutions are also important sources of community organization and mobilization, and many are flourishing in the face of, or perhaps in response to, processes of globalization that are perceived to undermine identity and autonomy.[15]

In the South, the rapid growth of CBOs, especially in Latin America, that address basic family consumption and income requirements in a general environment of survival has been evident since the 1980s. Many have managed to establish political freedoms and to escape from decades of repression, and/or to respond to the consequences of recession and structural adjustment. CBOs as interest associations have filled an institutional vacuum, providing basic services such as communal kitchens, milk for children, income-earning schemes and cooperatives in order to ensure that crises of poverty are met proactively. CBOs of this type are frequently run and controlled by impoverished women and are usually based on self-help

In 1998, in Asia, Africa and Latin America there were probably over 200,000 grassroots organizations

---

Box 8.3 Community-based organizations dealing with housing insecurity in the Philippines

The Kabalaka Homeowners Association is a local network of CBOs made up of around 1000 very poor households from around the city of Iloilo in The Philippines. This network has mobilized in response to the insecure tenure and housing conditions faced by its members, who were squatting illegally in informal settlements. Since 1997, they have collectively saved 2.5 million pesos that are being used to buy 4.4 hectares of land close to their original settlements. The community groups found this land themselves and researched its ownership, zoning and rights of way in preparation to purchasing it. In addition, the CBOs negotiated with the Philippines National Housing Authority (NHA) for help in developing these new sites through their Land Tenurial Assistance Programme, through which – once the land purchase has been finalized – the NHA will develop the land on the basis of the community's layout requirements, after which the people will build their own houses.

Source: Vincentian Missionaries Social Development Foundation Incorporated, 2001.

Box 8.4 Organizing for land and housing, social inclusion and human development, Quezon City, Philippines

Quezon City lies immediately to the north of Manila and is part of the national capital region of the Republic of the Philippines. It has a population of 2.3 million. A large number of the population lives in poor urban communities. In 1991, 50% of households were found to be below the official poverty line. On the north side of the city, straddling a major thoroughfare called Commonwealth Avenue, is an area of some 350 hectares known as the National Government Centre (NGC). This area was set aside during the 1940s and is now the home of the Philippines House of Representatives and a number of government departments. It is also home to a large number of urban dwellers living in poverty in largely unplanned and unauthorized settlements.

SAMASAMA is the largest of a number of people's organizations existing in the NGC, with a membership of about 12,000 families. It was formed in 1980 in response to evictions and demolitions by the Marcos regime that – through mass protest against armed police – it was successful in resisting. Its key objective has been to obtain secure and regularized tenure of the land on which its members have built their homes. Since 1982 it has been assisted in its work by the NGO Community Organization of the Philippines Enterprise (COPE). In 1988, SAMASAMA was officially designated the representative of the NGC residents on a National Government Centre Housing Committee (NGCHC), with 50% voting power on all decisions.

Currently, amidst rapid urbanization and lack of political will by the government in developing the NGC as a social housing site, the SAMASAMA has succeeded in getting 150 hectares proclaimed for on-site resettlement, successfully designing and implementing a social housing innovation called the People's Housing Alternative for Social Empowerment (PHASE), which was adopted and later revised by the government, who institutionalized the right of the people's organization to participate in the decision-making in the NGCHC. The leadership and general membership of SAMASAMA is comprised almost entirely of women, who are supported by their spouses and families.

It has also facilitated the setting up of 18 day-care centres; the installation of legal electricity and water connections to the communities within the 700 hectares of the NGC settlement; the dismantling of syndicates who prey on poor families; and the establishment of a credit and savings cooperative for its members. It formed the core of an anti-eviction federation in Metro Manila of poor families threatened with evictions. The majority of its women members supported the first political party of women that won a seat in congress, the Abanse Pinay, during the 2001 elections. These are highlights of its past and present work. It has worked with planners, architects, economists and the religious in its struggle to make a difference, to be heard, and to break out from poverty, ignorance and marginalization.

Source: UN-Habitat, Best Practices Database.

principles, though they may receive assistance from NGOs, churches and political parties. They contrast with the more traditional, male-led neighbourhood development organizations found in poor communities that are usually engaged in meeting community needs, such as water supply, sanitation systems, roads, garbage collection, schools, community and day-care centres, community health, neighbourhood vigilance, crime control, and other infrastructure and service needs.[16]

In the North, development practitioners, community leaders and government planners have been:

> ...seeking to soften the impact on community life of recession, de-industrialization, and economic and social restructuring. They sense the limits of traditional, macro-level economic development strategies, and they perceive co-operative forms of community organizing and community economic development as a

practical alternative for strengthening communities socially, as well as economically.[17]

Hence, as in the South, there has been a rapid growth in interest associations responding to specific needs generated by a crisis situation in the community, such as an industrial plant closure, or rises in drug use and crime. Again, many such organizations are formed and led by women; and not only are the numbers of CBOs of all types proliferating in both the North and the South, but traditional and newly created CBOs are beginning to organize horizontal networks among themselves. For example, Shack/Slum Dwellers International (SDI) is an international organization of the CBOs of the urban poor from 11 countries in Asia, Latin America and Africa who work to share ideas and experience, and lend each other support in their efforts to secure access to housing, infrastructure and land.[18] Such networks provide support and learning opportunities; strengthen their power to advocate changes in policy; improve fund-raising opportunities; increase membership; and generally increase the visibility of the multiple problems that CBOs are trying to tackle (see Box 8.5).

Working with CBOs

The diversity of residents' groups in slum communities has resulted in a wide range of strategies for acquiring resources. While some CBOs depend entirely upon voluntary labour and financial contributions to sustain their activities, most interact at some level with outside support organizations: governmental, religious, cultural, or other CBOs or NGOs. One important point of contact tends to be NGOs or grassroots support organizations that act to mobilize CBOs, lobby for resources on their behalf and implement initiatives within slums. A well-known example is the Society for the Protection of Area Resource Centres (SPARC), founded in 1984 in Mumbai to support community-based organizations of pavement dwellers, and subsequently expanded to give support to community organizations of the urban poor in India, more generally.[19] Another recent example is NAVIKU (Nairobi *Vikundi vya Kujisaidia*) (see Box 8.6). Direct contact with the state is also common – for instance, where the state itself has established the CBOs – when seeking partnerships within slum communities for the implementation of programmes and projects, or where politicians seek political support in return for much needed resources.

Just as there has been a tendency to overlook power and status differentials within the household, there has also been a tendency to idealize the concept of community, overlooking the heterogeneity within it: 'There is an assumption that democratic consensus will somehow overcome difference and bring the various segments in the community together to form a united front of community action.'[20] Communities are stratified along lines of social class, ethnicity, gender, sexual orientation, age, caste, religion, and cultural tradition, and so power and status within communities are shared unequally. Such inequalities are often apparent both within and between CBOs, and the extent to which community development organizations,

Traditional and newly created CBOs are beginning to organize horizontal networks among themselves, both national and international

such as residents' associations, community societies and neighbourhood committees, really represent the diverse interests of their communities has been the topic of considerable debate. In the context of increasing outside support for CBOs as a means of providing basic services and of acting as a force for empowerment and democratization, it has to be acknowledged that many CBOs are, themselves, profoundly undemocratic.

In response, during recent years there has been a growing demand that planned interventions in slum and other poor communities empower marginal groups to participate in community and institutional decision-making processes, either through their own social organizations or as representatives of local grassroots organizations or community-wide councils. Traditionally, support for community development in the South has primarily been aimed at securing an increase in the resources and productivity of the poor, whereas in the North it has been about the allocation of assets and power.[21] Over the last ten years, however, the latter is also talked about in relation to the South, and social dimensions, such as the need for community institution building, are added to environmental and economic goals. For collaborative partnership arrangements to emerge between the state, NGOs and CBOs, it is necessary to have strong self-managing community organizations and a less coercive approach on the part of state agencies and institutions.[22] Despite the current emphasis on partnership approaches, it is worth noting that a whole range of strategies (including conflicting approaches) can be vital in changing relationships, in forming leadership skills and, ultimately, in securing resources for the poor. It is obvious, however, that poor communities tend to have the least amount of bargaining power around the partnership table. As a result, CBOs frequently require the support of NGOs or other CBOs if they are to develop and implement strategies that build their power base and maximize their access to resources. Table 8.1 outlines a number of common social values and principles that are currently acknowledged to be essential to the growth of strong community organizations and community development.

Box 8.5 Shack/Slum Dwellers International (SDI)

Shack/Slum Dwellers International (SDI) is a voluntary association of like-minded people's organizations committed to a shared process of grassroots organization, problem solving and solution sharing. SDI was formed in the North-West Province of South Africa in May 1996. Today, it has many affiliates on three continents. These include:

- Umfelanda Wonye (South Africa Homeless People's Federation) – South Africa.
- Zimbabwe Federation of the Homeless – Zimbabwe.
- Twahangana – Namibia.
- Muungano Wa Wanavijiji (Slum Dwellers Collective) – Kenya.
- Enda-Graf – Senegal.
- National Slum Dwellers Federation (NSDF) – India.
- Mahila Milan (network of slum and pavement women) – India.
- Urban Poor Federations – Thailand.
- Society of Urban Poor Federations – Cambodia.
- Payatas Savings and Credit Federation – Philippines.
- Mutirao Groups in Belem – Brazil.

These organizations, often supported by NGOs, avail the network of their facilities, their time and contributions in kind. Most importantly, they share knowledge and solidarity across regional boundaries. For example, NSDF and Mahila Milan from India have developed a slum dwellers' enumeration process by which they generate records on names, faces, locations and living conditions of slum dwellers. This process produces information that can be used for negotiating services or as baseline data in slum upgrading projects. Persons thus enumerated are issued with an identity card, which can be used in a variety of ways:

- Proof of residence in case of upgrading.
- Proof of economic status in case of provision of subsidies or safety net measures, etc.

SDI groups from India have shared the enumeration process with counterparts in other countries – for example, in the slums of Nairobi, Kenya.

By involving the communities, a significant change has come about in dealing with the issues of poverty eradication. Using capacity building as a strategy, SDI has involved grassroots organizations, made up of vulnerable members of the society such as the homeless and landless women so that they are able to play a central role in their environmental development. Interactions through networking have begun to create a far-flung solidarity and to enable a rapid transfer of developmental knowledge, organizational skills and people's own resources from one context of urban poverty to another by way of sharing their problems and experiences.

Source: www.sdinet.org.

NON-GOVERNMENTAL ORGANIZATIONS (NGOs) IN ACTION

Defining NGOs

At face value, the simplest definition of an NGO is an organization that is the opposite of a government organization – independent from the state and state authority. However, such a definition is misleading and overly simplistic. Sometimes, the term NGO is used to

...mean all NGOs everywhere, including Northern NGOs based in one developed country that operate internationally, inter-national NGOs or networks... [and] Southern

NGOs from the Third World, and many other kinds of non-profit organizations throughout the world. The term also has numerous culturally specific meanings. In Western Europe, it generally means non-profit organizations that are active internationally. In the transitional countries of Europe and the former Soviet Union, it tends to mean all charitable and non-profit organizations. In the Third World, the term NGO generally refers to organizations involved in development, broadly defined.[23]

With the mushrooming of NGOs and expansion of their activities, the lines between different types of NGOs and between the non-government and government sectors have

Box 8.6 Nairobi Vikundi vya Kujisaidia (NAVIKU: self-help groups, Nairobi, Kenya)

Rapid urbanization has led to an alarming deterioration in the quality of life of city dwellers. Nairobi suffers from infrastructural deficiencies; poor sanitation and solid waste disposal; water shortages; polluted natural watercourses; frequent epidemics; inadequate health care; depletion of green areas; poor roads and transportation; dust and air pollution; proliferation of slums; growing illiteracy; and lack of support for the social and economic development of the disadvantaged communities. The aggregate of distress is especially debilitating for the urban poor who live in slums. Women and children bear the worst brunt as they continually manage their daily lives and chores in this environment.

Nairobi Vikundi Vya Kujisaidia (NAVIKU) is a Swahili title for 'Association of Self-help Groups in Nairobi'. NAVIKU was formed with a mission to strengthen and activate the existing programmes related to self-help groups in Nairobi because some of them were on the verge of extinction/collapse due to poor management and non-participation by members. NAVIKU has been able to mobilize some of its finances through registration fees (US$7) by member groups. The group has also been able to pool finances from the contributions made by members after the sale of various wares that they are involved in producing. Some member groups own houses that they rent out; from the money that they collect, a certain portion is paid to NAVIKU to finance some of its development activities. Most of the technical activities implemented by the umbrella organization have been in the form of seminars and workshops for the member groups; as such, members are imparted with organizational skills for the effective running of their respective groups. Nairobi City Council (NCC), Shelter Forum, UN-Habitat, the Small Town Development Programme (STDP), supported by GTZ, and Shelter 2000 facilitate these seminars. Of importance are the seminars organized by the NCC that were instrumental in forming NAVIKU, since the main theme of these seminars was the need for an organization to champion the rights of the inhabitants of informal settlements who are the majority members of NAVIKU.

Most community-based organizations (CBOs) that are also members of this umbrella organization have been revitalized and are posting positive gains in their activities due to improved production and, consequently, income generation (the current membership stands at 50 self-help groups). This was achieved by making the communities aware, through seminars and local '*barazas*', of the fact that they themselves were ultimately responsible for the success of their respective organizations, and any benefits accruing from such a success would go a long way to improving their livelihoods.

The other aim was to identify and promote income-generating activities. This was achieved by encouraging the member groups to participate in soap- and candle-making; preparing compost and charcoal from garbage waste; weaving; leatherwork; making fire-less cookers and lampshades; operating sanitation services; cattle rearing for milk production; and garbage collection. All of these activities have a ready market in the area where they are carried out and this has encouraged the member groups to involve themselves since they realized that they were/are receiving steady income from them. NAVIKU has been directly involved in the marketing of the wares produced by the member groups.

NAVIKU has also been involved in the pursuit of decent living by encouraging members to improve their shelter using the available building materials and provision of basic needs, such as clean drinking water, community health education, the hygienic disposal of solid waste and improved drainage in their living areas. NAVIKU has been involved in the sensitization of gender roles, and the rights and responsibilities of women who constitute the majority of members in most of the member groups. Women members are now knowledgeable about their rights, their role in development and the need for them to participate in policy-making at the grassroots level. The youth who were idle before the initiative began now engage in development activities, such as garbage collection and 'pay-as-you-use' toilets, and have even formed community savings schemes popularly known as 'merry-go-rounds'. In the process, NAVIKU has achieved its wider goal of a sustainable environment.

become increasingly blurred. This has spawned a host of attempts to distinguish between 'real' NGOs and their bogus counterparts. Much of this is done on the basis of the source of their funding, and/or the intent of their work. For example, it has been argued that:

> *Those set up by Third World government ministers, which work essentially with government departments and which receive their funding from official aid agencies, are hardly non-governmental... Neither are Northern-based agencies, financed overwhelmingly by their home governments and operating projects in conjunction with Southern governments. Furthermore, agencies whose primary motivation is religious or political, or which don't aim to help the poor, are not 'true NGOs'.*[24]

Some argue that NGOs should not be explicitly political. However, as NGO activity expands away from improving services and economic opportunities for the poor towards empowerment and capacity building of grassroots organizations, the ideal of political neutrality is increasingly exposed as false.

The commonly accepted definition of NGOs suggests that they are 'largely or entirely autonomous from central government funding and control: emanating from civil society...or from political impulses beyond state control and direction'.[25] This definition excludes churches and political parties. However, even this narrower definition of NGOs can be further broken down, as is illustrated by Table 8.2. In this light, NGOs are just one category of non-state actor (distinguished from, for example, criminal gangs, private companies, liberation movements or social movements); but unlike some other non-state actors, they belong within the benign liberal tradition – the quintessential NGOs are those

Table 8.1

Seven values and principles underpinning community development

1	Nurturing and mobilizing cooperative, responsible and active communities of men and women for the purpose of mutual aid, self-help, problem solving, social integration and social action.
2	Fostering the ideal of participatory democracy at all levels of society in order to counter apathy, frustration and resentment, which arise from feelings of powerlessness and oppression in the face of unresponsive power structures.
3	Relying upon the capacity and initiative of relevant groups and local communities to identify needs, define problems, and plan and execute appropriate courses of action, increasing leadership competency and reducing dependence on the state and professional interventions.
4	Mobilizing and deploying resources from within the community and outside (through partnerships with governments, NGOs, etc) in such a way as to ensure balanced, sustainable forms of development.
5	Promoting community integration around two sets of relations: social relations among diverse groups whose differing characteristics may cause conflict; and structural relations among those institutions (government, private, NGO and CBO) that address social challenges at the community level in order to avoid competition and duplication.
6	Organizing activities such as circles of solidarity that empower marginal or excluded population groups by linking them with the progressive forces in different social sectors and classes.
7	Giving the marginalized, excluded or oppressed the essential tools to enable them to critically analyse and become conscious of their situation in structural terms, so that they can envisage possibilities for change.

Source: Campfens, 1997, p24.

of liberal and cosmopolitan intent.[26] Those whose work concentrates upon poor slum communities tend to fall in this tradition, usually staffed by professionals who channel international and other development funds to community and grassroots organizations, helping communities other than their own to develop.[27]

The growth of NGOs

The history of civil society voluntary organizations that work to improve the lives of the poor dates from long before the 20th century in both the North and the South. However, in the North, the first NGOs with a concern for development arose after World War I and grew in strength and numbers after Word War II: 'Initially, these NGOs were engaged in relief work, primarily in war-torn Europe. They gradually shifted their attention to the Third World and also broadened it to include welfare activities – a natural extension of relief.'[28] During the 1950s and 1960s, the number of Northern NGOs multiplied and their focus moved progressively towards development activities. As it became apparent that welfare and relief work only attacked the symptoms of poverty, their focus began to shift toward increasing the capacity of poor men and women to meet their own needs, working with existing initiatives and organizations in villages and urban slums. New funding streams became available from Northern NGOs to local groups, many of which became significant NGOs in their own right. The homogeneity between NGOs pursuing similar agendas began to break down by the 1960s, with Southern NGOs becoming more assertive, as well as growing quickly in number and influence. During the 1970s, there

was a shift again, away from small-scale, self-help type projects towards promoting empowerment through raising the consciousness of the poor so that they could overcome their exploitation. The growing realization of the political nature of development, during the 1970s, led many NGOs to question their role and their financial dependence on Northern sources of funding and their relationship to their constituents. In the North, there was a growing body of advocacy work that was directed towards changing the exploitative structures (governments and companies) that were based within the North itself. This presented contradictions as these NGOs were dependent upon governments that were exacerbating poverty in the South in some way.

By the 1980s, Northern NGOs became less timid in their advocacy work, while, in the South, North–South networks began to flourish, increasing their analytical and advocacy strength. Some progressive Northern NGOs have helped to fund these networks, while rarely taking an active role in their operations. A more recent NGO trend is to engage in a range of activities that aim to bring about change in Southern official structures in order to create a more effective policy environment for their initiatives, concentrating especially upon the reforms needed by local government. They have realized that 'their projects by themselves can never hope to benefit more than a few chosen communities and that these projects are only likely to be sustainable when local public and private organizations are linked into a supportive national development system'.[29]

By 1996, there were at least 50,000 active NGOs working with poor communities in the South, reaching over 300 million people.[30] To understand the rapid growth of

1	Relief and welfare agencies, including missionary societies.
2	Technical innovation organizations that pioneer innovative approaches in specialist fields.
3	Public service contractors, mostly funded by Northern governments and that work closely with Southern governments and official aid agencies to implement components of official programmes.
4	Popular development agencies, Northern NGOs and Southern intermediary counterparts that concentrate on self-help, social development and grassroots democracy.
5	Grassroots development organizations and locally based Southern NGOs whose members are the poor and oppressed themselves, and which attempt to shape a popular development process. They often receive support from popular development agencies.
6	Advocacy groups and networks: organizations that have no field projects but that exist primarily for education and lobbying.

Source: Clark, 1991, pp40–41.

Table 8.2

Six types of NGOs

The rise of NGOs
and grassroots
organizations
reflects a
proliferation of local
self-help initiatives;
more fundamentally,
it is the product of
neo-liberal
economics and the
liberal democratic
agenda

NGOs in both North and South, 'No explanation can ignore state or national interest, nor broader structural changes in society that accompany such NGO activity'.[31] Their growth has been, in part, a response to the damaging effects of SAPs, resulting in increasing poverty and social exclusion, and growing numbers of the 'new poor'. The increase in the number and types of NGOs is also a response to new opportunities to work with donors, Northern NGOs and governments, making the work of many NGOs financially viable and more strategic. Successive increases in aid budgets have seen the funding opportunities for NGOs proliferate, frequently on the assumption that NGOs have the ability to reach the poor and be agile and innovative, in contrast with the supposedly 'corrupt' and 'bureaucratic' state.

The growing availability of direct funding from governments and donors to NGOs is just one result of broader ideological, political, technological and economic shifts at the global, as well as national levels. The rise of NGOs and grassroots organizations reflects a proliferation of local self-help initiatives; more fundamentally, it is the product of neo-liberal economics and the liberal democratic agenda.[32] Structural shifts in the global economy have seen successive rounds of multilateral trade liberalization, and rising flows of investment and finance. Keynesian economic policies have given way to monetarism, tilting the balance between the public and private in favour of the latter:

NGOs have not just
grown rapidly in
numbers over the
last four decades.
Their coverage, in
terms of population
and sectors, has also
grown markedly

> *...all that was not the state was now to be encouraged, and what the voluntary or private-sector organizations could do, the state should not do. This culminated in the neo-liberal agenda of the post-1980 world.*[33]

There has been a growing disillusionment with the state:

> *...the replacement of the image of the public servant as enlightened technocrat by that of the self-interested bureaucrat, together with resistance to rising levels of taxation and public expenditure, led governments to contract out public functions to private actors, converting companies and NGOs into agents in providing public services.*[34]

Service delivery through markets and private initiatives is held to be more efficient than through the state, while – because of their supposed cost-effectiveness in reaching the poorest – NGOs have become the preferred channel of official agencies wanting to provide welfare services to those who cannot be reached through markets. Furthermore, NGOs and grassroots organizations are seen as vehicles for liberal democratization and essential components of a thriving civil society, which, in turn, is seen as essential to the success of the agenda's economic dimension. NGOs are thus perceived to be effective vehicles for the delivery of the agenda's economic and political objectives, even though these two can pose many contradictions.[35]

Political change has also encouraged the proliferation of NGOs and other civil society groups. The diffusion of

international rivalry after the end of the Cold War has weakened the link between national solidarity and national security, favouring the emergence or strengthening of 'non-national identities' – for example, around ethnicity, particular causes such as civil rights and the environment, or diaspora populations.[36] The era of conventional state- and party-centred politics has waned in the face of a new world of social movements. These have been greatly assisted by technological progress and a communications revolution that has transformed the ability of non-state actors to develop cheap and easy international contact, while rising educational standards, increased international travel and the emergence of global media have widened the perspective of the elites and counter-elites.[37] These elites played a key role in NGO expansion. As idealistic young professionals, they benefited from widespread government investment in universities during the 1960s and have established or joined NGOs as a means of expressing their genuine commitment to the poor, and as an alternative to unemployment, dead-end government jobs or migration to developed countries. They have established thousands of NGOs and grassroots support organizations concerned with development, the environment, the role of women and primary health care, many of them working with slum communities.[38]

The range and diversity of NGOs

Northern, Southern, transnational and international NGOs have not just grown rapidly in numbers over the last four decades. Their coverage, in terms of population and sectors, has also grown markedly. Rural welfare projects for small groups no longer dominate all NGO portfolios; instead, many have extended into the provision of health, education, housing and credit services to millions who are increasingly located in cities and their slums (see Boxes 8.7 and 8.8). Many now assume some advocacy and lobbying roles, while some work exclusively in these areas, without project-based work. Those NGOs that do work directly with the organizations of poor men and women conduct a range of tasks, from direct service provision to capacity building for CBOs, to acting as a go-between to the outside world. They encourage CBOs to form networks, as well as provide technical innovations. The roles played by NGOs include:

- encouraging organizational pluralism between citizens and the state;
- supporting micro-enterprise development and institution strengthening with implications for equality;
- promoting political rights and civil liberties and providing legal aid (especially to women's CBOs);
- promoting bottom-up democratization;
- influencing other players in the independent sector; and
- broadening the ownership of capital through encouraging micro-enterprise development.[39]

Clearly, not all NGOs perform all of these roles, and as NGO numbers have proliferated, some have specialized in particular activities. In addition, many NGOs are no longer

Box 8.7 Popular Habitat Programme in San José, Costa Rica (FUPROVI)

This NGO-operated programme uses a self-help housing approach and a revolving fund system to provide quality housing and to achieve social development in a sustainable manner. After a financial slump during the 1980s, Costa Rica was faced with a major housing shortage. This resulted in the growth of slums in marginal areas in San José, the capital, and in other main cities, primarily affecting the lowest-income groups and exacerbating their social exclusion.

The Popular Habitat Programme was developed to address this crisis in 1988 by the Foundation for Housing Promotion (FUPROVI), a national NGO, with assistance from the Swedish government (providing a grant of US\$20 million). FUPROVI was founded in 1987 to support low-income households and improve their living conditions. Their approach is to build the skills and organizational abilities of low-income households and communities in order to find solutions for their own housing and community problems. Women-headed households are an important target group. FUPROVI sets out to promote housing construction and upgrading as a means of encouraging community development.

The programme initially consisted of the construction of new houses by means of mutual effort and help. Later, it was expanded to include programming, execution and administration of housing initiatives. The programme provides financial and technical support for infrastructure work, new housing and house improvement. It also incorporates environmental aspects such as reforestation, water treatment, sewage and refuse disposal, 'alternative housing' construction and urbanization.

The programme consists of four main areas – namely, low-income housing; community development; income generation; and sustainable development and institutional building. Within the low-income housing areas, the programme offers credit for building materials for housing improvements, infrastructure and service provision. It also offers guarantees for land tenure. Through its community development initiative, the programme provides advisory, training and technical assistance in social organization, building methods, and management and financial and legal aspects. Income-generation support is provided to families with commercial activities in the informal sector. Credit programmes

serve community banks, solidarity groups and individual micro-enterprises. Finally, the institutional building and training component disseminates the programme's operative structure and financial model. Training activities target communities, as well as governmental bodies and NGOs. The financial sustainability of the programme is based on a rotating fund, managed by FUPROVI, and is comprised of short-term recovery loans to families from Costa Rica's National Housing Financing System (SFNV); medium- and long-term recovery of other loans; return on invested funds; and additional direct-resource inputs. The main financial strategy of the programme has changed from providing subsidies to housing projects to the present system of offering families long-term low-interest credit to act as bridging finance until they qualify for a loan under the SFNV. FUPROVI offers preliminary loan finance to households, which is then transferred to the SFNV. This allows FUPROVI to recover its capital and to extend credit to other households.

So far, the programme has helped about 8000 families in 42 settlements in the metropolitan San José area and Limon province with new houses, or in improving old ones, or providing maintenance, basic services, land legalization and training. In achieving this, it has worked closely with other stakeholders, including government institutions (services, social assistance, financial), private financial organizations (saving loans, banks and co-operatives), other NGOs, international agencies and municipalities.

The programme has had an important impact on the Costa Rican housing problem, both quantitatively and qualitatively, demonstrating that it is possible to work with families from the lowest-income groups on a competitive and sustainable basis. It has promoted significant changes in policies, legislation and sectoral strategies. It has also brought about changes in awareness and public perception of self-help projects, as well as changes in the attitudes and organization of low-income groups. Several international agencies and institutions have shown an interest in the model of the Popular Habitat Programme, and other initiatives in Nicaragua, El Salvador, Guatemala and South Africa have adopted the programme's principles.

Source: UN-Habitat, Best Practices Database.

small organizations run by a number of professionals along informal lines, but are now larger, administratively complex organizations with high staff numbers and large turnovers. The latter is particularly true of Northern NGOs that now act as channels through which huge amounts of funding are passed on to their Southern counterparts. Some NGOs are members of formal umbrella organizations with written constitutions, annual general meetings and access to governments and international donors with whom they negotiate on behalf of their members (see Box 8.9). Although they often assist their member organizations through capacity-building activities, such formal networks are not generally involved in grassroots support. Instead, characteristic forms of activity can include direct lobbying of governments; participation in international conferences;

campaigns to address elites or the mass public; reliance on existing supporters within national political systems; financial contributions; intellectual efforts to shape and reshape the language of debate; and activities outside of the boundaries of conventional politics or the domestic legal order.

NGOs in informal networks are more likely than those in formal networks to interact with one another in the field, and they may provide grassroots support as a group. The two most common types of NGO network are service networks and support movements.[40] Service networks may be large or small, but they are consistently homogeneous, involving mainly grassroots support organizations and enabling NGOs to exchange and promote one another's professional capacities. In contrast, support networks are large,

Box 8.8 Increasing urban focus of NGOs

WaterAid is an international NGO that works in 15 countries in Africa and Asia. Like many NGOs with roots in rural development, it has become increasingly involved in work with urban poor communities. Its activities include water provision, sanitation and hygiene promotion and lobbying national policy-makers to ensure that the poor gain access to safe, affordable, accessible and sustainable water supplies, sanitation and hygiene-promotion services.

WaterAid's projects were initially all in rural areas until 1990, after which the organization began working in urban areas on a small scale in recognition of the crowded and unsanitary conditions faced by the growing populations living in urban slums, and due to the fact that illegal urban residents are not entitled to basic services, such as water and sanitation. Today, WaterAid has major urban projects in seven countries and is developing projects in five others. It aims to allocate around 30% of its funds to urban work in the future in order to work with the urban poor.

Source: www.wateraid.org.uk.

Box 8.9 CARE-Zambia: Project Urban Self-Help (PUSH II)

The CARE International country office in Zambia (CARE-Zambia) began Project Urban Self-Help (PUSH) in 1992 in four informal settlements of Lusaka and Livingstone that were characterized by high HIV/AIDS infection rates, 46% of the population living below the poverty level and an estimated 46% of the children being malnourished. Following a large-scale Participatory Appraisal and Needs Assessment (PANA) that explored the dimensions of poverty and identified priority issues, water was deemed to be of highest priority.

The identification of water as a priority area led PUSH to initiate plans for a water project that would ensure the sustainable provision of water for the community. Additional development programmes included gender training and indicators for the assessment of residential development committees (RDCs).

Community participation and ownership were emphasized throughout the process, with the RDCs playing a pivotal role in coordinating representation in decision-making processes. CARE-Zambia provided overall technical assistance in project start-up, design, monitoring, and evaluation and training. Financial resources were mobilized from the Lusaka County Council and community members through the establishment of two funds for monthly and annual charges that cover the running costs of the system and the replacement of assets. Human resources for the initiative were provided largely by the community themselves, with 80% of families providing voluntary labour for construction.

The Chipata water scheme was completed in February, benefiting 44,000 people. The project succeeded in improving integration between the community, area-based organizations (ABOs) and council authorities, due to their active involvement in the scheme from appraisal and design to construction. As a result of the project training initiatives, ABO members, council staff and other NGOs have shown improved capacity in leading community development initiatives, largely as a result of the participatory methodologies of PUSH II. In 1997, the Ministry of Local Government and Housing produced a policy paper on decentralization that recognizes RDCs as appropriate sub-district planning structures. This was an important outcome of the project as it provides communities with a viable mechanism of representation and acknowledges them as stakeholders in the consultative process and in future development initiatives.

Following the success of the water scheme, CARE-Zambia has undertaken the Programme of Support for Poverty Elimination and Community Transformation (PROSPECT), which seeks to ensure the long-term viability of the ABOs, and to help councils consolidate their capability to support them. Initiated in January 1998, PROSPECT seeks to develop institutions, water and infrastructure services, and to promote savings and loans. The goal of PROSPECT is to alleviate poverty in informal settlements in Lusaka and Livingstone. The purpose is to assist representative ABOs to develop, manage and maintain basic infrastructure and other services, with particular emphasis on vulnerable individuals. PROSPECT will extend over a five-year period to support project activities in 14 compounds, with a total of 600,000 beneficiaries.

Source: UN-Habitat, Best Practices Database.

heterogeneous and often amorphous systems of communication that include NGOs, universities, charities, community and grassroots organizations, and some individuals, such as journalists or academics who are interested in grassroots development. Whatever the type of NGO, it is clear that, over the last four decades:

> *...the climate of international opinion, be it that of states or informed public opinion, has been significantly affected by what these NGOs, linked to social change, have brought about... Activity, lobbying, protest by NGOs, their fundraising, their local groups, their letter writers, their hunger strikes and, not least, the actions and convictions of dogged individuals have made a difference world-wide.*[41]

The increasing power and decreasing autonomy of NGOs

The most significant change to affect the workings of NGOs has, perhaps, occurred during the last 20 years, and hinges on the relationship between NGOs and governments and other official bodies: 'The overall picture is one in which NGOs are seen as the "favoured child" of official agencies and something of a panacea for the problems of development'.[42] As noted above, in the context of neo-liberal economics and liberal democratic theory, NGOs have become key players in service delivery and the processes of democratization. These two roles are not necessarily compatible, and evidence of that incompatibility is usually found at the community level. When NGOs start to become more responsive to their funders than to poor men and women, their autonomy can be compromised and the real interests of the poor people whom they supposedly support and represent can be neglected.

Relations between governments and NGOs remain, however, far from uniform. NGO approaches to the state vary from active opposition (through protests, legal action, political activity and media exposure) to complementarity – filling the gaps left by the state – and to reform – seeking to improve the state through deliberate collaboration with government.[43] NGO actors and networks may have many levels of influence over the state, including direct links to domestic politics, influence over national policy-making in different states, an ability to set the agenda by influencing the language and discourse of national debates, and access to international institutions, as well as to national governments. Which strategy is taken depends upon the social and political context of a country at any one time. It would be wrong to suggest that all NGOs now seek to compliment or reform the state because many governments still undermine or explicitly repress the activities of their non-government sector, and pursue policies that are profoundly harmful to the poor. Therefore, the openings for NGOs to work with them are limited.

While some states favour such outright repression, a more common tactic is to make life difficult for NGOs. Legislation can make NGO registration bureaucratic and cumbersome in the extreme, or tax regulations can make it difficult for NGOs to survive financially. Some governments merely ignore the NGOs that function in their territory, while others seek to co-opt them. The desire to co-opt comes from the recognition of a need for the services provided by NGOs and of a need to control them politically.[44] Tactics of co-optation include small grants, dividing NGOs by selectively favouring some over others, and by governments creating their own NGOs – sometimes used as channels for large foreign and private-sector donations. Another government response to NGOs is to take advantage of them as a source of additional funds for development, passively accepting them in order to enhance government legitimacy at home and abroad, or to enhance security by diluting social dissatisfaction. However, cooperation with NGOs has become increasingly common over the last 20 years. This consists of ad hoc or more systematically planned partnerships and contracts. However, it is ad hoc cooperation that still predominates. Furthermore, policies of cooperation tend to be devised and pursued by individual government departments rather than across entire central, regional or local administrations.[45]

Despite the complex range of NGO–government relations in evidence in both the North and South, it is fair to say that, over the previous two decades, relations between states and NGOs have become much closer and, at times, too close, raising a number of potential problems. It is impossible to know how much of the increase in official funding to NGOs actually responds to NGO-expressed demands, rather than NGOs tailoring their projects and proposals to suit the official streams of funding available.[46] The knock-on effect of this trend is that local development efforts are being distorted in favour of non-radical NGOs who are willing to 'play the game'. In response, some radical NGOs have advocated the drawing up of an NGO charter or code of conduct to define the responsibilities that all NGOs ought to adopt in order to promote more democratic, equitable values and greater public awareness and political debate about development issues.[47]

Another disadvantage of the trend of contracting out public service provision to NGOs is that, in contrast to partnership approaches, it can reduce the potential for cross-fertilization and learning between government and non-government sectors. Indeed, it can reduce the capacity of the state as government departments are closed or downsized. An additional fear is that 'because service delivery tends to attract more official funding, there will be a growing rift between well-resourced service providers and poorly funded social mobilization agencies'.[48] This exposes the conflict that can exist between the political and economic roles that NGOs are being called on to play. Large-scale service delivery requires standardized procedures, structures that can handle large amounts of external funding, systems for speedy delivery and, often, hierarchical decision-making. In contrast, 'effective performance as an agent of democratization rests on organizational independence, closeness to the poor, representative structure, and a willingness to spend large amounts of time in awareness-raising and dialogue'.[49] It is difficult to combine these characteristics within the same organization;

to date, there is little evidence that alliances between service provider and social mobilization NGOs have developed to any extent. In shifting away from consciousness-raising and mobilization towards service delivery, NGOs are retreating from any serious role in addressing the structural causes of poverty and injustice.

However, it is not only service-delivery NGOs whose autonomy can be questioned. Virtually all NGOs, except those involved in hostile opposition to the state, have personal, financial and political ties of some sort to the state: 'the very participation in a policy debate, in an apparently open exchange of views, leads to erosion of an NGO's autonomy and programme in an effort, idealistically motivated, to keep the door open to states'.[50] Thus, the non-governmental merges with the governmental, and degrees of autonomy from state authority and control vary. The merging also occurs at international levels as NGOs interact with transnational networks of official bodies, as well as individual agencies: 'Non-state actors have learned to exploit the space between these multilateral institutions and their member states, developing a triangular relationship of "complex multilateralism" in which economic associations and social movements are also significant players.'[51]

Perhaps it is too easy to fuss about NGO autonomy and too easy to devise neat dichotomies between service-provider NGOs and social mobilization NGOs, and between autonomous NGOs and those compromised through their interaction with the state. The provision of services can, after all, be used as a vehicle through which to mobilize slum communities, increase their awareness of their rights and encourage the strengthening of community organizations. Similarly, if we recognize that poverty reduction and democratization will only come about on a significant scale through reforms in official structures, and not through multiplying the projects of autonomous NGOs, then the issue of state–NGO collaboration or interaction becomes irrelevant.[52] Instead, importance should be attached to the balance of benefits and costs that such collaboration brings to poor men and women:

> [NGOs] possess a remarkably widespread commitment to the idea that political empowerment from below can untie the negative connections among ignorance, malnutrition, inequality and powerlessness that now sustain poverty. Political and institutional sustainability ultimately depends, however, upon NGOs' impact on civil society and the ways in which NGOs and the state interact to promote both environmentally and politically sustainable development.[53]

URBAN-SECTOR CBOs AND NGOs

The series of United Nations conferences that were held during the 1990s highlighted the vast potential for effective cooperation with NGOs. This was evident from the far-reaching commitments of governments, with respect to

NGO approaches to the state vary from active opposition to complementarity, filling the gaps left by the state, and to reform, seeking to improve the state through deliberate collaboration with government

Over the previous two decades, relations between states and NGOs have become much closer and, at times, too close, raising a number of potential problems

NGOs have 'learned to exploit the space between multilateral institutions and their member states, developing a triangular relationship of "complex multilateralism" in which economic associations and social movements are also significant players'

Box 8.10 *The Habitat Agenda* **commitment on enablement and participation**

We commit ourselves to the strategy of enabling all key actors in the public, private and community sectors to play an effective role – at the national, state/provincial, metropolitan and local levels – in human settlements and shelter development.

We further commit ourselves to the objectives of:

- Enabling local leadership, promoting democratic rule, exercising public authority and using public resources in all public institutions at all levels in a manner that is conducive to ensuring transparent, responsible, accountable, just, effective and efficient governance of towns, cities and metropolitan areas.
- Establishing, where appropriate, favourable conditions for the organization and development of the private sector, as well as defining and enhancing its role in sustainable human settlements development, including through training.
- Decentralizing authority and resources, as appropriate, as well as functions and responsibilities to the level most effective in addressing the needs of people in their settlements.
- Supporting progress and security for people and communities, whereby every member of society is enabled to satisfy his or her basic human needs and to realize his or her personal dignity, safety, creativity and life aspirations.
- Working in partnership with youth in order to develop and enhance effective skills and provide education and training to prepare youth for current and future decision-making roles and sustainable livelihoods in human settlements management and development.
- Promoting gender-sensitive institutional and legal frameworks and capacity building at the national and local levels conducive to civic engagement and broad-based participation in human settlements development.
- Encouraging the establishment of community-based organizations, civil society organizations and other forms of non-governmental entities that can contribute to the efforts to reduce poverty and improve the quality of life in human settlements.
- Institutionalizing a participatory approach to sustainable human settlements development and management based on a continuing dialogue among all actors involved in urban development (the public sector, the private sector and communities), especially women, persons with disabilities and indigenous people, including the interests of children and youth.
- Fostering capacity building and training for human settlements planning, management and development at the national and local levels that includes education, training and institutional strengthening, especially for women and persons with disabilities.
- Promoting institutional and legal enabling frameworks at the national, sub-national and local levels for mobilizing financial resources for sustainable shelter and human settlements development.
- Promoting equal access to reliable information at the national, sub-national and local levels, utilizing, where appropriate, modern communications technology and networks.
- Ensuring the availability of education for all and supporting research aimed at building local capacity that promotes adequate shelter for all and sustainable human settlements development, given that the challenges make it necessary to increase the application of science and technology to problems related to human settlements.
- Facilitating participation by tenants in the management of public and community-based housing and by women and those belonging to vulnerable and disadvantaged groups in the planning and implementation of urban and rural development.

Source: United Nations Conference on Human Settlements, 1996, Chapter III: Commitments, paras 44, 45.

---

enablement, participation and partnerships (see Box 8.10). Speaking about the 'NGO revolution', Secretary-General of the United Nations Kofi Annan noted that 'the new global people-power is the best thing that has ever happened'.

A number of additional international conferences – namely, the Seoul International Conference of NGOs (October 1999), the World Civil Society Conference (WOCSOC, December 1999) and the Millennium Forum (May 2000) carried forward the work of transforming relations with NGOs into true partnerships. The Millennium Assembly recently resolved 'to work collectively for more inclusive political processes, allowing genuine participation by all citizens in all countries'.

The number of NGOs involved in *The Habitat Agenda* negotiation process prior to the Habitat II Conference in June 1996 was 2450. In the aftermath, only 1 per cent of those Habitat Partners proceeded to legitimize their consultative role in United Nations terms. In total, the number of NGOs officially registered by the United Nations at present is around 1400.

The urban-sector NGO profile reflects the global picture quite closely. Urban-sector NGOs are formed around the interests of citizens and neighbourhoods, and mainly take the form of issue-based alliances. It is estimated that there are close to 300 million people belonging to 2773 NGOs involved in human settlements issues.[54]

Table 8.3 shows the current estimated breakdown of urban-sector NGOs. The largest category is CBOs, followed by academics, women, human solidarity groups, the private sector, professionals and youth groups.

Currently, 39 per cent of the urban-sector NGOs belong to wider regional or international NGO networks. Many of these actors communicate through virtual networks: 32.7 per cent of the urban-sector NGOs currently have access to organizational email. Communication technology has greatly strengthened spontaneous, issue-based alliances within civil society. Most of the major *Habitat Agenda* partner networks are good examples of this new form of civic organization. While members of different forums and groups (such as women's groups and forums of professionals and researchers) perform their work through their own independent organizations, they join forces, when it is necessary, to air their concerns around a specific issue, usually without forming a solid formal structure.

Table 8.4 shows the distribution of the urban-sector NGOs by region. The Northern NGOs – probably because of their relatively longer tradition of democracy – take the lead, with 39 per cent of all. South Asia (14 per cent) and Caribbean and East African regions (with 12 per cent each) follow this. The regions with the weakest civic initiatives are Eastern Europe, accounting for only 3 per cent of the world total, the Middle East (5 per cent) and Central and Eastern Asia (6 per cent). Within the urban-sector NGO community, gender remains an important leadership challenge. Only 24 per cent of urban-sector NGOs have female executives. Only one third of urban-sector women organizations have women executives (74 organizations out of 241).

THE CHALLENGES FACED BY NGOs AND CBOs

While the climate has become markedly more favourable towards NGOs and CBOs over the last 20 years, in some states there is evidence of increasing criticism, political attack and even physical assault on NGOs and CBOs. As links between NGOs (and, hence, grassroots organizations) and foreign donors and governments have increased, those governments who are hostile to civil society mobilization can now accuse NGOs of being agents of foreign powers, seeking to subvert national development with Western ideas and strategies. This critique has frequently been levelled at the feminist and gender-equality movements, despite the fact that efforts to promote women's rights have long been initiated by citizens in the South through groups such as Development Alternatives for Women in a New Era (DAWN).[55] In more extreme cases, the protection that NGOs have enjoyed is being eroded by kidnapping, murder, theft, assault, and campaigns of hatred in the media: 'This may all be part of "global civil society"; but it is a society that is, in many ways, violent, contested and with an uncertain future.'[56] Thus, one of the challenges still faced by civil society organizations in some parts of the world is their very survival.

Competition among NGOs and CBOs is also increasing as they vie for government grants and contracts. This is likely to reduce NGO solidarity and collaboration, and may potentially undermine the political power of NGOs to stand in opposition to or to influence governments. The increasing reliance of NGOs on grant funding is argued, by some, to be a threat to the time-consuming skilled task of building up the capacities and capabilities of community organizations as 'many official agencies are unwilling to support the long-time horizons, slow, careful nurturing and gradual qualitative results which characterize successful institutional development'.[57] Allied to this is the challenge that NGOs and CBOs face in reaching the very poor, rather than working only with those with some asset base who can be more easily lifted out of poverty. Under pressure to meet

development targets and to answer to donors and governments, NGOs and CBOs may find it increasingly expedient to neglect the worst off. Where this is happening, the trend runs contrary to current efforts to recognize the heterogeneity of communities and the most vulnerable within them. Despite this, there still remains a tendency to trust that civil society organizations are automatically representative of the communities with whom they work.

A further challenge comes from the issue of scale. To date, the geographical coverage of NGOs and CBOs is patchy and incomplete, leaving some slum settlements, neighbourhoods, towns or whole regions to fend for themselves, depending upon the self-help strategies that their inhabitants can devise and on what weak governments can provide. Nevertheless, scaling-up NGO and CBO activities can jeopardize the quality of their work. Grant funding can facilitate interventions at a greater scale but can pose problems of bureaucratization as funders require increasingly complex appraisal and reporting requirements:

> When official agencies finance service delivery, they expect contracted outputs to be achieved and are less interested in a 'learning process'. Time and space for reflection may be reduced and the ability of NGOs to articulate approaches, ideas, language and values which run counter to official orthodoxies may also be compromised.[58]

All of this points to the need for both NGOs and CBOs to be able to prove their credentials and justify their actions. Ultimately, it is in the interest of these organizations to be ahead of the game in defining what are acceptable or legitimate activities as a means of defending themselves and increasing their legitimacy and influence.[59] Thus, one of the

Category	Percentage
Youth groups	5
Women's groups	8
Academics	11
Foundations	4
Human solidarity groups	7
Labour unions	1
Community-based organizations	49
Parliamentarians	1
Professional and researchers	5
Private sector associations	6

Source: UN-Habitat Partnership Section estimates.

Table 8.3

Main categories of urban-sector NGOs

While the climate has become markedly more favourable towards NGOs and CBOs over the last 20 years, in some states there is evidence of increasing criticism

Table 8.4

Urban-sector NGOs by region

Region	Number	Percentage
Latin America and the Caribbean	287	12
Western Europe and other states	912	39
Eastern Europe	71	3
Central and Eastern Asia	131	6
South Asia and Oceania	326	14
Middle East	118	5
West Africa	238	10
East Africa	274	12

Source: UN-Habitat Partnership Section estimates.

biggest challenges is to make civil society organizations accountable. Yet, it is only now that this is starting to happen and performance monitoring for these organizations is still in its infancy.

To date, evaluations of NGOs tend towards propaganda; where they are more rigorous, they are rarely made public. Performance monitoring and evaluation would enable not only the improvement of procedures, but may also lead to a questioning of the assumption that working with NGOs and CBOs is the best way to reduce costs, reach the poor and encourage democratization. Already, 'there is increasing evidence that NGOs and CBOs do not perform as effectively as had been assumed in terms of poverty-reach, cost-effectiveness, sustainability, popular participation (including gender), flexibility and innovation'.[60]

Despite some evidence to the contrary, for example, there is no empirical study that demonstrates a general case that the provision of services by NGOs is cheaper than public provision. Furthermore, even when it is cheap, it may often still fail to reach the very poor. The sustainability of large-scale service provision by NGOs has also been called into question by those who cite the large subsidies granted to NGOs that make the gap between private and public provision a self-perpetuating reality.[61] Furthermore, with regard to NGO and CBO progress in democratization processes, while there is evidence of some success at influencing policy reform at a local level:

> ...there is little evidence that NGOs and even CBOs are managing to engage in the formal political process successfully, without becoming embroiled in partisan politics and the distortions that accompany the struggle for state power.[62]

States can be adept at putting a ceiling on the types of activities that NGOs and CBOs perform, encouraging their participation in service provision, but capping their ability to have political influence.

Accountability is, therefore, not only a means by which NGOs and CBOs can be held responsible for their actions, but also a basis upon which there can be a more fundamental questioning of development strategies. Accountability requires a statement of goals, transparency of decision-making and relationships, honest reporting, and an appraisal process. It can emphasize issues of probity or performance, functional accountability or strategic accountability.[63] To whom NGOs and CBOs are accountable is, of course, a complex question because they deal not only with their constituents or beneficiaries, as well as their partners, members, staff and supporters, but also with their funders, trustees and governments. It is this multiple accountability that can lead to either too much or not enough accountability, and the fear is that accountability may be directed away from the grassroots and towards official agencies that hold the purse strings. Should this happen, monitoring and evaluation processes are likely to stress the short-term attainment of project objectives, time schedules and spending targets, with the process becoming one of auditing rather than learning.[64] Intellectually, those who work for NGOs and CBOs are 'well aware that money spent does not equate to development achieved, that all problems cannot be overcome through projects; but they also know that the public, the media and even their peers judge the worth of their organizations by this single, narrow measurement'.[65]

Accountability is also problematic due to the nature of what NGOs and CBOs are trying to do, especially in relation to empowerment and democratization, which are hard to measure:

> In addition, NGOs and CBOs are rarely able to control all (or even most) of the factors which influence the outcome of their work – macro-economic performance, state policy and the actions of other agencies are obvious examples.[66]

All of this makes the development of accountability procedures a huge challenge, but one that is essential to face. When it comes to the normative implications of analysis of the non-state sector, three issues merit attention:

> First, once we have escaped from the assumption that all non-state actors are benign, or preferable to states, we have to have a normative compass by which to assess these groups. The mere fact of their being 'non-state', even when we are satisfied that they are, does not answer the issue. One part of this compass would involve the attitude to the state itself and to the engagement with those positive functions that states perform. Another would be our, necessarily diverse, assessment of the policy goals of these NGOs. A third would be the very conformity of these 'non-state' entities to the democratic and good governance norms we increasingly insist on for governments themselves.[67]

Within the actor groups identified (governments, donors, NGOs and CBOs), there exists inertia, corruption, resistance to change and conflict. Equally, most groups contain within them champions of change and some degree of political will to formulate and implement policies that are aimed at poverty eradication and social justice. Turning the efforts of such champions into effective and sustained change on a large scale is an enormous challenge. It is here that partnerships among donors, governments and civil society can prove to be effective, with like-minded progressive individuals providing each other with sufficient support to foster broader political will that can then be translated into lasting change.

To whom NGOs and CBOs are accountable is a complex question. Accountability is, therefore, not only a means by which NGOs and CBOs can be held responsible for their actions, but also a basis upon which there can be a more fundamental questioning of development strategies

NOTES

1   This chapter draws mainly on a draft prepared by Patrick Wakely in collaboration with Elizabeth Riley. For other contributors, see the Acknowledgements.

2   White, 1994, p379.

3   White, 1994.

4   Carothers and Ottaway, 2000, p11.

5   Carothers and Ottaway, 2000, p11.

6   Carothers and Ottaway, 2000, p12.

7   Douglass, 1998, p121.

8   Douglass, 1998, p124.

9   Douglass, 1998, p123.

10 Douglass, 1998.

11 Douglass, 1998.

12 Barr, 1999.

13 Fisher, 1998, p6.

14 Fisher, 1998.

15 Campfens, 1997.

16 Campfens, 1997.

17 Campfens, 1997, pp18–19.

18 For more information, see:www.sdinet.org.

19 For more information, see www.sparcindia.org.

20 Campfens, 1997, p21.

21 Campfens, 1997.

22 Campfens, 1997.

23 Fisher, 1998, p5.

24 Clark, 1991, p53.

25 Josselin and Wallace, 2001, p3.

26 Halliday, 2001.

27 Fisher, 1998.

28 Fisher, 1998, p34.

29 Fisher, 1998, p39.

30 Fisher, 1998, p7.

31 Halliday, 2001, p29.

32 Edwards and Hulme, 1995.

33 Halliday, 2001, p25.

34 Josselin and Wallace, 2001, p9.

35 Edwards and Hulme, 1995.

36 Josselin and Wallace, 2001.

37 Josselin and Wallace, 2001.

38 Fisher, 1998.

39 Fisher, 1998.

40 Fisher, 1998.

41 Halliday, 2001, p29.

42 Edwards and Hulme, 1995, p5.

43 Clark, 1991.

44 Fisher, 1998.

45 Clark, 1991.

46 Clark, 1991.

47 Clark, 1991.

48 Edwards and Hulme, 1995, p7.

49 Edwards and Hulme, 1995, p7.

50 Halliday, 2001, p26.

51 Josselin and Wallace, 2001, p3.

52 Clark, 1991.

53 Fisher, 1998, p11.

54 UN-Habitat Partnership Section estimation.

55 DAWN, which promotes a Southern feminist critique of development, was founded by a group of feminists from the South in 1984.

56 Halliday, 2001, p23.

57 Edwards and Hulme, 1995, p8.

58 Edwards and Hulme, 1995, p8.

59 Clark, 1991.

60 Edwards and Hulme, 1995, p6.

61 Edwards and Hulme, 1995, p6.

62 Edwards and Hulme, 1995, p7.

63 Edwards and Hulme, 1995, p7.

64 Edwards and Hulme, 1995, p7.

65 Clark, 1991, p38.

66 Edwards and Hulme, 1995, p11.

67 Halliday, 2001, p35.

TOWARDS INCLUSIVE CITIES: RECONSIDERING DEVELOPMENT PRIORITIES[1]

The rapid and unprecedented growth in urban populations over the past 50 years that was documented in Chapter 2 will continue into the new millennium, but is now confined almost entirely to the cities of the developing world, where an extra 2 billion people will need to be provided with housing and services over the next 30 years.

The questions that the world needs to ask are where will these new urban residents live? Which land should they use? Which schools will their children go to? Where will they get their water? How will their rubbish be collected? Where should they vote? Who will protect them? In fact, very few politicians and policy-makers are even asking these questions. Macro-economic responses, in particular, are ignoring the urban situation and damaging the prospects for city economic growth and job creation. Already, 25 per cent of the developing world's urban population live below official poverty lines; and over 40 per cent of urban households in sub-Saharan Africa are in poverty. In most developing countries, conditions are worsening as inappropriate macro-economic policy and weak urban governance meet the impact of growing inequality, corruption and imbalances in resource allocation.

The challenges of urban poverty, appalling living conditions and bad governance do not arise because of a failure to provide technical and workable solutions – they arise because of narrow political and economic priorities that are not based on addressing human needs in an equitable or sustainable manner. This concentration of extreme poverty raises difficult policy issues that need to be addressed within an approach that integrates human rights into the development framework by emphasizing the promotion of freedom, well-being and the dignity of individuals, and the centrality of the person. This rights-based approach is underscored by evidence that political freedoms are associated with higher levels of growth. Indeed, the evidence shows that authoritarianism and the absence of civil liberties are associated with increased distortions in trade and labour markets that disproportionately harm the poor.

Slums, as indicated in the previous chapters, are the products of failed policies, bad governance, corruption, inappropriate regulation, dysfunctional land markets, unresponsive financial systems, and a fundamental lack of political will. Each of these failures adds to the load on people already deeply burdened by poverty, and also constrains the enormous opportunity for human development that urban life offers.

Older sectorial approaches sought to tackle urban problems in the traditional engineering-based manner, but with hopelessly inadequate resources to meet the huge and continuing problem of urban growth and rising urban poverty levels. In most cases, they used imported technology, equipment and capital, creating few local job opportunities, adding to balance of payments problems, and failing to address issues of asset management, upkeep and maintenance of the new assets, which were subject to chronic overuse and rapid degradation.

It has become increasingly clear that strategies to deal with urban poverty need to consider much more than the provision of housing and physical services. They need to consider questions of governance and political will; of ownership and rights; of social capital and access; of appropriate technology involving low-income people in economic and political activity; and of coordination and partnerships between all of the various partners in urban activities who are currently delivering to limited constituencies that must be extended by different means.

The new locally based strategies for poverty alleviation and urban improvement combine aspects of market-based enabling processes with new holistic anti-poverty and partnership approaches. They are conducted using longer-term plans and budgetary commitments, and must embody high levels of local commitment and local ownership to ensure sustainability of effort. Some of the recommended good practices for improving urban management include:

- *slum upgrading*, conducted through concerted strategies and involving self-help and local ownership as the recommended response to poor conditions and services in existing slums;
- improving *tenure security* as a means of bettering the lives of slum dwellers and improving their access to urban services, finance and income-generating opportunities;
- attention to the interaction of *land use, transport and infrastructure provision*, taking particular care that new construction benefits the poor as well as the affluent, and that adverse impacts and displacement are minimized for poor communities;
- increasing *employment opportunities* through support for the small enterprises and poverty alleviation measures, including the use of appropriate

technologies for infrastructure and housing provision that are affordable and provide work opportunities;

- mobilizing *urban finance* for enterprises and housing through micro-finance institutions and by facilitating the involvement of banks and other investment bodies in housing and infrastructure investment;
- an '*inclusive city*' approach by local authorities who are increasingly responsive and accountable to their citizens, seeking to benefit all constituents and embracing principles of good governance;
- forming *partnerships* between different levels of government, non-governmental organizations (NGOs) and the private sector, and citizens represented through community-based organizations (CBOs);
- establishing meaningful forms of inter-sectorial and cross-government *coordination* that permit the integration of top-down planning to meet national goals, with bottom-up participatory planning that brings local and grassroots needs to the forefront of the policy debate.

This chapter considers each of these eight areas in turn, in some detail, outlining the reasons for the conduct of these particular policies and the strengths and opportunities inherent in each strategy.

POLICY ISSUES AND STRATEGIES FOR INCLUSIVE CITIES

The main difference between earlier unsustainable approaches and the approaches of the present is that today's best practices are strategic, inclusive and holistic. Under the new paradigm, projects are now undertaken not because they deliver numbers of houses, kilometres of road or good benefit-to-cost ratios, but because they:

- benefit urban citizens, especially low-income people and vulnerable groups, and deliver worthwhile social outcomes that improve equity and participation;
- form part of larger strategies aimed at improving the overall well-being and operation of cities, not just today but for future generations; and
- involve all stakeholders, particularly marginalized groups, in conception and design, and often in construction and operation.

Inclusive strategies may be applied to all classes of urban inputs and outputs – to slum upgrading, housing tenure and rights, transport infrastructure, income generation, and municipal and housing finance. These are the subjects of this section.

From slum upgrading to cities without slums[2]

As stated in Chapter 7, the policy alternative that has come to be regarded as best practice in dealing with the problems

---

Box 9.1 Slum upgrading actions

Slum upgrading consists of physical, social, economic, organizational and environmental improvements undertaken cooperatively and locally among citizens, community groups, businesses and local authorities. Actions include:

- installing or improving basic infrastructure – for example, water supply and storage, sanitation/waste collection, rehabilitation of circulation, storm drainage and flood prevention, electricity, security lighting and public telephones;
- removing or mitigating environmental hazards;
- providing incentives for community management and maintenance;
- constructing or rehabilitating community facilities, such as nurseries, health posts and community open space;
- regularizing security of tenure;
- home improvement;
- relocating/compensating the small number of residents dislocated by the improvements;
- improving access to health care and education, as well as to social support programmes in order to address issues of security, violence, substance abuse, etc;
- enhancing income-earning opportunities through training and micro-credit;
- building social capital and the institutional framework to sustain improvements.

---

of existing slums is participatory slum upgrading – conducted not as a technical exercise, but as a political, social and organizational plan. To be sustainable and replicable, it has been found that slum upgrading must be undertaken within a framework that is inclusive and responsive to local conditions, while involving the considerable energy of the slum dwellers and their representative organizations. At the same time, it must be broad and conducted as part of a city and national plan that institutionalizes the activities in a continuous, rolling improvement, conducted within the scope and full legitimacy of the existing political system.

■ Lessons learned from past experiences of upgrading

Box 9.1 shows the local activities typically involved in slum upgrading. A fully operational slum upgrading plan is a broad intervention involving aspects of a complete poverty alleviation programme. Upgrading directly addresses some of the most egregious manifestations of urban policy and institutional failures; but these also have to be confronted by complementary efforts to correct these failures and to build positive channels for improving the economic prospects of the poor.

Important complementary components of a slum upgrading strategy may include:

- *Sectorial reforms*: reforming regulatory and policy regimes for housing, land and infrastructure markets should remove obstacles and disincentives to access for the poor. Pro-poor regulatory frameworks will eliminate inappropriate standards of provision that raise costs; encourage entry of new technologies and of small-scale and other competing suppliers; make subsidy policies more effective and better targeted; establish more equitable tariff and cost recovery systems; and facilitate active partnerships among private investors and utilities, community groups, NGOs and local governments to create practical solutions that are responsive to the needs of the urban poor.

- *Finance*: engaging private financial institutions leads to institution-based strategies that may extend access to credit for housing, services and business development to the poor, especially financing for developers, infrastructure providers and landlords, and micro-credit for households.
- *Jobs*: measures to support small-scale enterprise and to remove regulatory or other obstacles to the growth of the informal sector will increase employment, productivity and private investment among the urban poor.
- *Governance*: improved governance and management of cities at all levels should make local governments more responsive to the issues facing the poor.
- *Social capital and knowledge*: measures to facilitate and strengthen the organizational capacities of citizen groups and local governments will increase access to information and guidance on solutions to slum communities. Upgrading programmes have, in fact, in many cases proven a highly effective forum for community action, helping members to negotiate with local authorities and utility companies in order to define solutions that meet their demands. There is also evidence of broad social benefits for the community, such as reduced violence.
- *Other targeted activities*: other traditional measures to fight poverty, including social safety nets, public works employment, and the promotion of health care, training and educational opportunities also have an important place in an upgrading programme. Particular attention needs to be paid to child care for working parents, activities for vulnerable youth (including street children) and efforts to combat crime and violence.

Upgrading also needs to be complemented by policies to forestall the growth of future slums. Upgrading of slums addresses the backlog of urban neglect; but many cities – especially in Africa and Asia – will continue to face an onslaught of new urban residents over the next few decades. Without significant improvements in the housing provision system and the capacities of governments, civil society and the private sector to provide services for new residents, many of whom will be poor, the problems of slums will be magnified rather than lessened. Despite advances and improvements in city management, most cities in developing economies cannot keep pace with the increasing numbers of urban poor.

The improved performance of local government is necessary to manage future urban growth, particularly by:

- *Effectively carrying out basic land-use planning*: for example, setting aside basic rights of way for primary infrastructure reduces the costs of extending networks. Revising regulatory policies discourages the sprawl and settlement of unsafe or environmentally fragile areas.
- *More effectively mobilizing local resources*: cities with slums often have significant fiscal resources at their disposal, opportunities to mobilize private investment, technical knowledge and indigenous entrepreneurial talents. In the slums themselves, there is both nascent and active organizational dynamism and powerful self-interest, coupled with unrecognized or underutilized talent.

Considerable knowledge has been gained from past experience regarding what works best; but very few upgrading pilot projects have been scaled-up to city-wide or nation-wide programmes. In fact, urban slum conditions are qualitatively and quantitatively worsening worldwide. The lessons from this experience make it clear that moving from pilot slum-upgrading projects to city-wide and nation-wide scales of action is absolutely necessary. But this will require tackling critical development issues head on:

- *Good governance*: the capacity of local governments must be strengthened to carry out their responsibility for the equitable provision of infrastructure and services to all urban residents, while planning for future growth. The capacity of provincial, state and national authorities must be strengthened to ensure their critical normative roles, to establish facilitating policy environments, and to rid corruption from land markets and the provision of public services.
- *Legal system*: property rights and security of tenure are crucial in sustainable approaches to upgrading. Most residents of urban slums live without any form of secure tenure and under constant threat of eviction, which vitiates their ability to access credit and constrains their motivation to improve their homes and neighbourhoods.
- *Financial system*: coupled with security of tenure, access to credit is key to unleashing the vast potential of the urban poor to improve their living and working environments and livelihoods. Micro-credit and other facilities that expand access to credit to the poor can provide critical elements of institutional support in creating financially self-supporting and sustainable urban upgrading programmes.
- *Social framework*: community participation in the conception, development, financing, upgrading and maintenance of infrastructure and services is a critical element of sustainable programmes. Experience has shown that the most successful programmes address community priorities. Communities must be enfranchised through knowledge sharing and security of their civil rights.

With respect to infrastructure, experience has shown that the best solution is a city-wide approach, as opposed to the typical ad hoc settlement-by-settlement approach. This has successfully been done with three Indian cities, including one with a population of over 1 million (see Box 9.2).[3] Instead of focusing on individual settlements or on the city limits as the area for planning, the focus should be on the primary infrastructure networks, such as the water mains, road networks and/or sewerage system of the urban area.

Urban planning should aim to develop a city-wide infrastructure supply system that provides the possibility of individual household connections as and when they can afford it, and the possibility of community mobilization and self-help.[4] A number of key lessons have been learned from the implementation of city-wide approaches:[5]

- Infrastructure networks must be designed to ensure that basic services reach the entire population in an equitable manner.
- Infrastructure networks must be easy to maintain, repair and upgrade.
- Wasteful overlaps and uncoordinated services should be avoided by using an integrated and holistic approach to design.
- Care should be taken to ensure that the design makes provision for future growth and the expansion of informal settlements.
- Short-term measures to save money should not be used.
- Flexibility should be provided in order to ensure that the informal settlement dwellers can connect to the network as and when they can afford it.
- City-wide information on the informal settlements should be analysed before planning.
- Professional input is needed in most aspects of the work that is carried out since slum upgrading is more complex to plan and implement than conventional projects.
- The costs of infrastructure systems need to be assessed on the basis of both the capital costs and continuing maintenance.
- Working on a large scale enables solutions that are uneconomic at the local level.

■ The Cities Without Slums action plan

The Cities Without Slums action plan was launched in Berlin in December 1999 at the inaugural meeting of the Cities Alliance.[6] The World Bank and UN-Habitat are the founding members of the Cities Alliance – a major global alliance of cities and their development partners. The Cities Without Slums action plan constitutes part of the Millennium Development Goals (MDGs) and targets. The target on slums aims, by the year 2020, to have achieved a significant improvement in the lives of at least 100 million slum dwellers. Its implementation will require the international development community to adopt a new unity of effort that is focused on improving the living conditions and livelihoods of the urban poor. It calls for long-term commitment, a ratcheting up of resources and a coherence of priorities, programmes and organizational arrangements within each international development organization. It also engages committed local and national partners who are willing to make a concerted, results-driven attack on the slum

> **Box 9.2 Slum networking: Indore, India**
>
> In Indore, the slums were located on the watercourses of the city. The new infrastructure that was provided in the slums and linked to the rest of the city made it possible to clean up a river, as all the slum gutters were discharging into the river. The whole city did not have an underground sewerage system; by putting infrastructure down for the whole city, including the slums, the whole city benefited. Cross-subsidies for the network then became possible. By providing decent roads within, and on the perimeter of, slum areas, it became possible to complete linkages within the city's road network, which substantially improved traffic flows.
> *Source:* Diacon, 1997.

problem. The credibility and resources required for success depend upon a highly targeted effort of all partners to support the provision of basic services for the urban poor within the framework of country and city development strategies for the new millennium.

The action plan focuses upon upgrading the most squalid, unhealthy, unserved and vulnerable urban slums and squatter settlements. It builds upon successful community-based upgrading programmes, while addressing the broader policy and institutional issues that have often impeded their sustainability. By supporting those national and local authorities who are prepared to develop city-wide and nation-wide upgrading programmes, it hopes to set in motion a global movement that can transform the lives of significant numbers of the most vulnerable and marginalized urban residents. The action plan calls for:

- challenging donors, governments and slum communities to improve the lives of 5 to 10 million slum dwellers by 2005, and 100 million by 2020, in line with the Millennium Declaration;
- increasing investments aimed at providing basic services to the urban poor;
- leading a worldwide effort to move from pilot projects to city-wide and nation-wide upgrading, and to generate the required resources to do so; and
- investing in global knowledge, learning and capacity in slum upgrading, and reducing the growth of new slums.

The key activities of the plan are outlined in Box 9.3.

Tenure issues and access to land for the urban poor[7]

In most developing cities, the expansion of informal settlements over the last two decades has taken place in a context of accelerated globalization and structural adjustment policies. This has been combined with deregulation measures, privatization of urban services, massive state disengagement in the urban and housing sector, and attempts to integrate informal markets – including the land and housing markets – within the sphere of the formal market economy.[8] These policy measures, along with the lack of, or inefficiency of, corrective measures or safety net programmes, have tended to further increase inequalities in wealth and resource distribution at all levels.[9]

Box 9.3 Cities Without Slums action plan: six key actions necessary to meet the goal

1   *Strengthening in-country capacity* by restructuring policy and regulatory and operating frameworks, and eliminating legal/technical constraints from upgrading to scale; overcoming institutional bottlenecks; encouraging local commitment and resolve, including political understanding and buy-in; and strengthening learning and training.
2   *Preparing national/city upgrading programmes* by helping committed countries to design programmes for upgrading to scale.
3   *Supporting regional and global knowledge and learning* that capture and share the varied approaches and local practices to getting the job done; this entails the full involvement of the affected communities, the organizing networks of practice, and fielding specialists in order to help countries and cities upgrade to scale.
4   *Investing in slums*, with the appropriate basic infrastructure and municipal services identified, implemented and operated with the community.
5   *Strengthening partner capacity* to focus attention on the task, with emphasis on the resources, knowledge and tools to help governments and communities do the job well and to scale.
6   *Leadership and political buy-in* by the partners of the Cities Alliance to prioritize slum upgrading.

Source: Cities Alliance, 1999, p7. Available at: www.citiesalliance.org.

As a result, the urban poor and large segments of low- and low-to-medium-income groups have no choice but to rely on informal land and housing markets for access to land and shelter.[10] This situation has led to the rapid spatial expansion of irregular settlements. Informal land and housing delivery systems remain the only realistic alternative for meeting the needs of low-income households.[11]

The total number of squatters is tending to decrease in most developing cities, and unauthorized settlements are on the increase. This is a trend that has been observed for almost two decades: in many cities there is no longer free access to land for squatting purposes; but land can be accessed for unauthorized settlements by informal deals with the landowner. This reflects the ever increasing commodification of land delivery systems for the poor of the cities, and the fact that there is less and less public land available for occupation by squatters.[12]

■ Security of tenure: a key to the 'inclusive city'

Land tenure refers to the rights of individuals or groups in relation to land. The exact nature and content of these rights, the extent to which people have confidence that they will be honoured, and their various degrees of recognition by the public authorities and communities concerned will have a direct impact on how land will be used:[13]

> *Tenure often involves a complex set of rules, frequently referred to as a 'bundle of rights'. A given resource may have multiple users, each of whom has particular rights to the resource. Some users may have access to the entire 'bundle of rights', with full use and transfer rights. Other users may be limited in their use of the resources.*[14]

It is important to bear this definition of tenure in mind since it underlines both the diversity of rights to land and the existence of a wide range of options, from full ownership to less exclusive forms of possession and use. There is a possible coexistence in one place of forms of tenure that give access to different rights and a continuum between these different forms of tenure. This highlights the fact that ownership is only one form of tenure among many others.[15]

Populations living in irregular urban settlements are all confronted with the same set of inter-related problems: they have no access – or limited access only – to basic services, and they have no security of tenure. Their situation is precarious as they usually belong to the poorest segment of the urban population.[16]

Security of tenure describes an agreement between individuals or groups, with respect to land and residential property, that is governed and regulated by a legal and administrative framework. This legal framework is taken to include both customary and statutory systems. The security derives from the fact that the right of access to, and use of, the land and property is underwritten by a legitimate set of rules. The tenure can be affected in a variety of ways, depending upon constitutional and legal frameworks, social norms, cultural values and, to some extent, individual preference. In summary, a person or household can be said to have secure tenure when they are protected from involuntary removal from their land or residence, except in exceptional circumstances, and then only by means of a known and agreed legal procedure, which must itself be objective, equally applicable, contestable and independent. Such exceptional circumstances might include situations where the physical safety of life and property is threatened, or where the persons to be evicted have themselves taken occupation of the property by force or intimidation.[17]

Protection against forced evictions is a prerequisite for integrating irregular settlements within the city. For households living in irregular settlements, security of tenure offers a response to their immediate problem of forced removal or eviction.[18] It means recognizing and legitimizing the existing forms of tenure that prevail amongst poor communities, and creating space for the poorest populations to improve their quality of life. Security of tenure can be considered the main component of the right to housing, and an essential prerequisite for access to citizenship, as emphasized by the Global Campaign for Secure Tenure (GCST). Security of tenure is a fundamental requirement of the progressive integration of the urban poor within the city, and one of the basic components of the right to housing. It guarantees legal protection against forced eviction. The granting of secure tenure is one of the most important catalysts in stabilizing communities; improving shelter conditions; encouraging investment in home-based activities that play a major role in poverty reduction; reducing social exclusion; and improving access to urban services.[19] However, as most studies have stressed, tenure security is not, in itself, sufficient to break the poverty cycle. It forms only a part of a more comprehensive and integrated approach to informal settlement upgrading, as the case studies presented in this report confirm.

Chapters 5 and 6 considered the issues of security of tenure and legality in considerable detail, showing that

The urban poor and large segments of low- and low-to-medium-income groups have no choice but to rely on informal land and housing markets for access to land and shelter

Security of tenure can be considered the main component of the right to housing, and an essential prerequisite for access to citizenship

informal housing involves a wide range of situations and levels of precariousness. The social structure of irregular settlements is far from homogeneous within a single city or even within one settlement. Irregular settlements are not always exclusively occupied by the urban poor.[20] Middle-income households settle in these areas when the formal housing market cannot meet their demands; in such cases, a certain 'right to irregularity' may be recognized, with the situation being periodically set right through mass regularization using legal measures.

Some informal residential tenure arrangements can guarantee a reasonably good security of tenure. In communal or customary land delivery systems, recognition by the community itself and by the neighbourhood is often considered more important than recognition by public authorities. However, this arrangement can deteriorate under some circumstances – for instance, when the customary system is in crisis, or when there are leadership conflicts within the group of customary owners, especially between those who allocate the land and other members of the group.[21] Multiple allocations of the same plot can also generate a series of conflicts within the community (this may be the result of illicit land sales by unauthorized persons, a common phenomenon in the absence of any land information and record system). Major conflicts may arise between customary owners and public authorities about the ownership and use of the land, or about the legitimacy of the customary claim. In such cases, alliances often develop between customary owners and the community against the public authorities.[22]

Whatever the type of irregular settlement (for example, unauthorized land development on customary or private land, or squatter settlements on public or private land), four main factors contribute to protect households from eviction:

1   Length of occupation (older settlements enjoy a much better level of legitimacy and, thus, of protection than new settlements).
2   Size of the settlement (small settlements are more vulnerable than those with a large population).
3   Level and cohesion of community organization.
4   Support, which concerned communities may get from third-sector organizations, such as NGOs.

The current preoccupation with security of tenure issues by institutions that are responsible for urban land management and housing development programmes is, to a large extent, the result of lessons learned from the experience of recent years. Responses regarding access to land and housing for the urban poor have been well documented. They are primarily based on the regularization of irregular settlements, emphasizing tenure legalization and the provision of individual freehold.[23] Box 9.4 sums up conventional responses to irregularity.

Programmes combining tenure legalization and titling with programmes to provide serviced land, upgrading and improvements at settlement level have had limited success.[24] When large-scale allocation of property titles to

---

Box 9.4 Conventional responses to irregularity

Traditional responses have included the following:

- Tolerance by the public authorities of the existence of a dual formal/informal land delivery system, but the absence of a clear strategy regarding irregular settlements (this is the case in most sub-Saharan African countries). Responses may combine repression (forced eviction, harassment and various forms of pressure), tolerance (laissez-faire policies) and selective tenure regularization, according to the political context. It must be noted that there is always, in principle, a legal procedure that allows individual tenure regularization.[i]
- Attempts to adapt land law to the situation and needs of developing cities.[ii]
- Formal recognition and legitimization of the existence of informal land-delivery systems, only when they are considered as being controlled by customary owners in specific areas, and under specific conditions – most decisions by customary owners must be approved or authenticated by public authorities.[iii]
- Reduction of constraining planning and construction norms and standards.[iv] This also includes the integration of informal land and housing delivery systems within the sphere of formal activities through large-scale registration and tenure upgrading and legalization programmes.[v]
- The setting-up of a parallel alternative system, supposedly simpler and cheaper than the existing formal registration system. This may be based on simplified recording procedures. The entities in charge provide titles that are possible to mortgage. However, the mortgage value of such titles is less than that of freehold titles.[vi]
- Tentative top-down land-policy and institutional reforms.[vii]
- The cornerstone of regularization policies as implemented in some developing countries – such as Mexico during the 1990s[viii] – primarily based on the massive provision of individual freehold titles, or other forms of real rights. Rights can be transferred, inherited and mortgaged. Such responses require a series of complex procedures to identify the holders of rights and their beneficiaries; to resolve disputes; to delineate plots by surveying; to pay out compensation, if required; and to provide land registration and titling. Although this gives beneficiaries sound security of tenure, it is an expensive and time-consuming process, especially in contexts where the processing capacity of the administrations involved is limited, where land-related information is out of date or insufficient, and where centralized land registration procedures are complicated. Frequent incidents of corruption in administrations in charge of land management and allocation, and the low level of literacy amongst populations concerned, further aggravate the situation.

Sources: i Serageldin, 1990. ii McAuslan, 1998. iii Mosha, 1993; Mabogunje, 1992. iv Dowall, 1991. v Azuela, 1995; Varley, 1994. vi Zimmermann, 1998; Zevenbergen, 1998. vii Farvacque and McAuslan, 1992. viii Azuela, 1995; Varley, 1999.

---

households living in informal settlements has been made possible, it has often resulted in increased housing prices within the settlements, and/or in an increase in the cost of services, both of which have tended to exclude the poorest sections of the population. A critical analysis of the positive and negative consequences of increased formalization and commodification of the urban tenure process has increased.

Policies based on large-scale provision of land and housing by the public sector have been effective, in some cases, in reaching the poor, but only when carried out in a very determined way and in fairly special circumstances (for example, situations of housing scarcity and strong governments that can mobilize significant resources). Market-oriented responses tend to increase social urban segregation as the formal private sector responds much better and, often, almost exclusively to the needs of households in the upper-income bracket. Public–private partnerships in land and housing development cannot easily reach the poor unless heavy and well-targeted subsidies can be provided.

Centralized land registration and management systems and procedures, as well as existing legal and regulatory frameworks, cannot respond to the requirement of large-scale tenure regularization programmes in cities where up to 50 per cent of the urban population are living in irregular settlements. Governments rarely have sufficient human and financial resources to operate on a large scale. Shifting from projects to programmes and then to policies remains a major problem.

In spite of these problems, most countries opt in favour of private land and housing ownership, to the detriment of other options. This is due largely to conventional responses to the expansion of informal settlements that always reflect culturally and ideologically oriented development models.[25] Diagnoses of, and responses to, the situation regarding access to land and housing, and the perception of needs and rights, are primarily guided by Western forms of technical rationality and financial logic that have been designed by international finance institutions and aid agencies.[26]

The strategic role of market-oriented urban land and housing policies was repeatedly emphasized by the World Bank and the US Agency for International Development (USAID) during the 1990s.[27] Priority was given to tenure regularization of irregular settlements and to upgrading land tenure systems. The long-term objective has been to promote private ownership through the allocation of individual freehold/property titles. This may have a negative impact on the urban poor. On the one hand, these measures are expensive and may price the poor out of the land market. On the other hand, excluding informal or other landlords who normally provide low-cost housing removes both a ready source of capital, with some access to the formal sector, and the better political connections that this group may have in supporting neighbourhood upgrading in the longer term.

One of the basic hypotheses behind urban land policies, in general, and tenure reforms, in particular, is still that home-ownership and the provision of property titles is the only sustainable solution for providing security of tenure to the urban poor, while facilitating the integration of informal land markets within the framework of the formal economy. This convergence of diagnoses and responses has, as its starting point, a neo-liberal certainty that an increase in urban productivity will result from the unfettered development of the market economy through privatization, deregulation, decentralization and improvements in the financial system.[28]

The dominance of this paradigm is illustrated, at a global level, by the adoption of a standardized vocabulary and reference to the same notions and concepts (productivity, efficiency, deregulation, privatization). This vocabulary is by no means neutral and can be culturally insensitive in more traditional communities. Relations between urban stakeholders – including tenure relations – are seen by neo-liberals as being mainly organized around economic supply and demand. This view tends to 'de-

politicize perceptions and interpretations', and political actors are analysed as economic actors.[29]

It is now more and more frequently acknowledged that conventional responses to irregularities must be drastically redefined and reassessed.[30]

■ Alternative approaches to security of tenure

There are basically two approaches to secure tenure that differ but are not contradictory. The first emphasizes formal tenure regularization at the settlement level. Regularization policies are generally based on the delivery of individual freehold and, more rarely, of leasehold titles. However, the difficulty of finding legal forms of regularization that are compatible with constitutional rules and the legal framework, acceptable to the actors concerned, and in compliance with existing standards and procedures constitutes a major obstacle for many operations.

The second approach emphasizes security of tenure as the primary goal, rather than formalization and commodification. It does not require the provision of freehold individual title, although this is not excluded. Rather, it combines protective administrative or legal measures against forced evictions – including the provision of titles that can be upgraded, if required – with the provision of basic services. One of the objectives is to preserve the cohesion of beneficiary communities and to protect them against market pressures during and, more importantly, after the tenure upgrading process.[31] This approach must be understood as a first, but essential, step in an incremental process of tenure upgrading that can lead, at a later stage, to formal tenure regularization and the provision of formal rights. Unlike complicated, expensive and time-consuming tenure regularization programmes, security of tenure can be provided through simple legal and regulatory measures.[32] Box 9.5 shows the more recent alternative responses to irregularity.

The rapid integration of informal settlements within the broader community through conventional tenure regularization and the provision of freehold titles may hinder community cohesion, dissolve social links, and induce or accelerate segregation processes through market eviction. Measures that aim primarily at guaranteeing security of tenure, however, give communities time to consolidate their settlements with a view to further improving their tenure status.

This consolidation process involves improvements to the economic condition of households; the emergence of legitimate leadership at the community level; the identification of rights holders; and the resolution of conflicts within the community and between the community and other actors involved – such as landowners, local authorities, planning authorities and central administrations in charge of land management and registration, among many others. In addition, the time between the initial security guarantees and later delivery of formal property titles can be used to improve the quality of services in the settlement. It also gives households time to define a strategy, and to save or raise funds to pay for the next step in the tenure upgrading and regularization process.

The strategic role of market-oriented urban land and housing policies was repeatedly emphasized during the 1990s

The consolidation process involves improvements to the economic condition of households; the emergence of legitimate leadership at the community level; the identification of rights holders; and the resolution of conflicts

In addition, being given security of tenure without transferable or negotiable property titles lessens market pressures on the settlement and limits market evictions. This is an essential advantage of options that emphasize incremental regularization procedures, where occupants are granted occupancy rights that can, at a later stage, be incrementally upgraded to real rights, such as freehold or long-term leases, if so desired. Such an approach can be used both on vacant land and for regularizing irregular settlements.[33]

The question of the role of landlords remains somewhat unexplored. It is not an accident that a large proportion of low-income housing in the world is provided by private landlords. Many of these landlords are themselves quite poor, so the rental system actually provides a means of informal income generation, especially for women, and is often the only pension scheme available in slum communities.

On the other hand, the involvement of private landlords hastens commodification, higher land prices and the growth of high-density tenements and poor living conditions, as detailed in the 19th-century pejorative literature in which the slum reform movement was born. The 'slumlord', however, remains a figure of fear and derision. The question is whether this very substantial local capital can be accessed in ways that permit reasonable security for tenants, while avoiding the trap of concentrating the poor in ever worsening accommodation. This possibility has never really been investigated.

■ Diversity of situations and objectives requires diversity of responses

Although there has been a considerable shift towards implementing more flexible forms of security of tenure, which tend to stress user rights rather than ownership, programmes and policies have not yet been developed that can be applied at a national level. As emphasized in the New Delhi Declaration[34] and by the Habitat Agenda, there is a clear need to have a variety of responses available in order to cope with the diversity of local situations encountered.

There may be various objectives behind the provision of security of tenure, such as ensuring social peace (the prime political motivation of most governments), social justice, urban planning, or environmental and economic objectives such as the integration of informal practices within the sphere of the formal economy. The content of security of tenure policies depends upon the priorities given to these objectives and to the forms and types of irregularity encountered. Clearly, the responses and options available to deal with security of tenure cannot be seen only in technical terms. They depend upon a set of inter-related social, political, economic and technical factors:

- The principle of the right to housing and the legal measures to enforce this right frequently contradict constitutional principles regarding the protection of property rights. This is one of the main areas of conflict when tenure upgrading and regularization policies are implemented, as well as when providing the simplest forms of secure tenure.[35]

Box 9.5 Recent responses to irregularity

Recent shifts have focused on the following practices:

- Setting up a simplified registration system where tenure can be incrementally upgraded to real rights in accordance with the needs and resources of individual households and the processing capacity of administrations in charge (for example, in Namibia).[i] A system such as this must be compatible with formal registration procedures.
- Devising and adopting innovative tenure formulae that emphasize collective trust or cooperative ownership. In the context of most cities, this is an appropriate, though temporary, solution that has difficulty in resisting market pressures.
- Emphasizing partnerships between formal and informal actors.[ii]
- Emphasizing protection against evictions, whenever possible, through long-term lease and other measures that, firstly, give priority to the consolidation of occupancy rights rather than to the provision of property freehold titles, and, secondly, give priority to collective rather than individual interests. In different cities, these basic responses can be combined in different ways.[iii]

Accompanying measures are usually adopted in order to facilitate the implementation of these responses. Here, again, recent shifts indicate a new approach to tenure issues, with emphasis mainly on the following:[iv]

- Decentralization of land management responsibilities to local/municipal levels, with municipalities receiving sufficient resources (both human and financial) to carry out land registration and land allocation and use.[v]
- Attempts at integrating legal pluralism approaches within tenure policies.[vi]
- Reliance on community-based and grassroots organizations at settlement and city levels.[vii]
- Provision of basic services as a form of settlement recognition and as a tool for alleviating poverty.
- Improved access to credit for the urban poor through conventional and micro-finance systems.[viii]

Sources: i Fourie, 2000; Christiensen, 1995, 1999; UNECA, 1998b. ii Payne, 1999a. iii UNCHS (Habitat), 1996b; Durand-Lasserve, 2000a; Payne, 1999a. iv Fourie, 2000; UNCHS (Habitat), 1999a. v Rakodi, 1999. vi Benton, 1994; Tribillon, 1993. vii Abbott, 2002; Imparato, 2001. viii Aurejac and Cabannes, 1995.

- The respective responsibilities of central and local governments in relation to the implementation of security of tenure policies are, generally, clearly defined. More often than not, local entities have responsibilities regarding land and housing policies, but are hindered in carrying them out by their limited resources, both human and financial.[36]
- At city/municipal level, the options available regarding security of tenure policies depend upon the balance of power between various urban stakeholders, as well as on the political orientation of the municipality.
- Available options also depend upon the prevailing residential tenure systems in place, and also, to some extent, on the size of the population living in irregular settlements.
- At settlement/community level, the measures employed will depend upon the size of the community concerned, any political influence that may be involved, the age of the settlement and the level of community organization. Any or all of these factors can determine whether the claims and

The options available to deal with security of tenure cannot be seen only in technical terms

demands of communities are, in fact, put forward for consideration.

- The role of NGOs and civil society organizations must be considered in their local context.[37]

Inclusive infrastructure: making the connections between transport and housing security[38]

■ Dilemmas of housing security versus access

As Chapter 2 observed, one of the principal forces determining city structure and residential location is the trade-off between transport costs and space. For low-income households, the dilemma may be more stark: a trade-off between location and safety or security. In accessible parts of the city, the poor can often afford only precarious sites with insecure tenure. For example, a survey in central Bombay of pavement dwellers showed that 80 per cent walked to work ('they were willing to live in congested dwellings without safety or security just so they could walk to work').[39] Conversely, affordable sites that have more secure tenure tend to be located on the inaccessible periphery of the urban area and involve high commuting time and costs.[40] Most urban residents around the world face some form of this dilemma, but it is most acute for the poor. The poorest groups face major problems in achieving decent levels of either housing security or ease of access to opportunities, let alone both.

Transport is a key issue that affects accessibility – not just the availability of low-cost transport that may make a more distant location feasible, but also the redevelopment of inner-city areas for transport infrastructure, resulting in evictions of the urban poor through whose domiciles transport corridors tend to be routed.

Displacement for urban transport infrastructure is significant in many cities. The World Bank has identified transport as the largest single cause of resettlement in its portfolio of projects. For example, transport accounted for 25 per cent of active projects in 1993 that involved resettlement.[41] As an example, 67 per cent of the resettlement in the World Bank's Surabaya Urban Project was associated with the project's transport components.[42]

Transport-related displacement is likely to be most intense where motorization is increasing rapidly, where population densities are high, where weak legal institutions exist, and where large numbers of people have insecure tenure. Other factors that influence the incidence of evictions for transport infrastructure include transport policies emphasizing space-consuming transport infrastructure. The most space-efficient modes of transport are high-capacity public transport modes, while the private car is the most space wasting.

People evicted for transport infrastructure are disproportionately from among the most vulnerable groups in society and tend to have weak housing tenure arrangements. This is partly because low-income settlements naturally tend to be identified as low-cost, 'easily cleared' alignments for new transport routes.[43] It is also because the affluent have been better organized to redirect new

construction away from their homes, while the biases of officials tend to support their objections: 'why destroy good quality housing when we can eliminate the slums?' As well, along existing transport corridors, there are often strips of vacant land and higher-density housing where lower-income people congregate. A common location for informal settlements is on linear reserves of land (usually state owned) that have been earmarked for infrastructure of some kind, and which are particularly attractive for transport projects. It is difficult, if not impossible, for settlers to gain security of tenure on such infrastructure reserve land.[44]

Ideally, minimizing the number of households displaced could be advanced as an integral feature of infrastructure policy and practice. Cost-benefit and environmental-income assessments should take explicit account of a much broader range of the negative impacts of displacement on communities, beyond just the immediate cost of buying and clearing land.[45] Good models for resettlement policies can now be found in the improved involuntary resettlement policies of multilateral lending agencies, such as the World Bank, the Asian Development Bank (ASDB) and the Inter-American Development Bank (IADB), which seek to minimize displacements. For example, the ASDB policy on involuntary resettlement states that 'involuntary resettlement [should] be an integral part of project design, dealt with from the earliest stages of the project cycle... The absence of formal legal title to land by some affected groups should not be a bar to compensation'.[46]

■ Resistance to displacement and negotiated outcomes

Inevitably, evictions and displacements for transport projects have provoked resistance in many areas. The sheer size of some transport projects tends to bring resettlement issues to public attention, and the glare of publicity may prompt better approaches. Furthermore, the common involvement of international finance agencies or companies, international engineering consultants, construction companies and the like may provide activists with leverage, in some cases, if there is an opportunity to lobby the actors of other governments who have clout and can influence local authorities.

Increased commitment to negotiating with communities who are threatened with involuntary resettlement is one of the beneficial outcomes of better security of tenure and respect for housing rights. This should also bring transport benefits to the communities concerned, since such negotiations tend to take accessibility into account in their selection of relocation sites. In the case of the railway dwellers of Janjur Marg in Mumbai, 900 families were empowered to negotiate effectively with the authorities, resulting in their relocation to an accessible location of their choice, with transit accommodation available and with the entire community kept together.[47]

Unfortunately, a lack of openness in transport planning is a major obstacle to achieving good negotiated outcomes for low-income communities threatened with eviction as a result of transport projects. Open, transparent,

One of the principal forces determining city structure and residential location is the trade-off between transport costs and space

Cost-benefit assessments should take explicit account of the negative impacts of displacement on communities

Lack of openness in transport planning is a major obstacle to achieving good negotiated outcomes

consultative approaches to transport planning are rare. Statistics on urban transport are piecemeal and poor. In some cases, this seems to be part of a deliberate strategy to obfuscate and prevent analysis of transport alternatives.[48] Community-based organizations have difficulty in obtaining timely information on transport projects that threaten them. The traditional mistrust by many transport planners of community involvement needs to be overcome, and more open, inclusive forms of dialogue need to be institutionalized.

■ Increasing housing choice through greater mobility for the poor

In recent years, there has been heightened attention in the international development community to the question of daily mobility for the urban poor, and a growing consensus has emerged on at least a core set of policies for improving mobility and access.[49] For example, increasing levels of access to affordable public or private transport, and allowing road space for bicycles, may increase the opportunity spaces of poor people. All else being equal, increasing mobility in affordable ways should expand the shelter options of the urban poor and reduce the extent to which they are forced to live in precarious and insecure locations.

However, simply expanding mobility will not necessarily guarantee improvements for the poor. Caution is warranted when seeking mobility increases because if the mobility of higher-income groups increases faster than that of the poor, then recolonization by the affluent through land-use changes and the undermining of low-cost modes of transport can harm access levels for the poor.[50] In particular, if attempts to achieve greater mobility in low-income cities are to help the poor, then they must not focus on private vehicles.[51] For example, the traffic congestion in Manila along the main Epifanio de los Santos avenue (EDSA) ring road, which is among the worst in Asia, is currently being blamed on the growth of unregistered buses that transport large numbers of low-income people, rather than on increased automobile ownership and lack of provision of adequate transport infrastructure.

■ Impacts of transport and land-use regulation

Excessively high, often car-oriented, standards and requirements for transport infrastructure in building or urban design codes can significantly raise the cost of new developments, further taking them beyond the reach of the poor. Examples of transport-related standards that are often set at unrealistic and unnecessary levels include minimum road-width standards, minimum setbacks of structures from the road and minimum parking-supply requirements. The effects of these standards are analogous to the impact of unrealistic housing design standards, with similar cost impacts.

These standards may both reflect and affect attitudes to low-income settlements. As with other standards, transport-related standards may be used to legitimize or rationalize policies of removing 'substandard' housing.[52] Conversely, the standards reinforce negative attitudes to informal settlements. Unrealistically high standards for parking or street widths may place legal barriers in the way of regularizing or legalizing low-income settlements. Instead of setting one-size-fits-all standards, an alternative pragmatic approach would be to tackle specific problems on a case-by-case basis in negotiations with the communities involved. Vernacular settlements that have obtained secure tenure can gradually be upgraded *in situ*. 'Land readjustment' techniques have also become a common way of providing adequate rights of way and common facilities in low-income settlements without the need for wholesale eviction.

Lack of secure tenure often prevents low-income residents from benefiting from transport and other improvements that increase the accessibility of land parcels, and which may lead to increases in land values. For renters without protection against rent increases, and for others without secure tenure to the housing that they occupy, increases in land value are a direct threat that may lead to their eviction and the 'gentrification' of the area or its wholesale redevelopment. Increased tenure security is vital in order to allow poor people to retain affordable housing, rather than paying through rents and evictions for any transport improvements in their vicinity while owners and landlords are receiving windfall capital gains.

Certain transport-related policies can help to slow or prevent gentrification. In Surabaya during the 1980s, a conscious decision was made to prevent four-wheeled vehicle access into the interiors of low-income areas in the inner city. The policy is said to have been successful in slowing gentrification, while reducing congestion.[53] Parking restrictions and variations in other transport-related standards may also have similar potential.

Urban planning and housing policy can directly and indirectly affect accessibility through their impact on the viability of the modes of transport that are most important to the poor – namely, walking, cycling, other non-motorized vehicles (NMVs) and public transport. Only rarely have debates about the effects of urban land-use policy on transport included an emphasis on the implications for the urban poor, or possible synergies with urban-poor housing policy. The land-use patterns of low-income cities tend to be well suited to allowing adequate access with a low level of daily mobility as a result of high urban densities, intense mixing of land uses, and a high proportion of jobs located in inner areas and in concentrated corridors along main roads.[54] Unfortunately, land-use trends in many cities tend to undermine these pro-poor land-use features.[55] As motorization rises, developers increasingly locate new developments where they are easily accessible by private vehicle, even if this renders them less accessible for the poor who tend to rely on public transport and non-motorized transport.[56] Planning and housing policy-makers also often view 'traditional' or vernacular urban fabric in a negative light as being backward, associated with poverty, unsuited to modern modes of transport and in need of removal. Both access-oriented transport policies and a greater emphasis on *in situ* slum-upgrading policies, as urged by many housing-sector specialists, would do much to preserve the traditional access-oriented, mixed-use urban fabric.

There has been a long-standing debate on the potential for land-use planning to play an explicit role in achieving transport policy goals in the South. Successes in integrating land-use and pro-transit policies in Hong Kong, Singapore and Curitiba, Brazil, are often seen as exceptions among many failures. One option with good potential advocates a policy of densification via transfers of development rights (and/or the relaxation of floor-area ratio or plot-ratio standards), the proceeds of which help to fund social housing. This is done in the Brazilian cities of São Paulo and Curitiba. Ideally, the densification would be located in highly accessible, transit-oriented locations, as would the social housing; but this has not always happened in these Brazilian examples.[57] Similarly, the supply of accessible, yet affordable, housing could be boosted by more widespread use of land readjustment or land sharing, as is often practiced in Korea, Japan and Thailand.[58]

This also has the important advantage of resettling people on-site and avoiding many of the access problems that accompany relocation to remote sites. Insecure tenure increases the likelihood of involuntary resettlement for transport infrastructure, and reduces the ability of affected households to obtain proper relocation assistance and compensation. A widespread lack of security of tenure probably reduces the incentive for transport planners to make strong efforts to minimize displacement in transport infrastructure proposals. Conversely, any widespread increase in security of tenure by low-income residents might increase the pressure for transport infrastructure to be planned more carefully in order to minimize displacement. More secure tenure may also encourage communities to invest more in improving their local access infrastructure and services, such as local footpath improvements (including covering drains) and local access roads. This is – by analogy with other self-help improvements – observed to take place when security of tenure improves.

■ Impacts of the location of housing for the urban poor

The location of affordable low-income housing should be a major concern of urban policy, and should be explicitly considered in a wide variety of contexts, from resettlement location choices to large-scale planning and transport strategies for urban areas. Greater efforts need to be made to ensure that low-income housing is more accessible to income-generating opportunities and other vital sites of urban exchange.

As Chapter 2 has suggested, income-based residential segregation, where the rich and poor live considerable distances from each other, is likely to be associated with greater inequity of access than more spatially integrated patterns. 'There are... a number of services which plenty of the poor can pay to use individually, but which exclusively poor areas can't collectively attract (commercially) or finance (municipally).'[59] A particularly problematic pattern appears to be where most of the poor are in peripheral areas of large cities. Very time-consuming commutes for low-income people are the norm in certain cities, such as São Paulo, Mexico City, Kinshasa and Manila.[60] In some low-income

cities, especially in Africa, there is also a high incidence of long, time-consuming walking trips.[61]

Transport and housing policies can create pressures on the poor to be pushed towards urban peripheries. The most obvious example is involuntary relocation to inaccessible locations. For reasons of cost, governments frequently site housing for low-income households in peripheral areas. The sudden wrenching nature of such relocations tends to make transport-related problems more severe, including loss of jobs or income from informal enterprises, increased travel time and costs, and loss of community ties.[62] A further access-related problem is that many resettlements involve two steps, with the people, firstly, being moved into temporary accommodation and then only later to a permanent site. This further multiplies access problems and transport disruptions, especially if neither transit accommodation nor eventual resettlement sites are close to each other or to the original settlement.[63] Lack of accessible employment and other facilities prompts many of those who are resettled to return to locations close to their former residences and work places.[64]

Transport infrastructure agencies need 'best-practice' policies and practices on involuntary displacement. These should include the following:

- Policies should conform to international housing rights standards and minimize resettlement and its associated stresses.
- Project assessment needs to take full account of the range of impacts on people who are relocated.
- The transport planning process should be more open and should always include negotiation with affected communities in a timely, sincere and open fashion.
- Transport-related guidelines and standards for residential areas can be reviewed, especially those that affect the legality of unplanned settlements and the affordability of formal low-cost housing. For example, adopt a more realistic, flexible, case-by-case performance-based approach to transport-related standards, and make wider use of 'land readjustment' techniques to meet basic standards without the need for wholesale eviction.
- Community-based access and transport improvements that increase the legitimacy of settlements and, hence, strengthen informal tenure should be promoted.
- Taking greater account of the space consumption of transport modes and promoting space-saving modes may reduce displacements.
- Transport policy may also offer tactics that can slow or prevent gentrification, including that triggered by transport changes.
- Strict accessibility guidelines should be established on the location of public housing for the poor, sites-and-services projects and resettlement sites.

In summary, resettlement practice requires more attention to transport and access dimensions in order to reduce accessibility problems for the poor. A greater emphasis on

The location of affordable low-income housing should be a major concern of urban policy

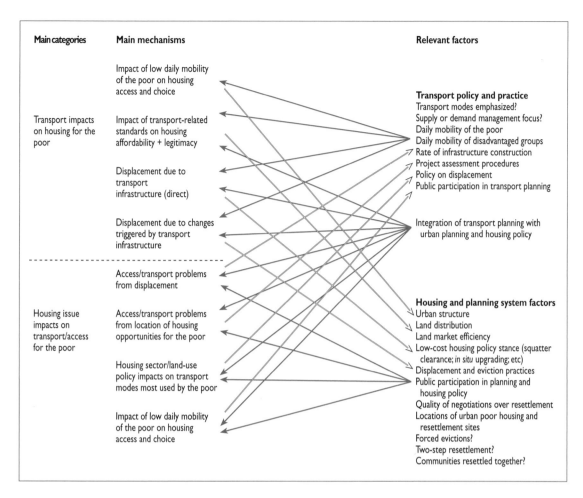

Figure 9.1

Linkages between
housing and transport

in situ upgrading, rather than eviction/redevelopment, would go a long way towards addressing these issues. Resettlement sites should preferably be located within a short distance of the original community; established communities should be kept together in the relocation process; and two-step resettlement should be avoided, whenever possible. In fact, respect for housing rights requires negotiated resettlement solutions with all displaced communities. This requires toleration and encouragement of community organizing, community development and empowerment efforts by CBOs and NGOs in low-income communities.

Improving the livelihoods of slum dwellers

■ Poverty, governance and empowerment[65]

The major objective of most international agencies today is the reduction of poverty, and poverty reduction is the major plank of the MDGs and Social Summit commitments. More than three-quarters of countries have poverty estimates, and more than two-thirds have plans for reducing poverty. However, fewer than one third have set targets for eradicating extreme poverty or substantially reducing overall poverty. This is a serious shortcoming. Many anti-poverty plans are, in fact, no more than vaguely formulated strategies. Only a minority of countries have genuine action plans with explicit targets, adequate budgets and effective organizations. Many countries do not have explicit poverty plans, but incorporate poverty within national planning –

and many national plans then appear to forget the topic.

Responsive and accountable institutions of governance may often be the missing link between anti-poverty efforts and poverty reduction. Even when a country seeks to implement pro-poor national policies and to target its interventions, faulty governance can nullify the impact. Reforms of governance institutions need to be emphasized before anti-poverty strategies can get off the ground.

Accountability in the use of public funds is crucial to poverty reduction efforts. The poor pay a high price for corruption. Programmes that target resources for poverty reduction are less likely to be bankrupted by the administrative costs of identifying and reaching the poor than by the diversion of a big part of the resources into other hands. If corruption were cleaned up at the same time that the poor organized themselves, many national poverty programmes would, undoubtedly, improve their performance in directing resources to the people who need them. Many problems of targeting are, in fact, problems of unaccountable, unresponsive governance institutions.

What the poor need, therefore, as much as resources for safety nets, are resources to build their own organizational capacity and to empower their constituencies. Ensuring resources for this capacity building is the direction in which support to civil society organizations is moving. Civil society organizations that arise outside of poor communities can play an important role in delivering essential goods and services, but they are less successful in directly representing the poor than those arising from within

Responsive and accountable institutions of governance may often be the missing link between anti-poverty efforts and poverty reduction

the communities themselves. Moreover, relying on these organizations for the delivery of goods and services may be inadvisable over the long term as, ultimately, it is more the responsibility of government.

A new generation of poverty programmes now focus on building community organizations in order to articulate people's needs and priorities, instead of concentrating on income-generating activities alone. Some of the greatest successes have been in mobilizing and organizing poor women. Experience confirms that, once afforded the opportunity, communities can quickly build their own organizations and develop their own leaders. Communities often start with small self-help groups and then combine these into larger area-based institutions in order to exert influence with local government or the private sector.

If the poor lack organization and power, the benefits of poverty programmes are unlikely to reach them – or, if they do, they may do no more than create a culture of dependence and charity. Effective focusing of resources follows from empowerment, not the other way around.

One way to focus resources is to adjust macro-economic policies to make growth more pro-poor. Another is to direct resources to sectors where the poor are employed. A third way is to allocate resources to poor areas or communities. To be effective, this third approach requires a geographical map of poverty based on a reliable set of human poverty indicators – and specific attention to the problems of leakage and appropriation by the middle class, with which area-based interventions are commonly associated. Countries need a comprehensive but workable monitoring system in order to gauge their progress against poverty and other MDGs, particularly service provision and slum conditions.

■ Generating employment from shelter development programmes and civil works[66]

A major problem with urban areas throughout the developing world is the lack of formal-sector jobs and a chronic excess supply of labour, which is exacerbated by the continual inflow of immigrants. Nevertheless, civil authorities typically use building and construction technologies designed for high-income countries in which labour is scarce, and which require expensive, imported oil-driven machinery. Productivity improvement is a major aim of labour-deficit technology and has been responsible for most innovation; but it is largely irrelevant in countries where wages are low and so many individuals are seeking work. There are many opportunities to use more labour-intensive appropriate or traditional technologies in improving urban conditions more cheaply, rather than through industrial approaches, while assisting with job creation; but this is rarely done.

As Chapter 6 has detailed, the informal sector provides more than half of the income-earning opportunities in many cities of the developing world. Its role in poverty alleviation and its considerable contribution to national incomes are widely recognized. The main characteristics of informal-sector enterprises are the small scale of their operations, their family ownership, and their labour-

intensive and adapted technology. The informal sector can be very effective in providing livelihoods and cheap goods and services for low-end consumers. However, at its worst, employment in the informal sector can be exploitative, with poor contractual relationships, unhealthy working conditions and low payment, while limiting the ability of governments to raise local revenue for vital services within poorer communities.

The continuing decline of formal urban income-earning opportunities in most developing countries under conditions of globalization and liberalization means that the deeply hostile attitude of many government officials to the informal sector must change. The informal sector must be taken seriously as a major and expanding part of the urban economy – one that is entwined with the key processes of enabling, empowerment and informal income generation.

The informal sector also provides a very large share of the new housing stock in developing countries, in terms of both numbers and value. This is a response to the inability of the formal market to satisfy effective demand. Formal housing markets in developing countries tend to function poorly because of bottlenecks in supply markets in land, finance, labour and materials, and because of poor regulatory frameworks, usually unadapted to local conditions, which make formal housing unaffordable to much of the urban population while preserving the formal system for the elite.

As well as providing better living conditions, a well-functioning housing-supply system has positive macro-economic impacts and can generate considerable employment, with substantial multiplier effects above and beyond the direct impact of construction, due to the long chains of intermediate inputs to construction. Construction activities tend to redistribute income to lower-paid workers in the construction industry. Housing construction has a low import content in most circumstances where local materials and fixtures are used, and much of its impact remains in the community where the building activity takes place.

Failures in the system of supply are endemic in housing markets, and may increase costs beyond the affordability thresholds of many poor households. Enabling strategies have sought to increase the supply of housing by removing impediments to supply and by involving small-scale enterprises and individual householders much more widely in the provision process.[67]

The poor have been left out of many housing efforts in the past. Formal construction, or even subsidized sites and services, have been more expensive than even the working poor can afford. New policies must respond to the gross poverty of many residents and provide for rental accommodation as well as owner occupation. A primary concern in housing demand should be to maximize income-earning opportunities and to minimize transport costs, which generally involve expensive, usually imported, fuel.

Clearly, as long as the informal sector is disadvantaged, the cheapest housing available is less efficiently provided than it need be. Legal, institutional and financial measures are required to integrate the informal sector progressively within the mainstream of the economy

A major problem with urban areas throughout the developing world is the lack of formal-sector jobs and a chronic excess supply of labour

Enabling strategies have sought to increase the supply of housing by removing impediments and involving enterprises and householders much more widely in the provision process

without removing its competitiveness. Land supply and the regulations governing buildings are important fields for government action to ease the supply of housing by the informal sector.

The construction of housing is particularly effective in providing work to low-income workers. However, there is a need for an adequate and continuous supply of skilled workers to perform and supervise the major trade tasks, and whose availability can be very influential in the efficiency of housing supply.

Demand that is created directly and indirectly in other sectors (for materials, equipment and their carriage) through the construction of housing is about four-fifths of the value of the housing, and is greater in the human-settlements sector than in most other industrial sectors. These backward linkages are inversely related to the cost of the housing and are greater for labour-intensive building operations than for those using capital equipment. In addition, self-help housing and upgrading activities are particularly effective for backward linkage employment generation.

Small-scale, relatively labour-intensive building-materials technologies are generally associated with larger multiplier effects than are large-scale, capital-intensive technologies because they tend to use locally manufactured machinery and local fuel, and are marketed and transported by smale-scale enterprises (SSEs). Most imported materials can be replaced by a local equivalent, which, in turn, can be produced in small-scale, labour-based plants. The difference in employment generation between large and small plants, and between equipment-based and labour-based technologies, can be very great (20-fold in the case of brick-making). The use of labour-intensive technologies in International Labour Organization (ILO) pilot and demonstration projects (particularly the Million Houses Programme in Sri Lanka) has produced encouraging results. However, despite several decades of research into adapting and improving local technologies, earth-based and labour-intensive technologies are often seen to be the poor relation of imported higher technology solutions.

Despite the intention that occupants in sites-and-services schemes should primarily use their own labour in constructing housing, most have used at least a proportion of paid labour through local SSEs and individual artisans. The renovation of housing in upgrading programmes, too, is ideally suited to small-scale contractors who use minimal equipment.

In the past, in sites-and-services and upgrading schemes, householders were expected to build or renovate their dwellings personally, or with the labour of family and friends. In practice, many have chosen to use contractors, who are likely to be more efficient and produce work of a higher standard. With this in mind, future upgrading projects should pay greater attention to assisting householders in carrying out management or development tasks through model contracts, advice on payment and quality control, and the settlement of disputes, and in empowering them to receive good value for money. Small contractors should also be enabled to carry out their task more efficiently (with access to materials, credit against staged payments,

insurance, site management, etc). Building regulations should also be altered to allow more affordable technologies.

Traditional building materials often require frequent, even annual, maintenance; but as they require only locally available materials and commonly held skills, this may be cost effective. More industrialized technologies present problems when maintenance is required.[68] However, even in this case, many maintenance tasks are well suited to SSEs. Construction projects, too, form a necessary part of the development process and can have considerable employment impacts for local communities.

The promotion of urban development should be a holistic process, involving all actors in the activities in which they are most effective and encompassing each sector in an integrated way. The role of individuals varies, from taking paid work generated by major works in local neighbourhoods, singly or through community groups, to acting as developers or as development consultants, creating partnerships between local authorities and community groups. As authorities are increasingly unable to provide services to all of the people, the need to involve communities not only in crisis management but also in planning and the provision of services is becoming widely recognized. Community involvement in servicing can provide positive inputs to social cohesion, and will result in additional care being taken of infrastructure for which the community is responsible. Training and empowering are necessary for the successful fulfilment of these roles.

The labour-based approach to road building is well tested through ILO initiatives. Two thousand work days can be created in building 1 kilometre of a 5 metre-wide earth road. While some road-building tasks on major roads require heavy equipment, work on minor gravel-enforced roads can be carried out with an appropriate mix of trained labourers and light equipment. In addition, wherever simple methods can be used, they may have significant poverty-alleviation effects, particularly in ensuring that money is disbursed locally and to the poorest workers. Even heavily trafficked roads have been successfully built in this way in Bangladesh. The training of supervisory staff is essential for successful labour-intensive public-works construction programmes.

There are many tasks in laying water pipes, drains and sewers that can be done by labour-based methods, but which are often done with heavy equipment. Community-based water-supply schemes are relatively common, particularly in rural areas. In urban areas, privatization or community control of water delivery and garbage disposal are becoming commonplace.

City authorities spend a significant portion of their budgets on solid-waste management; but few manage to keep up with the demand. There are considerable opportunities for labour-intensive composting and recycling operations that would provide employment and profit for many people, while making good use of existing resources and clearing the streets of garbage. The existing informal-sector rag-picking and scavenging operations require improvement in order to protect the operators and provide markets for recyclable materials: the *fellaheen* of Karachi

Land supply and the regulations governing buildings are important fields for government action to ease the supply of housing by the informal sector

The promotion of urban development should be a holistic process, involving all actors and encompassing each sector in an integrated way

have been a successful example of improved recycling that is carried out by labour-intensive methods.

While it may be assumed that the construction of transport infrastructure is necessarily a capital-intensive operation, the building of railways has historically been done by labour-based methods. In addition, public transport based on smaller buses, taxis and rickshaws has traditionally been cheaper, arguably more efficient, and a provider of more employment per trip than large municipal transport operations (although congestion and pollution remain a problem).

Communities have shown their ability to take on contracts for local infrastructure work. CBOs can be very effective in reducing urban poverty when they have been formed to represent people, to implement projects, to act as legal entities representing their communities, to raise and disburse money on behalf of the neighbourhoods, and to negotiate for services and contracts with public authorities. While, in the past, community initiatives in servicing relied upon unpaid labour, this is not ideal. Local participation should not be an excuse for exploitation, and all but the most local tasks should involve paid labour.

While many major works are capable of involving local participation, including the use of community contracts, such local participation should not lead to substandard remuneration or employment conditions. At the same time, while minor works usually involve some form of community contribution, this should come about as a result of negotiations with local authorities; and unpaid labour should not be used systematically.

Local government and other public-sector bodies should adopt a more supportive role towards the informal sector and SSEs, either in their own direct works or when contracting to the private sector. If shelter and infrastructure are to keep up with demand, partnerships between public authorities and the private sector must become part of local government culture.

Significant contributions have been recently made to equipping communities to carry out urban works and services in partnership with the public sector, and to successfully negotiate with service agencies. The ILO has been involved in promoting self-employment, SSEs and the informal sector for several decades. Its interventions have been targeted at eliminating inefficiencies in the labour market and at improving the efficiency of the enterprises. In addition, there has been a complementary focus on governments' attitudes towards, and abilities to deal with, informal-sector enterprises. Legislation affecting SSEs should aim to maximize their efficiency while progressively addressing labour standards issues to prevent exploitation and improve health and safety. Home-based enterprises should be recognized as important contributors to the poorest households' economies and to the country, as a whole. The best policy for current home-based enterprises is tolerance and non-intervention, while allowing them to be eligible for small business loans, training assistance, etc. Loans for small businesses could also be permitted to extend the home for business use.

Where public-sector agencies carry out development work, they should be encouraged to involve and engage contractors who use labour-intensive methods. International donors should take a lead in considering employment and poverty reduction throughout the implementation phase as a serious component in measuring project success. However, care must be taken to ensure that informal labour is not exploited or subject to unsafe working conditions.

Assistance targeted at SSEs and labour-based infrastructure works will largely involve the poorest workers. Legal, institutional and financial measures are required to integrate the informal sector within the mainstream of the economy without removing its competitiveness. Some forms of training, finance, servicing and involvement in government contracts should be offered to SSEs.

The public sector, NGOs and international donors have an important role as enablers and encouragers in the process of maximizing employment opportunities in providing housing and infrastructure during the coming decades. The future priorities of local and national governments – and of international development cooperation – must be to actively support and advocate poverty reduction strategies based on labour-intensive shelter delivery and using local resources, linking the goals of shelter for all and employment for all as a common strategy for poverty reduction.

Mobilizing finance for urban development[69]

■ Financing slum upgrading and shelter development: current challenges

In line with the principle of subsidiarity, whose theoretical roots can be traced to fiscal federalism as it has evolved in the West, municipal authorities have been assigned the role of providing a range of infrastructure services – primarily water and sewerage, solid waste management and city roads.[70] Under principles of neo-liberalism, responsibilities for a greater range of services are increasingly being decentralized to the local level.

In practice, municipal authorities in developing countries do not have the resources to meet their service obligations.[71] In particular, the capital expenditure per person per year has been extremely low in many developing countries, with expenditures averaging about US$35 per person in African cities in 1998 and falling below US$1 in smaller or poorer cities. In contrast, expenditure per person per year in Northern Europe is well above US$1,000.[72] Worse still, from the perspective of shelter delivery, municipal budgets have generally sidelined slums, with the bulk of resources directed at formal residential areas. Often, it is only during emergencies, such as disease outbreaks, that municipal authorities direct some of their resources towards service provision in slum areas.

Evolution of municipal policy for service delivery has mirrored policy changes at the centre. In developing countries, for instance, the initial post-independence period was characterized by state control of most areas of economic activity, from service provision to economic production, in line with the development orthodoxy of the day. More recently, especially since the 1980s, the role of the state has been redefined, with the major impetus for change coming from the Bretton Woods institutions through their structural adjustment programmes, or SAPs (see Chapter 3). This change has advocated the retreat of the state from direct production and service provision, whilst simultaneously seeking a more effective regulatory role for the state to ensure that markets and private firms perform to expectations.

This evolution of municipal policy, in response to pressure from donors, has its parallels in urban planning.[73] Until the 1960s, the usual response to the challenges of city growth was the 'master plan', a practice that was rooted in colonial town planning. The typical plan envisaged a central role for the city government in service provision, with little account taken of the budgetary implications for the public sector, or of the need to leverage resources from the private sector. In time, it became clear that plan implementation was generally not feasible as a result of declining resources and a rapidly growing city population.

The neo-liberal-mandated transition from public-sector service delivery to private sector-led provision has been difficult. In fact, the crafting of new policy responses has been overtaken in many cities by the informalization of service delivery, as municipal governments struggle to meet the needs of a rapidly growing and impoverished population. Generally, privatization has occurred by default, with informal enterprises filling profitable niches in the urban economy, while government has all but capitulated from any effective role, using the excuse of liberalization. In the absence of regulation and competition, service delivery to the consumer has been poor and expensive. In the water sector, for instance, a large proportion of impoverished slum dwellers pay exorbitant prices for water, bearing costs that far exceed those incurred by non-poor consumers with direct access to city networks.

A broad-sweeping assessment of the deterioration of service provision in developing country cities has concluded that:

> *In many African cities, most refuse is uncollected and piles of decaying waste are allowed to rot in streets and vacant lots. Schools are becoming so overcrowded that many students have only minimum contact with their teachers. A declining proportion of urban roads are tarmacked and drained, and many that are not turn into virtual quagmires during the rainy season. Basic drugs – once given out freely – have disappeared from public clinics, and professional medical care is extremely difficult to obtain, except for the rich. Public transport systems are seriously overburdened; and more and more people are obliged to live in unserviced plots in 'informal' housing, where clean drinking water must be directly purchased from water sellers at a prohibitive cost, and where telephones and electrical connections are scarcely available.*[74]

■ Improving municipal finance for investment in low-income residential areas

Cities in developing countries face a bewildering array of challenges in their efforts to deliver services, especially to the poorer segments of their inhabitants. These challenges, many of which are inter-linked, are as much a reflection of poor governance as they are of diminishing resources. They include poorly defined and ineffective inter-governmental fiscal relations, sometimes due to the reluctance of governments to decentralize, and sometimes due to a lack of capacity in dealing with complex inter-governmental arrangements that confound bureaucracies in even the most developed countries.[75]

The tension in inter-governmental relations can be traced to a diverse set of factors: the contest for political power and resources; the need for nation building in ethnically fragmented societies; and the desire for macro-economic control.[76] After independence, the typical post-colonial state was keen to consolidate power. Centralization has persisted, in spite of rhetoric to the contrary, and is borne out by empirical evidence. For instance, the local government share of total government expenditure in developing countries averaged 15 per cent during the late 1980s and early 1990s in contrast to 32 per cent for countries in the Organisation for Economic Co-operation and Development (OECD).[77]

In the absence of a clear and effective framework for inter-governmental relations, municipal authorities in developing countries have not been able to craft appropriate municipal finance policies. The result is policy drift, often characterized by ad hoc decisions and myopia. Thus, city administrations stumble from crisis to crisis, unable or unwilling to map out long-term development paths for municipal finance.

Declining resources at the municipal level are the result of many factors. One is the fall in financial transfers from the centre, the result of poor macro-economic performance and decreasing per capita tax revenues at the disposal of the state. Another is a narrowing tax base at the municipal level as a result of deepening poverty and the informalization of the urban economy. Yet another is the limited capacity of municipal authorities to collect local taxes, user charges and other fees.

Formal privatization of municipal services, including commercialization, has brought to the fore a number of challenges. Political elites feel threatened by the loss of existing channels of patronage, especially where either the management or ownership of municipal assets is transferred to the private sector;[78] weak regulatory regimes mean that municipal authorities are not able to regulate the behaviour of private firms, raising the risk of excluding poor households through higher prices for services, and risking reduced quality, reduced safety of service and poor employment practices; and the perception, often wrong, by municipal authorities that privatization will deprive them of revenue sources.

Corruption undermines development wherever it occurs, and it has substantially distorted decision-making within municipal governments, severely limiting their ability to respond rationally to city priorities.[79] Rent-seeking by officials most negatively affects the poor, who typically do not have the resources with which to pay bribes, while they are more likely to be required to pay 'speed money' or to be subject to harassment because of their vulnerability. Corruption has also diverted substantial resources away from municipal budgets for the development and maintenance of services. The combination of corruption, poor administration and incompetent financial management has sapped the ability of municipal governments to meet the needs of their constituents.

In addressing inter-governmental fiscal relations, the starting point should be to acknowledge that 'finance follows function'. In other words, if the political commitment to decentralize exists, the state must ensure that the functions devolved to municipal governments are accompanied by the requisite quantum of resources. Where there is no match between finance and function, decentralization remains within the realm of rhetoric.

A range of policy instruments can be used to improve municipal finance. To counter poor revenue collection, it is necessary to build the capacity of municipal authorities by using a variety of interventions: training staff; introducing better methods of financial management and control; developing better cadastres; and updating valuation rolls of landed properties. However, this managerial approach to 'fixing' capacity problems has its limitations, especially where corruption abounds, and these measures are only effective and sustainable where good governance prevails. Fighting corruption requires political will and a reform-minded government. Four areas of reform that are acknowledged as important are reducing the discretionary power of public officials; enforcing anti-corruption laws; reforming the public service; and increasing the accountability of government to citizens.[80] Decentralization could also help to curb corruption by pushing 'decision-making responsibility down to the levels at which people can more control their agents, or at which peer monitoring can operate'.[81] Nevertheless, patronage and the manipulation of funds are exceptionally common at the local level, and this may counter the benefits of improved visibility.

There are other issues, besides collection problems, that surround the generation of municipal revenue: inadequacy of the revenue sources assigned to local government; inefficient revenue sources whose yield does not cover collection costs;[82] and rigid and administratively demanding revenue sources with design flaws in pricing, collection and the maintenance of records.[83]

Municipal finance can benefit from carefully designed and implemented privatization. For instance, loss-making water utilities can be turned around through various forms of privatization. But there are some municipal services that do not readily lend themselves to privatization in the conventional sense, such as solid waste collection in slum areas. In the typical slum, the majority of residents are too poor to afford the prices charged by private service providers, even where competition exists. However, the potential exists to use non-market mechanisms, such as community-based efforts, working with or without municipal support.

If municipal governments do not design and manage privatization programmes properly, harmful social consequences could arise. These might include high prices for services, as well as inadequate output by the provider, particularly where competition is limited. Regulatory 'capture' by the private provider is also a danger to guard against since it undermines the ability of a municipal authority to act as an effective regulator. Private-sector transactions are rarely monitored or accountable outside of the organization, and pay-offs and semi-legal forms of corruption and crony arrangements are very common. The lack of robust cost data, a classic case of information asymmetry between provider and regulator, also tends to undermine the benefits of privatization, making it difficult to regulate natural monopolies such as water supply.[84]

■ Improving housing finance for low-income shelter development

Meeting the challenges of housing finance in the developing countries will not be an easy task. In low-income countries, perhaps the most critical challenge is how best to apply the lessons of micro-finance to housing. Whereas conventional micro-finance lends itself particularly well to trading enterprises, which typically require short-term loans, it is not well suited to housing, which is a long-lived asset with a high value relative to household income. For housing to be affordable, loan finance must be offered for relatively long periods, thus raising lending risks. At the same time, monthly loan payments, a requirement in formal lending, can be quite high relative to the income of the house buyer. For these reasons, it is not easy to directly apply conventional micro-finance practices to house finance, except where small loans are needed for incremental construction, house extensions and house repair.[85]

In South Africa, for instance, experience shows that 'the shorter term of micro-loans (typically no longer than three years) and the high rates of interest [have] limited the affordable loan sizes to US$1500, well below that necessary for the purchase of a new basic starter house, typically US$4000 to US$6000'.[86] By comparison, *crédit foncier* mortgage loans in the developed world typically have repayment periods of 20 to 30 years and permit the borrowing of three times the household income, on average.

However, in spite of the difficulties listed here, micro-finance approaches have been applied successfully in housing, if not always at scale. The most commonly cited example is the Grameen model; but other examples exist – for instance, the community mortgage programme in the Philippines;[87] and housing banks in Thailand and Jordan, which have been successful in providing mortgage funds to low-income borrowers and for informal housing. South Africa has also experimented with non-mortgage loans to establish a secondary market that targets a house cost range not normally addressed by standard mortgages.[88]

A second challenge is how to expand the outreach of formal housing finance so that it serves a wider clientele. While this is only possible when incomes have risen substantially, a number of measures can be taken to improve access to housing finance. At the macro level, housing will not

The combination of corruption, poor administration and incompetent financial management has sapped the ability of municipal governments to meet the needs of their constituents

attract adequate savings unless its returns are equivalent to returns in other sectors. As long as housing finance remains a regulated 'special circuit' with controlled interest rates, there will always be a capital shortage. Deregulating housing finance integrates it within the rest of the financial sector, enabling housing to attract savings on equal terms with other sectors and preventing the rationing of private finance.[89]

With deregulated markets, formal housing finance may never reach a substantial proportion of households. In many developing countries, especially in Africa, banking systems are rudimentary and are often confined only to the major urban centres and to formal housing. A large population in the smaller urban centres, and, indeed, in the sprawling slums of the large cities, is therefore poorly served or not served at all by the financial sector.[90]

There are many ways of devising lending instruments that are more attractive to borrowers. Examples include low start or progressive mortgages, which work well where the borrower's income increases over time; fixed interest loans that insulate the borrower from the adverse impacts of rapidly changing interest rates; low down payments and, therefore, high loan-to-value ratios, making it easier for the potential borrower to access loans; and loan guarantees that aim to reduce the risk of defaulting. Most of these measures, however, generally do not find favour with the lender, and are only offered under government patronage or guarantee.[91] Additionally, the small loans typically affordable by low-income borrowers are, in relative terms, expensive to process, administer and foreclose, making them unattractive to lenders. For these reasons, among others, governments generally have to intervene in the form of creating housing loan bodies, institutions or instruments, or in providing guarantees, not just in the developing world, but practically everywhere.

In general, developing countries need to diversify and strengthen housing finance by:

- encouraging the private sector to be involved in lending to a wider range of customers, so that the public sector does not have to bear the whole brunt of low-income housing finance;
- repositioning housing subsidies so that they target low-income groups.

Since it acts as a secure and profitable investment, housing benefits the financial market in other ways. It readily attracts individual savings, especially where a market-driven and properly regulated financial environment exists. Conversely, the prospect of owning a house encourages households to save with financial institutions, thus promoting savings mobilization and investment.

The solution now favoured by most developed countries is to facilitate the private financial system in order to provide funds for households that do not need subsidies – thereby eliminating the burden on the public budget – and to increase the number of households served by attracting substantial quantities of extra funds through a secondary mortgage market. Lending can be extended to households with somewhat lower incomes than the private market will

serve through interest, deposit subsidies or by supporting non-standard mortgage types. However, in practice, lending for owner-occupied housing remains unaffordable for the bottom 30 per cent of households, and other tenure solutions must be sought.

In some middle-income countries, an interesting development is the introduction of secondary markets that enable mortgage originators to sell the mortgage loans that they hold as assets to a third party in return for cash – following the example of the widespread secondary mortgage markets that operate in the US and are now operating in most other developed countries. The third party, usually a special institution established for that purpose, raises the funds to purchase the mortgages through the issuance of bonds or mortgage-backed securities. These securities are normally sold to institutional long-term investors, such as pension funds, using the mortgages as underlying collateral. This can permit a very substantial expansion of housing finance available to those further down the income distribution than is usual.

In developing countries, financial systems have rarely reached the sophistication or breadth of those of the West. Government-based lending organizations rarely offer innovative products, and subsidies, for the most part, pass to households that would be better served by a properly functioning private sector.

It is unlikely that any country can address the housing problems of low-income households solely through the use of market mechanisms. There is, therefore, a strong social case for public subsidies that target households with limited incomes and that aim to improve access to adequate housing. An important policy issue, therefore, is how to design subsidy programmes to target those in need, thus ensuring that resources are not wasted on the non-poor. But, in many countries, subsidies often fail this test as they do not systematically target low-income households. In these circumstances, there is a clear case for repositioning subsidies so that they more effectively achieve their social objective. It is equally important to ensure that subsidies do not distort the market, as often happens where interest rates are subsidized. Indeed, where subsidized financing is channelled through government institutions, private banks are reluctant to extend their lending to the segments served by government.[92]

Housing subsidies have been widely and successfully administered within the developed world, though there are few documented examples of success in the developing world. But the principles of good practice are clear. Firstly, potential beneficiaries should be means-tested to ensure successful targeting. Financial subsidies should be tied to the household and not to the dwelling, and should be regularly reviewed or tapered off, so that households receive the majority of the benefit when they most require a house. Secondly, subsidies should promote horizontal equity, which calls for equal treatment of households in similar circumstances, while they should be progressive, varying inversely with income. Thirdly, subsidies should be designed so that they distort housing markets as little as possible and cannot easily be directly appropriated by landlords or developers.

It is unlikely that any country can address the housing problems of low-income households solely through the use of market mechanisms

ENABLING LOCAL POLICY TO WORK

While national 'macro-policy' and globalization have very major effects on the economic and policy environment, especially that affecting employment, finance markets and the distribution of poverty, it is at the local level that many of the more visible and successful initiatives in income generation, shelter provision and poverty reduction have taken place. One reason that the local level has been neglected in poverty reduction efforts is that poverty has traditionally been defined in terms of income poverty. As a human development approach to poverty alleviation becomes more customary, the scope for local action to reduce poverty is expanding. There are at least six areas in which local authorities can have an impact on poverty reduction.[93]

1 Most local authorities control access to *land* and are responsible for land-use planning and regulation. The ease of access, and the cost and location of land available to the poor have a significant impact on their livelihoods.
2 Access to *infrastructure and basic services* highlights the linkages between the health costs incurred by the poor due to unsafe water supply and inadequate health care.
3 The degree of success in *local economic development* determines the resources available for capital investments in such things as improved access to land, infrastructure and services.
4 *Local economic policies* can be supportive of the poor by promoting labour-intensive work methods and providing support for SSEs and the informal sector.
5 *Access to justice* and the enforcement of laws can, if not enforced at the local level, adversely affect the poor (for example, corruption in public office, pollution control and personal safety in informal settlements).
6 Perhaps most significantly, *influencing local decision-making* greatly determines the 'pro-poorness' of local strategic planning, priority setting and capital investments. Progress in poverty reduction depends upon the quality of the participation of the urban poor in the decisions affecting their lives and on the responsiveness of urban planning and policy-making processes to the needs of the urban poor.

These and other local interventions make a major contribution to improving the situation of the urban poor in cities, especially when national or other higher-level policy has failed to provide adequate job opportunities and poverty reduction strategies. Progress in these areas is dependent, to a large extent, not only on resources but upon the way in which these resources are mobilized, organized and used through the general principles of good governance.

The concept of good governance is now recognized as an all-embracing concept covering effectiveness, inclusiveness and transparency in both government and civil society, and the Global Campaign on Urban Governance (GCUG) was launched by UN-Habitat in 1999 to promote these goals.[94] The campaign proceeds through normative debate to increase the capacity of local governments and other stakeholders to practice good urban governance. It has the 'inclusive city' as its theme, focusing attention on the needs of the urban poor and on other marginalized groups, and recognizing that participatory planning and decision-making are the strategic means for realizing this vision.

Good urban governance and the 'inclusive city'

The idea of the 'inclusive city' has global applicability. The notion of inclusion, however, has a different resonance in different parts of the world, with exclusion of specific vulnerable groups being more significant in some places, while exclusion of the poor majority is more important in others. In this connection, it is essential for all actors to discuss the question of 'who' in a particular city is excluded from 'what', and 'how'.

The inclusion of women and men on an equal basis is one theme that unites North and South. The GCUG has developed a three-pronged approach to addressing the issue of gender in good urban governance. Firstly, it argues that, based on the Universal Declaration of Human Rights and other internationally agreed human rights instruments, women and men are equally entitled to the benefits of urban citizenship. Secondly, it demonstrates and argues that urban planning and management is made more effective, equitable and sustainable through the equal participation of women and men in decision-making processes.[95] Finally, the GCUG specifically targets its interventions to be responsive to the needs of women, carefully monitoring the impact of these interventions.

The GCUG promotes various policies and practices, depending upon context, to strengthen inclusiveness. Again, these are likely to vary from country to country and from city to city. In some cities, the *welfare approach*, which stresses the importance of providing individuals and groups with the goods that they need in order to effectively participate in society – such as land and infrastructure – may be most appropriate. In others, the *human development approach*, which aims at empowering groups and individuals to strengthen their ability and willingness to participate in society, may be key. In other contexts, the *environmental approach*, which stresses the precautionary principle and concern for future generations, may be the desired entry point to the good urban governance debate. The *institutional approach*, which is concerned with the roles of actors and the institutional frameworks that determine the formal and informal incentives for inclusion, is of particular importance everywhere. A *rights-based approach*, which emphasizes the right to development and provides a framework for poverty reduction based on the full complement of civil, cultural, economic, political and social rights, underpins all of the other approaches.[96]

The implementation of these approaches must be grounded in the reality of urban planning and management. Good urban governance is characterized by the principles of

Good urban governance is characterized by the principles of sustainability, subsidiarity, equity, efficiency, transparency and accountability, civic engagement and citizenship, and security. These principles must be interdependent and mutually reinforcing

sustainability; subsidiarity; equity; efficiency; transparency and accountability; civic engagement and citizenship; and security. These principles must be interdependent and mutually reinforcing. These principles are summarized as follows.[97]

■ Sustainability in all dimensions of urban development

Cities must balance the social, economic and environmental needs of present and future generations.[98] This should include a clear commitment to urban poverty reduction. Leaders of all sections of urban society must have a long-term, strategic vision of sustainable human development and the ability to reconcile divergent interests for the common good.

■ Subsidiarity of authority and resources to the closest appropriate level

Responsibility for service provision should be allocated on the basis of the principle of subsidiarity – that is, at the closest appropriate level consistent with efficient and cost-effective delivery of services. This will maximize the potential for the inclusion of the citizenry in the process of urban governance. Decentralization and local democracy should improve the responsiveness of policies and initiatives to the priorities and needs of citizens. Cities and smaller devolved authorities should be empowered with sufficient resources and autonomy to meet their responsibilities.

■ Equity of access to decision-making processes and the basic necessities of urban life

The sharing of power leads to equity in the access to, and use of, resources. Women and men must participate as equals in all urban decision-making, priority-setting and resource-allocation processes. Inclusive cities provide everyone – whether the poor, young or older persons, religious or ethnic minorities, or the handicapped – with equitable access to nutrition; education; employment and livelihood; health care; shelter; safe drinking water; sanitation and other basic services.

■ Efficiency in the delivery of public services and in promoting local economic development

Cities must be financially sound and cost effective in their management of revenue sources and expenditures, the administration and delivery of services, and in the enablement of government, civil society, the private sector and communities to contribute formally or informally to the urban economy. A key element in achieving efficiency is to recognize and enable the specific contribution of women to the urban economy.

■ Transparency and accountability of decision-makers and stakeholders

The accountability of local authorities to their citizens is a fundamental tenet of good governance. In particular, there should be no place for corruption in cities. Corruption takes resources from those least able to afford the loss; it will undermine local government credibility and may deepen urban poverty. Transparency and accountability are essential to stakeholder understanding of local government and to clarifying precisely who is benefiting from decisions and actions. Access to information is fundamental to this understanding and to good governance. Laws and public policies should be applied in a transparent and predictable manner. Elected and appointed officials and other civil service leaders need to set an example of high standards of professional and personal integrity. Citizen participation is a key element in promoting transparency and accountability.

■ Civic engagement and citizenship

People are the principal wealth of cities; they are both the object and the means of sustainable human development. Civic engagement implies that living together is not a passive exercise: in cities, people must actively contribute to the common good. Citizens, especially women, must be empowered to participate effectively in decision-making processes. The civic capital of the poor must be recognized and supported.

■ Security of individuals and their living environment

Every individual has the inalienable right to life, liberty and security. Insecurity has a disproportionate impact in further marginalizing poor communities. Cities must strive to avoid human conflicts and natural disasters by involving all stakeholders in crime and conflict prevention, as well as disaster preparedness. Security also implies freedom from persecution and forced evictions, and provides for security of tenure. Cities should also work with social mediation and conflict-reduction agencies, and encourage cooperation between enforcement agencies and other social service providers.

Enhancing development potential through partnerships

As Chapter 8 has described, there is now a considerable experience with partnerships that bring together the public and the private sectors. However, it is only fairly recently that more broad-based partnerships have emerged in forms that intentionally extend to civil society, as well – including CBOs and other representative organizations of people living in poverty. Indeed, there is not yet a commonly accepted term to describe these new arrangements, which have been called, for example, multi-sector and tri-sector partnerships.[99]

The concept of partnerships with civil society featured in the work of UN-Habitat during most of the 1990s. It was one of the key commitments adopted by governments at the Habitat II Conference in 1996. It was also the subject of a special meeting jointly sponsored by the International Social Science Council (ISSC) and the United Nations Educational, Scientific and Cultural Organization (UNESCO) Programme on Management of Social Transformations (MOST), which was concerned with the place and effect of partnerships in inter-governmental relations, the contact between public and private spheres, and the relationships between government leaders and civil society.[100] The emerging literature on tri-sector partnerships suggests that the inclusion of civil society can bring about a transformation in opportunities for people living in poverty.[101]

Arguments in favour of partnership approaches generally rest upon a number of premises:[102]

- *Synergy*: this comprises the additional benefit gained when two or more partners act together to attain a common goal.
- *Transformation*: this includes the efforts made by one partner to change the other's worldview, behaviour and priorities.
- *Budget augmentation*: resources are pooled to increase the size or scope of activities that may be undertaken, and to avoid overlap.[103]
- *Diffusion of responsibility* for success or failure: shifting the blame can be attractive to government.[104] However, it can also be used as an argument against partnerships: it raises the question of whether the partnership approach can deliver accountability, along with balancing of efficiency and equity. There is also a risk that partnerships could become a system for co-opting NGOs who are intended to exert a countervailing force within the democratic process.
- *Reduction of open conflict*: this entails the creation of a more consensual decision-making climate, turning away from the monolithic attitude that is typical of administrative thinking. Partnerships, joint ventures and contracting with other public, private, voluntary and grassroots organizations may give development projects and services a broader base of community acceptance.[105]
- *Efficiency*: partnerships induce local authorities to be competitive, either directly with the private sector or through market surrogates, such as comparative performance measurement or benchmarking. These are systematically used to offer citizens quality services, while – at the same time – increasing efficiency within the bureaucracy.[106]

Many questions must be addressed in establishing partnerships such as which interests, and which players, will be included in partnerships, and who will be left outside? Who will be the leader within partnerships? Whose agendas will prevail?[107] The answers to these questions are likely to be different in each application, and the harmonious welding of effective partnerships will have a prime bearing on successful outcomes and processes.

More critical observations of partnerships in action suggest that:[108]

- The process may be anti-democratic. For example, urban regeneration partnerships in the UK were not democratically controlled and politically accountable, and were largely technocratic in nature.[109] Similarly, in the Cooperative Urban Renewal Programme in Seoul, Republic of Korea, the residents' association is not always established by general consensus of all the legitimate residents, but – in some cases – is manipulated by a select group of residents who invest major developmental interests in the project.[110]
- The process may be inequitable. In urban redevelopment in New York, Philadelphia and Chicago, the conventional public–private partnership (PPP) approach may have done little to improve the living conditions for a majority of the slum dwellers and, in fact, may have exacerbated inequality and urban dualism.[111]
- Policy formulations produced by complex constellations of partners may not be well coordinated with national priorities. This lack of coordination may make the long-term viability of such policies tenuous.
- PPPs may undertake ventures that are susceptible to the vagaries of business cycles. For example, many ambitious PPP ventures in urban development that were initiated during the economic boom in Japan and other Asian newly industrialized countries (NICs) languished after the bubble deflated.[112]

Enabling partnerships and inter-sectorial coordination in urban development planning and management involves a continuous process of monitoring and policy reformulation in order to adapt development concepts and approaches in the light of changing social, economic and functional needs.

Partnership approaches should be seen as part of a wider arsenal of approaches that also include, for example, participatory budgeting and Local Agenda 21 processes. A recent review of partnerships concludes that:[113]

- Partnerships cannot replace government. Partnerships should be subsumed under representative democratic systems.[114] The elected bodies must oversee partnerships and prevent them from becoming the prime policy-making institutions in their area of activity.
- Partnerships must not exclude marginalized groups. Governments at all levels – through elected representatives – have a special duty to look after vulnerable groups through traditional policy programmes and by encouraging them to organize.
- The Local Agenda 21 and the Habitat II partnerships may be regarded as embryos of broader and more open kinds of partnerships. Transnational partnerships at all levels are crucial in achieving consensus and a broad-ranging attack on problems associated with urbanization and globalization.[115]

'Partnership' is a loose umbrella term that covers many different types of arrangements. Examples in Africa that are involved in the exchange of experience and 'twinning' include horizontal municipal associations, such as the Union of African Towns (UVA); the United Towns Organization (UTO); and the International Association of Mayors and Leaders of Wholly or Partially French-speaking Capital Cities and Metropolitan Areas (AIMF).[116]

Partnerships are often formed in the context of infrastructure projects. The Sustainable Cities Programme supported by the UNDP and UN-Habitat offers one of the more successful models in this regard, bringing together not only the public and private sector, but also community organizations.[117]

Other forms of partnerships join local communities and universities, as in the case of Université Cheikh Anta Diop – the oldest university in Francophone Africa – in Dakar, Senegal.[118] There are many academic researchers who deliberately choose to work in partnership with neighbourhood groups and NGOs in community outreach. For example, in 1994, the US Department of Housing and Urban Development established the Office of University Partnerships (OUP) to encourage and support cooperation between institutions of higher education and low-income communities through grant programmes, interactive conferences and a clearing house for the dissemination of information.[119] Its goals are to:

- Recognize, reward, and build upon successful examples of universities' activities in local revitalization projects.
- Create the next generation of urban scholars and encourage them to focus their work on housing and community development policy.
- Create partnerships with other federal agencies to support innovative teaching, research and service partnerships.

By 2001, OUP had allocated more than US$64 million to 143 partnership initiatives.[120] Good examples may be found at the University of Illinois at Chicago[121] and the University of Pennsylvania.[122] Similar programmes exist in other countries.

A review of recent experiences may provide guidance for establishing and operating future partnerships. Lessons that emerge from these experiences are as follows.

■ Capacity building

The Community Animator Programme in Sri Lanka has been very successful in community capacity building.[123] Under its auspices, the National Housing Development Authority (NHDA) trained community workers from low-income areas, who then went back to offer support to Community Development Committees (CDCs) in promoting and establishing women's mutual help groups. More generally, women's active participation in decision-making, planning, implementation, operation and maintenance can significantly contribute to community capacity building.[124]

Greater capacity to act may be better achieved by slow learning rather than rapid replication of possibly inappropriate international models. The SPARC/Mahila Milan/National Slum Dwellers Alliance in Mumbai rejects temporal logic dictated by the 'project model', and relies upon precedent setting (for example, housing and toilet exhibitions) and self-census.[125]

Local government needs to play different roles at different levels. It must be a facilitator and enabler of community processes, a partner with the community, a technical adviser, and a client of national and international funding agencies.[126]

■ Low-income households as financial and political partners

Partnerships may be conducted between potential borrowers and lenders through CBOs to establish sources of credit for small-scale business. Collectivization and scaling-up of financial and social assets of poor households can create valuable resources for development.[127] Experience indicates that slum dwellers often are responsible partners, financially and otherwise, and micro-lending programmes typically have very low default rates.[128]

This model for credit delivery retains the advantages of the informal credit market (timely and flexible credit) and avoids the weaknesses of the informal delivery system (usury, exploitation), while encouraging household savings.[129] Cost recovery must be based on regular and affordable payments.[130] However, full capital cost recovery may not always be feasible; and recognition of this fact must inform anti-poverty policies.

If the partnership is government initiated, where government has created and used CBOs for cost-saving and control purposes, there may be lack of 'ownership' among the urban poor who may view their involvement more as an 'extractive' participation, rather than one of contribution and sharing.

The success of particular partnership 'models' may encourage international development organizations to associate themselves with the process, potentially making it difficult for approaches that are led by the poor.[131]

Weak organizational capacity of CBO leaders, owing to their lack of education, status and language skills, may be a problem when directly dealing with international donors. Abuse of the power vested in them by their constituency may sometimes occur.[132]

■ Local businesses, city elites and local media as partners

The local business elites of a city can substitute for, or supplement, international donor agencies in funding slum improvement projects.[133] In one case, as the partnership generated local pride and as self-help action reached wider publicity, it received significant support from the local media and, ultimately, international acclaim.[134]

■ NGOs as partners

Initially, prominent NGOs may operate in the forefront in order to obtain recognition of the abilities of the CBOs in the eyes of regulatory authorities and international donors, and to build confidence among the urban poor.[135] However, over time, the roles of NGO partners may recede more into the background, and people's organizations can begin to assume more responsibilities. There is a view that it is necessary to eliminate the monopoly of professional NGOs as intermediaries for aid money, in favour of a broader-based people-to-people mode of development ('the de-professionalizing of the aid business').[136]

Maintaining the required pace of the project may lead NGOs to compromise their commitment to local priorities, or their ability to work closely with local residents prior to and during the activity.[137]

■ Women's participation

Women frequently constitute a majority of participants in urban popular movements, and success often depends upon women's active involvement and their participation in leadership roles.[138] Women also play key roles in organizing and coordinating design, and in the construction stages.[139]

■ Self-help and management of projects

An analysis of partnerships in slums show that self-help by households living in poverty is widespread and present in almost every partnership reported.[140] Self-management by the communities may help to control corruption and autocracy,[141] and may also encourage the pooling of human expertise.[142]

Community action-planning workshops can be an effective way of developing workable solutions and prioritizing problems from the perspective of the community. A 'community contract' system by which the local government or an NGO contracts a CDC to build its service infrastructure project (rather than a private company) may result in cost savings and better quality of services.[143]

A municipal corporation may be able to keep construction costs lower than private contractors would, and may transfer the responsibility for maintenance either to the NGO partner or to local residents.[144]

■ Scaling-up and spreading the movement

Organizational replicability is important for 'spreading the movement'.[145] Effective strategies in this regard also include mobilization of local citizens (for example, a rally in front of national government offices in Korea) and international networking.[146]

■ Partnerships based on trust

While contracts are assumed to be more economically efficient, evidence is emerging that it is trust, rather than legal obligations *per se*, that significantly affect economic transactions and efficiency gains in partnership arrangements. Contract-based relationships may not be as effective in partnerships as trust.[147] Trust and credibility regarding roles, attitudes and modes of operation of all the stakeholders involved in the process (particularly local government) are required to bring any participatory planning process to a successful conclusion.[148]

■ Horizontal partnerships

In some cases, the external partners have relevant expertise and experience (for example, in areas such as wastewater management or planning), and they are able quickly and easily to demonstrate the benefits and drawbacks of some strategies over others.[149]

Effective policy coordination

Partnerships can extend the reach, resources and legitimacy of government; but the ultimate responsibility for achieving strategic goals of inclusive cities rests with government. Inevitably, government is fragmented horizontally by function, and vertically by level. The responsibility of bringing together planning processes that operate all of the way from national goal setting to local participatory governance, and that integrate inter-sectoral competition for scarce resources without undue overlap or neglect, are key aspects of government that are very difficult to successfully fulfil. Some of the major organizational and governance changes that will need to be to be pursued include:[150]

- Eliminating political opportunism that arises from short-term electoral interests to the detriment of long-term needs of the urban poor. Lack of political will also need to be overcome in order to achieve affective local action towards the realization of the goal of cities without slums.[151] This can be achieved through more effective community organization among the poor and engaging local and central government authorities with one voice.

- Overcoming the numerous conflicts in formulating and implementing settlements programmes. Such conflicts occur, for example, within the public sector – where different agencies with overlapping functional responsibilities or spatial jurisdictions jostle for position – or in the private sector – where industrial enterprises and land developers may have different objectives from each other – or between different stakeholders who have different priorities for investment and spending.

- Deepening democratic and participatory governance processes in order to eliminate inefficient bureaucracy and inertia that are often responsible for blocking and paralysing new innovations and initiatives.

- More effectively coordinating urban shelter policies with economic and social policies for creating employment opportunities and generating economic growth. The emphasis should be on the holistic improvement of the lives of the urban poor and on the mobilization and allocation of adequate resources.

- Ensuring that slum improvement and related shelter programmes focus not only on the activities to be conducted, but also on the roles of the different actors and the processes by which the contribution of each actor will be supported and coordinated.

- Recognizing existing diversities in local conditions, such as physical characteristics, levels of development, development goals, material resources and so on, by designing programmes with appropriate substantive focus, orientation, scale, organizational arrangement and time horizon.

Achieving all of these reforms requires not only political will at both the local and national levels, but also a strategic vision of the city. Strategic visioning is increasingly recognized as a prerequisite to realizing truly inclusive and liveable cities. The effectiveness of such a vision will depend upon the extent to which it is shared by all urban citizens, especially the poor and disadvantaged. This, in turn, will depend upon how seriously decision-making structures and processes are transformed and enabled to build the kind of broad consensus that is required for a shared vision of the city.

Strategic visioning is increasingly recognized as a prerequisite to realizing truly inclusive and liveable cities

NOTES

1　This chapter is based on contributions from many authors and institutions whose name are mentioned at the references to particular sections and in the Acknowledgements.

2　This section is sourced from Cities Without Slums: Action Plan (Cities Alliance, 1999).

3　Diacon, 1997.

4　Durand-Lasserve, 1998, pp241–242.

5　Diacon, 1977.

6　Cities Without Slums action plan was launched by Nelson Mandela in 1999 in Berlin. The action plan was subsequently endorsed by the heads of states attending the Millennium Summit in September 2000.

7　This section is based on a paper prepared by Alain Durand-Lasserve and Lauren Royston.

8　World Bank, 1991, 1993; Harris, 1992.

9　See Chapter 3. See also Pugh, 1993; Durand-Lasserve, 1994.

10　Hardoy and Satterthwaite, 1989; Skinner et al, 1987.

11　Mathey, 1992.

12　Baross and Van der Linden, 1990; Jones and Ward, 1994.

13　Fourie, 2000.

14　Fischer, 1995.

15　Fourie, 2000; Payne, 1997, 1999b.

16　Cobbett, 1999. It must be stressed that informality does not necessarily mean insecurity of tenure.

17　UNCHS (Habitat), 1999b.

18　For overview of studies in Bangkok, Manila, Karachi, Durban, see April issue of Environment and Urbanization, 1994.

19　UNCHS (Habitat), 1999b.

20　Fernandes, 1996.

21　Rochegude, 1998.

22　UNCHS (Habitat), 1999c; Rakodi, 1994.

23　Dowall and Giles, 1991.

24　Urban Management Programme, 1993, 1995.

25　Feder and Nisho, 1998; Rolnick, 1996.

26　Torstensson, 1994.

27　World Bank, 1991; Cohen and Sheema, 1992.

28　World Bank, 1991.

29　Hibou, 1998.

30　Ward, 1998.

31　Tribillon, 1995.

32　Cobbett, 1999.

33　Christiensen and Hoejaard, 1995; Fourie, 2000.

34　UNCHS (Habitat), 1996c.

35　Leckie, 1992, 1993.

36　See overview of community development and shelter improvement funding systems in the April issue of *Environment and Urbanization*, 1993.

37　African NGOs Habitat II Caucus.

38　This section draws primarily from a paper prepared by Paul Barter, Visiting Fellow, Department of Geography, National University of Singapore, and Brian Williams, Human Settlements Officer, United Nations Human Settlements Programme.

39　Gopalan, 1998.

40　This is not universally true. Many of the larger squatter estates, particularly in Africa, are peri-urban since the inner city has been effectively sealed off to the poor under colonialism.

41　World Bank, 1994.

42　World Bank, 1996.

43　Gannon and Liu, 1997.

44　See, for example, Mumbai's railway dwellers, discussed by Patel, 1999.

45　Hook, 1994.

46　Asian Development Bank, 1995, pp10–11.

47　Patel, 1999.

48　This is because of the extensive kickbacks associated with transport projects (NESDB Thailand, private communication).

49　Hook, 1998; World Bank, 2000; Koster, 2000.

50　Manning, 1984.

51　Linn, 1983.

52　Mabogunje et al, 1978.

53　See Professor Johan Silas's interview in Barter, 2002.

54　Thomson, 1977.

55　Hook and Replogle, 1996.

56　Manning, 1984.

57　Acioly, 2000.

58　Lloyd Jones, 2000.

59　Stretton, 1975, p106.

60　Poole et al, 1994; Gannon and Liu, 1997; UNCHS (Habitat), 1996c; UN-Habitat, 2002f. This depends upon the relative co-location of jobs and residences, and upon traffic congestion.

61　Godard, 1997.

62　Hook, 1998; Boonyabancha, 1983.

63　Patel, 1999.

64　Fernandes, 1998; Murphy and Pimple, 1995. This has also been observed in subsidized housing solutions, such as in South Africa, where some new owners have vacated their new houses after a short period.

65　This section is derived from UNDP, 2000b, pp8–15.

66　This section is based on studies carried out by the Shelter Branch of UN-Habitat. See also UNCHS (Habitat) and ILO, 1995.

67　Pugh, 1995.

68　For example, even single-storey, concrete industrialized construction is almost impossible to maintain without specialized equipment.

69　This section is based on the background paper prepared by James Mutero, housing finance consultant, Kenya.

70　'Decisions regarding services should rest with the entity of governance closest to the community that is able to deliver these services in a cost-effective way, while minimizing the externalization of environmental and social costs.' See UNCHS (Habitat), 1996a

71　See UNCHS (Habitat), 1996a.

72　UNCHS (Habitat), 1996c; UN-Habitat, 2002f.

73　UNCHS (Habitat), 1996a.

74　UNCHS (Habitat), 1996a.

75　Wunsch and Olowu, 1990.

76　Smoke, 2000.

77　Bahl and Linn, 1992. This has changed a good deal during the 1990s as a result of decentralization programmes, and a number of developing countries now generate and spend a good proportion of income at the local level.

78　Unless, of course, the political elites also control the private

organizations.

79　Rose-Ackerman, 1998.

80　Rose-Ackerman, 1998.

81　Stiglitz, 1999.

82　This is the case with property taxes in many smaller constituencies. For small municipalities in the Philippines, the return is typically about one third of the cost.

83　Smoke, 2000.

84　Noll et al, 2000.

85　Ferguson, 1999.

86　Porteous, 2000.

87　UNCHS (Habitat), 1996a, p373.

88　Porteous, 2000.

89　Deregulated finance systems may have their own problems, such as the savings and loans crisis in the US and the near collapse of some Australian banks following deregulation, until suitable prudential measures are put in place.

90　See, for instance, UNCHS (Habitat), 1990. Banks rarely have branches in slum areas, even in better-developed countries such as South Africa.

91　Fixed interest loans are, however, the norm in the US – one of a number of unusual features that has arisen because of the lack of a national banking system.

92　Struyck, 1986.

93　*Environment and Urbanization*, 2000.

94　See www.unchs.org/campaigns/governance/.

95　International Union of Local Authorities Worldwide Declaration on Women in Local Government (1998).

96　Statement by Mary Robinson, former UN High Commissioner for Human Rights, at the Special Dialogue on Poverty and the Enjoyment of Human Rights, 12 April 2000. See www.unhchr.ch.

97　'Good Urban Governance: A Normative Framework', Conference Room Paper of 26 February 2000; www.un-habitat.org/govern/.

98　From the 27 principles elaborated in the Rio Declaration on Environment and Development, 1992.

99　For example, Caplan et al, 2001.

100 Revisions of papers presented at this meeting were published in a special theme issue of *International Social Science Journal* (June, 2002).

101 See, for example, Baumann, 2001, in a special issue of *Environment and Urbanization* on the roles of civil society. See also Plummer, 2002; Edwards and Gaventa, 2001; Evans et al, 2001.

102 A useful recent discussion of partnership approaches can be found in Elander, 2002.

103 This was one of the primary forces that forged the partnership arrangement in the UNDP's Sustainable Cities Programme for the city of Chennai, India.

104 Jewson and MacGregor, 1997.

105 Banner, 2002.

106 Banner, 2002.

107 See, for example, Jewson and

MacGregor, 1997.

108 For a more extensive discussion, see Elander, 2002.

109 See UNDP, 2001.

110 Choe, 2002.

111 Levine, 1989.

112 Choe, 2002.

113 Elander, 2002.

114 See, also, the discussion in UNCHS (Habitat), 2001a, pp161–163.

115 See, for example, Edwards and Gaventa, 2001, for a collection of case studies of the roles of civil society in these transnational partnerships. See, also, UNCHS (Habitat), 2001a, pp171–176.

116 For a fuller discussion of 'twinning' or international municipal cooperation, see UNCHS (Habitat), 2001a, pp163–165.

117 UNCHS (Habitat), 2001a.

118 See Mbodj, 2002.

119 See, for example, Forsyth et al, 2000; Kleniewski, 1999; Wiewel et al, 1996. See, also, two special issues of *American Behavioral Scientist* (1999), vol 42(5), and (2000), vol 43(5).

120 Barbara Holland, Director, Office of University Partnerships, HUD, pers com).

121 See Mayfield et al, 1999; Wiewel and Lieber, 1998.

122 See Benson et al, 2000.

123 Russel and Vidler, 2000.

124 Rahman, 2002.

125 Appadurai, 2001.

126 Abbott, 2002.

127 Baumann, 2001.

128 Dutta, 2000.

129 Igel and Srinivas, 1996.

130 Rahman, 2002.

131 Patel et al, 2001.

132 Russel and Vidler, 2000.

133 Dutta, 2000.

134 Gwebu, 2002.

135 Patel et al, 2001.

136 Fowler, 1998.

137 Hobson, 2000.

138 Moctezuma, 2001.

139 Hobson, 2000; Rahman, 2002.

140 UN-Habitat Best Practices Database.

141 Moctezuma, 2001.

142 Ogu, 2000.

143 Russel and Vidler, 2000.

144 Hobson, 2000.

145 Moctezuma, 2001.

146 Rahman, 2002.

147 Fowler, 1998.

148 Rahardjo, 2000.

149 Hewitt, 2000.

150 Several studies during the 1990s have identified a wide range of obstacles to human settlements policy development.

151 Luke et al, 1988, p29.

LOOKING FORWARD – MOVING AHEAD

There is no point in free market-based development if the majority of human beings see it only on TV.[1]

TOWARDS CITIES WITHOUT SLUMS: TURNING THE DREAM INTO REALITY

The desirable future, as perceived by most people, is a world where everyone has the basic needs of life: where everyone has enough to eat, a decent home in sanitary and unpolluted surroundings, the opportunity to earn a decent living, access to health care and education, and the means to access the things that are important to them. What the people in cities throughout the world would like to have as a minimum is:

- the means of earning or obtaining a reasonable livelihood, preferably with a secure job under safe working conditions;
- affordable, adequate and appropriate housing, with security of tenure;
- access to clean water, basic sanitation and other urban services, along with a clean and attractive environment;
- the means to participate in broader society and have access to its opportunities; and
- responsive and honest government, justice and the means to redress wrongs.

To achieve the goal of 'cities without slums', all of these elements are necessary. More advanced countries have demonstrated, through a concerted programme of action, how these basic goals could be implemented to achieve a high quality of life.[2] The styles and methods by which this was achieved differed in that some countries had more government involvement than others; but all methods involved government, the private sector and civil society working together or negotiating solutions.

These basic requirements are now largely taken for granted in most of the developed world. However, perhaps half of the world's population does not have any of these minimum living conditions met. Of these disadvantaged people, half live in the slums of the developing world – and since the 1970s, these numbers have more than doubled. Both the proportion and numbers of slum dwellers will increase substantially in the next 30 years (in fact, the

numbers will probably double again) unless action is taken globally, nationally and locally to solve these problems.

Considerable advances have been made during the 1990s in most of the world regions, particularly in health care and education, because these areas have been targeted and acted upon by international and national agencies in a concerted and organized way.[3] Some progress has also been made in providing clean water and electricity. It is in the areas of employment generation, housing delivery and urban environmental management that progress has not been adequate to meet growing demand. Good governance has also continued to be sorely lacking in many places, with corruption and poor management widespread.

At present, there is little concerted effort to achieve these aims in the developing world; in fact, some of them are actually denied as legitimate goals by people in positions of authority. Where there is agreement, the means of reaching these aims has been hotly argued – so that the goals have not been explicitly targeted and indirect issues have taken precedence. There has also been considerable backsliding on the issues of employment and housing in a number of highly developed countries for the same reasons of denial, lack of consensus and application.

ACTION NEEDED TO TACKLE THE CURRENT TRENDS

If it is agreed that the major inadequacies in current policy are due to:

- lack of development planning, in general, and urban planning, in particular, for future population growth (both natural growth and rural influxes);
- lack of action to deal with the poor environmental and social conditions existing in present and future slum areas;
- inability of the market to provide adequate, secure housing at affordable prices for poor people; and
- loss of urban jobs when urban labour forces are swelling,

then the following actions are needed.

For *planning*, urban, housing and population policies based on housing rights and the right to a clean environment must be established at all levels. These policies should be directed at inclusive cities and poverty alleviation and should include formal mechanisms for participation. City governments should plan for future population growth by ensuring serviced land release in a timely fashion, either providing infrastructure or facilitating its provision by private firms. They should take account of the fact that many of the new arrivals will not have money to afford even the most basic formal-sector house or to pay for utilities on a regular basis.

For *environmental management and physical and social infrastructure* in existing slum areas, it has been established that participatory slum upgrading, conducted as part of a city-wide strategy, is the preferred solution. Improving water supply, basic sanitation, footpaths and roads is relatively inexpensive and programmes can often be conducted with the financial and labour resources of the people themselves, supplemented by local government or donor contributions. There are a number of pitfalls to be avoided by successful upgrading programmes. These can be summarized as follows:[4]

- Upgrading should be undertaken as part of a city-wide strategy and with the full involvement of local government, otherwise it will not be sustainable or replicable.
- Upgrading should involve the local people and civil society in the planning and possibly the implementation phases. Residents are then more likely to receive what they want and to assist in the maintenance and upkeep of facilities.
- An asset management approach must be used, setting in place mechanisms and procedures for operating or repairing the facilities in the longer term.
- Rapid commodification of regularized slum properties should be prevented through the adoption of appropriate tenure mechanisms.
- Attention must be paid to income generation, transport and empowerment of the beneficiaries to redress possible future problems.
- It may be the case that the poorest households cannot afford to pay for such services as water supply, sanitation or electricity. The government will then have to consider if it is prepared to subsidize capital or ongoing costs for minimum allocations to individuals or communities.

The biggest stumbling block to achieving cities without slums is, in fact, *housing*, because formal-sector housing is well beyond the reach of most slum dwellers and without formal housing, areas are usually automatically considered to be slums. Therefore, it is, strictly speaking, necessary for governments to follow the example of the highly developed countries and the few other countries that have achieved this goal by providing the funds to meet affordability constraints. This can be done through a variety of mechanisms ranging from largely private-sector enabling approaches to building more or less self-sustaining social housing sectors, or through hybrid approaches. These policies can result in very large building programmes that will eliminate housing shortage. However, before embarking on ambitious programmes, governments should consider the following:

- These programmes have only worked in places where there is a very strong social consensus that the housing problem must be solved, in places where governance is strong and efficient and the building sector is sufficiently developed.
- Subsidy programmes that are run in a half-hearted manner or with inadequate resources have always been seen as failures, and a substantial proportion of the population should be targeted. This requires a significant proportion of the national budget to be allocated to housing. Ultimately, the government must have good access to substantial revenues.
- The target group must be capable of paying the costs of operating the dwellings, including repair costs and the costs of utilities, and also should contribute to construction costs through individual savings when possible. Private lending institutions should also augment government funds.

For countries that cannot meet these rather stringent requirements – which would be the majority – formal-sector solutions are not appropriate. Countries with limited resources, therefore, need to develop programmes of appropriate technology using local materials, through assisted self-construction, ensuring that local artisans are available to assist with the critical parts of construction and facilitating local landlords in the provision of affordable, adequate housing.

The most difficult area of all, and the one upon which eradicating slums ultimately depends, is providing *income-earning opportunities*. In the end, families can only afford non-slum housing if they have good incomes. In a global environment where formal-sector urban jobs have been lost almost everywhere and where there are no proposals to improve the situation, the prospects are not promising. Since the major agencies adopted poverty reduction as their primary goal, anti-poverty programmes are under way all over the developing world, and these can help to strengthen the income-earning capacities and opportunities for poor people. Such programmes tend to target the poorest households, as they should, and are usually not sufficient to deliver the kinds of incomes necessary to pay for formal housing.

Development studies have suggested a number of ways of improving incomes – for example, encouraging more labour-intensive technologies for construction and upgrading programmes, since these are often more cost-effective than more commonly used mechanized approaches designed for countries with high labour costs; and allowing and facilitating small enterprises and non-governmental organizations (NGOs) to bid for these contracts rather than using large or foreign firms.[5] It is also imperative to take access to livelihood opportunities into account during slum relocations and other forms of improvement, especially transport policies, which tend to be designed for the benefit of the middle class.

It has to be remembered that slums have always been a part of market societies. In the long run, the goal of cities without slums is only going to be achieved in a predominantly market economy once a good majority of the urban work force has middle-class incomes. How to achieve this major aim of development is rooted in controversy and is somewhat beyond the scope of this report. However, global trends are definitely not heading in this direction, except for a few lucky countries. Until this is achieved, the principal goal cannot be the outright elimination of slums, but improving the lives of slum dwellers in the many ways that this report has suggested.

Each of the different urban stakeholders must take active roles in achieving these goals, as outlined in *The Habitat Agenda*:

- *Central governments* should formulate and implement national urban policies, population policies and comprehensive national housing policies that facilitate the ability of local or sub-national governments to carry out their mandate, based on housing rights and the right to a clean environment. They may reform local government regulation towards greater inclusiveness and participation, improving the ability of local governments to generate local financial resources – but retaining assistance to local governments with a poor revenue base. They should formulate and facilitate the implementation of nation-wide slum upgrading policies and strategies by up-scaling and replicating successful city experiences, mobilizing financial support to local authorities for innovative or continuing activities. Above all, their principal task is to position their country in the global system to permit economic growth and development that can benefit all citizens and not just a few.

- *Municipal authorities and local governments* must engage in more effective planning to limit the emergence of future slums and to ensure that conditions in future low-income housing areas are as favourable as possible. They should engage in programmes of city-wide slum upgrading rather than relocation and renewal, with scheduled rolling upgrades that reflect the needs of the local communities and involve their participation, while taking an asset management approach to the city's housing stock and infrastructure in order to ensure their long-term sustainability. They should adopt good and inclusive models of city governance, involving transparency and participation in planning decisions, and should aim to have sufficient revenue to be able to act independently in response to local priorities. While planning for broad economic growth and employment creation is essential, pro-poor economic policies should be adopted, including explicit support for livelihood activities of the poor, microcredit for small enterprises, and NGO or municipal 'safety-net' services for the most indigent.

- *Civil society* (NGOs and community-based organizations – CBOs) should support poor households to organize themselves into interest groups that can obtain resources for local funding and act to redress local problems, mediating between

communities and local authorities and providing local and national advocacy for slum dwellers and housing issues. They can provide and maintain basic infrastructure, such as water or community services, bid for income-earning projects in the place of large firms, and can channel national or international aid to poverty reduction and income-generation projects.

- *The private sector* (formal-sector enterprises) can help the urban poor by extending services into poorer or informal communities, by providing safe work places and adopting non-discriminatory policies in employment, by helping the urban poor to access credit for shelter improvement and for small enterprises, and through investment in low-income rental housing.

- *International organizations* can facilitate the dissemination and exchange of knowledge and experience, providing technical and financial support to national governments and local authorities – for example, through the Cities Alliance and other partnerships and programmes, and through loan guarantee schemes, grants and facilities that seek to improve urban conditions and governance. They also have a primary role in advocacy for the poorer countries of the world and their poorer citizens, seeking to minimize negative effects of global financial and trade arrangements on poor people and their living environments, and finding solutions that will distribute wealth fairly rather than impoverish low-income people.

Many of these activities are governance related, involving organization, planning and changes in attitude, and these alone can result in considerable improvements in the situation and quality of life of slum dwellers. The political will, organization and inclusiveness that constitute the foundation of good urban governance are very much a precondition for the successful adoption and implementation of pro-poor capital works and subsidy programmes of any kind. Without a refocusing of governance, the failures of the past will simply be repeated. Ultimately, however, like all significant social goals, 'cities without slums' requires the allocation of significant resources in the way that those countries that have achieved these goals have done.

With the great global urbanization project half completed, the resources, technology and experience of the North can be used to solve the situation much more rapidly than the way in which Northern countries solved their own urbanization problems, or their economic power can be used to make the situation worse by marginalizing the poorest countries in international dealings, and by sponsoring the division of the cities of the South into rich people who access the incomes, the technologies and advantages of the North and the majority who 'only see the market economy on television'. The choice is one that the world must make.

In conclusion, the world faces a very great challenge in improving the lives of the approximately 924 million existing slum dwellers and in providing jobs, housing and services for 2 billion future urban residents. Many existing slum dwellers live in degraded and marginalized conditions that are unacceptable. The numbers of new urban residents who will be arriving in the cities of the developing world are unprecedented and will put great pressure on city administrations that are already struggling with inadequate infrastructure and widespread poverty. A concerted international response is required to deal with the situation, and this demands a change in the processes and global organization of aid and the economy in order to deal with this huge challenge in a balanced, sustainable and inclusive way.

NOTES

1   President Aylwin of Chile, March 1994.

2   UNCHS (Habitat), 2001a, pp232–235.

3   UN-Habitat, 2003; UNCHS (Habitat), 1996a, pp24–27.

4   These issues are considered in detail in Chapter 7.

5   See Chapters 7 and 9 for detail.

PART IV

SUMMARY OF CITY CASE STUDIES

OVERVIEW OF CASE STUDIES[1]

A total of 29 city case studies on slums from around the world has been summarized and analysed on the basis of the following themes:[2]

- Origin of slums.
- Slum definition.
- Types of slums.
- Tenure types in slums.
- Slum dynamics.
- Slum socio-political characteristics.
- Policy actions proposed or taken.
- Policy impacts and development prospects.

The comparative analysis of these cities – despite their huge geographical, cultural, historic, economic, social and organizational differences – revealed a number of commonalties or correlations. Although each city is different and there is no such thing as a common solution, the case studies did indicate that similar issues perhaps warrant similarities in the required approaches for achieving results.

ORIGIN OF SLUMS

Almost without exception, slum formation in the 29 case study cities principally originated from four types of rapid urban population expansion that were primarily triggered by:

1 rural–urban migration;[3]
2 natural growth;[4]
3 combinations of natural and migratory growth;[5] or
4 population displacement following armed conflicts or internal strife and violence.[6]

Additionally, in some of the cities, demographic forces were compounded by urban-specific transformation processes with clear segregational implications, such as inner-city deterioration, gentrification and counter-urbanization.[7]

Surges in urban population and the often-related spatial segregation of urban population segments on socio-economic and ethnic grounds have become problematic in several of the studied cities for a variety of reasons, the most common being:

- a relatively long period of general *laisser-faire* attitude on the part of the urban authorities towards illegal occupation of urban lands and commensurate flouting

of building regulations and/or of urban zoning prescriptions; and
- a general failure of housing and land markets to provide for the land and housing requirements of rapidly growing urban low-income populations in a timely fashion and in sufficient numbers and locations.

In many of the studied cities, considerable political and institutional inertia allowed slums to expand to levels where their sheer magnitude overwhelmed the capacity of existing institutional arrangements to effectively address the issues. This inertia, perhaps, even overtook any political desirability for intervention. Wherever and whenever formal urban interventions took place to address issues such as urban degeneration, explosive growth of informal housing, or illegal urban land occupancy, all too often such interventions were ad hoc, marginal and insignificant in relation to the scale and scope of the issues at hand. The nature of such interventions appears to indicate that the phenomenon of slums and the related problems are generally little understood, and that public interventions – more often than not – address symptoms rather than the underlying causes. The number of cities that consider squatting, slums and informal housing developments as a highly undesirable and temporary phenomenon to be dealt with through various window-dressing exercises, rather than addressing core issues of urban poverty, is perhaps indicative of the general lack of understanding of the forces, trends and conditions that are causing the rapid growth of informal urbanization.

The world is faced with the reality that many large- and medium-sized cities are increasingly becoming areas of impoverished urban exclusion, surrounding comparatively small pockets of urban wealth. Frequently, this trend is the spatial outcome of mismatches and disconnections between national macro-policies and the absence of coherent connections with the policies at the city level. With the rise of the city as the predominant and preferred residential locus of the majority of the world population, the spatial translation of such policy disconnections is increasingly becoming visible and problematic through urban processes such as counter-urbanization, urban fragmentation, societal stratification, segregation and the explosive growth of informal forms of urban development beyond the control of city authorities. Any attempt to address the issues by merely fighting their spatial symptoms is a futile exercise that, at best, will give some temporary relief in small locations, and which, at worst, will lead to economic, social and political instability. Rather, the core issue of current policy mismatches, both at and between the national and the urban levels, should be addressed if any tangible impact is to be expected in terms of urban poverty alleviation and the general improvement of the living conditions in areas classified as slums. This is also a requisite to improving the general liveability of our cities.

SLUM DEFINITIONS

Of the 29 cities analysed, 8 lack any formal slum definition. On the basis of the limited sample, it was not possible to determine whether this is a result of political or institutional inertia, a lack of capacity, denial of the problem, or an indication that the magnitude of slum-related issues has become so enormous that even thinking about solutions at the urban level has ceased. Surely, any city that is seriously dedicated to effective urban-poverty alleviation strategies and to programmes aimed at upgrading the living conditions in its slums would, firstly, identify the target and its beneficiaries by defining what exactly constitutes a slum under local socio-economic conditions and under the municipal and/or national legislative system(s).

Of the 21 case study cities that have a definition of slums, the definitions vary to a large extent. The shortest definition is the one applied in Chengdu: 'Slums are shanties in low-lying areas.' Of the more elaborate definitions used by other cities, none is anywhere near comprehensive in terms of its coverage of the issues. This is unlikely to be a collective oversight; rather, it is the outcome of local-level political decisions.

It is perhaps useful to deconstruct the definitions into their components, as this will give indications of what is considered important by the local authorities. The separation of the issues covered by the various definitions is elaborated in Table 10.1.

It is revealing that the two most-referred to issues are the use of poor construction materials and the legality (or lack thereof) of land occupancy. Twelve (60 per cent) of the 21 cities with a slum definition include notions about the inadequacy of construction materials used, while 11 (55 per cent) in one way or another refer to the legal status of urban land occupancy. This is surprising in the sense that the vast majority of the slums in these cities are, to a large degree, the result of persistent *laissez-faire* attitudes on the part of the municipal authorities regarding irregular urban land occupancy and informal construction. In the case of Karachi, land legality issues are even the sole component of the slum definition. The implications of this could be that there may be a case for the development of urban policies that enhance the role and effectiveness of land-use planning and the enforcement of minimal construction standards at the urban level. This is, moreover, the case as land is the fundamental resource in any housing programme, while security of land ownership is the *sine qua non* for any investment in shelter. Clearly, with the majority of the definitions concerning themselves with the legality status of urban land use and construction, among the primary issues there seems to be a

need for increased or expanded land regulation – that is, at least at the political level.

Basic services (sanitation, water and, in some cases, electricity) supply are the runner-up in frequency, with nine cities (45 per cent) including these issues in their definition of slums. In the case of Nairobi, basic services and infrastructure are the sole criteria of the definition, which, strikingly enough, appears not to be a priority issue for the actual slum dwellers themselves.

What is perhaps the most striking aspect of the deconstruction of the slum definitions is that the term poverty only appears in the definitions applied in Ibadan and Manila, although in three other cities – Ibadan, Jakarta and Lusaka – the term 'low income' is part of the definition. It is unclear whether this is a deliberate disconnection of the two issues that are obviously two sides of the same coin, or whether, in many cases, the connection between poverty and slums simply has not been made. It must be said, however, that slum dwellers are not necessarily all poor, or poor by definition.

TYPES OF SLUMS

The case studies show that many cities do make distinctions between types of slums. In general, there is a clear separation between slums proper, on the one hand, and shanties or spontaneous housing and urban development, on the other. This distinction is often made on the basis of combinations of physical location and legality status of the built structure, urban zoning, land invasion and informal construction.

The term 'slum', or its equivalent local term, often refers to inner-city residential areas that were laid out and built several decades ago in line with the then prevailing urban planning, zoning and construction standards, but which, over time, have progressively become physically dilapidated and overcrowded to the point where they became the near exclusive residential zone for lowest-income groups.

The term 'informal settlement' often refers to illegal or semi-legal urbanization processes, or unsanctioned subdivisions of land at the (then) urban periphery where land invasion took place – often by squatters, who erected housing units usually without formal permission of the land owner and often with materials and building standards not in line with the criteria of the local building code. This type of slum is usually referred to as a shanty, or squatter settlement. Depending upon the local conditions, many local authorities recognize derivatives of this form of informal shelter as separate types of slums, such as informal settlements on vacant urban lots or on precarious urban sites along canals, on road reserves or adjacent to landfill areas.

Several of the cities without a formal slum definition nevertheless apply terms or concepts that denote different types of slum housing depending upon the construction type, location, legality status, etc. This is notably the case for Beirut, Colombo, Havana, Los Angeles, Lusaka, Mexico City, Moscow and Naples.

	No definition	Construction materials	Temporary nature	Construction legality	Land legality	Health and hygiene	Basic services	Infrastructure	Crowding	Poverty	Low income	Environment	Compactness	Crime and violence
Abidjan	X													
Ahmedabad		X	X			X	X		X				X	
Bangkok						X			X			X		X
Barcelona	X													
Beirut	X													
Bogotá				X	X									
Cairo		X		X	X		X							
Chengdu													X	
Colombo		X	X	X	X	X	X							
Durban		X	X				X							
Havana		X				X	X	X						
Ibadan		X							X	X	X			
Jakarta					X						X			
Karachi					X									
Kolkata		X	X				X		X					
Los Angeles		X			X				X					
Lusaka					X		X	X				X		
Manila		X				X			X	X				
Mexico City	X													
Moscow	X													
Nairobi							X	X						
Naples	X													
Newark	X													
Phnom Penh					X								X	
Quito				X	X									
Rabat-Salé		X			X									
Rio de Janeiro		X		X	X		X	X	X					
São Paulo		X				X	X	X	X					
Sydney	X													

Table 10.1

Issues covered in slum definitions

TENURE IN SLUMS

The tenure status of slum dwellers is as diverse as the variety in slum typology. Security of tenure can be tied to the legality of the physical structure and/or the legality of land ownership. It can be tied to residency permits or legal proof of some form of tenure. It can depend upon ration cards or other modes of urban registration. Yet, in many cases, security of tenure is a *de facto* recognition of tenure despite illegality of the structure, thus blurring the distinction between legal, semi-legal and illegal.

On the whole, there appears to be a greater degree of security of tenure in inner-city slums. This is perhaps the outcome of the original fully legal status of many of the inner-city tenement blocks, and degenerated and former middle-income residential areas. The land in such areas is frequently formally held with deeds to prove it. Insecurity of tenure tends, obviously, to increase with the degree of illegality – such as illegal land invasions, illegal subdivisions of land and illegal construction. The overriding factor, however, seems to be the attitude of the local authorities in granting *de facto* recognition of residency rights.

SLUM DYNAMICS

The growth or decline dynamics of slums is closely linked to variations in the rural and urban economy and to related poverty levels. It is clearly also a factor of demographics in terms of household formation rates, as well as the effectiveness of public interventions. More than half of the case study cities report that slum formation will continue.[8] Four cities reported decreasing slum formation.[9] In Barcelona, slums have formally ceased to exist; but the city is still an important destination for immigrants from other areas within Spain and, more recently, from overseas. These immigrants tend to cluster in areas with higher indices of social inequality and marginalization. Eight cities reported no or insufficient data on this topic.[10]

SLUM SOCIO-POLITICAL CHARACTERISTICS

Throughout the case studies, slum populations tend to have low average incomes, high levels of unemployment and relatively low levels of education. As a result, they are often stigmatized, leading to social discrimination. Notable exceptions are Bangkok – where only a minority of the slum dwellers is considered poor and stigmatization is, subsequently, less – and Havana – where slum dwellers have secure tenure and access to the same social infrastructure as non-slum dwellers.

The often pronounced urban isolation and victimization, difficult access to physical and social infrastructure and generally higher incidence of violence and crime generate patterns of depressed urban areas where the inhabitants, despite their heterogeneity, seek common interests on the basis of unsatisfied basic needs.

POLICY ACTIONS TAKEN OR PROPOSED

Three correlations in terms of slum development appeared among the cities covered by the case studies. Firstly, the cities with the worst slum conditions and the largest slum areas display a number of common features:

- There is a long history of unbridled urban growth that is not hampered by any national urban policy or regulatory interventions; more importantly, there is an absence of a coherent city-wide set of urban policies as the basis for public regulation.
- Urban interventions that address the issues of slums are frequently triggered only by external factors, such as land development and speculation, and health and safety threats to the wealthy, and are therefore mostly reactive, rather than proactive.
- Regardless of whether action is reactive or proactive, the absence or failure of coordinating mechanisms that set the roles and jurisdictions of various levels of government inevitably leads to governance gaps, jurisdiction overlaps, competency conflicts, duplication of functions, waste of precious resources, decentralization of problematic issues, and general confusion regarding the developmental directions to be followed.
- Subsequently, slum areas and related problems grow beyond local authorities' capacity to address them, to the point that acceptance, if not total fatalism, on the part of the local, regional and/or national government takes over and slums become 'an inevitable issue that cannot be dealt with at the local level.' In practice, this means that the control over the municipal area and the urban periphery is effectively handed over to spontaneous urbanization processes that are beyond the regulatory influence of the authorities.
- There is an absence of effective and tailored urban and other policy responses to address the underlying issues and their translation into new spatial regulatory and developmental policies.

Secondly, cities that have achieved a degree of success in addressing shelter-related urban issues tend to have recognized the issues and have related these issues to the need for city-wide, pro-poor policies as their starting point for interventions. In addition, such cities tend to have adhered, in a consistent and persistent way, to combinations of housing, urban and socio-economic policies over a period of several generations, while viewing these policies and their impacts in a framework of other macro-level policies.

Thirdly, although the above appears to indicate that the consistent application of policies does have tangible impacts, it should be noted that even under these conditions the issues of slums and urban poverty do not necessarily disappear. Rather, success in addressing low-income housing and shelter-related problems tends to serve as a new pull factor that extends the range of the city's migration collection basin further into the rural hinterlands and,

frequently, even into neighbouring or far-away countries. This, however, does not suggest that urban upgrading and the addressing of urban poverty are futile exercises. On the contrary, it indicates that urban policies can be highly successful. However, they need to be implemented within the context of broader urban-regional and macro-level socio-economic policies. Particularly where there are national or international components to the urbanization process, it would be unrealistic to expect that local-level urban policies alone can address all of the outcomes of migration patterns.

POLICY IMPACTS AND DEVELOPMENT PROSPECTS

The case studies clearly indicate that the world has largely begun to realize that forced evictions and slum clearance are no real option. Rather, wholesale urban renewal programmes, slum regularization, upgrading and community-based slum networking are increasingly attracting the attention of city managers worldwide. Administrative reforms for greater efficiency and reduction of corruption permit the implementation of pro-poor social policies with tangible successes in the area of social housing, transportation, education and public participation. In many cities of the developing world, however, the housing backlog is staggering, while urban populations continue to grow and current housing-delivery systems are hopelessly inadequate to even start addressing the issue.

The experiences of several cities indicate that inroads can be made with approaches that have a holistic character. These include *city-wide*, rather than ad hoc, slum improvement, environmental improvement, land regularization, housing finance provision, urban poverty reduction and partnerships with the private sector, NGOs and communities. The case studies further show the need for combining these actions with true decentralization and empowerment of local governments. Authority and resources need to be decentralized to government levels, allowing for the active involvement of both the beneficiaries and city managers in local priority setting, participatory decision-making and community-based involvement in implementation. However, if these processes are to succeed, a vital and crucial ingredient is the political will to make things happen.

There is no hope whatsoever for any municipality to even start addressing the issues related to slums if there is no clear recognition of their relation to urban poverty. Additionally, if there is no coherent city-wide set of urban policies to guide public interventions, whatever the actions undertaken, they will inevitably be ad hoc and ineffective in the long run in terms of scope and impacts.

Critical reflection on the lack of coherent housing, urban development and national macro-policies would help to reveal the reasons of world-wide failure to adequately address the spatial and socio-economic legacies of the past. Such a set of policies – particularly if they are founded on, and derived from, a coherent set of national urban policies linked to other national macro-policies – may go a long way to addressing slum and urban poverty issues. Urban policies cannot be effective if isolated from their national and international contexts. Critical reflection on policies would also be conducive to clarifying and framing the roles and jurisdictions of different levels of government, thus serving a clear purpose in resolving the current governance trap called 'decentralization', which all too frequently is used as the excuse to delegate difficult issues to a lower level.

Furthermore, to help balance the geographical distribution of urbanization, a strong set of national urban policies is necessary. The purpose of such policies would be to develop a balanced national urban hierarchy that can help to better spread urban growth, resulting from natural growth and rural to urban migration, while preventing unnecessary duplications of urban functions at the national level. The city, as the major venue for economic and political decision-making at the local, national and – increasingly – the international level, cannot afford to ignore the larger system of relationships.

NOTES

1   For the purposes of this report, 37 case studies were prepared, of which 29 were selected for summary in this part. The case study authors are listed in the Acknowledgements. Case study synopses, as well as an overview of case study major findings, have been prepared by Joseph Maseland of UN-Habitat.

2   Abidjan, Ahmedabad, Bangkok, Barcelona, Beirut, Bogotá, Cairo, Chengu, Colombo, Durban, Havana, Ibadan, Jakarta, Karachi, Kolkata, Los Angeles, Lusaka, Manila, Mexico City, Moscow, Nairobi, Naples, Newark, Phnom Penh, Quito, Rabat-Salé, Rio de Janeiro, São Paulo, Sydney.

3   Ahmedabad, Barcelona, Bogotá, Chengdu, Durban, Ibadan, Mexico City, Newark, Phnom Penh, Quito, Rabat-Salé, São Paulo and Sydney.

4   Abidjan, Bangkok, Cairo and Naples.

5   Havana, Jakarta, Karachi, Kolkata, Los Angeles, Lusaka, Manila, Nairobi, and Rio de Janeiro.

6   Beirut and, to a lesser extent, Bogotá.

7   Bogotá, Colombo, Ibadan, Mexico City, Naples, Newark, and Rabat-Salé.

8   Abidjan, Ahmedabad, Beirut, Bogotá, Cairo, Havana, Jakarta, Karachi, Kolkata, Los Angeles, Mexico City, Nairobi, Newark, Rabat-Salé, Rio de Janeiro and São Paulo.

9   Bangkok, Chengdu, Colombo and Naples.

10 Durban, Ibadan, Lusaka, Manila, Moscow, Phnom Penh, Quito and Sydney.

CASE STUDY HIGHLIGHTS

ABIDJAN, CÔTE D'IVOIRE

The growth of Abidjan – and, therefore, its slums – is associated with three phases. During the first phase, from the 1930s to the 1950s, Abidjan was set up as the colonial capital, economically linked to the Abidjan–Niger railway. The town consisted of three areas: the administrative centre and European quarters of Le Plateau, and two African districts: Treichville and Adjamé.

The second phase is associated with a number of socio-economic stimuli, including the opening of the Vridi canal and a deep-water port during the 1950s, and the establishment of industrial zones in the south-west and the commensurate growth of popular residential areas in the south.

The third phase is associated with sustained demographic growth from the 1960s onwards, and the emergence of new popular residential areas at the urban periphery.

Topographical factors, such as plateaux rising to 50 metres, added to spatial segregation of the urban area, placing major obstacles to urban structuring and functioning and considerable spatial imbalances between residential and working areas.

Slum dwellers represent one fifth of the Abidjan population. In response to a 1988 survey on why households chose to stay in slum areas, 23.7 per cent refused to answer. Among those who did answer, 69 per cent cited the cheaper cost of living; because they were born there or had family living in the slum (18 per cent); and proximity to work (8 per cent).

The case study recognizes three types of slums by area characteristics:

1   Areas distinguishable from formal residential areas only by their illegal land occupation forms: they primarily contain buildings of permanent materials and fair basic infrastructure. An example of such neighbourhoods is Zoe Bruno.
2   Poorly structured areas: these areas have more buildings of non-permanent materials and lower levels of infrastructure provision (for example, Vridi Canal, Zimbabwe and Blingue).
3   Irregular areas with largely non-permanent structures: these areas have little, if any, infrastructure (for example, Alliodan).

Similar to the tenure type of the Abidjan population at large, the majority of slum residents (75 per cent) are tenants, 18.7 per cent are owner occupiers and 5.8 per cent stay free of charge.

In 1995, the urban population of Abidjan had grown to 2.7 million, with an annual growth rate of 5 per cent (down from 11 per cent during the 1970s) and with a transnational demographic collection basin spanning a large area of West Africa. Despite the slowing down of growth, the numbers of urban poor, in absolute terms, will continue to rise in the foreseeable future.

The residents of slum quarters are highly heterogeneous, with 40 per cent of Côte d'Ivoire origin; 20 per cent from Burkina Faso; 9 per cent from Mali; 9 per cent from Ghana; and Togo and Bénin together accounting for 12.3 per cent. The density in slums varies from one area to another: Zimbabwe lies at the top with 340 inhabitants per hectare; Zoé Bruno has 254.5 inhabitants per hectare; and Vridi-Canal has 206 inhabitants per hectare. Blingué has the least dense concentration of 69.6 inhabitants per hectare. On the whole, slums are stigmatized and are the focus of unfavourable prejudice as dens of highwaymen, drug addicts and the hangouts of impoverished foreigners who are incapable of living within the city legally.

Although the authorities previously dealt with slums through outright clearance, slums are, today, the focus of sustained development efforts. Since the 1980s, slum regularization has been implemented with assistance from the World Bank, aiming at:

*   basic infrastructure provision;
*   improvement of land security;
*   development of economic activities; and
*   promotion of community development.

This new context provides more tolerance and, to some extent, prevents slum clearance. A shortcoming is the ad hoc nature of these interventions and the relative lack of participatory approaches.

Although the urban interventions of the public authorities have led to progress in some areas – notably, in the accessibility of social services – these efforts over the past few years have fallen well behind of expectations. In the absence of a comprehensive public policy on urban restructuring, slum regularization and the genuine involvement of all stakeholders, the slum issues to be faced and the number of poor will both remain significant. Unless public policy addresses the issues in a comprehensive manner, drawing on the capabilities and will of all stakeholders, many of the developmental efforts may remain largely marginal.

AHMEDABAD, INDIA

Ahmedabad has been a trading city throughout history. Eastern Ahmedabad, within the Ahmedabad Municipal Corporation (AMC) limits, but outside of the walled city, was the first area to industrialize, with textile mills near to the railway. The earliest low-income housing were the *chawls*, single-room housing units built for the industrial workers. During the late 19th and the early 20th centuries *chawls* mushroomed as the accommodation for the (migrant) workers. Controls kept rents extremely low, discouraging maintenance, and many *chawls* deteriorated rapidly. This was particularly the case following a crisis in the textile industry and the closure of the factories. From the 1950s onwards, urban growth largely took place in the eastern and, particularly, the western urban peripheries, where illegal occupation of marginal areas represents the housing option for newly arrived migrants and other economically weaker urban groups.

Although migrants who arrived after independence largely settled in informal settlements at the urban periphery, *chawls* are still present in large numbers. Eastern Ahmedabad has about 44 per cent of the total housing units in the AMC region, with 54.8 per cent of the total dwelling units in the category of *chawls* and slums. It accounts for 75 per cent of the chawl units and 47 per cent of the slum units in the city.

In the case study, a slum is defined as a compact area with a collection of poorly built tenements, mostly of a temporary nature, crowded together and usually with inadequate sanitary and with drinking water facilities in unhygienic conditions.

There are two dominant types of low-income residential areas found in the city: *chawls* or residential units, originally built in the mill premises for workers; and slums that represent illegal occupation of marginal areas of the city. The latter typically lack facilities and basic amenities and are found along riverfronts, in low-lying areas, on vacant private or government land.

Tenure patterns and percentages are unclear but are closely related to the possession of a ration card (71 to 75 per cent of households) and/or an AMC photo pass (2.5 to 10 per cent of households). Close to 28 per cent had neither and their tenure status remains undefined. These figures roughly appear to reflect the following percentages: owner (70 per cent), renter (about 20 per cent) and undefined (8 per cent).

The percentage of Ahmedabad *housing* categorized as slums increased from 17.2 per cent in 1961 to 22.8 per cent in 1971 and 25.6 per cent in 1991. It is estimated that 17.1 per cent of Ahmedabad's population lived in slums in 1971. This rose to an estimated 21.4 per cent in 1982. The last estimate, based on a population census for the year 1991, nevertheless indicates that 40 per cent of households lived in slums and *chawls*.

Muslims, scheduled castes (SCs) and other backward castes (OBCs) constitute 91 per cent of the slum households, and more than 95 per cent of slum dwellers are migrants, indicating how rural poverty levels are now spilling over into urban areas. Often fleeing rural inter-caste exploitation and debts, slum populations require their children to contribute to the household income. Victimized by the police, municipal authorities and the upper classes alike, this group represents a particularly vulnerable section of society.

A series of shifts to improve the conditions in low-income settlements have occurred since the 1950s. From initial slum clearance, the focus is now more on environmental and slum upgrading and community-based slum networking. With 40 per cent of its population of more than 3 million living in slums, the AMC functioned, until the early 1990, as a small welfare state. It deliberately made life easier for the poor by applying a regime that did not enforce anti-poor regulations, while tolerating squatter settlements on public and private land and allowing public space to be used for income-generating activities, with forced evictions rare. The AMC even constructed a small number of low-income houses.

An amendment to the Municipal Corporation Act during the 1970s obliged the AMC to spend 10 per cent of its revenue on improving basic services in slums and *chawls*. Based on a soft international loan, the AMC extended urban services to slums in its eastern suburbs. Under the Slum Improvement Partnership, the AMC now coordinates and facilitates the activities of other agencies, while picking up a considerable proportion of the costs in an effort to link slum upgrading with city-level service-delivery standards.

Nevertheless, the AMC had still failed to fully include many of the new insights in their overall urban planning. It is, in particular, their unwillingness to grant security of tenure for periods of longer than 10 years that sends out strong negative signals. Furthermore, the labyrinth of regulatory mechanisms and the complex procedures of the urban planning process have not helped the poor either. Although the AMC has not executed wholesale slum demolitions, public housing agencies have not provided city-level shelter programmes for the poor.

BANGKOK, THAILAND

Thailand has experienced low urbanization as rural–urban migration has been comparatively very low, and excess rural population invaded forestland rather than migrated to urban centres. In 1990, less than 19 per cent of the population lived in urban areas, and the rise to 31 per cent by 2001 was largely the result of the conversion of rural districts to urban municipalities. Bangkok's major growth took place after World War II, increasing by a factor of 3.5 between 1958 and 1999 to 5.6 million. It expanded well beyond its administrative boundaries, and today the Bangkok Metropolitan Region (BMR) refers to Bangkok proper and five adjacent provinces. The growth of slums, however, is less associated with rural–urban migration than with natural growth. Of Thailand's slum population, 62 per cent is concentrated in Bangkok proper and 22 per cent in the BMR. This is explained by the fact that the urbanization of the 1960s focused on Bangkok, and only later on the BMR via the highways and development corridors of the expanding city. With the exception of Pathum Thani, with large numbers of slum dwellers along the canals, there are comparatively few squatters in Bangkok (16 per cent) and very few street dwellers and homeless people.

The National Housing Authority (NHA) defines a slum as 'a dirty, damp, swampy or unhealthy area with overcrowded buildings and dwellings which can be harmful for health or lives or can be a source of unlawful or immoral actions, with a minimum number of 30 housing units per 1600 [square metres]'.

On the other hand, the BMA defines a slum as 'an overcrowded, non-orderly and dilapidated community with unample environment which can be harmful to health and lives and with a minimum of 15 housing units per 1600 [square metres]'.

While slums and squatter settlements are considered similar terms, squatter settlements are largely sited on illegally occupied lands, with slums being mostly on rented land. There are few cases where both land and house are owned by the dwellers.

Slum areas are on the decrease (1020 areas in 1985 and 866 in 2000). Many slums were demolished under the pressure of rising land prices, while few new slums could be established as alternative land use was more profitable. Furthermore, the proportion of slum dwellers decreased, despite growth in their absolute number. While, in 1974, 24 per cent of Bangkok's housing units were considered slums, in 1994 this number was estimated at a mere 6 per cent. This is believed to be largely the result of more affordable access to public and market housing, and the percentage that could not afford a house in the open market decreased from 80 per cent in 1980 to 50 per cent in 1993. An additional factor is that during the larger migration wave of the 1960s and 1970s, wood was a cheap and readily available building material. With a ban on tree felling, the dilapidated wooden slum house is slowly disappearing and more permanent materials are cheaper.

Crowding in Bangkok's slums is, on average, three times higher than in non-slum areas, with a dependent population of about 30 per cent (below 15 or over 60 years old). Almost 60 per cent of the population in slums were born in their existing slum. Although access to the formal housing market is now more affordable, about three-quarters of the current slum population cannot afford the approximately US$2000 (20 per cent) down payment for formal housing. However, only a minority of the slum dwellers are poor.

The chronology of low-income housing and slum policies during the last 54 years may be summarized as follows:

- *1948–1958*: The government constructed 3462 housing units for the urban population as part of its social welfare policy.
- *1960–1971*: Public housing in the form of high-rise apartments was built to replace slums; but funding restrictions limited the output.
- *1970s*: The establishment of the NHA in 1975 came along with international funding for slum improvements. This was largely non-productive due to too narrow physical objectives.
- *1980s*: The concept of land for housing the poor was introduced. The logic is that if land is given to the poor, they will have a sense of belonging and develop their own homes and community. As a result, there were some land-sharing and slum relocation projects.
- *1990s*: Slums became more recognized through the involvement of the people and the development of savings groups to generate loans for slum dwellers.

A well-planned Bangkok would have been possible if the high-rise development option had been more widely promoted and accepted. Instead, horizontal development with the commensurate costs of additional infrastructure became the norm. Revisiting this position to achieve more intensive land use is behind much of the slum clearance and evictions. The slum problem of Bangkok is fairly limited, with only 6 per cent of the total housing considered slum. Almost all households are connected to water and electricity; the education levels of slums dwellers are improving and few slum dwellers are below the poverty line. The issues of land use, land sharing and land renting as solutions to the unacceptable housing and living conditions should be further explored as a means of equitably and effectively dealing with Bangkok's slum issues.

BARCELONA, SPAIN

Barcelona, for legal reasons unable to expand beyond its medieval walls, became an intensely overcrowded city during the 19th century. After these restrictions were lifted, the old city gradually became an industrial district with many slums. During the 20th century, three major expansion bursts occurred in Barcelona:

1   The 1929 world exhibition brought about an urban boom, with an influx of immigrants without commensurate housing provision, leading to the creation of shanties around the town.
2   Industrialization from 1945 onwards created a new industrial ring around the town and drew a new wave of immigrants. A large quantity of poor-quality housing was built that rapidly developed into slums.
3   The 1970s saw a third ring of industrial and housing development on a metropolitan scale.

In Barcelona, there is no formal definition of a slum, as such areas ceased to formally exist. Nevertheless, there are areas in the city with higher indices of social inequality and there are marginalized people; but both are dispersed throughout the city and there are no ghettos as such.

There have been *slums* in the old city of Barcelona in one form or another for centuries, but the development of slum conditions with the typical degraded housing, lack of services and concentrations of social inequality in the old city date from the mid 19th-century expansion of the city, and the consequent out-migration of the high-income population from this area.

The *shantytowns*, which no longer exist, date from the rapid growth of the city's population during the 20th century, which was not accompanied by an adequate growth in housing. They largely concerned self-built structures without urban services, in areas of wasteland around the then edges of the city.

The slum conditions in some of the new *multifamily blocks* built from the 1950s onwards resulted from attempts to re-house the shantytown dwellers without dealing with essential problems relating to their social exclusion and, furthermore, from the breaking up of communities and mixing people from different communities in the same blocks.

At present, there are temporary *gypsy encampments* in areas of waste ground in and around the city. The inhabitants live in lorries and the settlements lack all formal urban services. These encampments are of a recurrent and temporary nature.

Although there are no longer believed to be slum areas or ghettos as such in Barcelona, there are areas with higher concentrations of marginalized people. The whole of the old city, and a large part of the periphery, is considered to be – if not a slum – at best, a disagreeable area, with a few exceptions of neighbourhoods that have been gentrified.

A significantly high proportion of the inhabitants of marginal areas are tenants (some 80 per cent), although reliable figures do not exist. Subletting is extremely common; especially in the marginal areas, the majority of tenants lack a written contract and have limited rights in the face of unscrupulous landlords. Tenancy with formal contract constitutes 26.5 per cent, while informal contracts constitute 47 per cent of the tenants in marginal areas.

Although Barcelona has lost population since the 1970s, it has not ceased to be an important destination for immigrants from other parts of Spain and, more recently, from overseas, mainly Latin America and North Africa.

The populations of the different areas with slum housing share certain basic characteristics: low average incomes and relatively low levels of education. However, the populations of the different areas vary in a number of respects with regard to other indicators.

Despite economic growth since the 1960s, the conditions in the slum areas improved very little until after the transition to democracy during the mid 1970s when, gradually, policies were introduced that were aimed at addressing the physical and social problems of the city. The following decades witnessed the eradication of all shantytowns, improvements in living conditions in the housing blocks, and, from the end of the 1980s, important improvements in many areas of the old city. Barcelona's municipal interventions have been instrumental in improving physical and socio-economic conditions in many (former) slum areas. Key to these successes were the combination of wholesale urban renewal programmes in specific areas, combined with major social components aimed at combating poverty. In general terms, public institutions (central, regional and local level) tended to deal with the major urban redevelopments, while NGOs worked at the individual household or community levels. Policy commitment, careful planning, coordination among agencies and participation of affected groups determined the success of the interventions.

The policies that are still underway and that are planned for the future, although often contentious in a number of ways, continue to have important effects in improving living conditions and reducing poverty.

BEIRUT, LEBANON

Prior to 1950, the growth of Beirut and its slums largely took place in waves associated with displacement and the establishment of camps or low-income housing for international refugees (from Armenia and Syria during the 1920s and Palestine around 1948). Historically, these are the oldest slums, although these camps have now all disappeared, except for the Palestinian camps that developed into the city's current main slums. Between 1950 and 1972, successive waves of rural-to-urban migration, notably from southern Lebanon and in the wake of military conflict, created slums:

* in the form of refugee camps;
* on peri-urban agricultural lands; and
* by the squatting of land.

During this period, the total population of Beirut quadrupled from 300,000 to 1,100,000.

A third in-migration wave, during the Civil War (1975 to 1990), consisted of displaced people who occupied empty buildings or entire neighbourhoods in Beirut that were abandoned for security reasons by the original occupants, or who squatted on large plots of vacant land.

No formal definition of the slum phenomenon exists; but for the purpose of the case study, the following definition was adopted: areas of the city where the majority of residents live in precarious economic and/or political conditions, with high levels of vulnerability, and where services and living conditions appear to be lower than in other sections of the city.

Due to the complex 20th-century history of Lebanon, slums are perhaps best categorized by the cause and period of their establishment. This leads to three categories:

1 Camps and low-income areas for international refugees (1920 to 1955).
2 Housing areas for rural–urban migrants (1950 to 1975).
3 Squatter settlements of the displaced during and after the Civil War (1975 to 1990).

The first two categories were nearly all located in the industrial north-east of Beirut. Shortly after 1975, most of these residents were evicted and they moved to squat in the southern suburbs on empty green areas and beach resorts. Their numbers were compounded by rural-to-urban migration waves in the wake of two Israeli invasions and the occupation of southern Lebanon, thus helping to create huge informal squatter settlements in the southern Beirut region. The camps and low-income areas have, over the years, developed into high-density areas with structures of permanent materials and reasonable levels of service provision. The illegal squatter settlements are also largely built of permanent materials, some on comparatively large plots of land. While land ownership is often legal, land subdivisions and construction violate various urban regulations and building codes.

Just as the slum typology is extremely diverse, so are tenure type and legality, which vary from UN-protected refugee camps, on the one hand – often with owner-occupied buildings on land rented by the UN – to illegal settlements with land squatting and illegally constructed buildings, on the other. Nevertheless, and perhaps as the outcome of a sustained lack of policy other than *laissez-faire*, all slums have become subject to a similar large-scale rental market. Since 1982, renting has become the primary method for accessing housing. Other options, including squatting inside camps or in informal settlements, both inside the city as in the suburbs, do exit.

The slum dynamics of the post-war era are basically not different from the conflict years. The 'return policies' of the Ministry of Displaced in the post-war era are aimed at ensuring the return of people. The ministry has paid indemnities and displaced most squatters from informal settlements, returning properties to their original owners. Many are returning; others choose to sell or rent to family, or, more often, rent to migrant workers, leading to congestion and unusually high percentages of a mobile male population. Poor living conditions prevail, particularly poor services, pollution and lack of social infrastructure. The general attitude of municipal authorities to such areas is hostile, as many residents are not voters and are considered 'illegal'. Currently, an estimated 20 per cent of Beirut lives in 24 listed slum areas, though this does not account for all those living in poverty and/or poor conditions, since many shacks are spread out over the city outside of the recognized slums.

Today, all of Beirut's slums display an increasingly similar demographic composition, housing heterogeneous populations that include members of migrant and displaced groups (but not refugees), as well as migrant labour and low-income Beirut families. New arrivals – especially migrant workers – are largely segregated, inevitably on the basis of their poverty, and they contribute to the homogenization of the socio-political characteristics of these areas. However, these new arrivals cannot hide the effects of the religious segregation generated by the civil war and other military conflicts that have led to major population reshuffling, and the partial or complete destruction of a number of slums. In those particular slums where evictions have occurred, post-war policies that encourage the return of displaced families are recreating new religious mixes, thus distinguishing them from other war slums where no such evictions have occurred. Displaced groups, city-wide, constitute roughly one third of the population and are generally young, with a higher number of children per household and higher illiteracy rates, and are engaged in low-skill menial employment or are unemployed.

Up to 1975, policy proposals in Lebanon often followed international trends brought by foreign experts along the hygienist and modernist schools. However, these proposals never materialized and, historically, policy actions were only taken (by international organizations) to resolve refugee settlement crises. Armenian refugees of the 1920s were housed in thousands of tents on empty terrain, situated in the north-eastern extremity of the city; but they were gradually relocated and consolidated over time in low-income neighbourhoods with better living conditions. In 1948, waves of Palestinian refugees occupied spaces in the camps vacated by Armenians before they were relocated on special United Nations-administered sites, where they were first allowed tents and, later, more permanent buildings. They remain, until today, in these special camp areas. During the 1920s, the Syriac population settled in self-help structures in the Syriac camp, in an area in eastern Beirut. Here they remained until 1995, when the Catholic Syriac Church decided to replace camp houses with a new building complex.

Despite a long history of serious income inequality in Lebanese society – that, to some extent, has been at the root of massive rural-to-urban migration – the period up to 1975 is characterized by a virtual lack of social policy or housing interventions. Public initiatives, such as the construction of two public housing projects in the Armenian quarters, depended upon specific individuals, rather than upon policy. Policies taken to address the internal population movements of the 1970s and 1980s were ineffective, slum clearance often took the form of political revenge, and upgrading initiatives never reached the level of implementation. During the 1990s, one project – Elissar – was proposed to relocate/upgrade a number of squatter settlements located on prime sea-front land. However, the project was never implemented and its social component was gradually downplayed, even in discussions about implementation. Thus, the civil war, and the (re)construction projects and policies in its wake, often generated new important patterns of displacement. Since the end of the civil war, several studies point out increases in poverty; currently, 25 per cent of the population lives below the poverty level.

Large-scale infrastructure projects are seen by central and local authorities as an appropriate occasion to halt slum development or even for slum clearance. Few, if any, upgrading projects have ever been undertaken, and slums are typically addressed with policies that call for their eradication. The highly visible southern suburb slums have been the focus of efforts, perhaps because the squatted lands have high market values, and because of the large numbers of people involved and the high political profile. Throughout Beirut, it is often the legal issue that is used as the justification not to intervene (for example, the illegal nature of developments and internal roads on private lands). When minor efforts are made to provide services, it is because of the slums' proximity to more 'regular' communities. With the current perception that many slum dwellers are 'illegal', and the associated lack of municipal representation or voter constituency, the outlook for the future is bleak.

BOGOTÁ, COLOMBIA

As in most cities around the world that host slums areas, the slums of Bogotá are largely the result of rapid population increase without the housing and services provision that such growth demands. During the past few decades, Bogotá has seen sustained, rapid demographic growth through waves of rural-to-urban migration in the wake of general impoverishment and violence. The Bogotá urban perimeter expanded rapidly through illegal subdivisions, occupation and the development of marginal areas by immigrants. Bogotá's inner-city slums, on the other hand, are mostly the result of urban transformation processes, whereby certain downtown areas underwent progressive social and physical deterioration and, increasingly, accommodated lower-hierarchy social strata and economic activities.

Slums are defined as spontaneous settlements on the city margins that started to show up during the first years of the accelerated urbanization process, and that were manifested as groups of shacks or provisional housing; as resident communities in precarious housing conditions; and as urban settlements in which the terrain's occupation and its development are conducted without any plan and without the corresponding permits and licences that are officially required.

The slums of Bogotá can be classified as the outcome of:

- unplanned and informal urbanization through subdivisions in peripheral and marginal areas, largely characterized by an initial lack of physical and social infrastructure, but which are often – within a few years – improved by the city administration or through self-help (or combinations thereof);
- squatter settlements with generally more dire physical and social circumstances (although this category historically has had a relatively low importance);
- inner-city urban deterioration zones that came about through the progressive move of 19th-century industrial, military and other functions adjacent to the traditional urban centre to more appropriate locations, and the social, economic and physical deterioration that followed in the wake of this urban abandonment.

Although the latter concerns a relatively small proportion of the urban area, these zones stand out by their strategic location and the gravity of their social conditions. They are primarily associated with crowded and dilapidated tenement houses, commercial room-renting in marginal housing and critical social situations of poverty, drugs and delinquency.

The tenure type in the slums is closely related to geographical location and type of housing. The inner-city slums are, typically, rental housing of dilapidated tenement blocks, whereas the squatter settlements and 'pirate neighbourhoods' of the peri-urban areas are owner-occupied. The latter tend to have a more transient nature in the sense that four decades of experience with this type of illegal urban expansion means that the very deficient conditions are often only the phenomena of the first few years. After this, gradual self-help and community improvements bring them to higher standards in terms of infrastructure and housing quality.

With an upward trend in the share of the population living below the poverty line – 19.4 per cent of the total population in 1994 and 23.0 per cent in 2000 – combined with a steady increase in urbanization and an increase of the population of Bogotá, it is expected that the proliferation of new slums will continue well into the future.

There is no clear information about social and urban homogeneity in the slum areas. There are, however, indications that the pronounced urban isolation in which the slum dwellers live – the difficulty of access to physical and social infrastructure – and the high levels of violence compared to other areas of the city, generate patterns of depressed urban areas where the inhabitants, despite their great heterogeneity, look for common interests originating from their unsatisfied basic needs. Where underlying social structures get stronger, there is a degree of empowerment that increases their ability to act and react. The non-slum dwellers would appear to view the impoverished urban groups as undesirables, expressed in the specific terms applied to describe them – *desechable* (disposable), *gamin* (street boy), *vagabundo* (tramp), *populacho* (commoner) – that are highly associated with delinquency, unproductiveness and uselessness.

During the past few years, remarkably effective actions involving urban regeneration and recuperation have been conducted in the central areas. New legal instruments and tools paved the way for reforms and political transformations at the local level and improved the quality of life for many population segments. In 2001 alone, urban improvement policies for Bogotá, including administrative reforms for greater efficiency and corruption reduction, have permitted the implementation of social policies with tangible successes in the areas of social housing, transportation, education and public participation.

With a dire need to address a growing housing deficit that currently stands at more than 500,000 units, and to stop the process of informal urbanization in the peri-urban areas, Bogotá has a daunting task before it. The combination of a growing political basis for real involvement of the affected communities and improved knowledge of the social problems of communities in the peri-urban areas will, perhaps, provide the all-important lessons for improving the living conditions in the slums, and may reflect the substantial change in political will and in the management of poverty within Bogotá.

CAIRO, EGYPT

Most Cairo slums resulted from explosive post-World War II population growth. But it wasn't until the mid 1960s that slums really started to appear, with little official resistance to informal and clearly illegal subdivision and construction on the agricultural lands at the urban fringes. Almost without exception, the slums started off from existing satellite villages because rural housing was unregulated, and uncontrolled development could thus be 'overlooked'. During the 1967 to 1973 period of military conflict, all formal development in Cairo froze as the war effort soaked up most of the financial resources available. Demographic growth, however, continued unabated, including evacuees from the Canal Zone, and informal settlement growth boomed. Substantial urban fringe areas, already largely subdivided, were sold during this period, expanding the urban limits. This was further compounded by expansion from the satellite villages.

The 1974 to 1985 oil boom in the Gulf States and the subsequent remittances of Egyptian workers there provided investments for the population groups attracted by Cairo's urban informal areas and caused further massive informal housing activity at the urban fringes.

During the period of 1986 to 2000, the process consolidated with a reduction in new land for residential purposes due to:

- the drying-up of foreign remittances;
- significant falls in population growth rates; and
- strict control over agricultural-to-residential land conversion.

Only recently, the Egyptian government has formally recognized the existence of 'deteriorated and underserved urban residential areas' and applies the term *aashiwa'i* (random) to them, indicating their unplanned and illegal nature.

The main slum types in Cairo are as follows:

- *Informal settlements on private, former agricultural lands.* These consist of private residences built on land purchased informally from farmers at the urban fringes on informally subdivided plots and without building permits. Housing is generally of a good, permanent type, often incremental and at places even high rise (10 to 14 storeys). Although initially ignored by the government, it has now become a criminal act to utilize scarce agricultural lands for residential purposes.
- *Informal settlements on desert state lands.* These consist of private residences built informally on state-owned, vacant desert land. Strictly speaking, this is land invasion and land squatting and construction without permits; but semi-legality emerged on the basis of customary rights and nominal land rents paid. Government policy is to grant *post-facto* legalization. Housing quality and crowding conditions tend to be worse that in informal settlements on private, former agricultural lands.
- *Deteriorated sections of the old city core.* These comprise pre-1860 sections of medieval Cairo, with a mixture of dilapidated and sound buildings, with the former buildings often being the result of ownership disputes and lack of maintenance resulting from tight rent controls and non-profitability of rental. Residents are generally very poor; but the population in these areas is declining as a result of increasing conversion

of residential into commercial spaces and the collapse of entire buildings due to lack of maintenance.

- *Deteriorated urban pockets.* Various inner-city areas of Cairo, notably those from the early 20th century, have pockets of dilapidated one- to three-storey structures that house poor families. These are characterized by insecure tenure and limited housing investment. They generally attract poor families seeking the cheapest possible housing solutions. Numerically, this group is very insignificant.

City-wide, the tenure types in slums can roughly be divided into 50 per cent owner-occupied and 50 per cent rented. No figures are available on current slum dynamics.[1]

In Cairo, urban poverty is not notably concentrated in particular geographic areas. Poor and ultra poor families are found mixed in with lower- and middle-income families in a wide number of older core neighbourhoods and in the vast informal areas of Greater Cairo. In most informal areas, there is a small percentage of well-off entrepreneurs and professionals. This spatial income heterogeneity is due to such historical factors as lack of residential mobility, rent control and imperfect real estate markets.

A 'Master Plan of Cairo' was published in 1956 that led, in 1958, to the Nasr City scheme, an ambitious desert fringe development organized through a public-sector concession company affiliated with the Ministry of Housing. A public housing programme was launched, and by 1965 the Cairo Governorate had constructed almost 15,000 units for low-income families. It was only during the period of 1974 to 1985 that the government started to address the booming informal areas by preserving state and agricultural lands from encroachments. The Egyptian government had only then officially recognized how vast the informal areas were, and that there were deteriorated or underserved urban residential areas, and launched its new towns policy. Starting in 1992, after some poorer urban areas were perceived as breeding grounds for political instability, the government finally launched a programme to improve informal or *aashwa'i* areas throughout Egypt.

Despite some successes in slowing down the further encroachment of Cairo on its urban fringes, informal building is still going on. In spite of the massive investments required and the rather limited success in attracting population to date, the policy of creating modern planned desert settlements remains the Government's ultimate solution to the phenomenon of urban informality, the idea being to offer alternatives which will absorb the millions who are in or would otherwise go to informal areas of Greater Cairo. Recent comparisons of satellite pictures indicate that informal encroachment on agricultural lands continues at a rate triple that of 'formal' expansion.

CHENGDU, CHINA

Since the 1950s, there have been three distinct types of slums in Chengdu, each corresponding to a specific phase in economic development and policy change. The first slums of Chengdu were formed on the banks of the Fu and Nan rivers. Originally established as low-rent flats on the fringe of the city, from the 1970s onwards they became inner-city slums with the growth of the city and the spontaneous settlement of rural migrants and returning youth sent to the countryside during the Cultural Revolution. Although by no means destitute, location, low levels of income and education and a poor living environment contributed to their social exclusion. These slums were eradicated during the late 1990s, together with other inner-city substandard housing, and the inhabitants benefited from favourable housing-and-relocation policies and strategies.

The second phase in slum formation in Chengdu came as a result of economic reforms starting in the late 1980s. These reforms created much sudden unemployment and poverty, and a new group of suburban poor whose employer-provided pre-1970s row housing and flats became substandard and are now considered slums. Although access to physical and social infrastructure is more or less guaranteed, and while the entire areas cannot be considered slums, they are often perceived as slums by association. The improvement of their living conditions is contingent upon new sources of employment.

Rapid urbanization and urban development during the 1990s have also created a category of about 1 million low-educated peri-urban dwellers known as the 'floating population'. Recruited on a temporary basis from the rural areas, most live in rental accommodation provided by farmers on the urban border. Although adequate in terms of size and structure, they are located outside the scope and coverage of municipal services. Therefore, their long-term social, economic and living conditions are of direct concern to the municipality in terms of public health and the environment. Their status as non-resident is cause for social exclusion, as is their role and share in petty crime and prostitution.

Slums are simply defined as shanties in low-lying areas. More than 60 per cent of Chengdu's slum housing belongs to those residing in them. Of the remaining 40 per cent, all had secure tenure; but many owners of the shanties did not have legally recognized property rights. The floating population tends to live on the fringe of the city either by renting their accommodation from farmers or by constructing sheds and shacks on uncontrolled or unused land. A small percentage is homeless, choosing to sleep in the inner city in such public places as bus and train stations.

The numbers of slums and slum dwellers in Chengdu are rapidly decreasing due to effective low-income housing and urbanization policies and strategies. Slum dwellers include those without income; those with no work ability (long illnesses, injuries or the handicapped); those with no one to care for them (retirees); those people waiting for new jobs owing to the collapse of their enterprises; low-paid employees with heavy family burdens; and people who receive relief funds.

Between 20 and 30 per cent of the population living in slums have a criminal record and tend to be treated as social outcasts. Residents of slum areas also tend to have less financial security. The combination of these two factors results in higher degrees of social discrimination.

Recently, China has been pursuing a deliberate policy to raise urbanization from 36 to 50 per cent in the coming years as a means of stimulating rural and urban economic development and productivity. The strategy is to focus on 18,000 existing secondary and tertiary towns through the development of markets, infrastructure and services. Since 1996, China has invested heavily in promoting employment, eradicating poverty, and setting up social security and holistic policies of city-wide upgrading and eradication of urban poverty and slums.

Chengdu started its lowest living standards guarantee system in 1997, and implemented it in all of its areas of jurisdiction. From 2001, it focused on poor living conditions in the city centre's single-storey houses, implementing a large-scale rehabilitation, relocation and 'low-rent housing programme'. The households whose living conditions are below the poverty line standards specified by the city government can apply for apartments appropriate to their needs, with the government paying the rent. In 2001, less than 500 households filed an application with the city government and were provided with appropriate houses. The city government has planned to provide 1000 households with new 'low-rent apartments' in 2002.

Chengdu's successes in poverty alleviation, slum eradication, urban transformation and environmental improvement of the city and its rivers is based on a holistic, city-wide approach that emphasizes the thorough understanding of the underlying causes of poverty. The eradication of inner-city slums involving 100,000 urban poor and the alleviation of their poverty were successfully carried out through an affordable housing policy involving one-time equity grants, and through parallel improvements to urban infrastructure, transport and the environment.

The participatory approach adopted in the slum relocation initiative, involving the residents themselves as well as other social groups and the public at large, was a key contributing factor to the success of the endeavour. Public meetings and consultations raised the awareness of citizens of the need to simultaneously address the issues of slums, urban poverty, urban renewal and environmental improvement.

The issue of migrant workers will still require more harmonized approaches to economic development, social services and welfare. While many migrant workers witness an increase in cash income by coming to work in the city or on the fringe of the city, they represent the most recent trend in urbanization. Most of them inhabit the grey area that falls between urban and rural jurisdictions, calling for a concerted approach to rural and urban development policies.

Another possible aspect to Chengdu's success is its three-tier local government management system that covers governance issues of a metropolitan area with unusual effectiveness. The first tier – the metro-level – is in charge of formulating macro-policies and overseeing their implementation by subordinate departments. The second tier – the district government and its subordinate departments – is in charge of implementing the policies established by the first tier. The third tier – neighbourhood committees – is in charge of specific political, social and economic affairs.

COLOMBO, SRI LANKA

Slums came into existence with the expansion of export trade associated with the rubber boom after World War II, especially during the Korean War in 1953. The character of Colombo changed in keeping with the new economic demands for warehousing, workers' housing and road networks. Colombo became more congested and the city elite moved out into more spacious residential areas in the suburbs. The central part of Colombo became characterized by predominantly low-income residential areas, mainly slums, and the northern and eastern parts contained most of the shanties. Slums and shanties are the most common types. Slums on the high lands of the old city consist of the oldest low-income housing – mostly from the 1930s and with a definite legal occupancy status. Shanties along canal banks and road reserves have emerged since independence in 1948 onwards, and consist of unauthorized and improvised shelter without legal rights of occupancy of the land and structures.

Although there are no formal definitions as such, four categories are recognized:

1   *Slums*: these are old deteriorating tenements or subdivided derelict houses. The slum tenements, built mostly of permanent materials, are very often single roomed and compactly arranged in back-to-back rows. The occupants have a definite legal status of occupancy.
2   *Shanties*: these consist of improvised and un-authorized shelter, constructed by the urban squatters on state or privately owned land, without any legal rights of occupancy. The areas are badly serviced and very often insanitary.
3   *Unserviced semi-urban neighbourhoods*: these are badly serviced residential areas in the suburban areas of Colombo and secondary towns. One difference from the squatter areas is that residents of these settlements have definite legal titles, and the sizes of the plots are relatively larger than the shanties.
4   *Labour lines*: these are derelict housing areas that belong to the local authority or government agencies, and that are occupied by temporary or casual labourers. These settlements are in an insanitary and derelict condition due to lack of maintenance over a long period of time.

About half of the urban poor have no security of tenure (unauthorized occupation or user permit only), 37 per cent have freehold and 13 per cent have leasehold.

Under the impacts of strong political will and effective housing improvement, regularization, community development and self-help efforts, the growth of slums and shanties has been brought under control, and clear impacts have been made in improving the general housing conditions of the urban poor.

Close to half of Colombo's urban population consists of communities that have been living in inadequate housing conditions for many years, and 16 per cent of the urban poor depend on poverty-relief assistance. Most economically active slum dwellers are unskilled workers or petty traders or hawkers. Youth unemployment rates are around 60 per cent, and some 20 per cent of households receive public financial assistance. All slum dwellers are subject to serious discrimination.

Prior to 1970, there was minimal government intervention as the housing of the poor either concerned privately owned or illegal property. Between 1970 and 1977, the government recognized and took action regarding the housing issues of the urban poor, including interventions in ensuring housing rights, direct housing construction and the provision of tenure rights. Between 1978 and 1994, a shift from provision towards enabling, recognition of the role of local authorities, promotion of community participation, and self-help and establishment of nation-wide housing programmes occurred. In this period, the One Hundred Thousand Houses, the One Million Houses and the 1.5 Million Houses programmes were established with strong political support from the central government. The post-1994 period saw interventions including the private sector in housing provision, urban renewal programmes and urban settlements improvement programmes.

The principles of the One Million Houses Programme clearly promoted an enabling environment (legal, institutional, financial and technical support) for people to improve their own houses. In particular, the institutional mechanism created by the government to implement the national housing programmes was very effective. The establishment of the National Housing Development Authority under the Ministry of Housing and Construction, with district offices of the authority for each administrative district of the country, and the linking of programme activities at local level through urban and rural local authorities, were notable initiatives in this context. Bottom-up information flow and decision-making processes were encouraged. Numerous shanty settlements have been regularized and improved, and very few shanties have been built in Colombo over the past 20 years.

DURBAN, SOUTH AFRICA

Durban's current pattern of informal settlement is largely a product of apartheid factors during the second half of the 20th century. The 1913 Land Act alienated Africans from most of the land, forcing them wholesale into wage employment for survival. During the 1930s, massive informal settlements formed just beyond the urban fringes. In addition, the creation, during the 1960s and 1970s, of 'independent states' adjacent to city boundaries, and including formal African residential areas, further spurred the growth of informal settlements along the urban edge. Informal settlements grew as a result of a lack of housing alternatives, as well as the devastating drought of the late 1970s and early 1980s, which forced people to seek livelihoods in urban areas.

Newer settlements that emerged during the late 1980s and early 1990s have tended to be smaller and more clandestine land invasions closer to the city centre – often within former Asian residential areas or on marginal land at risk from floods or landslides. In many cases, these newer settlements were developed by households who fled political violence.

Recent estimates have suggested that approximately 35 per cent of informal structures are located within pockets of formal settlements; 55 per cent are located on the periphery of formal settlements; and 10 per cent are peri-urban in location.

Slums are defined as erstwhile formal settlements that have degenerated to such an extent that there exists a need to rehabilitate them to acceptable levels. While there is no clear definitive statement of what an 'informal settlement' is, factors taken into consideration when 'classifying' an area as such comprise an evaluation of the nature of the structures, land-ownership, tenure situation, size of structures, access to services and land-use zoning.

The predominant form of inadequate housing in the city comprises informal settlements – characterized by constructions of varying degrees of permanence, with a variety of materials, including corrugated iron, plastic, timber and metal sheeting, or built with more traditional wattle and daub – that have developed on apartheid 'buffer strips': marginal land within established areas, or land that formerly lay beyond the city boundaries. Informal dwellings represent about 75 per cent of the metropolitan gross housing backlog of 305,000 units. The population living in informal areas is overwhelmingly African; indeed, nearly half of the African population of the entire municipal area lives in informal dwellings. Another form of inadequate housing comprises the dilapidated and crowded hostels developed to house and control (usually) male workers.

No data is available on the tenure in slums. Security of tenure is calculated from the general association of tenure with dwelling type and geographical location in the metropolitan area. It is estimated that 75 per cent of the households in Durban live in formal areas and have full security of tenure. Of the remaining 25 per cent, approximately 20 per cent (41,000 households) have a level of security of tenure derived from tribal land allocation systems; the rest (150,000 to 195,000 households) have little or no security of tenure. All informal dwellings that were in existence in Durban in 1996 were granted some status and security from arbitrary eviction by the local authority. The municipality resists new settlements, and attempts are made, with varying degrees of success, to keep vacant land free from occupation.

The 33 per cent of Durban's population who live in informal areas are overwhelmingly African. 44 per cent are male, 56 per cent female and 27.9 per cent of the households are female-headed. Informal settlements tend to be popularly regarded as incubators of vice and disease, harbouring 'those too lazy to work' and groups regarded as the 'undeserving poor'. The violence that erupted during 1984 in the slums was, in part, a struggle for the control of land, largely linked to the national struggle for democracy.

Between 1986 and 1992, 3228 people died of politicized urban violence in Durban; increasingly over the period, these deaths occurred in informal settlements.

The city has expanded its boundaries a number of times, largely driven by the regulatory impetus to gain control of burgeoning informal settlements that abut its borders and to protect and secure the economic privileges of the white population. Since 1996, there has been a dramatic transformation of local government focusing on issues of equity, including integrated development planning based on local-level community participation to develop a framework for better governance. The Long-Term Development Framework focuses on a development vision for the next 20 years; the Integrated Development Planning Process seeks to achieve better coordination; and the organizational transformation process of the council seeks to better reflect its development and democratic priorities. These initiatives, however, are still at an embryonic stage.

Critical reflection on housing, urban development and other policies reveals a failure to adequately address the spatial and socio-economic legacies of the past, and highlights the absence of policies that specifically deal with the issues they raise. Given lower-than-anticipated housing delivery rates and rapid population growth, a significant housing backlog remains the issue of the future. This is partly because responsibilities for implementation lie across different tiers of government, and partly because of the complexities associated with achieving coordinated public policy. Sectoral public policies that are pro-poor have far less impact when they are not implemented in a coordinated manner.

HAVANA, CUBA

The forced concentration of peasants around major Cuban cities in 1896 in order to cut their aid to Cuban patriots can be considered as the cause of contemporary squatter settlements. These settlements grew throughout the first half of the 20th century after Cuba's independence from Spain. During 1960 to 1961, the largest and worst shantytowns were demolished and their residents built housing through self-help and mutual aid. The remaining shantytowns – formerly called *barrios de indigentes* (indigent neighbourhoods) – were renamed 'unhealthy neighbour-hoods' to make clear that the issue was the quality of the housing and settlements, not the economic or social status of their residents. A second small wave of shantytown clearance and replacement occurred during the late 1960s and early 1970s as part of the creation of the 'Havana Green Belt'. But aside from those efforts, shantytowns were largely ignored in the belief that rapid new construction would replace them. Nevertheless, many shantytowns continued to grow and new settlements formed. By 1987, Havana had 15,975 units in shantytowns (less than 3 per cent of all Havana dwellings). By 2001, the city had 60 *barrios* and 114 *focos insalubres*, with a total of 21,552 units, representing one quarter of such units nationally. This 50 per cent growth was seen as the result of an increase in net migration to Havana, especially from the less developed eastern provinces.

Inner-city tenements are large mansions, boarding houses or hotels that are subdivided into single-room units, or multifamily dwellings originally built for workers with single-room units built around courtyards or along narrow alleys or passage ways. Most were built more than 70 years ago and have deteriorated substantially. In 2001, more than 60,000 units were located in tenements.

The generic term 'slum' (*tugurio*) is seldom used in Cuba. Substandard housing is, instead, described by housing type and conditions, building materials and settlement type. Most slum units are concentrated in the inner-city municipalities of Old Havana and Centro Habana and neighbourhoods such as Atarés, whereas shantytowns are at the urban periphery or along rivers, creeks and former railway lines.

The Cuban government regards three housing types as inherently substandard:

1   *Tenements*: the typical inner-city slum dwelling is in a tenement, usually a single room with shared bathing and sanitary facilities, although often upgraded and expanded to include indoor plumbing. Indeed, according to the 1981 census, 44 per cent of tenements had indoor water and that number continued to increase during the following two decades. Nevertheless, such additions are mostly done at the expense of scarce open space, natural light and ventilation. The great majority of these rooms are located in older multifamily buildings in central areas of Havana.
2   *Bohíos*: thatched-roof shacks, once common in rural areas, are now almost non-existent in Havana.
3   *Improvised housing*: these comprise dwelling units that are primarily built of scrap material. In 1996, there were 3574 units located in shantytowns that were categorized as 'improvised'.

Other types: a small but significant number of occupied units were converted from non-residential uses (stores, garages and warehouses). With the drop in tourism after the revolution, most of the cheap hotels and boarding houses became permanent dwellings. In 1981, some 34,000 units (6.5 per cent of the total) had been adapted from non-residential uses. Of these, two-fifths became 'houses', nearly one third became tenements and the rest were apartments.

Shantytowns consist of these substandard types of units, as well as many that have been upgraded to acceptable housing but remain within a settlement still considered a shantytown.

Following the 1959 revolution, all evictions were stopped, rents were reduced by 30 to 50 per cent, and land speculation was eliminated. The Urban Reform Law established the concept of housing as a public service and established two basic tenure forms: ownership and long-term leasehold of government-owned units, while prohibiting most private renting.[2] Most tenants became homeowners, amortizing the price of units with their rents. Residents of slum housing remained as long-term leaseholders but, by the mid 1960s, no longer paid rent.

Beginning in 1961, the government built housing and provided occupants with lifetime leases at rents of about 10 per cent of family income.

The most recent shantytown growth occurred during the 1990s in order to absorb a growing number of new migrants to the city. Inner-city tenements continued to deteriorate and, during the 1990s, between two and four total or partial building collapses a day occurred in the city. The greatest concentration of the worst housing conditions is found in five municipalities – Old Havana, Arroyo Naranjo, Centro Habana, San Miguel and 10 de Octubre – which together have two-thirds of all units in poor condition. These municipalities also have the highest proportions of units in fair and poor condition, with Old Havana having two-thirds and the others having 40 to 47 per cent.

In market economies, most of the poor live in slums and most slum dwellers are poor. However, in Cuba, this occurs less frequently because of relative tenure security, generally low-cost or free housing, and the restricted legal housing and land markets (despite the growth in informal ones). Moreover, people living in substandard housing have access to the same education, health care, job opportunities and social security as those who live in formerly privileged neighbourhoods. Cuban slums are quite socially diverse, and poverty is relatively dispersed.

The 1960s' sweeping policies also included urban reform, with housing legislation affecting nearly all urban residents through the distribution of vacant units, innovative construction programmes reaching small numbers of urban and rural households, and assistance to private builders. Urban and regional policies of the early 1960s were largely followed for the next quarter century and were designed to:

•   promote balanced regional growth, including designated growth poles;
•   diminish urban–rural differences by improving rural living conditions;
•   develop a network of urban and rural settlements of different sizes and functions; and
•   ensure rational land use through comprehensive urban planning.

At least until the early 1990s, these policies were largely successful, although there were contradictions and problems in achieving rational land use and in stabilizing the rural labour force. Despite fleeting anti-urban rhetoric during the late 1960s, Cuba sought to increase the urban proportion of its population, reaching 75 per cent by 2000.

The Cuban government has been notable for its commitment to devoting a large share of its resources to social needs. Long-standing policies that target more vulnerable populations have mitigated the effects of various crises, but have not been able to completely counteract centuries of inherited deficiencies and inequalities. Moreover, some argue that economic reform policies that helped to revive the economy also contributed to making life more difficult for at-risk sectors. Several decades of neglect of Havana have led to the increased deterioration of a large section of the housing stock and infrastructure.

Strongly centralized policies and persistent shortages of building materials have made residents' initiatives to address their own community housing problems more difficult, while vertical planning made it more difficult to coordinate development strategies at the community level.

IBADAN, NIGERIA

The intense crowding and subsequent deterioration of Ibadan's inner city took place over a long period, closely linked to socio-economic change and limited municipal budgets. The, in principle, well-planned town thus turned into a slum. In 1963, half of the city's core area consisted of slum dwellings, growing to 70 per cent of the town's total number of derelict housing in 1985. Problems of illegal squatting, conversion of functions and extremely poor levels of service provision are compounded by the apparent lack of financial capacity and political will to upgrade such a large area. In addition, people strongly oppose resettlement due to their strong attachment to the ancestral lands.

During the past 20 years, the planned city saw a growth of squatting areas along the urban fringes and in the crowded low- and medium-income residential areas of the first half of the 20th century. Massive cash injections in urban utilities and infrastructure during the 1970s oil boom attracted a flow of rural migrants and citizens of other African states. Considerable unplanned development thus occurred along the major traffic arteries in the northern, eastern and southern directions, resulting in urban areas entirely devoid of urban management and planning. Whatever facilities were provided in these relatively prosperous times rapidly declined due to overuse and lack of maintenance. Rapid development of makeshift shelters since the 1980s largely corresponds to general, nation-wide increases in poverty.

Slums are defined as those areas that are yet to develop in terms of good planning and settlement. Some of the characteristics of slums are that they lack infra-structural facilities, have no planned layout and the residents are predominantly poor and illiterate. Slums are areas that concentrate low-income earners, low-cost houses, possibly mud houses, no layout and poor inhabitants.

The three main slum types in Ibadan are:

1 *Inner city slums*: these consist of the oldest (19th-century) and lowest quality residences and are characterized by severe deterioration, the city's highest population density and no identifiable sanitation facilities. They house a very high percentage of indigenous Yoruba people.
2 *Squatting areas*: the low- and medium-income residential districts of the first half of the 20th century – although better controlled by the planning authorities – have attracted some illegal squatting by migrants from the 1970s and 1980s onwards. Squatting is highly organized and cannot be considered as spontaneous.
3 *Unplanned outskirts*: from the 1970s to the 1990s, land along the major traffic arteries has attracted slums in the north, the east and the south of the city. Here, at the outskirts of the city, 30 per cent of the derelict houses in Ibadan are found. Most of them have developed because a new labour market gave opportunities for employment, but without housing provision. Some spontaneous slums also exist in other parts of the city; but few data are available.

There are serious problems with migrants' access to land, partly because of discriminatory allocation of urban land, particularly with the last migration wave of the Hausa during the late 1970s. The uncertain political situation and the ethnic riots of the past 30 years are associated with loss of property. Migrants, therefore, prefer to rent in order to allow for a quick departure in emergency situations. There is, generally, a high percentage of poor and illiterate people; but the percentage varies from slum to slum.

Since the 1950s, Nigerian urban governance has had three separate levels of government that directly intervene: federal, state and local government. During the 1960s to the 1980s, the power of local authorities decreased. Local government largely viewed slums as inevitable and not an issue that could be addressed at the local level. Thus, only marginal interventions took place, if any. A series of interventions to improve slums and alleviate poverty took place from 1988 onwards. However, the failure to address weak local-level capacity to formulate strategies, programmes and projects, combined with rampant corruption and conflicts between various levels of governance, wasted most of the resources.

Multiple agencies responsible for generating urban policies have not been able to effect urban improvements. Rather, duplication of functions and lack of coordination has affected the entire city. Conflicts of jurisdiction and competence, the absence of effective coordination between levels of government, frequent bureaucratic changes, low priority for urban planning, and the commensurate lack of funding have caused delays and confusion in the execution of urban policies.

JAKARTA, INDONESIA

Jakarta became a post-independence boomtown, more than quadrupling in size to a population of 9.1 million between 1975 and 1995. It now has a metropolitan population approaching 12 million, though the actual figure of inhabitants is a matter of speculation. Population density is extremely high.

Indonesia uses the term *kampung*, which literally means 'village', but which has come to denote a poorer neighbourhood that is contained within a city. However, as it comprises a mix of lower and middle class and frequently contains permanent buildings, it is not really synonymous with slums. Squatters are few and most residents have some sort of title to the land. *Kampungs* are really remnants of original villages upon which cities have encroached and not vice versa. The controversial transmigration policies of the Suharto government may have eased the urban growth pressures; but rapid industrialization of the 1970s and

1980s has counterbalanced attempts to stem urban growth. Jakarta's growth is higher than the official figures, as it excludes seasonal migrants who may spend as much as ten months per year in Jakarta. It is estimated that 20 to 25 per cent of Jakarta residents live in *kampungs*, with an additional 4 to 5 per cent squatting illegally along riverbanks, empty lots and floodplains. Renters and squatters who have managed to set up homes in the 490 pockets of poverty in Jakarta are gradually being squeezed out due to sky-rocketing land prices and speculation. The past 20 years saw the land area occupied by *kampungs* in Jakarta reduced by 50 per cent. As a result, nearly half of the families have been relocated to Jakarta's outlying areas.

Population projections indicate that urban dwellers will surpass their rural counterparts as a percentage of the total between 2010 and 2015, rising to 60 per cent by 2025. At the same time, land prices and land speculation have dramatically reduced available land for low-income housing. Families who were pushed out set up residence in outlying areas, creating new squatter, illegal and semi-legal settlements.

Jakarta is a melting pot of the strong ethnic identities of Indonesians; but, fortunately, a sense of shared solidarity among the poor and the near poor tends to keep social and ethnic tensions that have disrupted Indonesia for the past half decade at bay – at least within the confines of the *kampungs*.

Since *kampungs* are not administrative entities, nobody really knows with any real degree of accuracy how many of Jakarta's inhabitants live in *kampungs*. Furthermore, not everyone living there is poor. For more than 30 years, the Suharto government sought to impose total control over the citizenry, co-opting traditional institutions and leadership and making them subservient to government-controlled structures. Crony capitalism became commonplace, increasing the gap between rich and poor. Corruption and nepotism came to flourish to the point where even the most menial of bureaucratic tasks would seldom be completed without a bribe. The period of prolonged economic growth under Suharto saw many new roads being built and a functioning public transportation system; sewer and drainage systems were also constructed, and the national electricity grid was extended into almost all regions. However, local government revenue fell increasingly short of needs, and infrastructure deteriorated rapidly through sheer lack of maintenance. The state-owned monopolies in water and sanitation, power and telecommunications were operated with an inefficiency remarkable even by most developing country standards. Government policies and programmes for housing have been entirely inadequate in meeting the needs of the urban poor; for all intents and purposes, the government abdicated its role in the provision of housing. The reform in the wake of Suharto's resignation did little to change politics at the local level.

KARACHI, PAKISTAN

During the 1940s and 1950s, due to migration from India following partition, extensive unorganized land invasion led to the establishment of extensive squatter settlements (*katchi abadis*) on the then Karachi periphery and on open urban lands. Traditional urban institutions based on clan, caste and religion quickly collapsed. The settlements densified over time as political instability prevented coherent urban planning. The 1950s saw sharp urban increases as infant mortality rates fell and rural-to-urban migration exploded when agricultural production was modernized. The military government shifted the squatter communities to two townships outside of Karachi. Squatter settlements within the city were bulldozed and the affected people moved to the storm drain lands that connected Karachi and the new townships. The 1960s and 1970s had increased rural–urban migration through urban pull factors. Under army rule, city institutions fell apart and the Karachi Master Plan could not be implemented due to social and political instability. From 1988 onwards, ethnic politics, conflict and violence drove industry to other parts of the country, greatly increasing unemployment in Karachi. In the absence of adequate housing programmes, homelessness and informal settlement has increased, as have densities in existing *katchi abadis*.

The government of Pakistan recognizes only two terms related to unserviced or underserviced settlements:

1   *Katchi abadis*: these are informal settlements created through squatting or informal subdivisions of state or private land.
2   *Slums*: these settlements consist of villages absorbed in the urban sprawl or the informal subdivisions created on community and agricultural land. Here, security of tenure is a rule; but there is no programme to improve conditions other than through political patronage.

The *katchi abadis* are of two types:

1   Settlements established through unorganized invasion of state lands at the time of partition; most of them were removed and relocated during the 1960s or have been regularized.
2   Informal subdivisions of state land (ISD), further divided into:
    –   notified *katchi abadis*: settlements earmarked for regularization through a 99-year lease and local government infrastructure development; and
    –   non-notified *katchi abadis*: settlements not to be regularized because they are on valuable land required for development, or on unsafe lands.

The slums can also be divided into two types:

1   Inner-city, traditional pre-independence working-class areas now densified and with inadequate infrastructure.
2   *Goths* or old villages now part of the urban sprawl; those within or near the city centre have become

formal – others have developed informally into inadequately serviced high-density working-class areas.

Notified *katchi abadis* have secure tenure based on 99-year leases; the un-notified ones have no security of tenure and are scheduled for removal. *Goths* have secure tenure, while ISD on agricultural lands only have secure tenure if declared *katchi abadis*.

Although little specific survey information is available on slum dynamics, it is clear that slums are on the rise, notably to the west and north of Karachi, as extensions of existing ISDs. Estimates indicate an increase of close to 50 per cent between 1988 and 2000 from 3.4 to 5 million people.

Estimates indicate that about half of Karachi lives in *katchi abadis*. Most individuals are employed in the informal sector. An existing analysis of 20 ISD households is too limited an example to draw city-wide conclusions about socio-political characteristics of the 'typical' slum dweller.

The first major slum upgrading and poverty alleviation programme was proposed for the 1988 to 1993 period. The programme largely failed to meet its targets and regularized only 1 per cent of the *katchi abadis* per year due to faulty land records, corruption and non-inclusion of grassroots organizations.

The Social Action Programme of 1993 supported NGOs for infra-structural improvements, but failed largely due to lack of capacity.

Although notable successes have been achieved in terms of regularization and infra-structural work (comparatively high electricity and water connections to many of Karachi's slum areas), too little has been done to effectively address poverty and poor shelter conditions. The impact of more recent programmes is still unclear due to a lack of effective impact monitoring other than yearly reviews based on the feedback of the very agencies that implement the programmes.

KOLKATA, INDIA

The slums of Kolkata can be divided into three groups: the older, up to 150 years old, ones in the heart of the city are associated with early urbanization. The second group dates from the 1940s and 1950s and emerged as an outcome of industrialization-based rural–urban migration, locating themselves around industrial sites and near infra-structural arteries. The third group came into being after the independence of India and took vacant urban lands and areas along roads, canals and on marginal lands. In 2001, 1.5 million people, or one third of Kolkata's population, lived in 2011 registered and 3500 unregistered slums.

The 1956 Slum Act defines slums as 'those areas where buildings are in any respect unfit for human habitation'. The Calcutta Municipal Council Act of 1980 defines *bustees* as 'an area of land not less than 700 square metres occupied by, or for the purposes of, any collection of huts or other structures used or intended to be used for human habitation'. The Central Statistics Organization

defines slums as an area 'having 25 or more *katcha* structures, mostly of temporary nature, or 50 or more households residing mostly in *katcha* structures huddled together or inhabited by persons with practically no private latrine and inadequate public latrine and water facilities'.

There is a host of different slum types, primarily divided into two categories:

1   *Registered slums* (*bustees*): these slums are recognized by the Calcutta Municipal Corporation (CMC) on the basis of land title; since 1980, they have been taken over by the CMC for letting/lease to slum dwellers.
2   *Unregistered slums*: this comprises slums on the land encroaching settlements.

The *bustee*-type generally has some form of secure tenure or ownership rights based on land rent or lease, with structures built by the slum dwellers, or house rental/lease of structures built by third parties.

Tenure security is, in principle, not available to the unregistered land encroaching settlements on road sides (*jhupri*), along canals (*khaldhar*) or on other vacant land (*udbastu*).

It is envisaged that the number of urban poor will increase considerably in the near future due to natural growth and in-migration, combined with a lack of well-planned and long-term intervention strategies.

Over 40 per cent of Kolkata's slum residents have been slum dwellers for two generations or longer, and more than half originate from the Kolkata hinterland. With the majority engaged in the informal sector, with average monthly earnings of between 500 and 1700 rupees and a household size of five to six persons, some three-quarters of the Kolkata slum population are below the poverty line.

The standard of living of the slum dwellers caused concern even during colonial rule. For a long time, slums were treated as an eyesore and a nuisance to be dealt with for reasons of safety, security, and the health and hygiene of the urban elite. Policy interventions focused mostly on clearance and removal. The First, Second and Third Five-Year Plans laid emphasis on slum eradication and removal. Various attempts were made to address the issue in alternative ways; but all failed for different reasons.

The Environment Improvement in Urban Sector (EIUS) scheme, in operation since 1974, has been partially successful in improving the living environment of slum dwellers; but it has not helped in preventing the growth of new slums through migration or natural increase. The scheme suffers from lack of community involvement in planning, implementation and monitoring of the programme. Another initiative that has generally been effective in reducing urban poverty is the National Slum Development Programme (NSDP).

Although some considerable successes have been achieved, there is a long way to go for Kolkata in terms of addressing the issues related to urban poverty and slums. There is an urgent need to establish clear long-term strategies that address such issues as:

- land titles in *bustees*;
- unauthorized new slums around canal and roads;
- greater effectiveness of urban poverty-eradication programmes;
- public awareness-building programmes on slum population;
- the role of each actor and stakeholder;
- poverty reduction approaches to slum improvement;
- inadequate municipal institutional arrangements, including coordination of the activities of various actors.

LOS ANGELES, US

Los Angeles's history is one of both ethnic diversity and segregation. Founded as an outpost of New Spain in 1781 and incorporated as a city in 1850 after the annexation of California to the US, it did not attract many residents until the railroad reached it in 1876. Ethnic minorities who worked as railroad labourers were part of an imported underclass who lived in segregated residential areas. From around 1900, the Los Angeles port at San Pedro began to gain in significance, setting the stage for poor port workers settling in the harbour area. By 1945, Los Angeles (LA) had assumed great economic prominence and witnessed commensurate demographic growth. Much of the housing stock was, however, recorded with restrictive ethnic covenants, providing a framework for enduring ethnic segregation. This was compounded by:

- discriminatory lending and federal subsidy practices that increased the racial segregation in the metropolis, at large, and in the inner-city areas in particular;
- reductions in public transport that virtually isolated the poor; and
- industrial plant closings that diminished economic opportunities for residents of low-income areas of the city.

Ultimately, this history of segregation contributed to the conditions that led to the 1992 Los Angeles civil unrest – the largest urban uprising ever in the US.

The city does not officially use the word 'slum'. However, Los Angeles slums exist both as individual buildings and as disinvested neighbourhoods, encompassing 20 per cent of the LA area and some 43 per cent of the population. These slums share the following general characteristics:

- Deteriorated physical housing conditions.
- Low levels of resident income.
- Low levels of private investment and property maintenance.

High-density disinvested areas: this generally consists of pre-1930s, brick construction tenement-style housing stock with poor light and air circulation and located near the inner city.

Mid-density disinvested areas: this mostly consists of post-World War II, poorly constructed and/or maintained multifamily dwellings, scattered over each section of the city.

Low-density disinvested areas: these are mostly single-family housing units and low-cost expansions of liveable space, often garage dwellings. Nearly half of the residents of slum neighbourhoods live in low-density areas, reflecting the high proportion of single-family dwellings in the city.

Mixed-density disinvested areas: these areas comprise a mix of the above densities within the same neighbourhood.

Los Angeles is distinctive from most US cities in housing tenure as the majority of its residents are tenants, with less than 40 per cent of households owning their homes. In all disinvested areas, the vast majority of slum dwellers are renters: high density comprise 92.8 per cent; mid density comprise 85.5 per cent; low density comprise 62.2 per cent; and mixed density comprise 83.8 per cent.

In the wake of the urban unrest of the 1990s, the migration of wealthy and white residents from Los Angeles intensified, even though the urban economy rebounded during the late 1990s. Poverty, however, did not decline, as employment was largely low-wage employment and a steady stream of immigrants occupies these low-paying jobs. With rents rising sharply and low-income residents choosing overcrowding rather than homelessness, residential structures are increasingly deteriorating and decaying. The growth in poverty during the coming decades is, therefore, as likely to continue as the growth of disinvested urban areas in Los Angeles.

The residents of LA's disinvested areas are overwhelmingly (two-thirds) Latino, with African Americans the second largest group (one fifth), followed by Asian/Pacific Islanders (one tenth) and a small Caucasian population group. A long history of civil unrest and violent urban riots is an expression of frustration with the slow improvement of race relations and lack of equal access to economic opportunities. The largest urban uprising in the US took place in Los Angeles and was centred in the disinvested communities; it was very noticeable in these areas of the city that there was a lack of employment opportunities, adequate retail services and adequate and affordable housing.

There are three categories of policy intervention and action to improve slums and alleviate poverty:

1   Locational targeting, made up of national, regional and city policies and programmes to eradicate or upgrade slums.
2   Socio-economic targeting, consisting of national, regional and city policies and programmes to eradicate and alleviate poverty.
3   Non-governmental interventions, consisting of community- and NGO-based programmes to improve slums and eradicate/alleviate poverty.

Due to the economic segregation within Los Angeles, locational targeting of housing and community development programmes that focus on low-income areas and low-income households typically reach the same groups. Socio-economic targeting provides combinations of targeted tax benefits, low-interest loans and some grants to support neighbourhood revitalization efforts. Non-governmental and community-based interventions roughly come in two groups: the consumer side (tenants' organizations, advocacy groups) and housing producers (non-profit developers, community development organizations).

Considerable impacts have been made during the past half decade, resulting from partnerships in the development and implementation stages of new slum housing policies. Largely as the result of pressure from community leaders and political activists, the LA local authorities revamped their building code enforcement in the city through better inspection, collection and data management of the city's rental housing stock. As a result of these new tools and increased transparency of information, approximately 90 per cent of landlords are now complying with repair requirements, and an estimated US$450 million of private funding has been invested in housing in the disinvested areas of the city over the past four years.

LUSAKA, ZAMBIA

The slums of Lusaka owe their origins to the neglect of providing low-cost public housing and to short-sighted urban and housing policies, both during colonial and post-independence times. Lusaka's population grew most rapidly after 1948. The city quadrupled in size between 1963 and 1980 as a result of rural–urban migration, natural growth and extension of the city boundaries. In the absence of sufficient public low-cost housing, and with non-insistence on statutory building standards, the urban growth resulted in a series of housing crises and the growth of unauthorized settlements at the urban periphery. This was exacerbated by highly centralized forms of governance that did not delegate decision-making and revenue-raising powers to the local level.

A distinction is made between two types of slum:

1 *Early self-help housing*: this comprises low-income housing as it emerged on specifically allocated lands on the outskirts of Lusaka, with communal water provision, located just outside of the municipal boundaries in the post-1948 period.
2 *Unauthorized housing*: this comprises all other informal subdivisions, land squatting, etc, largely on privately owned lands zoned for agricultural purposes and without essential physical or social infrastructure.

Generally, there is security of tenure for the early self-help (improved and authorized) settlements and regularized former unauthorized settlements. There remains a serious lack of security of tenure for unauthorized housing settlements.

The bulk of the residents of the low-income housing areas are predominantly unskilled and semi-skilled and work mainly in the informal sector (piecework and small-scale trading activities). A few young men and women engage in criminal and anti-social activities.

The 1948 African Housing Ordinance, designed to stabilize the urban population, allowed African workers in urban centres to live with their families.

The second National Development Plan (1972 to 1976) recognized unauthorized housing as an asset that required improvement and was followed by the 1974 Improvement Area Act to pave the way for upgrading.

The Draft Decentralization Policy of 1997 (which has remained a draft since) attempts to address the failures of local-government financing and autonomy arrangements.

The successive post-independence governments have also failed to come up with permanent solutions to inadequate low-income housing in a rapidly growing city. Although the Improvement Areas Act of 1974 has shown that the solution to the critical housing shortage can be best resolved with the involvement of the residents of the slum areas, the government does not seem to have grasped the essential lessons that should have been learned from the upgrading projects. Participatory approaches are more likely to help deliver decent housing at an affordable cost to both the individuals and the government, while the traditional public provision of low-cost housing failed to deliver improved housing for the bulk of the population. This was especially the case during the period of 1966 to 1970, when enormous public resources were devoted to providing public housing.

The major problem confronting the slum areas of Lusaka today is not poor housing quality, but the sustainable provision of essential infrastructure and services, as well as effective solid waste management. Other less perceived problems are insecurity and overcrowding.

Finding answers to the problems faced by the residents of the slums of Lusaka requires concerted efforts by a more proactive and progressive leadership at all levels. Above all, it requires a more autonomous local authority, with full control over the affairs of the city, including its finances and management. Bringing that about requires the acceptance that essential urban services can only be effectively delivered by an autonomous and democratically elected and decentralized local authority.

MANILA, PHILIPPINES

Segregation has a long history in Metro Manila. As a Spanish enclave during the Spanish colonial period, native inhabitants lived in the suburbs of what are now the districts of Tondo, Sta Cruz, Quiapo and Sampaloc. The Chinese lived in the *parian*, a district that became part of the present Binondo.

Slums are now scattered over 526 communities in all cities and municipalities of Metro Manila, housing 2.5 million people on vacant private or public lands, usually along rivers, near garbage dumps, along railroad tracks, under bridges and beside industrial establishments. Slums alongside mansions in affluent residential areas are also not uncommon. Although there are relatively large slum communities, the settlement pattern of the Metro Manila urban poor is generally dispersed, located wherever there is space and opportunity.

Slums are defined as buildings or areas that are deteriorated, hazardous, insanitary or lacking in standard conveniences. Slums are also defined by the squalid, crowded or insanitary conditions under which people live, irrespective of the physical state of the building or area. Under such definitions, slum dwellers are identified as the urban poor: individuals or families residing in urban and urbanizable areas whose income or combined household income falls below the poverty threshold.

Slums cannot be clearly classified by location as they are so dispersed over Metro Manila; but they can broadly be classified by construction type:

- Temporary shelter made from salvaged materials.
- Semi-permanent shelter.
- Permanent shelter.

There is an additional category that is referred to as 'professional squatters' and is defined as individuals or groups who occupy lands without the owner's consent and who have sufficient income for legitimate housing. The term also applies to those previously awarded lots or housing by the government, but who sold, leased or transferred the same and settled illegally in the same place or in another urban area as *non-bona fide* occupants and intruders on land for social housing. The term does not apply to individuals or groups who rent land and housing from 'professional squatting syndicates'. Professional squatting syndicates are the informal and illegal organizations that covertly coordinate the activities of professional squatters.

Expenses on housing primarily involve mortgages or rents; but 'squatters' typically spend nothing on a regular basis on housing. However, most squatters incur initial housing investments to pay for 'land rights' and to build their house.

On average, three-quarters of the households in Manila's slums are long-term residents of the area (more than five years). The settlements average 19.2 years in age and often are 40 years old, or older. The majority of the households migrated to these areas from other cities within the metro or the city. The majority of the urban poor households have been living in Metro Manila for nearly two decades. Half of the population in slums are employed in the formal sector. Informal employment largely consists of domestic help, tricycle driving, construction labour, self-employment, factory labour and vending.

Metro Manila consists of 12 cities, 5 municipalities and 1694 *barangays*, governed by their respective local government units (LGUs). The Local Government Code (LGC) mandates the LGUs to provide efficient and effective governance and to promote general welfare within their respective territorial jurisdictions. The LGUs are relatively autonomous. The Metropolitan Manila Development Authority (MMDA) was created in order to ensure the effective delivery of metro-wide services; the adoption and implementation of policies, standards, rules and regulations, as well as programmes and projects to rationalize and optimize land use and provide direction to urban growth and expansion; the rehabilitation and development of slum and blighted areas; the development of shelter and housing facilities; and the provision of necessary social services.

With increased decentralization, the participation of NGOs and people's organizations (POs) in the planning, implementation and monitoring of LGU-led projects has increased. The LGC prescribed the formation of local development councils or special bodies to serve as venues for representing communities, through their organizations, to express their views on issues affecting them.

The 1987 Bill of Rights grants all citizens the right of access to affordable housing. In 1986, the government was turned into 'enabler' and 'facilitator', and the Urban Development and Housing Act (UDHA) was passed. The UDHA provides for comprehensive and integrated urban development and housing, while, under the communal upgrading scheme – the Zonal Improvement Programme – the government can expropriate land for resale to the residents after developing the site and introducing basic services and facilities. The government established a viable home financing system through the revival of home financing institutions, while funding for long-term mortgages that would be affordable even to those below the poverty line was sourced from insurance funds administered by the social security system.

The strength of Metro Manila's approaches lies in the holistic character of metro-wide action for slum improvement, regularization, housing finance, poverty alleviation and partnerships with NGOs and CBOs The long-term effectiveness of this approach is, despite the enormity of Manila's slum issues, likely to show that persistent adherence to urban-wide policy will lead to satisfactory results.

MEXICO CITY, MEXICO

Historically, urban segregation in Mexico City was caused by topography and colonial land use, with the flood-prone areas to the east of the city being occupied by the lower classes. With high immigration and birth rates during the greater part of the 20th century, the city's population grew to 18 million, of which over 60 per cent are currently considered to be 'poor' or 'moderately poor'. The built-up area expanded from 23 square kilometres to 154,710 square kilometres between 1900 and 2000, engulfing surrounding towns and villages and invading steep hillsides and dried-up lake beds on which slums developed. Initially, highly crowded one- or two-roomed rented tenements, called *vecindades*, provided housing for the poor. With intensive industrialization and concurrent urbanization after 1940, peripherally located *colonias populares* – irregular settlements comprised of self-built and mainly owner-occupied dwellings – emerged as the leading lower-middle and low-income housing option.

The immense scale of Mexico City's housing poverty and the highly complex, dynamic processes preclude general official or unofficial definitions of slums comparable to the English word. Instead, terms such as *colonias populares* (lower class neighbourhoods) are used. Recently, 'areas with high marginalization indices' have been identified.

The following five types of slum are identifiable:

1. *Colonias populares*: the most critical housing conditions are in the newer or unconsolidated irregular settlements, or *colonias populares*, resulting from unauthorized land development and construction, with deficits in urban services, often in high-risk areas and with dubious property titles. Most settlements have been improved to varying degrees as property is regularized, infrastructure and services put in and houses solidly built. Yet, the *colonias* never become completely regular. Legalized properties become irregular again through intestate inheritance, dilapidation or fiscal problems. Irregular settlements constitute roughly half of the urbanized area and house more than 60 per cent of the population.

2. *Inner-city rental slums (vecindades)*: these slums date from the late 19th century and comprise houses abandoned by the wealthy and converted into tenements for the poor, providing the model for purpose-built cheap rental housing. After the 1940s, the production of rented *vecindades* continued in the peripheral irregular settlements; but here, unlike in the inner city, the landlords are often slum dwellers themselves. About 10 per cent of all housing in Mexico City is in *vecindades*.

3. *Ciudades perdidas*: this is a broad concept referring to small-scale pockets of shanty housing on vacant land or undesirable urban locations. These are no longer quantitatively important as a form of slum.

4. *Cuartos de azotea*: these are servants' quarters and makeshift accommodation on the roofs of apartments or early public housing. They are almost invariably well located in central areas and provide 0.4 per cent of all of Mexico City's housing units.

5. *Deteriorated public housing projects*: many formally produced, subsidized owner-occupied housing projects built for the working classes have become highly deteriorated, with overcrowding and other social problems. As much as 15 per cent of Mexico City's population now live in government-financed housing projects of variable quality.

The vast majority of the precarious settlements' occupants are homeowners. Only 7 per cent of the housing in the worst areas are rented, compared to a metropolitan average of 17.3 per cent. In the central areas, the traditional *vecindades* and other rental accommodation continue to lose population and to be destroyed due to ageing and land-use changes. Apart from the highly successful housing reconstruction programme after the 1985 earthquake, further projects for repopulating the city centre have had limited impact since they are severely hampered by a lack of viable finance and land for development.

Many public housing projects throughout the city are becoming slums. Inadequate self-administration of these projects has led to lack of maintenance, invasion and degradation of public space, structurally dangerous alterations and bad neighbourhood relations. All of this is aggravated by the original cheap construction, low space standards and the increasing impoverishment of their working-class occupants, smitten by unemployment, alcohol and drug dependency, social violence and high crime rates.

Irregular settlements continue to develop in a more dispersed and differentiated manner, especially in the metropolitan municipalities. The city is growing disproportionately to demographic increase, accommodating smaller families and an ageing population. Nevertheless, most of the city has been built now, and what happens within existing *colonias* will determine the quality of future habitat for the majority of the poor. The original problems here of precarious construction, risks from landslides or flooding and insufficient services are compounded by deterioration and overcrowding. The advantages of irregular settlements are flexibility and relatively large plots that accommodate extended families and second or third generations. In the last decade, financial subsidies have been directed at formal commercial developments of mass-produced tiny single-family houses on the extreme outskirts of the city.

About two-thirds of Mexico City's population live in *colonias populares*; but by no means should all be considered to be 'slum dwellers'. In fact, most *colonias* contain some degree of social heterogeneity. The distinguishing characteristic of hopeless slums is not so much the poverty of all of their inhabitants, but, rather, the absence of middle- and high-income families.

Local government policy towards irregular settlement formation has generally been of a *laissez faire* or even encouraging nature, with some notable exceptions of mass evictions. Once established, a *colonia popular* will normally encounter few problems in obtaining electricity, although basic infrastructure may take longer, depending upon the terrain, the location of the settlement, the political climate and other localized factors. The costs are covered by the inhabitants and the local governments, with federal subsidies for certain items in the case of some specific upgrading programmes. Since 2001, the federal district government (governing the half of Mexico City that is the nation's capital) has run an innovative programme providing credits for home improvements and new extensions to owner occupiers in the more impoverished *colonias populares*. This is part of a wider policy of social investment, including monthly cash subsidies for the over-70s and the disabled, school breakfasts and community crime-prevention measures. The housing programme accounts for about one quarter of the social budget. In addition, the social prosecutor of the same federal district government runs a scheme called Housing Projects Rescue, consisting of non-repayable grants for the maintenance and repair of public housing. Similar projects might be implemented in Mexico City's metropolitan municipalities, though these have yet to be devised. An evaluation of the immediate and longer-term effects of credits for home improvement, as well as the housing project rescue scheme, is premature.

In spite of recent decentralization policies, power and resources are highly concentrated in central government. Throughout most of the 20th century, political power was virtually monopolized by the Revolutionary Institutional

Party (PRI). Political reform began during the late 1970s, slowly at first, with electoral successes of opposition parties being limited to lower levels of government, but gathering momentum towards the end of the century. The replacement of the traditional one-party clientism by competitive electioneering has altered the unwritten rules governing access to benefits and basic necessities, such as housing credits, urban services, regularization programmes and social subsidies. The role of political intermediaries has been undermined or transformed. Political reform is combined with new social policies that replace collective targeting and aspirations of global coverage through the individualization of benefits, with the aim of 'targeting the most needy'. The practical effects are, however, uneven and it is unlikely that what the needy most require is the kind of housing subsidies that are provided, and even less likely that they will obtain them.

MOSCOW, RUSSIAN FEDERATION

Since 1924, five-year plans provided national economic and urban development that was aimed at providing equal services for all. Muscovites primarily live in flats in multi-storey buildings. Moscow's population has tripled during the last 70 years and, in spite of massive municipal housing construction, there are still some people who live in shared flats, or in outdated or dilapidated buildings.

Shared flats with communal services, built between 1920 and 1955, were designed to house the needy on the basis of one family per room. Despite enormous efforts – more than 80 per cent of Moscow's housing was built during the past 30 to 40 years – about 15 per cent of the registered population still live in shared flats.

Dilapidated buildings are generally five-storey high blocks of apartments, built from pre-fabricated concrete panels during the mid 1950s. That first generation of industrial housing was followed by an improved second (mid 1960s) and a still better third generation (1980s) of mass-type housing. Due to poor maintenance and shortage of living space, about 36 per cent of Moscow's housing stock is physically or otherwise 'out of date'.

Squatter flats resulted from illegal subleasing of municipal or private housing. The post-1994 easing of the 'urban employment access to housing requirement' made Moscow the number one migration destination, including a considerable percentage of refugees.

No formal definition of slum is given, as it is generally considered that the city does not have slums, but has *communal* (shared) flats, *dilapidated buildings* and *deteriorated houses*.

Several types of accommodation in Moscow do not meet contemporary standards for housing:

- *Communal flats* (*communalky*): these are apartments that are used by two or more families who share the kitchen and other facilities (including hostels, dormitories and hotels).

- *Outdated and dilapidated buildings* (*vethi* and *avariyni*): this typically comprises the first generation of mass housing, now outdated in terms of quality of construction and facilities. Residents are entitled to housing improvement or free alternative accommodation, but queues are long and move slowly according to availability of municipal housing stock.
- *Deteriorated houses*: these are primarily post-World War II structures that are recognized as damaged or otherwise unsuitable for constant habitation.

Before 1992, almost all houses in Moscow were state owned, municipal or corporate. There were practically no private houses in Moscow for 70 years. In ten years, two-thirds of the housing stock became private through privatization and new construction. Poor people generally stay in state-owned flats that they rent or lease.

'Low-income citizens' are defined through the criterion of 'cost of living', representing a minimum basket of consumption materials and services 'necessary for preservation of health and maintenance of ability to live of the people' – this is estimated as 2900 rubles (about US$90) per person (during the year 2002). Moscow provides financial assistance to families with actual per person income lower than the cost of living in the city, and to families *with minor children, students and youth, veterans of the Great Patriotic war, older citizens and invalids (handicapped).*

'Needy for dwelling' people have the right to apply for housing improvement at the expense of the city. In Moscow, a family is considered in need for housing purposes if there are less than 9 square metres of floor area per person.

Moscow's poor population is also made up of illegal immigrants, refugees and seasonal workers. As the collection basin is, in principle, the entire territory of the former USSR, little specific socio-political characteristics can be attributed to this wide array of people.

The main purpose of the federal programme Dwellings for 2002–2010 is a transition to sustainable development in the housing sphere, ensuring availability of housing accommodation to the citizens, as well as a safe and comfortable urban environment. This housing reform programme comprises modernizing municipal housing and resettling citizens from shabby and dilapidated housing stock. The reforms are aimed at:

- implementing a transition to sustainable development;
- undertaking the necessary legal, taxation, privatization, housing finance and registration changes.

With accumulated public- and private-sector resources and according to the Law on Moscow Master Plan, the following changes in housing reconstruction and development are envisaged for the following 20 years:

- liquidation of shared flats and existing dilapidated housing stock by 2010;
- increase of housing stock from 176 up to 220 million–230 million square metres;

- decrease and stabilization of the total share of physically amortized and of out-of-date residential stock from 36 to 15 per cent through substitution of apartments of the first generation and by increase of annual of reconstruction;
- improvement of maintenance and operating performances of residential buildings (at the expense of increase of high-quality housing stock and a decrease of low-quality residential stock);
- improvement of the urban environment, and of socio-psychological and ecological comfort; and
- increase in the efficiency of urban territories through mixed-use development, and increase of residential and mixed residential densities.

Much of Moscow's current housing crisis is inherited from the past, exacerbated by problems inherent to the current politico-philosophical shifts of the transitional period. In both cases, the housing sector did not receive sufficient resources. Largely dependent on subsidies and unsatisfactory financing, expensive maintenance and an environment with a general absence of economic incentives or market competition, the housing crisis does not come as a surprise. In order to work itself out of these problems, considerable institutional and social reorganizations may be required.

Necessary new directions include, but are not limited to:

- finding a new balance between private and municipal roles;
- better access to housing finance;
- privatization of housing to pave the way for more owner/tenant rights in order to ease the burden on the state;
- an overhaul of municipal finance;
- the creation of more public–private partnerships;
- the establishment of resident community-based organizations to improve public control over the maintenance and effective use of government subsidies;
- subsidies going directly to recipients rather than to agencies in order to stimulate competition for maintenance services; and
- municipal support for NGO interventions.

NAIROBI, KENYA

The roots for the formation of Nairobi's slums can be traced back to the pre-independence period when the urban layout was based on government-sanctioned population segregation into separate enclaves for Africans, Asians and Europeans.[3] During this period, slums essentially developed because of the highly unbalanced allocation of public resources towards the housing and infra-structural needs of the separate sections. The post-colonial period saw a relaxation of the colonial residential segregation policies, and major population shifts occurred, notably rural-to-urban migration, with little obstruction to the proliferation of urban shacks

'as long as they were not located near the central business district'. Slums sprang up all over the town in the proximity of employment. Spatial segregation during this period continued to be reinforced, but this time more as socio-economic and cultural stratification. The post-independence period also saw rapid urban population growth without corresponding housing provision, and poor population resettlement due to new developments and extension of city boundaries that included rural parts within urban boundaries, often changing the characteristics of the settlements.

There is no official definition of slums or informal settlements, and the terms slums and informal settlement are often used interchangeably. City authorities, however, view lack of basic services and infrastructure as characteristics of slums, an aspect that slum dwellers do not emphasize.

Slums accommodate the majority of Nairobi's population and are generally of two types:

1 Squatter settlements.
2 Illegal subdivisions of either government or private land.

A number of slums are located on land that is unsuitable for construction, and all have high to very high population densities, with up to 2300 persons per hectare. Slums and informal settlements are widely located across the city, typically in proximity to areas with employment opportunities.

The majority of structures are let on a room-to-room basis and the majority of households occupy single rooms.[4] Several studies indicate that 56 to 80 per cent of the slum households rent from private-sector landlords (who, in the past, often had the political connections that helped them to protect their investments).

Between 1971 and 1995, the number of informal settlement villages within the Nairobi divisional boundaries rose from 50 to 134, while the estimated total population of these settlements increased from 167,000 to some 1,886,000 individuals. In terms of percentage of the total Nairobi population, the share of informal-settlement village inhabitants rose from one third to an estimated 60 per cent. Today, both natural growth and rural-to-urban migration continue to contribute to the growth of Nairobi's informal settlements villages.

Slums house urban residents who earn low incomes and have limited assets. Employment is largely low skill (domestic help, waiter, bar maid, guard), often on a casual basis (construction labour), small business owners (kiosk owner, newspaper seller) and other income-generating activities. Discrimination, especially along ethnic lines, exists, with most ethnic groups living in (sub) communities of their own ethnic background. Clashes between ethnic groups have been experienced. Slums are not a major source of urban unrest, although they constitute areas with a higher concentration of crime, violence and victimization.

There is a lack of a clear policy that would facilitate and guide urban development in Kenya, and urban interventions are largely made on an ad hoc basis. Most slums are located on unplanned sites that are unsuitable for housing, and their residents are exposed to different forms of pollution. In some slums, housing and infrastructure programmers are being put in place through joint efforts of the government, donors and civil society organizations. These interventions have had mixed results.

Several policy-sensitive initiatives have been undertaken and institutions and facilities have been established to address the issue of slums, including the enabling strategy, the Nairobi Informal Settlements Coordination Committee, Nairobi Situation Analysis, the Poverty Reduction Strategy Paper and the Local Authority Transfer Fund. They address a series of themes, including settlement upgrading, community participation and improved access to services. The outcomes of these interventions are an increased housing stock and expanded community opportunities and participation, as well as a host of less fortunate aspects. These include:

- Proliferation of new slums.
- Exclusion of particular population groups.
- Subsidy and affordability mismatches.
- Top-down approaches.
- Gentrification.
- Erroneous focus and failing partnerships.
- Non-replicability of efforts.

It is perhaps also the lack of a precise definition of the concept 'slum' that contributes to the lack of effective and tailored policy response. Additionally, in the face of the failure to establish coherent and effective Nairobi-wide urban policies, the outlook for the situation in slums appears to be rather bleak.

NAPLES, ITALY

Slum areas of Naples are geographically divided into:

- *Historic residential periphery*: this consists of public-housing workers' quarters on the then rural areas bordering industrial plants of the early 1900s that have since closed. The older buildings are in a dilapidated state, while recent construction is of poor quality.
- *Recent public city*: this comprises two zones that were planned during the 1960s for dormitory-style public housing, now housing large numbers of residents with low socio-economic status in areas rife with organized crime activities.
- *Unauthorized city*: this is made up of areas of unauthorized construction from the 1970s and 1980s on agricultural lands (no construction permits and violating zoning; illegal but not informal expansion or construction of single-family homes). Quite a few urban areas saw this spontaneous type of development. There may be a scarcity or lack of services; but these areas, nevertheless, constitute a rich urban landscape.

- *Decaying central pockets*: this comprises some areas of the historic centre with high levels of decay, in terms of housing and social indicators, that have, at the same time, a solid and rich urban fabric.

In Naples, the concept of ghetto (a completely decayed and impoverished neighbourhood with a homogeneous social makeup in terms of income and profession) is not an appropriate one to describe the identified slum areas. In each of such areas the relationship between exclusion and poverty and relative wealth varies. Some are being renewed and there are residents who are decidedly not low income. Deep poverty can even be found in areas that are not included among the slums, although such cases do not comprise the majority.

There is no official definition of slums, or of specific decaying areas, even though the debate over this question has been raging for the past century in Naples. However, as in most European cities, the term 'slum' can be used in Naples to describe a habitat where housing maintenance is poor, where social city services (health, education, social and cultural facilities) are lacking, where incomes are low and where social indicators are clearly below the city average.

Except for a few gypsy camps on the edge of the city, there are no cases of informal housing built with precarious materials, nor are there areas with significant numbers of dwellings without public services. Most of the illegal structures are actually associated with middle-class neighbourhoods. Perhaps the best candidate for a slum label is the basso, a ground-floor dwelling with a door onto the street that serves as the only source of light and ventilation. Usually it is just one room divided to create a kitchen and bathroom.

There is insufficient data on slum tenure, although there are indications that in the slum areas only one third are owner occupiers.

Population is more or less stable, a result of negative natural growth compensated by a positive migratory balance. Population movements are no longer to the urban periphery but, rather, to towns in the province. The areas of Scampia and Ponticelli (recent public city-type areas) are slowly growing.

There is no data on the income of slum inhabitants, while there are fairly reliable figures for the social, employment and crime situation. The sectorial nature of policies that support the vulnerable social segments, largely implemented by national structures through various ministries, does not allow for data to be compared even for the same zone. The increase in the number of interventions conducted by NGOs has led to greater knowledge of the situation; but there has been no centralization that might help to share data.

The population decline in Naples between 1981 and 1991 was sharp, especially in the historic centre areas (particularly, Pendino, Porto and Vicaria), with the exception of the Scampia, S. Pietro, Pianura, Chiaiano and Ponticelli neighbourhoods. Within the former central areas, the decay of the ancient housing stock has allowed low-income classes to stay in private homes, while those with the means to leave preferred to go elsewhere. In the latter case, the smaller drop in population can be explained by the low income of the residents of these quarters. In fact, the exodus from the city mostly involved young middle-class white-collar families and stably employed blue-collar families, and was most evident in middle-class, central and hilltop residential neighbourhoods.

The main policies for urban slum areas are national programmes that support employment and entrepreneurship. The late 1990s saw the launch of the Urban Renewal and Local Sustainable Development Programme (PRUSST). This funds the planning of projects with the support of local owners and private capital for promoting the recovery and improvement of urban aspects of the cities; promoting social services offered in city slum areas; the creation of services and infrastructure; and renovation and renewal, taking advantage of the existing urban landscape and construction patterns.

The Naples City Social Plan is trying to create a shift from government, which is the exclusive province of the state, to local governance. With a long history of highly permissive urban governance forms, Naples had become a haven of illegal (not informal) construction that flaunted construction permit systems, land zoning and building regulations. This is hardly surprising: during the three decades to 1993, the city had 26 different city councils that were characterized by serious governance discontinuity.

Rises in unemployment were particularly sharp during the 1970s, in the wake of the closing down of major industrial plants, and during the mid 1990s, when central government interventions ceased, demonstrating how almost the entire southern Italian economy had become overdependent upon public funds. Insufficient growth of the service sector could not make up for the job losses. Combined with the prolific presence of organized crime, it is little wonder that the city is in a somewhat precarious position.

It is premature to evaluate the results of the Naples City Social Plan. Overall, changes taking place in Naples show how deep social and urban decay remains. Considering that these conditions are the result of countless inter-playing factors, urban renewal can only take place with a comprehensive plan of social, urban and environmental reorganization, matched by measures aimed at increasing and improving the services needed to attract economic activity and to integrate those segments of the population that currently face increasing marginalization, within the social and economic fabric of the city. Naples needs to develop a city-wide holistic plan that simultaneously places its urban economy within the national economy, while developing an overall urban strategy to help address urban and socio-economic issues alike.

NEWARK, US

Although Newark is a city on the rise, it remains a troubled city with highly unequal opportunities. During the 1960s and 1970s, Newark experienced an exodus of the middle class and the wealthy to the suburbs, leaving the working class and poor behind in the city. Today, Newark and the surrounding suburbs have reached extremes in ethnic segregation, exacerbated by a declining municipal tax base with grave consequences on service delivery and the quality of life in the city. Record rates of immigration, notably from South America, have made up for the exodus of the better-off groups in terms of urban population. The city is highly densely populated, with 11,500 persons per square mile. The city suffered major employment losses between the 1970s and 1990s and most neighbourhoods contain evidence of poverty, dis-investment and abandonment. An estimated 170,000 households in Metro Newark have 'worst case' housing needs, defined as renters with less than 50 per cent of the area's median income, spending more than half of their income on rent, or living in severely inadequate housing, while not receiving government housing assistance. Today, 4000 households are on the public housing waiting list, which has been closed for years, and the wait for rental assistance is ten years.

The housing stock in poor neighbourhoods includes a small number of high-rise multifamily buildings, some low-rise public housing blocks dating from the 1940s and 1950s, new public housing developments consisting of town homes, and older wood-frame houses for one to four families. Because of the city's old housing stock, 90 per cent of the housing units are likely to be contaminated with poisonous lead paints.

The tenure type is largely rental, although the North Broadway neighbourhood has an uncharacteristically high 35 per cent owner-occupier rate. With the recent economic slump, unemployment has risen to 11.4 per cent and is double the state average. Nearly 30 per cent of Newark residents are poor. The most affordable housing clearly under-serves the needy. Although considerable neighbourhood upgrading is in process, the poorest are not directly benefiting.

Many of the city's poorest sections are racially segregated, with pluralities of either blacks or Hispanics and small white populations. For example, of the three neighbourhoods profiled, two of them have black populations that make up 89 per cent of the neighbourhood's households. In the third neighbourhood, the black population declined from 56 per cent to 31 per cent during the 1990s, while the Hispanic population grew from 40 per cent to 60 per cent. More and more immigrants arrive from South America – notably, Argentina, Brazil, Chile, Colombia and Ecuador.

For more than 20 years, the Newark Housing Authority has been transforming its housing stock, reflecting shifts in federal housing policies from the 1990s, rooted in concerns about concentrated poverty and a belief in market forces. Nearly all high-rise housing has been demolished and replaced with town units of lower density, while some low-rise complexes have been renovated. Poor neighbourhoods also receive assistance through state programmes. The focus of federal programmes shifted to lower-density mixed-income communities; but whether such mixed-income communities will improve the neighbourhood environment, while providing a better quality of life, remains to be seen.

Encouraging housing (re)development has also been a priority of the current mayoral administration, with particular attention to increasing the home-ownership rate.

Two state policies have addressed the problem of regional disparities. Both stem from court battles, one related to housing inequity and the other to school inequity. In theory, if housing affordability and school quality were more equally distributed across the region, Newark would not endure the level of need that it endures today. The city's strategy for economic development has been described as largely relying on ad hoc deals secured with tax abatements, rather than carried out according to a master plan. In addition, fighting crime has been a key concern. Long-range trends show the crime rate declining, although 2001 and 2002 saw increases in homicides. City leaders see crime reduction as integral to successful economic development and home-ownership.

In some respects, elements of city governance can be characterized as anti-democratic. Some have characterized city government as exclusionary and/or dis-empowering, noting that grassroots community organizations have had little success in penetrating the city hall or in influencing development policy, and that a set of well-established non-profit organizations receive regular funding, effectively keeping them from criticizing the administration. Over the years, city officials have been convicted or accused of corrupt practices, including extortion, taking pay-offs, theft and fraud.

PHNOM PENH, CAMBODIA

At the end of the Pol Pot regime, returnees to Phnom Penh were authorized to occupy buildings on a first-come, first-served basis. The few professionals alive occupied vacant dwellings close to the places of employment in the civil service. These new owners took many centrally located buildings, which some then subdivided and sold, even in the absence of formal titles. Once all buildings were occupied, people started to settle on vacant lands, creating the communities that are now considered illegal.

Low-income settlements were created by:

* rural migrants fleeing the countryside because of indebtedness or lack of economic opportunities;
* refugees returning from camps; and
* internally displaced persons.

Most came to Phnom Penh for economic reasons and settled close to where they could earn a living. Afterwards, the slum population increased through natural growth, through migration by relatives of existing slum dwellers and through seasonal migrants. People who move regularly in and out because of floods account for seasonal variation in settlements sizes.

Two types of slums may be recognized:

1   *Squatter settlements*: these consist of dwellers and housing units on illegally occupied private or public lands.

2   *Urban poor settlements*: these comprise low-income families with some sort of recognized occupancy.

However, there exists no clear distinction between legal and illegal occupancy in Phnom Penh as all private ownership of land was abolished in 1974, and no clear ownership system has since been implemented. Almost no one has full ownership title and most city dwellers could be considered squatters.

Slums on public lands largely developed along wider streets, railway tracks, riversides and *boengs* (water reservoirs). On private lands, slums tend to consist of squatting in dilapidated, multiple-occupancy buildings. Increasingly, there is also rooftop squatting in and around the city centre, while, since 1995, rural migrants have formed squatter settlements at the urban periphery on marginal public lands. Most slums are made of low-cost, recycled materials (paper, palm leaves and old wood). These structures are vulnerable to winds and heavy rains, and can be easily destroyed by fire. Those who own brick and cement houses are typically financially better off.

The land tenure situation in Phnom Penh is complex as there is no clear distinction between legal and illegal occupancy and/or ownership. Although, recently, some have been granted social concessions by the government, no family yet holds any certificate of ownership. Families with a registration book may feel more secure than those without, but it does not give them any strong claim to ownership. These unclear rights of tenure make eviction a constant threat. Most low-income settlers are officially regarded as squatters. Yet, at least 75 per cent consider themselves owners of the plot that they purchased from the local authorities or previous owner, who themselves may not have had ownership rights. Transactions are recorded on handwritten receipts; although without any legal authority, it is often enough to claim compensation in case of municipal relocation. Renters are either short-term seasonal migrants or the poorest of the poor who cannot afford to purchase in a squatter settlement and rent on a weekly or monthly basis, with the constant threat of eviction by their slum landlord.

Until 1999, the Municipality of Phnom Penh (MPP) kept a rigid position of not recognizing 'squatters' as legitimate inhabitants of the city, and its agencies did not support development activities to reach slum dwellers. Rather, they evicted squatters, often violently, without compensation or support to relocate. The municipal efforts to develop tourism in Phnom Penh led to the removal of many slum communities.

Nevertheless, in 1999, the MPP and UN-Habitat, after consultations with NGOs and community-based organizations (CBOs), developed an Urban Poverty Reduction Strategy (UPRS) to improve access to basic social and physical infrastructure, enhancing economic opportunities and strengthening participatory governance mechanisms.

In 2000, Prime Minister Hun Sen redefined squatter dwellers as 'temporary residents', while publicly recognizing their economic value to the city. He emphasized that helping them to rebuild new, liveable communities in locations outside of the city had become a priority of the municipality. This change of status coincided with a first step of implementing the UPRS.

The term 'squatter', long used in Phnom Penh to classify most inhabitants of low-income settlements, conveys much more than a connotation of illegality. In Khmer, it refers to 'people living in anarchy', and is strongly linked to immorality, disorder and criminality. At the official level, this gives the MPP grounds to refuse dialogue with squatters and not to acknowledge the legitimacy of their claims for public recognition. This official view is quite widely shared by the middle and upper classes, who consider squatters an aesthetic nuisance to the city and a threat to public order, all feelings based on the same stereotypes of anarchy and reinforced by a poorly informed media. Relations between the MPP and poor communities remain tense as, until recently, the MPP did not engage in dialogue with representatives of squatters, who were considered illegal. In this way, the most vulnerable populations are not included in the political process.

MPP governance is severely restricted by the limited authority to plan and finance its activities. Although the MPP officially gained financial autonomy in 1998, its budget remains constrained as a national law predefines all lines, the minister of interior must approve the budget and the national assembly ratifies it. In addition, the city has little power or incentive to raise its own revenue.

The UPRS, however, suggests that poor communities in Phnom Penh can improve their living conditions and prospects for human development, provided that:

* they receive security of tenure, education, training, credit and technical advice;
* the MPP removes legal, procedural, financial and practical barriers to self-improvement;
* urban poor communities, the government, NGOs and the private sector develop partnerships;
* decisions on policies and programmes that affect the urban poor are made at the lowest possible level of government, in close consultation with those affected;
* harassment by corrupt officials and the current lack of legal recourse by slum dwellers is redressed; and
* the general perception of the problem of illegal squatters rises above the level of 'places where anarchy and confusion reign'.

QUITO, ECUADOR

Between 1950 and 2001, Quito grew from 200,000 to 1.4 million inhabitants and evolved from a centrally oriented city to an urban agglomeration through the incorporation of minor urban centres and the peripheral area. The urban structure has been conditioned by the scarcity of flat land, topographic irregularities of the surrounding mountain system and the numerous east–west slopes.

The phenomenon of popular neighbourhoods in Quito is relatively recent. It started during the mid 1970s as a result of massive migration to Quito. Low-income populations

seeking housing settled on the peripheral areas of the city, in deteriorated houses in the historical centre, and also in houses located in nearby towns. This process has consolidated during the last decade. Recent settlements located in areas of irregular topography, in the northern and southern peripheries of the city, are composed of dwellings such as huts, hovels and small houses, built with inadequate materials. There is no drinking water, no sewage and few of these dwellings possess latrines. The rubbish collection service is nonexistent or inefficient, and the main or secondary access roads are in poor condition, as is the street lighting.

The municipality defines slums as *barrios ilegales* – illegal settlements, meaning that these neighbourhoods don't possess an official approval and an urbanization licence.

In Quito, there are three main types of slums:

1   *Barrios periféricos*: these are popular neighbourhoods located on the urban edge.
2   *Conventillos*: these comprise deteriorated tenements in the historic centre.
3   *Rural neighbourhoods*: these house low-income families who commute to the urban area.

Most low-income households are located in the *barrios periféricos*. Many of the urban slum dwellers do not own the land on which they live and only some 24 per cent have secure tenure. However, the urban periphery neighbourhoods developed through the subdivision of agricultural plots, and most of these residents own the house and land. Only an estimated 10 per cent of them are in rented accommodation.

Income poverty, low levels of education, high unemployment rates and unsatisfied basic services affect a massive 82 per cent of the slum dwellers. Slum dwellers' perception of their status, however, is one of forthcoming integration through strategies for the progressive upgrading of living conditions and social inclusion.

Since 1993, the Law of the Metropolitan District of Quito (LDMQ) has provided a wider legal framework than the traditional municipal competencies. Applicable only to the urban and rural management of the Metro Quito, the LDMQ has generated important administrative changes with respect to decentralization.

The Quito local government, apart from strong investments in conventional infrastructure, is undertaking a massive process of land regularization and has adopted two innovative strategies to upgrade slums:

1   A programme to provide security of tenure has delivered property deeds to 13,000 families.
2   A metropolitan land and housing enterprise, conceived as a public–private partnership, intends to regulate the prices of land through direct participations in the market.

In 1996, approximately 200 poor families invaded and built their slums on a piece of public land zoned as a park near the historic area of Quito. For over six years the problem was untouched until a new municipal administration took office and developed a process of negotiation. In a very short time, the municipality was able to provide another plot of land and a private company built several blocks of flats to accommodate all of the families. The project was financed with a loan from a cooperative owned by the Chamber of Commerce, with further financial support provided by the Ministry of Housing and Urban Development. An NGO provided technical support and the required international seed money. The invaders are now moving to their new apartments and the city has recovered the land.

Quito's urban planning process has largely been motivated by technical rationality, although it was, in practice, often based on legitimization of *de facto* situations. Weak enforcement of land zoning and other regulatory controls have been at the root of today's problems, together with lack of sufficient involvement of the underprivileged groups. After 30 or 40 years of attempted solutions to Quito's slums and poverty problems, it seems clear that unilateral and small-scale efforts have lower success rates. Results were also limited when authorities and public entities adopted an authoritarian position that failed to include the communities and their organizations.

The lesson learned is that slum improvement and poverty alleviation efforts require precise targeting from the supply side, rather than coping with the situation from the demand side. Undesirable urbanization aspects and gradual construction of houses have been permitted for too long as an alternative to the difficulties posed by economic crises. Recent experiences, however, indicate that partnerships and agreement among stakeholders can lead to adequate solutions if executed in combination with political will and perseverance.

RABAT-SALÉ, MOROCCO

In Rabat-Salé, a slum is defined as any settlement of precarious housing either on private plots of land, or with the settlers being provisionally tolerated on publicly owned plots of land. The main categories in Rabat-Salé are:

- *Médinas*: these are the old neighbourhoods of the pre-colonial city. Their deterioration resulted from the out-migration of middle and well-off classes and of economic activities. This double loss impoverished the neighbourhoods. Lack of maintenance of houses that were rented room by room led to a rapid deterioration. The médinas continued to constitute a source of informal and irregular employment that allowed underprivileged populations to live and work there, attracting poor external populations. Médinas are comparatively well preserved and, although damaged in part, other sections have been rehabilitated. For some, the only problem is general urban development.
- *Intra-muros*: these shanties are slums with precarious buildings in sheet metal or adobe that date from the 1960s on rented or squatted plots of land. They emerged as spontaneous settlements on easily occupied lands near industrial or agricultural activities. Originally peripheral, they should have been integrated as the town was developing. These slums have been gradually and partially rebuilt with more permanent material. They have better urban integration, with some services and self-improvements of tertiary road, rail and waterways and organized garbage collection. However illegal, those slums that have existed for a long time are often tolerated by the authorities.
- *Peripheral slums*: these emerged in a similar way to the *intra-muros*, on easily accessible community land or near economic activity. However, their history is less marked by formal and structured interventions. They are still able to accommodate new populations because of lower densities. Their sheer numbers force the authorities to tolerate them.
- *Illegal districts*: these are groups of concrete buildings that more or less resemble traditional low-cost buildings built on purchased plots of land but without any permit. They are deprived of basic services and infrastructure. However, depending upon age and stage of legalization, their situations do vary. This is why it is difficult to consider them as similar to the previous categories, and to the 'slums' category in general. They are primarily designed in anticipation of legality. Populations in illegal districts are more heterogeneous than in the former categories, both in terms of origins and in socio-economic terms. Today, the oldest formations of illegal neighbourhoods are completely integrated within the urban environment. The first settlements were on rented or leased lands. The most recent settlements (since the 1970s) started as subdivided agricultural properties. The majority of the population is of lower-middle class, for whom these neighbourhoods were the only access to home-ownership.

The main policy on people living in slums involves resettling them in public housing estates; more rarely does the policy involve restructuring. Until quite recently, no differentiation was made between urbanized and peripheral slums. Urban policies never had the objective of improving slums or their social conditions. Interventions tried either to get rid of slums as obstacles to urban development or to minimize their impacts on the urban landscape and on the city image. In the past, reasons to 'clean up' slums and force their inhabitants to reception sites have included: political or security imperatives; the need to undertake big infrastructure works; urban modernization or improvement requirements; land or property pressures; and accidents or natural catastrophes. These sites are generally less central than the primary settlements (often outside of the urban area) and quite often lack adequate services. Alternatively, urban cosmetic operations that were meant to hide the unsightly or disturbing effects of slums, and to encapsulate them by limiting their expansion, were carried out.

During the 1970s and 1980s, some more positive interventions took place, prompted by the conviction that improvement *in situ* can resolve the problems of the poor in a more efficient way because it is adapted to their real conditions. These interventions came in two categories:

1   *Limited improvements*: neither part of programmes nor formal policy, they are mainly in the form of daily political management, and ad hoc negotiations involving elected representatives, local authorities, private agencies and populations regarding NGO and community-based action.
2   *Restructuring*: this encompasses upgrading projects implemented on a large scale and decided at the national level as policy popularized during the1970s and 1980s. The interventions brought basic infrastructure and services to existing shantytowns, regularized occupational status and allowed the occupants to build on their plots. From then on, the site is considered as integrated within the formal city. The best known operation is the Urban Development Project that integrated spatial and physical upgrading with social, economic or institutional improvements. This restructuring soon raised disputes, was called into question and was abandoned at the end of the 1980s. The central contentious issue concerned the quality of the final product – housing – as well as neighbourhoods.

The rapid evolution of legal urbanization around slums has generated strong pressures for their eradication. This pressure is sharply felt by the inhabitants and deepens the feelings of extreme marginalization. Cleaning up interventions, except for the recovered urban space ready for new urban development, does not achieve any improvement in housing conditions for the previous inhabitants. Confidence in resettlement as the perceived unique and best answer to the slum issue has entirely ceased during the last 15 years.

The only hope for Rabat-Salé lies in the steady promotion of regularization interventions, combined with massive basic infrastructure and services provision to underserved areas. This can only happen if Morocco is prepared to seriously step up its national- and local-level interventions in a holistic approach to urban poverty alleviation and to support social programmes that help slum inhabitants to emerge from their marginalization and societal exclusion. To achieve this, the general perception of slum dwellers has to be considerably improved nation-wide, and far greater emphasis must be given to participation and partnerships that involve all stakeholders and beneficiaries. Coherent urban policy must be promulgated as a start to creating a national system of urban governance that includes all sections of society.

RIO DE JANEIRO, BRAZIL

The history of Rio's slums is a long story of industrial and infrastructure development, high fertility rates and urbanization that persistently led to the displacement of the urban poor. Segregation initially took place in and along the urban periphery, reinforced during the late 1920s by Rio's first urban plan. The 1930s and 1950s saw mass construction of cheap housing in the suburbs, away from the city and its infrastructure. From the 1950s onwards, the suburbs became so crowded that only swamps, mangrove areas, steep hills and riverbanks were left for occupation. Lack of affordable housing and of a suitable mass transportation system promoted the further spread of *favelas* all over Rio, and the eastern parts in particular. The 1960s saw massive slum clearance, notably for speculative construction. By the 1970s, 13 per cent of the city population lived in slums. The 1980s saw not much change other than the promotion of self-construction and improvement that would hopefully lead to regularization. Despite the development of a new municipal housing policy during the 1990s, the magnitude and complexity of the issues faced are so enormous that slum issues continue to increase, as does the socio-spatial segregation of Rio's poor.

Sub-normal settlements (*aglomerado subnormal*) are settlements with the following characteristics:

* Residential settlement with more than 50 inhabitants.
* Houses of precarious materials or raw appearance due to lack of external finishes.
* Houses built without legal permit on land owned by someone else or whose status is unknown.
* Houses built in areas deprived of official street names and numbering, lacking infrastructure and services.

Four types of slums are identified:

1   *Favelas*: these are highly consolidated residential areas of self-construction on invaded public and private land and without infrastructure. They exist in large numbers all over Rio.
2   *Loteamentons*: these comprise illegal subdivisions of land not in compliance with planning rules or infrastructure. They are considered irregular if submitted for regularization by the planning authorities and clandestine if they have not. They are located mainly in the eastern part of Rio.
3   *Invasoes*: these consist of irregular occupation of public or private land still in the process of consolidation. They are frequently located on riverbanks, swamps, hills or in residual public areas, such as under viaducts and along roads throughout Rio.
4   *Cortiços*: these comprise social housing formed by one or more buildings located on a single plot, or shared rooms in a single building. The rooms are rented or sublet without contract. The dwellers share bathrooms, kitchen and sometimes even electrical appliances. Houses lack ventilation and lighting, they are frequently overcrowded, and one room may house many people while accommodating multiple uses. Services are deficient, and they are mainly located in the city centre.

Throughout the city, different types of illegality are often mixed, and it is difficult, in many cases, to recognize boundaries. There is no specific data on slum tenure. However, most slums are illegal, leaving the inhabitants without secure tenure. In practice, however, eviction is a low risk and a lively real-estate sector operates within slums. There is no visible end to growth.

A number of significant slum programmes are currently operating. The Programa Favela-Bairro follows the basic approach of urbanizing *favelas* and, at the same time, promotes social programmes of health and education. It does not cover the construction of housing units – unless in cases of resettlement – and it is focused on the improvement of the social inclusion of neighbourhoods.

The recently launched *Programa de Arrendamento Residencial* (PAR) reserved about US$1.1 billion for new dwellings in the metropolitan regions of Brazil. It supports public and public–private partnerships. Its key feature is the establishment of a 180-month rental contract, with an acquisition option, without interest.

State governments also have programmes of housing finance and urbanization. At the local government level, two types of private–public partnership can be discerned:

1   *Mobilization of municipal and community resources*: this encompasses local authority efforts to mobilize resources for low-income housing, and the use of small individual savings channelled through cooperatives and associations.
2   *Special funds*: these are created by local authorities with resources coming from (i) the municipal budget; (ii) urban instruments; (iii) national and state funds; (iv) payments and refunds of housing loans; and (v) mortgages given to housing projects.

Despite being innovative, programmes have been difficult to implement given:

*   excessive and time-consuming administrative requirements;
*   the exclusion of many potential candidates;
*   lack of banks at the municipal level to speed up the process of resource mobilization; and
*   difficulties for developers to use alternative technologies for sanitation, paving and housing.

The Favela-Bairro programme perhaps constitutes a best practice example in housing policy. Its innovative aspect is the introduction of social projects within the urbanization programme. By promoting articulation between several sectors of the municipal administration, it has managed to go forward in the required procedures for land ownership – one of the main demands of the population living in sub-normal settlements. The continuity of the programme will allow the improvement of some managerial aspects and structures, consolidating the key idea of integration between areas of social exclusion and the formal boroughs of the city – a segregation that is characteristic of the city at present.

SÃO PAULO, BRAZIL

São Paulo, a small trading town until the mid 19th century, slowly grew in importance through coffee exports. By the turn of the 20th century, the city was socially divided between the geographically high and low areas, with the wealthy in the higher central districts – the places of formal urban interventions – and the poor on the floodplains and along the railways.

Between 1930 and 1980, urbanization accelerated greatly, with an intense process of migration from the countryside, building on the existing socio-spatial segregation. At the end of the 1970s, the pattern of a wealthy centre and poor periphery began to change with, initially, different urban social groupings living in adjacent areas as a result of steadily growing numbers of poor migrants in all areas of the city. The 'lost decade' of the 1980s saw spiralling growth of shantytowns in the urban periphery, known as *favelas*, and inner-city slum tenements, known as *cortiços*. The *cortiço* was the dominating São Paulo slum type until the beginning of the 1980s, when the *favela* broke out of its traditional urban periphery confines and spread all over the city to become the new dominant type of slum. They did so by occupying just about every empty or unprotected urban lot and on lands where building is difficult, or of limited interest to the formal market. *Favelas* and *cortiços* have the following characteristics:

*   *Favela*: these are agglomerations of dwellings with limited dimensions, built with inadequate materials (old wood, tin, cans and even cardboard) distributed irregularly in lots, almost always lacking urban and social services and equipment, and forming a complex social, economic, sanitary, educational and urban order.
*   *Cortiço*: this is a unit used as a collective multifamily dwelling, totally or partially presenting the following characteristics: (i) made up of one or more buildings constructed on an urban lot; (ii) subdivided in several rented, sublet or ceded units on any ground whatsoever; (iii) several functions performed in the same room; (iv) common access and use of non-constructed spaces and sanitary installations; (v) in general, precarious circulation and infrastructure; and (vi) overcrowded population.

The *favela* is, in general, a squatter settlement type of accommodation – an owner-occupied structure located on an invaded lot and without security of tenure – while the *cortiço* is, generally, inner-city, dilapidated rental accommodation. The *cortiço*'s origin dates back to the 19th century as the *legal*, market alternative of popular housing. The *favela* is a much younger phenomenon and represents the *illegal* market alternative, utilizing invasion and squatting of open and unprotected lands. Unlike the *cortiço* dweller, who is subject to the laws of the market, to rent and to payment for services, *favela* dwellers are seen as having 'an easy life', not paying for anything.

The *favela* is largely owner-occupied, albeit often on squatted or invaded lands, whereas the *cortiço* is predominantly private-sector rental accommodation. Although figures depend upon the methodology applied, *favela* inhabitants now roughly outnumber *cortiço* dwellers at a rate of 3:1.

The industrial deconcentration of the 1980s caused medium-sized Brazilian cities to grow at rates much above those of the metropolises.[5] In large metropolises, this caused lower central area population growth rates or even a decrease. The peripheral areas, however, continued to grow at almost double the national urban rate. São Paulo's transformation from an industrial into a service metropolis was responsible for considerable further economic and social polarization and a rapidly growing income gap between the richest and the poorest. This process continues to fuel the growth and emergence of *favelas* and, as a whole, tenure patterns are therefore changing accordingly.

Both *favelas* and *cortiços* are popularly seen as a space for the city's 'shady characters, bums, troublemakers and dirty'. The medical metaphors 'cancer' and 'wound' are recurrent. The prejudice is quite ingrained, especially among neighbours, who see their property devalued by the slum. The image of the São Paulo *favela* dweller is confused with that of the 'marginal' and not so much with the crook or trafficker, as, for instance, in Rio de Janeiro.

The year 1971 saw the establishment of the first overall master plan for São Paulo, intended to establish guidelines for all municipal policies and urban zoning. The plan, however, did not cater for the peripheral areas, effectively excluding thousands from planning and public investments. A 1988 constitutional amendment expanded municipal decentralization and autonomy. However, in the face of insufficient national and federal fund disbursements to the local level, this had comparatively little impact. The latter is, moreover, the case as highly polarized local-level politics – with often opposing public policy priorities – tend to cancel each other out.

The *favelas*, however, had emerged during the 1970s as a target for limited public policy. Nevertheless, this largely involved cheap voter-drawing attempts rather than structurally addressing the issues. During the early 1990s, the *favelas* for the first time became the target of widespread action with a programme that served 41,000 families in its first two years. In the programme's ten-year existence, some US$322 million was invested. The *cortiço*, however, did not see any similar attention until recently when the central area real-estate price recovered and profitable activities started in these areas.

Currently, a new action plan for *favelas* is being implemented, which aims to reach 52,000 slum dwellers in the next three years with legalization of tenure and upgrading of slum areas, and to network with other social programmes.

The impact of all of these efforts is multiple, although not always convergent, and very little evaluated. It is therefore difficult to find out what their real impacts are. Programmes are frequently paralysed by changes in public administration and subsequent policy swings. Additionally,

neither state nor federal investments in poverty reduction reach São Paulo for technical reasons. Public policies conducted in highly unequal and polarized countries such as Brazil produce their own conflicts, tensions and impasses, since a common development project for all social classes is no longer easily visualized.

SYDNEY, AUSTRALIA

Since the 1840s, Sydney's housing development has historically followed a cyclical pattern of booms – in which large areas of poor quality housing were hastily erected on vacant land – and busts, in which poverty and misery combined with rapidly deteriorating and unserviced housing to create traditional slum areas. The first economic and population boom during the 1850s was followed by a depression during the 1860s, in which Sydney's first large slum areas emerged.

From 1906, the resident population began to fall in inner-city slum areas and some areas were razed to make way for commercially profitable redevelopments, especially factories and warehouses. Secondary employment centres began to be constructed further afield as the city expanded. The post-World War II wave of assisted immigration tripled Sydney's population within 50 years. Huge new, sprawling single-family homes in suburban areas were built, assisted by housing loans at concessional interest rates, and home-ownership rates soared to 70 per cent by 1960. The construction of urban services at these low densities was expensive and providers had a great deal of trouble keeping up. By 1970, it appeared that the whole inner-city area would be completely redeveloped for business purposes and that the working-class inhabitants would be displaced. However, inner-city areas with their historical precincts came to be seen as better located and more colourful than suburbia, and most inner-city slum areas were steadily redeveloped, sometimes by building new houses, but more often by refurbishing. The wave of gentrification spread south over the next 30 years to encompass much of the south Sydney local government area, though improvement has been patchy and still eludes some areas. Land became too expensive for industry and much of it has relocated to the outer west. The century-long population flow out of the inner areas has reversed: between 1995 and 2000, the population of Sydney's inner suburbs grew by an average of 15 per cent each year, which was among the fastest growth rates in the country.

There is no official definition of slums. The term is regarded as offensive and is rarely used. Three types of area with relatively dilapidated housing are considered:

1   Inner-city former slums, now partly gentrified.
2   Extensive public-sector estates toward the periphery.
3   Areas with cheap housing, centred about 20 kilometres to the south-west of the central business district (CBD), where many new immigrants and other disadvantaged groups live.

Accommodation in the inner areas are mostly private rental, though with an increasing proportion of homeowners and some public housing. The estates are primarily public housing, with some 'right-to-buy' ownership and private rental. In some places, housing associations are becoming established. The immigrant areas have a good proportion of home-ownership and public housing, but private rental is increasing.

Apart from a few run-down suburban blocks and areas, Sydney no longer has any slums as is normally conceived, although there are many areas where disadvantaged people live in high concentrations. Its traditional inner-city slum areas have moved from squalor to mixed-income status, with high proportions both of advantaged and disadvantaged people and culturally disparate groups. The city is shaped by multiculturalism and a fairly profound spatial separation of social and income groups – mediated through globalization – through which the slums of the future might possibly emerge. There are large deteriorating tracts of poorly maintained public housing estates near the outskirts that form the focus of most social interventions for the disadvantaged. To the south-west of Sydney stretch some 60 kilometres of flat suburban sprawl, standing in sharp contrast to the wealth and privilege of the northern suburbs. Here, the bulk of population increase is taking place, where the new immigrants increasingly settle, and the disadvantaged can find affordable housing and support mechanisms. The city is fairly clearly dividing between a 'new economy' around the CBD area, and an 'old economy' of poor households ringed by suburban families to the west.

During the 1980s and 1990s, the gap between the rich and the poor widened considerably, although in absolute terms everyone was better off. With regard to the three 'slum' types:

1   Despite gentrification and the impact of higher income or shared professional households, low-income people still live in significant concentrations in inner Sydney. It is the middle class and families that are absent in their usual numbers.

2   Market rent policies have caused average incomes to fall rapidly in the old public housing estates, and most people are on pensions and benefits. Single mothers are particularly prevalent.

3   Ethnic groups improve their status with time and move to better suburbs, so that successive waves of new immigrants tend to occupy the cheapest housing – currently, Vietnamese, Lebanese and Somalis. Studies have shown no essential difference between second-generation immigrants and the general population.

The two major governmental housing programmes are public housing (mostly post-1945) and rent assistance (since the late 1980s), as well as very large programmes of concessional housing loans to lower middle-income groups from 1945 to 1990 – although these have become less necessary due to low interest rates and secondary mortgage markets. From the late 1970s, public housing became 'welfare housing' and is now restricted almost entirely to the most disadvantaged groups, who are heavily subsidized. During the late 1980s, it became obvious that public housing construction was never going to keep up with increasing demand, and that the majority of disadvantaged people would remain in the private rental sector. Rent assistance has become the largest housing programme, with national outlays of about US$700 million, compared with US$550 million for public housing. Housing policy has been in something of an impasse for a decade, with the Commonwealth unwilling to take responsibility for the public housing deficit from the states (which would enable the states to expand the stock).

The marginalization of public housing has resulted in many social problems on the larger estates, and the lack of rent-paying middle-class households has reduced operational funds below the level required for sustainability. Almost no new public housing is being constructed in Sydney, with capital funds now devoted to upgrading existing estates. In the meantime, with continuing work-force restructuring, family breakdown and population ageing contributing to polarization, the demand for public housing continues to grow. Some joint ventures with the private sector to build more affordable housing have been tried, but these have been small scale. Cooperation between tenants and a housing association in one estate to police social problems and improve run-down housing has reduced social problems considerably. Joint programmes between state departments of housing, health, education and social welfare to provide a comprehensive improvement strategy for problem areas are taking place.

NOTES

1   However, the following circumstantial indications may be helpful. With a labour force growth rate of 3 per cent due to the large youth bulge in the population pyramid now reaching working age, it must be assumed that household formation is perhaps also in the region of 3 per cent. As the informal sector absorbs about half of the city's labour, and while this percentage is growing, the indications perhaps hint at a new possible growth in informal settlement formation.

2   The goal was eventually to make housing free.

3   Although the segregation by ethnicity was government sanctioned, there are indications that, at least initially, there was also a voluntary cultural segregation.

4   All of those households covered in the rapid survey except one were renting.

5   Between 100,000 and 500,000 inhabitants.

PART V

STATISTICAL ANNEX

■ **General disclaimer**

The designations employed and presentation of the data do not imply the expression of any opinion whatsoever on the part of the Secretariat of the United Nations concerning the legal status of any country, city or area or of its authorities, or concerning the delimitation of its frontiers or boundaries.

DATA TABLES

Regional-Level Data

A.1   Demographic indicators   246
A.2   Housing indicators   247
A.3   Economic and social indicators   248

Country-Level Data

Demographic indicators and household projections
B.1   Size and growth of total population and households   249
B.2   Urbanization trends, size and growth of urban and rural population   252
Housing and infrastructure indicators
B.3   Housing-ownership and water and toilet facilities, selected countries   255
B.4   Access to improved water sources and sanitation   258
B.5   Energy and transport   260
Economic and social indicators
B.6   Economic development indicators   262
B.7   Social indicators   264

City-Level Data

Demographic indicators and household projections
C.1   Urban agglomerations: population size and growth rate   267
C.2   Households' living conditions, selected cities   273
Housing and infrastructure indicators
C.3   Housing indicators, selected cities   274
C.4   Environmental infrastructure, selected cities   277
C.5   Transport and environment indicators, selected cities   280
Economic and social indicators
C.6   Social indicators, selected cities   283
C.7   Urban governance indicators, selected cities   287

TECHNICAL NOTES

The Statistical Annex comprises 17 tables covering three broad categories: (i) demographic indicators and households data; (ii) housing and housing infrastructure indicators; and (iii) economic and social indicators. These tables are divided into three sections presenting data at the regional, country and city levels. Tables A.1 to A.3 present regional-level data grouped by selected criteria of geographic, economic and development aggregation. Tables B.1 to B.7 contain country-level data and Tables C.1 to C.7 are devoted to city-level data. Data have been compiled from various international sources, from national statistical offices and from the United Nations.

EXPLANATION OF SYMBOLS

The following symbols have been used in presenting data throughout the Statistical Annex:

Category not applicable   ..
Data not available   ...
Magnitude zero   –

COUNTRY GROUPINGS AND STATISTICAL AGGREGATES

More developed regions: All countries and areas of Europe and Northern America, as well as Australia, Japan and New Zealand.

Less developed regions: All countries and areas of Africa, Latin America, Asia (excluding Japan), and Oceania (excluding Australia and New Zealand).

Least developed countries (LDCs): The United Nations currently designates 49 countries as LDCs: Afghanistan, Angola, Bangladesh, Benin, Bhutan, Burkina Faso, Burundi, Cambodia, Cape Verde, Central African Republic, Chad, Comoros, Democratic Republic of the Congo, Djibouti, Equatorial Guinea, Eritrea, Ethiopia, Gambia, Guinea, Guinea-Bissau, Haiti, Kiribati, Lao People's Democratic Republic, Lesotho, Liberia, Madagascar, Malawi, Maldives, Mali, Mauritania, Mozambique, Myanmar, Nepal, Niger, Rwanda, Samoa, Sao Tome and Principe, Senegal, Sierra Leone, Solomon Islands, Somalia, Sudan, Togo, Tuvalu, Uganda, United Republic of Tanzania, Vanuatu, Yemen, Zambia.

Landlocked developing countries (LLDCs): Afghanistan, Armenia, Azerbaijan, Bhutan, Bolivia, Botswana, Burkina Faso, Burundi, Central African Republic, Chad, Ethiopia, Kazakhstan, Kyrgyzstan, Lao People's Democratic Republic, Lesotho, Malawi, Mali, Mongolia, Nepal, Niger, Paraguay, Rwanda, Swaziland, Tajikistan, TFYR Macedonia, Turkmenistan, Uganda, Uzbekistan, Zambia, Zimbabwe.

Small island developing states (SIDS): Antigua and Barbuda, Aruba, Bahamas, Bahrain, Barbados, Belize, Cape Verde, Comoros, Cook Islands, Cuba, Cyprus, Dominica, Dominican Republic, Fiji, Grenada, Guinea-Bissau, Guyana, Haiti, Jamaica, Kiribati, Maldives, Malta, Marshall Islands, Mauritius, Micronesia (Federated States of), Nauru, Netherlands Antilles, Niue, Palau, Papua New Guinea, Saint Kitts and Nevis, Saint Lucia, Samoa, Sao Tome and Principe, Seychelles, Singapore, Solomon Islands, Saint Vincent and the Grenadines, Suriname, Tokelau, Tonga, Trinidad and Tobago, Tuvalu, United States Virgin Islands, Vanuatu.

United Nations Regional Groups[1]

African States: Algeria, Angola, Benin, Botswana, Burkina Faso, Burundi, Cameroon, Cape Verde, Central African Republic, Chad, Comoros, Congo, Côte d'Ivoire, Democratic Republic of Congo, Djibouti, Egypt, Equatorial Guinea, Eritrea, Ethiopia, Gabon, Gambia, Ghana, Guinea, Guinea-Bissau, Kenya, Lesotho, Liberia, Libyan Arab Jamahiriya, Madagascar, Malawi, Mali, Mauritania, Mauritius, Morocco, Mozambique, Namibia, Niger, Nigeria, Rwanda, Sao Tome and Principe, Senegal, Seychelles, Sierra Leone, Somalia, South Africa, Sudan, Swaziland, Togo, Tunisia, Uganda, United Republic of Tanzania, Zambia, Zimbabwe.

Asian States: Afghanistan, Bahrain, Bangladesh, Bhutan, Brunei Darussalam, Cambodia, China, Cyprus, Democratic People's Republic of Korea, Fiji, India, Indonesia, Iran, Iraq, Japan, Jordan, Kazakhstan, Kuwait, Kyrgyzstan, Lao People's Democratic Republic, Lebanon, Malaysia, Maldives, Marshall Islands, Micronesia (Federated States of), Mongolia, Myanmar, Nauru, Nepal, Oman, Pakistan, Palau, Papua New Guinea, Philippines, Qatar, Republic of Korea, Samoa, Saudi Arabia, Singapore, Solomon Islands, Sri Lanka, Syrian Arab Republic, Tajikistan, Thailand, Tonga, Turkmenistan, Tuvalu, United Arab Emirates, Uzbekistan, Vanuatu, Viet Nam, Yemen.

Eastern European States: Albania, Armenia, Azerbaijan, Belarus, Bosnia and Herzegovina, Bulgaria, Croatia, Czech Republic, Georgia, Hungary, Latvia, Lithuania, Poland, Republic of Moldova, Romania, Russian Federation, Serbia and Montenegro, Slovakia, Slovenia, TFYR Macedonia, Ukraine.

Latin American and Caribbean States: Antigua and Barbuda, Argentina, Bahamas, Barbados, Belize, Bolivia, Brazil, Chile, Colombia, Costa Rica, Cuba, Dominica, Dominican Republic, Ecuador, El Salvador, Grenada, Guatemala, Guyana, Haiti, Honduras, Jamaica, Mexico, Nicaragua, Panama, Paraguay, Peru, Saint Kitts and Nevis, Saint Lucia, Saint Vincent and the Grenadines, Suriname, Trinidad and Tobago, Uruguay, Venezuela.

Western Europe and Other States: Andorra, Australia, Austria, Belgium, Canada, Denmark, Finland, France, Germany, Greece, Iceland, Ireland, Israel, Italy, Liechtenstein, Luxembourg, Malta, Monaco, Netherlands, New Zealand, Norway, Portugal, San Marino, Spain, Sweden, Switzerland, Turkey, United Kingdom.

United Nations Regional Commissions

Economic Commission for Africa (UNECA): Algeria, Angola, Benin, Botswana, Burkina Faso, Burundi, Cameroon, Cape Verde, Central African Republic, Chad, Comoros, Congo, Côte d'Ivoire, Democratic Republic of Congo, Djibouti, Egypt, Equatorial Guinea, Eritrea, Ethiopia, Gabon, Gambia, Ghana, Guinea, Guinea-Bissau, Kenya, Lesotho, Liberia, Libyan Arab Jamahiriya, Madagascar, Malawi, Mali, Mauritania, Mauritius, Morocco, Mozambique, Namibia, Niger, Nigeria, Rwanda, Sao Tome and Principle, Senegal, Seychelles, Sierra Leone, Somalia, South Africa, Sudan, Swaziland, Togo, Tunisia, Uganda, United Republic of Tanzania, Zambia, Zimbabwe.

Economic and Social Commission for Asia and the Pacific (UNESCAP):[2] Afghanistan, Armenia, Australia, Azerbaijan, Bangladesh, Bhutan, Brunei Darussalam, Cambodia, China, Democratic Peoples Republic of Korea, Fiji, France, Georgia, India, Indonesia, Iran, Japan, Kazakhstan, Kiribati, Kyrgyzstan, Lao People's Democratic Republic, Malaysia, Maldives, Marshall Islands, Micronesia (Federated States of), Mongolia, Myanmar, Nauru, Nepal, Netherlands, New Zealand, Pakistan, Palau, Papua New Guinea, Philippines, Republic of Korea, Russian Federation, Samoa, Singapore, Solomon Islands, Sri Lanka, Tajikistan, Thailand, Tonga, Turkey, Turkmenistan, Tuvalu, United Kingdom, United States, Uzbekistan, Vanuatu, Viet Nam.

Associate Members: American Samoa, Cook Islands, French Polynesia, Guam, Hong Kong SAR of China, Macao SAR of China, New Caledonia, Niue, Northern Marianas.

Economic and Social Commission for Western Asia (UNESCWA):[3] Bahrain, Egypt, Iraq, Jordan, Kuwait, Lebanon, Oman, Palestine, Qatar, Saudi Arabia, Syrian Arab Republic, United Arab Emirates, Yemen.

Economic Commission for Latin America and the Caribbean (UNECLAC):[4] Antigua and Barbuda, Argentina, Bahamas, Barbados, Belize, Bolivia, Brazil, Canada, Chile, Colombia, Costa Rica, Cuba, Dominica, Dominican Republic, Ecuador, El Salvador, France, Grenada, Guatemala, Guyana, Haiti, Honduras, Italy, Jamaica, Mexico, Netherlands, Nicaragua, Panama, Paraguay, Peru, Portugal, Saint Kits and Nevis, Saint Lucia, Saint Vincent and the Grenadines, Spain, Suriname, Trinidad and Tobago, United Kingdom, United States, Uruguay, Venezuela.

Associate Members: Anguilla, Aruba, British Virgin Islands, Montserrat, Netherlands Antilles, Puerto Rico, United States Virgin Islands.

Economic Commission for Europe (ECE):[5] Albania, Andorra, Armenia, Austria, Azerbaijan, Belarus, Belgium, Bosnia and Herzegovina, Bulgaria, Canada, Croatia, Cyprus, Czech Republic, Denmark, Estonia, Finland, France, Georgia, Germany, Greece, Hungary, Iceland, Ireland, Israel, Italy, Kazakhstan, Kyrgzstan, Latvia, Liechtensten, Lithuania, Luxembourg, Malta, Monaco, Netherlands, Norway, Poland, Portugal, Republic of Moldova, Romania, Russian Federation, San Marino, Serbia and Montenegro, Slovakia, Slovenia, Spain, Sweden, Switzerland, TFYR Macedonia, Tajikistan, Turkey, Turkmenistan, Ukraine, United Kingdom, United States, Uzbekistan.

Countries in the Human Development Aggregates[6]

High human development (*HDI 0.800 and above*):[7] Antigua and Barbuda, Argentina, Australia, Austria, Bahamas, Bahrain, Barbados, Belgium, Brunei Darussalam, Canada, Chile, Hong Kong SAR of China, Costa Rica, Croatia, Cyprus, Czech Republic, Denmark, Estonia, Finland, France, Germany, Greece, Hungary, Iceland, Ireland, Israel, Italy, Japan, Kuwait, Latvia, Lithuania, Luxembourg, Malta, Netherlands, New Zealand, Norway, Poland, Portugal, Qatar, Republic of Korea, Saint Kitts and Nevis, Seychelles, Singapore, Slovakia, Slovenia, Spain, Sweden, Switzerland, Trinidad and Tobago, United Arab Emirates, United Kingdom, United States, Uruguay.

Medium human development (*HDI 0.500–0.799*): Albania, Algeria, Armenia, Azerbaijan, Belarus, Belize, Bolivia, Botswana, Brazil, Bulgaria, Cambodia, Cameroon, Cape Verde, China, Colombia, Comoros, Congo, Cuba, Dominica, Dominican Republic, Ecuador, Egypt, El Salvador, Equatorial Guinea, Fiji, Gabon, Georgia, Ghana, Grenada, Guatemala, Guyana, Honduras, India, Indonesia, Iran (Islamic Republic of), Jamaica, Jordan, Kazakhstan, Kenya, Kyrgyzstan, Lebanon, Lesotho, Libyan Arab Jamahiriya, Malaysia, Maldives, Mauritius, Mexico, Mongolia, Morocco, Myanmar, Namibia, Nicaragua, Oman, Panama, Papua New Guinea, Paraguay, Peru, Philippines, Republic of Moldova, Romania, Russian Federation, Saint Lucia, Saint Vincent and the Grenadines, Samoa, Sao Tome and Principe, Saudi Arabia, Solomon Islands, South Africa, Sri Lanka, Suriname,

Swaziland, Syrian Arab Republic, Tajikistan, TFYR Macedonia, Thailand, Tunisia, Turkey, Turkmenistan, Ukraine, Uzbekistan, Vanuatu, Venezuela, Viet Nam, Zimbabwe.

Low human development (*HDI below 0.500*):[8] Angola, Bangladesh, Benin, Bhutan, Burkina Faso, Burundi, Central African Republic, Chad, Côte d'Ivoire, Democratic Republic of the Congo, Djibouti, Eritrea, Ethiopia, Gambia, Guinea, Guinea-Bissau, Haiti, Lao People's Democratic Republic, Madagascar, Malawi, Mali, Mauritania, Mozambique, Nepal, Niger, Nigeria, Pakistan, Rwanda, Senegal, Sierra Leone, Sudan, Togo, Uganda, United Republic of Tanzania, Yemen, Zambia.

Countries in the income aggregates[9]

High income (*GNP per capita of US$9266 or more in 2000*): Australia, Austria, Bahamas, Barbados, Belgium, Brunei Darussalam, Canada, Hong Kong SAR of China, Cyprus, Denmark, Finland, France, Germany, Greece, Iceland, Ireland, Israel, Italy, Japan, Kuwait, Luxembourg, Malta, Netherlands, New Zealand, Norway, Portugal, Qatar, Singapore, Slovenia, Spain, Sweden, Switzerland, United Arab Emirates, United Kingdom, United States.

Medium income (*GNP per capita of US$756-US$9265 in 2000*): Albania, Algeria, Antigua and Barbuda, Argentina, Bahrain, Belarus, Belize, Bolivia, Botswana, Brazil, Bulgaria, Cape Verde, Chile, China, Colombia, Costa Rica, Croatia, Cuba, Czech Republic, Djibouti, Dominica, Dominican Republic, Ecuador, Egypt, El Salvador, Equatorial Guinea, Estonia, Fiji, Gabon, Grenada, Guatemala, Guyana, Honduras, Hungary, Iran (Islamic Republic of), Jamaica, Jordan, Kazakhstan, Latvia, Lebanon, Libyan Arab Jamahiriya, Lithuania, Malaysia, Maldives, Mauritius, Mexico, Morocco, Namibia, Oman, Panama, Papua New Guinea, Paraguay, Peru, Philippines, Poland, Republic of Korea, Romania, Russian Federation, Saint Kitts and Nevis, Saint Lucia, Saint Vincent and the Grenadines, Samoa, Saudi Arabia, Seychelles, Slovakia, South Africa, Sri Lanka, Suriname, Swaziland, Syrian Arab Republic, TFYR Macedonia, Thailand, Trinidad and Tobago, Tunisia, Turkey, Turkmenistan, Uruguay, Vanuatu, Venezuela.

Low income (*GNP per capita of US$755 or less in 2000*): Angola, Armenia, Azerbaijan, Bangladesh, Benin, Bhutan, Burkina Faso, Burundi, Cambodia, Cameroon, Central African Republic, Chad, Comoros, Congo, Côte d'Ivoire, Democratic Republic of the Congo, Eritrea, Ethiopia, Gambia, Georgia, Ghana, Guinea, Guinea-Bissau, Haiti, India, Indonesia, Kenya, Kyrgyzstan, Lao People's Democratic Republic, Lesotho, Madagascar, Malawi, Mali, Mauritania, Mongolia, Mozambique, Myanmar, Nepal, Nicaragua, Niger, Nigeria, Pakistan, Republic of Moldova, Rwanda, Sao Tome and Principe, Senegal, Sierra Leone, Solomon Islands, Sudan, Tajikistan, Togo, Uganda, Ukraine, United Republic of Tanzania, Uzbekistan, Viet Nam, Yemen, Zambia, Zimbabwe.

Regional aggregates for Millennium Development Goal (MDG) indicators

At the December 2001 and March and April 2002 expert groups on Millennium Development Goal (MDG) indicators, the appropriate country and area classification for regional aggregates was discussed. It was agreed and affirmed that regional aggregates of agencies' series would conform as much as possible to the United Nations Statistics Division (UNSD)/Population Division (PD) classification in the UNSD 'M/49' code book. Many agencies followed this plan in preparing their series for use in the Secretary-General's first monitoring report (A/57/270); but in a few cases the data were too complex and there was insufficient time to do the recalculations with confidence.

UNSD requested that those regional estimates not originally submitted according to the UNSD/PD classification be recalculated for this purpose. This will enable UNSD to provide regional estimates on its MDG indicators' site according to a comparable classification. The importance of this harmonization is twofold: firstly, to avoid confusing the user with varying classifications that are difficult to compare, and, secondly, and very substantively, to allow for inter-regional comparisons of regional aggregates. The UNSD Regional Classification provides the list of regions and sub-regions, as well as of countries included in each of them.

United Nations Statistics Division (UNSD) regional classification

Developed regions

Europe: Albania, Andorra, Austria, Belarus, Belgium, Bosnia and Herzegovina, Bulgaria, Channel Islands, Croatia, Czech Republic, Denmark, Estonia, Faeroe Islands, Finland, France, Germany, Greece, Hungary, Iceland, Ireland, Isle of Man, Italy, Latvia, Liechtenstein, Lithuania, Luxembourg, Malta, Monaco, Netherlands, Norway, Poland, Portugal, Republic of Moldova, Romania, Russian Federation, San Marino, Serbia and Montenegro, Slovakia, Slovenia, Spain, Sweden, Switzerland, TFYR Macedonia, Ukraine, United Kingdom.

Other: Canada, United States, Australia, New Zealand, Japan.

Developing regions

Northern Africa: Algeria, Egypt, Libyan Arab Jamahiriya, Morocco, Tunisia, Western Sahara.

Sub-Saharan Africa: Angola, Benin, Botswana, Burkina Faso, Burundi, Cameroon, Cape Verde, Central African Republic, Chad, Comoros, Congo, Côte d'Ivoire, Democratic Republic of the Congo, Djibouti, Equatorial Guinea, Eritrea, Ethiopia, Gabon, Gambia, Ghana, Guinea, Guinea-Bissau, Kenya, Lesotho, Liberia, Madagascar, Malawi, Mali, Mauritania, Mauritius, Mayotte, Mozambique, Namibia, Niger, Nigeria, Réunion, Rwanda, Sao Tome and Principe, Senegal, Seychelles, Sierra Leone, Somalia, South Africa, Sudan, Swaziland, Togo, Uganda, United Republic of Tanzania, Zambia, Zimbabwe.

Latin America and the Caribbean: Anguilla, Antigua and Barbuda, Argentina, Aruba, Bahamas, Barbados, Belize, Bermuda, Bolivia, Brazil, British Virgin Islands, Cayman Islands, Chile, Colombia, Costa Rica, Cuba, Dominica, Dominican Republic, Ecuador, El Salvador, Falkland Islands (Malvinas), French Guiana, Grenada, Guadeloupe, Guatemala, Guyana, Haiti, Honduras, Jamaica, Martinique, Mexico, Montserrat, Netherlands Antilles, Nicaragua, Panama, Paraguay, Peru, Puerto Rico, Saint Kitts and Nevis, Saint Lucia, St Vincent and the Grenadines, Suriname, Trinidad and Tobago, Turks and Caicos Islands, Uruguay, United States Virgin Islands, Venezuela.

Eastern Asia: China, Hong Kong SAR of China, Macao SAR of China, Democratic People's Republic of Korea, Republic of Korea, Mongolia.

South-central Asia: Afghanistan, Bangladesh, Bhutan, India, Iran (Islamic Republic of), Kazakhstan, Kyrgyzstan, Maldives, Nepal, Pakistan, Sri Lanka, Tajikistan, Turkmenistan, Uzbekistan.

Southeast Asia: Brunei Darussalam, Cambodia, Indonesia, Lao People's Democratic Republic, Malaysia, Myanmar, Philippines, Singapore, Thailand, Timor-Leste, Viet Nam.

Western Asia: Armenia, Azerbaijan, Bahrain, Cyprus, Georgia, Iraq, Israel, Jordan, Kuwait, Lebanon, Occupied Palestinian Territory, Oman, Qatar, Saudi Arabia, Syrian Arab Republic, Turkey, United Arab Emirates, Yemen.

Oceania: American Samoa, Cook Island, Fiji, French Polynesia, Guam, Kiribati, Marshall Islands, Micronesia (Federated States of), Nauru, Niue, New Caledonia, Northern Mariana Islands, Palau, Papua New Guinea, Samoa, Solomon Islands, Tokelau, Tonga, Tuvalu, Vanuatu.

NOMENCLATURE AND ORDER OF PRESENTATION

Tables A.1 to A.3 contain regional, income and development aggregates data. Tables B.1 to B.7 and C.1 to C.6 contain national- and city-level data, respectively. In these tables, the countries or areas are listed in English alphabetical order within the macro-regions of Africa, Asia, Europe, Latin America, Northern America and Oceania. Countries or area names are presented in the form commonly used within the United Nations Secretariat for statistical purposes. Due to space limitations, the short name is used – for example, the United Kingdom of Great Britain and Northern Ireland is referred to as 'United Kingdom', the United States of America as 'United States'.

DEFINITION OF STATISTICAL TERMS

Access to improved drinking water supply: 'Improved' water supply technologies are household connection, public standpipe, borehole, protected dug well, protected spring, rainwater collection. Availability of at least 20 litres per person per day from a source within 1 kilometre of the user's dwelling. 'Not improved' are unprotected well, unprotected spring, vendor-provided water, bottled water (based on concerns about the quantity of supplied water, not concerns over the quality of water), tanker truck-provided water.

Access to improved sanitation: 'Improved' sanitation technologies are connection to a public sewer, connection to septic system, pour-flush latrine, simple pit latrine, ventilated improved pit latrine. The excreta disposal system is considered adequate if it is private or shared (but not public) and if it hygienically separates human excreta from human contact. 'Not improved' are service or bucket latrines (where excreta are manually removed), public latrines, latrines with an open pit.

Access to water: Percentage of households with access to water. Access is defined as having water located within 200 metres of the dwelling. It refers to housing units where the piped water is available within the unit and to those where it is not available to occupants within their housing unit, but is accessible within the range of 200 metres. This assumes that access to piped water within that distance allows occupants to provide water for household needs without being subjected to extreme effort.

Adult illiteracy rate: Percentage of people aged 15 and over who cannot, with understanding, read and write a short, simple statement about their everyday life.

Civil society involvement or **Citizen participation in major planning decisions:** Based on responses (yes/no) to the following questions. Do cities involve the civil society in a formal participatory process prior to new major roads and highway proposals (A)?; alteration in zoning (B)?; and major public projects (C)?

Commercial energy production: Commercial forms of primary energy – petroleum (crude oil, natural gas liquids and oil from non-conventional sources); natural gas; solid fuels (coal, lignite and other derived fuels); and primary electricity, all converted into oil equivalents.

Commercial energy use: Apparent consumption, which is equal to indigenous production plus imports and stock changes, minus exports and fuels supplied to ships and aircraft engaged in international transport.

Conventional dwelling: A room or suite of rooms and its accessories in a permanent building or structurally separated part thereof that, by the way it has been built, rebuilt or converted, is intended for habitation by one household and is not, at the time of the enumeration, used wholly for other purposes. It should have a separate access to a street (direct or via a garden or grounds) or to a common space within the building (staircase, passage, gallery and so on). Examples of dwellings are houses, flats, suites of rooms, apartments. Therefore, the essential elements of a conventional dwelling are (i) a room or suite of rooms; (ii) located in a permanent building; (iii) with separate access to a street or to a common space; (iv) intended to be occupied by one household, equipped with the following facilities within dwelling: (v) kitchen or other space for cooking, (vi) fixed bath or shower, (vii) toilet and (viii) piped water. *Basic dwelling*: A housing unit that has some but not all of the essential facilities of a conventional dwelling. It is a permanent structure or a part of a permanent structure. Hence, it may be a room or a suite of rooms in a permanent building; but it is without some of the conventional dwelling facilities, such as kitchen, fixed bath or shower, piped water or toilet. In a number of countries or areas, a certain proportion of the housing inventory comprises such housing units, which possess some but not all of the characteristics of conventional dwellings. Therefore, basic dwellings are more or less conventional from the point of view of permanency of structure, but lack some of the housing facilities identified as essential (the four types being cooking facilities, bathing facilities, piped water and toilet). *Temporary housing unit*: A structure that, by the way in which it has been built, is not expected to maintain its durability for as long a period of time as (but has some of the facilities of) a conventional dwelling. This category also refers to a traditional and typical type of housing unit that does not have all of the characteristics of conventional or basic dwellings, but is considered somewhat suitable from the point of view of climate and tradition. This is especially the case in many tropical and subtropical rural areas where housing units have been constructed or built with locally available raw materials, such as bamboo, palm, straw or any similar materials. Such units often have mud walls, thatched roofs and so forth, and may be expected to last only for a limited time (from a few months to ten years), although occasionally they may last for longer periods. *Marginal housing unit*: A unit that does not have many of the features of a conventional dwelling and is generally characterized as unfit for human habitation, but that is used for the purpose of habitation. Therefore, it is neither a permanent structure nor one equipped with any of the essential facilities. These units are characterized by the fact that they are either makeshift shelters constructed of waste materials and generally considered unfit for habitation (for example, squatters' huts) or places that are not intended for human habitation although in use for that purpose (barns, warehouses, natural shelters and so on). Under almost all circumstances, such places of abode represent unacceptable housing. *Collective living quarters*: Include structurally separate and independent places of abode intended for habitation by large groups of individuals or several households and occupied at the time of the census. Such quarters usually have certain common facilities, such as

cooking and toilet installations, baths, lounge rooms or dormitories, which are shared by the occupants. They may be further classified into hotels, rooming houses and other lodging houses, institutions and camps.

Decentralization: Based on responses (all/some) to the following questions. Can the local government, without permission from higher governments set local tax levels (for example, property tax) (A)? Set user charges for services (B)?

Disaster prevention and mitigation instruments: Based on responses (yes/no) to the following questions. In the city, are there building codes (A)? Hazard mapping (B)? Natural disaster insurance for public and private buildings (C)? Building codes includes anti-cyclonic and anti-seismic building standards. They should be based on hazard and vulnerability assessment. Hazard mapping is a simple and effective way of ensuring that hazard maps are recorded and updated on a regular basis. The maps shall cover the entire city and its boundaries, be available to the public and be as recent as possible (less than five years' old).

Gross capital formation: Consists of outlays on additions to the fixed assets of the economy plus net changes in the level of inventories. Fixed assets include land improvements (for example, fences, ditches, drains), plant, machinery and equipment purchases, and the construction of roads, railways and the like, including schools, offices, hospitals, private residential dwellings, and commercial and industrial buildings. Inventories are stocks of goods held by firms to meet temporary or unexpected fluctuations in production or sales, and 'work in progress'. According to the 1993 System of National Accounts (SNA), net acquisitions of valuables are also considered capital formation.

Gross domestic product (GDP): At purchaser prices, this is the sum of the gross value added by all resident producers in the economy plus any product taxes, minus any subsidies not included in the value of the products. It is calculated without making deductions for depreciation of fabricated assets or for depletion and degradation of natural resources. *GDP per capita:* GDP divided by the mid-year population. Growth is calculated from constant price GDP data in local currency.

Gross school enrolment ratio: Number of students, by sex, enrolled in a level of education whether or not they belong in the relevant age group for that level, as a percentage of the population in the relevant group for that level.

Household: Estimations and projections prepared by UN-Habitat. Household statistics were collected through the Human Settlements Statistical Questionnaires. The concept of household is based on the arrangements made by persons, individually or in groups, for providing themselves with food or other essentials for living. A household may be either:

1   A one-person household – that is to say, a person who makes provision for his or her own food or other essentials for living without combining with any other person to form a part of a multiperson household; or

2   A multiperson household – that is to say, a group of two or more persons living together who make common provision for food or other essentials for living. The persons in the group may pool their incomes and may, to a greater or lesser extent, have a common budget; they may be related or unrelated persons or constitute a combination of persons both related and unrelated. This concept of household is known as the 'housekeeping' concept. It does not assume that the number of households and housing units is equal. Although the concept of housing unit implies that it is a space occupied by one household, it may also be occupied by more than one household or by a part of a household (for example, two nuclear households that share one housing unit for economic reasons or one household in a polygamous society routinely occupying two or more housing units).

Household connections: Percentage of households that, within their housing unit, are connected to piped water (A), sewerage (B), electricity (C) and telephone (D).

Household final consumption expenditure: The market value of all goods and services, including durable products (such as cars, washing machines and home computers), purchased by households. It excludes purchases of dwellings but includes imputed rent for owner-occupied dwellings. It also includes payments and fees to governments to obtain permits and licences. Here, household consumption expenditure includes the expenditures of non-profit institutions serving households, even when reported separately by the country. In practice, household consumption expenditure may include any statistical discrepancy in the use of resources relative to the supply of resources.

Household projection methods: Determined by availability and reliability of data. The five types of projection approaches followed by the lists of countries, for which the respective approach has been applied, are:

1   *Total headship rate-based projection:* Albania, Algeria, Austria, Bangladesh, Belarus, Benin, Bolivia, Botswana, Brazil, Brunei Darussalam, Bulgaria, Burkina Faso, Cambodia, Cape Verde, China Macau SAR, Colombia, Cyprus, Denmark, Dominican Republic, Ecuador, Estonia, Fiji, Finland, France, French Polynesia, Gambia, Georgia, Germany, Greece, Guatemala, Haiti, Honduras, Hungary, Ireland, Italy, India, Indonesia, Iraq, Japan, Jamaica, Kazakhstan, Kenya, Kuwait, Latvia, Lesotho, Libyan Arab Jamahiriya, Lithuania, Luxembourg, Malaysia, Maldives, Malta, Madagascar, Malawi, Mali, Mauritius, Mexico, Netherlands, New Caledonia, Nicaragua, Niger, Pakistan, Poland, Paraguay, Peru, Portugal, Republic of Korea, Rwanda, Singapore, Solomon Islands, South Africa, Spain, Sudan, Switzerland, Thailand, Tunisia, Turkey, Venezuela, Viet Nam, United Republic of Tanzania, United States, Yemen, Zambia and Zimbabwe.

2   *Headship size rate-based projection:* Armenia, Argentina, Australia, Azerbaijan, Bahamas, Bahrain, Barbados, Belgium, Belize, Burundi, Canada, Central African Republic, Chile, Congo, Costa Rica, El Salvador, Egypt, Guadeloupe, Guam, Guyana, Iran (Islamic Republic of), Israel, Jordan, Kyrgyzstan, Liberia, Martinique, Morocco, Netherlands Antilles, Nepal, New Zealand, Norway, Panama, Philippines, Puerto Rico, Republic of Moldova, Réunion, Romania, Russian Federation, Serbia and Montenegro, Samoa, Sweden, Syrian Arab Republic, Tajikistan, Trinidad and Tobago, Turkmenistan, Vanuatu, Ukraine, United Kingdom, Uruguay and Uzbekistan.

3   *Estimation on country level not possible:* Afghanistan, Angola, Bosnia and Herzegovina, Democratic People's Republic of Korea, Lebanon, Occupied Palestinian Territory, Sierra Leone, Timor-Leste and Western Sahara.

4   *Estimation on the basis of one data point:* Cameroon, Comoros, Côte d'Ivoire, Croatia, Czech Republic, Democratic Republic of the Congo, Eritrea, Ethiopia, Gabon, Ghana, Guinea, Guinea-Bissau, Iceland, Mauritania, Mongolia, Mozambique, Myanmar, Namibia, Nigeria, Oman, Papua New Guinea, Qatar, Senegal, TFYR Macedonia, Slovakia, Slovenia, Suriname, Togo, Uganda and United Arab Emirates.

5   *Estimation with no data point:* Bhutan, Chad, Djibouti, Equatorial Guinea, Lao People's Democratic Republic, Saudi Arabia, Somalia and Swaziland.

The following countries or areas are not included in the total number of households calculated for regions and other aggregates: American Samoa, Andorra, Anguilla, Antigua and Barbuda, Aruba, Bermuda, British Virgin Islands, Cayman Islands, Channel Islands, Cook Islands, Dominica, Faeroe Islands, Falklands, French Guiana, Gibraltar, Greenland, Grenada, Holy See, Isle of Man, Liechtenstein, Marshall Islands, Micronesia (Federated States of), Monaco, Montserrat, Nauru, Northern Mariana Islands, Palau, Pitcairn, Seychelles, Sao Tome and Principe, Saint Helena, Saint Kitts and Nevis, Saint Lucia, Saint Pierre and Miquelon, Saint Vincent, San Marino, Tokelau, Tonga, Tuvalu, Turks and Caicos Islands, United States Virgin Islands, Wallis and Futuna Islands.

For the following countries the estimates are extremely rough and cannot be interpreted on their own; they have only been calculated for completeness reasons on the aggregate (regional and global) level: Afghanistan, Angola, Bosnia and Herzegovina, Democratic People's Republic of Korea, Lebanon, Occupied Palestinian Territory, Sierra Leone, Timor-Leste and Western Sahara.

Housing price-to-income ratio: Ratio of the median free-market price of a dwelling unit and the median annual household income. *Rent-to-income ratio*: Ratio of the median annual rent of a dwelling unit and the median annual household income of renters.

Housing rights: Based on responses (yes/no) to the following questions. Does the constitution or national law promote the full and progressive realization of the right to adequate housing (A)? Does it include protections against eviction (B)?

Impediments to women: Based on responses (considerable/some/none) to the following questions. Are there impediments to women owning land (A)? Are there impediments to women inheriting land and housing (B)? Are there impediments to women taking mortgages in their own name (C)?

Labour force: Total labour force comprises people who meet the International Labour Organization (ILO) definition of the economically active population – all people who supply labour for the production of goods and services during a specified period. It includes both the employed and unemployed. While national practices vary in the treatment of such groups as the armed forces and seasonal or part-time workers, the labour force generally includes the armed forces, the unemployed and first-time job-seekers, but excludes homemakers and other unpaid caregivers and workers in the informal sector.

Level of urbanization: Percentage of the population residing in places classified as urban. Urban and rural settlements are defined in the national context and vary among countries (the definitions of urban are generally national definitions incorporated within the latest census).

Life expectancy at birth: Number of years a newborn infant would live if prevailing patterns of mortality at the time of birth were to stay the same throughout the child's life.

Literacy rate: Percentage of people aged 15 and above who can, with understanding, both read and write a short, simple statement on their everyday life.

Local environmental planning: Based on responses (yes/no) to the following questions. Has the city established a long-term strategic planning initiative for sustainable development, involving key partners (A)? Is this process institutionalized and/or has there been any legislative change to support cities to engage in sustainable development planning processes (B)? Is the city implementing local environmental action plans involving key partners (C)?

Local government revenue and expenditures: Total annual *local government revenue* from all sources in US dollars, both capital and recurrent, divided by population (three-year average) and capital expenditure in US dollars per person, by all local governments in the metropolitan area, averaged over the last three years. *Per capita*

expenditures include both fixed capital and plant as per the capital account.

Motor vehicles: Include cars, buses, and freight vehicles but not two-wheelers. Population figures refer to the mid-year population during the year for which data are available.

Ownership: *Owner:* A household that owns the living quarters it occupies, whether used wholly or partly for own occupation by the owner. This may include living quarters being purchased in installments or mortgaged, according to national legal systems and practice. Other arrangements, such as living quarters in co-operatives and housing associations, may also be included, depending upon national practices. *Tenant in publicly owned housing unit:* A household residing in a housing unit it does not own, but is owned by a public institution (disregarding whether or not the institution is sponsored by central or local government). These institutions may be co-operatives, housing associations or government agencies. *Tenant in privately owned housing unit:* A household residing in a housing unit that it does not own, but is owned by the private sector. This includes households renting a housing unit from individuals – for example, a landlord – or units owned by a private corporation.

Persons in housing units: Number of persons resident in housing units. *Persons per room:* Figures are derived by dividing the number of occupants by the number of rooms in a given housing unit. The number of rooms is obtained by multiplying the number of units by the number of rooms in the unit. The calculations were done by the Secretariat.

Poor households: Percentage of women and men-headed households situated below the locally defined poverty line. The poverty line is usually an 'absolute' poverty line, taken as the income necessary to afford a minimum nutritionally adequate diet, plus essential non-food requirements, for a household of a given size.

Population, total: Mid-year population estimates for the world, region, countries or areas. The Population Division of the United Nations Department of Economic and Social Affairs updates, every two years, population estimates and projections by incorporating new data, new estimates and new analysis of data on population, fertility, mortality and international migration. Data from new population censuses and/or demographic surveys are used to verify and update old estimates of population or demographic indicators, or to make new ones and to check the validity of the assumptions made in the projections. Total population refers to the estimates and projections (medium variant) of the total population for each country region and major area. *Annual growth rate*, calculated by UN-Habitat, refers to the average annual percentage change of population (r) during the indicated period (t) for each country, major regions and global totals. The formula used throughout the Annex is as follows: $r = [(1/t) \times \ln(A2/A1)] \times 100$, where 'A1' is a value at any given year; 'A2' is a value at any given year later than the year of 'A1'; 't' is the year interval between 'A1' and 'A2'; and 'ln' is the natural logarithm function.

Population, urban and rural: Mid-year estimates and projections (medium variant) of the population residing in human settlements classified as urban or rural.

Poverty definitions: *National poverty rate:* Percentage of the population living below the national poverty line. National estimates are based on population-weighted subgroup estimates from household surveys. Survey year is the year in which the underlying data were collected. *Population below US$1 a day* and *Population below US$2 a day:* Percentages of the population living on less than US$1.08 a day and US$2.15 a day at 1993 international prices (equivalent to US$1 and US$2 in 1985 prices, adjusted for purchasing power parity). Poverty rates are comparable across countries, but as result of revisions in purchasing power parity (PPP) exchange rates, they cannot be compared with poverty rates reported in previous editions for individual countries.

PPP (purchasing power parity) gross national income: Gross national income (GNI) converted to international dollars using purchasing power parity rates. An international dollar has the same purchasing power over GNI as a US dollar has in the United States.

Refugees, asylum-seekers and others concern: Data are provided by governments based on their own definitions and methods of collection. Total asylum-seekers, refugees and others of concern to the United Nations High Commissioner for Refugees (UNHCR) include the following. *Refugees:* Persons recognized as refugees under the international conventions, in accordance with the UNHCR Statute; persons allowed to stay on humanitarian grounds and those granted temporary protection. *Asylum-seekers:* Persons whose application for refugee status is pending in the asylum procedure or who are otherwise registered as asylum-seekers. The total number of asylum-seekers is underestimated, due to a lack of data from a number of countries. *Returned refugees:* Refugees who have returned to their country of origin during the year. *Internally displaced persons (IDPs):* Persons who are displaced within their country and to whom UNHCR extends protection or assistance, generally pursuant to a special request by a competent organ of the United Nations. *Returned IDPs:* IDPs of concern to UNHCR who have returned to their place of origin during the year.

Roads: Motorways, highways, main or national roads, and secondary or regional roads. A motorway is a road specially designed and built for motor vehicles that separates the traffic flowing in opposite directions. *Total road network:* Includes motorways, highways and main or national roads, secondary or regional roads, and all other roads in a country. *Paved roads:* Roads surfaced with crushed stone (macadam) and hydrocarbon binder or bitumized agents, with concrete, or with cobblestones, as a percentage of all of the country's roads measured in length.

Solid waste disposal: Percentage of solid waste disposed: to sanitary landfill (A), incinerated (B), disposed to open dump (C), recycled (D), burned openly (E), other (F).

Squatter household: A household that built a structure it occupies on land on which it does not have a title. Squatter settlements are usually built on the fringes of large cities, without a predetermined plan and without any legal validation. Most of the structures of these settlements usually fall into the category of 'marginal housing unit', although they may also consist of more solid structures.

Toilet inside housing unit: An installation, either flush or non-flush located within walls that constitute a housing unit. *Toilet outside unit:* Units where either a flush or a non-flush toilet is available to occupants, but is located outside of the housing unit walls. *Flush toilet:* An installation provided with piped water that permits humans to discharge their wastes and from which the wastes are flushed by water. A non-flush toilet is not equipped with piped water.

Traditional fuel use: Includes estimates of the consumption of fuel-wood, charcoal, bagasse, and animal and vegetable wastes. *Total energy use:* Commercial energy use and traditional fuel use.

Transparency and accountability: Based on responses (yes/no) to the following questions at the city level. Is there regular independent auditing of municipal accounts (A)? Published contracts and tenders for municipal services (B)? Sanctions against faults of civil servants (C)? Laws on disclosure of potential conflicts of interest (D)?

Transport used for work trips: Percentage of work trips undertaken by private car (A); train, tram or ferry (B); bus or minibus (C); other (motorcycle, bicycle and other non-motorized modes) (D). When several modes of transport are used for a given trip, the principal mode is selected.

Travel time: Average time in minutes for a one-way work trip. This is an average over all modes of transport.

Type of living quarters: Living quarters are structurally separate and independent places of abode. They may (i) have been constructed, built, converted or arranged for human habitation provided that they are not used wholly for other purposes and that, in the case of improvised housing units and collective living quarters, they are occupied at the time of the enumeration; or (ii) although not intended for habitation, actually be in use for such a purpose. Living quarters are either housing units or collective living quarters. *Housing unit:* A separate and independent place of abode intended for habitation by a single household, or one not intended for habitation but occupied as living quarters by a household at the time of the enumeration. It may be an occupied or vacant dwelling, an occupied mobile or improvised housing unit or any other place occupied as living quarters by a household at the time of the census. This category includes housing of various levels of permanency and acceptability.

Value added: The net output of an industry after adding up all outputs and subtracting intermediate inputs. The industrial origin of value added is determined by the International Standard Industrial Classification (ISIC) revision 3. Agriculture includes forestry and fishing. Industry comprises mining, manufacturing (also reported as a separate subgroup), construction, electricity, water, and gas. Manufacturing refers to industries. Services sector is derived as a residual (from GDP, less agriculture and industry) and may not properly reflect the sum of service output, including banking and financial services.

Under-five mortality: Percentage of female children and male children who die before reaching their fifth birthday. Child mortality = (number of deaths for children below five years of age during the year)/(average number of live births during the last five years).

Urban agglomeration: The contours of contiguous territory without regard to administrative boundaries. It comprises the city or town proper and also the suburban fringe lying outside of, but adjacent to, the city boundaries. Table B.1 contains revised estimates and projections for all urban agglomerations comprising 750,000 or more inhabitants in the year 2000. *Annual growth rate:* Average annual percentage change of population during the indicated period for each country's major regions and global totals.

Wastewater treated: Percentage of all wastewater undergoing some form of treatment.

Water consumption: Average consumption of water in litres per day per person, for all domestic uses (excludes industrial use) in settlements. Data in Table C.4 column 'A' refer to the city average, while column 'B' data refer to water consumption in informal settlements.

Water price, median: Median price paid per 1000 litres of water in US dollars, at the time of year when water is most expensive.

Water supply system: 'Housing units with piped water inside the housing unit' refers to the existence of water pipes within the walls that constitute a housing unit. Water can be piped from the community source – that is, one that is subject to inspection and control by public authorities. Water can be also piped into the unit from a private source, such as a pressure tank, a pump or some other installation. The category 'piped water outside unit, but within 200 metres' refers to units where the piped water is not available to occupants within the unit they reside in, but is accessible within the range of 200 metres, assuming that access to piped water within that distance allows occupants to provide water for household needs without being subjected to

extreme effort. 'Other' refers to units that do not have access to piped water at all, whose occupants depend upon springs or wells, or to units where piped water is located beyond 200 metres.

Women-headed household: Households headed by women. In identifying the members of a household, a common approach is to identify, first, the household head or reference person and then the remaining members of the household according to their relationship to the head or reference person. The head of household is defined as that person in the household who is acknowledged as such by other members. However, it is recognized that national practices in identifying household headship vary significantly on the basis of customs and cultural traditions.

SOURCES OF DATA

The Statistical Data Tables have been compiled from the following UN-Habitat databases: Human Settlements Statistics Database, Global Urban Observatory (GUO) Database, CitiBase and Habitat's Household Projections Project.

Various statistical publications from the United Nations and other international organizations have been used as well. Notable among them are International Energy Agency (IEA), *Energy Balances of OECD Countries,* Paris, various years. ILO (2003) *Economically Active Population Estimates and Projections: 1950–2010,* 4th edition, Geneva. International Road Federation (IRF) (2001) *World Road Statistics 2001*, Geneva. Organisation for Economic Co-operation and Development (OECD) *International Development Statistics*, CD-ROM, various years, Paris. United Nations (2001) *Compendium of Human Settlements Statistics 2001* (United Nations publication sales No E01.XVII5), New York. United Nations (2001) *World Urbanization Prospects: The 2001 revision*. United Nations Educational, Scientific and Cultural Organization (UNESCO) (2002), *Estimated Illiteracy Rate and Illiterate Population Aged 15 Years and Older, by Country, 1970–2015: July 2002 Assessment*. Institute for Statistics (UIS), Montreal. UNHCR (2002) *Statistical Yearbook 2001*, Geneva. United Nations Human Settlements Programme (UN-Habitat) (2002) *Global Urban Indicators Database 2*. UNSD (2002) *Energy Statistics Yearbook 2002*, New York. UNSD *National Accounts Statistics: Main Aggregates and Detailed Tables*, parts 1 and 2, various years, New York. World Bank (2002) *World Development Indicators, 2002*. World Health Organization (WHO) and United Nations Children's Fund (UNICEF), Water Supply and Sanitation Collaborative Council (2000) *Global Water Supply and Sanitation Assessment, 2000 Report*, Geneva and New York. World Resources Institute (2000) *World Resources 2000–2001*, Washington, DC.

NOTES

1. All members of the General Assembly arranged in Regional Groups. According to the *United Nations Handbook 2002*, this grouping is unofficial and has been developed to take account of the purposes of General Assembly Resolution 1991 (XVIII) (1963), 33/138 (1978) and 2847 (XXVI) (1971). The US is not a member of any regional group, but attends meetings of the Western European and Other States Group (WEOG) as an observer and is considered to be a member of that group for electoral purposes. Turkey participates fully in both the Asian and WEOG groups, but for electoral purposes is considered a member of WEOG only. Israel became a full member of WEOG on a temporary basis on 28 May 2000. As of 31 May 2002, Estonia and Kiribati were not members of any regional group. In addition to Member States, there is also a non-Member State, the Holy See, that has observer status in the United Nations. By General Assembly Resolution 52/250 (1998), the General Assembly conferred upon Palestine, in its capacity as observer, additional rights and privileges of participation. These included, *inter alia*, the right to participation in the general debate of the General Assembly, but did not include the right to vote or to put forward candidates.

2. UNESCAP has 52 Member States and 9 Associate Members.

3. The members of UNESCWA consist of Member States of the United Nations situated in Western Asia. There are 13 members.

4. UNECLAC has 41 Member States and 7 Associate Members.

5. The UNECE is composed of the European Members of the United Nations and US, Canada, Israel and the Central Asian and Caucasian Republics of the former USSR. The Holy See, which is not a member of the United Nations, participates in UNECE activities in a consultative capacity. Provision is also made for participation by representatives of other Member States of the United Nations inter-governmental and non-governmental organizations (NGOs) in activities of concern to them.

6. As classified by the United Nations Development Programme (UNDP); see *Human Development Reports* for detail.

7. 53 countries or areas.

8. 36 countries or areas.

9. As classified by the World Bank; see *World Development Reports* for detail.

METHODOLOGICAL NOTES

SLUM DWELLER ESTIMATIONS AT THE GLOBAL AND REGIONAL LEVELS

The Millennium Declaration has outlined detailed development goals that were further elaborated in the 'Road Map towards the Implementation of the United Nations Millennium Declaration'. The Road Map contains 8 goals, 18 targets and 48 indicators. Millennium Development Goal 7, Target 11 (MDG T 11) is: 'By 2020, to have achieved a significant improvement in the lives of 100 million slum dwellers'. Reporting on the MDG T 11 requires a global and regional estimation of the number of slum dwellers. Similar country estimates are required as part of the country-level MDG reports.

This report presents the first attempt to monitor the MDG T 11. This exercise uses currently available data to monitor the target. These data were not designed or collected with the objective of monitoring the MDG T 11. Accordingly, there is added uncertainty in the results provided. The ability to monitor progress – or the lack of progress – in reaching the target is no better than the quality of the data. It is therefore important to understand whether the data are of sufficient quality to meet policy needs. Before turning to the indicators used to track the MDG T 11, some of the properties of indicators are examined. The key properties in the context of the MDG indicators are:

* Is the indicator conceptually the right measure of the target?
* Are the data available?
* Are the data accurate?
* Is the coverage of the indicator sufficient for global and regional estimates?
* Are the available data consistent over time?

Departing from these questions, for each MDG target one or more indicators were specified.[1] The indicators identified to monitor MDG T 11 are Indicator 31, Proportion of urban population with access to improved sanitation; and Indicator 32, Proportion of households with access to secure tenure.[2] It was noted, in general, that 'the indicator might not capture the whole spectrum of a target, but only one or few aspects. This is caused by the difficulty of using one number to express a complex phenomenon and/or the difficulty of reaching agreement on a definition of multidimensional concerns, such as poverty' or slum dwelling.[3]

Research on estimating the number of slum dwellers started with an attempt to measure the phenomenon of 'secure tenure'. Secure tenure is the concept of 'protection from involuntary removal from land or residence except through due legal process'. *The indicator should be a proxy for the concern expressed in the target.* The MDG T 11 is to improve the lives of 100 million slum dwellers; therefore, the indicator should relate directly to that objective. Insecure tenure is commonly associated with being a slum dweller. However, the lack of data based on a specific and operational definition of secure tenure made direct estimation from the indicator impossible.[4] Initial efforts attempted unsuccessfully to use tenure status data (owner, renter and squatter) as a proxy measure. It was proposed that the attribute of secure tenure would be demonstrated in household behaviour. The proposition was that households with secure tenure could be measured by a proxy index that included information about the dwelling structure, access to urban infrastructure and legality of the residence. The strategy, then, was to combine several measurements for which data were available into a 'secure tenure index' and then to use this composite index to estimate the number of slum dwellers.

Foundations of the Secure Tenure Index

The Secure Tenure Index is a summary measure of the manifestation of security of tenure in cities. It hypothesizes the physical result of security of tenure in the city. Where secure tenure exists, there will be comparatively more dwelling unit assets and amenities. The characteristic variables for the Secure Tenure Index include the following:[5]

* Proportion of households with access to water (within 200 metres).
* Proportion of permanent structures in the housing stock.
* Proportion of housing that is in compliance with local regulations.
* Proportion of households connected to a sewer.
* Proportion of households connected to electricity.

The Urban Indicators Programme provided a source of data for the estimation. During 1995 to 1996, data were collected for the base year 1993 (*Global Urban Indicators Database* (GUID) 1993) from 237 cities. During 2000 to

Variable in the PCA	Correlation coefficient
Proportion of permanent structures	.835
Proportion of structures in compliance	.829
Proportion of households with access to water	.819
Proportion of households with sewer connection	.757
Proportion of households with electricity connection	.743

Table 11.1

Component loadings

2001, data were collected for the base year 1998 (GUID 1998) from 232 cities.[6] The data are city summary data and the unit of analysis is the city. The Urban Indicators Programme intends to collect similar data at approximately five-year intervals and will contain data that are suitable for global and regional estimates, thus meeting the criteria for monitoring the MDG T 11.[7]

In addition to the above data sets, numerous local studies of cities and slums have been used to verify estimates made at the city level. These data were used to illustrate and confirm the findings of the secure tenure-based proxy estimates of slum dwellers and, in some cases, to update the data in the Urban Indicators Database. The Urban Indicators data were first reviewed and improved to compensate for non-response and missing data. The sources of the secondary data and a detailed examination of the methodology referred to here are found in an earlier report.[8]

The data from the 1993 Urban Indicators and the 1998 Urban Indicators cities were not collected from a probability sample of cities and were not intended to be used for global or regional estimates of the urban condition. However, adjustments could be made to the data so that these estimates could be made. The adjustments necessary would correct the distributions of the reporting cities to reflect the true underlying distribution of cities by size and region. This required the introduction of a weighting factor calculated from a global list of cities that represented the statistical universe of all cities. The weighting factors considered the global distribution of cities by size and major regional areas. The distribution of cities from the Urban Indicators Programme was compared with the distribution of cities from the global list of cities. Weighting factors were then calculated for each major region and size in order to permit initial estimates of the global situation.[9]

The Principal Components Analysis (PCA) for the Secure Tenure Index

Principal Components Analysis (PCA) is a multivariate statistical procedure commonly used in the development of an index. A PCA solution reduces the contributing variables (the five variables noted above) into sets of variables that are highly correlated with one another, but unrelated to other sets of correlated variables. The PCA 'extracts' these sets of variables by examining the correlation matrix of all the variables. Those variables that are highly correlated are said to form a Principal Component. The adequacy of the PCA solution can be measured by several standard statistical tests. Tests performed on the PCA suggested that the use of PCA to form an index was justified.

PCA confirms that the variables identified as components of the hypothesized secure tenure were related and together form a common component or index. PCA simplifies a complex phenomenon represented by many variables into (a) parsimonious component(s) that well represents all of the contributing characteristics to the phenomenon. The five characteristic variables measured the same underlying phenomenon. The result was that a single component was formed that explains the underlying complexity of secure tenure. Since it is a composite measure of the (i) infrastructure condition, (ii) permanency of structure and (iii) legality of the dwelling, it is a also good estimator of slum conditions. The index was therefore proposed as an alternative proxy measure for estimating the number of slum dwellers.

Statistically, the final PCA solution explained 64 per cent of the variance and was deemed adequate for calculating the secure tenure index. The component loadings showing how each variable loads onto the solution are presented in Table 11.1. The loadings are the correlation coefficients of the variables to the Principal Component. These loadings range from –1 to +1, ranging from an absolute negative correlation to an absolute positive correlation. A value near zero indicates that there is no relationship between the variable and the Principal Component. From Table 11.1, it is shown that each of the variables is positively correlated to the component and each contributes approximately equally to the component. During the development of the index, many different solutions were posited and proved viable. A single component solution was selected as it is most easily scaled from 1 to 100 and is therefore more intuitively appealing. A single component also had the advantage of a simple definition.

The reduction of the contributing variables to a component is accomplished through the calculation of a component score. The component score is a linear combination of the component score coefficient for the variable with the standardized value of the variable. In this case, the component score coefficient is equivalent to regression weights obtained when the component is regressed on the variables. The result is that each city has a component score that represents a linear combination of the five variables. The component score is the basis for the Secure Tenure Index. The final Secure Tenure Index is the calculated 'normalized' component score that has a range from 0 to 100.[10] The resulting index is an intuitively suitable index that tracks well with other indicators, such as under-five mortality rate, solid waste disposal and wastewater treatment.

The Secure Tenure Index is a proxy for the percentage of households with inadequate housing attributes. The baseline year (1993) estimate of global slum dwellers is 712 million. The straight-line projection for 2001 is 837 million.[11] Data by region are presented in Table A.2 of the Statistical Annex.

The estimation procedure is work in progress. In October 2002, UN-Habitat convened an Expert Group Meeting (EGM) to address problems relevant to the estimation methodology. It was recognized that no universal definition of slum or secure tenure existed. EGM participants fulfilled the stated objectives to contribute to the development of indicators for the MDG T 11, which aims *to significantly improve the lives of at least 100 million slum dwellers by the year 2020*. Assembling in working groups for two days, participants accomplished this objective, first, by formulating an operational definition for 'slums' and 'secure tenure'. It was agreed that while 'secure tenure' (Indicator 31) is an important indicator for measuring the existence of slums, four other criteria should be equally considered. The EGM adopted five indicators to measure the 'improvement in the lives of 100 million slum dwellers by the year 2020', as specified in the Cities without Slums MDG T 11:

1   Proportion of urban population with sustainable access to an improved water source.
2   Proportion of urban population with access to improved sanitation.
3   Proportion of urban population with secure tenure.
4   Proportion of urban population with durable housing units.
5   Proportion of urban population with sufficient living area.

A new slum definition has been applied to a revised estimation, completed in March 2003, as part of monitoring the MDG. The new estimates are at the country level and are based on national household survey data. There is a comparative wealth of data from household surveys conducted in developing countries. More than 290 surveys (Demographic and Health Surveys (DHS), Joint Monitoring Programme (JMP) and Multiple Indicator Cluster Surveys (MICS)) have been analysed. In countries where there were no DHS or MICS, UN-Habitat relied on census data, other sources of national data or made estimates based on similar-country experience. For Europe, Japan, Canada, the US (American Housing Survey) and Australia, published reports on the quality of housing have been consulted as a guide to estimation.

When using the household level data, we applied the new definition of a slum household. As agreed during the EGM, a household was not deemed to be a slum household if it had *one or more* of the following attributes:

•   Security of tenure.
•   Structural quality/durability of dwellings.
•   Access to safe water.
•   Access to sanitation facilities.
•   Sufficient-living area.

Definitions of the attributes are as follows.

Security of tenure: The right of all individuals and groups to effective protection by the state against arbitrary forced evictions. This can be indicated in two ways:

1   Evidence of documentation that can be used as proof of secure tenure status.
2   Either *de facto* or perceived/protection from forced evictions.

Structural quality/durability of dwellings: A house is considered as 'durable' if it is built on a non-hazardous location and has a structure permanent and adequate enough to protect its inhabitants from the extremes of climatic conditions such as rain, heat, cold and humidity.

Generally, a housing structure is considered durable when certain strong building materials are used for roof, walls and floor. Even though some houses may be built with materials classified as durable, the dwellers may still not enjoy adequate protection against weather and climate due to the overall state of a dwelling. Alternatively, a material may not look durable, in the modern sense, but is, in the traditional sense, when combined with skills of repair. Such cases are vernacular housing made of natural materials in villages, maintained by its residents annually. The observation of the building material has therefore to be supplemented by an observation of the state of repair of a house. Adequate shelter is thus operationalized in terms of building material in combination with state of repair. Both indicators can be observed by an enumerator in the field.

Durability of building materials is, to a very large extent, subject to local conditions as well as to local construction and maintenance traditions and skills. Which materials are considered durable under local conditions has to be determined by local experts. This is also true for the common problem that dwellings in the semi-urban outskirts of cities of developing countries often follow rural construction patterns by using materials that can be considered non-durable under urban conditions.

In addition, compliance with local regulations and the quality of the location form part of the definition. These two indicators cannot be easily observed as they require specific knowledge about the legal condition and the land-use plan, as well as skills to determine hazardous areas.

Access to safe water: A household is considered to have access to safe drinking water if it has a sufficient amount of water for family use, at an affordable price, available to household members without being subject to extreme effort, especially to women and children. Households with piped water to the dwelling or plot also should receive safe water reliably at a reasonable cost.

This category also includes urban families who use non-piped safe and affordable water sources at a sufficient quantity that is available without excessive physical effort and time.

Access to sanitation facilities: A household is considered to have access to sanitation if an excreta disposal system, either in the form of a private toilet or a public toilet shared with a reasonable number of people, is available to household members. Households who are included in this category use well-functioning private/public latrines that are (i) connected to non-clogged sewer systems; or (ii) connected to septic tanks with sufficient capacity; or (iii) households that share a public latrine with no more than one household.

Table 11.2

List of indicators
corresponding to
The Habitat Agenda key
areas of commitment

I: Shelter
1. Provide security of tenure
Indicator 1: tenure types
Indicator 2: evictions
2. Promote the right to adequate housing
Checklist 1: housing rights
Indicator 3: housing price-to-income ratio
3. Provide equal access to land
Indicator 4: land price-to-income ratio
4. Promote equal access to credit
Indicator 5: mortgage and non-mortgage
5. Promote access to basic services
Indicator 6: access to water
Indicator 7: household connections

II: Social development and eradication of poverty
6. Provide equal opportunities for a safe and healthy life
Indicator 8: under-five mortality
Indicator 9: crime rates
Checklist 2: urban violence
7. Promote social integration and support disadvantaged groups
Indicator 10: poor households
8. Promote gender equality in human settlements development
Indicator 11: female–male gaps

III: Environmental management
9. Promote geographically balanced settlement structures
Indicator 12: urban population growth
10. Manage supply and demand for water in an effective manner
Indicator 13: water consumption
Indicator 14: price of water
11. Reduce urban pollution
Indicator 15: air pollution
Indicator 16: wastewater treated
Indicator 17: solid waste disposal
12. Prevent disasters and rebuild settlements
Checklist 3: disaster prevention and mitigation instruments
13. Promote effective and environmentally sound transportation system
Indicator 18: travel time
Indicator 19: transport modes
14. Support mechanisms to prepare and implement local environmental plans and local Agenda 21 initiatives
Checklist 4: local environmental plans

IV: Economic development
15. Strengthen small and micro-enterprises, particularly those developed by women
Indicator 20: informal employment
16. Encourage public–private sector partnership and stimulate productive employment opportunities
Checklist 5: public–private partnerships
Indicator 21: city product
Indicator 22: unemployment

V: Governance
17. Promote decentralization and strengthen local authorities
Checklist 6: level of decentralization
18. Encourage and support participation and civic engagement
Checklist 7: citizen involvement in major planning decisions
19. Ensure transparent, accountable and efficient governance of towns, cities and metropolitan areas
Checklist 8: transparency and accountability
Indicator 23: local government revenue and expenditures

VI: International cooperation
20. Enhance international cooperation and partnerships
Checklist 9: engagement in international cooperation

Sufficient living area: A house is considered to provide a sufficient living area for the household members if there are three or less people per room.

Applications of these definitions to specific data surveys, such as the data from the DHSs, were considered on a country-by-country basis. The application of the definition depends upon the type of questions and categories of response that are available from the household survey data. The definitions are applicable to urban areas, rather than rural ones. In the past, a single standard has been applied to assess the adequacy of water and sanitation. It was found that rural definitions applied to urban areas can statistically mask critical problems. For example, a 'traditional pit latrine' can be acceptable in the rural areas, but is unacceptable in densely populated urban areas and is a common problem in slum areas.

As can be seen in Table 11.1, surveys used in the estimation were primarily the DHS, JMP or MICS, or a number of local variants of these. In some countries, there were multiple rounds of surveys that could be consulted. Each survey type may have a different way of categorizing safe water and sanitation. As much as was possible, an attempt was made to ensure that there was a consistent categorization across surveys. Firstly, for each country, the summary survey report was consulted. If there were anomalies in the report, then the household-level data itself was accessed so that categories could be regrouped and double counting of households prevented.

The EGM slum definition counts a household as a slum household if there are one or more of the five attributes. In the earlier estimation method, a composite index based on summary city data was used. The new EGM definition has broadened the interpretation of slums and is not a composite index. It has resulted in a higher count. Due to the change in slum definition, the two estimations are not comparable.

The new estimation methodology proceeded in stages. The first stage of the estimate examined only access to safe water and sanitation. This was done because these data have been proved to be the most influential attributes. In stage two, the attribute of overcrowding was added. The number of persons per room was calculated and those households with three or more persons per room counted as slum dwellings in accord with the definition.[12] Precautions were taken to avoid the double counting of households with more than one attribute.

Stages 3 and 4 of the estimation included two more components - condition of housing and security of tenure. However, these stages added only marginally to the final estimates because the attributes are highly correlated in slum dwellings. The primary purpose of the estimates is to provide country-level slum improvement targets for the Millennium Project, Task Force 8 on 'Improving the Lives of Slum Dwellers: An Action Plan'. The 2003 estimates using the new slum definition appear in Chapter 1 (Table 1.3) and in this Annex (Table A.1).

THE *GLOBAL URBAN INDICATORS DATABASES*

Tables C.3 to C.6 of the Statistical Annex are drawn on the *Global Urban Indicators Databases*. The Urban Indicators Programme was established following decisions of the United Nations Commission on Human Settlements to continue and extend the work of the UNCHS (Habitat)/World Bank Housing Indicators Programme, which collected housing indicators in principal cities of 53 countries during 1991 and 1992. Following an EGM in Nairobi in January 1994, a more extensive set of urban indicators was established covering the whole range of urban issues. A first *Global Urban Indicators Database* was produced in 1996.[13] This database collected information on 237 cities worldwide and was perhaps the first sample of urban indicators on a global basis. The second *Global Urban Indicators Database* was produced in 2001 and published in 2002.[14]

The sample of cities that submitted indicators was reasonably well distributed between regions, in line with urban population, except that Africa was over-sampled and the return from the most rapidly developing economies of East and Southeast Asia was poor.

The present collection, conducted by UN-Habitat, like all previous indicator efforts, has operated under a relatively low-cost model that does not require a formal international network. Cities are invited to participate. In those cities that respond, a consultant is hired whom the local government usually recommends. This consultant has the responsibility for obtaining the data, making estimates of data that are not directly available (using UN-Habitat or their own methodology), documenting the results and providing other reports, as necessary.

This methodology, in theory, has the advantage of independence and control in that the consultants are removed from political influence, and can also be required to correct their data, document their methods and explain divergences with other sources. In practice, however, the problems have been (i) sample design and (ii) quality control.

The Habitat Agenda and Resolutions 15/6 and 17/1 of the United Nations Commission on Human Settlements required the development of an indicators system representing the minimum data required to monitor changes in conditions in human settlements post-Habitat II. UN-Habitat developed an indicators system that contains a set of 23 key indicators and 9 checklists of qualitative data. These are the minimum data required for reporting on shelter and urban development, consistent with the 20 key areas of commitment in the universal-reporting format.

The indicators are designed to measure performances and trends in the 20 selected key areas, and to measure progress in implementing *The Habitat Agenda*. Indicators provide a comprehensive picture of cities, which – with other indicators that may be chosen by countries – provide a quantitative, comparative base for the condition of cities, and show progress towards achieving urban objectives.

The resultant *Global Urban Indicators Database 2* was prepared for Istanbul +5.[15] It assesses urban conditions and trends during the two years, 1993 and 1998, and evaluates progress made between 1993 and 1998. It was the main source of information for analysing urban conditions, trends and progress for the Istanbul +5 meeting, held in June 2001.

Data compiled in the Global Urban Indicators Database have been checked and corrected where possible. However, some results need to be taken with caution as they may conflict with other expert opinions available on the issues addressed.

NOTES

1   United Nations, 2002a.

2   The indicators used to measure and track the MDG have been provided by several specialized agencies and funds, and by international finance institutions. A meeting of relevant agencies (organized by UNSD in March 2002) identified for each indicator either a single agency or an agency team to provide the data.

3   This was discussed at the 'Expert Group meeting on the Monitoring of the Millennium Development Goals (MDGs) of the Millennium Declaration', New York, 29–30 April 2002.

4   An Expert Group Meeting convened by UN-Habitat in October 2002 resulted in identifying guidelines for the definition of secure tenure and slums.

5   Bazoglu and Biau, 2001. The constituent variables of this index are in compliance with the corporate thinking in UN-Habitat that was developed via a series of task-force meetings. Participants at that meeting were Daniel Biau, Farouk Tebbal, Nefise Bazoglu, Eduardo Moreno, Guenter Karl, Christine Auclair, Inge Jenssen and Gulelat Kebede.

6   These data are available from the UN-Habitat website at www.unhabitat.org.

7   The 1993 data includes reports on 46 indicators. This was reduced to 23 indicators for the 1998 data collection round. The next round of data collection for the urban indicators will enumerate a Global Sample of Cities that have been selected with probability of selection proportional to size (PPS) and will be administered to approximately 350 cities.

8   Herr and Karl, 2002.

9   United Nations Secretariat, Department of Economic and Social Affairs, Population Division, provided the geographic standards for development category, major area and region classifications that were applied to the Urban Indicators data.

10   The Human Development Index calculates its 'dimension indices' in a similar manner.

11   Based on recent population estimations and projections. See United Nations, 2002b.

12   United Nations, 1976, p43, is the source of this indicator.

13   UNCHS (Habitat), 1996c.

14   UN-Habitat, 2002f.

15   UN-Habitat, 2002f.

TABLE A.I

Demographic Indicators

	Total population			Level of urbanization (%)		Urban population		Rural population		Estimated urban slum population[7]	
	Estimates and projections (000)		Growth rate (%)			Estimates and projections (000)		Estimates and projections (000)		(000)	(%)
	2000	2020	2000–2020	2000	2020	2000	2020	2000	2020	2001	2001
WORLD TOTAL	6,056,710	7,579,281	1.1	47.2	55.9	2,861,758	4,236,926	3,194,957	3,342,349	923,986	31.6
WORLD MAJOR AGGREGATES											
More developed regions	1,191,303	1,217,602	0.1	75.3	79.9	897,640	973,362	293,666	244,241	54,068	6.0
Less developed regions	4,865,407	6,361,679	1.3	40.4	51.3	1,964,118	3,263,564	2,901,291	3,098,108	869,918	43.0
Least developed countries	667,613	1,079,351	2.4	25.6	37.6	171,185	405,652	496,430	673,697	140,114	78.2
Landlocked developing countries	323,540	504,819	2.2	26.8	34.1	86,841	171,941	236,704	332,876	47,303	56.5
Small island developing states	51,205	64,073	1.1	57.5	63.5	29,459	40,680	21,745	23,393	7,321	24.4
UNITED NATIONS REGIONAL GROUPS											
African States	792,647	1,229,684	2.2	37.1	47.8	294,468	588,293	498,180	641,394	187,562	61.3
Asian States	3,573,098	4,460,877	1.1	36.6	47.9	1,306,801	2,138,887	2,266,302	2,321,987	539,917	40.1
Eastern European States	353,718	323,813	-0.4	66.3	70.1	234,583	227,150	119,135	96,659	15,482	6.6
Latin American and Caribbean States	513,385	657,261	1.2	75.4	81.8	387,152	537,887	126,232	119,374	127,438	32.3
Western European and Other States	448,786	472,685	0.3	76.7	81.5	344,240	385,117	104,543	87,570	38,990	9.6
UNITED NATIONS REGIONAL COMMISSIONS											
UNECA	792,647	1,229,684	2.2	37.1	47.7	294,468	588,293	498,180	641,394	187,562	61.3
UNESCAP	4,183,773	5,080,572	1.0	42.6	52.3	1,782,074	2,655,575	2,401,703	2,424,997	565,388	31.3
UNESCWA	165,577	259,567	2.2	55.0	60.9	91,129	158,179	74,449	101,383	33,296	35.3
UNECLAC	1,073,736	1,274,139	0.9	76.5	82.0	821,209	1,045,274	252,523	228,864	153,350	18.4
UNECE	1,188,378	1,242,329	0.2	72.8	77.1	812,720	890,211	328,305	287,451	76,344	8.8
HUMAN DEVELOPMENT AGGREGATES											
High human development[1]	1,063,353	1,142,472	0.4	78.5	83.2	834,644	950,368	228,707	192,107	102,576	11.6
Medium human development[2]	4,048,122	4,912,689	1.0	42.6	53.6	1,724,450	2,632,487	2,323,676	2,280,197	636,657	36.3
Low human development[3]	839,485	1,364,686	2.4	29.7	41.4	249,544	565,565	589,942	799,119	207,903	79.4
INCOME AGGREGATES											
High income[4]	878,484	941,720	0.3	79.1	83.4	694,682	785,778	183,802	155,945	39,477	5.6
Medium income[5]	2,675,336	3,141,076	0.8	51.2	63.8	1,370,922	2,002,632	1,304,413	1,138,441	430,477	30.7
Low income[6]	2,397,140	3,337,051	1.7	31.0	40.8	743,034	1,360,010	1,654,110	1,977,037	432,080	56.5
GEOGRAPHICAL AGGREGATES											
Developed regions	1,191,275	1,217,576	0.1	75.3	79.9	897,612	973,336	293,666	244,241	54,068	6.0
Europe	727,276	694,852	-0.2	73.4	77.6	534,035	539,510	193,243	155,344	33,062	6.2
Other	463,999	522,724	0.6	78.4	83.0	363,577	433,826	100,423	88,897	21,006	5.7
Developing regions	4,865,393	6,361,663	1.3	40.4	51.3	1,964,118	3,263,564	2,901,277	3,098,092	869,918	43.0
Northern Africa	143,054	189,692	1.4	51.7	59.7	73,925	113,270	69,128	76,423	21,355	28.2
Sub-Saharan Africa	650,572	1,041,282	2.4	34.0	45.7	221,302	476,136	429,272	565,148	166,208	71.9
Latin America and the Caribbean	518,935	663,824	1.2	75.4	81.8	391,455	543,293	127,476	120,528	127,567	31.9
Eastern Asia	1,353,978	1,534,831	0.6	38.2	55.1	516,757	845,715	837,223	689,116	193,824	36.4
South-central Asia	1,480,868	1,980,687	1.5	29.8	37.8	440,880	748,842	1,039,990	1,231,843	262,354	58.0
South-eastern Asia	522,121	661,054	1.2	37.5	51.1	196,029	337,607	326,093	323,449	56,781	28.0
Western Asia	188,275	279,058	2.0	64.7	69.8	121,766	194,904	66,510	84,145	41,331	33.1
Oceania	7,590	11,235	2.0	26.4	33.8	2,004	3,797	5,585	7,440	499	24.1

Notes: 1 HDI 0.800 and above. 2 HDI 0.500–0.799. 3 HDI below 0.500. 4 GNP per capita of US$9266 or more in 2000. 5 GNP per capita of US$756–US$9265. 6 GNP per capita of US$755 or less in 2000.
7 The 2003 Assessment.

TABLE A.2

Housing Indicators

	Urban population (%) with access to				Number of households (000)						
	improved water sources*		improved sanitation*		Estimates and projections			5-year increments			
	1990	2000	1990	2000	2000	2010	2020	2000–2005	2005–2010	2010–2015	2015–2020
WORLD TOTAL	94.0	95.0	81.0	85.0	1,542,424	1,901,127	2,252,746	172,363	186,333	177,222	174,397
WORLD MAJOR AGGREGATES											
More developed regions	99.9	99.9	99.9	99.9	465,664	518,624	556,357	27,075	25,886	20,897	16,836
Less developed regions	92.4	94.8	87.1	88.1	1,076,760	1,382,503	1,696,389	145,288	160,447	156,325	157,561
Least developed countries	81.1	81.0	68.4	71.6	110,572	145,876	190,936	16,565	18,738	20,587	24,473
Landlocked developing countries	92.0	94.0	72.1	82.0	57,557	73,346	94,781	7,244	8,546	9,882	11,553
Small island developing states	…	…	…	…	12,256	14,797	17,319	1,203	1,342	1,290	1,232
UNITED NATIONS REGIONAL GROUPS											
African States	88.1	86.4	81.3	80.4	153,559	207,359	276,365	27,541	30,244	30,508	38,498
Asian States	93.0	96.0	83.0	87.0	820,402	1,033,231	1,245,118	100,646	112,334	107,388	104,499
Eastern European States	99.9	99.9	99.9	99.0	134,934	149,251	157,528	8,159	7,793	4,136	4,141
Latin American and Caribbean States	92.8	94.9	85.0	86.2	125,891	159,151	192,720	16,519	16,907	16,800	16,769
Western European and Other States	98.7	99.1	99.4	99.6	304,170	186,841	375,807	19,018	18,683	18,074	170,892
UNITED NATIONS REGIONAL COMMISSIONS											
UNECA	88.1	86.4	81.3	80.4	153,559	207,359	276,365	27,541	30,244	30,508	38,498
UNESCAP	93.0	96.0	83.0	87.0	1,069,337	1,317,807	1,556,634	118,651	129,822	122,086	116,741
UNESCWA	97.0	98.0	96.0	97.6	27,038	36,545	47,610	4,468	5,039	5,154	5,911
UNECLAC	92.8	94.9	85.0	86.2	341,737	401,819	459,903	29,821	30,260	29,949	28,135
UNECE	99.9	99.9	99.0	92.9	424,928	474,452	511,013	24,833	24,693	20,213	16,348
HUMAN DEVELOPMENT AGGREGATES											
High human development[1]	99.9	99.9	99.9	99.9	401,079	447,870	486,790	23,983	22,805	21,014	17,906
Medium human development[2]	92.0	95.0	88.0	89.0	989,144	1,246,666	1,492,531	123,008	134,518	125,229	120,636
Low human development[3]	83.2	87.9	76.0	81.1	142,479	194,568	258,899	24,159	27,930	29,880	34,451
INCOME AGGREGATES											
High income[4]	99.9	99.9	99.9	99.9	341,945	380,576	412,774	19,717	18,912	17,419	14,779
Medium income[5]	92.0	95.0	88.0	89.0	733,357	923,880	1,102,777	90,332	100,191	91,072	87,825
Low income[6]	80.1	79.6	76.0	77.8	457,400	584,649	722,669	61,101	66,150	67,632	70,388
GEOGRAPHICAL AGGREGATES											
Developed regions	99.9	99.9	99.9	99.9	465,664	518,624	556,357	27,075	25,886	20,897	16,836
Europe	99.9	99.9	99.9	99.9	288,461	316,151	330,754	14,325	13,367	8,759	5,844
Other	99.9	99.9	99.9	99.9	177,203	202,472	225,603	12,750	12,519	12,138	10,993
Developing regions	92.4	94.8	87.1	88.1	1,076,760	1,382,503	1,696,443	145,292	160,452	156,330	157,610
Northern Africa	98.0	97.0	87.0	87.0	26,578	34,374	41,867	3,818	3,977	3,674	3,819
Sub-Saharan Africa	85.9	84.9	80.2	80.4	126,981	177,016	234,787	23,745	26,290	26,859	30,912
Latin America and the Caribbean	92.8	94.9	85.0	86.2	127,263	160,886	194,493	16,621	17,003	16,902	16,705
Eastern Asia	93.8	94.2	60.3	69.5	377,827	483,604	591,130	47,518	58,257	54,495	53,031
South-central Asia	88.9	96.7	47.8	65.9	261,950	329,914	396,273	33,410	34,556	33,926	32,433
South-eastern Asia	92.6	90.8	70.1	75.8	119,835	149,779	178,760	14,924	15,023	14,734	14,247
Western Asia	98.0	98.1	96.7	97.9	34,852	45,068	56,811	5,073	5,141	5,518	6,225
Oceania	88.1	76.5	91.7	87.2	1,474	1,862	2,322	183	205	222	238

Notes: * Provisional data. 1 HDI 0.800 and above. 2 HDI 0.500–0.799. 3 HDI below 0.500. 4 GNP per capita of US$9266 or more in 2000. 5 GNP per capita of US$756–US$9265. 6 GNP per capita of US$755 or less in 2000.

TABLE A.3

Economic and Social Indicators

	PPP GNI per capita (US$)	Labour force Total (000)		Labour force Women (%)		Illiteracy rate Male (%)		Illiteracy rate Female (%)		Population in poverty Below US$1 per day*	Population in poverty Below US$2 per day*
	2000*	2000	2010	2000	2010	2000	2015	2000	2015	%	%
WORLD TOTAL	7,482	2,946,397	3,408,248	40.6	41.2	18.0	13.1	32.0	23.1	19.4	42.0
WORLD MAJOR AGGREGATES											
More developed regions	22,223	601,041	617,205	44.7	45.6	0.8	0.4	1.6	0.7	...	...
Less developed regions	3,751	2,345,356	2,791,043	39.5	40.2	19.5	13.9	34.7	24.7	25.7	60.4
Least developed countries	1,145	311,803	402,372	43.1	43.0	37.7	28.0	57.7	43.1	34.6	75.8
Landlocked developing countries	1,675	147,401	188,343	43.8	43.8	32.2	24.7	47.0	36.1	31.0	63.1
Small island developing states	...	22,901	26,920	39.1	40.2	18.2	14.1	22.1	16.6	4.2	20.4
UNITED NATIONS REGIONAL GROUPS											
African States	2,143	341,762	440,697	40.6	41.0	30.7	20.4	48.7	32.5	33.0	63.9
Asian States	4,337	1,799,775	2,087,731	39.9	40.5	18.7	13.6	35.3	25.6	26.6	65.0
Eastern European States	7,288	183,273	184,942	47.7	47.7	0.5	0.3	1.0	0.5	3.3	18.9
Latin American and Caribbean States	7,096	220,379	267,739	35.0	37.0	10.3	6.9	12.5	7.7	14.1	32.8
Western European and Other States	21,330	211,940	220,609	41.6	42.8	...	...	...	...	...	...
UNITED NATIONS REGIONAL COMMISSIONS											
UNECA	..	341,762	440,697	40.6	41.0	30.7	20.4	48.7	32.5	33.0	63.9
UNESCAP	..	2,120,577	2,423,409	41.0	41.5	17.7	13.0	33.5	24.4	25.2	62.2
UNESCWA	..	55,900	77,531	26.4	29.9	28.6	20.9	53.1	39.1	5.4	48.7
UNECLAC	..	495,708	559,456	40.1	41.4	8.8	6.0	10.8	6.8	13.7	32.0
UNECE	..	554,521	578,574	45.2	46.0	0.8	0.4	1.7	0.7	3.1	19.3
HUMAN DEVELOPMENT AGGREGATES											
High human development[1]	24,955	526,727	553,721	42.9	44.3	2.1	1.3	3.5	1.7	...	...
Medium human development[2]	4,076	2,009,511	2,320,849	40.2	40.6	14.8	10.0	28.1	18.9	22.3	55.7
Low human development[3]	1,222	367,752	480,336	40.0	40.7	39.2	27.9	61.1	44.7	39.4	79.7
INCOME AGGREGATES											
High income[4]	27,667	437,851	455,789	43.2	44.5	2.5	1.6	4.6	2.2	...	...
Medium income[5]	5,597	1,386,754	1,559,553	42.1	42.5	8.8	4.9	18.8	10.7	13.4	40.4
Low income[6]	1,986	1,079,385	1,339,564	37.8	38.6	29.0	21.4	48.2	35.9	36.6	77.4
GEOGRAPHICAL AGGREGATES											
Developed regions	22,223	601,041	617,205	44.7	45.6	0.8	0.4	1.6	0.7	3.3	18.6
Europe	16,357	359,355	359,696	44.8	45.4	0.8	0.4	1.6	0.7	3.3	18.6
Other	31,214	241,686	257,509	44.5	45.9	...	...	...	...	...	...
Developing regions	3,751	2,345,356	2,791,043	39.5	50.5	19.5	13.9	34.7	24.7	25.7	60.4
Northern Africa	4,089	53,648	71,466	31.1	37.2	30.5	21.6	53.0	37.9	2.3	21.3
Sub-Saharan Africa	1,685	288,411	369,582	42.3	42.3	30.7	20.2	47.7	31.4	42.7	73.5
Latin America and the Caribbean	7,096	222,351	269,969	35.0	37.0	10.3	6.9	12.4	7.7	13.6	33.2
Eastern Asia	4,497	803,571	869,910	44.8	44.9	7.6	3.1	21.3	10.7	11.6	34.9
South-central Asia	2,430	642,787	798,606	33.4	34.9	32.5	24.9	54.6	42.7	20.8	57.8
South-eastern Asia	3,771	259,236	313,924	42.7	43.6	7.4	4.5	14.4	8.0	12.0	52.2
Western Asia	6,467	72,492	93,933	32.6	34.7	16.6	12.0	37.4	27.4	5.3	19.4
Oceania	2,180	2,860	3,653	41.1	42.6	25.2	18.9	37.3	27.5	...	...

Notes * Provisional data. 1 HDI 0.800 and above. 2 HDI 0.500–0.799. 3 HDI below 0.500. 4 GNP per capita of US$9266 or more in 2000. 5 GNP per capita of US$756–US$9265. 6 GNP per capita of US$755 or less in 2000.

TABLE B.1

Size and Growth of Total Population and Households

	Total population							Number of households					
	Estimates and projections (000)				Annual growth rate (%)			Estimates and projections (000)		5-year increments (000)			
	1990	2000	2010	2020	1990–2000	2000–2010	2010–2020	2000	2020	2000–2005	2005–2010	2010–2015	2015–2020
WORLD	5,254,820	6,056,715	6,825,736	7,579,278	1.42	1.20	1.05	1,575,277	2,304,624	175,650	190,376	182,769	180,552
AFRICA	619,477	793,627	996,960	1,230,975	2.48	2.28	2.11	173,413	307,453	28,397	32,368	34,299	38,977
Algeria	24,855	30,291	35,635	40,418	1.98	1.62	1.26	4,966	7,932	747	724	729	765
Angola	9,570	13,134	17,765	24,263	3.17	3.02	3.12	...	...	...	...	...	...
Benin	4,655	6,272	8,278	10,697	2.98	2.78	2.56	1,054	2,035	205	235	254	287
Botswana	1,240	1,541	1,628	1,767	2.18	0.55	0.82	367	526	44	30	37	47
Burkina Faso	9,008	11,535	15,764	21,667	2.47	3.12	3.18	1,633	2,431	150	177	219	252
Burundi	5,636	6,356	8,662	11,085	1.20	3.10	2.47	1,530	2,911	177	380	389	435
Cameroon	11,614	14,876	18,347	22,121	2.47	2.10	1.87	3,360	6,890	715	801	919	1,095
Cape Verde	341	427	522	608	2.24	2.01	1.52	91	167	16	18	20	22
Central African Republic	2,945	3,717	4,430	5,369	2.33	1.75	1.92	751	1,298	108	125	143	172
Chad	5,829	7,885	10,689	14,275	3.02	3.04	2.89	1,113	1,753	128	147	173	193
Comoros	527	706	939	1,197	2.93	2.85	2.43	98	184	20	20	22	24
Congo	2,230	3,018	4,084	5,464	3.03	3.02	2.91	703	1,589	149	188	244	306
Côte d'Ivoire	12,582	16,013	19,625	23,353	2.41	2.03	1.74	2,857	4,973	395	537	544	641
Dem. Republic of the Congo	36,999	50,948	71,272	98,621	3.20	3.36	3.25	10,797	22,905	1,627	2,682	3,510	4,289
Djibouti	504	632	679	747	2.27	0.71	0.96	134	219	9	23	25	27
Egypt	56,223	67,884	79,260	89,686	1.88	1.55	1.24	13,410	21,935	2,063	2,264	2,091	2,108
Equatorial Guinea	352	457	605	787	2.61	2.82	2.63	103	210	19	24	29	34
Eritrea	3,103	3,659	5,097	6,382	1.65	3.32	2.25	726	1,500	179	165	197	232
Ethiopia	47,509	62,908	79,853	100,944	2.81	2.39	2.34	12,303	23,145	1,865	2,339	2,975	3,664
Gabon	935	1,230	1,568	1961	2.74	2.43	2.24	310	531	43	50	58	71
Gambia	928	1,303	1,626	1933	3.39	2.22	1.73	164	309	35	33	36	40
Ghana	15,138	19,306	23,938	28,755	2.43	2.15	1.83	4,163	8,397	841	1,000	1,134	1,258
Guinea	6139	8,154	9,996	12,681	2.84	2.04	2.38	1,115	1,871	85	213	215	242
Guinea-Bissau	946	1199	1531	1940	2.37	2.44	2.37	139	219	18	19	21	23
Kenya	23,574	30,669	36,941	42,695	2.63	1.86	1.45	7,238	13,361	1,485	1,575	1,470	1,592
Lesotho	1,682	2,035	2127	2177	1.90	0.44	0.23	412	647	52	50	59	74
Liberia	2,144	2,913	4,682	6,516	3.07	4.75	3.30	307	953	295	112	96	144
Libyan Arab Jamahiriya	4,311	5,290	6,531	7,510	2.05	2.11	1.40	789	1,087	99	87	53	59
Madagascar	11,956	15,970	21,096	27,319	2.89	2.78	2.58	3,280	5,896	454	553	795	814
Malawi	9,434	11,308	14,024	17,507	1.81	2.15	2.22	1,743	1,773	...	...	...	...
Mali	8,778	11,351	15,234	20,389	2.57	2.94	2.92	1,827	3,328	271	326	413	492
Mauritania	1,992	2,665	3,577	4,708	2.91	2.94	2.75	373	598	49	52	59	65
Mauritius[1]	1,057	1,161	1,256	1,341	0.94	0.78	0.66	279	344	18	16	19	12
Morocco	24,624	29,878	35,324	39,833	1.93	1.67	1.20	5,390	8,034	663	667	603	710
Mozambique	13,645	18,292	21,649	25,673	2.93	1.68	1.71	3,228	3,816	176	69	77	266
Namibia	1,375	1,757	2,097	2,547	2.45	1.77	1.94	321	421	38	19	15	28
Niger	7,707	10,832	15,550	21,853	3.40	3.62	3.40	1,307	2,096	153	180	223	233
Nigeria	85,953	113,862	146,935	184,248	2.81	2.55	2.26	28,009	57,073	6,903	7,494	7,047	7,619
Réunion	604	721	809	879	1.77	1.15	0.82	198	289	22	23	25	22
Rwanda	6,766	7,609	9,425	11,662	1.17	2.14	2.13	1,468	3,474	797	352	390	467
Saint Helena[2]	6	6	7	7	0.84	0.83	0.84	...	...	...	...	...	...
Sao Tome and Principe	115	138	164	193	1.84	1.73	1.62	...	...	...	...	...	...
Senegal	7,327	9,421	12,051	15,023	2.51	2.46	2.20	928	1,708	148	179	213	240
Seychelles	70	80	91	103	1.46	1.28	1.23	...	...	...	...	...	...
Sierra Leone	4,061	4,405	6,283	8,036	0.81	3.55	2.46	...	...	...	...	...	...
Somalia	7,163	8,778	13,065	18,112	2.03	3.98	3.27	1,271	2,664	270	315	348	460
South Africa	36,376	43,309	45,140	43,977	1.74	0.41	-0.26	12,228	20,985	3,713	2,969	1,129	947
Sudan	24,818	31,095	38,667	46,114	2.25	2.18	1.76	3,315	5,167	258	519	516	559
Swaziland	769	925	987	1,076	1.84	0.65	0.86	212	488	65	75	66	69
Togo	3,453	4,527	5,826	7,383	2.71	2.52	2.37	957	1,888	166	203	258	303
Tunisia	8,156	9,459	10,629	11,841	1.48	1.17	1.08	2,023	2,879	246	235	198	177
Uganda	17,245	23,300	32,588	45,787	3.01	3.35	3.40	3,987	7,557	482	783	1,019	1,284
United Republic of Tanzania	26,043	35,119	44,062	54,875	2.99	2.27	2.19	5,977	8,826	554	669	768	858
Western Sahara	178	252	331	404	3.46	2.74	1.99	...	...	...	...	...	...
Zambia	8,049	10,421	12,989	16,833	2.58	2.20	2.59	1,665	2,648	192	196	270	324
Zimbabwe	10,241	12,627	15,028	17,632	2.09	1.74	1.60	2,940	4,724	418	403	443	520
ASIA	3,164,081	3,672,342	4,144,937	4,581,584	1.49	1.21	1.00	854,709	1,297,511	105,831	116,663	111,595	108,713
Afghanistan	13,675	21,765	31,308	40,206	4.65	3.64	2.50	...	...	...	...	...	...
Armenia	3,545	3,787	3,807	3,789	0.66	0.05	-0.05	680	695	-2	18	8	-8
Azerbaijan	7,175	8,041	8,498	8,935	1.14	0.55	0.50	1,561	1,954	83	128	121	61
Bahrain	490	640	744	843	2.67	1.50	1.25	100	135	9	9	10	7
Bangladesh	110,025	137,439	167,926	197,642	2.22	2.00	1.63	24,136	37,654	4,062	3,702	2,708	3,046
Bhutan	1,696	2,085	2,707	3,453	2.06	2.61	2.44	370	686	59	72	86	98
Brunei Darussalam	257	328	388	445	2.45	1.68	1.37	54	70	5	5	4	2
Cambodia	9,630	13,104	16,630	20,529	3.08	2.38	2.11	2,210	3,969	378	437	454	490
China[3]	1,155,305	1,275,133	1,366,215	1,446,092	0.99	0.69	0.57	360,982	568,637	45,770	56,867	53,162	51,856
China, Hong Kong SAR[4]	5,705	6,860	7,659	8,365	1.84	1.10	0.88	1,979	2,787	317	221	158	112
China, Macau SAR[5]	372	444	481	516	1.77	0.80	0.69	154	253	32	25	23	19
Cyprus	681	784	841	885	1.41	0.70	0.51	200	232	13	10	7	3
Dem. People's Rep. of Korea	19,956	22,268	23,688	25,158	1.10	0.62	0.60	...	...	...	...	...	...
Georgia	5,460	5,262	4,956	4,584	-0.37	-0.60	-0.78	1,343	1,359	-48	22	23	18

TABLE B.I

continued

	Total population							Number of households					
	Estimates and projections (000)				Annual growth rate (%)			Estimates and projections (000)		5-year increments (000)			
	1990	2000	2010	2020	1990–2000	2000–2010	2010–2020	2000	2020	2000–2005	2005–2010	2010–2015	2015–2020
India	844,886	1,008,937	1,164,020	1,291,290	1.77	1.43	1.04	185,929	273,303	21,655	22,440	22,407	20,871
Indonesia	182,474	212,092	237,711	261,897	1.50	1.14	0.97	52,040	74,484	5,871	5,732	5,484	5,357
Iran (Islamic Republic of)	58,435	70,330	80,809	93,512	1.85	1.39	1.46	15,154	26,332	3,115	2,892	2,909	2,262
Iraq	17,271	22,946	29,917	37,054	2.84	2.65	2.14	2,722	4,302	295	340	363	583
Israel	4,514	6,040	7,249	8,097	2.91	1.82	1.11	1,661	2,391	216	187	173	153
Japan	123,537	127,096	128,220	125,958	0.28	0.09	-0.18	48,520	55,069	2,578	1,824	1,198	949
Jordan	3,254	4,913	6,423	7,941	4.12	2.68	2.12	652	1,255	123	143	158	180
Kazakhstan	16,742	16,172	15,800	16,073	-0.35	-0.23	0.17	5,710	7,343	314	439	439	442
Kuwait	2,143	1,914	2,473	3,017	-1.13	2.56	1.99	260	423	57	50	32	24
Kyrgyzstan	4,395	4,921	5,510	6,162	1.13	1.13	1.12	936	1,143	25	58	63	62
Lao People's Dem. Republic	4,132	5,279	6,611	8,053	2.45	2.25	1.97	983	1,838	155	205	238	257
Lebanon	2,713	3,496	4,017	4,409	2.54	1.39	0.93	…	…	…	…	…	…
Malaysia	17,845	22,218	26,146	29,608	2.19	1.63	1.24	4,748	7,802	705	700	849	799
Maldives	216	291	393	516	2.99	3.00	2.74	40	76	8	9	9	10
Mongolia	2,216	2,533	2,869	3,291	1.34	1.24	1.37	532	794	70	82	61	49
Myanmar	40,517	47,749	52,990	57,756	1.64	1.04	0.86	9,893	13,809	1,226	1,003	832	856
Nepal	18,142	23,043	28,922	35,449	2.39	2.27	2.03	4,266	7,641	701	829	892	953
Occupied Palestian Territory	2,154	3,191	4,525	6,194	3.93	3.49	3.14	…	…	…	…	…	…
Oman	1,785	2,538	3,515	4,745	3.52	3.26	3.00	359	655	62	74	73	87
Pakistan	109,811	141,256	181,385	227,781	2.52	2.50	2.28	15,609	28,843	2,601	3,174	3,599	3,861
Philippines	61,040	75,653	89,888	101,424	2.15	1.72	1.21	15,661	27,131	2,487	2,804	2,980	3,199
Qatar	453	565	653	727	2.21	1.43	1.08	106	123	6	6	3	1
Republic of Korea	42,869	46,740	49,623	51,409	0.86	0.60	0.35	14,180	18,659	1,329	1,062	1,091	997
Saudi Arabia	15,400	20,346	27,588	36,095	2.78	3.04	2.69	2,898	4,949	457	452	520	622
Singapore	3,016	4,018	4,604	4,879	2.87	1.36	0.58	728	764	17	11	12	-4
Sri Lanka	17,022	18,924	20,699	22,057	1.06	0.90	0.64	3,867	4,987	360	289	242	230
Syrian Arab Republic	12,386	16,189	20,781	25,456	2.68	2.50	2.03	2,550	4,555	490	553	473	489
Tajikistan	5,303	6,087	6,618	7,602	1.38	0.84	1.39	1,104	1,546	85	114	111	132
Thailand	54,736	62,806	69,681	75,097	1.38	1.04	0.75	15,840	21,034	1,501	1,476	1,147	1,070
Timor-Leste	740	737	1,019	1,161	-0.04	3.24	1.30	…	…	…	…	…	…
Turkey	56,098	66,668	75,145	82,887	1.73	1.20	0.98	15,779	24,505	2,406	2,001	2,123	2,195
Turkmenistan	3,668	4,737	5,651	6,448	2.56	1.76	1.32	605	799	33	44	40	78
United Arab Emirates	2,014	2,606	3,056	3,364	2.58	1.59	0.96	829	1,042	75	74	40	24
Uzbekistan	20,515	24,881	28,538	32,496	1.93	1.37	1.30	4,224	5,920	392	494	421	388
Viet Nam	66,074	78,137	88,684	100,205	1.68	1.27	1.22	17,678	27,859	2,579	2,650	2,734	2,217
Yemen	11,590	18,349	27,359	40,036	4.59	3.99	3.81	3,152	8,236	831	1,074	1,391	1,788
EUROPE	**721,981**	**727,304**	**713,211**	**694,877**	**0.07**	**-0.20**	**-0.26**	**289,735**	**332,310**	**14,446**	**13,442**	**8,812**	**5,875**
Albania	3,289	3,134	3,311	3,565	-0.48	0.55	0.74	652	766	-4	38	42	38
Andorra	53	86	126	165	4.90	3.81	2.71	…	…	…	…	…	…
Austria	7,729	8,080	7,953	7,735	0.44	-0.16	-0.28	3,318	3,846	174	153	125	76
Belarus	10,260	10,187	9,819	9,508	-0.07	-0.37	-0.32	3,134	3,291	99	86	9	-37
Belgium	9,967	10,249	10,296	10,244	0.28	0.05	-0.05	4,259	4,792	159	152	133	90
Bosnia and Herzegovina	4,308	3,977	4,269	4,244	-0.80	0.71	-0.06	…	…	…	…	…	…
Bulgaria	8,718	7,949	7,185	6,467	-0.92	-1.01	-1.05	3,285	3,322	40	41	-7	-38
Channel Islands	142	144	144	141	0.18	-0.02	-0.21	…	…	…	…	…	…
Croatia	4,517	4,654	4,650	4,577	0.30	-0.01	-0.16	1,624	1,704	48	32	5	-4
Czech Republic	10,306	10,272	10,138	9,895	-0.03	-0.13	-0.24	4,375	4,694	130	114	78	-3
Denmark	5,140	5,320	5,374	5,365	0.34	0.10	-0.02	2,470	2,737	57	65	81	65
Estonia	1,571	1,393	1,253	1,127	-1.20	-1.06	-1.06	582	608	13	18	-3	-2
Faeroe Islands	47	46	51	54	-0.22	0.90	0.62	…	…	…	…	…	…
Finland	4,986	5,172	5,187	5,165	0.36	0.03	-0.04	2,247	2,600	108	94	88	62
France	56,735	59,238	61,203	62,412	0.43	0.33	0.20	24,176	28,114	1,170	1,086	920	763
Germany	79,433	82,017	81,353	79,864	0.32	-0.08	-0.18	35,888	38,901	962	1,050	654	347
Gibraltar	27	27	26	25	-0.03	-0.18	-0.33	…	…	…	…	…	…
Greece	10,160	10,610	10,579	10,325	0.43	-0.03	-0.24	3,902	4,392	236	140	79	35
Holy See[6]	1	1	1	1	-0.50	-	-	…	…	…	…	…	…
Hungary	10,365	9,968	9,489	9,021	-0.39	-0.49	-0.51	3,978	4,052	36	33	27	-22
Iceland	255	279	297	312	0.92	0.61	0.50	111	152	10	10	11	10
Ireland	3,515	3,803	4,201	4,594	0.79	1.00	0.89	1,225	1,632	120	104	89	93
Isle of Man	67	75	81	84	1.11	0.78	0.34	…	…	…	…	…	…
Italy	56,719	57,530	56,390	53,861	0.14	-0.20	-0.46	22,542	23,891	605	401	277	66
Latvia	2,671	2,421	2,288	2,161	-0.98	-0.56	-0.57	871	851	-6	11	-8	-18
Liechtenstein	29	33	36	38	1.23	0.98	0.66	…	…	…	…	…	…
Lithuania	3,722	3,696	3,594	3,483	-0.07	-0.28	-0.31	1,305	1,500	63	68	44	19
Luxembourg	382	437	490	546	1.34	1.16	1.08	165	208	13	11	10	8
Malta	360	390	405	416	0.80	0.37	0.27	132	167	11	10	8	7
Monaco	30	33	36	38	1.09	0.81	0.53	…	…	…	…	…	…
Netherlands	14,952	15,864	16,313	16,507	0.59	0.28	0.12	6,814	8,060	341	335	324	245
Norway	4,241	4,469	4,614	4,733	0.52	0.32	0.26	1,987	2,468	106	123	132	119
Poland	38,111	38,605	38,253	37,741	0.13	-0.09	-0.13	13,052	14,345	625	429	219	21
Portugal	9,899	10,016	10,082	9,940	0.12	0.07	-0.14	3,649	4,021	144	88	85	56
Republic of Moldova	4,364	4,295	4,190	4,110	-0.16	-0.25	-0.19	1,250	1,454	64	71	44	26
Romania	23,207	22,438	21,819	21,026	-0.34	-0.28	-0.37	7,956	8,424	227	275	39	-73

Russian Federation	148,292	145,491	136,976	129,687	-0.19	-0.60	-0.55	65,782	81,557	5,707	5,305	2,738	2,025
San Marino	23	27	29	32	1.35	1.04	0.72	...	...	...	...	...	...
Serbia and												
Montenegro	10,156	10,552	10,404	10,192	0.38	-0.14	-0.21	3,411	3,944	174	146	117	97
Slovakia	5,256	5,399	5,430	5,384	0.27	0.06	-0.08	2,032	2,350	117	99	73	28
Slovenia	1,918	1,988	1,955	1,890	0.36	-0.16	-0.34	723	773	28	20	5	-3
Spain	39,303	39,910	39,569	38,272	0.15	-0.09	-0.33	12,693	13,039	326	100	4	-85
Sweden	8,559	8,842	8,703	8,571	0.33	-0.16	-0.15	4,285	5,158	201	253	255	164
Switzerland	6,834	7,170	7,073	6,860	0.48	-0.14	-0.31	3,303	4,028	207	199	182	137
TFYR Macedonia[7]	1,909	2,034	2,072	2,076	0.63	0.18	0.02	547	670	36	32	28	27
Ukraine	51,891	49,568	45,239	41,478	-0.46	-0.91	-0.87	15,855	18,072	704	749	471	294
United Kingdom	57,561	59,415	60,262	60,946	0.32	0.14	0.11	24,881	30,171	1,274	1,426	1,381	1,210
LATIN AMERICA AND THE CARIBBEAN	**440,354**	**518,809**	**594,312**	**663,687**	**1.64**	**1.36**	**1.10**	**127,264**	**194,494**	**16,621**	**17,002**	**16,902**	**16,706**
Anguilla	8	11	15	18	2.97	2.44	1.91	...	...	...	...	...	...
Antigua and Barbuda	63	65	67	69	0.33	0.30	0.27	...	...	...	...	...	...
Argentina	32,527	37,032	41,474	45,347	1.30	1.13	0.89	10,557	15,012	1,075	1,104	1,127	1,148
Aruba	66	101	138	176	4.22	3.16	2.45	...	...	...	...	...	...
Bahamas	255	304	341	376	1.76	1.15	0.97	70	85	4	4	4	3
Barbados	257	267	277	283	0.39	0.34	0.24	85	104	5	5	5	4
Belize	186	226	268	306	1.98	1.70	1.30	48	87	8	9	11	11
Bolivia	6,573	8,329	10,229	12,193	2.37	2.06	1.76	1,616	2,596	205	230	261	284
Brazil	147,957	170,406	191,444	210,577	1.41	1.16	0.95	45,228	66,578	5,841	5,562	5,082	4,866
British Virgin Islands	17	24	30	34	3.16	2.27	1.38	...	...	...	...	...	...
Cayman Islands	26	38	52	66	3.73	3.05	2.37	...	...	...	...	...	...
Chile	13,100	15,211	17,010	18,774	1.49	1.12	0.99	4,133	6,573	533	610	638	658
Colombia	34,970	42,105	49,159	55,999	1.86	1.55	1.30	8,776	14,616	1,324	1,411	1,550	1,555
Costa Rica	3,049	4,024	4,857	5,592	2.77	1.88	1.41	1,026	1,881	210	219	212	214
Cuba	10,629	11,199	11,514	11,721	0.52	0.28	0.18	4,053	5,361	311	374	332	292
Dominica	71	71	70	70	-0.11	-0.06	-0.01	...	...	...	...	...	...
Dominican Republic	7,061	8,373	9,621	10,565	1.70	1.39	0.94	2,090	3,269	281	306	303	289
Ecuador	10,264	12,646	14,898	16,903	2.09	1.64	1.26	3,107	5,408	545	567	591	598
El Salvador	5,112	6,278	7,441	8,493	2.06	1.70	1.32	1,677	2,972	290	304	338	363
Falkland Islands (Malvinas)	2	2	3	3	1.32	1.16	1.02	...	...	...	...	...	...
French Guiana	116	165	223	290	3.48	3.01	2.62	...	...	...	...	...	...
Grenada	91	94	96	99	0.30	0.28	0.25	...	...	...	...	...	...
Guadeloupe	391	428	460	480	0.91	0.71	0.43	140	192	13	13	13	12
Guatemala	8,749	11,385	14,631	18,002	2.63	2.51	2.07	1,791	3,070	261	298	343	378
Guyana	731	761	763	728	0.39	0.04	-0.47	182	216	9	8	9	8
Haiti	6,907	8,142	9,500	10,905	1.65	1.54	1.38	1,583	2,584	228	272	240	261
Honduras	4,870	6,417	7,962	9,419	2.76	2.16	1.68	1,187	2,315	236	271	304	318
Jamaica	2,369	2,576	2,821	3,113	0.84	0.91	0.99	506	566	15	14	17	14
Martinique	360	383	402	416	0.62	0.48	0.34	127	162	9	10	9	8
Mexico	83,223	98,872	112,884	124,975	1.72	1.33	1.02	22,970	34,767	2,945	2,972	2,993	2,887
Montserrat	11	4	5	7	-10.51	3.22	2.47	...	...	...	...	...	...
Netherlands Antilles	188	215	234	249	1.37	0.83	0.64	68	97	7	7	8	7
Nicaragua	3,824	5,071	6,493	7,926	2.82	2.47	1.99	833	1,700	176	193	235	263
Panama	2,398	2,856	3,266	3,622	1.75	1.34	1.03	707	1,113	97	103	104	101
Paraguay	4,219	5,496	6,980	8,570	2.65	2.39	2.05	1,165	2,357	248	286	317	341
Peru	21,569	25,662	29,885	33,757	1.74	1.52	1.22	5,650	8,649	736	776	760	727
Puerto Rico	3,528	3,915	4,250	4,512	1.04	0.82	0.60	1,177	1,514	86	79	85	86
Saint Kitts and Nevis	42	38	36	35	-0.85	-0.64	-0.45	...	...	...	...	...	...
Saint Lucia	131	148	163	174	1.17	0.99	0.66	...	...	...	...	...	...
Saint Vincent and the Grenadines	106	113	120	126	0.69	0.59	0.49	...	...	...	...	...	...
Suriname	402	417	433	440	0.38	0.38	0.17	104	138	8	7	11	9
Trinidad and Tobago	1,215	1,294	1,358	1,420	0.63	0.48	0.45	296	362	25	21	13	8
Turks and Caicos Islands	12	17	23	29	3.68	3.01	2.34	...	...	...	...	...	...
United States Virgin Islands	104	121	134	146	1.48	1.05	0.85	...	...	...	...	...	...
Uruguay	3,106	3,337	3,566	3,771	0.72	0.66	0.56	1,023	1,290	59	64	69	75
Venezuela	19,502	24,170	28,716	32,911	2.15	1.72	1.36	5,288	8,859	831	904	918	917
NORTHERN AMERICA	**282,598**	**314,113**	**341,904**	**369,934**	**1.06**	**0.85**	**0.79**	**119,986**	**158,468**	**9,362**	**9,844**	**10,078**	**9,197**
Bermuda	59	63	67	71	0.66	0.62	0.57	...	...	...	...	...	...
Canada	27,701	30,757	33,216	35,598	1.05	0.77	0.69	12,690	18,171	1,360	1,399	1,430	1,292
Greenland	56	56	57	58	0.12	0.16	0.17	...	...	...	...	...	...
Saint Pierre and Miquelon	6	7	7	8	0.68	0.69	0.61	...	...	...	...	...	...
United States	254,776	283,230	308,557	334,200	1.06	0.86	0.80	107,296	140,297	8,002	8,445	8,648	7,905
OCEANIA	**26,330**	**30,521**	**34,411**	**38,221**	**1.48**	**1.20**	**1.05**	**10,170**	**14,388**	**993**	**1,057**	**1,084**	**1,084**
American Samoa	47	68	91	117	3.60	3.02	2.44	...	...	...	...	...	...
Australia[8]	16,888	19,138	21,029	22,745	1.25	0.94	0.78	7,269	10,108	688	714	727	709
Cook Islands	18	20	21	22	0.68	0.66	0.63	...	...	...	...	...	...
Fiji	724	814	896	943	1.17	0.97	0.51	156	222	18	17	16	15
French Polynesia	195	233	271	303	1.78	1.48	1.14	54	80	6	7	7	6
Guam	134	155	191	226	1.47	2.07	1.71	37	50	2	3	4	3
Kiribati	72	83	94	106	1.44	1.30	1.16	...	...	...	...	...	...
Marshall Islands	44	51	58	65	1.41	1.28	1.14	...	...	...	...	...	...
Micronesia (Fed. States of)	94	123	155	188	2.61	2.33	1.95	...	...	...	...	...	...
Nauru	9	12	15	18	2.60	2.24	1.88	...	...	...	...	...	...
New Caledonia	171	215	258	297	2.30	1.81	1.41	56	80	6	5	6	6
New Zealand	3,360	3,778	4,041	4,223	1.17	0.67	0.44	1,428	1,958	122	137	135	137
Niue	2	2	2	2	-1.45	-1.06	-0.68	...	...	...	...	...	...

TABLE B.1

continued

	Total population							Number of households					
	Estimates and projections (000)				Annual growth rate (%)			Estimates and projections (000)		5-year increments (000)			
	1990	2000	2010	2020	1990–2000	2000–2010	2010–2020	2000	2020	2000–2005	2005–2010	2010–2015	2015–2020
Northern Mariana Islands	44	73	106	141	5.02	3.79	2.84	...	...	...	...	...	...
Palau	15	19	23	28	2.32	2.01	1.70	...	...	...	...	...	...
Papua New Guinea	3,762	4,809	5,989	7,327	2.46	2.19	2.02	1,028	1,643	130	148	161	176
Pitcairn	-	-	-	-	0.30	-	-	...	...	...	...	...	...
Samoa	160	159	168	190	-0.10	0.58	1.24	36	57	4	5	6	7
Solomon Islands	319	447	619	828	3.40	3.24	2.91	73	136	13	15	17	18
Tokelau	2	1	1	1	-0.99	-	-	...	...	...	...	...	...
Tonga	96	99	103	107	0.34	0.38	0.42	...	...	...	...	...	...
Tuvalu	9	10	12	13	1.45	1.28	1.11	...	...	...	...	...	...
Vanuatu	149	197	252	313	2.75	2.47	2.16	34	54	4	5	5	5
Wallis and Futuna Islands	14	14	15	16	0.55	0.55	0.56	...	...	...	...	...	...

Notes: 1 Including Agalega, Rodrigues and Saint Brandon. 2 Including Ascension and Tristan da Cunha. 3 For statistical purposes, the data for China do not include Hong Kong and Macao Special Administrative Regions (SAR) of China. 4 As of 1 July 1997, Hong Kong became a SAR of China. 5 As of 20 December 1999, Macao became a SAR of China. 6 Refers to the Vatican City State.
7 The former Yugoslav Republic of Macedonia. 8 Including Christmas Island, Cocos (Keeling) Islands and Norfolk Island.

Sources: United Nations, *World Urbanization Prospects: The 2001 revision*; UN-Habitat, *Household Projections*, 2nd revision.

TABLE B.2

Urbanization Trends, Size and Growth of Urban and Rural Population

	Level of urbanization (%)			Urban population					Rural population				
				Estimates and projections (000)			Annual growth rate (%)		Estimates and projections (000)			Annual growth rate (%)	
	2000	2010	2020	2000	2010	2020	2000–2010	2010–2020	2000	2010	2020	2000–2010	2010–2020
WORLD	**47.2**	**51.5**	**55.9**	**2,861,756**	**3,513,700**	**4,236,927**	**2.05**	**1.87**	**3,194,959**	**3,312,036**	**3,342,351**	**0.36**	**0.09**
AFRICA	**37.2**	**42.7**	**47.9**	**295,228**	**425,596**	**589,408**	**3.66**	**3.26**	**498,400**	**571,364**	**641,567**	**1.37**	**1.16**
Algeria	57.1	62.6	67.5	17,311	22,323	27,301	2.54	2.01	12,980	13,312	13,117	0.25	-0.15
Angola	34.2	40.8	47.4	4,492	7,251	11,490	4.79	4.60	8,642	10,514	12,773	1.96	1.95
Benin	42.3	49.7	55.9	2,651	4,111	5,981	4.39	3.75	3,621	4,168	4,716	1.41	1.24
Botswana	49.0	53.5	58.6	756	871	1,036	1.42	1.74	786	757	731	-0.37	-0.35
Burkina Faso	16.5	20.5	26.0	1,905	3,235	5,630	5.29	5.54	9,630	12,529	16,037	2.63	2.47
Burundi	9.0	12.5	16.7	569	1,079	1,856	6.40	5.42	5,787	7,583	9,228	2.70	1.96
Cameroon	48.9	56.0	61.5	7,277	10,283	13,611	3.46	2.80	7,599	8,064	8,510	0.59	0.54
Cape Verde	62.2	71.6	75.3	266	374	457	3.42	2.01	161	148	150	-0.85	0.14
Central African Republic	41.2	46.5	52.8	1,531	2,061	2,834	2.97	3.19	2,186	2,369	2,535	0.80	0.68
Chad	23.8	28.1	34.2	1,876	3,005	4,877	4.71	4.84	6,010	7,685	9,398	2.46	2.01
Comoros	33.2	39.4	45.9	235	370	549	4.54	3.96	471	569	648	1.88	1.29
Congo	65.4	70.6	74.4	1,974	2,884	4,064	3.79	3.43	1,045	1,201	1,400	1.39	1.53
Côte d'Ivoire	43.6	48.2	53.7	6,984	9,465	12,540	3.04	2.81	9,029	10,160	10,813	1.18	0.62
Dem. Republic of the Congo	30.3	36.0	42.6	15,427	25,629	41,997	5.08	4.94	35,521	45,643	56,624	2.51	2.16
Djibouti	84.0	86.0	87.7	531	584	655	0.95	1.15	101	95	92	-0.61	-0.36
Egypt	42.7	44.0	48.2	28,970	34,871	43,252	1.85	2.15	38,914	44,389	46,434	1.32	0.45
Equatorial Guinea	48.2	57.9	63.9	220	351	503	4.66	3.62	237	255	284	0.73	1.09
Eritrea	18.7	23.2	29.3	685	1,184	1,867	5.47	4.55	2,973	3,913	4,515	2.75	1.43
Ethiopia	15.5	19.5	24.8	9,762	15,564	25,080	4.66	4.77	53,146	64,290	75,864	1.90	1.66
Gabon	81.4	87.5	89.6	1,002	1,372	1,758	3.15	2.48	228	196	204	-1.53	0.38
Gambia	30.7	37.1	43.8	399	604	846	4.13	3.37	903	1,022	1,087	1.24	0.61
Ghana	36.1	39.9	45.3	6,963	9,545	13,021	3.15	3.11	12,342	14,393	15,735	1.54	0.89
Guinea	27.5	32.5	38.6	2,242	3,252	4,896	3.72	4.09	5,912	6,743	7,785	1.32	1.44
Guinea-Bissau	31.5	39.4	46.3	378	603	898	4.67	3.98	821	928	1,042	1.22	1.16
Kenya	33.4	42.9	50.8	10,234	15,857	21,710	4.38	3.14	20,435	21,084	20,985	0.31	-0.05
Lesotho	28.0	35.6	42.2	569	757	919	2.86	1.94	1,466	1,370	1,258	-0.68	-0.85
Liberia	44.9	50.9	56.8	1,308	2,384	3,703	6.00	4.40	1,605	2,298	2,813	3.59	2.02
Libyan Arab Jamahiriya	87.6	89.7	90.9	4,635	5,858	6,829	2.34	1.53	654	673	681	0.28	0.12
Madagascar	29.5	36.1	42.8	4,710	7,610	11,679	4.80	4.28	11,261	13,486	15,640	1.80	1.48
Malawi	14.7	18.8	24.0	1,665	2,638	4,201	4.60	4.65	9,643	11,386	13,306	1.66	1.56
Mali	30.2	37.2	44.2	3,427	5,668	9,007	5.03	4.63	7,924	9,566	11,383	1.88	1.74
Mauritania	57.7	69.7	76.9	1,539	2,491	3,619	4.82	3.73	1,126	1,086	1,089	-0.36	0.03
Mauritius[1]	41.3	45.3	51.7	480	570	693	1.72	1.97	682	686	648	0.07	-0.57
Morocco	55.5	61.7	66.7	16,571	21,796	26,583	2.74	1.99	13,307	13,528	13,250	0.16	-0.21
Mozambique	32.1	43.4	52.1	5,874	9,397	13,382	4.70	3.53	12,419	12,251	12,291	-0.14	0.03
Namibia	30.9	36.3	42.8	542	762	1,089	3.40	3.57	1,214	1,335	1,458	0.95	0.88
Niger	20.6	26.1	32.3	2,228	4,054	7,068	5.99	5.56	8,604	11,496	14,785	2.90	2.52
Nigeria	44.1	52.1	58.3	50,175	76,559	107,428	4.23	3.39	63,687	70,376	76,819	1.00	0.88
Réunion	71.4	77.1	80.9	515	624	711	1.92	1.29	206	185	168	-1.07	-0.96
Rwanda	6.2	7.7	10.4	468	728	1,218	4.42	5.15	7,141	8,697	10,444	1.97	1.83
Saint Helena[2]	70.6	79.0	81.7	4	5	6	1.96	1.17	2	1	1	-2.52	-0.52
Sao Tome and Principe	47.0	53.5	59.2	65	88	114	3.03	2.64	73	76	79	0.42	0.31
Senegal	47.4	54.3	60.2	4,469	6,549	9,037	3.82	3.22	4,952	5,503	5,986	1.06	0.84
Seychelles	63.8	70.4	74.2	51	64	77	2.25	1.76	29	27	27	-0.72	-0.15

Sierra Leone	36.6	43.4	49.9	1,614	2,729	4,008	5.25	3.84	2,791	3,554	4,028	2.42	1.25
Somalia	27.5	32.6	39.2	2,413	4,262	7,102	5.69	5.11	6,365	8,804	11,010	3.24	2.24
South Africa	56.9	64.2	69.6	24,629	28,975	30,624	1.63	0.55	18,680	16,165	13,353	-1.45	-1.91
Sudan	36.1	45.0	51.8	11,231	17,383	23,887	4.37	3.18	19,864	21,284	22,228	0.69	0.43
Swaziland	26.4	30.2	35.6	244	298	384	2.01	2.52	681	689	693	0.12	0.05
Togo	33.4	39.3	45.9	1,510	2,292	3,390	4.17	3.92	3,017	3,534	3,992	1.58	1.22
Tunisia	65.5	71.3	75.2	6,198	7,576	8,909	2.01	1.62	3,261	3,052	2,933	-0.66	-0.40
Uganda	14.2	18.2	23.5	3,299	5,936	10,740	5.87	5.93	20,001	26,652	35,047	2.87	2.74
United Republic of Tanzania	32.3	42.2	49.4	11,327	18,573	27,091	4.95	3.78	23,792	25,489	27,784	0.69	0.86
Western Sahara	95.4	97.5	98.0	240	323	396	2.96	2.04	12	8	8	-3.48	-0.22
Zambia	39.6	42.6	48.4	4,128	5,539	8,151	2.94	3.86	6,293	7,449	8,682	1.69	1.53
Zimbabwe	35.3	42.5	49.1	4,459	6,380	8,652	3.58	3.05	8,168	8,648	8,980	0.57	0.38
ASIA	**37.5**	**43.0**	**48.7**	**1,375,519**	**1,783,600**	**2,231,108**	**2.60**	**2.24**	**2,296,822**	**2,361,337**	**2,350,476**	**0.28**	**-0.05**
Afghanistan	21.9	27.0	33.3	4,762	8,443	13,392	5.73	4.61	17,003	22,864	26,814	2.96	1.59
Armenia	67.2	68.5	71.4	2,545	2,609	2,705	0.25	0.36	1,242	1,199	1,084	-0.35	-1.01
Azerbaijan	51.9	52.5	56.0	4,173	4,461	5,005	0.67	1.15	3,868	4,037	3,929	0.43	-0.27
Bahrain	92.2	94.4	95.3	590	702	803	1.74	1.34	50	42	40	-1.76	-0.39
Bangladesh	25.0	31.1	37.7	34,354	52,223	74,432	4.19	3.54	103,085	115,703	123,209	1.15	0.63
Bhutan	7.1	9.9	13.5	149	268	465	5.87	5.52	1,936	2,439	2,989	2.31	2.03
Brunei Darussalam	72.2	76.9	80.1	237	299	357	2.31	1.78	91	90	89	-0.17	-0.10
Cambodia	16.9	22.8	29.5	2,216	3,796	6,052	5.39	4.66	10,889	12,833	14,477	1.64	1.21
China[3]	35.8	45.2	53.4	456,340	617,348	771,861	3.02	2.23	818,793	748,866	674,231	-0.89	-1.05
China, Hong Kong SAR[4]	100.0	100.0	100.0	6,860	7,659	8,365	1.10	0.88	-	-	-	-	-
China, Macau SAR[5]	98.8	99.0	99.1	439	476	511	0.81	0.70	5	5	5	-0.37	-0.48
Cyprus	69.9	73.0	76.2	548	614	674	1.13	0.94	236	227	210	-0.38	-0.75
Dem. People's Rep. of Korea	60.2	63.5	67.9	13,415	15,046	17,074	1.15	1.26	8,854	8,642	8,085	-0.24	-0.67
Georgia	56.3	59.2	63.9	2,962	2,935	2,929	-0.09	-0.02	2,300	2,021	1,654	-1.29	-2.00
India	27.7	30.3	34.7	279,045	352,246	447,535	2.33	2.39	729,893	811,774	843,755	1.06	0.39
Indonesia	41.0	50.9	58.4	86,943	120,986	153,006	3.30	2.35	125,149	116,725	108,891	-0.70	-0.69
Iran (Islamic Republic of)	64.0	70.6	75.5	45,023	57,032	70,574	2.36	2.13	25,307	23,777	22,938	-0.62	-0.36
Iraq	67.5	67.7	70.1	15,493	20,268	25,971	2.69	2.48	7,453	9,649	11,082	2.58	1.39
Israel	91.6	93.0	93.9	5,535	6,738	7,604	1.97	1.21	505	511	493	0.11	-0.35
Japan	78.8	80.5	82.6	100,089	103,211	104,039	0.31	0.08	27,007	25,009	21,920	-0.77	-1.32
Jordan	78.7	80.1	82.2	3,867	5,147	6,524	2.86	2.37	1,046	1,275	1,416	1.98	1.05
Kazakhstan	55.8	56.7	60.2	9,031	8,960	9,677	-0.08	0.77	7,142	6,840	6,396	-0.43	-0.67
Kuwait	96.0	96.7	97.1	1,838	2,391	2,930	2.63	2.03	76	82	87	0.66	0.65
Kyrgyzstan	34.4	34.7	38.3	1,692	1,912	2,360	1.22	2.11	3,229	3,598	3,801	1.08	0.55
Lao People's Dem. Republic	19.3	24.2	30.2	1,018	1,602	2,436	4.54	4.19	4,261	5,009	5,618	1.62	1.15
Lebanon	89.7	92.1	93.1	3,138	3,700	4,102	1.65	1.03	359	316	306	-1.26	-0.33
Malaysia	57.4	63.8	68.6	12,758	16,680	20,325	2.68	1.98	9,461	9,466	9,283	0.00	-0.19
Maldives	27.6	32.3	38.3	80	127	197	4.58	4.42	211	266	319	2.32	1.82
Mongolia	56.6	58.0	61.6	1,434	1,663	2,027	1.48	1.98	1,100	1,206	1,264	0.93	0.47
Myanmar	27.7	33.4	40.0	13,220	17,712	23,121	2.92	2.67	34,529	35,278	34,635	0.21	-0.18
Nepal	11.8	15.6	20.4	2,730	4,523	7,245	5.05	4.71	20,313	24,399	28,203	1.83	1.45
Occupied Palestinian Territory	66.8	70.0	73.5	2,132	3,167	4,550	3.96	3.62	1,059	1,358	1,644	2.49	1.91
Oman	76.0	80.8	83.9	1,928	2,841	3,982	3.88	3.38	610	674	762	1.00	1.23
Pakistan	33.1	36.9	42.4	46,757	66,966	96,534	3.59	3.66	94,499	114,418	131,247	1.91	1.37
Philippines	58.6	66.1	71.4	44,295	59,398	72,452	2.93	1.99	31,358	30,490	28,972	-0.28	-0.51
Qatar	92.7	94.5	95.4	524	617	694	1.63	1.19	41	36	33	-1.35	-0.83
Republic of Korea	81.9	86.7	89.2	38,269	43,024	45,877	1.17	0.64	8,471	6,599	5,531	-2.50	-1.76
Saudi Arabia	86.2	90.0	91.6	17,531	24,837	33,054	3.48	2.86	2,815	2,751	3,041	-0.23	1.00
Singapore	100.0	100.0	100.0	4,018	4,604	4,879	1.36	0.58	-	-	-	-	-
Sri Lanka	22.8	26.8	33.2	4,314	5,552	7,312	2.52	2.75	14,610	15,147	14,745	0.36	-0.27
Syrian Arab Republic	51.4	55.4	60.6	8,324	11,519	15,435	3.25	2.93	7,865	9,262	10,021	1.63	0.79
Tajikistan	27.6	27.9	32.8	1,681	1,845	2,491	0.93	3.00	4,406	4,773	5,111	0.80	0.68
Thailand	19.8	22.3	26.7	12,453	15,517	20,080	2.20	2.58	50,352	54,164	55,017	0.73	0.16
Timor-Leste	7.5	8.4	11.1	55	86	129	4.44	4.08	682	933	1,031	3.14	1.00
Turkey	65.8	69.9	73.7	43,844	52,491	61,060	1.80	1.51	22,824	22,654	21,826	-0.07	-0.37
Turkmenistan	44.8	47.5	53.0	2,122	2,683	3,416	2.35	2.41	2,616	2,968	3,032	1.26	0.21
United Arab Emirates	86.7	90.5	92.4	2,260	2,765	3,107	2.02	1.17	346	291	257	-1.75	-1.24
Uzbekistan	36.7	37.1	40.7	9,140	10,574	13,212	1.46	2.23	15,740	17,965	19,284	1.32	0.71
Viet Nam	24.1	28.8	34.7	18,816	25,547	34,770	3.06	3.08	59,321	63,137	65,436	0.62	0.36
Yemen	24.7	28.5	34.4	4,534	7,789	13,775	5.41	5.70	13,815	19,569	26,260	3.48	2.94
EUROPE	**73.4**	**75.1**	**77.6**	**534,061**	**535,949**	**539,532**	**0.04**	**0.07**	**193,242**	**177,263**	**155,344**	**-0.86**	**-1.32**
Albania	42.3	48.7	54.9	1,326	1,614	1,956	1.97	1.92	1,808	1,697	1,608	-0.63	-0.54
Andorra	92.4	91.3	91.3	79	115	151	3.69	2.71	7	11	14	5.16	2.71
Austria	67.3	69.3	72.9	5,436	5,515	5,639	0.14	0.22	2,643	2,438	2,096	-0.81	-1.51
Belarus	69.4	71.3	74.2	7,073	7,001	7,053	-0.10	0.07	3,114	2,818	2,455	-1.00	-1.38
Belgium	97.3	97.9	98.2	9,976	10,076	10,058	0.10	-0.02	273	220	186	-2.15	-1.67
Bosnia and Herzegovina	43.0	47.9	53.8	1,709	2,046	2,285	1.80	1.10	2,269	2,223	1,959	-0.20	-1.26
Bulgaria	67.5	68.2	70.9	5,363	4,901	4,585	-0.90	-0.67	2,587	2,284	1,882	-1.24	-1.94
Channel Islands	28.9	30.0	34.2	42	43	48	0.35	1.08	103	101	93	-0.17	-0.82
Croatia	57.7	62.1	66.8	2,686	2,887	3,056	0.72	0.57	1,967	1,763	1,522	-1.09	-1.47
Czech Republic	74.5	75.4	77.6	7,653	7,645	7,680	-0.01	0.05	2,619	2,492	2,215	-0.50	-1.18
Denmark	85.1	85.3	86.2	4,527	4,584	4,627	0.12	0.09	793	790	739	-0.03	-0.67
Estonia	69.4	70.2	72.8	967	880	821	-0.94	-0.70	427	373	306	-1.35	-1.96
Faeroe Islands	37.9	43.4	49.4	18	22	27	2.24	1.92	29	29	27	-0.02	-0.51
Finland	59.0	59.0	59.9	3,050	3,059	3,093	0.03	0.11	2,122	2,129	2,072	0.03	-0.27
France	75.4	77.2	79.6	44,649	47,268	49,705	0.57	0.50	14,588	13,935	12,707	-0.46	-0.92
Germany	87.5	89.2	90.5	71,798	72,595	72,303	0.11	-0.04	10,218	8,758	7,561	-1.54	-1.47
Gibraltar	100.0	100.0	100.0	27	26	25	-0.18	-0.33	-	-	-	-	-
Greece	60.1	63.1	67.4	6,376	6,672	6,959	0.45	0.42	4,234	3,908	3,366	-0.80	-1.49
Holy See[6]	100.0	100.0	100.0	1	1	1	0.00	0.00	-	-	-	-	-
Hungary	64.5	67.6	71.3	6,434	6,418	6,428	-0.03	0.02	3,534	3,071	2,593	-1.40	-1.69
Iceland	92.5	93.8	94.7	258	279	296	0.76	0.59	21	18	17	-1.34	-1.05
Ireland	59.0	62.1	66.1	2,244	2,608	3,037	1.50	1.52	1,559	1,593	1,557	0.22	-0.23
Isle of Man	76.6	79.3	82.0	58	64	69	1.13	0.66	18	17	15	-0.48	-1.01
Italy	66.9	69.0	72.6	38,512	38,906	39,092	0.10	0.05	19,018	17,485	14,769	-0.84	-1.69
Latvia	60.4	60.4	60.7	1,463	1,383	1,312	-0.56	-0.52	957	905	848	-0.56	-0.65

TABLE B.2

continued

	Level of urbanization (%)			Urban population Estimates and projections (000)			Annual growth rate (%)		Rural population Estimates and projections (000)			Annual growth rate (%)	
	2000	2010	2020	2000	2010	2020	2000–2010	2010–2020	2000	2010	2020	2000–2010	2010–2020
Liechtenstein	21.4	23.7	28.2	7	9	11	1.99	2.39	26	27	28	0.69	0.05
Lithuania	68.5	70.2	73.2	2,532	2,525	2,548	-0.03	0.09	1,164	1,069	935	-0.85	-1.35
Luxembourg	91.5	94.3	95.5	400	462	522	1.45	1.21	37	28	25	-2.78	-1.34
Malta	90.9	93.0	94.2	355	377	392	0.60	0.39	35	28	24	-2.27	-1.59
Monaco	100.0	100.0	100.0	33	36	38	0.81	0.53	-	-	-	-	-
Netherlands	89.5	90.5	91.6	14,197	14,767	15,116	0.39	0.23	1,667	1,546	1,392	-0.75	-1.05
Norway	74.7	77.5	80.2	3,339	3,576	3,798	0.69	0.60	1,130	1,038	936	-0.86	-1.04
Poland	62.3	64.8	68.5	24,069	24,805	25,834	0.30	0.41	14,536	13,448	11,906	-0.78	-1.22
Portugal	64.4	74.7	79.0	6,453	7,536	7,850	1.55	0.41	3,563	2,546	2,090	-3.36	-1.97
Republic of Moldova	41.6	43.3	47.7	1,786	1,814	1,961	0.16	0.78	2,509	2,375	2,148	-0.55	-1.00
Romania	55.1	57.4	61.5	12,360	12,532	12,927	0.14	0.31	10,078	9,287	8,099	-0.82	-1.37
Russian Federation	72.9	73.3	75.0	106,063	100,358	97,308	-0.55	-0.31	39,428	36,618	32,380	-0.74	-1.23
San Marino	90.2	91.7	92.7	24	27	29	1.19	0.84	3	2	2	-0.53	-0.67
Serbia and Montenegro	51.6	53.7	57.8	5,443	5,583	5,892	0.25	0.54	5,109	4,821	4,300	-0.58	-1.14
Slovakia	57.4	60.0	64.5	3,100	3,257	3,475	0.49	0.65	2,299	2,173	1,909	-0.56	-1.29
Slovenia	49.2	50.0	53.9	978	979	1,018	0.01	0.40	1,010	977	872	-0.34	-1.14
Spain	77.6	79.9	82.3	30,974	31,633	31,499	0.21	-0.04	8,936	7,936	6,773	-1.19	-1.58
Sweden	83.3	83.7	84.9	7,364	7,286	7,274	-0.11	-0.02	1,478	1,417	1,296	-0.42	-0.89
Switzerland	67.4	68.3	71.1	4,834	4,833	4,875	0.00	0.09	2,337	2,240	1,985	-0.42	-1.21
TFYR Macedonia[7]	59.4	60.5	63.9	1,208	1,254	1,326	0.37	0.56	826	818	749	-0.10	-0.87
Ukraine	67.9	69.2	72.0	33,657	31,299	29,867	-0.73	-0.47	15,911	13,941	11,612	-1.32	-1.83
United Kingdom	89.5	90.3	91.3	53,162	54,394	55,670	0.23	0.23	6,253	5,867	5,276	-0.64	-1.06
LATIN AMERICA AND THE CARIBBEAN	**75.4**	**79.0**	**81.8**	**391,342**	**469,755**	**543,166**	**1.83**	**1.45**	**127,467**	**124,558**	**120,521**	**-0.23**	**-0.33**
Anguilla	100.0	100.0	100.0	11	15	18	2.44	1.91	-	-	-	-	-
Antigua and Barbuda	36.8	40.5	46.5	24	27	32	1.26	1.65	41	40	37	-0.30	-0.79
Argentina	88.2	89.6	90.8	32,662	37,160	41,196	1.29	1.03	4,370	4,314	4,151	-0.13	-0.38
Aruba	50.8	53.7	58.9	51	74	104	3.72	3.37	49	64	72	2.54	1.28
Bahamas	88.5	90.9	92.0	269	310	346	1.41	1.09	35	31	30	-1.17	-0.30
Barbados	50.0	55.6	61.1	134	154	173	1.41	1.19	134	123	110	-0.85	-1.09
Belize	48.0	49.9	54.1	109	134	165	2.09	2.12	118	135	140	1.34	0.42
Bolivia	62.4	67.6	71.9	5,193	6,917	8,765	2.87	2.37	3,136	3,312	3,427	0.55	0.34
Brazil	81.2	86.0	88.9	138,287	164,724	187,281	1.75	1.28	32,119	26,720	23,297	-1.84	-1.37
British Virgin Islands	61.1	68.7	73.3	14	20	25	3.45	2.02	9	9	9	0.07	-0.18
Cayman Islands	100.0	100.0	100.0	38	52	66	3.05	2.37	-	-	-	-	-
Chile	85.8	88.2	89.8	13,049	14,997	16,868	1.39	1.18	2,162	2,014	1,906	-0.71	-0.55
Colombia	75.0	79.6	82.8	31,566	39,129	46,341	2.15	1.69	10,538	10,031	9,659	-0.49	-0.38
Costa Rica	59.0	64.1	68.8	2,374	3,115	3,847	2.72	2.11	1,649	1,742	1,745	0.54	0.02
Cuba	75.3	77.3	79.7	8,435	8,898	9,344	0.53	0.49	2,764	2,616	2,377	-0.55	-0.96
Dominica	71.0	74.4	77.6	50	52	54	0.40	0.42	20	18	16	-1.29	-1.35
Dominican Republic	65.4	70.9	74.8	5,475	6,818	7,905	2.19	1.48	2,898	2,803	2,660	-0.33	-0.52
Ecuador	63.0	67.3	71.4	7,967	10,025	12,066	2.30	1.85	4,679	4,873	4,837	0.41	-0.07
El Salvador	60.3	69.9	75.6	3,786	5,204	6,423	3.18	2.10	2,492	2,237	2,070	-1.08	-0.78
Falkland Islands (Malvinas)	80.8	84.8	87.3	2	2	3	1.65	1.31	-	-	-	-1.17	-0.76
French Guiana	75.1	76.4	78.7	124	170	228	3.19	2.92	41	52	62	2.45	1.60
Grenada	37.9	43.9	50.3	35	42	50	1.75	1.61	58	54	49	-0.74	-0.96
Guadeloupe	99.6	99.8	99.9	426	459	479	0.74	0.44	2	1	-	-8.77	-4.30
Guatemala	39.7	43.5	49.4	4,515	6,358	8,885	3.42	3.35	6,870	8,273	9,117	1.86	0.97
Guyana	36.3	41.0	47.2	276	313	344	1.26	0.93	485	450	384	-0.74	-1.58
Haiti	35.7	42.3	48.8	2,906	4,014	5,325	3.23	2.83	5,236	5,486	5,580	0.47	0.17
Honduras	52.7	61.2	66.7	3,384	4,873	6,280	3.65	2.54	3,033	3,089	3,139	0.18	0.16
Jamaica	56.1	61.0	65.9	1,445	1,722	2,052	1.75	1.76	1,131	1,099	1,061	-0.29	-0.35
Martinique	94.9	96.9	97.7	364	390	406	0.69	0.41	19	12	10	-4.47	-2.50
Mexico	74.4	76.6	79.2	73,531	86,500	99,017	1.62	1.35	25,341	26,384	25,958	0.40	-0.16
Montserrat	13.0	15.1	19.3	-	1	1	4.72	4.97	3	4	5	2.98	1.96
Netherlands Antilles	69.2	71.4	74.8	149	167	186	1.15	1.10	66	67	63	0.07	-0.61
Nicaragua	56.1	60.3	65.1	2,847	3,912	5,156	3.18	2.76	2,225	2,580	2,769	1.48	0.71
Panama	56.3	59.6	64.0	1,606	1,948	2,317	1.93	1.73	1,249	1,318	1,305	0.54	-0.10
Paraguay	56.0	62.3	67.3	3,077	4,348	5,766	3.46	2.82	2,420	2,632	2,804	0.84	0.63
Peru	72.8	76.3	79.3	18,674	22,798	26,778	2.00	1.61	6,988	7,088	6,979	0.14	-0.16
Puerto Rico	75.2	78.5	81.3	2,945	3,337	3,666	1.25	0.94	970	912	846	-0.61	-0.76
Saint Kitts and Nevis	34.1	36.8	42.6	13	13	15	0.11	1.02	25	23	20	-1.04	-1.41
Saint Lucia	37.8	41.0	46.9	56	67	82	1.82	1.99	92	96	93	0.46	-0.39
Saint Vincent and the Grenadines	54.8	64.8	70.1	62	78	88	2.26	1.28	51	42	38	-1.90	-1.15
Suriname	74.1	79.6	82.5	309	345	363	1.09	0.53	108	89	77	-1.99	-1.40
Trinidad and Tobago	74.1	77.9	80.7	959	1,058	1,146	0.98	0.80	335	301	275	-1.09	-0.91
Turks and Caicos Islands	45.2	49.9	55.9	8	11	16	4.01	3.48	9	11	13	2.11	1.06
United States Virgin Islands	46.4	49.7	54.5	56	67	80	1.72	1.77	65	68	66	0.42	-0.16
Uruguay	91.9	93.8	94.8	3,067	3,343	3,575	0.86	0.67	270	222	196	-1.94	-1.27
Venezuela	86.9	89.1	90.7	21,010	25,594	29,842	1.97	1.54	3,160	3,122	3,068	-0.12	-0.17
NORTHERN AMERICA	**77.4**	**79.8**	**82.3**	**242,999**	**272,759**	**304,503**	**1.16**	**1.10**	**71,114**	**69,145**	**65,431**	**-0.28**	**-0.55**
Bermuda	100.0	100.0	100.0	63	67	71	0.62	0.57	-	-	-	-	-
Canada	78.7	80.8	83.0	24,206	26,841	29,552	1.03	0.96	6,551	6,375	6,046	-0.27	-0.53
Greenland	82.0	84.2	86.2	46	48	50	0.43	0.40	10	9	8	-1.14	-1.15
Saint Pierre and Miquelon	92.1	93.1	93.9	6	7	7	0.79	0.69	1	1	-	-0.63	-0.63
United States	77.2	79.7	82.2	218,678	245,796	274,823	1.17	1.12	64,553	62,761	59,376	-0.28	-0.55

OCEANIA	74.1	75.7	76.4	22,607	26,041	29,209	1.41	1.15	7,913	8,370	9,012	0.56	0.74
American Samoa	52.7	57.9	63.2	36	53	74	3.97	3.32	32	38	43	1.85	1.10
Australia[8]	90.7	94.0	95.4	17,361	19,764	21,690	1.30	0.93	1,777	1,265	1,054	-3.40	-1.82
Cook Islands	59.0	61.0	64.7	12	13	14	0.99	1.22	8	8	8	0.15	-0.36
Fiji	49.4	56.7	62.8	402	508	592	2.34	1.53	411	388	351	-0.59	-0.99
French Polynesia	52.7	52.9	56.0	123	143	170	1.51	1.71	110	128	134	1.45	0.46
Guam	39.2	43.4	49.9	61	83	113	3.09	3.09	94	108	113	1.35	0.50
Kiribati	38.2	42.8	48.5	32	40	51	2.45	2.41	51	54	55	0.53	0.12
Marshall Islands	65.8	67.9	71.2	34	39	46	1.59	1.61	17	19	19	0.63	0.08
Micronesia (Fed. States of)	28.3	32.3	38.4	35	50	72	3.63	3.67	88	105	116	1.76	1.01
Nauru	100.0	100.0	100.0	12	15	18	2.24	1.88	-	-	-	-	-
New Caledonia	76.9	85.4	89.0	166	220	264	2.85	1.82	50	38	33	-2.77	-1.43
New Zealand	85.8	86.9	88.1	3,243	3,510	3,722	0.79	0.59	535	530	501	-0.09	-0.57
Niue	32.8	36.6	42.0	1	1	1	0.05	0.70	1	1	1	-1.65	-1.57
Northern Mariana Islands	52.7	54.5	58.5	38	58	83	4.12	3.55	34	48	59	3.40	1.92
Palau	69.5	69.5	71.1	13	16	20	2.01	1.93	6	7	8	2.01	1.17
Papua New Guinea	17.4	20.3	24.6	836	1,217	1,806	3.75	3.94	3,973	4,772	5,521	1.83	1.46
Pitcairn	-	-	-	-	-	-	-	-	-	-	-	-	-
Samoa	22.1	25.1	30.7	35	42	58	1.88	3.25	124	126	132	0.17	0.46
Solomon Islands	19.7	25.5	31.7	88	158	263	5.84	5.09	359	461	565	2.48	2.03
Tokelau	-	-	-	-	-	-	-	-	1	1	1	-	-
Tonga	32.7	35.8	40.9	32	37	44	1.27	1.76	67	66	63	-0.08	-0.41
Tuvalu	52.2	60.9	66.5	5	7	9	2.83	1.98	5	5	4	-0.73	-0.41
Vanuatu	21.7	25.9	31.5	43	65	99	4.25	4.11	154	187	214	1.91	1.38
Wallis and Futuna Islands	-	-	-	-	-	-	-	-	14	15	16	0.55	0.56

Notes: A figure of 0 means the population was below 500 persons. 1 Including Agalega, Rodrigues and Saint Brandon. 2 Including Ascension and Tristan da Cunha. 3 For statistical purposes, the data for China do not include Hong Kong and Macao Special Administrative Regions (SAR) of China. 4 As of 1 July 1997, Hong Kong became a SAR of China. 5 As of 20 December 1999, Macao became a SAR of China. 6 Refers to the Vatican City State. 7 The former Yugoslav Republic of Macedonia. 8 Including Christmas Island, Cocos (Keeling) Islands and Norfolk Island.

Source: United Nations, *World Urbanization Prospects: The 2001 Revision.*

TABLE B.3

Housing Ownership and Water and Toilet Facilities, Selected Countries

			Occupied housing units						Housing units with	
			All households			Women-headed households			piped water	toilet inside
		Year	Number	Owner occupied (%)	Tenants* (%)	Number	Owner occupied (%)	Tenants* (%)	(%)	(%)
AFRICA										
Benin[1]	Total	1994	832,526	59.4	23.4	...	...	...	...	21.0
Benin[1]	Urban	1994	306,780	39.7	27.6	...	...	...	...	...
Benin[1]	Rural	1994	525,746	70.9	20.9	...	...	...	...	...
Botswana[2]	Total	1996	276,209	...	...	...	...	...	77.0	...
Botswana[2]	Urban	1996	...	...	...	...	...	...	100.0	...
Botswana[2]	Rural	1996	...	...	...	...	...	...	53.1	...
Egypt[3]	Total	1996	12,702,600	69.3	30.7	...	...	...	63.2	...
Egypt[3]	Urban	1996	5,839,877	49.1	50.9	...	...	...	86.3	...
Egypt[3]	Rural	1996	6,862,723	86.6	13.4	...	...	...	43.6	...
Gambia	Total	1993	116,001	61.3	8.5	18,415	60.9	8.0	15.7	71.2
Gambia	Urban	1993	54,042	34.9	10.5	10,463	44.0	8.2	32.0	79.3
Gambia	Rural	1993	61,959	84.3	6.8	7,952	83.1	7.6	1.5	64.1
Lesotho	Total	1996	370,972	84.3	...	108,893	...	...	47.8	45.7
Lesotho	Urban	1996	79,452	...	...	...	...	...	...	...
Lesotho	Rural	1996	291,520	...	...	...	...	...	...	...
Libyan Arab Jamahiriya[4]	Total	1995	711,837	40.6	21.6	...	...	...	89.0	93.4
Libyan Arab Jamahiriya[4]	Urban	1995	545,998	...	...	...	...	...	91.1	...
Libyan Arab Jamahiriya[4]	Rural	1995	88,921	...	...	...	...	...	77.3	...
Niger	Total	1998	1,129,126	77.6	1.0	...	...	...	15.0	1.2
Niger	Urban	1998	182,969	39.7	3.9	...	...	...	81.1	6.0
Niger	Rural	1998	946,157	84.9	0.4	...	...	...	2.2	0.3
Sengal[5]	Total	1994	777,931	66.7	14.2	152,197	...	...	47.6	42.4
Sengal[5]	Urban	1994	330,828	49.3	...	89,797	...	...	80.0	77.4
Sengal[5]	Rural	1994	447,103	79.7	...	62,450	...	...	23.6	16.4
Seychelles[6]	Total	1997	17,878	74.7	11.7	8,564	74.8	...	85.0	86.3
Seychelles[6]	Rural	1997	...	...	...	...	...	...	80.9	83.4
South Africa[7]	Total	1996	9,059,571	76.8	21.6	3,428,796	80.1	18.2	43.9	87.2
South Africa[7]	Urban	1996	5,426,873	74.3	24.0	1,726,059	71.7	26.6	66.0	95.9
South Africa[7]	Rural	1996	3,632,698	80.4	18.0	1,702,737	88.7	9.7	10.9	74.0
Saint Helena	Total	1998	1,577	78.8	7.4	...	...	...	95.2	99.7
Saint Helena	Urban	1998	280	61.4	10.4	...	...	...	99.6	100.0
Saint Helena	Rural	1998	1,297	82.5	6.7	...	...	...	94.2	99.7
Tunisia	Total	1994	1,704,805	77.4	13.7	...	...	...	...	...
Tunisia	Urban	1994	1,093,243	70.7	20.2	...	...	...	...	...
Tunisia	Rural	1994	611,562	89.5	2.1	...	...	...	...	...
Zimbabwe[8]	Total	1997	2,510,410	58.7	3.8	822,912	...	...	...	...
Zimbabwe[8]	Urban	1997	926,210	31.3	9.6	...	...	...	...	...
Zimbabwe[8]	Rural	1997	1,584,200	74.8	0.5	...	...	...	...	...
ASIA										
Armenia[9]	Total	1998	...	90.6	5.9	...	91.3	6.3	66.7	61.4
Armenia[9]	Urban	1998	...	89.4	7.2	...	90.5	7.6	91.7	90.1
Armenia[9]	Rural	1998	...	92.5	3.8	...	93.1	3.6	28.1	17.4

TABLE B.3

continued

			Occupied housing units						Housing units with	
			All households			Women-headed households			piped water	toilet inside
		Year	Number	Owner occupied (%)	Tenants* (%)	Number	Owner occupied (%)	Tenants* (%)	(%)	(%)
Azerbaijan[10]	Total	1998	1,479,504	76.1	23.9	...	...	...	...	41.1
Azerbaijan[10]	Urban	1998	897,283	62.2	37.8	...	...	...	...	66.0
Azerbaijan[10]	Rural	1998	582,221	97.5	2.5	...	...	...	...	2.7
Cambodia[11]	Total	1998	...	95.3	2.6	...	...	...	...	...
Cambodia[11]	Urban	1998	...	88.4	3.9	...	...	...	...	...
Cambodia[11]	Rural	1998	...	96.5	2.3	...	...	...	...	...
China, Hong Kong SAR[12]	Total	1996	1,855,553	43.6	36.4	504,294	38.2	45.5	...	...
China, Macau SAR	Total	1996	119,966	72.9	4.6	26,170	70.0	2.0	99.6	99.5
Cyprus	Total	1992	184,161	69.3	10.6	25,645	51.5	16.8	95.3	91.0
Cyprus	Urban	1992	124,673	64.7	12.1	17,592	45.9	19.8	98.1	96.2
Cyprus	Rural	1992	59,488	78.9	7.5	8,053	63.7	10.1	89.4	80.2
Iran (Islamic Republic of)[13]	Total	1996	12,280,539	72.7	2.5	...	...	...	87.2	98.4
Iran (Islamic Republic of)[13]	Urban	1996	7,929,830	66.7	2.6	...	...	...	96.3	99.6
Iran (Islamic Republic of)[13]	Rural	1996	4,350,709	83.5	2.4	...	...	...	70.8	96.2
Israel[14]	Total	1995	1,587,000	62.5	5.5	468,940	54.8	8.0	...	...
Israel[14]	Urban	1995	1,490,525	62.5	5.6	447,315	54.5	8.1	...	...
Israel[14]	Rural	1995	96,475	62.1	3.6	21,625	60.0	4.3	...	...
Japan[15]	Total	1993	40,773,300	59.8	7.1	8,170,000	43.8	10.5	...	97.2
Japan[15]	Urban	1993	32,941,900	54.7	7.5	...	...	...	...	96.7
Japan[15]	Rural	1993	7,853,300	...	...	...	...	...	...	99.3
Kazakhstan[16]	Total	1998	...	...	6.3	...	...	...	61.4	...
Kazakhstan[16]	Urban	1998	...	...	8.9	...	...	...	87.6	...
Kazakhstan[16]	Rural	1998	...	...	2.5	...	...	...	21.5	...
Pakistan	Total	1998	19,344,232	...	...	...	...	...	27.4	...
Pakistan	Urban	1998	6,240,469	...	...	...	...	...	58.3	...
Pakistan	Rural	1998	13,103,763	...	...	...	...	...	12.7	...
Republic of Korea[17]	Total	1995	9,204,929	74.9	25.1	...	...	...	97.3	99.4
Republic of Korea[17]	Urban	1995	6,562,695	70.5	29.5	...	...	...	98.1	99.4
Republic of Korea[17]	Rural	1995	2,642,234	85.7	14.3	...	...	...	95.0	99.6
Singapore[18]	Total	1995	773,722	90.2	...	...	...	...	...	...
Syrian Arab Republic	Total	1994	2,196,084	...	...	...	...	...	88.5	...
Syrian Arab Republic	Urban	1994	1,181,158	...	...	...	...	...	97.5	...
Syrian Arab Republic	Rural	1994	1,014,926	...	...	...	...	...	78.0	...
Thailand[19]	Total	1996	15,002,591	82.8	13.3	...	75.4	4.5	18.7	90.5
Thailand[19]	Urban	1996	3,046,293	53.0	41.0	...	...	...	48.1	84.9
Thailand[19]	Rural	1996	11,956,299	90.4	6.3	...	...	...	11.2	92.0
Turkey[20]	Total	1994	13,382,841	69.0	1.8	1,051,854	75.4	0.2	...	...
Turkey[20]	Urban	1994	7,515,762	56.1	1.6	601,929	68.1	0.1	...	...
Turkey[20]	Rural	1994	5,867,079	85.4	1.9	449,925	85.1	0.4	...	...
EUROPE										
Austria[21]	Total	1999	2,972,222	50.0	11.2	968,654	36.5	15.2	99.7	96.0
Austria[21]	Urban	1999	2,171,457	40.4	14.4	787,960	30.9	17.7	99.7	95.4
Austria[21]	Rural	1999	800,765	75.9	2.6	180,694	60.6	4.2	99.8	98.4
Bulgaria	Total	1992	2,950,873	89.8	9.3	...	...	...	89.4	59.0
Bulgaria	Urban	1992	1,977,184	86.3	12.5	...	...	...	96.4	82.4
Bulgaria	Rural	1992	973,689	96.9	2.8	...	...	...	75.2	11.4
Channel Island	Total	1996	21,862	69.5	9.8	5,932	55.9	16.0	...	...
Estonia[22]	Total	1998	657,000	76.1	7.7	356,100	74.9	7.6	...	...
Estonia[22]	Urban	1998	524,400	73.8	8.8	283,700	72.1	8.6	...	...
Estonia[22]	Rural	1998	132,600	85.1	3.4	72,400	85.9	3.9	...	...
Finland[23]	Total	1998	2,247,206	65.4	14.4	...	...	...	...	...
Finland[23]	Urban	1998	1,422,984	59.6	17.8	...	...	...	...	...
Finland[23]	Rural	1998	824,222	75.3	8.6	...	...	...	...	...
Germany	Total	1998	34,865,300	40.2	59.8	10,675,800	26.8	73.2	100.0	...
Germany[24]	Total	1996	3,863,502	89.1	9.9	...	...	...	87.6	...
Germany[24]	Urban	1996	2,490,481	85.3	13.6	...	...	...	93.7	...
Hungary[25]	Rural	1996	1,373,021	85.3	13.6	...	...	...	76.8	...
Isle of Man	Total	1996	29,377	...	...	...	...	...	...	...
Isle of Man	Urban	1996	21,623	...	...	...	...	...	...	...
Isle of Man	Rural	1996	7,754	...	...	...	...	...	...	...
Lithuania	Total	1999	1,306,061	93.6	2.5	...	...	...	74.5	72.9
Lithuania	Urban	1999	890,208	91.6	2.8	...	...	...	89.7	89.5
Lithuania	Rural	1999	415,853	97.8	1.9	...	...	...	41.9	37.6
Malta[26]	Total	1995	119,479	68.0	28.3	25,051	...	...	...	98.2
Netherlands[27]	Total	1998	6,641,200	49.8	33.7	2,843,300	45.6	36.3	100.0	...
Netherlands[27]	Urban	1998	4,406,900	42.5	37.6	1,960,200	39.1	39.8	100.0	...
Netherlands[27]	Rural	1998	2,234,400	64.2	26.0	883,200	60.2	28.5	100.0	...
Norway[28]	Total	1990	1,751,363	78.2	21.8	600,353	71.3	28.7	...	100.0
Norway[28]	Urban	1990	1,300,372	78.2	21.8	463,806	71.6	28.4	...	100.0
Norway[28]	Rural	1990	439,216	78.1	21.9	133,442	70.5	29.5	...	100.0
Poland[29]	Total	1995	12,498,473	50.3	21.9	4,396,312	...	...	90.2	79.0
Poland[29]	Urban	1995	8,383,622	38.7	24.9	3,282,931	...	...	97.1	89.6
Poland[29]	Rural	1995	4,114,851	73.8	15.9	1,113,381	...	...	76.0	57.5

LATIN AMERICA AND THE CARIBBEAN

Bolivia	Total	1997	1,822,785	70.2	...	329,784	67.6	...	64.9	59.1
Bolivia	Urban	1997	1,094,237	59.8	...	228,448	59.9	...	88.8	78.1
Bolivia	Rural	1997	728,548	85.8	...	101,336	85.0	...	29.1	30.8
Brazil[30]	Total	1998	41,839,703	74.0	11.8	9,675,173	74.6	9.5	84.7	91.0
Brazil[30]	Urban	1998	33,993,829	74.2	8.9	8,601,559	73.6	9.0	92.8	96.9
Brazil[30]	Rural	1998	7,845,874	73.2	24.0	1,073,614	82.8	13.7	49.7	65.5
Colombia[31]	Total	1993	7,159,842	63.5	...	1,749,420	65.6	...	79.7	84.9
Colombia[31]	Urban	1993	5,384,656	60.6	...	1,447,461	62.7	...	93.5	95.1
Colombia[31]	Rural	1993	1,775,186	72.2	...	301,959	79.8	...	38.0	54.0
Costa Rica[32]	Total	1997	715,264	67.5	15.9	...	...	...	97.8	89.5
Costa Rica[32]	Urban	1997	341,136	57.0	19.9	...	...	...	99.9	98.0
Costa Rica[32]	Rural	1997	374,128	77.1	12.3	...	...	...	96.1	82.5
Dominican Republic[33]	Total	1993	1,629,616	71.2	...	534,850	...	...	67.2	...
Guatemala[34]	Total	1994	1,591,823	...	...	...	...	...	62.7	35.2
Guatemala[34]	Urban	1994	604,029	...	...	...	...	...	87.8	73.3
Guatemala[34]	Rural	1994	987,794	...	...	...	...	...	47.4	11.9
Mexico[35]	Total	1996	20,199,398	78.0	...	3,287,122	75.6	...	57.3	71.1
Mexico[35]	Urban	1996	15,318,401	74.3	...	2,738,112	72.6	...	69.9	84.5
Mexico[35]	Rural	1996	4,880,997	89.7	...	549,010	90.3	...	17.6	29.2
Nicaragua[36]	Total	1998	631,326	54.8	...	185,352	57.4	...	44.5	25.0
Nicaragua[36]	Urban	1998	386,047	54.1	...	135,970	57.0	...	51.0	26.0
Nicaragua[36]	Rural	1998	245,279	56.0	...	49,382	58.6	...	21.4	1.0
Saint Lucia[37]	Total	1999	33,079	72.4	1.3	...	...	...	47.8	35.7
Uruguay	Total	1996	975,056	...	...	...	...	...	76.8	95.6
Uruguay	Urban	1996	887,032	...	...	...	...	...	83.3	96.4
Uruguay	Rural	1996	88,024	...	...	...	...	...	9.0	87.5

NORTHERN AMERICA

Canada[38]	Total	1998	11,690,200	62.4	5.7	5,442,600	59.1	7.5	99.8	99.8
Canada[38]	Urban	1998	9,730,000	58.6	5.8	4,593,900	55.2	7.9	...	99.8
Canada[38]	Rural	1998	1,960,000	81.0	4.9	848,700	80.2	5.3	...	99.5
Greenland	Total	1999	20,350	...	...	...	...	...	...	...
Greenland	Urban	1999	17,467	...	...	...	...	...	...	...
Greenland	Rural	1999	2,883	...	...	...	...	...	...	...
United States[39]	Total	1997	99,487,000	65.8	1.9	28,852,000	51.2	4.6	99.6	99.7
United States[39]	Urban	1997	71,317,000	59.3	2.4	22,838,000	45.7	5.2	99.7	99.7
United States[39]	Rural	1997	28,170,000	82.4	0.6	6,013,900	71.7	2.1	99.4	99.7

OCEANIA

Australia[40]	Total	1966	...	...	...	1,276,064	60.5	1.3	92.8	63.2
Australia[40]	Urban	1966	...	...	...	267,210	59.2	1.1	98.2	63.3
Australia[40]	Rural	1966	...	...	...	223,720	66.9	1.1	84.3	63.0
Pitcairn	Rural	1999	15	86.7	6.7	5	80.0	20.0	100.0	...
Tonga[41]	Total	1996	15,670	83.3	14.9	3,003	86.0	12.6	84.6	...
Tonga[41]	Urban	1996	3,665	...	...	...	...	...	...	...
Tonga[41]	Rural	1996	12,529	...	...	...	...	...	...	...

Notes: * Data refer to tenants in publicly-owned housing units unless otherwise specified. 1 Data reported in percentages only. 2 Data for Housing units with toilet inside as reported; the total differs from the sum of categories. 3 Data for Tenants refer to tenant households in both publicly-owned and privately-owned housing units. 4 Data for Owner occupied includes housing units with bank loans. Collective living quarters not included in totals shown. 5 Data for Tenants refer to tenant households in both publicly-owned and privately-owned housing units. Data as reported; the total shown may differ from the sum of its parts. Data for Housing units with toilet inside include piped water from shared public tap. Data for Housing units with toilet inside non-flush toilets connected to sewage and pit latrine. 6 Data as reported; the total shown may differ from the sum of its parts. Data for Housing units with piped water include 14,254 households with access to treated piped water. 7 Data for Tenants refer to tenant households in both publicly-owned and privately-owned housing units. Data for Housing units with toilet inside include chemical toilet, pit latrine and bucket latrine. 8 Data reported in percentages only. Data as reported; the total shown may differ from the sum of its parts. 9 Data reported in percentages only and are based on the results of an integrated survey of 3600 households. 10 Data on the total number of households are extracted from a different table of the original questionnaire. 11 Data reported in percentages only. Data for Tenants refer to households occupying units rent-free. Data for Owner occupied refers to households occupying units and paying rent. 12 Households refer to domestic households only. 13 Data for Housing units with toilet inside refer to households in conventional dwellings only. 14 Households residing in Kibbutz community settlements not included. Data for Households includes data for East Jerusalem and Israeli residents in certain other territories under occupation by Israeli military forces since June 1967. 15 Data as reported; the total shown may differ from the sum of its parts. No data are reported for rural areas. Data for Women-headed households refer to 1998 and are based on preliminary findings. 16 Data reported in percentages only and are based on a sample survey of 6000 households. Data for Households provided as percentages only. 17 Data for Tenants refer to tenant households in both publicly-owned and privately-owned housing units. 18 All data refer to resident private households. 19 Data for Tenants refer to tenant households in both publicly-owned and privately-owned housing units. Data for Housing units with toilets inside refer to the year 1994. 20 Data for Tenants refer to households that live in a house which belongs to government or workplace of one of the household members. 21 Data for Owner occupied includes tenant households in housing units owned by non-profit building associations and official dwellings or other tenure. Data refer to private households only. Data for Households refer to the year 1991. 22 Data as reported; the total shown may differ from the sum of its parts. Source of data is the Household Budget Survey. Data are estimates. A woman-headed household is one where a woman is the household member with the largest income. 23 Data as reported; the total shown may differ from the sum of its parts. Data for Tenants refer to state-subsidized (government) rental housing. Data for Owner occupied refer to other rental housing. Data for Housing units with piped water refer to dwellings. 24 Data for Tenants refer to tenant households in both publicly-owned and privately-owned housing units. Data as reported; the total shown may differ from the sum of its parts. 25 Data for Tenants refer to tenant households in both publicly-owned and privately-owned housing units. Data as reported; the total shown may differ from the sum of its parts. Data for Housing units with piped water/toilet inside are based on 2% sample and refer to households in conventional dwellings only. Data on households refer to a 2% sample. Data do not include households in collective living quarters. 26 Data for Tenants refer to tenant households in both publicly-owned and privately-owned housing units. Data include households occupying housing units free of charge and non-respondents. The Population and Housing Census of 26 November 1995 distinguished between private and institutional households. Data in this table refer to private one-person and multi-person households only. 27 Data for Housing units with piped water refer to the year 1993. 28 Data for Tenants refer to tenant households in both publicly-owned and privately-owned housing units. Women-headed households refer to households where women are the main income earners. Data for Housing units with toilet inside include 11,775 households with no information on urban/rural. Data refer to conventional housing units and 11,775 households are without information. 29 Housing units with toilet inside include flush toilets from community source and local flush toilets from private source. 30 Data for Owner occupied refer to housing units owned by one of the occupants and housing units that are not completely paid for. Data for Tenants refer to housing units that are offered to occupants free of charge. Data for Owner occupied refer to tenants who rent the unit they occupy, irrespective of ownership. 31 No distinction between inside and outside toilet. 32 Data for Housing units with piped water as reported and Housing units with toilet inside (Rural); the total differs from the sum of the categories. 33 Source of data is the owner household statistical estimates for 1993. Data for Women-headed households refer only to units owned by female family heads.

34 Data for Housing units with toilet inside refer to household with latrines. 35 No distinction between inside and outside toilet. Data for Households refer to the year 1995. 36 Data for Households refer to the year 1995. 37 Data as reported; the total shown may differ from the sum of its parts. Data for Households refer to the year 1991. 38 Data as reported; the total shown may differ from the sum of its parts. Data for Housing units with piped water/toilet inside refer to the year 1997. 39 Data for Housing units with piped water as reported; the total differs from the sum of the categories. 40 Data for Tenants refer to households occupying units free of rent. Data for Owner occupied refer to households renting their housing units. Data for Housing units with piped water/toilet inside refer to the year 1998. 41 Data reported are only for those households headed by Tongans (including part-Tongans). Data for Tenants include households that rent either a publicly or privately-owned housing unit and those that occupy a housing unit rent-free. One household may have two or more sources of water supply available. For example, a household may have piped water as well as have its own water tank. There is no distinction between households and living quarters. Data on urban refer to Nuku'alofa.

Source: United Nations, *Compendium of Human Settlements Statistics 2001.*

TABLE B.4

Access to Improved Water Sources and Sanitation

	Access to improved drinking water sources (%)						Access to improved sanitation (%)					
	Total		Urban		Rural		Total		Urban		Rural	
	1990	2000	1990	2000	1990	2000	1990	2000	1990	2000	1990	2000
WORLD	77	82	94	95	64	71	51	61	81	85	28	40
AFRICA	60	64	88	86	46	50	59	60	81	80	49	48
Algeria	...	89	...	94	...	82	...	92	...	99	...	81
Angola	...	38	...	34	...	40	...	44	...	70	...	30
Benin	...	63	...	74	...	55	20	23	46	46	6	6
Botswana	93	95	100	100	88	90	60	66	87	88	41	43
Burkina Faso	...	42	...	66	...	37	...	29	...	39	...	27
Burundi	69	78	96	91	67	77	87	88	65	68	89	90
Cameroon	51	58	78	78	32	39	77	79	97	92	64	66
Cape Verde	...	74	...	64	...	89	...	71	...	95	...	32
Central African Republic	48	70	71	89	35	57	24	25	38	38	16	16
Chad	...	27	...	31	...	26	18	29	70	81	4	13
Comoros	88	96	97	98	84	95	98	98	98	98	98	98
Congo	...	51	...	71	...	17	...	...	...	14	...	...
Côte d'Ivoire	80	81	97	92	69	72	46	52	70	71	29	35
Dem. Republic of the Congo	...	45	...	89	...	26	...	21	...	54	...	6
Djibouti	...	100	...	100	...	100	...	91	...	99	...	50
Egypt	94	97	97	99	92	96	87	98	96	100	79	96
Equatorial Guinea	...	44	...	45	...	42	...	53	...	60	...	46
Eritrea	...	46	...	63	...	42	...	13	...	66	...	1
Ethiopia[1]	25	24	80	81	17	12	8	12	24	33	6	7
Gabon	...	86	...	95	...	47	...	53	...	55	...	43
Gambia	...	62	...	80	...	53	...	37	...	41	...	35
Ghana	53	73	85	91	36	62	61	72	56	74	64	70
Guinea	45	48	72	72	36	36	55	58	94	94	41	41
Guinea-Bissau	...	56	...	79	...	49	44	56	87	95	33	44
Kenya	45	57	91	88	31	42	80	87	91	96	77	82
Lesotho	...	78	...	88	...	74	...	49	...	72	...	40
Libyan Arab Jamahiriya	71	72	72	72	68	68	97	97	97	97	96	96
Madagascar	44	47	85	85	31	31	36	42	70	70	25	30
Malawi	49	57	90	95	43	44	73	76	96	96	70	70
Mali	55	65	65	74	52	61	70	69	95	93	62	58
Mauritania	37	37	34	34	40	40	30	33	44	44	19	19
Mauritius	100	100	100	100	100	100	100	99	100	100	100	99
Morocco	75	80	94	98	58	56	58	68	88	86	31	44
Mozambique	...	57	...	81	...	41	...	43	...	68	...	26
Namibia	72	77	98	100	63	67	33	41	84	96	14	17
Niger	53	59	65	70	51	56	15	20	71	79	4	5
Nigeria	53	62	83	78	37	49	53	54	69	66	44	45
Rwanda	...	41	...	60	...	40	...	8	...	12	...	8
Senegal	72	78	90	92	60	65	57	70	86	94	38	48
Sierra Leone	...	57	...	75	...	46	...	66	...	88	...	53
South Africa	86	86	99	99	73	73	86	87	93	93	80	80
Sudan	67	75	86	86	60	69	58	62	87	87	48	48
Togo	51	54	82	85	38	38	37	34	71	69	24	17
Tunisia	75	80	91	92	54	58	76	84	96	96	48	62
Uganda	45	52	81	80	40	47	...	79	...	93	...	77
United Republic of Tanzania	38	68	76	90	28	57	84	90	84	99	84	86
Zambia	52	64	88	88	28	48	63	78	86	99	48	64
Zimbabwe	78	83	99	100	69	73	56	62	70	71	50	57
ASIA	72	80	94	93	63	73	26	46	59	74	12	31
Afghanistan	...	13	...	19	...	11	...	12	...	25	...	8
Azerbaijan	...	78	...	93	...	58	...	81	...	90	...	70
Bangladesh	94	97	99	99	93	97	41	48	81	71	31	41
Bhutan	...	62	...	86	...	60	...	70	...	65	...	70
Cambodia	...	30	...	54	...	26	...	17	...	56	...	10
China[2]	71	75	99	94	60	66	17	40	56	69	2	27
Cyprus	100	100	100	100	100	100	100	100	100	100	100	100
Dem. People's Rep. of Korea	...	100	...	100	...	100	...	99	...	99	...	100
Georgia	...	79	...	90	...	61	...	100	...	100	...	99
India	68	84	88	95	61	79	16	28	44	61	6	15
Indonesia	71	78	92	90	62	69	47	55	66	69	38	46
Iran (Islamic Republic of)	...	92	...	98	...	83	...	83	...	86	...	79
Iraq	...	85	...	96	...	48	...	79	...	93	...	31
Jordan	97	96	99	100	92	84	98	99	100	100	95	98
Kazakhstan	...	91	...	98	...	82	...	99	...	100	...	98
Kyrgyzstan	...	77	...	98	...	66	...	100	...	100	...	100
Lao People's Dem. Republic	...	37	...	61	...	29	...	30	...	67	...	19
Lebanon	...	100	...	100	...	100	...	99	...	100	...	87
Malaysia	...	...	...	...	...	94	...	...	...	...	...	98
Maldives	...	100	...	100	...	100	...	56	...	100	...	41
Mongolia	...	60	...	77	...	30	...	30	...	46	...	2
Myanmar	...	72	...	89	...	66	...	64	...	84	...	57
Nepal	67	88	93	94	64	87	20	28	69	73	15	22
Occupied Palestian Territory	...	86	...	97	...	86	...	100	...	100	...	100
Oman	37	39	41	41	30	30	84	92	98	98	61	61
Pakistan	83	90	96	95	77	87	36	62	77	95	17	43

Philippines	87	86	93	91	82	79	74	83	85	93	63	69
Republic of Korea	...	92	...	97	...	71	...	63	...	76	...	4
Saudi Arabia	...	95	...	100	...	64	...	100	...	100	...	100
Singapore	100	100	100	100	...	...	100	100	100	100	...	...
Sri Lanka	68	77	91	98	62	70	85	94	94	97	82	93
Syrian Arab Republic	...	80	...	94	...	64	...	90	...	98	...	81
Tajikistan	...	60	...	93	...	47	...	90	...	97	...	88
Thailand	80	84	87	95	78	81	79	96	95	96	75	96
Turkey	79	82	83	81	72	86	87	90	97	97	70	70
Uzbekistan	...	85	...	94	...	79	...	89	...	97	...	85
Viet Nam	55	77	86	95	48	72	29	47	52	82	23	38
Yemen	...	69	...	74	...	68	32	38	69	89	21	21
EUROPE	**...**	**97**	**...**	**100**	**...**	**89**	**...**	**...**	**...**	**...**	**...**	**...**
Albania	...	97	...	99	...	95	...	91	...	99	...	85
Andorra	...	100	...	100	...	100	...	100	...	100	...	100
Austria	100	100	100	100	100	100	100	100	100	100	100	100
Belarus	...	100	...	100	...	100	...	...	...	...	...	...
Bulgaria	...	100	...	100	...	100	...	100	...	100	...	100
Denmark	...	100	...	100	...	100	...	...	...	...	...	...
Estonia	...	...	...	...	...	...	...	...	...	93	...	...
Finland	100	100	100	100	100	100	100	100	100	100	100	100
Hungary	99	99	100	100	98	98	99	99	100	100	98	98
Malta	100	100	100	100	100	100	100	100	100	100	100	100
Monaco	...	100	...	100	...	100	...	100	...	100	...	100
Netherlands	100	100	100	100	100	100	100	100	100	100	100	100
Norway	100	100	100	100	100	100	...	...	100	...	...	...
Republic of Moldova	...	92	...	97	...	88	...	99	...	100	...	98
Romania	...	58	...	91	...	16	...	53	...	86	...	10
Russian Federation	...	99	...	100	...	96	...	...	...	...	...	...
Serbia and Montenegro	...	98	...	99	...	97	...	100	...	100	...	99
Slovakia	...	100	...	100	...	100	...	100	...	100	...	100
Slovenia	100	100	100	100	100	100	...	...	100	...	...	...
Sweden	100	100	100	100	100	100	100	100	100	100	100	100
Switzerland	100	100	100	100	100	100	100	100	100	100	100	100
Ukraine	...	98	...	100	...	94	...	99	...	100	...	98
United Kingdom	100	100	100	100	100	100	100	100	100	100	100	100
LATIN AMERICA AND THE CARIBBEAN	**82**	**86**	**92**	**94**	**58**	**66**	**72**	**77**	**85**	**86**	**41**	**52**
Antigua and Barbuda	...	91	...	95	...	89	...	95	...	98	...	94
Argentina	94	...	97	...	73	...	82	...	87	...	47	...
Bahamas	...	97	...	98	...	86	...	100	...	100	...	100
Barbados	...	100	...	100	...	100	...	100	...	100	...	100
Belize	...	92	...	100	...	82	...	50	...	71	...	25
Bolivia	71	83	91	95	47	64	52	70	73	86	26	42
Brazil	83	87	93	95	54	53	71	76	82	84	38	43
Chile	90	93	98	99	49	58	97	96	98	96	92	97
Colombia	94	91	98	99	84	70	83	86	96	96	55	56
Costa Rica	...	95	...	99	...	92	...	93	...	89	...	97
Cuba	...	91	...	95	...	77	...	98	...	99	...	95
Dominica	...	97	...	100	...	90	...	83	...	86	...	75
Dominican Republic	83	86	92	90	71	78	66	67	70	70	60	60
Ecuador	71	85	82	90	58	75	70	86	88	92	49	74
El Salvador	66	77	88	91	48	64	73	82	87	89	62	76
Grenada	...	95	...	97	...	93	...	97	...	96	...	97
Guatemala	76	92	88	98	69	88	70	81	82	83	62	79
Guyana	...	94	...	98	...	91	...	87	...	97	...	81
Haiti	53	46	59	49	50	45	23	28	33	50	19	16
Honduras	83	88	89	95	78	81	61	75	88	93	41	55
Jamaica	93	92	98	98	87	85	99	99	99	99	99	99
Mexico	80	88	90	95	52	69	70	74	87	88	26	34
Nicaragua	70	77	93	91	44	59	76	85	97	95	53	72
Panama	...	90	...	99	...	79	...	92	...	99	...	83
Paraguay	63	78	80	93	46	59	93	94	96	94	91	93
Peru	74	80	88	87	42	62	60	71	77	79	21	49
Saint Kitts and Nevis	...	98	...	...	...	...	...	96	...	...	...	...
Saint Lucia	...	98	...	...	...	...	...	89	...	...	...	...
Saint Vincent and the Grenadines	...	93	...	...	...	...	...	96	...	...	...	...
Suriname	...	82	...	93	...	50	...	93	...	99	...	75
Trinidad and Tobago	91	90	...	...	...	...	99	99	...	...	...	...
Uruguay	...	98	...	98	...	93	...	94	...	95	...	85
Venezuela	...	83	...	85	...	70	...	68	...	71	...	48
NORTHERN AMERICA	**99**	**99**	**99**	**99**	**99**	**99**	**99**	**99**	**99**	**99**	**99**	**99**
Canada	100	100	100	100	99	99	100	100	100	100	99	99
United States	100	100	100	100	100	100	100	100	100	100	100	100
OCEANIA	**40**	**48**	**88**	**76**	**32**	**40**	**82**	**74**	**92**	**87**	**80**	**71**
Australia	100	100	100	100	100	100	100	100	100	100	100	100
Fiji	...	47	...	43	...	51	...	43	...	75	...	12
Kiribati	...	48	...	82	...	25	...	48	...	54	...	44
New Zealand	...	...	100	100	...	...	...	...	...	...	...	...
Palau	...	79	...	100	...	20	...	100	...	100	...	100
Papua New Guinea	40	42	88	88	32	32	82	82	92	92	80	80
Samoa	...	99	...	95	...	100	...	99	...	95	...	100
Solomon Islands	...	71	...	94	...	65	...	34	...	98	...	18
Tonga	...	100	...	100	...	100	...	100	...	100	...	100
Vanuatu	...	88	...	63	...	94	...	100	...	100	...	100

Notes: 1 Data for the year 1993. 2 For statistical purposes the data for China do not include Hong Kong and Macao Special Administrative Regions and Taiwan province of China.

Sources: World Health Organization (WHO); United Nations Children's Fund (UNICEF).

TABLE B.5

Energy and Transport

	Traditional fuel (% of energy use)		Commercial energy				Motor vehicles				Roads	
			Production (kt of oil equivalent)*		Use per capita (kg of oil equivalent)**		per 1000 people		per km of road		Total road network (km)	Paved roads (%)
	1980	1997	1980	1999	1980	1999	1990	2000	1990	2000	1995–2000***	1995–2000***
AFRICA												
Algeria	1.9	1.5	66,741	142,883	647	944	...	...	...	...	104,000	68.9
Angola	64.9	69.7	11,301	43,644	628	595	19	...	...	...	51,429	10.4
Benin	85.4	89.2	1,212	1,556	394	323	3	...	2	...	6,787	20.0
Botswana	35.7	...	...	...	...	...	19	70	3	11	10,217	55.0
Burkina Faso	91.3	87.1	...	...	...	...	4	...	3	...	12,506	16.0
Burundi	97.0	94.2	...	...	...	...	...	...	...	...	14,480	7.1
Cameroon	51.7	69.2	6,707	12,109	421	419	10	...	3	...	34,300	12.5
Central African Republic	88.9	87.5	...	...	...	...	1	...	...	...	23,810	2.7
Chad	95.9	97.6	...	...	...	...	5	...	...	...	33,400	0.8
Congo	77.8	53.0	4,024	14,079	516	245	18	...	3	...	12,800	9.7
Côte d'Ivoire	52.8	91.5	2,419	5,973	447	388	23	...	6	...	50,400	9.7
Dem.Republic of the Congo	73.9	91.7	8,697	14,860	324	293	...	...	...	...	157,000	...
Egypt	4.7	3.2	34,168	58,460	391	709	29	...	33	...	64,000	78.1
Eritrea	...	96.0	...	...	...	...	1	...	1	...	4,010	21.8
Ethiopia	89.6	95.9	10,575	17,176	295	290	1	2	2	3	31,571	12.0
Gabon	30.8	32.9	9,441	17,842	2,158	1,342	26	...	4	...	8,464	9.9
Gambia	72.7	78.6	...	...	...	...	14	...	5	...	2,700	35.4
Ghana	43.7	78.1	3,305	5,540	375	377	...	...	...	...	39,409	29.6
Guinea	71.4	74.2	...	...	...	...	4	...	1	...	30,500	16.5
Guinea-Bissau	80.0	57.1	...	...	...	...	7	...	2	...	4,400	10.3
Kenya	76.8	80.3	7,891	12,129	589	499	13	...	5	...	63,942	12.1
Lesotho	...	...	...	...	...	...	11	...	4	...	5,940	18.3
Liberia	62.5	89.7	...	...	...	...	15	...	4	...	10,600	6.2
Libyan Arab Jamahiriya	2.3	0.9	96,550	73,420	2,364	2,370	...	...	...	...	83,200	57.2
Madagascar	78.4	84.3	...	...	...	...	6	...	2	...	49,827	11.6
Malawi	90.6	88.6	...	...	...	...	4	...	4	...	28,400	18.5
Mali	86.7	88.9	...	...	...	...	4	...	2	...	15,100	12.1
Mauritania	0.0	0.0	...	...	...	...	9	...	3	...	7,660	11.3
Mauritius	59.1	36.1	877	615	247	352	60	98	35	49	1,926	97.0
Morocco	5.2	4.0	877	615	247	352	37	52	15	21	57,707	56.4
Mozambique	43.7	91.4	7,413	7,067	668	404	4	...	2	...	30,400	18.7
Namibia	...	...	...	270	...	645	71	...	1	2	66,467	8.3
Niger	79.5	80.6	...	...	...	...	6	...	4	5	10,100	7.9
Nigeria	66.8	67.8	148,479	178,822	743	705	33	...	21	14	194,394	30.9
Rwanda	89.8	88.3	...	...	...	...	2	...	1	2	12,000	8.3
Senegal	50.8	56.2	1,046	1,684	347	318	11	...	6	8	14,576	29.3
Sierra Leone	90.0	86.1	...	...	...	...	10	3	4	2	11,330	7.9
Somalia	78.6	...	...	...	...	...	2	...	1	...	22,100	11.8
South Africa	4.9	43.4	73,169	143,993	2,372	2,597	160	143	26	11	362,099	20.3
Sudan	86.9	75.1	7,089	17,034	435	503	9	...	21	28	11,900	36.3
Swaziland	...	...	...	...	...	...	72	70	18	17	3,247	...
Togo	35.7	71.9	562	1,015	284	313	24	...	11	...	7,520	31.6
Tunisia	16.1	12.4	6,966	7,120	612	811	48	...	19	40	18,997	64.8
Uganda	93.6	89.7	...	...	...	...	2	5	...	4	27,000	6.7
United Republic of Tanzania	92.0	91.4	9,502	14,269	553	457	5	...	2	2	88,200	4.2
Zambia	37.4	72.7	4,198	5,784	793	626	15	...	3	...	66,781	...
Zimbabwe	27.6	25.2	5,793	8,322	921	821	...	...	...	...	18,338	47.4
ASIA												
Afghanistan	63.0	75.6	...	...	...	...	...	...	...	...	21,000	13.3
Armenia	...	0.0	1,263	646	...	485	5	...	2	...	15,918	96.3
Azerbaijan	...	0.0	14,821	19,037	...	1,575	52	49	7	16	24,981	92.3
Bangladesh	81.3	46.0	6,745	14,474	99	139	1	1	...	1	207,486	9.5
Cambodia	100.0	89.3	...	...	...	...	1	6	...	31	12,323	16.2
China	8.4	5.7	608,625	1,056,963	604	868	5	...	4	11	1,402,698	22.4
China, Hong Kong SAR	0.9	0.7	39	48	1,079	2,661	66	78	253	287	1,831	100.0
Dem. People's Rep. of Korea	3.1	1.4	29,135	54,198	1,856	2,658	...	...	...	...	31,200	6.4
Georgia	...	1.0	1,504	739	...	512	107	63	27	15	20,362	93.5
India	31.5	20.7	222,418	409,788	353	482	4	8	2	3	3,319,644	45.7
Indonesia	51.5	29.3	128,996	226,378	404	658	16	25	10	14	342,700	46.3
Iran (Islamic Republic of)	0.4	0.7	81,142	229,406	996	1,651	34	...	14	...	167,157	56.3
Iraq	0.3	0.1	136,643	131,754	925	1,263	14	...	6	...	45,550	84.3
Israel	0.0	0.0	153	615	2,208	3,029	210	270	74	107	16,281	100.0
Japan	0.1	1.6	43,281	104,223	2,967	4,070	469	560	52	62	1,161,894	46.0
Jordan	0.0	0.0	1	286	786	1,028	60	...	26	...	7,245	100.0
Kazakhstan	...	0.2	76,799	64,668	...	2,374	76	86	8	12	81,331	94.7
Kuwait	0.0	0.0	91,636	104,291	8,908	8,984	...	...	...	...	4,450	80.6
Kyrgyzstan	...	0.0	2,190	1,301	...	504	44	39	10	10	18,500	91.1
Lao People's Dem. Republic	72.3	88.7	...	...	...	...	9	...	3	...	21,716	13.8
Lebanon	2.4	2.5	178	161	841	1,280	321	336	183	...	7,300	84.9
Malaysia	15.7	5.5	18,202	73,411	884	1,878	124	200	26	69	65,877	75.8
Mongolia	14.4	4.3	...	...	...	...	21	30	1	2	49,250	3.5
Myanmar	69.3	60.5	9,513	13,943	280	273	...	...	...	...	28,200	12.2
Nepal	94.2	89.6	4,630	7,035	330	358	...	...	...	...	13,223	30.8
Occupied Palestinian Territory	...	...	...	...	...	...	...	...	...	...	...	...
Oman	0.0	...	15,090	54,504	905	3,607	130	...	9	...	32,800	30.0

Pakistan	24.4	29.5	20,997	44,091	308	444	6	8	4	4	254,410	43.0
Philippines	37.0	26.9	10,670	19,681	442	549	10	31	4	11	201,994	21.0
Republic of Korea	4.0	2.4	9,644	31,852	1,082	3,871	79	238	60	128	86,990	74.5
Saudi Arabia	0.0	0.0	533,071	448,735	3,773	4,204	165	...	19	...	151,470	30.1
Singapore	0.4	0.0	...	64	2,511	5,742	130	132	142	170	3,066	100.0
Sri Lanka	53.5	46.5	3,209	4,547	308	406	20	34	4	7	96,695	95.0
Syrian Arab Republic	0.0	0.0	9,502	34,205	614	1,143	26	30	10	11	43,381	23.1
Tajikistan	...	...	1,986	1,381	...	543	3	...	1	...	27,767	82.7
Thailand	40.3	24.6	11,182	38,499	488	1,169	46	...	36	...	64,600	97.5
Turkey	20.5	3.1	17,077	26,903	707	1,093	50	85	8	14	385,960	34.0
Turkmenistan	...	...	8,034	26,331	...	2,677	...	...	...	...	24,000	81.2
United Arab Emirates	0.0	...	89,716	135,681	5,860	9,977	121	...	52	...	1,088	100.0
Uzbekistan	...	0.0	4,615	55,109	...	2,024	...	...	...	...	81,600	87.3
Viet Nam	49.1	37.8	18,364	44,858	364	454	...	...	...	...	93,300	25.1
Yemen	0.0	1.4	60	20,247	167	184	34	...	8	...	67,000	11.5

EUROPE

Albania	13.1	7.3	3,428	865	1,142	311	11	44	3	10	18,000	39.0
Austria	1.2	4.7	7,561	9,520	3,022	3,513	421	536	30	22	200,000	100.0
Belarus	...	0.8	2,566	3,475	...	2,381	61	135	13	20	74,385	89.0
Belgium	0.2	1.6	7,986	13,766	4,682	5,735	423	497	30	35	148,216	78.2
Bosnia and Herzegovina	...	10.1	...	705	...	518	114	...	24	...	21,846	52.3
Bulgaria	0.5	1.3	7,737	9,056	3,236	2,218	163	266	39	60	37,286	94.0
Croatia	...	3.2	...	3,721	...	1,864	...	...	...	44	28,123	84.6
Czech Republic	0.6	1.6	41,208	27,952	4,618	3,754	246	363	46	67	55,408	100.0
Denmark	0.4	5.9	896	23,642	3,852	3,773	368	411	27	31	71,591	100.0
Estonia	...	13.8	6,951	2,762	...	3,286	211	394	22	11	51,411	20.1
Finland	4.3	6.5	6,912	15,402	5,317	6,461	441	462	29	31	77,900	64.5
France	1.3	5.7	46,799	127,617	3,485	4,351	494	564	32	38	894,000	100.0
Germany	0.3	1.3	185,628	132,961	4,602	4,108	405	...	53	...	230,735	99.1
Greece	3.0	4.5	3,696	9,812	1,628	2,552	248	348	22	31	117,000	91.8
Hungary	2.0	1.6	14,935	11,491	2,703	2,512	212	272	21	15	188,203	43.4
Ireland	0.0	0.2	1,894	2,513	2,495	3,726	270	...	10	14	92,500	94.1
Italy	0.8	1.0	19,644	27,754	2,456	2,932	529	591	99	73	479,688	100.0
Latvia	...	26.2	261	1,497	...	1,586	135	260	6	9	73,202	38.6
Lithuania	...	6.3	...	3,540	...	2,138	159	322	12	17	75,243	91.3
Netherlands	0.0	1.1	71,821	59,054	4,593	4,686	405	427	58	58	116,500	90.0
Norway	0.4	1.1	55,716	209,765	4,593	5,965	458	505	22	25	91,454	76.0
Poland	0.4	0.8	122,224	83,394	3,458	2,416	168	286	18	33	364,656	68.3
Portugal	1.2	0.9	1,481	1,940	1,054	2,365	222	348	34	...	68,732	86.0
Republic of Moldova	...	0.5	35	63	...	656	53	70	17	24	12,657	87.0
Romania	1.3	5.7	52,587	27,859	2,933	1,622	72	154	11	17	198,603	49.5
Russian Federation	...	0.8	748,647	950,589	...	4,121	87	153	14	48	532,393	67.4
Serbia and Montenegro	...	1.5	...	10,096	...	1,258	137	190	31	36	49,805	62.3
Slovakia	...	0.5	3,418	5,136	4,221	3,335	194	260	57	33	42,717	86.7
Slovenia	...	1.5	...	2,985	...	3,277	306	455	42	46	20,177	99.9
Spain	0.4	1.3	15,636	30,691	1,834	3,005	360	472	43	53	663,795	99.0
Sweden	7.7	17.9	16,132	34,489	4,803	5,769	464	478	29	21	212,402	78.4
Switzerland	0.9	6.0	7,030	11,805	3,301	3,738	491	526	46	54	71,011	...
TFYR Macedonia	...	6.1	...	...	...	...	132	...	30	...	8,684	63.8
Ukraine	...	0.5	109,708	81,923	...	2,973	63	...	19	...	169,491	96.7
United Kingdom	0.0	3.3	196,792	281,674	3,573	3,871	400	418	64	62	371,913	100.0

LATIN AMERICA AND THE CARIBBEAN

Argentina	5.9	4.0	38,813	81,932	1,490	1,727	181	181	27	30	215,471	29.4
Bolivia	19.3	14.0	4,374	6,020	455	562	41	...	6	8	53,790	6.5
Brazil	35.5	28.7	62,372	133,654	917	1,068	88	...	8	17	1,724,929	5.5
Chile	12.3	11.3	5,801	7,668	867	1,688	81	135	13	25	79,814	19.4
Colombia	15.9	17.7	18,040	77,142	680	676	...	51	...	19	112,988	14.4
Costa Rica	26.3	54.2	767	1,322	669	818	87	133	7	14	35,892	22.0
Cuba	27.9	30.2	4,227	5,242	1,536	1,117	37	32	16	6	60,858	49.0
Dominican Republic	27.5	14.3	1,327	1,491	613	904	75	...	48	...	12,600	49.4
Ecuador	26.7	17.5	11,745	21,730	651	705	35	46	8	14	43,197	18.9
El Salvador	52.9	34.5	1,623	2,136	553	651	33	61	14	36	10,029	19.8
Guatemala	54.6	62.0	2,503	4,566	550	548	...	57	...	45	14,118	34.5
Haiti	80.7	74.7	1,877	1,578	392	265	...	...	...	...	4,160	24.3
Honduras	55.3	54.8	1,315	1,817	530	522	22	62	9	28	13,603	20.4
Jamaica	5.0	6.0	224	641	1,115	1,597	...	...	...	...	18,700	70.1
Mexico	5.0	4.5	149,359	221,771	1,464	1,543	119	151	41	44	329,532	32.8
Nicaragua	49.2	42.2	910	1,482	532	539	19	10	5	8	19,032	11.0
Panama	26.6	14.4	529	704	934	835	75	113	18	27	11,400	34.6
Paraguay	62.0	49.6	1,605	6,741	671	773	...	...	...	...	29,500	9.5
Peru	15.2	24.6	14,655	11,659	675	519	...	43	...	15	72,900	12.8
Puerto Rico	0.0	...	...	...	...	...	...	...	...	...	14,400	100.0
Trinidad and Tobago	1.4	0.8	13,141	16,079	3,579	6,205	...	...	...	...	8,320	51.1
Uruguay	11.1	21.0	763	961	906	976	138	174	45	63	8,983	90.0
Venezuela	0.9	0.7	139,392	209,707	2,317	2,253	...	...	...	...	96,155	33.6

NORTHERN AMERICA

Canada	0.4	4.7	207,417	366,554	7,848	7,929	605	581	20	19	901,903	35.3
United States	1.3	3.8	1,553,263	1,687,886	7,973	8,159	758	760	30	34	6,304,193	58.8

OCEANIA

Australia	3.8	4.4	86,096	212,204	4,790	5,690	530	...	11	13	811,603	38.7
New Zealand	0.2	0.8	5,485	15,143	2,959	4,770	524	540	19	29	92,053	62.8
Papua New Guinea	65.4	62.5	...	...	...	...	...	...	...	...	19,600	3.5

Notes: * kt of oil equivalent is 1000 metric tons of oil equivalent. ** kg of oil equivalent is 1 kilogramme of oil equivalent. *** Data for Total road network and Paved roads are for the latest year available in the period shown.

Sources: World Bank, *World Development Indicators 2002*; International Energy Agency (IEA); United Nations Statistics Division (UNSD), *Energy Statistics Yearbook*; International Road Federation (IRF), *World Road Statistics*.

TABLE B.6

Economic Development Indicators

	PPP* gross national income	Labour force				Agriculture value added		Industry value added		Manufacturing value added		Services value added		Gross capital formation	
	Per capita US$	Total (000)		Women (%)		% of GDP		% of GDP		% of GDP		% of GDP		% of GDP	
	2000	2000	2010	2000	2010	1990	2000	1990	2000	1990	2000	1990	2000	1990	2000
AFRICA															
Algeria[1]	5,040	10,458	15,089	27.6	34.4	11	9	48	60	11	8	40	31	29	24
Angola[1]	1,180	5,941	7,840	46.2	45.9	18	6	41	76	5	3	41	18	12	28
Benin	980	2,835	3,825	48.1	47.7	36	38	13	14	8	9	51	48	14	20
Botswana	7,170	673	723	45.6	43.6	5	4	56	44	5	5	39	52	32	20
Burkina Faso[1]	970	5,486	7,116	49.2	48.1	32	35	22	17	16	12	45	48	21	28
Burundi[1]	580	3,344	4,728	49.3	48.1	56	51	19	18	13	9	25	31	15	9
Cameroon	1,590	6,104	7,800	37.9	38.7	25	44	29	20	15	11	46	36	18	16
Cape Verde	...	174	235	39.7	40.0	...	...	...	...	...	...	...	...	...	...
Central African Republic[1]	1,160	1,752	2,055	46.5	45.8	48	55	20	20	11	9	33	26	12	11
Chad	870	3,614	4,816	44.9	45.5	29	39	18	14	14	11	53	47	16	17
Comoros	...	331	448	43.2	42.6	...	...	...	...	...	...	...	...	...	...
Congo	570	1,232	1,641	43.4	43.5	13	5	41	71	8	3	46	24	16	24
Côte d'Ivoire	1,500	6,531	8,262	32.7	33.8	32	29	23	22	21	19	44	48	7	12
Dem. Republic of the Congo	...	20,686	28,415	43.4	42.9	30	...	28	...	11	...	42	...	9	...
Egypt	3,670	25,790	34,083	30.6	33.6	19	17	29	34	18	19	52	49	29	24
Equatorial Guinea	...	189	246	35.4	36.2	...	...	...	...	...	...	...	...	...	...
Eritrea	960	1,825	2,583	47.3	47.2	29	17	19	29	13	15	52	54	5	38
Ethiopia	660	27,781	34,651	41.8	41.5	49	52	13	11	8	7	38	37	12	14
Gabon	5,360	555	672	44.5	44.8	7	6	43	53	6	4	50	40	22	26
Gambia[1]	1,620	668	843	45.1	45.3	29	38	13	13	7	5	58	49	22	17
Ghana[1]	1,910	9,508	12,434	50.3	49.6	45	35	17	25	10	9	38	39	14	24
Guinea	1,930	4,047	4,938	47.2	46.9	24	24	33	37	5	4	43	39	18	22
Guinea-Bissau	710	549	685	40.6	40.7	61	59	19	12	8	10	21	29	30	18
Kenya	1,010	15,816	19,648	46.5	46.5	29	20	19	19	12	13	52	61	20	13
Lesotho[1]	2,590	864	909	36.6	36.3	24	17	33	44	14	16	43	39	53	40
Liberia	...	1,172	1,686	39.6	39.3	...	...	...	...	...	...	...	...	...	...
Libyan Arab Jamahiriya	...	1,794	2,372	23.4	27.4	...	...	...	...	...	...	...	...	...	...
Madagascar	820	7,632	10,163	44.6	44.6	32	35	14	13	12	...	53	52	17	16
Malawi	600	5,445	6,656	48.5	47.3	45	42	29	19	19	14	26	39	23	13
Mali	780	5,558	7,170	45.6	45.0	46	46	16	17	9	4	39	37	23	23
Mauritania	1,630	1,180	1,546	43.7	43.2	30	22	29	31	10	9	42	47	20	30
Mauritius[2]	9,940	507	567	32.7	34.6	12	6	32	32	24	24	56	62	31	26
Morocco	3,450	11,780	15,084	34.7	36.0	18	14	32	32	18	18	50	54	25	24
Mozambique[1]	800	9,586	11,295	48.3	48.0	37	24	18	25	10	13	44	50	16	34
Namibia[1]	6,410	695	841	41.4	41.1	11	11	35	28	13	11	54	61	35	24
Niger[1]	740	5,000	6,994	43.3	43.4	35	39	16	18	7	7	49	44	8	11
Nigeria	800	45,129	59,569	35.5	36.4	33	30	41	46	6	4	26	25	15	23
Réunion	...	297	351	43.4	45.0	...	...	...	...	...	...	...	...	...	...
Rwanda	930	4,134	5,147	48.5	47.9	33	44	25	21	19	12	42	35	15	15
Senegal	1,480	4,179	5,440	43.0	43.3	20	18	19	27	13	18	61	55	14	20
Sierra Leone	480	1,632	2,300	36.7	38.2	47	47	20	30	4	5	33	23	9	8
Somalia	...	3,757	5,405	43.3	43.3	65	...	...	...	5	...	...	...	16	...
South Africa[1]	9,160	18,028	18,992	38.3	38.1	5	3	40	31	24	19	55	66	12	15
Sudan	1,520	12,207	16,069	29.5	31.9	...	37	...	18	...	9	...	45	...	14
Swaziland	4,600	342	370	35.4	36.2	14	17	43	44	35	33	44	39	20	20
Togo	1,410	1,913	2,514	39.9	39.9	34	38	23	22	10	10	44	40	27	21
Tunisia	6,070	3,826	4,838	31.9	34.2	16	12	30	29	17	18	54	59	32	27
Uganda[1]	1,210	11,397	15,450	47.2	47.1	57	42	11	19	6	9	32	38	13	18
United Republic of Tanzania	520	18,088	23,089	49.1	48.5	46	45	18	16	9	7	36	39	26	18
Zambia	750	4,398	5,538	42.9	42.4	21	27	51	24	36	13	28	49	17	18
Zimbabwe	2,550	5,630	6,917	43.8	43.4	16	18	33	25	23	16	50	57	17	13
ASIA															
Afghanistan	...	8,872	12,657	35.3	36.6	...	...	...	...	...	...	...	...	...	...
Armenia	2,580	1,924	2,223	49.2	48.8	17	25	52	36	33	24	31	39	47	19
Azerbaijan	2,740	3,625	4,477	44.4	44.7	...	19	...	38	...	7	...	43	...	26
Bahrain	...	299	371	20.7	24.3	...	...	...	...	...	...	...	...	...	...
Bangladesh	1,590	69,611	88,727	41.9	42.5	29	25	21	24	13	15	50	51	17	23
Bhutan	...	1,005	1,311	39.7	40.0	...	...	...	...	...	...	...	...	...	...
Brunei Darussalam	...	148	191	35.1	38.2	...	...	...	...	...	...	...	...	...	...
Cambodia	1,440	6,401	8,579	52.0	50.9	56	37	11	20	5	6	33	42	8	15
China	3,920	762,942	824,808	45.3	45.2	27	16	42	51	33	35	31	33	35	37
China, Hong Kong SAR	25,590	3,716	4,157	38.6	39.5	-	-	25	14	18	6	74	85	27	28
China, Macau SAR	...	231	271	42.0	42.8	...	...	...	...	...	...	...	...	...	...
Cyprus	...	385	427	38.7	39.6	...	...	...	...	...	...	...	...	...	...
Dem. People's Rep. of Korea	...	11,421	12,238	43.2	43.6	...	...	...	...	...	...	...	...	...	...
Georgia	2,680	2,647	2,684	46.8	46.9	32	32	33	13	24	7	35	55	31	15
India	2,340	442,156	535,102	32.3	33.3	31	25	28	27	17	16	41	48	25	24
Indonesia	2,830	102,561	125,241	40.4	42.5	20	17	38	47	18	26	42	36	31	18
Iran (Islamic Republic of)	5,910	24,169	34,832	26.4	33.4	24	19	29	22	12	16	48	59	29	20
Iraq	...	6,339	8,999	19.8	23.2	...	...	...	...	...	...	...	...	...	...
Israel	19,330	2,589	3,308	41.7	44.1	...	...	...	...	...	...	...	...	25	19
Japan	27,080	68,369	67,217	41.4	43.2	2	1	39	32	27	22	58	66	33	26
Jordan	3,950	1,566	2,239	23.8	29.0	8	2	28	25	15	16	64	73	32	20
Kazakhstan	5,490	7,998	8,347	47.2	47.3	27	9	45	43	9	18	29	48	32	14
Kuwait	18,690	807	1,260	22.9	31.7	1	...	52	...	12	...	47	...	18	11
Kyrgyzstan	2,540	2,163	2,745	47.3	46.9	34	39	36	26	28	6	30	34	24	16
Lao People's Dem. Republic[1]	1,540	2,625	3,440	46.7	46.7	61	53	15	23	10	17	24	24	...	24

Lebanon	4,550	1,256	1,656	29.5	31.9	...	12	...	22	...	10	...	66	18	18
Malaysia	8,330	9,432	11,888	37.6	39.9	15	11	42	45	24	33	43	44	32	26
Maldives	...	123	172	43.1	43.6	...	...	...	...	...	...	...	...	...	...
Mongolia	1,760	1,295	1,654	47.1	47.8	17	33	30	19	...	5	52	48	38	30
Myanmar	...	25,682	30,124	43.5	43.8	57	60	11	9	8	7	32	31	13	13
Nepal	1,370	10,870	13,746	39.4	40.1	52	40	16	22	6	10	32	37	18	24
Occupied Palestinian Territory	...	673	1,065	11.4	15.4	...	8	...	27	...	15	...	66	...	33
Oman	...	721	1,088	17.1	26.1	3	...	58	...	4	...	39	...	13	...
Pakistan	1,860	52,077	70,896	29.1	33.8	26	26	25	23	17	15	49	51	19	16
Philippines	4,220	31,355	40,277	37.9	39.3	22	16	34	31	25	23	44	53	24	18
Qatar	...	313	354	16.3	21.8	...	...	...	...	...	...	...	...	...	...
Republic of Korea	17,300	23,966	26,782	41.4	43.4	9	5	43	43	29	31	48	53	38	29
Saudi Arabia	11,390	6,095	8,919	18.1	26.1	6	7	50	48	8	10	43	45	20	16
Singapore	24,910	2,013	2,248	39.1	39.7	-	-	34	34	27	26	65	66	37	31
Sri Lanka	3,460	8,540	9,810	34.1	36.6	26	20	26	27	15	17	48	53	23	28
Syrian Arab Republic	3,340	5,165	7,652	26.9	29.8	28	24	24	30	20	27	48	46	17	21
Tajikistan	1,090	2,400	3,186	45.0	46.4	33	19	38	26	25	23	29	55	25	20
Thailand	6,320	37,379	41,637	46.9	46.6	12	10	37	40	27	32	50	49	41	23
Timor-Leste	...	380	608	44.5	44.7	...	...	...	...	...	...	...	...	...	...
Turkey	7,030	31,212	37,366	37.6	40.1	18	16	30	25	20	15	52	59	24	24
Turkmenistan	3,800	2,047	2,710	45.9	46.0	32	27	30	50	...	40	38	23	40	40
United Arab Emirates	...	1,362	1,596	13.0	17.4	2	...	64	...	8	...	35	...	20	...
Uzbekistan	2,360	10,756	14,365	46.9	46.7	33	35	33	23	...	10	34	42	32	11
Viet Nam	2,000	40,880	49,083	48.3	48.1	37	24	23	37	19	18	40	39	13	27
Yemen	770	5,514	8,249	29.3	29.8	24	15	27	46	9	7	49	38	15	19
EUROPE															
Albania	3,600	1,558	1,745	41.3	42.1	36	51	48	26	42	12	16	23	29	19
Austria	26,330	3,733	3,649	41.0	42.1	4	2	34	33	23	21	62	65	25	24
Belarus	7,550	5,410	5,595	49.5	49.1	24	15	47	37	39	31	29	47	27	23
Belgium	27,470	4,222	4,194	41.0	42.1	2	2	33	27	...	20	65	72	22	22
Bosnia and Herzegovina	...	1,859	2,034	38.2	38.4	...	12	...	26	...	16	...	62	...	20
Bulgaria	5,560	4,100	3,788	48.1	47.4	18	15	51	28	...	17	31	58	26	17
Croatia	7,960	2,196	2,179	44.2	45.0	10	9	34	33	28	23	56	58	14	22
Czech Republic	13,780	5,765	5,599	47.3	46.7	6	4	49	41	...	...	45	55	25	30
Denmark	27,250	2,935	2,812	46.6	47.0	4	3	27	26	18	17	69	71	20	22
Estonia	9,340	769	724	49.5	48.9	17	6	50	27	42	16	34	67	30	26
Finland	24,570	2,602	2,475	48.0	48.4	7	4	34	34	23	25	60	62	29	20
France	24,420	26,836	27,310	45.1	46.2	4	3	30	26	21	19	66	71	23	21
Germany	24,920	40,299	39,898	42.4	43.4	2	1	38	31	28	23	60	68	22	23
Greece	16,860	4,626	4,724	37.8	39.6	11	8	28	24	...	12	61	68	23	22
Hungary	11,990	4,769	4,536	44.6	44.8	15	6	39	34	23	25	46	61	25	31
Iceland	...	158	173	45.6	45.7	...	...	...	...	...	...	...	...	...	...
Ireland	25,520	1,605	1,863	35.0	37.7	9	4	35	36	28	28	56	60	21	23
Italy	23,470	25,437	24,528	38.6	39.9	4	3	34	30	25	21	63	68	22	20
Latvia	7,070	1,330	1,333	49.5	49.0	22	4	46	25	34	14	32	70	40	27
Lithuania	6,980	1,925	1,981	48.1	47.9	27	8	31	33	21	21	42	59	33	21
Luxembourg	...	184	202	37.5	39.1	...	...	...	...	...	...	...	...	...	...
Malta	...	148	156	27.7	30.1	...	...	...	...	...	...	...	...	...	...
Netherlands	25,850	7,357	7,391	40.6	42.4	5	3	31	27	...	17	64	70	24	22
Norway	29,630	2,314	2,387	46.6	47.4	4	2	35	43	13	...	61	55	23	22
Poland	9,000	19,975	20,681	46.4	46.6	8	4	50	36	...	21	42	60	26	27
Portugal	16,990	5,103	5,110	44.1	45.0	9	4	31	31	...	19	60	66	28	28
Republic of Moldova	2,230	2,180	2,310	48.7	47.1	31	28	39	20	...	16	30	52	25	22
Romania	6,360	10,718	10,738	44.7	44.9	20	13	50	36	...	27	30	51	30	19
Russian Federation	8,010	78,041	78,068	49.1	49.2	17	7	48	39	...	...	35	54	30	17
Serbia and Montenegro	...	5,054	5,190	42.9	43.7	...	...	...	...	...	...	...	...	...	14
Slovakia	11,040	2,966	3,072	47.8	47.1	7	4	59	31	...	22	33	65	33	30
Slovenia	17,310	1,020	985	46.5	46.5	6	3	46	38	35	28	49	58	17	28
Spain	19,260	17,575	17,748	37.4	38.8	7	4	34	31	...	20	59	66	27	26
Sweden	23,970	4,793	4,746	48.1	48.3	3	2	32	29	...	...	64	69	23	18
Switzerland	30,450	3,807	3,749	40.5	42.0	...	2	...	30	...	...	...	68	28	20
TFYR Macedonia	5,020	937	1,015	42.2	43.4	9	12	46	33	36	21	46	55	19	17
Ukraine	3,700	25,274	24,709	48.9	48.7	26	14	45	38	36	34	30	48	27	19
United Kingdom	23,550	29,775	30,299	43.7	44.9	2	1	35	29	23	18	63	70	20	18
LATIN AMERICA AND THE CARIBBEAN															
Argentina	12,050	14,996	18,704	33.2	39.0	8	5	36	28	27	18	56	68	14	16
Bahamas	...	156	182	46.8	47.8	...	...	...	...	...	...	...	...	...	...
Barbados	...	147	158	46.3	45.6	...	...	...	...	...	...	...	...	...	...
Belize	...	79	99	24.1	27.3	...	...	...	...	...	...	...	...	...	...
Bolivia	2,360	3,391	4,410	37.8	38.7	26	22	20	15	17	13	54	63	13	18
Brazil	7,300	79,247	89,647	35.5	35.5	8	7	39	29	25	24	53	64	20	21
Chile	9,100	6,211	7,590	33.6	38.2	9	11	41	34	20	16	50	56	25	23
Colombia	6,060	18,213	22,957	39.1	41.2	17	14	38	31	21	14	45	56	19	12
Costa Rica	7,980	1,629	2,045	31.1	34.4	18	9	29	31	22	24	53	59	27	17
Cuba	...	5,552	5,929	39.5	41.4	...	7	...	46	...	37	...	47	...	10
Dominican Republic	5,710	3,625	4,500	30.8	34.5	13	11	31	34	18	17	55	55	25	24
Ecuador	2,910	4,948	6,483	28.0	31.5	13	10	38	40	19	17	49	50	17	17
El Salvador	4,410	2,703	3,283	36.3	43.6	17	10	26	30	22	23	57	60	14	17
Guadeloupe	...	203	216	45.3	45.4	...	...	...	...	...	...	...	...	...	...
Guatemala	3,770	4,142	5,792	29.1	35.8	26	23	20	20	15	13	54	57	14	17
Guyana	...	320	344	35.3	37.8	...	...	...	...	...	...	...	...	...	...
Haiti[1]	1,470	3,513	4,270	43.6	43.3	32	28	21	20	15	7	48	51	12	11
Honduras	2,400	2,405	2,971	31.9	40.6	22	18	26	32	16	20	51	51	23	35
Jamaica	3,440	1,284	1,497	47.5	47.6	6	6	43	31	20	13	50	62	28	27
Martinique	...	187	200	47.1	47.0	...	...	...	...	...	...	...	...	...	...
Mexico	8,790	40,724	51,864	33.2	35.2	8	4	28	28	21	21	64	67	23	23
Netherlands Antilles	...	99	105	42.4	41.9	...	...	...	...	...	...	...	...	...	...

TABLE B.6

continued

	PPP* gross national income Per capita US$	Labour force Total (000)		Labour force Women (%)		Agriculture value added % of GDP		Industry value added % of GDP		Manufacturing value added % of GDP		Services value added % of GDP		Gross capital formation % of GDP	
	2000	2000	2010	2000	2010	1990	2000	1990	2000	1990	2000	1990	2000	1990	2000
Nicaragua¹	2,080	1,981	2,647	36.2	42.6	31	32	21	23	17	14	48	45	19	34
Panama¹	5,680	1,205	1,386	35.3	39.8	9	7	15	17	9	8	76	76	17	30
Paraguay¹	4,450	2,075	2,817	30.0	32.2	28	21	25	27	17	14	47	52	23	22
Peru	4,660	9,713	12,715	31.3	34.2	7	8	23	27	15	14	70	65	16	20
Puerto Rico	...	1,483	1,709	37.4	40.3	1	...	42	...	40	...	57	...	...	...
Suriname	...	159	193	33.3	36.3	...	...	...	...	...	...	...	...	...	...
Trinidad and Tobago	8,220	578	681	37.4	40.2	3	2	46	43	9	8	51	55	13	19
Uruguay	8,880	1,502	1,654	42.0	43.8	9	6	35	27	28	17	56	67	12	14
Venezuela	5,740	9,881	12,921	34.8	37.6	5	5	50	36	20	14	44	59	10	18
NORTHERN AMERICA															
Canada¹	27,170	16,559	17,794	45.9	46.8	3	...	33	...	18	...	64	...	21	20
United States	34,100	145,105	159,723	46.0	47.0	...	...	...	...	...	...	...	...	18	21
OCEANIA															
Australia³	24,970	9,770	10,733	44.0	45.6	3	3	28	26	14	13	68	71	22	24
Fiji	...	324	401	30.6	36.9	...	...	...	...	...	...	...	...	...	...
New Zealand	18,530	1,883	2,042	45.4	46.7	7	...	28	...	19	...	65	...	19	21
Papua New Guinea¹	2,180	2,313	2,950	41.9	42.7	29	26	30	44	9	9	41	30	24	18
Solomon Islands	...	223	302	46.6	46.4	...	...	...	...	...	...	...	...	...	...

Notes: * PPP is purchasing power parity. 1 The estimate is based on regression; others are extrapolated from the International Comparison Programme benchmark estimates. 2 Data for Labour force include Agalesca, Rodrigues and Saint Brandon. 3 Data for Labour force include Christmas Island, Cocos (Keeling) Islands and Norfolk Island.

Sources: World Bank, *World Development Indicators 2002*; International Labour Organization (ILO); Organisation for Economic Co-operation and Development (OECD); United Nations Statistics Division (UNSD), *National Accounts Statistics: Main Aggregates and Detailed Tables.*

TABLE B.7

Social Indicators

	Household final consumption expenditure % of GDP		Illiteracy rate Male (%)	Female (%)	Male (%)	Female (%)	Population below the poverty line — National Year	Rural	Urban	Total	International Survey year	Below $1 a day	Below $2 a day	Refugees and assylum-seekers* (000)
	1990	2000	2000	2000	2015	2015		(%)	(%)	(%)		(%)	(%)	2001
AFRICA														
Algeria	57	42	23.7	43.0	12.7	26.0	1995	30.3	14.7	22.6	1995	<2	15.1	169
Angola	36	17	...	...	...	...		...	...	...		...	...	228
Benin	87	82	47.9	76.4	30.1	61.7	1995	...	...	33.0		...	...	5
Botswana	39	58	25.5	20.2	15.5	10.0		...	...	...	1985–86	33.3	61.4	4
Burkina Faso	77	76	66.1	85.9	51.7	71.7		...	...	...	1994	61.2	85.8	1
Burundi	95	93	43.9	59.6	33.6	38.2	1990	...	...	36.2		...	...	126
Cameroon	67	69	20.9	36.3	10.5	18.0	1984	32.4	44.4	40.0	1996	33.4	64.4	44
Cape Verde	...	...	15.5	34.3	9.7	20.8		...	...	...		...	...	...
Central African Republic	86	81	40.3	65.1	25.0	41.7		...	...	...	1993	66.6	84.0	53
Chad	89	91	48.4	66.0	28.8	40.6	1995–96	67.0	63.0	64.0		...	...	17
Comoros	...	...	36.8	51.3	34.7	48.4		...	...	...		...	...	0
Côte d'Ivoire	72	71	40.5	62.8	29.4	46.0	1995	...	...	36.8	1995	12.3	49.4	129
Dem. Republic of the Congo	79	...	26.9	49.8	13.8	27.7		...	...	...		...	...	367
Djibouti	...	...	24.4	45.6	14.0	27.2		...	...	...		...	...	24
Egypt	73	73	33.4	56.2	26.0	42.3	1995–96	23.3	22.5	22.9	1995	3.1	52.7	23
Equatorial Guinea	...	...	7.5	25.6	2.8	10.6		...	...	...		...	...	...
Eritrea	98	132	32.7	55.5	21.4	40.5	1993–94	...	...	53.0		...	...	36
Ethiopia	74	78	52.9	69.0	38.4	48.8		...	...	...	1995	31.3	76.4	162
Gabon	50	62	...	...	...	...		...	...	...		...	...	19
Gambia	76	83	56.3	70.3	38.2	52.2	1992	...	...	64.0	1998	59.3	82.9	8
Ghana	85	81	19.7	36.8	9.9	19.3	1992	34.3	26.7	31.4	1999	44.8	78.5	14
Guinea	73	77	...	...	...	...	1994	...	...	40.0		...	...	179
Guinea-Bissau	87	95	45.9	76.5	29.2	54.2	1991	...	...	48.7		...	...	8
Kenya	67	78	11.1	24.0	5.0	10.1	1992	46.4	29.3	42.0	1994	26.5	62.3	252
Lesotho	139	101	27.4	6.4	18.6	2.7	1993	53.9	27.8	49.2	1993	43.1	65.7	-
Liberia	...	...	29.8	63.3	17.5	46.5		...	...	...		...	...	253
Libyan Arab Jamahiriya	...	...	9.2	31.9	3.2	17.4		...	...	...		...	...	12
Madagascar	86	87	26.4	40.3	17.6	26.2	1993–94	77.0	47.0	70.0	1999	49.1	83.3	-
Malawi	72	82	25.5	53.5	18.4	38.4	1990–91	...	...	54.0		...	...	6
Mali	80	79	64.2	84.0	51.6	72.6		...	...	...	1994	72.8	90.6	9
Mauritania	69	68	49.3	69.9	44.4	60.8	1989–90	...	...	57.0	1995	28.6	68.7	30
Mauritius	65	66	12.2	18.8	8.7	11.7	1992	...	...	10.6		...	...	-
Morocco	65	63	38.2	63.9	28.1	48.1	1998–99	27.2	12.0	19.0	1990–91	<2	7.5	3
Mozambique	101	79	40.0	71.3	24.4	49.5		...	...	...	1996	37.9	78.4	6
Namibia	46	54	17.2	18.8	10.1	8.5		...	...	...	1993	34.9	55.8	33
Niger	84	84	76.2	91.5	65.4	83.8	1989–93	66.0	52.0	63.0	1995	61.4	85.3	1

Nigeria	56	45	27.8	43.9	14.1	22.9	1992–93	36.4	30.4	34.1	1997	70.2	90.8	7
Réunion	...	...	14.4	10.5	8.0	4.7		...	...	...		...	...	
Rwanda	84	88	26.4	39.6	15.6	21.1	1993	...	...	51.2	1983–85	35.7	84.6	58
Senegal	76	79	52.7	72.3	40.0	56.7	1992	40.4	...	33.4	1995	26.3	67.8	26
Sierra Leone	82	91	...	...	...	...	1989	76.0	53.0	68.0	1989	57.0	74.5	103
Somalia	112							...	...	...		...	...	52
South Africa	63	64	14.0	15.4	9.3	10.2		...	...	...	1993	11.5	35.8	30
Sudan	...	85	30.8	53.8	20.4	34.8		...	...	...		...	...	354
Swaziland	62	75	19.2	21.4	11.7	12.2	1995	...	...	40.0		...	...	1
Togo	71	83	27.7	57.5	14.8	36.7	1987–89	...	...	32.3		...	...	12
Tunisia	58	60	18.6	39.4	8.4	23.9	1990	21.6	8.9	14.1	1995	<2	10.0	-
Uganda	92	87	22.5	43.2	14.2	27.2	1993	...	...	55.0		...	...	201
United Republic of Tanzania	81	84	16.1	33.5	8.2	16.3	1993	49.7	24.4	41.6	1993	19.9	59.7	670
Zambia	64	86	14.8	28.5	8.8	15.4	1993	88.0[1]	46.0[1]	86.0	1998	63.7	87.4	285
Zimbabwe	63	63	7.2	15.4	2.4	6.4	1990–91	31.0	10.0	25.5	1990–91	36.0	64.2	9

ASIA

Afghanistan	...	...	...	...	...	...		...	...	...		...	...	1,226
Armenia	46	96	0.7	2.4	0.4	1.0		...	...	...	1996	7.8	34.0	264
Azerbaijan	...	59	...	...	...	...	1995	...	...	68.1	1995	<2	9.6	587
Bahrain	...	...	9.1	17.4	5.0	8.4		...	...	...		...	...	-
Bangladesh	86	78	50.6	69.8	44.3	61.7	1995–96	39.8	14.3	35.6	1996	29.1	77.8	22
Bhutan	...	...	...	...	...	...		...	...	...		...	...	...
Brunei Darussalam	...	...	5.4	11.9	2.8	5.8		...	...	...		...	...	...
Cambodia	91	92	19.8	42.8	15.8	29.3	1997	40.1	21.1	36.1		...	...	1
China	50	47	7.9	22.1	3.2	11.1	1998	4.6	<2	4.6	1999	18.8	52.6	295
China, Hong Kong SAR	57	58	3.1	10.8	2.0	5.1		...	...	...		...	...	2
China, Macau SAR	...	...	3.2	9.0	1.5	5.2		...	...	...		...	...	...
Cyprus	...	...	1.3	4.6	0.6	1.3		...	...	...		...	...	2
Dem. People's Rep. of Korea	...	...	...	...	...	...		...	...	...		...	...	...
Georgia	65	82	...	...	...	...	1997	9.9	12.1	11.1	1996	<2	<2	272
India	66	65	31.6	54.6	23.5	41.1	1994	36.7	30.5	35.0	1997	44.2	86.2	170
Indonesia	59	67	8.2	18.1	3.9	8.9	1999	...	...	27.1	1999	7.7	55.3	74
Iran (Islamic Republic of)[5]	62	52	17.0	31.1	8.1	17.4		...	...	...		...	...	1,868
Iraq	...	...	45.1	76.7	40.3	70.9		...	...	...		...	...	131
Israel	56	59	3.0	7.3	1.3	2.9		...	...	...		...	...	5
Japan	53	56	...	...	...	...		...	...	...		...	...	4
Jordan	74	81	5.1	15.7	1.8	6.2	1997	...	...	11.7	1997	<2	7.4	6
Kazakhstan	52	63	0.3	0.9	0.2	0.3	1996	39.0	30.0	34.6	1996	<2	15.3	120
Kuwait	57	41	16.1	20.4	11.6	12.8		...	...	...		...	...	139
Kyrgyzstan	71	77	...	...	...	...	1997	64.5	28.5	51.0		...	...	10
Lao People's Dem. Republic	...	82	23.8	46.6	16.1	31.8	1933	53.0	24.0	46.1	1997	26.3	73.2	-
Lebanon	140	88	7.9	19.7	4.1	11.5		...	...	...		...	...	6
Malaysia	52	43	8.6	16.6	4.5	7.9	1989	...	...	15.5		...	...	51
Maldives	...	...	3.0	3.2	1.4	1.4		...	...	...		...	...	...
Mongolia	58	66	1.4	1.7	1.2	0.9	1955	33.1	38.5	36.3	1995	13.9	50.0	...
Myanmar	89	87	11.1	19.5	9.4	13.4		...	...	...		...	...	-
Nepal	83	75	40.6	76.0	26.8	57.9	1995–96	44.0	23.0	42.0	1995	37.7	82.5	131
Occupied Palestinian Territory	...	92	...	...	...	...		...	...	...		...	...	-
Oman	27	...	19.9	38.4	8.4	17.9		...	...	...		...	...	-
Pakistan[6]	74	77	42.6	72.1	31.6	58.4	1991	36.9	28.0	34.0	1996	31.0	84.7	2,199
Philippines	72	63	4.9	5.2	2.5	2.5	1997	50.7	21.5	36.8		...	...	2
Qatar	...	...	19.6	16.9	14.7	9.0		...	...	...		...	...	-
Republic of Korea	53	58	0.9	3.6	0.4	1.1		...	...	...	1993	<2	<2	-
Saudi Arabia	40	33	17.0	33.1	9.5	17.0		...	...	...		...	...	246
Singapore	46	40	3.8	11.7	1.9	5.1		...	...	...		...	...	-
Sri Lanka	76	72	5.6	11.0	4.0	6.7	1995–96	...	...	25.0	1995	6.6	45.4	683
Syrian Arab Republic	69	62	11.7	39.6	6.3	25.5		...	...	...		...	...	4
Tajikistan	74	76	0.4	1.2	0.2	0.4		...	...	...		...	...	18
Thailand	57	60	2.9	6.1	1.5	3.3	1992	15.5	10.2	13.1	1998	<2	28.2	111
Timor-Leste	...	...	...	...	...	...		...	...	...		...	...	18
Turkey	69	69	6.6	23.5	2.9	13.4		...	...	...	1994	2.4	18.0	8
Turkmenistan	49	34	...	...	...	...		...	...	...	1998	12.1	44.0	14
United Arab Emirates	39	...	25.2	20.9	19.9	12.1		...	...	...		...	...	1
Uzbekistan	61	64	0.4	1.2	0.3	0.5		...	...	...	1993	3.3	26.5	41
Viet Nam	86	69	5.5	9.3	4.7	5.8	1993	57.2	25.9	50.9		...	...	16
Yemen	74	58	32.5	74.7	18.8	48.9	1992	19.2	18.6	19.1	1998	15.7	45.2	72

EUROPE

Albania	61	92	7.9	23.0	3.1	11.5	1996	28.9[2]	15.0	...		...	...	-
Austria[7]	55	57	...	...	...	...		...	...	...		...	...	30
Belarus	47	59	0.2	0.4	0.2	0.2	2000	...	...	41.9	1998	<2	<2	36
Belgium	55	54	...	...	...	...		...	...	...		...	...	13
Bosnia and Herzegovina	...	110	...	...	...	...		...	...	...		...	...	570
Bulgaria	60	71	1.0	2.1	0.5	0.9		...	...	...	1997	<2	21.9	5
Croatia	74	57	0.7	2.7	0.4	0.8		...	...	...	1998	<2	<2	68
Czech Republic	49	54	...	...	...	...		...	...	...	1996	<2	<2	13
Denmark[7]	49	48	...	...	...	...		...	...	...		...	...	73
Estonia	62	58	0.2	0.2	0.3	0.2	1995	14.7	6.8	8.9	1998	<2	5.2	-
Finland[7]	51	50	...	...	...	...		...	...	...		...	...	13
France	55	55	...	...	...	...		...	...	...		...	...	166
Germany[8]	55	58	...	...	...	...		...	...	...		...	...	989
Greece	72	71	1.5	4.1	0.7	1.4		...	...	...		...	...	13
Hungary	61	64	0.5	0.8	0.3	0.5	1993	...	...	8.6	1998	<2	7.3	7
Ireland[7]	58	49	...	...	...	...		...	...	...		...	...	14
Italy[7]	58	60	1.1	2.0	0.5	0.8		...	...	...		...	...	9
Latvia	53	63	0.2	0.2	0.2	0.2		...	...	...	1998	<2	8.3	-
Lithuania	57	64	0.3	0.5	0.2	0.3		...	...	...	1996	<2	7.8	-
Malta	...	...	8.7	7.3	5.4	3.2		...	...	...		...	...	-
Netherlands[7]	49	50	...	...	...	...		...	...	...		...	...	231

TABLE B.7

continued

| | Household final consumption expenditure % of GDP | | Illiteracy rate | | | | Population below the poverty line | | | | | | | Refugees and assylum-seekers* (000) |
| | | | | | | | National | | | | International | | | |
	1990	2000	Male (%) 2000	Female (%) 2000	Male (%) 2015	Female (%) 2015	Year	Rural (%)	Urban (%)	Total (%)	Survey year	Below $1 a day (%)	Below $2 a day (%)	2001
Norway[7]	49	43	...	...	...	...		...	...	...		...	...	50
Poland	48	64	0.3	0.3	0.2	0.2	1993	...	...	23.8	1998	<2	<2	1
Portugal	62	63	5.3	10.1	1.9	3.7		...	...	...	1994	<2	<2	-
Republic of Moldova	58	89	0.5	1.7	0.2	0.3	1997	26.7	...	23.3	1997	11.3	38.4	1
Romania	66	74	1.0	2.7	0.6	1.0	1994	27.9	20.4	21.5	1994	2.8	27.5	2
Russian Federation	49	46	0.3	0.6	0.2	0.3	1994	...	...	30.9	1998	7.1	25.1	1,140
Serbia and Montenegro	...	79	...	...	...	...		...	...	...		...	...	777
Slovakia	54	53	...	...	...	...		...	...	...	1992	<2	<2	4
Slovenia	55	55	0.3	0.4	0.3	0.3		...	...	...	1998	<2	<2	7
Spain[7]	60	59	1.5	3.2	0.8	1.4		...	...	...		...	...	7
Sweden[7]	49	50	...	...	...	...		...	...	...		...	...	164
Switzerland	57	61	...	...	...	...		...	...	...		...	...	84
TFYR Macedonia	72	82	...	...	...	...		...	...	...		...	...	169
Ukraine	57	58	0.3	0.5	0.2	0.2	1995	...	...	31.7	1999	2.9	31.0	10
United Kingdom[7]	63	65	...	...	...	...		...	...	...		...	...	187
LATIN AMERICA AND THE CARIBBEAN														
Argentina	77	71	3.2	3.2	2.3	2.0	1993	...	...	17.6		...	...	4
Bahamas	...	...	5.5	3.7	4.3	2.6		...	...	...		...	...	...
Barbados	...	...	0.3	0.3	0.2	0.2		...	...	...		...	...	...
Belize	...	...	6.7	6.8	3.6	2.9		...	...	...		...	...	1
Bolivia	77	74	8.1	20.8	3.6	10.9	1995	79.1	29.3[3]	...	1999	14.4	34.3	-
Brazil	59	63	13.0	13.2	8.8	7.6	1990	32.6	13.1	17.4	1998	11.6	26.5	4
Chile	62	63	4.1	4.4	2.3	2.4	1998	...	...	21.2	1998	<2	8.7	-
Colombia	66	67	8.4	8.4	5.2	4.6	1992	31.2	8.0	17.7	1998	19.7	36.0	720
Costa Rica	61	67	4.5	4.4	2.8	2.5	1992	25.5	19.2	22.0	1998	12.6	26.0	11
Cuba	...	70	3.2	3.4	1.5	1.7		...	...	...		...	...	1
Dominican Republic	80	78	16.3	16.3	12.0	11.2	1992	29.8	10.9	20.6	1996	3.2	16.0	...
Ecuador	69	62	6.8	10.1	3.8	5.7	1994	47.0	25.0	35.0	1995	20.2	52.3	4
El Salvador	89	88	18.5	23.9	12.8	16.3	1992	55.7	43.1	48.3	1998	21.0	44.5	-
Guatemala	84	84	24.0	38.9	15.9	29.1	1989	71.9	33.7	57.9	1998	10.0	33.8	1
Guyana	...	...	1.1	1.9	0.5	0.6		...	...	...		...	...	...
Haiti	93	100	48.0	52.2	36.3	38.1	1995	66.0	...	65.0[4]		...	...	...
Honduras	66	66	25.1	25.0	17.9	16.2	1993	51.0	57.0	53.0	1998	24.3	45.1	-
Jamaica	62	68	17.1	9.3	11.8	5.1	2000	...	...	18.7	1996	3.2	25.2	...
Martinique	...	...	3.0	2.2	1.3	0.9		...	...	...		...	...	...
Mexico	70	68	6.7	10.9	4.0	6.3	1998	...	...	10.1	1998	15.9	37.7	15
Netherlands Antilles	...	...	3.5	3.4	2.6	2.4		...	...	...		...	...	...
Nicaragua	59	88	33.8	33.3	29.2	28.3	1993	76.1	31.9	50.3		...	...	-
Panama	60	61	7.5	8.8	4.5	5.7	1997	64.9	15.3	37.3	1998	14.0	29.0	2
Paraguay	77	83	5.6	7.8	3.6	4.3	1991	28.5	19.7	21.8	1998	19.5	49.3	-
Peru	74	71	5.3	14.8	2.9	8.4	1997	64.7	40.4	49.0	1996	15.5	41.4	1
Puerto Rico	...	...	6.4	6.0	4.4	3.6		...	...	...		...	...	...
Suriname	...	...	...	...	...	...		...	...	...		...	...	...
Trinidad and Tobago	59	56	1.1	2.3	0.5	0.9	1992	20.0	24.0	21.0	1992	12.4	39.0	...
Uruguay	70	75	2.9	2.0	1.8	1.1		...	...	...	1989	<2	6.6	-
Venezuela	62	63	7.0	8.0	4.0	3.8	1989	...	...	31.3	1998	23.0	47.0	-
NORTHERN AMERICA														
Canada[9]	57	58	...	...	...	...		...	...	...		...	...	175
United States[9]	67	68	...	...	...	...		...	...	...		...	...	912
OCEANIA														
Australia[9]	59	60	...	...	...	...		...	...	...		...	...	69
FIJI	...	...	5.1	9.2	2.4	4.3		...	...	...		...	...	...
New Zealand[9]	63	64	...	...	...	...		...	...	...		...	...	7
Papua New Guinea	59	66	29.4	43.2	21.7	31.4		...	...	...		...	...	5
Samoa	...	...	1.1	1.7	0.7	0.9		...	...	...		...	...	...

Notes: * Data for Refugees and assylum-seekers refer to the total assylum-seekers, refugees and others of concern to UNCHR. There is a total population of concern of 22 whose nationality falls under the category various/unknown. 1 Data refer to the year 1991. 2 Data refer to the year 1994. 3 Data refer to the year 1993. 4 Data refer to the year 1987. 5 According to the government, the number of Afghans is estimated to be some 2.3 million. 6 According to the government, the number of Afghans is estimated to be some 3.3 million. 7 Refugee estimate provided by UNHCR, based on ten years of refugee arrivals and asylum-seeker recognition. 8 In addition to the 85,553 asylum cases pending at the administrative level, some 107,000 claims were pending at the courts. 9 Refugee estimate provided by UNHCR, based on five years of refugee arrivals and asylum-seeker recognition.

Sources: World Bank, *World Development Indicators 2002*; United Nations Educational, Scientific and Cultural Organization (UNESCO); United Nations Commissioner for Refugees (UNHCR), *Statistical Yearbook 2001*.

TABLE C.1

Urban Agglomerations: Population Size and Growth Rate

		Estimates and projections (000)						Annual rate of growth (%)					Share in country's urban population (%)	
		1990	1995	2000	2005	2010	2015	1990–1995	1995–2000	2000–2005	2005–2010	2010–2015	2000	2015
AFRICA														
Algeria	Algiers	1,908	2,295	2,761	3,269	3,741	4,142	1.85	1.85	1.69	1.35	1.02	15.95	16.71
Angola	Luanda	1,644	2,149	2,697	3,362	4,166	5,144	2.68	2.27	2.20	2.14	2.11	60.03	56.07
Burkina Faso	Ouagadougou	594	700	831	1,014	1,284	1,659	1.63	1.71	2.00	2.36	2.56	43.59	38.86
Cameroon	Douala	1,001	1,317	1,642	1,972	2,297	2,607	2.74	2.21	1.83	1.53	1.26	22.57	21.90
Cameroon	Yaoundé	823	1,117	1,420	1,720	2,009	2,281	3.05	2.40	1.92	1.55	1.27	19.52	19.16
Congo	Brazzaville	826	1,055	1,306	1,589	1,901	2,259	2.45	2.13	1.96	1.80	1.73	66.15	65.83
Côte d'Ivoire	Abidjan	2,189	2,880	3,790	4,557	5,316	6,076	2.75	2.75	1.84	1.54	1.34	54.27	55.46
Dem. Republic of the Congo	Kinshasa	3,445	4,236	5,054	6,231	7,899	9,883	2.07	1.77	2.09	2.37	2.24	32.76	29.94
Dem. Republic of the Congo	Lubumbashi	671	809	965	1,201	1,540	1,950	1.88	1.76	2.19	2.49	2.36	6.25	5.91
Egypt	Alexandria	3,063	3,277	3,506	3,751	4,019	4,330	0.67	0.67	0.67	0.69	0.75	12.10	11.21
Egypt	Cairo	8,296	8,860	9,462	10,094	10,767	11,531	0.66	0.66	0.65	0.65	0.69	32.66	29.85
Egypt	Shubra El-Kheima	765	847	937	1,032	1,129	1,234	1.01	1.01	0.97	0.90	0.89	3.23	3.19
Ethiopia	Addis Ababa	1,791	2,173	2,645	3,238	3,988	4,932	1.93	1.97	2.02	2.08	2.13	27.09	24.99
Ghana	Accra	1,376	1,603	1,868	2,170	2,510	2,890	1.53	1.53	1.50	1.46	1.41	26.82	25.84
Guinea	Conakry	877	1,039	1,232	1,446	1,724	2,073	1.70	1.70	1.60	1.75	1.85	54.95	51.74
Kenya	Nairobi	1,380	1,756	2,233	2,825	3,500	4,168	2.41	2.41	2.35	2.14	1.75	21.82	22.09
Libyan Arab Jamahiriya	Benghazi	624	725	829	931	1,024	1,099	1.51	1.33	1.17	0.95	0.71	17.87	17.23
Libyan Arab Jamahiriya	Tripoli	1,297	1,518	1,733	1,940	2,122	2,265	1.58	1.32	1.13	0.90	0.65	37.39	35.52
Madagascar	Antananarivo	931	1,226	1,603	2,063	2,596	3,190	2.75	2.68	2.52	2.30	2.06	34.04	33.60
Mali	Bamako	737	906	1,114	1,378	1,719	2,143	2.07	2.07	2.13	2.21	2.21	32.49	29.79
Morocco	Casablanca	2,685	2,994	3,357	3,778	4,217	4,605	1.09	1.14	1.18	1.10	0.88	20.26	18.98
Morocco	Fes	684	787	907	1,042	1,179	1,300	1.41	1.42	1.38	1.23	0.98	5.48	5.36
Morocco	Marrakech	580	693	822	960	1,095	1,210	1.77	1.71	1.56	1.31	1.00	4.96	4.99
Morocco	Rabat	1,161	1,374	1,616	1,876	2,126	2,339	1.68	1.63	1.49	1.25	0.95	9.75	9.64
Mozambique	Maputo	776	921	1,094	1,316	1,593	1,899	1.72	1.72	1.85	1.91	1.76	18.62	16.75
Niger	Niamey	447	587	775	1,031	1,369	1,789	2.73	2.78	2.85	2.83	2.68	34.81	33.22
Nigeria	Ibadan	1,227	1,361	1,549	1,816	2,159	2,542	1.04	1.29	1.59	1.73	1.63	3.09	2.77
Nigeria	Lagos	4,765	6,485	8,665	11,134	13,627	15,966	3.08	2.90	2.51	2.02	1.58	17.27	17.41
Nigeria	Ogbomosho	623	702	809	957	1,146	1,356	1.19	1.42	1.69	1.80	1.68	1.61	1.48
Senegal	Dakar	1,401	1,708	2,078	2,510	2,987	3,481	1.98	1.96	1.89	1.74	1.53	46.50	44.86
Sierra Leone	Freetown	581	681	800	1,023	1,257	1,506	1.59	1.60	2.46	2.05	1.81	49.57	45.33
Somalia	Mogadishu	779	941	1,157	1,483	1,919	2,444	1.88	2.07	2.49	2.58	2.42	47.93	44.20
South Africa	Cape Town	2,322	2,603	2,930	3,213	3,377	3,458	1.14	1.18	0.92	0.50	0.24	11.90	11.54
South Africa	Durban	1,673	2,032	2,391	2,719	2,921	3,020	1.94	1.63	1.28	0.72	0.33	9.71	10.08
South Africa	East Rand	1,360	1,457	1,552	1,631	1,673	1,703	0.69	0.64	0.49	0.26	0.17	6.30	5.68
South Africa	Johannesburg	2,077	2,463	2,950	3,399	3,679	3,811	1.71	1.80	1.42	0.79	0.35	11.98	12.72
South Africa	Port Elizabeth	849	921	1,006	1,079	1,122	1,150	0.81	0.89	0.70	0.39	0.25	4.09	3.84
South Africa	Pretoria	1,060	1,292	1,590	1,874	2,059	2,152	1.98	2.07	1.64	0.94	0.44	6.46	7.18
Sudan	Khartoum	1,828	2,249	2,742	3,343	4,013	4,687	2.08	1.98	1.99	1.83	1.55	24.41	22.69
Tunisia	Tunis	1,568	1,722	1,892	2,070	2,249	2,414	0.94	0.94	0.90	0.83	0.71	30.52	29.19
Uganda	Kampala	755	955	1,213	1,560	2,047	2,706	2.35	2.39	2.51	2.72	2.79	36.78	33.77
United Republic of Tanzania	Dar es Salaam	1,313	1,657	2,115	2,702	3,375	4,080	2.32	2.44	2.45	2.22	1.90	18.67	17.91
Zambia	Lusaka	974	1,317	1,653	1,978	2,314	2,733	3.02	2.27	1.80	1.57	1.66	40.03	40.86
Zimbabwe	Bulawayo	570	699	824	964	1,130	1,314	2.03	1.64	1.57	1.60	1.50	18.47	17.50
Zimbabwe	Harare	1,048	1,410	1,791	2,186	2,598	3,013	2.97	2.39	1.99	1.73	1.48	40.16	40.14
ASIA														
Afghanistan	Kabul	1,565	2,048	2,602	3,358	4,364	5,397	2.69	2.40	2.55	2.62	2.13	54.64	50.42
Armenia	Yerevan	1,210	1,305	1,407	1,453	1,478	1,490	0.75	0.75	0.32	0.17	0.08	55.28	56.07
Azerbaijan	Baku	1,751	1,847	1,948	2,015	2,072	2,137	0.53	0.53	0.34	0.28	0.31	46.69	45.45
Bangladesh	Chittagong	2,265	2,942	3,651	4,468	5,389	6,360	2.62	2.16	2.02	1.87	1.66	10.63	10.11
Bangladesh	Dhaka	6,621	9,407	12,519	15,921	19,393	22,766	3.51	2.86	2.40	1.97	1.60	36.44	36.18
Bangladesh	Khulna	973	1,205	1,442	1,731	2,081	2,467	2.14	1.79	1.83	1.84	1.71	4.20	3.92
Bangladesh	Rajshahi	517	757	1,035	1,348	1,676	2,003	3.81	3.14	2.64	2.18	1.78	3.01	3.18
Cambodia	Phnom Penh	594	810	1,070	1,237	1,460	1,766	3.10	2.79	1.45	1.65	1.91	48.29	36.41
China[1]	Anshan	1,442	1,448	1,453	1,459	1,500	1,592	0.04	0.04	0.04	0.28	0.59	0.32	0.23
China[1]	Anshun	658	721	789	864	954	1,057	0.91	0.91	0.91	0.98	1.03	0.17	0.15
China[1]	Baotou	1,229	1,273	1,319	1,367	1,442	1,554	0.36	0.36	0.36	0.53	0.75	0.29	0.22
China[1]	Beijing	10,819	10,829	10,839	10,849	11,099	11,671	0.01	0.01	0.01	0.23	0.50	2.38	1.67
China[1]	Benxi	938	947	957	967	1,000	1,065	0.10	0.10	0.10	0.34	0.64	0.21	0.15
China[1]	Changchun	2,192	2,604	3,093	3,673	4,315	4,944	1.72	1.72	1.72	1.61	1.36	0.68	0.71
China[1]	Changde	1,180	1,273	1,374	1,483	1,615	1,774	0.76	0.76	0.76	0.86	0.94	0.30	0.25
China[1]	Changsha	1,329	1,536	1,775	2,051	2,359	2,674	1.45	1.45	1.45	1.40	1.25	0.39	0.38
China[1]	Changzhou	730	804	886	976	1,082	1,202	0.97	0.97	0.97	1.03	1.05	0.19	0.17
China[1]	Chengdu	2,955	3,120	3,294	3,478	3,720	4,030	0.54	0.54	0.54	0.67	0.80	0.72	0.58
China[1]	Chifeng	987	1,036	1,087	1,140	1,215	1,318	0.48	0.48	0.48	0.64	0.81	0.24	0.19
China[1]	Chongqing	3,123	4,073	4,900	5,695	6,572	7,440	2.66	1.85	1.50	1.43	1.24	1.07	1.07
China[1]	Dalian	2,472	2,549	2,628	2,709	2,843	3,048	0.30	0.30	0.30	0.48	0.70	0.58	0.44
China[1]	Daqing	997	1,035	1,076	1,117	1,181	1,275	0.38	0.38	0.38	0.56	0.76	0.24	0.18
China[1]	Datong	1,277	1,220	1,165	1,112	1,141	1,210	-0.46	-0.46	-0.46	0.25	0.58	0.26	0.17
China[1]	Dongguan	1,737	1,514	1,319	1,150	1,179	1,250	-1.38	-1.38	-1.38	0.25	0.58	0.29	0.18
China[1]	Fushun	1,388	1,400	1,413	1,425	1,471	1,565	0.09	0.09	0.09	0.32	0.62	0.31	0.22
China[1]	Fuxin	743	764	785	807	846	910	0.27	0.27	0.27	0.48	0.73	0.17	0.13
China[1]	Fuyu	945	984	1,025	1,068	1,131	1,223	0.41	0.41	0.41	0.58	0.78	0.22	0.18
China[1]	Fuzhou	1,396	1,396	1,397	1,398	1,434	1,519	0.00	0.00	0.00	0.25	0.58	0.31	0.22
China[1]	Guangzhou	3,918	3,906	3,893	3,881	3,973	4,192	-0.03	-0.03	-0.03	0.24	0.54	0.85	0.60
China[1]	Guiyang	1,665	2,054	2,533	3,124	3,784	4,418	2.10	2.10	2.10	1.92	1.55	0.56	0.63
China[1]	Handan	1,769	1,879	1,996	2,120	2,279	2,481	0.60	0.60	0.60	0.73	0.85	0.44	0.36

TABLE C.1

continued

		Estimates and projections (000)						Annual rate of growth (%)					Share in country's urban population (%)	
		1990	1995	2000	2005	2010	2015	1990–1995	1995–2000	2000–2005	2005–2010	2010–2015	2000	2015
China[1]	Hangzhou	1,476	1,621	1,780	1,955	2,159	2,388	0.94	0.94	0.94	0.99	1.01	0.39	0.34
China[1]	Harbin	2,991	2,959	2,928	2,898	2,968	3,135	-0.11	-0.11	-0.11	0.24	0.55	0.64	0.45
China[1]	Hefei	1,100	1,169	1,242	1,320	1,421	1,550	0.61	0.61	0.61	0.74	0.87	0.27	0.22
China[1]	Hengyang	702	749	799	853	921	1,008	0.65	0.65	0.65	0.77	0.90	0.18	0.14
China[1]	Heze	1,201	1,386	1,600	1,847	2,123	2,406	1.44	1.44	1.44	1.39	1.25	0.35	0.34
China[1]	Huaian	1,113	1,171	1,232	1,297	1,385	1,504	0.51	0.51	0.51	0.66	0.82	0.27	0.22
China[1]	Huaibei	536	682	814	946	1,094	1,246	2.41	1.77	1.50	1.46	1.31	0.18	0.18
China[1]	Huainan	1,228	1,289	1,354	1,422	1,515	1,643	0.49	0.49	0.49	0.64	0.81	0.30	0.24
China[1]	Huhehaote	938	958	978	998	1,040	1,114	0.20	0.20	0.20	0.42	0.69	0.21	0.16
China[1]	Hunjiang	722	746	772	798	841	907	0.33	0.33	0.33	0.53	0.76	0.17	0.13
China[1]	Huzhou	1,028	1,052	1,077	1,102	1,152	1,235	0.23	0.23	0.23	0.44	0.70	0.24	0.18
China[1]	Jiamusi	660	759	874	1,006	1,155	1,311	1.41	1.41	1.41	1.38	1.26	0.19	0.19
China[1]	Jiaxing	741	766	791	817	861	928	0.33	0.33	0.33	0.52	0.75	0.17	0.13
China[1]	Jilin	1,320	1,376	1,435	1,496	1,585	1,712	0.42	0.42	0.42	0.58	0.77	0.31	0.25
China[1]	Jinan	2,404	2,484	2,568	2,654	2,791	2,996	0.33	0.33	0.33	0.50	0.71	0.56	0.43
China[1]	Jingmen	1,017	1,083	1,153	1,228	1,324	1,445	0.63	0.63	0.63	0.75	0.88	0.25	0.21
China[1]	Jining	871	942	1,019	1,101	1,203	1,323	0.78	0.78	0.78	0.88	0.96	0.22	0.19
China[1]	Jinxi	1,350	1,568	1,821	2,115	2,443	2,775	1.50	1.50	1.50	1.44	1.27	0.40	0.40
China[1]	Jinzhou	736	784	834	888	958	1,047	0.62	0.62	0.62	0.76	0.89	0.18	0.15
China[1]	Jixi	836	890	949	1,012	1,092	1,194	0.64	0.64	0.64	0.76	0.89	0.21	0.17
China[1]	Kaifeng	693	730	769	810	866	942	0.52	0.52	0.52	0.67	0.84	0.17	0.13
China[1]	Kaohsiung	1,380	1,421	1,463	1,506	1,580	1,697	0.29	0.29	0.29	0.48	0.71	0.32	0.24
China[1]	Kunming	1,612	1,656	1,701	1,748	1,830	1,962	0.27	0.27	0.27	0.46	0.70	0.37	0.28
China[1]	Lanzhou	1,618	1,673	1,730	1,788	1,882	2,024	0.33	0.33	0.33	0.51	0.73	0.38	0.29
China[1]	Leshan	1,070	1,103	1,137	1,172	1,231	1,324	0.30	0.30	0.30	0.49	0.73	0.25	0.19
China[1]	Linqing	696	787	891	1,009	1,143	1,286	1.24	1.24	1.24	1.25	1.18	0.20	0.18
China[1]	Linyi	1,741	2,085	2,498	2,992	3,540	4,076	1.81	1.81	1.81	1.68	1.41	0.55	0.58
China[1]	Liuan	1,481	1,641	1,818	2,015	2,242	2,491	1.03	1.03	1.03	1.07	1.05	0.40	0.36
China[1]	Liupanshui	1,845	1,932	2,023	2,118	2,252	2,435	0.46	0.46	0.46	0.61	0.78	0.44	0.35
China[1]	Liuzhou	751	835	928	1,031	1,150	1,283	1.05	1.05	1.05	1.10	1.09	0.20	0.18
China[1]	Luoyang	1,202	1,321	1,451	1,594	1,762	1,951	0.94	0.94	0.94	1.00	1.02	0.32	0.28
China[1]	Mianyang	876	965	1,065	1,174	1,302	1,446	0.98	0.98	0.98	1.03	1.05	0.23	0.21
China[1]	Mudanjiang	751	775	801	827	871	939	0.32	0.32	0.32	0.52	0.75	0.18	0.13
China[1]	Nanchang	1,262	1,474	1,722	2,012	2,335	2,661	1.55	1.55	1.55	1.49	1.30	0.38	0.38
China[1]	Nanchong	619	860	1,055	1,226	1,417	1,614	3.30	2.04	1.50	1.45	1.30	0.23	0.23
China[1]	Nanjing	2,611	2,674	2,740	2,806	2,931	3,132	0.24	0.24	0.24	0.43	0.66	0.60	0.45
China[1]	Nanning	1,159	1,233	1,311	1,395	1,502	1,639	0.62	0.62	0.62	0.74	0.87	0.29	0.23
China[1]	Neijiang	1,289	1,340	1,393	1,449	1,532	1,653	0.39	0.39	0.39	0.56	0.76	0.31	0.24
China[1]	Ningbo	1,142	1,157	1,173	1,188	1,231	1,313	0.13	0.13	0.13	0.36	0.64	0.26	0.19
China[1]	Pingxiang	1,388	1,444	1,502	1,562	1,653	1,783	0.39	0.39	0.39	0.56	0.76	0.33	0.26
China[1]	Qingdao	2,102	2,206	2,316	2,431	2,589	2,801	0.48	0.48	0.48	0.63	0.79	0.51	0.40
China[1]	Qiqihar	1,401	1,418	1,435	1,452	1,503	1,601	0.12	0.12	0.12	0.35	0.63	0.31	0.23
China[1]	Shanghai	13,342	13,112	12,887	12,665	12,944	13,598	-0.17	-0.17	-0.17	0.22	0.49	2.82	1.95
China[1]	Shantou	885	1,020	1,176	1,356	1,558	1,767	1.42	1.42	1.42	1.39	1.26	0.26	0.25
China[1]	Shenyang	4,655	4,741	4,828	4,916	5,105	5,429	0.18	0.18	0.18	0.38	0.61	1.06	0.78
China[1]	Shenzhen	875	995	1,131	1,285	1,460	1,645	1.28	1.28	1.28	1.28	1.19	0.25	0.24
China[1]	Shijiazhuang	1,372	1,483	1,603	1,733	1,890	2,076	0.78	0.78	0.78	0.87	0.94	0.35	0.30
China[1]	Suining	1,260	1,341	1,428	1,520	1,639	1,788	0.63	0.63	0.63	0.75	0.87	0.31	0.26
China[1]	Suqian	1,061	1,123	1,189	1,258	1,350	1,470	0.57	0.57	0.57	0.71	0.85	0.26	0.21
China[1]	Suzhou	875	1,017	1,183	1,376	1,592	1,813	1.51	1.51	1.51	1.46	1.30	0.26	0.26
China[1]	Taian	1,413	1,457	1,503	1,550	1,628	1,749	0.31	0.31	0.31	0.49	0.72	0.33	0.25
China[1]	Taichung	754	847	950	1,066	1,200	1,344	1.15	1.15	1.15	1.18	1.14	0.21	0.19
China[1]	Taipei	2,711	2,629	2,550	2,473	2,534	2,678	-0.31	-0.31	-0.31	0.24	0.55	0.56	0.38
China[1]	Taiyuan	2,225	2,318	2,415	2,516	2,664	2,871	0.41	0.41	0.41	0.57	0.75	0.53	0.41
China[1]	Tangshan	1,485	1,575	1,671	1,773	1,905	2,074	0.59	0.59	0.59	0.72	0.85	0.37	0.30
China[1]	Tianjin	8,785	8,969	9,156	9,346	9,716	10,319	0.21	0.21	0.21	0.39	0.60	2.01	1.48
China[1]	Tianmen	1,484	1,625	1,779	1,948	2,146	2,371	0.91	0.91	0.91	0.97	1.00	0.39	0.34
China[1]	Tianshui	1,040	1,111	1,187	1,269	1,372	1,501	0.66	0.66	0.66	0.78	0.90	0.26	0.21
China[1]	Tongliao	674	727	785	847	924	1,017	0.76	0.76	0.76	0.87	0.96	0.17	0.15
China[1]	Wanxian	1,414	1,577	1,759	1,963	2,195	2,447	1.09	1.09	1.09	1.12	1.08	0.39	0.35
China[1]	Weifang	1,152	1,217	1,287	1,360	1,458	1,586	0.55	0.55	0.55	0.69	0.84	0.28	0.23
China[1]	Wenzhou	604	987	1,269	1,475	1,705	1,940	4.90	2.52	1.50	1.45	1.29	0.28	0.28
China[1]	Wuhan	3,833	4,451	5,169	6,003	6,923	7,833	1.50	1.50	1.50	1.43	1.24	1.13	1.12
China[1]	Wulumuqi	1,161	1,282	1,415	1,562	1,733	1,924	0.99	0.99	0.99	1.04	1.04	0.31	0.28
China[1]	Wuxi	1,009	1,066	1,127	1,192	1,278	1,391	0.56	0.56	0.56	0.70	0.85	0.25	0.20
China[1]	Xian	2,873	2,995	3,123	3,257	3,448	3,714	0.42	0.42	0.42	0.57	0.74	0.68	0.53
China[1]	Xiangxiang	853	880	908	936	985	1,061	0.31	0.31	0.31	0.51	0.74	0.20	0.15
China[1]	Xiantao	1,361	1,482	1,614	1,758	1,929	2,126	0.85	0.85	0.85	0.93	0.97	0.35	0.30
China[1]	Xianyang	737	813	896	988	1,096	1,218	0.98	0.98	0.98	1.04	1.05	0.20	0.17
China[1]	Xiaoshan	1,113	1,119	1,124	1,130	1,164	1,236	0.05	0.05	0.05	0.29	0.61	0.25	0.18
China[1]	Xinghua	1,497	1,526	1,556	1,587	1,652	1,766	0.19	0.19	0.19	0.40	0.66	0.34	0.25
China[1]	Xintai	1,306	1,315	1,325	1,334	1,375	1,461	0.07	0.07	0.07	0.31	0.61	0.29	0.21
China[1]	Xinyi	884	927	973	1,022	1,089	1,182	0.48	0.48	0.48	0.64	0.82	0.21	0.17
China[1]	Xinyu	608	701	808	932	1,071	1,216	1.42	1.42	1.42	1.39	1.27	0.18	0.17
China[1]	Xuanzhou	769	796	823	851	898	968	0.34	0.34	0.34	0.53	0.76	0.18	0.14
China[1]	Xuzhou	944	1,329	1,636	1,901	2,197	2,497	3.43	2.08	1.50	1.45	1.28	0.36	0.36
China[1]	Yancheng	1,352	1,453	1,562	1,678	1,823	1,997	0.72	0.72	0.72	0.82	0.91	0.34	0.29
China[1]	Yantai	838	1,320	1,681	1,953	2,256	2,564	4.54	2.41	1.50	1.45	1.28	0.37	0.37

Country	City													
China[1]	Yichun (Heilongjiang)	882	893	904	916	949	1,012	0.12	0.12	0.12	0.35	0.65	0.20	0.15
China[1]	Yichun (Jiangxi)	836	854	871	890	928	994	0.21	0.21	0.21	0.42	0.69	0.19	0.14
China[1]	Yixing	1,065	1,086	1,108	1,129	1,177	1,259	0.20	0.20	0.20	0.41	0.68	0.24	0.18
China[1]	Yiyang	1,062	1,194	1,343	1,510	1,700	1,904	1.17	1.17	1.17	1.19	1.13	0.29	0.27
China[1]	Yongzhou	946	1,019	1,097	1,182	1,287	1,413	0.74	0.74	0.74	0.85	0.94	0.24	0.20
China[1]	Yueyang	1,078	1,143	1,213	1,286	1,383	1,507	0.59	0.59	0.59	0.72	0.86	0.27	0.22
China[1]	Yulin	1,323	1,436	1,558	1,691	1,850	2,037	0.82	0.82	0.82	0.90	0.96	0.34	0.29
China[1]	Yuyao	794	821	848	876	923	995	0.33	0.33	0.33	0.52	0.75	0.19	0.14
China[1]	Yuzhou	1,073	1,122	1,173	1,226	1,303	1,411	0.45	0.45	0.45	0.61	0.79	0.26	0.20
China[1]	Zaoyang	962	1,039	1,121	1,210	1,319	1,450	0.76	0.76	0.76	0.86	0.95	0.25	0.21
China[1]	Zaozhuang	1,793	1,916	2,048	2,189	2,365	2,582	0.66	0.66	0.66	0.78	0.88	0.45	0.37
China[1]	Zhangjiakou	720	796	880	973	1,082	1,204	1.01	1.01	1.01	1.06	1.07	0.19	0.17
China[1]	Zhangjiangang	793	838	886	936	1,004	1,094	0.55	0.55	0.55	0.70	0.85	0.19	0.16
China[1]	Zhanjiang	1,049	1,198	1,368	1,562	1,780	2,008	1.33	1.33	1.33	1.31	1.20	0.30	0.29
China[1]	Zhaodong	797	824	851	879	926	998	0.33	0.33	0.33	0.52	0.75	0.19	0.14
China[1]	Zhengzhou	1,752	1,905	2,070	2,250	2,464	2,711	0.83	0.83	0.83	0.91	0.96	0.45	0.39
China[1]	Zibo	2,484	2,578	2,675	2,775	2,928	3,148	0.37	0.37	0.37	0.54	0.73	0.59	0.45
China[1]	Zigong	977	1,023	1,072	1,123	1,195	1,295	0.46	0.46	0.46	0.62	0.80	0.23	0.19
China, Hong Kong SAR[2]	Hong Kong	5,701	6,210	6,860	7,271	7,659	8,025	0.86	1.00	0.58	0.52	0.47	..	..
Dem. People's Rep. of Korea	Nampo	580	808	1,022	1,185	1,288	1,359	3.31	2.35	1.47	0.84	0.53	7.62	8.49
Dem. People's Rep. of Korea	Pyongyang	2,473	2,865	3,124	3,300	3,442	3,580	1.47	0.86	0.55	0.42	0.39	23.29	22.38
Georgia	Tbilisi	1,277	1,382	1,406	1,406	1,406	1,406	0.79	0.17	-	-	-	47.46	47.96
India	Agra	933	1,095	1,293	1,526	1,757	1,990	1.60	1.66	1.66	1.41	1.25	0.46	0.50
India	Ahmedabad	3,255	3,790	4,427	5,171	5,893	6,612	1.52	1.55	1.55	1.31	1.15	1.59	1.67
India	Allahabad	830	928	1,035	1,153	1,269	1,400	1.12	1.09	1.09	0.95	0.98	0.37	0.35
India	Amritsar	701	814	955	1,121	1,284	1,452	1.50	1.60	1.60	1.36	1.23	0.34	0.37
India	Asansol	728	891	1,065	1,272	1,479	1,686	2.03	1.78	1.78	1.51	1.31	0.38	0.43
India	Aurangabad	569	708	868	1,065	1,265	1,461	2.19	2.04	2.04	1.72	1.44	0.31	0.37
India	Bangalore	4,036	4,745	5,567	6,533	7,469	8,391	1.62	1.60	1.60	1.34	1.16	2.00	2.12
India	Bhopal	1,031	1,218	1,425	1,667	1,905	2,148	1.67	1.57	1.57	1.34	1.20	0.51	0.54
India	Chandigarh	564	667	791	937	1,083	1,232	1.68	1.70	1.70	1.45	1.28	0.28	0.31
India	Coimbatore	1,088	1,239	1,420	1,628	1,830	2,044	1.30	1.36	1.36	1.17	1.10	0.51	0.52
India	Delhi	8,207	10,093	12,441	15,335	18,215	20,884	2.07	2.09	2.09	1.72	1.37	4.46	5.27
India	Dhanbad	805	915	1,046	1,195	1,341	1,497	1.28	1.33	1.33	1.15	1.10	0.37	0.38
India	Durg-Bhilainagar	673	782	906	1,049	1,190	1,337	1.50	1.47	1.47	1.26	1.17	0.32	0.34
India	Faridabad	593	779	1,018	1,331	1,662	1,977	2.74	2.68	2.68	2.22	1.74	0.36	0.50
India	Ghaziabad	492	675	928	1,277	1,662	2,027	3.15	3.19	3.19	2.64	1.98	0.33	0.51
India	Guwahati	572	675	797	941	1,084	1,230	1.66	1.66	1.66	1.42	1.27	0.29	0.31
India	Gwalior	706	779	855	939	1,021	1,120	0.98	0.94	0.94	0.84	0.92	0.31	0.28
India	Hubli-Dharwad	639	705	776	854	931	1,023	0.97	0.96	0.96	0.86	0.94	0.28	0.26
India	Hyderabad	4,193	4,825	5,445	6,146	6,812	7,513	1.40	1.21	1.21	1.03	0.98	1.95	1.89
India	Indore	1,088	1,314	1,597	1,942	2,288	2,626	1.89	1.95	1.95	1.64	1.38	0.57	0.66
India	Jabalpur	880	982	1,100	1,234	1,363	1,508	1.10	1.14	1.14	1.00	1.01	0.39	0.38
India	Jaipur	1,478	1,826	2,259	2,796	3,339	3,860	2.11	2.13	2.13	1.78	1.45	0.81	0.97
India	Jamshedpur	817	938	1,081	1,246	1,408	1,578	1.37	1.42	1.42	1.22	1.14	0.39	0.40
India	Jodhpur	654	739	833	939	1,042	1,157	1.22	1.20	1.20	1.05	1.04	0.30	0.29
India	Kanpur	2,001	2,294	2,641	3,040	3,427	3,826	1.36	1.41	1.41	1.20	1.10	0.95	0.96
India	Kochi (Cochin)	1,103	1,229	1,340	1,461	1,578	1,721	1.09	0.86	0.86	0.77	0.87	0.48	0.43
India	Kolkata (Calcutta)	10,890	11,925	13,058	14,299	15,452	16,747	0.91	0.91	0.91	0.78	0.80	4.68	4.22
India	Kozhikode (Calicut)	781	835	875	917	960	1,030	0.66	0.47	0.47	0.46	0.70	0.31	0.26
India	Lucknow	1,614	1,906	2,221	2,589	2,947	3,312	1.66	1.53	1.53	1.30	1.17	0.80	0.84
India	Ludhiana	1,006	1,183	1,368	1,583	1,793	2,011	1.62	1.46	1.46	1.25	1.15	0.49	0.51
India	Madras	5,338	5,836	6,353	6,915	7,445	8,068	0.89	0.85	0.85	0.74	0.80	2.28	2.03
India	Madurai	1,073	1,132	1,187	1,245	1,305	1,398	0.53	0.48	0.48	0.47	0.69	0.43	0.35
India	Meerut	824	975	1,143	1,340	1,534	1,733	1.68	1.59	1.59	1.35	1.22	0.41	0.44
India	Mumbai (Bombay)	12,308	14,111	16,086	18,337	20,455	22,577	1.37	1.31	1.31	1.09	0.99	5.76	5.69
India	Mysore	640	708	776	851	925	1,014	1.01	0.92	0.92	0.83	0.92	0.28	0.26
India	Nagpur	1,637	1,849	2,089	2,359	2,621	2,902	1.22	1.22	1.22	1.05	1.02	0.75	0.73
India	Nashik	700	886	1,117	1,408	1,708	1,997	2.35	2.31	2.31	1.93	1.56	0.40	0.50
India	Patna	1,087	1,331	1,658	2,066	2,483	2,883	2.03	2.20	2.20	1.84	1.49	0.59	0.73
India	Pune (Poona)	2,430	2,978	3,655	4,485	5,318	6,112	2.03	2.05	2.05	1.70	1.39	1.31	1.54
India	Rajkot	638	787	974	1,205	1,442	1,672	2.10	2.13	2.13	1.79	1.48	0.35	0.42
India	Ranchi	607	712	844	999	1,155	1,312	1.60	1.69	1.69	1.44	1.28	0.30	0.33
India	Solapur	613	720	853	1,012	1,170	1,330	1.60	1.70	1.70	1.45	1.28	0.31	0.34
India	Srinagar	730	833	954	1,093	1,229	1,374	1.31	1.36	1.36	1.17	1.12	0.34	0.35
India	Surat	1,469	1,984	2,699	3,672	4,729	5,715	3.01	3.08	3.08	2.53	1.89	0.97	1.44
India	Thiruvananthapuram	801	853	885	918	954	1,018	0.63	0.37	0.37	0.38	0.65	0.32	0.26
India	Tiruchchirapalli	705	768	837	914	988	1,080	0.86	0.87	0.87	0.78	0.89	0.30	0.27
India	Vadodara	1,096	1,273	1,465	1,686	1,901	2,127	1.49	1.40	1.40	1.20	1.12	0.52	0.54
India	Varanasi (Benares)	1,013	1,106	1,199	1,300	1,398	1,522	0.87	0.81	0.81	0.73	0.85	0.43	0.38
India	Vijayawada	821	914	999	1,093	1,184	1,294	1.07	0.89	0.89	0.80	0.89	0.36	0.33
India	Visakhapatnam	1,018	1,168	1,309	1,468	1,623	1,794	1.37	1.15	1.15	1.00	1.00	0.47	0.45
Indonesia	Bandar Lampung (Tanj)	567	720	915	1,145	1,382	1,595	2.39	2.39	2.24	1.89	1.43	1.05	1.16
Indonesia	Bandung	2,460	2,896	3,409	4,008	4,646	5,245	1.63	1.63	1.62	1.48	1.21	3.92	3.81
Indonesia	Jakarta	7,650	9,161	11,018	13,156	15,341	17,268	1.80	1.85	1.77	1.54	1.18	12.67	12.55
Indonesia	Malang	620	698	787	896	1,023	1,155	1.20	1.20	1.29	1.33	1.22	0.91	0.84
Indonesia	Medan	1,537	1,699	1,879	2,103	2,371	2,655	1.01	1.01	1.13	1.20	1.13	2.16	1.93
Indonesia	Palembang	1,033	1,212	1,422	1,671	1,940	2,200	1.60	1.60	1.61	1.50	1.26	1.64	1.60
Indonesia	Semarang	804	795	787	814	877	969	-0.11	-0.11	0.33	0.75	0.99	0.91	0.70
Indonesia	Surabaja	2,062	2,253	2,461	2,727	3,055	3,407	0.89	0.89	1.03	1.13	1.09	2.83	2.48
Indonesia	Tegal	550	650	762	896	1,042	1,186	1.67	1.60	1.61	1.52	1.29	0.88	0.86
Indonesia	Ujung Pandang	816	926	1,051	1,202	1,375	1,552	1.27	1.27	1.34	1.35	1.21	1.21	1.13
Iran (Islamic Republic of)	Ahvaz	688	784	871	968	1,074	1,188	1.30	1.05	1.05	1.04	1.01	1.93	1.86
Iran (Islamic Republic of)	Esfahan	1,094	1,230	1,381	1,552	1,737	1,929	1.17	1.16	1.16	1.12	1.05	3.07	3.02
Iran (Islamic Republic of)	Karaj	394	779	1,044	1,200	1,368	1,538	6.83	2.93	1.39	1.31	1.17	2.32	2.41
Iran (Islamic Republic of)	Mashhad	1,681	1,854	1,990	2,135	2,302	2,498	0.98	0.70	0.70	0.75	0.82	4.42	3.92
Iran (Islamic Republic of)	Qom	625	744	888	1,061	1,247	1,428	1.75	1.77	1.77	1.62	1.36	1.97	2.24
Iran (Islamic Republic of)	Shiraz	946	1,030	1,124	1,227	1,341	1,471	0.85	0.87	0.87	0.89	0.92	2.50	2.31
Iran (Islamic Republic of)	Tabriz	1,058	1,165	1,274	1,393	1,526	1,674	0.96	0.90	0.90	0.91	0.93	2.83	2.63

TABLE C.1

continued

		Estimates and projections (000)						Annual rate of growth (%)					Share in country's urban population (%)	
		1990	1995	2000	2005	2010	2015	1990–1995	1995–2000	2000–2005	2005–2010	2010–2015	2000	2015
Iran (Islamic Republic of)	Teheran	6,360	6,687	6,979	7,285	7,669	8,178	0.50	0.43	0.43	0.51	0.64	15.50	12.82
Iraq	Baghdad	4,039	4,433	4,865	5,359	5,923	6,549	0.93	0.93	0.97	1.00	1.00	31.40	28.44
Iraq	Mosul	744	917	1,131	1,371	1,611	1,835	2.09	2.09	1.92	1.61	1.30	7.30	7.97
Israel	Tel-Aviv-Yafo	1,790	1,897	2,001	2,126	2,266	2,392	0.58	0.53	0.60	0.64	0.54	36.15	33.17
Japan	Hiroshima	842	855	866	871	875	876	0.15	0.13	0.06	0.04	0.02	0.87	0.84
Japan	Kitakyushu	2,487	2,619	2,750	2,844	2,902	2,926	0.52	0.49	0.34	0.20	0.08	2.75	2.81
Japan	Kyoto	1,760	1,804	1,849	1,876	1,893	1,899	0.25	0.25	0.15	0.09	0.03	1.85	1.83
Japan	Nagoya	2,948	3,055	3,157	3,225	3,267	3,283	0.36	0.33	0.21	0.13	0.05	3.15	3.16
Japan	Osaka	11,035	11,043	11,013	11,013	11,013	11,013	0.01	-0.03	-	-	-	11.00	10.59
Japan	Sapporo	1,561	1,685	1,813	1,914	1,976	2,002	0.76	0.74	0.54	0.32	0.13	1.81	1.93
Japan	Sendai	743	839	953	1,050	1,113	1,139	1.22	1.27	0.97	0.58	0.23	0.95	1.10
Japan	Tokyo	25,081	25,785	26,444	26,849	27,093	27,190	0.28	0.25	0.15	0.09	0.04	26.42	26.16
Jordan	Amman	940	986	1,148	1,309	1,478	1,654	0.48	1.52	1.32	1.21	1.13	29.68	28.37
Kazakhstan	Almaty	1,124	1,127	1,130	1,130	1,130	1,144	0.03	0.03	-	-	0.12	12.52	12.33
Kuwait	Kuwait City	896	859	879	935	1,028	1,136	-0.43	0.23	0.61	0.95	0.99	47.83	42.35
Lebanon	Beirut	1,582	1,823	2,070	2,276	2,416	2,500	1.42	1.27	0.95	0.60	0.34	65.96	63.98
Malaysia	Kuala Lumpur	1,120	1,236	1,379	1,542	1,717	1,882	0.98	1.10	1.12	1.08	0.92	10.81	10.15
Mongolia	Ulan Bator	572	661	764	838	912	993	1.45	1.45	0.93	0.85	0.85	53.28	54.09
Myanmar	Mandalay	615	683	770	877	1,004	1,134	1.04	1.20	1.30	1.35	1.22	5.83	5.59
Myanmar	Yangon	3,316	3,853	4,393	4,965	5,610	6,258	1.50	1.31	1.22	1.22	1.09	33.23	30.85
Pakistan	Faisalabad	1,520	1,805	2,142	2,535	2,992	3,526	1.71	1.71	1.69	1.66	1.64	4.58	4.38
Pakistan	Gujranwala	923	1,106	1,325	1,581	1,877	2,223	1.81	1.81	1.77	1.72	1.69	2.83	2.76
Pakistan	Hyderabad	950	1,077	1,221	1,394	1,613	1,891	1.25	1.25	1.33	1.46	1.59	2.61	2.35
Pakistan	Karachi	7,147	8,468	10,032	11,830	13,871	16,197	1.70	1.70	1.65	1.59	1.55	21.46	20.10
Pakistan	Lahore	3,970	4,653	5,452	6,379	7,458	8,721	1.59	1.59	1.57	1.56	1.57	11.66	10.82
Pakistan	Multan	953	1,097	1,263	1,460	1,702	2,000	1.41	1.41	1.45	1.53	1.62	2.70	2.48
Pakistan	Peshawar	769	905	1,066	1,256	1,481	1,750	1.64	1.64	1.63	1.65	1.67	2.28	2.17
Pakistan	Rawalpindi	1,087	1,286	1,521	1,796	2,119	2,500	1.68	1.68	1.66	1.65	1.66	3.25	3.10
Philippines	Davao	856	1,179	1,146	1,179	1,258	1,365	3.20	-0.29	0.29	0.65	0.81	2.59	2.06
Philippines	Metro Manila	7,973	9,402	9,950	10,684	11,618	12,579	1.65	0.57	0.71	0.84	0.79	22.46	19.01
Republic of Korea	Ansan	249	487	984	1,555	1,998	2,230	6.70	7.04	4.58	2.50	1.10	2.57	4.99
Republic of Korea	Inch'on	1,785	2,272	2,884	3,137	3,213	3,270	2.41	2.39	0.84	0.24	0.18	7.54	7.32
Republic of Korea	Kwangju	1,122	1,249	1,379	1,379	1,379	1,395	1.08	0.99	-	-	0.12	3.60	3.12
Republic of Korea	P'ohang	314	493	790	1,036	1,192	1,275	4.53	4.71	2.72	1.40	0.68	2.06	2.86
Republic of Korea	Puch'on	651	771	900	917	917	929	1.69	1.54	0.18	-	0.13	2.35	2.08
Republic of Korea	Pusan	3,778	3,813	3,830	3,830	3,830	3,857	0.09	0.04	-	-	0.07	10.01	8.64
Republic of Korea	Seoul	10,544	10,256	9,888	9,888	9,888	9,918	-0.28	-0.37	-	-	0.03	25.84	22.21
Republic of Korea	Songnam	534	842	1,353	1,779	2,045	2,184	4.55	4.74	2.74	1.39	0.66	3.54	4.89
Republic of Korea	Suwon	628	748	876	895	895	907	1.75	1.58	0.22	-	0.13	2.29	2.03
Republic of Korea	Taegu	2,215	2,434	2,675	2,675	2,675	2,698	0.94	0.94	-	-	0.09	6.99	6.04
Republic of Korea	Taejon	1,036	1,256	1,522	1,597	1,603	1,624	1.92	1.92	0.48	0.04	0.13	3.98	3.64
Republic of Korea	Ulsan	673	945	1,340	1,593	1,725	1,800	3.40	3.49	1.73	0.80	0.42	3.50	4.03
Saudi Arabia	Dammam	409	591	764	932	1,107	1,278	3.68	2.56	1.99	1.72	1.44	4.36	4.42
Saudi Arabia	Jidda	1,743	2,494	3,192	3,859	4,535	5,183	3.59	2.47	1.90	1.62	1.34	18.21	17.94
Saudi Arabia	Mecca	856	1,120	1,335	1,550	1,800	2,063	2.68	1.76	1.49	1.49	1.36	7.61	7.14
Saudi Arabia	Medina	529	722	891	1,058	1,241	1,429	3.11	2.10	1.71	1.60	1.41	5.08	4.94
Saudi Arabia	Riyadh	2,326	3,453	4,549	5,589	6,602	7,536	3.95	2.76	2.06	1.66	1.32	25.95	26.08
Singapore	Singapore	3,016	3,476	4,018	4,384	4,604	4,756	1.42	1.45	0.87	0.49	0.33	..	..
Syrian Arab Republic	Aleppo	1,554	1,870	2,229	2,622	3,046	3,489	1.85	1.76	1.63	1.50	1.36	26.78	25.96
Syrian Arab Republic	Damascus	1,732	1,920	2,144	2,425	2,775	3,170	1.03	1.10	1.23	1.35	1.33	25.76	23.59
Syrian Arab Republic	Homs	565	680	811	958	1,120	1,291	1.85	1.77	1.66	1.56	1.43	9.75	9.61
Thailand	Bangkok	5,901	6,596	7,372	8,140	8,937	9,816	1.11	1.11	0.99	0.93	0.94	59.20	55.89
Turkey	Adana	906	997	1,091	1,154	1,215	1,288	0.96	0.90	0.56	0.52	0.58	2.49	2.27
Turkey	Ankara	2,538	2,833	3,155	3,379	3,575	3,778	1.10	1.08	0.69	0.56	0.55	7.20	6.66
Turkey	Bursa	822	981	1,166	1,317	1,442	1,551	1.77	1.72	1.22	0.91	0.73	2.66	2.73
Turkey	Gaziantep	595	674	757	819	875	933	1.24	1.17	0.78	0.66	0.65	1.73	1.65
Turkey	Istanbul	6,544	7,662	8,953	9,946	10,722	11,362	1.58	1.56	1.05	0.75	0.58	20.42	20.03
Turkey	Izmir	1,740	1,965	2,214	2,393	2,548	2,704	1.22	1.19	0.78	0.63	0.59	5.05	4.77
United Arab Emirates	Dubai	478	651	886	1,029	1,145	1,229	3.08	3.08	1.50	1.06	0.71	39.21	41.55
Uzbekistan	Tashkent	2,074	2,111	2,148	2,197	2,277	2,428	0.18	0.18	0.22	0.36	0.64	23.50	20.72
Viet Nam	Hai Phong	1,471	1,570	1,676	1,814	2,007	2,269	0.65	0.65	0.79	1.01	1.23	8.91	7.60
Viet Nam	Hanoi	3,127	3,424	3,751	4,140	4,624	5,227	0.91	0.91	0.99	1.11	1.23	19.93	17.51
Viet Nam	Ho Chi Minh City	3,996	4,296	4,619	5,021	5,555	6,251	0.72	0.72	0.84	1.01	1.18	24.55	20.94
Yemen	Sana'a	678	965	1,327	1,777	2,328	3,028	3.53	3.19	2.92	2.70	2.63	29.27	29.35
EUROPE														
Austria	Vienna	2,055	2,060	2,065	2,068	2,069	2,069	0.03	0.02	0.01	0.01	0.00	37.98	37.15
Belarus	Minsk	1,617	1,692	1,667	1,667	1,667	1,667	0.46	-0.15	-	-	-	23.57	23.75
Belgium	Brussels	1,148	1,140	1,135	1,135	1,135	1,135	-0.07	-0.05	-	-	-	11.38	11.27
Bulgaria	Sofia	1,191	1,191	1,187	1,187	1,187	1,187	0.01	-0.03	-	-	-	22.14	25.13
Croatia	Zagreb	849	981	1,067	1,124	1,161	1,183	1.45	0.84	0.52	0.32	0.19	39.74	39.75
Czech Republic	Prague	1,207	1,214	1,203	1,203	1,203	1,203	0.05	-0.09	-	-	-	15.71	15.70
Denmark	Copenhagen	1,337	1,335	1,332	1,330	1,330	1,330	-0.02	-0.02	-0.02	-	-	29.43	28.89
Finland	Helsinki	872	943	937	937	937	937	0.78	-0.06	-	-	-	30.73	30.68
France	Lille	960	976	991	1,007	1,022	1,036	0.16	0.16	0.16	0.15	0.13	2.22	2.14
France	Lyon	1,265	1,309	1,353	1,394	1,425	1,446	0.34	0.34	0.30	0.22	0.15	3.03	2.98
France	Marseille	1,233	1,261	1,290	1,318	1,341	1,358	0.23	0.23	0.21	0.17	0.13	2.89	2.80
France	Paris	9,329	9,478	9,630	9,753	9,828	9,858	0.16	0.16	0.13	0.08	0.03	21.57	20.32
France	Toulouse	654	705	761	812	849	871	0.76	0.76	0.64	0.45	0.26	1.70	1.80

Country	City													
Germany	Aachen	1,001	1,040	1,060	1,069	1,070	1,070	0.39	0.19	0.08	0.02	-	1.48	1.48
Germany	Berlin	3,288	3,317	3,319	3,320	3,320	3,320	0.09	0.01	0.00	0.00	-	4.62	4.58
Germany	Bielefeld	1,201	1,262	1,294	1,307	1,310	1,310	0.49	0.25	0.10	0.02	-	1.80	1.81
Germany	Bremen	840	866	880	885	886	886	0.31	0.15	0.06	0.01	-	1.23	1.22
Germany	Hamburg	2,540	2,624	2,664	2,680	2,683	2,683	0.33	0.15	0.06	0.01	-	3.71	3.70
Germany	Hannover	1,230	1,267	1,283	1,290	1,291	1,291	0.29	0.13	0.05	0.01	-	1.79	1.78
Germany	Karlsruhe	912	954	977	986	988	988	0.45	0.23	0.09	0.02	-	1.36	1.36
Germany	Munich	2,134	2,237	2,291	2,313	2,317	2,317	0.47	0.24	0.09	0.02	-	3.19	3.19
Germany	Nuremberg	1,106	1,160	1,189	1,201	1,204	1,204	0.48	0.25	0.10	0.02	-	1.66	1.66
Germany	Rhein-Main[3]	3,456	3,605	3,681	3,712	3,718	3,718	0.42	0.21	0.08	0.02	-	5.13	5.13
Germany	Rhein-Neckar[4]	1,503	1,570	1,605	1,618	1,621	1,621	0.44	0.22	0.09	0.02	-	2.23	2.24
Germany	Rhein-Ruhr Middle[5]	2,700	3,030	3,233	3,317	3,335	3,335	1.16	0.65	0.26	0.05	-	4.50	4.60
Germany	Rhein-Ruhr North[6]	6,353	6,482	6,531	6,550	6,554	6,554	0.20	0.07	0.03	0.01	-	9.10	9.04
Germany	Rhein-Ruhr South[7]	2,855	2,984	3,050	3,077	3,082	3,082	0.44	0.22	0.09	0.02	-	4.25	4.25
Germany	Saarland[8]	878	888	891	892	892	892	0.11	0.03	0.01	0.00	-	1.24	1.23
Germany	Stuttgart	2,485	2,608	2,672	2,698	2,703	2,703	0.48	0.24	0.10	0.02	-	3.72	3.73
Greece	Athens	3,070	3,093	3,116	3,131	3,137	3,138	0.08	0.07	0.05	0.02	0.00	48.87	46.04
Greece	Thessaloniki	746	768	789	806	817	825	0.30	0.27	0.21	0.14	0.10	12.38	12.11
Hungary	Budapest	2,009	1,911	1,819	1,819	1,819	1,819	-0.50	-0.50	-	-	-	28.27	28.32
Ireland	Dublin	916	947	985	1,028	1,083	1,149	0.32	0.40	0.43	0.52	0.59	43.88	40.71
Italy	Florence	820	778	778	778	778	778	-0.53	-	-	-	-	2.02	1.99
Italy	Genoa	943	890	890	890	890	890	-0.58	-	-	-	-	2.31	2.28
Italy	Milan	4,603	4,251	4,251	4,251	4,251	4,251	-0.79	-	-	-	-	11.04	10.90
Italy	Naples	3,210	3,012	3,012	3,012	3,012	3,012	-0.64	-	-	-	-	7.82	7.72
Italy	Rome	2,807	2,649	2,649	2,649	2,649	2,649	-0.58	-	-	-	-	6.88	6.79
Italy	Turin	1,394	1,294	1,294	1,294	1,294	1,294	-0.75	-	-	-	-	3.36	3.32
Latvia	Riga	892	833	761	761	761	761	-0.69	-0.91	-	-	-	52.00	56.57
Netherlands	Amsterdam	1,053	1,102	1,105	1,110	1,113	1,115	0.45	0.03	0.04	0.03	0.01	7.78	7.46
Netherlands	Rotterdam	1,047	1,078	1,078	1,080	1,082	1,082	0.29	0.00	0.02	0.02	0.01	7.59	7.24
Norway	Oslo	684	729	779	807	822	836	0.64	0.66	0.35	0.19	0.17	23.34	22.69
Poland	Gdansk	857	875	893	900	906	913	0.20	0.20	0.09	0.07	0.07	3.71	3.61
Poland	Katowice	3,357	3,425	3,494	3,523	3,540	3,547	0.20	0.20	0.08	0.05	0.02	14.52	14.02
Poland	Krakow	806	832	859	874	884	892	0.31	0.31	0.17	0.12	0.09	3.57	3.53
Poland	Lodz	1,030	1,041	1,053	1,054	1,056	1,061	0.11	0.11	0.01	0.02	0.04	4.38	4.19
Poland	Warsaw	2,165	2,219	2,274	2,302	2,318	2,325	0.25	0.25	0.12	0.07	0.03	9.45	9.19
Portugal	Lisbon	2,434	3,363	3,861	4,232	4,472	4,544	3.23	1.38	0.92	0.55	0.16	59.83	58.46
Portugal	Porto	1,107	1,615	1,940	2,189	2,347	2,400	3.78	1.83	1.21	0.70	0.22	30.06	30.88
Romania	Bucharest	2,054	2,040	2,001	2,001	2,001	2,001	-0.07	-0.19	-	-	-	16.19	15.75
Russian Federation	Chelyabinsk	1,125	1,084	1,045	1,008	1,008	1,008	-0.37	-0.37	-0.37	-	-	0.99	1.02
Russian Federation	Ekaterinburg	1,338	1,277	1,218	1,162	1,162	1,162	-0.47	-0.47	-0.47	-	-	1.15	1.18
Russian Federation	Kazan	1,089	1,076	1,063	1,051	1,051	1,051	-0.12	-0.12	-0.12	-	-	1.00	1.07
Russian Federation	Krasnoyarsk	901	870	840	811	811	811	-0.35	-0.35	-0.35	-	-	0.79	0.82
Russian Federation	Moscow	8,837	8,599	8,367	8,141	8,141	8,141	-0.27	-0.27	-0.27	-	-	7.89	8.25
Russian Federation	Nizhni Novgorod	1,420	1,376	1,332	1,290	1,290	1,290	-0.32	-0.32	-0.32	-	-	1.26	1.31
Russian Federation	Novosibirsk	1,416	1,368	1,321	1,276	1,276	1,276	-0.35	-0.35	-0.35	-	-	1.25	1.29
Russian Federation	Omsk	1,149	1,161	1,174	1,187	1,187	1,187	0.11	0.11	0.11	-	-	1.11	1.20
Russian Federation	Perm	1,072	1,031	991	952	952	952	-0.40	-0.40	-0.40	-	-	0.93	0.97
Russian Federation	Rostov-on-Don	1,016	1,014	1,012	1,009	1,009	1,009	-0.02	-0.02	-0.02	-	-	0.95	1.02
Russian Federation	Saint Petersburg	4,944	4,787	4,635	4,488	4,488	4,488	-0.32	-0.32	-0.32	-	-	4.37	4.55
Russian Federation	Samara	1,238	1,184	1,132	1,083	1,083	1,083	-0.45	-0.45	-0.45	-	-	1.07	1.10
Russian Federation	Saratov	901	891	881	871	871	871	-0.11	-0.11	-0.11	-	-	0.83	0.88
Russian Federation	Tolyatti	644	705	771	843	886	899	0.89	0.89	0.89	0.50	0.14	0.73	0.91
Russian Federation	Ufa	1,084	1,093	1,102	1,110	1,110	1,110	0.08	0.08	0.08	-	-	1.04	1.13
Russian Federation	Ulyanovsk	647	748	864	999	1,098	1,144	1.45	1.45	1.45	0.95	0.41	0.81	1.16
Russian Federation	Volgograd	998	999	1,000	1,000	1,000	1,000	0.01	0.01	0.01	-	-	0.94	1.01
Russian Federation	Voronezh	888	903	918	934	934	934	0.17	0.17	0.17	-	-	0.87	0.95
Serbia and Montenegro	Belgrade	1,322	1,483	1,673	1,673	1,673	1,680	1.15	1.20	-	-	0.04	30.74	29.37
Spain	Barcelona	2,913	2,819	2,729	2,729	2,729	2,729	-0.33	-0.33	-	-	-	8.81	8.62
Spain	Madrid	4,172	4,072	3,976	3,976	3,976	3,976	-0.24	-0.24	-	-	-	12.84	12.56
Sweden	Göteborg	729	753	778	803	808	808	0.32	0.32	0.32	0.06	-	10.56	11.12
Sweden	Stockholm	1,487	1,548	1,612	1,678	1,700	1,704	0.40	0.40	0.40	0.13	0.02	21.89	23.47
Switzerland	Zürich	834	926	939	945	947	947	1.05	0.14	0.06	0.02	0.01	19.43	19.55
Ukraine	Dnepropetrovsk	1,169	1,149	1,069	1,069	1,069	1,069	-0.18	-0.72	-	-	-	3.18	3.50
Ukraine	Donetsk	1,104	1,089	1,007	1,007	1,007	1,007	-0.13	-0.79	-	-	-	2.99	3.30
Ukraine	Kharkov	1,591	1,558	1,416	1,416	1,416	1,416	-0.21	-0.95	-	-	-	4.21	4.64
Ukraine	Kiev	2,582	2,626	2,499	2,499	2,499	2,499	0.17	-0.50	-	-	-	7.42	8.19
Ukraine	Lvov	789	801	764	764	764	764	0.15	-0.47	-	-	-	2.27	2.50
Ukraine	Odessa	1,089	1,050	931	931	931	931	-0.36	-1.20	-	-	-	2.77	3.05
Ukraine	Zaporozhye	880	879	813	813	813	813	-0.01	-0.79	-	-	-	2.41	2.66
United Kingdom	Birmingham	2,301	2,272	2,272	2,272	2,272	2,272	-0.13	-	-	-	-	4.27	4.13
United Kingdom	Leeds	1,449	1,433	1,433	1,433	1,433	1,433	-0.11	-	-	-	-	2.69	2.61
United Kingdom	Liverpool	831	876	915	939	949	951	0.53	0.43	0.26	0.10	0.02	1.72	1.73
United Kingdom	London	7,653	7,640	7,640	7,640	7,640	7,640	-0.02	-	-	-	-	14.37	13.90
United Kingdom	Manchester	2,282	2,252	2,252	2,252	2,252	2,252	-0.13	-	-	-	-	4.24	4.10
United Kingdom	Tyneside (Newcastle)	877	933	981	1,011	1,023	1,026	0.62	0.50	0.30	0.12	0.02	1.85	1.87

LATIN AMERICA AND THE CARIBBEAN

Country	City													
Argentina	Buenos Aires	11,180	11,620	12,024	12,439	12,844	13,185	0.39	0.34	0.34	0.32	0.26	36.81	33.59
Argentina	Córdoba	1,188	1,278	1,368	1,458	1,542	1,613	0.73	0.68	0.64	0.56	0.45	4.19	4.11
Argentina	Mendoza	758	842	934	1,025	1,104	1,165	1.06	1.03	0.93	0.75	0.54	2.86	2.97
Argentina	Rosario	1,105	1,189	1,279	1,370	1,453	1,523	0.73	0.73	0.68	0.59	0.46	3.92	3.88
Argentina	San Miguel de Tucumán	611	694	792	889	972	1,032	1.27	1.32	1.16	0.89	0.60	2.42	2.63
Bolivia	La Paz	1,062	1,267	1,460	1,662	1,879	2,098	1.77	1.42	1.30	1.23	1.10	28.11	26.76
Bolivia	Santa Cruz	616	833	1,062	1,286	1,492	1,676	3.02	2.42	1.91	1.49	1.16	20.45	21.37
Brazil	Belém	1,295	1,465	1,658	1,877	2,031	2,158	1.24	1.24	1.24	0.79	0.61	1.20	1.22
Brazil	Belo Horizonte	3,339	3,755	4,224	4,752	5,110	5,395	1.18	1.18	1.18	0.73	0.54	3.05	3.05
Brazil	Brasilia	1,550	1,768	2,016	2,299	2,503	2,667	1.31	1.31	1.31	0.85	0.64	1.46	1.51
Brazil	Campinas	1,342	1,595	1,895	2,251	2,532	2,752	1.72	1.72	1.72	1.18	0.83	1.37	1.56
Brazil	Campo Grande	495	638	821	1,057	1,269	1,437	2.53	2.53	2.53	1.83	1.24	0.59	0.81
Brazil	Curitiba	1,934	2,226	2,562	2,949	3,233	3,457	1.41	1.41	1.41	0.92	0.67	1.85	1.96

TABLE C.1

continued

		Estimates and projections (000)						Annual rate of growth (%)					Share in country's urban population (%)	
		1990	1995	2000	2005	2010	2015	1990–1995	1995–2000	2000–2005	2005–2010	2010–2015	2000	2015
Brazil	Fortaleza	2,218	2,608	3,066	3,605	4,018	4,338	1.62	1.62	1.62	1.09	0.76	2.22	2.46
Brazil	Goiânia	898	1,001	1,117	1,245	1,333	1,409	1.09	1.09	1.09	0.68	0.55	0.81	0.80
Brazil	Maceió	600	729	886	1,076	1,234	1,359	1.95	1.95	1.95	1.36	0.97	0.64	0.77
Brazil	Manaus	962	1,188	1,467	1,811	2,101	2,328	2.11	2.11	2.11	1.49	1.02	1.06	1.32
Brazil	Natal	584	686	806	947	1,057	1,147	1.61	1.61	1.61	1.10	0.81	0.58	0.65
Brazil	Porto Alegre	2,949	3,328	3,757	4,240	4,573	4,838	1.21	1.21	1.21	0.76	0.56	2.72	2.74
Brazil	Recife	2,814	3,068	3,346	3,648	3,828	3,986	0.87	0.87	0.87	0.48	0.40	2.42	2.26
Brazil	Rio de Janeiro	9,689	10,159	10,652	11,170	11,342	11,543	0.47	0.47	0.47	0.15	0.18	7.70	6.54
Brazil	Salvador	2,409	2,793	3,238	3,754	4,138	4,436	1.48	1.48	1.48	0.97	0.70	2.34	2.51
Brazil	Santos	1,077	1,169	1,270	1,379	1,444	1,506	0.82	0.82	0.82	0.46	0.42	0.92	0.85
Brazil	São José dos Campos	633	784	972	1,205	1,403	1,560	2.15	2.15	2.15	1.52	1.06	0.70	0.88
Brazil	São Luís	665	803	968	1,167	1,330	1,459	1.87	1.87	1.87	1.30	0.93	0.70	0.83
Brazil	São Paulo	15,100	16,469	17,962	19,591	20,514	21,229	0.87	0.87	0.87	0.46	0.34	12.99	12.02
Brazil	Teresina	571	696	848	1,034	1,187	1,310	1.98	1.98	1.98	1.39	0.98	0.61	0.74
Chile	Santiago	4,572	5,029	5,467	5,867	6,216	6,495	0.95	0.84	0.71	0.58	0.44	41.90	40.71
Colombia	Barranquilla	1,244	1,396	1,683	1,918	2,134	2,323	1.15	1.87	1.31	1.06	0.85	5.33	5.42
Colombia	Bogotá	4,970	5,716	6,771	7,596	8,334	8,970	1.40	1.69	1.15	0.93	0.74	21.45	20.95
Colombia	Bucaramanga	648	777	937	1,069	1,192	1,302	1.81	1.87	1.32	1.09	0.88	2.97	3.04
Colombia	Cali	1,591	1,819	2,233	2,583	2,896	3,158	1.34	2.06	1.46	1.14	0.87	7.08	7.38
Colombia	Cartagena	576	667	845	1,002	1,144	1,262	1.48	2.36	1.71	1.32	0.98	2.68	2.95
Colombia	Cucuta	520	637	772	883	987	1,080	2.03	1.91	1.35	1.11	0.90	2.44	2.52
Colombia	Medellín	2,147	2,403	2,866	3,237	3,575	3,872	1.13	1.76	1.22	0.99	0.80	9.08	9.04
Costa Rica	San José	767	858	961	1,080	1,211	1,343	1.13	1.13	1.17	1.15	1.03	40.47	38.57
Cuba	Havana	2,108	2,183	2,256	2,306	2,342	2,365	0.35	0.33	0.22	0.16	0.10	26.74	25.89
Dominican Republic	Santiago de los Caballeros	643	718	804	897	988	1,064	1.10	1.13	1.10	0.96	0.74	14.68	14.37
Dominican Republic	Santo Domingo	1,952	2,242	2,563	2,889	3,177	3,397	1.38	1.34	1.20	0.95	0.67	46.82	45.89
Ecuador	Guayaquil	1,491	1,843	2,118	2,359	2,592	2,819	2.12	1.39	1.08	0.94	0.84	26.58	25.50
Ecuador	Quito	1,088	1,376	1,616	1,832	2,037	2,228	2.35	1.61	1.26	1.06	0.90	20.28	20.16
El Salvador	San Salvador	970	1,140	1,341	1,533	1,707	1,877	1.62	1.62	1.34	1.08	0.95	35.42	32.12
Guatemala	Guatemala City	1,676	2,577	3,242	3,869	4,542	5,268	4.30	2.30	1.77	1.60	1.48	71.80	69.88
Haiti	Port-au-Prince	1,134	1,427	1,769	2,117	2,487	2,864	2.30	2.14	1.80	1.61	1.41	60.86	61.53
Honduras	Tegucigalpa	711	814	949	1,120	1,311	1,492	1.36	1.53	1.66	1.57	1.29	28.04	26.65
Mexico	Ciudad Juárez	809	997	1,239	1,462	1,646	1,781	2.10	2.17	1.66	1.18	0.79	1.68	1.92
Mexico	Culiacán	606	690	750	796	842	892	1.30	0.83	0.60	0.56	0.57	1.02	0.96
Mexico	Guadalajara	3,011	3,431	3,697	3,889	4,072	4,265	1.31	0.75	0.50	0.46	0.46	5.03	4.59
Mexico	León	961	1,127	1,293	1,432	1,551	1,654	1.60	1.38	1.02	0.80	0.64	1.76	1.78
Mexico	Mérida	664	765	849	915	977	1,038	1.42	1.04	0.76	0.65	0.60	1.15	1.12
Mexico	Mexicali	607	690	771	837	897	954	1.29	1.11	0.82	0.69	0.62	1.05	1.03
Mexico	Mexico City	15,311	16,791	18,066	18,934	19,694	20,434	0.92	0.73	0.47	0.39	0.37	24.57	22.01
Mexico	Monterrey	2,594	2,961	3,267	3,502	3,710	3,906	1.32	0.98	0.70	0.58	0.51	4.44	4.21
Mexico	Puebla	1,699	1,932	1,888	1,888	1,922	1,997	1.28	-0.23	-	0.18	0.38	2.57	2.15
Mexico	Querétaro	561	671	798	909	1,003	1,079	1.79	1.72	1.31	0.98	0.73	1.08	1.16
Mexico	San Luis Potosí	665	774	857	924	985	1,046	1.52	1.02	0.75	0.65	0.60	1.17	1.13
Mexico	Tijuana	761	1,017	1,297	1,564	1,781	1,937	2.91	2.43	1.87	1.30	0.84	1.76	2.09
Mexico	Toluca	835	981	1,455	1,979	2,423	2,707	1.61	3.94	3.07	2.02	1.11	1.98	2.92
Mexico	Torreón	882	954	1,012	1,053	1,099	1,157	0.78	0.59	0.40	0.43	0.51	1.38	1.25
Nicaragua	Managua	735	870	1,009	1,166	1,342	1,529	1.68	1.49	1.45	1.41	1.30	35.45	33.85
Panama	Panama City	848	998	1,173	1,299	1,424	1,543	1.62	1.62	1.02	0.92	0.80	73.04	72.44
Paraguay	Asunción	928	1,081	1,262	1,472	1,711	1,959	1.53	1.55	1.54	1.50	1.35	41.03	38.79
Peru	Lima	5,826	6,667	7,443	8,185	8,843	9,388	1.35	1.10	0.95	0.77	0.60	39.86	37.82
Puerto Rico	San Juan	1,226	1,305	1,388	1,466	1,532	1,584	0.62	0.62	0.55	0.44	0.33	47.12	45.13
Uruguay	Montevideo	1,274	1,299	1,324	1,352	1,383	1,411	0.19	0.19	0.21	0.22	0.20	43.16	40.74
Venezuela	Barquisimeto	743	828	923	1,005	1,085	1,164	1.09	1.09	0.85	0.76	0.71	4.39	4.19
Venezuela	Caracas	2,867	3,007	3,153	3,261	3,403	3,587	0.47	0.47	0.34	0.43	0.53	15.01	12.91
Venezuela	Ciudad Guayana	494	628	799	966	1,111	1,223	2.40	2.40	1.90	1.40	0.96	3.80	4.40
Venezuela	Maracaibo	1,351	1,603	1,901	2,172	2,408	2,604	1.71	1.71	1.33	1.03	0.78	9.05	9.37
Venezuela	Maracay	795	935	1,100	1,249	1,383	1,498	1.62	1.62	1.27	1.01	0.80	5.24	5.39
Venezuela	Valencia	1,129	1,462	1,893	2,320	2,682	2,948	2.58	2.58	2.03	1.45	0.95	9.01	10.61
NORTHERN AMERICA														
Canada	Calgary	738	809	953	1,070	1,164	1,228	0.92	1.63	1.16	0.84	0.54	3.94	4.36
Canada	Edmonton	831	859	944	1,004	1,056	1,101	0.33	0.95	0.61	0.51	0.41	3.90	3.90
Canada	Montréal	3,154	3,306	3,480	3,566	3,659	3,754	0.47	0.52	0.24	0.26	0.26	14.38	13.32
Canada	Ottawa	918	998	1,081	1,135	1,185	1,231	0.84	0.80	0.49	0.43	0.38	4.47	4.37
Canada	Toronto	3,807	4,197	4,752	5,157	5,471	5,679	0.98	1.24	0.82	0.59	0.37	19.63	20.14
Canada	Vancouver	1,559	1,789	2,049	2,247	2,404	2,513	1.38	1.36	0.92	0.68	0.44	8.46	8.92
United States	Atlanta	2,174	2,464	2,706	2,874	2,994	3,100	1.25	0.94	0.60	0.41	0.35	1.24	1.19
United States	Austin	568	671	759	821	864	903	1.68	1.23	0.78	0.51	0.44	0.35	0.35
United States	Baltimore	1,893	1,968	2,053	2,140	2,224	2,308	0.39	0.42	0.41	0.39	0.37	0.94	0.89
United States	Boston	2,778	2,842	2,934	3,039	3,149	3,260	0.23	0.32	0.35	0.35	0.35	1.34	1.25
United States	Buffalo-Niagra Falls	953	963	990	1,028	1,073	1,119	0.10	0.27	0.38	0.42	0.42	0.45	0.43
United States	Chicago	6,792	6,849	6,989	7,181	7,390	7,603	0.08	0.20	0.27	0.29	0.28	3.20	2.92
United States	Cincinnati	1,215	1,265	1,323	1,382	1,441	1,500	0.41	0.45	0.44	0.42	0.40	0.61	0.58
United States	Cleveland	1,676	1,692	1,735	1,796	1,867	1,940	0.10	0.25	0.35	0.38	0.38	0.79	0.75
United States	Columbus	948	1,007	1,067	1,121	1,172	1,222	0.61	0.57	0.50	0.44	0.42	0.49	0.47
United States	Dallas	3,220	3,612	3,937	4,163	4,323	4,465	1.15	0.86	0.56	0.38	0.32	1.80	1.72
United States	Denver	1,522	1,610	1,698	1,778	1,852	1,924	0.56	0.53	0.46	0.41	0.38	0.78	0.74
United States	Detroit	3,695	3,726	3,809	3,927	4,058	4,193	0.08	0.22	0.30	0.33	0.33	1.74	1.61

Country	City													
United States	Fort Lauderdale	1,245	1,364	1,471	1,555	1,624	1,689	0.92	0.75	0.56	0.43	0.39	0.67	0.65
United States	Houston	2,915	3,166	3,386	3,556	3,690	3,816	0.83	0.67	0.49	0.37	0.33	1.55	1.47
United States	Indianapolis	917	960	1,008	1,056	1,104	1,151	0.46	0.49	0.47	0.44	0.42	0.46	0.44
United States	Jacksonville	742	816	883	937	982	1,025	0.95	0.79	0.59	0.47	0.43	0.40	0.39
United States	Kansas City	1,280	1,373	1,460	1,536	1,602	1,667	0.70	0.62	0.50	0.42	0.39	0.67	0.64
United States	Las Vegas	706	863	995	1,083	1,139	1,188	2.02	1.42	0.84	0.51	0.42	0.46	0.46
United States	Los Angeles	11,456	12,418	13,213	13,766	14,154	14,494	0.81	0.62	0.41	0.28	0.24	6.04	5.57
United States	Louisville	755	763	785	816	853	891	0.11	0.28	0.40	0.44	0.44	0.36	0.34
United States	Memphis	827	857	894	935	977	1,020	0.36	0.43	0.45	0.44	0.43	0.41	0.39
United States	Miami-Hialeah	1,923	2,081	2,224	2,339	2,434	2,524	0.79	0.66	0.50	0.40	0.36	1.02	0.97
United States	Milwaukee	1,227	1,247	1,285	1,335	1,391	1,448	0.16	0.30	0.38	0.41	0.40	0.59	0.56
United States	Minneapolis	2,088	2,238	2,378	2,494	2,593	2,688	0.70	0.60	0.48	0.39	0.36	1.09	1.03
United States	New Orleans	1,039	1,050	1,079	1,120	1,168	1,217	0.10	0.27	0.38	0.42	0.42	0.49	0.47
United States	New York	16,056	16,343	16,732	17,147	17,551	17,944	0.18	0.24	0.25	0.23	0.22	7.65	6.90
United States	Norfolk	1,341	1,681	1,963	2,140	2,245	2,329	2.26	1.55	0.86	0.48	0.37	0.90	0.90
United States	Oklahoma City	787	845	901	951	995	1,039	0.71	0.64	0.53	0.46	0.43	0.41	0.40
United States	Orlando	897	1,076	1,226	1,326	1,392	1,449	1.82	1.30	0.78	0.49	0.40	0.56	0.56
United States	Philadelphia	4,225	4,305	4,427	4,571	4,721	4,873	0.19	0.28	0.32	0.32	0.32	2.02	1.87
United States	Phoenix	2,024	2,353	2,623	2,804	2,925	3,029	1.51	1.09	0.67	0.42	0.35	1.20	1.16
United States	Pittsburgh	1,676	1,692	1,735	1,796	1,867	1,939	0.10	0.25	0.35	0.38	0.38	0.79	0.75
United States	Portland	1,176	1,253	1,328	1,395	1,456	1,516	0.63	0.58	0.49	0.43	0.40	0.61	0.58
United States	Providence	848	878	916	957	1,000	1,044	0.35	0.42	0.45	0.44	0.43	0.42	0.40
United States	Riverside	1,185	1,466	1,699	1,848	1,938	2,013	2.13	1.47	0.84	0.48	0.38	0.78	0.77
United States	Sacramento	1,106	1,270	1,408	1,506	1,576	1,640	1.38	1.03	0.67	0.46	0.40	0.64	0.63
United States	Salt Lake City	793	853	911	962	1,007	1,051	0.74	0.66	0.54	0.46	0.43	0.42	0.40
United States	San Antonio	1,134	1,230	1,318	1,391	1,453	1,513	0.81	0.69	0.54	0.44	0.40	0.60	0.58
United States	San Diego	2,367	2,716	3,002	3,197	3,329	3,445	1.37	1.00	0.63	0.41	0.34	1.37	1.32
United States	San Francisco	3,641	3,866	4,077	4,253	4,404	4,548	0.60	0.53	0.42	0.35	0.32	1.86	1.75
United States	San Jose	1,440	1,540	1,635	1,717	1,790	1,860	0.67	0.60	0.49	0.41	0.39	0.75	0.71
United States	Seattle	1,754	1,938	2,097	2,217	2,311	2,397	1.00	0.79	0.56	0.41	0.37	0.96	0.92
United States	St. Louis	1,949	2,008	2,084	2,166	2,250	2,335	0.30	0.37	0.39	0.38	0.37	0.95	0.90
United States	Tampa	1,719	1,904	2,064	2,184	2,276	2,362	1.02	0.81	0.56	0.41	0.37	0.94	0.91
United States	Washington, DC	3,380	3,687	3,952	4,151	4,305	4,446	0.87	0.69	0.49	0.36	0.32	1.81	1.71
United States	West Palm Beach	805	989	1,143	1,244	1,309	1,363	2.07	1.45	0.85	0.50	0.41	0.52	0.52
OCEANIA														
Australia	Adelaide	1,019	1,041	1,064	1,094	1,133	1,173	0.21	0.22	0.29	0.35	0.35	6.13	5.65
Australia	Brisbane	1,303	1,453	1,622	1,790	1,930	2,027	1.09	1.10	0.99	0.75	0.49	9.34	9.75
Australia	Melbourne	3,003	3,112	3,232	3,363	3,494	3,605	0.36	0.38	0.40	0.38	0.32	18.61	17.35
Australia	Perth	1,123	1,221	1,329	1,438	1,533	1,605	0.84	0.85	0.79	0.64	0.45	7.66	7.72
Australia	Sydney	3,524	3,696	3,907	4,124	4,319	4,467	0.48	0.56	0.54	0.46	0.34	22.51	21.50
New Zealand	Auckland	870	976	1,102	1,244	1,340	1,403	1.15	1.22	1.22	0.74	0.46	33.98	38.74

Notes: 1 For statistical purposes, the data for China do not include Hong Kong and Macao Special Administrative Regions (SAR) of China. 2 As of 1 July 1997, Hong Kong became a SAR of China. 3 The Rhein-Main agglomeration includes Darmstadt, Frankfurt am Main, Offenbach and Wiesbaden. 4 The Rhein-Neckar agglomeration includes Ludwigshafen am Rhein, Heidelberg, Mannheim, Frankenthal (Pfalz), Neustadt an der Weinstrasse and Speyer. 5 The Rhein-Ruhr Middle agglomeration includes Düsseldorf, Mönchengladbach, Remscheid, Solingen and Wuppertal. 6 The Rhein-Ruhr North agglomeration includes Duisburg, Essen, Krefeld, Mühlheim an der Ruhr, Oberhausen, Bottrop, Gelsenkirchen, Bochum, Dortmund, Hagen, Hamm and Herne. 7 The Rhein-Ruhr South agglomeration includes Bonn, Cologne and Leverkusen. 8 The Saarland agglomeration includes Neunkirchen, Saarbrücken and Saarlouis.

Source: United Nations, *World Urbanization Prospects, 2001 Revision.*

TABLE C.2

Household Living Conditions, Selected Cities

				Distribution by size of housings units								Persons per room in housing unit								
		Year	Total number*	1	2	3	4	5	6	7	8+	Average	1	2	3	4	5	6	7	8+
AFRICA																				
Egypt[1]	Alexandria	1996	3,321,844	5.7	12.4	38.5	31.4	12.0	...	...	...	1.3	3.5	2.0	1.4	1.1	0.9	...	...	...
Egypt[1]	Cairo	1996	6,735,172	7.0	11.5	37.3	33.4	10.8	...	...	...	1.2	3.5	2.0	1.4	1.0	0.8	...	...	...
Egypt[1]	Giza	1996	2,203,688	4.7	9.0	39.5	37.1	9.7	...	...	...	1.2	3.6	2.1	1.4	1.0	0.8	...	...	...
Egypt[1]	Shubra El-Kheima	1996	869,853	5.6	10.1	44.8	35.0	4.5	...	...	...	1.4	3.7	2.2	1.5	1.1	1.0	...	...	...
ASIA																				
Azerbaijan	Baku	1998	1,721,372	9.5	36.5	41.2	12.8	...	...	...	...	1.6	2.1	1.6	1.5	1.5	...	...	...	...
Azerbaijan	Giandja	1998	279,043	18.9	35.4	30.5	15.2	...	...	...	...	2.1	3.0	2.1	1.9	1.8	...	...	...	...
Azerbaijan[2]	Mingecheviz	1998	86,294	6.5	30.2	37.2	26.1	...	...	...	...	1.7	2.1	1.7	1.6	1.9	...	...	...	...
Azerbaijan	Sumgait	1998	320,731	15.1	39.1	40.8	5.0	...	...	...	...	2.0	2.7	2.1	1.7	1.6	...	...	...	...
Cyprus[3]	Larnaka	1992	59,832	0.2	1.6	3.2	17.1	30.8	31.5	10.4	4.9	0.6	1.3	0.7	0.6	0.7	0.7	0.6	0.6	0.5
Cyprus[3]	Limassol	1992	135,469	0.2	1.4	5.2	14.5	29.9	36.6	7.9	4.2	0.6	1.3	0.8	0.7	0.7	0.7	0.6	0.5	0.5
Cyprus[3]	Nicosia	1992	175,310	0.1	1.2	3.1	11.9	25.9	34.5	16.3	6.9	0.6	1.2	0.7	0.6	0.6	0.6	0.6	0.5	0.5
Cyprus[3]	Patos	1992	32,251	0.4	2.4	5.5	14.2	26.6	35.0	11.1	4.7	0.7	1.3	0.8	0.7	0.7	0.7	0.6	0.5	0.5
Pakistan[4]	Islamabad	1998	524,359	11.7	28.6	25.4	13.9	7.5	12.7	...	...	2.0	4.4	3.0	2.1	1.7	1.3	1.2	...	...
Syrian Arab Republic[3]	Aleppo	1994	2,959,053	5.5	25.1	32.7	20.5	9.2	4.2	1.3	1.3	2.1	4.6	3.0	2.2	1.7	1.4	1.2	1.1	1.4
Syrian Arab Republic[3]	Damascus	1994	1,384,017	3.8	16.4	27.2	24.2	14.5	6.8	2.4	3.9	1.7	4.0	2.5	1.9	1.5	1.3	1.2	1.2	1.6
Syrian Arab Republic[3]	Homs	1994	1,205,785	3.3	18.7	29.5	26.1	13.1	5.1	1.5	2.3	2.0	4.4	2.9	2.2	1.8	1.5	1.4	1.4	1.5
Syrian Arab Republic[3]	Lattakia	1994	741,372	4.9	18.4	31.4	26.4	11.7	4.0	1.2	1.7	1.7	3.9	2.5	1.9	1.5	1.3	1.2	1.1	1.0
Turkey[3]	Adana	1994	1,018,248	1.4	12.3	54.0	28.4	3.2	0.2	...	0.2	1.4	3.5	2.2	1.5	1.1	1.0	0.8	...	0.8
Turkey[3]	Ankara	1994	2,669,550	0.4	7.2	35.2	53.0	2.2	0.2	...	1.8	1.2	5.5	1.8	1.4	1.1	0.9	0.8	...	0.6
Turkey[3]	Istanbul	1994	7,362,804	0.6	9.1	45.7	37.1	4.3	1.9	...	1.0	1.2	4.0	2.0	1.3	1.1	1.0	1.1	...	0.5
Turkey[3]	Izmir	1994	1,902,831	0.7	11.2	41.6	39.7	2.2	0.7	...	1.3	1.1	3.6	1.9	1.3	0.9	0.8	0.8	...	1.0
EUROPE																				
Finland[5]	Espoo	1998	201,335	5.3	19.2	28.4	26.8	13.5	4.1	1.8	...	0.8	1.2	0.8	0.9	0.8	0.7	0.6	0.5	...
Finland[5]	Helsinki	1998	523,443	14.5	30.2	27.6	17.9	6.7	1.8	0.7	...	0.8	1.2	0.8	0.8	0.7	0.6	0.5	0.4	...
Finland[5]	Tampere	1998	185,796	10.9	29.5	27.9	20.2	7.6	2.2	0.8	...	0.8	1.2	0.8	0.8	0.7	0.6	0.6	0.5	...
Finland[5]	Turku	1998	165,042	12.3	29.4	25.8	18.3	6.5	1.9	0.9	...	0.8	1.2	0.8	0.7	0.7	0.6	0.5	0.4	...
Netherlands	Amsterdam	1998	706,100	4.0	16.2	35.0	29.7	9.3	3.6	1.2	0.9	0.6	1.0	0.6	0.5	0.6	0.6	0.5	0.3	0.4
Netherlands	Rotterdam	1998	555,600	1.8	9.4	31.7	32.9	16.7	4.5	1.8	1.3	0.6	1.1	0.6	0.5	0.6	0.6	0.6	0.5	0.3

TABLE C.2

continued

| | | Year | Total number* | Distribution by size of housings units | | | | | | | | | Persons per room in housing unit | | | | | | | |
				1	2	3	4	5	6	7	8+	Average	1	2	3	4	5	6	7	8+
Netherlands	The Hague	1998	437,200	1.9	10.7	26.5	33.8	15.1	5.8	2.6	3.5	0.6	1.0	0.6	0.6	0.6	0.6	0.5	0.4	0.4
Netherlands	Utrecht	1998	218,700	6.1	9.0	22.6	33.7	19.8	5.6	2.0	1.1	0.6	1.1	0.6	0.5	0.6	0.5	0.4	0.3	0.3
Poland6	Krakow	1995	719,520	...	18.1	32.6	36.2	13.1	...	...	...	0.9	...	1.1	1.0	0.9	0.8	...	...	...
Poland6	Lodz	1995	811,652	...	24.9	42.6	24.2	8.3	...	...	...	0.8	...	1.0	0.8	0.8	0.8	...	...	...
Poland6	Warsaw	1995	1,635,557	...	19.1	33.7	35.5	11.7	...	...	...	0.9	...	1.0	0.9	0.8	0.8	...	...	...
Poland6	Wroclaw	1995	618,469	...	16.4	28.7	31.4	23.5	...	...	...	0.9	...	1.1	0.9	0.8	0.8	...	...	...
United Kingdom2	London	1996	7,050,000	0.6	2.5	9.5	20.1	26.3	20.6	9.3	11.0	0.5	1.1	0.6	0.5	0.5	0.5	0.5	0.5	0.4
LATIN AMERICA AND THE CARIBBEAN																				
Brazil2	Belo Horizonte	1998	3,978,856	0.6	2.6	7.2	14.0	19.2	17.2	14.3	24.9	0.7	2.3	1.5	1.1	0.9	0.8	0.7	0.6	0.5
Brazil2	Brasília	1998	1,927,737	1.4	4.5	6.7	12.4	20.5	17.8	12.5	24.3	0.7	2.2	1.5	1.1	0.8	0.8	0.7	0.6	0.5
Brazil2	Rio de Janeiro	1998	10,382,082	0.7	2.0	6.7	18.5	36.2	17.5	7.9	10.4	0.6	2.3	1.2	1.0	0.7	0.7	0.6	0.5	0.4
Brazil2	São Paulo	1998	17,119,420	0.6	4.3	14.5	18.9	24.4	14.3	7.8	15.1	0.6	2.8	1.6	1.1	0.9	0.8	0.6	0.6	0.5
Colombia7	Barranquilla	1993	988,657	7.6	14.7	18.8	22.0	18.0	19.0	...	...	1.3	3.6	2.2	1.6	1.3	1.1	1.0	...	...
Colombia7	Bogotá	1993	4,934,591	13.6	20.8	17.2	20.2	12.8	15.3	...	...	1.2	3.0	1.9	1.3	1.0	0.9	0.8	...	...
Colombia7	Cali	1993	1,666,378	11.3	15.4	16.7	21.3	17.3	17.9	...	...	1.2	3.0	1.9	1.4	1.1	0.9	0.8	...	...
Colombia7	Medellín	1993	1,621,489	6.9	13.1	16.7	20.2	18.4	24.7	...	...	1.1	3.2	1.9	1.3	1.0	0.9	0.8	...	...
Nicaragua	Jinotepe	1995	25,034	10.3	28.2	26.1	16.6	9.4	5.1	2.3	2.0	1.8	4.8	2.6	2.0	1.5	1.3	1.1	0.8	0.9
Nicaragua	Leon	1995	123,687	26.1	30.1	22.4	12.0	5.2	2.4	0.9	1.0	2.3	5.0	2.7	2.0	1.6	1.4	1.1	1.1	0.9
Nicaragua	Managua	1995	862,240	25.5	28.2	23.2	13.4	5.8	2.4	0.8	0.6	2.2	4.6	2.6	1.9	1.5	1.3	1.1	1.0	0.9
Nicaragua	Matagalpa	1995	59,349	17.6	28.8	25.2	15.6	6.7	3.1	1.6	1.4	2.0	4.8	2.6	1.9	1.6	1.3	1.1	1.0	0.9
Saint Lucia8	Castries	1999	13,179	6.9	23.7	25.0	22.3	13.0	5.5	3.7		...	...	...	...	...	...	...	...	...
Saint Lucia8	Gros Islet	1999	3,656	4.5	22.0	24.7	24.4	14.4	5.6	4.5		...	...	...	...	...	...	...	...	...
Saint Lucia8	Soufriere	1999	1,905	6.6	20.5	20.2	24.7	19.0	6.1	2.9		...	...	...	...	...	...	...	...	...
Saint Lucia8	Vieux-Fort	1999	3,097	7.2	21.1	26.6	24.6	12.1	5.0	3.4		...	...	...	...	...	...	...	...	...
Uruguay	Montevideo	1996	1,282,277	7.3	17.6	32.7	23.0	10.7	4.5	1.9	2.2	1.0	2.7	1.4	1.0	0.9	0.8	0.7	0.6	0.7
Uruguay	Paysandu	1996	73,737	9.3	15.6	30.1	24.7	12.8	4.5	1.6	1.4	1.1	3.1	1.6	1.2	0.9	0.8	0.7	0.6	0.6
Uruguay	Rivera	1996	62,391	7.7	15.7	30.9	25.7	12.0	4.8	1.8	1.4	1.0	2.8	1.5	1.1	0.9	0.8	0.7	0.6	0.5
Uruguay	Salto	1996	92,030	8.0	14.2	30.9	27.6	11.8	4.1	1.9	1.5	1.2	3.5	1.9	1.2	1.0	0.9	0.7	0.6	0.6
NORTHERN AMERICA																				
Canada	Calgary	1996	813,925	0.4	1.2	4.2	8.2	13.7	14.8	15.1	42.5	0.4	1.2	0.7	0.5	0.5	0.5	0.4	0.4	0.4
Canada	Montreal	1996	3,272,810	0.6	1.5	5.3	14.6	22.6	18.6	13.5	23.3	0.5	1.1	0.6	0.5	0.5	0.5	0.5	0.4	0.4
Canada	Ottawa	1996	994,110	0.5	1.4	5.3	9.6	13.8	16.8	16.9	35.7	0.4	1.2	0.7	0.5	0.5	0.5	0.5	0.4	0.4
Canada	Toronto	1996	4,218,470	1.0	2.7	7.7	11.2	13.1	14.8	13.9	35.6	0.5	1.3	0.9	0.6	0.6	0.5	0.5	0.5	0.5

Notes: * Data for Total number refer to the number of persons resident in housing units. 1 Data for the category 5 rooms refer to housing units with 5+ rooms. 2 Data as reported; the total differs from the sum of categories. 3 The total differs from the sum of categories and that difference refers to the category not stated. 4 Data for total occupied housing units and total number of occupants are provisional and are estimated based on advanced sample tabulation of census data. Data for the category 6 rooms refer to housing units with 6+ rooms. 5 Data as reported; the total differs from the sum of categories. Data for the category 7 rooms refer to housing units with 7+ rooms. 6 Data for the category 2 rooms also include housing units with 1 room. Data for the category 5 rooms refer to housing units with 5+ rooms. 7 Data for the category 6 rooms refer to housing units with 6+ rooms. 8 Estimated data. Data for the category 7 rooms refer to housing units with 7+ rooms.

Source: UNSD and UNCHS (Habitat), *Compendium of Human Settlements Statistics 2001*.

TABLE C.3

Housing Indicators, Selected Cities

| | | Housing price* to income (ratio) | Rent** to income (ratio) | Access to water*** (%) | In-house connections† (%) | | | | Housing rights | | | | |
| | | | | | | | | | Legal provisions†† | | Impediments to women††† None (x) Some (o) Considerable (+) | | |
					A	B	C	D	A	B	A	B	C
AFRICA													
Algeria	Algiers	..	..	..	..	..	..	..	Yes	Yes	x	x	x
Benin	Cotonou	..	..	70.0	45.0	13.0	50.0	18.6	Yes	No	o	o	x
Benin	Parakou	2.9	36.3	90.0	20.0	3.4	45.3	..	Yes	No	o	o	x
Benin	Porto-Novo	2.9	..	85.0	35.0	..	60.0	6.4	Yes	No	o	o	x
Botswana	Gaborone	..	..	100.0					No	No	o	o	o
Burkina Faso	Bobo-Dioulasso	..	..	72.0	24.0	..	29.3	5.7	Yes	Yes	..	..	..
Burkina Faso	Koudougou	..	..	79.0	30.0	..	25.8	7.4	Yes	Yes	..	..	..
Burkina Faso	Ouagadougou	..	..	77.0	30.0	..	47.1	10.7	Yes	Yes	..	..	..
Burundi	Bujumbura	7.5	..	95.0	25.8	61.7	56.7	18.9	Yes	Yes	o	+	o
Cameroon	Douala	13.4	..	84.4	34.2	1.2	94.9	9.4	Yes	Yes	o	+	o
Cameroon	Yaounde	..	..	84.4	34.2	1.2	94.9	9.4	Yes	Yes	o	+	o
Central African Republic	Bangui	..	..	30.0	30.6	..	17.8	11.1	Yes	No	o	o	+
Chad	N'Djamena	..	21.0	22.0	42.0	..	13.3	6.0	Yes	Yes	o	x	+
Congo	Brazzaville	..	..	96.6	55.5	0.1	52.3	18.4	Yes	No	+	+	o
Congo	Pointe-Noire	..	..	74.3	66.5	3.1	43.6	12.0	Yes	No	o	o	+
Côte d'Ivoire	Abidjan	18.0	9.9	92.1	26.3	14.6	40.7	5.0	Yes	Yes	x	x	o
Côte d'Ivoire	Yamoussoukro	..	..	79.0	7.9	5.7	10.5	6.6	Yes	Yes	+	+	x
Dem. Rep. of Congo	Kinshasa	..	..	72.3	72.3	..	66.2	1.2	Yes	Yes	x	o	o
Egypt	Ismailia	5.4	21.0	99.6	99.6	95.5	99.8	80.0	Yes	Yes	x	x	x
Egypt	Tanta	23.1	25.3	..	..	..	..	..	Yes	Yes	x	x	x
Ethiopia	Addis Ababa	..	..	..	32.3	0.0	49.4	15.7	Yes	Yes	x	x	x
Gabon	Libreville	..	..	60.0	55.0	..	95.0	45.0	Yes	Yes	o	o	o
Gabon	Port-Gentil	..	..	..	48.0	..	..	..	Yes	No	+	+	+
Gambia	Banjul	11.4	12.4	79.0	22.5	12.4	24.0	..	Yes	No	x	x	x
Ghana	Accra	14.0	21.1	..	..	..	..	..	Yes	No	x	x	x
Ghana	Kumasi	11.6	20.8	65.0	65.0	..	95.0	51.0	Yes	No	x	x	x

Country	City													
Guinea	Conakry	..	..	79.5	29.7	32.3	53.8	5.6	Yes	Yes	x	o	x
Kenya	Kisumu	8.5	..	93.3	38.0	31.0	49.0	..	Yes	Yes	o	o	x
Kenya	Mombasa	..	..	100.0	..	..	..	..	Yes	Yes	o	o	x
Kenya	Nairobi	..	..	..	..	..	..	..	Yes	Yes	o	o	x
Lesotho	Maseru	..	..	70.0	41.0	10.0	13.0	10.0	Yes	No	+	x	o
Liberia	Monrovia	28.0	..	46.0	..	..	..	..	Yes	Yes	x	x	x
Libyan Arab Jamahiriya	Tripoli	0.8	..	97.0	97.0	89.9	99.0	6.3	Yes	Yes	x	x	x
Madagascar	Antananarivo	13.9	30.0	89.0	38.5	27.5	73.0	14.5	Yes	Yes	x	x	x
Malawi	Lilongwe	..	..	60.0	65.0	12.0	50.0	10.0	Yes	Yes	x	o	..
Mali	Bamako	..	..	82.3	38.4	1.5	61.2	3.0	Yes	Yes	o	o	x
Mauritania	Nouakchott	5.4	..	16.0	..	..	..	..	Yes	No	x	x	x
Morocco	Casablanca	..	..	95.0	83.0	93.0	91.0	..	Yes	Yes	o	o	o
Morocco	Rabat	..	..	95.9	92.8	97.2	52.0	..	Yes	Yes	o	o	o
Mozambique	Maputo	20.0	..	49.6	21.8	25.6	37.8	13.6	Yes	Yes	+	x	x
Namibia	Windhoek	..	..	97.0	97.0	90.0	..	..	Yes	Yes	o	o	x
Niger	Maradi	..	..	..	14.6	..	14.1	..	Yes	Yes	o	x	+
Niger	Niamey	..	..	..	33.2	..	51.0	3.7	Yes	Yes	o	x	+
Nigeria	Ibadan	..	..	25.7	25.7	12.1	41.4	..	..	..	x	x	x
Nigeria	Lagos	..	..	25.7	..	..	41.4	..	..	..	x	x	x
Rwanda	Kigali	11.4	..	79.0	36.0	20.0	57.0	6.0	Yes	Yes	x	+	x
Senegal	Bignona	2.5	5.8	38.9	17.6	..	25.3	8.0	Yes	No	o	x	o
Senegal	Dakar	3.5	14.6	91.4	77.0	43.1	89.3	40.8	Yes	Yes	x	x	x
Senegal	Thies	2.9	17.3	64.1	57.2	1.2	74.2	12.8	Yes	No	o	x	o
South Africa	Durban	..	..	..	..	..	..	..	Yes	Yes	..	..	..
South Africa	East Rand	..	..	20.0	40.0	43.0	38.0	..	Yes	Yes	o	o	..
South Africa	Port Elizabeth	10.6	..	100.0	74.0	73.0	..	..	Yes	Yes	..	..	..
Togo	Lome	..	8.3	80.0	..	70.0	51.0	18.0	Yes	Yes	x	x	x
Togo	Sokode	1.4	7.1	70.0	6.0	45.0	31.0	10.0	Yes	Yes	x	x	x
Tunisia	Tunis	5.0	20.3	97.4	75.2	47.2	94.6	26.8	Yes	Yes	x	x	x
Uganda	Entebbe	10.4	..	56.0	48.0	13.0	42.0	..	Yes	Yes	o	+	o
Uganda	Jinja	15.4	6.0	78.0	65.0	43.0	55.0	5.0	Yes	Yes	o	+	o
Zimbabwe	Bulawayo	..	..	100.0	100.0	100.0	98.0	..	Yes	Yes	x	x	x
Zimbabwe	Chegutu	3.4	..	..	100.0	68.0	9.0	3.0	Yes	No	x	x	x
Zimbabwe	Gweru	..	..	100.0	100.0	100.0	90.0	60.9	Yes	No	x	o	x
Zimbabwe	Harare	..	..	100.0	100.0	100.0	88.0	42.0	Yes	Yes	o	o	x
Zimbabwe	Mutare	..	..	100.0	88.0	88.0	74.0	4.0	Yes	No	x	x	x

ASIA

Country	City													
Armenia	Yerevan	4.0	6.6	97.9	97.9	98.0	100.0	88.1	No	No	..	..	..
Bangladesh	Chittagong	8.1	9.2	100.0	44.0	..	95.0	..	Yes	Yes	x	x	x
Bangladesh	Dhaka	16.7	..	99.1	60.0	22.0	90.0	7.0	Yes	Yes	x	x	x
Bangladesh	Sylhet	6.0	..	100.0	28.8	..	93.0	39.6	Yes	Yes	x	x	x
Bangladesh	Tangail	13.9	4.6	100.0	11.6	..	90.0	11.5	Yes	Yes	x	x	x
Cambodia	Phnom Penh	8.9	..	85.4	44.7	74.9	75.5	40.0	Yes	No	o	o	o
Georgia	Tbilisi	9.4	..	91.9	..	98.0	100.0	57.9	..	..	x	x	x
India	Alwar	..	..	..	..	..	..	..	Yes	Yes	..	..	..
India	Bangalore	13.8	..	82.9	22.5	20.8	98.3	44.5	Yes	Yes	x	x	x
India	Chennai	7.7	14.6	94.0	51.3	55.5	..	60.4	Yes	Yes	x	x	x
India	Delhi	..	..	78.6	58.5	55.0	82.2	0.0	Yes	Yes	+	+	+
India	Mysore	4.7	26.1	92.5	44.4	68.0	82.8	33.6	Yes	Yes	x	x	x
Indonesia	Bandung	7.6	..	90.0	..	55.0	99.0	..	Yes	Yes	x	x	x
Indonesia	Jakarta	14.6	..	91.4	50.3	64.8	99.0	..	Yes	Yes	x	x	x
Indonesia	Semarang	..	..	89.7	34.0	..	85.2	..	Yes	Yes	x	x	x
Indonesia	Surabaya	3.4	19.0	94.3	40.9	55.8	89.2	70.8	Yes	Yes	x	x	x
Iraq	Baghdad	..	..	..	..	..	..	..	No	No	x	x	x
Japan	Tokyo	5.6	2.5	100.0	100.0	100.0	100.0	99.2	Yes	Yes	x	x	x
Jordan	Amman	6.1	16.7	98.0	97.7	81.3	98.5	62.0	Yes	Yes	x	x	x
Kazakhstan	Astana	8.6	9.9	94.3	84.1	83.9	100.0	58.3	Yes	No	x	x	x
Kuwait	Kuwait	6.5	27.8	100.0	100.0	98.0	100.0	98.0	Yes	Yes	x	x	x
Kyrghyzstan	Bishkek	..	..	75.0	29.7	23.3	99.9	19.8	Yes	Yes	x	x	x
Lao PDR	Vientiane	23.2	10.0	95.0	87.0	..	100.0	86.8	Yes	Yes	x	x	x
Lebanon	Sin El Fil	8.3	28.6	80.0	80.0	30.0	98.0	80.0	Yes	Yes	x	x	x
Malaysia	Penang	7.2	4.9	99.9	99.1	..	100.0	98.0	Yes	Yes	x	x	x
Mongolia	Ulaanbaatar	7.8	..	90.3	60.0	60.0	100.0	90.0	Yes	Yes	x	x	x
Myanmar	Yangon	8.3	15.4	95.0	77.8	81.2	85.0	17.3	No	No	x	x	x
Nepal	Butwal	10.3	..	80.0	33.7	..	80.0	10.0	Yes	No	x	x	x
Nepal	Pokhara	21.6	34.0	80.0	41.4	..	75.0	11.3	Yes	No	x	x	x
Occupied Palestine Territory	Gaza	5.4	..	..	85.4	37.9	99.0	37.7	Yes	Yes	+	+	o
Oman	Muscat	..	..	80.0	80.0	90.0	89.0	53.0	Yes	Yes	x	x	x
Pakistan	Karachi	13.7	..	89.5	82.4	85.0	98.4	..	No	No	+	+	+
Pakistan	Lahore	7.1	23.3	100.0	96.4	78.0	97.1	70.0	No	No	+	+	+
Philippines	Cebu	13.3	..	98.2	41.4	92.3	80.0	25.0	Yes	Yes	x	x	x
Qatar	Doha	..	..	..	..	..	..	..	No	No	x	x	x
Republic of Korea	Hanam	3.7	13.9	81.1	81.1	67.9	100.0	100.0	Yes	Yes	o	o	o
Republic of Korea	Pusan	4.0	..	99.9	97.9	69.4	100.0	100.0	Yes	Yes	o	o	o
Republic of Korea	Seoul	5.7	..	99.9	99.9	98.6	100.0	..	Yes	Yes	o	o	o
Singapore	Singapore	3.1	2.0	100.0	100.0	100.0	100.0	100.0	Yes	No	x	x	x
Sri Lanka	Colombo	..	..	..	22.9	76.0	96.0	26.0	Yes	Yes	o	x	x
Syrian Arab Republic	Damascus	10.3	..	98.4	98.4	71.0	95.0	9.9	Yes	Yes	x	x	x
Thailand	Bangkok	8.8	22.2	..	99.0	100.0	99.8	59.7	Yes	No	x	x	x
Thailand	Chiang Mai	6.8	25.0	99.0	95.0	60.0	100.0	75.0	Yes	No	o	o	o
Turkey	Ankara	4.5	24.0	97.0	97.0	98.5	100.0	..	Yes	Yes	x	x	x
Viet Nam	Hanoi	..	..	100.0	70.0	50.0	100.0	60.0	Yes	Yes	x	x	x
Viet Nam	Ho Chi Minh	..	..	90.0	59.0	30.0	99.7	21.2	Yes	Yes	x	x	x
Yemen	Sana'a	..	..	30.4	30.4	9.4	96.0	..	Yes	Yes	x	x	x

EUROPE

Country	City													
Albania	Tirana	..	..	62.6	62.6	..	99.5	12.6	Yes	Yes	x	x	x
Belarus	Minsk	..	..	..	99.3	98.4	100.0	87.2	Yes	Yes	x	x	x

TABLE C.3

continued

| | | Housing price* to income (ratio) | Rent** to income (ratio) | Access to water*** (%) | In-house connections† (%) | | | | Housing rights | | | | |
| | | | | | | | | | Legal provisions†† | | Impediments to women††† None (x) Some (o) Considerable (+) | | |
					A	B	C	D	A	B	A	B	C
Bosnia and Herzegovina	Sarajevo	..	..	95.0	95.0	90.0	100.0	..	No	No	x	x	x
Bulgaria	Bourgas	5.1	3.9	100.0	100.0	93.0	100.0	144.4	Yes	Yes	x	x	x
Bulgaria	Sofia	13.2	..	100.0	95.4	90.5	100.0	89.0	Yes	Yes	x	x	x
Bulgaria	Troyan	3.7	2.0	100.0	99.0	82.0	100.0	44.8	Yes	Yes	x	x	x
Bulgaria	Veliko Tarnovo	5.4	3.3	100.0	98.4	97.6	100.0	96.0	Yes	Yes	x	x	x
Croatia	Zagreb	7.8	..	98.0	97.5	96.9	99.7	94.0	Yes	Yes	o	o	o
Czech Republic	Brno	..	..	99.5	99.5	95.6	100.0	68.5	Yes	Yes	x	x	x
Czech Republic	Prague	..	..	100.0	98.9	99.7	100.0	99.5	Yes	Yes	x	x	x
Estonia	Riik	..	..	91.6	91.6	90.2	98.0	55.0	Yes	Yes	x	x	x
Estonia	Tallin	6.4	7.0	98.0	98.1	98.1	100.0	85.5	Yes	Yes	x	x	x
Germany	Berlin	..	..	100.0	99.9	..	..	..	..	..	..	..	..
Germany	Cologne	4.3	..	100.0	100.0	..	..	..	..	..	..	..	..
Germany	Duisburg	3.2	..	100.0	100.0	..	..	..	..	..	..	..	..
Germany	Erfurt	2.6	..	100.0	100.0	..	..	..	..	..	..	..	..
Germany	Freiburg	..	..	100.0	100.0	..	..	..	..	..	..	..	..
Germany	Leipzig	3.2	..	100.0	100.0	..	..	..	..	..	..	..	..
Germany	Wiesbaden	..	..	100.0	100.0	..	..	..	..	..	..	..	..
Hungary	Budapest	3.6	11.8	100.0	98.3	90.7	100.0	84.0	Yes	No	x	x	x
Italy	Aversa	3.5	..	100.0	..	..	..	..	..	..	x	x	x
Latvia	Riga	4.7	0.9	99.9	95.0	93.0	99.9	90.0	No	No	x	x	x
Lithuania	Vilnius	20.0	..	89.4	89.4	89.1	100.0	77.0	No	Yes	o	x	x
Netherlands	Amsterdam	7.8	17.5	100.0	100.0	100.0	100.0	..	..	..	..	..	..
Netherlands	Eindhoven	5.6	16.5	100.0	100.0	100.0	100.0	..	..	..	x	x	x
Netherlands	Meppel	4.5	15.9	100.0	100.0	100.0	100.0	..	..	..	x	x	x
Poland	Bydgoszcz	4.3	18.8	94.9	94.6	87.1	100.0	84.9	Yes	Yes	x	x	x
Poland	Gdansk	4.4	7.4	100.0	98.7	94.0	99.6	56.2	Yes	Yes	x	x	x
Poland	Katowice	1.7	5.2	100.0	99.1	94.4	100.0	75.2	Yes	Yes	x	x	x
Poland	Poznan	5.8	18.4	100.0	94.9	96.4	99.9	85.5	Yes	Yes	x	x	x
Republi of Moldova	Chisinau	..	..	100.0	100.0	95.0	100.0	83.0	Yes	Yes	o	o	+
Russian Federation	Astrakhan	5.0	13.8	100.0	81.0	79.0	100.0	51.0	Yes	Yes	x	x	x
Russian Federation	Belgorod	4.0	6.4	100.0	90.0	89.0	100.0	51.0	Yes	Yes	x	x	x
Russian Federation	Kostroma	6.9	12.4	100.0	88.0	84.0	100.0	46.3	Yes	Yes	x	x	x
Russian Federation	Moscow	5.1	5.2	100.0	99.8	99.8	100.0	100.0	Yes	Yes	x	x	x
Russian Federation	Nizhny Novgorod	6.9	7.8	100.0	98.4	98.0	100.0	63.7	Yes	Yes	x	x	x
Russian Federation	Novomoscowsk	4.2	7.1	100.0	99.0	93.0	100.0	62.0	Yes	Yes	x	x	x
Russian Federation	Omsk	3.9	12.8	100.0	87.0	87.0	100.0	41.0	Yes	Yes	x	x	x
Russian Federation	Pushkin	9.6	7.2	100.0	99.0	99.0	100.0	89.0	Yes	Yes	x	x	x
Russian Federation	Surgut	4.5	8.8	100.0	98.4	98.4	100.0	50.1	Yes	Yes	x	x	x
Russian Federation	Veliky Novgorod	3.4	11.1	100.0	97.0	96.7	100.0	51.1	Yes	Yes	x	x	x
Serbia and Montenegro	Belgrade	13.5	..	99.0	95.0	86.0	99.6	86.0	Yes	Yes	x	x	..
Slovenia	Ljubljana	7.8	17.3	100.0	100.0	100.0	100.0	97.0	Yes	Yes	x	x	x
Spain	Madrid	..	..	100.0	..	..	..	..	Yes	Yes	x	x	x
Spain	Pamplona	..	..	100.0	100.0	..	100.0	..	Yes	Yes	x	x	x
Sweden	Amal	2.9	..	100.0	100.0	100.0	100.0	..	Yes	Yes	x	x	x
Sweden	Stockholm	6.0	..	100.0	100.0	100.0	100.0	..	Yes	Yes	x	x	x
Sweden	Umea	5.3	..	100.0	100.0	100.0	100.0	..	Yes	Yes	x	x	x
Switzerland	Basel	12.3	19.4	100.0	100.0	100.0	100.0	99.0	Yes	Yes	o	x	x
United Kingdom	Belfast	3.6	6.9	100.0	100.0	100.0	100.0	..	..	Yes	o	x	x
United Kingdom	Birmingham	3.4	12.5	100.0	100.0	100.0	100.0	..	..	Yes	x	x	x
United Kingdom	Cardiff	3.2	13.2	100.0	100.0	100.0	100.0	..	..	Yes	o	x	x
United Kingdom	Edinburgh	3.5	11.7	100.0	100.0	100.0	100.0	..	..	Yes	o	x	x
United Kingdom	London	4.7	15.6	100.0	100.0	100.0	100.0	..	..	Yes	o	x	x
United Kingdom	Manchester	3.0	12.3	100.0	100.0	100.0	100.0	..	..	Yes	o	x	x
LATIN AMERICA AND THE CARIBBEAN													
Argentina	Buenos Aires	5.1	..	100.0	100.0	98.1	100.0	70.4	Yes	No	..	..	..
Argentina	Comodoro Rivadavia	..	..	99.0	98.0	93.0	99.9	..	Yes	No	x	x	x
Argentina	Córdoba	6.8	5.4	100.0	98.7	40.1	99.3	80.0	Yes	No	x	x	x
Argentina	Rosario	5.7	..	..	97.8	66.8	92.9	75.7	Yes	No	x	x	x
Barbados	Bridgetown	4.4	..	100.0	98.0	4.5	99.0	78.0	Yes	Yes	x	x	x
Belize	Belize City	..	..	..	..	..	..	..	Yes	No	o	x	o
Bolivia	Santa Cruz de la Sierra	..	..	47.4	52.6	33.3	97.7	59.1	Yes	Yes	x	x	x
Brazil	Belém	..	..	..	..	..	..	..	Yes	Yes	x	x	x
Brazil	Icapui	4.5	9.6	85.0	88.0	..	90.0	33.0	Yes	Yes	x	x	x
Brazil	Maranguape	..	..	90.0	73.0	..	..	..	Yes	Yes	x	x	x
Brazil	Porto Alegre	..	..	99.0	99.0	87.0	100.0	..	Yes	Yes	x	x	x
Brazil	Recife	12.5	25.9	97.1	89.3	41.0	99.8	29.1	Yes	Yes	x	x	x
Brazil	Rio de Janeiro	..	..	..	87.7	79.8	10.0	..	Yes	Yes	x	x	x
Brazil	São Paulo	..	24.3	98.0	98.0	95.0	99.9	78.9	Yes	Yes	x	x	x
Chile	Gran Concepcion	..	..	100.0	99.7	90.7	95.0	69.1	Yes	No	x	x	x
Chile	Santiago de Chile	..	..	100.0	100.0	99.2	99.2	72.8	Yes	No	x	x	x
Chile	Tome	..	..	78.4	91.7	51.9	98.0	57.6	Yes	No	x	x	x
Chile	Valparaiso	..	..	98.0	98.0	91.8	97.0	62.5	Yes	No	x	x	o
Chile	Vina del mar	..	..	97.1	97.1	97.0	98.0	64.9	Yes	No	x	x	x
Colombia	Armenia	5.0	..	100.0	90.0	50.0	98.7	97.1	Yes	Yes	o	x	x
Colombia	Marinilla	8.5	..	100.0	97.7	92.8	100.0	65.0	Yes	Yes	x	x	x
Colombia	Medellín	..	..	99.9	99.9	98.5	99.5	86.9	Yes	Yes	x	x	x
Cuba	Baracoa	..	..	89.0	83.0	3.0	93.0	32.0	Yes	Yes	x	x	x
Cuba	Camaguey	..	..	72.0	72.0	47.0	97.0	..	Yes	Yes	x	x	x

Cuba	Cienfuegos	4.0	..	100.0	100.0	73.0	100.0	8.7	Yes	Yes	x	x	x
Cuba	Havana	8.5	..	100.0	100.0	85.0	100.0	14.0	Yes	Yes	x	x	x
Cuba	Pinar Del Rio	..	..	..	97.0	48.0	99.6	..	Yes	Yes	x	x	x
Cuba	Santa Clara	..	..	95.0	95.0	42.0	99.7	43.2	Yes	Yes	x	x	x
Dominican Republic	Santiago de los Caballeros	..	..	80.0	75.0	80.0	..	71.0	Yes	Yes	x	x	x
Ecuador	Ambato	..	..	85.0	89.5	80.5	90.6	86.8	Yes	Yes	x	x	x
Ecuador	Cuenca	4.6	..	98.0	96.8	92.2	97.0	48.0	Yes	Yes	o	o	o
Ecuador	Guayaquil	3.4	16.1	77.0	70.0	42.0	99.0	44.0	Yes	Yes	x	x	o
Ecuador	Manta	..	28.0	70.0	70.0	52.0	98.0	40.0	Yes	Yes	o	o	o
Ecuador	Puyo	2.1	15.8	89.4	80.0	30.0	90.0	60.0	Yes	Yes	x	x	x
Ecuador	Quito	2.4	13.3	89.4	85.0	70.0	96.2	55.3	Yes	Yes	x	x	x
Ecuador	Tena	1.6	..	80.0	80.0	60.0		..	Yes	Yes	x	x	o
El Salvador	San Salvador	3.5	37.0	81.5	81.5	79.7	97.7	70.1	No	No	+	+	+
Guatemala	Quetzaltenango	4.3	..	90.0	60.0	55.0	80.0	40.0	Yes	Yes	o	x	o
Jamaica	Kingston	..	..	..	96.6	..	88.1	..	No	No	..	..	..
Jamaica	Montego Bay	..	..	78.0	78.0	..	86.0	..	No	No	..	..	..
Mexico	Ciudad Juarez	1.4	..	92.0	89.2	77.0	96.0	45.0	Yes	Yes	x	x	x
Nicaragua	Leon	..	..	..	78.2	..	83.8	20.6	..	..	..	..	..
Panama	Colon	14.2	24.5	100.0	..	..	..	..	Yes	Yes	x	x	o
Paraguay	Asuncion	10.7	..	..	46.2	8.2	86.4	17.0	Yes	No	o	x	x
Peru	Cajamarca	3.9	34.9	86.0	86.0	69.0	81.0	38.0	Yes	No	x	x	x
Peru	Huanuco	30.0	24.0	54.0	57.0	28.0	80.0	32.0	Yes	Yes	x	x	x
Peru	Huaras	6.7	..	90.0	..	..	71.0	..	Yes	Yes	x	x	+
Peru	Iquitos	5.6	..	72.5	72.5	60.3	82.3	62.3	Yes	Yes	x	x	o
Peru	Lima	8.7	..	81.1	75.2	71.5	99.0	..	Yes	Yes	o	x	x
Peru	Tacna	4.0	..	87.0	64.6	58.3	73.7	15.8	Yes	Yes	..	..	..
Peru	Tumbes	..	29.0	85.0	60.0	35.0	80.0	25.0	Yes	Yes	x	x	x
Trinidad and Tobago	Port of Spain	..	..	..	..	..	..	..	..	..	..	..	..
Uruguay	Montevideo	5.6	31.1	99.3	97.6	79.1	99.7	75.1	Yes	No	x	x	x
NORTHERN AMERICA													
Canada	Hull	..	18.7	100.0	100.0	100.0	100.0	100.0	Yes	Yes	x	x	x
United States	Atlanta	2.10	29.0	99.8	99.6	100.0	100.0	90.3	Yes	Yes	x	x	x
United States	Birmingham-USA	..	24.0	99.8	99.8	100.0	100.0	..	Yes	Yes	x	x	x
United States	Boston	2.90	31.0	100.0	99.9	100.0	100.0	..	Yes	Yes	x	x	x
United States	Des Moines	..	..	..	..	..	..	..	Yes	Yes	x	x	x
United States	Hartford	2.50	29.0	99.8	100.0	100.0	100.0	90.0	Yes	Yes	x	x	x
United States	Minneapolis-St. Paul	2.10	28.0	100.0	99.8	100.0	100.0	100.0	Yes	Yes	x	x	x
United States	New York	2.70	28.0	100.0	100.0	100.0	100.0	96.0	Yes	Yes	x	x	x
United States	Providence	2.50	29.0	100.0	99.9	100.0	100.0	..	Yes	Yes	x	x	x
United States	Salt Lake	2.80	27.0	100.0	100.0	100.0	99.9	..	Yes	Yes	x	x	x
United States	San Jose	..	..	100.0	99.9	100.0	100.0	..	Yes	Yes	x	x	x
United States	Seattle	3.00	28.0	100.0	100.0	100.0	100.0	92.1	Yes	Yes	x	x	x
United States	Tampa	2.10	30.0	100.0	100.0	100.0	100.0	..	Yes	Yes	x	x	x
United States	Washington, DC	2.30	26.0	100.0	100.0	100.0	99.9	..	Yes	Yes	x	x	x
OCEANIA													
Samoa	Apia	10.0	36.0	69.0	60.0	..	98.0	96.0	Yes	Yes	x	x	x

Notes: * Housing price-to-income ratio: ratio of the median free-market price of a dwelling unit and the median annual household income. ** Rent-to-income ratio: per cent ratio of the median annual rent of a dwelling unit and the median annual household income of renters. *** Percentage of households with access to water within 200 metres. † Percentage of households which, within their housing unit, are connected to: (A) piped water; (B) sewerage; (C) electricity; (D) telephone. †† Responses (yes/no) to the questions: (A) Does the Constitution or national law promote the full and progressive realization of the right to adequate housing? (B) Does the Constitution or national law include protections against eviction? ††† Responses (none/some/considerable) to the questions: (A) Are there impediments to women owning land? (B) Are there impediments to women inheriting land and housing? (C) Are there impediments to women taking mortgages in their own name?

Source: UN-Habitat (2002), *Global Urban Indicators Database 2 (1998 data).*

TABLE C.4

Environmental Infrastructure, Selected Cities

		Water consumption* (litres/person/day)		Median price of water (US$/m³)	Waste water treated (%)	Solid waste disposal (%)					
		A	B			Incinerated	Sanitary landfill	Open dump	Recycled	Burned openly	Other
AFRICA											
Algeria	Algiers	150.0	100.0	0.08	80.0	..	..	..	..	..	..
Benin	Cotonou	36.4	..	0.39	70.0	-	-	75.0	20.0	-	5.0
Benin	Parakou	60.4	..	0.39	..	-	-	90.0	5.0	-	5.0
Benin	Porto-Novo	26.4	..	0.39	..	-	-	70.0	25.0	-	5.0
Botswana	Gaborone	239.0	..	..	95.0	-	-	99.0	1.0	-	-
Burkina Faso	Bobo-Dioulasso	27.0	..	..	..	..	..	..	..	..	..
Burkina Faso	Koudougou	27.0	..	..	..	..	..	..	..	..	..
Burkina Faso	Ouagadougou	39.0	..	..	18.5	7.0	-	55.0	12.0	25.0	1.0
Burundi	Bujumbura	82.4	30.0	0.08	21.3	-	15.0	33.4	-	27.4	24.2
Cameroon	Douala	40.0	20.0	0.33	5.0	0.6	65.4	26.0	8.0	-	-
Cameroon	Yaounde	40.0	15.0	0.33	24.2	0.3	66.9	31.0	1.8	-	-
Central African Republic	Bangui	55.0	30.0	3.33	0.1	-	-	80.0	-	20.0	-
Chad	N'Djamena	17.5	10.0	2.50	20.9	..	76.0	..	-	45.0	-
Congo	Brazzaville	30.0	25.0	..	..	-	0.8	40.0	16.2	38.0	5.0
Congo	Pointe-Noire	30.0	25.0	..	..	0.8	5.3	23.2	26.2	36.1	8.4
Côte d'Ivoire	Abidjan	40.0	20.0	1.19	45.0	10.0	-	72.0	3.0	-	15.0
Côte d'Ivoire	Yamoussoukro	37.0	..	0.48	25.0	-	-	100.0	-	-	-
Dem. Rep. of Congo	Kinshasa	25.0	20.0	..	..	5.8	15.9	15.5	4.9	32.5	18.5
Egypt	Ismailia	444.0	..	0.03	35.0	-	-	80.0	-	-	20.0
Egypt	Tanta	259.0	..	..	..	..	..	..	..	..	..
Ethiopia	Addis Ababa	16.9	..	..	..	-	10.8	21.8	-	-	67.4

TABLE C.4

continued

		Water consumption* (litres/person/day)		Median price of water (US$/m³)	Waste water treated (%)	Solid waste disposal (%)					
		A	B			Incinerated	Sanitary landfill	Open dump	Recycled	Burned openly	Other
Gabon	Libreville	160.0	120.0	0.57	44.0	-	70.0	10.0	-	15.0	5.0
Gabon	Port-Gentil	160.0	120.0	0.60	25.0	-	65.0	6.0	-	25.0	4.0
Gambia	Banjul	9.3	6.8	1.20	..	-	96.0	-	-	2.5	1.5
Ghana	Accra	9.0	6.5	1.20	0.0	..	..	..	..	..	..
Ghana	Kumasi	9.1	6.3	0.75	..	-	98.0	-	-	0.8	1.2
Guinea	Conakry	20.0	..	..	..	5.0	70.0	15.0	5.0	5.0	-
Kenya	Kisumu	20.0	..	..	65.0	-	-	30.0	-	7.0	63.0
Kenya	Mombasa	16.0	10.0	..	49.5	-	55.0	-	-	-	45.0
Kenya	Nairobi	17.7	..	2.18	52.0	..	25.0	-	1.0	3.0	1.3
Lesotho	Maseru	40.0	..	0.23	..	..	..	..	..	..	..
Liberia	Monrovia	30.0	..	0.03	0.0	-	-	100.0	-	-	-
Libyan Arab Jamahiriya	Tripoli	404.0	..	0.05	40.0	-	15.0	65.0	20.0	-	-
Madagascar	Antananarivo	..	..	0.12	..	..	..	..	..	..	..
Malawi	Lilongwe	100.0	60.0	..	0.0	..	..	22.0	..	3.0	..
Mali	Bamako	54.0	31.0	..	..	-	2.0	95.0	-	-	3.0
Mauritania	Nouakchott	35.0	20.0	0.62	..	3.0	..	28.0	1.0	6.0	2.0
Morocco	Casablanca	..	..	0.72	..	3.0	7.0	90.0	-	-	-
Morocco	Rabat	..	..	0.60	..	7.0	8.0	85.0	-	-	-
Mozambique	Maputo	67.0	..	0.41	5.0	-	-	100.0	-	-	-
Namibia	Windhoek	139.0	30.0	0.79	100.0	3.0	92.5	-	4.5	-	-
Niger	Maradi	24.0	..	0.34	..	..	..	..	..	..	..
Niger	Niamey	45.0	..	0.34	..	..	..	..	..	..	..
Nigeria	Ibadan	..	..	..	..	..	..	..	..	..	..
Nigeria	Lagos	45.0	22.5	..	..	..	..	..	..	..	..
Rwanda	Kigali	81.0	29.0	1.00	20.0	-	-	16.0	-	84.0	-
Senegal	Bignona	44.0	..	0.12	0.0	-	-	100.0	-	-	-
Senegal	Dakar	70.5	..	0.61	3.5	-	-	100.0	-	-	-
Senegal	Thies	44.0	..	0.18	0.0	-	-	100.0	-	-	-
South Africa	Durban	..	..	..	..	..	..	..	..	..	..
South Africa	East Rand	113.0	..	..	80.0	..	..	..	..	..	..
South Africa	Port Elizabeth	110.0	25.0	2.39	..	0.1	99.9	-	-	-	-
Togo	Lome	73.0	..	0.33	..	-	-	25.0	-	10.0	65.0
Togo	Sokode	7.0	4.0	0.40	0.0	-	-	100.0	-	-	-
Tunisia	Tunis	..	..	0.30	83.0	2.0	80.0	12.0	5.0	1.0	-
Uganda	Entebbe	25.0	..	1.60	30.0	2.0	-	75.0	-	20.0	3.0
Uganda	Jinja	100.0	40.0	0.50	30.0	1.5	34.0	35.0	2.5	17.0	10.0
Zimbabwe	Bulawayo	87.0	..	..	80.0	1.0	65.0	2.0	5.0	..	1.0
Zimbabwe	Chegutu	160.0	..	0.63	69.0	5.0	-	75.0	3.0	15.0	2.0
Zimbabwe	Gweru	100.0	..	..	95.0	6.0	40.0	13.0	16.0	4.0	21.0
Zimbabwe	Harare	..	..	0.10	..	..	..	..	..	..	..
Zimbabwe	Mutare	139.0	..	..	100.0	-	97.7	-	2.3	-	-
ASIA											
Armenia	Yerevan	250.0	50.0	0.10	35.7	-	-	35.0	-	65.0	-
Bangladesh	Chittagong	96.0	48.0	0.09	0.0	..	..	70.0	0.5	..	..
Bangladesh	Dhaka	160.0	..	0.50	..	-	-	50.0	35.0	..	15.0
Bangladesh	Sylhet	96.0	48.0	1.37	0.0	..	..	45.0	0.5	..	..
Bangladesh	Tangail	..	..	..	0.0	-	-	83.0	-	..	17.0
Cambodia	Phnom Penh	..	..	0.21	0.0	-	-	74.0	15.0	5.0	6.0
Georgia	Tbilisi	..	..	0.19	0.0	..	..	..	..	..	..
India	Alwar	..	..	..	..	..	..	..	..	..	..
India	Bangalore	68.8	40.0	0.20	82.9	-	-	60.8	14.5	-	24.7
India	Chennai	70.0	45.0	0.08	70.0	-	-	100.0	-	-	-
India	Delhi	136.0	45.0	..	73.2	-	99.5	-	-	-	0.5
India	Mysore	124.2	80.0	0.06	13.0	-	-	100.0	-	-	-
Indonesia	Bandung	130.0	..	0.85	23.4	-	78.6	-	-	16.3	5.1
Indonesia	Jakarta	161.6	..	0.18	15.7	-	77.7	-	-	-	22.3
Indonesia	Semarang	137.4	..	0.09	0.0	-	74.3	-	-	-	25.7
Indonesia	Surabaya	138.6	34.7	0.85	0.0	-	70.0	-	30.0	-	-
Iraq	Baghdad	..	..	..	..	..	..	..	..	..	..
Japan	Tokyo	84.0	..	..	..	78.0	8.6	0.1	10.3	-	3.0
Jordan	Amman	84.0	..	0.53	54.3	-	100.0	-	-	-	-
Kazakhstan	Astana	..	..	0.23	93.0	..	..	..	..	..	..
Kuwait	Kuwait	379.0	..	1.26	..	9.0	82.0	2.0	-	2.0	5.0
Kyrghyzstan	Bishkek	135.0	..	0.04	15.0	-	-	100.0	-	-	-
Lao PDR	Vientiane	161.0	..	0.06	20.0	..	..	..	..	..	..
Lebanon	Sin El Fil	..	..	..	..	-	82.0	-	6.0	-	12.0
Malaysia	Penang	384.0	..	0.08	20.0	10.0	-	80.0	10.0	-	-
Mongolia	Ulaanbaatar	160.0	3.2	0.32	96.0	5.0	5.0	90.0	-	-	-
Myanmar	Yangon	160.0	50.0	0.81	0.0	-	-	86.0	14.0	-	-
Nepal	Butwal	75.0	..	0.03	0.0	..	-	94.0	6.0	..	..
Nepal	Pokhara	80.0	..	0.03	0.0	-	-	76.7	15.9	7.4	-
Occupied Palestine Territory	Gaza	80.0	..	0.41	..	..	..	..	..	..	..
Oman	Muscat	..	..	..	..	..	..	..	..	..	..
Pakistan	Karachi	132.0	63.0	0.25	10.0	-	-	51.0	12.0	20.0	17.0
Pakistan	Lahore	320.0	..	0.09	0.0	-	70.0	25.0	-	5.0	-
Philippines	Cebu	225.0	..	0.50	..	-	100.0	-	-	-	-
Qatar	Doha	..	..	..	..	..	..	..	..	..	..
Republic of Korea	Hanam	286.0	..	0.33	80.8	3.0	67.0	-	30.0	-	-

Republic of Korea	Pusan	384.0	..	0.35	69.4	14.5	41.2	-	44.3	-	-
Republic of Korea	Seoul	409.0	..	0.33	98.6	5.0	57.0	-	38.0	-	-
Singapore	Singapore	166.2	..	0.32	100.0	66.3	33.7	-	-	-	-
Sri Lanka	Colombo	..		0.03	10.0	-	-	100.0	-	-	-
Syrian Arab Republic	Damascus	270.0	..	0.20	3.0	4.0	46.0	6.0	21.0	16.0	7.0
Thailand	Bangkok	352.0	..	0.19	..	-	99.0	-	-	-	1.0
Thailand	Chiang Mai	200.0	100.0	0.45	70.0	2.0	98.0	-	-	-	-
Turkey	Ankara	138.0	..	1.06	80.0	-	-	92.0	0.8	0.8	6.5
Viet Nam	Hanoi	100.0	..	0.90	..	-	65.0	-	15.0	-	20.0
Viet Nam	Ho Chi Minh	200.0	..	..	..	..	..	..	..	..	..
Yemen	Sana'a	75.0	40.0	0.90	30.0	-	-	95.0	5.0	-	-
EUROPE											
Albania	Tirana	130.0	..	0.05	..	-	-	-	-	100.0	-
Belarus	Minsk	358.0	..	..	100.0	-	100.0	-	-	-	-
Bosnia and Herzegovina	Sarajevo	165.0	..	0.90	..	..	..	..	..	..	..
Bulgaria	Bourgas	112.0	..	0.35	93.0	-	100.0	-	-	-	-
Bulgaria	Sofia	150.0	..	0.17	94.0	-	0.2	77.0	22.8	-	-
Bulgaria	Troyan	121.0	..	0.10	..	-	-	73.0	9.0	4.0	14.0
Bulgaria	Veliko Tarnovo	114.0	..	0.22	50.0	-	-	94.0	6.0	-	-
Croatia	Zagreb	145.3	..	0.67	..	-	-	85.0	13.0	-	2.0
Czech Republic	Brno	131.8	..	0.78	100.0	100.0	-	-	-	-	-
Czech Republic	Prague	110.0	..	0.81	..	..	..	..	..	..	..
Estonia	Riik	144.0	..	..	..	..	..	..	..	..	..
Estonia	Tallin	138.0	..	0.51	99.6	-	23.9	74.3	-	-	1.8
Germany	Berlin	178.0	..	0.20	100.0	..	..	..	..	..	..
Germany	Cologne	247.0	..	0.20	100.0	..	..	..	..	..	..
Germany	Duisburg	200.0	..	0.23	100.0	..	..	..	..	..	..
Germany	Erfurt	210.0	..	0.30	97.5	..	..	..	..	..	..
Germany	Freiburg	203.0	..	0.19	100.0	..	..	..	..	..	..
Germany	Leipzig	200.0	..	0.23	100.0	..	..	..	..	..	..
Germany	Wiesbaden	188.0	..	0.35	99.7	..	..	..	..	..	..
Hungary	Budapest	184.0	..	0.35	87.5	64.7	35.3	-	-	-	-
Italy	Aversa	..		3.00	90.0	-	-	98.8	1.2	-	-
Latvia	Riga	166.0	..	0.57	83.3	-	-	92.0	-	-	8.0
Lithuania	Vilnius	73.0	..	0.77	53.9	..	..	..	..	..	..
Netherlands	Amsterdam	..		2.87	..	-	1.0	-	30.0	69.0	-
Netherlands	Eindhoven	..		1.98	..	-	1.0	-	30.0	69.0	-
Netherlands	Meppel	..		1.76	..	-	1.0	-	30.0	69.0	-
Poland	Bydgoszcz	133.9	..	0.29	28.4	-	-	99.8	0.2	-	-
Poland	Gdansk	129.9	..	0.34	100.0	0.0	-	96.5	3.5	-	-
Poland	Katowice	149.0	..	0.54	67.0	-	-	85.0	1.5	-	13.5
Poland	Poznan	145.0	..	0.32	78.0	1.1	..	81.7	17.2	..	..
Republi of Moldova	Chisinau	..		0.25	71.2	..	..	..	..	..	..
Russian Federation	Astrakhan	200.0	..	0.08	92.0	-	-	86.4	13.6	-	..
Russian Federation	Belgorod	200.0	..	0.05	95.9	..	5.0	89.0	-	-	..
Russian Federation	Kostroma	250.0	..	0.04	95.9	-	-	86.1	13.9	-	..
Russian Federation	Moscow	235.0	..	..	98.1	1.2	66.2	24.0	8.0	0.6	-
Russian Federation	Nizhny Novgorod	230.0	..	0.05	97.6	-	-	90.2	9.8	-	-
Russian Federation	Novomoscowsk	225.0	..	0.09	97.0	-	-	97.1	2.9	-	-
Russian Federation	Omsk	300.0	..	0.07	89.0	-	-	100.0	-	-	-
Russian Federation	Pushkin	220.0	..	0.15	100.0	-	-	90.0	10.0	-	-
Russian Federation	Surgut	320.0	..	0.40	93.2	-	-	100.0	-	-	-
Russian Federation	Veliky Novgorod	325.0	..	0.04	95.0	-	2.0	97.0	1.0	-	-
Serbia and Montenegro	Belgrade	385.0	..	0.13	20.0	-	-	99.3	0.7	-	-
Slovenia	Ljubljana	179.0	..	0.28	98.0	-	92.0	-	8.0	-	-
Spain	Madrid	172.5	..	0.73	100.0	-	46.0	-	54.0	-	-
Spain	Pamplona	136.1	..	0.38	79.0	1.8	82.0	-	16.2	-	-
Sweden	Amal	143.0	..	1.98	100.0	-	71.0	-	29.0	-	-
Sweden	Stockholm	198.0	..	1.49	100.0	74.0	1.0	-	25.0	-	-
Sweden	Umea	153.0	..	1.75	100.0	78.0	1.0	-	21.0	-	-
Switzerland	Basel	380.0	..	..	100.0	58.0	27.0	-	15.0	-	-
United Kingdom	Belfast	..		..	..	-	-	-	4.0	-	96.0
United Kingdom	Birmingham	..		..	100.0	53.0	43.0	-	4.0	-	-
United Kingdom	Cardiff	..		..	..	-	95.0	-	5.0	-	-
United Kingdom	Edinburgh	..		..	..	..	..	..	..	..	..
United Kingdom	London	..		..	..	23.0	72.0	-	5.0	-	-
United Kingdom	Manchester	..		..	..	-	92.0	-	3.0	-	5.0
LATIN AMERICA AND THE CARIBBEAN											
Argentina	Buenos Aires	270.0	..	..	0.0	-	100.0	-	-	-	-
Argentina	Comodoro Rivadavia	440.0	..	0.35	10.0	-	-	100.0	-	-	-
Argentina	Córdoba	340.0	..	0.36	49.1	0.1	99.6	..	0.3	-	-
Argentina	Rosario	171.8	..	0.17	0.6	0.1	71.9	25.2	-	2.7	-
Barbados	Bridgetown	230.0	..	0.75	7.0	..	..	..	..	..	..
Belize	Belize City	..		..	..	..	..	..	..	..	..
Bolivia	Santa Cruz de la Sierra	122.0	..	..	53.0	2.0	60.0	30.0	2.0	2.0	3.0
Brazil	Belém	..		..	..	..	..	..	..	..	..
Brazil	Icapui	120.0	..	0.67	..	-	-	75.0	-	15.0	10.0
Brazil	Maranguape	150.0	..	0.45	..	-	96.0	2.0	2.0	-	-
Brazil	Porto Alegre	202.4	..	0.51	..	-	92.0	-	7.6	..	0.4
Brazil	Recife	185.0	..	0.72	33.0	-	75.0	24.0	1.0	..	..
Brazil	Rio de Janeiro	209.0	..	..	..	..	73.2	-	22.0	0.7	4.1
Brazil	São Paulo	159.6	108.7	0.52	..	-	99.0	-	1.0	-	-
Chile	Gran Concepcion	179.0	30.0	0.28	5.7	-	100.0	-	-	-	-
Chile	Santiago de Chile	..		0.34	3.3	-	100.0	-	-	-	-
Chile	Tome	144.0	..	0.20	57.0	-	91.6	-	2.2	0.8	5.4
Chile	Valparaiso	166.3	..	0.45	100.0	-	100.0	-	-	-	-
Chile	Vina del mar	170.0	12.0	0.46	92.9	-	89.0	3.0	8.0	-	-
Colombia	Armenia	..		0.58	0.0	-	-	96.0	-	-	4.0
Colombia	Marinilla	125.5	..	..	..	-	88.5	-	11.5	-	-

TABLE C.4

continued

		Water consumption* (litres/person/day)		Median price of water (US$/m³)	Waste water treated (%)	Solid waste disposal (%)					
		A	B			Incinerated	Sanitary landfill	Open dump	Recycled	Burned openly	Other
Colombia	Medellin	141.5	..	0.18	..	-	75.0	7.0	10.0	3.0	5.0
Cuba	Baracoa	225.0	..	1.00	..	-	-	100.0	-	-	-
Cuba	Camaguey	203.0	..	..	..	-	-	100.0	-	-	-
Cuba	Cienfuegos	230.0	..	0.85	2.2	-	80.0	20.0	-	-	-
Cuba	Havana	100.0	..	1.30	..	-	100.0	-	-	-	-
Cuba	Pinar Del Rio	125.0	..	..	..	10.0	60.0	10.0	-	20.0	-
Cuba	Santa Clara	225.0	..	..	..	-	70.0	30.0	-	-	-
Dominican Republic	Santiago de los Caballeros	..	..	..	80.0	..	..	100.0	..	100.0	..
Ecuador	Ambato	220.0	..	0.11	0.0	-	-	95.0	5.0	-	-
Ecuador	Cuenca	246.0	..	..	82.0	-	88.0	-	5.0	-	7.0
Ecuador	Guayaquil	244.0	109.0	0.51	9.0	-	94.0	0.3	0.3	1.2	4.2
Ecuador	Manta	40.5	..	0.66	..	..	..	..	..	..	..
Ecuador	Puyo	420.0	..	0.04	..	-	-	90.0	10.0	-	-
Ecuador	Quito	..	..	..	..	-	-	70.0	20.0	-	10.0
Ecuador	Tena	190.0	..	0.11	0.0	-	-	90.0	5.0	-	5.0
El Salvador	San Salvador	..	..	..	..	-	81.1	18.9	-	-	-
Guatemala	Quetzaltenango	120.0	..	0.16	..	-	60.0	30.0	5.0	5.0	-
Jamaica	Kingston	..	..	..	20.0	..	..	..	..	..	..
Jamaica	Montego Bay	..	..	..	15.0	..	..	..	..	..	..
Mexico	Ciudad Juarez	336.4	..	0.26	..	-	89.0	2.0	8.0	1.0	-
Nicaragua	Leon	..	..	..	..	..	..	..	..	..	..
Panama	Colon	496.0	..	0.21	0.0	-	90.0	10.0	-	-	-
Paraguay	Asuncion	200.0	90.0	0.40	0.0	0.2	..	..	4.0	..	91.0
Peru	Cajamarca	160.0	..	0.64	62.0	-	95.0	1.5	-	-	3.5
Peru	Huanuco	..	..	..	..	-	100.0	-	-	-	-
Peru	Huaras	120.0	..	0.33	..	-	-	100.0	-	-	-
Peru	Iquitos	119.8	..	0.23	..	-	64.0	15.0	-	8.0	13.0
Peru	Lima	108.0	..	0.34	4.0	-	57.0	34.0	7.0	2.0	-
Peru	Tacna	201.0	90.0	0.43	64.0	-	-	50.0	-	50.0	-
Peru	Tumbes	150.0	..	0.59	..	70.0	..	..	..	20.0	10.0
Trinidad and Tobago	Port of Spain	..	..	..	..	..	..	..	..	..	..
Uruguay	Montevideo	173.1	..	0.62	34.0	0.2	-	99.8	-	-	-
NORTHERN AMERICA											
Canada	Hull	397.0	..	0.29	100.0	-	91.9	-	8.1	-	-
United States	Atlanta	403.0	..	..	..	..	..	..	..	..	..
United States	Birmingham-USA	393.0	..	..	..	..	..	..	..	..	..
United States	Boston	252.0	..	..	..	..	..	..	..	..	..
United States	Des Moines	226.0	..	..	..	..	..	..	..	..	..
United States	Hartford	284.0	..	..	..	..	..	..	..	..	..
United States	Minneapolis-St. Paul	281.0	..	..	..	..	..	..	..	..	..
United States	New York	448.0	..	..	..	..	..	..	..	..	..
United States	Providence	246.0	..	..	..	..	..	..	..	..	..
United States	Salt Lake	668.0	..	..	..	..	..	..	..	..	..
United States	San Jose	343.0	..	..	..	..	..	..	..	..	..
United States	Seattle	476.0	..	..	..	..	..	..	..	..	..
United States	Tampa	327.0	..	..	..	..	..	..	..	..	..
United States	Washington, DC	396.0	..	..	..	..	..	..	..	..	..
OCEANIA											
Samoa	Apia	..	..	0.10	0.0	..	..	..	..	..	..

Note: * Average consumption of water, in litres per person per day, for all domestic uses (excludes industrial use): (A) city average; (B) city average in informal settlements.

Source: UN-Habitat (2002), *Global Urban Indicators Database 2 (1998 data)*.

TABLE C.5

Transport and Environmental Indicators, Selected Cities

		Travel time per work-trip (minutes)	Transport used for work trips* (%)				Disaster prevention and mitigation measures**			Local environmental planning***		
			Car	Train	Bus	Other	A	B	C	A	B	C
AFRICA												
Algeria	Algiers	..	..	..	..	..	Yes	Yes	No	Yes	Yes	Yes
Benin	Cotonou	..	90.0	-	-	10.0	Yes	No	No	Yes	Yes	Yes
Benin	Parakou	45	80.0	-	-	20.0	Yes	No	No	Yes	Yes	Yes
Benin	Porto-Novo	50	83.0	-	-	17.0	Yes	No	No	Yes	Yes	Yes
Botswana	Gaborone	..	..	..	..	..	No	No	No	No	No	No
Burkina Faso	Bobo-Dioulasso	..	..	..	..	..	No	No	No	No	No	No
Burkina Faso	Koudougou	..	..	..	..	..	No	No	No	No	No	No
Burkina Faso	Ouagadougou	..	63.4	-	2.2	34.4	No	Yes	No	Yes	Yes	No
Burundi	Bujumbura	25	12.4	-	48.2	39.4	No	No	Yes	Yes	No	Yes
Cameroon	Douala	40	..	..	..	..	Yes	Yes	Yes	Yes	No	No
Cameroon	Yaounde	45	30.0	-	42.3	27.7	Yes	Yes	Yes	Yes	No	Yes
Central African Republic	Bangui	60	3.7	-	66.3	30.0	Yes	Yes	Yes	No	No	No

Country	City											
Chad	N'Djamena	..	17.0	-	35.0	48.0	No	No	No	Yes	Yes	Yes
Congo	Brazzaville	20	19.0	-	55.0	26.0	No	No	Yes	Yes	Yes	Yes
Congo	Pointe-Noire	30	8.0	-	55.0	37.0	No	No	Yes	Yes	Yes	Yes
Côte d'Ivoire	Abidjan	45	..	..	..	..	Yes	No	No	Yes	Yes	No
Côte d'Ivoire	Yamoussoukro	20	..	..	..	..	Yes	No	No	Yes	Yes	No
Dem. Rep. of Congo	Kinshasa	57	13.0	42.0	30.0	15.0	Yes	Yes	Yes	Yes	Yes	Yes
Egypt	Ismailia	30	..	..	..	..	Yes	Yes	Yes	No	No	No
Egypt	Tanta	50	..	..	..	..	Yes	Yes	No	No	No	No
Ethiopia	Addis Ababa	..	4.2	..	12.6	83.3	No	No	No	Yes	No	Yes
Gabon	Libreville	30	-	55.0	25.0	20.0	No	No	No	Yes	Yes	Yes
Gabon	Port-Gentil	45	..	..	..	..	No	No	No	Yes	Yes	Yes
Gambia	Banjul	22	19.5	-	54.9	25.6	No	No	No	Yes	Yes	Yes
Ghana	Accra	21	34.7	4.0	50.0	11.3	Yes	Yes	Yes	Yes	Yes	Yes
Ghana	Kumasi	21	22.2	0.6	50.0	27.2	Yes	Yes	Yes	Yes	Yes	Yes
Guinea	Conakry	45	22.0	-	25.5	52.5	Yes	No	Yes	Yes	Yes	Yes
Kenya	Kisumu	24	21.1	-	43.5	35.5	Yes	Yes	Yes	No	No	No
Kenya	Mombasa	20	2.1	-	47.0	50.9	Yes	Yes	Yes	Yes	Yes	Yes
Kenya	Nairobi	57	6.0	1.0	70.0	23.0	Yes	Yes	Yes	No	No	No
Lesotho	Maseru	15	3.0	-	47.0	50.0	Yes	Yes	No	Yes	Yes	Yes
Liberia	Monrovia	60	10.0	-	80.0	10.0	Yes	Yes	Yes	Yes	Yes	Yes
Libyan Arab Jamahiriya	Tripoli	20	81.0	-	18.0	1.0	Yes	Yes	No	Yes	Yes	Yes
Madagascar	Antananarivo	60	7.0	-	60.0	33.0	Yes	Yes	Yes	Yes	Yes	Yes
Malawi	Lilongwe	5	6.0	-	27.0	67.0	Yes	No	No	Yes	Yes	Yes
Mali	Bamako	30	24.9	-	12.2	62.9	No	No	No	Yes	Yes	Yes
Mauritania	Nouakchott	50	16.5	-	45.0	38.5	No	No	No	Yes	Yes	No
Morocco	Casablanca	30	..	..	..	..	Yes	Yes	No	Yes	Yes	Yes
Morocco	Rabat	20	40.0	-	40.0	20.0	Yes	Yes	No	Yes	Yes	Yes
Mozambique	Maputo	60	6.5	-	80.0	13.5	No	No	Yes	Yes	Yes	No
Namibia	Windhoek	20	..	..	..	..	No	No	Yes	Yes	Yes	Yes
Niger	Maradi	15	..	..	..	..	Yes	Yes	Yes	No	No	Yes
Niger	Niamey	30	..	..	..	..	Yes	Yes	Yes	No	No	Yes
Nigeria	Ibadan	45	45.0	0.5	45.0	9.5	Yes	No	Yes	Yes	Yes	Yes
Nigeria	Lagos	60	51.0	2.5	45.5	..	Yes	No	Yes	Yes	Yes	Yes
Rwanda	Kigali	45	12.0	-	32.0	56.0	No	Yes	Yes	Yes	Yes	Yes
Senegal	Bignona	10	1.7	-	-	98.3	Yes	Yes	Yes	Yes	Yes	Yes
Senegal	Dakar	30	8.1	1.3	77.2	13.4	Yes	Yes	Yes	No	No	No
Senegal	Thies	12	18.2	-	59.3	22.6	Yes	Yes	Yes	Yes	Yes	Yes
South Africa	Durban	..	..	..	..	..	No	No	No	No	No	No
South Africa	East Rand	..	..	..	..	..	Yes	Yes	Yes	Yes	Yes	Yes
South Africa	Port Elizabeth	35	52.4	1.8	45.8	-	No	No	No	No	No	No
Togo	Lome	30	45.0	-	40.0	15.0	Yes	Yes	No	Yes	Yes	Yes
Togo	Sokode	15	60.0	-	10.0	30.0	Yes	Yes	No	Yes	Yes	Yes
Tunisia	Tunis	..	..	..	..	..	Yes	Yes	Yes	Yes	No	Yes
Uganda	Entebbe	20	35.0	-	65.0	-	No	No	No	No	No	Yes
Uganda	Jinja	12	18.0	-	49.0	33.0	Yes	No	Yes	Yes	Yes	Yes
Zimbabwe	Bulawayo	15	22.8	-	74.9	2.3	Yes	Yes	Yes	Yes	Yes	Yes
Zimbabwe	Chegutu	22	19.0	-	20.0	61.0	No	No	No	Yes	No	Yes
Zimbabwe	Gweru	15	..	..	..	..	Yes	No	Yes	Yes	Yes	Yes
Zimbabwe	Harare	45	18.0	-	32.0	50.0	No	No	No	Yes	Yes	Yes
Zimbabwe	Mutare	20	12.0	-	70.0	18.0	Yes	No	No	Yes	No	Yes
ASIA												
Armenia	Yerevan	30	2.0	11.5	72.5	14.0	Yes	Yes	Yes	No	No	No
Bangladesh	Chittagong	45	4.0	1.0	25.0	70.0	Yes	Yes	No	Yes	Yes	Yes
Bangladesh	Dhaka	45	4.6	0.0	9.2	86.2	Yes	Yes	No	Yes	Yes	Yes
Bangladesh	Sylhet	50	1.3	-	10.0	88.7	Yes	Yes	No	Yes	Yes	Yes
Bangladesh	Tangail	30	..	..	..	..	Yes	Yes	No	Yes	Yes	No
Cambodia	Phnom Penh	45	87.3	-	0.2	12.5	No	No	No	Yes	No	Yes
Georgia	Tbilisi	..	..	..	..	..	Yes	Yes	No	No	No	No
India	Alwar	..	..	..	..	..	No	No	No	No	No	No
India	Bangalore	30	39.6	-	35.7	24.7	Yes	Yes	No	Yes	No	Yes
India	Chennai	23	42.0	11.0	25.0	22.0	Yes	No	No	Yes	No	No
India	Delhi	..	24.6	0.4	62.0	13.0	No	No	No	No	No	No
India	Mysore	20	39.1	-	0.1	60.8	Yes	No	No	No	No	No
Indonesia	Bandung	30	82.0	..	..	..	No	Yes	Yes	Yes	No	Yes
Indonesia	Jakarta	..	..	..	..	..	No	Yes	Yes	Yes	No	Yes
Indonesia	Semarang	..	..	..	..	..	No	Yes	Yes	Yes	No	Yes
Indonesia	Surabaya	35	80.0	-	17.8	2.2	Yes	No	No	Yes	No	No
Iraq	Baghdad	..	..	..	..	..	No	No	No	No	No	No
Japan	Tokyo	45	..	..	..	..	Yes	Yes	Yes	Yes	Yes	Yes
Jordan	Amman	25	51.0	-	21.0	28.0	Yes	No	Yes	No	No	No
Kazakhstan	Astana	27	30.0	28.0	34.0	8.0	Yes	Yes	Yes	No	No	No
Kuwait	Kuwait	10	68.0	-	21.0	11.0	Yes	Yes	Yes	Yes	Yes	Yes
Kyrghyzstan	Bishkek	35	5.0	35.4	59.6	0.0	Yes	Yes	Yes	Yes	Yes	Yes
Lao PDR	Vientiane	27	41.8	-	2.1	56.1	Yes	Yes	No	Yes	Yes	Yes
Lebanon	Sin El Fil	10	25.0	-	50.0	25.0	No	Yes	No	No	No	No
Malaysia	Penang	40	42.0	-	55.0	3.0	Yes	No	Yes	Yes	Yes	Yes
Mongolia	Ulaanbaatar	30	10.0	21.0	59.0	10.0	Yes	Yes	Yes	Yes	Yes	Yes
Myanmar	Yangon	45	16.7	3.7	65.0	14.7	Yes	No	Yes	Yes	Yes	Yes
Nepal	Butwal	15	10.0	-	15.0	75.0	No	Yes	No	Yes	Yes	No
Nepal	Pokhara	20	11.0	-	14.0	75.0	Yes	Yes	No	Yes	No	No
Occupied Palestine Territory	Gaza	..	..	..	..	..	Yes	No	No	No	No	No
Oman	Muscat	20	..	..	..	..	Yes	Yes	Yes	Yes	Yes	Yes
Pakistan	Karachi	..	16.5	-	41.0	39.5	Yes	No	No	No	No	No
Pakistan	Lahore	..	..	..	..	..	Yes	No	No	No	No	No
Philippines	Cebu	35	..	..	..	..	Yes	No	Yes	Yes	Yes	Yes
Qatar	Doha	..	..	..	..	..	No	No	No	No	No	No
Republic of Korea	Hanam	..	..	..	..	..	Yes	Yes	Yes	Yes	Yes	Yes
Republic of Korea	Pusan	42	37.1	6.6	32.5	23.8	Yes	Yes	No	Yes	Yes	Yes
Republic of Korea	Seoul	60	20.1	32.3	38.8	8.8	No	Yes	Yes	Yes	Yes	Yes

TABLE C.5

continued

		Travel time per work-trip (minutes)	Transport used for work trips* (%)				Disaster prevention and mitigation measures**			Local environmental planning***		
			Car	Train	Bus	Other	A	B	C	A	B	C
Singapore	Singapore	30	25.1	14.5	38.7	21.7	No	Yes	Yes	Yes	Yes	Yes
Sri Lanka	Colombo	25	23.7	8.1	65.0	3.2	Yes	No	Yes	Yes	Yes	Yes
Syrian Arab Republic	Damascus	40	15.0	-	32.6	52.4	Yes	Yes	Yes	No	No	No
Thailand	Bangkok	60	58.7	1.0	27.0	13.3	No	Yes	No	Yes	Yes	Yes
Thailand	Chiang Mai	30	94.1	-	5.0	0.9	Yes	No	No	No	Yes	No
Turkey	Ankara	32	20.0	6.3	..	15.9	Yes	Yes	No	No	No	No
Viet Nam	Hanoi	30	64.4	-	2.0	33.6	No	No	No	Yes	Yes	Yes
Viet Nam	Ho Chi Minh	25	74.0	-	2.0	24.0	No	No	No	Yes	Yes	Yes
Yemen	Sana'a	20	20.0	-	78.0	2.0	Yes	Yes	No	No	No	No
EUROPE												
Albania	Tirana	25	..	..	..	..	No	No	Yes	No	No	No
Belarus	Minsk	..	..	..	..	..	No	No	No	No	No	Yes
Bosnia and Herzegovina	Sarajevo	12	..	57.0	43.0	..	Yes	Yes	Yes	Yes	No	No
Bulgaria	Bourgas	32	6.0	0.1	61.0	33.0	Yes	Yes	Yes	Yes	Yes	Yes
Bulgaria	Sofia	32	21.0	26.0	53.0	-	Yes	Yes	Yes	Yes	Yes	Yes
Bulgaria	Troyan	22	18.0	-	44.0	38.0	Yes	Yes	No	Yes	Yes	Yes
Bulgaria	Veliko Tarnovo	30	2.4	-	45.8	51.8	Yes	Yes	No	Yes	Yes	Yes
Croatia	Zagreb	31	37.5	35.9	20.4	6.2	Yes	Yes	Yes	Yes	Yes	Yes
Czech Republic	Brno	25	25.0	29.0	21.0	25.0	Yes	Yes	Yes	Yes	No	Yes
Czech Republic	Prague	22	33.0	-	54.5	12.5	No	No	No	Yes	Yes	Yes
Estonia	Riik	..					Yes	Yes	Yes	Yes	Yes	Yes
Estonia	Tallin	35					Yes	Yes	Yes	Yes	Yes	Yes
Germany	Berlin	..	..	..	..	..	No	No	No	No	No	No
Germany	Cologne	..	..	..	..	..	No	No	No	No	No	No
Germany	Duisburg	..	..	..	..	..	No	No	No	No	No	No
Germany	Erfurt	..	..	..	..	..	No	No	No	No	No	No
Germany	Freiburg	..	..	..	..	..	No	No	No	No	No	No
Germany	Leipzig	..	..	..	..	..	No	No	No	No	No	No
Germany	Wiesbaden	..	..	..	..	..	No	No	No	No	No	No
Hungary	Budapest	..	..	..	..	..	Yes	No	Yes	No	No	No
Italy	Aversa	..	..	..	..	..	Yes	No	Yes	No	No	No
Latvia	Riga	..	..	..	..	..	Yes	No	Yes	Yes	Yes	Yes
Lithuania	Vilnius	37	22.3	29.1	23.2	25.5	No	No	No	Yes	Yes	Yes
Netherlands	Amsterdam	..	..	..	..	..	No	No	No	No	No	No
Netherlands	Eindhoven	..	..	..	..	..	No	No	No	No	No	No
Netherlands	Meppel	..	..	..	..	..	No	No	No	No	No	No
Poland	Bydgoszcz	18	42.5	10.5	24.0	..	No	No	Yes	Yes	Yes	Yes
Poland	Gdansk	20	43.0	32.9	23.4	0.7	Yes	Yes	Yes	Yes	Yes	Yes
Poland	Katowice	36	46.2	9.4	19.9	24.6	No	Yes	Yes	Yes	Yes	Yes
Poland	Poznan	25	33.0	30.0	21.0	16.0	Yes	Yes	No	Yes	Yes	Yes
Republi of Moldova	Chisinau	23	15.0	-	80.0	5.0	Yes	No	Yes	Yes	Yes	Yes
Russian Federation	Astrakhan	35	16.0	31.0	35.0	18.0	Yes	Yes	Yes	Yes	No	Yes
Russian Federation	Belgorod	25	..	..	..	..	Yes	Yes	Yes	Yes	Yes	Yes
Russian Federation	Kostroma	20	5.0	19.5	48.0	27.5	Yes	Yes	Yes	Yes	Yes	Yes
Russian Federation	Moscow	62	15.0	63.7	21.0	0.3	Yes	Yes	Yes	Yes	Yes	Yes
Russian Federation	Nizhny Novgorod	35	17.0	37.3	41.7	4.0	Yes	Yes	Yes	Yes	Yes	Yes
Russian Federation	Novomoscowsk	25	5.0	22.5	38.9	33.6	Yes	Yes	Yes	Yes	Yes	Yes
Russian Federation	Omsk	43	9.5	16.5	69.0	5.0	Yes	Yes	Yes	Yes	Yes	No
Russian Federation	Pushkin	15	6.0	-	60.2	33.8	Yes	Yes	Yes	Yes	Yes	Yes
Russian Federation	Surgut	57	1.5	-	81.0	17.5	No	No	No	Yes	Yes	Yes
Russian Federation	Veliky Novgorod	30	9.5	-	75.0	15.5	Yes	Yes	Yes	Yes	Yes	Yes
Serbia and Montenegro	Belgrade	40	12.5	18.8	53.0	..	Yes	No	Yes	No	No	No
Slovenia	Ljubljana	30	43.0	0.1	20.0	36.9	Yes	Yes	Yes	Yes	Yes	No
Spain	Madrid	32	60.0	-	16.0	24.0	Yes	Yes	Yes	No	No	No
Spain	Pamplona	..	..	..	..	..	Yes	Yes	No	Yes	No	Yes
Sweden	Amal	..	..	..	..	..	Yes	Yes	Yes	Yes	Yes	Yes
Sweden	Stockholm	28	35.1	34.5	13.8	16.6	Yes	Yes	Yes	Yes	Yes	Yes
Sweden	Umea	16	..	..	..	..	Yes	Yes	Yes	Yes	Yes	Yes
Switzerland	Basel	..	..	..	..	..	Yes	Yes	Yes	Yes	Yes	No
United Kingdom	Belfast	..	..	..	..	..	No	No	No	No	No	No
United Kingdom	Birmingham	20	73.9	1.4	9.1	15.6	No	No	No	No	No	No
United Kingdom	Cardiff	20	81.0	0.3	5.7	13.0	No	No	No	No	No	No
United Kingdom	Edinburgh	20	69.9	2.4	13.0	14.7	No	No	No	No	No	No
United Kingdom	London	24	..	..	..	..	No	No	No	No	No	No
United Kingdom	Manchester	19	71.8	1.9	8.1	18.0	No	No	No	No	No	No
LATIN AMERICA AND THE CARIBBEAN												
Argentina	Buenos Aires	42	33.5	16.4	42.2	..	Yes	Yes	Yes	Yes	No	Yes
Argentina	Comodoro Rivadavia	29	44.0	-	36.0	20.0	Yes	Yes	Yes	Yes	No	Yes
Argentina	Córdoba	32	26.5	2.9	40.9	..	Yes	Yes	Yes	Yes	Yes	Yes
Argentina	Rosario	22	..	..	..	..	No	Yes	Yes	Yes	No	No
Barbados	Bridgetown	..	..	..	..	..	Yes	Yes	Yes	Yes	Yes	No
Belize	Belize City	..	..	..	..	..	No	Yes	Yes	No	No	No
Bolivia	Santa Cruz de la Sierra	29	..	..	..	..	No	Yes	No	Yes	Yes	No
Brazil	Belém	..	..	..	..	..	No	No	No	No	No	No
Brazil	Icapui	30	6.0	..	1.0	93.0	Yes	No	No	No	No	No
Brazil	Maranguape	20	5.0	-	30.0	..	No	No	No	Yes	Yes	Yes
Brazil	Porto Alegre	..	..	..	..	..	Yes	Yes	Yes	Yes	Yes	Yes
Brazil	Recife	35	28.6	1.8	44.2	25.4	Yes	Yes	Yes	Yes	Yes	Yes
Brazil	Rio de Janeiro	..	..	..	..	..	Yes	Yes	Yes	Yes	No	Yes

Brazil	São Paulo	40	42.0	6.0	37.0	15.0	Yes	Yes	Yes	Yes	No	Yes
Chile	Gran Concepcion	35	19.6	-	56.5	23.9	Yes	Yes	Yes	Yes	No	Yes
Chile	Santiago de Chile	38	14.1	4.0	55.8	26.2	Yes	Yes	Yes	No	No	Yes
Chile	Tome	..	..	..	..	..	No	No	No	No	Yes	No
Chile	Valparaiso	..	42.0	19.0	36.0	3.0	No	No	No	No	No	No
Chile	Vina del mar	..	..	..	..	..	Yes	Yes	Yes	No	No	Yes
Colombia	Armenia	60	31.0	-	41.9	27.2	Yes	No	No	Yes	Yes	Yes
Colombia	Marinilla	15	14.3	-	18.4	67.3	Yes	Yes	Yes	Yes	Yes	Yes
Colombia	Medellín	35	21.9	4.8	33.1	40.2	Yes	Yes	Yes	Yes	Yes	No
Cuba	Baracoa	..	..	..	..	..	Yes	Yes	Yes	No	No	No
Cuba	Camaguey	60	2.5	-	2.1	95.4	Yes	Yes	Yes	No	No	No
Cuba	Cienfuegos		..	..	..	..	Yes	Yes	Yes	No	No	No
Cuba	Havana		6.5	1.0	57.1	35.4	Yes	Yes	Yes	No	No	No
Cuba	Pinar Del Rio	..	..	..	..	..	Yes	Yes	Yes	No	No	No
Cuba	Santa Clara	48	30.3	3.2	4.1	62.4	Yes	Yes	Yes	No	No	No
Dominican Republic	Santiago de los Caballeros	30	..	..	..	..	Yes	Yes	Yes	Yes	No	Yes
Ecuador	Ambato	..	..	..	..	..	Yes	Yes	No	Yes	Yes	Yes
Ecuador	Cuenca	25	..	..	..	..	Yes	Yes	No	No	No	Yes
Ecuador	Guayaquil	45	10.7	-	89.3	-	No	Yes	No	Yes	Yes	Yes
Ecuador	Manta	30	..	..	..	..	No	Yes	No	Yes	Yes	Yes
Ecuador	Puyo	15	..	..	..	..	No	No	No	Yes	No	Yes
Ecuador	Quito	33	..	..	..	..	Yes	Yes	No	Yes	Yes	No
Ecuador	Tena	5	..	..	..	..	Yes	Yes	No	Yes	Yes	Yes
El Salvador	San Salvador	..	29.0	..	..	2.0	Yes	Yes	Yes	No	No	No
Guatemala	Quetzaltenango	15	..	..	..	..	No	No	Yes	Yes	No	Yes
Jamaica	Kingston	..	..	..	..	..	Yes	Yes	Yes	No	No	No
Jamaica	Montego Bay	..	..	..	..	..	Yes	No	Yes	No	No	No
Mexico	Ciudad Juarez	23	51.3	-	23.7	25.0	No	Yes	Yes	Yes	No	Yes
Nicaragua	Leon	15	..	..	56.0	..	Yes	Yes	No	No	No	No
Panama	Colon	15	..	..	..	..	Yes	Yes	Yes	No	No	No
Paraguay	Asuncion	25	49.8	..	..	..	Yes	Yes	No	Yes	Yes	Yes
Peru	Cajamarca	20	22.0	..	20.0	58.0	Yes	Yes	No	No	No	No
Peru	Huanuco	20	17.5	..	45.0	..	No	Yes	No	Yes	No	No
Peru	Huaras	15	..	..	..	..	No	Yes	No	No	No	No
Peru	Iquitos	10	35.0	-	25.0	40.0	No	Yes	Yes	Yes	Yes	Yes
Peru	Lima	..	16.9	-	82.2	0.9	Yes	Yes	Yes	Yes	No	Yes
Peru	Tacna	25	37.5	-	66.0	1.0	Yes	Yes	Yes	No	No	Yes
Peru	Tumbes	20	25.0	..	..	5.0	Yes	Yes	No	Yes	Yes	Yes
Trinidad and Tobago	Port of Spain	..	56.2	-	43.8	-	No	No	No	No	No	No
Uruguay	Montevideo	45	26.9	-	59.6	13.5	No	No	Yes	Yes	No	Yes
NORTHERN AMERICA												
Canada	Hull	..	73.3	-	16.3	10.4	Yes	Yes	Yes	Yes	Yes	Yes
United States	Atlanta	26	..	..	..	..	Yes	Yes	Yes	Yes	Yes	Yes
United States	Birmingham-USA	23	..	..	..	..	Yes	Yes	Yes	Yes	Yes	Yes
United States	Boston	25	..	..	..	..	Yes	Yes	Yes	Yes	Yes	Yes
United States	Des Moines	18	..	..	..	..	Yes	Yes	Yes	Yes	Yes	Yes
United States	Hartford	21	..	..	..	..	Yes	Yes	Yes	Yes	Yes	Yes
United States	Minneapolis-St. Paul	21	..	..	..	..	Yes	Yes	Yes	Yes	Yes	Yes
United States	New York	35	..	..	..	..	Yes	Yes	Yes	Yes	Yes	Yes
United States	Providence	19	..	..	..	..	Yes	Yes	Yes	Yes	Yes	Yes
United States	Salt Lake	20	..	..	..	..	Yes	Yes	Yes	Yes	Yes	Yes
United States	San Jose	23	..	..	..	..	Yes	Yes	Yes	Yes	Yes	Yes
United States	Seattle	24	..	..	..	..	Yes	Yes	Yes	Yes	Yes	Yes
United States	Tampa	22	..	..	..	..	Yes	Yes	Yes	Yes	Yes	Yes
United States	Washington, DC	30	..	..	..	..	Yes	Yes	Yes	Yes	Yes	Yes
OCEANIA												
Samoa	Apia	..	..	..	..	..	Yes	No	Yes	No	Yes	No

Notes: * Car = private car. Train = train, tram or ferry. Bus = bus or minibus. Other = motorcycle, bicycle and other non-motorized modes. When several modes of transport are used for a given trip, the following hierarchy is used to determine the principal mode: (1) train; (2) tram or ferry; (3) bus or minibus; (4) car; (5) taxi or motorcycle; (6) bicycle or other non-motorized modes. ** Responses (yes/no) to the following questions: In the city, are there: (A) building codes? (B) hazard mapping? (C) natural disaster insurance for public and private buildings? *** Responses (yes/no) to the following questions: (A) Has the city established a long-term strategic planning initiative for sustainable development, involving key partners? (B) Is this process institutionalized and/or has there been any legislative change to support cities to engage in sustainable development planning processes? (C) Is the city implementing local environmental action plans involving key partners?

Source: UN-Habitat (2002), *Global Urban Indicators Database 2 (1998 data).*

TABLE C.6

Social Indicators, Selected Cities

		Households below the poverty line	Life expectancy at birth (years)		Under-five mortality	Gross school enrolment ratios (%)				Literacy rate (%)	
						Primary		Secondary			
		(%)	Female	Male	(%)	Female	Male	Female	Male	Female	Male
AFRICA											
Algeria	Algiers	..	71.0	68.0	4.0	..	..	..	..	76.3	86.4
Benin	Cotonou	35.0	60.6	55.9	8.2	74.3	78.3	27.7	39.2	70.0	94.0
Benin	Parakou	35.0	62.2	58.0	10.1	74.3	120.3	26.5	39.3	54.0	79.0
Benin	Porto-Novo	22.0	59.5	54.6	12.0	..	..	37.1	49.8	75.0	90.0
Botswana	Gaborone	54.1	67.1	63.1	10.5	49.7	50.3	52.6	47.4	66.9	70.3
Burkina Faso	Bobo-Dioulasso	12.2	..	..	21.0	..	..	..	..	..	..
Burkina Faso	Koudougou	23.1	..	..	21.0	..	..	..	..	..	..
Burkina Faso	Ouagadougou	12.2	..	..	21.0	..	..	..	..	..	..
Burundi	Bujumbura	66.5	53.7	52.3	..	81.5	81.6	43.3	44.0	64.2	80.1
Cameroon	Douala	19.7	..	..	15.0	..	..	..	..	..	..

TABLE C.6

continued

		Households below the poverty line	Life expectancy at birth (years)		Under-five mortality	Gross school enrolment ratios (%)				Literacy rate (%)	
						Primary		Secondary			
		(%)	Female	Male	(%)	Female	Male	Female	Male	Female	Male
Cameroon	Yaounde	30.0	..	..	15.0	..	..	..	..	..	..
Central African Republic	Bangui	49.0	..	..	16.2	50.0	..	27.0	..	..	..
Chad	N'Djamena	..	50.0	48.0	17.2	64.4	45.6	16.5	8.0	..	..
Congo	Brazzaville	21.7	56.0	52.0	12.2	36.0	41.8	6.8	8.2	12.0	31.0
Congo	Pointe-Noire	25.0	56.0	52.0	14.3	26.4	26.6	28.1	23.8	15.0	28.0
Côte d'Ivoire	Abidjan	..	60.0	55.0	9.0	61.7	81.7	14.8	29.8	36.8	63.3
Côte d'Ivoire	Yamoussoukro	..	60.0	65.0	..	34.5	45.0	7.0	18.1	36.8	63.3
Dem. Rep. of Congo	Kinshasa	22.9	51.0	50.0	14.1	36.0	48.7	9.2	21.9	..	..
Egypt	Ismailia	9.7	67.7	66.6	3.6	47.6	52.4	49.2	50.8	78.1	89.6
Egypt	Tanta	..	..	..	5.6	48.5	51.5	51.0	49.0	..	..
Ethiopia	Addis Ababa	..	61.5	57.8	17.1	83.5	86.1	44.1	53.0	..	..
Gabon	Libreville	30.0	56.5	53.3	14.4	72.9	86.0	72.9	86.0	60.5	80.3
Gabon	Port-Gentil	30.0	56.5	53.3	14.0	..	..	..	..	60.5	80.3
Gambia	Banjul	40.0	57.0	54.0	..	56.3	64.2	..	..	37.0	63.0
Ghana	Accra	..	69.0	66.2	9.6	..	..	..	..	74.5	87.3
Ghana	Kumasi	26.0	69.0	66.2	9.6	..	..	..	..	74.5	87.3
Guinea	Conakry	9.0	41.0	46.0	..	63.8	82.3	..	..	..	..
Kenya	Kisumu	58.2	66.3	62.8	12.4	..	..	..	..	81.4	91.7
Kenya	Mombasa	33.5	..	..	12.4	..	..	..	..	..	..
Kenya	Nairobi	46.6	60.9	57.6	12.4	..	..	..	..	..	..
Lesotho	Maseru	..	52.3	47.7	..	76.0	67.0	76.0	70.0	..	..
Liberia	Monrovia	..	53.0	50.0	..	72.5	72.9	..	..	26.0	40.0
Libyan Arab Jamahiriya	Tripoli	..	71.0	69.0	2.7	..	..	..	..	72.8	89.6
Madagascar	Antananarivo	54.2	0.6	0.6	13.9	64.0	67.0	..	..	..	..
Malawi	Lilongwe	..	44.6	41.4	22.9	..	..	..	..	31.0	52.0
Mali	Bamako	16.2	58.7	55.3	..	41.0	59.0	35.0	65.0	71.2	71.2
Mauritania	Nouakchott	25.0	54.3	52.3	14.8	83.5	87.6	14.2	19.2	..	..
Morocco	Casablanca	11.9	74.4	70.1	6.1	..	..	..	..	..	..
Morocco	Rabat	11.7	74.0	70.0	6.1	..	..	..	..	..	..
Mozambique	Maputo	47.8	61.7	54.6	..	132.8	136.7	26.2	27.0	77.4	92.9
Namibia	Windhoek	..	..	..	6.5	52.0	48.0	52.5	47.5	67.0	66.0
Niger	Maradi	..	56.0	55.0	25.0	..	..	..	..	..	..
Niger	Niamey	..	56.0	55.0	25.0	..	..	..	..	53.0	67.0
Nigeria	Ibadan	53.0	55.5	52.0	11.9	..	..	..	..	13.1	17.2
Nigeria	Lagos	53.0	55.5	52.0	11.9	..	..	..	..	13.1	17.2
Rwanda	Kigali	65.0	50.0	47.0	..	50.0	71.0	..	..	45.0	57.0
Senegal	Bignona	65.0	58.2	60.2	..	92.0	105.0	..	..	23.7	44.7
Senegal	Dakar	38.2	58.2	60.2	..	86.0	88.9	..	..	47.7	74.7
Senegal	Thies	48.7	58.2	60.2	..	59.4	78.8	..	..	23.7	44.7
South Africa	Durban	..	..	..	..	..	..	..	..	..	..
South Africa	East Rand	..	..	..	..	..	..	..	..	..	..
South Africa	Port Elizabeth	..	..	..	3.7	..	..	..	..	..	..
Togo	Lome	20.0	60.0	54.0	14.4	52.0	55.0	..	..	75.0	94.0
Togo	Sokode	33.0	53.0	51.0	9.5	75.9	90.3	..	..	50.0	74.0
Tunisia	Tunis	..	74.2	70.6	3.2	47.2	52.8	50.2	49.8	59.2	80.0
Uganda	Entebbe	..	..	..	17.0	43.0	53.0	53.0	45.0	93.6	98.0
Uganda	Jinja	..	51.0	47.0	17.0	94.0	95.0	51.0	76.0	53.0	77.0
Zimbabwe	Bulawayo	..	..	..	12.5	..	..	..	..	..	..
Zimbabwe	Chegutu	..	..	..	12.5	..	..	..	..	..	..
Zimbabwe	Gweru	..	..	..	12.5	..	..	..	..	..	..
Zimbabwe	Harare	..	..	..	12.5	..	..	48.6	54.4	..	..
Zimbabwe	Mutare	..	..	..	12.5	..	..	..	..	..	..
ASIA											
Armenia	Yerevan	58.2	76.2	69.3	1.5	..	..	..	..	100.0	100.0
Bangladesh	Chittagong	..	..	..	9.6	93.0	94.0	..	..	..	..
Bangladesh	Dhaka	44.3	60.9	61.7	9.6	77.9	80.4	62.3	65.9	60.3	60.3
Bangladesh	Sylhet	..	..	..	9.6	93.6	86.9	..	..	..	..
Bangladesh	Tangail	50.0	..	..	9.6	..	..	..	..	..	..
Cambodia	Phnom Penh	16.4	69.0	64.0	11.5	74.1	82.2	8.3	12.7	57.0	79.5
Georgia	Tbilisi	54.7	76.8	68.5	..	..	..	..	..	99.0	99.0
India	Alwar	..	..	..	..	..	..	..	..	..	..
India	Bangalore	18.6	..	..	4.9	..	..	..	..	..	..
India	Chennai	20.5	68.5	65.0	3.7	49.5	50.5	50.7	49.3	69.0	72.0
India	Delhi	16.0	..	..	2.6	..	..	..	..	76.0	91.0
India	Mysore	18.8	..	..	..	96.1	93.6	69.7	74.3	..	..
Indonesia	Bandung	2.0	..	..	4.0	..	..	..	..	..	..
Indonesia	Jakarta	6.6	..	..	2.4	97.6	98.9	95.7	..	97.3	99.2
Indonesia	Semarang	24.8	..	..	3.9	98.1	97.7	92.9	..	91.4	97.5
Indonesia	Surabaya	0.9	..	..	3.9	..	..	..	..	..	..
Iraq	Baghdad	..	..	..	12.5	..	..	..	..	..	..
Japan	Tokyo	0.0	84.1	77.5	3.9	100.0	100.0	100.0	100.0	100.0	100.0
Jordan	Amman	17.7	71.3	68.6	2.9	91.2	91.7	63.4	62.4	86.9	95.5
Kazakhstan	Astana	18.8	74.0	63.0	0.5	..	..	89.0	94.0	100.0	100.0
Kuwait	Kuwait	6.9	72.0	70.0	1.3	..	..	..	..	78.6	85.4
Kyrghyzstan	Bishkek	51.0	71.2	63.1	4.4	..	..	..	..	96.2	98.4
Lao PDR	Vientiane	19.0	..	..	7.5	52.7	47.4	54.9	45.2	78.9	92.2
Lebanon	Sin El Fil	..	..	..	3.2	..	..	..	..	..	..
Malaysia	Penang	6.1	74.6	69.6	0.7	..	..	..	..	82.0	91.0

Mongolia	Ulaanbaatar	30.0	63.9	59.7	4.3	100.0	100.0	74.2	64.7	97.1	99.1
Myanmar	Yangon	..	64.6	60.6	7.2	99.8	92.2	57.7	53.3	88.7	90.6
Nepal	Butwal	..	57.8	60.5	..	49.7	53.7	85.3	74.3	25.6	58.8
Nepal	Pokhara	20.0	50.0	55.0	2.1	88.0	83.3	35.4	26.6	42.0	66.2
Occupied Palestine Territory	Gaza	38.0	73.1	69.9	..	21.5	24.4	22.1	21.8	76.9	90.4
Oman	Muscat	..	72.0	70.0	2.5	..	..	..	..	..	..
Pakistan	Karachi	35.0	65.0	63.0	12.0	58.7	60.9	67.3	70.6	64.2	72.0
Pakistan	Lahore	28.0	65.0	63.0	6.3	66.2	68.5	73.3	71.9	65.1	72.7
Philippines	Cebu	..	71.6	67.6	3.8	..	..	..	..	..	..
Qatar	Doha	..	..	..	..	..	..	..	..	..	..
Republic of Korea	Hanam	1.5	65.9	77.7	0.2	98.8	97.9	99.9	99.9	..	..
Republic of Korea	Pusan	2.1	65.9	77.7	0.8	95.9	94.9	99.7	99.8	..	..
Republic of Korea	Seoul	1.1	65.9	77.7	0.2	98.8	97.9	99.9	99.9	..	..
Singapore	Singapore	4.0	79.2	75.0	..	93.0	100.0	100.0	100.0	89.2	96.8
Sri Lanka	Colombo	18.0	..	..	..	..	..	..	..	..	..
Syrian Arab Republic	Damascus	..	..	..	3.2	46.0	62.0	..	..	89.0	96.0
Thailand	Bangkok	15.9	79.0	76.0	3.3	..	..	..	..	95.1	98.4
Thailand	Chiang Mai	9.7	71.0	66.0	3.3	..	..	..	..	90.0	93.0
Turkey	Ankara	14.9	..	..	4.2	..	..	..	..	..	..
Viet Nam	Hanoi	2.1	69.6	64.9	4.2	..	..	..	..	89.0	95.1
Viet Nam	Ho Chi Minh	10.6	69.6	64.9	4.2	..	..	..	..	89.5	95.1
Yemen	Sana'a	..	..	..	9.6	..	..	..	..	..	..

EUROPE

Albania	Tirana	18.7	76.0	70.0	..	48.4	51.6	48.0	52.0	50.1	49.9
Belarus	Minsk	17.9	76.0	65.1	1.0	..	..	..	..	..	..
Bosnia and Herzegovina	Sarajevo	..	..	..	1.4	..	..	..	..	..	..
Bulgaria	Bourgas	..	74.8	67.9	1.0	..	..	..	..	99.0	99.0
Bulgaria	Sofia	55.0	74.3	67.1	1.3	..	..	..	..	99.5	99.8
Bulgaria	Troyan	6.4	74.5	67.6	0.5	100.0	100.0	100.0	100.0	99.8	..
Bulgaria	Veliko Tarnovo	..	74.3	67.1	1.5	..	..	..	..	..	..
Croatia	Zagreb	2.5	77.0	68.0	..	..	..	..	..	99.5	99.9
Czech Republic	Brno	11.0	77.6	70.8	0.6	..	..	..	..	100.0	100.0
Czech Republic	Prague	1.1	78.1	71.1	0.6	100.0	100.0	96.7	99.5	99.7	99.7
Estonia	Riik	3.6	76.0	64.7	..	100.0	100.0	100.0	100.0	100.0	100.0
Estonia	Tallin	1.9	73.8	62.5	..	100.0	100.0	100.0	100.0	100.0	100.0
Germany	Berlin	15.8	..	..	0.1	78.4	87.7	..	..	..	..
Germany	Cologne	11.2	..	..	0.1	80.6	87.9	..	..	..	..
Germany	Duisburg	11.2	..	..	0.1	69.9	85.6	..	..	..	..
Germany	Erfurt	6.8	..	..	0.3	..	..	88.9	88.3	..	..
Germany	Freiburg	8.5	..	..	0.1	..	..	95.2	96.5	..	..
Germany	Leipzig	11.2	..	..	0.1	69.9	85.6	..	..	..	..
Germany	Wiesbaden	6.3	..	..	0.1	..	..	81.2	89.0	..	..
Hungary	Budapest	..	75.5	67.9	0.9	..	..	..	..	..	..
Italy	Aversa	14.2	..	..	0.6	..	..	..	..	..	..
Latvia	Riga	..	75.9	65.2	1.4	..	..	..	..	99.7	100.0
Lithuania	Vilnius	16.0	76.9	66.5	1.1	..	..	..	..	100.0	100.0
Netherlands	Amsterdam	..	..	..	1.0	..	..	..	..	100.0	100.0
Netherlands	Eindhoven	..	..	..	..	..	..	..	..	100.0	100.0
Netherlands	Meppel	..	..	..	..	..	..	..	..	100.0	100.0
Poland	Bydgoszcz	8.0	76.5	68.8	1.4	98.0	98.8	91.0	90.0	99.0	99.0
Poland	Gdansk	4.9	77.0	69.0	0.6	99.4	99.4	100.0	100.0	99.9	99.9
Poland	Katowice	3.6	76.6	67.8	1.2	100.0	100.0	100.0	87.7	99.5	98.5
Poland	Poznan	5.9	76.7	69.3	0.8	99.7	99.3	96.3	97.8	99.9	99.9
Republi of Moldova	Chisinau	..	..	..	2.2	..	..	..	..	..	..
Russian Federation	Astrakhan	34.4	72.6	60.0	2.6	100.0	99.0	98.0	93.0	97.4	99.6
Russian Federation	Belgorod	19.9	75.4	64.5	1.5	99.0	99.0	100.0	100.0	97.9	99.8
Russian Federation	Kostroma	26.7	73.0	61.5	2.0	100.0	98.0	100.0	100.0	98.8	99.8
Russian Federation	Moscow	17.6	73.8	62.8	1.6	100.0	100.0	100.0	100.0	97.6	99.7
Russian Federation	Nizhny Novgorod	21.5	73.7	61.4	1.6	100.0	99.0	100.0	100.0	98.2	99.8
Russian Federation	Novomoscowsk	23.0	71.2	58.1	1.9	100.0	100.0	100.0	100.0	96.7	99.4
Russian Federation	Omsk	25.2	73.7	63.0	1.8	100.0	100.0	100.0	100.0	97.6	99.7
Russian Federation	Pushkin	27.2	74.4	63.8	1.4	100.0	100.0	100.0	100.0	99.4	99.9
Russian Federation	Surgut	15.3	74.3	63.4	1.5	100.0	99.0	100.0	98.0	97.3	99.5
Russian Federation	Veliky Novgorod	18.8	71.9	57.9	1.4	100.0	100.0	100.0	100.0	98.9	99.9
Serbia and Montenegro	Belgrade	48.0	74.5	68.8	1.3	98.7	97.5	94.0	89.0	97.9	99.6
Slovenia	Ljubljana	5.5	78.0	71.0	0.7	94.7	94.6	94.0	89.5	100.0	100.0
Spain	Madrid	9.9	82.7	75.2	0.6	100.0	100.0	98.3	98.1	98.1	99.3
Spain	Pamplona	3.9	..	..	0.7	100.0	100.0	87.4	88.1	99.3	99.6
Sweden	Amal	3.4	81.2	75.5	0.5	100.0	100.0	..	..	..	..
Sweden	Stockholm	5.6	75.8	81.4	0.5	100.0	100.0	..	..	..	..
Sweden	Umea	4.6	81.5	76.7	0.5	100.0	100.0	..	..	..	..
Switzerland	Basel	7.1	82.5	76.5	..	..	..	..	..	..	..
United Kingdom	Belfast	..	..	..	0.5	100.0	100.0	100.0	100.0	..	..
United Kingdom	Birmingham	..	..	..	0.9	100.0	100.0	100.0	100.0	78.0	80.0
United Kingdom	Cardiff	..	..	..	0.8	100.0	100.0	100.0	100.0	77.0	75.0
United Kingdom	Edinburgh	..	..	..	0.7	100.0	100.0	100.0	100.0	78.0	76.0
United Kingdom	London	..	..	..	0.7	100.0	100.0	100.0	100.0	78.0	80.0
United Kingdom	Manchester	..	..	..	0.8	100.0	100.0	100.0	100.0	78.0	80.0

LATIN AMERICA AND THE CARIBBEAN

Argentina	Buenos Aires	4.4	..	..	4.2	..	..	..	..	..	..
Argentina	Comodoro Rivadavia	17.6	74.0	67.3	..	..	..	..	..	97.8	98.4
Argentina	Córdoba	26.8	78.7	71.6	4.0	..	..	..	..	..	..
Argentina	Rosario	27.2	75.7	71.7	0.3	98.8	99.1	..	..	98.0	98.0
Barbados	Bridgetown	9.0	..	..	..	..	..	..	..	..	..
Belize	Belize City	18.8	71.8	68.2	3.2	69.9	79.2	67.9	58.8	75.0	75.0
Bolivia	Santa Cruz de la Sierra	40.1	67.7	64.2	7.8	86.8	92.0	51.0	52.5	..	..
Brazil	Belém	..	..	..	4.0	..	..	..	..	..	..
Brazil	Icapui	..	..	..	4.0	30.2	27.9	4.9	2.9	12.0	9.8
Brazil	Maranguape	40.5	..	..	4.0	..	..	..	..	..	..

TABLE C.6

continued

		Households below the poverty line (%)	Life expectancy at birth (years)		Under-five mortality (%)	Gross school enrolment ratios (%)				Literacy rate (%)	
						Primary		Secondary			
			Female	Male		Female	Male	Female	Male	Female	Male
Brazil	Porto Alegre	..	76.2	66.2	4.0	92.3	93.0	57.4	51.0	..	..
Brazil	Recife	44.4	..	..	5.8	..	..	..	..	86.7	89.6
Brazil	Rio de Janeiro	17.0	..	..	4.0	..	..	..	..	..	..
Brazil	São Paulo	6.5	76.2	67.3	2.0	..	..	..	..	92.2	94.7
Chile	Gran Concepcion	19.8	78.4	72.4	1.4	..	..	..	..	..	..
Chile	Santiago de Chile	4.7	..	..	..	..	..	..	..	..	..
Chile	Tome	16.9	..	..	1.2	..	..	..	..	..	..
Chile	Valparaiso	18.2	..	..	..	49.6	51.0	51.3	47.2	..	..
Chile	Vina del mar	11.6	..	..	..	..	..	..	..	..	..
Colombia	Armenia	17.9	65.4	72.6	3.2	47.3	52.7	46.4	53.6	8.0	12.0
Colombia	Marinilla	31.3	71.3	64.0	2.8	41.8	43.3	35.9	31.2	81.0	77.0
Colombia	Medellín	..	72.5	62.5	..	95.9	94.0	98.0	85.8	..	..
Cuba	Baracoa	..	..	..	0.9	..	..	..	..	..	..
Cuba	Camaguey	..	..	..	0.9	..	..	..	..	..	..
Cuba	Cienfuegos	..	..	..	0.9	..	..	..	..	..	..
Cuba	Havana	..	..	..	0.9	..	..	..	..	..	..
Cuba	Pinar Del Rio	..	78.0	74.0	6.5	..	..	..	..	..	..
Cuba	Santa Clara	..	..	..	0.9	..	..	..	..	..	..
Dominican Republic	Santiago de los Caballeros	40.0	..	..	6.1	..	..	..	..	..	..
Ecuador	Ambato	..	..	..	3.7	..	..	..	..	..	..
Ecuador	Cuenca	..	75.0	66.1	..	94.6	97.5	64.5	67.7	93.2	97.5
Ecuador	Guayaquil	48.0	71.2	67.4	3.7	98.8	98.9	75.3	68.6	97.8	98.2
Ecuador	Manta	25.0	68.0	64.0	4.3	..	..	..	..	..	..
Ecuador	Puyo	..	50.3	61.0	3.7	..	..	..	..	..	..
Ecuador	Quito	11.5	77.1	71.7	3.7	100.0	100.0	94.2	97.3	95.6	..
Ecuador	Tena	..	64.8	56.6	3.7	..	..	..	..	..	..
El Salvador	San Salvador	27.4	74.7	70.1	3.2	..	..	..	..	..	..
Guatemala	Quetzaltenango	..	67.2	62.9	4.6	..	..	..	..	..	..
Jamaica	Kingston	10.1	..	..	2.4	..	..	..	..	..	..
Jamaica	Montego Bay	13.4	..	..	2.4	..	..	..	..	..	..
Mexico	Ciudad Juarez	70.0	75.0	70.0	4.9	..	..	..	..	..	..
Nicaragua	Leon	28.3	..	..	3.5	..	..	..	..	..	..
Panama	Colon	21.3	75.0	69.6	2.5	..	..	..	..	..	..
Paraguay	Asuncion	9.8	72.0	67.5	2.6	..	..	..	..	89.3	93.0
Peru	Cajamarca	60.0	68.0	70.0	5.0	..	..	..	..	..	..
Peru	Huanuco	..	..	..	5.5	..	..	..	..	..	..
Peru	Huaras	..	82.0	75.0	4.7	..	..	..	..	..	..
Peru	Iquitos	46.3	67.5	62.4	5.0	39.7	36.0	37.0	41.0	41.1	48.4
Peru	Lima	..	80.0	74.0	4.7	..	..	..	..	..	..
Peru	Tacna	14.7	70.9	65.9	..	49.0	51.1	49.8	50.2	92.0	92.0
Peru	Tumbes	26.0	75.0	80.0	3.7	..	..	..	..	..	..
Trinidad and Tobago	Port of Spain	..	..	..	2.8	..	..	..	..	89.8	85.8
Uruguay	Montevideo	15.4	76.1	68.6	1.9	100.0	100.0	100.0	93.9	98.3	98.6
NORTHERN AMERICA											
Canada	Hull	..	81.4	75.7	0.1	..	..	..	..	..	..
United States	Atlanta	11.0	..	..	0.2	..	..	..	..	..	..
United States	Birmingham-USA	13.2	..	..	0.3	..	..	..	..	..	..
United States	Boston	9.3	..	..	0.1	..	..	..	..	..	..
United States	Des Moines	8.2	..	..	0.2	..	..	..	..	..	..
United States	Hartford	9.3	..	..	0.2	..	..	..	..	..	..
United States	Minneapolis-St. Paul	7.7	..	..	0.2	..	..	..	..	..	..
United States	New York	20.4	..	..	0.2	..	..	..	..	..	..
United States	Providence	11.5	..	..	0.2	..	..	..	..	..	..
United States	Salt Lake	8.9	..	..	0.2	..	..	..	..	..	..
United States	San Jose	9.0	..	..	0.1	..	..	..	..	..	..
United States	Seattle	7.8	..	..	0.1	..	..	..	..	..	..
United States	Tampa	13.6	..	..	0.2	..	..	..	..	..	..
United States	Washington, DC	8.2	..	..	0.2	..	..	..	..	..	..
OCEANIA											
Samoa	Apia	38.9	71.9	65.4	1.9	92.7	95.5	89.6	76.0	98.9	99.1

Source: UN-Habitat (2002), *Global Urban Indicators Database 2 (1998 data).*

TABLE C.7

Urban Governance Indicators, Selected Cities

		Local government				Transparency and accountability[**]				Participation of civil society involvement[***]		
		Decentralization[*]		Revenue	Expenditures	A	B	C	D	A	B	C
		A	B	(US$ per capita)								
AFRICA												
Algeria	Algiers	None	None	..	..	Yes	Yes	Yes	Yes	No	No	No
Benin	Cotonou	None	All	8.7	3.9	Yes	Yes	Yes	Yes	Yes	Yes	Yes
Benin	Parakou	None	All	..	..	Yes	Yes	Yes	Yes	Yes	Yes	Yes
Benin	Porto-Novo	None	All	4.1	0.2	Yes	Yes	Yes	Yes	Yes	Yes	Yes
Botswana	Gaborone	None	Some	..	..	Yes	Yes	Yes	Yes	Yes	Yes	Yes
Burkina Faso	Bobo-Dioulasso	..	..	..	..	No	No	No	No	No	No	No
Burkina Faso	Koudougou	..	..	..	..	No	No	No	No	No	No	No
Burkina Faso	Ouagadougou	All	None	..	..	Yes	Yes	No	No	Yes	No	Yes
Burundi	Bujumbura	None	None	7.5	6.0	No	Yes	Yes	No	No	No	No
Cameroon	Douala	None	None	..	..	Yes	Yes	Yes	Yes	No	No	No
Cameroon	Yaounde	None	None	..	..	Yes	Yes	Yes	Yes	Yes	Yes	Yes
Central African Republic	Bangui	None	None	..	..	No	Yes	No	No	No	No	No
Chad	N'Djamena	Some	All	..	..	Yes	Yes	Yes	Yes	Yes	Yes	Yes
Congo	Brazzaville	Some	Some	0.9	0.3	No	Yes	Yes	Yes	No	No	No
Congo	Pointe-Noire	Some	Some	..	..	No	Yes	Yes	No	No	No	No
Côte d'Ivoire	Abidjan	None	None	15.2	2.2	Yes	Yes	Yes	Yes	Yes	Yes	Yes
Côte d'Ivoire	Yamoussoukro	None	None	6.9	1.5	Yes	Yes	Yes	Yes	Yes	Yes	Yes
Dem. Rep. of Congo	Kinshasa	None	None	0.1	0.0	No	Yes	Yes	No	No	No	No
Egypt	Ismailia	None	Some	..	..	Yes	Yes	Yes	No	Yes	Yes	Yes
Egypt	Tanta	None	None	..	..	Yes	Yes	Yes	No	No	Yes	Yes
Ethiopia	Addis Ababa	..	..	36.2	21.0	No	No	No	No	No	No	No
Gabon	Libreville	None	Some	..	..	No	Yes	Yes	Yes	Yes	Yes	Yes
Gabon	Port-Gentil	None	Some	..	..	No	No	No	No	Yes	Yes	Yes
Gambia	Banjul	All	Some	..	..	Yes	Yes	Yes	Yes	Yes	Yes	Yes
Ghana	Accra	Some	Some	..	..	Yes	Yes	Yes	Yes	Yes	Yes	Yes
Ghana	Kumasi	None	All	..	0.7	Yes	Yes	Yes	Yes	Yes	Yes	Yes
Guinea	Conakry	Some	Some	..	..	Yes	Yes	Yes	Yes	Yes	Yes	Yes
Kenya	Kisumu	Some	Some	7.6	8.1	No	Yes	Yes	Yes	No	Yes	No
Kenya	Mombasa	Some	Some	..	..	No	Yes	Yes	Yes	No	Yes	No
Kenya	Nairobi	Some	Some	7.0	21.3	No	Yes	Yes	Yes	No	Yes	No
Lesotho	Maseru	None	Some	..	..	No	No	No	No	No	No	No
Liberia	Monrovia	Some	All	..	..	Yes	No	Yes	Yes	No	No	No
Libyan Arab Jamahiriya	Tripoli	Some	All	30.6	15.3	Yes	Yes	Yes	Yes	Yes	Yes	Yes
Madagascar	Antananarivo	All	Some	..	..	No	Yes	Yes	Yes	No	Yes	Yes
Malawi	Lilongwe	None	Some	..	..	Yes	Yes	Yes	Yes	No	No	No
Mali	Bamako	None	None	..	..	Yes	Yes	Yes	No	Yes	Yes	Yes
Mauritania	Nouakchott	None	None	..	..	Yes	Yes	Yes	Yes	No	No	No
Morocco	Casablanca	Some	Some	..	..	Yes	Yes	Yes	Yes	Yes	Yes	Yes
Morocco	Rabat	Some	Some	..	..	Yes	Yes	Yes	Yes	Yes	Yes	Yes
Mozambique	Maputo	None	None			No	No	No	No	No	No	No
Namibia	Windhoek	Some	None	..	..	Yes	Yes	Yes	Yes	Yes	Yes	Yes
Niger	Maradi	None	Some	..	..	No	No	Yes	No	Yes	Yes	Yes
Niger	Niamey	None	Some	..	..	Yes	No	No	No	Yes	No	No
Nigeria	Ibadan	Some	Some	9.5	8.9	Yes	Yes	Yes	Yes	Yes	Yes	Yes
Nigeria	Lagos	Some	Some	2.3	1.9	Yes	Yes	Yes	Yes	Yes	Yes	Yes
Rwanda	Kigali	Some	Some	..	..	No	Yes	Yes	No	Yes	No	Yes
Senegal	Bignona	None	None	..	..	Yes	Yes	Yes	No	No	No	No
Senegal	Dakar	All	All	..	..	Yes	Yes	Yes	No	Yes	No	No
Senegal	Thies	None	None	..	..	Yes	Yes	Yes	No	No	No	No
South Africa	Durban	..	..	..	..	No	No	No	No	No	No	No
South Africa	East Rand	None	Some	..	..	No	No	No	No	Yes	Yes	Yes
South Africa	Port Elizabeth	..	..	..	..	No	No	No	No	No	No	No
Togo	Lome	Some	Some			Yes	Yes	Yes	No	No	No	Yes
Togo	Sokode	Some	Some	0.9	0.7	Yes	Yes	Yes	No	No	No	Yes
Tunisia	Tunis	None	Some	28.1	..	Yes	Yes	Yes	No	Yes	Yes	No
Uganda	Entebbe	Some	Some	207.0	207.0	Yes	Yes	Yes	No	Yes	Yes	Yes
Uganda	Jinja	All	All	5.6	4.7	Yes	Yes	Yes	Yes	Yes	Yes	Yes
Zimbabwe	Bulawayo	Some	Some	2.2	0.3	Yes	Yes	Yes	No	Yes	Yes	Yes
Zimbabwe	Chegutu	None	None	..	..	Yes	Yes	Yes	Yes	No	No	No
Zimbabwe	Gweru	None	None	355.4	356.3	Yes	Yes	Yes	Yes	Yes	Yes	Yes
Zimbabwe	Harare	Some	Some	..	..	Yes	Yes	Yes	Yes	Yes	Yes	Yes
Zimbabwe	Mutare	None	None	..	..	Yes	Yes	Yes	Yes	Yes	Yes	Yes
ASIA												
Armenia	Yerevan	..	All	..	..	No	No	No	No	No	No	Yes
Bangladesh	Chittagong	None	None	8.4	9.1	Yes	Yes	Yes	No	No	No	No
Bangladesh	Dhaka	None	None	..	4.2	No	No	No	No	No	No	No
Bangladesh	Sylhet	None	None	..	..	Yes	Yes	Yes	No	No	Yes	No
Bangladesh	Tangail	Some	Some	..	..	Yes	Yes	No	No	No	Yes	No
Cambodia	Phnom Penh	None	Some	5.2	5.2	No	Yes	Yes	No	No	No	No
Georgia	Tbilisi	Some	Some	..	..	No	Yes	No	No	No	No	No
India	Alwar	None	None	..	..	No	No	No	No	No	No	No
India	Bangalore	None	Some	25.3	26.4	Yes	Yes	Yes	Yes	No	Yes	No
India	Chennai	None	All	..	..	Yes	Yes	Yes	Yes	Yes	Yes	Yes
India	Delhi	None	None	..	..	No	No	No	No	No	No	No
India	Mysore	None	All	7.3	7.2	Yes	Yes	Yes	Yes	Yes	Yes	Yes
Indonesia	Bandung	Some	All	21.0	18.8	Yes	Yes	Yes	No	No	No	No
Indonesia	Jakarta	None	Some	90.7	87.6	Yes	Yes	Yes	Yes	Yes	Yes	Yes

TABLE C.7

continued

		Local government				Transparency and accountability**				Participation of civil society involvement***		
		Decentralization*		Revenue	Expenditures	A	B	C	D	A	B	C
		A	B	(US$ per capita)								
Indonesia	Semarang	None	None	23.0	19.6	Yes	Yes	Yes	Yes	Yes	Yes	Yes
Indonesia	Surabaya	Some	Some	15.0	32.0	Yes	Yes	Yes	Yes	No	Yes	Yes
Iraq	Baghdad	None	None	..	..	No	No	No	No	No	No	No
Japan	Tokyo	Some	Some	807.2	804.5	Yes	Yes	Yes	Yes	Yes	Yes	Yes
Jordan	Amman	None	None	56.7	56.7	Yes	Yes	Yes	No	Yes	Yes	No
Kazakhstan	Astana	None	All	..	..	No	Yes	Yes	Yes	No	No	No
Kuwait	Kuwait	None	None			Yes	Yes	Yes	Yes	No	No	No
Kyrghyzstan	Bishkek	All	Some	671.4	571.2	No	Yes	Yes	Yes	Yes	No	Yes
Lao People's Dem. Rep.	Vientiane	Some	Some	..	..	Yes	Yes	Yes	No	Yes	Yes	Yes
Lebanon	Sin El Fil	None	None	..	..	Yes	Yes	Yes	Yes	No	No	No
Malaysia	Penang	Some	Some		..	Yes	Yes	Yes	Yes	Yes	Yes	Yes
Mongolia	Ulaanbaatar	Some	All	4.4	5.0	Yes	Yes	Yes	Yes	Yes	Yes	Yes
Myanmar	Yangon	Some	Some	..	..	Yes	Yes	Yes	Yes	Yes	Yes	Yes
Nepal	Butwal	All	All	..	..	Yes	Yes	Yes	No	Yes	No	Yes
Nepal	Pokhara	All	All	..	..	Yes	Yes	Yes	No	Yes	No	Yes
Occupied Palestine Territory	Gaza	None	None			Yes	Yes	Yes	Yes	Yes	Yes	Yes
Oman	Muscat	None	None	5.4	6.5	Yes	Yes	Yes	Yes	Yes	No	No
Pakistan	Karachi	None	None	104.4	105.7	Yes	Yes	No	No	No	No	No
Pakistan	Lahore	None	None	37.7	38.4	Yes	Yes	No	No	No	No	No
Philippines	Cebu	All	All	4.1	3.0	Yes	Yes	Yes	Yes	Yes	Yes	Yes
Qatar	Doha	None	None			No	No	No	No	No	No	No
Republic of Korea	Hanam	Some	All	458.0	716.0	Yes	Yes	Yes	Yes	Yes	Yes	Yes
Republic of Korea	Pusan	Some	All	744.0	469.3	Yes	Yes	Yes	Yes	Yes	Yes	Yes
Republic of Korea	Seoul	Some	All	865.1	742.2	Yes	Yes	Yes	Yes	Yes	Yes	Yes
Singapore	Singapore	None	None	4637.9	3725.0	Yes	Yes	Yes	Yes	Yes	Yes	Yes
Sri Lanka	Colombo	Some	Some	2.2	1.6	Yes	Yes	Yes	Yes	Yes	Yes	Yes
Syrian Arab Republic	Damascus	All	All	..	..	Yes	Yes	Yes	Yes	Yes	Yes	Yes
Thailand	Bangkok	Some	Some	108.1	96.4	Yes	Yes	No	No	Yes	Yes	Yes
Thailand	Chiang Mai	Some	Some	106.3	105.2	No	No	No	No	No	No	No
Turkey	Ankara	None	Some	173.4	173.4	Yes	Yes	Yes	No	No	No	No
Viet Nam	Hanoi	Some	Some	309.8	59.6	No	Yes	Yes	Yes	Yes	Yes	Yes
Viet Nam	Ho Chi Minh	Some	Some	266.0	260.0	No	Yes	Yes	Yes	No	No	Yes
Yemen	Sana'a	None	None	110.0	138.0	Yes	Yes	Yes	Yes	No	No	No
EUROPE												
Albania	Tirana	Some	None	..	..	No	No	No	No	No	No	No
Belarus	Minsk	..	..	..	..	No	No	No	No	No	No	No
Bosnia and Herzegovina	Sarajevo	All	Some	490.4	479.1	Yes	Yes	Yes	No	Yes	Yes	Yes
Bulgaria	Bourgas	None	Some	150.9	150.9	Yes	Yes	Yes	Yes	Yes	Yes	Yes
Bulgaria	Sofia	All	Some	..	..	No	No	No	No	Yes	Yes	Yes
Bulgaria	Troyan	Some	None	..	..	Yes	Yes	No	No	Yes	Yes	Yes
Bulgaria	Veliko Tarnovo	All	Some	..	..	Yes	Yes	Yes	No	No	No	No
Croatia	Zagreb	Some	Some	..	..	Yes	Yes	Yes	Yes	No	No	Yes
Czech Republic	Brno	Some	Some	..	..	Yes	Yes	Yes	Yes	Yes	Yes	Yes
Czech Republic	Prague	Some	Some	..	..	Yes	Yes	Yes	Yes	Yes	Yes	Yes
Estonia	Riik	All	All	..	..	No	No	No	No	No	No	No
Estonia	Tallin	All	All	316.4	298.8	Yes	Yes	Yes	Yes	Yes	Yes	Yes
Germany	Berlin	..	..			No	No	No	No	No	No	No
Germany	Cologne	..	..	3531.0	3599.0	No	No	No	No	No	No	No
Germany	Duisburg	..	..	3273.0	3476.0	No	No	No	No	No	No	No
Germany	Erfurt	..	..	2552.0	2550.0	No	No	No	No	No	No	No
Germany	Freiburg	..	..	2803.0	2884.0	No	No	No	No	No	No	No
Germany	Leipzig	..	..	3273.0	3476.0	No	No	No	No	No	No	No
Germany	Wiesbaden	..	..	3609.0	3837.0	No	No	No	No	No	No	No
Hungary	Budapest	..	..			No	No	No	No	No	No	No
Italy	Aversa	Some	Some	..	..	Yes	Yes	Yes	Yes	No	No	No
Latvia	Riga	Some	All	233.0	218.0	Yes	Yes	Yes	Yes	Yes	Yes	Yes
Lithuania	Vilnius	Some	Some	253.6	249.2	Yes	Yes	Yes	Yes	Yes	Yes	Yes
Netherlands	Amsterdam	None	None			No	No	No	No	No	No	No
Netherlands	Eindhoven	..	..	..	..	No	No	No	No	No	No	No
Netherlands	Meppel	..	..	..	..	No	No	No	No	No	No	No
Poland	Bydgoszcz	All	All	339.1	377.1	Yes	Yes	Yes	Yes	Yes	Yes	Yes
Poland	Gdansk	All	All	452.0	479.0	Yes	Yes	Yes	Yes	Yes	Yes	Yes
Poland	Katowice	Some	Some	437.0	431.0	Yes	Yes	Yes	Yes	Yes	Yes	Yes
Poland	Poznan	All	All	476.6	510.6	Yes	Yes	Yes	Yes	No	No	Yes
Republi of Moldova	Chisinau	Some	All	15.9	..	Yes	No	No	Yes	Yes	No	Yes
Russian Federation	Astrakhan	Some	Some	126.0	10.0	Yes	Yes	Yes	Yes	Yes	Yes	Yes
Russian Federation	Belgorod	Some	Some	131.0	8.0	Yes	Yes	Yes	Yes	Yes	Yes	Yes
Russian Federation	Kostroma	Some	Some	180.0	7.0	No	No	No	No	No	No	No
Russian Federation	Moscow	Some	Some	596.0	116.0	Yes	Yes	Yes	Yes	Yes	Yes	Yes
Russian Federation	Nizhny Novgorod	Some	Some	236.0	14.0	Yes	Yes	Yes	Yes	Yes	Yes	Yes
Russian Federation	Novomoscowsk	Some	Some	151.0	11.0	Yes	Yes	Yes	Yes	Yes	Yes	Yes
Russian Federation	Omsk	Some	Some	205.0	8.0	Yes	Yes	Yes	Yes	Yes	Yes	Yes
Russian Federation	Pushkin	Some	Some	..	..	Yes	Yes	Yes	Yes	Yes	Yes	Yes
Russian Federation	Surgut	Some	Some	923.0	97.0	Yes	Yes	Yes	Yes	Yes	Yes	Yes
Russian Federation	Veliky Novgorod	Some	Some	212.0	21.0	Yes	Yes	Yes	Yes	Yes	Yes	Yes
Serbia and Montenegro	Belgrade	None	None	178.6	180.2	No	No	No	No	No	No	No
Slovenia	Ljubljana	Some	Some	176.9	142.1	Yes	Yes	Yes	Yes	Yes	Yes	Yes
Spain	Madrid	Some	Some	547.0	547.0	Yes	Yes	Yes	No	Yes	Yes	Yes

Country	City	A*	B*			A**	B**	C**	D**	A***	B***	C***
Spain	Pamplona	Some	Some	546.7	483.5	Yes	Yes	Yes	Yes	Yes	Yes	Yes
Sweden	Amal	All	All	4835.0	4790.0	Yes	Yes	Yes	Yes	Yes	Yes	Yes
Sweden	Stockholm	All	All	5450.0	5602.0	Yes	Yes	Yes	Yes	Yes	Yes	Yes
Sweden	Umea	All	All	4942.0	4835.0	Yes	Yes	Yes	Yes	Yes	Yes	Yes
Switzerland	Basel	Some	All	..	..	No	Yes	Yes	Yes	Yes	Yes	Yes
United Kingdom	Belfast	..	..	..	..	No	No	No	No	No	No	No
United Kingdom	Birmingham	None	None	..	..	No	No	No	No	No	No	No
United Kingdom	Cardiff	..	..	..	..	No	No	No	No	No	No	No
United Kingdom	Edinburgh	..	..	..	..	No	No	No	No	No	No	No
United Kingdom	London	..	..	..	..	No	No	No	No	No	No	No
United Kingdom	Manchester	..	..	..	..	No	No	No	No	No	No	No
LATIN AMERICA AND THE CARIBBEAN												
Argentina	Buenos Aires	All	All	243.1	258.0	Yes	Yes	Yes	Yes	Yes	Yes	Yes
Argentina	Comodoro Rivadavia	All	All	332.0	30.0	Yes	Yes	Yes	Yes	No	No	No
Argentina	Córdoba	All	All	256.4	267.2	Yes	Yes	Yes	Yes	No	No	No
Argentina	Rosario	None	Some	809.0	802.7	Yes	Yes	Yes	Yes	Yes	No	Yes
Barbados	Bridgetown	..	..			No	No	No	No	No	No	No
Belize	Belize City	..	..	..	..	Yes	Yes	Yes	Yes	Yes	No	No
Bolivia	Santa Cruz de la Sierra	None	None	64.4	29.3	Yes	Yes	Yes	Yes	No	No	Yes
Brazil	Belém	..	..	185.9	186.7	No	Yes	Yes	No	Yes	Yes	Yes
Brazil	Icapui	Some	Some	918.1	..	Yes	Yes	Yes	Yes	Yes	Yes	Yes
Brazil	Maranguape	None	Some	133.8	140.9	No	Yes	Yes	Yes	Yes	Yes	Yes
Brazil	Porto Alegre	All	All	134.4	17.4	Yes	Yes	Yes	Yes	Yes	Yes	Yes
Brazil	Recife	Some	Some	334.8	40.3	Yes	Yes	Yes	No	Yes	Yes	Yes
Brazil	Rio de Janeiro	Some	Some	50.5	142.6	Yes	Yes	Yes	No	Yes	No	Yes
Brazil	São Paulo	All	All	446.1	102.7	Yes	Yes	Yes	Yes	Yes	Yes	Yes
Chile	Gran Concepcion	None	Some	115.9	..	Yes	Yes	Yes	No	No	Yes	Yes
Chile	Santiago de Chile	Some	All	..	..	Yes	Yes	Yes	Yes	No	Yes	No
Chile	Tome	None	Some	66.3	72.4	No	Yes	Yes	No	No	Yes	No
Chile	Valparaiso	Some	All	105.8	105.9	Yes	Yes	Yes	No	Yes	No	Yes
Chile	Vina del mar	Some	Some	71.6	66.1	Yes	Yes	Yes	Yes	Yes	Yes	Yes
Colombia	Armenia	All	Some	102.9	39.2	Yes	Yes	Yes	Yes	Yes	Yes	Yes
Colombia	Marinilla	All	All	30.7	27.3	Yes	Yes	Yes	Yes	Yes	Yes	Yes
Colombia	Medellin	Some	All	403.4	154.0	Yes	Yes	Yes	No	No	No	No
Cuba	Baracoa	Some	Some	..	..	No	No	Yes	No	Yes	Yes	Yes
Cuba	Camaguey	Some	Some	..	..	No	No	Yes	No	Yes	Yes	Yes
Cuba	Cienfuegos	Some	Some	..	..	No	No	Yes	No	Yes	Yes	Yes
Cuba	Havana	Some	Some	..	..	No	No	Yes	No	Yes	Yes	Yes
Cuba	Pinar Del Rio	Some	Some	..	..	No	No	No	No	No	No	No
Cuba	Santa Clara	Some	Some	..	..	No	No	Yes	No	Yes	Yes	Yes
Dominican Republic	Santiago de los Caballeros	..	..	82.2	82.3	No	Yes	No	No	No	No	No
Ecuador	Ambato	None	All	9.0	8.4	Yes	Yes	Yes	Yes	No	No	No
Ecuador	Cuenca	..	All	37.9	12.4	Yes	Yes	Yes	Yes	Yes	Yes	Yes
Ecuador	Guayaquil	None	All	87.3	43.6	Yes	Yes	Yes	No	Yes	No	No
Ecuador	Manta	All	All	22.3	0.5	No	No	No	No	No	No	No
Ecuador	Puyo	None	All	18.7	21.7	Yes	Yes	Yes	Yes	No	No	Yes
Ecuador	Quito	None	All	102.1	48.8	Yes	Yes	Yes	Yes	No	No	No
Ecuador	Tena	None	All	17.4	23.8	Yes	Yes	Yes	No	Yes	No	Yes
El Salvador	San Salvador	..	..	..	..	No	No	No	No	No	No	No
Guatemala	Quetzaltenango	None	All	..	..	Yes	Yes	Yes	Yes	No	No	Yes
Jamaica	Kingston	Some	Some	58.6	..	No	No	No	No	No	No	No
Jamaica	Montego Bay	..	..	..	..	No	No	No	No	No	No	No
Mexico	Ciudad Juarez	None	None	67.6	22.9	Yes	Yes	Yes	No	Yes	Yes	Yes
Nicaragua	Leon	..	..	..	..	No	No	No	No	No	No	No
Panama	Colon	Some	Some	5.5	0.3	No	Yes	Yes	No	No	No	No
Paraguay	Asuncion	None	All	87.0	13.0	Yes	Yes	Yes	No	Yes	Yes	Yes
Peru	Cajamarca	All	Some	18.3	18.3	Yes	Yes	Yes	No	Yes	Yes	Yes
Peru	Huanuco	None	Some	4.9	1.7	Yes	Yes	Yes	No	No	No	Yes
Peru	Huaras	None	Some	44.9	17.0	Yes	Yes	Yes	Yes	No	No	No
Peru	Iquitos	All	Some	9.4	5.5	Yes	Yes	Yes	Yes	Yes	Yes	Yes
Peru	Lima	None	Some	63.4	11.5	Yes	Yes	Yes	Yes	Yes	Yes	Yes
Peru	Tacna	None	Some	2.6	2.7	Yes	Yes	Yes	Yes	No	No	No
Peru	Tumbes	..	..	..	..	No	Yes	Yes	No	No	No	No
Trinidad and Tobago	Port of Spain	..	..	..	..	No	No	No	No	No	No	No
Uruguay	Montevideo	Some	Some	230.0	56.0	Yes	Yes	Yes	No	Yes	No	Yes
NORTHERN AMERICA												
Canada	Hull	All	All	1113.0	1098.0	Yes	Yes	No	Yes	Yes	Yes	Yes
United States	Atlanta	All	All	1902.0	553.0	Yes	Yes	Yes	Yes	Yes	Yes	Yes
United States	Birmingham-USA	All	All	1427.0	234.0	Yes	Yes	Yes	Yes	Yes	Yes	Yes
United States	Boston	All	All	2668.0	701.0	Yes	Yes	Yes	Yes	Yes	Yes	Yes
United States	Des Moines	All	All	1854.0	424.0	Yes	Yes	Yes	Yes	Yes	Yes	Yes
United States	Hartford	All	All	2442.0	276.0	Yes	Yes	Yes	Yes	Yes	Yes	Yes
United States	Minneapolis-St. Paul	All	All	2066.0	626.0	Yes	Yes	Yes	Yes	Yes	Yes	Yes
United States	New York	All	All	3962.0	934.0	Yes	Yes	Yes	Yes	Yes	Yes	Yes
United States	Providence	All	All	1169.0	99.0	Yes	Yes	Yes	Yes	Yes	Yes	Yes
United States	Salt Lake	All	All	1308.0	463.0	Yes	Yes	Yes	Yes	Yes	Yes	Yes
United States	San Jose	All	All	2232.0	889.0	Yes	Yes	Yes	Yes	Yes	Yes	Yes
United States	Seattle	All	All	2232.0	889.0	Yes	Yes	Yes	Yes	Yes	Yes	Yes
United States	Tampa	All	All	1738.0	358.0	Yes	Yes	Yes	Yes	Yes	Yes	Yes
United States	Washington, DC	All	All	2379.0	658.0	Yes	Yes	Yes	Yes	Yes	Yes	Yes
OCEANIA												
Samoa	Apia	None	None	..	..	No	No	No	No	Yes	Yes	Yes

Notes: * Responses (all/none/some) to the following questions: Can the local government, without permission from higher governments: (A) set local tax levels (property tax etc)? (B) set user charges for services?

** Responses (yes/no) to the following questions: At the city level, are there: (A) regular independent auditing of municipal accounts? (B) published contracts and tenders for municipal services? (C) sanctions against faults of civil servants? (D) laws on disclosure of potential conflicts of interest? *** Civil society involvement in or citizen participation in major planning decisions. Responses (yes/no) to the following questions: Are cities involving the civil society in a formal participatory process prior to: (A) new major roads and highway proposals? (B) alteration in zoning? (C) major public projects?

Source: UN-Habitat (2002), *Global Urban Indicators Database 2 (1998 data).*

REFERENCES

Abate, G, W Kogi-Makau et al (2000) 'Health seeking and hygiene behaviours predict nutritional status of pre-school children in a slum area of Addis Ababa, Ethiopia' *Ethiopian Medical Journal* **38**(4): 253–265

Abbott (2002) 'A method-based planning framework for informal settlement upgrading' *Habitat International* **26**(3): 317–333

Abrams, C (1964) *Man's Struggle for Shelter in an Urbanizing World*. MIT Press, Cambridge, MA

Acioly, C C Jr (2000) 'Can urban management deliver the sustainable city? Guided densification in Brazil versus informal compactness in Egypt' in M Jenks and R Burgess (eds) *Compact Cities: Sustainable Urban Forms for Developing Countries*. Spon Press, London and New York, pp127–140

Ackroyd, P (2000) *London, The Biography*. Chatto and Windus, London

African Economic Research Bulletin, Financial, Economic and Technical Series (1997) **36**: 7

African NGOs Habitat II Caucus (1996) *Citizenship and Urban Development in Africa. Popular Cities for their Inhabitants*. Prepared for Habitat II, Istanbul

Agbola, T and A M Jinadu (1997) 'Forced eviction and forced relocation in Nigeria: The experience of those evicted from Maroko in 1990' *Environment and Urbanization* **9**(2): 271–288

Aitken, B, A Harrison and R Lipsey (1996) 'Wages and foreign ownership: A comparative study of Mexico, Venezuela, and the United States' *Journal of International Economics* **42**: 345–371

Albert, M (2000) 'A Q&A on the WTO, IMF, World Bank, and activism' *Znet*, January, www.zmag.org/zmag//articles/jan2000albert.htm

Alcock, P (1997) *Understanding Poverty*, second edition. Macmillan, Basingstoke

Ali, S M and S Sirivardana (1996) 'Towards a new paradigm for poverty eradication in South Asia' *International Social Science Journal* **48**(2): 201–218

Amaral, M R (1994) 'Community organisation, housing improvements and income generation' *Habitat International* **18**: 81–97

Amis, P (1984) 'Squatters or tenants: The commercialisation of unauthorized housing in Nairobi' *World Development* **12**: 87–96

Amis, P (1990) 'Administrative control or market mechanisms: The economics of commercialised

rental housing in Nairobi' in UNCHS (Habitat) *Rental Housing: Proceedings of an Expert Group Meeting*. UNCHS (Habitat), Nairobi, pp86–96

Amis, P (1995) 'Making sense of urban poverty' *Environment and Urbanization* **7**(1): 145–159

Amis, P (2002a) 'Municipal government, urban economic growth and poverty reduction: Identifying the transmission mechanisms between growth and poverty' in C Rakodi and T Lloyd-Jones (eds) *Urban Livelihoods: A People-centred Approach to Reducing Poverty*. Earthscan, London, pp97–111

Amis, P (2002b) 'Thinking about chronic urban poverty', CPRC Working Paper 12. University of Birmingham, www.chronicpoverty.org/pdfs/urbanareas.pdf

Amis, P and S Kumar (2000) 'Urban economic growth, infrastructure and poverty in India: Lessons from Visakhapatnam' *Environment and Urbanization* **12**(1): 185–196

Amis, P and C Rakodi (1995) 'Urban poverty: Concepts, characteristics and policies' *Habitat International* **19**: 403–405

Amole, B, D Korboe et al (1993) 'The family house in West Africa: A forgotten resource for policy makers?' *Third World Planning Review* **15**(4): 355–372

Andersson, R (1999) '"Divided Cities" as a policy-based notion in Sweden' *Housing Studies* **14**(5): 601–624

Angel, S (1983) 'Land tenure for the urban poor' in S Angel et al (eds) *Land for Housing the Poor*. Select Books, Singapore

Angel, S (2001) 'Comments on Hernando De Soto's "the Mystery of capital", round table discussion' *Interplan*, June, http://interplan.org/pdf/Solly.pdf

Ansari, J H and N von Einsiedel (eds) (1998) *Urban Land Management. Improving Policies and Practices in Developing Countries of Asia*. Urban Management Programme, IBH Publishing, Oxford and New Delhi and Calcutta

Appadurai, A (2001) 'Deep democracy: Urban governmentality and the horizon of politics' *Environment and Urbanization* **13**(2): 23–43

Arandel, C and M El Batran (1997) 'The informal housing development process in Egypt', DPU Working Paper 82. Development Planning Unit, University College, London

Arblaster, L and M Hawtin (1993) *Heath, Housing and Social Policy*. Socialist Health Association, London

Aryeety, E and M Nissanke (1997) 'Asia and Africa in the global economy:

Economic policies and external performance in South-east Asia and sub-Saharan Africa 1998', Paper presented at the United Nations University-African Economic Research Consortium Conference on Asia and Africa in the Global Economy, Tokyo, 3–4 August 1998

Asian Development Bank (1995) *Involuntary Resettlement*, ADB Policy Paper R1-79-95, August. Asian Development Bank, Manila

Asian Development Bank (2001) *Cities Data Book for the Asia Pacific*. Asian Development Bank, Manila

Atoh, M (2000) 'The coming of a hyper-aged and depopulating society and population policies: The case of Japan', Expert Group Meeting on Policy Responses to Population Ageing and Population Decline. United Nations Population Division, October

Augé, M (1999) *An Anthropology of Contemporary Worlds*. Stanford University Press, Stanford

Aurejac, P and Y Cabannes (1995) 'Accompagnement et financement d'initiatives communautaires locales. Enseignements des expériences en Amérique latine et en Asie des opérations de construction ou d'amélioration de l'habitat menées à l'initiative ou avec le concours d'associations populaires de quartier', GRET-PSH, Paris

Auyero, J (1999) '"This is a lot like the Bronx, isn't it?" Lived experiences of marginality in an Argentine slum' *International Journal of Urban and Regional Research* **23**(1): 45–69

Azizi, M M (1995) 'The provision of urban infrastructure in Iran: An empirical evaluation' *Urban Studies* **32**: 507–522

Azuela, A (1995) 'La propriété, le logement et le droit, in Régularisations de propriétés' *Les Annales de la Recherche Urbaine* **66**: 5–11. Plan Urbain, Ministère de l'Equipement, des Transports et du Tourisme

Badcock, B (1984) *Unfairly Structured Cities*. Basil Backwell, London

Badcock, B (1986) 'Land and housing policy in Chinese urban development, 1978–86' *Planning Perspectives* **1**: 147–170

Bahl, R W and J Linn (1992) *Urban Public Finance in Developing Countries*. Oxford University Press, New York

Baldacci, E, L de Mello and G Inchauste (2002) *Financial Crises, Poverty and Income Distribution*. International Monetary Fund WP 02/4

Banerji, R (2000) 'Poverty and primary schooling: Field studies from Mumbai and Delhi' *Economic and

Political Weekly* **35**(10): 795–802

Banner, G (2002) 'Community governance and the new central-local partnership' *International Social Science Journal* **54**(172): 217–231

Barasa, F S and E S M Kaabwe (2001) 'Fallacies in policy and strategies of skills training for the informal sector: Evidence from the Jua Kali sector in Kenya' *Journal of Education and Work* **14**(3): 329–353

Baross, P and J Van der Linden J (eds) (1990) *The Transformation of Land Supply Systems in Third World Cities*. Avebury, Aldershot

Barr, A (1999) *Familiarity and Trust: An Experimental Investigation*. Centre for the Study of African Economies, University of Oxford, Oxford

Barter, P A (2002) 'Transport and Housing Security in the Klang Valley, Malaysia' *Singapore Journal of Tropical Geography [Singapore]* **23**(3): 268–287

Baulch, B (1996) 'The new poverty agenda: A disputed consensus' *IDS Bulletin* **27**: 1–10

Baum, S (1997) 'Australia: A global city? Testing the social polarisation thesis' *Urban Studies* **34**: 1881–1902

Baumann, T (1998) *South Africa's Housing Policy – Construction of Development or Development of Construction?* Report to Homeless International

Baumann, T (2001) 'Shack/Slum Dwellers International and banks' *Environment and Urbanization* **13**(2): 139–143

Bayart, J-F, S Ellis and B Hibou (1999) *The Criminalization of the State in Africa*. Indiana University Press, Indianapolis/James Currey, London

Bazoglu, N and D Biau (2001) 'Measuring slums: A composite index', Paper presented at the Cities Alliance Consultative Group Meeting, Kolkata, 11 December

Beall, J (2002) 'Globalisation and social exclusion in cities: Framing the debate with lessons from Africa and Asia' *Environment and Urbanization* **14**(1): 41–51

Becker, C M, A M Hamer and A R Morrison (1994) *Beyond Urban Bias in Africa*. James Currey, London

Benton, L (1994) 'Beyond legal pluralism: Towards a new approach to law in the informal sector' *Social and Legal Studies* **3**: 223–242

Berger, M (1996) 'An introduction' in M Buvinic (ed) *Women's Ventures: Assistance to the Informal Sector in Latin America*. Kumerian Press, West Hartford, CT

Berry, B (1991) *Long Wave Rhythms in Economic Development and*

Political Behavior. Johns Hopkins, Baltimore

Berry, B J L and J D Kasarda (1977) *Contemporary Urban Ecology*. Macmillan, New York

Berry, S (1995) 'Stable prices, unstable values: Some thoughts on monetization and the meaning of transactions in West African economies' in J Guyer (ed) *Money Matters: Instability, Values and Social Payments in the Modern History of West African Communities*. Heinemann, Portsmouth, NH/James Currey, London

Bingham, R D and Z Zhang (1997) 'Poverty and economic morphology of Ohio central-city neighborhoods' *Urban Affairs Review* 32(6): 766–796

Blong, R (1992) 'Some perspectives on geological hazards' in G McCall, D Laming and S Scott (eds) *Geohazards: Natural and Man-made*. Chapman and Hall, London, pp209–216

Bloom, D E and J G Williamson (1998) 'Demographic transitions and economic miracles in emerging Asia' *World Bank Economic Review* 12: 419–55

BMZ (German Ministry for Economic Cooperation and Development) (2000) *Making a Future for Cities: Development Policy in the Urban Century*. BMZ Special Paper No 015. BMZ, Bonn, p46

Bolt, G, J Burgers et al (1998) 'On the social significance of spatial location: Spatial segregation and social inclusion' *Netherlands Journal of Housing and the Built Environment* 13(1): 83–95

Boltho, A and G Toniolo (1999) 'The assessment: The twentieth century – achievements, failures, lessons' *Oxford Review of Economic Policy* 15: 1–17

Boone, P (1996) 'Politics and the effectiveness of foreign aid' *European Economic Review* 40: 289–329

Boonyabancha, S (1983) 'The causes and effects of slum eviction in Bangkok' in S Angel, R W Archer, S Tanphiphat, and E A Wegelin (eds) *Land For Housing the Poor*. Select Books, Bangkok, pp254–280

Booth, C (1892) *Life and Labour of the People in London*. Macmillan, London

Boris, E and E Prügl (1996) *Homeworkers in Global Perspective: Invisible No More*. Routledge, New York

Bourdieu, P (1990) *The Logic of Practice*. Polity Press, Cambridge

Brenner, N (1998a) 'Beyond state-centrism? Space, territory and geographical scale' *Globalization Studies, Theory and Society* 28(1): 39–78

Brenner, N (1998b) 'Between fixity and motion: Accumulation, territorial organization and the historic geography of spatial scales' *Environment and Planning* D: Society and Space 16: 459–481

Breton, R (1964) 'Institutional completeness of ethnic communities and the personal relations of immigrants' *American Journal of Sociology* 70: 193–205

Briggs, J and D Mwamfupe (2000) 'Peri-urban development in an era of structural adjustment in Africa: The city of Dar es Salaam, Tanzania' *Urban Studies* 37: 797–809

Briggs, X D S (1998) 'Brown kids in white suburbs: Housing mobility and the many faces of social capital' *Housing Policy Debate* 9(1): 177

Bromley, R and C Gerry (1979) *Casual Work and Poverty in Third World Cities*. John Wiley and Sons, Chichester

Brooks-Gunn, J, G Duncan and J L Aber (eds) (1997) *Neighborhood Poverty: Volume 1: Context and Consequences for Children*. Russell Sage Foundation, New York

Brooks-Gunn, J, G Duncan, P Klebanov and N Sealand (1993) 'Do neighborhoods influence child and adolescent outcomes?' *American Journal of Sociology* 99(2): 353–395

Brotchie, J et al (eds) (1985) *The Future of Urban Form: The Impact of New Technology*. Croom Helm, London

Brotchie, J F, P Hall and P W Newton (eds) (1987) *The Spatial Impact of Technological Change*. Croom Helm, London

Brueckner, J K and Y Zenou (1999) 'Harris-Todaro models with a land market' *Regional Science and Urban Economics* 29: 317–339

Bruno, M, M Ravallion and L Squire (1997) 'Equity and growth in developing countries: Old and new perspectives on the policy issues', World Bank Policy Research Working Paper 1563. World Bank, Washington, DC, http://econ.worldbank.org/files/451_wps1563.pdf

Burby, R and W Rohe (1989) 'Deconcentration of public housing: Effects of residents' satisfaction with their living environment and their fear of crime' *Urban Affairs Quarterly* 25: 117–141

Burgers, J (1996) 'No polarisation in Dutch cities? Inequality in a corporatist country' *Urban Studies* 33: 99–105

Burgess, E W (1925) 'The growth of the city: An introduction to a research project' in R E Park, E W Burgess and McKenzie (eds) *The City*. The University of Chicago Press, Chicago, pp47–62

Burgess, R (1978) 'Petty commodity housing or dweller control? A critique of John Turner's views on housing policy' *World Development* 6(9/10): 1105–1133

Burgess, R (1992) 'Helping some to help themselves: Third World housing policies and development strategies' in K Mathéy (ed) *Beyond Self-Help Housing*. Mansell, London

Bussolo, M and H-B Solignac Lecomte (1999) *Trade Liberalisation and Poverty*. ODI Poverty Briefing

Caldeira, T P R (1996a) *Building up Walls: The New Pattern of Spatial Segregation in Sao Paulo*. UNESCO, pp55–66

Caldeira, T P R (1996b) 'Fortified enclaves: The new urban segregation' *Public Culture* 8: 303–328

Cambodia (2000) *Education Reform in Cambodia*, www.moeys.gov.kh/education_reform_in_cambodia/strategic_analysis/chapter7.htm

Campfens, H (1997) 'International review of community development' in H Campfens (ed) *Community Development Around the World, Practice, Theory, Research,*

Training. Pact Publications, New York

Caplan, K, S Heap, A Nicol, J Plummer, S Simpson and J Weiser (2001) 'Flexibility by design: Lessons from multi-sector partnerships in water and sanitation projects', Water and Sanitation Cluster, Business Partners for Development, London, www.bpd-waterandsanitation.org/english/docs/flexibility.pdf

Carney, D (1998) 'Implementing the sustainable rural livelihoods approach' in D Carney (ed) *Sustainable Rural Livelihoods: What Contribution Can We Make?* Department for International Development, London, pp3–23

Carney, D (1999) *Approaches to Sustainable Livelihoods for the Rural Poor*. ODI Poverty Briefing, London

Carothers, T and M Ottaway (2000) 'The burgeoning world of civil society aid' in M Ottaway and T Carothers (eds) *Funding Virtue, Civil Society Aid and Democracy Promotion*. Carnegie Endowment for International Peace, Washington, DC

Carroll, T F (1992) *Intermediary NGOs, the Supporting Link in Grassroots Development*. Kumarian Press, Bloomfield, CT

Carter, D M (1997) *States of Grace: Senegalese in Italty and the New European Immigration*. University of Minnesota Press, Minneapolis; London

Cashin, P, P Mauro, C Patillo and R Sahay (2001) 'Macroeconomic policies and poverty reduction. Stylized facts and an overview of research', IMF Working Paper 01/135. International Monetary Fund, www.imf.org/external/pubs/ft/wp/2001/wp01135.pdf

Castells, M (1996a) *The Rise of the Network Society*. Blackwell Publishers, Malden, MA

Castells, M (1996b) 'The net and the self: Working notes to a critical theory of information society' *Critical Anthropology* 16(1): 9–38

Castells, M (1997) *The Power of Identity*. Blackwell, Oxford

Castells, M, L Goh and R Y W Kwok (1990) *The Shep Kik Mei Syndrome: Economic Development and Public Housing in Hong Kong and Singapore*. Pion, London

Chambers, R (1997) *Whose Reality Counts? Putting the first last*. Intermediate Technology Publications, London

Chang, H-J (2002) 'The real lesson for developing countries from the history of the developed world: Freedom to choose' *History and Policy*, Policy Paper 9, www.historyandpolicy.org/main/policy-paper-09.htm

Chant, S (1997) *Women-Headed Households: Diversity and Dynamics in the Developing World*. Macmillan, Basingstoke

Chen, M, J Sebstad et al (1999) 'Counting the invisible workforce: The case of home-based workers' *World Development* 27(3): 603–610

Chen, S and M Ravallion (2001) 'How did the world's poorest fare in the 1990s?' *Review of Income and Wealth* 47: 283–300

Chiquier, L (1999) 'Secondary mortgage facilities: A case study of

Malaysia's Cagamas Berhad', Financial Sector Development Department, World Bank

Choe, S-C (2002) 'The promise and pitfalls of public-private partnerships in Korea' *International Social Science Journal* 54(172): 191–204

Christiensen, S F and P D Hoejgaard (1995) *How to Provide Secure Tenure for Informal Urban Settlers*. Ministry of Lands, Resettlement and Rehabilitation, Namibia

Christiensen, S F, P D Hoejgaard and W Werner (1999) 'Innovative land surveying and land registration in Namibia', DPU Working Paper 93, May. Development Planning Unit, University College, London

Churchill, A (1980) *Shelter*. World Bank, Washington, DC

CIDA (Canadian International Development Agency) (1998) *An Urbanizing World: Statement on Sustainable Cities*. CIDA, Quebec

Cinar, E M (1994) 'Unskilled urban migrant women and disguised employment: Home working women in Istanbul, Turkey' *World Development* 22(3): 369–380

Cities Alliance (1999) *Cities Without Slums: Action Plan for Moving Slum Upgrading to Scale*. The World Bank/UNCHS (Habitat), Washington, DC, www.citiesalliance.org

'Civil Society Engaging Multilateral Institutions: At the Crossroads' (1999) Montreal International Forum – FIM, Fall 1999, 1(1)

Clark, J (1991) *Democratizing Development: The Role of Voluntary Organizations*. Earthscan, London

Cobbett, W (1999) 'Towards securing tenure for all' *Habitat Debate* 5(3): 40

Cohen, M (1983) *Learning by Doing: World Bank Lending for Urban Development, 1972–1982*. World Bank, Washington, DC

Cohen, M (2001) 'Urban assistance and the material world: Learning by doing at the World Bank' *Environment and Urbanization* 13(1): 37–60

Cohen, M and S Cheema (1992) 'The new agendas' in N Harris (ed) *Cities in the 90s. The Challenge for Developing Countries*. Overseas Development Administration, Development Planning Unit, University College London Press, London, pp9–42

COHRE (Centre on Housing Rights and Evictions) (1999) *Forced Evictions: A Manual for Action and Human Rights*, No 3. COHRE, Geneva

COHRE (2002) *Forced Evictions. Violation of Human Rights*, No 8. COHRE, Geneva

Collier, P (1998) *Social Capital and Poverty*. World Bank, Washington, DC

Congdon, P (1995) 'Socio-economic structure and health in London' *Urban Studies* 32: 523–549

Congressional Budget Office (1997) 'The role of foreign aid in development', www.cbo.gov/showdoc.cfm?index=8&sequence=0

Constantin, F (1996) 'L'informal international ou la subversion de la territorialité' *Cultures and Conflicts* 21/22: 311–346

Cooper, F (1994) 'Conflict and connection: Rethinking colonial African history' *American*

Historical Review **99**(5): 1516–1545

Cornea, G A and S Kiiski (2001) 'Trends in income distribution in the post World War II period: Evidence and interpretation', Discussion Paper 2001-89. World Institute for Development Economics Research, www.wider.unu.edu/publications/dps/dp2001-89.pdf

Coulton, C J and S Pandey (1992) 'Geographic concentration of poverty and the risk to children in urban neighborhoods' *American Behavioral Scientist* **35**: 238–257

Courmont, V (2001) 'Poverty, a few definitions' *Villes en Développement* **53**: 4

Cragg, M and M Epelbaum (1995) 'Why has wage dispersion grown in Mexico? Is it the incidence of reforms or the growing demand for skills?' *Journal of Development Economics* **51**(1): 99–116

Cuervo, J C and D H O K Hin (1998) 'Todaro migration and primacy models: Relevance to the urbanization of the Philippines' *Cities* **15**(4): 245–256

Curry-Stevens, A (2001) *When Markets Fail People: Exploring the widening gap between rich and poor in Canada.* Centre for Social Justice, University of Toronto, Toronto, www.socialjustice.org/pubs/pdfs/winlose.pdf

Cutler, D and E Glaeser (1997) 'Are ghettos good or bad?' *Quarterly Journal of Economics* **112**: 827–872

DANIDA (Danish International Development Agency) (2000) *Byer i dansk udviklingssamarbeijde* [Towns in Danish Development Cooperation]. Danish Royal Ministry of Foreign Affairs, Copenhagen

Daniels, L (1999) 'The role of small enterprises in the household and national economy in Kenya: A significant contribution or a last resort?' *World Development* **27**(1): 55–65

De Coulanges, F (1873) *The Ancient City: A Study of the Religion, Laws, and Institutions of Greece and Rome*, translated by Willard Small, 1901, 12th edition. Lothrop, Lee and Shepard, Boston, MA

de la Barra, X (1998) 'Poverty: The main cause of ill health in urban children' *Health Education and Behavior* **25**: 46–59

De Soto, H (1989) *The Other Path: The Invisible Revolution in the Third World.* IB Taurus, London

De Soto, H (2000) *The Mystery of Capital: Why Capitalism Triumphs in the West and Nowhere Else.* Basic Books, New York

De Zoysa, I, N Bhandari, N Akhtari and M K Bhan (1998) 'Careseeking for illness in young infants in an urban slum in India' *Social Science & Medicine* **47**(12): 2101–2111

Deane, P (1965) *The First Industrial Revolution.* Cambridge University Press, Cambridge

Deininger, K and H Binswanger (1998) *The Evolution of the World Bank's Land Policy.* World Bank, http://wbln0018.worldbank.org/Networks/ESSD/icdb.nsf/

Dennis, R (1995) 'Landlords and housing in depression' *Housing Studies* **10**: 305–324

DeSouza, R M (1997) 'Housing and environmental factors and their effects on the health of children in the slums of Karachi, Pakistan' *Journal of Biosocial Science* **29**(3): 271–281

Develtere, P and P van Durme (1999–2000) 'Social exclusion, the informal sector and the social economy' *Courier*, December 1999–January 2000: 68–70

Develtere, P and P van Durme (2000) 'Social exclusion, the informal sector and the social economy' Dossier, europa.eu.int/comm/development/publicat/courier/courier-178/en/en-053-ni.pdf

DFID (Department for International Development) (2001) *Meeting the Challenge of Poverty in Urban Areas. Strategies for Achieving the International Development Targets.* DFID, London

DHA (Department for Humanitarian Affairs) (1993) *Natural Disasters.* DHA, Geneva, pp26–27

Diacon, D (1997) *Slum Networking. An Innovative Approach to Urban Development,* Building and Social Housing Foundation, London

Diko, J and A G Tipple (1992) 'Migrants build at home: Long distance housing development by Ghanaians in London' *Cities* **9**(6): 288–294

Dinham, B and S Sarangi (2002) 'The Bhopal gas tragedy 1984 to ?: The evasion of corporate responsibility' *Environment and Urbanization* **14**(1): 89–99

Doebele, W A (1975) 'The private market and low income urbanization in developing countries: The "pirate" subdivision of Bogotá', World Bank Discussion Paper D75-11. World Bank, Washington, DC

Dolinskaya, I (2001) 'Explaining Russia's output collapse: Aggregate sources and regional evidence', IMF Working Paper 01/16. International Monetary Fund, www.imf.org/external/pubs/ft/wp/2001/wp0116.pdf

Dollar, D and A Kraay (2000) 'Growth is good for the poor', Seminar Series 2000-35, International Monetary Fund

Douglass, M (1998) 'World city formation on the Asia Pacific Rim' in M Douglass and J Friedmann (eds) *Cities for Citizens.* John Wiley and Sons, Chichester

Dowall, D E (1991) 'Less is more: The benefits of minimal land development regulation' in *Regularizing the Informal Land Development Process.* 2: Discussion papers, pp9–20. Office of Housing and Urban Programs, US Agency for International Development, Washington, DC

Dowall, D E and G Clarke (1991) 'Urban management and land: A framework for reforming urban land policies in developing countries', Urban Management Programme Policy Paper 7. UMP, Washington, DC

Drakakis-Smith, D (1967) 'Urban renewal in an Asian context: A case study in Hong Kong' *Urban Studies* **13**: 295–305

Drakakis-Smith, D (1976) 'Some perspectives on slum and squatter settlements in Ankara', Paper presented to Institute of British Geographers Annual Conference, January, Lanchester Polytechnic, Coventry

Drakakis-Smith, D (1981) *Urbanization, Housing and the Development Process.* Croom Helm, London

Dreier, P and J Atlas (1995) 'US housing problems, politics and policies in the 1980s' *Housing Studies* **10**: 245–269

Drennan, M P, E Tobier and J Lewis (1996) 'The interruption of income convergence and income growth in large cities in the 1980s' *Urban Studies* **33**: 63–82

Ducci, M E (2000) 'Santiago: Territorios, anhelos y temores. Efectos sociales y espaciales de la expansión urbana' *EURE* **26**(79): 149

Duebel A (2000) *Separating Homeownership Subsidies from Finance: Traditional Mortgage Market Policies, Recent Reform Experiences and Lessons for Subsidy Reform.* Land and Real Estate Initiative Background series 14. World Bank, Washington, DC, www.worldbank.org/urban/publicat/background14.pdf

Dunning, J (1993) *Multinational Enterprises and the Global Economy.* Addison-Wesley, New York

Durand-Lasserve, A (1993) *Conditions de mise en place des systemes d'information foncière dans les villes d'Afrique Sub-Saharienne Francophone.* Programme de Gestion Urbaine. Document de travail no 8. PNUD-Banque Mondiale.

Durand-Lasserve, A (1994) 'Researching the relationship between economic liberalization and changes to land markets and land prices: The case of Conakry, Guinea, 1985, 1991' in G Jones and P Ward (eds) *Methodology for Land and Housing Market Analysis.* University College Press, London, pp55–69

Durand-Lasserve, A (2000) 'Security of land tenure for the urban poor in developing cities: Home ownership ideology v/s efficiency and equity', Paper presented at the global conference on the urban future, *Urban 21*, Berlin, 4–6 July

Durand-Lasserve, A and L Royston (2002) 'International trends and country contexts: From tenure regularization to tenure security' in A Durand-Lasserve and L Royston (eds) *Holding Their Ground: Secure Land Tenure for the Urban Poor in Developing Countries.* Earthscan, London

Durand-Lasserve, A and L Royston (eds) (2002a) *Holding Their Ground: Secure Land Tenure for the Urban Poor in Developing Countries.* Earthscan, London

Dutta, S S (2000) 'Partnerships in urban development: A review of Ahmedabad's experience' *Environment and Urbanization* **14**(1): 13–26

Dwyer, D J (ed) (1975) *People and Housing in Third World Cites.* Longman, London

Dwyer, D J (1987) 'Urban housing and planning in China,' *Transactions of Institute of British Geographers* **11**: 479–489

Easterlow, D, S J Smith and S Mallinson (2000) 'Housing for health: The role of owner occupation' *Housing Studies* **15**: 367–386

The Economist (1993) 'Breaking the cycle: Government role in economic growth. A Survey of Nigeria' *The Economist* **328**(7825): 3

Edwards M and J Gaventa (2001) *Global Citizen Action.* Lynne Rienner Publishers, Boulder, CO

Edwards, M and D Hulme (1995) 'NGO performance and accountability: Introduction and overview' in M Edwards and D Hulme (eds) *Non-governmental Organisations: Performance and Accountability. Beyond the Magic Bullet.* Earthscan, London, pp3–16

Elander, I (2002) 'Partnerships and urban governance' *International Social Science Journal* **54**(172): 191–204

Elbadawi, I and B Ndulu (1996) 'Long run development and sustainable growth in sub-Saharan Africa' in M Lundahl and B Ndulu (eds) *New Directions in Development Economics.* Routledge, London

Elliott, D S, W J Wilson and D Huizinga (1996) 'The effects of neighborhood disadvantage on adolescent development' *Journal of Research in Crime and Delinquency* **33**: 389–426

Ellis, S and J MacGaffey (1996) 'Research on sub-Saharan Africa's unrecorded international trade: Some methodological and conceptual problems' *African Studies Review* **39**(2): 19–41

Elmhirst, R (1999) 'Space, identity politics and resource control in Indonesia's transmigration programme' *Political Geography* **18**(7): 813–835

El-Raey, M, Y Fouda and P Gal (2000) 'GIS for environmental assessment of the impacts of urban encroachment on Rosetta Region, Egypt', *Environmental Monitoring and Assessment* **60**(2): 217–233

Environment and Urbanization (2000) 'Towards more pro-poor local government in urban areas' (Editorial) *Environment and Urbanization* **11**(1): 3–11

Epstein, T S and D Jezeph (2001) 'Development – There is another way: A rural–urban partnership development paradigm' *World Development* **29**(8): 1443–1454

Erdogan, N, G Saglamer, V Dokmeci and A Dikbas (1996) 'Socioenvironmental determinants of social interactions in a squatter settlement in Istanbul' *Journal of Architectural and Planning Research* **13**(4): 329–336

Escobar, S (1996) 'Small-scale commerce in the city of La Paz, Bolivia' in M Buvinic (ed) *Women's Ventures: Assistance to the Informal Sector in Latin America.* Kumerian Press, West Hartford, CT

European Commission (2000) *Guidelines for Sustainable Urban Development*, draft, February

Evans, P et al (2001) *Livable Cities: The Politics of Urban Livelihood and Sustainability.* University of California Press, Berkeley

Farvacque, C and P McAuslan (1992) 'Reforming urban land policies and institutions in developing countries', Urban Management Programme Policy Paper 5. World Bank, Washington, DC

Feder, G and A Nisho (1998) 'The benefits of land registration and titling: Economic and social perspectives' *Land Use Policy* **15**(1): 25–43

Ferguson, B (1996) 'The environmental impacts and public costs of unguided informal settlement: The case of Montego Bay' *Environment and Urbanization* **8**(2): 171–193

Ferguson, B (1999) 'Micro-finance of housing: A key to housing the low or moderate-income majority? *Environment and Urbanization* 11: 185–199

Fernandes, E (1996) *Law and Urban Change in Brazil*. Avebury, Aldershot

Fernandes, K (ed) (1998) 'Forced evictions and housing rights abuses in Asia' Second Report 1996–97, *Eviction Watch Asia*. CP Press, Karachi

Fieldhouse, E A (1999) 'Ethnic minority unemployment and spatial change: The case of London' *Urban Studies* 36: 1569–1596

Fiori, J and R Ramirez (1992) 'Notes on the self-help housing critique: Towards a conceptual framework for the analysis of self-help housing policies in developing countries' in K Mathéy (ed) *Beyond Self-Help Housing*. Mansell, London

Fiori, J, E Riley and R Ramirez (2000) *Urban Poverty Alleviation through Environmental Upgrading in Rio de Janeiro: Favela Bairro*. Development Planning Unit, University College, London

Fischer, J E (1995) 'Local land tenure and natural resource management systems in Guinea: Research findings and policy options', USAID-Guinea. Land Tenure Center, University of Wisconsin-Madison

Fisher, J (1998) *Nongovernments, NGOs and the Political Development of the Third World*. Kumarian Press, Bloomfield, CT

Flanagan, P and T Kanaley (1996) 'Urbanisation in Asia: Challenges and opportunities for Australia', Paper presented to the Royal Australian Planning Institute, Perth

Flood, J (1984) 'Rental gradients in Melbourne', Papers of the 8th meeting of the ANZ Regional Science Association, pp231–245

Flood, J (1997) 'Urban and housing indicators' *Urban Studies* 34(10): 1635–1665

Flood, J (2000a) 'Urban indicators for Thailand', Working Paper 2. Urban Area Definition

Flood, J (2000b) 'Sydney divided: Factorial ecology revisited. Residential differentiation in Australian cities', Paper presented to ANZRSA Annual Meeting, Hobart, December 2000; to Population Conference, Melbourne, December; and to South Africa Cities Forum, November 2002

Flood, J (2000c) 'Three ring circus: Axial and radial distribution of incomes and social groups in Sydney. Residential differentiation in Australian cities. Working Paper 1, Urban Frontiers', Paper presented to Population Conference, Melbourne, November

Flood, J (2001) *Istanbul + 5: Analysis of the data collection*. Report for UNCHS (Habitat)

Flood, J (2003) 'Estimating population in urban slums', Paper presented to Making Cities Work: The International Conference of the European Network on Housing Research, Tirana, May

Flood, J and P Jones (1990) 'The determinants of internal migration in Australia' in M T Gordon and B L J Gordon (eds) *Regional Modelling and Regional Planning*. Institute of Industrial Economics, Newcastle, pp213–232

Flood, J, C Maher, P W Newton and J R Roy (1992) *The Determinants of Internal Migration in Australia*. DBCE, Melbourne

Flood, J and J Yates (1989) 'Housing subsidies and income distribution' *Housing Studies* 4: 193–210

Forrest, R and A Murie (1988) *Selling the Welfare State: The Privatisation of Public Housing*. Routledge, London and New York

Fourie, C (2000) *Best Practices Analysis on Access to Land and Security of Tenure*. United Nations Centre for Human Settlements. Land Management Series No 8

Fowler, A (1998) 'Authentic NGDO partnerships: Dead end or way ahead?' *Development and Change* 29: 137–159

Freeman, J (2000) 'Welcome NGOs! You are now members of the New Establishment' *The Earth Times*, 16 March

Frijns, J and B Van Vliet (1999) 'Small-scale industry and cleaner production strategies' *World Development* 27(6): 967–983

Fujita, M (1989) *Urban Economic Theory: Land Use and City Size*. Cambridge University Press, Cambridge

Fukuyama, F (1992) *The End of History and the Last Man*. Free Press, New York

Fukuyama, F (1995) *Trust: The Social Virtues and the Creation of Prosperity*. Free Press, New York

Funkhouser, E (1996) 'The urban informal sector in Central America: Household survey evidence' *World Development* 24(11): 1737–1751

Gallagher, R (1992) *The Rickshaws of Bangladesh*. The University Press, Dhaka

Galster, G and A Zobel (1998) 'Will dispersed housing programmes reduce social problems in the US?' *Housing Studies* 13: 749–759

Gannon, C A and Z Liu (1997) 'Poverty and transport', Discussion Paper, TWU Papers TWU-30. Transportation, Water and Urban Development Department, World Bank, Washington, DC

Gans, H J (1962) *The Urban Villagers*. The Free Press, New York

Gaubatz, P (1999) 'China's urban transformation: Patterns and processes of morphological change in Beijing, Shanghai and Guangzhou' *Urban Studies* 36: 1495–1521

Gilbert, A G (1999) 'A home is for ever? Residential mobility and home ownership in self-help settlements' *Environment and Planning A*, 31: 1073–1091

Gilbert, A G (2001) 'On the mystery of capital and the myths of Hernando de Soto: What difference does legal title make?', Mimeo. University College, London

Gilbert, A G (2002) 'Helping the poor through housing subsidies: Lessons from Chile, Columbia and South Africa', Mimeo. University College, London

Gilbert, A and J Gugler (1992) *Cities, Poverty and Development Urbanization in the Third World*. Oxford University Press, Oxford

Godard, X (1997) 'Transport and mobility strategy for urban poverty reduction: The western African experience', Paper presented to the International Forum on Urban Poverty, Florence, 9–13 November. UNCHS (Habitat), Nairobi

Goddard, M (2001) 'From rolling thunder to reggae: Imagining squatter settlements in Papua New Guinea' *Contemporary Pacific* 13(1): 1–32

Goethert, R and N Hamdi (1988) *A Community Based Process in Programming and Development*. Intermediate Technology Development, London

Goetz, E G (2000) 'The politics of poverty deconcentration and housing demolition' *Journal of Urban Affairs* 22(2): 157–173

Goetz, E G (2002) 'Forced relocation vs voluntary mobility: The effects of dispersal programmes on households' *Housing Studies* 17: 107–123

Goldsmith, Sir J (1994) 'Testimony before the Senate Commerce Committee on the Subject of the Uruguay Round of GATT', www.hartford-hwp.com/archives/25a/004.html

Gong, X and A van Soest (2002) 'Wage differentials and mobility in the urban labor market: A panel data analysis for Mexico' *Labour Economics* 9: 513–529

Gopalan, P (1998) 'Circumscribed existence: Women's mobility and settlements development', Note prepared for discussion at the SUSTRAN Network General Assembly, 2–5 June 1998, Manila, Swayam Shikshan Prayog (SSP), Mumbai

Gough, K V (1998) 'Houses for sale? The self-help housing market in Pereira, Columbia' *Housing Studies* 13: 149–160

Grimes, O F (1976) *Housing for Low Income Urban Families*. Johns Hopkins University Press, Baltimore and London

Grootaert, C (1998) *Social Capital: The Missing Link*. World Bank, Washington, DC

Guha Sapir, D (1996) 'Health and nutrition among the urban poor: The case of the Calcutta slums' in Dasgupta, Chen and Krishnan (eds) *Health, Poverty and Development in India*. Oxford University Press, Delhi

Gupta, S, H Davoodi and R Alonso-Terme (1998) 'Does corruption affect income inequality and poverty?', IMF Working Paper 98/76, International Monetary Fund, www.imf.org/external/pubs/ft/wp/wp9876.pdf

Gwebu, Thando D (2002) 'Urban water scarcity management: Civic vs. state response in Bulawayo' *Habitat International* 26(3): 417–431

Haddad, L, M T Ruel and J L Garrett (1999) 'Are urban poverty and undernutrition growing? Some newly assembled evidence' *World Development* 27: 1891–1904

Hahnel, R (2001) 'Understanding the global economy and the current global economy crisis', www.zmag.org/instructionals/globalecon/index.htm

Hall, P (1997) 'Regeneration policies for peripheral housing estates: Inward and outward-looking approaches' *Urban Studies* 34: 873–890

Halliday, J (2001) 'The romance of non-state actors' in D Josselin and W Wallace (eds) *Non-State Actors in World Politics*. Palgrave, Basingstoke

Hamdi, N and R Goethert (1997) *Action Planning for Cities: A Guide for Community Practices*. John Wiley and Sons, New York

Hamnett, C (1994) 'Social polarisation in global cities: Theory and evidence' *Urban Studies* 31: 401–424

Hannah, L, K-H Kim and E S Mills (1993) 'Land use controls and housing prices in Korea' *Urban Studies* 30: 147–156

Hanson, G and A Harrison (1995) 'Trade, technology and wage inequality in Mexico', NBER Working Paper No 5110, May. National Bureau of Economic Research, http://papers.nber.org/papers/w5110

Hardoy, J, D Mitlin and D Satterthwaite (2001) *Environmental Problems in an Urbanizing World: Finding Solutions for Cities in Africa, Asia and Latin America*. Earthscan, London

Hardoy, J E and D Satterthwaite (1989) *Squatter Citizen: Life in the Urban Third World*, Earthscan, London

Harris, N (ed) (1992) *Cities in the 90s: The Challenge for Developing Countries. Overseas Development Administration*. Development Planning Unit. University College London Press, London

Harris, R (1999) 'Slipping through the cracks: The origins of aided self-help housing 1918–53' *Housing Studies* 14: 281–309

Hart, K (1970) 'Small-scale entrepreneurs in Ghana and development planning' *Journal of Development Planning*, July

Harth, A, U Herlyn et al (1998) 'Segregation in Eastern German cities: Gentrification, downgrading of large estates, and suburbanization' *Netherlands Journal of Housing and the Built Environment* 13(4): 421–438

Hegedus, J and I Tosics, I (1998) 'Rent reform: Issues for the countries of Eastern Europe and the Newly Independent States' *Housing Studies* 13: 657–678

Held, D, A McGrew, D Goldblat and J Perraton (1999) *Global Transformations*. Polity Press, Cambridge, MA

Herbst, J (1996) 'Responding to state failure in Africa' *International Security* 21(3): 120–144

Herr, H and G Karl (2002) 'Estimating global slum dwellers, monitoring the Millennium Development Goal 7, Target 11', Paper presented at the UN Working Group on the MDGs, May

Hewitt, W E (2000) 'International municipal cooperation: An enabling approach to development for small and intermediate urban centres' *Third World Planning Review* 22(3): 335–360

Heywood, G M, P J Kolsky and D Butler (1997) 'Modelling drainage performance in an Indian catchment' *Journal of the Chartered Institution of Water and Environmental Management* 11(1): 31–38

Hibou, B (1998) 'Banque mondiale: Les méfaits du cathéchisme économique' *Politique Africaine* 71, Les coopérations dans la nouvelle géopolitique, pp 58–74

Hill, O (1883) *Homes of the London Poor*, http://digital.library.upenn.edu/webbin/book/titlestart (first edition published 1875)

Hirshfield, A and K J Bowers (1997) 'The effect of social cohesion on levels of recorded crime in disadvantaged areas' *Urban Studies* **34**: 1275–1295

Hirst, P Q and G Thompson (1996) *Globalisation in Question: The International Economy and the Possibilities of Governance*. Blackwell Publishers, Cambridge, MA

Hobson, J (2000) 'Sustainable sanitation: Experiences in Pune with a municipal–NGO–community partnership' *Environment and Urbanization* **12**(2): 53–62

Hodges, A (2001) *Angola from Afro-Stalinism to Petro-Diamond Capitalism*. Indiana University Press, Bloomington, IN

Hook, W (1994) 'Counting on cars, counting out people: A critique of the World Bank's Economic Assessment Procedures for the Transport Sector and their Environmental Implications', ITDP Policy Paper 1-0194. Institute for Transportation and Development Policy, New York

Hook, W (1998) 'Transport and Development Policy for the United Nations Development Program', Unpublished draft document, UNDP. Institute for Transportation and Development Policy, New York

Hook, W and M Replogle (1996) 'Motorization and non-motorized transport in Asia: Transport system evolution in China, Japan and Indonesia' *Land Use Policy* **13**(1), 69–84

Hopkins, A G (1973) *An Economic History of West Africa*. Columbia University Press, New York

Howell, J (1997) 'The Chinese economic miracle and urban workers' *European Journal of Development Research* **9**: 148–175

Huchzermeyer M (2001) 'Housing for the poor? Negotiated housing policy in South Africa' *Habitat International* **25**: 303–331

Huchzermeyer, M (2002) 'Evaluating tenure intervention in informal settlements in South Africa' in A Durand-Lasserve and L Royston (eds) *Holding Their Ground: Secure Land Tenure for the Urban Poor in Developing Countries*. Earthscan, London, pp182–194

Human Rights, the United Nations and Non-governmental Organizations: A report of the International Human Rights Council, The Carter Centre, 1998

Humphreys, C and W Jaeger (1989) 'Africa's adjustment and growth' *Finance and Development*, June: 6–8

Igel, B and H Srinivas (1996) 'The co-optation of low-income borrowers by informal credit suppliers: A credit delivery model for squatter housing' *Third World Planning Review* **18**(3): 287–305

Illife, J (1987) *The African Poor*. Cambridge University Press, Cambridge

ILO (International Labour Organization) (1972) *Employment, Income and Equality: A Strategy for Increasing Productive Employment in Kenya*. ILO, Geneva

ILO (1993) *Official Bulletin of the 15th International Conference of Labour Statisticians* **LXXVI**. ILO, Geneva, pp178–188

ILO (2002) *Global Prospects Report 2002: A Future Without Child Labour*. ILO, Vienna

IMF (International Monetary Fund) and World Bank (2002) *Poverty Reduction, Growth, and Debt Sustainability in Low-Income CIS Countries*. IMF and World Bank, February, p9

Imparato, I and J Ruster (2001) *Participatory Urban Upgrading: A Road Map for Going to Scale. Lessons from Latin America*. The World Bank, Washington, DC

Ineichin, B (1993) *Homes and Health*. E N and F Spon, London

Jaffee, D M and B Renaud (1996) 'Strategies to develop mortgage markets in transition economies', Policy Research Working Paper 1697. World Bank, Washington, DC

Jargowsky, P A (1996a) 'Beyond the street corner: The hidden diversity of high-poverty neighborhoods' *Urban Geography* **17**(7): 579–603

Jargowsky, P A (1996b) 'Take the money and run: Economic segregation in US metropolitan areas' *American Sociological Review* **61**: 984–998

Jargowsky, P A (1997) *Poverty and Place: Ghettos, Barrios, and the American City*. Russell Sage Foundation, New York

Jenkins, R (1997) 'Structural adjustment and Bolivian industry' *European Journal of Development Research* **9**: 107–128

Jessop, B (1999) 'Reflections on globalization and its (il)logics' in P Dicken et al (eds) *The Logic of Globalization*. Routledge, London

Jewson, N and S MacGregor (1997) 'Transforming cities: Social exclusion and the reinvention of partnership' in N Jewson and S Macgregor (eds) *Transforming Cities: Contested Governance and New Spatial Divisions*. Routledge, London, pp1–18

Jones, G and P Ward (eds) (1994) *Methodology for land and housing market analysis*. UCL Press, London

Jones, S (1999) 'Defining urban poverty: An overview' in S Jones and N Nelson (eds) *Urban Poverty in Africa*, Intermediate Technology Publications, London

Josselin, D and W Wallace (2001) 'Non-state actors in world politics: A framework' in D Josselin and W Wallace (eds) *Non-State Actors in World Politics*. Palgrave, Basingstoke

Kalim, S I (1990) 'Rent-control legislation and its impacts in Karachi' in UNCHS (Habitat) *Rental Housing: Proceedings of an Expert Group Meeting*. UNCHS (Habitat), Nairobi, pp186–196

Kalter, E and H E Khor (1990) 'Mexico's experience with adjustment' *Finance and Development*, December: 22–25

Kamete, A Y, A Tostensen and I Tvedten (2001) *From Global Village to Urban Globe. Urbanisation and Poverty in Africa: Implications for Norwegian Aid Policy*. CMI Reports. Chr. Michelsen Institute, Bergen

Kanbur, R and N Lustig (1999) 'Why is Inequality Back on the Agenda?', Paper presented to the World Bank Conference on Development Economics, April

Kanji, N (1995) 'Gender, poverty and economic adjustment in Harare, Zimbabwe' *Environment and Urbanization* **7**: 37–55

Kaplinsky, R (2001) 'Is globalisation all it's cracked up to be?' *Review of International Political Economy* **8**: 45–65

Kaufman, J E and J E Rosenbaum J E (1992) 'The education and employment of low-income black youth in white suburbs' *Educational Evaluation and Policy Analysis* **14**: 229–240

Keare, D A and S Parris (1982) 'Evaluation of shelter programs for the urban poor: Principal findings', World Bank Staff Working Paper 547. World Bank, Washington, DC

Keare, D and S Parris (1983) *Evaluation of Shelter Projects for the Urban Poor*. World Bank, Washington, DC

Kearns, A (2002) 'Response: From residential disadvantage to opportunity? Reflections on British and European policy and research' *Housing Studies* **17**: 145–150

Kessides, C (1997) *World Bank Experience with the Provision of Infrastructure Services for the Urban Poor*. World Bank, Washington, DC

Kesteloot, C (1995) 'The creation of socio-spatial marginality in Brussels: A tale of flexibility, geographical competition and guestworker's neighbourhoods' in C Hadjimichalis and D Sadler (eds) *Europe at the Margins: New Mosaics of Inequality*. John Wiley and Sons, Chichester

Kesteloot, C and H Meert (1999) 'Informal spaces: The geography of informal economic activities in Brussels' *Housing Studies* **14**: 232–251

Kiang, H C (1999) *Cities of Aristocrats and Bureaucrats: The Development of Chinese Cityscapes*. University of Hawai'i Press, Honolulu

Killias, M (1993) 'International correlations between gun ownership and rates of homicide and suicide' *Canadian Medical Association Journal* **148**: 1723, www.unicri.it/icvs/publications/understanding_files/19_GUN%20OWNERSHIP.pdf, London

Killick, T (1999) *Adjustment, Income Distribution and Poverty in Africa: A Research Guide*. African Economic Research Consortium, Nairobi, www.odi.org.uk/briefing/pov5.html

King, A D (1976) *Colonial Urban Development: Culture, Social Power and Environment*. Routledge and Kegan Paul, London, Henley and Boston

King, A D (1990) *Urbanism, Colonialism and the World Economy: Cultural and Spatial Foundations of the World Urban System*. Routledge, London

Kloosterman, R C and J P van der Leun (1999) 'Just for starters: Commercial gentrification by immigrant entrepreneurs in Amsterdam and Rotterdam Neighbourhoods' *Housing Studies* **14**: 679–701

Knox, P L and P Taylor (eds) (1995) *World Cities in a World System*. Cambridge University Press, Cambridge

Koster, J H (2002) 'The Delft low-cost mobility statement' *World Transport Policy and Practice* **6**(3): 18–20

Krantz, B, E Oresjo et al (eds) (1999) *Large Scale Housing Estates in North West Europe: Problems, Interventions, Experiences*. Delft University Press, Delft

Krueckeberg, D and K Paulsen (2002) 'Evaluating the experience of Brazilian, South African and Indian Urban Tenure Programmes' in A Durand-Lasserve and L Royston (eds) *Holding Their Ground: Secure Land Tenure for the Urban Poor in Developing Countries*. Earthscan, London

Krugman, P (1996) *Pop Internationalism*. MIT Press, Cambridge, MA

Krugman, P and A J Venables (1995) 'Globalisation and the inequality of nations' *The Quarterly Journal of Economics* **110**(4): 857–880

Kumar, S (1996a) 'Landlordism in Third World urban low income settlements: A case for further research' *Urban Studies* **33**: 753–782

Kumar, S (1996b) 'Subsistence and petty capitalist landlords: A theoretical framework for the analysis of landlordism in Third World low income settlements' *International Journal of Urban and Regional Research* **20**: 317–329

Kumar, S (2001) 'Embedded tenures: Private renting and housing policy in Surat, India' *Housing Studies* **16**: 425–443

Lacroux, S (1997) 'The Habitat II land initiative: Access to land and security of tenure as conditions for sustainable development' *Habitat Debate* **3**(2): 1,4 (www.unchs.org/HD/hdjun97/land.htm#initiat)

Laquian, A A (ed) (1971) *Rural-urban Migrants and Metropolitan Development*. Centre for Community Studies, Toronto

Laubé, E (1994) *Le rôle du locatif privé dans l'habitat populaire. Pour un renouveau des politiques du logement (Peshawar, N'Djamena, Calcutta, Dhaka, Conakry, Abidjan)*. DPhil, Université de Paris VIII Saint-Denis, Institut Français d'Urbanisme, Paris

Leckie, S (1992) *From Housing Needs to Housing Rights: An Analysis of the Right to Adequate Housing under International Human Rights Law*. Human Settlements Programme, International Institute for Environment and Development, London

Leckie, S (1995) *When Push Comes to Shove. Forced Evictions and Human Rights*. Habitat International Coalition, Geneva

Lee, J (2000) 'From welfare housing to home ownership: The dilemma of China's housing reform' *Housing Studies* **15**: 61–76

Lee, L, E Petrovia, M Shapiro, and R Struyk (1998) 'Housing maintenance and management in Russia during the reforms' *Housing Studies* **13**: 679–696

Lee, M (2002) 'The global divide' *Behind the Numbers* **4**(2), Canadian Centre for Policy Alternatives

Lee, P (1999) 'Where are the socially excluded? Continuing debates in the identification of poor neighbourhoods' *Regional Studies* **33**(5): 483–487

Lee, P and A Murie (1999) 'Spatial and social divisions within British cities: Beyond residualisation' *Housing Studies* **14**(5): 625–640

Lee, S L, L L Yuan and T K Poh (1993) 'Shelter for all: Singapore's strategy for full home ownership by the year 2000' *Habitat International* **17**: 85–103

Levin, C E, M T Ruel, S S Morris, D G Maxwell, M Armar-Klemesu and C Ahiadeke (1999) 'Working women in an urban setting: Traders, vendors and food security in Accra' *World Development* **27**: 1977–1991

Levine, M V (1989) 'The politics of partnership: Urban redevelopment since 1945' in G D Squire (ed) *Unequal Partnership*. Rutgers University Press, New Brunswick, pp26–28

Lewis, D and T Wallace (2000) (eds) *New Roles and Relevance, Development NGOs and the Challenge of Change*. Kumarian Press, Bloomfield, CT

Liebow, E (1967) *Tally's Corner*. Little, Brown and Co, Boston, MA

Lin, G C S (1999) 'State policy and spatial restructuring in China' *Journal of Urban and Regional Research* **23**: 670–695

Linn, J F (1983) *Cities in Developing Countries: Policies for their Equitable and Efficient Growth*. World University Press, Oxford

Lipsey, B and F Sjöholm (2001) 'Foreign direct investment and wages in Indonesian manufacturing', NBER Working Paper 8299. National Bureau of Economic Research, http://papers.nber.org/papers/w8299

Lipton, M (1980) 'Family, fungibility, and formality: Rural advantages of informal non-farm enterprise versus the urban-formal state' in S Amin (ed) *Human Resources, Employment, and Development, Volume 5, Developing Countries*. Macmillan, London

Lloyd, P (1979) *Slums of Hope? Shanty Towns of the Third World*. Penguin, London

Lloyd Jones, A (2000) 'Compact city policies for megacities: Core areas and metropolitan regions' in M Jenks and R Burgess (eds) *Compact Cities: Sustainable Urban Forms for Developing Countries*. Spon Press, London and New York, pp37–52

Logan, J R (2002) *The Suburban Advantage*. Lewis Mumford Center for Comparative Urban and Regional Research, http://mumford1.dyndns.org/cen2000/CityProfiles/SuburbanReport/page1.html

Logan, J R, Y Bian and F Bian (1999) 'Housing inequality in urban China in the 1990s' *International Journal of Urban and Regional Research* **23**: 7–25

Lokshin, M and M Ravallion (2000) *Short-Lived Shocks with Long-Lived Impacts? Household Income Dynamics in a Transition Economy*. World Bank, June

Lord, J D and G S Rent (1987) 'Residential satisfaction in scattered-site public housing projects' *The Social Science Journal* **24**: 287–302

Lowry, S (1991) *Housing and Health*. BM, London

Luke, J S, C Ventriss, B J Reed and C M Reed (1988) *Managing Economic Development. A Guide to State and Local Leadership Strategies*. Jossey-Bass Publishers, San Francisco and London

Luna, E M, O P Ferrer and U Ignacio Jr (1994) *Participatory Action Planning for the Development of Two PSF Projects*. University of the Philippines, Manila

Mabogunje, A L (1990) 'Urban planning and the post-colonial state in Africa: A research overview' *African Studies Review* **33**(2): 121–203

Mabogunje, A L (1992) 'Perspective on urban land and urban management policies in sub-Saharan Africa', World Bank Technical Paper 196. World Bank, Washington, DC

Mabogunje, A L, J E Hardoy and R P Misra (1978) *Shelter Provision in Developing Countries: The Influence of Standards and Criteria*. John Wiley and Sons, Chichester

Mackay, C J (1999) 'Housing Policy in South Africa: The challenge of delivery' *Housing Studies* **14**: 387–400

Maclennan, D and A More (1997) 'The future of social housing: Key economic questions' *Housing Studies* **12**: 531–548

Madanipour, A, G Cars et al (eds) (1998) *Social Exclusion in European Cities: Processes, Experiences and Responses*. Jessica Kingsley, London

Maddison, A (1995) *Monitoring the World Economy, 1820–1992*. OECD, Paris

Maddison, A (2001) *The World Economy: A Millennium Perspective*. OECD, Paris

Madon, S and S Sahay (2002) 'An information-based model of NGO mediation for the empowerment of slum dwellers in Bangalore', *Information Society* **18**(1): 13–19

Maldonado, C (1995) 'The informal sector: Legalisation or laissez-faire?' *International Labour Review* **34**(6): 705

Malpezzi, S (1984) 'Rent controls: An international comparison', Paper presented to American Real Estate and Urban Economics Association. Centre for Economic Research, University of Wisconsin-Madison

Malpezzi, S (1989) *Rental Housing in Developing Countries: Issues and Constraints*. Urban Development Division, World Bank, Washington, DC

Malpezzi, S and G Ball (1991) *Rent Control in Developing Countries*. World Bank, Washington, DC

Malpezzi, S and S Mayo (1987) 'User cost and housing tenure in developing countries' *Journal of Development Economics* **25**: 197–220

Mangin, W (1967) 'Latin American squatter settlements: A problem and a solution' *Latin American Research Review* **2**: 65–68

Manning, I (1984) 'Beyond Walking Distance: The gains from speed in Australian Urban Travel', Urban Research Unit, Australian National University, Canberra

Marris, R (1999) *Ending Poverty*. Thames and Hudson, London

Marsh, A and D Mullins (1998) 'The social exclusion perspective and housing studies: Origins, applications and limitations' *Housing Studies* **13**: 749–759

Marsh, A, D Gordon, P Heslop, and C Pantazis (2000) 'Housing deprivation and health' *Urban Studies* **15**: 411–428

Massey, D and M Eggers (1990) 'The ecology of inequality: Minorities and the concentration of poverty' *American Journal of Sociology* **95**: 1153–1188

Massey, D S and N A Denton (1993) *American Apartheid: Segregation and the Making of the Underclass*. Harvard University Press, Cambridge, Massachusetts

Mathey, K (1992) *Beyond Self-help Housing*. Mansell, London and New York

Maxwell, S (1999) *The Meaning and Measurement of Poverty*. ODI Poverty Briefing, London

Maxwell, S (2001) 'Innovative and important, yes, but also instrumental and incomplete: The treatment of redistribution in the "new poverty agenda"' *Journal of International Development* **13**(3): 331–343

Mayo, S K and D J Gross (1987) 'Sites and services – and subsidies: The Economics of low-cost housing in developing countries' *The World Bank Economic Review* **1**(2): 301–335

Mazur, Jay (2000) 'Labor's New Internationalism (Globalization's Dark Side)' *Foreign Affairs*, January–February: 79–93

Mbodj, El Hadj (2002) 'Les perspectives de partenariat entre les villes africaines' *Revue internationale des sciences sociales* **LIV**(172): 259–263

McAuslan, P (1998) 'Urbanisation, law and development: A record of research' in E Fernandes and A Varley (eds) *Illegal Cities: Law and Urban Change in Developing Countries*. Zed Books Ltd, London, pp 18–52

McElroy, S A (1999) 'In situ accretion and urban transformation on the periphery: Social and physical changes in Villa El Salvador, 1971–1998 (Peru)', University of California, Santa Barbara

Meehan, E (1989) 'Low income housing: The ownership question' *Journal of Housing* **45**: 105–109

Mehta, A (2001) 'Chronic poverty in India', Overview Paper presented to the Centre for Research on Chronic Poverty Research Workshop

Meier, J E (2000) '"On the margins": The emergence and growth of informal settlements in the greater Cape Town area, 1939–1960 (South Africa)', University of Florida, Florida

Melchior, A, K Telle, and H Wiig (2000) 'Globalisation and inequality: World income distribution and living standards, 1960–1998', Royal Norwegian Ministry of Foreign Affairs, Studies on Foreign Policy Issues, Report 6B: 2000, October

Mezzera, J (1996) 'Excess labour supply and the urban informal sector: An analytical framework' in M Buvinic (ed) *Women's Ventures: Assistance to the Informal Sector in Latin America*. Kumarian Press, Boulder, CO, pp45–64

Mhone, G (1995) *The Impact of Structural Adjustment on the Urban Informal Sector in Zimbabwe*. International Labour Office, Geneva

Michael, M S (1997) 'Why free trade may hurt developing countries' *Review of International Economics* **5**: 179–187

Mies, M (1986) *Indian Women in Subsistence and Agricultural Labour*. International Labour Organization, Geneva

Milanovic, B (1998) *Income, Inequality and Poverty during the Transition*. World Bank, Washington, DC

Milanovic B (1999a). 'True world income distribution, 1988 and 1993: First calculations, based on household surveys alone', (draft) World Bank, http://econ.worldbank.org/files/978_wps2244.pdf; see also (2002) *Economic Journal* **112**: 51–92

Milanovic, B (1999b) 'On the threshold of the Third Globalization: why Liberal Capitalism might fail?' (draft) World Bank, www.worldbank.org/research/inequality/globalization/thirdglob.pdf

Milanovic, B (2002a) 'Worlds apart: The twentieth century promise that failed', (draft) World Bank, www.worldbank.org/research/inequality/pdf/Maksense4.pdf

Milanovic, B (2002b) 'The two faces of globalisation: Against globalisation as we know it', (draft) World Bank, www.worldbank.org/research/inequality/globalisation/twofaces.pdf

Milbert, I with the collaboration of V Peat (1999) *What Future for Urban Cooperation? Assessment of Post Habitat II Strategies*. The Graduate Institute of Development Studies (IUED, Institut Universitaire d'Etudes du Développement), Swiss Agency for Development and Cooperation (SDC), Geneva, Bern

Moavenzadeh, F (1987) 'The construction industry' in L Rodwin (ed) *Shelter, Settlement and Development*. Allen and Unwin, Boston

Moctezuma, P (2001) 'Community-based organization and participatory planning in Southeast Mexico City' *Environment and Urbanization* **13**(2): 117–133

Moser, C (1978) 'Informal sector or petty commodity production: Dualism or dependence in urban development' *World Development* **6**: 1041–1064

Moser, C (1995) 'Urban social policy and poverty reduction' *Environment and Urbanization* **7**(1): 159–173

Moser, C (1996) 'Confronting crisis: A summary of household responses to poverty and vulnerability in four poor urban communities', Environmentally Sustainable Development Studies and Monographs Series, No 7. World Bank, Washington, DC

Moser, C, A J Herbert and R E Makonnen (1993) 'Urban poverty in the context of structural adjustment: Recent evidence and policy responses', Discussion Paper DP No 4. Urban Development Division, World Bank, Washington, DC

Mosha, A C (1993) *An evaluation of the effectiveness of national land policies and instruments in improving supply of and access to land for human settlement development in Botswana*. Report prepared for the UNCHS (Habitat)

Mumford, L (1961) *The City in History: Its Origins, Its Transformations, and Its Prospects*. Harcourt Brace, New York

Mumtaz, B (2001) 'Why cities need slums' *Habitat Debate* **7**(3): 20–21

Mumtaz, B and E Wegelin (2001)
'Guiding Cities: The
UNDP/UNCHS/World Bank Urban
Management Programme'. DPU
and Institute for Housing and
Urban Development Studies,
Rotterdam

Murie, A (1997) 'The social rented
sector, housing and the welfare
state in the UK' *Housing Studies*
12: 437–462

Murie, A and S Musterd (1996) 'Social
segregation, housing tenure and
social change in Dutch cities in the
late 1980s' *Urban Studies* 33:
495–516

Murphy, D (1990) *A Decent Place to
Live: Urban Poor in Asia*. Asian
Coalition for Housing Rights.
Habitat International Coalition,
Asia. Bangkok

Murphy, D and M Pimple (1995)
*Eviction Watch Asia: Forced
Evictions and Housing Rights
Abuses in Asia*. Asian Coalition for
Housing Rights and Urban Poor
Associates, Quezon City, The
Philippines

Musterd, S and W Ostendorf (eds)
(1998) *Urban Segregation and the
Welfare State: Inequality and
Exclusion in Western Cities*.
Routledge, London

Musterd, S, H Priemus and R van
Kempen (1999) 'Towards
undivided cities: The potential of
economic revitalisation and
housing redifferentiation' *Housing
Studies* 14: 585–600

Muth, R F (1969) *Cities and Housing:
The Spatial Pattern of Urban
Residential Land Use*. The
University of Chicago Press,
Chicago

Narayan, D (1995) *The Contribution of
People's Participation: Evidence
from 121 Rural Water Supply
Projects*. World Bank, Washington,
DC

Noll, R G et al (2000) 'Reforming urban
water systems in developing
countries', Discussion Paper No
99-32. Stanford Institute for
Economic Policy Research, Stanford
University

Norconsult (1996) *A Spatial
Development Framework for
Thailand. Volume 2: Key Analysis*.
NESDB, Bangkok

Notzon, F C, Y M Komarov, S P
Ermakov, C T Sempos, J S Marks
and E V Sempos (1998) 'Causes of
declining life expectancy in Russia'
Journal of the AMA 279: 793–800

Observatoire Geopolitique des Drogues
(1999) 'World Geopolitics of
Drugs' *Annual Report 1997/98*

Ogu, V I (2000) 'Stakeholders'
partnership approach to
infrastructure provision and
management in developing world
cities: Lessons from the
Sustainable Ibadan project' *Habitat
International* 24: 517–533

O'Hare, G (2001) 'New horizons for
Rio's favelas' *Geography* 86: 61–75

O'Hare, G, D Abbott and M Barke
(1998) 'A review of slum housing
policies in Mumbai' *Cities* 15(4):
269–283

Oruwari, Y (1990) 'Conditions of low-
income housing, with special
reference to rental stock and
rental-housing strategies in
Nigeria' in UNCHS (Habitat) *Rental
Housing: Proceedings of an Expert
Group Meeting*, pp32–43

Otiso, K M (2000) 'The voluntary
sector in urban service provision

and planning in Nairobi City,
Kenya', University of Minnesota,
Minnesota

Ould-Mey, M (1994) 'Global
adjustment and implications for
peripheral states' *Third World
Quarterly* 15(2): 319–362

Packer, J E (1971) *The Insulae of
Imperial Ostia*. American Academy
in Rome, Rome

Park, R (1948) *The Harp of the South*.
Angus & Robertson, Sydney

Parker, J C and T R Torres (1994) *Micro
and Small Enterprises in Kenya:
Results of the 1993 National
Baseline Survey*. USAID, Nairobi

Parkinson, M (1998) *Combating Social
Exclusion: Lessons from Area-Based
Programmes in Europe*. Policy
Press, Bristol

Parnell, S (1997) 'South African cities:
Perspectives from the ivory tower
of urban studies' *Urban Studies*
34: 891–906

Parnell, S and D Hart (1999) 'Self-help
housing as a flexible instrument of
state control in 20th-century
South Africa' *Housing Studies* 14:
367–386

Patel, S (1999) 'Revisiting participation:
"Win–Win" strategies in
negotiations with railway
authorities and squatters, Mumbai,
India' *Transport and
Communications Bulletin for Asian
and the Pacific* 69: 79–87

Patel, S, S Burra and C D'Cruz (2001)
'Shack/Slum Dwellers International
(SDI); foundations to treetops'
Environment and Urbanization
13(2): 45–59

Patel, S, C d'Cruz et al (2002) 'Beyond
evictions in a global city: People-
managed resettlement in Mumbai'
Environment and Urbanization
14(1): 159–172

Payne, G (1997) *Urban Land Tenure and
Property Rights in Developing
Countries. A Review*. Intermediate
Technology Publications/Overseas
Development Administration
(ODA), London

Payne, G (ed) (1999a) *Making Common
Ground: Public–Private Partnerships
in Land for Housing*. Intermediate
Technology Publications, London

Payne, G (1999b) 'Urban land tenure
policy options: Titles or rights?',
Paper presented to the
International Research Group on
Law and Urban Space/Centre for
Applied Legal Studies workshop on
Facing the Paradox: Redefining
Property in the Age of
Liberalization and Privatization,
Johannesburg, 29–30 July

Payne, G (2001) 'Urban land tenure
policy options: Titles or rights?'
Habitat International 25(3):
415–429

Payne, G (ed) (2002) *Land, Rights and
Innovation*. ITDG, London

Peattie, L R (1987) 'An idea in currency
and how it grew: The informal
sector' *World Development* 15:
851–860

Peil, M (1976) 'African squatter
settlements: A comparative study'
Urban Studies 131: 155–166

Phang, S-Y (2001) 'Housing policy,
wealth formation and the
Singapore economy' *Housing
Studies* 16: 443–460

Pikholz, L (1997) 'Managing politics
and storytelling: Meeting the
challenge of upgrading informal
housing in South Africa' *Habitat
International* 21(4): 377–396

Pirenne, H (1956) *Medieval Cities:*

*Their Origins and the Revival of
Trade*. Double Day Anchor, Garden
City, NY

Plummer, J (2002) *Focusing
Partnerships: A Sourcebook for
Municipal Capacity-building in
Public–private Partnerships*.
Earthscan, London

Polyani, K (1944) *The Great
Transformation: The Political and
Economic Origins of Our Time*.
Rinehart, New York

Poole et al (1994) *Moving People:
Transport Policy in the Cites of
Brazil*. International Development
Research Centre, Ottawa

Porteous, D (2000) 'Coming second?
Secondary market development in
developing countries: A case study'
Housing Finance International
15(1): 18–25

Porter, M (1998) 'Clusters and the new
economics of competition' *Harvard
Business Review*,
November–December

Potts, D (1995) 'Shall we go home?
Increasing urban poverty in African
cities and migration processes' *The
Geographical Journal* 161: 245–264

Potts D (1997) 'Urban lives: Adopting
new strategies and adopting new
rural links' in C Rakodi (ed) *The
Urban Challenge in Africa: Growth
and Management of its Large
Cities*. United Nations University
Press, Tokyo

Power, A (1997) *Estates on the Edge:
The Social Consequences of Mass
Housing in Northern Europe*.
MacMillan, London

PREALC (1975) 'Situacion y
perspectivas del empleo en
Paraguay. Santiago', Programa
Regional del Empleo para America
Latina y el Caribe

Priemus, H (1998) 'Redifferentiation of
the urban housing stock in the
Netherlands: A strategy to prevent
spatial segregation?' *Housing
Studies* 14: 301–310

Priemus, H and F Dielemann (1997)
'Social rented housing: Recent
changes in Western Europe –
Introduction' *Urban Studies* 12:
421–425

Priemus, H and F Dielemann (1999)
'Social housing finance in the
European Union: Developments
and prospects' *Urban Studies* 36:
623–633

Pritchett, L (1997) 'Divergence, big
time' *Journal of Economic
Perspectives* 11: 3–17

Pugh, C (1985) 'Housing and
development in Singapore'
Contemporary Southeast Asia 6:
275–307

Pugh, C (1987) 'Housing in Singapore:
The effective ways of the
unorthodox' *Environment and
Behavior* 19: 211–230

Pugh, C (1993) 'Housing policy
development in developing
countries: The World Bank and
internationalisation', an article
proposed to *Cities*. [Published in
1994 – *Cities* 11(3): 159–180]

Pugh, C (1994) 'The idea of
enablement in housing sector
development: The political
economy of housing for developing
countries' *Cities* 11: 357–371

Pugh, C (1995) 'The role of the World
Bank in housing' in B C Aldrich
and R S Sandhu (eds) *Housing the
Urban Poor. Policy and Practice in
Developing Countries*. Zed Books,
London, pp34–92

Pugh, C (1997) 'The changing roles of
self-help in housing and urban
policies 1950–1996' *Third World
Planning Review* 19: 91–109

Pugh, C (2000) 'Squatter settlements:
Their sustainability, architectural
contributions, and socio-economic
roles' *Cities* 17(5): 325–337

Querrien, A (2000) 'La stratégie
urbaine de la Banque mondiale:
Villes en développement:
"Stratégies de coopération
urbaine"' *Bulletin de la coopération
française pour le développement
urbain, l'habitat et l'aménagement
spatial* 48, June: 4–5

Rahardjo, T (2000) 'The Semarang
Environmental Agenda: A stimulus
to targeted capacity building
among the stakeholders' *Habitat
International* 24(4): 443–453

Rahman, M M (2002) 'Problems of the
NGOs in housing the urban poor
in Bangladesh' *Habitat International*
26(3): 433–451

Raj, M and B Mitra (1990) 'Households,
housing and home based economic
activities in low income
settlements' in P Niented (ed)
*Housing and Income in Third
World Urban Development*. Aspect
Publishing, London

Rakodi, C (1994) 'Property markets in
African cities', Draft, mimeo,
provided by the author

Rakodi, C (1995) 'Rental tenure in the
cities of developing countries'
Urban Studies 32(4–5): 791–811

Rakodi, C (1999) *Economic Growth,
Well-being and Governance in
Africa's Towns and Cities: Policy
Priorities and Challenges*.
Department of City and Regional
Planning, Cardiff University,
Cardiff

Ranciere, J (1998) 'The cause of the
Other' *Parallax* 1: 25–31

Randel, J and T German (1996) *The
Realities of Aid. An Independent
Review of International Aid*.
Earthscan, London

Rao, V and M Walton (eds) (2003
forthcoming) *Culture and Public
Action: How Cultural Factors Affect
an Unequal World*. World
Bank/Stanford University Press,
Palo Alto, CA

Rashid, S F (2000) 'The urban poor in
Dhaka City: Their struggles and
coping strategies during the floods
of 1998' *Disasters* 24(3): 240–253

Ravallion, M (2002) *Who Is Protected?
On the incidence of fiscal
adjustment*. World Bank,
Washington, DC

Ravallion, M and S Chen (1997) 'What
can new survey data tell us about
recent changes in distribution and
poverty?' *World Bank Economic
Review* 11: 357–382

Reddy, S G and T W Pogge (2002) *How
Not to Count the Poor*. Columbia
University, www.columbia.edu/
~sr793/count.pdf

Renaud, B (1997) 'Financial
liberalization and the privatization
of housing finance institutions',
Paper presented to the
International Symposium marking
the 30th anniversary of the Kore
Housing Bank, Seoul, 7 July 1997

Renaud, B (1999) 'Access to housing
finance: World trends' Urban
Upgrading in Latin America
Workshop, World Bank, September

Rich, J and A Wallace-Hadrill (eds)
(1991) *City and Country in the
Ancient World*. Routledge, London
and New York

Riddell, J B (1997) 'Structural adjustment programmes and the city in tropical Africa' *Urban Studies* **34**(8): 1297–1307

Riis, J (1891) *How the Other Half Lives: Studies Among the Poor*. Sampson Low, Marston, Searle and Rivington, London

Riis, J (1902) *The Battle with the Slum*. MacMillan, New York

Rimmer, P J (1996) 'International transport and communications interactions between Pacific Asia's emerging world cities' in F C Lo and Y M Yeung (eds) *Emerging World Cities in Pacific Asia*. United Nations University Press, Tokyo

Roberts, A (2001) 'NGOs: New gods overseas' *The Economist*, Millennium edition entitled 'The World in 2001', January 2001

Robinson, J (1977) 'What are the questions?' *Journal of Economic Literature* **15**(4): 1318–1339

Rochegude, A (1998) *Décentralisation, acteurs locaux et fonciers; mise en perspective juridique des textes sur la décentralisation et le foncier*. Ministère Délégué à la Coopération et à la Francophonie. Laboratoire d'anthropologie juridique de Paris

Rojas, E (2001) 'The long road to housing sector reform: Lessons from the Chilean housing experience' *Housing Studies* **16**: 461–484

Rolnick, R (1996) 'Urban legislation and informal land markets: The perverse link', Paper presented to the Department of Urban Studies and Planning, MIT Informal Land Market Seminar, November

Rose-Ackerman, S (1998) 'Corruption and development', Annual World Bank Conference on Development Economics 1997, World Bank, Washington, DC

Roy, A (1999) 'Paupers and patrons: Class, gender, and regime politics in Calcutta's rural–urban transformation (India)', University of California, Berkeley

RSA, Department of Housing (2001) 'The South African housing policy: Operationalizing the right to adequate housing', Paper presented at Istanbul + 5, New York, June

Ruel, M T, L Haddad and J L Garrett (1999) 'Some urban facts of life: Implications for research and policy' *World Development* **27**: 1917–1938

Russel, S and E Vidler (2000) 'The rise and fall of government – Community partnerships for urban development: Grassroots testimony from Colombo' *Environment and Urbanization* **12**(1): 73–86

Rust, K and S Rubenstein (eds) (1996) *A Mandate to Build: Developing Consensus Around a National Housing Policy in South Africa*. Raven Press, Johannesburg

Sanchez-Jankowski, M (1999) 'The concentration of African-American poverty and the dispersal of the working class: An ethnographic study of three inner city areas' *International Journal of Urban and Regional Research* **23**: 619–637

Sanderson, D (2000) 'Third World cities: Sitting on a time bomb' *Humanitarian Affairs Review* **11**: 32–36

Sanyal, B (1988) 'The urban informal sector revisited: Some notes on the relevance of the concept in the 1980s' *Third World Planning Review* **10**: 65–83

Sarel, M (1997) 'How macroeconomic factors affect income distribution: The cross-country evidence', IMF Working Paper 97/152. International Monetary Fund, www.imf.org/external/pubs/ft/wp/wp97152.pdf

Sassen, S (1998) 'Cracked casings: Notes towards an analytic for studying transnational processes', Workshop on the Sociology and Cultures of Globalization. Council on Advanced Studies in the Humanities and Social Sciences, University of Chicago, Chicago

Sassen, S (1999) *Globalization and its Discontents: Essays on the New Mobility of People and Money*. New Press, New York

Satterthwaite, D (1998) 'The constraints on aid and development assistance agencies giving a high prioroty to basic needs', PhD thesis, London School of Economics and Political Sciences, London

Satterthwaite, D (2001) 'The scale and nature of urban poverty in low and middle income nations', Urban Poverty Conference Paper, Lusaka, 5–9 February

Schubeler, P (1996) *Conceptual framework for municipal solid waste management in low-income countries* (in collaboration with Karl Wehrle and Jurg Christen) UNDP/UNCHS/World Bank-UMP, Nairobi

Schultz, T P (1998) 'Inequality in the distribution of personal income in the world: How it is changing and why' *Journal of Population Economics* **11**: 307–344

SDC (Swiss Agency for Development and Cooperation) (1995) *Challenges of Urbanisation in Developing Countries: The Role of Switzerland*. Contribution to Swiss National Report, Habitat II. SDC, Bern

Sen, A (1997) *On Economic Inequality*. Oxford University Press, Oxford

Serageldin, M (1990) 'Regularizing the Informal Land Development Process', Working Paper, Office of Housing and Urban Programs. US Agency for International Development, Washington, DC

Server, O B (1996) 'Corruption: A major problem for urban management' *Habitat International* **20**: 23–41

Sethuraman, S V (1976) 'The informal sector: Concept, measurement and policy' *International Labour Review* **114**: 69–81

Sethuraman, S V (ed) (1981) *Urban Informal Sector in Developing Countries: Employment, Poverty and Environment*. ILO, Geneva

Sethuraman, S V (1985) 'Basic needs and the informal sector: The case of low-income housing in developing countries' *Habitat International* **9**(3/4): 299–316

Sethuraman, S V and A Ahmed (1992) 'Urbanisation, employment and environment' in A S Bhalla (ed) *Environment, Employment and Development*. ILO, Geneva, pp121–140

Shapiro, A L (1985) *Housing the Poor of Paris, 1850–1902*. University of Wisconsin Press, Madison

Sherman, L W, D Gottfredson, D MacKenzie, J Eck, P Reuter and S Bushway (1998) *Preventing Crime: What Works, What Doesn't, What's Promising*. A report to the United States Congress, prepared for the National Institute of Justice, Department of Criminology and Criminal Justice University of Maryland, www.ncjrs.org/works/

Shevky, E and W Bell (1955) *Social Area Analysis*. University of California Press, Berkeley

Shevky, E and M Williams (1949) *The Social Areas of Los Angeles: Analysis and Typology*. University of California Press, Berkeley

SIDA (Swedish International Development Cooperation Agency) (1995) *Towards an Urban World: Urbanisation and Development Assistance*. SIDA, Stockholm

Sik, E and C Wallace (1999) 'The development of open air markets in East-Central Europe' *The European Journal of Development Research*, pp697–714

Sit, V F S (1995) *Beijing: The Nature and Planning of a Chinese Capital City*. John Wiley and Sons, New York

Sjoberg, G (1960) *The Preindustrial City: Past and Present*. Free Press, New York

Skinner, R J, J L Taylor and A E Wegelin (1987) 'Shelter upgrading for the urban poor. Evaluation of third world experience', International Year of Shelter for the Homeless, UNCHS (Habitat) and Institute for Housing Studies. Island Publishing House, Manila

Smoke, P J (1994) *Local Government Finance in Developing Countries: The Case of Kenya*. Oxford University Press, Nairobi, p28

Smoke, P J (2000) 'Fiscal decentralization in developing countries: A review of current concepts and practice', Paper prepared for United Nations Research Institute for Social Development

Souza, P R (1979) *Emprego e salarios*. Hucitec, Sao Paolo

Srinivasan, S (1997) 'Breaking rural bonds through migration: The failure of development for women in India' *Journal of Comparative Family Studies* **28**(1): 89–102

Stern, N (2000) 'Globalisation and poverty', Address to Institute of Economic and Social Research, Indonesia

Stiglitz, J (1998) 'Responding to economic crises: Policy alternatives for equitable recovery and development', Address to the North-South Institute Seminar, Ottawa, October, www.worldbank.org/html/extdr/extme/jssp092998.htm

Stiglitz, J E (1999) 'Whither Reform? Ten Years of the Transition' in B Pleskovic and J E Stiglitz (eds) *Annual World Bank Conference of Development Economics 1999*. World Bank, Washington, DC, pp27–56

Stiglitz, J (2000) 'What I learned at the world economic crisis' *The Insider*, www.tnr.com/041700/stiglitz041700.html

Storper, M (1997) *The Regional World: Territorial Development in a Global Economy*. Guildford, New York

Stren, R (1975) 'Urban policy and performance in Kenya and Tanzania' *Journal of Modern African Studies* **13**: 267–294

Stretton, H (1975) *Ideas for Australian Cities*, 2nd edition. Georgian House, Melbourne

Struyck, R J (1986) *Finance and Housing Quality in Two Developing Countries*. The Urban Institute Press, Washington, DC

Subbarao, K, J Braithwaite and J Jalan (1995) 'Protecting the poor during adjustment and transitions', HCO Working Papers, World Bank, www.worldbank.org/html/extdr/hnp/hddflash/hcwp/hrwp049.html

Sutcliffe, M (1996) 'The fragmented city: Durban, South Africa' *International Social Science Journal* **147**: 67–72

Suttles, G D (1972) *The Social Construction of Communities*. University of Chicago Press, Chicago

Swaminathan, M (1997) 'The determinants of earnings among low-income workers in Bombay: An analysis of panel data' *Journal of Development Studies* **33**(4): 535–551

Tacoli, C (1999) 'Rural–urban interaction, urban governance, partnership and poverty', Supplementary Theme Paper, International Development Department, School of Public Policy, University of Birmingham, Birmingham

Taylor, M (1998) 'Combating the social exclusion of housing estates' *Housing Studies* **13**(6): 819–832

Taylor, P (1999) 'Democratising cities: Habitat's global campaign on urban governance' *Habitat Debate* **5**(4): 1–5

Te Velde, T W and O Morrissey (2001) 'Foreign ownership and wages: Evidence from five African countries', Research Paper 01/19. Centre for Research in Economic Development and International Trade, University of Nottingham, Nottingham

Tebbal, F (2002) 'Les politiques de réduction de l'habitat insalubre au niveau international. Bilan et perspectives. Le point de vue du Programme des Nations Unies pour les etablissements Humains (ONU-HABITAT)', Paper presented to the international conference Which Housing for Tomorrow? Emerging Practices for the Poor, Ministry for the Management of Land, Urbanism, Habitat and Environment. Casablanca, Marocco, 12–14 June

Tebbal, F and K Ray (2001) 'Housing the Urban Poor' *Habitat Debate*, September

Thapan, M (1997) 'Linkages between culture, education and women's health in urban slums' *Economic and Political Weekly* **32** (43): Ws83–Ws88

The Netherlands Ministry of Foreign Affairs (1994) *Urban Poverty Alleviation*. Sector Policy Document of Development Cooperation, No 5, The Hague

Thomas, S and S Canagarajah (2002) 'Poverty in a wealthy economy: The case of Nigeria', IMF Working Paper 02/114. International Monetary Fund, www.imf.org/external/pubs/ft/wp/2002/wp02114.pdf

Thomas, V and A Chhibber (1989) 'Experience with policy reforms under adjustment' *Finance and Development*, March: 28–31

Thomson, J M (1977) *Great Cities and Their Traffic*. Victor Gollancz Ltd, London

Tienda, M (1991) 'Poor people and poor places: Deciphering neighborhood effects on poverty outcomes' in J Huber (ed) *Macro-Micro Linkages in Sociology*. University of Chicago, Population Research Centre/Sage Publications, Chicago, pp204–212

Tipple, A G (1976) 'Self-help housing policies in a Zambian mining town' *Urban Studies* **13**: 167–169

Tipple, A G (1994) 'The need for new urban housing in sub-Saharan Africa: Problem or opportunity' *African Affairs* **93**: 587–608

Tipple, A G (2000) *Extending Themselves: User Initiated Transformations of Government Built Housing in Developing Countries.* Liverpool University Press, Liverpool

Tipple, A G and D Korboe (1998) 'Housing Policy in Ghana: Towards a supply-oriented approach' *Habitat International* **22**(3): 245–257

Tipple, A G and K G Willis (1991) 'Tenure choice in a West African city' *Third World Planning Review* **13**(1): 27–46

Tipple, A G, D Korboe et al (1999) *Housing Supply in Ghana: A Study of Accra, Kumasi and Berekum.* Pergamon, Oxford

Tokman, V E (1978) 'A model of labour migration and urban unemployment in less-developed countries' *American Economic Review* March: **84**(2): 255–260

Tokman, V E (1992) *Beyond Regulation: The Informal Economy in Latin America.* Lynne Rienner, Boulder, Colorado

Torstensson, J (1994) 'Property rights and economic growth: An empirical study' *Kyklos* **47**(2): 231–247

Tribillon, J-F (1993) *Villes africaines. Nouveau manuel d'aménagement foncier.* La Défense, ADEF, Paris

Tribillon, J-F (1995) 'Contourner la propriété par l'équipement des villes africaines, Régularisations de propriétés' *Les Annales de la Recherche Urbaine* **66**: 118–123

Turner, J (1966) *Uncontrolled Urban Settlements: Problems and Policies.* UN Centre for Housing, Building and Planning, New York. University of Pittsburgh Press, Pittsburgh

Turner, J F C (1976) *Housing by People: Towards Autonomy in Building Environments.* Pantheon Books, New York/Marion Boyars, LondonTurner, J F C and R Fichter (eds) (1972) *Freedom to Build.* Macmillan, New York

Twigg J and M Bhatt (eds) (1998) *Understanding Vulnerability: South Asian Perspectives.* Intermediate Technology, London

Uganda, Government of (2001) *The National Report, Istanbul +5,* Uganda

UNCHS (Habitat) (United Nations Centre for Human Settlements (Habitat)) (1982) *Survey of Slums and Squatter Settlements.* Tycooly International, Dublin

UNCHS (Habitat) (1988) *A New Agenda for Human Settlements* HS/130/88E. UNCHS (Habitat), Nairobi

UNCHS (Habitat) (1989) *Improving Income and Housing: Employment Generation in Low-income Settlements.* UNCHS (Habitat), Nairobi

UNCHS (Habitat) (1990a) *Finance for Shelter and Services as a Component of the Global Strategy for Shelter to the Year 2000* HS/220/91E. UNCHS (Habitat), Nairobi

UNCHS (Habitat) (1990b) *Financing Human Settlements Development and Management in Developing Countries: A Comparative Overview of Case Studies.* UNCHS (Habitat), Nairobi

UNCHS (Habitat) (1991a) *Report of the Inter-Regional Workshop on Integration of Housing Finance into the National Finance Systems of Developing Countries. Goa, India, 10–14 June 1991,* UNCHS (Habitat), Nairobi

UNCHS (Habitat) (1991b) *Report on the Workshop on Land Registration and Land Information Systems.* UNCHS (Habitat), Nairobi

UNCHS (Habitat) (1991c) *Evaluation of Experience with Initiating Enabling Shelter Strategies.* UNCHS (Habitat), Nairobi

UNCHS (Habitat) (1991d) *Human Settlements Development through Community Participation.* UNCHS (Habitat), Nairobi

UNCHS (Habitat) (1996a) *An Urbanizing World: Global Report on Human Settlements 1996.* Oxford University Press, Oxford

UNCHS (Habitat) (1996b) *Global Conference on Access to Land and Security of Tenure as a Condition for Sustainable Shelter and Urban Development.* Preparation document for Habitat II Conference. New Delhi, India, 17–19 January

UNCHS (Habitat) (1996c) *Global Urban Indicators Database: Version 1.* UNCHS (Habitat), Nairobi

UNCHS (Habitat) (1996d) *Women in Human Settlements Development and Management.* UNCHS (Habitat), Nairobi

UNCHS (Habitat) (1998) *Proceedings of the International Conference on Urban Poverty* (International Forum on Urban Poverty, 9–13 November 1997, Florence, Italy). UNCHS (Habitat), Nairobi

UNCHS (Habitat) (1999a) *Implementing the Habitat Agenda: Adequate Shelter for All. Global Campaign for Secure Tenure.* UNCHS (Habitat), Nairobi

UNCHS (Habitat) (1999b) *Urban Poverty in Africa: Selected Countries' Experiences.* Africa Forum on Urban Poverty. UNCHS (Habitat), Nairobi

UNCHS (Habitat) (2001a) *Cities in a Globalizing World: Global Report on Human Settlements 2001.* UNCHS (Habitat)/Earthscan, London

UNCHS (Habitat) (2001b) *Implementing the Habitat Agenda. The 1996–2001 Experience.* Report on the Istanbul +5 Thematic Committee 25th Special Session of the United Nations General Assembly, New York, 6–8 June. UNCHS (Habitat), Nairobi

UNCHS (Habitat) (2001c) *State of the World's Cities 2001.* UNCHS (Habitat), Nairobi

UNCHS (Habitat) and Burkina Faso Government (1999) *Aménagement foncier urbain et gouvernance locale en Afrique sub-saharienne. Enjeux et opportunités après la Conférence Habitat II.* Rapport du Colloque régional des professionnels africains. Ouagadougou, Burkina Faso, 20–23 April

UNCHS (Habitat) and International Labour Office (ILO) (1995) *Shelter Provision and Employment Generation.* UNCHS (Habitat)/ILO, Geneva

UNCTAD (United Nations Conference on Trade and Development) (1998) *Foreign Direct Investment in Africa: Performance and Potential.* UNCTAD, Geneva

UNCTAD (2002) *The Least Developed Countries Report 2002.* UNCTAD, Geneva/New York

UNDP (United Nations Development Programme) (1991) 'Cities, people and poverty: Urban development cooperation for the 1990s', UNDP Strategy Paper. UNDP, New York

UNDP (1992) *Human Development Report 1992: Global Dimensions of Human Development.* UNDP/Oxford University Press, New York

UNDP (1996) *Uzbekistan Human Development Report,* Chapter 3, 'Urban Concerns'. UNDP

UNDP (1999) *Human Development Report 1999: Globalization with a Human Face.* UNDP/Oxford University Press, New York

UNDP (2000a) *Human Development Report 2000: Human Rights and Human Development.* UNDP/Oxford University Press, New York

UNDP (2000b) *Overcoming Human Poverty: UNDP Poverty Report 2000.* UNDP, New York

UNDP (2001) *Human Development Report 2001: Making New Technologies Work for Human Development.* UNDP/Oxford University Press, New York

UNDP (2002) *Human Development Report 2002: Deepening Democracy in a Fragmented World.* UNDP/Oxford University Press, New York

UNECA (United Nations Economic Commission for Africa (1998a) *African Economic Report 1998.* UNECA, Addis Ababa

UNECA (1998b) *An Integrated Geo-Information (GIS) with Emphasis on Cadastre and Land Information Systems (LIS) for Decision-Makers in Africa.* Expert Group Meeting, Addis Ababa, Ethiopia, November

UNECA (1999) *Economic Report for Africa.* UNECA, Addis Ababa

UNECA (2002a) *Economic Report on Africa 2002.* UNECA, Addis Ababa

UNECA (2002b) *Harnessing Technology for Sustainable Development: ECA Policy Research Report.* UNECA, Addis Ababa

UNEP (United Nations Environment Programme) (1999) *Global Environment Outlook 2000.* UNEP/Earthscan, London

UNEP (2002) *Global Environment Outlook 3.* UNEP/Earthscan, London

UNESCAP (United Nations Economic and Social Commission for Asia and the Pacific) (1990) *Case Studies on Metropolitan Fringe Development with Focus on Informal Land Subdivisions.* UNESCAP, Bangkok,

UNESCAP (1997) *Urban Land Policies for the Uninitiated.* UNESCAP, Bangkok, www.unescap.org/huset/land_policies/index.htm

UNESCAP (2001) *Synthesis of National Reports on the Implementation of the Habitat Agenda in the Region,* Report to Istanbul +5. UNESCAP, Bangkok,

UN-Habitat (United Nations Human Settlements Programme) (2002a) 'Cities without slums', HSP/WUF/1/DLG/I/Paper 4, First World Urban Forum, 29 April–3 May, Nairobi. UN-Habitat, Nairobi, www.unhabitat.org/cdrom/unhabitat_cdrom/html/documents/dlg1paper4.pdf

UN-Habitat (2002b) 'Monitoring urban conditions and trends', HSP/WUF/1/DLG/I/Paper 9, First World Urban Forum, 29 April–3 May, Nairobi. UN-Habitat, Nairobi, www.unhabitat.org/cdrom/unhabitat_cdrom/html/documents/dlg1paper9.pdf

UN-Habitat (2002c) 'Expert group meeting on slum indicators, October', Revised Draft Report. UN-Habitat, Nairobi

UN-Habitat (2002d) 'Defining slums: Towards an operational definition for measuring slums', Background Paper 2, Expert Group Meeting on Slum Indicators, October. UN-Habitat, Nairobi

UN-Habitat (2002e) 'Global city sampling: Secure tenure, slums and global sample of cities, Background Paper 3, Expert Group Meeting on Slum Indicators, October. UN-Habitat, Nairobi

UN-Habitat (2002f) *Global Urban Indicators Database: Version 2.* UN-Habitat, Nairobi

UN-Habitat (2003) *Water and Sanitation in the World's Cities: Local Action for Global Goals.* UN-Habitat/Earthscan, London

UNODCCP (United Nations Office for Drug Control and Crime Prevention) (1999) *Global Illicit Drug Trends 1999.* UNODCCP, New York, www.drugwarfacts.org/interdic.htm

United Nations (1976) *World Housing Survey 1974: An Overview of the State of Housing, Building and Planning within Human Settlements.* Department of Economic and Social Affairs, United Nations, New York

United Nations (2001) *Report of the Executive Director of the United Nations Centre for Human Settlements on the Review and Appraisal of Progress Made in the Implementation of the Habitat Agenda.* 25th special session of the General Assembly, June. United Nations

United Nations (2002a) 'Millennium Development Goals, Targets and Indicators', DESA Technical Version identifying data sources, 31 May. Department of Economic and Social Affairs, United Nations

United Nations (2002b) *World Urbanization Prospects: The 2001 Revision. Data Tables and Highlights.* ESA/P/WP.173. Population Division, Department of Economic and Social Affairs, United Nations Secretariat, New York, www.un.org/esa/population/publications/wup2001/wup2001dh.pdf

United Nations Conference on Human Settlements (Habitat II) (1996) *The Habitat Agenda.* Chapter II: Goals and Principles, Chapter III: Commitments, and Chapter IV: Global Plan of Action. UNCHS (Habitat), Nairobi, www.unchs.org/istanbul+5/agenda.htm

United Nations Handbook 2002 (2002) New Zealand Ministry of Foreign Affairs and Trade, Wellington

United Nations Millennium Declaration, A/55/L.2 adopted at 55th session under agenda item 61(b) called 'The Millennium Assembly of the United Nations'

United Nations Population Division (2001) *World Population Prospects 2000*. United Nations, New York

United Nations Population Division (2002) *World Urbanization Prospects: The 2001 Revision, Data Tables and Highlights*. United Nations, New York, www.un.org/esa/population/publications/wup2001/wup2001dh.pdf

United States Bureau of the Census (1998–2001) *Money Income in the United States and Poverty in the United States*. US Department of Commerce, Washington, DC

United States Conference of Mayors (2001) *A Status Report on Hunger and Homelessness in America's Cities: A 27-City Survey*. US Conference of Mayors, Washington, DC

Urban Management Programme (1989) *Land Development Policies; Analysis and Synthesis Report*. Nairobi

Urban Management Programme and French Ministry of Foreign Affairs (1993) *Managing the Access of the Poor to Urban Land: New Approaches for Regularisation Policies in the Developing Countries*: 1. Synthesis of main findings. 2. Summary of case studies. 3. Conclusion and recommendations of the Seminar. Mexico, February

Urban Management Programme, French Ministry of Foreign Affairs, GTZ, Germany (1995) *Urban Land Management, Regularisation Policies and Local Development in Africa and the Arab States*. Abidjan, 21–24 March. Land Management Series 4

Urban Resources (2001) *Report on the Past and Current Experience of People's Participation in the Local Development Councils*. Final report of PAGF Study. DILG, Manila

USAID (United States Agency for International Development) (1984) *Urban Development Policy*, www.usaid.gov/pubs/ads/200/urban_dev/urbandev.pdf

USAID (1991) *Regularizing the Informal Land Development Process: vol 1 Background Paper; vol 2 Discussion Papers*. Office of Housing and Urban Programs, USAID, Washington, DC

USAID (2001) *Making Cities Work: USAID's Urban Strategy*. An initiative launched by the Administrator and prepared by the Urbanization Task Force, USAID, Washington, DC, www.makingcitieswork.org/docs/MCWurbanstrategy01.pdf

Van Huyck, A P (1968) 'The housing threshold for lowest income groups: The case of Inida' in J D Herbert and A P Van Huyck (eds) *Urban Planning in the Developing Countries*. Praeger, New York, pp64–108

Van Kempen, R and H Priemus (1999) 'Undivided cities in the Netherlands: Present situation and political rhetoric' *Housing Studies* **14**: 659–677

van Vliet–, W (1997) *Affordable Housing and Urban Redevelopment in the United States: Learning from success and failure*. Sage Publications, Thousand Oaks, California

van Vliet–, W (2002) 'Cities in a globalizing world: From engines of growth to agents of change' *Environment and Urbanization* **14**(1): 31–40

Varela-Michel, M (1997) *Cultural Adaptation and Rural Migrant Housing (Mexico)*. Mcgill University, Montreal

Varley, A (1994) 'Clientelism or technocracy? The political logic of urban land regularisation' in N Harvey and I P Tauris (eds) *Mexico: The Dilemma of Transition*. University of London, London

Varley, A (1998) 'The political uses of illegality: Evidence from urban Mexico' in E Fernandes and A Varley (ed) *Illegal Cities: Law and Urban Change in Developing Countries*, Zed Books, London and New York

Varley, A (1999) 'New models of urban land regularisation in Mexico: Decentralisation and democracy vs. Clientilism', Paper presented to N-aerus International Workshop on Concepts and Paradigms of Urban Management in the Context of Developing Countries, Venice, 11–12 March, http://obelix.polito.it/forum/n-aerus

Vega, C A and D Kruijt (1994) *The Convenience of the Miniscule: Informality and Microenterprise in Latin America*. Thela Publishers, Amsterdam

Viloria, J, D G Williams and J Didier (1998) *Urban Community Upgrading*. World Bank, Washington, DC

Vincentian Missionaries Social Development Foundation Incorporated (VMSDFI) Manila (2001) 'Meet the Philippines Homeless People's Federation' *Environment and Urbanization* **13**(2): 73–84

Wallace, R, D Wallace, J E Ullmann, and H Andrews (1999) 'Deindustrialisation, inner-city decay, and the hierarchical diffusion of AIDS in the USA: How neoliberal and cold war policies magnified the ecological niche for emerging infections and created a national security crisis' *Environment and Planning* **4**: 113–139

Wallace-Hadrill, A (1994) *Houses and Society in Pompeii and Herculaneum*. Princeton University Press, Princeton

Wandeler, K D and A Khanaiklang (1992) 'Low-income rental and rent-free housing' in K S Yap (ed) *Low Income Housing in Bangkok: A Review of Housing Submarkets*. Asian Institute of Technology, Bangkok, Human Settlements Development (HSD) Monograph 25, pp115–136

Wang, Y P (1995a) 'Public sector housing in urban China 1949–88: The case of Xian' *Housing Studies* **10**: 57–82

Wang, Y P (1995b) 'Private sector housing in urban China since 1949' *Housing Studies* **10**: 119–137

Wang, Y P (2000) 'Housing reform and its impacts on the urban poor in China' *Housing Studies* **15**: 845–864

Wang, Y P and Murie A (1998) *Housing Policy and Practice in China*.

Macmillan, London

Ward, P M (ed) (1982) *Self-help Housing: A Critique*. Mansell, London

Ward, P (1998) 'International forum on regularisation and land markets' *Land Lines, Newsletter of the Lincoln Institute of Land Policy* **10**(4): 1–4

Ward, P and G Macoloo (1992) 'Articulation theory and self-help housing practice in the 1990s' *International Journal of Urban and Regional Research* **16**(1): 60–80

Weber, M (1921(1958)) *The City* (translated by D Martindale and G Neuwirth from the original which appeared in *Archiv für Sozialwissenschaft und Sozialpolitik* **47**: 621 ff.). Free Press, New York

Wee, A (1972) 'Some social implications of rehousing programmes in Singapore' in D J Dwyer (ed) *The City as a Center of Change in Asia*. Hong Kong University Press, Hong Kong, pp216–20

Wegelin, E A (1978) *Urban Low-income Housing and Development*. Kluwer Academic Publishers, Dordrecht

Werlin, H (1999) 'The slum upgrading myth' *Urban Studies* **36**: 1569–1596

Westendorff, D and D Eade (eds) (2002) *Development and Cities: Development in Practice Reader*. UNRISD/Oxfam, Oxford

White, G (1994) 'Civil society, democratization and development (I): Clearing the analytical ground' *Democratization* **1**(3): 375–390

Willis, K G and A G Tipple (1991) 'Economics of multihabitation: Housing conditions, household occupancy, and household structure under rent control, inflation and non-marketability of property rights' *World Development* **19**(12): 1705–1720

Wilson, D, H Margulis and J Ketchum (1994) 'Spatial aspect of housing abandonment in the 1990s: The Cleveland experience' *Housing Studies* **9**: 493–510

Wilson, W J (1987) *The Truly Disadvantaged: The Inner City, the Underclass, and Public Policy*. University of Chicago Press, Chicago

Wong, A and S Yeh (eds) (1985) *Housing a Nation*. Singapore Housing and Development Board, Singapore

Wood, A and C Ridao-Cano (1996) 'Skill, trade and international inequality', IDS Working Paper, vol 47. Institute of Development Studies, University of Sussex, Brighton

Wood, A and C Ridao-Cano (1999) 'Skill, trade and international inequality' *Oxford Economic Papers* **51**: 89–119

Woodruff, C (2001) 'Review of de Soto's *The Mystery of Capital*' *Journal of Economic Literature* **39**(4): 1215–1223

World Bank (1975) *Sites and Services Projects*. World Bank, Washington, DC

World Bank (1991) 'Urban policy and economic development. An agenda for the 1990s', World Bank Policy Paper. World Bank, Washington, DC

World Bank (1993) 'Housing: enabling markets to work. With technical supplements', World Bank Policy Paper. World Bank, Washington, DC

World Bank (1994a) 'Resettlement and Development' in *Bankwide Review of Projects Involved Involuntary Resettlement 1986–1993*. Environment Department, World Bank, Washington, DC

World Bank (1994b) *Twenty Years of Lending for Urban Development, 1972–1992*. Operations Evaluation Department, Report No 13117. World Bank, Washington, DC

World Bank (1995) *Indonesia: Impact Evaluation Report: Enhancing the Quality of Life in Urban Indonesia: The Legacy of Kampung Improvement Program*. Report 4747-IND. World Bank, Washington, DC

World Bank (1996) *Sustainable Transport: Priorities for Policy Reform*. World Bank, Washington, DC

World Bank (1999a) *A Strategic View of Urban and Local Government Issues: Implications for the Bank*. Transportation, Water and Urban Development Department, Urban Development Division, draft. World Bank, Washington, DC

World Bank (1999b) *World Development Report 1999/2000: Entering the 21st Century*. Oxford University Press, New York, www.worldbank.org/wdr/2000/fullreport.html

World Bank (2000a) *Cities in Transition. World Bank Urban and Local Government Strategy*. Infrastructure Group Urban Development, World Bank, Washington, DC

World Bank (2000b) *Draft Urban Transport Strategy Review, As Revised on 16 October 2000*, http://wbln0018.worldbank.org/oed/oeddoclib.nsf/3b01efb621e65 53785256885007d98b9/13 (last accessed 11 January 2001)

World Bank (2000c) *World Development Report 2000/2001: Attacking Poverty*. World Bank/Oxford University Press, New York, www.worldbank.org/poverty/wdrpoverty/report/index.htm

World Bank (2001a) *African Poverty at the Millennium*. World Bank, Washington, DC

World Bank (2001b) *World Development Report 2002: Building Institutions for Markets*. World Bank/Oxford University Press, New York, http://econ.worldbank.org/files/2404_61606_00_fm.pdf

World Bank (2001c) *Transition – The First Ten Years: Analysis and Lessons for Eastern Europe and the Former Soviet Union*. World Bank, Washington, DC, p8

World Bank (2002a) *African Development Indicators 2002*. World Bank, Washington, DC

World Bank (2002b) *Globalization, Growth, and Poverty. Building an Inclusive World Economy*. A World Bank Policy Research Report. World Bank, Washington, DC/Oxford University Press, New York

World Bank (2002c) *Improving the Lives of the Poor through Investment in Cities. An Update on the Performance of the World Bank's Urban Portfolio*, draft, May 7. Operations Evaluation Department, Sector and Thematic Evaluation. World Bank, Washington, DC

World Bank (2002d) 'Glossary of urban upgrading', www.worldbank.org

[http://web.mit.edu/urbanupgrading/
upgrading/resources/glossary.html],
accessed 20 August 2002

World Bank (2003) *World Development
Report 2003: Sustainable
Development in a Dynamic World –
Transforming Institutions, Growth,
and Quality of Life.* World Bank,
Washington, DC/Oxford University
Press, New York,
http://econ.worldbank.org/wdr/wdr
2003/

Wratten, E (1995) 'Conceptualizing
urban poverty' *Environment and
Urbanization* **7**: 11–37

WRI (World Resources Institute) (1999)
*World Resources Report
1998–1999.* World Resources
Institute, Washington, DC

WRI (2000) *World Resources Report
2000–2001.* World Resources
Institute, Washington, DC

Wunsch, J and Olowu, D (1990) *The
Failure of the Centralized State:
Institutions and Self-Governance in
Africa.* Westview Press, Boulder,
CO

Wyly, E K (1999) 'Continuity and
change in the restless urban
landscape' *Economic Geography*
75: 309

Xie, Z K (1999) *Breakthrough: The
Activities of Housing Reform in
China.* Social Sciences
Documentation Pubication, Beijing

Yahya, S, E Agevi et al (2001) *Double
Standards, Single Purpose.* ITDG
Publishing, London

Yeh, S (ed) (1975) *Public Housing in
Singapore.* Singapore University
Press, Singapore

Zamberia, A M (1999) 'The state civil
society partnership in the provision
of water and sanitation for the
urban poor: The case of Kibera,
Nairobi', Dissertation, K F
Schuessler Institute for Social
Research. Indiana University,
Indiana

Zevenbergen, J (1998) 'Is title
registration really the panacea for
defective land administration in
developing countries?' in
*Proceedings of the International
Conference on Land tenure in the
Developing World, with a focus on
Southern Africa.* University of Cape
Town, 27–28 January, pp570–580

Zhu, G L (ed) (1998) *Analysis on All
Social Strata in Modern China.*
Tianjian People's Press, Tianjian

Zhu, J M (2000) 'The changing mode of
housing provision in transitional
China' *Urban Affairs Review* **35**:
502–519

Zimmermann, W (1998) *Facing the
Challenge of Implementing a New
Land Policy. Lessons learned in the
context of international
cooperation,* Proceedings of the
International Conference on Land
tenure in the Developing World,
with a focus on Southern Africa,
27–28 January, University of Cape
Town, pp581–587

INDEX

Aachen, Germany 271
abandoned cities 22–23, 27–28
Abidjan, Côte d'Ivoire xxx, 200, 267, 274, 277, 281, 284, 287
absolute poverty 30
access
communications technology 41–42
credit 100, 108, 134
decision-making 183
differential 58
education xxx, 70
equity 183
limited 59
low-cost labour 67–68
peripheral slums 90
policy 173, 182
privatization 45
sanitation 8, 12, 234, 243
security dilemmas 172
services 5, 6, 11, 70, 113
small slums 91
social capital 6
space 20
tenure 167–172
water 7–8, 12, 113–114, 234, 243
accountability 161–162, 175, 183, 238
Accra, Ghana 110, 267, 275, 278, 281, 284, 287
accumulation 101
Adana, Turkey 270, 273
Addis Ababa, Ethiopia 267, 274, 277, 281, 284, 287
Adelaide, Australia 273
adequacy 112, 114–115, 119–192
adult illiteracy rates 234
aetiology of slums xxxiii
affluence 39, 74, 76, 104, 115
affordability xxviii, 111, 123–128, 202
Afghanistan 249, 253, 258, 260, 262, 265
Africa, 249, 252, 255, 258, 260, 262, 264
banking systems 181
child labour 99
East 161
economic stagnation 43
extreme poverty 31
housing 107, 111–112
income 7
informal sector 103
labour force 97
Northern xxv, 14–15, 31, 97, 112, 113, 115, 233
populations 5, 14
poverty 39
rent levels 110–111
services 114, 178, 179
slum estimations 2, 3, 13
structural adjustment 46
sub-Saharan xxv, 14–15, 60, 84, 103, 106, 112, 113, 115, 233
unemployment 99
West 89, 161
women-headed households 29
see also South Africa
age 28, 85–88
agglomeration 49
aglomerado subnormal 225
Agra, India 269
agriculture 97, 206
Ahmedabad, India xxx, 151, 201, 269
Ahvaz, Iran (Islamic Republic of) 269

aid
actors 135, 136–144
agencies 48–49, 52
failure 137
financial impact 145
MDGs 8
rental tenure 109
self-help 130–131
AIDS 8, 73
Albania 250, 253, 259, 261, 263, 265
Aleppo, Syrian Arab Republic 270, 273
Alexandra, Egypt 132, 259, 273
Algeria 249, 252, 258, 260, 262, 264
Algiers, Algeria 267, 274, 277, 280, 283, 287
Allahabad, India 269
Almaty, Kazakhstan 270
allowances 124
Alonso-Muth-Mills model 18
Alwar, India 275, 278, 281, 284, 287
Amal, Sweden 276, 279, 282, 285, 289
Ambato, Ecuador 277, 280, 283, 286, 289
American Samoa 251, 255
Amman, Jordan 270, 275, 278, 281, 284, 288
Amritsar, India 269
Amsterdam, Netherlands 65, 271, 273, 276, 279, 282, 285, 288
Andorra 250, 253, 259
Angola 39, 249, 252, 258, 260, 262, 264
Anguilla 251, 254
Ankara, Turkey 270, 273, 275, 279, 282, 285, 288
Ansan, Republic of Korea 270
Anshan, China 267
Anshun, China 267
Antananarivo, Madagascar 267, 275, 278, 281, 284, 287
Antigua and Barbuda 251, 254, 259
apartheid 208–209
Apia, Samoa 277, 280 , 283, 286, 289
Argentina 251, 254, 259, 261, 263, 266
Armenia 249, 253, 255, 260, 262, 265
Armenia, Colombia 276, 279, 283, 286, 289
articulation 51, 53
Aruba 251, 254
Asansol, India 269
Ashaiman, Ghana 90
Asia, 249, 253, 255, 258, 260, 262, 265
Central 3, 30, 37, 107, 161
child labour 99
Eastern 3, 7, 14–15, 97, 161, 234
Eastern Asia xxv, 30, 31
economic growth 36
informal sector 103
and the Pacific 111–112, 113, 115, 141
slum dweller estimations 2, 3, 13–15
South 7, 31, 97, 161
South-central xxv, 14–15, 234
Southeast xxv, 14–15, 97, 149, 234
tenure 107
unemployment 99
urban populations 5
Western xxv, 14–15, 97, 234
see also tiger economies

Astana, Kazakhstan 275, 278, 281, 284, 288
Astrakhan, Russian Federation 276, 279, 282, 285, 288
Asunción, Paraguay 272, 277, 280, 283, 286, 289
asylum-seekers 238
Athens, Greece 271
Atlanta, United States 272, 277, 280, 283, 286, 289
attitudes
affluent 104
civil society 148
historical context 65
immigration 27
informal sector 60, 103
political 195, 196
transport standards 173
Auckland, New Zealand 273
Aurangabad, India 269
Austin, United States 272
Australia 19, 20, 23, 30, 65–66, 123, 128, 227–228, 251, 255, 257, 259, 261, 264, 266
Austria 106, 250, 253, 256, 259, 261, 263, 265
autonomy 158–159
Aversa, Italy 276, 279, 282, 285, 288
Aviles, Spain 124
Azerbaijan 249, 253, 256, 258, 260, 262, 265

backward linkages 177
Baghdad, Iraq 270, 275, 278, 281, 284, 288
Bahamas 251, 254, 259, 263, 266
Bahrain 249, 253, 262, 265
Baku, Azerbaijan 267, 273
Baltimore, United States 272
Bamako, Mali 267, 275, 278, 281, 284, 287
Bandar Lampung (Tanj), Indonesia 269
Bandung, Indonesia 269, 275, 278, 281, 284, 287
Bangalore, India xxv, 15, 269, 275, 278, 281, 284, 287
Bangkok, Thailand xxvi, xxx, 197, 201–202, 270, 275, 279, 282, 285, 288
Bangladesh 149, 249, 253, 258, 260, 262, 265
Bangui, Central African Republic 274, 277, 280, 284, 287
Banjul, Gambia 274, 278, 281, 284, 287
banking see credit; finance; loans
Baotou, China 267
Baracoa, Cuba 276, 280, 283, 286, 289
Barbados 251, 254, 259, 263, 266
Barcelona, Spain 80, 202–203, 271
Barquisimeto, Venezuela 272
Barranquilla, Colombia 272, 274
barrios ilegales 223
Basel, Switzerland 276, 279, 282, 285, 289
basic dwellings 235
bassos 220
Beijing, China 267
Beirut, Lebanon xxix, 80, 90, 203–204, 270
Belarus 250, 253, 259, 261, 263, 265
Belém, Brazil 271, 276, 279, 282, 285, 289

Belfast, United Kingdom 276, 279, 282, 285, 289
Belgium 250, 253, 261, 263, 265
Belgorod, Russian Federation 276, 279, 282, 285, 288
Belgrade, Serbia and Montenegro 271, 276, 279, 282, 285, 288
Belize 251, 254, 259, 263, 266
Belize City, Belize 276, 279, 282, 285, 289
Belo Horizonte, Brazil 271, 274
Benghazi, Libyan Arab Jamahiriya 267
Benin 249, 252, 255, 258, 260, 262, 264
Benxi, China 267
Berlin, Germany 271, 276, 279, 282, 285, 288
Bermuda 251, 254
best practices 132–133, 164–165, 174–175
Bhopal, India 69, 269
Bhutan 249, 253, 258, 262, 265
bias 46
bid rent curves 18
Bielefeld, Germany 271
Bignona, Senegal 275, 278, 281, 284, 287
bilateral agencies 135, 136, 142–145
Birmingham, United Kingdom 271, 276, 279, 282, 285, 289
Birmingham, United States 277, 280, 283, 286, 289
Bishkek, Kyrghyzstan 275, 278, 281, 284, 288
Bobo-Dioulasso, Burkina Faso 274, 277, 280, 283, 287
Bogotá, Colombia xxvi, xxx, 81, 88, 205, 272, 274
bohíos 210
Bolivia 104, 251, 254, 257, 259, 261, 263, 266
Bombay see Mumbai, India
boom and bust economies 3, 35–39, 53, 64–65, 227
Bosnia and Herzegovina 250, 253, 261, 263, 265
Boston, United States 272, 277, 280, 283, 286, 279
Botswana 249, 252, 255, 258, 260, 262, 264
bottom-up globalization 3, 47
Bourgas, Bulgaria 276, 279, 282, 285, 288
Brasília, Brazil 271, 274
Brazil 223–224, 251, 254, 257, 259, 261, 263, 266
income differentials 96
participatory relocation 132
social inclusion 133
squatter settlements 83
Brazzaville, Congo 267, 274, 277, 281, 284, 287
Bremen, Germany 271
Bridgetown, Barbados 276, 279, 282, 285, 289
Brisbane, Australia 273
British Virgin Islands 251, 254
Brno, Czech Republic 276, 279, 282, 285, 288
bright lights phenomenon 26, 51
broken windows theory 75–76
Brunei Darussalam 249, 253, 262, 265

Brussels, Belgium 270
Bucaramanga, Colombia 272
Bucharest, Romania 271
Budapest, Hungary 271, 276, 279, 282, 285, 288
budget augmentation 184
Buenos Aires, Argentina 271, 276, 279, 282, 285, 289
Buffalo-Niagra Falls, United States 272
building materials 177, 202, 209, 243
see also structural aspects, construction
Bujumbura, Burundi 274, 277, 280, 283, 287
Bulawayo, Zimbabwe 267, 275, 278, 281, 284, 287
Bulgaria 250, 253, 256, 259, 261, 263, 265
bureaucracy 107, 112
Burkina Faso 249, 252, 258, 260, 262, 264
Burgess spatial schema 18
Bursa, Turkey 270
Burundi 249, 252, 258, 260, 262, 264
business centres 22
bust *see* boom and bust economies
bustees 213
Butwal, Nepal 275, 278, 281, 285, 288
Bydgoszcz, Poland 276, 279, 282, 285, 288

Cairo, Egypt xxvi, xxx, 84, 93, 205–206, 267, 273
Cajamarca, Peru 277, 280, 283, 286, 289
Calcutta *see* Kolkata, India
Calgary, Canada 272, 274
Cali, Colombia 272, 274
Camaguey, Cuba 276, 280, 283, 286, 289
Cambodia 83, 88, 92, 134, 222–223, 249, 253, 256, 258, 260, 262, 265
Cameroon 249, 252, 258, 260, 262, 264
Campinas, Brazil 271
Campo Grande, Brazil 271
Canada 35, 36, 251, 254, 257, 259, 261, 264, 266
Canton, China 63
capability poverty 29
capacity 144–145, 168, 175–176, 185, 198
see also empowerment
Cape Town, South Africa 267
Cape Verde 249, 252, 258, 262, 264
capital
    flight 42
    flows 34
    gross 235
    housing subsidies 127–128
    informal sector 100, 102
    landlords 60, 110
    poverty 29
    secure tenure 107
    social 6, 29, 166
capitalism 35–36, 64–65, 102
Caracas, Venezuela 272
Cardiff, United Kingdom 276, 279, 282, 285, 289
Caribbean countries *see* Latin America and the Caribbean
Cartagena, Colombia 272
Casablanca, Morocco 267, 275, 278, 281, 284, 287
cash grant schemes 127
Castries, Saint Lucia 274
casual work 101
Cayman Islands 251, 254
CBOs *see* community-based organizations
CDI *see* City Development Index
Cebu, Philippines 275, 278, 281, 285, 288
Central African Republic 249, 252, 258, 260, 262, 264
censuses 13
Central Asia *see* Asia, Central
central locations *see* inner-cities
centralization 18–19, 170, 179

Chad 249, 252, 258, 260, 262, 264
Chandigarh, India 269
Changchun, China 267
Changde, China 267
Changsha, China 267
Changzhou, China 267
Channel Islands 250, 253, 256
chawls 81, 201
Chegutu, Zimbabwe 275, 278, 281, 284, 287
Chelyabinsk, Russian Federation 271
Chengdu, China xxvi, 82, 87, 196, 206–208, 267
Chennai, India 275, 278, 281, 284, 287
Chiang Mai, Thailand 275, 279, 282, 285, 288
Chicago model 2, 17–18, 27, 81
Chicago, United States 21, 272
Chifeng, China 267
child mortality 8, 72, 74, 239
    see also disease; health; life expectancy; mortality
children 60, 77, 99
Chile 121, 127–128, 251, 254, 259, 261, 263, 266
China 126, 249, 253, 258, 260, 262, 265
    low-income housing xxvii
    poverty alleviation 3
    public housing 120–121
    spatial separation 63
    tenure 107
    urbanization 126
Chisinau, Republic of Moldova 276, 279, 282, 285, 288
Chittagong, Bangladesh 267, 275, 278, 281, 284, 287
Chongqing, China 267
chronic poverty 29–30
Cienfuegos, Cuba 277, 280, 283, 286, 289
Cincinnati, United States 272
CIS *see* Commonwealth of Independent States
cities
    abandoned 22–23, 27–28
    child mortality 8, 72, 74, 239
    concentric zones 18
    fragmentation 2
    globalization and trade 40–43
    growth projections 3
    historic 79
    image 70–71
    inclusion 164–188, 198
    inequality 133–136
    market-driven forces 17
    secure tenure 171
    threshold population xxxi
    urban increments 25
    without slums 5–7, 167, 168, 189
    see also inner-cities; urban areas
Cities Alliance 7, 139–140
Cities Without Slums action plan xxxii, xxxiii, 7, 140, 167, 168
Ciudad Guayana, Venezuela 272
Ciudad Juárez, Mexico 272, 277, 280, 283, 286, 289
civic engagement 183
civil society 69, 120, 148–163, 175–176, 191, 234
civil works 176–178
clearance xxviii, 125, 209, 212
    see also eviction
Cleveland, United States 272
Coimbatore, India 269
Cologne, Germany 276, 279, 282, 285, 288
Colombia 251, 254, 257, 259, 261, 263, 266
Colombo, Sri Lanka 275, 279, 282, 285, 288
Colon, Panama 277, 280, 283, 286, 289
Columbus, United States 272
Comodoro Rivadavia, Argentina 276, 279, 282, 285, 289
Comoros 249, 252, 258, 262, 264
Conakry, Guinea 267, 275, 278, 281, 284, 287

Congo 249, 252, 258, 260, 262
co-location 71–72
Cook Islands 251, 255
co-optation 158–159
coalitions xxxii
cohesion 72
collaboration 48, 51
collective living quarters 235
collective solidarity 47
Colombia xxx, 81, 88, 133, 205
Colombo, Sri Lanka xxvi, xxx, 89, 208
colonialism 22, 36, 47, 81, 200, 219
colonias populares 216–217
Comecon countries 37, 41
command economies 124
commercial energy
    production 260–261
    consumption per capita 260–261
commodities 40, 136, 168
Commonwealth of Independent States (CIS) 39, 59
communal flats 218
communications 3, 34, 41–42, 48, 53, 160
communism 36, 37, 126
communities
    capacity building 175–176
    cooperation 51–52, 150, 185
    development 155
    diversity 152–153
    eviction 92
    gated 20
    household relationships 150
    improvement 93, 95
    infrastructure 178
    negotiated outcomes 172–173
    participation 71, 158, 177
    power 152–153
    risk and crime 75–76
    secure tenure 171–172
community-based organizations (CBOs) 139, 148, 151–153
community funds 134
competition 18, 44, 90, 101, 103, 133–135, 161
complementary efforts 165–166
component score coefficients 242
concentric zones 18
conflicts 169, 184, 186, 203–204, 206, 211
congestion 64
    see also overcrowding
Congo, Democratic Republic of 46
consolidation 51, 87, 88, 94, 170
construction
    bilateral agencies 144
    durability of dwellings 243
    failures xxv, 176
    government 123
    housing reform 218–219
    industry 68
    informal 104
    slum definitions 196
    small-scale enterprise 60
    support 109
    see also building materials, structural aspects
consumption 100–101, 113, 236, 239
continuity 130–131
contracts 177, 178, 186
controlling cities 22
conventional dwellings 234–235
convergence 136–139
cooperation
    actors 135
    bilateral 136
    communities 150, 185
    decentralized 142
    EU 139
    government and NGO 159
    inter-sectoral 122
    international 145–146, 244
    partnerships 171, 184
    promotion 141–142
    tenants and housing associations 228
    transurban 50–52
coordination
    inclusive cities 165, 167

international actors 145–146
    lack of 198
    multiple agencies 211
    partnerships 184
    policy 186–187
    subsidiarity 49
Copenhagen, Denmark 270
Córdoba, Argentina 271, 276, 279, 282, 285, 289
correlation matrices 242
corruption 31, 44, 175, 179–180, 183, 212
cortiços 225
Costa Rica 157, 251, 254, 257, 259, 261, 263, 266
costs
    environmental risk 70
    formal sector 103
    housing 21, 130, 190
    institutional 101
    living 218
    recovery 44, 45, 185
Côte d'Ivoire 200, 249, 252, 258, 260, 262, 264
Cotonou, Benin 274, 277, 280, 283, 287
creation of income 96
credit
    access 100, 108, 134
    home improvement 217
    housing finance 180–181
    partnerships 185
    programmes xxx–xxxi
    women 103, 149
    see also banking; loans
crime xxvi, xxviii, 20, 58, 59, 75–77, 83
Croatia 250, 253, 261, 263, 265
cross-sectoral interventions 141
cross-subsidization 45
CSOs *see* civil society organizations
cuartos de azotea 217
Cuba 41, 86, 197, 209–211, 251, 254, 259, 261, 263, 266
Cucuta, Colombia 272
Cuenca, Ecuador 277, 280, 283, 286, 289
cuidades perdidas 217
Culiacán, Mexico 272
cultural aspects 21–22, 50, 71, 75, 85, 129
Curitiba, Brazil 174, 271
customary tenure 84, 106, 109, 168, 169
cyclical growth patterns 35–36
Cyprus 249, 253, 256, 258, 262, 265
Czech Republic 250, 253, 261, 263, 265

Dakar, Senegal 133, 267, 275, 278, 281, 284, 287
Dalian, China 267
Dallas, United States 272
Damascus, Syrian Arab Republic 270, 273, 275, 279, 282, 285, 288
Dammam, Saudi Arabia 270
Daqing, China 267
Dar es Salaam, Tanzania, United Republic of 46, 267
Datong, China 267
Davao, Philippines 270
de facto ownership 60, 83, 84, 87, 107–108, 197
death rates *see* mortality rates
decaying central pockets 220
decentralization
    cooperation 142
    development 198
    governance 6, 44
    inclusive cities 183
    MDP 140
    services 178, 180
    statistical terms 235
    see also subsidiarity
decision-making xxvii, 149, 150, 182, 183, 184
declining areas 9, 27–28, 80
    see also deterioration
definitions
    CBOs 151

civil society 148
informal sector 100–101
NGOs 153–155
operational 12
poverty xxvi, 29–30, 196
slums 1–2, 8–16, 196, 197, 202, 243–244
statistical terms 234–239
tenure 168
degeneration 209
Delhi, India 269, 275, 278, 281, 284, 287
demand subsidies 123–124, 127
Democratic People's Rep. of Korea 249, 253, 258, 260, 262, 265
democratic processes 23–28, 156, 158, 162, 184, 186
Democratic Republic of Congo 249, 252, 258, 260, 262, 264
Denmark 250, 253, 259, 261, 263, 265
Denver, United States 272
Des Moines, United States 277, 280, 283, 286, 289
density 11, 12, 174, 214, 221
dependency rates 28
depopulation 2, 27–28
deposit gap 128
deregulation 43–44, 137, 181
desert state lands 206
despair, slums of xxvi, 9
deterioration
broken windows theory 75–76
inner-cities 80–81, 89, 206, 220
public housing 9, 86–87, 217
services 179
slum creation 79–82, 95
trade terms 40
see also declining areas
Detroit, United States 272
devaluation 42
developed countries
crime 76
informal sector 103
mortality 72–73
populations 14–15
regional classifications 231, 233
self-help programmes 127
tenure security 108
unemployment 98
developing countries
cities without slums xxviii, 189
crime 76
dependency rates 28
health expenditure 74
informal sector 102, 103
infrastructure 114
inner-city redevelopment 81
international trade 41
labour markets 99
mortality rates 72–73
negligence 129–130
policy 178–179
populations xxv, 2, 13, 14
post-modern cities 22–23
public housing 124–125
regional classifications 233
squatter settlements 82
statistical aggregates 231
terminology 9
development
community 153, 155
dynamics 92–95
economic 244
environmental management 114
EU 139
housing 112, 202
human xxxi, 152, 182, 232–233
inclusive cities 164–188
infrastructure 121
inter-institutional programmes 139–140
life expectancy 72
partnerships 8, 183–186
planning xxxi
policy xxxii, 31, 123–147, 182, 198–199
secure tenure 107
services xxviii

shelter 176–178
social 244
waste management 115
water 113
see also improvement
Dhaka, Bangladesh 79, 103, 267, 275, 278, 281, 284, 287
Dhanbad, India 269
differential power 39
diffusion 40, 47–48, 184
dilapidated buildings 218
direct factors 22, 47
disadvantage 19, 20, 22–23, 112, 228
disarticulation 50
disaster prevention 235
discrimination 27, 93–95, 197, 207, 223, 227
disease xxx, 8, 73, 74–75
see also child mortality; health; life expectancy; mortality
disinvested areas 214
disparate populations 71
displacement
involuntary 174
migration 26
resistance to 172–173
statistical terms 238
transport 172
see also eviction; resettlements
dissimilarity index 20
distribution 26, 96, 106–107
diversity
communities 152–153
CSOs 120
inclusive cities 171–172
NGOs 156–158
policy 186–187
social 58, 59, 62, 66–67
spatial forms 84–85
tenure 197
divided cities 20
Djibouti 249, 252, 258, 264
Dnepropetrovsk, Ukraine 271
Doha, Qatar 275, 278, 281, 285, 288
domestic service xxx, 101–102, 102
Dominica 251, 254, 259
Dominican Republic 251, 254, 257, 259, 261, 263, 266
Donetsk, Ukraine 271
Dongguan, China 267
Douala, Cameroon 267, 274, 277, 280, 283, 287
downsizing 37
drinking water *see* water
duplication 49
Dubai, United Arab Emirates 270
Dublin, Ireland 271
Duisburg, Germany 276, 279, 282, 285, 288
durability of dwellings 243
Durban, South Africa xxvi, 83, 208–209, 267, 275, 278, 281, 284, 287
Durg-Bhilainagar, India 269

earth movements 69
East Africa *see* Africa, East
Eastern Asia *see* Asia, Eastern
Eastern Europe *see* Europe, Eastern
East Rand, South Africa 267, 5, 278, 281, 284, 287
ecological aspects 17–19, 19–20
see also Chicago model
economic aspects
access 59
boom and bust 35–39
crime 76
development 183, 244
dynamics 96–117
globalization 6, 34–55
governance 51
growth 36–39
informality 100–104
inner-city redevelopment 81
macro- 164
policy 182, 207
slum attributes 67
social objectives 145
stagnation 28, 43

trade 41–43
unemployment 98
see also financial aspects
Ecuador xxix, 85, 102, 223–224, 251, 254, 259, 261, 263, 266
Edinburgh, United Kingdom 276, 279, 282, 285, 289
Edmonton, Canada 272
education
access xxx, 70
crime 76
diversity 67
inequality 39
informal sector 104
intervention 129
low-cost labour 68
MDGs 8
efficiency 44–45, 184
Egypt xxx, 10, 84, 93, 132, 205–206, 249, 252, 255, 258, 260, 262, 264
Eindhoven, Netherlands 276, 279, 282, 285, 288
Ekaterinburg, Russian Federation 271
El Salvador 251, 254, 259, 261, 263, 266
emigration 28
employment
central slums 80, 88
crime 76
generating 176–178
globalization 52
informal sector 96, 102, 103, 176
opportunities 60, 164–165, 166, 176
structural adjustment 46
self 98, 100, 104
social clustering 21
urbanization xxxi, xxxii
women 91, 99
see also labour markets; occupation; unemployment
empowerment 175–176
see also capacity
enablement xxvi, 131, 160
Entebbe, Uganda 275, 278, 281, 284, 287
enterprise 59, 62, 70, 100, 101–102, 177, 178
entrepôt free-trade ports 35
entrepreneurs 101
entry fees 83
environmental aspects
externalities 69–70
inclusive cities 182
international actors 143
management 114, 244
multilateral agencies 143–144
planning 237
policy 190
risk 11, 62
security 183
sustainability 7–8
environmental aspects
disaster prevention and mitigation measures 280–283
equality 8, 144
see also inequality
Equatorial Guinea 249, 252, 258, 262, 264
equity 183
eradication *see* clearance; eviction
estates 81–82, 86–87
ethnicity 19, 22, 27, 63, 124, 228
Erfurt, Germany 276, 279, 282, 285, 288
Eritrea 249, 252, 258, 260, 262, 264
Esfahan, Iran (Islamic Republic of) 269
Espoo, Finland 273
Estonia 250, 253, 256, 259, 261, 263, 265
Ethiopia 249, 252, 258, 260, 262, 264
EU *see* European Union
Europe 250, 253, 256, 259, 261, 263, 265
Eastern 30, 31, 37, 107, 161, 231–232
inclusion 124
inner-city slums 81

liberalization 3
Northern 178
populations xxv, 14–15
regional classifications 233
tenure security 108
urbanization 2
Western 37, 107, 149, 161, 232
European Union (EU) 139, 143, 144
evaluation 162
eviction
civil society 69
failures 104
political responses xxvi, 130, 131
scale 91, 92
security xxviii, 168, 169, 170, 171
urbanization 120
see also displacement; resettlement
exclusion
cities 133–135, 182
crime xxvi, 77
economic growth 39
governance 222
planning 227
public rental estates 106
social 11, 12, 20–21
zoning 21
expenditure 43, 74, 121, 128, 236, 237
exports 40–41, 43, 46
extensions 84, 104
externalities 69–70
extreme poverty xxvi, 23–24, 30–31
see also poverty

factorial ecology 19–20
Faeroe Islands 250, 253
Faisalabad, Pakistan 270
Falkland Islands (Malvinas) 251, 254
families 19–20, 71, 79, 89, 203
famine 26
Faridabad, India 269
favelas 225, 226–227
FDI *see* foreign direct investment
Fes, Morocco 267
Fiji 251, 255, 259, 264, 266
financial aspects
access 6–7
accountability 175
banking 181
capital 29
constraints 145
deregulation 43–44
development funds 134
housing xxxii, 125, 180–182
international actors 144, 145
low-income partnerships 185
micro 121–122, 180
mobilization 120, 178–182, 226
multilateral agencies 137–139
municipal 179–180
regeneration 66
trade 41–43
upgrading 95, 166, 178–179
urban 142–143, 165
women xxx–xxxi
see also economic aspects; funding
Finland 250, 253, 256, 259, 261, 263, 265
fires 69
flexibility 167
floating population 207
floods 69
Florence, Italy 271
forced savings 125, 127
foreign direct investment (FDI) 43
formal sector
employment xxxi
globalization 52
home ownership 105, 108, 111–112
informal linkages xxvii, 42–43, 57, 58, 100–104, 136
integration 136
market structures 64
titling 108
formalization programmes 107
formation of slums xxv–xxvi, 195–196, 197
Fort Lauderdale, United States 273

Fortaleza, Brazil 272
France 250, 253, 261, 263, 265
fragmentation 2
France 74–75
free trade 40
Freetown, Sierra Leone 267
Freiburg, Germany 276, 279, 282, 285, 288
French Guiana 251, 254
French Polynesia 251, 255
functionality 137
funding 154, 156, 157, 159, 161
    see also financial aspects
Fushun, China 267
Fuxin, China 267
Fuyu, China 267
Fuzhou, China 267

Gabon 249, 252, 258, 260, 262, 264
Gaborone, Botswana 274, 277, 280, 283, 287
Gambia 249, 252, 255, 258, 260, 262, 264
garbage dumps 69
gated communities xxvi, 20, 21
Gaza, Occupied Palestine Territory 275, 278, 281, 285, 288
Gaziantep, Turkey 270
Gdansk, Poland 271, 276, 279, 282, 285, 288
GDP *see* gross domestic product
Genoa, Italy 271
gender 8, 66, 97–98, 107, 144, 182
    see also women
gentrification 22, 23, 80–81, 83, 89, 173, 174, 227, 228
    see also redevelopment
geographical areas 9–10, 161, 206
geographical information systems (GIS) 13
Georgia 249, 253, 258, 260, 262, 265
Germany 250, 253, 256, 261, 263, 265
Ghana 46, 82, 90, 104, 110, 111, 249, 252, 258, 260, 262, 264
Ghaziabad, India 269
Giandja, Azerbaijan 273
Gibraltar 250, 253
Gini coefficient 37, 38
GIS *see* geographical information systems
Giza, Egypt 273
global aspects
    declining areas 28
    development partnerships 8, 183–186
    inequality 2, 38
    knowledge 168
    labour force 97–98
    policy 6
    population xxiii, 5
    poverty 2, 30
    trade 40
Global Campaign for Secure Tenure xxviii, 138, 143
Global Urban Indicators Database 245
globalization 2, 3, 6, 34–55, 46–53
Goiânia, Brazil 272
Göteborg, Sweden 271
goths 212–213
governance
    adequacy 115
    economic 51
    exclusion 222
    failure 5–6
    inclusivity xxvii, 120, 182–183
    indicators 242
    informal sector xxvii, 98
    local 135, 223
    policy 186–187
    poverty 31, 175
    upgrading 131, 166
governments
    decentralization 43–46
    informal sector 178
    institutions 103
    local 135, 166, 191, 198, 207–208, 223, 237
    NGOs 121, 153–154, 158–159
    partnerships 142, 184

post-independence 212–214, 215, 219
    relations 170, 179–180, 223
    responsibilities 171, 186, 191
    services 6, 123
    weakening of 48–49
Gran Concepcion, Chile 276, 279, 283, 286, 289
grassroots organizations *see* community-based organizations
Greece 250, 253, 261, 263, 265
Greenland 251, 254, 257
Grenada 251, 254, 259
Gros Islet, Saint Lucia 274
gross capital formation 235, 262–266
gross domestic product (GDP) 36, 37, 96, 235
gross school enrolment ratios 235, 283–286
growth 3, 35–39, 52–53, 96–99, 101, 167, 237
Guadalajara, Mexico 272
Guadeloupe 251, 254, 263
Guam 251, 255
Guangzhou, China 267
Guatemala 251, 254, 257, 259, 261, 263, 266
Guatemala City, Guatemala 272
Guayaquil, Ecuador 272, 277, 280, 283, 286, 289
Guinea 249, 252, 258, 260, 262, 264
Guinea-Bissau 249, 252, 258, 260, 262, 264
Guiyang, China 267
Gujranwala, Pakistan 270
Guwahati, India 269
Guyana 251, 254, 259, 263, 266
Gwalior, India 269
Gweru, Zimbabwe 275, 278, 281, 284, 287
gypsy communities 124, 203

Habitat II *see* United Nations Conference on Human Settlements, second
Habitat Agenda 7, 104, 107, 124, 129, 131, 138, 140, 160, 171, 191, 244, 245
Hai Phong, Viet Nam 270
Haiti 251, 254, 259, 261, 263, 266
Hamburg, Germany 271
Hanam, Republic of Korea 275, 278, 281, 285, 288
Handan, China 267
Hangzhou, China 268
Hannover, Germany 271
Hanoi, Viet Nam 270, 275, 279, 282, 285, 288
Harare, Zimbabwe 267, 275, 278, 281, 284, 287
Harbin, China 268
Hartford, United States 277, 280, 283, 286, 289
Havana, Cuba xxvi, 41, 86, 197, 209–211, 272, 277, 280, 283, 286, 289
hazardous locations 11
headship size rate-based projections 236
health 58, 59, 71, 72–75, 143–144
    see also child mortality; disease; life expectancy; mortality
hedge funds 42
Hefei, China 268
Helsinki, Finland 270, 273
Hengyang, China 268
Herculaneum, Italy 63
heritage 85
Heze, China 268
hierarchical structures 62–63
high-rise development 202
high-risk zones xxx
Hiroshima, Japan 270
historical context
    cities 70–71, 85–86, 89
    inequality 35–39
    NGOs 155–156
    residential periphery 220
    slums 9, 128–133

social stratification 62–67
HIV/AIDS 8, 73
Ho Chi Minh City, Viet Nam 270, 275, 279, 282, 285, 288
holistic approaches xxxii, 198, 216
Holy See 250, 253
home improvement credits 217
home-working 90, 104
Homs, Syrian Arab Republic 270, 273
Honduras 251, 254, 259, 261, 263, 266
Hong Kong, China SAR 249, 253, 256, 260, 262, 265, 269
hope, slums of xxvi, 9
horizontal partnerships 186
hostels 81
households
    below the poverty line 283–286
    differences 120
    final consumption expenditure 264–266
    global inequality 38
    heads 29, 66, 239
    management 148–151
    national surveys 243
    number 247, 249–252, 273–274
    poverty 30, 237
    statistical terms 235–236
    total 255–257
    women headed 255–257
housing
    adequacy 114–115
    costs 21, 130, 190
    deterioration 9
    disadvantage 111–112
    economic position of slums 58
    failures xxvii, 195
    families 89
    finance xxxii, 7, 180–182
    health 59, 74
    inadequate 68
    income 111, 128, 207, 236–237
    informal 68, 100, 104
    insecurity 151
    international actors 144
    interventions 120–121, 123–128
    management xxvii, 82
    mobility 173
    peripheral slums 90
    planning 104
    policy 190, 210
    public 9, 59, 120–121, 124–125, 126, 130
    quality 11, 115
    reform 129, 138, 218–219
    rights 216, 237, 274–277
    security 172
    self-help 157, 215
    subsidies 124, 127–128
    transport 172–175
    unauthorized 11, 26
    working men's 18
housing price to income ratio 274–277
housing units 255–257, 273–274
Houston, United States 273
Huaian, China 268
Huaibei, China 268
Huainan, China 268
Huanuco, Peru 277, 280, 283, 286, 289
Huaras, Peru 277, 280, 283, 286, 289
Hubli-Dharwad, India 269
Huhehaote, China 268
Hull, Canada 277, 280, 283, 286, 289
human development xxxi, 152, 182
human development index (HDI), country aggregates 232–233
human rights *see* rights
Hungary 250, 253, 256, 259, 261, 263, 265
hunger 7, 8
Hunjiang, China 268
Huzhou, China 268
Hyderabad, India 269
Hyderabad, Pakistan 270

Ibadan, Nigeria xxvi, 86, 211, 267, 275, 278, 281, 284, 287
Icapui, Brazil 276, 279, 282, 285, 289

Iceland 250, 253, 263
illegal settlements
    building structures 11
    city of 23
    opportunities 94
    political will 195
    spatial forms 79, 82–83, 83–84
    subdivisions 106
    trade 41
    vulnerability 92
    see also informal sector; squatter settlements
illiteracy rate 248, 264–266
image 70–71
immigration
    adequacy 115
    congestion 64
    depopulation 28
    policy 27
    segregation 124
improvements xxv, 85–86, 93–95, 121, 125–127, 132–133, 217, 224–225, 234
    see also development; upgrading
improvised housing 210
in-country capacity 168
in-migration *see* migration
inadequate housing 11, 68
Inch'on, Republic of Korea 270
incentives 95
incipient slum creation 95
inclusion xxvii–xxviii, 120, 124, 133, 135–136, 152, 164–188, 198
income
    country aggregates 233
    creation and distribution 27, 96
    cyclical growth patterns 36
    globalization 52
    housing 111, 128, 207, 236–237
    inequality xxvii, 38, 42, 53, 97–98
    informal sector xxvi
    opportunities 190–191
    poverty 7, 29, 30
    segregation 11, 20
independent enterprises 101
India 167, 213, 250, 253, 258, 260, 262, 265
    community funds 134
    diversity 67
    enumeration processes 153
    minority groups 151
    networks 167
    pavement communities 92
    rented accommodation 80, 81–82
    trends xxv, 15
    upgrading schemes 130
Indianapolis, United States 275
indicators
    economic 96
    global database 244, 245
    health 73, 74
    housing 112
    MDGs 7–8, 241
    slum definition 12
    urban 242
individual improvements 93
Indonesia 173, 211–212, 250, 253, 258, 260, 262, 265
Indore, India 167, 269
Industrial Revolution 63, 65
industrialization xxix, 114
industry
    deconcentration 227
    housing 81–82, 86–87, 201
    location 21, 49
    participation 97
    pollution 69
    subsidies 49
    tied worker's housing 82
inequality
    communities 133–136, 152–153
    education 39
    global 2, 52
    households 120, 149
    income xxvii, 53, 97
    poverty 3, 5, 34–43
    regional 38
    socio-economic 17–23
    spatial 20, 124

trade 40
see also equality
inequitability 184
infant mortality *see* child mortality
infectious disease *see* disease
informal sector
    city 23
    consolidation 87
    credit 108
    definitions 196
    employment xxxi, 96, 102, 103,
        176
    enterprise 121–122
    formal linkages xxvii, 57, 58,
        100–104, 136
    government 178
    housing 104, 176–177, 190
    income xxvi
    infrastructure access 114
    labour 60, 68
    landlords 110
    networks 3–4, 53, 157
    opportunities 29
    ownership 105–106
    security of tenure 169
    services 70, 113
    settlements 11, 59, 196, 206, 208,
        219
    spatial expansion 167–168
    urban population 5
    vulnerability 92
    see also illegal settlements; squatter
        settlements
information 39, 41–43, 167
infrastructure
    access to 59, 114
    city-wide approaches 167
    deficiency 25, 26
    development 121
    inclusivity 120, 164, 172–175, 178
    investment xxviii
    partnerships 185
    policy 182, 190
    regional 113
    revenue 212
    upgrading 127
injury 73
inner-cities
    deterioration 205, 206, 220
    eradication 207
    historic aspects 85–86
    illegal settlements 84
    industry location 21
    population 66
    redevelopment 81, 227
    rental slums 217
    slums 58, 59, 80–81, 88–89, 196
    social stratification 63–66
    tenure security 197
    vacation of 18
    see also central slums; cities; urban
        areas
innovative approaches xxxiii
Iquitos, Peru 277, 280, 283, 286, 289
Iran (Islamic Republic of) 250, 253,
        256, 258, 260, 262, 265
Iraq 250, 253, 258, 260, 262, 265
Ireland 250, 253, 261, 263, 265
insecurity 47–48, 53, 75, 76, 98,
        107–109, 151, 241
Islamabad, Pakistan 273
Isle of Man 250, 253, 256
Ismailia, Egypt 274, 277, 281, 284, 287
Israel 250, 253, 256, 260, 262, 265
Istanbul, Turkey 270, 273
institutional aspects 6–7, 101, 103,
        139–142, 143, 166, 182
integration xxvii, 50–52, 124, 136,
        141, 168, 174
inter-country inequality 38
inter-governmental relations 179–180
inter-institutional aspects 139–142
inter-sectoral cooperation 122
international level
    actors 135, 136–144, 145
    aid agencies 48–49
    cooperation 145–146, 244
    interventions 4, 6
    liberalization 36

migration 27
organizations 191
trade 34, 40, 41
transurban cooperation 50
internationalization 50–51
interventions
    cross-sectoral 141
    division by potential 79–80
    failures 71–72, 195, 200, 213
    housing 120–121, 123–128
    impacts 6
    improved slums 93
    regeneration 65–66
    urban fringes 206
    see also policy
intra-household relationships 30, 120,
        150
intra-muros 224
invasoes 225
investment
    Africa 43
    Asia 37
    cities without slums 168
    inequality 42
    municipal finance 179–180
    rent freezing 80
    secure tenure 107
    subsidiarity 49
    upgrading xxviii
irregularity 169, 170, 171, 200, 217
isolation 89, 205
Italy 63, 82, 84, 220–221, 250, 253,
        261, 263, 265
Izmir, Turkey 270, 273

Jabalpur, India 269
Jacksonville, United States 273
Jaipur, India 269
Jakarta, Indonesia xxvi, 130, 211–212,
        269, 275, 278, 281, 284, 287
Jamaica 251, 254, 259, 261, 263, 266
Jamshedpur, India 269
Japan 37, 250, 253, 256, 260, 262, 265
Jiamusi, China 268
Jiaxing, China 268
Jidda, Saudi Arabia 270
Jilin, China 268
Jinan, China 268
Jingmen, China 268
Jining, China 268
Jinja, Uganda 275, 278, 281, 284, 287
Jinotepe, Nicaragua 274
Jinxi, China 268
Jinzhou, China 268
Jixi, China 268
Jodhpur, India 269
Johannesburg, South Africa 267
Jordan 250, 253, 258, 260, 262, 265
jobless growth theory 101
jobs *see* employment; income

Kabul, Afghanistan 267
Kaifeng, China 268
Kampala, Uganda 267
kampungs 211–212
Kanpur, India 269
Kansas City, United States 273
Kaohsiung, China 268
Karachi, Pakistan xxvi, 91, 132, 196,
        212–213, 270, 275, 278, 281,
        285, 288
Karaj, Iran (Islamic Republic of) 269
Karlsruhe, Germany 271
katchi abadis 212
Katowice, Poland 271, 276, 279, 282,
        285, 288
Kazakhstan 250, 253, 256, 258, 260,
        262, 265
Kazan, Russian Federation 271
Kenya xxix, 13, 83, 103, 154, 196,
        219–220, 249, 252, 258, 260,
        262, 264
Keynesianism 36, 124
Kharkov, Ukraine 271
Khartoum, Sudan 267
Khulna, Bangladesh 267
Kiev, Ukraine 271
Kigali, Rwanda 275, 278, 281, 284,
        287

Kingston, Jamaica 277, 280, 283, 286,
        289
Kinshasa, Democratic Rep. of Congo
        267, 274, 277, 281, 284, 287
Kiribati 251, 255, 259
Kisumu, Kenya 275, 278, 281, 284,
        287
Kitakyushu, Japan 270
Kitwe, Zambia 127
knowledge 144–145, 166, 168
Kochi (Cochin), India 269
Kolkata, India xxvi, xxix, 11, 130,
        213–214, 269
Kostroma, Russian Federation 276, 279,
        282, 285, 288
Koudougou, Burkina Faso 274, 277,
        280, 283, 287
Kozhikode (Calicut), India 269
Krakow, Poland 271, 274
Krasnoyarsk, Russian Federation 271
Kuala Lumpur, Malaysia 270
Kumasi, Ghana 275, 278, 281, 284,
        287
Kunming, China 268
Kuwait 250, 253, 260, 262, 265
Kuwait City, Kuwait 270, 275, 278,
        281, 284, 288
Kwangju, Republic of Korea 270
Kyoto, Japan 270
Kyrgyzstan 250, 253, 258, 260, 262,
        265

La Paz, Bolivia 104, 271
labour
    based approaches 177
    conditions 60, 99
    deregulation 43–44
    free trade 42–43
    growth 96–99
    hollowing out 98
    informal 100, 101, 103
    lines 208
    low-cost 67–68
    statistical terms 237
    see also employment
labour force 248, 262–264
LAC *see* Latin America and the
        Caribbean
lack of growth theory 101
Lagos, Nigeria 267, 275, 278, 281,
        284, 287
Lahore, Pakistan 270, 275, 278, 281,
        285, 288
land
    acquisition 131
    costs 21
    formal markets 64, 112, 195
    inclusive cities 164
    invasion 82
    management xxviii, 143
    policy 169
    public 121
    registration 112
    use 83–84, 173–174
    see also tenure
landlocked developing countries
        (LLDCs) 14, 231
landlords 58, 60, 64, 109–110, 171
landowners 83–84
Lanzhou, China 268
Lao People's Democratic Republic 250,
        253, 258, 260, 262, 265
Laos 103, 134
large-scale settlements 90–91
Larnaka, Cyprus 273
Las Vegas, United States 273
Latin America xxv
    economic growth 36
    extreme poverty 31
    GDP 37
    informal sector 103–104
    labour force participation 97
    slum estimations 2, 3, 13
    unemployment 99
Latin America and the Caribbean (LAC)
        251, 254, 257, 259, 261, 263,
        266
    crime xxviii
    housing 111–112

infrastructure 113
NGOs 161
population xxv
regional classifications 232, 234
rents 110
slum dweller estimations 13–15
tenure 107
UMP 141
unemployment 99
waste management 115
Lattakia, Syrian Arab Republic 273
Latvia 250, 253, 261, 263, 265
LDCs *see* least developed countries
leadership 168
least developed countries (LDCs)
    housing quality 112
    inequality 39, 43
    international trade 41
    populations 14
    structural adjustment 46
    statistical aggregates 231
    unskilled workers 42
    waste 59
Lebanon 80, 90, 203–204, 250, 253,
        258, 260, 263, 265
Leeds, United Kingdom 271
legal aspects
    de facto 83
    definitions 196
    failure 6–7
    land 196
    reform 210
    settlements 94
    social clustering 21
    tenure 108, 168, 169
    upgrading 166
    vulnerability 92
    see also security of tenure
legislation 74–75, 80, 85, 89, 129,
        158–159, 178
legitimization 224
Leipzig, Germany 276, 279, 282, 285,
        288
lending *see* credit
León, Mexico 272
Leon, Nicaragua 274, 277, 280, 283,
        286, 289
Leshan, China 268
Lesotho 249, 252, 255, 258, 260, 262,
        264
leverage 68
liberalization
    CIS 59
    cooperation 136
    financial systems 42
    inequality 38, 39
    international 36
    living conditions 3
    mortgages 108
    NGOs 156
    poverty 2
    trade 45
    transitional countries 37
Liberia 249, 252, 260, 262, 264
Libreville, Gabon 274, 278, 281, 284,
        287
Libyan Arab Jamahiriya 249, 252, 255,
        258, 260, 262, 264
Liechtenstein 250, 254
life expectancy 28, 63, 72, 74, 237,
        283–286
lifestyle 19–20
Lille, France 270
Lilongwe, Malawi 275, 278, 281, 284,
        287
Lima, Peru 272, 277, 280, 283, 286,
        289
Limassol, Cyprus 273
linkages 47–53, 57, 175, 177
    see also relationships
Linqing, China 268
Linyi, China 268
Lisbon, Portugal 271
literacy rate 237, 283–286
Lithuania 250, 254, 256, 261, 263,
        265
Liuan, China 268
Liupanshui, China 268
Liuzhou, China 268

Liverpool, United Kingdom 271
living conditions 3, 11, 175–178, 189, 207, 218, 244
Ljubljana, Slovenia 276, 279, 282, 285, 288
LLDCs *see* landlocked developing countries
loans xxx–xxxi, 6–7, 134, 180
  see also banking; credit
local level
  actors 135
  diffusion 47–48
  disarticulation 50
  employment 176–178
  environmental planning 237
  globalization 46–53
  governments 135, 166, 191, 198, 207–208, 223, 237
  informal sector 101
  inter-institutional programmes 139–140
  policy 6, 128–133, 182–187
  regulations 21
  upgrading 165
localization 63
location
  co- 71–72
  housing estates 82, 86
  inclusive infrastructure 172, 174–175
  informal sector 98
  resettlement xxviii, 175
  risk 69
  security 79
  services 72, 80, 90, 208
  slum characteristics 11, 12
  subsidies 49
  territoriality 88–90
  see also spatial forms
Lodz, Poland 271, 274
Lome, Togo 275, 278, 281, 284, 287
London, United Kingdom 271, 274, 276, 279, 282, 285, 289
Los Angeles, United States xxvi, 214–215, 273
Louisville, United States 273
loteamentos 225
low-cost labour 67–68
low-income households 172, 207, 218
Luanda, Angola 39, 267
Lubumbashi, Democratic Republic of Congo 267
Lucknow, India 269
Ludhiana, India 269
Luoyang, China 268
Lusaka, Zambia xxvi, 215, 267
Luxembourg 250, 254, 263
Lvov, Ukraine 271
Lyon, France 270

Macau , China SAR 249, 253, 256, 262, 265
Maceió, Brazil 272
macro-economic responses 164
Madagascar 249, 252, 258, 260, 262, 264
Madras, India 269
Madrid, Spain 271, 276, 279, 282, 285, 288
Madurai, India 269
maintenance xxvii, 126, 131
Malang, Indonesia 269
Malawi 249, 252, 258, 260, 262, 264
Malaysia 250, 253, 258, 260, 263, 265
Maldives 250, 253, 258, 263, 265
Mali 249, 252, 258, 260, 262, 264
Malta 250, 254, 256, 259, 263, 265
management
  environmental 114, 244
  household 148–151
  housing xxvii, 82
  land xxviii, 143
  large slums 90
  local government 207–208
  partnerships 186
  urban 142–143
Managua, Nicaragua 272, 274
Manaus, Brazil 272
Manchester, United Kingdom 271, 276,

279, 282, 285, 289
Mandalay, Myanmar 270
Manila (Metro Manila), Philippines xxvi, 10, 69, 114, 125, 130, 173, 215–216, 270
Manta, Ecuador 277, 280, 283, 286, 289
Maputo, Mozambique 267, 275, 278, 281, 284, 287
Maracaibo, Venezuela 272
Maracay, Venezuela 272
Maradi, Niger 275, 278, 281, 284, 287
Maranguape, Brazil 276, 279, 282, 285, 289
marginal housing units 235
marginalization 52, 53, 71, 203, 225, 228
market mechanisms
  failure 143, 195
  housing 181
  land 64
  large slums 90–91
  reliance on 119
  security of tenure 169, 170
  social contradictions 145
Marinilla, Colombia 276, 279, 283, 286, 289
Marrakech, Morocco 267
marriage xxx
Marseille, France 270
Marshall Islands 251, 255
Martinique 251, 254, 263, 266
Maseru, Lesotho 275, 278, 281, 284, 287
Mashhad, Iran (Islamic Republic of) 269
Matagalpa, Nicaragua 274
maternal health 8
Mauritania 249, 252, 258, 260, 262, 264
Mauritius 249, 252, 258, 260, 262, 264
MDGs *see* Millennium Development Goals
MDP *see* Municipal Development Programme
Mecca, Saudi Arabia 270
Medan, Indonesia 269
Medellín, Colombia 133, 272, 274, 276, 280, 283, 286, 289
Medina, Saudi Arabia 270
médinas 224

Meerut, India 269
megacities 25, 26
Melbourne, Australia 273
Memphis, United States 273
Mendoza, Argentina 271
Meppel, Netherlands 276, 279, 282, 285, 288
Mérida, Mexico 272
methodology 241–245
Mexicali, Mexico 272
Mexico 251, 254, 257, 259, 261, 263, 266
Mexico City, Mexico xxvi, xxix, 91, 94, 216–218, 272
Miami-Hialeah, United States 273
Mianyang, China 268
Micronesia (Federated States of) 251, 255
micro-enterprises 60, 101
micro-finance approaches 121–122, 180
Middle East 31, 112, 113, 115, 161
migration
  inner-cities 81
  international 27
  low-cost labour 67–68
  rural–urban xxviii, xxix, 2, 24, 25–27, 29, 203, 207
  transurban cooperation 50
Milan, Italy 271
Millennium Development Goals (MDGs) xxv, xxvi, 7–8, 13, 141, 233, 241, 243
Milwaukee, United States 273
Mingecheviz, Azerbaijan 273
mini political economies 149
minimal state approach 137

Minneapolis-St. Paul, United States 273, 277, 280, 283, 286, 289
Minsk, Belarus 270, 275, 279, 282, 285, 288
mobility 29–30, 68, 173
mobilization
  finance 120, 178–182, 226
  local 166
  NGOs 159
  political 61, 68–69
  resource 166, 226
  subsidiarity 49
  see also action
model housing 65
modernism 65
Mogadishu, Somalia 267
Mombasa, Kenya 275, 278, 281, 284, 287
Monaco 250, 254, 259
Mongolia 250, 253, 258, 260, 263, 265
monitoring 162, 241, 244
Monrovia, Liberia 275, 278, 281, 284, 287
Montego Bay, Jamaica 277, 280, 283, 286, 289
Monterrey, Mexico 272
Montevideo, Uruguay 272, 274, 277, 280, 283, 286, 289
Montreal, Canada 36, 272, 274
Montserrat 251, 254
Morocco 81, 87, 93, 224–225, 249, 252, 258, 260, 262, 264
mortality 23–24, 72–73, 283–286
  see also child mortality; disease; health; life expectancy
mortgages 108, 125, 180, 181
Moscow, Russian Federation xxvi, 95, 218–219, 271, 276, 279, 282, 285, 288
mosaic post-modern cities 22–23
Mosul, Iraq 270
motorization 173
motor vehicles 260–261
Mozambique 249, 252, 258, 260, 262, 264
Mudanjiang, China 268
Multan, Pakistan 270
multi-centred cities 22
multi-criteria approaches 13
multidimensional methods 13
multifamily blocks 203
multilateral agencies 135, 136–145
multinational corporations 48
Mumbai, India 80, 81, 92, 152, 172, 185, 269
Munich, Germany 271
Municipal Development Programme (MDP) 140
municipal aspects xxxi, 49, 135, 178, 179–180, 191, 223
Muscat, Oman 275, 278, 281, 285, 288
music 71
Mutare, Zimbabwe 275, 278, 281, 284, 287
Myanmar 250, 253, 258, 260, 263, 265
Mysore, India 269, 275, 278, 281, 284, 287

Nagoya, Japan 270
Nagpur, India 269
Nairobi, Kenya xxvi, xxix, 13, 83, 154, 196, 219–220, 267, 275, 278, 281, 284, 287
Namibia 134, 249, 252, 258, 260, 262, 264
Nampo, Democratic People's Republic of Korea 269
Nanchang, China 268
Nanchong, China 268
Nanjing, China 268
Nanning, China 268
Naples, Italy xxvi, 82, 84, 220–221, 271
Nashik, India 269
Natal, Brazil 272
national level
  actors 135

affordability 123–128
crime 76
development policies xxxii
globalization 46
governments 3, 48–49
household surveys 243
informal sector 103
NGOs 156
policy xxvi, 6, 128–133, 198–199
upgrading programmes 168
Nauru 251, 255
N'Djamena, Chad 274, 277, 281, 284, 287
negative externalities 69–70, 71
neglect 120
negligence 129–130
negotiation 172–173, 224
Neijiang, China 268
neo-classical models 18–19
neo-liberalism 2–3, 6, 36, 53, 123, 156
Nepal 250, 253, 258, 260, 263, 265
Netherlands 36, 65, 124, 250, 254, 256, 259, 261, 263, 265
Netherlands Antilles 251, 254, 263, 266
networks
  CBOs 152
  globalization 3–4
  informal sector 53, 135
  inter-institutional 141–142
  migrant 68
  NGOs 157, 160
  North-South 155
  reciprocity 150
  research 144
  services 113–115
  transurban cooperation 51
New Caledonia 251, 255
New Orleans, United States 273
new settlements 59, 87–88
New York, United States 65, 273, 277, 280, 283, 286, 289
New Zealand 251, 255, 259, 261, 264, 266
Newark, United States xxvi, 221–222, 273, 277, 280, 283, 286, 289
NGOs *see* non-governmental organizations
Niamey, Niger 267, 275, 278, 281, 284, 287
Nicaragua 251, 254, 257, 259, 261, 264, 266
Nicosia, Cyprus 273
Niger 249, 252, 255, 258, 260, 262, 264
Nigeria 39, 103, 249, 252, 258, 260, 262, 265
Ningbo, China 268
Niue 251, 255
Nizhni Novgorod, Russian Federation 271, 276, 279, 282, 285, 288
nomenclature 234
non-governmental organizations (NGOs) xxvii, 70, 121, 148, 153–160, 185–186
non-housing poverty reduction programmes 29
Norfolk, United States 273
Northern Africa *see* Africa, Northern
Northern America 251, 254, 257, 259, 261, 264, 266
Northern countries 155, 157, 161
Northern Mariana Islands 252, 255
Norway 250, 254, 256, 259, 261, 263, 266
Nouakchott, Mauritanie 275, 278, 281, 284, 287
Novomoscowsk, Russian Federation 276, 279, 282, 285, 288
Novosibirsk, Russian Federation 271
Nuremberg, Germany 271

occupation xxvi, 2, 63, 66–67
  see also employment; opportunities
Occupied Palestinian Territory 250, 253, 258, 260, 263, 265
Oceania xxv, 14–15, 161, 234, 251, 255, 257, 259, 261, 264, 266
Odessa, Ukraine 271

OECD *see* Organisation for Economic
Co-operation and Development
Ogbomosho, Nigeria 267
Oklahoma City, United States 273
old city centres 85, 202–204
Oman 250, 253, 258, 260, 263, 265
Omsk, Russian Federation 271, 276, 279, 282, 285, 288
One Million Houses Programme, Colombo 208
opportunities
employment 60, 164–165, 166, 176
globalization 52
income 190–191
inequality 221
informal sector 29, 102
mobility 173
political 186
spatial forms 84–85
tenure 94
oppositional cultures 75
Organisation for Economic Co-operation and Development (OECD) countries 98
organizational aspects 90, 186–187
organized crime xxvi, 83
original city centres 85, 202–204
Orlando, United States 273
Osaka, Japan 270
Oslo, Norway 271
Ottawa, Canada 272, 274
Ouagadougou, Burkina Faso 267, 274, 277, 280, 283, 287
outdated buildings 218
overcrowding xxx, 11, 12, 244
see also congestion
ownership
de facto 60
home 105, 108, 111–112
illegal 83–84
improvement 95
opportunities 94
partnerships 185
private 170
state 218
statistical terms 237
women 60
see also security of tenure; tenure

Pacific countries 99, 111–112, 113, 115, 141
Pakistan 212–213, 91, 132, 196, 212–213, 250, 253, 256, 258, 261, 263, 265
Palau 252, 255, 259
Palembang, Indonesia 269
Pamplona, Spain 276, 279, 282, 285, 289
Panama 251, 254, 259, 261, 264, 266
Panama City, Panama 272
pandemics 73–74
Papua New Guinea 252, 255, 259, 261, 264, 266
Paraguay 251, 254, 259, 261, 264, 266
Parakou, Benin 274, 277, 280, 283, 287
Paris, France 270
participation
approaches 207
communities 71, 158, 178
decision-making xxvii
enabling policies 131
governance 121, 186
improvement 132–133
intervention 71–72
labour force 97
NGOs 121, 160
people xxxiii
planning 234
trade theories 40
urban development 177
partnerships
broad-based xxxiii
capacity 168
CBOs 153
cooperation 171, 184
global development 8
governments and NGOs 121

inclusive cities 165, 183–186
inter-institutional programmes 139–140
policy 122, 184
promotion 141–142
public–private 123–124, 138–139, 184, 226
see also relationships
Patna, India 269
Patos, Cyprus 273
Paysandu, Uruguay 274
pedestrian globalization 47
Penang, Malaysia 275, 278, 281, 284, 288
pension funds 42
perceptions 3, 53, 76, 109–110
period of adjustment theory 101
peripheral areas 79, 90, 205–206, 211, 220, 223, 224, 226–227
Perm, Russian Federation 271
Perth, Australia 273
Peru 82, 107, 251, 254, 259, 261, 264, 266
Peshawar, Pakistan 270
Philadelphia, United States 273
Philippines 103, 130, 151, 152, 173, 215–216, 250, 253, 259, 261, 263, 265
Phnom Penh, Cambodia xxvi, 83, 88, 92, 222–223, 267, 275, 278, 281, 284, 287
Phoenix, United States 273
piecework 90
Pinar Del Rio, Cuba 277, 280, 283, 287, 289
Pingxiang, China 268
Pitcairn 252, 255, 257
Pittsburgh, United States 273
planning
development xxxii
ethnic separations 22
exclusion 227
historical context 65, 66
inadequacy 114–115
informal 104
land-use 166, 174
local 182, 237
municipal 179, 182
participation 234
policy actions xxviii, 189–190
restrictions 44
transport 172–174
urban xxxii, 51, 166–167
urbanization 205
P'ohang, Republic of Korea 270
Pointe-Noire, Congo 274, 277, 281, 284, 287
Pokhara, Nepal 275, 278, 281, 285, 288
Poland 250, 254, 256, 261, 263, 266
policy
adequacy 119–192
anti-poverty 45
coordination 186–187
crime 75
development xxvii, xxviii, 31, 123–147, 198–199
employment 221
enabling 131
failures 6, 189, 209, 215
housing 190, 210
immigration 27
inclusive cities 165–182
lack of 219–220
land provision 169
municipal 178–179, 182–187
national development xxxii
partnerships 122, 184
planning xxviii, 189–190
retreat of the state 43–44
rights xxvi, 164
shift xxvi, 143
spatial outcomes 195–196
stagnation 53
see also interventions
political aspects
eviction xxvi, 130, 131
influence 135–136
land invasion 82

mobilization 61, 68–69
NGOs 154, 156
opportunism 186
partnerships 185
slum improvement 93
will xxvii, 5–6, 115, 186, 195, 196, 198
pollution xxx, 69
Pompeii, Italy 63
population
below the poverty line 264–266
estimates and projections 246, 252–255
global xxv–xxvi, 5
growth rate 246, 249–255
immigration 64
in poverty 248
increments 24–25
international actors 144
slum dweller estimations xxv, 2, 12–15
urban xxi, 66, 200, 238
Port Elizabeth, South Africa 267, 275, 278, 281, 284, 287
Port of Spain, Trinidad and Tobago 277, 280, 283, 286, 289
Port-au-Prince, Haiti 272
Port-Gentil, Gabon 274, 278, 281, 284, 287
Portland, United States 273
Porto Alegre, Brazil 272, 276, 279, 282, 286, 289
Porto, Portugal 271
Porto-Novo, Benin 274, 277, 280, 283, 287
Portugal 250, 254, 261, 263, 266
post-independence governments 212–214, 215, 219
post-modernism 2, 22–23
poverty
alleviation 3, 31, 213, 246
changes 2
characteristics 11, 12
crime 76
definitions xxvi, 29–30, 196
health 71, 74
households 29, 148–149, 237
inequality 3, 5, 17, 34–43
international agencies 144
location 174–175
macro-economic responses 164
MDGs 7, 8
national plans 175
spatial concentration 20–22
statistical terms 238
structural adjustment 45–46
subletting 110
tenure 170
urbanization xxxi–xxxii, 28–31
vulnerability 120
see also extreme poor; vulnerability
power 39, 48–49, 68–69, 149, 152–153, 158–159, 217–218
Poznan, Poland 276, 279, 282, 285, 288
Prague, Czech Republic 270, 276, 279, 282, 285, 288
pre-independence countries 219
prejudice 9–10
Pretoria, South Africa 70, 267
prices
commodities 40
globalization 52
houses 111
income ratios 236–237
land 112
privatization 44
public sector 45
water 239
primary education, MDGs 8
principal components analysis 242–244
priorities 115, 136–139
private sector
home rental 105
NGOs 156
post-modern cities 23
public partnerships 123–124, 184
roles 191
privatization 43, 44–46, 137, 179, 180

production 26, 40, 100–101
professional squatters 216
professionalization 98
profit 101, 110, 151
progressing settlements 9, 80
Providence, United States 273, 277, 280, 283, 286, 289
proxy measurements 13, 242
Puch'on, Republic of Korea 270
public sector
estates 81–82, 86–87
health 143
housing 9, 59, 120–121, 124–125, 126, 130, 190, 210, 217, 228
land 121
partnerships 123–124, 138–139, 184
services 162
Puebla, Mexico 272
Puerto Rico 251, 254, 261, 264, 266
pull factors 25–26
Pune (Poona) India 67, 269
purchasing power parity 238, 248, 262–264
Pusan, Republic of Korea 270, 275, 279, 281, 285, 288
push factors 25–26
Pushkin, Russian Federation 276, 279, 282, 285, 288
Puyo, Ecuador 277, 280, 283, 286, 289
Pyongyang, Democratic People's Republic of Korea 269

Qatar 250, 253, 263, 265
Qingdao, China 268
Qiqihar, China 268
Qom, Iran (Islamic Republic of) 269
Querétaro, Mexico 272
Quetzaltenango, Guatemala 277, 280, 283, 286, 289
Quezon City, Philippines 152
Quito, Ecuador xxvi, xxix, 85, 102, 223–224, 272, 277, 280, 283, 286, 289

Rabat-Salé, Morocco xxvi, 93, 224–225, 267, 275, 278, 281, 284, 287

racheting of inequality 3, 35–36
Rajkot, India 269
Rajshahi, Bangladesh 267
Ranchi, India 269
Rawalpindi, Pakistan 270
recent slums 87–88, 220
Recife, Brazil 272, 276, 279, 282, 286, 289
reciprocity 150
recycling 177–178
redevelopment 80–81, 227
see also gentrification
reform 43–44, 65, 165–166, 207, 210, 218
refugees 27, 203, 204, 240, 264–266
regeneration 66, 205
regional level
crime 76
declining areas 28
disarticulation 50
GDP 37
housing 111–112
inequality 38
infrastructure 113
knowledge 168
populations 14–16
tenure 107, 109
urban NGOs 161
waste management 115
registration 112, 171, 213, 222
see also security of tenure
regularization xxv, 69, 121, 127, 169–170, 200, 223, 225
see also security of tenure
regulations
construction 243
crime 76
informal sector 103
land-use 173–174
local policy 182
planning 104

reform 43–44, 165–166
removal 121
social clustering 21
relationships
business 48
community 75
governmental 158–159, 170,
179–180, 223
household 149–150
informal 100
race 214
tenure insecurity 107–109
transurban 51
see also linkages; partnerships
relative poverty 30
religious groups 65
relocation 89, 91, 132, 174, 204, 207,
212, 224
see also resettlement
remittance 150
rent to income ratio 274–277
rented accommodation
assistance 228
control 80, 85, 89, 95, 106, 108,
110
informal 106, 109–111
inner-cites 217
levels 18, 110
private 105
public 106
repair bills 125
replication *see* scaling up
Republic of Korea 250, 253, 256, 259,
261, 263, 265
Republic of Moldova 250, 254, 259,
261, 263, 266
rescue organizations 24
research and training institutions 142,
144–145
resettlement xxvi, xxviii, 124, 125,
131–132, 150, 172, 174–175,
224
see also displacement; eviction;
relocation
residency 66
residential differentiation 2, 17–22
residual cities 22–23
responsibility 48–49, 149, 171, 178,
183, 184, 186
restrictive covenants 21
restructuring 225
retirement cities 23
retreat of the state 43–46
Réunion 249, 252, 262, 265
revenue 60–61, 113, 180, 212, 237
revolving fund systems 157
Rhein-Main, Germany 271
Rhein-Neckar, Germany 271
Rhein-Ruhr Middle, Germany 271
Rhein-Ruhr North, Germany 271
Rhein-Ruhr South, Germany 271
Riga, Latvia 271, 276, 279, 282, 285,
288
rights
home rental 105
housing 129, 138, 216, 237
inclusive cities 182–183
irregularity 169
policy approaches xxvi, 164
property 171
public rental 106
tenure xxviii, 105, 109, 143
see also security of tenure; tenure
Riik, Estonia 276, 279, 282, 285, 288
Rio de Janeiro, Brazil xxvi, 87,
225–226, 272, 274, 276, 279,
282, 286, 289
risk xxx, 11, 26, 62, 69, 75–76, 77, 83
Rivera, Uruguay 274
Riverside, United States 273
Riyadh, Saudi Arabia 270
roads 177, 238, 260–261
roles 156, 171, 191
Romania 250, 254, 259, 261, 263, 266
Rome, Italy 271
Rosario, Argentina 271, 276, 279, 282,
285, 289
Rostov-on-Don, Russian Federation 271
Rotterdam, Netherlands 271, 273

rural areas
population xxvi, 2, 24–25, 26, 201,
238
poverty comparisons 30
urban interaction 97, 203
rural–urban migration xxviii, xxix, 2,
24, 25–27, 29, 203, 207
Russian Federation 37, 39, 95,
218–219, 251, 254, 259, 261,
263, 266
Rwanda 249, 252, 258, 260, 262, 265

Saarland, Germany 271
Sacramento, United States 273
Saint Helena 249, 252, 255
Saint Kitts and Nevis 251, 254, 259
Saint Lucia 251, 254, 257, 259
Saint Petersburg, Russian Federation
271
Saint Pierre and Miquelon 251, 254
Saint Vincent and the Grenadines 251,
254, 259
Salt Lake City, United States 273, 277,
280, 283, 286, 289
Salto, Uruguay 274
Salvador, Brazil 272
Samambaia, Brazil 132
Samara, Russian Federation 271
Samoa 252, 255, 259, 266
San Antonio, United States 273
San Diego, United States 273
San Francisco, United States 273
San José, Costa Rica 157, 272
San Jose, United States 273, 277, 280,
283, 286, 289
San Juan, Puerto Rico 272
San Luis Potosí, Mexico 272
San Marino 251, 254
San Miguel de Tucumán, Argentina 271
San Salvador, El Salvador 272, 277,
280, 283, 286, 289
Sana'a, Yemen 270, 275, 279, 282,
285, 288
sanitation 8, 12, 234, 243
access to 258–259
Santo Andre, Brazil 133
Santo Domingo, Dominican Republic
272
Santos, Brazil 272
São José dos Campos, Brazil 272
São Luís, Brazil 272
São Paulo, Brazil xxvi, xxx, 83, 89, 132,
174, 226–227, 272, 274, 276,
279, 283, 286, 289
Sao Tome and Principe 249, 252
Sapporo, Japan 270
Sarajevo, Bosnia and Herzegovina 276,
279, 282, 285, 288
Saratov, Russian Federation 271
saucer cities 22
Saudi Arabia 250, 253, 259, 261, 263,
265
savings xxx–xxxi, 125, 127, 134, 181
scale 90–91, 103–104, 161
scaling up xxvii, 161, 166, 186
scattered slum islands 89–90, 91
SDI *see* Shack/Slum Dwellers
International
Seattle, United States 273, 277, 280,
283, 286, 289
secondary mortgage markets 181
sectoral reform 165–166
Secure Tenure Index 12–13, 241–242,
242–244
security
guards 101, 102
inclusive infrastructure 172
individual 183
job 98
location 79
poor and rich contrast 59
squatter settlements 83
subdivisions 106
see also vulnerability
security of tenure
case study summaries 197
definitions 243
formal-informal housing 105–109
global campaign 138, 143

inclusive cities xxvii–xxviii, 164,
168–174
index 241–242
MDGs 8, 241
regularization contrast 120
slum characteristics 11, 12
see also ownership; regularization;
tenure
segregation
clustering 20–21
ethnicity 63
index 20
oppositional cultures 75
planned ethnic separations 22
spatial 124
self-help approaches
building programmes xxvi, 125–127
employment 98, 100, 104
housing 157, 215
partnerships 186
in situ upgrading 130–131
Semarang, Indonesia 269, 275, 278,
281, 284, 288
Sendai, Japan 270
Senegal 133, 249, 252, 255, 258, 260,
262, 265
Seoul, Republic of Korea 270, 275,
279, 281, 285, 288
Serbia and Montenegro 251, 254, 259,
261, 263, 266
servants quarters 217
services
access 5, 6, 12, 70, 113
Africa 114, 178, 179
congestion 64
development land xxviii
health 74
inclusion 133, 183
income 126
informal settlements 70, 87, 113
labour 60, 97
lack of 11
location 72, 80, 90, 208
multilateral agencies 143
networks 157
NGOs 159, 162
policy 182
privatization 44–46
responsibilities 178–179
revenue 60–61
rural and urban contrast 26, 27
slum definitions 196
small slums 91
social clustering 21
squatter settlements 83
tenure and security 105
welfare 156
Seychelles 249, 252, 255
Shanghai, China 268
Shantou, China 268
shantytowns 203, 208
shelter development programmes
176–182, 186
Shenyang, China 268
Shenzhen, China 268
Shijiazhuang, China 268
Shiraz, Iran (Islamic Republic of) 269
Shubra El-Kheima, Egypt 267, 273
SIDS *see* small island developing states
Sierra Leone 249, 253, 258, 260, 262,
265
Sin El Fil, Lebanon 275, 278, 281, 284,
288
Singapore xxvii, 121, 124, 125, 250,
253, 256, 259, 261, 263, 265,
270, 275, 279, 282, 285, 288
single-issue organizations 151
sites-and-services schemes 127, 137
size 11, 25, 26, 82–83, 90–91
see also scale; small-scale aspects
Slovakia 251, 254, 259, 261, 263, 266
Slovenia 251, 254, 259, 261, 263, 266
small island developing states (SIDS)
14, 231
small-scale enterprises (SSEs) 60,
82–83, 91, 100, 177, 178, 217
socio-economic aspects 17–23
socio-political characteristics 197
Sofia, Bulgaria 270, 276, 279, 282,

285, 288
Sokode, Togo 275, 278, 281, 284, 287
Solapur, India 269
solid waste disposal 238
solidarity 47–48, 212
Solomon Islands 252, 255, 259, 264
Somalia 249, 253, 260, 262, 265
Songnam, Republic of Korea 270
Soufriere, Saint Lucia 274
South Africa xxv, 128–129, 249, 253,
255, 258, 260, 262, 265
community funds 134
cost recovery 44
hostels 81
informal settlements 83
loans 180
low-income housing xxvii
responses to slums 121
services 70
subsidies 128, 129
South Asia *see* Asia, South
Southern countries 155, 157
southern growth triangle 50
space 20
Spain 80, 124, 202–203, 251, 254,
261, 263, 266
spatial aspects
concentration 20–22
expansion 167–168
forms 79–95
inequality 20, 124
organization 17–22
policy 195–196
separation 63, 124, 228
unemployment 98
see also location; segregation
specialist services 70
squatter settlements
definitions 196
professional 216
relocation 132
statistical terms 238
tenure 105–106, 107, 109
territoriality 79, 82–83
upgrading 127
worldwide 60
see also illegal settlements; informal
sector
Sri Lanka 89, 185, 208, 250, 253, 259,
261, 263, 265
Srinagar, India 269
SSEs *see* small-scale enterprises
St. Louis, United States 273
stagnation 53
standards xxv, 104, 115, 129, 173,
174, 207
status 19, 21–22, 63, 149, 201, 228
stigmatization 65, 197
Stockholm, Sweden 271, 276, 279,
282, 285, 289
strategic visioning 187
stratification 62–67
structural adjustment
CBOs 151
housing xxvii
informal sector 6, 102–103
neo-liberalism 3
NGOs 156
poverty 37, 45–46
World Bank 137
structural aspects 12, 40, 102, 200,
243
see also building materials;
construction
Stuttgart, Germany 271
sub-normal settlements 225
sub-Saharan Africa *see* Africa, sub-
Saharan
subcontracting 101
subdivisions 83–84, 85, 86, 106, 210,
225
subletting 106, 110, 111, 203, 218
subsidiarity 48–49, 183
see also decentralization
subsidies
demand 123–124, 127, 129
housing 127–128, 181–182
improvements 121, 217
locating industry 49

policy actions 190
post-war 130
privatization 45
substandard housing 11
suburban city 22, 23
Sudan 249, 253, 258, 260, 262, 265
sufficient living area 244
Suining, China 268
Sumgait, Azerbaijan 273
support
   CBOs 151–153
   community development 153
   construction sector 109
   informal sector 103
   intra-household 150
   multilateral agencies 136–139
   networks 68, 157
   participation 131
Suqian, China 268
Surabaya (Surabaja), Indonesia 173, 269, 275, 278, 281, 284, 288
Surat, India 269
Surgut, Russian Federation 276, 279, 282, 285, 288
Suriname 251, 254, 259, 264, 266
sustainability 7–8, 23–31, 137, 183
Suwon, Republic of Korea 270
Suzhou, China 268
Swaziland 249, 253, 260, 262, 265
Sweden 251, 254, 259, 261, 263, 266
Switzerland 251, 254, 259, 261, 263, 266
Sydney, Australia xxvi, 19, 20, 23, 65–66, 123, 227–228, 273
Sylhet, Bangladesh 275, 278, 281, 284, 287
Syrian Arab Republic 250, 253, 256, 259, 261, 263, 265

Tabriz, Iran (Islamic Republic of) 269
Tacna, Peru 277, 280, 283, 286, 289
Taegu, Republic of Korea 270
Taejon, Republic of Korea 270
Taian, China 268
Taichung, China 268
Taipei, China 268
Taiyuan, China 268
Tajikistan 250, 253, 259, 261, 263, 265
Tallin, Estonia 276, 279, 282, 285, 288
Tamil Nadu, India 81–82
Tampa, United States 273, 277, 280, 283, 286, 289
Tampere, Finland 273
Tangail, Bangladesh 275, 278, 281, 284, 287
Tangshan, China 268
Tanta, Egypt 274, 277, 281, 284, 287
Tanzania, United Republic of 46, 249, 253, 258, 260, 262, 265
targeted housing subsidies 127
Tashkent, Uzbekistan 270
taxation 21, 26–27, 43, 101, 103, 108, 179
Tbilisi, Georgia 269, 275, 278, 281, 284, 287
technology 100
Tegal, Indonesia 269
Tegucigalpa, Honduras 272
Teheran, Iran (Islamic Republic of) 270
Tel-Aviv-Yafo, Israel 270
televisions xxx
temporary housing units 235
temporary residents 222–223
Tena, Ecuador 277, 280, 283, 286, 289
tenants 228, 237
tenements 81, 89, 210
tenure
   access 167–172
   distribution 106–107
   diversity 197
   international actors 143
   opportunities 94
   regularization 69, 170
   rights xxviii, 105, 109, 143
   status 201
   see also land; ownership; rented accommodation; rights; security of tenure

Teresina, Brazil 272
terminology 9–10
territoriality 79–95
TFYR Macedonia 251, 254, 261, 263, 266
Thailand xxx, 83, 88, 92, 97, 132, 134, 197, 201–202, 250, 253, 256, 259, 261, 263, 265
The Hague, Netherlands 274
Thessaloniki, Greece 271
Thies, Senegal 275, 278, 281, 284, 287
Thiruvananthapuram, India 269
three-tier local governments 207
threshold populations xxxi
Tianjin, China 268
Tianmen, China 268
Tianshui, China 268
Tibet 63
tied worker's housing 82, 86–87
tiger economies 36, 37–38, 45, 124–125
   see also Asia
Tijuana, Mexico 272
Timor-Leste 250, 253, 263, 265
Tirana, Albania 275, 279, 282, 285, 288
Tiruchchirapalli, India 269
titling systems 107–108, 169
Togo 249, 253, 258, 260, 262, 265
toilet inside housing unit 238, 243
Tokelau 252, 255
Tokyo, Japan 270, 275, 278, 281, 284, 288
Toluca, Mexico 272
Tolyatti, Russian Federation 271
Tome, Chile 276, 279, 283, 286, 289
Tonga 252, 255, 257, 259
Tongliao, China 268
Toronto, Canada 272, 274
Torreón, Mexico 272
Toulouse, France 270
trade
   barrier reduction 43
   domination 3
   globalization 40–43
   inequality 39
   international 34
   liberalization 45
   weapons 76
traditional fuel 260–261
training institutions 142
transferable property titles 170, 171
transitional countries
   inequality 38, 39
   international trade 41
   liberalization 37
   ownership 107
   poverty 2
   unemployment 99
transparency 183, 238
transport
   environmental risk 69
   housing 172–175
   inclusive cities 164
   infrastructure 178
   peripheral slums 90
   post-modern cities 22
   work trips 238, 280–283
transurban cooperation 50–52
travel time 238
trickle-down effects 40, 52
Trinidad and Tobago 251, 254, 259, 261, 264, 266
Tripoli, Libyan Arab Jamahiriya 267, 275, 278, 281, 284, 287
Troyan, Bulgaria 276, 279, 282, 285, 288
trust 47, 186
Tumbes, Peru 277, 280, 283, 286, 289
Tunis, Tunisia 267, 275, 278, 281, 284, 287
Tunisia 249, 253, 255, 258, 260, 262, 265
Turin, Italy 271
Turkey 250, 253, 256, 259, 261, 263, 265
Turkmenistan 250, 253, 261, 263, 265
Turks and Caicos Islands 251, 254
Turku, Finland 273

Tuvalu 252, 255
Tyneside (Newcastle), United Kingdom 271

Ufa, Russian Federation 271
Uganda 103, 249, 253, 258, 260, 262, 265
Ujung Pandang, Indonesia 269
UK *see* United Kingdom
Ukraine 251, 254, 259, 261, 263, 266
Ulaanbaatar, Mongolia 275, 278, 281, 285, 288
Ulan Bator, Mongolia 270
Ulsan, Republic of Korea 270
Ulyanovsk, Russian Federation 271
Umea, Sweden 276, 279, 282, 285, 289
UMP *see* Urban Management Programme
unauthorized cities 220
unauthorized housing 26, 215
unconventional trade 41
under-five mortality 239
unemployment 53, 75, 76, 96, 98–99, 212, 221
   see also employment
United Arab Emirates 250, 253, 261, 263, 265
United Kingdom (UK) 36, 74, 251, 254, 259, 261, 263, 266
United Nations 136–137, 138, 141, 143, 144
   conferences xxxi, 1, 7, 136, 159
United Nations Conference on Human Settlements
   first (Vancouver, 1976) xxxi
   second (Habitat II) (Istanbul, 1996) xxxi, 112, 136, 141, 160, 183
   see also Habitat Agenda
United States of America (US), 251, 254, 257, 259, 261, 264, 266
   chronic poverty 29
   crime 76
   economy 37, 39
   industry location 21
   partnerships 185
   public health 75
   segregation 20, 124
United States Virgin Islands 251, 254
universities 185
unplanned outskirts 211
unserviced semi-urban neighbourhoods 208
unskilled workers 22, 42
upgrading
   contractors 177
   failures 213
   financing 178–179
   guidelines 142
   impact 93
   inclusive cities 164, 165–168
   inter-institutional programmes 139–140
   peripheral slums 90
   policy actions 190
   scaling up xxvii
   in situ xxvi, 130–131
   squatter slums 127
   tenure and opportunities 94
   World Bank 137
   see also improvements, development
urban
   slum population 246
urban agglomerations
   growth rate 267–273
   population, estimates and projections 267–273
urban areas
   agglomeration 239
   CBOs and NGOs 159–162
   crime 75–77
   development 23, 120, 177, 178–182, 183
   form 22–23
   management 142–143, 164–165
   planning xxxii, 51, 166–167
   population xxv–xxvi, 5, 14, 24–25, 200, 238

transformation processes 205
urban governance
   local government 287–289
   transparency and accountability 287–289
   participation of civil society 287–289
Urban Indicators Index 242
Urban Management Programme (UMP) 140, 141
urbanization
   determining factors 25–26
   employment xxxi, xxxii
   favelas 226
   historical context 64
   inner-city slums 59
   levels of 201, 207, 237, 246, 252–255
   planning 205
   population xxv, xxxi, xxxii, 2
   sustainability 23–31
   trends 17–33
Uruguay 251, 254, 257, 259, 261, 264, 266
US *see* United States of America
Utrecht, Netherlands 274
Uzbekistan 250, 253, 259, 261, 263, 265

Vadodara, India 269
Valencia, Venezuela 272
Valparaiso, Chile 276, 279, 283, 286, 289
value 173, 239
value added
   agriculture 262–264
   industry 262–264
   manufacturing 262–264
   services 262–264
Vancouver, Canada 272
Vanuatu 252, 255, 259
Varanasi (Benares), India 269
vecindades 217
Veliko Tarnovo, Bulgaria 276, 279, 282, 285, 288
Veliky Novgorod, Russian Federation 276, 279, 282, 285, 288
Venezuela 251, 254, 259, 261, 264, 266
Vienna, Austria 106, 270
Vientiane, Lao People's Democratic Republic 275, 278, 281, 284, 288
Viet Nam 134, 250, 253, 259, 261, 263, 265
Vieux-Fort, Saint Lucia 274
Vijayawada, India 269
Villa el Salvador, Peru 82
Vilnius, Lithuania 276, 279, 282, 285, 288
Vina del mar, Chile 276, 279, 283, 286, 289
violence *see* crime
Visakhapatnam, India 269
visioning 187
Volgograd, Russian Federation 271
Voronezh, Russian Federation 271
vulnerability 29, 92, 120, 150–151, 161, 172
   see also security

wages *see* income
Wallis and Futuna Islands 252, 255
Wanxian, China 268
Warsaw, Poland 271, 274
Washington, DC, United States 273, 277, 280, 283, 286, 289
waste xxx, 59, 69, 114, 177, 238, 239
   water treated 277–280
   solid disposal 277–280
water
   access to 7–8, 12, 113–114, 234, 243, 258–259, 274–277
   consumption 239, 277–280
   development 113
   disease xxx
   employment 177
   median price of 277–280
   provision 44, 158, 179, 239

WaterAid 158
weapons trade 76
Weifang, China 268
weighting factors 242
Wenzhou, China 268
welfare 43, 156, 182, 201, 228
West Africa *see* Africa, West
West Palm Beach, United States 273
Western Asia *see* Asia, Western
Western Sahara 249, 253
Wiesbaden, Germany 276, 279, 282, 285, 288
Windhoek, Namibia 275, 280, 281, 284, 287
within-country inequality 38
women
    credit xxx–xxxi, 103, 149
    employment 91, 99
    household heads 29, 66, 239
    impediments 237
    income inequality 97–98
    informal sector 102, 103, 104
    international actors 144

MDGs 8
NGOs 161
    ownership 60
    participation 186
    vulnerability 151
    see also gender
work *see* labour
working men's housing 18
World Bank 127, 137–138, 141, 143, 144
worldling 51
Wroclaw, Poland 274
Wuhan, China 268
Wulumuqi, China 268
Wuxi, China 268

Xian, China 268
Xiangxiang, China 268
Xiantao, China 268
Xianyang, China 268
Xiaoshan, China 268
Xinghua, China 268
Xintai, China 268

Xinyi, China 268
Xinyu, China 268
Xuanzhou, China 268
Xuzhou, China 268

Yamoussoukro, Côte d'Ivoire 274, 277, 281, 284, 287
Yancheng, China 268
Yangon, Myanmar 270, 275, 278, 281, 285, 288
Yantai, China 268
Yaoundé, Cameroon 267, 274, 277, 280, 284, 287
Yemen 250, 253, 259, 261, 263, 265
Yerevan, Armenia 267, 275, 278, 281, 284, 287
Yichun (Heilongjiang), China 269
Yichun (Jiangxi), China 269
Yixing, China 269
Yiyang, China 269
Yongzhou, China 269
young people 98
youth crime 75, 76

Yueyang, China 269
Yulin, China 269
Yuyao, China 269
Yuzhou, China 269

Zagreb, Croatia 270, 276, 279, 282, 285, 288
Zambia 127, 158, 215, 249, 253, 258, 260, 262, 265
Zaoyang, China 269
Zaozhuang, China 269
Zaporozhye, Ukraine 271
Zhangjiakou, China 269
Zhangjiangang, China 269
Zhanjiang, China 269
Zhaodong, China 269
Zhengzhou, China 269
Zibo, China 269
Zigong, China 269
Zimbabwe 134, 150, 249, 253, 255, 258, 260, 262, 265
Zürich, Switzerland 271

DATE DUE

Demco, Inc. 38-293